Managerial Accounting

Creating Value in a Dynamic Business Environment

Eleventh Edition

Ronald W. Hilton
Cornell University

David E. Platt
University of Texas at Austin

MANAGERIAL ACCOUNTING: CREATING VALUE IN A DYNAMIC BUSINESS ENVIRONMENT, ELEVENTH EDITION
International Edition 2017

10 09 08 07 06 05 04 03 02
20 19 18
CTP MPM

When ordering this title, use ISBN 978-981-3151-65-9 or MHID 981-3151-65-X

Printed in Singapore

www.mhhe.com

Ronald W. Hilton:
To Meg, Brad, Molly, Tim, Kerry, and Liliana.

David E. Platt:
To Nancy, Evan, and Hannah.

Praise for *MANAGERIAL ACCOUNTING*

"Extremely comprehensive, easy to read managerial accounting textbook that provides well-designed integrated examples along with coverage of service-based companies."

—Angela Sandberg, Jacksonville State University

"I am loving the book, and I see the students learning the concepts a lot quicker than my previous experience."

—Patti Brown, The University of Texas at Austin

"I would describe it as the Cadillac of core management accounting textbooks."

—Bill Wempe, Texas Christian University

"This is an excellent text—well balanced, well organized, and up to date with current topics, including service industries and state-of-the-art manufacturing environments. I highly recommend it also for the excellent examples and illustrations through focus companies and contrasting companies."

—John C. Anderson, San Diego State University

"I've been using this text since its second edition, and it gets better each year with continuous improvement."

—Steve G. Green, United States Air Force Academy

"Well written with good explanations of the 'why' and 'how'."

—Christa Morgan, Georgia Perimeter College

"Major strength is how it relates managerial accounting to the general management function and reveals the managerial accountant as an important member of the management team."

—Linda C. Bowen, University of North Carolina–Chapel Hill

"The book goes beyond covering the basics and organizes and integrates contemporary topics nicely."

—Harrison McCraw, State University of West Georgia

"Well written, well organized and excellent end of chapter problems."

—Kathleen Sevigny, Boston College

"The technology supplements and instructor resources are top-notch and very appropriate for our students."

—Marilyn Okleshen, Minnesota State University–Mankato

"The book is very thorough, well written, and still remains student-friendly. The supplements are outstanding."

—Ben Baker, Davidson College

"A solid, well-written, user-friendly book; can't go wrong with it!"

—Rochelle Greenberg, Florida State University

Hilton & Platt *Managerial Accounting*: After 11 editions, one of the most enduring and respected managerial accounting books on the market.

Keeping pace with the speed of modern business, the authors combine their experience and expertise to make sure *Managerial Accounting* is the most relevant, accurate, and up-to-date textbook in the field. *Managerial Accounting* continues to focus and update content to bridge accounting and management practices.

About the Authors

© Jon Reis Photography

Ronald W. Hilton is a Professor Emeritus of Accounting at Cornell University. With bachelor's and master's degrees in accounting from The Pennsylvania State University, he received his PhD from The Ohio State University. A Cornell faculty member since 1977, Professor Hilton also has taught accounting at Ohio State and the University of Florida, where he held the position of Walter J. Matherly Professor of Accounting. Prior to pursuing his doctoral studies, Hilton worked for Peat, Marwick, Mitchell and Company and served as an officer in the United States Air Force.

Professor Hilton is a member of the Institute of Management Accountants and has been active in the American Accounting Association. He has served as associate editor of *The Accounting Review* and as a member of its editorial board. Hilton also has served on the editorial board of the *Journal of Management Accounting Research*. He has been a member of the resident faculties of both the Doctoral Consortium and the New Faculty Consortium sponsored by the American Accounting Association. With wide-ranging research interests, Hilton has published articles in many journals, including the *Journal of Accounting Research, The Accounting Review, Management Science, Decision Sciences*, the *Journal of Economic Behavior and Organization*, *Contemporary Accounting Research*, and the *Journal of Mathematical Psychology*. He also has published a monograph in the *AAA Studies in Accounting Research* series, and he is a co-author of *Cost Management: Strategies for Business Decisions, Budgeting: Profit Planning and Control*, and *Cost Accounting: Concepts and Managerial Applications*. Professor Hilton's current research interests focus on contemporary cost management systems and international issues in managerial accounting. In recent years, he has toured manufacturing facilities and consulted with practicing managerial accountants in North America, Europe, Asia, and Australia.

© Eva Reavley

David E. Platt is the Associate Dean for Undergraduate Programs at the McCombs School of Business, University of Texas at Austin. He earned his BS in Economics from the Wharton School at the University of Pennsylvania, his MBA in Marketing from Syracuse University, and his PhD in Accounting from Cornell University. After earning his CPA while working for Pricewaterhouse Coopers, he spent several years doing financial and product management at a supply chain systems integrator. Dr. Platt currently teaches a variety of managerial accounting courses at UT, including the sophomore-level Fundamentals of Managerial Accounting, and has received teaching awards at both the undergraduate and graduate levels. He directed UT–Austin's Center for International Business Education and Research (CIBER) and has served as a chair of the Partnership in International Management, a consortium of leading graduate business schools worldwide. He has been a visiting lecturer at the Sorbonne Graduate Business School, and has delivered training for companies in the U.S., Europe, Latin America, and China.

How Does Hilton & Platt 11e Prepare Students for the Businesses of Today and Tomorrow?

Managerial Accounting.

Business is always changing: new technologies, new models, new global competitors. And students, despite being more technologically adept every year, need a framework for all of that change so that they can hit the ground running in their careers. To keep up, managers must be able to interpret the rapid flow of information and make the right decisions. Assisted by the tools of managerial accounting, and by managerial accounting professionals, managers will work side by side in global cross-functional teams to make the complex decisions that today's dynamic business environment requires of them. The goal of *Managerial Accounting* is to acquaint students of business with the fundamental tools of managerial decision making and to provide a context for understanding and reacting to the dramatic ways in which business is changing. The emphasis throughout the text is on using accounting information to help manage an organization, while explaining concepts in a way that students can relate to. They should not only be able to produce accounting information, but also understand how managers are likely to use and react to the information in a range of businesses.

"It is a well-written book with numerous well-selected cases, allowing students to see the contemporary business operations and practices in the real world."

—Dennis Hwang, Bloomsburg University

Relevant.

Focus Companies provide a powerful strategy for fostering learning, and the integration of Focus Companies throughout the Hilton & Platt text is unmatched by other managerial accounting books. Each chapter introduces important managerial accounting topics within the context of a realistic company. Students see the immediate impact of managerial accounting decisions on companies and gain exposure to different types of organizations.

"The company story acts as a hook to get students interested in the chapter material."
—Michele Matherly, University of North Carolina at Charlotte

"I like the mix of company types."
—Barbara Durham, University of Central Florida

"Balanced, time-proven approach to managerial accounting."
—Michael Flores, Wichita State University

Balanced.

Hilton & Platt *Managerial Accounting* offers the most balanced coverage of service and manufacturing companies. The authors recognize that students will be working in a great variety of business environments and will benefit from exposure to diverse types of companies. A wide variety of examples from retail, service, manufacturing, and nonprofit organizations are included.

"A nice intro textbook, with multiple perspectives on the behavioral aspects of managerial accounting. Touches many modern issues facing the field."
Theodore Rodgers, Emory University

"Perhaps what sets Hilton & Platt apart from the competition is its recognition that the world consists of more than manufacturing firms and that managerial accounting plays a significant role in service and not-for-profit organizations."
—Lanny Solomon, University of Missouri–Kansas City

Contemporary.

Hilton & Platt continues to be the leader in presenting the most contemporary coverage of managerial accounting topics. The traditional tools of managerial accounting such as budgeting and product costing have been updated with current approaches. Emerging topics such as environmental cost management, monetizing the Internet, and time-driven activity-based costing are also discussed.

"Very current with managerial accounting topics (RFID, . . ., ABC, outsourcing, decision making)."
—Maggie Houston, Wright State University

Flexible.

Managerial Accounting is written in a modular format allowing topics to be covered in the order you want. For example, some instructors prefer to cover contribution-margin approaches to decision making and/or relevant costs early in the course. So Chapter 6 (cost behavior and estimation), Chapter 7 (CVP), and Chapter 14 (relevant costs) are written so they can be covered immediately after Chapter 2, which introduces basic cost concepts. A table showing the text's flexibility is in the Introduction to the Instructor's Manual.

How Does Hilton & Platt 11e Help Students Learn Managerial Accounting in the Context of Business?

FOCUS COMPANIES

Students need to see the relevance of managerial accounting information in order to actively engage in learning the material. Ron Hilton and Dave Platt use their years working as managers and consultants to create Focus Companies that illustrate key concepts, and students immediately see the significance of the material and become excited about the content.

Whenever the Focus Company is presented in the chapter, its logo is shown so the student sees its application to the text topic.

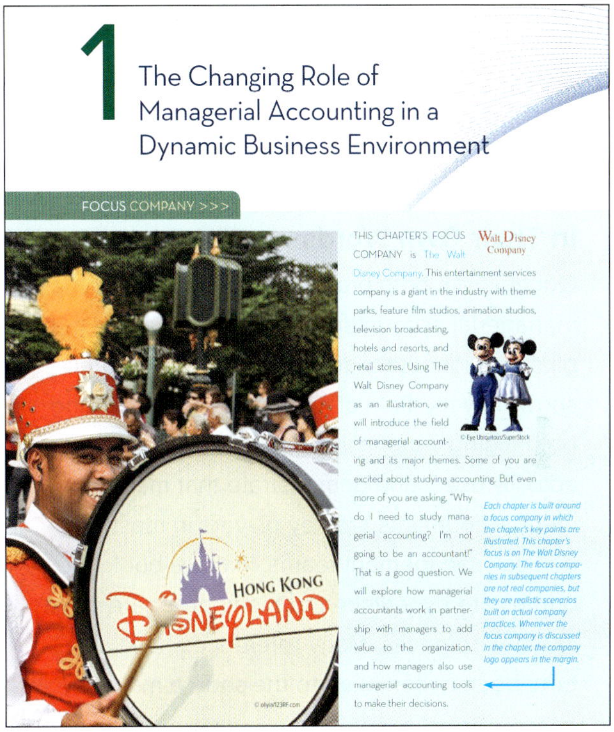

> *"I like the 'Focus on the Company' at the beginning of each chapter and this type of boxed info throughout each chapter."*
>
> —Anna Cianci, Drexel University

CONTRAST COMPANIES

A Contrast Company is also introduced in each chapter. In most cases these highlight an industry different from that of the Focus Company. This feature allows even greater emphasis on service-industry firms and other nonmanufacturing environments. It also helps demonstrate the wide applicability of the managerial accounting techniques being taught.

Real-World Examples

The Hilton & Platt text provides a variety of thought-provoking, real-world examples to focus students on managerial accounting tools and professionals as an essential part of the management process. Featured organizations include Amazon, Ford Motor Company, Southwest Airlines, Whole Foods Market, General Electric, FedEx, and many others. These companies are highlighted in blue in the text.

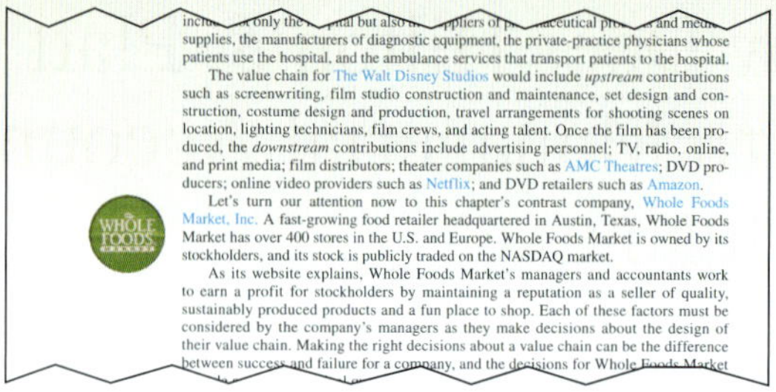
supplies, the manufacturers of diagnostic equipment, the private-practice physicians whose patients use the hospital, and the ambulance services that transport patients to the hospital.

The value chain for The Walt Disney Studios would include *upstream* contributions such as screenwriting, film studio construction and maintenance, set design and construction, costume design and production, travel arrangements for shooting scenes on location, lighting technicians, film crews, and acting talent. Once the film has been produced, the *downstream* contributions include advertising personnel; TV, radio, online, and print media; film distributors; theater companies such as AMC Theatres; DVD producers; online video providers such as Netflix; and DVD retailers such as Amazon.

Let's turn our attention now to this chapter's contrast company, Whole Foods Market, Inc. A fast-growing food retailer headquartered in Austin, Texas, Whole Foods Market has over 400 stores in the U.S. and Europe. Whole Foods Market is owned by its stockholders, and its stock is publicly traded on the NASDAQ market.

As its website explains, Whole Foods Market's managers and accountants work to earn a profit for stockholders by maintaining a reputation as a seller of quality, sustainably produced products and a fun place to shop. Each of these factors must be considered by the company's managers as they make decisions about the design of their value chain. Making the right decisions about a value chain can be the difference between success and failure for a company, and the decisions for Whole Foods Market

"Great graphics, exhibits, and illustrations to keep the computer generation interested."

—Kathy Sevigny, Boston University

In Their Own Words

Quotes from both practicing managers and managerial accountants are included in the margins throughout the text. These actual quotes show how the field of management accounting is changing, emphasize how the concepts are actually used, and demonstrate that management accountants are key players in most companies' management teams. In the e-book, the quotes are hyperlinked to the appropriate point in the References. Many references have, in turn, been hyperlinked to the source material.

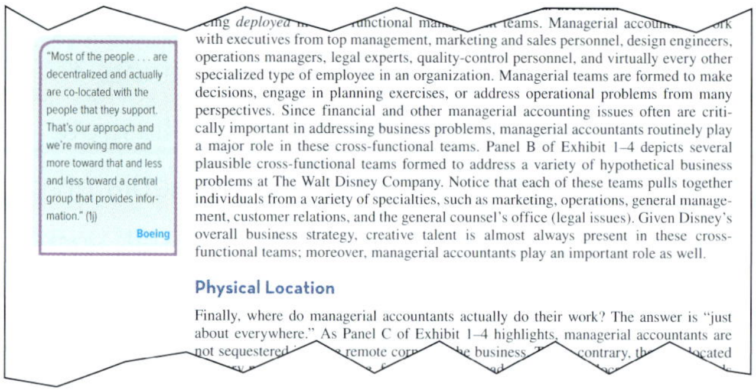
"Most of the people . . . are decentralized and actually are co-located with the people that they support. That's our approach and we're moving more and more toward that and less and less toward a central group that provides information." (1j)

Boeing

with executives from top management, marketing and sales personnel, design engineers, operations managers, legal experts, quality-control personnel, and virtually every other specialized type of employee in an organization. Managerial teams are formed to make decisions, engage in planning exercises, or address operational problems from many perspectives. Since financial and other managerial accounting issues often are critically important in addressing business problems, managerial accountants routinely play a major role in these cross-functional teams. Panel B of Exhibit 1–4 depicts several plausible cross-functional teams formed to address a variety of hypothetical business problems at The Walt Disney Company. Notice that each of these teams pulls together individuals from a variety of specialties, such as marketing, operations, general management, customer relations, and the general counsel's office (legal issues). Given Disney's overall business strategy, creative talent is almost always present in these cross-functional teams; moreover, managerial accountants play an important role as well.

Physical Location

Finally, where do managerial accountants actually do their work? The answer is "just about everywhere." As Panel C of Exhibit 1–4 highlights, managerial accountants are

Management Accounting Practice

The managerial accounting practices of well-known, real-world organizations are highlighted in these boxes. They stimulate student interest and provide a springboard for classroom discussion.

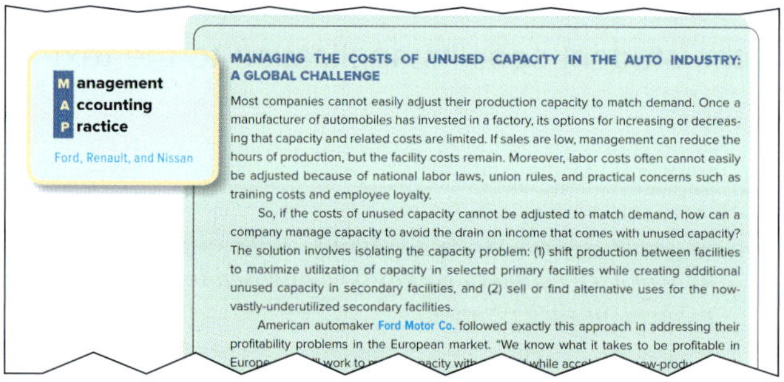
Management Accounting Practice

Ford, Renault, and Nissan

MANAGING THE COSTS OF UNUSED CAPACITY IN THE AUTO INDUSTRY: A GLOBAL CHALLENGE

Most companies cannot easily adjust their production capacity to match demand. Once a manufacturer of automobiles has invested in a factory, its options for increasing or decreasing that capacity and related costs are limited. If sales are low, management can reduce the hours of production, but the facility costs remain. Moreover, labor costs often cannot easily be adjusted because of national labor laws, union rules, and practical concerns such as training costs and employee loyalty.

So, if the costs of unused capacity cannot be adjusted to match demand, how can a company manage capacity to avoid the drain on income that comes with unused capacity? The solution involves isolating the capacity problem: (1) shift production between facilities to maximize utilization of capacity in selected primary facilities while creating additional unused capacity in secondary facilities, and (2) sell or find alternative uses for the now-vastly-underutilized secondary facilities.

American automaker Ford Motor Co. followed exactly this approach in addressing their profitability problems in the European market. "We know what it takes to be profitable in

"Good extras within chapters—ethics at the end of each chapter, MAPs throughout chapter, the Focus vs. In Contrast real world examples."

—Mike Thomas, Humboldt State University

Focus on Ethics

This feature is included in most chapters. Focus on Ethics poses an ethical dilemma, then asks tough questions that underscore the importance of ethical management. Some of these are based on real-world incidents while others are fictional but based on well-established anecdotal evidence.

Focus on Ethics

DID BOEING EXPLOIT ACCOUNTING RULES TO CONCEAL COST OVERRUNS AND PRODUCTION SNAFUS?

Aircraft manufacturers use job-order costing to determine the cost of an airplane. As this chapter discusses, supply chain management and production controls are also important tools used by manufacturers to manage production costs. As *BusinessWeek* reports, however, things don't always go according to plan.

For three years, Boeing's top management had been seeking a merger with McDonnell-Douglas Corporation, whose board of directors was reluctant to approve the deal. Finally, the deal went through, and the world's largest aerospace company was born—"the first manufacturer ever with the ability to build everything that flies, from helicopters and fighter jets to space stations."

Unfortunately, "a disaster was quietly unfolding inside Boeing's sprawling factories—one that would ultimately wind

In May of 2002, *BusinessWeek* reported the results of its three-month investigation, which "reconstructed this hidden chapter in the company's history—and analyzed its current implications." The *BusinessWeek* article alleges that "new details supplied by several inside witnesses indicate that Boeing did more than simply fail to tell investors about its production disaster. It also engaged in a wide variety of aggressive accounting techniques that papered over the mess. Critics say the company should have taken charges for the assembly-line disaster in the first half of 1997, even if it meant jeopardizing the McDonnell merger. They also claim that Boeing took advantage of the unusual flexibility provided by *program accounting*—a system that allows the huge upfront expense of building a plane to be spread out over several years—to cover up cost overruns and to book savings from efficiency initiatives that never panned out. 'Boeing managed its earnings to the point where it got caught,' says Debra A. Smith, a partner at Constraints Management, a Seattle-area manufacturing

How Can My Students Use Hilton & Platt 11e to Master the Concepts of Managerial Accounting?

End-of-Chapter Assignment Material

Each chapter includes an extensive selection of assignment material, including Review Questions, Exercises, Problems, and Cases. Our problem and case material conforms to AECC and AACSB recommendations and facilitates class discussions and projects.

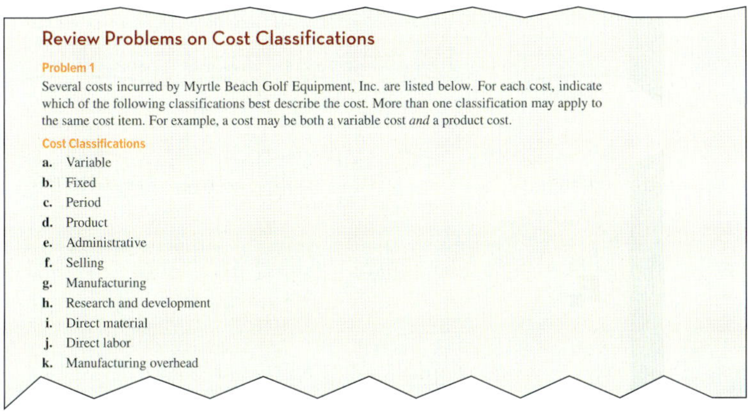

Review Problems on Cost Classifications

Problem 1

Several costs incurred by Myrtle Beach Golf Equipment, Inc. are listed below. For each cost, indicate which of the following classifications best describe the cost. More than one classification may apply to the same cost item. For example, a cost may be both a variable cost *and* a product cost.

Cost Classifications

a. Variable
b. Fixed
c. Period
d. Product
e. Administrative
f. Selling
g. Manufacturing
h. Research and development
i. Direct material
j. Direct labor
k. Manufacturing overhead

Review Problems present both a problem and a complete solution, allowing students to review the entire problem-solving process.

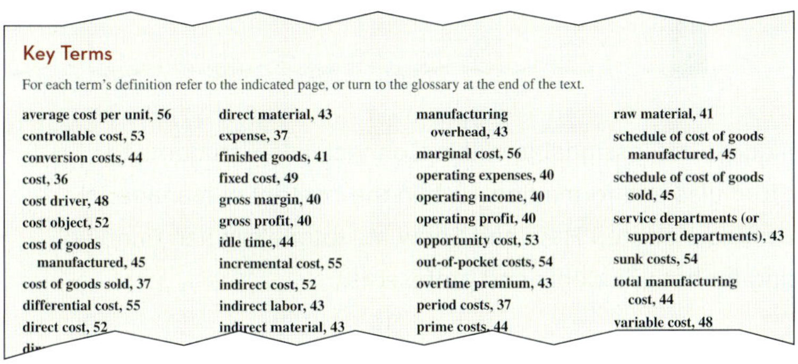

Key Terms

For each term's definition refer to the indicated page, or turn to the glossary at the end of the text.

average cost per unit, 56	**direct material, 43**	**manufacturing overhead, 43**	**raw material, 41**
controllable cost, 53	**expense, 37**	**marginal cost, 56**	**schedule of cost of goods manufactured, 45**
conversion costs, 44	**finished goods, 41**	**operating expenses, 40**	**schedule of cost of goods sold, 45**
cost, 36	**fixed cost, 49**	**operating income, 40**	**service departments (or support departments), 43**
cost driver, 48	**gross margin, 40**	**operating profit, 40**	**sunk costs, 54**
cost object, 52	**gross profit, 40**	**opportunity cost, 53**	**total manufacturing cost, 44**
cost of goods manufactured, 45	**idle time, 44**	**out-of-pocket costs, 54**	**variable cost, 48**
cost of goods sold, 37	**incremental cost, 55**	**overtime premium, 43**	
differential cost, 55	**indirect cost, 52**	**period costs, 37**	
direct cost, 52	**indirect labor, 43**	**prime costs, 44**	
	indirect material, 43		

Key Terms are bolded in the text and linked to their definition in the eBook version. In the print version, they are repeated at the end of the chapter with page references. The book also includes a complete Glossary of Key Terms (fully hyper-linked in the eBook).

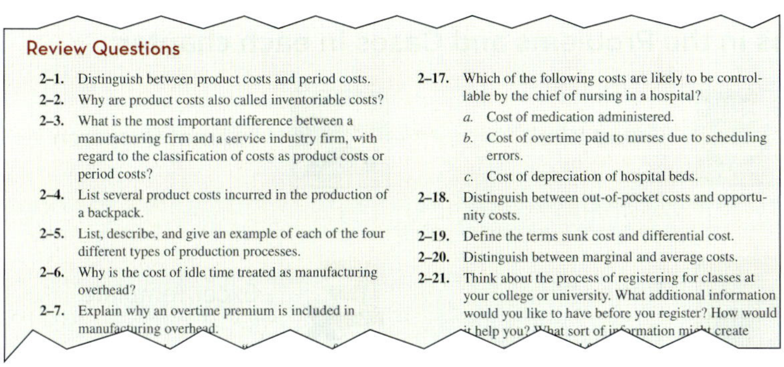

Review Questions

2–1. Distinguish between product costs and period costs.
2–2. Why are product costs also called inventoriable costs?
2–3. What is the most important difference between a manufacturing firm and a service industry firm, with regard to the classification of costs as product costs or period costs?
2–4. List several product costs incurred in the production of a backpack.
2–5. List, describe, and give an example of each of the four different types of production processes.
2–6. Why is the cost of idle time treated as manufacturing overhead?
2–7. Explain why an overtime premium is included in manufacturing overhead.
2–17. Which of the following costs are likely to be controllable by the chief of nursing in a hospital?
a. Cost of medication administered.
b. Cost of overtime paid to nurses due to scheduling errors.
c. Cost of depreciation of hospital beds.
2–18. Distinguish between out-of-pocket costs and opportunity costs.
2–19. Define the terms sunk cost and differential cost.
2–20. Distinguish between marginal and average costs.
2–21. Think about the process of registering for classes at your college or university. What additional information would you like to have before you register? How would it help you? What sort of information might create

Review Questions, Exercises, Problems, and Cases are comprehensive in covering the points in the chapter. They exhibit a wide range of difficulty, and the Instructor's Manual provides guidance for the instructor on the difficulty level and time required for each problem. Numerous adapted CMA and CPA problems are included.

> *"Best selection of problems of any text: a large number of problems, problems at all levels, including many interesting, different problems that challenge students, and often interesting real world applications."*
>
> **—Lynda Thoman, Purdue University**

EXCEL® Spreadsheets Spreadsheet applications are essential to contemporary accounting practice. Students must recognize the power of spreadsheets and know how accounting data are presented in them. Excel applications are discussed where appropriate in the text.

Several exercises and problems in each chapter include an optional requirement for students to **Build a Spreadsheet** to develop the solution.

> *"Use of spreadsheets [is a strength]."*
> —Ralph Greenberg, Temple University

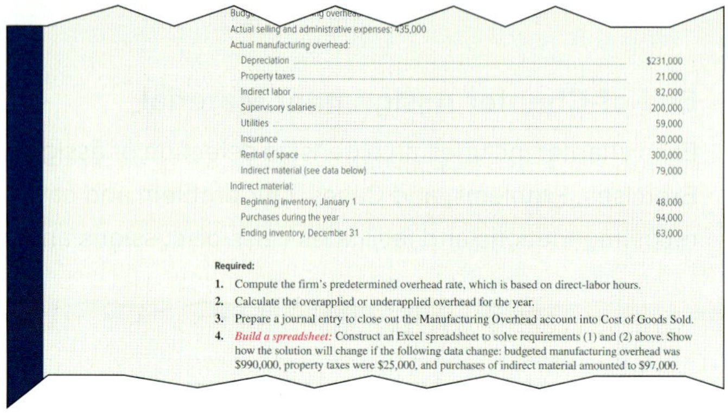

Actual selling and administrative expenses: 435,000

Actual manufacturing overhead:

Depreciation	$231,000
Property taxes	21,000
Indirect labor	82,000
Supervisory salaries	200,000
Utilities	59,000
Insurance	30,000
Rental of space	300,000
Indirect material (see data below)	79,000
Indirect material:	
Beginning inventory, January 1	48,000
Purchases during the year	94,000
Ending inventory, December 31	63,000

Required:

1. Compute the firm's predetermined overhead rate, which is based on direct-labor hours.
2. Calculate the overapplied or underapplied overhead for the year.
3. Prepare a journal entry to close out the Manufacturing Overhead account into Cost of Goods Sold.
4. *Build a spreadsheet:* Construct an Excel spreadsheet to solve requirements (1) and (2) above. Show how the solution will change if the following data change: budgeted manufacturing overhead was $990,000, property taxes were $25,000, and purchases of indirect material amounted to $97,000.

Many problems can be solved using the Excel spreadsheet templates found in Connect. An Excel logo appears in the margin next to these problems for easy identification.

> *"Good description of managerial accounting tools. Easy to read and understand. Strength is in the end-of-chapter problems—good variety and lots of them."*
> —Priscilla Wisner, Thunderbird School of Global Management

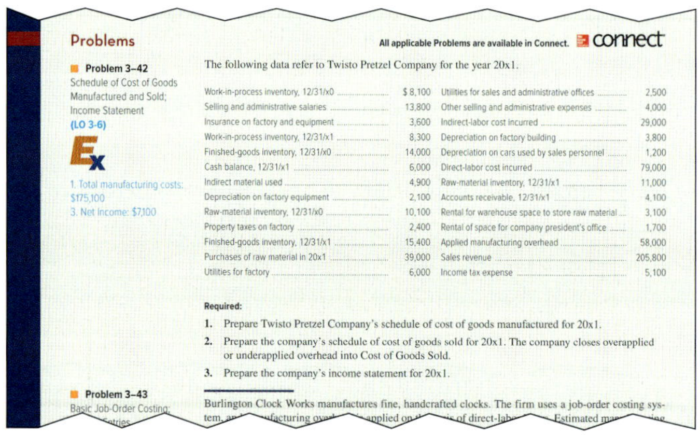

Problems

All applicable Problems are available in Connect. connect

Problem 3–42
Schedule of Cost of Goods Manufactured and Sold; Income Statement
(LO 3-6)

1. Total manufacturing costs: $175,100
3. Net income: $7,100

The following data refer to Twisto Pretzel Company for the year 20x1.

Work-in-process inventory, 12/31/x0	$ 8,100	Utilities for sales and administrative offices	2,500
Selling and administrative salaries	13,800	Other selling and administrative expenses	4,000
Insurance on factory and equipment	3,600	Indirect-labor cost incurred	29,000
Work-in-process inventory, 12/31/x1	8,300	Depreciation on factory building	3,800
Finished-goods inventory, 12/31/x0	14,000	Depreciation on cars used by sales personnel	1,200
Cash balance, 12/31/x1	6,000	Direct-labor cost incurred	79,000
Indirect material used	4,900	Raw-material inventory, 12/31/x1	11,000
Depreciation on factory equipment	2,100	Accounts receivable, 12/31/x1	4,100
Raw-material inventory, 12/31/x0	10,100	Rental for warehouse space to store raw material	3,100
Property taxes on factory	2,400	Rental of space for company president's office	1,700
Finished-goods inventory, 12/31/x1	15,400	Applied manufacturing overhead	58,000
Purchases of raw material in 20x1	39,000	Sales revenue	205,800
Utilities for factory	6,000	Income tax expense	5,100

Required:

1. Prepare Twisto Pretzel Company's schedule of cost of goods manufactured for 20x1.
2. Prepare the company's schedule of cost of goods sold for 20x1. The company closes overapplied or underapplied overhead into Cost of Goods Sold.
3. Prepare the company's income statement for 20x1.

Problem 3–43
Basic Job-Order Costing;

Burlington Clock Works manufactures fine, handcrafted clocks. The firm uses a job-order costing sys-

NEW! Excel Simulations Simulated Excel questions, assignable within Connect, allow students to practice their Excel skills—such as basic formulas and formatting—within the content of managerial accounting. These questions feature animated, narrated Help and Show Me tutorials (when enabled), as well as automatic feedback and grading for both students and professors.

Icons identify key business areas in the Problems and Cases in each chapter:

Ethical Issues

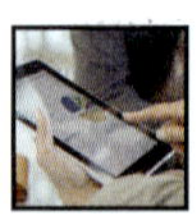
Group Work

Internet Research

International Setting

Business Communication

Excel Template

What's New in the 11th Edition?

New and Updated Companies and Content

Chapter 3, which introduces product costing, features a new focus company, Blue River Paddle Boards. This company produces recreational water sports products and continues the authors' commitment to keeping the example companies fresh and relevant for students.

Chapter 5, on activity-based costing (ABC), introduces time-driven activity-based costing via that chapter's contrast company, Immunity Medical Center. The use of a health care organization shows how this important topic extends beyond manufacturing into one of today's most important and high-profile industries. In addition, it continues the text's leadership in providing in-depth examples showing the applicability of managerial accounting outside of manufacturing.

We also incorporated the topic of "big data" into the text. The challenges and opportunities of big data, though in large part beyond the scope of this text, are introduced to provide students with greater perspective on the origins and analysis of data for decision making, and hopefully to alert them to the relevance of a topic they will encounter in subsequent courses. The challenges and opportunities of big data are summarized in Chapter 6, and an example of its relevance to activity-based costing is provided in a MAP (Management Accounting Practice) box in Chapter 5.

Updated Pedagogy

Many chapters include revisions of pedagogy, streamlined and condensed explanations, and the addition of more current examples and references from the popular business press. In the prior edition, we enhanced budgeting pedagogy by placing it first into a nonmanufacturing setting before subsequently addressing the complexities of the manufacturing environment. In an analogous fashion, in Chapter 5 of the 11th edition we begin activity-based costing in the manufacturing setting where it is most easily understood, after which we use the specific version of ABC called time-driven ABC to show how the technique applies in a service environment (health care).

End-of-Chapter Assignment Material

The end-of-chapter assignment material has been heavily revised. Virtually all of the quantitative exercises, problems, and cases contain data different from that used in the 10th edition. In addition, the authors updated many of the products and services produced by the companies featured both in the text and in the assignment material. In the e-book, the Key Figures that are provided for most Problems and Cases in the text have been integrated as "poptips," remaining hidden until the student clicks on a small icon to pop up the answer that is selectively provided to help students make sure they are on the right track.

Service Industry Examples

Despite the recent resurgence in U.S. manufacturing, the service industry continues to play a dominant role in the economy. As noted above regarding Companies and Pedagogy, the authors have continued their track record of finding and integrating examples from service industry organizations. Widely acknowledged as having the most service industry focus of any managerial accounting text, the 11th edition widens the margin even further.

In Their Own Words

The authors continually work to update many of the quotations in this popular feature, keeping them fresh and relevant for today's students. Many of the quotations are new in this edition. These quotes from practicing managers and managerial accountants portray the important role managerial accounting plays in today's dynamic business environment.

Management Accounting Practice (MAPs)

Many of these real-world examples have been revised and updated to make them more current, and several new examples have been added. For example, in Chapter 2 the Affordable Care Act has been included in a MAP to connect this cutting-edge topic to managing health care costs.

Your feedback is crucial in improving each new edition of *Managerial Accounting.* In response to your suggestions, you will find revised coverage of key topical areas, new pedagogy for the most challenging topics, and new assignment material in the 11th edition.

Instructor Supplements

Assurance of Learning Ready Many educational institutions today are focused on the notion of assurance of learning, an important element of some accreditation standards. Hilton & Platt *Managerial Accounting,* 11e is designed specifically to support your assurance of learning initiatives with a simple, yet powerful, solution. Each test bank question for *Managerial Accounting,* 11e maps to a specific chapter learning outcome/objective listed in the text. You can use our test bank software and Connect to easily query for learning outcomes/objectives that directly relate to the learning objectives for your course. You can then use the reporting features of Connect to aggregate student results in similar fashion, making the collection and presentation of assurance of learning data simple and easy.

AACSB Statement McGraw-Hill Education is a proud corporate member of AACSB International. Recognizing the importance and value of AACSB accreditation, we have sought to recognize the curricula guidelines detailed in AACSB standards for business accreditation by connecting selected questions in Hilton & Platt *Managerial Accounting* 11e with the general knowledge and skill guidelines found in the AACSB standards. The statements contained in Hilton & Platt 11e are provided only as a guide for the users of this text. The AACSB leaves content coverage and assessment clearly within the realm and control of individual schools, the mission of the school, and the faculty. The AACSB charges schools with the obligation of doing assessment against their own content and learning goals. While Hilton & Platt 11e and its teaching package make no claim of any specific AACSB qualification or evaluation, we have labeled selected questions according to the six general knowledge and skills areas. The labels or tags within Hilton & Platt 11e are as indicated. There are, of course, many more within the test bank, the text, and the teaching package which might be used as a "standard" for your course. However, the labeled questions are suggested for your consideration.

connect Connect houses all the instructor resources you need to administer your course, including:

- Solutions Manual
- Test Bank
- Instructor PowerPoint® slides
- Instructor's Manual
- Excel Spreadsheet Solutions
- Supplementary Chapter Solutions

> *"The available website accompanying the text offers some challenging and helpful aids for students."*
> **—Melvin Houston, Wayne State University**

Instructor's Manual This comprehensive manual includes step-by-step, explicit instructions on how the text can be used to implement alternative teaching methods. It also provides guidance for instructors who use the traditional lecture method. The guide includes lesson plans and demonstration problems with student work papers, as well as solutions.

Solutions Manual Prepared by the authors, the solutions manual contains complete solutions to all the text's end-of-chapter review questions, exercises, problems, and cases. The solutions manual also includes a discussion of the issues in each of the chapter-by-chapter Focus on Ethics pieces.

Excel Spreadsheet Templates This resource includes solutions to spreadsheet problems found in the text end-of-chapter material.

PowerPoint Presentations A complete set of Instructor PowerPoints follows the chapter-by-chapter content.

Test Bank This test bank contains multiple choice questions, essay questions, and short problems. Each test item is coded for level of diffculty, learning objective, AACSB, AICPA, and Bloom's.

McGraw-Hill Education **connect**®

Required=Results

McGraw-Hill Connect®
Learn Without Limits

Connect is a teaching and learning platform that is proven to deliver better results for students and instructors.

Connect empowers students by continually adapting to deliver precisely what they need, when they need it, and how they need it, so your class time is more engaging and effective.

73% of instructors who use **Connect** require it; instructor satisfaction **increases** by 28% when **Connect** is required.

Connect's Impact on Retention Rates, Pass Rates, and Average Exam Scores

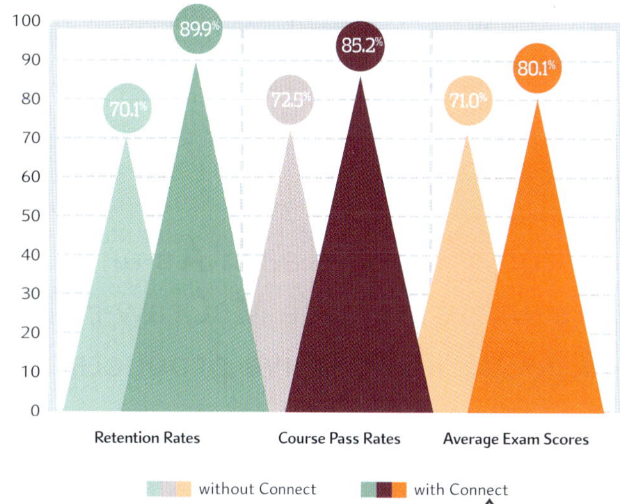

Using Connect improves passing rates by **12.7%** and retention by **19.8%.**

Analytics

Connect Insight®

Connect Insight is Connect's new one-of-a-kind visual analytics dashboard that provides at-a-glance information regarding student performance, which is immediately actionable. By presenting assignment, assessment, and topical performance results together with a time metric that is easily visible for aggregate or individual results, Connect Insight gives the user the ability to take a just-in-time approach to teaching and learning, which was never before available. Connect Insight presents data that helps instructors improve class performance in a way that is efficient and effective.

Impact on Final Course Grade Distribution

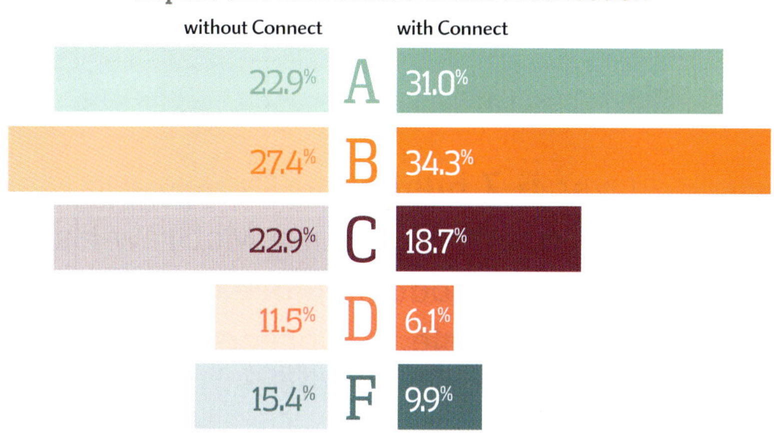

Acknowledgments

We Are Grateful

We would like to express our appreciation to the many people who have provided assistance in the development of this textbook. First, our gratitude goes to the thousands of managerial accounting students we have had the privilege to teach over many years. Their enthusiasm, comments, and questions have challenged us to clarify our thinking about many topics in managerial accounting.

Second, we express our sincere thanks to the following professors who provided extensive reviews and contributions for this and prior editions:

Dr. Kathie J. Shaffer, CMA, *Frostburg State University*
Linda Brown, *St. Ambrose University*
Russell Calk, *New Mexico State University*
Chiaho Chang, *Montclair State University*
Anna Cianci, *Drexel University*
Deb Cosgrove, *University of Nebraska at Lincoln*
William Eichenauer, *Northwest State Community College*
Amanda Farmer, *University of Georgia*
Leslie Fletcher, *Georgia Southern University*
Waqar Ghani, *Saint Joseph's University*
Marybeth Govan, *Sinclair Community College*
Ralph Greenberg, *Temple University*
Rochelle Greenberg, *Florida State University*
Maggie Houston, *Wright State University*
Melvin Houston, *Wayne State University*
Dennis Hwang, *Bloomsburg University*
Mike Metzcar, *Indiana Wesleyan University*
Christa Morgan, *Georgia Perimeter College*
Karl Putnam, *University of Texas at El Paso*
Theodore Rodgers, *Emory University*
Casey Rowe, *Purdue University, West Lafayette*
Angela Sandberg, *Jacksonville State University*
Kathleen Sevigny, *Boston College*
Lynda Thoman, *Purdue University*
Michael Thomas, *Humboldt State University*
John C. Anderson, *San Diego State University*
Jeffrey Archambault, *Marshall University*
Florence Atiase, *University of Texas at Austin*
Rowland Atiase, *University of Texas at Austin*
Ben Baker, *Davidson College*
K. R. Balachandran, *Stern School of Business, New York University*
Frederick Bardo, *Shippensburg University*
Joseph Beams, *University of New Orleans*
Michael Blue, *Bloomsburg University*
Linda Bowen, *University of North Carolina*
Richard Brody, *University of New Haven*
Wayne Bremser, *Villanova University*
Richard Campbell, *University of Rio Grande*
Gyan Chandra, *Miami University*
Marilyn Ciolino, *Delgado Community College*
Paul Copley, *James Madison University*
Maureen Crane, *California State University, Fresno*
Stephen Dempsey, *University of Vermont*
Patricia Derrick, *George Washington University*
Martha Doran, *San Diego State University*
Allan Drebin, *Northwestern University*
Barbara Durham, *University of Central Florida*
James Emig, *Villanova University*
Robert Eskew, *Purdue University*
Andrew Felo, *Pennsylvania State University at Great Valley*
Michael Flores, *Wichita State University*
Kimberly Frank, *University of Nevada at Las Vegas*
Alan Friedberg, *Florida Atlantic University*
Steve G. Green, *United States Air Force Academy*
Edward Goodhart, *Shippensburg University*
Denise Guithues Amrhein, *Saint Louis University*
Sueann Hely, *West Kentucky Community & Technical College*
Susan B. Hughes, *University of Vermont*
Paul Juras, *Wake Forest University*
Sherrie Koechling, *Lincoln University*
Stacey Konesky, *Kent State University*
Christy Larkin, *Bacone College*
James Lasseter, Jr. *University of South Florida*
Angelo Luciano, *Columbia College*
Lois Mahoney, *Eastern Michigan University*
Ana Marques, *University of Texas at Austin*
Scott Martens, *University of Minnesota*
Maureen Mascha, *Marquette University*
Michele Matherly, *University of North Carolina at Charlotte*
Harrison McCraw, *State University of West Georgia*
Sanjay Mehrotra, *Northwestern University*
Jamshed Mistry, *Worcester Polytechnic Institute*
Hamid Mohammadi, *St. Xavier University*
Cynthia Nye, *Bellevue University*
Marilyn Okleshen, *Minnesota State University*
Mohamed Onsi, *Syracuse University*
Samuel Phillips, *Shenandoah University*
Thomas H. Ramsey, *Wake Forest University*
Frederick Rankin, *Washington University*
Roy Regel, *University of Montana at Missoula*
Laura Rickett, *Kent State University*
Don Samelson, *Colorado State University*
Angela Sandberg, *Jacksonville State University*
Rebecca Sawyer, *University of North Carolina at Wilmington*
Pamela Schwer, *St. Xavier University*
Thomas Selling, *Thunderbird, The Garvin School of International Management*
Lanny Solomon, *University of Missouri at Kansas City*
Wendy Tietz, *Kent State University*
Ralph Tower, *Wake Forest University*
Mark Turner, *Stephen F. Austin State University*
Michael Tyler, *Barry University*
Bill Wempe, *Texas Christian University*
James Williamson, *San Diego State University*
Priscilla Wisner, *Thunderbird, The Garvin School of International Management*
Richard Young, *Ohio State University*

We want to thank *Beth Woods, Ilene Persoff and Helen Roybark* for their thorough checking of the content and solutions manual for accuracy and completeness.

The supplements are a great deal of work to prepare. We appreciate the efforts of those who developed them, since these valuable aids make teaching the course easier for everyone who uses the text. Thank you to *Luann Bean,* Florida Institute of Technology; *Julie Hankins,* User Euphoria; *Patti Lopez,* Valencia College; *Ilene Persoff,* Long Island University; *Dr. Kay Poston,* Francis Marion University*; Dr. Helen Roybark, Ph.D., CPA, CFE,* Radford University; *Linda Schain,* Hofstra University*; Debbie Schmidt-Johnson,* Cerritos College*;* and *Beth Woods* for their contributions to the ancillary products.

We are indebted to *Professors Roland Minch, Michael Maher,* and *David Solomons* for allowing the use of their case materials in the text. The source for the actual company information in Chapters 1 and 2 regarding The Walt Disney Company, Whole Foods Market, Caterpillar, Walmart, and Southwest Airlines is the companies' published annual reports and other public materials available on their company websites.

Finally, we wish to express our gratitude to the fine people at McGraw-Hill who so professionally guided this book through the publication process. In particular, we wish to acknowledge *Tim Vertovec, Pat Plumb, Erin Quinones, Pat Frederickson, Brian Nacik, Kristine Tibbetts, Cheryl Osgood, Debra Kubiak,* and *Daryl Horrocks.*

Ronald W. Hilton

David E. Platt

Focus Company and Contrast Company Used in Each Chapter

Chapter Title	Focus Company	Focus Company Logo	Focus Company Industry	Contrast Company
1. The Changing Role of Managerial Accounting in a Dynamic Business Environment	The Walt Disney Company	Walt Disney Company	Entertainment company	Whole Foods Market, Inc. (grocery retailer)
2. Basic Cost Management Concepts	Comet Computer; Southwest Airlines, Walmart, and Caterpillar	Comet Cometcomp.com	Computer manufacturer with heavy reliance on Internet sales; airline, retailer, and manufacturer, respectively	Midas, Inc. (automotive service company)
3. Product Costing and Cost Accumulation in a Batch Production Environment	Blue River Paddle Boards	Blue River PADDLE BOARDS	Manufacturer of stand-up paddle boards and related equipment	Small World Advertising (Ad and Public Relations Firm)
4. Process Costing and Hybrid Product-Costing Systems	MVP Sports, Wisconsin Division	MVP Sports Equipment Company	Manufacturer of baseball gloves	MVP Sports, Minnesota Division
5. Activity-Based Costing and Management	Patio Grill Company	Patio Grill company	Manufacturer of gas barbeque grills	Immunity Medical Center (health care services)
6. Activity Analysis, Cost Behavior, and Cost Estimation	Donut Desire	DONUT DESIRE	Food service; donut shops in Toronto, Ontario, Canada	Constellation Communications Technology (satellite manufacturer)
7. Cost-Volume-Profit Analysis	Seattle Contemporary Theater	SEATTLE CONTEMPORARY THEATER	Nonprofit arts organization	Digital: Time (digital clock manufacturer)
8. Variable Costing and the Costs of Quality and Sustainability	FitDat.com	fit dat	Designer and manufacturer of fitness monitors	FitDat.com (manufacturer)
9. Financial Planning and Analysis: The Master Budget	Snowcap Music Festivals	Snowcap Music Festivals	Producer of music festivals	FestiChair.com (manufacturer and Internet retailer)

Focus Company and Contrast Company Used in Each Chapter

Chapter Title	Focus Company	Focus Company Logo	Focus Company Industry	Contrast Company
10. Standard Costing and Analysis of Direct Costs	DCdesserts.com		Producer of fresh fancy desserts, with complete reliance on e-commerce for both sales and purchasing	Forest Home National Bank (financial services company)
11. Flexible Budgeting and Analysis of Overhead Costs	DCdesserts.com		Producer of fresh fancy desserts, with complete reliance on e-commerce for both sales and purchasing	Upstate Auto Rentals (vehicle rental services company)
12. Responsibility Accounting, Operational Performance Measures, and the Balanced Scorecard	Aloha Hotels and Resorts		Hotel chain	Forest Home National Bank (financial services company)
13. Investment Centers and Transfer Pricing	Suncoast Food Centers		Retail grocery chain	Food Processing Division (food processor)
14. Decision Making: Relevant Costs and Benefits	Worldwide Airways		Airline company	International Chocolate Company (chocolate manufacturer)
15. Target Costing and Cost Analysis for Pricing Decisions	Sydney Sailing Supplies		Manufacturer of sailboats in Sydney, Australia	Marine Services Division (marina contractor)
16. Capital Expenditure Decisions	City of Mountainview		City government	High Country Department Stores (retailer)
17. Allocation of Support Activity Costs and Joint Costs	Riverside Clinic		Health care provider	International Chocolate Company (chocolate manufacturer)

Brief Contents

Contents photo credits:
Chapter 1, © Eye Ubiquitous/SuperStock;
Chapter 2, © Robert Mora/Alamy RF;
Chapter 3, © SpaceExpert/Shutterstock.com RF;
Chapter 4, © Photodisc/Getty Images RF;
Chapter 5, © Ingram Publishing/SuperStock RF;
Chapter 6, © Photodisc/PunchStock RF;
Chapter 7, © Ingram Publishing/Alamy RF;
Chapter 8, © Haiyin Wang/Alamy RF;
Chapter 9, © phaitoons/Getty Images RF;
Chapter 10, © Iconotec/Glow Images RF;
Chapter 11, © Yvonne Duivenvoorden/Getty Images RF;
Chapter 12, © PhotoLink/Getty Images RF;
Chapter 13, © Brand X Pictures/PunchStock RF;
Chapter 14, © Ilene MacDonald/Alamy RF;
Chapter 15, © TONO BALAGUER/123RF.com;
Chapter 16, NPS Photo by Robb Hannawacker;
Chapter 17, © Siede Preis/Getty Images RF;

Contents

3 Product Costing and Cost Accumulation in a Batch Production Environment 80

4 Process Costing and Hybrid Product-Costing Systems 136

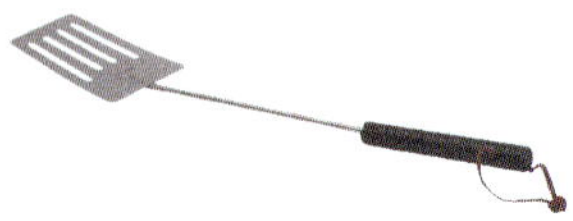

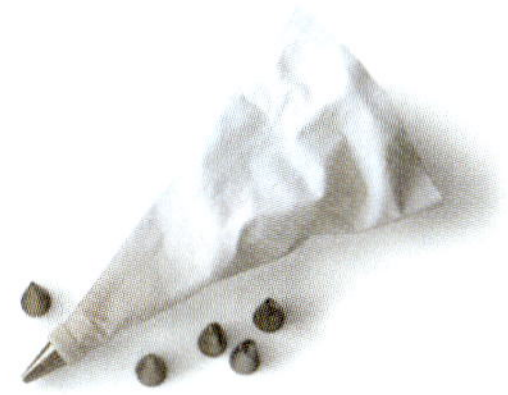

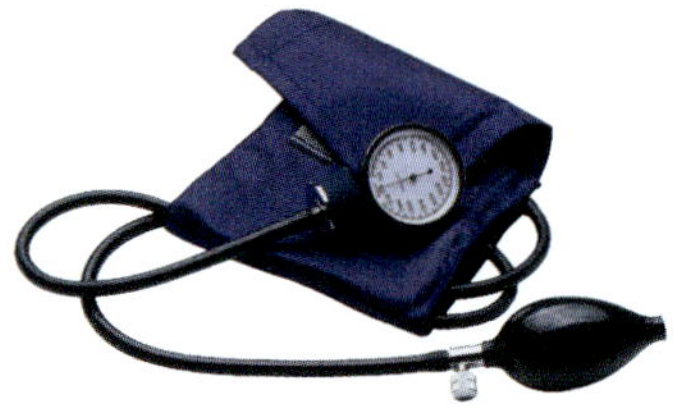

Managerial Accounting

Creating Value in a Dynamic Business Environment

1 The Changing Role of Managerial Accounting in a Dynamic Business Environment

FOCUS COMPANY >>>

© ollyia/123RF.com

Walt Disney Company

THIS CHAPTER'S FOCUS COMPANY is The Walt Disney Company. This entertainment services company is a giant in the industry with theme parks, feature film studios, animation studios, television broadcasting, hotels and resorts, and retail stores. Using The Walt Disney Company as an illustration, we will introduce the field of managerial accounting and its major themes. Some of you are excited about studying accounting. But even more of you are asking, "Why do I need to study managerial accounting? I'm not going to be an accountant!" That is a good question. We will explore how managerial accountants work in partnership with managers to add value to the organization, and how managers also use managerial accounting tools to make their decisions.

© Eye Ubiquitous/SuperStock

Each chapter is built around a focus company in which the chapter's key points are illustrated. This chapter's focus is on The Walt Disney Company. The focus companies in subsequent chapters are not real companies, but they are realistic scenarios built on actual company practices. Whenever the focus company is discussed in the chapter, the company logo appears in the margin.

<<< IN CONTRAST

© Ed Endicott/Alamy

In contrast to the entertainment services setting of The Walt Disney Company, we will turn our attention to Whole Foods Market, Inc. This fast-growing food retailer has over 400 stores around North America and Europe. A leader in the area of corporate social responsibility, Whole Foods Market is frequently faced with challenging decisions that require them to balance the need to run a profitable business and satisfy their investors against the cost of their much-publicized commitment to organic foods and sustainable production. We will explore managerial accounting's contribution to Whole Foods Market's efforts to sell products that are more costly to produce in a competitive market while still achieving appropriate returns for investors.

Each chapter also includes a contrast company. In most cases, the contrast company will present a key chapter topic in an industry that is different from that of the focus company. In this chapter, the focus company (Walt Disney) is an entertainment services company, whereas the contrast company (Whole Foods Market) is a food retailer.

© Scott Olson/Getty Images

After completing this chapter, you should be able to:

Learning Objectives highlight the key topics to be covered in the chapter. They are repeated in the margin of the text where they are discussed. Also, each end-of-chapter assignment lists its learning objectives in the margin.

1-1 Define managerial accounting and describe its role in the management process.

1-2 Explain four fundamental management processes that help organizations attain their goals.

1-3 List and describe five objectives of managerial accounting activity.

1-4 Explain the major differences between managerial and financial accounting.

1-5 Describe the accounting and finance structure in an organization.

1-6 Describe the roles of an organization's chief financial officer (CFO) or controller, treasurer, and internal auditor.

1-7 Understand and explain the value chain concept.

1-8 Explain how investments in capacity affect managerial decision making.

1-9 Discuss the professional organizations and certifications in the field of managerial accounting.

1-10 Describe the ethical responsibilities and ethical standards that apply to managerial accounting.

Many different kinds of organizations affect our daily lives. Manufacturers, retailers, service industry firms, agribusiness companies, nonprofit organizations, and government agencies provide us with a vast array of goods and services. All of these organizations have two things in common. First, every organization has a set of *goals* or objectives. An airline, such as Quantas or Southwest Airlines, might specify profitability and customer service as its goals. The New York Police Department's goals would include public safety and security coupled with cost minimization. Second, in pursuing an organization's goals, managers need *information*. The information needs of management range across financial, production, marketing, legal, and environmental issues. Generally, the larger the organization, the greater management's need for information.

In this chapter, we will explore the role of managerial accounting within the overall management process. In the remaining chapters, we will expand our study by exploring the many concepts and tools used in managerial accounting.

Managerial Accounting: A Business Partnership with Management

Learning Objective 1-1

Define managerial accounting and describe its role in the management process.

Managerial accounting is the process of identifying, measuring, analyzing, interpreting, and communicating information in pursuit of an organization's goals. Managerial accounting is an integral part of the management process, and managerial accountants are important strategic partners in an organization's management team. But note that the actions listed above are not done just by accountants: all managers use the tools of managerial accounting. That is why you are here—even if you are not planning to be an accountant!

An organization's management team seeks to create value for the organization by managing resources, activities, and people to achieve the organization's goals effectively and efficiently. Managerial accounting provides tools and perspectives that help managers accomplish this, and for that reason it is important that every business student study it.

Managerial accountants are specialists in using the tools of managerial accounting to help the organization and its managers run the operation effectively. Their knowledge builds from the material in this textbook to include advanced tools as well as knowledge and techniques specific to a company and its industry.

"We are looked upon as business advisors, more than just accountants, and that has a lot to do with the additional analysis and the forward-looking goals we are setting." (1a)[1]
Caterpillar

The role of managerial accounting is very different now than it was years ago. In the past, managerial accountants were organized into support departments, often physically separated from the managers for whom they provided reports and information. Now, rather than isolate managerial accountants in a separate department, companies usually locate them in the operating departments where they are working with other managers to make decisions and resolve operational problems. Managerial accountants, often carrying the job title of "analyst," take on leadership roles on their teams and are sought out for the valuable information they provide. The role of the accountant in leading-edge companies "has been transformed from number cruncher and financial historian to being business partner and trusted advisor."[2] And the tools of managerial accounting are used by all managers.

Managing Resources, Activities, and People

Walt Disney Company

The owners, directors, or trustees of an organization set its goals, generally with the help of management. For example, The Walt Disney Company's goals are set by its board of directors, who are elected by the company's stockholders. The overall goal of The Walt Disney Company, according to a recent annual report, may be expressed as a commitment to creative excellence and corporate citizenship coupled with strict financial discipline in order to maximize value to the company's shareholders.[3]

Learning Objective 1-2

Explain four fundamental management processes that help organizations attain their goals.

In pursuing its goals, an organization acquires *resources* (for example, funding, patents, and buildings), hires *people,* and then engages in an organized set of *activities.* It is up to the management team to make the best use of the organization's resources, activities, and people in achieving the organization's goals. In trying to accomplish this, the day-to-day work of the management team comprises four activities:

1. Decision making
2. Planning
3. Directing operational activities
4. Controlling

[1]*In Their Own Words* Throughout the text, you will find these quotes from both practicing managers and managerial accountants. Collectively they portray the important role managerial accounting plays in today's dynamic business environment. The references for these quotes appear at the end of the text. The references are organized by chapter; thus reference (1a) relates to the first quote in Chapter 1, and so forth.

[2]Gary Siegel, "The Image of Corporate Accountants," *Strategic Finance* 82, no. 2 (August 2000), p. 71.

[3]The Walt Disney Company, which is discussed in this chapter, is, of course, a real company. However, the subsequent focus organizations around which chapters are built are not real organizations. They are, rather, realistic settings in which to discuss business and managerial accounting issues. In most cases, they are based on real organizations. Similarly, each chapter includes a discussion of a contrast company. Some of these contrast companies, such as food retailer Whole Foods Market, Inc., in this chapter, are real companies. Others, however, are fictitious companies that are based on real organizations. These realistic illustrations and scenarios are intended to help students connect the business and managerial accounting issues discussed in this book to everyday life.

Decision Making

Several years ago, Disney's board of directors decided that one of the company's growth objectives would be to expand its theme park operations in Florida. It was not immediately clear, however, what would be the best way to accomplish that goal. Would it be best to expand one of the company's three existing theme parks—the Magic Kingdom, Epcot, or Disney's Hollywood Studios? Or should the company branch out in an entirely new direction with a brand new theme park attraction? How would each of these alternative courses of action mesh with the company's other goals of bringing the best in creative entertainment to its customers and maintaining sound financial discipline? Disney's top management team had to *make a decision* about the best way to expand the company's Florida operations, which entailed *choosing among the available alternatives.*

Planning

"What I need is someone who can analyze data, see problems and figure out solutions . . . [just doing] debits and credits and financial statements doesn't really help me." (1b)

Tente Casters Inc

In Their Own Words

These quotes are from practicing managers or managerial accountants. The quotes show how various managerial accounting concepts are actually used and that managerial accountants are key players in most companies.

Disney's top management team decided to expand the company's Florida operations by building an entirely new theme park named Disney's Animal Kingdom. Created and designed by Walt Disney's Imagineering Division, this 500-acre theme park would offer guests wide-ranging adventures and tell the fascinating stories of all animals—ancient and present-day, real and imagined. Now the detailed planning phase began. How would the Animal Kingdom's many attractions designed by the Imagineering Division be laid out and organized? What food and beverage operations would be appropriate? How many employees would be needed on a day-to-day basis? What supplies would be required to run the park? How much would electricity and other utilities cost? How much would running the park during a typical year cost? Finally, how should the park's admission be priced given predicted attendance? Disney's management team had to *plan* for running the Animal Kingdom, which meant *developing a detailed financial and operational description of anticipated operations.*

Directing Operational Activities

Now the theme park has been built, equipped, and staffed. How many cashiers should be on duty on Saturday morning? How much food should be ordered each day? How much cash will be needed to meet the payroll, pay the utility bills, and buy maintenance supplies next month? All of these questions fall under the general heading of *directing operational activities,* which means *running the organization on a day-to-day basis.*

Controlling

The theme park has operated for several years now. Is the company's goal being accomplished? More specifically, have the theme park's operations adhered to the plans developed by management for achieving the goal? In seeking to answer these questions, management is engaged in *control,* which means *ensuring that the organization operates in the intended manner and achieves its goals.*

How Managerial Accounting Adds Value to the Organization

Managers need information for all of the managerial activities described in the preceding section. That information comes from a variety of sources, including economists, financial experts, marketing and production personnel, accountants, and the organization's managerial accounting system.

Objectives of Managerial Accounting Activity

Managerial accounting activity comprises a set of tools, systems and perspectives that add value to an organization by supporting five major objectives:

Learning Objective 1-3

List and describe five objectives of managerial accounting activity.

1. Providing information for decision making and planning.
2. Assisting managers in directing and controlling operational activities.
3. Motivating managers and other employees toward the organization's goals.
4. Measuring the performance of activities, subunits, managers, and other employees within the organization.
5. Assessing the organization's competitive position, and working with other managers to ensure the organization's long-run competitiveness in its industry.

Although financial data make up a large part of the inputs and outputs of a managerial accounting system, there is a strong trend toward the presentation of nonfinancial data as well. Managerial accounting systems supply all kinds of information to management in support of management's role in directing the organization's activities. Measuring, managing, and continually improving operational activities are critical to an organization's success. As we will see in subsequent chapters, contemporary managerial accounting systems are focusing more and more on the activities that occur at all levels of the organization.

To illustrate the objectives of managerial accounting activity, let us continue with the example of Disney's Animal Kingdom.

"In five years [we will become] even more strategic. Really understanding the ins and outs of all the organizations, and really trying to be visionary—understanding what is happening to our business." (1c)
Hewlett-Packard

Providing Information for Decision Making and Planning For virtually all major decisions, Disney's management team would rely heavily on managerial accounting information. For example, the *decision* to establish the new theme park would be influenced by estimates of the costs of building the Animal Kingdom and maintaining it throughout its life. The theme park's managers also would rely on managerial accounting data in formulating plans for the park's operations. Prominent in those *plans* would be a budget detailing the projected revenues and costs of providing entertainment.

Because of the complexity and importance of this decision, Disney's managerial accountants were key participants in the management team as decisions were made and plans formulated for the theme park's operations.

"What we're seeing is less transactional and more decision support type of work. More analytical, more . . . option analysis. Looking at the whole spectrum of options in helping management make decisions." (1d)
Boeing

Assisting Managers in Directing and Controlling Operational Activities Directing and controlling day-to-day operations require a variety of data about the process of providing entertainment services. For example, in *directing* operational activities, the park's management team would need data about customer food-service demand patterns in order to make sure appropriate staffing was provided in the theme park's various food venues. In *controlling* operations, management would compare actual costs incurred with those specified in the budget.

Managerial accounting information often assists management through its **attention-directing function.** Managerial accounting reports rarely solve a decision problem. However, managerial accounting information often directs managers' attention to an issue that requires their skills. To illustrate, suppose Disney's Animal Kingdom incurred electricity costs that significantly exceeded the budget. This fact does not explain why the budget was exceeded, nor does it tell management what action to take, but it does direct management's attention to the situation. Suppose that upon further investigation, the accounting records reveal that Disney's electric rates have increased substantially. This information will help management in framing the decision problem. Should steps be taken to conserve electricity? Should they seek out a different electric power provider? Perhaps management should consider investing in a more sophisticated air conditioning system to manage the Florida heat.

Management Accounting Practice

Facebook, Walmart, Amazon, Coursera, and edX

The managerial accounting practices of well-known, real-world organizations are highlighted in these boxes. You'll see how topics in the chapter are actually used. Actual companies are indicated in blue whenever they are referenced.

USING MANAGERIAL ACCOUNTING TO MONETIZE THE INTERNET

Monetizing the Internet means finding a way to generate revenues from users in order to make a profit after the costs of providing the Internet service or content. Creating a successful revenue model is one of the biggest challenges faced by Internet companies. Here are some examples of how companies are using managerial accounting as they try to monetize the Internet.

Facebook

Four months after **Facebook**'s initial public offering (IPO) of its stock on May 18, 2012, with its shares trading more than 50% below their $38 per share initial offering price, investors were demanding answers to a question they had begun asking soon after the IPO: "How will [Facebook] continue to monetize its more than 900 million users on a consistent basis?"[4] Many changes in Facebook's site during the following months were intended to do exactly that, with managerial accountants analyzing the costs and benefits of different courses of action. For example, design changes in March 2013 were intended to "help the company increase monetization by improving its ability to target content to users with increased precision based on 'likes.'"[5] A few years later, Facebook stock was trading for almost three times the IPO price.

Walmart

Walmart was slow to embrace Internet sales because of their investment in bricks-and-mortar stores. But they see an opportunity to use it in conjunction with their stores to provide what competitor **Amazon** cannot. "Customers who buy some of the more than 1.5 million products on **Walmart.com** can have them shipped free to a local Walmart, where new service desks at the front of some stores make it easier for customers to retrieve their stuff."[6] A managerial accounting cost analysis showed the initiative to be profitable, so Walmart is now experimenting with other innovations to take advantage of their retail infrastructure. Still, "Walmart has been repeatedly outgunned and outsmarted by Amazon's price-matching, robot-utilizing, competition-crushing machine," and with just a fraction of Amazon's online presence, the managerial accountants there are going to be busy analyzing initiatives for some time to come.[7]

Higher Education

Many view the Internet as the solution to the high cost of higher education, and companies like **Coursera** and **edX** have sprung up to deliver MOOCs (massive open online courses). While their effectiveness is yet to be proven, their efficiency in bringing content to thousands of users appeals to many. But there is one unsolved problem: even if it proves to be effective, no one has yet figured out how to monetize MOOCs! "All of this could well add up to the future of higher education—if anyone can figure out how to make money."[8]

Motivating Managers and Other Employees Toward the Organization's Goals

Organizations have goals. However, organizations also are made up of people who have goals of their own. The goals of individuals are diverse, and they do not always match

[4]Steven Russolillo and Kaitlyn Kiernan, "MarketBeat: Facebook Shares Fall Below $30," *Wall Street Journal*, May 29, 2012.

[5]Andrew Tonner, "What Does Facebook's Redesign Mean for Investors?" *The Motley Fool*, March 7, 2013, http://www.fool.com/investing/general/2013/03/07/what-does-facebooks-redesign-mean-for-investors.aspx.

[6]M. Bustillo and G. A. Fowler, "Wal-Mart Uses Its Stores To Get an Edge Online," *The Wall Street Journal*, December 15, 2009, p. B1.

[7]Hiroko Tabuchi, "Wal-Mart, Lagging in Online Sales, is Strengthening E-Commerce," *NYTimes.com*, June 5, 2015.

[8]Tamar Lewin, "Students Rush to Web Classes, But Profits May Be Much Later," *New York Times*, January 7, 2013, p. A1.

those of the organization. A key purpose of managerial accounting is to motivate managers and other employees to direct their efforts toward achieving the organization's goals. One means of achieving this purpose is through budgeting. In establishing a budget for Disney's Animal Kingdom, top management indicates how resources are to be allocated and what activities are to be emphasized. When actual operations do not conform to the budget, the managerial accounting system will highlight the deviation from plan, and managerial accounting tools will help the theme park's managers to analyze and explain the reasons for the deviation.

Measuring the Performance of Activities, Subunits, Managers, and Other Employees within the Organization One means of motivating people toward the organization's goals is to measure their performance in achieving those goals. Such measurements then can be used as the basis for rewarding performance through positive feedback, promotions, and pay raises. For example, most large corporations compensate their executives, in part, on the basis of the profit achieved by the subunits they manage. In other organizations, managers are rewarded on the basis of operational measures, such as product quality, sales, or on-time delivery. At Disney's Animal Kingdom, for example, management could be rewarded, in part, on the basis of growth in attendance at the theme park.

In addition to measuring the performance of people, the managerial accounting system measures the performance of an organization's subunits, such as divisions, product lines, geographical territories, and departments. These measurements help the subunits' managers obtain the highest possible performance level in their units. Such measurements also help top management decide whether a particular subunit is a viable economic investment. For example, it may turn out that a particular attraction at Disney's Animal Kingdom is too costly an activity to continue, despite the efforts of a skilled management team.

Assessing the Organization's Competitive Position, and Working with Other Managers to Ensure the Organization's Long-Run Competitiveness in Its Industry The business environment often changes very rapidly. These changes result from global competition, rapidly advancing technology, and improved communication systems, such as social media. The activities that make an enterprise successful today may no longer be sufficient next year. A crucial role of managerial accounting is to continually assess how an organization stacks up against the competition, with an eye toward continuously improving. Among the questions asked in assessing an organization's competitive position are the following:

- How well is the organization doing in its internal operations and business processes?
- How well is the organization doing in the eyes of its customers? Are their needs being served as well as possible?
- How well is the organization doing from the standpoint of innovation, learning, and continuously improving operations? Is the organization a trendsetter that embraces new products, new services, and new technology? Or is it falling behind?
- How well is the organization doing financially? Is the enterprise viable as a continuing entity?

"You want to be on the team. You want to be the business consultant. You want to be thought of as a value-adding department versus just someone who closes the books." (1e)

Qwest
(now part of **CenturyLink**)

The Balanced Scorecard

One example of a managerial accounting tool that is used to assess competitive position and ensure long-run competitiveness is a management framework called the *balanced scorecard*.[9]

---

[9]The balanced scorecard concept was developed by Robert S. Kaplan and David P. Norton. See Robert S. Kaplan and David P. Norton, *The Strategy-Focused Organization: How Balanced Scorecard Companies Thrive in the New Business Environment* (Boston: Harvard Business School Press, 2001).

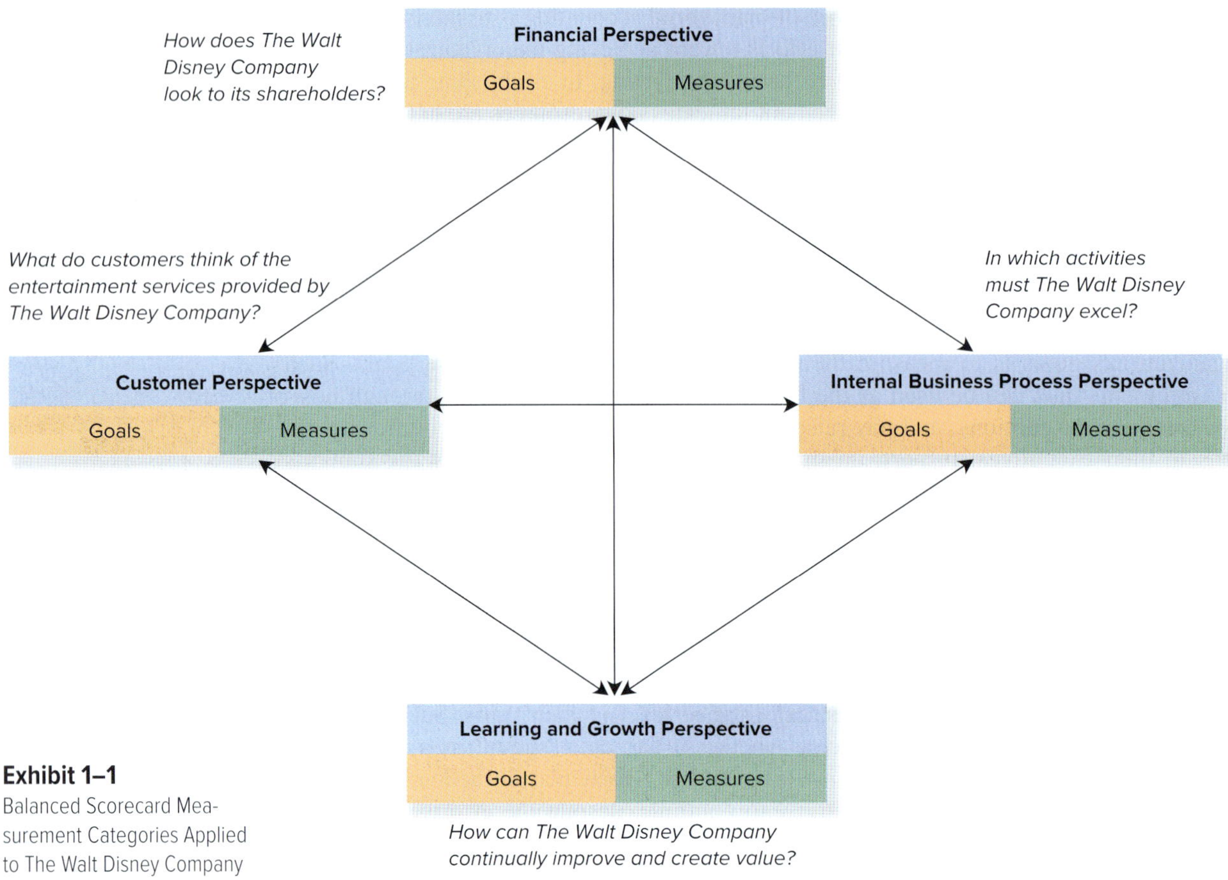

Exhibit 1–1
Balanced Scorecard Measurement Categories Applied to The Walt Disney Company

Depicted in Exhibit 1–1 for The Walt Disney Company, the **balanced scorecard** is a model of business performance evaluation that includes several types of financial and nonfinancial performance measures.

If an organization is to remain viable in a changing and ever more competitive business environment, its managers need to continually ask the questions emphasized in the balanced scorecard. The Walt Disney Company is no exception.

- Disney's management team must be concerned with the quality of the company's business processes as well as its entertainment services.
- Management must continually monitor the needs of its customers and assess their level of satisfaction with the services provided.
- The company's overall financial strength also must be prominent in management's thinking.
- Management must ask if the company possesses the skills it needs to continually adapt as the entertainment industry changes.

The balanced scorecard is an important managerial accounting concept. We will provide an extensive discussion of the balanced scorecard in Chapter 12.

Managerial Accounting in Different Types of Organizations

Organizations need information the way humans need food: without this basic fuel, they cannot sustain the activities that make them vital. This is true whether they are profit-seeking or nonprofit enterprises and regardless of the activities they pursue.

As a result, managerial accounting information is vital in all types of organizations. Ford (manufacturing), J.Crew (retail), GoDaddy.com (Internet), American Airlines (transportation), Marriott Hotels (tourism), Goldman Sachs (financial services), The University of Texas (education), The American Red Cross (nonprofit), M. D. Anderson Cancer Center (health care), and the U.S. Department of Defense (government) all have managerial accountants who provide information to management. Moreover, the five basic purposes of managerial accounting activity are relevant in each of these organizations, and all managers in those companies and industries are using managerial accounting tools.

"[A CFO should] be a strategic partner to the chief executive officer and the business . . . For CFOs of high-growth tech companies, the key is managing growth and balancing growth and profitability." (1f)

Trulia Inc.

Managerial versus Financial Accounting

Learning Objective 1-4

Explain the major differences between managerial and financial accounting.

Take another look at the major objectives of managerial accounting activity. Notice that the focus in each of these objectives is on *managers*. Thus, the focus of *managerial accounting* is on the needs of managers *within* the organization, rather than interested parties outside the organization.

Financial accounting, by contrast, is the use of accounting information for reporting to parties outside the organization. The annual report distributed by McDonald's Corporation or Facebook to its stockholders is an example of the output from a financial accounting system. Users of financial accounting information include current and prospective stockholders, lenders, investment analysts, unions, consumer groups, and government agencies.

There are many similarities between managerial accounting information and financial accounting information because they both draw upon data from an organization's core *accounting system*. This is the system of procedures, personnel, and computers used to accumulate and store financial data in the organization. One part of the overall accounting system is the **cost accounting system,** which accumulates data about the costs of producing goods and services. These data are used in both managerial and financial accounting. For example, production cost data typically are used in helping managers evaluate the pricing of different products or services, which is a managerial accounting use. However, production cost data also are used to value inventory on a manufacturer's balance sheet, which is a financial accounting use.

Exhibit 1–2 depicts the relationships among an organization's core accounting system, its cost accounting system, and uses of the data for managerial accounting and financial accounting purposes. Although similarities do exist between managerial and financial accounting, the differences are even greater. Exhibit 1–3 lists the most important differences.

Where Do We Find Managerial Accountants in an Organization?

Learning Objective 1-5

Describe the accounting and finance structure in an organization.

As we discussed earlier, every manager must have an understanding of basic managerial accounting concepts and tools. However, complex decisions such as the one to open Disney's Animal Kingdom usually receive the support of expert managerial accountants. To have a good understanding of where these experts can be found in a large organization, we must answer three questions:

- Where are managerial accountants *located in an organization chart?*
- How are managerial accountants *deployed to support decision making?*
- In what *physical location* do managerial accountants actually do their work?

Although most business schools have separate departments dedicated to teaching the skills of accounting and finance, in companies accounting and finance personnel are often part of the same organizational units. Take a look at Exhibit 1–4, which portrays the

Exhibit 1–2
Managerial Accounting, Financial Accounting, and Cost Accounting

Accounting System
(one part of the organization's management information system)

Accumulates data for use in both financial and managerial accounting

Cost Accounting System
(one part of the organization's overall accounting system)

Accumulates cost information

Managerial Accounting
Information for decision making, planning, directing, and controlling an organization's operations, and assessing its competitive position

Internal Users of Information
Managers at all levels in the organization

© Purestock/SuperStock RF

Financial Accounting
Published financial statements and other financial reports

External Users of Information
Stockholders, financial analysts, lenders, unions, consumer groups, and governmental agencies

© Royalty-Free/Corbis

Exhibit 1–3
Differences between Managerial and Financial Accounting

	Managerial Accounting	**Financial Accounting**
Users of Information	Managers, *within the organization.*	Interested parties, *outside the organization.*
Regulation	*Not required* and *unregulated,* since it is intended only for management.	*Required* and must conform to generally accepted accounting principles. *Regulators* include the International Accounting Standards Board, the Financial Accounting Standards Board (U.S.), and the U.S. Securities and Exchange Commission.
Source of Data	The organization's *core accounting system, plus various other sources,* provide financial data as well as nonfinancial data such as product defect rates, quantities of material and labor used in production, occupancy rates in hotels, and average take-off delays in airlines.	Almost exclusively drawn from the organization's *core accounting system,* which accumulates financial information.
Nature of Reports and Procedures	*Reports often focus on subunits* within the organization, such as departments, divisions, geographical regions, or product lines. Based on a combination of historical data, estimates, and projections of future events.	*Published reports focus on the enterprise in its entirety.* Generally consolidated from the reports of geographic or business segment divisions, and based almost exclusively on historical transaction data.

A. Organization Chart for The Walt Disney Company

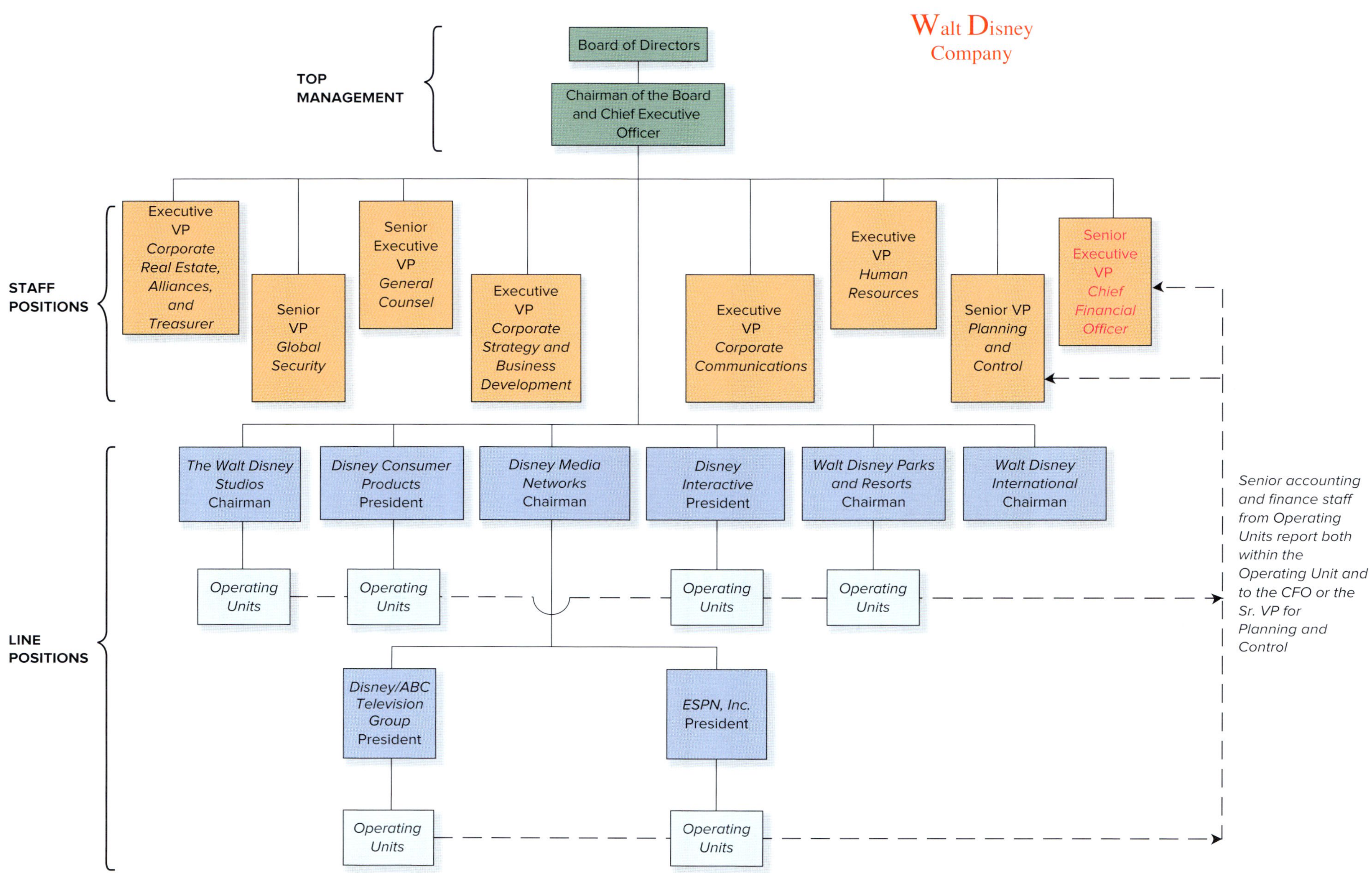

Exhibit 1–4
Managerial Accountants in The Walt Disney Company

Exhibit 1–4 *continued*

B. Deployment of Managerial Accountants in Cross-Functional Management Teams

Hypothetical Planning Team for Disney's Animal Kingdom

Marketing Manager, Walt Disney Parks and Resorts Worldwide	Creative Talent, Walt Disney Imagineering	Operations Manager, Walt Disney World Resort	Managerial Accountants, Walt Disney World Resort

Hypothetical Planning Team for New Attractions at California's Disneyland Resort

Assistant General Manager, Disneyland Resort	Operations Manager, Disneyland Resort	Manager of Customer Relations, Walt Disney Parks and Resorts Worldwide	Creative Talent, Walt Disney Imagineering	Managerial Accountants, Disneyland Resort

Hypothetical Decision-Making Team for a New Line of Disney Products to Be Sold at Disney Stores

Marketing Manager, Disney Consumer Products	Operations Manager, Disney Consumer Products	Creative Talent, Walt Disney Imagineering	Marketing Personnel, Disney Interactive Media Group	Managerial Accountants, Disney Consumer Products

Hypothetical Decision-Making Team for Hotel to Be Built near the Tokyo Disney Resort

Assistant General Manager, Tokyo Disney Resort	Assistant General Manager for Disney Yacht Club Resort at Walt Disney World	Creative Talent, Walt Disney Imagineering	Staff Lawyers, Office of the General Counsel	Managerial Accountants, Walt Disney Parks and Resorts Worldwide and Tokyo Disney Resort

organization, deployment, and physical location of the accounting and finance organization, including managerial accountants, in The Walt Disney Company.

Organization Chart

"[Managerial accountants] need to be strongly partnered with the line management. They need to be proactive. They need to have a broad sense of business. It's not strictly accounting. It's looking at the full spectrum and range of business." (1g)
Boeing

First, let's focus on panel A in Exhibit 1-4, which depicts The Walt Disney Company's organization structure.[10] Notice that the company is led by its board of directors, which represent the interests of the company's stockholders. The company's leading executive is its chief executive officer (CEO). The CEO is generally a member of the Board of Directors and sometimes, as is currently the case at Disney, also serves as the chairman of the Board of Directors. Other times, a board member who is not part of company management will hold the position of chairman.

Line and Staff Positions The other positions in Disney's organization chart are of two types: line positions and staff positions. Managers in **line positions** are *directly* involved in the provision of goods or services. For example, Disney's line positions include the president of Disney Consumer Products (producing and selling products

[10]The information for the organization chart comes from *The Walt Disney Company Fact Book*, available at http://thewaltdisneycompany.com/investors/shareholder-information.

Exhibit 1–4 *continued*

C. Managerial Accountants Physically Located Throughout the Enterprise

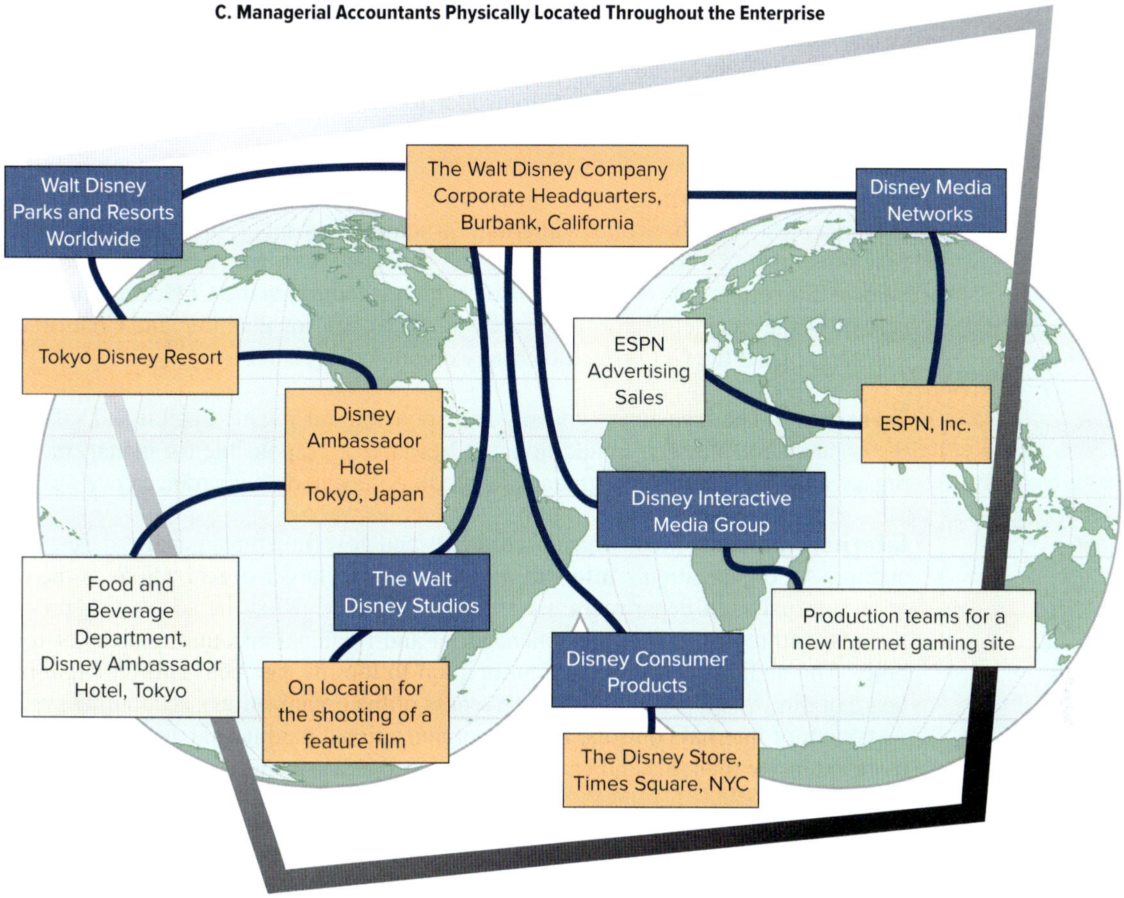

based on the Disney brand and characters), the president of the ESPN sports cable channel, and the chairman of Walt Disney Parks and Resorts (operating Disney's theme parks around the world and its cruise line). Also in line positions would be the thousands of managers in the various operating units of the divisions shown in the organization chart. For example, the general manager of Disney's Animal Kingdom in the Walt Disney World Resort, the production manager for SportsCenter on ESPN, and the manager of the Disney Store in the Mall of America in Minnesota, would all be in line positions.

Managers in **staff positions** supervise activities that support Disney's overall mission, but they are only *indirectly* involved in operational activities. Disney's staff positions include the general counsel, the executive VP for human resources, and the chief financial officer (CFO), among others.

CFO or Controller In many organizations, the designation given to the executive responsible for all accounting and finance functions is the **chief financial officer (CFO).** Sometimes called the **controller** in smaller companies or the **comptroller** in nonprofit or governmental organizations, the CFO is the organization's top managerial and financial accountant. The CFO has responsibility for supervising the accounting and finance specialists throughout the company and for preparing the information and reports used in both managerial and financial accounting. As the organization's chief managerial accountant, the CFO interprets accounting information for line managers and participates as an integral member of the management team. Most CFOs and controllers are involved in planning and decision making at all levels and across all functional areas of the enterprise. This broad role has enabled many managerial accountants to rise to the top of their organizations. Former

Learning Objective 1-6

Describe the roles of an organization's chief financial officer (CFO) or controller, treasurer, and internal auditor.

"One role [of the CFO] is classic finance to focus Intel on driving profits and compliance with all laws world-wide. The other role is to be a sounding board for [the CEO] and other senior managers in terms of our strategies and opportunities." (1h)

Intel Corp.

accountants have served as top executives in such companies as General Motors, Singer, General Electric, and Fruehauf.

In addition to the CFO or controller for the entire corporation, most companies, including The Walt Disney Company, have divisional controllers. Thus, Disney's detailed organization chart would show a controller for Disney/ABC Television Group, Disneyland Paris, The Walt Disney Studios, and so forth.

In recent years, an increasing awareness of the importance of planning, budgeting, and analysis of performance has caused some larger organizations to adopt a variation on the model just described. In this alternate structure, a subset of the managerial accounting functions relating to financial planning and analysis are overseen by a *chief performance analyst*. Sometimes the chief performance analyst reports to the CFO. But often, as in the case of Disney's chief performance analyst, the Sr. VP for Planning and Control, the unit is separate from the CFO (see the Disney organization chart).

"Historically the career path in finance had been very linear across the traditional finance roles. . . . It's not linear anymore." (1i)

IBM

Treasurer The **treasurer** typically is responsible for raising capital and safeguarding the organization's assets. In addition, the treasurer is responsible for management of the organization's cash and investments, its credit policy, and its insurance coverage.

Internal Auditor Most large corporations and governmental agencies have an internal auditor. An organization's **internal auditor,** who in larger organizations is the director of an internal audit department, is responsible for reviewing the accounting procedures, records, and reports in both the managerial and financial accounting areas of responsibility. The auditor then expresses an opinion to top management and the organization's board of directors regarding the effectiveness of the organization's accounting system and its system of internal controls. In some organizations, the internal auditor's role is much more extensive than this and can include a broad assessment of company operations.

Cross-Functional Deployment

On a formal organization chart, accountants generally are in a staff capacity, as explained in the preceding section. However, managerial accountants are increasingly being *deployed* in cross-functional management teams. Managerial accountants work with executives from top management, marketing and sales personnel, design engineers, operations managers, legal experts, quality-control personnel, and virtually every other specialized type of employee in an organization. Managerial teams are formed to make decisions, engage in planning exercises, or address operational problems from many perspectives. Since financial and other managerial accounting issues often are critically important in addressing business problems, managerial accountants routinely play a major role in these cross-functional teams. Panel B of Exhibit 1–4 depicts several plausible cross-functional teams formed to address a variety of hypothetical business problems at The Walt Disney Company. Notice that each of these teams pulls together individuals from a variety of specialties, such as marketing, operations, general management, customer relations, and the general counsel's office (legal issues). Given Disney's overall business strategy, creative talent is almost always present in these cross-functional teams; moreover, managerial accountants play an important role as well.

"Most of the people . . . are decentralized and actually are co-located with the people that they support. That's our approach and we're moving more and more toward that and less and less toward a central group that provides information." (1j)

Boeing

Physical Location

Finally, where do managerial accountants actually do their work? The answer is "just about everywhere." As Panel C of Exhibit 1–4 highlights, managerial accountants are not sequestered in some remote corner of the business. To the contrary, they are located in every part of an enterprise, from corporate headquarters to the locations where goods and services are being produced. At Disney, for example, managerial accountants would be present on location when a feature film is being produced, near the ESPN production studio when decisions are made about deploying sports commentators, and in the various Disney hotels, such as the Disney Ambassador Hotel in Tokyo.

© Getty Images RF

© Comstock Images/Getty Images RF

© McGraw-Hill Education. Andrew Resek, photographer

© Stockbyte RF

Managerial accounting information is vital in all types of organizations. Managerial accountants act as strategic business partners in support of management's roles in decision making and directing operational activities. Pictured here (clockwise, from top left) are a manufacturer, a financial services firm, a nonprofit municipal fire department, and a retailer. How would managerial accounting be important in each of these organizations?

The Operational Context of Managerial Accounting

As we have discussed, managerial accounting concepts and techniques are applied throughout an organization, sometimes by professional managerial accountants and other times by managers in other fields who are using managerial accounting techniques. This means that managerial accounting concepts and techniques are applied in every imaginable part of a company's operations. This includes not only the obvious accounting and finance areas, but also sales, marketing, production and operations, customer service, product development, and human resource management.

We can put these many and varied applications of managerial accounting into context by thinking of the organization as the sum of the activities it performs to produce its goods and services and the decisions that need to be made to support each of those activities.

Managerial Accounting and the Value Chain

Learning Objective 1-7

Understand and explain the value chain concept.

How are the goods and services that we all consume created? Usually many activities are involved in securing basic raw materials and turning them into valuable products or services. The set of linked, value-creating activities, ranging from securing basic raw materials and energy to the ultimate delivery of products and services, is called the **value chain.** Different companies define their value chains in different ways, depending on their strategies, but the bottom line is this: Customers must "value" the activities in the value chain, because unless customers are willing to pay the cost of those activities *plus* an appropriate amount of profit, the company will fail.

Although there may be only one organization involved in a particular value chain, usually there are many. San Francisco General Hospital's value chain, for example, would include not only the hospital but also the suppliers of pharmaceutical products and medical supplies, the manufacturers of diagnostic equipment, the private-practice physicians whose patients use the hospital, and the ambulance services that transport patients to the hospital.

The value chain for The Walt Disney Studios would include *upstream* contributions such as screenwriting, film studio construction and maintenance, set design and construction, costume design and production, travel arrangements for shooting scenes on location, lighting technicians, film crews, and acting talent. Once the film has been produced, the *downstream* contributions include advertising personnel; TV, radio, online, and print media; film distributors; theater companies such as AMC Theatres; DVD producers; online video providers such as Netflix; and DVD retailers such as Amazon.

© Ed Endicott/Alamy

Let's turn our attention now to this chapter's contrast company, Whole Foods Market, Inc. A fast-growing food retailer headquartered in Austin, Texas, Whole Foods Market has over 400 stores in the U.S. and Europe. Whole Foods Market is owned by its stockholders, and its stock is publicly traded on the NASDAQ market.

As its website explains, Whole Foods Market's managers and accountants work to earn a profit for stockholders by maintaining a reputation as a seller of quality, sustainably produced products and a fun place to shop. Each of these factors must be considered by the company's managers as they make decisions about the design of their value chain. Making the right decisions about a value chain can be the difference between success and failure for a company, and the decisions for Whole Foods Market include answering critical questions like:

- Which value chain activities must a grocery store include?
- Are there activities that other grocery stores don't include in their value chain that would provide a competitive advantage?
- Which activities must they provide themselves and which can be outsourced to others?
- How much can each value chain activity cost?

The major steps in the value chain for Whole Foods Market, Inc. are depicted in Exhibit 1–5. They include the following:

- Supplier development (sustainable, organic, and local suppliers).
- Agricultural and nonagricultural production.
- Managing and distributing inventory.
- Marketing and customer service.
- In-store production.
- Store retail operations.
- Community stewardship.

Notice that Whole Foods Market does not execute every step in this value chain itself. Except for in-store production, like prepared meals and baked goods, Whole Foods Market does not produce what it sells. As the company states in its Core Values, "We are not a fully self-sustaining ecosystem. There are hundreds of other businesses that we depend

Supplier development

Source: Ken Hammond/USDA-NRCS

Agricultural and non-agricultural production

© small_frog/Getty Images RF

Managing and distributing inventory

© Thinkstock/Corbis RF

Marketing and customer service

© Patrick T. Fallon/Bloomberg/Getty Images

In-store production and retailing

© Nadine Hutton/Bloomberg/Getty Images

Community stewardship

© Yellow Dog Productions RF

Exhibit 1–5

The Whole Foods Market value chain consists of a myriad of activities, from production through sales, and beyond.

© Ed Endicott/Alamy

on to assist us in creating an outstanding retail shopping experience for our customers."[11] What Whole Foods Market does do is establish the variety and standards for its products, outsource the production of those products, market the products, and distribute them to retail stores where they are sold, in some cases adding value through in-store production.

Now compare in your mind the Whole Foods Market value chain to the one for your biggest local grocery chain. Would its supplier development and community stewardship efforts be so large and significant that they warrant being included as the first and last steps in the value chain? This is a strategic choice that Whole Foods Market has made, and as a result it has to generate profits from customers that are adequate to support significant and costly efforts in these areas. For example, their website notes that the Whole Foods Market Local Producer Loan Program "provides up to $25 million in low-interest loans to independent local farmers and food artisans," and that "Overall, our community giving well exceeds 5% of our total net profits each year." But these elements of the value chain have to be supported by customer spending because "We recognize that profits are essential to creating capital for growth, prosperity, opportunity, job satisfaction and job security."

Supporting these elements of the value chain while still making a profit is why Whole Foods Market is sometimes jokingly called "Whole Paycheck"! But by understanding their customers and the value chain activities that they are willing to pay for, Whole Foods Market consistently covers its costs and makes a nice return for stockholders.

In order for any organization to most effectively achieve its goals, it is important for its managers to understand the *entire* value chain in which their organization participates. This understanding can help managers ask, and answer, important questions about their organization's strategy. Should the company concentrate on only a narrow link in the value chain, such as retail operations? Or should it expand its operational scope to include in-store production? Are there opportunities to acquire suppliers, and good reasons to do so?

---

[11]The quotes in these paragraphs are from the Whole Foods Market website at www.wholefoodsmarket.com/mission-values/core-values/declaration-interdependence.

These questions involve fundamental, strategic issues about how an organization can best meet its goals. Although many factors affect such decisions, one important factor concerns the costs incurred when companies compete based on the same set of value chain activities. In order for a company to achieve a sustainable competitive advantage, it must either (1) perform one or more activities in the value chain at the same quality level as its competitors, but at a lower cost, or (2) perform its value chain activities at a higher quality level than its competitors, but at no greater cost. Understanding the value chain, and the factors that cause costs to be incurred in each activity in the value chain, is a crucial step in the development of a firm's strategy. These cost-causing factors are called **cost drivers,** and we will have much more to say about them throughout the text. The overall recognition of the importance of cost relationships among the activities in the value chain, and the process of managing those cost relationships to the firm's advantage, is called **strategic cost management.** Issues in strategic cost management will arise in a variety of contexts as we pursue our study of managerial accounting.

Capacity and Capacity Costs

Learning Objective 1-8

Explain how investments in capacity affect managerial decision making.

A key challenge in providing useful managerial accounting information is understanding and correctly analyzing an organization's capacity and the costs of providing that capacity. By **capacity** we mean the upper limit on the amount of goods or services that an organization can produce in a specified period of time. For example, how many iPhones can Apple's suppliers manufacture in a month? Or how many people can Disney's Magic Kingdom effectively accommodate in a day? Or how many cell phone calls or text messages can Verizon process in an hour?

© Ed Endicott/Alamy

Managers at Whole Foods Market must make many decisions about the amount of capacity to provide. Each activity in their value chain brings capacity challenges, from how many supplier development managers to hire, to the size of the next store to be opened, to the staffing levels in each existing store.

For example, the company must spend money to train and employ cashiers. Every dollar spent on cashiers is a dollar of profit that will not be earned for stockholders, so Whole Foods Market does not want to schedule one hour more of cashier time than it has to. But if shoppers find checkout lines that are too long because there are not enough cashiers available to work, they will not find the shopping environment to be enjoyable and might go elsewhere to shop for groceries. Every grocery item that they buy somewhere else represents lost profit to Whole Foods Market. But how to balance the lost profit on groceries against the cost of providing cashiers, especially when hiring and orienting a new employee and then training that employee as a cashier is such a significant investment. This is the capacity dilemma faced by Whole Foods Market's managers and accountants.

We will develop some tools in a later chapter to help describe this problem more precisely and to make this decision. But let's begin in this chapter by considering a very simple example of how to think about the costs of capacity.

There are various concepts of an organization's capacity. *Theoretical capacity* refers to the upper limit on production of goods or services if everything works perfectly. This means that no cashiers miss time for illness, no cash registers break down, there are no unexpected interruptions such as power outages or severe storms, and so forth. Most managers believe that a more useful measure of capacity is **practical capacity,** which allows for normal occurrences such as equipment (cash register) downtime and worker (cashier) fatigue or illness.

"One of the problems today is that we rely on all these computer reports—we know what customers buy, and how rapid the sell-through is on any given item—but no report will tell you how much they would have bought if things had been different." (1k)

Macy's

Important questions for the managerial accounting system to address are: (1) What is an organization's *practical capacity?* (2) What are the costs of the *resources supplied* to provide that capacity? and (3) How have those *resources* been *used?*

To explore these issues, let's focus on a familiar scenario, the pizza business. Some of Whole Foods Market's bigger stores include a "pizza bar," where pizzas can be purchased whole or by the slice. Let's suppose you have taken a part-time job there making pizzas. You work the 6:00 to 8:00 p.m. shift three evenings a week, Monday, Wednesday, and Friday. In addition to the great fringe benefit of getting to eat the occasional free slice of pizza with your favorite toppings, you receive a wage of $11 an hour. So each evening that you work, you make $22.

After some training and a little experience, you can make a pizza in about six minutes. This includes picking up a premeasured lump of pizza dough, patting it out, twirling it ostentatiously over your head a few times, putting it down, covering it with pizza sauce, applying the cheese and other toppings, and tossing it in the oven. Making a pizza with "the works" takes longer than a plain cheese pizza, but for the typical combination of pizzas made on a typical evening, it averages out to six minutes. Also, the six-minute average time required per pizza allows for occasional mistakes, retrieving more toppings from the deli when they run out, taking short cell-phone calls, and other normal disruptions. You have no scheduled break during your short two-hour shift, so on a busy evening you could make as many as 20 pies (120 minutes available ÷ the average 6 minutes per pizza).

So, using the terminology discussed above, the cost of the labor *resources supplied* for your two-hour shift is $22, and the *practical capacity* of that two-hour shift is 20 pizzas made.

Now suppose that during the first week of October, you experience very different levels of demand on your three evening shifts. Monday night football causes a steady demand for pizzas, and you make 20 of them that evening. Wednesday evening is pretty slow, and you make just 10 pizzas. Friday evening, which is normally very busy, is unusually slow because of a traffic jam that keeps many customers from reaching the store. You make just one pizza.

Now we can calculate the cost of your labor for a pizza during each of your three shifts. One fairly simple answer is to divide your labor cost per shift by the number of pizzas you made in each shift, as follows:

Shift	Labor Cost	Pizzas Made	Cost per Pizza
Monday	$22.00	20	$ 1.10
Wednesday	22.00	10	2.20
Friday	22.00	1	22.00

Let's stop and think about this. Does this analysis make any sense? Most accountants and managers would argue that it does not make much sense to say that Monday's pizzas cost $1.10 each for your labor, Wednesday's cost $2.20 each, and the one you made Friday cost $22.00! This result highlights the problem of confusing the cost of a resource *supplied* with the cost of a resource *used.* The cost of your labor resource *supplied* during each shift was $22.00, but the cost of your labor resource *used* varied from shift to shift due to widely different demand levels.

The cost of your labor resource *used* should be computed as shown in column (c) of the following table. Moreover, the cost of your labor resource used *per pizza* is a constant $1.10 per pizza, regardless of demand, as calculated in column (d). Finally, the cost of your labor resource *unused* (i.e., the cost of unused capacity) is calculated in column (e).

To best understand the table, start with column (a) and work across.

(a) Shift	(b) Cost of Labor Resource Supplied	(c) Cost of Labor Resource Used	(d) Cost of Labor Resource Used per Pizza	(e) Cost of Labor Resource Unused (i.e., cost of unused capacity)
Monday	$22.00	$22.00 [$22 × (20 ÷ 20)]	$1.10 ($22.00 ÷ 20)	$ 0.00
Wednesday	22.00	11.00 [$22 × (10 ÷ 20)]	1.10 ($11.00 ÷ 10)	11.00
Friday	22.00	1.10 [$22 × (1 ÷ 20)]	1.10 ($1.10 ÷ 1)	20.90

(b) 2 hours × $11.00 per hour
(c) $22.00 × (pizzas made ÷ pizzas in practical capacity)
(d) cost of labor resource used ÷ pizzas made
(e) $22.00 − cost of labor resource used

Seems obvious, doesn't it? But it is not uncommon for managers to mistakenly act like all the money spent on production should be divided up over the products or services produced, without considering whether some of that spending was for resources *supplied but unused.*

The moral of the story is that it is very important to distinguish among the cost of resources supplied [column (b) above], the cost of resources used [column (c) above], and the cost of resources unused [column (e) above], which is the same as the cost of unused capacity. An important task for any management team, including the one at Whole Foods Market, is to understand and manage the cost of capacity. Providing them data about the costs of unused capacity gives them an important tool.[12]

M anagement
A ccounting
P ractice

Ford, Renault, and Nissan

MANAGING THE COSTS OF UNUSED CAPACITY IN THE AUTO INDUSTRY: A GLOBAL CHALLENGE

Most companies cannot easily adjust their production capacity to match demand. Once a manufacturer of automobiles has invested in a factory, its options for increasing or decreasing that capacity and related costs are limited. If sales are low, management can reduce the hours of production, but the facility costs remain. Moreover, labor costs often cannot easily be adjusted because of national labor laws, union rules, and practical concerns such as training costs and employee loyalty.

So, if the costs of unused capacity cannot be adjusted to match demand, how can a company manage capacity to avoid the drain on income that comes with unused capacity? The solution involves isolating the capacity problem: (1) shift production between facilities to maximize utilization of capacity in selected primary facilities while creating additional unused capacity in secondary facilities, and (2) sell or find alternative uses for the now-vastly-underutilized secondary facilities.

American automaker **Ford Motor Co.** followed exactly this approach in addressing their profitability problems in the European market. "We know what it takes to be profitable in Europe. . . . We'll work to match capacity with demand while accelerating new-product development." A few months after that statement, Ford announced that it would move production of vehicles and components from three underutilized plants in Europe to other facilities and close the plants. "The closings include . . . a 48-year-old plant in Genk [Belgium] that builds cars and minivans. . . . Production of those models will shift to Ford's plant in Valencia, Spain."[13]

Renault SA and **Nissan Motor Co.**, French and Japanese companies, respectively, have used their unusual alliance to manage capacity across the two companies. Each company owns a substantial portion of the other, and they share a CEO, Carlos Ghosn. Nissan recently began manufacturing a vehicle for the U.S. market at "a Renault Samsung Motors plant in Busan, South Korea . . . [that had] been operating at half of its capacity of 300,000 vehicles a year." Meanwhile, with Renault struggling to manage decreased demand in Europe due to weakness in that market, Nissan is considering "shifting some of its [production] workload to Renault's underutilized French facilities" as a way of absorbing strong demand for their products elsewhere.[14]

---

[12]This is, of course, a very simple illustration, because it focuses on a single resource, i.e., the cost of one employee's labor. Even an operation as simple as making pizzas involves many resources, such as pizza ingredients, multiple employees, buildings and equipment, and advertising. Imagine how much more complicated capacity issues are for a major airline or a large manufacturer. Nevertheless, by exploring the concepts of capacity and the cost of capacity in a very simple scenario, you should have an initial understanding of this critical issue. For another example, see D. Welch and I. Rowley, "Risky Business at Nissan," *BusinessWeek*, November 2, 2009, p. 34.

[13]Keith Naughton, "Ford Profit Squeezed by Excess Plant Capacity in Europe," *Bloomberg.com*, July 19, 2012; and Keith Naughton and Alex Webb, "Ford to Cut 5,700 Jobs with Three European Plan Closings," *Bloomberg.com*, October 25, 2012.

[14]David Pearson, "Renault Mulls Making Nissan Cars," *Wall Street Journal*, January 18, 2013.

Cost Management Systems

The explosion in technology we are experiencing, coupled with significant worldwide competition, is forcing managers to produce high-quality goods and services, provide outstanding customer service, and do so at the lowest possible cost. To help managers cope with this high-pressure environment, many companies have moved away from a historical cost accounting perspective and toward a proactive *cost management* perspective. A **cost management system** is a management planning and control system with the following objectives.

- Measure the cost of the resources consumed in performing the organization's significant *activities* and measure the unused capacity of those resources.
- Identify and eliminate **non-value-added costs.** These are the costs of *activities* that can be eliminated with no deterioration of product quality, performance, or perceived value.
- Determine the efficiency and effectiveness of all major *activities* performed in the enterprise.
- Identify and evaluate new *activities* that can improve the future performance of the organization.

Notice the emphasis in a cost management system on the organization's activities. This emphasis, sometimes called **activity accounting,** is crucial to the goal of producing quality goods and services at the lowest possible cost. In keeping with the focus on activities, managerial accountants have developed a system for determining the cost of producing goods or services called **activity-based costing (ABC).** In an ABC system, the costs of the organization's significant activities are accumulated and then assigned to goods or services in accordance with how the activities are used in the production of those goods and services. An ABC system helps management understand the causal linkages between activities and costs.

Using an activity-based costing system to improve the operations of an organization is called **activity-based management,** or **ABM.** We will have considerably more to say about activity-based costing, activity-based management, and the role of cost management systems throughout the text.

Managerial Accounting as a Career

Learning Objective **1-9**

Discuss the professional organizations and certifications in the field of managerial accounting.

As we have discussed, managerial accountants are found throughout the organization and, as such, they are often in touch with its many practices and procedures. In most businesses, managerial accountants interact frequently with engineers, sales personnel, finance specialists, production staff, and managers at all levels. To perform their duties effectively, managerial accountants must be knowledgeable not only in accounting but in the other major business disciplines as well. Moreover, strong oral and written communication skills are critically important for the success of any professional, including managerial accountants.

Professional Organizations

Many managerial accountants and members of the corporate finance and accounting team are Certified Public Accountants (CPAs) and members of the American Institute of CPAs. However, the CPA designation was designed primarily to assure the competence of those working *outside* of companies and passing judgments about the reliability of accounting reports for the "public," particularly investors and regulators.

To focus on best practices and new developments in accounting and finance *inside* of companies, the managerial accounting profession also has its own certifications and organizations. The Institute of Management Accountants (IMA) has over 80,000 members and publishes a practitioner-oriented journal about managerial accounting practice entitled *Strategic Finance*. Other professional organizations in which managerial accountants hold membership include Financial Executives International (for senior financial executives), the Institute of Internal Auditors, and the American Accounting Association (for academics).

The primary professional association for managerial accountants outside of the U.S. is the Chartered Institute of Management Accountants (CIMA). CIMA has offices throughout Europe and Asia, and it publishes educational e-journals to support its 100,000-plus members who are located in over 150 countries. There are also associations for the certified managerial accountants of various individual countries, including the Certified Management Accountants of Canada and the Institute of Certified Management Accountants, Australia.

Professional Certification

"[We] look for a combination of solid accounting skills, the ability to think strategically, and strong business ethics. If someone is a CMA, we can be more comfortable that the person has mastered these aspects of the profession." (1l)
Microsoft

In keeping with the importance of their role and the specialized knowledge they must possess, managerial accountants can earn a professional certification similar to the CPA. Since 1972, the IMA has administered the **Certified Management Accountant (CMA)** program. Requirements for becoming a CMA include meeting specified educational requirements and passing the rigorous CMA examination. In addition, the American Institute of CPAs has teamed with CIMA to offer an experience- and examination-based certification called the **Chartered Global Management Accountant (CGMA).**[15] Canada, Great Britain, and many other countries also have professional certification programs for their managerial accountants. In addition to validating their skills, the CMA, CGMA, and other certifications bring managerial accountants a very tangible benefit: a recent study of managerial accountants practicing in the U.S. showed professionals with a certification earning over 30% more in average total compensation than their noncertified peers.[16]

Managerial Accounting and the Ethical Climate of Business

Learning Objective 1-10

Describe the ethical responsibilities and ethical standards that apply to managerial accounting.

Who among us is not shocked and dismayed by the seemingly endless stream of corporate and investment scandals that we have experienced in the 21st century? And the headlines keep on coming. Many of the cases involve mismanagement, some are characterized by alleged ethical lapses, and in some instances there is alleged criminal behavior. Who is to blame? According to most observers, there is plenty of blame to go around: greedy corporate executives, managers who make overreaching business deals, lack of oversight by various companies' boards of directors (particularly the boards' audit committees), substandard work by external auditors, lack of sufficient probing by Wall Street analysts and the financial press, and some accountants who have been all too willing to push the envelope on aggressive accounting to (or beyond) the edge. Several financial executives have filed guilty pleas on felony charges. Others have been convicted by juries. Some are serving time in prison. Some observers have wondered if the confidence of the investing public can ever be regained.

One important lesson from these scandals is that not only is unethical behavior in business wrong in a moral sense, but it also can be disastrous from the standpoint of the economy. We cannot have managers lying, stealing, perpetrating frauds, and making up accounting rules as they go without seriously disrupting business. Thus, ethical behavior by managers in general, and accountants in particular, is not a luxury or a discretionary "good thing to do." It is an absolute necessity to the smooth functioning of the economy.

[15]For information about the CMA program, visit the IMA website at imanet.org. For more about the CGMA certification, visit cgma.org.

[16]Denis Desroches, Raef Lawson, and Kip Krumwiede, "IMA 2014 Salary Survey," Online at http://www.imanet.org/docs/default-source/salary-survey/us.pdf.

Sorting out the details of the major scandals would take us well beyond the subject matter of this text. Most of the purely accounting issues in these cases involve financial accounting (external reporting) rather than managerial accounting (internal reporting). But remember we said earlier that in a company's finance and accounting organization many of the same individuals are involved in both types of accounting. In the notorious Enron case, for example, the courts concluded that a massive fraud was perpetrated on the investing public by creating so-called related parties with names like Raptor for the sole purpose of hiding debt and overstating earnings. Yet the same alleged fraud must have been perpetrated on many at Enron itself. Surely not all of the company's thousands of employees knew of these accounting schemes. So ultimately, what may have been largely financial (external) accounting misstatements almost certainly resulted in misstated managerial (internal) accounting reports as well.[17]

> "At the end of the day, as the CFO, everything is about your credibility, about being thoughtful and honest and fiduciarily responsible." (1m)
>
> **Perrigo Co.**

The chaos in corporate governance and accounting spawned a movement for reform. Congress passed the Sarbanes-Oxley Act in 2002, which, among other things, requires companies to establish, assess, and regularly report on their internal controls over financial reporting. This legislation also created the Public Company Accounting Oversight Board (PCAOB) to establish auditing standards and provide for an audit quality review process. Appendix I covers the Sarbanes-Oxley Act and its implications for managerial accounting.

In business schools, and in the accounting profession, the importance of education on ethical issues is widely embraced.[18] To this end, a significant *ethical issue in managerial accounting* will be addressed at the end of most chapters. The goal of these *Focus on Ethics* pieces is to help you see that although legitimate ethical issues do arise in the daily practice of business and accounting, guidelines for addressing these problems exist and can be applied. With this in mind our *Focus on Ethics* piece for this chapter will be a summary of the Institute of Management Accountants' *Statement of Ethical Professional Practice.*

Focus on Ethics *These scenarios discuss ethical issues and underscore the importance of ethical behavior in mangerial accounting. For easy reference in future* Focus on Ethics *examples, as well as problems and cases that include ethical issues to be resolved, the* IMA Statement of Ethical Professional Practice *can also be found on the last page of the book.*

All financial professionals, including managerial accountants and others practicing managerial accounting techniques, have an obligation to themselves, their colleagues, and their organizations to adhere to high standards of ethical conduct. In recognition of this obligation, the IMA has developed the following ethical standards for its members. Note especially that it is not only a set of principles, but it also includes a section on resolving ethical conflicts.

[17]Greg Stohr, "Enron's Skilling Rejected by Top U.S. Court on Conviction," *Bloomberg* (April 16, 2012), http://www.bloomberg.com/news/2012-04-16/enron-s-skilling-rejected-by-top-u-s-court-on-conviction.html.

[18]Joann Lublin and Kara Scannell, "Critics See Some Good from Sarbanes-Oxley," *The Wall Street Journal*, July 30, 2007, p. B1; and John Hodowanitz and Steven A. Solieri, "Guarding the Guardians," *Strategic Finance* 87, no. 2 (August 2005), pp. 47–53.

Focus on Ethics

IMA STATEMENT OF ETHICAL PROFESSIONAL PRACTICE

Members of IMA shall behave ethically. A commitment to ethical professional practice includes overarching principles that express our values, and standards that guide our conduct.

Principles

IMA's overarching ethical principles include: Honesty, Fairness, Objectivity, and Responsibility. Members shall act in accordance with these principles and shall encourage others within their organizations to adhere to them.

Standards

A member's failure to comply with the following standards may result in disciplinary action.

I. Competence

Each member has a responsibility to:

1. Maintain an appropriate level of professional expertise by continually developing knowledge and skills.
2. Perform professional duties in accordance with relevant laws, regulations, and technical standards.

3. Provide decision support information and recommendations that are accurate, clear, concise, and timely.
4. Recognize and communicate professional limitations or other constraints that would preclude responsible judgment or successful performance of an activity.

II. Confidentiality

Each member has a responsibility to:

1. Keep information confidential except when disclosure is authorized or legally required.
2. Inform all relevant parties regarding appropriate use of confidential information. Monitor subordinates' activities to ensure compliance.
3. Refrain from using confidential information for unethical or illegal advantage.

III. Integrity

Each member has a responsibility to:

1. Mitigate actual conflicts of interest. Regularly communicate with business associates to avoid apparent conflicts of interest. Advise all parties of any potential conflicts.
2. Refrain from engaging in any conduct that would prejudice carrying out duties ethically.
3. Abstain from engaging in or supporting any activity that might discredit the profession.

IV. Credibility

Each member has a responsibility to:

1. Communicate information fairly and objectively.
2. Disclose all relevant information that could reasonably be expected to influence an intended user's understanding of the reports, analyses, or recommendations.
3. Disclose delays or deficiencies in information, timeliness, processing, or internal controls in conformance with organization policy and/or applicable law.

Resolution of Ethical Conflict

In applying the Standards of Ethical Professional Practice, you may encounter problems identifying unethical behavior or resolving an ethical conflict. When faced with ethical issues, you should follow your organization's established policies on the resolution of such conflict. If these policies do not resolve the ethical conflict, you should consider the following courses of action:

1. Discuss the issue with your immediate supervisor except when it appears that the supervisor is involved. In that case, present the issue to the next level. If you cannot achieve a satisfactory resolution, submit the issue to the next management level. If your immediate superior is the chief executive officer or equivalent, the acceptable reviewing authority may be a group such as the audit committee, executive committee, board of directors, board of trustees, or owners. Contact with levels above the immediate superior should be initiated only with your superior's knowledge, assuming he or she is not involved. Communication of such problems to authorities or individuals not employed or engaged by the organization is not considered appropriate, unless you believe there is a clear violation of the law.
2. Clarify relevant ethical issues by initiating a confidential discussion with an IMA Ethics Counselor or other impartial advisor to obtain a better understanding of possible courses of action.
3. Consult your own attorney as to legal obligations and rights concerning the ethical conflict.

Chapter Summary

Each chapter's summary is built around the learning objectives, which appear at the beginning of the chapter.

LO1-1 Define managerial accounting and describe its role in the management process. Managerial accounting is the process of identifying, measuring, analyzing, interpreting, and communicating information in pursuit of an organization's goals. Managerial accounting concepts and tools are used by all managers, and professional managerial accountants are important strategic partners in an organization's management team.

LO1-2 Explain four fundamental management processes that help organizations attain their goals. In pursuing its goals, an organization acquires resources, hires employees, and then engages in an organized set of activities. It is up to the management team to make the best use of the organization's resources, employees, and activities in achieving the organization's goals. The four fundamental management processes are (1) decision making, (2) planning, (3) directing operational activities, and (4) controlling.

LO1-3 List and describe five objectives of managerial accounting activity. Five objectives of managerial accounting activity are (1) providing information for decision making and planning, (2) assisting managers in directing and controlling operational activities; (3) motivating managers and other employees to achieve the organization's goals; (4) measuring the performance of activities, subunits, managers, and other employees within the organization; and (5) assessing the organization's competitive position and working with other managers to ensure the organization's long-run competitiveness in its industry.

LO1-4 Explain the major differences between managerial and financial accounting. The users of managerial accounting information are managers inside the organization. Managerial accounting information is not mandatory, is unregulated, and draws on data from the core accounting system as well as other data sources. The users of financial accounting information are interested parties outside the organization. Financial accounting information is required, is regulated, and is based almost entirely on historical transaction data.

LO1-5 Describe the accounting and finance structure in an organization. Every manager must understand basic managerial accounting concepts and tools. Managerial accounting specialists, called managerial accountants or analysts, occupy staff positions in an organization chart. They are deployed as members of cross-functional teams, which address a variety of managerial decisions. Managerial accountants are physically located throughout an enterprise alongside the managers with whom they work closely.

LO1-6 Describe the roles of an organization's chief financial officer (CFO) or controller, treasurer, and internal auditor. The organization's top managerial and financial accountant is called the chief financial officer or controller. The treasurer is responsible for raising capital and safeguarding the organization's assets. An organization's internal auditor is responsible for reviewing the accounting procedures, records, and reports and sometimes makes a broad performance evaluation of management.

LO1-7 Understand and explain the value chain concept. The value chain is the set of linked, value-creating activities, ranging from securing basic raw materials and energy to the ultimate delivery of products and services. Understanding the value chain, its activities, and the costs and strategic benefits of those activities is a crucial step in the development of an organization's strategy.

LO1-8 Explain how investments in capacity affect managerial decision making. Capacity is the upper limit on the amount of goods or services that an organization can produce in a specified period of time. Practical capacity of resources supplied takes into account normal work disruptions, and based on this number the cost of resources used and unused can be measured. Costs information may be distorted if no adjustment is made for unused capacity.

LO1-9 Discuss the professional organizations and certifications in the field of managerial accounting. As professionals, managerial accountants may undergo a process to certify their expertise and, if successful, may enjoy the benefits of membership in one or more professional organizations, such as the Institute of Management Accountants (IMA).

LO1-10 Describe the ethical responsibilities and ethical standards that apply to managerial accounting. Managerial accountants are expected to display a commitment to ethical professional practice characterized by the overarching principles of honesty, fairness, objectivity, and responsibility. These principles, which are codified in the "IMA Statement of Ethical Professional Practice," can be applied to all managerial accounting concepts and practices.

Key Terms

For each term's definition refer to the indicated page, or turn to the glossary at the end of the text.

activity accounting, 23
activity-based costing (ABC), 23
activity-based management (ABM), 23
attention-directing function, 7
balanced scorecard, 10
capacity, 20
Certified Management Accountant (CMA), 24
chief financial officer (CFO), 15
controller (or comptroller), 15
cost accounting system, 11
cost drivers, 20
cost management system, 23
financial accounting, 11
internal auditor, 16
line positions, 14
managerial accountants, 5
managerial accounting, 4
non-value-added costs, 23
practical capacity, 20
staff positions, 15
strategic cost management, 20
treasurer, 16
value chain, 18

Review Questions

1–1. According to some estimates, the volume of electronic commerce transactions exceeds $3 trillion. Business-to-business transactions account for almost half of this amount. What changes do you believe are in store for managerial accounting as a result of the explosion in e-commerce?

1–2. List two plausible goals for each of these organizations: Amazon.com, American Red Cross, General Motors, Walmart, the City of Seattle, and Hertz.

1–3. List and define the four basic management activities.

1–4. Give examples of each of the four primary management activities in the context of a national fast-food chain such as Burger King.

1–5. Give examples of how each of the objectives of managerial accounting activity would be important in an airline company such as American Airlines.

1–6. List and describe four important differences between managerial and financial accounting.

1–7. Distinguish between cost accounting and managerial accounting.

1–8. Distinguish between line and staff positions. Give two examples of each in a university setting.

1–9. Distinguish between the following two accounting positions: controller and treasurer.

1–10. How could your college or university use the concepts in the balanced scorecard? List two possible performance measures that would be relevant to a college or university, for each of the balanced scorecard's four areas.

1–11. What does the following statement by a managerial accountant at Caterpillar imply about where in the organization the managerial accountants are located? "[We] are a partner with all of the other functions in the business here." (*Source:* see reference (1a))

1–12. What is meant by the following statement? "Managerial accounting often serves an attention-directing role."

1–13. What is the chief difference between manufacturing and service industry firms?

1–14. Explain the following terms: practical capacity, cost of resources supplied, cost of resources used, and cost of resources unused.

1–15. Evaluate the following statement: "If a resource has unused capacity, that capacity is lost forever."

1–16. Define and explain the significance of the term *CMA*.

1–17. Briefly explain what is meant by each of the following ethical standards for managerial accountants: competence, confidentiality, integrity, and credibility.

1–18. What is meant by the term *non-value-added costs?*

1–19. Managerial accounting is an important part of any enterprise's management information system. Name two other information systems that supply information to management.

1–20. Can managerial accounting play an important role in a nonprofit organization? Explain your answer.

1–21. A large manufacturer of electronic machinery stated the following as one of its goals: "The company should become the low-cost producer in its industry." How can managerial accounting help the company achieve this goal?

1–22. What do you think it means to be a professional? In your view, are managerial accountants professionals?

1–23. Name several activities in the value chain of (*a*) a manufacturer of cotton shirts and (*b*) an airline.

1–24. Define the term *strategic cost management.*

Exercises

All applicable Exercises are available in Connect. connect

Exercise 1–25
Managerial Accounting and Decision Making
(LO 1-1, 1-2, 1-3)

Give an example of managerial accounting information that could help a manager make each of the following decisions.

1. The president of Budget Car Rental is deciding whether to add luxury cars to the rental car fleet.
2. The production manager in a Volvo Trucks plant is deciding whether to have routine maintenance performed on a machine weekly or biweekly.
3. The manager of a Target store is deciding how many security personnel to employ for the purpose of reducing shoplifting.
4. The Miami-Dade County board of representatives is deciding whether to build an addition onto one of the county libraries.

Exercise 1–26
Objectives of Managerial Accounting Activity
(LO 1-3, 1-4)

For each of the following activities, explain which of the objectives of managerial accounting activity is involved. In some cases, several objectives may be involved.

1. Developing a bonus reward system for the managers of the various offices of the AAA (American Automobile Association) Travel Agency.
2. Comparing the actual and planned cost of a consulting engagement completed by an engineering firm such as Allied Engineering.
3. Determining the cost of manufacturing a tennis racket at Wilson Sporting Goods.

4. Measuring the cost of the inventory of digital cameras on hand in a Best Buy store.
5. Estimating the annual operating cost of a newly proposed Wells Fargo branch bank.
6. Measuring the following costs incurred during one month in a Hyatt Regency hotel:
   a. Wages of table-service personnel.
   b. Property taxes.
7. Comparing a Sheraton Hotel's room rate structure, occupancy rate, and restaurant patronage with industry averages.

Exercise 1–27
Contributions of Managerial Accounting; Use of Internet
(LO 1-1, 1-3, 1-5)

This icon indicates use of the Internet.

Use the Internet to access the Web site for one of the following companies, or any other company of your choosing.

Delta Air Lines	www.delta.com
Pepsico	www.pepsico.com
Procter & Gamble	www.pg.com
Apple	www.apple.com
Walmart	www.walmart.com

Required: Find the management discussion and analysis portion of the firm's most recent online annual report. Then briefly discuss how managerial accounting can contribute to the company's financial goals.

Exercise 1–28
Value Chain; Use of Internet
(LO 1-7)

The tablet icon indicates group work.

Use the Internet to access the Web site for one of the following companies, or any other company of your choosing.

Avis Car Rental	www.avis.com
Expedia.com	www.expedia.com
Holland America Line	www.hollandamerica.com
Levi Strauss & Co.	www.levistrauss.com
Nokia	www.nokia.com
Regal Entertainment Group	www.regmovies.com

Required: After perusing the company's website, work as a group to list several key activities you believe would be in the company's value chain.

Problems

All applicable Problems are available in Connect.

Problem 1–29
Managing a Retail Business; Cross-Functional Teams; E-Commerce
(LO 1-5, 1-6, 1-8)

The pen icon indicates that a written response is needed.

Dave Nelson recently retired at age 48, courtesy of the numerous stock options he had been granted while president of WowzaShops.com, an Internet start-up company. He soon moved to Montana to follow his dream of living in the mountains and Big Sky Country. Nelson, always the entrepreneur, began a sporting-goods store shortly after relocating. The single store soon grew to a chain of four outlets throughout the sparsely populated state. As Nelson put it, "I can't believe how fast we've expanded. It's basically uncontrolled growth—growth that has occurred in spite of what we've done."

Although business has been profitable, the chain did have its share of problems. Store traffic was somewhat seasonal, with a slowdown occurring as winter approached. Nelson therefore added ski equipment and accessories to his product line. The need to finance required inventories, which seemed to be bulging, left cash balances at very low levels, occasionally giving rise to short-term bank loans.

Part of Nelson's operation focused on canoe building and white-water rafting trips. Reports from the company's financial accounting system seemed to indicate that these operations were losing money because of increasing costs, although Nelson could not be sure. "The traditional income statement is not too useful in assessing the problem," he noted. "Also, my gut feeling is that we are not dealing with the best suppliers in terms of quality of goods, delivery reliability, and prices." Additional complications were caused by an increasingly competitive marketplace, with many former customers now buying merchandise and booking river excursions via the Internet, through catalogs received in the mail, or through businesses that advertised heavily in outdoor magazines.

Nelson's background is marketing, and he appeared somewhat puzzled on how to proceed. The company's chief financial officer (CFO) would be an obvious asset in terms of addressing these problems. Unfortunately, she knew her numbers but lacked key knowledge of general business operations. The same could be said for other executives who managed somewhat in "silos," becoming experts in a narrow facet of the company but, in general, lacking a big-picture outlook for the firm.

Required:

1. Explain how the CFO and managerial accounting could assist Nelson in addressing the company's problems.
2. Would a cross-functional team be useful here? Briefly discuss.
3. Many resources in the sporting-goods company would present significant capacity issues. List three such resources and describe their capacity issues in light of the company's operations.

Problem 1–30
Balanced Scorecard; Airline
(LO 1-3)

Susan Lopez, a consultant with Deloitte & Young, has just begun an engagement at Four Corners Airlines, which is based in Santa Fe, New Mexico. The company has fallen on hard times of late despite record profits for the rest of the airline industry. Management is somewhat set in its ways and could probably use some "new blood," as the most recent hire to the firm's executive team was 12 years ago.

In Lopez's first meeting with the team, the airline's chief executive officer commented that "all that mattered in this industry were load factors—the percentage of seats sold on scheduled flights. If load factors were adequate, everything else would take care of itself." Lopez noted that while this measure was important, other, broader facets of operation were significant as well. She asked if any of the management team had heard of the balanced scorecard, and received dead silence as a response.

Based on her experiences with other engagements, including two that involved airlines, Lopez was convinced that the balanced scorecard could provide benefits in helping to solve the airline's woes. After a presentation about the philosophy of the balanced scorecard, Four Corners Airlines' management team accepted her idea, feeling that a shift in operating philosophy was needed for survival.

Required:

1. What is a *balanced scorecard,* and what are its typical key elements?
2. Lopez wants to assemble a committee to prepare the airline's balanced scorecard. List several of the company's functional areas (e.g., marketing) that should be represented on the committee.
3. Identify a number of measures to evaluate the key elements that you specified in requirement 1. Measures would include items such as load factors, number of passenger complaints, percentage of on-time arrivals, and so forth.
4. Do you see any problems with management's prior focus on only one measure (i.e., load factor)? Briefly explain.

Problem 1–31
Quality Control; Ethical Behavior
(LO 1-6, 1-7, 1-9, 1-10)

The balance icon identifies an ethical issue.

AccuSound Corporation manufactures printed circuits for stereo amplifiers. A common product defect is a "drift" caused by failure to maintain precise heat levels during the production process. Rejects from the 100 percent testing program can be reworked to acceptable levels if the defect is drift. However, in a recent analysis of customer complaints, Marie Allen, the assistant controller, and the quality control engineer determined that normal rework does not bring the circuits up to standard. Sampling showed that about half of the reworked circuits will fail after extended amplifier operation. The incidence of failure in the reworked circuits is projected to be about 10 percent over five years.

Unfortunately, there is no way to determine which reworked circuits will fail, because testing will not detect the problem. The rework process could be changed to correct the problem, but the cost-benefit analysis for the suggested change indicates that it is not economically feasible. AccuSound's marketing analyst has indicated that this problem will have a significant impact on the company's reputation and customer satisfaction. Consequently, the board of directors would interpret this problem as having serious negative implications for the company's profitability.

Allen included the circuit failure and rework problem in her report prepared for the upcoming quarterly meeting of the board of directors. Due to the potential adverse economic impact, Allen followed a long-standing practice of highlighting this information. After reviewing the reports to be presented, the plant manager and his staff complained to the controller that he should control his people better. "We can't upset the board with this kind of material. Tell Allen to tone that down. Maybe we can get it by the board in this meeting and have some time to work on it. People who buy those cheap systems and play them that loud shouldn't expect them to last forever."

The controller called Allen into his office and said, "Marie, you'll have to bury this one. The probable failure of reworks can be mentioned briefly in the oral presentation, but it should not be mentioned or highlighted in the advance material mailed to the board."

Allen feels strongly that the board will be misinformed on a potentially serious loss of income if she follows the controller's orders. Allen discussed the problem with the quality control engineer, who simply remarked, "That's your problem, Marie."

Required:

1. Discuss the ethical considerations that Marie Allen should recognize in deciding how to proceed.
2. Explain what ethical responsibilities should be accepted by (*a*) the controller, (*b*) the quality control engineer, and (*c*) the plant manager.
3. What should Marie Allen do? Explain your answer.

(CMA, adapted)

Problem 1–32
Role of the Divisional Controller; Retailer
(LO 1-4, 1-6, 1-9, 1-10)

Urban Elite Apparel designs women's apparel and sells it through retail outlets across the country. All of the company's clothing lines are manufactured by contract manufacturers around the world. A division manager is responsible for each of the company's retail divisions. Each division's controller, assigned by the corporate controller's office, manages the division's accounting system and provides analysis of financial information for the division manager. The division manager evaluates the performance of the division controller and makes recommendations for salary increases and promotions. However, the final responsibility for promotion evaluation and salary increases rests with the corporate controller.

Each of Urban Elite Apparel's divisions is responsible for product design, sales, pricing, operating expenses, and profit. However, corporate management exercises tight control over divisional financial operations. For example, all capital expenditure above a modest amount must be approved by corporate management. The method of financial reporting from the division to corporate headquarters provides further evidence of the degree of financial control. The division manager and the division controller submit to corporate headquarters separate and independent commentary on the financial results of the division. Corporate management states that the division controller is there to provide an independent view of the division's operations, not as a spy.

Required:

1. Discuss the arrangements for line and staff reporting in Urban Elite Apparel.
2. The division manager for Urban Elite Apparel has a "dual reporting" responsibility. The controller is responsible both to the division manager, who makes recommendations on salary and promotion, *and* to the corporate controller, who has the final say in such matters.
   a. Identify and discuss the factors that make the division controller's role difficult in this type of situation.
   b. Discuss the effect of the dual reporting relationship on the motivation of the divisional controller.

(CMA, adapted)

Case

Case 1–33
Disclosure of Confidential Information; Ethics; Software Developer
(LO 1-1, 1-3, 1-6, 1-9, 1-10)

Progressive Applications Corporation, a developer and distributor of business applications software, has been in business for five years. The company's main products include programs used for list management, billing, and accounting for the mail order shopping business. Progressive's sales have increased steadily to the current level of $25 million per year. The company has 250 employees.

Andrea Nolan joined Progressive approximately one year ago as accounting manager. Nolan's duties include supervision of the company's accounting operations and preparation of the company's financial statements. No one has noticed that in the past six months Progressive's sales have ceased to rise and have actually declined in the two most recent months. This unexpected downturn has resulted in cash shortages. Compounding these problems, Progressive has had to delay the introduction of a new product line due to delays in documentation preparation.

Progressive contracts most of its printing requirements to Web Graphic Inc., a small company owned by Rob Borman. Borman has dedicated a major portion of his printing capacity to Progressive's requirements because Progressive's contracts represent approximately 50 percent of Web Graphic's business. Nolan has known Borman for many years; as a matter of fact, she learned of Progressive's need for an accounting manager through Borman.

While preparing Progressive's most recent financial statements, Nolan became concerned about the company's ability to maintain steady payments to its suppliers; she estimated that payments to all vendors, normally made within 30 days, could exceed 75 days. Nolan is particularly concerned about payments to Web Graphic; she knows that Progressive had recently placed a large order with Web Graphic for the printing of the new product documentation, and she knows that Web Graphic will soon be placing an order for the special paper required for Progressive's documentation. Nolan is considering telling Borman about Progressive's cash problems; however, she is aware that a delay in the printing of the documentation would jeopardize Progressive's new product.

Required:

1. Describe Nolan's ethical responsibilities in this situation.
2. Independent of your answer to requirement (1), assume that Nolan learns that Borman of Web Graphic has decided to postpone the special paper order required for Progressive's printing job. Nolan believes Borman must have heard rumors about Progressive's financial problems from some other source because she has not talked to Borman. Should Nolan tell the appropriate Progressive officials that Borman has postponed the paper order? Explain your answer.
3. Independent of your answers to the first two requirements, assume that Borman has decided to postpone the special paper order because he has learned of Progressive's financial problems from some source other than Nolan. In addition, Nolan realizes that Jim Grason, Progressive's purchasing manager, knows of her friendship with Borman. Now Nolan is concerned that Grason may suspect she told Borman of Progressive's financial problems when Grason finds out Borman has postponed the order. Describe the steps that Nolan should take to resolve this situation.

(CMA, adapted)

2 Basic Cost Management Concepts

FOCUS COMPANY >>>

© Caia Images/Glow Images RF

THIS CHAPTER'S FOCUS COMPANY is the Comet Computer Company, a US-based company that produces tablet and laptop computers in its plant in Hanoi, Vietnam. Most of the company's sales are made online through its website, cometcomp.com.

© Robert Mora/Alamy RF

This manufacturer/retailer combines many standardized components in different ways to produce several computer models popular with its customer base. In this chapter, we will introduce many of the issues involved in understanding and managing the costs of running this or any business.

© Ken Wolter/123RF.com

In contrast to the manufacturing/retail setting of the Comet Computer Company, we also explore the cost issues covered in the context of a service company, Midas, Inc. One of the world's largest automotive service companies, Midas has more than 2,000 company-owned or franchised automotive service locations worldwide. Midas' management, like that of any other company, must understand its costs in order to be successful in a competitive business environment.

© Juice Images/Alamy RF

After completing this chapter, you should be able to

2-1 Explain what is meant by the word *cost.*

2-2 Distinguish among product costs, period costs, and expenses.

2-3 Describe the role of costs in published financial statements.

2-4 List and describe four types of manufacturing processes.

2-5 Give examples of three types of manufacturing costs.

2-6 Prepare a schedule of cost of goods manufactured, a schedule of cost of goods sold, and an income statement for a manufacturer.

2-7 Understand the importance of identifying an organization's cost drivers.

2-8 Describe the behavior of variable and fixed costs, in total and on a per-unit basis.

2-9 Distinguish among direct, indirect, controllable, and uncontrollable costs.

2-10 Define and give examples of an opportunity cost, an out-of-pocket cost, a sunk cost, a differential cost, a marginal cost, and an average cost.

The process of management involves formulating strategy, planning, control, decision making, and directing operational activities. Managers cannot perform these functions effectively without high-quality managerial accounting information. Much of this information focuses on the costs incurred in the organization. For example, in *formulating its overall strategy,* Southwest Airlines' management team considered the cost savings necessary to succeed as a low-price, no-frills airline. In *planning* Southwest's routes and flight schedules, managers must consider aircraft fuel costs, salaries of flight crews, and airport landing fees. *Controlling* the costs of manufacturing heavy equipment requires that Caterpillar's managers and accountants carefully measure and manage production costs. In *making decisions* about locating a new store, Walmart managers need information about the cost of building, maintaining, equipping, and staffing the store. Finally, to *direct operational activities,* managers in all three of these companies need information about the cost of salaries, utilities, security, and a host of other goods and services.

What Do We Mean by a Cost?

Learning Objective 2-1

Explain what is meant by the word *cost.*

Each of the examples in the preceding paragraph focuses on costs of one type or another. An important first step in studying managerial accounting is to create a framework for thinking about the various types of costs incurred by organizations and how those costs are actively managed.

At the most basic level, a **cost** may be defined as the sacrifice made, usually measured by the resources expended, or given up, to achieve a particular purpose. If we look more carefully, though, we find that the word *cost* can have different meanings depending on the context in which it is used. Cost data that are classified and recorded in a particular way for one purpose may be inappropriate for another use. For example, the costs incurred in producing gasoline last year are important in measuring ExxonMobil's income for the year. However, those costs may not be useful in planning the company's refinery operations for the next year if the cost of oil has changed significantly or if the methods of producing gasoline have improved.

The important point is that different cost concepts and classifications are used for different purposes. Understanding these concepts and classifications helps managers to be sure that they are receiving cost data that is useful and relevant. The purpose of this chapter is to enable the users of this text to gain a firm grasp of the cost terminology used in companies, and which will be used throughout the text.

Product Costs, Period Costs, and Expenses

Learning Objective **2-2**

Distinguish among product costs, period costs, and expenses.

One important way of classifying costs is by the timing of their recognition as expenses for financial reporting. An **expense** is defined as the cost incurred when a resource (asset) is used up for the purpose of generating revenue.

The resource used up can be:

- cash, expended directly;
- a promise to use up cash in the future, recognized as a liability (accounts payable); or
- the reduction in value of a recorded asset such as plant and equipment (via depreciation) or inventory (via cost of goods sold).

"We are expected to say, 'Here are the costs, and this is why the costs are what they are, and this is how they compare to other things, and here are some suggestions where we could possibly improve.'" (2a)
Caterpillar

The terms *product cost* and *period cost* are used to describe the timing with which various expenses are recognized.

A **product cost** is a cost assigned to inventory, to goods that are either purchased or manufactured for resale. The product cost is used to value the inventory of manufactured goods or merchandise until the goods are sold. In the period of the sale, when the inventory asset is reduced, the product costs that have been recorded are reclassified as an expense called **cost of goods sold.**

- The product cost of merchandise inventory acquired by a retailer or wholesaler for resale consists of the purchase cost of the inventory plus any shipping charges paid by them.
- The product cost of manufactured inventory includes all of the costs incurred in its manufacture. For example, the labor cost of a production employee at Texas Instruments is included as a product cost of the calculators manufactured.

Exhibit 2–1 illustrates the relationship between product costs and cost-of-goods-sold expense.

Another term for product cost is **inventoriable cost,** since a product cost is stored as the cost of inventory until the goods are sold. In addition to retailers, wholesalers, and manufacturers, the concept of product cost is relevant to other producers of inventoriable goods. Agricultural firms, lumber companies, and mining firms are examples of nonmanufacturers that produce inventoriable goods. Apples, timber, coal, and other such goods are inventoried at their product cost until the time period during which they are sold.

All costs that are not product costs are called **period costs.** These costs are identified with the period of time in which they are incurred rather than with units of purchased or produced goods. Period costs are recognized as expenses during the time period in which they are incurred. All research and development, selling, and administrative costs are treated as period costs. This is true in manufacturing, retail, and service industry firms.

Research and development costs include all costs of developing new products and services. The costs of running laboratories, building prototypes of new products, and testing new products are all classified as research and development (or R&D) costs. *Selling costs* include salaries, commissions, and travel costs of sales personnel, shipping costs incurred by a manufacturer, and the costs of advertising and promotion.[1] *Administrative costs* refer

[1]Generally accepted accounting principles (GAAP) allow producers to elect to treat shipping costs as a cost of goods sold, in which case they would be a product cost. However, this is not the standard treatment. Physical distribution is one of the four Ps of marketing, and accordingly shipping is usually treated as a selling cost. In this book, shipping cost incurred by a producer will always be a period cost.

Exhibit 2–1
Product Costs and Cost of Goods Sold

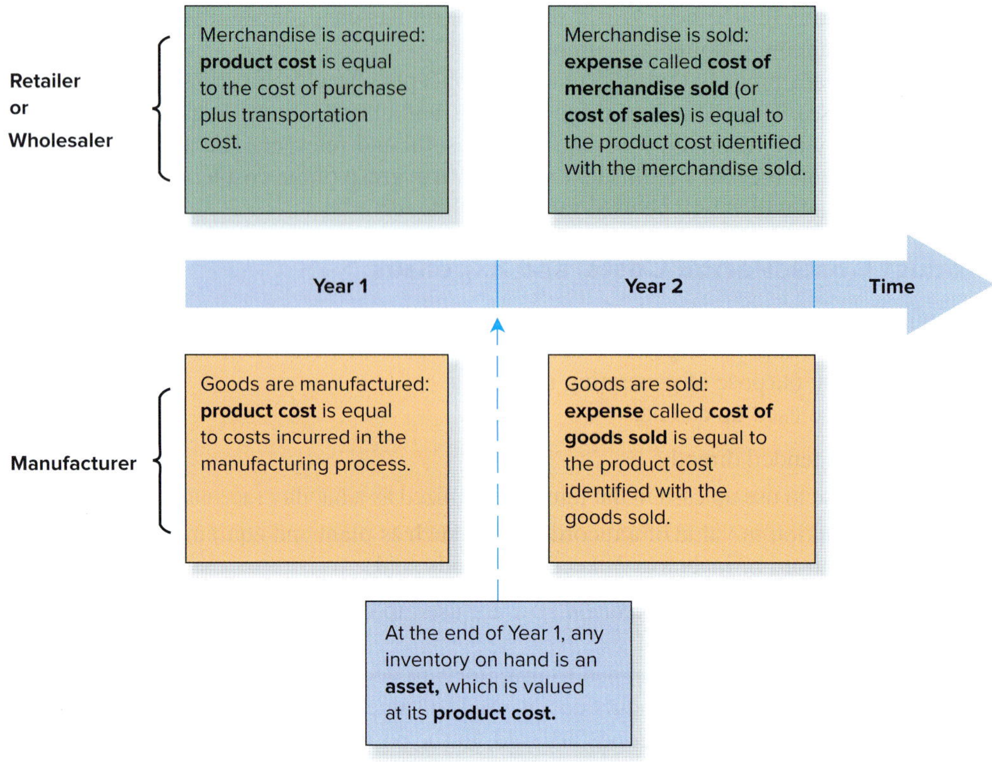

to all costs of running the organization as a whole. The salaries of top-management personnel and the costs of the accounting, legal, and public relations activities are examples of administrative costs.

Exhibit 2–2 illustrates the nature of period costs.

Costs on Financial Statements

Learning Objective 2-3

Describe the role of costs in published financial statements.

We can see the distinction between product costs and period costs by examining financial statements from three different types of firms.

Income Statement

Exhibit 2–3 displays recent income statements, in highly summarized form, from Caterpillar, Southwest, and Walmart. These companies are from three different industries. Caterpillar,

Exhibit 2–2
Period Costs

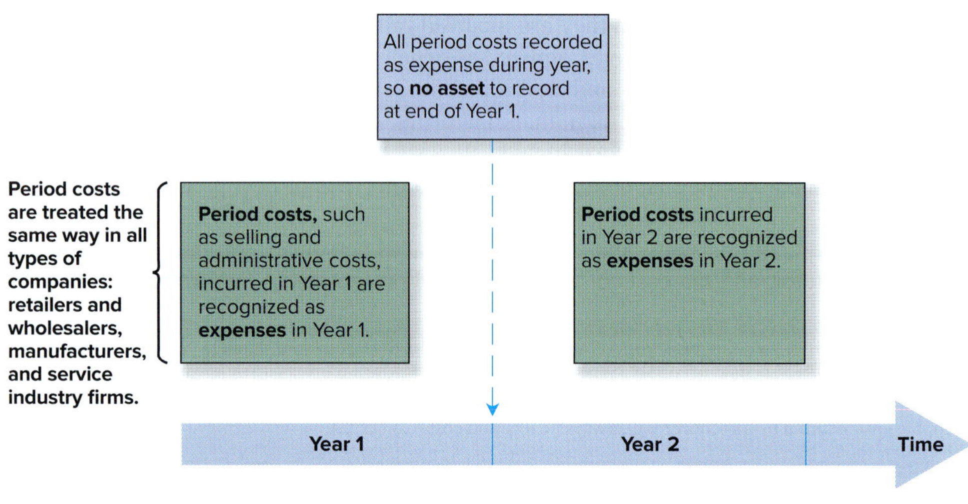

based in Peoria, Illinois, is a heavy equipment manufacturer. Walmart is a large retail firm with its headquarters in Bentonville, Arkansas, and merchandising operations throughout most of the nation. Southwest Airline, a major air carrier based in Dallas, Texas, represents the service industry.

Exhibit 2–3
Income Statements from Three Different Industries (all figures in thousands of dollars)

© Taina Sohlman/Shutterstock.com RF

CATERPILLAR INC.
Statement of Income for a Recent Year

Value measured by product costs → (Less: Cost of products sold)

Total sales and revenues	$ 55,184,000
Less: Cost of products sold	40,391,000
Gross profit	$ 14,793,000
Less: Operating costs :	
Selling, general, and administrative expenses	$ 5,697,000
Research and development expenses	2,135,000
Other operating expenses	1,633,000
Total operating costs	$ 9,465,000
Operating profit	$ 5,328,000
Less: Other expenses	245,000
Consolidated profit before taxes	$ 5,083,000
Provision for income taxes	1,380,000
Profit of consolidated companies	$ 3,703,000

© niloo138/123RF.com

WAL-MART STORES, INC.
Statement of Income for a Recent Year

Value measured by product costs → (Less: Cost of sales)

Total revenues	$485,651,000
Less: Cost of sales	365,086,000
Gross profit	$120,565,000
Less: Operating, selling, general, and administrative expenses	93,418,000
Operating income	$ 27,147,000
Less: Interest expense, net	2,348,000
Income from continuing operations before income taxes	$ 24,799,000
Provision for income taxes	(7,985,000)
Income from discontinued operations, net of tax	285,000
Consolidated net income	$ 17,099,000

© iStock.com/rypson RF

SOUTHWEST AIRLINES CO.
Statement of Income for a Recent Year

Operating revenue:	
Passenger	$ 17,658,000
Freight	175,000
Other	772,000
Total operating revenue	$ 18,605,000
Less: Operating expenses:	
Salaries, wages, and benefits	$ 5,434,000
Fuel and oil	5,293,000
Maintenance materials and repairs	978,000
Aircraft rentals	295,000
Landing fees and other rentals	1,111,000
Depreciation and amortization	938,000
Acquisition and integration	126,000
Other operating expenses	2,205,000
Total operating expenses	$ 16,380,000

(continued)

Exhibit 2–3
(concluded)

SOUTHWEST AIRLINES CO. Statement of Income for a Recent Year	
Operating income	$ 2,225,000
Other expenses (income):	
Interest expense	$ 130,000
Capitalized interest	(23,000)
Interest income	(7,000)
Other (gains) losses, net	309,000
Total other expenses (income)	$ 409,000
Income before income taxes	$ 1,816,000
Provision for income taxes	680,000
Net income	$ 1,136,000

Selling and administrative costs are always period costs on any type of company's income statement. For example, Caterpillar lists $5.697 billion of selling, general, and administrative expenses on its income statement in Exhibit 2–3.

For Caterpillar, the costs of manufactured inventory are product costs. All costs incurred in manufacturing finished products are stored in inventory until the time period when the products are sold. Then the product costs of the inventory sold become cost of goods sold, an expense on the income statement.

Product costs for Walmart include all costs of acquiring merchandise inventory for resale. These product costs are classified as inventory until the time period during which the merchandise is sold. Then these costs become cost of sales (cost of goods sold).

There are no inventoried product costs at Southwest Airlines. Although this firm does engage in the production of air transportation services, its service output is consumed as soon as it is produced. Service industry firms, such as Southwest Airlines, JPMorgan Chase & Co., Sheraton Hotels & Resorts, State Farm Insurance, and Subway, generally refer to the costs of producing services as **operating expenses.** Operating expenses are treated as period costs and as such are expensed during the period in which they are incurred. Southwest Airlines includes costs such as employee wages, aviation fuel, and aircraft maintenance in operating expenses for the period.

Gross Profit and Operating Income Notice that the manufacturer and retailer income statements above include an item called gross profit, and all three income statements include a subtotal called *operating income* (or *operating profit*). These two views of profitability differ from net income and are very important to managers and investors in understanding whether the company is successful in its core mission of producing and selling goods and services profitably.

Gross profit (sometimes called **gross margin**) is the portion of revenues left after deducting just the costs that have been classified as cost of sales (cost of goods sold), without considering any other costs of operating the company. This profit number provides a view of profitability that is specific to the production process: how much money are we receiving for our goods and services after covering the costs of producing them?

Operating income (operating profit) goes one step further to report the profit remaining from revenues after deducting both cost of sales *and* all period costs of operations. Operating income is a very important profit number for managers because it represents the profits resulting from operations, taking into account all costs of the operations but not the effects of financing, taxes, or any other unusual business events. Why omit these items from operating income? Because they are affected by many factors beyond just the process of producing and selling goods and services: how the company chooses to raise the financing it needs, the tax strategy it follows, and unusual occurrences that

Exhibit 2–4
Partial Balance Sheets for a Manufacturer and a Retailer (all figures in thousands of dollars)

© Taina Sohlman/Shutterstock.com RF

© niloo138/123RF.com

CATERPILLAR INC.
Partial Balance Sheet at the End of a Recent Year

Current assets:	
Cash and short-term investments	$ 7,341,000
Receivables (net)	16,764,000
Inventories	12,205,000
Other current assets	2,557,000
Total current assets	$38,867,000

Value measured by product costs → Inventories

WAL-MART STORES, INC.
Partial Balance Sheet at the End of a Recent Year

Current assets:	
Cash and cash equivalents	$ 9,135,000
Receivables (net)	6,778,000
Inventories	45,141,000
Prepaid expenses and other current assets	2,224,000
Total current assets	$63,278,000

Value measured by product costs → Inventories

are unrelated to regular operations (for example, the "Income from discontinued operations" shown in the Walmart income statement). By omitting these items, we see a clearer picture of the profit earned from operating the core business of the company, which is the outcome most relevant for most managers.

Throughout this textbook, we will usually view a company's profitability from the gross profit and operating income perspectives, and will discuss or compute net income only when we wish to consider the effect of a decision on taxes.

> "A key focus is on the levers within our control to manage the pace of expenses." (2b)
> **Google Inc.**

Balance Sheet

Since retailers, wholesalers, and manufacturers sell inventoriable products, their balance sheets are also affected by product costs. Exhibit 2–4 displays the current-assets section from recent balance sheets of Caterpillar and Walmart. Included in the current-assets section of each of these balance sheets is inventory. Manufacturers, such as Caterpillar, have three types of inventory. **Raw-material** inventory includes all materials before they are placed into production. **Work-in-process** inventory refers to manufactured products that are only partially completed at the date when the balance sheet is prepared. **Finished-goods** inventory refers to manufactured goods that are complete and ready for sale. The values of the work-in-process and finished-goods inventories are measured by their product costs.

On the Walmart balance sheet, the cost of merchandise on store shelves and in warehouses, but not yet sold, is recorded as inventories.

> "Inventory management will continue to be an ongoing focus for us." (2c)
> **Walmart**

Manufacturing Operations and Manufacturing Costs

Learning Objective 2-4
List and describe four types of manufacturing processes.

Although there are tens of thousands of manufacturing firms, their basic production processes can be classified into four standard types. The nature of the product and the manufacturing process define the manufacturing costs incurred. Therefore, the management team is in a better position to manage these costs if they understand the relationship between the production process and the types of costs incurred. Exhibit 2–5 defines and describes the four standard categories of manufacturing processes.[2]

[2]The exhibit is based on the widely-recognized Hayes-Wheelwright production process matrix. A variant of the assembly process is *mass customization,* in which the manufacturer uses inventoried parts to build products to customer specification.

Exhibit 2–5
Types of Production Processes

Type of Production Process	Description of Process	Example of Manufacturer
Job Shop	Low production volume; little standardization; one-of-a-kind products. Habitat for Humanity (custom home builder).	 © Kriss Russell/Getty Images RF
Batch	Multiple products; low volume; high product diversity; some customization. Caterpillar (batch production of heavy equipment).	 © Matthew Lloyd/Bloomberg/Getty Images
Assembly	A few major products; higher volume; lower diversity; minimal customization. Ford (automobile assembly line).	 © Bill Pugliano/Getty Images
Continuous Flow	High production volume; highly standardized commodity products. ExxonMobil (production of gasoline, a continuous-flow product).	 © Royalty-Free/Corbis

"What I need [from an accountant] is someone who can analyze data, see problems, and figure out solutions." (2d)
Tente Casters

We will study the role of managerial accounting and cost management in each of these manufacturing processes. This chapter will focus on an assembly operation. Chapter 3 will examine managerial accounting techniques used in job-shop and batch-processing operations. Chapter 4 will focus on the system used to record and manage costs in a continuous-flow production environment.

Assembly Manufacturing

Comet
cometcomp.com

To illustrate an assembly production environment, let's focus on Comet Computer Company, a manufacturer of computers and peripheral devices.[3] Comet purchases computer parts such as motherboards, computer chips, hard drives, and displays, and then assembles these parts into a variety of devices, such as tablet computers, laptops, and desktop computers. Comet sells many models of computers mainly through its website, cometcomp.com.

Let's look at the types of manufacturing costs incurred by Comet and other manufacturers.

Manufacturing Costs

Learning Objective 2-5

Give examples of three types of manufacturing costs.

To assist managers in planning, decision making, and cost management, managerial accountants classify costs by the functional area of the organization to which costs relate. Some examples of functional areas are manufacturing, marketing, administration, and research and development. Manufacturing costs are further classified into the following

[3]As mentioned at the beginning of Chapter 1, the focus organizations around which the remaining chapters in the text are built are not real organizations. They are, however, realistic settings in which to discuss business and managerial accounting issues. In most cases they are based on real organizations. These realistic illustrations are intended to help students connect the business and managerial accounting issues discussed in this book to the management process and to everyday life.

three categories: direct material, direct labor, and manufacturing overhead, which is sometimes referred to more generally as production overhead.

Direct Material Material that is consumed in the manufacturing process, is physically incorporated in the finished product, and can be traced to products relatively easily is called **direct material.** Examples include the sheet metal in a Subaru automobile and the microprocessor chips in a Comet computer.

Some students are confused by the seemingly interchangeable use of the terms *raw material* and *direct material.* However, there is a difference: *before* material is entered into the production process, it is called *raw* material; *after* it enters production, it becomes *direct* material.

Direct Labor The cost of salaries, wages, and fringe benefits for personnel who work directly on the manufactured products is classified as **direct-labor cost.** Examples include the wages of personnel who assemble Comet computers in Hanoi, Vietnam, and those who operate the equipment in one of Royal Dutch Shell's refineries.

The cost of fringe benefits associated with any labor spending classified as direct labor should also be classified as direct-labor costs. Fringe benefits include the costs of providing health insurance, making pension and social security contributions, and other non-salary benefits provided by the employer to the employee.

Manufacturing Overhead All other costs of manufacturing are classified as **manufacturing overhead** (also known as *production overhead*), which includes three types of costs: indirect material, indirect labor, and other manufacturing costs.

Indirect Material

The cost of materials that are required for the production process but do not become an integral part of the finished product are classified as **indirect material** costs. An example is the cost of drill bits used in a metal-fabrication department at Ford Motor Company. The drill bits wear out and are discarded, but they do not become part of the product.

Materials that do become an integral part of the finished product but are insignificant in cost are also often classified as indirect material. For example, the various machine screws used in assembling Comet computers are so inexpensive that it is not worth tracing their costs to specific products as direct materials. Instead, they are added to the cost of indirect materials and become part of manufacturing overhead cost.

Indirect Labor

The costs of personnel who do not work directly on the product, but whose services are necessary for the manufacturing process, are classified as **indirect labor.** At Comet Computer Company, such personnel include production department supervisors, quality control inspectors, and assembly plant security guards.

> "If you just simply have [an employee] performing an [assembly] operation, that's direct labor. But when you put in a robot to do the job, which we're all doing, then you've got to have an engineer to make sure the [robot] is programmed right. So now it becomes indirect labor." (2e)
>
> **Chrysler**

Other Manufacturing Costs

All other manufacturing costs that are neither material nor labor costs are classified as manufacturing overhead. These costs include various costs of the plant such as depreciation of building and equipment, property taxes, insurance, and utilities such as electricity, as well as the costs of operating service departments. **Service departments,** also known as **support departments,** are those that do not work directly on manufacturing products but are necessary for the manufacturing process to occur, such as equipment-maintenance departments. In some firms, departments are referred to as *work centers.*

Other manufacturing overhead costs include overtime premiums and the cost of idle time. An **overtime premium** is the *extra* compensation paid to an employee who works beyond the time normally scheduled. For most nonmanagement employees in the United

States and Canada, government regulations require that overtime work be paid at one and one-half times the regular rate of pay ("time and a half"). So the overtime premium portion is the extra one-half of regular pay.

Suppose a technician who assembles Comet computers earns $16 per hour. The technician works 48 hours during a week and overtime is paid after the the scheduled time of 40 hours. The overtime pay scale is time and a half, or 150 percent of the regular wage. The technician's compensation for the week is classified as follows:

Direct-labor cost ($16 × 48)	$768
Overhead (overtime premium: ½ × $16 × 8)	64
Total compensation paid	$832

Only the *extra* compensation of $8 per hour is classified as overtime premium. The regular wage of $16 per hour is treated as direct labor, even for the eight overtime hours.

Idle time is time that is not spent productively by an employee due to such events as equipment breakdowns or new setups of production runs. Such idle time is an unavoidable feature of most manufacturing processes. The cost of an employee's idle time is classified as overhead so that it may be spread across all production jobs, rather than being associated with a particular production job. Suppose that during one 40-hour shift, a machine breakdown resulted in idle time of 1½ hours and a power failure idled workers for an additional ½ hour. If an employee earns $14 per hour, the employee's wages for the week will be classified as follows:

Direct-labor cost ($14 × 38)	$532
Overhead (idle time: $14 × 2)	28
Total compensation paid	$560

Overtime premiums and the cost of idle time should be classified as manufacturing overhead, rather than associated with a particular production job, because the particular job on which idle time or overtime may occur tends to be selected at random. Suppose that to meet holiday demand, Comet must schedule computer production in November for 10 hours per day instead of eight hours. The overtime premium paid only during the extra two hours is actually a result of *all* of the computers needing to be produced each day and not just the ones that happen to be produced during hours 9 and 10. Similarly, if a power failure occurs during one of several production jobs, the idle time that results is not due to the job that happens to be in process at the time. The power failure is a random event, and the resulting cost should be treated as a cost of all of the department's production.

As summarized in Exhibit 2–6 **total manufacturing cost** includes direct material, direct labor, and manufacturing overhead. Direct labor and manufacturing overhead are often called **conversion costs,** since they are the costs of "converting" raw material into finished products. Direct material and direct labor are often referred to as **prime costs.**

Exhibit 2–6
Total Manufacturing Cost

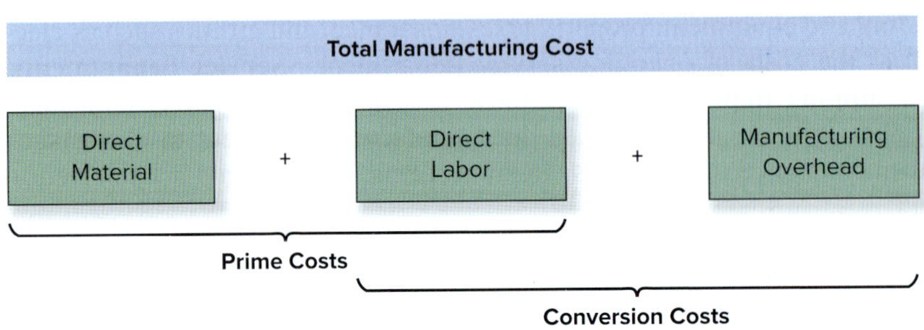

Manufacturing Cost Flows

Learning Objective 2-6

Prepare a schedule of cost of goods manufactured, a schedule of cost of goods sold, and an income statement for a manufacturer.

Direct material, direct labor, and manufacturing overhead are called product costs because they are assigned to products and stored in inventory until the time period when the manufacturer's products are sold. Manufacturers have product-costing systems to keep track of the flow of these costs from the time production begins until finished products are sold. This flow of manufacturing costs is depicted in Exhibit 2–7. As material is consumed in production, the cost of these direct materials is removed from the raw-material inventory account and added to work-in-process inventory. Similarly, the costs of payroll classified as direct labor and manufacturing overhead expenditures, as discussed in the previous section, are accumulated in work in process.

When products are finished, their costs are transferred from work-in-process inventory to finished-goods inventory. The total cost of direct material, direct labor, and manufacturing overhead transferred from work-in-process inventory to finished-goods inventory is called the **cost of goods manufactured.**[4] The costs then are stored in finished goods until the time period when the products are sold. At that time, the costs of those products are transferred from finished goods to cost of goods sold, which is an expense of the period when the sale is made. Exhibit 2–7 concentrates on the conceptual basis of a product-costing system. The detailed procedures and accounts used to keep track of product costs are covered in Chapters 3 and 4.

"In my mind, cost accountants are going to be business analysts." (2f)
Boeing

Manufacturers generally prepare a **schedule of cost of goods manufactured** and a **schedule of cost of goods sold** to summarize the flow of manufacturing costs during an accounting period. These schedules are intended for internal use by management and not made available to the public. The Excel spreadsheets in Exhibit 2–8 show these two schedules along with an income statement for Comet Computer Company.[5] Notice the extremely low inventories of raw material, finished goods, and work in process in these schedules. With annual sales of $700 million, Comet's year-end inventory of raw material is only $5,020,000, which is less than 1 percent of sales. Work-in-process inventory ($100,000) and finished-goods inventory ($190,000) are even lower. These low inventories, relative to sales volume, are characteristic of manufacturers using an online sales business model.

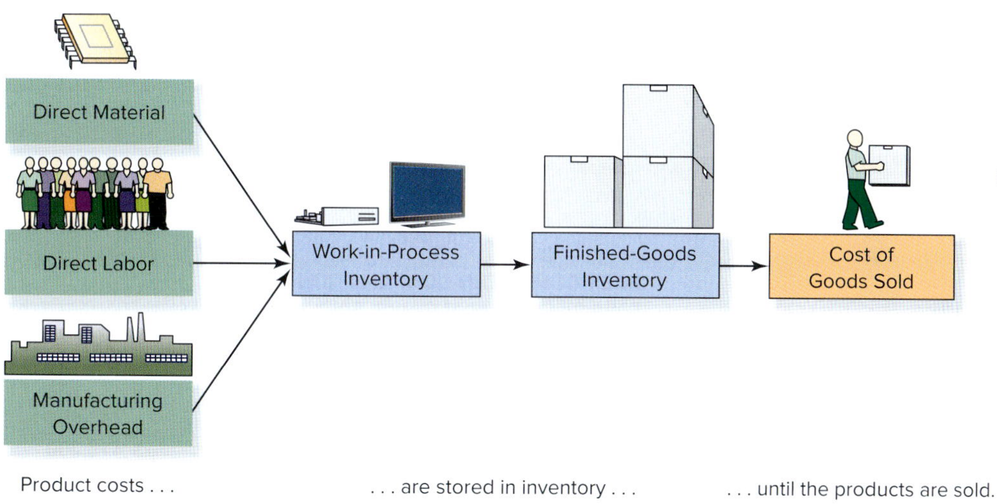

Exhibit 2–7
Flow of Manufacturing Costs

Comet
Cometcomp.com

[4]Do not confuse cost of goods manufactured with total manufacturing cost for the period. Cost of goods manufactured, as indicated, is the cost of goods completed and transferred from work-in-process inventory to finished-goods inventory. However the total manufacturing cost is the sum of direct material, direct labor, and manufacturing overhead incurred during the period, i.e. the spending on manufacturing. Some of that spending may still be in work-in-process inventory and so not part of what is traditionally called cost of goods manufactured.

[5]Some numerical displays in the text will be presented as Excel spreadsheets, since this tool is widely used in business.

Exhibit 2–8
Manufacturing Cost Schedules

Comet
Cometcomp.com

Comet Computer Corporation - Excel

H28 =H26-H27

COMET COMPUTER CORPORATION
Schedule of Cost of Goods Manufactured
For the Year Ended December 31, 20x2 (in thousands)

Direct material:		
Raw-material inventory, January 1	$ 6,000	
Add: Purchases of raw material	134,000	
Raw material available for use	$ 140,000	
Deduct: Raw-material inventory, December 31	5,020	
Raw material used		$ 134,980
Direct labor		50,000
Manufacturing overhead:		
Indirect material	$ 10,000	
Indirect labor	40,000	
Depreciation on factory	90,000	
Depreciation on equipment	70,000	
Utilities	15,000	
Insurance	5,000	
Total manufacturing overhead		230,000
Total manufacturing costs		$ 414,980
Add: Work-in-process inventory, January 1		120
Subtotal		$ 415,100
Deduct: Work-in-process inventory, December 31		100
Cost of goods manufactured*		$ 415,000

*Formula used to compute cost of goods manufactured: Beg inventory of WIP + Total manufacturing costs - End inventory of WIP = Cost of goods manufactured

Cost of Goods Manufactured

Comet Computer Corporation - Excel

H9 =H7-H8

COMET COMPUTER CORPORATION
Schedule of Cost of Goods Sold
For the Year Ended December 31, 20x2 (in thousands)

Finished-goods inventory, January 1	$ 200
Add: Cost of goods manufactured*	415,000
Cost of goods available for sale	$ 415,200
Finished-goods inventory, December 31	190
Cost of goods sold**	$ 415,010

*From the Schedule of Cost of Goods Manufactured

**Formula used to compute cost of goods sold: Beg inventory of FG + Cost of goods manufactured - End inventory of FG = Cost of goods sold

Cost of Goods Sold

(continued)

Exhibit 2–8
(concluded)

COMET COMPUTER CORPORATION	
Income Statement	
For the Year Ended December 31, 20x2 (in thousands)	
Sales revenue	$ 700,000
Less: Cost of goods sold*	415,010
Gross margin	$ 284,990
Selling and administrative expenses	174,490
Operating income	$ 110,500
Income tax expense	30,000
Net Income	$ 80,500
*From the Schedule of Cost of Goods Sold	

Non-Manufacturing Production Costs

Service industry firms and many nonprofit organizations are also engaged in production. What distinguishes these organizations from manufacturers is that a service is consumed as it is produced, whereas a manufactured product can be stored in inventory. Such businesses as Westin Hotels & Resorts, Bank of America, Delta Air Lines, the Chicago Bulls, and UnitedHealthcare are in the business of producing services. Similarly, nonprofit organizations such as the American Red Cross and the Houston Grand Opera Association also are engaged in service production. While less commonly observed in service firms, the same cost classifications used in manufacturing companies can be applied. For example, Air France produces air transportation services. Direct material includes such costs as jet fuel, aircraft parts, and food and beverages. Direct labor includes the salaries of the flight crew and the wages of aircraft-maintenance personnel. Overhead costs include depreciation of baggage-handling equipment, insurance, overtime premium for flight crew, and airport landing fees.

Notice that service firms can have direct material and direct labor costs just as manufacturing firms do. These costs can be traced to the company's service outputs, so they comprise part of the Operating Expenses that match with the Operating Revenues from the sale of services (see Exhibit 2–3). But as noted earlier, they are not product costs but rather they are period costs that are recorded in the accounting period of the expenditure. The reason? Services cannot be inventoried for future sale like a tangible product, so their costs don't flow though the work-in-process and finished-goods inventory accounts like products do.

The process of recording and classifying costs is important in service industry firms and nonprofit organizations for the same reasons as in manufacturing firms. Cost analysis is used in pricing banking and health care services, selecting car-rental agency locations, setting enrollment targets in universities, and determining cost reimbursements in hospitals. As such organizations occupy an ever-growing role in our economy, applying managerial accounting to their activities will take on ever-greater importance.

Basic Cost Management Concepts: Different Costs for Different Purposes

An understanding of cost concepts is absolutely critical to cost management. Moreover, different perspectives on costs are important in different managerial situations. The phrase *different costs for different purposes* is often used to convey the notion that different characteristics of costs can be important to understand in a variety of managerial circumstances. In this section, we will briefly discuss the work of several cross-functional management teams at Comet Computer Company, each of which is focusing on a particular management challenge. Through our discussion of these cost management teams' work, we will explore some of the key cost terms and concepts used in managerial accounting and cost management.

Cost Drivers

Learning Objective **2-7**

Understand the importance of identifying an organization's cost drivers.

Cometcomp.com

One of the most important cost concepts involves the way a cost changes in relation to changes in the activities of the organization. The kinds of activities that cause costs to be incurred are often called *cost drivers.*

One of Comet Computer Company's cost management teams was formed to understand and reduce the costs incurred by Comet. The team consisted of an engineer, a production manager, a purchasing manager, and a managerial accountant. After identifying the various costs incurred by Comet, the team's next step was to identify the reasons for the spending. A **cost driver** is a characteristic of an activity or event that causes costs to be incurred. In most organizations, different types of costs respond to widely differing cost drivers. For example, in a manufacturing firm, the cost of assembly labor would be driven by the quantity of products manufactured as well as the number of parts in each product. In contrast, the cost of machine setup labor would be driven by the number of production runs. The cost of material-handling labor would be driven by material-related factors such as the quantity and size of raw material used, the number of parts in various products, and the number of raw-material shipments received.

© Joe Raedle/Getty Images

Cost drivers in the airline industry are complex. The distance flown by an airplane and its passenger load drive costs, but so do a variety of other factors such as staffing rules, airport efficiency, even the weather.

In identifying a cost driver, the manager or accountant should consider the extent to which a cost or pool of costs varies in accordance with the cost driver. The higher the correlation between the cost and the cost driver, the more accurate will be the resulting understanding of cost behavior. Another important consideration is the cost of measuring the cost driver. Thus, there is a cost-benefit trade-off in the identification of cost drivers. As the number of cost drivers used in explaining an organization's cost behavior increases, the accuracy of the resulting information is likely to increase. However, the cost of identifying and tracking the information will increase also. The concept of a cost driver will be an important aspect of many of the topics discussed in subsequent chapters.

Variable and Fixed Costs

Learning Objective **2-8**

Describe the behavior of variable and fixed costs, in total and on a per-unit basis.

Cometcomp.com

After identifying costs and cost drivers for Comet Computer Company's operations, the cost management team went on to examine the relationship of various costs to the activities performed. Such a relationship is referred to as *cost behavior* and will be the focus of Chapter 6. At this juncture, though, let's look at two types of cost behavior identified at Comet Computer Company: *variable* and *fixed costs.*

Variable Costs A **variable cost** changes, in total, in direct proportion to a change in the level of activity (or cost driver). If activity increases by 20 percent, total variable cost increases by 20 percent also. For example, the cost of sheet metal used by

Chrysler will increase by approximately 5 percent if automobile production increases by 5 percent. The cost of napkins and other paper products used at a Chipotle Mexican Grill will increase by roughly 10 percent if the number of guests increases by 10 percent.

At Comet Computer Company, the cost management team identified direct material as a variable cost. One purchased component, a high-definition LCD display screen, costs $100 per laptop computer manufactured. The cost behavior for this direct material cost is graphed and tabulated in Exhibit 2–9.

Panel A of Exhibit 2–9 displays a graph of this variable cost. As this graph shows, *total* variable cost increases proportionately with activity. When activity doubles, from 10 to 20 laptops, total variable cost doubles, from $1,000 to $2,000. However, the variable cost *per unit* remains the same as activity changes. The variable cost associated with each unit of activity is $100, whether it is the first unit, the fourth, or the eighteenth. The table in panel B of Exhibit 2–9 illustrates this point.

To summarize, as activity changes, total variable cost increases or decreases proportionately with the activity change, but unit variable cost remains the same.

Fixed Costs A **fixed cost** remains unchanged in total as the level of activity (or cost driver) varies. If activity increases or decreases by 20 percent, total fixed cost remains the same. Examples of fixed costs include depreciation of plant and equipment at a Nike factory, the cost of property taxes at a Hyatt hotel, and the salary of a subway train operator employed by the New York City Transit Authority.

Comet Computer Company's cost management team identified the salary of the manager of Internet sales operations as a fixed cost. Her $150,000 annual salary does not vary with the number of units produced or sold.

This fixed cost is graphed in panel A of Exhibit 2–10.

Exhibit 2–9
Variable Cost

A. Graph of Total Variable Cost

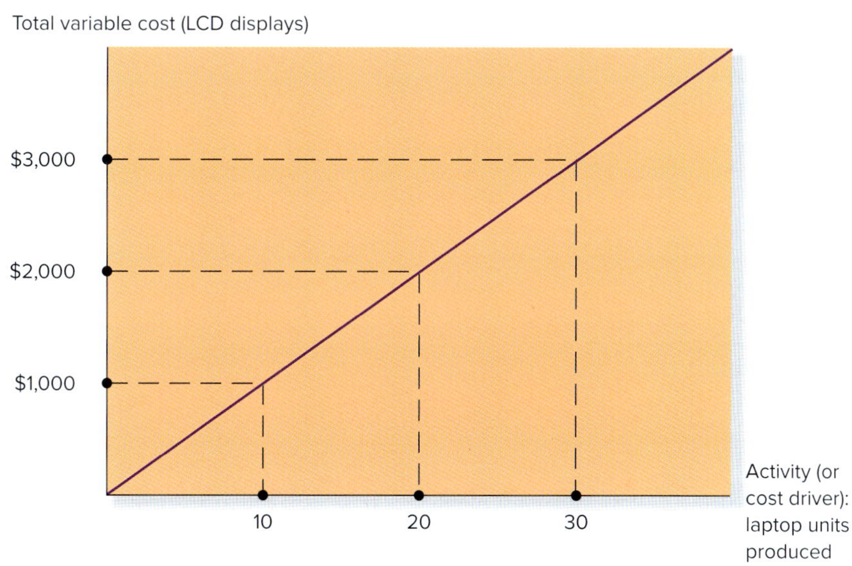

B. Tabulation of Variable Cost

Activity (or cost driver)	Variable Cost per Unit	Total Variable Cost
1	$100	$ 100
4	100	400
18	100	1,800
30	100	3,000

Exhibit 2–10
Fixed Cost

A. Graph of Total Fixed Cost

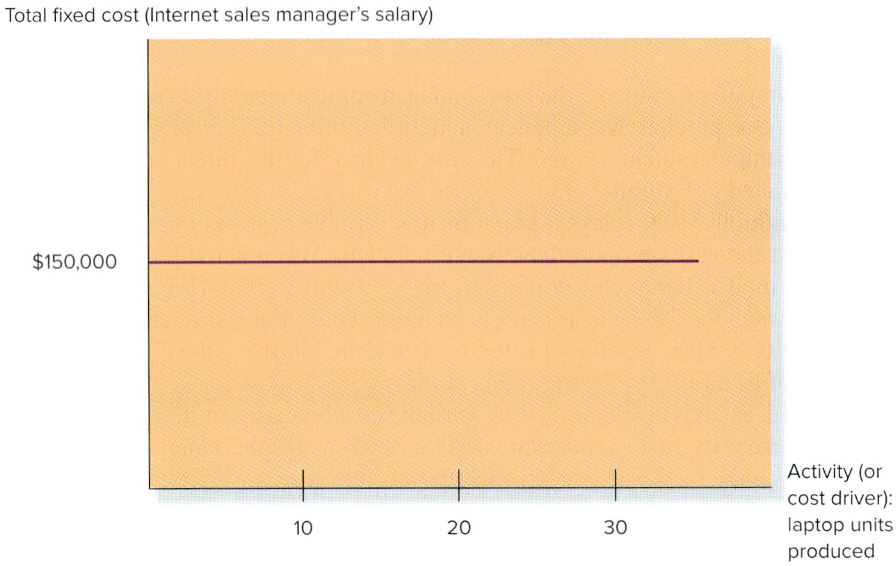

B. Tabulation of Fixed Cost

Activity (or cost driver)	Variable Cost per Unit	Total Fixed Cost
1	$150,000	$150,000
2	75,000	150,000
5	30,000	150,000
10	15,000	150,000
20	7,500	150,000
30	5,000	150,000

C. Graph of Unit Fixed Cost

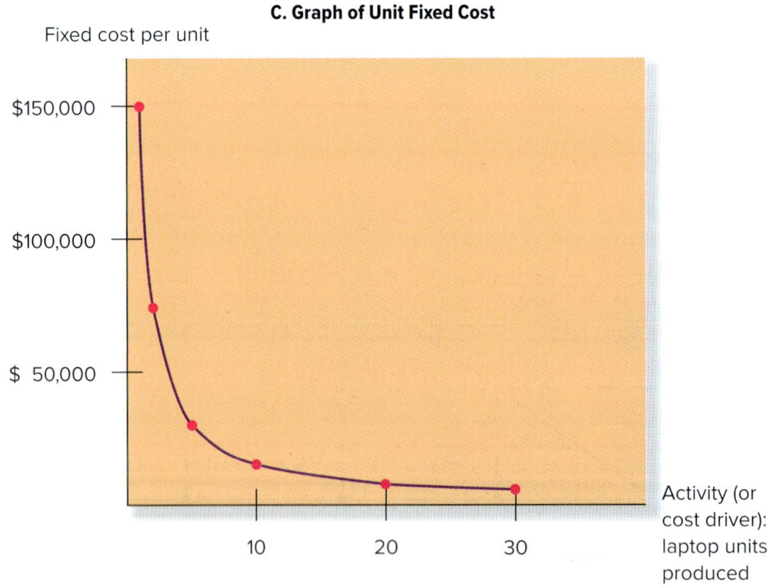

From the graph in panel A of Exhibit 2–10, it is apparent that *total* fixed cost remains unchanged as activity changes. When activity triples, from 10 to 30 units, total fixed cost remains constant at $150,000. However, the fixed cost *per unit* does change as activity changes. If the activity level is only 1 unit, then the fixed cost per unit is $150,000 per unit ($150,000 ÷ 1). If the activity level is 10 units, then the fixed cost per unit declines

MANAGING HEALTH CARE COSTS THROUGH COST BEHAVIOR

Health care costs occupy an ever-greater share of U.S. GDP, so an understanding of these costs takes on greater and greater importance. One area of misunderstanding is the cost behavior of health care costs: which of these costs are variable and which ones are largely fixed? According to two leading cost experts, it is a myth that most health care costs are fixed. "Many health care system participants, including economists and accountants, believe that most costs in health care are fixed because so much care is delivered using shared staff, space and equipment. The result of this misguided thinking is that cost reduction efforts tend to focus on only the small fraction of costs seen as variable." But a focus on only the costs that are clearly variable, such as drugs and supplies, cannot make enough headway in solving the overall cost management problem in health care.

A careful analysis of costs reveals that personnel costs, which account for at least 50 percent of health care costs, are only fixed in the short run and might be more productively viewed as variable over a longer term of management. "Hospital executives can set the quantity, mix and compensation of their employees each year. Personnel costs are fixed only when executives allow them to be." Another prominent health care cost is space, and according to these two cost experts, space costs are also fixed only over a short to medium horizon. "If demand for space is reduced, units can be consolidated into smaller space, and excess space can be repurposed, sold, or subleased. Similarly, equipment costs can be avoided if changes in processes, treatment protocols, or patient mix eliminate the demand for the resources."[6]

The controversial Affordable Care Act (ACA), which has as its goal to extend the reach of health care in the US, includes many elements intended to shift cost behavior. For example, by increasing the number of individuals covered by health insurance, the ACA hopes to shift high cost-per-visit emergency room treatment to less costly office visits, a reduction in unit variable cost.

The ACA also includes an initiative called *bundled payments* wherein all of the various treatments related to a particular episode of care are paid for at a flat payment rate. Today, if an athlete hurts his knee, there are separate anesthesiologists, nurses, physical therapists, etc. Under bundled payments, there would be one set payment for all aspects of treatment. For the patient and those who pay his bills, the cost would be made more fixed than it is today (but with increased financial risk to the providers).

The bottom line is that if health care costs are to be controlled, they must first be understood. This includes understanding the correct classification of costs as variable or fixed, the appropriate period of analysis (which is not always one year), and the correct unit of analysis (which is not always one treatment). No wonder reining in the cost of health care is such a challenge!

Management
Accounting
Practice

Health Care Industry
Affordable Care Act

to $15,000 per unit ($150,000 ÷ 10). The behavior of total fixed cost and unit fixed cost is illustrated by the table in panel B of Exhibit 2–10.

Another way of viewing the change in unit fixed cost as activity changes is in a graph, as shown in panel C of Exhibit 2–10. Unit fixed cost declines steadily as activity increases. Notice that the decrease in unit fixed cost when activity changes from 1 to 10 units is much larger than the decrease in unit fixed cost when activity changes from 10 to 20 units, which in turn is somewhat larger than the decrease from 20 to 30 units. Thus, the amount of the change in unit fixed cost declines as the activity level increases.

To summarize, as the activity level increases, total fixed cost remains constant but unit fixed cost declines. As you will see in subsequent chapters, it is vital in managerial accounting to thoroughly understand the behavior of both total fixed costs and unit fixed costs.

[6]Robert S. Kaplan and Michael E. Porter, "How to Solve the Crisis in Health Care," *Harvard Business Review*, September 2011, p. 60.

Cost Accountability

An important objective of managerial accounting is to assist managers in understanding and controlling costs. Sometimes cost management is facilitated by tracing costs to the department or work center in which the cost was incurred. Such tracing of costs to departments is known as *responsibility accounting.*

Comet
Cometcomp.com

Comet Computer Company formed a cost management and control team to refine the company's responsibility accounting system. The team consisted of an engineer, the production scheduling manager, the assistant manager of quality control, the manager of human resources, and a managerial accountant. The ultimate objective of the team was to develop a responsibility accounting system that would assist management in understanding and controlling costs as well as reducing costs whenever possible. We will study cost management systems and cost reduction in considerable detail in Chapter 5 and responsibility accounting in Chapter 12. For now, let's focus on a couple of cost concepts that are useful in these areas of managerial accounting.

Learning Objective 2-9

Distinguish among direct, indirect, controllable, and uncontrollable costs.

Direct and Indirect Costs An entity, such as a particular product, service, or department, to which a cost is assigned is called a **cost object.** A cost that can be traced to a particular cost object is called a **direct cost** of that cost object.

For example, the cost of paint used in the painting department of a Toyota plant is a direct cost of the painting department. At the same time, it is also a direct cost of the car that Toyota is manufacturing, and as we saw earlier, when the cost object is a product or service and the direct cost is a material, we call it *direct material.* Similarly, the salary of an auto mechanic is a direct cost of the automotive repair department in a Walmart store, and it is also *direct labor,* a direct cost of the service being sold (the cost object).

A cost that is not directly traceable to a particular cost object is called an **indirect cost** of that cost object. For example, the costs of national advertising for Walt Disney World are indirect costs of each of the departments or subunits of the recreational complex, such as the Magic Kingdom and Epcot. The salary of a General Electric Company plant manager is an indirect cost of each of the plant's production departments. The plant manager's duties are important to the smooth functioning of each of the plant's departments, but there is no way to trace a portion of the plant manager's salary cost to each department.

Whether a cost is a direct cost or an indirect cost of a department often depends on which department is under consideration. A cost can be a direct cost of one department or subunit in the organization but an indirect cost of other departments. While the salary of a General Electric Company plant manager is an *indirect* cost of the plant's departments, the manager's salary is a *direct* cost of the plant that he manages.

Comet Computer Company's cost management and control team determined that many of the company's costs were traceable to departments or to specific activities of those departments. In the purchasing department, for example, costs were traced not just to the department, but to the specific activities of identifying vendors, qualifying vendors, securing design specifications from the engineering design department, negotiating prices, placing orders, expediting orders, receiving materials and components, inspecting materials, and releasing materials to the material-handling operation.

An important objective of a cost management system is to trace as many costs as possible directly to the activities that cause them to be incurred. Sometimes called *activity accounting,* this process is vital to management's objective of eliminating *non-value-added costs.* These are costs of activities that can be eliminated without deterioration of product quality, performance, or perceived value. (We will study the elimination of non-value-added costs in greater detail in Chapter 5.)

For the typical business unit, which had responsibility for profits, less than one-third of overhead costs were directly in its control. (2g)
Kraft Foods

Controllable and Uncontrollable Costs Another cost classification that can be helpful in cost control indicates the controllability of a cost item by a particular manager. If a manager can control or heavily influence the level of a cost, then that cost is

Exhibit 2–11
Controllable and Uncontrollable Costs

Cost Item	Manager	Classification
Cost of raw material used to produce computer chips in an Intel factory	Supervisor of the production department for computer chips	Controllable (The production supervisor can exercise some control over the quantity of material used by ensuring that waste and defective units are minimized.)
Cost of food used in a Subway restaurant	Restaurant manager	Controllable (The restaurant manager exercises some control over the quantity of food used by scheduling production to ensure that excess food is not produced and wasted.)
Cost of national advertising for the Alamo car rental company	Manager of the Alamo rental agency at the Orlando airport	Uncontrollable
Cost of national accounting and data processing operations for Target	Manager of a Target store in Gainesville, Florida	Uncontrollable

classified as a **controllable cost** of that manager. Costs that a manager cannot influence significantly are classified as *uncontrollable costs* of that manager. Many costs are not completely under the control of any individual. In classifying costs as controllable or uncontrollable, managerial accountants generally focus on a manager's ability to influence costs. The question is not, Who controls the cost? but, Who is in the best position to influence the level of a cost item? Exhibit 2–11 lists several cost items along with their typical classification as controllable or uncontrollable.

Comet Computer's cost management and control team was able to designate many of Comet's costs as controllable or uncontrollable by various managers. Take the cost of raw materials and components, for example. The team determined that the *quantity* of materials used was largely controllable by the production supervisor, but the *price* of the materials was influenced more by the purchasing manager.

Economic Cost Concepts

Learning Objective 2-10

Define and give examples of an opportunity cost, an out-of-pocket cost, a sunk cost, a differential cost, a marginal cost, and an average cost.

Another of Comet Computer Company's interdisciplinary management teams was formed to take a close look at which of the raw materials and components used in Comet's products should be manufactured by Comet and which ones should be outsourced (purchased from outside vendors).[7] This outsourcing action team consisted of the assistant manager of purchasing, a product design engineer, a product group sales manager, and a managerial accountant. As the team pursued its assignment, its members soon found that they were once again dealing with several different cost concepts.

In addition to accounting cost classifications, such as product costs and period costs, the team's members also found themselves using economic concepts in classifying costs. Such concepts are often useful in helping managers decide what cost information is relevant to the decisions faced by the organization. Several of the most important economic cost concepts are discussed next.

Comet
Cometcomp.com

Opportunity Costs An **opportunity cost** is defined as the benefit that is sacrificed when the choice of one action precludes taking an alternative course of action. If your favorite band is playing downtown on Saturday night, but a college football game you want to watch is on TV at the same time, the opportunity cost of seeing the band perform live is the foregone pleasure of watching the game live.

Opportunity costs arise in many business decisions. For example, suppose a baseball manufacturer receives a special order for softballs from the city of Boston. If the firm accepts the softball order, it will not have enough productive capacity (labor or machine time) to produce its usual output of baseballs for sale to a large chain of sporting-goods

[7]The outsourcing decision, as well as several other common management decisions, is covered in detail in Chapter 14.

stores. The opportunity cost of accepting the softball order is, in part, the forgone benefit from the baseball production that cannot be achieved, measured by the potential revenue from the baseball sales minus the variable cost of manufacturing the baseballs. But it also includes all foregone future benefit caused by damage to the relationship with its sporting-goods customer. Calculating and considering such opportunity costs can be very difficult, but also very important in making the right decision.

Opportunity costs also arise in personal decisions, as in the music vs. football example above. More significantly, the opportunity cost of a student's college education includes the salary that is forgone as a result of not taking a full-time job during the student's years in college.[8]

From an economic perspective, a dollar of opportunity cost associated with an action should be treated as equivalent to a dollar of out-of-pocket cost. **Out-of-pocket costs** are those that require the payment of cash or other assets as a result of their incurrence. The out-of-pocket costs associated with the softball order consist of the manufacturing costs required to produce the softballs. In making the decision to accept or reject the softball order, the firm's management should consider *both* the out-of-pocket cost and the opportunity cost of the order.

Studies by behavioral scientists and economists have shown that many people have a tendency to ignore or downplay the importance of opportunity costs. For example, try the following experiment on your friends who are basketball fans. First, ask them if they would pay the going price of $1,000 for a ticket to the basketball Final Four. Then ask them, if they were to win that same ticket to the Final Four, would they be willing to sell it for $1,000? You are likely to find that many of them would not pay $1,000 for the ticket, but they also would not sell the ticket they won for $1,000! In other words, they refuse to incur the $1,000 *out-of-pocket cost* of buying the Final Four ticket, effectively saying, "I'd rather have $1,000 than see the game in person." However, they are willing to incur the $1,000 *opportunity cost* of going to the game rather than sell the ticket: "I'd rather see the game in person than have $1,000." An interesting contradiction!

Behavior such as that illustrated in the Final Four example is economically inconsistent. And surprisingly common! Ignoring or downplaying the importance of opportunity costs can result in inconsistent and faulty business decisions.[9]

Comet Computer's outsourcing action team found that the opportunity cost of using constrained production resources (such as space, machine time, and employee time) to produce a computer component in-house was an important factor to consider in deciding whether to outsource the component.[10]

Sunk Costs **Sunk costs** are costs that have been incurred in the past. Consequently, they do not affect future costs and cannot be changed by any current or future action. Examples of such costs include the acquisition cost of equipment previously purchased and the manufacturing cost of inventory on hand. Regardless of the current usefulness of the equipment or the inventory, the costs of acquiring them cannot be changed by any prospective action. Hence, these costs are irrelevant to all future decisions.

Suppose, for example, that a university's parking and traffic department purchased a system of software and 10 tablet computers last spring to support the ticketing and

---

[8]Not to worry. Studies consistently show that college graduates out-earn high school graduates by a significant amount ("well over $1 million…during their working lives" for the average four-year degree), easily enough benefit to offset the cost of a college education, including opportunity costs, for most people. Jaison R. Abel and Richard Deitz, "Do the Benefits of College Still Outweigh the Costs?" *Current Issues in Economics and Finance,* Federal Reserve Bank of New York, volume 20, number 3 (2014).

[9]This problem is called the *endowment effect*. For an interesting discussion of behaviorial problems in decision making, including an entire chapter on the endowment effect, see Daniel Kahneman, *Thinking, Fast and Slow,* Farrar, Straus, and Giroux (2011).

[10]The details of the outsourcing decision, including its relevant costs and the role of opportunity costs, are covered in Chapter 14.

enforcement process. Soon after the hardware's six-month warranty expired, traffic officers began complaining that the tablets are unreliable and overly sensitive to damp, cold winter weather. Their supervisor requests that the parking and traffic director junk the tablet-based system and replace them with units custom-designed for parking and traffic enforcement. The director responds by insisting, "We can't afford to junk the tablet system! We paid $14,000 for it just last spring."

This illustration is a typical example of the inappropriate attention paid to sunk costs. The $14,000 paid for the tablet-based system is sunk. No future decision about the tablet computers or the office's procedures can affect that cost. Future decisions should be based on future costs, such as the cost of weather-proofing the tablets, the cost of replacing them with the custom-designed units, and the cost of training new traffic officers if the current ones get fed up with the tablet system and quit.

Although it is incorrect, from an economic perspective, to allow sunk costs to affect future decisions, people often do so. It is human nature to attempt to justify past decisions. When there is a perceived need to demonstrate competence, either to themselves or to others, managers may seek to justify their decisions. The response of the parking and traffic director that "We can't afford to junk the tablet system!" may represent the director's need to justify her past decision to purchase the system. It is important for managers and accountants to be aware of such behavioral tendencies.

Comet Computer's outsourcing action team encountered a sunk cost as it considered outsourcing production of a component called a monitor interface unit (MIU). The team discovered that the automatic insertion robot used to insert components into the MIU was difficult to maintain and expensive to operate. Nevertheless, the department supervisor was inclined to keep the robot and continue in-house production of the MIU, because, as he put it, "Comet paid an arm and a leg for this robot." The team was able to demonstrate that the robot's acquisition cost was a sunk cost and was irrelevant to the outsourcing decision. We will explore sunk costs in more detail in Chapter 14.

Differential Costs A **differential cost** is the amount by which the cost differs under two alternative actions. Suppose, for example, that a county government is considering two competing sites for a new recycling center. If the northern site is chosen, the annual cost of transporting recyclable waste to the site is projected at $285,000. If the southern site is selected, annual transportation charges are expected to be $240,000. The annual differential cost of transporting refuse is calculated as follows:

Annual cost of transporting refuse to northern site	$285,000
Annual cost of transporting refuse to southern site	240,000
Annual differential cost	$ 45,000

The increase in cost from one alternative to another is called an **incremental cost.** In the landfill example, the annual incremental cost of selecting the northern site is $45,000. Differential or incremental costs are found in a variety of economic decisions. The additional cost incurred by Gulliver's Travels, a travel agency, in locating a new office in the suburbs is the incremental cost of the new business location. The difference in the total cost incurred by the travel agency with and without the suburban location is the differential cost of the decision whether to establish the new office. Decisions about establishing new airline routes, adding additional shifts in a manufacturing firm, or increasing the nursing staff in a hospital all involve differential costs.

At Comet Computer, the outsourcing action team estimated that the differential cost between outsourcing the production of the MIU and producing it in-house would be $200,000 annually in favor of outsourcing, based on current projections of annual production. We will explore differential costs in more detail in Chapter 14.

Exhibit 2–12
Marginal Cost of Producing Laptop Computers at Comet Computer Company

Comet
Cometcomp.com

Number of Laptop Computers Produced	Total Cost of Producing Laptops	Marginal Cost of Producing a Laptop
1	$ 2,000	Difference is $1,900 → Marginal cost of 2nd laptop is $1,900
2	3,900	
10	18,000	Difference is $1,690 → Marginal cost of 11th laptop is $1,690
11	19,690	
100	150,000	Difference is $995 → Marginal cost of 101st laptop is $995
101	150,995	

Marginal Costs and Average Costs A special case of the differential-cost concept is the **marginal cost**, which is the incremental cost of producing one additional unit. The additional cost incurred by Comet Computer when one additional high-performance laptop computer is made is the marginal cost of manufacturing the computer. The table in Exhibit 2–12 shows how marginal cost can change across different ranges of production quantities.

Marginal costs typically differ across different ranges of production quantities because the efficiency of the production process changes. At Comet Computer, the marginal cost of producing a laptop computer declines as output increases. It is much more efficient for the company to manufacture 101 computers than to make only one.

It is important to distinguish between *marginal costs* and *average costs*. In the Comet Computer example, the marginal cost of the second computer is $1,900. However, the average cost per unit when two laptops are manufactured is $3,900 divided by 2, or $1,950. Similarly, the marginal cost of the eleventh laptop is $1,690, but the average cost per unit when 11 laptops are produced is $1,790 (calculated by dividing $19,690 by 11). What is the marginal cost of the 101st laptop computer? The average cost per unit when 101 laptops are manufactured?[11]

To summarize, the marginal cost of production is the extra cost incurred when one more unit is produced. The **average cost per unit** is the total cost, for whatever quantity is manufactured, divided by the number of units manufactured. Marginal costs and average costs arise in a variety of economic situations. A University of Texas dean might be interested in the marginal cost of educating one additional student, and a Toyota executive might want to know the marginal cost of producing one more Toyota Prius. An Amtrak route manager might be interested in the average cost per mile on the Washington, D.C., to New York City route.

Costs and Benefits of Information

> "If you can't communicate information to the individual, then the information is. . .lost. So, your communication skills are very important." (2h)
>
> **Abbott Labs**

Many different cost concepts have been explored in this chapter. An important task for managers, and for the managerial accountants who support them, is to determine which of these cost concepts is most appropriate in each situation. The accountant strives to *communicate* the cost information to the user in the most effective manner possible, and to structure the organization's accounting information system to record data that will be useful for a variety of purposes. The benefits of measuring and classifying costs in a particular way are realized through the improvements in planning, control, and decision making that the information facilitates.

Another important task of the manager and accountant is to weigh the benefits of providing information against the costs of generating, communicating, and using that information. Some accountants, eager to show that they have not overlooked anything, tend to provide managers with too much information. But when managers receive more

[11] Marginal cost of the 101st laptop computer is $995 (from Exhibit 2–12). Average cost per unit when 101 laptops are produced is $1,495 ($150,995 ÷ 101).

HOW AIRLINES MAKE MONEY TODAY

Understanding costs is crucial in running any business. This is particularly true in the airline industry, which is beset by fluctuating fuel costs, staffing challenges, and intense competition to keep airfares low. *The Wall Street Journal* asked US Airways (now part of American Airlines) "to crunch airline expenses down to the percentages that an individual passenger pays, taking a hard look at the costs of running an airline. [The company] created a hypothetical flight of 100 passengers. Each one paid the average $146 fare for a domestic flight plus $18 each in fees and add-ons." The airline's bottom line was that "there is very little wiggle room on the plane for profit." On this hypothetical flight of 100 passengers, "it takes fares and fees from 99 seats to cover all costs." The breakdown? It takes 29 seats to cover fuel costs, 20 seats for salaries, 16 seats to cover the costs of ownership, 14 for government fees and taxes, 11 seats for maintenance, and 9 seats to cover other assorted costs. That leaves a meager one passenger's seat to cover the airline's profit.[12]

Little wonder, then, that airlines have been adding various other fees at a record pace. The president of an airline consulting firm put it like this: "It's a very crucial part of the profit picture... without [fees] you would not be looking at a profitable airline industry."[13]

Management
Accounting
Practice

Airline Industry
American Airlines

data than they can utilize effectively, *information overload* occurs. Struggling to process large amounts of information, managers may be unable to recognize the most important facts. In deciding how much and what type of information to provide, managerial accountants should consider these human limitations.

Costs in the Service Industry

© Ken Wolter/123RF.com

The cost terms and concepts that we have studied in this chapter are just as relevant in the service industry as in a manufacturing firm like Comet Computer Company. Here we will explore those cost issues in the context of a well-known automotive service company.

Midas, Inc. is one of the world's largest providers of automotive service, including exhaust systems, brakes, air conditioning, suspension, tires, and routine maintenance services. The company has over 1,000 franchised auto service shops in the United States and more than 2,000 worldwide. In recent years, Midas has undergone some significant changes. First, the company intentionally transitioned from an under-car repair specialist to a full-service, "total car care" automotive repair and maintenance provider. Second, Midas sold its exhaust system manufacturing business to concentrate fully on automotive service provision. To this end, Midas has established relationships with automobile parts vendors who distribute their products directly to Midas auto service shops.

A typical Midas automotive maintenance and repair shop has at least 4,000 square feet and six service bays. Midas supports the franchise dealer network with business managers who assist franchisees with operations, retail initiatives, training, and monitoring of the franchise agreement.[14]

Now let's think about a typical Midas-owned auto service shop to explore the various cost issues we have studied in a service-industry environment.

---

[12]Scott McCartney, "How Airlines Spend Your Airfare," *The Wall Street Journal*, June 7, 2012, pp. D1, D2.

[13]Martha C. White, "More Fees Propel Airlines' Profits, and Embitter Travelers," *The New York Times*, July 27, 2015, p. B1.

[14]Data are from historical Midas, Inc. annual reports and the company website. Midas, Inc. was acquired in 2012 by a subsidary of Sumitomo Corporation.

© Hill Street Studios/Blend Images/Getty Images RF

Product and Period Costs Midas service shops purchase auto parts and supplies, such as exhaust pipes, brake pads, oil filters, and engine oil, from vendors. These costs are stored in inventory as *product costs* (or *inventoriable costs*) until the time period when they are consumed in the repair process. At that time, these *product costs* become part of *cost of services* (or *operating expenses,* as discussed earlier*),* an *expense.* All of a Midas shop's other costs are *period costs,* and they are expensed as *operating expenses* during the period they are incurred. Examples of these period costs include employee salaries and wages, utilities, and depreciation on equipment and facilities.

Variable and Fixed Costs The costs incurred in the Midas service shop that vary directly with activity are *variable costs.* For example, the cost of lubricant, engine oil, and oil filters is a variable cost, because it varies in proportion to the number of lube-oil-filter (LOF) jobs the shop provides. Thus, a likely *cost driver* for this cost would be the number of LOF jobs performed. In contrast, any costs that do not tend to vary with service activity are *fixed costs.* Examples include the Midas shop's managerial salaries, depreciation on equipment and facilities, insurance, and property taxes.

Direct and Indirect Costs Consider a typical service and repair job. The customer has requested a routine lube-oil-filter job and an exhaust system repair, which requires a new muffler. The *direct costs* of this service and repair job (the *cost object*) include the parts and supplies used (lubricant, engine oil, oil filter, and a new muffler) and the wages of the automotive service technician for the time spent on this job. The many *indirect costs* of this service job include the shop manager's salary, the depreciation on the building, and local media advertising purchased by the franchise.

Now consider a different cost object—this Midas shop. For this cost object, the shop manager's salary is a direct cost of the Midas shop. However, the Midas CEO's salary is an indirect cost of this particular shop.

Controllable and Uncontrollable Costs Costs that are *controllable* by the manager of this Midas auto shop include local advertising, assuming the shop manager is responsible for such local ad buys. A cost that is partially controllable by the manager might include heating costs. Although the manager has little control over electricity or heating oil prices, the manager can ensure that the shop's heating system is properly maintained and the windows and doors have the proper weather stripping. Many of the shop's costs are largely *uncontrollable* by the shop manager. The depreciation, insurance, and property taxes on the building, for example, are the result of Midas policies regarding location and shop size.

Opportunity, Out-of-Pocket, and Sunk Costs These cost types all are represented in the Midas auto service business. Suppose the Midas shop manager decides to shut down one of the service bays on a particular day to inspect and maintain the lift and other equipment. Any customer business that is lost that day due to a shortage of service bays would be an *opportunity cost* of the shut-down decision. (Note that such an opportunity cost does not necessarily mean the shut-down decision was a poor one. The opportunity cost of any lost business could well be exceeded by the additional operating costs that could be incurred if the service bay was not properly maintained.) The wages paid to service technicians and utility costs are examples of *out-of-pocket costs*. The money spent last year to replace an auto lift is an example of a *sunk cost*.

Differential, Marginal, and Average Costs Suppose the Midas shop owns a small van to make short runs to pick up auto parts needed on short notice. The van needs to be replaced, and two vehicles are under consideration. The difference in the cost of these two alternative vehicles is a *differential cost* of the vehicle replacement decision. The cost of performing one additional lube-oil-filter (LOF) job in a given time period is the *marginal cost* of that type of service. The total cost of all LOF jobs in a time period, divided by the number of jobs, is the average cost of an LOF job.

To summarize, although manufacturers, like Lululemon, Motorola, or Renault, and service-industry firms, like Allstate, Enterprise Rent-a-Car, or Midas, are in very different businesses, they all must understand their costs in order to be successful in a competitive environment.

Focus on Ethics

WAS WORLDCOM'S CONTROLLER JUST FOLLOWING ORDERS?

Through a series of mergers and acquisitions, WorldCom, Inc. grew to become the nation's second-largest long-distance telecommunications company. WorldCom's core communication services included network data transmission over public and private networks. Trouble arose for WorldCom because of the immense overcapacity in the telecommunications industry due to overly optimistic growth projections during the Internet boom. The combination of overcapacity, decreased demand, and high fixed costs still poses a serious problem for many of the major players in the industry.

In June 2002, the company disclosed that it had overstated earnings for 2001 and the first quarter of 2002 to the tune of $3.8 billion. The overstatement arose because the company incorrectly classified period expenses as capital expenditures. This maneuver had two major effects on the company's financial statements: the company's assets were artificially inflated and the capitalization allowed the company to spread the recognition of its expenses into the future, which increased net income in the current period. The expenses in question related to line costs—the fees that WorldCom pays outside providers for access to their communications networks. In addition, the company announced in July 2002 that it had also manipulated reserve accounts, which affected another $3.8 billion in earnings in 1999 and 2000.

The problems at WorldCom were discovered during an internal audit and brought to the attention of the company's new auditors, KPMG. A different firm, Arthur Andersen, served as WorldCom's auditors during the period covered by the alleged accounting scandal. Arthur Andersen maintained that the details of the accounting fraud were kept from them by senior WorldCom management. The firm's controller and chief financial officer (CFO), who was a former KPMG employee, were fired after the alleged accounting frauds were revealed. WorldCom's CEO maintained that he knew nothing of the accounting decisions made by the CFO, but many observers question how almost $8 billion in expenses could slip by senior management.[15]

According to an Associated Press article that ran on September 27, 2002, "the former controller of WorldCom, Inc. pleaded guilty to securities fraud charges, saying he was instructed by 'senior management,' to falsify records. His plea was the first admission of guilt" to come out of what was at the time the largest corporate accounting scandal in U.S. history.[16] Subsequently, Worldcom's CFO pleaded guilty to his part in the accounting scandal.[17] In March of 2005, the company's CEO was convicted by a jury of nine criminal counts in the accounting fraud, including conspiracy and securities fraud.[18]

The CFO and controller were the top two financial and managerial accountants in the WorldCom organization. They were ultimately responsible for all of the company's financial and managerial accounting reports. (Note that this case also involves the alleged intentional misclassification of period costs.) What ethical issues are involved here? What do you make of the controller's assertion that he was just following orders given by senior management? What steps should WorldCom's controller have taken? (Review the Institute of Management Accountants' Statement of Ethical Professional Practice at the end of Chapter 1.)

---

[15]Jared Sandberg, Rebecca Blumenstein, and Shawn Young, "WorldCom Admits $3.8 Billion Error in Its Accounting—Firm Ousts Financial Chief and Struggles for Survival; SEC Probe Likely to Widen," *The Wall Street Journal,* June 26, 2002, p. A1; Jared Sandberg, Deborah Solomon, and Rebecca Blumenstein, "Disconnected: Inside WorldCom's Unearthing of a Vast Accounting Scandal," *The Wall Street Journal,* June 27, 2002, p. A1; and Jared Sandberg, "Leading the News: Was Ebbers Aware of Accounting Move at His WorldCom?" *The Wall Street Journal,* July 1, 2002, p. A3.

[16]Devlin Barrett, "Ex-WorldCom Exec Pleads Guilty," Associated Press, September 27, 2002 (as it appeared in the *Ithaca Journal*). See also Kurt Eichenwald and Simon Romero, "Plea Deals Are Seen for Three WorldCom Executives," *The New York Times*, August 29, 2002, pp. C1, C4.

[17]T. Richardson, "Worldcom CFO Lied, He Admits in Court," *The Register*, February 17, 2005, www.theregister.co.uk.

[18]A. Latour, S. Young, and L. Yuan, "Ebbers Is Convicted in Massive Fraud," *The Wall Street Journal*, March 16, 2005, p. A1.

Chapter Summary

LO2-1 Explain what is meant by the word *cost*. The word *cost* can have a variety of meanings in different situations. In general, a cost is the sacrifice made, usually measured by the resources given up, to achieve a particular purpose.

LO2-2 Distinguish among product costs, period costs, and expenses. A product cost is a cost assigned to manufactured or purchased goods. Period costs are those associated with the period of time in which they are incurred. An expense is the cost incurred when a resource (asset) is used up for the purpose of generating revenue.

LO2-3 Describe the role of costs in published financial statements. The cost of goods sold is an expense on the income statement. Inventory on the balance sheet is measured at its cost, as are all assets.

LO2-4 List and describe four types of manufacturing processes. The four basic types of manufacturing processes are job shop, batch, assembly line, and continuous flow.

LO2-5 Give examples of three types of manufacturing costs. Manufacturing costs are categorized as direct-material, direct-labor, and manufacturing-overhead (which is also known as production overhead).

LO2-6 Prepare a schedule of cost of goods manufactured, a schedule of cost of goods sold, and an income statement for a manufacturer. These accounting schedules, which are illustrated in the chapter, provide information to management about the costs incurred in a production operation.

LO2-7 Understand the importance of identifying an organization's cost drivers. A cost driver is any activity or event that causes costs to be incurred. Understanding the cost drivers in an organization is an essential component of managing those costs.

LO2-8 Describe the behavior of variable and fixed costs, in total and on a per-unit basis. As activity in an organization increases, a variable cost increases proportionately to activity in total, but remains constant on a per-unit basis. In contrast, as activity in an organization increases, a fixed cost remains constant in total but decreases on a per-unit basis.

LO2-9 Distinguish among direct, indirect, controllable, and uncontrollable costs. Direct and indirect costs refer to the ability of the accountant to trace costs to various departments in the organization. The terms *controllable* and *uncontrollable* are used to describe the extent to which a manager can influence a cost.

LO2-10 Define and give examples of an opportunity cost, an out-of-pocket cost, a sunk cost, a differential cost, a marginal cost, and an average cost. An opportunity cost is the benefit forgone because the choice of one action precludes another action. An out-of-pocket cost requires the payment of cash or other assets. Sunk costs are costs incurred in the past that cannot be altered by a current or future decision. A differential (or incremental) cost refers to the difference in the costs incurred under two alternative actions. A marginal cost is the cost of producing one additional unit. Finally, the average cost per unit is the total cost for whatever quantity is produced, divided by the number of units produced.

Review Problems on Cost Classifications

Problem 1

Several costs incurred by Myrtle Beach Golf Equipment, Inc. are listed below. For each cost, indicate which of the following classifications best describe the cost. More than one classification may apply to the same cost item. For example, a cost may be both a variable cost *and* a product cost.

Cost Classifications

a. Variable
b. Fixed
c. Period
d. Product
e. Administrative
f. Selling
g. Manufacturing
h. Research and development
i. Direct material
j. Direct labor
k. Manufacturing overhead

Cost Items

1. Metal used in golf clubs.
2. Salary of the plant manager.
3. Cost of electricity used to air condition the factory.
4. Commissions paid to sales personnel.
5. Wages paid to employees who assemble golf bags.
6. Salary of an engineer who is working on a prototype of a new self-driving golf cart.
7. Depreciation on the laptop used by the company president's executive assistant.

Problem 2

Listed below are several costs incurred in the loan department of Suwanee Bank and Trust Company. For each cost, indicate which of the following classifications best describe the cost. More than one classification may apply to the same cost item.

Cost Classifications

a. Controllable by the loan department manager
b. Uncontrollable by the loan department manager
c. Direct cost of the loan department
d. Indirect cost of the loan department
e. Differential cost
f. Marginal cost
g. Opportunity cost
h. Sunk cost
i. Out-of-pocket cost

Cost Items

1. Salary of the loan department manager.
2. Cost of office supplies used in the loan department.
3. Cost of the department's desktop computers purchased by the loan department manager last year.
4. The portion of general advertising cost of the bank that has been allocated to the loan department.
5. Revenue that the loan department would have generated for the bank if a branch loan office had been located downtown instead of in the next county.
6. Difference in the cost incurred by the bank when one additional loan application is processed.

Solutions to Review Problems

Problem 1

1. a, d, g, i
2. b, d, g, k
3. a, d, g, k
4. a, c, f
5. a, d, g, j
6. b, c, h
7. b, c, e

Problem 2

1. b, c, i
2. a, c, i
3. a, c, h
4. b, d, i
5. g
6. e, f

Key Terms

For each term's definition refer to the indicated page, or turn to the glossary at the end of the text.

average cost per unit, 56
controllable cost, 53
conversion costs, 44
cost, 36
cost driver, 48
cost object, 52
cost of goods manufactured, 45
cost of goods sold, 37
differential cost, 55
direct cost, 52
direct-labor cost, 43
direct material, 43
expense, 37
finished goods, 41
fixed cost, 49
gross margin, 40
gross profit, 40
idle time, 44
incremental cost, 55
indirect cost, 52
indirect labor, 43
indirect material, 43
inventoriable cost, 37
manufacturing overhead, 43
marginal cost, 56
operating expenses, 40
operating income, 40
operating profit, 40
opportunity cost, 53
out-of-pocket costs, 54
overtime premium, 43
period costs, 37
prime costs, 44
product cost, 37
raw material, 41
schedule of cost of goods manufactured, 45
schedule of cost of goods sold, 45
service departments (or support departments), 43
sunk costs, 54
total manufacturing cost, 44
variable cost, 48
work-in-process, 41

Review Questions

2–1. Distinguish between product costs and period costs.

2–2. Why are product costs also called inventoriable costs?

2–3. What is the most important difference between a manufacturing firm and a service industry firm, with regard to the classification of costs as product costs or period costs?

2–4. List several product costs incurred in the production of a backpack.

2–5. List, describe, and give an example of each of the four different types of production processes.

2–6. Why is the cost of idle time treated as manufacturing overhead?

2–7. Explain why an overtime premium is included in manufacturing overhead.

2–8. What is meant by the phrase "different costs for different purposes"?

2–9. Give examples to illustrate how the city of Tampa could use cost information in planning, controlling costs, and making decisions.

2–10. Distinguish between fixed costs and variable costs.

2–11. How does the fixed cost per unit change as the level of activity (or cost driver) increases? Why?

2–12. How does the variable cost per unit change as the level of activity (or cost driver) increases? Why?

2–13. Distinguish between volume-based and operations-based cost drivers in the airline industry.

2–14. Would each of the following characteristics be a volume-based or an operations-based cost driver in a college: (a) number of students, (b) number of disciplines offered for study, and (c) urban versus rural location?

2–15. List three direct costs of the food and beverage department in a hotel. List three indirect costs of the department.

2–16. List three costs that are likely to be controllable by a city's airport manager. List three costs that are likely to be uncontrollable by the manager.

2–17. Which of the following costs are likely to be controllable by the chief of nursing in a hospital?

a. Cost of medication administered.

b. Cost of overtime paid to nurses due to scheduling errors.

c. Cost of depreciation of hospital beds.

2–18. Distinguish between out-of-pocket costs and opportunity costs.

2–19. Define the terms sunk cost and differential cost.

2–20. Distinguish between marginal and average costs.

2–21. Think about the process of registering for classes at your college or university. What additional information would you like to have before you register? How would it help you? What sort of information might create information overload for you?

2–22. Two years ago the manager of a large department store purchased new bar code scanners costing $39,000. A salesperson recently tried to sell the manager a new computer-integrated checkout system for the store. The new system would save the store a substantial amount of money each year. The recently purchased scanners could be sold in the secondhand market for $19,000. The store manager refused to listen to the salesperson, saying, "I just bought those scanners. I can't get rid of them until I get my money's worth out of them." *(a)* What type of cost is the cost of purchasing the old bar code scanners? *(b)* What common behavioral tendency is the manager exhibiting?

2–23. Indicate whether each of the following costs is a direct cost or an indirect cost of the restaurant in a hotel.

a. Cost of food served.

b. Chef's salary and fringe benefits.

c. Part of the cost of maintaining the grounds around the hotel, which is allocated to the restaurant.

d. The portion of the cost of advertising the hotel that has been allocated to the restaurant.

Exercises

All applicable Exercises are available in Connect.

Exercise 2–24
Cost of Goods Manufactured and Sold; Missing Data
(LO 2-1, 2-3, 2-6)

For each case below, find the missing amount.

	Case I	Case II	Case III
Beginning inventory of finished goods	?	$12,000	$ 7,000
Cost of goods manufactured during period	$419,000	$95,000	?
Ending inventory of finished goods	98,000	8,000	21,000
Cost of goods sold	405,000	?	304,000

Exercise 2–25
Idle Time
(LO 2-5)

A foundry employee worked a normal 40-hour shift, but four hours were idle due to a small fire in the plant. The employee earns $18 per hour.

Required:

1. Calculate the employee's total compensation for the week.
2. How much of this compensation is a direct-labor cost? How much is overhead?

Exercise 2–26
Overtime Cost
(LO 2-5)

A loom operator in a textiles factory earns $16 per hour. By contract, the employee earns $24 (time and a half) for overtime hours. The operator worked 45 hours during the first week of May, and overtime is paid after the usual 40 hours.

Required:

1. Compute the loom operator's compensation for the week.
2. Calculate the employee's total overtime premium for the week.
3. How much of the employee's total compensation for the week is direct-labor cost? How much is overhead?

Exercise 2–27
Manufacturing Processes; Use of Internet
(LO 2-4)

Not all manufacturing processes fall neatly into the structure presented in the chapter. One variation is called *mass customization.* Search the term mass customization on the Internet.

Required: Select and read several articles about mass customization. Then briefly explain (1) how mass customization relates to the structure of manufacturing processes discussed in the chapter, (2) whether you believe mass customization would be the best type of manufacturing process for a gaming computer manufacturer like Falcon Northwest, and (3) what effect this choice would have on Falcon Northwest's costs.

Exercise 2–28
Cost Classifications
(LO 2-2, 2-8, 2-9)

Consider the following costs that were incurred during the current year:

1. Tire costs incurred by Ford Motor Company.
2. Sales commissions paid to the sales force of Dell Inc.
3. Wood glue consumed in the manufacture of Rooms To Go furniture.
4. Hourly wages of refinery security guards employed by ExxonMobil.
5. The salary of a financial vice president of Hewlett Packard.
6. Advertising costs of Coca-Cola.
7. Straight-line depreciation on factory machinery of Boeing Corporation.
8. Wages of assembly-line personnel of Whirlpool Corporation.
9. Delivery costs incurred by Ben & Jerry's for a shipment of their ice cream to a grocery store.
10. Newsprint consumed in printing *The New York Times.*
11. Plant insurance costs of Texas Instruments.
12. LED costs incurred in light-bulb manufacturing of GE Lighting.

Required: Evaluate each of the preceding and determine whether the cost is (a) a product cost or a period cost, (b) variable or fixed in terms of behavior, and (c) for the product costs only, whether the cost is properly classified as direct material, direct labor, or manufacturing overhead. Item 1 is done as an example:

1. Tire costs: Product cost, variable, direct material

Exercise 2–29
Schedules of Cost of Goods Manufactured and Sold; Income Statement
(LO 2-1, 2-3, 2-6)

Alexandria Aluminum Company, a manufacturer of recyclable soda cans, had the following inventory balances at the beginning and end of 20x1.

Inventory Classification	January 1, 20x1	December 31, 20x1
Raw material	$ 60,000	$ 70,000
Work in process	120,000	115,000
Finished goods	150,000	165,000

During 20x1, the company purchased $250,000 of raw material and spent $400,000 on direct labor. Manufacturing overhead costs were as follows:

Indirect material	$ 10,000
Indirect labor	25,000
Depreciation on plant and equipment	100,000
Utilities	25,000
Other	30,000

Sales revenue was $1,105,000 for the year. Selling and administrative expenses for the year amounted to $110,000. The firm's tax rate is 40 percent.

Required:

1. Prepare a schedule of cost of goods manufactured.
2. Prepare a schedule of cost of goods sold.
3. Prepare an income statement.
4. *Build a spreadsheet:* Construct an Excel spreadsheet to solve all of the preceding requirements. Show how both cost schedules and the income statement will change if the following data change: direct labor is $390,000 and utilities cost $35,000.

Exercise 2–30
Fixed and Variable Costs; Automobile Service; Missing Data
(LO 2-1, 2-8)

Mighty Muffler, Inc. operates an automobile service facility that specializes in replacing mufflers on compact cars. The following table shows the costs incurred during a month when 600 mufflers were replaced.

	Muffler Replacements		
	500	600	700
Total costs:			
Fixed costs	a	$42,000	b
Variable costs	c	30,000	d
Total costs	e	$72,000	f
Cost per muffler replacement:			
Fixed cost	g	h	i
Variable cost	j	k	l
Total cost per muffler replacement	m	n	o

Required: Fill in the missing amounts, labeled (a) through (o), in the table.

Exercise 2–31
Fixed, Variable, Marginal, and Average Costs; Hotel
(LO 2-1, 2-8, 2-10)

A hotel pays the phone company $100 per month plus $.25 for each call made. During January 6,000 calls were made. In February 5,000 calls were made.

Required:

1. Calculate the hotel's phone bills for January and February.
2. Calculate the cost per phone call in January and in February.

3. Separate the January phone bill into its fixed and variable components.
4. What is the marginal cost of one additional phone call in January?
5. What was the average cost of a phone call in January?

Exercise 2–32
Economic Characteristics of Costs
(LO 2-1, 2-10)

This icon indicates international setting.

Martin Shrood purchased a vacant lot outside of London for £13,500, because he heard that a shopping mall was going to be built on the other side of the road. He figured that he could make a bundle by putting in a fast-food outlet on the site. As it turned out, the rumor was false. A sanitary landfill was located on the other side of the road, and Martin's land was worthless. (£ denotes the British monetary unit, pounds sterling.)*

Required: With respect to the economic characteristics of costs, what type of cost is the £13,500 that Martin paid for the vacant lot?

Exercise 2–33
Differential Cost
(LO 2-1, 2-10)

Orbital Communications, Inc. manufactures communications satellites used in TV signal transmission. The firm currently purchases one component for its satellites from a European firm. An Orbital Communications engineering team has found a way to use the company's own component, part number A200, instead of the European component. However, the Orbital Communications component must be modified at a cost of $500 per part. The European component costs $8,900 per part. Orbital Communications' part number A200 costs $5,100 before it is modified. Orbital Communications currently uses 10 of the European components per year.

Required: Calculate the annual differential cost between Orbital Communications' two production alternatives.

Exercise 2–34
Computing Costs; Government Agency
(LO 2-1, 2-9, 2-10)

The state Department of Education owns a computer system, which its employees use for word processing and keeping track of education statistics. The governor's office recently began using this computer also. As a result of the increased usage, the demands on the computer soon exceeded its capacity. The director of the Department of Education was soon forced to lease several personal computers to meet the computing needs of her employees. The annual cost of leasing the equipment is $14,000.

Required:

1. What type of cost is this $14,000?
2. Should this cost be associated with the governor's office or the Department of Education? Why?

Exercise 2–35
Economic Characteristics of Costs
(LO 2-1, 2-10)

Suppose you paid $150 for a ticket to see your university's football team compete in a bowl game. Someone offered to buy your ticket for $400, but you decided to go to the game.

Required:

1. What did it really cost you to see the game?
2. What type of cost is this?

Exercise 2–36
Marginal Costs
(LO 2-1, 2-10)

List the costs that would likely be included in each of the following marginal-cost calculations.

1. The marginal cost of one additional passenger on an American Airlines flight.
2. The marginal cost of serving one additional customer in a Chipotle Mexican Grill.
3. The marginal cost of United Airlines adding a flight from Honolulu to Seattle.
4. The marginal cost of keeping a Wells Fargo branch bank open one additional hour on Saturdays.
5. The marginal cost of manufacturing one additional Burton snowboard.

*Although the euro is used in most European markets, Great Britain still uses the British pound sterling.

Problems

All applicable Problems are available in Connect.

connect

Problem 2–37
Content of Financial Statements and Reports
(LO 2-3, 2-4)

Consider the following cost items:

1. Salaries of players on the Boston Red Sox.
2. Year-end completed goods of Levi Strauss jeans.
3. Executive compensation costs at Home Depot.
4. Advertising costs for Sony.
5. Costs incurred during the period to insure a Ford plant against fire and flood losses.
6. Current year's depreciation on a Carnival Cruise Line ship.
7. The cost of printer ink and paper used during the period by Shutterfly.
8. Assembly-line wage cost incurred at a Kona bicycle plant.
9. Year-end production in process at Lenovo computer manufacturer.
10. The cost of products sold to customers of a Target store.
11. The cost of products sold to distributors of carpet manufacturer Shaw Floors.

Required:

1. Evaluate the costs just cited, and determine whether the associated dollar amounts would be found on the firm's balance sheet, income statement, or schedule of cost-of-goods-manufactured. (Note: In some cases, more than one answer will apply.)
2. What major asset will normally be insignificant for service enterprises and relatively substantial for retailers, wholesalers, and manufacturers? Briefly discuss.
3. Briefly explain the major differences between income statements of service enterprises versus those of retailers, wholesalers, and manufacturers.

Problem 2–38
Financial Statement Elements: Manufacturer
(LO 2-5, 2-6)

2. Cost of goods manufactured: $913,200
4. Net income: $154,420

The following selected information was extracted from the 20x1 accounting records of Lone Oak Products:

Raw material purchases	$ 175,000
Direct labor	254,000
Indirect labor	109,000
Selling and administrative salaries	133,000
Building depreciation*	80,000
Other selling and administrative expenses	195,000
Other factory costs	344,000
Sales revenue ($130 per unit)	1,495,000

*Seventy-five percent of the company's building was devoted to production activities; the remaining 25 percent was used for selling and administrative functions.

Inventory data:

	January 1	December 31
Raw material	$ 15,800	$18,200
Work in process	35,700	62,100
Finished goods*	111,100	97,900

*The January 1 and December 31 finished-goods inventory consisted of 1,350 units and 1,190 units, respectively.

Required:

1. Calculate Lone Oak's manufacturing overhead for the year.
2. Calculate Lone Oak's cost of goods manufactured.
3. Compute the company's cost of goods sold.
4. Determine net income for 20x1, assuming a 30% income tax rate.
5. Determine the number of completed units manufactured during the year.
6. ***Build a spreadsheet:*** Construct an Excel spreadsheet to solve all of the preceding requirements. Show how the solution will change if the following data change: indirect labor is $115,000 and other factory costs amount to $516,000.

Problem 2–39
Inventory Estimates; Partial Data
(LO 2-5, 2-6)

Direct material used: $40,000

On April 12, after the close of business, Singh & Sons had a devastating fire that destroyed the company's work-in-process and finished-goods inventories. Fortunately, all raw materials escaped damage because materials owned by the firm were stored in another warehouse. The following information is available:

Sales revenue through April 12	$330,000
Income before taxes through April 12	68,000
Direct labor through April 12	120,000
Cost of goods available for sale, April 12	275,000
Work-in-process inventory, January 1	21,000
Finished-goods inventory, January 1	37,000
Gross margin	30% of sales

The firm's accountants determined that the cost of direct materials used normally averages 25 percent of prime costs (i.e., direct material + direct labor). In addition, manufacturing overhead is 50 percent of the firm's total production costs.

Required: Singh & Sons is in the process of negotiating a settlement with its insurance company. Prepare an estimate of the cost of work-in-process and finished-goods inventories that were destroyed by the fire.

Problem 2–40
Financial-Statement Elements; Cost Behavior
(LO 2-5, 2-6, 2-8)

2. Net income: $168,000

Mason Corporation began operations at the beginning of the current year. One of the company's products, a refrigeration element, sells for $185 per unit. Information related to the current year's activities follows.

Variable costs per unit:	
Direct material	$ 20
Direct labor	37
Manufacturing overhead	48
Annual fixed costs:	
Manufacturing overhead	$600,000
Selling and administrative	860,000
Production and Sales activity:	
Production (units)	24,000
Sales (units)	20,000

Mason carries its finished-goods inventory at the average unit cost of production and is subject to a 30 percent income tax rate. There was no work in process at year-end.

Required:

1. Determine the cost of the December 31 finished-goods inventory.
2. Compute Mason's net income for the current year ended December 31.
3. If next year's production decreases to 23,000 units and general cost behavior patterns do not change, what is the likely effect on:
   a. The direct-labor cost of $37 per unit? Why?
   b. The fixed manufacturing overhead cost of $600,000? Why?
   c. The fixed selling and administrative cost of $860,000? Why?
   d. The average unit cost of production? Why?

Problem 2–41
Incomplete Data; Manufacturing Costs
(LO 2-2, 2-5)

Ex

This icon indicates that an Excel spreadsheet template is provided on the text's website.

Net income, case A: $110,000

Determine the missing amounts in each of the following independent cases.

	Case A	Case B	Case C
Beginning inventory, raw material	?	$20,000	$15,000
Ending inventory, raw material	$90,000	?	$30,000
Purchases of raw material	100,000	85,000	?
Direct material	70,000	95,000	?
Direct labor	?	100,000	125,000
Manufacturing overhead	250,000	?	160,000
Total manufacturing costs	520,000	345,000	340,000

(continued)

	Case A	Case B	Case C
Beginning inventory, work in process	35,000	20,000	?
Ending inventory, work in process	?	35,000	5,000
Cost of goods manufactured	525,000	?	350,000
Beginning inventory, finished goods	50,000	40,000	?
Cost of goods available for sale	?	?	370,000
Ending inventory, finished goods	?	?	25,000
Cost of goods sold	545,000	330,000	?
Sales	?	?	480,000
Gross margin	255,000	170,000	?
Selling and administrative expenses	?	75,000	?
Income before taxes	150,000	?	90,000
Income tax expense	40,000	45,000	?
Net income	?	?	55,000

Problem 2–42
Cost Terminology
(LO 2-2, 2-5, 2-10)

1(a). Total prime costs:$2,680,000
1(d). Manufacturing overhead:$534,000

The following cost data for the year just ended pertain to Sentiments, Inc., a greeting card manufacturer:

Direct material	$2,100,000
Advertising expense	99,000
Depreciation on factory building	115,000
Direct labor: wages	485,000
Cost of finished goods inventory at year-end	115,000
Indirect labor: wages	140,000
Production supervisor's salary	45,000
Service department costs*	100,000
Direct labor: fringe benefits	95,000
Indirect labor: fringe benefits	30,000
Fringe benefits for production supervisor	9,000
Total overtime premiums paid	55,000
Cost of idle time: production employees§	40,000
Administrative costs	150,000
Rental of office space for sales personnel†	15,000
Sales commissions	5,000
Product promotion costs	10,000

*All services are provided to manufacturing departments.

§Cost of idle time is an overhead item; it is not included in the direct-labor wages given above.

†The rental of sales space was made necessary when the sales offices were converted to storage space for raw material.

Required:

1. Compute each of the following costs for the year just ended: (a) total prime costs, (b) total manufacturing overhead costs, (c) total conversion costs, (d) total product costs, and (e) total period costs.
2. One of the costs listed above is an opportunity cost. Identify this cost, and explain why it is an opportunity cost.

Problem 2–43
Schedules of Cost of Goods Manufactured and Sold; Income Statement
(LO 2-1, 2-3, 2-5, 2-6)

2. Cost of goods sold: $580,000

The following data refer to San Fernando Fashions Company for the year 20x2:

Sales revenue	$950,000
Work-in-process inventory, December 31	30,000
Work-in-process inventory, January 1	40,000
Selling and administrative expenses	150,000
Income tax expense	90,000
Purchases of raw material	180,000
Raw-material inventory, December 31	25,000
Raw-material inventory, January 1	40,000
Direct labor	200,000

(continued)

Utilities: plant	40,000
Depreciation: plant and equipment	60,000
Finished-goods inventory, December 31	50,000
Finished-goods inventory, January 1	20,000
Indirect material	10,000
Indirect labor	15,000
Other manufacturing overhead	80,000

Required:

1. Prepare San Fernando Fashions' schedule of cost of goods manufactured for the year.
2. Prepare San Fernando Fashions' schedule of cost of goods sold for the year.
3. Prepare San Fernando Fashions' income statement for the year.
4. *Build a spreadsheet:* Construct an Excel spreadsheet to solve all of the preceding requirements. Show how both cost schedules and the income statement will change if raw-material purchases amounted to $190,000 and indirect labor was $20,000.

Problem 2–44
Direct and Indirect Labor
(LO 2-1, 2-3, 2-5, 2-9)
2. Total cost of wages: $624

Highlander Cutlery manufactures kitchen knives. One of the employees, whose job is to cut out wooden knife handles, worked 48 hours during a week in January. The employee earns $12 per hour for a 40-hour week, and overtime is paid after 40 hours. For additional hours, the employee is paid an overtime rate of $18 per hour. The employee's time was spent as follows:

Regular duties involving cutting out knife handles	38 hours
General shop cleanup duties	9 hours
Idle time due to power outage	1 hour

Required:

1. Calculate the total cost of the employee's wages during the week described above.
2. Determine the portion of this cost to be classified in each of the following categories:

   a. Direct labor
   b. Manufacturing overhead (idle time)
   c. Manufacturing overhead (overtime premium)
   d. Manufacturing overhead (indirect labor)

Problem 2–45
Cost Classifications
(LO 2-5, 2-8, 2-9)

Cape Cod Shirt Shop manufactures T-shirts and decorates them with custom designs for retail sale on the premises. Several costs incurred by the company are listed below. For each cost, indicate which of the following classifications best describe the cost. More than one classification may apply to the same cost item.

Cost Classifications

a. Variable
b. Fixed
c. Period
d. Product
e. Administrative
f. Selling
g. Manufacturing
h. Research and development
i. Direct material
j. Direct labor
k. Manufacturing overhead

Cost Items

1. Cost of fabric used in T-shirts.
2. Wages of shirtmakers.

3. Cost of new sign in front of retail T-shirt shop.
4. Wages of the employee who repairs the firm's sewing machines.
5. Cost of electricity used in the sewing department.
6. Wages of T-shirt designers and painters.
7. Wages of sales personnel.
8. Depreciation on sewing machines.
9. Rent on the building. Part of the building's first floor is used to make and paint T-shirts. Part of it is used for the retail sales shop. The second floor is used for administrative offices and storage of raw material and finished goods.
10. Cost of daily advertisements in local media.
11. Wages of designers who experiment with new fabrics, paints, and T-shirt designs.
12. Cost of hiring a pilot to fly along the beach pulling a banner advertising the shop.
13. Salary of the owner's secretary.
14. Cost of repairing the gas furnace.
15. Cost of insurance for the production employees.

Problem 2–46
Overtime Premiums and Fringe Benefit Costs; Airline
(LO 2-1, 2-3, 2-5, 2-9, 2-10)

Heartland Airways operates commuter flights in three Midwestern states. Due to a political convention held in Topeka, the airline added several extra flights during a two-week period. Additional cabin crews were hired on a temporary basis. However, rather than hiring additional flight attendants, the airline used its current attendants on overtime. Monica Gaines worked the following schedule on August 10. All of Gaines's flights on that day were extra flights that the airline would not normally fly.

Regular time:	2 round-trip flights between Topeka and St. Louis (8 hours)
Overtime:	1 one-way flight from Topeka to Kansas City (3 hours)

Gaines earns $12 per hour and is paid time and a half when working overtime. Fringe benefits cost the airline $3 per hour for any hour worked, regardless of whether it is a regular or overtime hour.

Required:

1. Compute the direct cost of compensating Gaines for her services on the flight from Topeka to Kansas City.
2. Compute the cost of Gaines's services that is an indirect cost.
3. How should the cost computed in requirement (2) be treated for cost accounting purposes?
4. Gaines ended her workday on August 10 in Kansas City. However, her next scheduled flight departed Topeka at 11:00 a.m. on August 11. This required Gaines to "dead-head" back to Topeka on an early-morning flight. This means she traveled from Kansas City to Topeka as a passenger, rather than as a working flight attendant. Since the morning flight from Kansas City to Topeka was full, Gaines displaced a paying customer. The revenue lost by the airline was $82. What type of cost is the $82? To what flight, if any, is it chargeable? Why?

Problem 2–47
Variable Costs; Graphical and Tabular Analyses
(LO 2-8, 2-9)

San Diego Sheet Metal, Inc. incurs a variable cost of $40 per pound for raw material to produce a special alloy used in manufacturing aircraft.

Required:

1. Draw a graph of the firm's raw material cost, showing the total cost at the following production levels: 10,000 pounds, 20,000 pounds, and 30,000 pounds.
2. Prepare a table that shows the unit cost and total cost of raw material at the following production levels: 1 pound, 10 pounds, and 1,000 pounds.

Problem 2–48
Fixed Costs; Graphical and Tabular Analyses
(LO 2-8, 2-9)

Hightide Upholstery Company manufactures a special fabric used to upholster the seats in power boats. The company's annual fixed production cost is $100,000.

Required:

1. Draw a graph of the company's fixed production cost showing the total cost at the following production levels of upholstery fabric: 10,000 yards, 20,000 yards, 30,000 yards, and 40,000 yards.
2. Prepare a table that shows the unit cost and the total cost for the firm's fixed production costs at the following production levels: 1 yard, 10 yards, 10,000 yards, and 40,000 yards.

3. Prepare a graph that shows the unit cost for the company's fixed production cost at the following production levels: 10,000 yards, 20,000 yards, 30,000 yards, and 40,000 yards.

Problem 2–49
Direct, Indirect, Controllable, and Uncontrollable Costs
(LO 2-1, 2-3, 2-9)

For each of the following costs, indicate whether the amount is a direct or indirect cost of the equipment maintenance department. Also indicate whether each cost is at least partially controllable by the department supervisor.

1. Cost of plant manager's salary, which is allocated to the maintenance department.
2. Cost of property taxes allocated to the maintenance department.
3. Cost of electricity used in the maintenance department.
4. Depreciation on the building space occupied by the maintenance department.
5. Idle time of maintenance department employees.

Problem 2–50
Product Costs and Period Costs
(LO 2-1, 2-2, 2-3)

Indicate for each of the following costs whether it is a product cost or a period cost.

1. Wages of aircraft mechanics employed by an airline.
2. Wages of drill-press operators in a manufacturing plant.
3. Cost of food in a microwavable dinner.
4. Cost incurred by a department store chain to transport merchandise to its stores.
5. Cost of grapes purchased by a winery.
6. Depreciation on pizza ovens in a pizza restaurant.
7. Cost of plant manager in a computer production facility.
8. Wages of security personnel in a department store.
9. Cost of utilities in a manufacturing facility.

Problem 2–51
Fixed and Variable Costs; Forecasting
(LO 2-7, 2-8)

Direct material, 20x2 forecast: $3,600,000

Water Technology, Inc. incurred the following costs during 20x1. The company sold all of its products manufactured during the year.

Direct material	$3,000,000
Direct labor	2,200,000
Manufacturing overhead:	
Utilities (primarily electricity)	140,000
Depreciation on plant and equipment	230,000
Insurance	160,000
Supervisory salaries	300,000
Property taxes	210,000
Selling costs:	
Advertising	195,000
Sales commissions	90,000
Administrative costs:	
Salaries of top management and staff	372,000
Office supplies	40,000
Depreciation on building and equipment	80,000

During 20x1, the company operated at about half of its capacity, due to a slowdown in the economy. Prospects for 20x2 are slightly better. Jared Lowes, the marketing manager, forecasts a 20 percent growth in sales over the 20x1 level.

Required: Categorize each of the costs listed above as to whether it is most likely variable or fixed. Forecast the 20x2 cost amount for each of the cost items listed above.

Problem 2–52
Economic Charactersitics of Costs
(LO 2-4, 2-10)

The following terms are used to describe various economic characteristics of costs.

a. Opportunity cost
b. Out-of-pocket cost
c. Sunk cost

d. Differential cost

e. Marginal cost

f. Average cost

Required: Choose one of the terms listed above to characterize each of the amounts described below.

1. The cost of feeding 500 children in a public school cafeteria is $800 per day, or $1.60 per child per day. What economic term describes this $1.60 cost?
2. The cost of including one extra child in a day-care center.
3. The cost of merchandise inventory purchased two years ago, which is now obsolete.
4. The management of a high-rise office building uses 2,500 square feet of space in the building for its own management functions. This space could be rented for $250,000. What economic term describes this $250,000 in lost rental revenue?
5. The cost of building an automated assembly line in a factory is $800,000. The cost of building a manually operated assembly line is $375,000. What economic term is used to describe the difference between these two amounts?
6. Referring to the preceding question, what economic term is used to describe the $800,000 cost of building the automated assembly line?
7. The cost incurred by a computer manufacturer to produce one more unit in its most popular line of laptop computers.

Problem 2–53
Cost Classifications; Hotel
(LO 2-1, 2-3, 2-9, 2-10)

Several costs incurred by Bayview Hotel and Restaurant are given in the following list. For each cost, indicate which of the following classifications best describe the cost. More than one classification may apply to the same cost item.

Cost Classifications

a. Direct cost of the food and beverage department

b. Indirect cost of the food and beverage department

c. Controllable by the kitchen manager

d. Uncontrollable by the kitchen manager

e. Controllable by the hotel general manager

f. Uncontrollable by the hotel general manager

g. Differential cost

h. Marginal cost

i. Opportunity cost

j. Sunk cost

k. Out-of-pocket cost

Cost Items

1. The cost of general advertising by the hotel, which is allocated to the food and beverage department.
2. The cost of food used in the kitchen.
3. The difference in the total cost incurred by the hotel when one additional guest is registered.
4. The cost of space (depreciation) occupied by the kitchen.
5. The cost of space (depreciation) occupied by a sauna next to the pool. The space could otherwise have been used for a magazine and bookshop.
6. The profit that would have been earned in a magazine and bookshop, if the hotel had one.
7. The discount on room rates given as a special offer for a "Labor Day Getaway Special."
8. The wages earned by table-service personnel.
9. The salary of the kitchen manager.
10. The cost of the refrigerator purchased 13 months ago. The unit was covered by a warranty for 12 months, during which time it worked perfectly. It stopped cooling after 13 months, despite an original estimate that it would last five years.

11. The hotel has two options for obtaining fresh pies, cakes, and pastries. The goodies can be purchased from a local bakery for approximately $1,600 per month, or they can be made in the hotel's kitchen. To make the pastries on the premises, the hotel will have to hire a part-time pastry chef. This will cost $600 per month. The cost of ingredients will amount to roughly $700 per month. Thus, the savings from making the goods in the hotel's kitchen amount to $300 per month.
12. The cost of dishes broken by kitchen employees.
13. The cost of leasing a computer used for reservations, payroll, and general hotel accounting.
14. The cost of a pool service that cleans and maintains the hotel's swimming pool.
15. The wages of the hotel's maintenance employees, who spent 11 hours (at $14 per hour) repairing the dishwasher in the kitchen.

Problem 2–54
Interpretation of Accounting Reports
(LO 2-1, 2-3)

Refer to Exhibit 2–3, and answer the following questions.

Required:

1. List the major differences between the income statements shown for Caterpillar, Inc., Walmart Stores, Inc., and Southwest Airlines Company.
2. Explain how cost-accounting data were used to prepare these income statements.
3. On the income statement for Southwest Airlines Company, where would the ticket agents' salaries be shown? Where would the costs of the computer equipment used to keep track of reservations be included on the statement?
4. On the income statement for Walmart Stores, Inc., where would the cost of newspaper advertising be shown? How about the cost of merchandise?
5. Refer to the income statement for Caterpillar, Inc. Where would the salary of the brand manager who plans advertising for Caterpillar equipment be shown? How about the salary of a production employee? Where would the cost of the raw materials used in the company's products be included on the statement?

Problem 2–55
Marginal Costs and Average Costs
(LO 2-7, 2-10)
6. $370

Roberta Coy makes custom mooring covers for boats. Each mooring cover is hand sewn to fit a particular boat. If covers are made for two or more identical boats, each successive cover generally requires less time to make. Coy has been approached by a local boat dealer to make mooring covers for all of the boats sold by the dealer. Coy has developed the following cost schedule for mooring covers made to fit 17-foot outboard power boats.

Mooring Covers Made	Total Cost of Covers
1	$ 450
2	850
3	1,210
4	1,540
5	1,850

Required: Compute the following:

1. Marginal cost of second mooring cover.
2. Marginal cost of fourth mooring cover.
3. Marginal cost of fifth mooring cover.
4. Average cost if two mooring covers are made.
5. Average cost if four mooring covers are made.
6. Average cost if five mooring covers are made.

Problem 2–56
Cost Classifications; Government Agency
(LO 2-3, 2-8, 2-9, 2-10)

The Department of Natural Resources is responsible for maintaining the state's parks and forest lands, stocking the lakes and rivers with fish, and generally overseeing the protection of the environment. Several costs incurred by the agency are listed below. For each cost, indicate which of the following classifications best describe the cost. More than one classification may apply to the same cost item.

Cost Classifications

a. Variable
b. Fixed

c. Controllable by the department director
d. Uncontrollable by the department director
e. Differential cost
f. Marginal cost
g. Opportunity cost
h. Sunk cost
i. Out-of-pocket cost
j. Direct cost of the agency
k. Indirect cost of the agency
l. Direct cost of providing a particular service
m. Indirect cost of providing a particular service

Cost Items

1. Cost of the automobiles used by the department's rangers. These cars were purchased by the state, and they would otherwise have been used by the state police.
2. Cost of live-trapping and moving beaver that were creating a nuisance in recreational lakes.
3. The department director's salary.
4. Cost of containing naturally caused forest fires, which are threatening private property.
5. Cost of the fish purchased from private hatcheries, which are used to stock the state's public waters.
6. The difference between (a) the cost of purchasing fish from private hatcheries and (b) the cost of running a state hatchery.
7. Cost of producing literature that describes the department's role in environmental protection. This literature is mailed free, upon request, to schools, county governments, libraries, and private citizens.
8. Cost of sending the department's hydroengineers to inspect one additional dam for stability and safety.
9. Cost of operating the state's computer services department, a portion of which is allocated to the Department of Natural Resources.
10. Cost of administrative supplies used in the agency's head office.
11. Cost of providing a toll-free number for the state's residents to report environmental problems.
12. The cost of replacing batteries in sophisticated monitoring equipment used to evaluate the effects of acid rain on the state's lakes.
13. Cost of a ranger's wages, when the ranger is giving a talk about environmental protection to elementary school children.
14. Cost of direct-mailing to 1 million state residents a brochure explaining the benefits of voluntarily recycling cans and bottles.
15. The cost of producing a TV show to be aired on public television. The purpose of the show is to educate people on how to spot and properly dispose of hazardous waste.

Problem 2–57
Unit Costs; Profit-Maximizing Output
(LO 2-7, 2-8, 2-10)

2. Output of 20,000 bottles, profit: $26,000

The controller for Canandaigua Vineyards, Inc. has predicted the following costs at various levels of wine output.

	Wine Output (.75 Liter Bottles)		
	10,000 Bottles	**15,000 Bottles**	**20,000 Bottles**
Variable production costs	$ 37,000	$ 55,500	$ 74,000
Fixed production costs	100,000	100,000	100,000
Fixed selling and administrative costs	40,000	40,000	40,000
Total	$177,000	$195,500	$214,000

The company's marketing manager has predicted the following prices for the firm's fine wines at various levels of sales.

	Wine Sales		
	10,000 Bottles	**15,000 Bottles**	**20,000 Bottles**
Sales price per .75 liter bottle	$18.00	$15.00	$12.00

Required:

1. Calculate the unit costs of wine production and sales at each level of output. At what level of output is the unit cost minimized?
2. Calculate the company's profit at each level of production. Assume the company will sell all of its output. At what production level is profit maximized?
3. Which of the three output levels is best for the company?
4. Why does the unit cost of wine decrease as the output level increases? Why might the sales price per bottle decline as sales volume increases?

Problem 2–58
Variable and Fixed Costs; Make or Buy a Component
(LO 2-8, 2-10)

Hoboken Industries currently manufactures 30,000 units of part MR24 each month for use in production of several of its products. The facilities now used to produce part MR24 have a fixed monthly cost of $150,000 and a capacity to produce 84,000 units per month. If the company were to buy part MR24 from an outside supplier, the facilities would be idle, but its fixed costs would continue at 40 percent of their present amount. The variable production costs of part MR24 are $11 per unit.

Required:

1. If Hoboken Industries continues to use 30,000 units of part MR24 each month, it would realize a net benefit by purchasing part MR24 from an outside supplier only if the supplier's unit price is less than what amount?
2. If Hoboken Industries is able to obtain part MR24 from an outside supplier at a unit purchase price of $12.875, what is the monthly usage at which it will be indifferent between purchasing and making part MR24?

(CMA, adapted)

Cases

Case 2–59
Economic Characteristics of Costs; Closing a Department; Ethics
(LO 2-1, 2-9, 2-10)

CompTech, Inc. manufactures printers for use with home computing systems. The firm currently manufactures both the electronic components for its printers and the plastic cases in which the devices are enclosed. Jim Cassanitti, the production manager, recently received a proposal from Universal Plastics Corporation to manufacture the cases for CompTech's printers. If the cases are purchased outside, CompTech will be able to close down its Printer Case Department. To help decide whether to accept the bid from Universal Plastics Corporation, Cassanitti asked CompTech's controller to prepare an analysis of the costs that would be saved if the Printer Case Department were closed. Included in the controller's list of annual cost savings were the following items:

Building rental (The Printer Case Department occupies one-sixth of the factory building, which CompTech rents for $177,000 per year.)	$29,500
Salary of the Printer Case Department supervisor	$50,000

In a lunchtime conversation with the controller, Cassanitti learned that CompTech was currently renting space in a warehouse for $39,000. The space is used to store completed printers. If the Printer Case Department were discontinued, the entire storage operation could be moved into the factory building and occupy the space vacated by the closed department. Cassanitti also learned that the supervisor of the Printer Case Department would be retained by CompTech even if the department were closed. The supervisor would be assigned the job of managing the assembly department, whose supervisor recently gave notice of his retirement. All of CompTech's department supervisors earn the same salary.

Required:

1. You have been hired as a consultant by Cassanitti to advise him in his decision. Write a memo to Cassanitti commenting on the costs of space and supervisory salaries included in the controller's cost analysis. Explain in your memo about the "real" costs of the space occupied by the Printer Case Department and the supervisor's salary. What types of costs are these?
2. Independent of your response to requirement (1), suppose that CompTech's controller had been approached by his friend Jack Westford, the assistant supervisor of the Printer Case Department.

Westford is worried that he will be laid off if the Printer Case Department is closed down. He has asked his friend to understate the cost savings from closing the department, in order to slant the production manager's decision toward keeping the department in operation. Comment on the controller's ethical responsibilities.

Case 2–60
Understanding Cost Concepts
(LO 2-7, 2-8, 2-10)

1(a). 60,000 copies

You just started a summer internship with the successful management consulting firm of Kirk, Spock, and McCoy. Your first day on the job was a busy one, as the following problems were presented to you.

Required: Supply the requested comments in each of the following independent situations.

1. FastQ Company, a specialist in printing, has established 500 convenience copying centers throughout the country. In order to upgrade its services, the company is considering three new models of laser copying machines for use in producing high-quality copies. These high-quality copies would be added to the growing list of products offered in the FastQ shops. The selling price to the customer for each laser copy would be the same, no matter which machine is installed in the shop. The three models of laser copying machines under consideration are 1024S, a small-volume model; 1024M, a medium-volume model; and 1024G, a large-volume model. The annual rental costs and the operating costs vary with the size of each machine. The machine capacities and costs are as follows:

	Copier Model		
	1024S	**1024M**	**1024G**
Annual capacity (copies)	100,000	350,000	800,000
Costs:			
Annual machine rental	$ 8,000	$ 11,000	$ 20,000
Direct material and direct labor	.02	.02	.02
Variable overhead costs	.12	.07	.03

a. Calculate the volume level in copies where FastQ Company would be indifferent to acquiring either the small-volume model laser copier, 1024S, or the medium-volume model laser copier, 1024M.

b. The management of FastQ Company is able to estimate the number of copies to be sold at each establishment. Present a decision rule that would enable FastQ Company to select the most profitable machine without having to make a separate cost calculation for each establishment. (*Hint:* To specify a decision rule, determine the volume at which FastQ would be indifferent between the small and medium copiers. Then determine the volume at which FastQ would be indifferent between the medium and large copiers.)

2. Alderon Enterprises is evaluating a special order it has received for a ceramic fixture to be used in aircraft engines. Alderon has recently been operating at less than full capacity, so the firm's management will accept the order if the price offered exceeds the costs that will be incurred in producing it. You have been asked for advice on how to determine the cost of two raw materials that would be required to produce the order.

a. The special order will require 800 gallons of endor, a highly perishable material that is purchased as needed. Alderon currently has 1,200 gallons of endor on hand, since the material is used in virtually all of the company's products. The last time endor was purchased, Alderon paid $5.00 per gallon. However, the average price paid for the endor in stock was only $4.75. The market price for endor is quite volatile, with the current price at $5.50. If the special order is accepted, Alderon will have to place a new order next week to replace the 800 gallons of endor used. By then the price is expected to reach $5.75 per gallon.

Using the cost terminology introduced in this chapter, comment on each of the cost figures mentioned in the preceding discussion. What is the real cost of endor if the special order is produced?

b. The special order also would require 1,500 kilograms of tatooine, a material not normally required in any of Alderon's regular products. The company does happen to have 2,000 kilograms of tatooine on hand, since it formerly manufactured a ceramic product that used the material. Alderon recently received an offer of $14,000 from Solo Industries for its entire supply of tatooine. However, Solo Industries is not interested in buying any quantity less than Alderon's entire 2,000-kilogram stock. Alderon's management is unenthusiastic about Solo's offer, since Alderon paid $20,000 for the tatooine. Moreover, if the tatooine were purchased at today's market price, it would cost $11.00 per kilogram. Due to the volatility of the tatooine, Alderon will need to get rid of its entire supply one way or another. If the material is not used in production or sold, Alderon will have to pay $1,000 for each 500 kilograms that is transported away and disposed of in a hazardous waste disposal site.

Using the cost terminology introduced in this chapter, comment on each of the cost figures mentioned in the preceding discussion. What is the real cost of tatooine to be used in the special order?

3. A local PBS station has decided to produce a TV series on state-of-the-art manufacturing. The director of the TV series, Justin Tyme, is currently attempting to analyze some of the projected costs for the series. Tyme intends to take a TV production crew on location to shoot various manufacturing scenes as they occur. If the four-week series is shown in the 8:00–9:00 P.M. prime-time slot, the station will have to cancel a wildlife show that is currently scheduled. Management projects a 10 percent viewing audience for the wildlife show, and each 1 percent is expected to bring in donations of $10,000. In contrast, the manufacturing show is expected to be watched by 15 percent of the viewing audience. However, each 1 percent of the viewership will likely generate only $5,000 in donations. If the wildlife show is canceled, it can be sold to network television for $25,000.

   Using the cost terminology introduced in this chapter, comment on each of the financial amounts mentioned in the scenario above. What are the relative merits of the two shows regarding the projected revenue to the station?

(CMA, adapted)

3 Product Costing and Cost Accumulation in a Batch Production Environment

FOCUS COMPANY >>>

© Mana Photo/Shutterstock.com RF

THIS CHAPTER'S FOCUS COMPANY is Blue River Paddle Boards, a small manufacturer of stand-up paddle boards (SUPs) and related equipment based in Chattanooga, Tennessee. Blue River Paddle Boards uses job-order costing to accumulate the costs of each of its products. Job-order costing is well suited to companies like Blue River Paddle Boards that manufacture relatively small numbers of distinct products. In a job-order costing system, direct material, direct labor, and manufacturing overhead are first assigned to each production job, such as a set number of paddle boards of a particular type. Then the cost of the production job is averaged across the number of units in the job.

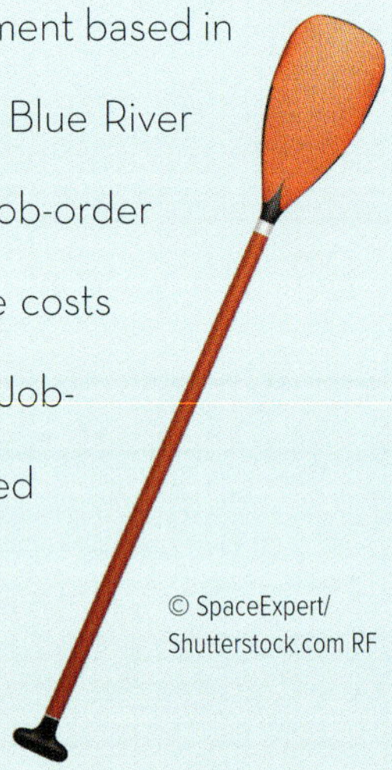

© SpaceExpert/ Shutterstock.com RF

<< IN CONTRAST

SMALL WORLD ADVERTISING In contrast to the manufacturing setting of Blue River Paddle Boards, we explore job-order costing in a service industry environment. Small World Advertising is an advertising and public relations firm in Portland, Oregon, that helps for-profit socially-oriented ventures craft their message and communicate it to consumers. The firm has two managing partners, six artistic and communication staff associates, and an office support staff. Costs of a typical Small World Advertising project include direct professional labor cost of partners and associates as well as overhead applied based on direct professional labor used in the project.

After completing this chapter, you should be able to:

3-1 Discuss the role of product and service costing in manufacturing and non-manufacturing firms.

3-2 Diagram and explain the flow of costs through the manufacturing accounts used in product costing.

3-3 Distinguish between job-order costing and process costing.

3-4 Compute a predetermined overhead rate and explain its use in job-order costing for job-shop and batch-production environments.

3-5 Prepare journal entries to record the costs of direct material, direct labor, and manufacturing overhead in a job-order costing system.

3-6 Prepare a schedule of cost of goods manufactured, a schedule of cost of goods sold, and an income statement for a manufacturer.

3-7 Describe the two-stage allocation process used to assign manufacturing overhead costs to production jobs.

3-8 Describe the process of project costing used in service industry firms and nonprofit organizations.

Product and Service Costing

Learning Objective 3-1

Discuss the role of product and service costing in manufacturing and nonmanufacturing firms.

Product costing is the assignment of production costs to all output of the organization, whether items manufactured, goods merchandised (resold), or services delivered. A **product-costing system** accumulates the costs incurred in a production process and assigns those costs to the organization's outputs. There are important distinctions between the costing of different types of outputs and we will highlight them as they arise. In referring to these outputs, we follow the standard approach of using the word "product" to refer to physical items manufactured or merchandised, and services to refer to outputs that are less tangible in nature.

Product costing produces data that are needed for a variety of purposes in financial accounting, managerial accounting, and cost management.

Use in Financial Accounting In financial accounting, product costs are needed to value inventory on the balance sheet and to compute cost-of-goods-sold expense on the income statement. Under generally accepted accounting principles, inventory is valued at its cost until it is sold. Then the cost of the inventory becomes cost of goods sold, an expense of the period in which it is sold.

Although services are not inventoried like products are, their costs still appear on the income statement and are matched to the corresponding sales revenues. A product-costing system is used to accumulate the costs of services delivered, which are then recorded on the income statement as cost of services.

Because product costs must be developed for financial accounting, these same costs are often used for decisions inside the organization as well. However, the simple approaches to product costing that are allowed for financial accounting are often inadequate to support effective decision making.

Use in Managerial Accounting Inside of organizations, product and service costs are needed to help managers with planning and to provide them with high-quality data for decision making. While product costs are interesting for what they tell us about the amount of resources expended to create a particular product or service, they are critical for what they tell us about how the organization earns its profits, which is just the difference between what we can sell output for and what we report as the cost of that output. If we are interested in the relative profitability of different products and services, and we usually are, the way that we choose to assign costs to them helps to define our perception of those outputs as successful or unsuccessful.

The word "choose" in that last sentence is the key. Most people believe that the cost of a product or service is a very objective number that anyone could agree on, given the right information about material costs, labor costs, and so on. But, in reality, product cost is a slippery concept. Suppose, for example, that a bakery buys 1,000 kilograms of sugar in early December for $1.00 per kilogram and another 1,000 kilograms of sugar in late December for $0.80 per kilogram, with both purchases stored in the same storage silo. When they use the sugar from that silo to make cakes during the first week of January, what cost for sugar should be reflected in the product cost of a cake?

- The average cost of sugar in the silo is $0.90 per kilogram.
- The silo is filled from the top and emptied from the bottom, so the sugar used in the first week of January is probably from the first purchase that was put into the silo, costing $1.00 per kilogram.
- The company uses last-in-first-out (LIFO) inventory accounting in its financial accounting system, so the financial accounting system will claim that the cost of sugar is the most recent market price of $0.80 per kilogram.

Each of these costs is right in its own way, and depending upon how the costing system is designed, any one of these costs could be used in calculating the product cost, and therefore the profit, of the cakes produced and sold.

If measuring and interpreting a direct cost, like sugar, is that ambiguous, imagine how many ways there might be to assign an indirect product cost, like the cost of a production-scheduling computer or the salary of a quality control supervisor. Maybe that product cost number isn't so objective after all! And if the cost number isn't objective, neither is the profit number.

Decisions about product prices, service charge rates, the mix of products to be produced, and the quantity of output to be manufactured or delivered are among those for which product cost information is needed. Moreover, controlling and reducing production costs is a frequent goal in organizations, but the organization will find it impossible to accomplish that goal without a clear and reasonably accurate measure of the costs to make its products and deliver its services. And finally, the profits that are derived from the product cost information are used to measure performance and make resource-allocation decisions that can lead to success or failure of a product. All else equal, which product gets more of the advertising budget? The one that appears to be making money for the company.

Thus, product costs provide crucial data for a variety of managerial purposes. The issues that arise in assigning product costs, and especially the indirect manufacturing (production) overhead costs, are the topic of this chapter, as well as Chapters 4 and 5.

"[We are] constantly focused on capital efficiency and cost management." (3a)

Exxon

Use in Reporting to Interested Organizations In addition to financial statement preparation and internal decision making, there is an ever-growing need for product cost information in relationships between firms and various outside organizations. Public utilities, such as electric and gas companies, record product costs to justify rate increases that must be approved by state regulatory agencies. Hospitals keep track of the costs of medical procedures that are reimbursed by insurance companies or by the federal government under the Medicare program. Manufacturing firms often sign cost-plus contracts with the government, where the contract price depends on the cost of manufacturing the product.

Product Costing in Nonmanufacturing Firms

As indicated above, the need for product costs is not limited to manufacturing firms. Merchandising companies include the costs of buying and transporting merchandise in their product costs. Nonmanufacturing producers of inventoriable goods, such as those in mining, oil and gas, and agriculture, also record the costs of producing their goods. The role of product costs in these companies is identical to that in manufacturing firms. For example, the pineapples grown and sold by Del Monte are inventoried at their product cost until they are sold. Then the product cost becomes cost-of-goods-sold expense.

"We now have better information on how people spend their time and can compare actual [cost] versus what was allocated in the budget." (3b)

Habitat for Humanity Greater San Francisco

Service Firms and Nonprofit Organizations The production output of service firms and nonprofit organizations consists of services that are consumed as they are produced. Although services cannot be stored as inventory and sold later like manufactured goods, such organizations need information about the costs of producing services. Banks, insurance companies, restaurants, airlines, law firms, hospitals, city governments and non-governmental organizations (NGOs) that provide charitable support all record the costs of producing various services for the purposes of planning, cost control, and decision making. For example, in making a decision about adding a flight from Chicago to Houston, United Airlines' management needs to know the cost of flying the proposed route. Before building a new branch bank, Wells Fargo's management would want to know the cost of maintaining the branch, as well as the additional revenue to be generated. And the American Red Cross needs to know the cost of the emergency services it has provided in order to assess its cost-effectiveness and report to donors.

Flow of Costs in Manufacturing Firms

Learning Objective 3-2

Diagram and explain the flow of costs through the manufacturing accounts used in product costing.

As introduced in Chapter 2, manufacturing costs generally consist of direct material, direct labor, and manufacturing overhead. The product-costing systems used by manufacturing firms employ several manufacturing accounts. As production takes place, all manufacturing costs are added (debited) to the *Work-in-Process Inventory* (WIP) account. Work in process is a partially completed inventory. A debit to the account increases the cost-based valuation of the asset represented by the unfinished products. As soon as products are completed, their product costs are transferred from WIP to *Finished-Goods Inventory* (FGI). This is accomplished by a reduction (credit) to WIP and an increase (debit) to FGI. During the time period when the finished products are sold, the product cost of the inventory sold is removed (credited) from Finished Goods and added (debited) to *Cost of Goods Sold* (COGS), which is an expense of the period in which the sale occurred. To formally summarize income and capture all of the items that will be recorded on the income statement, COGS is closed into the Income Summary account (debit Income Summary, credit COGS) at the end of the accounting period, along with all other expenses and revenues of the period. Exhibit 3–1 depicts the flow of costs through the manufacturing accounts.

Exhibit 3–1
Flow of Costs through Manufacturing Accounts

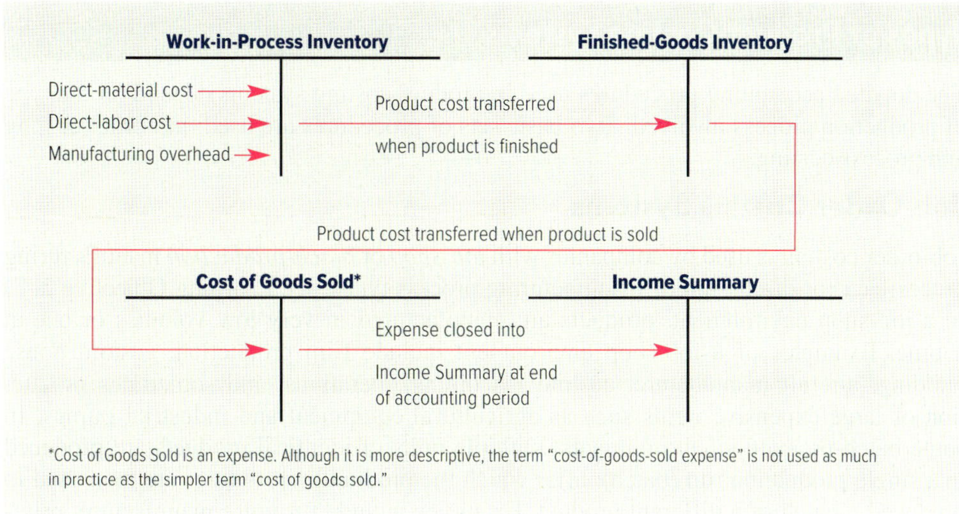

*Cost of Goods Sold is an expense. Although it is more descriptive, the term "cost-of-goods-sold expense" is not used as much in practice as the simpler term "cost of goods sold."

Example of Manufacturing Cost Flows Suppose that the Bradley Paper Company incurred and applied the following manufacturing costs during 20x1.

Direct material	$30,000
Direct labor	20,000
Manufacturing overhead	40,000

During 20x1, products costing $60,000 were finished and products costing $25,000 were sold for $32,000. Exhibit 3–2 shows the flow of costs through the Bradley Paper Company's manufacturing accounts and the effect of the firm's product costs on its balance sheet and income statement.

Exhibit 3–2
Example of Manufacturing Cost Flows for Bradley Paper Company

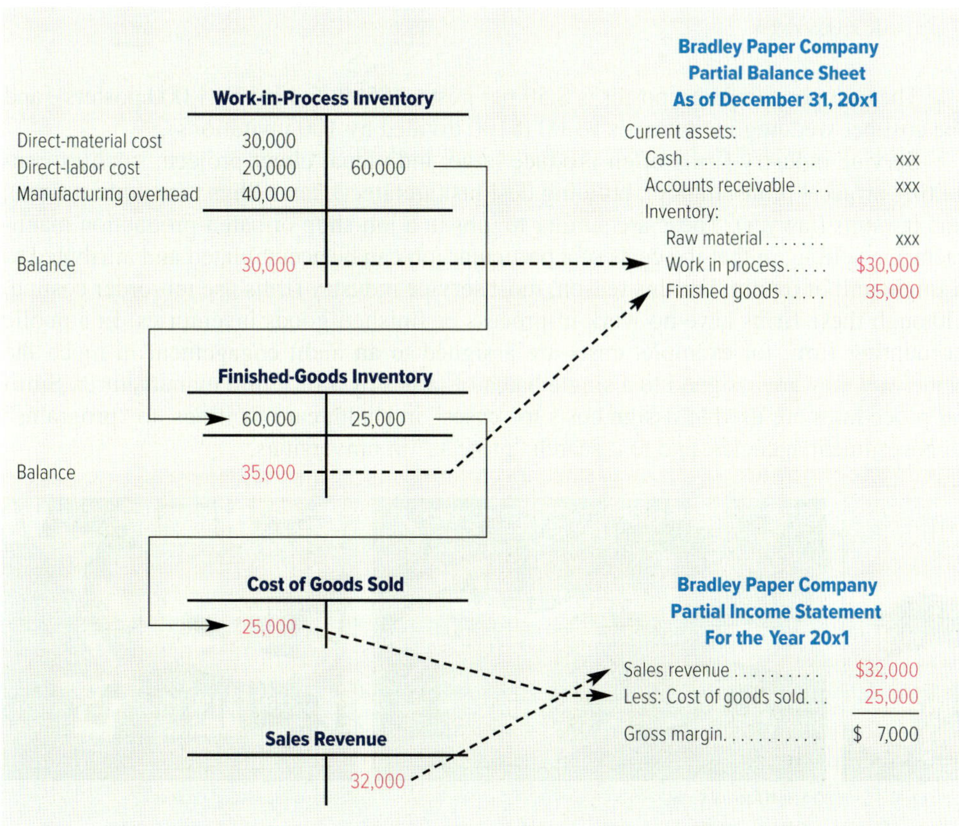

Types of Product-Costing Systems

The detailed accounting procedures used in product-costing systems depend on the type of production process involved. Two basic sets of procedures are used: job-order costing and process costing.

Job-Order Costing Systems

Learning Objective 3-3

Distinguish between job-order costing and process costing.

Job-order costing is used by companies with *job-shop* or *batch-production* manufacturing processes. (For discussion of manufacturing process types, see Learning Objective 2-4.) In a job-shop environment, products are manufactured in very low volumes or one at a time. Examples of a job-shop environment include film production, custom house building, aircraft manufacture, custom machining operations, and sometimes production of large expensive items such as agricultural equipment and industrial pumps. In some batch-production environments, multiple units of identical products are produced in a single production run (batch), after which the production resources are then used to produced a batch of a different product. Examples include furniture manufacture, printing, commercial baking, and injection molding of plastic objects. These batch-production environments would use job-order costing as well.

In **job-order costing,** each distinct batch of production is called a *job* or *job order.* The cost-accounting procedures are designed to assign costs to each job. Then the costs assigned to each job are averaged over the units of production in the job to obtain an average cost per unit. For example, suppose that AccuPrint worked on two printing jobs during October, and the following costs were incurred.

	Job A27 (1,000 campaign posters)	Job B39 (100 wedding invitations)
Direct material	$100	$ 36
Direct labor	250	40
Manufacturing overhead	150	24
Total manufacturing cost	$500	$100

"Many shipping lines are struggling to make money, so cost leadership is key to survival." (3c)
Drewry Shipping Consultants

The cost per campaign poster is $.50 per poster ($500 divided by 1,000 posters), and the cost per wedding invitation is $1.00 ($100 divided by 100 invitations).

Service industry firms often produce large, individual client projects, such as consulting projects (consultancy), building designs (architect), tax filings (accounting firm), and lawsuits (lawyer). These are similar to jobs in a job-shop or batch-production manufacturing setting, in that the costs of a particular job can be accumulated and attributed to a single unit of output. For this reason, most service industry firms use job-order costing, although these firms have no work-in-process or finished-goods inventories. In a public accounting firm, for example, costs are assigned to an audit engagement in much the same way they are assigned to a single batch of tables by a furniture manufacturer. Similar procedures are used to assign costs to "cases" in health care facilities, to "programs" in government agencies, and to research "projects" in universities.

© Creatas Images RF

© Sergio Azenha/Alamy

© Radius Images/Getty Images RF

The cost-accounting system keeps track of production costs as they flow from raw material, through work in process and finished goods, and into cost of goods sold.

Process-Costing Systems

A **process-costing system** accumulates all the production costs for a large number of units of output, and then these costs are averaged over all of the units. Process costing is used by companies that produce large numbers of identical units in a *continuous-flow* manufacturing process. Firms that produce chemicals, gasoline, and electricity are among those using continuous-flow manufacturing processes and process costing. In addition, some *batch-production* environments use process costing. This occurs when the manufacturing process requires that the product be produced in discrete batches rather than continuous flow, but batch after batch of identical products are produced (in contrast to the job-order costing discussion above, where products change between batches). Such products include microchips, beer, and processed food, and in this setting there is no need to trace costs to specific batches of production, because the products in the different batches are identical.

For example, suppose the Silicon Valley Company produced 40,000 microchips during November. The following manufacturing costs were incurred in November.

Direct material	$1,000
Direct labor	2,000
Manufacturing overhead	3,000
Total manufacturing cost	$6,000

The cost per microchip is $0.15 (total manufacturing cost of $6,000 ÷ 40,000 units produced).

Summary of Product-Costing System Alternatives

The distinction between job-order and process costing hinges on the type of production process involved. Job-order costing systems assign costs to distinct production jobs that are significantly different. Then an average cost is computed for each unit of product in each job. Process-costing systems average costs over a large number of identical (or very similar) units of product.[1]

The remainder of this chapter examines the details of job-order costing. The next chapter covers process costing.

Accumulating Costs in a Job-Order Costing System

To illustrate job-order costing, we will focus on Blue River Paddle Boards, Inc. Nestled in the foothills of the Appalachian Mountains outside of Chattanooga, Tennessee, Blue River Paddle Boards was founded by two 28-year-old outdoor enthusiasts. Friends since college, Julia Pieterse and Darius Wilson seized on the growing interest in one of their favorite hobbies, standup paddle boarding, to start a company manufacturing and selling standup paddle boards (SUPs) and related equipment. After three years of operation, the two founders have ridden the wave to a small but financially sound business.

Blue River PADDLE BOARDS

In a job-order costing system, costs of direct material, direct labor, and manufacturing overhead are assigned to each production job. These costs comprise the *inputs* of the product-costing *system.* As costs are incurred, they are added to the Work-in-Process Inventory account in the ledger. To keep track of the manufacturing costs assigned to *each job,* a subsidiary ledger is maintained. The subsidiary ledger account assigned to each job is a document called a **job-cost record.**

---

[1]Recall that the assembly-line production process, also introduced in Learning Objective 2-4, was discussed in a very basic form in Chapter 2. On more complex assembly lines, each unit produced is often different in some way from the ones preceding and following it. For example, Honda produces cars and light trucks on the same assembly line in Ohio. This kind of assembly line needs a hybrid of job-order and process costing called *operation costing* that is discussed in Chapter 4.

Job-Cost Record

An example of a job-cost record is displayed in Exhibit 3–3. At this juncture, focus on the major sections and headings, which are printed in blue. (For now just ignore the detailed entries, printed in black, which will be explained in due course.)

This job-cost record is for job S116, consisting of 80 units of standard 12' standup paddle boards (SUPs), produced during November 20x1. Three major sections on the job-cost record are used to accumulate the costs of direct material, direct labor, and manufacturing overhead assigned to the job. The other two sections are used to record the total cost and average unit cost for the job, and to keep track of units shipped to customers. Although we will visualize the job-cost record as a paper document upon which the entries for direct material, direct labor, and manufacturing overhead are written, it will generally exist as an Excel spreadsheet or, in larger companies, as a dedicated costing system in the company's administrative computing system.

Exhibit 3–3
Job-Cost Record: Blue River Paddle Boards, Inc.

Blue River PADDLE BOARDS

JOB-COST RECORD

Job Number S116
Date Started Nov. 1, 20x1
Description 80 standard 12' SUPs
Date Completed Nov. 22, 20x1
Number of Units Completed 80

Direct Material				
Date	**Requisition Number**	**Quantity**	**Unit Price**	**Cost**
11/1	803 - EPS Foam Core	2,500 sq ft	$4.00	$10,000
11/8	805 - Fiberglass/parts kit	80 units	$100	$8,000

Direct Labor				
Date	**Time Card Number**	**Hours**	**Rate**	**Cost**
Various dates	Various time cards	600	$20	$12,000

Manufacturing Overhead				
Date	**Cost Driver (Activity Base)**	**Quantity**	**Application Rate**	**Cost**
11/30	Machine hours	2,000	$9.00	$18,000

Cost Summary	
Cost Item	**Amount**
Total direct material	$18,000
Total direct labor	12,000
Total manufacturing overhead	18,000
Total cost	$48,000
Unit cost	$600

Shipping Summary			
Date	**Units Shipped**	**Units Remaining in Inventory**	**Cost Balance**
11/30	60	20	$12,000

The procedures used to accumulate the costs of direct material, direct labor, and manufacturing overhead for a job constitute the *set of activities* performed by the job-order costing *system*. These procedures are discussed next.

Direct-Material Costs

As raw materials are needed for producing a batch of SUPs, they are transferred from the raw-materials storage area to the production department. To authorize the release of materials, the production department supervisor completes a **material requisition form** and presents it to the raw-materials storage supervisor. A copy of the material requisition form goes to the cost accounting department. There it is used as the basis for transferring the cost of the requisitioned material from the Raw-Material Inventory account to the Work-in-Process Inventory account, and for entering the direct-material cost on the job-cost record for the production job in process. A document such as the material requisition form, which is used as the basis for an accounting entry, is called a **source document.** Exhibit 3–4 shows an example of a material requisition form.

In many production facilities, the production supervisor who needs raw materials would enter the information into the computer system, which would then generate the material requisition. The requisition would be automatically transmitted to computers in the warehouse and in the cost accounting department. Such automation reduces the flow of paperwork, minimizes clerical errors, and speeds up the supply chain and product-costing processes.

Supply Chain Management An organization's **supply chain** refers to the flow of all goods, services, and information into and out of the organization. The supply chain at Blue River Paddle Boards would look like this:

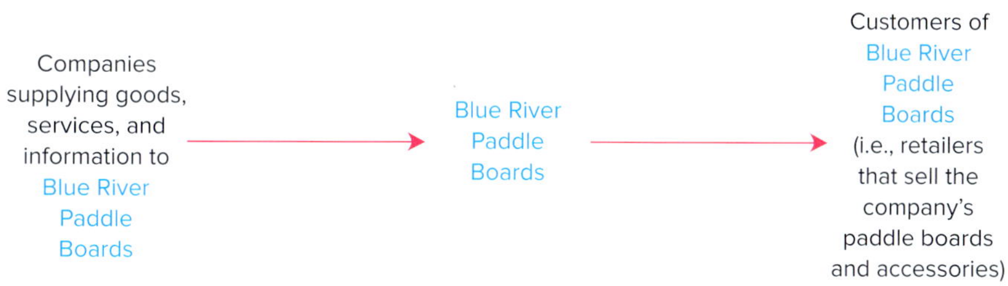

A supply chain often includes many companies and other organizations. *Supply chain management* means proactively working with some or all of the organizations in a company's supply chain to improve service and to manage or reduce costs. For example, Blue River's managers might work with the vendor supplying carbon fiber for their deluxe SUPs to improve delivery schedules or reduce material costs. Blue River's managers also might consult with retailers to provide input on more effective in-store displays for the company's SUP accessories or more timely information about the retailers' restocking needs.

Exhibit 3–4
Material Requisition Form

Material-Requisition Number 352 Date 1/28/x1
Job Number to Be Charged J621 Department Finishing
Department Supervisor Timothy Williams

Item	Quantity	Unit Cost	Amount
Fin kits	5 units	$35.00	$175
Epoxy resin	2 gallons	$50.00	$100

Material-Requirements Planning For products and product components that are produced routinely, the required materials are known in advance. For these products and components, material requisitions are based on a **bill of materials** that lists all of the materials needed.

In complex manufacturing operations, in which production takes place in several stages, highly-automated *material-requirements planning* (or *MRP*) systems are generally used for materials management. MRP is an operations-management tool that assists managers in scheduling production in each stage of the manufacturing process. Such careful planning ensures that, at each stage in the production process, the required subassemblies, components, or partially processed materials will be ready for the next stage. MRP systems, which are generally computerized, include files that list all of the component

Management Accounting Practice

Caterpillar, Inc., and the U.S. Marine Corps

SUPPLY CHAIN MANAGEMENT

Supply chain management has become a critically important issue in many companies and other organizations and the choices made in managing supplies of inventory can have wide-reaching implications for the managerial accounting that measures their costs and performance. Here are several examples of how organizations are managing their supply chains to get or provide better service at lower costs.

Caterpillar, Inc.—The Inventory "Bullwhip Effect"

Managing the supply chain is particularly critical for management during an economic slump and as the economy starts to emerge from a downturn. As Caterpillar, Inc., began to anticipate the end of the most recent economic recession, "it told its steel suppliers that it will more than double its purchases of the metal" within a year, even if there is no increase in sales of Caterpillar's own products. "In fact, the heavy equipment manufacturer has been boosting orders to suppliers for everything from big tires and hydraulic tubes to shatter-proof glass." Why would Caterpillar be making such a large inventory resupply effort even in the face of nearly flat sales? The phenomenon is called "the bullwhip effect."

"This phenomenon occurs when companies significantly cut or add inventories. Economists call it a bullwhip because even small increases in demand can cause a big snap in the need for parts and materials further down the supply chain. The bullwhip has broad implications [for the economy as] companies rush to fill orders while also restocking warehouse shelves. It touches everyone from retailers to the industrial companies that supply" the many resources needed to manufacture more products. "The manner in which companies, large and small, respond to market shifts determines which ones emerge first" from an economic downturn and start to grow again.[2]

U.S. Marine Corps

The U.S. Marine Corps "knew they had problems. When a soldier at Camp Pendleton would put in an order for a spare part, it took him a week to get it—from the other side of the base. Private companies, meanwhile, were greasing their supply chains to provide just-in-time delivery, and the Marines knew they could do better. So the Corps sketched a 10-year tech strategy in logistics, to ensure that 173,000 Marines have what they need when they need it. To execute, the Corps hired consultants and studied companies like Walmart and United Parcel Service." The Corps "aims to reduce inventory by half, saving up to $200 million. Taking a page from Unilever and Swissair, the Corps is developing better relations with suppliers to make sure they have access to hard-to-get items like tank parts. And with advice from Caterpillar, the Marines have been upgrading warehouses, adding gadgets like hand-held wireless scanners for real-time inventory placement and tracking."[3]

[2]Timothy Aeppel, *The Wall Street Journal*, January 27, 2010, p. A1. For more on Caterpillar, see D. DeFreitas, J. Gillette, R. Fink, and W. Cox, "Getting Lean and Mean at Caterpillar," *Strategic Finance*, January, 2013, pp. 24–33.

[3]For up-to-date information on the Marine Corps logistic Command's supply chain management mission, see www.logcom.usmc.mil. The information above is based on Faith Keenan, "The Marines Learn New Tactics—From Walmart," *BusinessWeek*, December 24, 2001, p. 74.

parts and materials in inventory and all of the parts and materials needed in each stage of the production process. They automatically generate materials requisitions and other process documentation based on the flow of production.

The scale and complexity of operations at Blue River Paddle Boards are, so far, small enough that an MRP system is not needed.

Direct-Labor Costs

The assignment of direct-labor costs to jobs is based on time records completed by production employees. A **time record** is a form that records the amount of time an employee spends on each production job. The time record is the source document used in the cost-accounting department as the basis for adding direct-labor costs to Work-in-Process Inventory and to the job-cost records for the various jobs in process. In most factories, a computerized timekeeping system is used. Employees indicate that they have begun work on a job, either on a computer or by scanning a bar code on the job paperwork, and the system automatically records the time they begin and stop work on each job and transmits the information to the accounting department.

Exhibit 3–5 displays an example of a time record. As the example shows, most of the employee's time was spent working on two different production jobs. In the accounting department (or the computerized costing system), the time spent on each job will be multiplied by the employee's wage rate, and the cost will be recorded in Work-in-Process Inventory and on the appropriate job-cost records. The employee also spent one-half hour on shop cleanup duties. This time will be classified by the accounting department as indirect labor, and its cost will be included in manufacturing overhead.

Manufacturing-Overhead Costs

It is relatively simple to trace direct-material and direct-labor costs to production jobs, but manufacturing overhead is not easily traced to jobs. Correctly applying overhead is the greatest challenge in correctly reporting and interpreting product costs.

By definition, manufacturing overhead is a heterogeneous pool of indirect production costs, such as indirect material, indirect labor, utility costs, and depreciation. These costs often bear no obvious relationship to individual jobs or units of product, but they must be incurred for production to take place. Therefore, they are legitimately part of the cost of production and it is necessary to assign manufacturing-overhead costs to jobs in order to have a complete picture of product costs. This process of assigning manufacturing-overhead costs to production jobs is called **overhead application** (or sometimes **overhead absorption**).

Overhead Application For product-costing information to be useful, it must be provided to managers on a timely basis, and it must fairly represent the costs incurred to help create the products or services whose cost is being measured and reported. This leads to two of the main challenges in applying overhead costs effectively.

First, suppose the cost-accounting department waited until the end of an accounting period so that the *actual* costs of manufacturing overhead could be determined before applying overhead costs to the firm's products. The result would be very accurate overhead application. However, the information might be useless because it was not available to managers for planning, control, and decision making during the period.

Exhibit 3–5
Time Record

Blue River PADDLE BOARDS

Employee Name: Ron Bradley Date: 12/19/x1
Employee Number: 12 Department: Finishing

Time Started	Time Stopped	Job Number
8:00	11:30	A267
11:30	12:00	Shop cleanup
1:00	5:00	J122

Second, suppose a company leases a raw-material warehouse for which it makes lease payments at the beginning of each quarter. Should a payment made on April 1 apply only to the products produced that day? That week? No, that payment is incurred to support production of products during the next three months. Or suppose a company located in Canada has just paid its January utility bill. Should the cost of that bill, which is probably much higher than the average monthly cost for the year because of the need to heat the facility, be assigned only to that month's production, resulting in higher than average product costs and lower than average product margins during that month? Most people would say no. So how do we make the costs of manufacturing overhead match up the way we think they should with the products and services produced?

Learning Objective **3-4**

Compute a predetermined overhead rate and explain its use in job-order costing for job-shop and batch-production environments.

Predetermined Overhead Rate The solution to these problems, for most organizations, is to apply overhead to products on the basis of estimates made at the beginning of the accounting period, taking into account the costs and activities of the entire year (which for most companies matches a full business and reporting cycle).[4] This full-cycle approach:

1. allows a timely but reasonable approximation to substitute for actual costs (the approximation is later corrected to actual cost);
2. combines costs that are only incurred sporadically (like the quarterly lease payments) and applies them to all production throughout the year; and
3. dampens the effects of cyclicality that are associated with causes unrelated to production (like the weather), instead applying the costs in a way that reflects the annual average.

This approach works by computing, in advance, a rate for expected manufacturing overhead that is then used in applying overhead costs throughout the period. To begin, the accounting department chooses some measure of productive activity to use as the basis for overhead application. In traditional product-costing systems, this measure is usually some **volume-based cost driver** (or **activity base**), such as direct-labor hours, direct-labor cost, or machine hours. The term *volume-based* refers to the fact that the cost driver chosen is something that will assign costs roughly in proportion to the amount (volume) of products produced. For example, twice as many units produced will require twice as many direct-labor hours, and twice as many direct-labor hours will assign twice as much manufacturing overhead cost.

Once the cost driver has been chosen, an estimate is made of (1) the amount of manufacturing overhead that will be incurred during the year, and (2) the amount of the cost driver (or activity base) that will be used or incurred during the same year. Then a **predetermined overhead rate**, which will be used throughout the year to apply manufacturing overhead costs to production, is computed as follows:

$$\text{Predetermined overhead rate} = \frac{\text{Budgeted manufacturing-overhead cost}}{\text{Budgeted amount of cost driver (or activity base)}}$$

Blue River PADDLE BOARDS

For example, Blue River Paddle Boards has chosen machine hours as its cost driver (or activity base). For the year 20x1, the firm estimates that overhead cost will amount to \$360,000 and that total machine hours used will be 40,000 hours. The 40,000 budgeted machine hours represent the company's *practical capacity* for production. This means that 40,000 machine hours are expected to be available for production under normal operating conditions. Recall from the discussion in Learning Objective 1-8 that normal operating conditions allow for such issues as routine machine maintenance, employee fatigue, and so forth.

[4]Other time periods than a year can be used. For example, some companies consider costs and activities quarter-by-quarter. But for the vast majority of companies, the process is an annual one, and we follow that approach here for simplicity of presentation.

The predetermined overhead rate for Blue River Paddle Boards is computed as follows:

$$\frac{\text{Predetermined}}{\text{overhead rate}} = \frac{\$360,000}{40,000 \text{ hours}} = \$9.00 \text{ per machine hour}$$

In our discussion of the predetermined overhead rate, we have emphasized the term *cost driver,* because increasingly this term is replacing the more traditional term *activity base.* Furthermore, we have emphasized that *traditional* product-costing systems tend to rely on a *single, volume-based cost driver.* We will introduce more elaborate product-costing systems based on multiple cost drivers later in this chapter, and this topic is examined in greater detail in Chapter 5.

Applying Overhead Costs Now that we know the predetermined overhead rate, what do we do with it? Recall that the predetermined overhead rate is expressed per unit of the cost driver chosen (per direct-labor hour, for example, or per machine hour). Because of this, if we can observe the quantity of the cost driver required by a particular job, we can multiply it by the predetermined overhead rate to determine the amount of overhead cost applied to the job.

For example, suppose Blue River Paddle Boards job number D38 requires 30 machine hours. The overhead applied to the job is computed as follows:

Predetermined overhead rate	$ 9
Machine hours required by job D38	× 30
Overhead applied to job D38	$270

The $270 of applied overhead will be added to Work-in-Process Inventory and recorded on the job-cost record as part of the cost of job D38. The accounting entries made to add manufacturing overhead to Work-in-Process Inventory may be made daily, weekly, or monthly. The interval will be chosen by the company to be consistent with the time typically required to process production jobs. But regardless of that interval, at the end of an accounting period entries will be made to record all manufacturing costs incurred to date in Work-in-Process Inventory. This is necessary to properly value Work-in-Process Inventory on the balance sheet.

Summary of Event Sequence in Job-Order Costing

The flowchart in Exhibit 3–6 summarizes the sequence of activities performed by the job-order costing system. The role of each document used in job-order costing also is summarized at the bottom of the flowchart.

Illustration of Job-Order Costing

Blue River PADDLE BOARDS

Learning Objective 3-5

Prepare journal entries to record the costs of direct material, direct labor, and manufacturing overhead in a job-order costing system.

Now let's examine the accounting entries made by Blue River Paddle Boards, during November of 20x1. The company worked on two production jobs for standup paddle boards (SUPs):

Job number D42: 80 deluxe 14' SUPs

Job number S116: 80 standard 12' SUPs

The job numbers designate these as the 42nd deluxe (carbon fiber displacement hull) SUP production job and the 116th standard (fiberglass planing hull) SUP production job undertaken by Blue River. The events of November are described below along with the associated accounting entries.

Exhibit 3–6
Summary of Event Sequence in a Job-Order Costing System

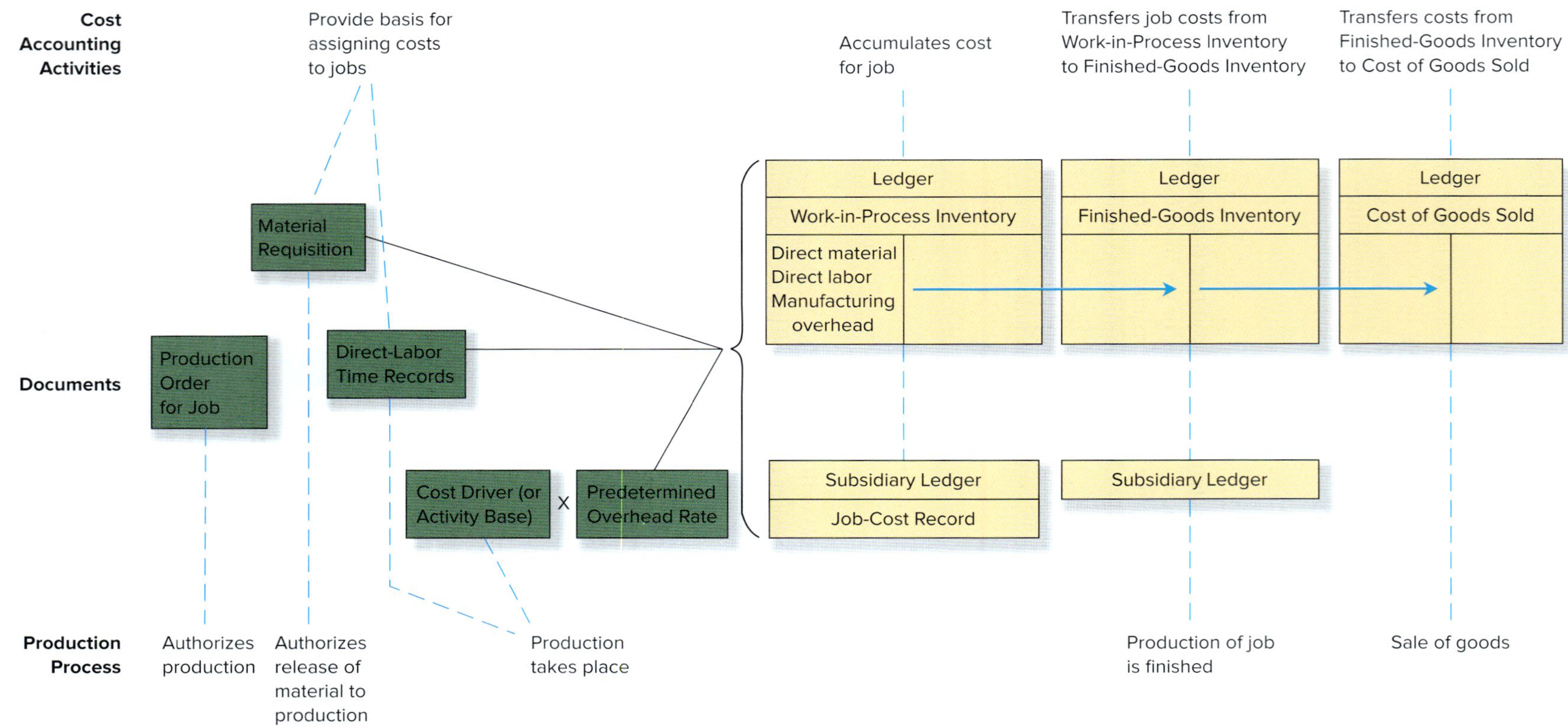

Purchase of Material

During November, the company purchased, on account, raw-material stocks of foam core, skin material (fiberglass and carbon fiber), and various SUP parts, costing $38,000. The journal entry to record these purchases would be, in total,

(1) Raw-Material Inventory	38,000	
Accounts Payable		38,000

The postings of this and all subsequent journal entries to the ledger are shown in Exhibit 3–11. In reality, it is likely that the various raw materials would have been purchased in several different transactions, with each transaction recorded as a separate journal entry.

Use of Direct Material

On November 1, the following material requisitions were submitted to begin production on the cores of the SUPs.

Requisition number 802: (for job number D42)	3,000 square feet of hi-density XPS (extruded polystyrene) foam core, at $8 per square foot, for a total of $24,000
Requisition number 803: (for job number S116)	2,500 square feet of EPS (expanded polystyrene) foam core, at $4.00 per square foot, for a total of $10,000

On November 8, additional material requisitions were submitted in preparation for laying the skin on the SUPs for these production jobs.

Requisition number 804: (for job number D42)	80 carbon fiber/parts kits, at $250 per unit, for a total of $20,000
Requisition number 805: (for job number S116)	80 fiberglass/parts kits, at $100 per unit, for a total of $8,000

The following journal entries record the release of these raw materials to production.

(2a) Work-in-Process Inventory	34,000	
Raw-Material Inventory		34,000

(2b) Work-in-Process Inventory	28,000	
Raw-Material Inventory		28,000

The associated ledger postings are shown in Exhibit 3–11. These direct-material costs are also recorded on the job-cost record for each job. The job-cost record for job number S116 is displayed in Exhibit 3–3. Since the job-cost record for job number D42 is similar, it is not shown.

Use of Indirect Material

On November 15, the following material requisition was submitted.

Requisition number 826:	4 gallons of epoxy resin, at $50 per gallon, for a total cost of $200

Epoxy resin is used in the production of all types of SUPs manufactured by Blue River. Since the cost incurred is relatively small and it affects all paddle boards, no attempt is made to trace the cost of epoxy resin to specific jobs. Rather, it is stocked in the production area and additional epoxy resin is requisitioned from manufacturing-supplies storage when needed. It is considered an indirect material, and its cost is included in manufacturing overhead. The company accumulates all manufacturing-overhead costs in the Manufacturing Overhead account. All actual overhead costs are recorded by debiting this account. The account is debited when indirect materials are requisitioned, when indirect-labor costs are incurred, when utility bills are paid, when depreciation is recorded on manufacturing equipment, and so forth. The journal entry made to record the usage of epoxy resin is as follows:

(3) Manufacturing Overhead	200	
Manufacturing Supplies Inventory		200

The posting of this journal entry to the ledger is shown in Exhibit 3–11. No entry is made on any job-cost record for the usage of epoxy resin, since its cost is not traced to individual production jobs.

© Ascent Xmedia/Getty Images

This small production facility records the cost of manufacturing paddle boards and surf boards, which are manufactured singly and in small batches. Direct material, direct labor, and manufacturing-overhead costs are tracked.

Use of Direct Labor

At the end of November, the cost accounting department uses the labor time records filed during the month to determine the following direct-labor costs of each job.

Direct labor: job number D42	$19,000
Direct labor: job number S116	12,000
Total direct labor	$31,000

The journal entry made to record these costs is as follows:

(4) Work-in-Process Inventory	31,000	
Wages Payable		31,000

The associated ledger posting is shown in Exhibit 3–11. These direct-labor costs also are recorded on the job-cost record for each job. The job-cost record for job number S116 is displayed in Exhibit 3–3. Only one direct-labor entry is shown on the job-cost record. In practice, there would be numerous entries made on different dates at a variety of wage rates for different employees.

Use of Indirect Labor

The analysis of labor time records undertaken on November 30 also revealed the following use of indirect labor:

Indirect labor: not charged to any particular job, $14,000

This cost comprises the production supervisor's salary and the wages of various employees who spent some of their time on maintenance and general cleanup duties during November. The following journal entry is made to add indirect-labor costs to manufacturing overhead:

(5) Manufacturing Overhead	14,000	
Wages Payable		14,000

No entry is made on any job-cost record, since indirect-labor costs are not traceable to any particular job. In practice, journal entries (4) and (5) are usually combined into one compound entry as follows:

Work-in-Process Inventory	31,000	
Manufacturing Overhead	14,000	
Wages Payable		45,000

Manufacturing-Overhead Costs Incurred

The following manufacturing-overhead costs were associated with indirect production resources provided during November:

Manufacturing overhead:	
Rent on factory building	$ 5,000
Depreciation on equipment	6,000
Utilities (electricity and natural gas)	4,750
Property taxes	2,500
Insurance	2,000
Total	$20,250

The following compound journal entry is made on November 30 to record these costs:

(6) Manufacturing Overhead	20,250	
Prepaid Rent		5,000
Accumulated Depreciation—Equipment		6,000
Accounts Payable (utilities and property taxes)		7,250
Prepaid Insurance		2,000

The entry is posted in Exhibit 3–11. No entry is made on any job-cost record because manufacturing-overhead costs are not traceable to any particular job.

Application of Manufacturing Overhead

Various manufacturing-overhead costs were incurred during November, and these costs were accumulated by debiting the Manufacturing Overhead account. However, no manufacturing-overhead costs have yet been added to Work-in-Process Inventory or recorded on the job-cost records. The application of overhead to the firm's products is based on a predetermined overhead rate. This rate was computed by the accounting department at the beginning of 20x1 as follows:

$$\text{Predetermined overhead rate} = \frac{\text{Budgeted total manufacturing overhead for 20x1}}{\text{Budgeted total machine hours for 20x1}}$$

$$= \frac{\$360,000}{40,000 \text{ hours}} = \$9.00 \text{ per machine hour}$$

As explained previously, the 40,000 budgeted machine hours represent the company's annual practical capacity for production.

Factory machine-usage records indicate the following actual usage of machine hours during November:

Machine hours used: job number D42	1,800 hours
Machine hours used: job number S116	2,000 hours
Total machine hours	3,800 hours

The total manufacturing overhead applied to Work-in-Process Inventory during November is calculated as follows:

	Machine Hours		Predetermined Overhead Rate		Manufacturing Overhead Applied
Job number D42	1,800	×	$9.00	=	$16,200
Job number S116	2,000	×	$9.00	=	18,000
Total manufacturing overhead applied					$34,200

The following journal entry is made to add **applied manufacturing overhead** to Work-in-Process Inventory.

(7) Work-in-Process Inventory	34,200	
Manufacturing Overhead		34,200

The entry is posted in Exhibit 3–11, and the manufacturing overhead applied to job number S116 is entered on the job-cost record in Exhibit 3–3.

Summary of Overhead Accounting

As the following time line shows, three concepts are used in accounting for overhead. Overhead is *budgeted* at the *beginning* of the accounting period, it is *applied during* the period, and *actual* overhead is measured at the *end* of the period.

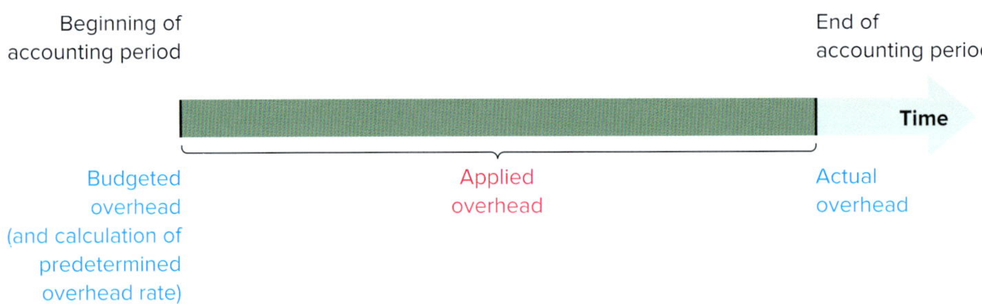

Exhibit 3–7 summarizes the accounting procedures used for manufacturing overhead. The left side of the Manufacturing Overhead account is used to accumulate **actual manufacturingoverhead** costs as they are incurred throughout the accounting

Exhibit 3–7
Manufacturing Overhead Account

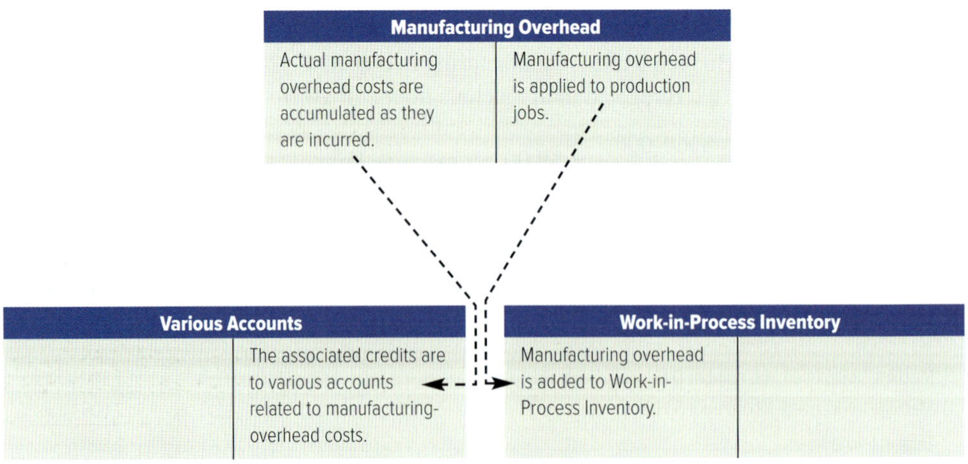

period. The actual costs incurred for indirect material, indirect labor, factory rental, equipment depreciation, utilities, property taxes, and insurance are recorded as debits to the account.

The right side of the Manufacturing Overhead account is used to record overhead *applied* to Work-in-Process Inventory.

While the left side of the Manufacturing Overhead account accumulates *actual* overhead costs, the right side applies overhead costs using the predetermined overhead rate, based on *estimated* overhead costs. The estimates used to calculate the predetermined overhead rate will generally prove to be incorrect to some degree. Consequently, there will usually be a nonzero balance in the Manufacturing Overhead account at the end of the year. This balance is usually relatively small, and its disposition is covered later in this illustration.

"As production processes are becoming more automated, manufacturing overhead is becoming a greater and greater portion of total manufacturing costs. This is true of almost all manufacturing firms." (3d)

Chrysler

Selling and Administrative Costs

During November, Blue River Paddle Boards incurred selling and administrative costs as follows:

Rental of sales and administrative offices	$ 1,500
Salaries of sales personnel	4,000
Salaries of management	8,000
Advertising	1,000
Office supplies used	300
Total	$14,800

Recall from Learning Objective 2-2 that selling and administrative costs are period costs, not product costs. Since these are not manufacturing costs, they are not added to Work-in-Process Inventory. They are instead treated as expenses of the accounting period in which they are incurred, and the following journal entry is made.

(8) Selling and Administrative Expenses	14,800	
Wages Payable		12,000
Accounts Payable		1,000
Prepaid Rent		1,500
Office Supplies Inventory		300

The entry is posted in Exhibit 3–11.

Completion of a Production Job

Job number S116 was completed during November, whereas job number D42 remained in process into December. As the job-cost record in Exhibit 3–3 indicates, the total cost of job number S116 was $48,000. The following journal entry records the transfer of these job costs from Work-in-Process Inventory to Finished-Goods Inventory.

(9) Finished-Goods Inventory	48,000	
Work-in-Process Inventory		48,000

The entry is posted in Exhibit 3–11.

Sale of Goods

Sixty of the standard 12' SUPs manufactured in job number S116 were sold for $900 each during November. The cost of each unit sold was $600, as shown on the job-cost record in Exhibit 3–3. The following journal entries are made.

(10) Accounts Receivable	54,000	
Sales Revenue		54,000

(11) Cost of Goods Sold	36,000	
Finished-Goods Inventory		36,000

These entries are posted in Exhibit 3–11.

The remainder of the manufacturing costs for job number S116 remain in Finished-Goods Inventory until some subsequent accounting period when the units are sold. Therefore, the cost balance for job number S116 remaining in inventory is $12,000 (20 units remaining times $600 per unit). This balance is shown on the job-cost record in Exhibit 3–3.

Underapplied and Overapplied Overhead

Blue River PADDLE BOARDS

During November, Blue River Paddle Boards incurred total *actual* manufacturing-overhead costs of $34,450, but only $34,200 of overhead was *applied* to Work-in-Process Inventory. The amount by which actual overhead exceeds applied overhead, called **underapplied overhead,** is calculated below.

Actual manufacturing overhead*	$34,450
Applied manufacturing overhead†	34,200
Underapplied overhead	$ 250

*Sum of debit entries in the Manufacturing-Overhead account: $200 + $14,000 + $20,250 = $34,450. See Exhibit 3–11.

†Applied overhead: $9.00 per machine hour × 3,800 machine hours.

If actual overhead had been less than applied overhead, the difference would have been called **overapplied overhead.** Underapplied or overapplied overhead is caused by errors in the estimates of overhead and activity used to compute the predetermined overhead rate. In this illustration, Blue River Paddle Boards' predetermined rate was underestimated by a small amount. Now, the estimation error needs to be corrected, in order to accurately report the *actual* amount of manufacturing overhead cost.

Disposition of Underapplied or Overapplied Overhead At the end of an accounting period, the company has two alternatives for the disposition of underapplied or overapplied overhead. Under the most common alternative, the underapplied or overapplied overhead is closed into Cost of Goods Sold. This is the method used by Blue River Paddle Boards, and the required journal entry is shown below.

(12) Cost of Goods Sold	250	
Manufacturing Overhead		250

This entry, which is posted in Exhibit 3–11, brings the balance in the Manufacturing Overhead account to zero. The account is then clear to accumulate manufacturing-overhead costs incurred in the next accounting period. Journal entry (12) has the effect of increasing cost-of-goods-sold expense. This reflects the fact that the cost of the units sold had been underestimated due to the slightly underestimated predetermined overhead rate. If the manufacturing overhead had been overapplied, meaning that more had been applied than was actually incurred, then the journal entry would have been reversed: a debit to zero out Manufacturing Overhead and a credit to reduce Cost of Goods Sold. Most companies use this approach of recording the entire amount to Cost of Goods Sold because it is simple and the amount of underapplied or overapplied overhead is usually small. Moreover, most firms wait until the end of the year to close underapplied or overapplied overhead into Cost of Goods Sold, rather than making the entry monthly as in this illustration.

Proration of Underapplied or Overapplied Overhead Some companies use a more accurate, but more complicated, procedure called **proration** to dispose of underapplied or overapplied overhead. This approach recognizes that underestimation or overestimation of the predetermined overhead rate affects not only Cost of Goods Sold, but also Work-in-Process Inventory and Finished-Goods Inventory. As the following diagram shows, applied overhead passes through all three of these accounts. Therefore, all three accounts are affected by any inaccuracy in the predetermined overhead rate.

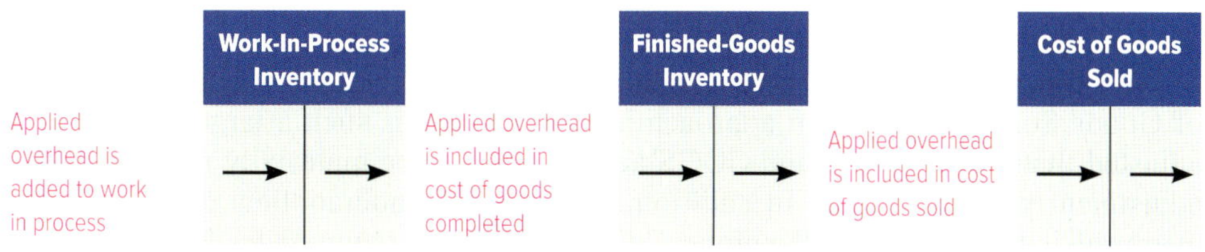

When proration is used, underapplied or overapplied overhead is allocated among the three accounts shown above. The amount of the current period's applied overhead remaining in each account is usually the basis for the proration procedure. In the Blue River Paddle Boards illustration, the amounts of applied overhead remaining in the three accounts on November 30 are determined as follows:

Applied Overhead Remaining in Each Account on November 30

Account	Explanation	Amount	Percentage*	Calculation of Percentages
Work in Process	Job D42 only	$16,200	47.37%	16,200 ÷ 34,200
Finished Goods	¼ of units in job S116	4,500	13.16%	4,500 ÷ 34,200
Cost of Goods Sold	¾ of units in job S116	13,500	39.47%	13,500 ÷ 34,200
Total overhead applied in November		$34,200	100.00%	

*Rounded

Using the percentages calculated above, the proration of Blue River Paddle Boards' underapplied overhead is determined as follows:

Account	Underapplied Overhead	×	Percentage	=	Amount Added to Account
Work in Process	$250	×	47.37%	=	$118.43
Finished Goods	250	×	13.16%	=	32.90
Cost of Goods Sold	250	×	39.47%	=	98.67
Total underapplied overhead prorated					$250.00

If Blue River Paddle Boards had chosen to prorate underapplied overhead, the following journal entry would have been made.

Work-in-Process Inventory	118.43	
Finished-Goods Inventory	32.90	
Cost of Goods Sold	98.67	
Manufacturing Overhead		250.00

Since this is *not* the method used by Blue River Paddle Boards in our continuing illustration, this entry is *not* posted to the ledger in Exhibit 3–11.

Although most firms record all underapplied or overapplied overhead in Cost of Goods Sold, the proration approach is used if there is such a large amount to be adjusted that the inventory and COGS accounts would be materially misstated if the adjustment were not made. In addition, proration of underapplied and overapplied overhead is used by a small number of firms that are required to do so under the rules specified by the *Cost Accounting Standards Board (CASB).* This federal agency develops mandatory cost-accounting standards for large government contractors, but the standards set forth by the agency apply only to firms receiving multi-million dollar government contracts.

Schedule of Cost of Goods Manufactured

Learning Objective 3-6

Prepare a schedule of cost of goods manufactured, a schedule of cost of goods sold, and an income statement for a manufacturer.

The Excel spreadsheet in Exhibit 3–8 displays the November **schedule of cost of goods manufactured** for Blue River Paddle Boards. The schedule details the costs of direct material, direct labor, and manufacturing overhead *applied* to work in process during November and shows the change in Work-in-Process Inventory. The **cost of goods manufactured,** shown in the last line of the schedule, is $48,000. This is the amount transferred from Work-in-Process Inventory to Finished-Goods Inventory during November, as recorded in journal entry number (9).

Schedule of Cost of Goods Sold

A **schedule of cost of goods sold** for Blue River Paddle Boards is displayed as an Excel spreadsheet in Exhibit 3–9. This schedule shows the November cost of goods sold and details the changes in Finished-Goods Inventory during the month. The Excel spreadsheet in Exhibit 3–10 displays the company's November income statement. As the income statement shows, income before taxes is $2,950, from which estimated income tax expense of $1,035 is subtracted, yielding net income of $1,915.

Posting Journal Entries to the Ledger

All of the journal entries in the Blue River Paddle Boards illustration are posted to the ledger in Exhibit 3–11. An examination of these T-accounts provides a summary of the cost flows discussed throughout the illustration.

Exhibit 3–8
Schedule of Cost of Goods Manufactured

Blue River PADDLE BOARDS

Blue River Paddle Boards - Excel

H31 | =H29-H30

		G	H
1	**BLUE RIVER PADDLE BOARDS, INC.**		
2	**Schedule of Cost of Goods Manufactured**		
3	**For the Month Ended November 30, 20x1**		
4			
5	Direct material:		
6	Raw-material inventory, November 1	$ 30,000	
7	Add: November purchases of raw material	38,000	
8	Raw material available for use	$ 68,000	
9	Deduct: Raw-material inventory, November 30	6,000	
10	Raw material used		$ 62,000
11			
12	Direct labor		31,000
13			
14	Manufacturing overhead:		
15	Indirect material	$ 200	
16	Indirect labor	14,000	
17	Rent on factory building	5,000	
18	Depreciation on equipment	6,000	
19	Utilities	4,750	
20	Property taxes	2,500	
21	Insurance	2,000	
22	Total actual manufacturing overhead	$ 34,450	
23	Deduct: Underapplied overhead*	250	
24	Overhead applied to work in process		34,200
25			
26	Total manufacturing costs		$ 127,200
27	Add: Work-in-process inventory, November 1		4,000
28			
29	Subtotal		$ 131,200
30	Deduct: Work-in-process inventory, November 30		83,200
31	Cost of goods manufactured		$ 48,000

*The schedule of cost of goods manufactured lists the manufacturing costs appplied to work in process. Therefore, the underapplied overhead, $250, must be deducted from total actual overhead to arrive at the amount of overhead applied to work in process during November. If there had been overapplied overhead, the balance would have been added to total manufacturing overhead.

Cost of Goods Manufactured | Cost of G...

Further Aspects of Overhead Application

Actual and Normal Costing

Most firms use a predetermined overhead rate, based on overhead and activity estimates for a relatively long time period. When direct material and direct labor are added to Work-in-Process Inventory at their actual amounts, but overhead is applied to Work-in-Process Inventory using a *predetermined overhead rate,* the product-costing system is referred to as **normal costing.** This approach, which takes its name from the use of a predetermined overhead rate that is *normalized* over a fairly long period, is used in the Blue River Paddle Boards illustration.

> "We use an actual costing system for the costs incurred in producing a feature film." (3e)
> **The Walt Disney Company**

A few companies use **actual costing,** a system in which direct material and direct labor are added to work-in-process inventory at their actual amounts, and actual overhead is allocated to work in process using an *actual overhead rate* computed at the *end* of each accounting period. Note that even though an actual overhead rate is used, the amount of

Exhibit 3–9
Schedule of Cost of Goods Sold

Blue River PADDLE BOARDS

BLUE RIVER PADDLE BOARDS, INC.
Schedule of Cost of Goods Sold
For the Month Ended November 30, 20x1

Finished-goods inventory, November 1	$ 12,000
Add: Cost of goods manufactured*	48,000
Cost of goods available for sale	$ 60,000
Deduct: Finished-goods inventory, November 30	24,000
Cost of goods sold	$ 36,000
Add: Underapplied overhead**	250
Cost of goods sold (adjusted for underapplied overhead)	$ 36,250

*From the Schedule of Cost of Goods Manufactured in Exhibit 3-8.

**The company closes underapplied or overapplied overhead into cost of goods sold. Hence, the $250 balance in underapplied overhead is added to the cost of goods sold for the month.

overhead assigned to each production job is still an allocated amount. Overhead costs, which are by definition indirect costs, cannot be traced easily to individual production jobs.

Although actual costing may seem at first glance like the approach most companies would follow, since it avoids the estimation associated with using a predetermined overhead rate, it is actually quite rare. This is because it suffers from several significant drawbacks.

- *Cyclicality*. Costs can vary from one part of the year to another for reasons that have nothing to do with the products or services being produced. Example: In Texas, utility bills tend to be very high in summer and relatively low in winter, because of the need to air condition the production space during the summer months. In Minnesota, the opposite is true, with heating costs causing winter months to be more costly. Actual costing would cause products and services produced in some months to appear more costly, and therefore less profitable, than those produced in other months. Most companies choose not to change their perception of product profitability based on the time of production.

Exhibit 3–10
Income Statement

Blue River PADDLE BOARDS

BLUE RIVER PADDLE BOARDS, INC.
Income Statement
For the Month Ended November 30, 20x1

Sales revenue	$ 54,000
Less: Cost of goods sold*	36,250
Gross margin	$ 17,750
Selling and administrative expenses	14,800
Operating income	$ 2,950
Income tax expense (estimated)	1,035
Net income	$ 1,915

*From the Schedule of Cost of Goods Sold in Exhibit 3-9.

Exhibit 3–11
Ledger Accounts for Blue River Paddle Boards Illustration*

Blue River PADDLE BOARDS

Accounts Receivable

	Debit	Credit	
Bal.	11,000		
(10)	54,000		

Accounts Payable

	Debit	Credit	
		3,000	Bal.
		38,000	(1)
		7,250	(6)
		1,000	(8)

Prepaid Insurance

	Debit	Credit	
Bal.	2,000	2,000	(6)

Wages Payable

	Debit	Credit	
		10,000	Bal.
		31,000	(4)
		14,000	(5)
		12,000	(8)

Prepaid Rent

	Debit	Credit	
Bal.	5,000		
		5,000	(6)
		1,500	(8)

Office Supplies Inventory

	Debit	Credit	
Bal.	900	300	(8)

Manufacturing Supplies Inventory

	Debit	Credit	
Bal.	750	200	(3)

Accumulated Depreciation: Equipment

	Debit	Credit	
		105,000	Bal.
		6,000	(6)

Raw-Material Inventory

	Debit	Credit	
Bal.	30,000	34,000	(2a)
(1)	38,000	28,000	(2b)

Manufacturing Overhead

	Debit	Credit	
(3)	200	34,200	(7)
(5)	14,000	250	(12)
(6)	20,250		

Work-in-Process Inventory

	Debit	Credit	
Bal.	4,000	48,000	(9)
(2a)	34,000		
(2b)	28,000		
(4)	31,000		
(7)	34,200		

Cost of Goods Sold

	Debit	Credit	
(11)	36,000		
(12)	250		

Finished-Goods Inventory

	Debit	Credit	
Bal.	12,000	36,000	(11)
(9)	48,000		

Selling and Administrative Expenses

	Debit	Credit	
(8)	14,800		

Sales Revenue

	Debit	Credit	
		54,000	(10)

*The numbers in parentheses relate T-account entries to the associated journal entries. The numbers in color are the November 1 account balances.

- *Large Payments.* Payments for some overhead costs are not spread evenly throughout the year, causing some production periods to have higher actual costs than others. Example: Companies can sometimes negotiate a better deal if they will agree to pay a lease on a quarterly or annual basis, rather than monthly. Actual costing would cause products or services produced in the payment months to appear more costly and less profitable than those produced in the "off" months when no payment is made.

- *Timeliness.* Companies want to receive cost information when it is still useful to them for decision making. However, actual overhead cost information is often only available after the production period has passed. Only when actual costs are at last known can the actual overhead rate be computed. Example: Utility bills often arrive only monthly, after the production month is over and some days or even weeks have passed in the following month.

Actual and normal costing may be summarized as follows:

ACTUAL COSTING Work-in-Process Inventory		
Actual direct-material costs		
Actual direct-labor costs		
Overhead applied:		
Actual overhead rate (computed at *end* of period)	×	*Actual* amount of cost driver used (e.g., direct-labor hours)

NORMAL COSTING Work-in-Process Inventory		
Actual direct-material costs		
Actual direct-labor costs		
Overhead applied:		
Predetermined overhead rate (computed at *beginning* of period)	×	*Actual* amount of cost driver used (e.g., direct-labor hours)

Choosing the Cost Driver for Overhead Application

Manufacturing overhead includes various indirect manufacturing costs that vary greatly in their relationship to the production process. If a single, volume-based cost driver (activity base) is used in calculating the predetermined overhead rate, it should be some productive input that is common across all of the firm's products. If, for example, all of the firm's products require direct labor, but only some products require machine time, direct-labor hours would usually be a preferable cost driver. If machine time were used as the cost driver, products not requiring machine time would not be assigned any overhead cost.

When selecting a volume-based cost driver, the goal is to choose an input that varies in a pattern that is most similar to the pattern with which overhead costs vary. Products that indirectly cause large amounts of overhead costs also should require large amounts of the cost driver, and vice versa. During periods when the cost driver is at a low level, the overhead costs incurred should be low. Thus, there should be a correlation between the incurrence of overhead costs and use of the cost driver.

> "Direct labor is becoming less and less appropriate as a basis for the application of manufacturing overhead." (3f)
>
> **Chrysler**

Limitation of Direct Labor as a Cost Driver In traditional product-costing systems, the most common volume-based cost drivers are direct-labor hours and direct-labor cost. However, there is a trend away from using direct labor as the overhead application base. Many production processes are becoming increasingly automated, through the use of robotics and computer-integrated manufacturing systems. Increased automation brings two results. First, manufacturing-overhead costs represent a larger proportion of total production costs. Second, direct labor decreases in importance as a factor of production. As direct labor declines in importance as a productive input, it becomes less appropriate as a cost driver. For this reason, some firms have switched to machine hours, process time, or throughput time as cost drivers that better reflect the pattern in which overhead costs are incurred. **Throughput time** (also known as **cycle time**) is the average amount of time required to convert raw materials into finished goods ready to be shipped to customers. Throughput time includes the time required for material handling, production processing, inspection, and packaging.

Departmental Overhead Rates

In the Blue River Paddle Boards illustration presented earlier in this chapter, all of the firm's manufacturing overhead was combined into a single cost pool. Then the overhead was applied to products using a single predetermined overhead rate based on machine hours. Since only one overhead rate is used in Blue River's entire factory, it is known as a **plantwide overhead rate.** In some production processes, the relationship between overhead costs and the firm's products differs substantially across production departments. In such cases, the firm may use **departmental overhead rates,** which differ across production departments. This usually results in a more accurate assignment of overhead costs to the firm's products. An even more accurate assignment of overhead costs can be achieved with *activity-based costing (ABC),* which is covered extensively in Chapter 5.

Two-Stage Cost Allocation

Learning Objective **3-7**

Describe the two-stage allocation process used to assign manufacturing overhead costs to production jobs.

When a company uses departmental overhead rates, the assignment of manufacturing-overhead costs to production jobs is accomplished in two stages, comprising what is called **two-stage cost allocation.** In the first stage, all manufacturing-overhead costs are assigned to the production departments, such as machining and assembly. In the second stage, the overhead costs that have been assigned to each production department are applied to the production jobs that pass through the department. Let's examine this two-stage process in more detail.

Stage One In the first stage, all manufacturing-overhead costs are assigned to the firm's production departments. However, stage one often involves two different types of allocation processes. First, all manufacturing-overhead costs are assigned to **departmental overhead centers.** This step is called **cost distribution** (or sometimes **cost allocation**). For example, the costs of heating a factory with natural gas would be distributed among all of the departments in the factory, possibly in proportion to the cubic feet of space in each department. In the cost distribution step, manufacturing-overhead costs are assigned to *both* production departments and service departments. **Service departments,** such as equipment-maintenance and material-handling departments, are departments that do not work directly on the firm's products but are necessary for production to take place.

Second, all service department costs are reassigned to the production departments through a process called **service department cost allocation.** In this step, an attempt is made to allocate service department costs on the basis of the relative proportion of each service department's output that is used by the various production departments. For example, production departments with more equipment would be allocated a larger share of the maintenance department's costs.

At the conclusion of stage one, all manufacturing-overhead costs have been assigned to the production departments.

Stage Two In the second stage, all of the manufacturing-overhead costs accumulated in each production department are assigned to the production jobs on which the department has worked. This process is called overhead application (or sometimes overhead absorption). In stage two, each production department has its own predetermined overhead rate. These rates often are based on different cost drivers.

The two-stage process of assigning overhead costs to production jobs is portrayed in Exhibit 3–12. Notice the roles of cost distribution, service department cost allocation, and overhead application in the exhibit. The techniques of overhead distribution and service department cost allocation will be covered later in the text. In this chapter, we are focusing primarily on the process of overhead application.[5]

"To figure out the relationship between the price you charge and the profitability that results, you have to . . . take into consideration reject rates, machine maintenance, insurance, rent, utilities and inventory carrying costs, just to name a few expenses." (3g)

Goltz Group

[5]One might legitimately ask why this is called two-stage cost allocation when there are three types of allocation involved. The term *two-stage allocation* is entrenched in the literature and in practice. It stems from the fact that there are two *cost objects,* or entities, to which costs are assigned: production *departments* in stage one and production *jobs* in stage two.

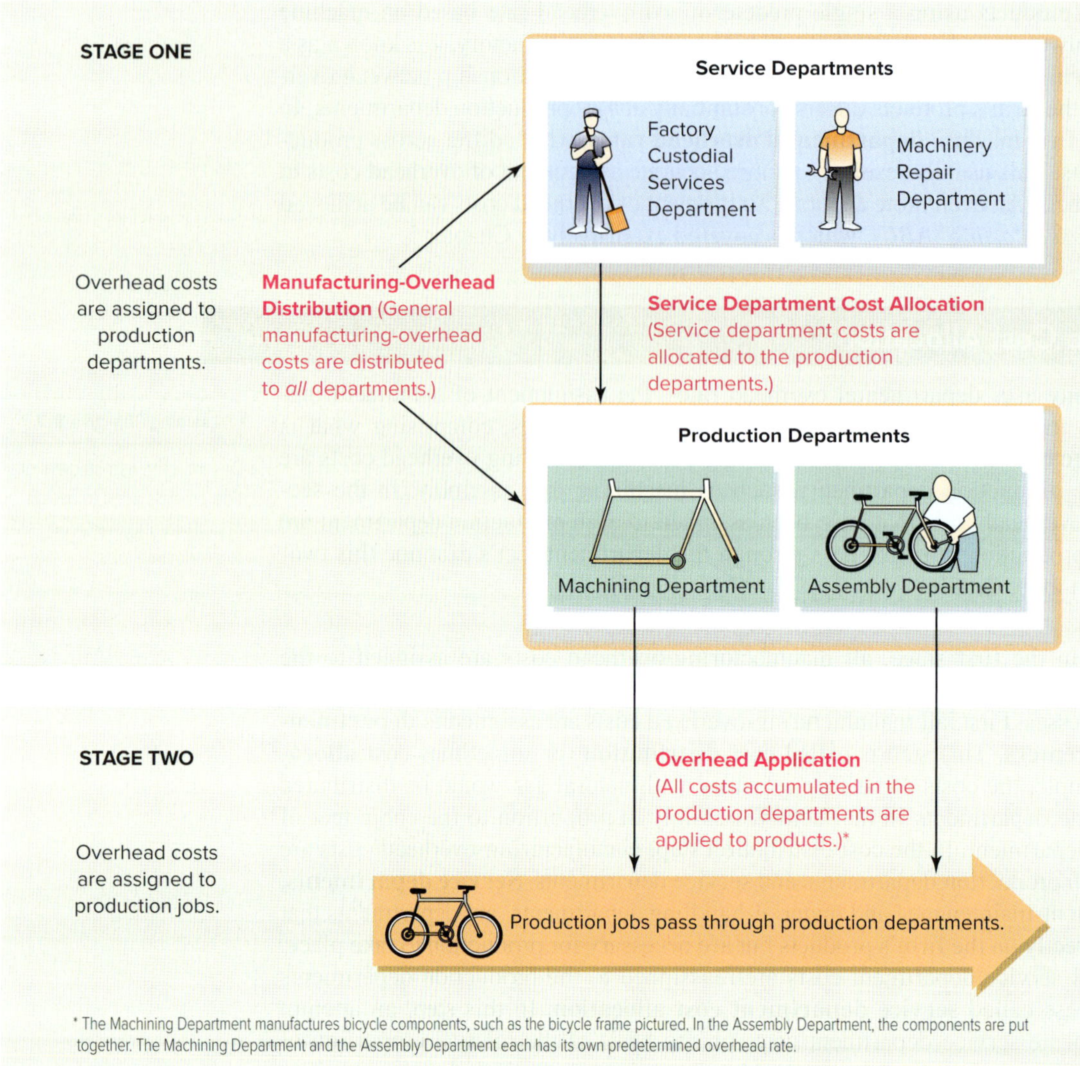

Exhibit 3–12
Developing Departmental Overhead Rates Using Two-Stage Allocation

Project Costing: Job-Order Costing in Nonmanufacturing Organizations

Learning Objective 3-8

Describe the process of project costing used in service industry firms and nonprofit organizations.

Job-order costing is also used in service industry companies and other nonmanufacturing organizations. However, rather than referring to production "jobs," such organizations use terminology that reflects their operations. For example, hospitals such as the The Children's Hospital of Philadelphia assign costs to "cases," and consulting firms like McKinsey & Company track "engagement" costs. Law firms assign costs to cases, while government agencies typically refer to "programs" or "missions." The need for cost accumulation exists in these and similar organizations for the same reasons found in manufacturing firms. For example, a mission to launch a commercial satellite at SpaceX is assigned a cost for the purposes of planning, cost control, and pricing of the launch service.

SMALL WORLD ADVERTISING

To illustrate the cost-accumulation system used in a service industry firm, let's turn our attention to Small World Advertising, an advertising and public relations agency located in Portland, Oregon. This small ad agency, whose mission is to help for-profit socially-oriented ventures achieve success by crafting an effective message and communicating it memorably to consumers, has two managing partners who pay themselves annual salaries of $100,000 each. An artistic and communications staff of six associates works on client engagements, and the associates earn $50,000 per year. Generous fringe benefits are provided to help retain these talented professionals, and cost of benefits averages 40 percent of compensation for all employees. Small World Advertising's direct professional labor budget is as follows:

Partner salaries	$200,000
Partner benefits (40%)	80,000
Total partner compensation	$280,000
Artistic and communications associate salaries	$300,000
Associate benefits (40%)	120,000
Total associate compensation	$420,000

The ad agency's annual overhead budget, which totals $756,000, appears in Exhibit 3–13. The overhead budget includes the costs of the support staff, artistic and photographic

Exhibit 3–13
Small World Advertising: Annual Overhead Budget

SMALL WORLD ADVERTISING

Small World Advertising - Excel

F36 =SUM(F8:F35)

SMALL WORLD ADVERTISING
Annual Overhead Budget
For the Year 20x6

	1st Quarter	2nd Quarter	3rd Quarter	4th Quarter	Year
Support staff:					
Receptionist	$ 8,000	$ 8,000	$ 8,000	$ 8,000	$ 32,000
Secretarial	17,500	17,500	17,500	17,500	70,000
Accounting	10,000	10,000	10,000	10,000	40,000
Custodial	7,250	7,250	7,250	7,250	29,000
Support staff benefits	17,100	17,100	17,100	17,100	68,400
Artistic supplies	40,000	40,000	40,000	40,000	160,000
Photographic supplies	30,000	30,000	30,000	30,000	120,000
Office:					
Computer	5,000	5,000	5,000	5,000	20,000
Photocopying	3,750	3,750	3,750	3,750	15,000
Office supplies	4,500	4,500	4,500	4,500	18,000
Postage	525	525	525	525	2,100
Utilities:					
Electricity	3,250	3,250	3,250	3,250	13,000
Heat/air conditioning	4,000	4,000	4,000	4,000	16,000
Internet access	375	375	375	375	1,500
Cable TV	500	500	500	500	2,000
Telephone	775	775	775	775	3,100
Trash collection	600	600	600	600	2,400
Other	625	625	625	625	2,500
Building rent	12,500	12,500	12,500	12,500	50,000
Insurance	3,750	3,750	3,750	3,750	15,000
Advertising	5,000	5,000	5,000	5,000	20,000
Vehicle maintenance	1,000	1,000	1,000	1,000	4,000
Depreciation					
Equipment	3,000	3,000	3,000	3,000	12,000
Vehicles	5,000	5,000	5,000	5,000	20,000
Other	5,000	5,000	5,000	5,000	20,000
Total overhead	$ 189,000	$ 189,000	$ 189,000	$ 189,000	$ 756,000

Overhead Budget

> "Every research contract negotiated between Cornell and the federal government includes an overhead component to cover the university's indirect costs." (3h)
>
> **Cornell University**

supplies, office operation, utilities, rent, insurance, advertising, vehicle maintenance, and depreciation. Small World's accountant has estimated that one-third of the budgeted overhead cost is incurred to support the ad agency's two partners, and two-thirds of it goes to support the artistic and communications associates. Thus, the following two overhead rates are calculated.

$$\frac{\text{Budgeted annual partner support overhead}}{\text{Budgeted annual partner compensation}} = \frac{\$756,000 \times 1/3}{\$280,000} = 90\%$$

$$\frac{\text{Budgeted annual associate support overhead}}{\text{Budgeted annual associate compensation}} = \frac{\$756,000 \times 2/3}{\$420,000} = 120\%$$

Based on the calculations above, overhead is assigned to each advertising engagement at the rate of 90 percent of partner direct professional labor plus 120 percent of associate direct professional labor. During May, Small World Advertising completed an advertising project for EyeStyle Global, a company that sells eyeglasses and for each pair sold donates one pair of glasses to nonprofit agencies in low-income countries. The contract required $1,800 in direct material, $1,200 of partner direct professional labor, and $2,000 of artistic staff direct professional labor (these labor costs include the cost of benefits). The total cost of the contract is computed as follows:

Contract MJH0207: Advertising Program for EyeStyle Global

Direct material	$1,800
Direct professional labor (partner)	1,200
Direct professional labor (associate)	2,000
Applied overhead:	
Partner support ($1,200 × 90%)	1,080
Associate support ($2,000 × 120%)	2,400
Total cost	$8,480

The total contract cost of $8,480 includes actual direct material and direct professional labor costs, and applied overhead based on the predetermined overhead rates for partner support costs and artistic and communications associate support costs. The contract cost can be used by the firm in controlling costs, for planning cash flows and operations, and as one informational input in its contract-pricing decisions. In addition to the contract cost, the firm also should consider the demand for its advertising services and the prices charged by its competitors.

The discussion above provides only a brief overview of cost-accumulation procedures in service industry and nonprofit organizations. The main point is that job-order costing systems are used in a wide variety of organizations, and these systems provide important information to managers for planning, decision making, and control.

Focus on Ethics

DID BOEING EXPLOIT ACCOUNTING RULES TO CONCEAL COST OVERRUNS AND PRODUCTION SNAFUS?

Aircraft manufacturers use job-order costing to determine the cost of an airplane. As this chapter discusses, supply chain management and production controls are also important tools used by manufacturers to manage production costs. As *BusinessWeek* reports, however, things don't always go according to plan.

For three years, Boeing's top management had been seeking a merger with McDonnell-Douglas Corporation, whose board of directors was reluctant to approve the deal. Finally, the deal went through, and the world's largest aerospace company was born—"the first manufacturer ever with the ability to build everything that flies, from helicopters and fighter jets to space stations."

Unfortunately, "a disaster was quietly unfolding inside Boeing's sprawling factories—one that would ultimately wind up costing billions of dollars, cause several executives to lose their jobs, and lead to claims of accounting fraud. Facing an unprecedented surge in orders because of a booming economy, workers were toiling around the clock, pushing the assembly line to the breaking point. At the same time, the company was struggling to overhaul outdated production methods. These pressures were building up to what was, in essence, a manufacturing nervous breakdown. In the weeks after the merger announcement, parts shortages and overtime approached all-time highs. As costs went through the roof, the profitability of airliners such as the 777 swooned. A special team formed to study the crisis issued a report with a blunt conclusion: 'Our production system is broken.'"

Had investors "understood the scope of the problems, the stock would probably have tumbled and the McDonnell deal—a stock swap that hinged on Boeing's ability to maintain a lofty share price—would have been jeopardized."

In May of 2002, *BusinessWeek* reported the results of its three-month investigation, which "reconstructed this hidden chapter in the company's history—and analyzed its current implications." The *BusinessWeek* article alleges that "new details supplied by several inside witnesses indicate that Boeing did more than simply fail to tell investors about its production disaster. It also engaged in a wide variety of aggressive accounting techniques that papered over the mess. Critics say the company should have taken charges for the assembly-line disaster in the first half of 1997, even if it meant jeopardizing the McDonnell merger. They also claim that Boeing took advantage of the unusual flexibility provided by *program accounting*—a system that allows the huge upfront expense of building a plane to be spread out over several years—to cover up cost overruns and to book savings from efficiency initiatives that never panned out. 'Boeing managed its earnings to the point where it got caught,' says Debra A. Smith, a partner at Constraints Management, a Seattle-area manufacturing consultancy, and a former senior auditor at Deloitte & Touche who worked on the company's account during the early 1980s. 'Boeing basically decided in the short run that [managing earnings] was a lesser evil than losing the merger,' adds Smith. At a time when investors are asking themselves how far Corporate America can be trusted, the Boeing saga provides rich new evidence that companies have much greater leeway to manipulate their numbers than most people suspect."[6]

Boeing allegedly used a system they called *program accounting* to spread their huge cost overruns across several years, thereby propping up earnings and the company's share price. After the merger with McDonnell-Douglas, however, the truth came out in the form of much lower earnings.

What is your view of how Boeing handled its cost overruns, its production problems, and the merger with McDonnell-Douglas? Did the company's top executives act ethically? How about their accountants?

[6]Stanley Holmes and Mike France, "Boeing's Secret: Did the Aircraft Giant Exploit Accounting Rules to Conceal a Huge Factory Snafu?" *Businessweek,* May 20, 2002, pp. 110–120. Also see Andy Pasztor and Anne Soueo, "Boeing Could Pay Large Penalty to Settle Probes, Avoid Prosecution," *The Wall Street Journal,* September 17, 2005, pp. A1, A8. Unrelated to the ethical issues described above, Boeing has experienced more recent setbacks relating to the grounding of its 787 Dreamliner, due to problems with the aircraft's lithium-ion batteries. As this book goes to press, the problem had apparently been solved, and several airlines had resumed their flights of the Dreamliner. See Christopher Drew, "United Joins in Grounded Dreamliners' Return to the Skies," *The New York Times* (online), May 20, 2013, p. 1

Chapter Summary

LO3-1 Discuss the role of product and service costing in manufacturing and nonmanufacturing firms. Product costing is the process of accumulating the costs of a production process and assigning them to the firm's products. Product costs are needed for three major purposes: (1) to value inventory and cost of goods sold in financial accounting; (2) to provide managerial accounting information to managers for planning, cost control, and decision making; and (3) to provide cost data to various organizations outside the firm.

LO3-2 Diagram and explain the flow of costs through the manufacturing accounts used in product costing. The costs of direct material, direct labor, and manufacturing overhead are first entered into the Work-in-Process Inventory account. When goods are completed, the accumulated manufacturing costs are transferred from Work-in-Process Inventory to Finished-Goods Inventory. Finally, these product costs are transferred from Finished-Goods Inventory to Cost of Goods Sold when sales occur.

LO3-3 Distinguish between job-order costing and process costing. Job-order costing is used by firms that engage in either job-shop or batch-production operations. Such firms produce relatively small numbers of dissimilar products. Process costing is used by companies that produce relatively large numbers of nearly identical products.

LO3-4 Compute a predetermined overhead rate and explain its use in job-order costing for job-shop and batch-production environments. Overhead is applied to production jobs using a predetermined overhead rate, which is based on estimates of manufacturing overhead (in the numerator) and the level of some cost driver or activity base (in the denominator).

LO3-5 Prepare journal entries to record the costs of direct material, direct labor, and manufacturing overhead in a job-order costing system. Journal entries, as illustrated in the chapter, are used to track the flow of manufacturing costs through the various accounts, such as Raw-Material Inventory, Work-in-Process Inventory, Finished-Goods Inventory, and Cost of Goods Sold. Two methods for periodically adjusting overapplied and underapplied overhead are described and illustrated.

LO3-6 Prepare a schedule of cost of goods manufactured, a schedule of cost of goods sold, and an income statement for a manufacturer. These accounting schedules, which are illustrated in the chapter, provide information to management about the costs incurred in a production operation.

LO3-7 Describe the two-stage allocation process used to assign manufacturing overhead costs to production jobs. In stage one, cost distribution and service-department cost allocation are used to assign all manufacturing overhead costs to production departments. In stage two, cost application is used to assign overhead costs from production departments to production jobs using a predetermined overhead rate.

LO3-8 Describe the process of project costing used in service industry firms and nonprofit organizations. Job-order costing methods are used in a variety of service industry firms and nonprofit organizations. Accumulating costs of projects, contracts, cases, programs, or missions provides important information to managers in such organizations as hospitals, law firms, and government agencies.

Review Problem on Job-Order Costing

Piedmont Paint Company uses a job-order costing system, and the company had two jobs in process at the beginning of the current year. Job JY65 currently has a cost of $134,400 assigned to it, and job DC66 currently has a cost of $85,600 assigned to it. The following additional information is available.

- The company applies manufacturing overhead on the basis of machine hours. Budgeted overhead and machine activity (based on practical capacity) for the year were $1,344,000 and 16,000 hours, respectively.
- The company worked on four jobs during the first quarter. Direct materials used, direct labor incurred, and machine hours consumed were as follows:

Job No.	Direct Material	Direct Labor	Machine Hours
JY65	$33,600	$ 56,000	1,200
DC66	—	35,200	700
SG78	70,400	104,000	2,000
RG82	24,000	14,080	500

- Manufacturing overhead during the first quarter included charges for depreciation ($54,400), indirect labor ($96,000), indirect materials used ($8,000), and other factory costs ($223,200).
- Piedmont Paint Company completed job JY65 and job DC66. Job DC66 was sold on account, producing a profit of $55,520 for the firm.

Required:

1. Determine Piedmont Paint Company's predetermined overhead application rate.
2. Prepare journal entries as of March 31 to record the following. (*Note:* Use summary entries where appropriate by combining individual job data.)
   a. The issuance of direct material to production and the direct labor incurred.
   b. The manufacturing overhead incurred during the quarter.
   c. The application of manufacturing overhead to production.
   d. The completion of jobs JY65 and DC66.
   e. The sale of job DC66.
3. Determine the cost of the jobs still in production as of March 31.
4. Did the finished-goods inventory increase or decrease during the first quarter? By how much?
5. Was manufacturing overhead under- or overapplied for the first quarter of the year? By how much?

Solutions to Review Problems

1. Predetermined overhead rate = budgeted overhead ÷ budgeted machine hours
   = $1,344,000 ÷ 16,000 = $84 per machine hour

2.

(a)	Work-in-Process Inventory	128,000*	
	Raw-Material Inventory		128,000
	Work-in-Process Inventory	209,280†	
	Wages Payable		209,280
	*$33,600 + $70,400 + $24,000 = $128,000		
	†$56,000 + $35,200 + $104,000 + $14,080 = $209,280		
(b)	Manufacturing Overhead	381,600	
	Accumulated Depreciation		54,400
	Wages Payable		96,000
	Manufacturing Supplies Inventory		8,000
	Miscellaneous Accounts		223,200
(c)	Work-in-Process Inventory	369,600*	
	Manufacturing Overhead		369,600
	*(1,200 + 700 + 2,000 + 500) × $84 = $369,600		
(d)	Finished-Goods Inventory	504,400*	
	Work-in-Process Inventory		504,400
	*Job JY65: $134,400 + $33,600 + $56,000 + (1,200 × $84) = $324,800		
	Job DC66: $85,600 + $35,200 + (700 × $84) = $179,600		
	$504,400 = $324,800 + $179,600		
(e)	Accounts Receivable	235,120*	
	Sales Revenue		235,120
	*$179,600 + $55,520 = $235,120		
	Cost of Goods Sold	179,600	
	Finished-Goods Inventory		179,600

3. Job SG78 and RG82 are in production as of March 31:

Job SG78: $70,400 + $104,000 + (2,000 × $84)	$342,400
Job RG82: $24,000 + $14,080 + (500 × $84)	80,080
Total	$422,480

4. Finished-goods inventory increased by $324,800 ($504,400 − $179,600).
5. The company's actual overhead amounted to $381,600, whereas applied overhead totaled $369,600. Thus, overhead was underapplied by $12,000.

Key Terms

For each term's definition refer to the indicated page, or turn to the glossary at the end of the text.

Review Questions

3–1. List and explain four purposes of product costing.

3–2. Explain the difference between job-order and process costing.

3–3. How is the concept of product costing applied in service industry firms?

3–4. What are the purposes of the following documents: (*a*) material requisition form, (*b*) labor time record, and (*c*) job-cost record.

3–5. Why is manufacturing overhead applied to products when product costs are used in making pricing decisions?

3–6. Explain the benefits of using a predetermined overhead rate instead of an actual overhead rate.

3–7. Describe one advantage and one disadvantage of prorating overapplied or underapplied overhead.

3–8. Describe an important cost-benefit issue involving accuracy versus timeliness in accounting for overhead.

3–9. Explain the difference between actual and normal costing.

3–10. When a single, volume-based cost driver (or activity base) is used to apply manufacturing overhead, what is the managerial accountant's primary objective in selecting the cost driver?

3–11. Describe some costs and benefits of using multiple overhead rates instead of a plantwide overhead rate.

3–12. Describe the process of two-stage cost allocation in the development of departmental overhead rates.

3–13. Define each of the following terms, and explain the relationship among them: (*a*) overhead cost distribution, (*b*) service department cost allocation, and (*c*) overhead application.

3–14. Describe how job-order costing concepts are used in professional service firms, such as law practices and consulting firms.

3–15. What is meant by the term *cost driver?* What is a *volume-based cost driver?*

3–16. Describe the flow of costs through a product-costing system. What special accounts are involved, and how are they used?

3–17. Give an example of how a hospital, such as the Mayo Clinic, might use job-order costing concepts.

3–18. Why are some manufacturing firms switching from direct-labor hours to machine hours or throughput time as the basis for overhead application?

3–19. What is the cause of overapplied or underapplied overhead?

3–20. Briefly describe two ways of closing out overapplied or underapplied overhead at the end of an accounting period.

3–21. Describe how a large retailer such as Lowes would assign overhead costs to products.

3–22. Explain how a non-profit organization like Doctors Without Borders might assign overhead costs to their operations in a particular refugee camp.

Exercises

All applicable Exercises are available in Connect.

Exercise 3–23
Job-Order versus Process Costing
(LO 3-1, 3-3)

For each of the following companies, indicate whether job-order or process costing is more appropriate.

1. Manufacturer of swimming pool chemicals.
2. Manufacturer of custom hot tubs and spas.
3. Architectural firm.
4. Manufacturer of ceramic tile.
5. Producer of yogurt.
6. Manufacturer of custom tool sheds.
7. Manufacturer of papers clips.
8. Engineering consulting firm.
9. Manufacturer of balloons.
10. Manufacturer of custom emergency rescue vehicles.

Exercise 3–24
Fixed and Variable Costs; Overhead Rate; Agribusiness
(LO 3-1, 3-4)

The controller for Tender Bird Poultry, Inc. estimates that the company's fixed overhead is $100,000 per year. She also has determined that the variable overhead is approximately $.10 per chicken raised and sold. Since the firm has a single product, overhead is applied on the basis of output units, chickens raised and sold.

Required:

1. Calculate the predetermined overhead rate under each of the following output predictions: 200,000 chickens, 300,000 chickens, and 400,000 chickens.
2. Does the predetermined overhead rate change in proportion to the change in predicted production? Why?

Exercise 3–25
Basic Journal Entries in Job-Order Costing
(LO 3-5)

Finley Educational Products started and finished job number B67 during June. The job required $4,600 of direct material and 40 hours of direct labor at $17 per hour. The predetermined overhead rate is $5 per direct-labor hour.

Required: Prepare journal entries to record the incurrence of production costs and the completion of job number B67.

Exercise 3–26
Job-Order Costing; Feature Film Production; Use of Internet
(LO 3-1, 3-3)

Visit the website of a film producer, such as Disney, MGM, or Warner Brothers.

Walt Disney Studios	www.disney.com
MGM	www.mgm.com
Warner Brothers	www.warnerbros.com

Required: Read about one of the company's recent (or upcoming) film releases. Then discuss why or why not job-order costing would be an appropriate costing method for feature film production. Would your answer be any different depending on the type of film being produced (e.g., animation in a studio versus filming on location in Timbuktu)?

Exercise 3–27
Job-Order Costing Basics
(LO 3-2, 3-4, 3-5, 3-6)

Bodin Company manufactures finger splints for kids who get tendonitis from playing video games. The firm had the following inventories at the beginning and end of the month of January.

	January 1	January 31
Finished goods	$125,000	$117,000
Work in process	235,000	251,000
Raw material	134,000	124,000

The following additional data pertain to January operations.

Raw material purchased	$191,000
Direct labor	300,000
Actual manufacturing overhead	175,000
Actual selling and administrative expenses	115,000

The company applies manufacturing overhead at the rate of 60 percent of direct-labor cost. Any overapplied or underapplied manufacturing overhead is accumulated until the end of the year.

Required: Compute the following amounts.

1. The company's prime cost for January.
2. The total manufacturing cost for January.
3. The cost of goods manufactured for January.
4. The cost of goods sold for January.
5. The balance in the manufacturing overhead account on January 31. Debit or credit?

(CMA, adapted)

Exercise 3–28
Cost Relationships; Normal Costing System
(LO 3-2, 3-4, 3-6)

McAllister, Inc. employs a normal costing system. The following information pertains to the year just ended.

- Total manufacturing costs were $2,500,000.
- Cost of goods manufactured was $2,425,000.
- Applied manufacturing overhead was 30 percent of total manufacturing costs.
- Manufacturing overhead was applied to production at a rate of 80 percent of direct-labor cost.
- Work-in-process inventory on January 1 was 75 percent of work-in-process inventory on December 31.

Required:

1. Compute the total direct-labor cost for the year.
2. Calculate the total cost of direct material used during the year.
3. Compute the value of the company's work-in-process inventory on December 31.

(CMA, adapted)

Exercise 3–29
Job-Cost Record
(LO 3-2, 3-3, 3-4)

Garrett Toy Company incurred the following costs in April to produce job number TB78, which consisted of 1,000 teddy bears that can walk, talk, and play cards.

Direct Material:

4/1/20x0 Requisition number 101: 400 yards of fabric at $.80 per yard

4/5/20x0 Requisition number 108: 500 cubic feet of stuffing at $.30 per cubic foot

Direct Labor:

From employee time cards for 4/1/20x0 through 4/8/20x0: 500 hours at $12 per hour

Manufacturing Overhead:

Applied on the basis of direct-labor hours at $2.00 per hour.

On April 30, 700 of the bears were shipped to a local toy store.

Required: Prepare a job-cost record using the information given above. (Use Exhibit 3–3 as a guide.)

Exercise 3–30
Schedule of Cost of Goods Manufactured
(LO 3-2, 3-4, 3-6)

Crunchem Cereal Company incurred the following actual costs during 20x1.

Direct material used	$275,000
Direct labor	120,000
Manufacturing overhead	252,000

The firm's predetermined overhead rate is 210 percent of direct-labor cost. The January 1 inventory balances were as follows:

Raw material	$30,000
Work in process	39,000
Finished goods	42,000

Each of these inventory balances was 10 percent higher at the end of the year.

Required:

1. Prepare a schedule of cost of goods manufactured for 20x1.
2. What was the cost of goods sold for the year?
3. ***Build a spreadsheet:*** Construct an Excel spreadsheet to solve all of the preceding requirements. Show how the solution will change if the following data change: direct material used amounted to $281,000 and raw-material inventory on December 31 was $28,000.

Exercise 3–31
Manufacturing Cost Flows
(LO 3-2, 3-5, 3-6)

Reimel Furniture Company, Inc. incurred the following costs during 20x2.

Direct material used	$174,000
Direct labor	324,000
Manufacturing overhead applied	180,000

During 20x2, products costing $120,000 were finished, and products costing $132,000 were sold on account for $195,000. There were no purchases of raw material during the year. The beginning balances in the firm's inventory accounts are as follows:

Raw material	$227,000
Work in process	18,000
Finished goods	30,000

Required:

1. Prepare T-accounts to show the flow of costs through the company's manufacturing accounts during 20x2.
2. Prepare a partial balance sheet and a partial income statement to reflect the information given above. (*Hint:* See Exhibit 3–2.)

Exercise 3–32
Basic Manufacturing Cost Flows
(LO 3-2, 3-6)

Selected data concerning the past year's operations of the Ozarks Manufacturing Company are as follows:

	Inventories	
	Beginning	**Ending**
Raw material	$71,000	$ 81,000
Work in process	80,000	30,000
Finished goods	90,000	110,000
Other data:		
Direct material used		$326,000
Total manufacturing costs charged to production during the year (includes direct material, direct labor, and manufacturing overhead applied at a rate of 60% of direct-labor cost)		686,000
Cost of goods available for sale		826,000
Selling and administrative expenses		31,500

Required:

1. What was the cost of raw materials purchased during the year?
2. What was the direct-labor cost charged to production during the year?
3. What was the cost of goods manufactured during the year?
4. What was the cost of goods sold during the year?

(CMA, adapted)

Exercise 3–33
Proration of Underapplied Overhead
(LO 3-5)

Sweet Tooth Confectionary incurred $157,000 of manufacturing overhead costs during the year just ended. However, only $141,000 of overhead was applied to production. At the conclusion of the year, the following amounts of the year's applied overhead remained in the various manufacturing accounts.

	Applied Overhead Remaining in Account on December 31
Work-in-Process Inventory	$35,250
Finished-Goods Inventory	49,350
Cost of Goods Sold	56,400

Required: Prepare a journal entry to close out the balance in the Manufacturing Overhead account and prorate the balance to the three manufacturing accounts.

Exercise 3–34
Overapplied or Underapplied Overhead
(LO 3-4, 3-5)

The following information pertains to Trenton Glass Works for the year just ended.

Budgeted direct-labor cost: 75,000 hours (practical capacity) at $16 per hour
Actual direct-labor cost: 80,000 hours at $17.50 per hour
Budgeted manufacturing overhead: $997,500
Actual selling and administrative expenses: 435,000

Actual manufacturing overhead:	
Depreciation	$231,000
Property taxes	21,000
Indirect labor	82,000
Supervisory salaries	200,000
Utilities	59,000
Insurance	30,000
Rental of space	300,000
Indirect material (see data below)	79,000
Indirect material:	
Beginning inventory, January 1	48,000
Purchases during the year	94,000
Ending inventory, December 31	63,000

Required:

1. Compute the firm's predetermined overhead rate, which is based on direct-labor hours.
2. Calculate the overapplied or underapplied overhead for the year.
3. Prepare a journal entry to close out the Manufacturing Overhead account into Cost of Goods Sold.
4. ***Build a spreadsheet:*** Construct an Excel spreadsheet to solve requirements (1) and (2) above. Show how the solution will change if the following data change: budgeted manufacturing overhead was $990,000, property taxes were $25,000, and purchases of indirect material amounted to $97,000.

Exercise 3–35
Predetermined Overhead Rate; Various Cost Drivers
(LO 3-4)

The following data pertain to the Oneida Restaurant Supply Company for the year just ended.

Budgeted sales revenue	$205,000
Actual manufacturing overhead	340,000
Budgeted machine hours (based on practical capacity)	10,000
Budgeted direct-labor hours (based on practical capacity)	20,000
Budgeted direct-labor rate	$ 14
Budgeted manufacturing overhead	$364,000
Actual machine hours	11,000
Actual direct-labor hours	18,000
Actual direct-labor rate	$ 15

Required:

1. Compute the firm's predetermined overhead rate for the year using each of the following common cost drivers: (*a*) machine hours, (*b*) direct-labor hours, and (*c*) direct-labor dollars.
2. Calculate the overapplied or underapplied overhead for the year using each of the cost drivers listed above.

Exercise 3–36
Actual versus Normal Costing
(LO 3-4, 3-5)

Refer to the data for the preceding exercise for Oneida Restaurant Supply Company. Prepare a journal entry to add to work-in-process inventory the total manufacturing overhead cost for the year, assuming:

1. The firm uses actual costing.
2. The firm uses normal costing, with a predetermined overhead rate based on machine hours.

Exercise 3–37
Project Costing; Interior Decorating
(LO 3-1, 3-8)

Design Arts Associates is an interior decorating firm in Berlin. The following costs were incurred in the firm's contract to redecorate the mayor's offices.

Direct material used	3,500 euros
Direct professional labor	6,000 euros

The firm's budget for the year included the following estimates:

Budgeted overhead	400,000 euros
Budgeted direct professional labor	250,000 euros

Overhead is applied to contracts using a predetermined overhead rate calculated annually. The rate is based on direct professional labor cost.

Required: Calculate the total cost of the firm's contract to redecorate the mayor's offices. (Remember to express your answer in terms of euros.)

Exercise 3–38
Choice of a Cost Driver for Overhead Application
(LO 3-1, 3-4)

Suppose you are the controller for a company that produces handmade glassware.

1. Choose a volume-based cost driver upon which to base the application of overhead. Write a memo to the company president explaining your choice.
2. Now you have changed jobs. You are the controller of a microchip manufacturer that uses a highly automated production process. Repeat the same requirements stated above.

Exercise 3–39
Cost Drivers; Different Production Methods
(LO 3-4, 3-5)

Laramie Leatherworks, which manufactures saddles and other leather goods, has three departments. The Assembly Department manufactures various leather products, such as belts, purses, and saddlebags, using an automated production process. The Saddle Department produces handmade saddles and uses very little machinery. The Tanning Department produces leather. The tanning process requires little in the way of labor or machinery, but it does require space and process time. Due to the different production processes in the three departments, the company uses three different cost drivers for the application of manufacturing overhead. The cost drivers and overhead rates are as follows:

	Cost Driver	Predetermined Overhead Rate
Tanning Department	Square feet of leather	$3 per square foot
Assembly Department	Machine time	$9 per machine hour
Saddle Department	Direct-labor time	$4 per direct-labor hour

The company's deluxe saddle and accessory set consists of a handmade saddle, two saddlebags, a belt, and a vest, all coordinated to match. The entire set uses 100 square feet of leather from the Tanning Department, 3 machine hours in the Assembly Department, and 40 direct-labor hours in the Saddle Department.

Required: Job number DS-20 consisted of 20 deluxe saddle and accessory sets. Prepare journal entries to record applied manufacturing overhead in the Work-in-Process Inventory account for each department.

Exercise 3–40
Two-Stage Allocation
(LO 3-1, 3-7)

Refer to Exhibit 3–12, which portrays the three types of allocation procedures used in two-stage allocation. Give an example of each of these allocation procedures in a hospital setting. The ultimate cost object is a patient-day of hospital care. This is one day of care for one patient. (*Hint:* First think about the various departments in a hospital. Which departments deal directly with patients; which ones are service departments and do not deal directly with patients? What kinds of costs does a hospital incur that should be distributed among all of the hospital's departments? Correct hospital terminology is not important here. Focus on the *concepts* of cost allocation portrayed in Exhibit 3–12.)

Exercise 3–41
Overhead Application in a Service Industry Firm
(LO 3-8)

Refer to the illustration of overhead application in the Small World Advertising example. Suppose the firm used a single cost driver, total staff compensation, to apply overhead costs to each advertising engagement.

Required:

1. Compute the total budgeted staff compensation: both partner and associate staff compensation.
2. Compute Small World's overhead rate on the basis of this single cost driver.
3. Recalculate the applied overhead for the EyeStyle Global engagement.
4. Compare the applied overhead using the single cost driver with the applied overhead computed using the two cost drivers used in the text illustration.

Problems

All applicable Problems are available in Connect. connect

Problem 3–42
Schedule of Cost of Goods Manufactured and Sold; Income Statement
(LO 3-6)

Ex

1. Total manufacturing costs: $175,100
3. Net income: $7,100

The following data refer to Twisto Pretzel Company for the year 20x1.

Work-in-process inventory, 12/31/x0	$ 8,100	Utilities for sales and administrative offices	2,500
Selling and administrative salaries	13,800	Other selling and administrative expenses	4,000
Insurance on factory and equipment	3,600	Indirect-labor cost incurred	29,000
Work-in-process inventory, 12/31/x1	8,300	Depreciation on factory building	3,800
Finished-goods inventory, 12/31/x0	14,000	Depreciation on cars used by sales personnel	1,200
Cash balance, 12/31/x1	6,000	Direct-labor cost incurred	79,000
Indirect material used	4,900	Raw-material inventory, 12/31/x1	11,000
Depreciation on factory equipment	2,100	Accounts receivable, 12/31/x1	4,100
Raw-material inventory, 12/31/x0	10,100	Rental for warehouse space to store raw material	3,100
Property taxes on factory	2,400	Rental of space for company president's office	1,700
Finished-goods inventory, 12/31/x1	15,400	Applied manufacturing overhead	58,000
Purchases of raw material in 20x1	39,000	Sales revenue	205,800
Utilities for factory	6,000	Income tax expense	5,100

Required:

1. Prepare Twisto Pretzel Company's schedule of cost of goods manufactured for 20x1.
2. Prepare the company's schedule of cost of goods sold for 20x1. The company closes overapplied or underapplied overhead into Cost of Goods Sold.
3. Prepare the company's income statement for 20x1.

Problem 3–43
Basic Job-Order Costing; Journal Entries
(LO 3-4, 3-5)

1. Predetermined overhead rate: $12 per hour

Burlington Clock Works manufactures fine, handcrafted clocks. The firm uses a job-order costing system, and manufacturing overhead is applied on the basis of direct-labor hours. Estimated manufacturing overhead for the year is $240,000. The firm employs 10 master clockmakers, who constitute the direct-labor force. Each of these employees is expected to work 2,000 hours during the year, which represents each employee's practical capacity. The following events occurred during October.

a. The firm purchased 3,000 board feet of mahogany veneer at $11 per board foot.
b. Twenty brass counterweights were requisitioned for production. Each weight cost $23.
c. Five gallons of glue were requisitioned for production. The glue cost $20 per gallon. Glue is treated as an indirect material.
d. Depreciation on the clockworks building for October was $8,000.
e. A $400 utility bill was paid in cash.
f. Time cards showed the following usage of labor:

Job number G60: 12 grandfather clocks, 1,000 hours of direct labor
Job number C81: 20 cuckoo clocks, 700 hours of direct labor
The master clockmakers (direct-labor personnel) earn $20 per hour.

g. The October property tax bill for $910 was received but has not yet been paid in cash.

h. The firm employs laborers who perform various tasks such as material handling and shop cleanup. Their wages for October amounted to $2,500.

i. Job number G60, which was started in July, was finished in October. The total cost of the job was $14,400.

j. Nine of the grandfather clocks from job number G60 were sold in October for $1,500 each.

Required:

1. Calculate the firm's predetermined overhead rate for the year.
2. Prepare journal entries to record the events described above.

Problem 3–44
Manufacturing Cost Flows; Analysis of T-Accounts
(LO 3-2, 3-5)

Perfecto Pizza Company produces microwavable pizzas. The following accounts appeared in Perfecto's ledger as of December 31.

Raw-Materials Inventory

Bal. 1/1	21,000		
	?	?	
Bal. 12/31	36,000		

Accounts Payable

		2,500	Bal. 1/1
	136,500	?	
		1,000	Bal. 12/31

Work-in-Process Inventory

Bal. 1/1	17,000		
Direct material	?	?	
Direct labor	?		
Manufacturing overhead	?		
Bal. 12/31	19,000		

Finished-Goods Inventory

Bal. 1/1	12,000		
	?	?	
Bal. 12/31	20,000		

Manufacturing Overhead

	?	?	

Cost of Goods Sold

	710,000		

Wages Payable

		2,000	Bal. 1/1
	147,000	?	
		5,000	Bal. 12/31

Sales Revenue

		?	

Accounts Receivable

Bal. 1/1	11,000		
	?	806,000	
Bal. 12/31	15,000		

Additional information:

a. Accounts payable is used only for direct-material purchases.

b. Underapplied overhead of $2,500 for the year has not yet been closed into cost of goods sold.

Required: Complete the T-accounts by computing the amounts indicated by a question mark.

Problem 3–45
Job-Order Costing; Journal Entries
(LO 3-2, 3-4, 3-5)

4. Finished-goods inventory increased by $203,000

Stellar Sound, Inc. which uses a job-order costing system, had two jobs in process at the start of 20x1: job no. 64 ($84,000) and job no. 65 ($53,500). The following information is available:

a. The company applies manufacturing overhead on the basis of machine hours (based on practical capacity). Budgeted overhead and machine activity for the year were anticipated to be $840,000, and 16,000 hours, respectively.

b. The company worked on four jobs during the first quarter. Direct materials used, direct labor incurred, and machine hours consumed were as follows:

Job No.	Direct Material	Direct Labor	Machine Hours
64	$21,000	$35,000	1,200
65	—	22,000	700
66	44,000	65,000	2,000
67	15,000	8,800	500

c. Manufacturing overhead during the first quarter included charges for depreciation ($34,000), indirect labor ($60,000), indirect materials used ($5,000), and other factory costs ($139,500).

d. Stellar Sound completed job no. 64 and job no. 65. Job no. 65 was sold on account, producing a profit of $34,700 for the firm.

Required:

1. Determine the company's predetermined overhead application rate.
2. Prepare journal entries as of March 31 to record the following. (*Note:* Use summary entries where appropriate by combining individual job data.)
   a. The issuance of direct material to production and the direct labor incurred.
   b. The manufacturing overhead incurred during the quarter.
   c. The application of manufacturing overhead to production.
   d. The completion of jobs no. 64 and no. 65.
   e. The sale of job no. 65.
3. Determine the cost of the jobs still in production as of March 31.
4. Did the finished-goods inventory increase or decrease during the first quarter? By how much?
5. Was manufacturing overhead under- or overapplied for the first quarter of the year? By how much?

Problem 3–46
Job-Order Costing; Focus on Manufacturing Overhead
(LO 3-2, 3-4, 3-5)

1. Predetermined overhead rate: 130% of direct labor cost
6. Cost of goods sold: $15,309,300

Finlon Upholstery, Inc. uses a job-order costing system to accumulate manufacturing costs. The company's work-in-process on December 31, 20x1, consisted of one job (no. 2077), which was carried on the year-end balance sheet at $156,800. There was no finished-goods inventory on this date.

Finlon applies manufacturing overhead to production on the basis of direct-labor cost. (The budgeted direct-labor cost is the company's practical capacity, in terms of direct-labor hours, multiplied by the budgeted direct-labor rate.) Budgeted totals for 20x2 for direct labor and manufacturing overhead are $4,200,000 and $5,460,000, respectively. Actual results for the year follow.

Direct material used	$ 5,600,000
Direct labor	4,350,000
Indirect material used	65,000
Indirect labor	2,860,000
Factory depreciation	1,740,000
Factory insurance	59,000
Factory utilities	830,000
Selling and administrative expenses	2,160,000
Total	$17,664,000

Job no. 2077 was completed in January 20x2; there was no work in process at year-end. All jobs produced during 20x2 were sold with the exception of job no. 2143, which contained direct-material costs of $156,000 and direct-labor charges of $85,000. The company charges any under- or overapplied overhead to Cost of Goods Sold.

Required:

1. Determine the company's predetermined overhead application rate.
2. Determine the additions to the Work-in-Process Inventory account for direct material used, direct labor, and manufacturing overhead.
3. Compute the amount that the company would disclose as finished-goods inventory on the December 31, 20x2, balance sheet.
4. Prepare the journal entry needed to record the year's completed production.
5. Compute the amount of under- or overapplied overhead at year-end, and prepare the necessary journal entry to record its disposition.
6. Determine the company's 20x2 cost of goods sold.
7. Would it be appropriate to include selling and administrative expenses in either manufacturing overhead or cost of goods sold? Briefly explain.

Problem 3–47
Job-Order Costing in a Consulting Firm
(LO 3-1, 3-2, 3-4, 3-8)

1. Traceable costs: $2,500,000

JLR Enterprises provides consulting services throughout California and uses a job-order costing system to accumulate the cost of client projects. Traceable costs are charged directly to individual clients; in contrast, other costs incurred by JLR, but not identifiable with specific clients, are charged to jobs by using a predetermined overhead application rate. Clients are billed for directly chargeable costs, overhead, and a markup.

JLR's director of cost management, Brent Dean, anticipates the following costs for the upcoming year:

	Cost	Percentage of Cost Directly Traceable to Clients
Professional staff salaries	$2,500,000	80%
Administrative support staff	300,000	60%
Travel	250,000	90%
Photocopying	50,000	90%
Other operating costs	100,000	50%
Total	$3,200,000	

The firm's partners desire to make a $640,000 profit for the firm and plan to add a percentage markup on total cost to achieve that figure.

On March 10, JLR completed work on a project for Martin Manufacturing. The following costs were incurred: professional staff salaries, $41,000; administrative support staff, $2,600; travel, $4,500; photocopying, $500; and other operating costs, $1,400.

Required:

1. Determine JLR's total traceable costs for the upcoming year and the firm's total anticipated overhead.
2. Calculate the predetermined overhead rate. The rate is based on total costs traceable to client jobs.
3. What percentage of cost will JLR add to each job to achieve its profit target?
4. Determine the total cost of the Martin Manufacturing project. How much would Martin be billed for services performed?
5. Notice that only 50 percent of JLR's other operating cost is directly traceable to specific client projects. Cite several costs that would be included in this category and difficult to trace to clients.
6. Notice that 80 percent of the professional staff cost is directly traceable to specific client projects. Cite several reasons that would explain why this figure isn't 100 percent.

Problem 3–48
Job-Order Costing; Focus on Overhead and Cost Drivers
(LO 3-2, 3-4, 3-5, 3-7)

Garcia, Inc. uses a job-order costing system for its products, which pass from the Machining Department, to the Assembly Department, to finished-goods inventory. The Machining Department is heavily automated; in contrast, the Assembly Department performs a number of manual-assembly

2. Ending work-in-process inventory cost: $153,530

activities. The company applies manufacturing overhead using machine hours in the Machining Department and direct-labor cost in the Assembly Department. The following information relates to the year just ended:

	Machining Department	Assembly Department
Budgeted manufacturing overhead	$4,000,000	$3,080,000
Actual manufacturing overhead	4,260,000	3,050,000
Budgeted direct-labor cost (based on practical capacity)	1,500,000	5,600,000
Actual direct-labor cost	1,450,000	5,780,000
Budgeted machine hours (based on practical capacity)	400,000	100,000
Actual machine hours	425,000	110,000

The data that follow pertain to job no. 775, the only job in production at year-end.

	Machining Department	Assembly Department
Direct material	$24,500	$ 6,700
Direct labor	27,900	58,600
Machine hours	360	150

Selling and administrative expense amounted to $2,500,000.

Required:

1. Assuming the use of normal costing, determine the predetermined overhead rates used in the Machining Department and the Assembly Department.
2. Compute the cost of the company's year-end work-in-process inventory.
3. Determine whether overhead was under- or overapplied during the year in the Machining Department.
4. Repeat requirement (3) for the Assembly Department.
5. If the company disposes of under- or overapplied overhead as an adjustment to Cost of Goods Sold, would the company's Cost of Goods Sold account increase or decrease? Explain.
6. How much overhead would have been charged to the company's Work-in-Process account during the year?
7. Comment on the appropriateness of the company's cost drivers (i.e., the use of machine hours in Machining and direct-labor cost in Assembly).

Problem 3–49
Journal Entries in Job-Order Costing
(LO 3-4, 3-5)

1. Predetermined overhead rate: $20 per machine hour

MarineCo, Inc. manufactures outboard motors and an assortment of other marine equipment. The company uses a job-order costing system. Normal costing is used, and manufacturing overhead is applied on the basis of machine hours. Estimated manufacturing overhead for the year is $1,464,000, and management estimates the firm's practical capacity at 73,200 machine hours.

Required:

1. Calculate MarineCo's predetermined overhead rate for the year.
2. Prepare journal entries to record the following events, which occurred during April.
   a. The firm purchased marine propellers from Peninsula Marine Corporation for $7,850 on account.
   b. A requisition was filed by the Gauge Department supervisor for 300 pounds of clear plastic. The material cost $0.60 per pound when it was purchased.
   c. The Motor Testing Department supervisor requisitioned 300 feet of electrical wire, which is considered an indirect material. The wire cost $.10 per foot when it was purchased.
   d. An electric utility bill of $800 was paid in cash.
   e. Direct-labor costs incurred in April were $75,000.
   f. April's insurance cost was $1,800 for insurance on the cars driven by sales personnel. The policy had been prepaid in March.
   g. Metal tubing costing $3,000 was purchased on account.
   h. A cash payment of $1,700 was made on outstanding accounts payable.

i. Indirect-labor costs of $21,000 were incurred during April.

j. Depreciation on equipment for April amounted to $7,000.

k. Job number G22, consisting of 50 tachometers, was finished during April. The total cost of the job was $1,100.

l. During April, 7,000 machine hours were used.

m. Sales on account for April amounted to $176,000. The cost of goods sold in April was $139,000.

Problem 3–50
Schedule of Cost of Goods Manufactured and Sold; Income Statement
(LO 3-5, 3-6)

2. Cost of goods sold (adjusted for underapplied overhead): $1,770,000

The following data refers to Huron Corporation for the year 20x2.

Sales revenue	$2,105,000	Indirect material used	45,000
Raw-material inventory, 12/31/x1	89,000	Depreciation on factory equipment	60,000
Purchases of raw material in 20x2	731,000	Insurance on factory and equipment	40,000
Raw-material inventory, 12/31/x2	59,000	Utilities for factory	70,000
Direct-labor cost incurred	474,000	Work-in-process inventory, 12/31/x1	-0-
Selling and administrative expenses	269,000	Work-in-process inventory, 12/31/x2	40,000
Indirect labor cost incurred	150,000	Finished-goods inventory, 12/31/x1	35,000
Property taxes on factory	90,000	Finished-goods inventory, 12/31/x2	40,000
Depreciation on factory building	125,000	Applied manufacturing overhead	577,500
Income tax expense	25,000		

Required:

1. Prepare Huron's schedule of cost of goods manufactured for 20x2.
2. Prepare the company's schedule of cost of goods sold for 20x2. The company closes overapplied or underapplied overhead into Cost of Goods Sold.
3. Prepare the company's income statement for 20x2.
4. ***Build a spreadsheet:*** Construct an Excel spreadsheet to solve all of the preceding requirements. Show how the solution will change if the following data change: sales revenue was $2,115,000, applied manufacturing overhead was $580,000, and utilities amounted to $78,000.

Problem 3–51
Interpreting the Schedule of Cost of Goods Manufactured
(LO 3-2, 3-6)

Refer to the schedule of cost of goods manufactured prepared for Huron Corporation in the preceding problem.

Required:

1. How much of the manufacturing costs incurred during 20x2 remained associated with work-in-process inventory on December 31, 20x2?
2. Suppose the company had increased its production in 20x2 by 20 percent. Would the direct-material cost shown on the schedule have been larger or the same? Why?
3. Answer the same question as in requirement (2) for depreciation on the factory building.
4. Suppose only half of the $60,000 in depreciation on equipment had been related to factory machinery, and the other half was related to selling and administrative equipment. How would this have changed the schedule of cost of goods manufactured?

Problem 3–52
Cost of Goods Manufactured; Prime and Conversion Costs
(LO 3-2, 3-6)

1. Cost of goods manufactured: $348,000

Marco Polo Map Company's cost of goods sold for March was $345,000. March 31 work-in-process inventory was 90 percent of March 1 work-in-process inventory. Manufacturing overhead applied was 50 percent of direct-labor cost. Other information pertaining to the company's inventories and production for the month of March is as follows:

Beginning inventories, March 1:	
Raw material	$ 17,000
Work in process	40,000
Finished goods	102,000
Purchases of raw material during March	113,000
Ending inventories, March 31:	
Raw material	26,000
Work in process	?
Finished goods	105,000

Required:

1. Prepare a schedule of cost of goods manufactured for the month of March.
2. Prepare a schedule to compute the prime costs (direct material and direct labor) incurred during March.
3. Prepare a schedule to compute the conversion costs (direct labor and manufacturing overhead) charged to work in process during March.

(CMA, adapted)

Problem 3–53
Proration of Overapplied or Underapplied Overhead
(LO 3-2, 3-4, 3-5, 3-6)

3. Underapplied overhead: $6,000

Midnight Sun Apparel Company uses normal costing, and manufacturing overhead is applied to work-in-process on the basis of machine hours. On January 1 of the current year, there were no balances in work-in-process or finished-goods inventories. The following estimates were included in the current year's budget.

Total budgeted manufacturing overhead	$235,000
Total budgeted machine hours	47,000

During January, the firm began the following production jobs:

A79:	1,000 machine hours
N08:	2,500 machine hours
P82:	500 machine hours

During January, job numbers A79 and N08 were completed, and job number A79 was sold. The actual manufacturing overhead incurred during January was $26,000.

Required:

1. Compute the company's predetermined overhead rate for the current year.
2. How much manufacturing overhead was applied to production during January?
3. Calculate the overapplied or underapplied overhead for January.
4. Prepare a journal entry to close the balance calculated in requirement (3) into Cost of Goods Sold.
5. Prepare a journal entry to prorate the balance calculated in requirement (3) among the Work-in-Process Inventory, Finished-Goods Inventory, and Cost of Goods Sold accounts.

Problem 3–54
Ethical Issues; Underapplication of Manufacturing Overhead
(LO 3-1, 3-2, 3-4, 3-6)

Marc Jackson has recently been hired as a cost accountant by Offset Press Company, a privately held company that produces a line of offset printing presses and lithograph machines. During his first few months on the job, Jackson discovered that Offset has been underapplying factory overhead to the Work-in-Process Inventory account, while overstating expenses through the General and Administrative Expense account. This practice has been going on since the start of the company, which is in its sixth year of operation. The effect in each year has been favorable, having a material impact on the company's tax position. No internal audit function exists at Offset, and the external auditors have not yet discovered the underapplied factory overhead.

Prior to the sixth-year audit, Jackson had pointed out the practice and its effect to Mary Brown, the corporate controller, and had asked her to let him make the necessary adjustments. Brown directed him not to make the adjustments, but to wait until the external auditors had completed their work and see what they uncovered.

The sixth-year audit has now been completed, and the external auditors have once again failed to discover the underapplication of factory overhead. Jackson again asked Brown if he could make the required adjustments and was again told not to make them. Jackson, however, believes that the adjustments should be made and that the external auditors should be informed of the situation.

Since there are no established policies at Offset Press Company for resolving ethical conflicts, Jackson is considering one of the following three alternative courses of action:

- Follow Brown's directive and do nothing further.
- Attempt to convince Brown to make the proper adjustments and to advise the external auditors of her actions.
- Tell the Audit Committee of the Board of Directors about the problem and give them the appropriate accounting data.

Required:

1. For each of the three alternative courses of action that Jackson is considering, explain whether or not the action is appropriate.
2. Independent of your answer to requirement (1), assume that Jackson again approaches Brown to make the necessary adjustments and is unsuccessful. Describe the steps that Jackson should take in proceeding to resolve this situation.

(CMA, adapted)

Problem 3–55
Predetermined Overhead Rate; Different Time Periods; Pricing
(LO 3-4)

4. Predetermined rate: $4.44 per hour (rounded)

Troy Electronics Company calculates its predetermined overhead rate on a quarterly basis. The following estimates were made for the current year.

	Estimated Manufacturing Overhead	Estimated Direct-Labor Hours	Quarterly Predetermined Overhead Rate (per direct-labor hour)
First quarter	$100,000	25,000	?
Second quarter	80,000	16,000	?
Third quarter	50,000	12,500	?
Fourth quarter	70,000	14,000	?
Total	$300,000	67,500	

The firm's main product, part number A200, requires $100 of direct material and 20 hours of direct labor per unit. The labor rate is $15 per hour.

Required:

1. Calculate the firm's *quarterly* predetermined overhead rate for each quarter.
2. Determine the cost of one unit of part number A200 if it is manufactured in January versus April.
3. Suppose the company's pricing policy calls for a 10 percent markup over cost. Calculate the price to be charged for a unit of part number A200 if it is produced in January versus April.
4. Calculate the company's predetermined overhead rate for the year if the rate is calculated *annually*.
5. Based on your answer to requirement (4), what is the cost of a unit of part number A200 if it is manufactured in January? In April?
6. What is the price of a unit of part A200 if the predetermined overhead rate is calculated annually?

Problem 3–56
Overhead Application Using a Predetermined Overhead Rate
(LO 3-2, 3-4, 3-5, 3-6)

2. Cost of job 77: $200,675
6. Underapplied overhead for November: $4,575

Tiana Shar, the controller for Bondi Furniture Company, is in the process of analyzing the overhead costs for the month of November. She has gathered the following data for the month.

Labor	
Direct-labor hours:	
Job 77	3,500
Job 78	3,000
Job 79	2,000
Labor costs:	
Direct-labor wages	$204,000
Indirect-labor wages	15,000
Supervisory salaries	6,000
Material	
Inventories, November 1:	
Raw material and supplies	$ 10,500
Work in process (job 77)	54,000
Finished goods	112,500
Purchases of raw material and supplies:	
Raw material	$135,000
Supplies (indirect material)	15,000

(continued)

Direct material and supplies requisitioned for production:	
Job 77	$ 45,000
Job 78	37,500
Job 79	25,500
Supplies (indirect material)	12,000
Total	$120,000
Other	
Building occupancy costs (heat, light, depreciation, etc.)	
Factory facilities	$ 6,400
Sales offices	1,600
Administrative offices	1,000
Total	$ 9,000
Production equipment costs:	
Power	$ 4,100
Repairs and maintenance	1,500
Depreciation	1,500
Other	1,000
Total	$ 8,100

The firm's job-order costing system uses direct-labor hours (measured at practical capacity) as the cost driver for overhead application. In December of the preceding year, Shar had prepared the following budget for direct-labor and manufacturing-overhead costs for the current year. The plant is theoretically capable of operating at 150,000 direct-labor hours per year. However, Shar estimates that the practical capacity is 120,000 hours in a typical year.

	Manufacturing Overhead	
Direct-Labor Hours	**Variable**	**Fixed**
100,000	$325,000	$216,000
120,000	390,000	216,000
140,000	455,000	216,000

During November the following jobs were completed:

Job 77	Side chairs
Job 78	End tables

Required: Assist Shar by making the following calculations.

1. Calculate the predetermined overhead rate for the current year.
2. Calculate the total cost of job 77.
3. Compute the amount of manufacturing overhead applied to job 79 during November.
4. What was the total amount of manufacturing overhead applied during November?
5. Compute the actual manufacturing overhead incurred during November.
6. Calculate the overapplied or underapplied overhead for November.

(CMA, adapted)

Problem 3–57
Comprehensive Job-Order Costing Problem
(LO 3-2, 3-4, 3-5, 3-6)

1. Predetermined overhead rate: $21 per direct-labor hour
4. Total actual overhead: $33,900
7. Income (loss): $(1,625)

Scholastic Brass Corporation manufactures brass musical instruments for use by high school students. The company uses a normal costing system, in which manufacturing overhead is applied on the basis of direct-labor hours. The company's budget for the current year included the following predictions.

Budgeted total manufacturing overhead	$426,300
Budgeted total direct-labor hours (based on practical capacity)	20,300

During March, the firm worked on the following two production jobs:

Job number T81, consisting of 76 trombones

Job number C40, consisting of 110 cornets

The events of March are described as follows:

a. One thousand square feet of rolled brass sheet metal were purchased on account for $5,000.

b. Four hundred pounds of brass tubing were purchased on account for $4,000.

c. The following requisitions were submitted on March 5:

Requisition number 112: 250 square feet of brass sheet metal at $5 per square foot (for job number T81)

Requisition number 113: 1,000 pounds of brass tubing, at $10 per pound (for job number C40)

Requisition number 114: 10 gallons of valve lubricant, at $10 per gallon

All brass used in production is treated as direct material. Valve lubricant is an indirect material.

d. An analysis of labor time cards revealed the following labor usage for March.

Direct labor: Job number T81, 800 hours at $20 per hour

Direct labor: Job number C40, 900 hours at $20 per hour

Indirect labor: General factory cleanup, $4,000

Indirect labor: Factory supervisory salaries, $9,000

e. Depreciation of the factory building and equipment during March amounted to $12,000.

f. Rent paid in cash for warehouse space used during March was $1,200.

g. Utility costs incurred during March amounted to $2,100. The invoices for these costs were received, but the bills were not paid in March.

h. March property taxes on the factory were paid in cash, $2,400.

i. The insurance cost covering factory operations for the month of March was $3,100. The insurance policy had been prepaid.

j. The costs of salaries and fringe benefits for sales and administrative personnel paid in cash during March amounted to $8,000.

k. Depreciation on administrative office equipment and space amounted to $4,000.

l. Other selling and administrative expenses paid in cash during March amounted to $1,000.

m. Job number T81 was completed on March 20.

n. Half of the trombones in job number T81 were sold on account during March for $700 each.

The March 1 balances in selected accounts are as follows:

Cash	$ 10,000
Accounts Receivable	21,000
Prepaid Insurance	5,000
Raw-Material Inventory	149,000
Manufacturing Supplies Inventory	500
Work-in-Process Inventory	91,000
Finished-Goods Inventory	220,000
Accumulated Depreciation: Buildings and Equipment	102,000
Accounts Payable	13,000
Wages Payable	8,000

Required:

1. Calculate the company's predetermined overhead rate for the year.
2. Prepare journal entries to record the events of March.
3. Set up T-accounts, and post the journal entries made in requirement (2).

4. Calculate the overapplied or underapplied overhead for March. Prepare a journal entry to close this balance into Cost of Goods Sold.
5. Prepare a schedule of cost of goods manufactured for March.
6. Prepare a schedule of cost of goods sold for March.
7. Prepare an income statement for March.

Problem 3–58
Job-Cost Record; Continuation of Preceding Problem
(LO 3-2, 3-4, 3-6)

Total cost of job T81: $34,050

Refer to the preceding problem regarding Scholastic Brass Corporation. Complete the following job-cost record for job number T81. (Assume that all of the direct-labor hours for job T81 occurred during the week of 3/8 through 3/12.)

SCHOLASTIC BRASS CORPORATION:
JOB-COST RECORD

Job Number T81 ____________ **Description** ____________
Date Started ____________ **Date Completed** ____________
Number of Units Completed ____________

Direct Material				
Date	**Requisition Number**	**Quantity**	**Unit Price**	**Cost**

Direct Labor				
Date	**Time Card Number**	**Hours**	**Rate**	**Cost**
3/8 to 3/12	3–08 through 3–12			

Manufacturing Overhead				
Date	**Cost Driver (Activity Base)**	**Quantity**	**Application Rate**	**Cost**
3/8 to 3/12				

Cost Summary	
Cost Item	**Amount**
Total direct material Total direct labor Total manufacturing overhead	
Total cost	
Unit cost	

Shipping Summary			
Date	**Units Shipped**	**Units Remaining in Inventory**	**Cost Balance**

Problem 3–59
Flow of Manufacturing Costs; Incomplete Data
(LO 3-2, 3-4, 3-5)

5. $80,000

Conundrum Corporation manufactures furniture. Due to a fire in the administrative offices, the accounting records for November of the current year were partially destroyed. You have been able to piece together the following information from the ledger.

Raw-Materials Inventory

	40,000
Bal. 11/30 45,000	

Accounts Payable

	12,000 Bal. 10/31

Work-in-Process Inventory

Bal. 10/31 8,000	

Finished-Goods Inventory

Bal. 10/31 35,000	

Manufacturing Overhead

60,000	

Cost of Goods Sold

Wages Payable

	1,500 Bal. 11/30

Sales Revenue

Accounts Receivable

Bal. 10/31 8,000	

Upon examining various source documents and interviewing several employees, you were able to gather the following additional information.

a. Collections of accounts receivable during November amounted to $205,000.

b. Sales revenue in November was 120 percent of cost of goods sold. All sales are on account.

c. Overhead is applied using an annual predetermined overhead rate using direct-labor hours (based on practical capacity).

d. The budgeted overhead for the current year is $720,000.

e. Budgeted direct-labor cost for the current year is $960,000. The direct-labor rate is $20 per hour.

f. The accounts payable balance on November 30 was $1,000. Only purchases of raw material are credited to accounts payable. A payment of $81,000 was made on November 15.

g. November's cost of goods sold amounted to $180,000.

h. The November 30 balance in finished-goods inventory was $5,000.

i. Payments of $79,500 were made to direct-labor employees during November. The October 31 balance in the Wages Payable account was $1,000.

j. The *actual* manufacturing overhead for November was $60,000.

k. An analysis of the furniture still in process on November 30 revealed that so far these items have required 500 hours of direct labor and $20,500 of direct material.

Required: Calculate the following amounts. Then complete the T-accounts given in the problem.

1. Sales revenue for November.
2. November 30 balance in accounts receivable.
3. Cost of raw material purchased during November.
4. November 30 balance in work-in-process inventory.
5. Direct labor added to work in process during November.

6. Applied overhead for November.
7. Cost of goods completed during November.
8. Raw material used during November.
9. October 31 balance in raw-material inventory.
10. Overapplied or underapplied overhead for November.

Problem 3–60
Plantwide versus Departmental Overhead Rates; Product Pricing
(LO 3-1, 3-4, 3-7)

1. Total budgeted overhead (departments A and B): $800,000
3. Departmental overhead rate, Department A: $26 per direct-labor hour

TeleTech Corporation manufactures two different color printers for the business market. Cost estimates for the two models for the current year are as follows:

	Basic System	Advanced System
Direct material	$ 400	$ 800
Direct labor (20 hours at $15 per hour)	300	300
Manufacturing overhead*	400	400
Total	$1,100	$1,500

*The predetermined overhead rate is $20 per direct-labor hour.

Each model of printer requires 20 hours of direct labor. The basic system requires 5 hours in department A and 15 hours in department B. The advanced system requires 15 hours in department A and 5 hours in department B. The overhead costs budgeted in these two production departments are as follows:

	Department A	Department B
Variable cost	$16 per direct-labor hour	$4 per direct-labor hour
Fixed cost	$200,000	$200,000

The firm's management expects to operate at a level of 20,000 direct-labor hours in each production department during the current year. (This estimate is based on the practical capacity of each department.)

Required:

1. Show how the company's predetermined overhead rate was determined.
2. If the firm prices each model of color printer at 10 percent over its cost, what will be the price of each model?
3. Suppose the company were to use departmental predetermined overhead rates. Calculate the rate for each of the two production departments.
4. Compute the product cost of each model using the departmental overhead rates calculated in requirement (3).
5. Compute the price to be charged for each model, assuming the company continues to price each product at 10 percent above cost. Use the revised product costs calculated in requirement (4).
6. Write a memo to the president of TeleTech Corporation making a recommendation as to whether the firm should use a plantwide overhead rate or departmental rates. Consider the potential implications of the overhead rates and the firm's pricing policy. How might these considerations affect the firm's ability to compete in the marketplace?

Cases

Case 3–61
Interpreting Information from a Job-Order Costing System
(LO 3-2, 3-3, 3-4, 3-6)

3. Finished-goods inventory, 12/31: 13,400 units
4. Actual manufacturing overhead: $4,392,000

CompuFurn, Inc. manufactures furniture for computer work stations. CompuFurn uses a job-order costing system and employs absorption costing. ComuFurn's work-in-process inventory on November 30 consisted of the following jobs.

Job No.	Description	Units	Accumulated Cost
CC723	Computer caddy	20,000	$ 900,000
CH291	Chair	15,000	431,000
PS812	Printer stand	25,000	250,000
Total			$1,581,000

On November 30, the company's finished-goods inventory, which is evaluated using the first-in, first-out (FIFO) method, consisted of four items.

Item	Quantity and Unit Cost	Accumulated Cost
Computer caddy	7,500 units @ $64 each	$ 480,000
Chair	19,400 units @ $35 each	679,000
Printer stand	21,000 units @ $55 each	1,155,000
Desk	11,200 units @ $102 each	1,142,400
Total		$3,456,400

At the end of November, the balance in CompuFurn's Materials Inventory account, which includes both raw materials and purchased parts, was $668,000. Additions to and requisitions from the materials inventory during the month of December included the following.

Additions	Raw Materials	Purchased Parts
Purchases	$242,000	$396,000
Requisitions:		
Job CC723	51,000	104,000
Job CH291	3,000	10,800
Job PS812	124,000	87,000
Job DS444 (5,000 desks)	65,000	187,000

CompuFurn applies manufacturing overhead on the basis of machine hours. The company's manufacturing overhead budget for the year totaled $4,500,000. The company planned to use 900,000 machine hours during this period, which is the firm's estimated practical capacity. Through the first 11 months of the year, a total of 830,000 machine hours were used, and actual manufacturing overhead amounted to $4,140,000.

During the month of December, machine hours and labor hours consisted of the following:

Account	Machine Hours	Labor Hours	Labor Cost
CC723	12,000	11,600	$122,400
CH291	4,400	3,600	43,200
PS812	19,500	14,300	200,500
DS444	14,000	12,500	138,000
Indirect labor	—	3,000	29,400
Supervision	—	—	57,600
Total	49,900	45,000	$591,100

The jobs completed in December and the unit sales for that month are as follows:

Job No.	Production Items	Quantity Completed	Item	Quantity Shipped
CC723	Computer caddy	20,000	Computer caddy	17,500
CH291	Chair	15,000	Chair	21,000
DS444	Desks	5,000	Printer stand	18,000
			Desk	6,000

Required:

1. Describe when it is appropriate for a company to use a job-order costing system.
2. Calculate the balance in CompuFurn, Inc.'s Work-in-Process Inventory account as of December 31.
3. Calculate the cost of the chairs in CompuFurn, Inc.'s finished-goods Inventory as of December 31.
4. Actual manufacturing overhead incurred in December amounted to $252,000. Calculate CompuFurn's overapplied or underapplied overhead for the year.
5. Explain two alternative accounting treatments for overapplied or underapplied overhead balances when using a job-order costing system.

(CMA, adapted)

■ **Case 3–62**

Cost Flows in a Job-Order Costing System; Schedule of Cost of Goods Manufactured; Automation

(LO 3-2, 3-3, 3-4, 3-5, 3-6)

3. Manufacturing overhead applied in December: $90,000

6. Cost of goods manufactured: $2,968,800

FiberCom, Inc., a manufacturer of fiber optic communications equipment, uses a job-order costing system. Since the production process is heavily automated, manufacturing overhead is applied on the basis of machine hours using a predetermined overhead rate. The current annual rate of $15 per machine hour is based on budgeted manufacturing overhead costs of $1,200,000 and a budgeted activity level of 80,000 machine hours (the company's estimated practical capacity). Operations for the year have been completed, and all of the accounting entries have been made for the year except the application of manufacturing overhead to the jobs worked on during December, the transfer of costs from Work-in-Process to Finished-Goods for the jobs completed in December, and the transfer of costs from Finished Goods to Cost of Goods Sold for the jobs that have been sold during December. Summarized data as of November 30 and for the month of December are presented in the following table. Jobs T11-007, N11-013, and N11-015 were completed during December. All completed jobs except Job N11-013 had been turned over to customers by the close of business on December 31.

	Work-in-Process	December Activity		
Job No.	Balance November 30	Direct Material	Direct Labor	Machine Hours
T11-007	$ 87,000	$ 1,500	$ 4,500	300
N11-013	55,000	4,000	12,000	1,000
N11-015	-0-	25,600	26,700	1,400
D12-002	-0-	37,900	20,000	2,500
D12-003	-0-	26,000	16,800	800
Total	$142,000	$95,000	$80,000	6,000

Operating Activity	Activity through November 30	December Activity
Actual manufacturing overhead incurred:		
Indirect material	$ 125,000	$ 9,000
Indirect labor	345,000	30,000
Utilities	245,000	22,000
Depreciation	385,000	35,000
Total overhead	$1,100,000	$96,000
Other data:		
Raw-material purchases*	$ 965,000	$98,000
Direct-labor costs	$ 845,000	$80,000
Machine hours	73,000	6,000

Account Balances at Beginning of Year	January 1
Raw-material inventory*	$105,000
Work-in-process inventory	60,000
Finished-goods inventory	125,000

*Raw-material purchases and raw-material inventory consist of both direct and indirect materials. The balance of the Raw-Material Inventory account as of December 31 of the year just completed is $85,000.

Required:

1. Explain why manufacturers use a predetermined overhead rate to apply manufacturing overhead to their jobs.
2. How much manufacturing overhead would FiberCom have applied to jobs through November 30 of the year just completed?
3. How much manufacturing overhead would have been applied to jobs during December of the year just completed?
4. Determine the amount by which manufacturing overhead is overapplied or underapplied as of December 31 of the year just completed.
5. Determine the balance in the Finished-Goods Inventory account on December 31 of the year just completed.
6. Prepare a Schedule of Cost of Goods Manufactured for FiberCom, Inc. for the year just completed. (*Hint:* In computing the cost of direct material used, remember that FiberCom includes both direct and indirect material in its Raw-Material Inventory account.)

(CMA, adapted)

4 Process Costing and Hybrid Product-Costing Systems

FOCUS COMPANY >>>

© Comstock Images/Getty Images RF

THIS CHAPTER'S FOCUS COMPANY is the MVP Sports Equipment Company. The company's Wisconsin Division manufactures baseball gloves in its Milwaukee plant. MVP's Wisconsin Division uses a product-costing method called process costing. Under process costing, direct material and conversion costs (direct labor and manufacturing overhead) are first assigned to each of the processes (or departments) used in the manufacturing operation. Then, the costs of each process (or department) are assigned to the units worked on in the department. Process costing is used by manufacturing companies that produce relatively large numbers of similar products.

© Photodisc/Getty Images RF

<<< IN CONTRAST

In contrast to the process-costing system used in MVP's Wisconsin Division, we explore a different product-costing system in the company's Minnesota Division. This MVP division manufactures two types of basketballs in its Minneapolis plant. The professional basketballs are covered with genuine leather, whereas the scholastic basketballs are covered with imitation leather. Except for the different exterior material, though, each basketball requires the same production steps. MVP's Minnesota Division uses a product-costing system called operation costing, which is well suited to its production environment.

After completing this chapter, you should be able to:

4-1 List and explain the similarities and important differences between job-order and process costing.

4-2 Prepare journal entries to record the flow of costs in a process-costing system with sequential production departments.

4-3 Prepare a table of equivalent units under weighted-average process costing.

4-4 Compute the cost per equivalent unit under the weighted-average method of process costing.

4-5 Analyze the total production costs for a department under the weighted-average method of process costing.

4-6 Prepare a departmental production report under weighted-average process costing.

4-7 Describe how an operation costing system accumulates and assigns the costs of direct-material and conversion activity in a batch manufacturing process.

We have seen that a product-costing system performs two primary functions:

1. Accumulating production costs.
2. Assigning those production costs to the firm's products.

Product costs are needed for the purposes of planning, cost management, decision making, and reporting to various outside organizations, such as governmental regulatory agencies.

Job-order costing was described in Chapter 3. This type of product-costing system is used when relatively small numbers of products are produced in distinct batches or job orders and these products differ significantly from each other. This chapter covers **process-costing systems.** Process costing is used in repetitive production environments, where large numbers of identical or very similar products are manufactured in a continuous flow. Industries using process costing include paper, petroleum, chemicals, textiles, food processing, lumber, and electronics.

Comparison of Job-Order Costing and Process Costing

Learning Objective 4-1

List and explain the similarities and important differences between job-order and process costing.

In many ways, job-order costing and process costing are similar. Both product-costing systems have the same ultimate purpose—assignment of production costs to units of output. Moreover, the flow of costs through the manufacturing accounts is the same in the two systems.

Flow of Costs

Exhibit 4–1 displays the flow of costs in two process-costing situations: one with a single production department and one with two production departments used in sequence. The same accounts are used in this process-costing illustration as were used in job-order costing in the preceding chapter. As the illustration shows, direct-material, direct-labor, and manufacturing-overhead costs are added to a Work-in-Process Inventory account.

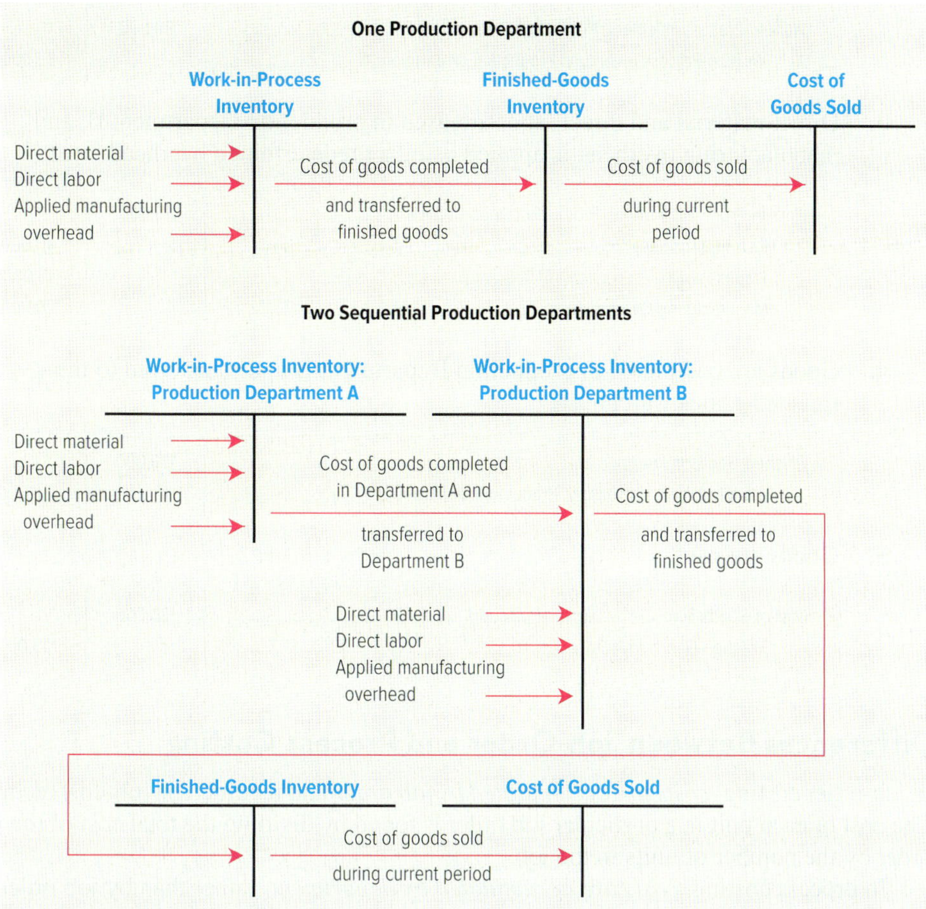

Exhibit 4–1
Flow of Costs in Process-Costing Systems

As goods are finished, costs are transferred to Finished-Goods Inventory. During the period when goods are sold, the product costs are transferred to Cost of Goods Sold. In the two-department case, when goods are finished in the first production department, costs accumulated in the Work-in-Process Inventory account for production Department A are transferred to the Work-in-Process Inventory account for production Department B.

Learning Objective 4-2

Prepare journal entries to record the flow of costs in a process-costing system with sequential production departments.

The journal entries for the case of two sequential production departments, as illustrated in Exhibit 4–1, are as follows. (The numbers used in the journal entries are assumed for the purpose of showing the form of the entries.)

1. As direct material and direct labor are used in production Department A, these costs are added to the Work-in-Process Inventory account for Department A. Overhead is applied using a predetermined overhead rate. The predetermined overhead rate is computed in the same way in job-order and process costing.

Work-in-Process Inventory: Production Department A	100,000	
Raw-Material Inventory		50,000
Wages Payable		20,000
Manufacturing Overhead		30,000

2. When production Department A completes its work on some units of product, these units are transferred to production Department B. The costs assigned to these goods are transferred from the Work-in-Process Inventory account for Department A to the Work-in-Process Inventory account for Department B. In Department B, the costs assigned to these partially completed products are called **transferred-in costs.**

"Process-based costing provided our first opportunity to convert the functional budget into process costing. It allowed us to look at what drives the costs of the individual processes." (4a)

John Deere Health Care, Inc.

Work-in-Process Inventory: Production Department B	80,000	
Work-in-Process Inventory: Production Department A		80,000

3. Direct material and direct labor are used in production Department B, and manufacturing overhead is applied using a predetermined overhead rate.

Work-in-Process Inventory: Production Department B	75,000	
Raw-Material Inventory		40,000
Wages Payable		15,000
Manufacturing Overhead		20,000

4. Goods are completed in production Department B and transferred to the finished-goods warehouse.

Finished-Goods Inventory	130,000	
Work-in-Process Inventory: Production Department B		130,000

5. Goods are sold.

Cost of Goods Sold	125,000	
Finished-Goods Inventory		125,000

Differences Between Job-Order and Process Costing

Learning Objective 4-1

List and explain the similarities and important differences between job-order and process costing.

In job-order costing, *costs are accumulated by job order* and recorded on job-cost records. The cost of each unit in a particular job order is found by dividing the total cost of the job order by the number of units in the job.

In process costing, *costs are accumulated by department,* rather than by job order or batch. The cost per unit is found by averaging the total costs incurred over the units produced. Exhibit 4–2 summarizes this key difference between job-order and process costing.

Equivalent Units: A Key Concept

Learning Objective 4-3

Prepare a table of equivalent units under weighted-average process costing.

Material, labor, and overhead costs often are incurred at different rates in a production process. Direct material is usually placed into production at one or more discrete points in the process. In contrast, direct labor and manufacturing overhead, called *conversion costs,* usually are incurred continuously throughout the process. When an accounting period ends, the partially completed goods that remain in process generally are at different stages of completion with respect to material and conversion activity. For example, the in-process units may be 75 percent complete with respect to conversion, but they may already include all of their direct materials. This situation is portrayed in Exhibit 4–3.

Equivalent Units

The graphical illustration in Exhibit 4–3 supposes there are 1,000 physical units in process at the end of an accounting period. Each of the physical units is 75 percent complete with respect to conversion (direct labor and manufacturing overhead). How much conversion activity has been applied to these partially completed units? Conversion activity occurs uniformly throughout the production process. Therefore, the amount of conversion activity required to do 75 percent of the conversion on 1,000 units is *equivalent* to the amount of conversion activity required to do all of the conversion on 750 units. This number is computed as follows:

$$\begin{matrix}\text{1,000 partially completed} \\ \text{physical units in process}\end{matrix} \times \begin{matrix}\text{75\% complete with} \\ \text{respect to conversion}\end{matrix} = \text{750 equivalent units}$$

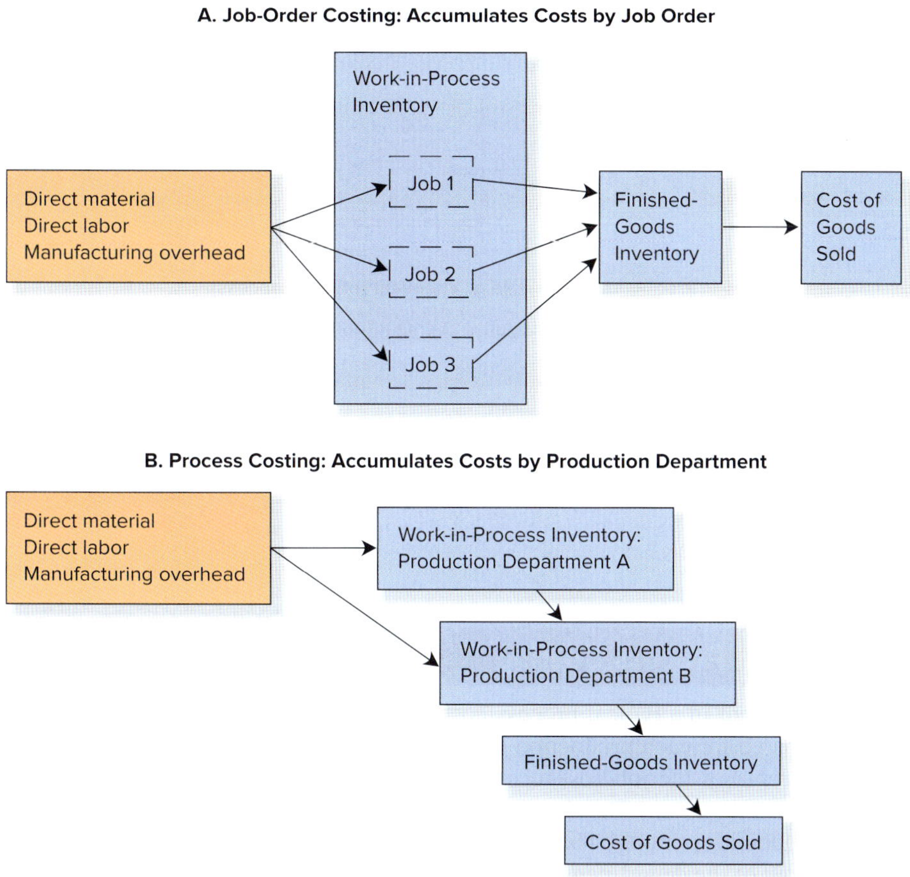

Exhibit 4–2
Comparison of Job-Order and Process Costing

The term **equivalent units** is used in process costing to refer to the amount of manufacturing activity that has been applied to a batch of physical units. The *1,000 physical units* in process represent *750 equivalent units* of conversion activity.

The term *equivalent units* also is used to measure the amount of direct materials represented by the partially completed goods. Since direct materials are incorporated at the beginning of the production process, the *1,000 physical units* represent *1,000 equivalent units of direct material* (1,000 physical units × 100% complete with respect to direct materials).

The most important feature of process costing is that the costs of direct material and conversion are assigned to equivalent units rather than to physical units. Refer again to Exhibit 4–3. For simplicity, suppose that the only production activity of the current accounting period was to start work on the 1,000 physical units and complete 75 percent of the required conversion activity. Assume that the costs incurred were $1,500 for conversion (direct labor and manufacturing overhead) and $5,000 for direct material. These costs would then be assigned as follows:

$$\frac{\$1{,}500 \text{ conversion cost}}{750 \text{ equivalent units of conversion}} = \begin{array}{c}\$2.00 \text{ per equivalent unit} \\ \text{for conversion}\end{array}$$

$$\frac{\$5{,}000 \text{ direct-material cost}}{1{,}000 \text{ equivalent units of direct material}} = \begin{array}{c}\$5.00 \text{ per equivalent unit} \\ \text{for direct material}\end{array}$$

This is a highly simplified example because there is no work-in-process inventory at the beginning of the accounting period and no goods were completed during the period. Nevertheless, it illustrates the important concept that under process costing, costs are assigned to equivalent units rather than physical units.

> "Operations [managers] have a keen interest in cost management. To truly manage costs, you must look at the processes involved." (4b)
>
> **John Deere Health Care, Inc.**

Exhibit 4–3
Direct Material and Conversion Activity in a Typical Production Process

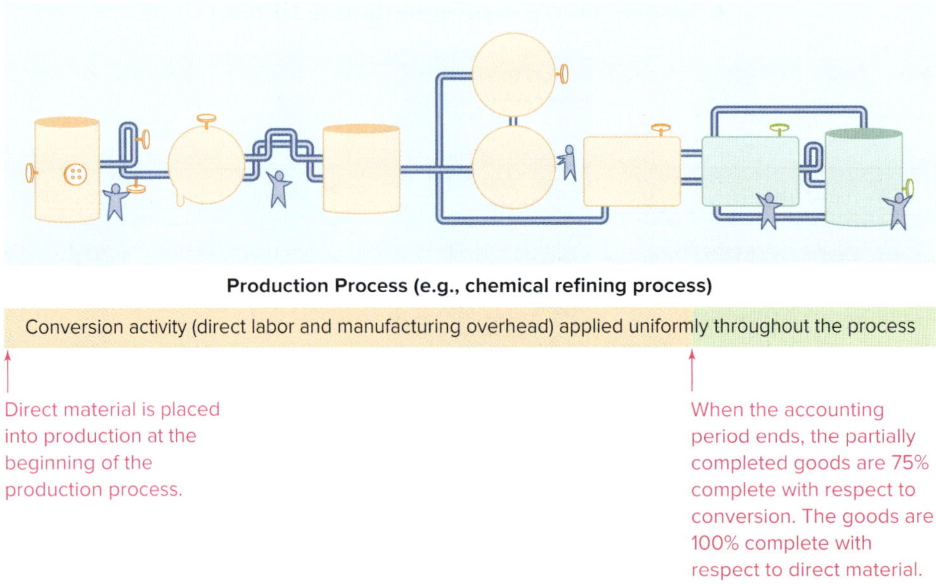

Illustration of Process Costing

The key document in a typical process-costing system is the **departmental production report,** prepared for each production department at the end of every accounting period. This report replaces the job-cost record, which is used to accumulate costs by job in a job-order costing system. The departmental production report summarizes the flow of production quantities through the department, and it shows the amount of production cost transferred out of the department's Work-in-Process Inventory account during the period. The following four steps are used in preparing a departmental production report.

1. Analysis of physical flow of units.
2. Calculation of equivalent units (for direct material and conversion activity).
3. Computation of unit costs (i.e., the cost per equivalent unit for direct material and conversion).
4. Analysis of total costs (determine the cost to be removed from work in process and transferred either to the next production department or to finished goods).

The method of process costing that we will focus on in this chapter is called the **weighted-average method.** *This method is almost always used in practice* by companies

© Royalty-Free/Corbis

© Eric Martin, photographer/Iconotec RF

Process costing is used in the wine industry. First, raw material (in this case, grapes) is harvested and entered into production. Then conversion costs are incurred in the production process. At the end of the accounting period, partially completed units of wine remain in process as the wine ages.

Exhibit 4–4
Basic Data for Illustration—Cutting Department

MVP Sports Equipment Company - Excel

B22 =SUM(B20:B21)

	A	B	C
1	Information for Illustration	Amount	
2			
3	Work in process, March 1 - 20,000 units		
4	Direct material: 100% complete, cost of*	$ 50,000	
5	Conversion: 10% complete, cost of*	7,200	
6	Balance in work in process, March 1*	$ 57,200	
7			
8	Units started during March	30,000	units
9			
10	Units completed during March and transferred out of the Cutting Department	40,000	units
11			
12	Work in process, March 31	10,000	units
13	Direct material: 100% complete		
14	Conversion: 50% complete		
15			
16	Costs Incurred during March:		
17	Direct material	$ 90,000	
18			
19	Conversion costs:		
20	Direct labor	$ 86,000	
21	Applied manufacturing overhead**	107,500	
22	Total conversion costs	$ 193,500	
23			
24	*These costs were incurred during the prior month, February		
25			
26	**(Predetermined overhead rate) x (Direct labor cost) = 125% x $86,000 = $107,500		

Cutting Department

using process costing. There is another process-costing method called the *first-in, first-out,* or *FIFO, method.* This method is covered in some cost accounting courses, but it is rarely used in practice.[1]

Basic Data for Illustration

The Wisconsin Division of MVP Sports Equipment Company manufactures baseball gloves in its Milwaukee plant. In the Cutting Department, direct material consisting of imitation leather is placed into production at the beginning of the process. Direct-labor and manufacturing overhead costs are incurred uniformly throughout the process. The material is rolled to make it softer and then cut into the pieces needed to produce baseball gloves. The predetermined overhead rate used in the Cutting Department is 125 percent of direct-labor *cost.*

The Excel spreadsheet in Exhibit 4–4 presents a summary of the activity and costs in the Cutting Department during March. The direct-material and conversion costs listed in Exhibit 4–4 for the March 1 work in process consist of costs that were incurred during February. These costs were assigned to the units remaining in process at the end of February.

Based on the data in Exhibit 4–4, the Cutting Department's Work-in-Process Inventory account has the following balance on March 1.

Work-in-Process Inventory: Cutting Department		
March 1 balance	57,200	

[1]The FIFO method of process costing is also covered in a supplement to this text titled *Process Costing: The First-In, First-Out Method.* This supplement is available to students and instructors in the Connect Library.

Management Accounting Practice

NEW YORK WINE INDUSTRY

The New York State wine industry, the second largest in the United States after California, contributes nearly $4.5 billion to the state's economy annually. The Empire State's 30 thousand acres of vineyards and 212 wineries produce over 200 million bottles of wine each year. New York wineries in the Finger Lakes region, in the Hudson Valley, along the Lake Erie shoreline, in the Niagara escarpment area, and on Long Island constitute the fastest-growing segment of New York's two largest industries: agriculture and tourism.

Wine production provides an excellent example of process costing. The processes used in a typical Finger Lakes area vineyard are as follows:[2]

- *Trimming:* At the end of a growing season, the vines are trimmed, which helps prepare them for the next harvest.
- *Tying:* The vines are tied onto wires to help protect them from the weather. (This also occurs at the end of the season.)
- *Hilling:* Dirt is piled up around the roots to further protect them.
- *Conditioning:* In the spring, dirt is leveled back from the roots.
- *Untying:* The vines are untied from the wires to allow them freedom to grow during the spring and summer months.
- *Chemical spraying:* The vines are sprayed in the spring to protect them from disease and insects.
- *Harvesting:* The highest-quality grapes are picked by hand to minimize damage.
- *Stemming and crushing:* Batches of grapes are loaded into a machine, which gently removes the stems and mildly crushes them.
- *Pressing:* After removal from the stemmer/crusher, the juice runs freely from the grapes.
- *Filtering:* The grapes are crushed mechanically to render more juice from them.
- *Fermentation:* This process varies, depending on the type of wine. For example, riesling grape juice is placed in stainless-steel tanks for fermentation. Chardonnay grape juice undergoes a two-stage fermentation process in oak barrels.
- *Aging:* Again, this process varies. Riesling wines are aged in the stainless-steel tanks for approximately a year. Chardonnays are aged in the oak barrels for about two years.
- *Bottling:* A machine bottles the wine and corks the bottles.
- *Labeling:* Each bottle is labeled with the name of the vintner, vintage, and variety.
- *Packing:* The bottles are packed in 12-bottle cases.
- *Case labeling:* The cases are stamped with the same information as is on the bottles.
- *Shipping:* The wine is shipped to wine distributors and retailers.

The following journal entry is made during March to add the costs of direct material, direct labor, and manufacturing overhead to Work-in-Process Inventory.

Work-in-Process Inventory: Cutting Department	283,500	
Raw-Material Inventory		90,000
Wages Payable		86,000
Manufacturing Overhead		107,500

[2]Based on the author's research, and D.J. Groom, "Wine Industry Important to New York State," *Syracuse Post-Standard,* January 10, 2010.

Weighted-Average Method of Process Costing

We now present the four steps used to prepare a departmental production report using weighted-average process costing.

Step 1: Analysis of Physical Flow of Units The first step is to prepare a table summarizing the physical flow of production units during March. The table is shown in Exhibit 4–5 and reflects the following inventory formula.

$$\begin{pmatrix}\text{Physical units}\\ \text{in beginning}\\ \text{work in process}\end{pmatrix} + \begin{pmatrix}\text{Physical}\\ \text{units}\\ \text{started}\end{pmatrix} - \begin{pmatrix}\text{Physical units}\\ \text{completed and}\\ \text{transferred out}\end{pmatrix} = \begin{pmatrix}\text{Physical units}\\ \text{in ending work}\\ \text{in process}\end{pmatrix}$$

Step 2: Calculation of Equivalent Units The second step in the process-costing procedure is to calculate the equivalent units of direct material and conversion activity. A table of equivalent units, displayed in Exhibit 4–6, is based on the table of physical flows prepared in step 1 (Exhibit 4–5). The 40,000 physical units that were completed and transferred out of the Cutting Department were 100 percent complete. Thus, they represent 40,000 equivalent units for both direct material and conversion. The 10,000 units in the ending work-in-process inventory are complete with respect to direct material, and they represent 10,000 equivalent units of direct material. However, they are only 50 percent complete with respect to conversion. Therefore, the ending work-in-process inventory represents 5,000 equivalent units of conversion activity (10,000 physical units × 50% complete).

Learning Objective 4-3

Prepare a table of equivalent units under weighted-average process costing.

As Exhibit 4–6 indicates, the total number of equivalent units is calculated:

$$\begin{pmatrix}\text{Equivalent units of}\\ \text{activity in units completed}\\ \text{and transferred out}\end{pmatrix} + \begin{pmatrix}\text{Equivalent units of}\\ \text{activity in ending}\\ \text{work in process}\end{pmatrix} = \begin{pmatrix}\text{Total}\\ \text{equivalent units}\\ \text{of activity}\end{pmatrix}$$

Exhibit 4–5

Step 1: Analysis of Physical Flow of Units—Cutting Department

	Physical Units
Work in process, March 1	20,000
Units started during March	30,000
Total units to account for	50,000
Units completed and transferred out during March	40,000
Work in process, March 31	10,000
Total units accounted for	50,000

Exhibit 4–6

Step 2: Calculation of Equivalent Units—Cutting Department (weighted-average method)

	Physical Units	Percentage of Completion with Respect to Conversion	Equivalent Units: Direct Material	Equivalent Units: Conversion
Work in process, March 1	20,000	10%		
Units started during March	30,000			
Total units to account for	50,000			
Units completed and transferred out during March	40,000	100%	40,000	40,000
Work in process, March 31	10,000	50%	10,000	5,000
Total units accounted for	50,000			
Total equivalent units			50,000	45,000

Note that the total equivalent units of activity, for both direct material and conversion, exceeds the activity accomplished in the current period alone. Since only 30,000 physical product units were started during March and direct material is added at the beginning of the process, only 30,000 equivalent units of direct material were actually placed into production during March. However, the total number of equivalent units of direct material used for weighted-average process costing is 50,000 (see Exhibit 4–6). The other 20,000 equivalent units of direct material were actually entered into production during the preceding month. *This is the key feature of the weighted-average method. The number of equivalent units of activity is calculated without making a distinction as to whether the activity occurred in the current accounting period or the preceding period.*

Learning Objective 4-4

Compute the cost per equivalent unit under the weighted-average method of process costing.

Step 3: Computation of Unit Costs The third step in the process-costing procedure, calculating the cost per equivalent unit for both direct material and conversion activity, is presented in Exhibit 4–7. The cost per equivalent unit for direct material is computed by dividing the total direct-material cost, including the cost of the beginning work in process *and* the cost incurred during March, by the total equivalent units (from step 2, Exhibit 4–6). An analogous procedure is used for conversion costs.

Learning Objective 4-5

Analyze the total production costs for a department under the weighted-average method of process costing.

Step 4: Analysis of Total Costs Now we can complete the process-costing procedure by determining the total cost to be transferred out of the Cutting Department's Work-in-Process Inventory account and into the Stitching Department's Work-in-Process Inventory account. Exhibit 4–8 provides the required calculations. For convenience, the computations in step 3 are repeated in Exhibit 4–8. At the bottom of Exhibit 4–8, a check is made to be sure that the total costs of $340,700 have been fully accounted for in the cost of goods completed and transferred out and the balance remaining in work-in-process inventory.

The calculations in Exhibit 4–8 are used as the basis for the following journal entry to transfer the cost of goods completed and transferred out of the Cutting Department.

Work-in-Process Inventory: Stitching Department	290,400	
Work-in-Process Inventory: Cutting Department		290,400

On March 31, the Cutting Department's Work-in-Process Inventory account appears as follows. The March 31 balance in the account agrees with that calculated in Exhibit 4–8.

Work-in-Process Inventory: Cutting Department			
March 1 balance	57,200		
March cost of direct material, direct labor, and applied manufacturing overhead	283,500	290,400	Cost of goods completed and transferred out of the Cutting Department
March 31 balance	50,300		

Exhibit 4–7

Step 3: Computation of Unit Costs—Cutting Department (weighted-average method)

	Direct Material	Conversion	Total
Work in process, March 1 (from Exhibit 4–4)	$ 50,000	$ 7,200	$ 57,200
Costs incurred during March (from Exhibit 4–4)	90,000	193,500	283,500
Total costs to account for	$140,000	$200,700	$340,700
Equivalent units (from step 2, Exhibit 4–6)	50,000	45,000	
Costs per equivalent unit	$2.80	$4.46	$7.26
	↑	↑	↑
	$\frac{\$140,000}{50,000}$	$\frac{\$200,700}{45,000}$	$2.80 + $4.46

MVP Sports Equipment Company

Exhibit 4–8
Step 4: Analysis of Total Costs—Cutting Department (weighted-average method)

MVP Sports Equipment Company

	Direct Material	Conversion	Total
Work in process, March 1 (from Exhibit 4–4)	$ 50,000	$ 7,200	$ 57,200
Costs incurred during March (from Exhibit 4–4)	90,000	193,500	283,500
Total costs to account for	$140,000	$200,700	$340,700
Equivalent units (from step 2, Exhibit 4–6)	50,000	45,000	
Costs per equivalent unit	$2.80	$4.46	$7.26
	↑ $\frac{\$140{,}000}{50{,}000}$	↑ $\frac{\$200{,}700}{45{,}000}$	↑ $2.80 + $4.46

Cost of goods completed and transferred out of the Cutting Department during March:		
(Number of units transferred out) × (Total cost per equivalent unit)	40,000 × $7.26	$290,400
Cost remaining in March 31 work-in-process inventory in the Cutting Department:		
Direct material:		
(Number of equivalent units of direct material) × (Cost per equivalent unit of direct material)	10,000 × $2.80	$ 28,000
Conversion:		
(Number of equivalent units of conversion) × (Cost per equivalent unit of conversion)	5,000 × $4.46	22,300
Total cost of March 31 work in process		$ 50,300
Check: Cost of goods completed and transferred out		$290,400
Cost of March 31 work-in-process inventory		50,300
Total costs accounted for		$340,700

Departmental Production Report We have now completed all four steps necessary to prepare the March production report for the Cutting Department. The report, which is displayed in Exhibit 4–9, simply combines the tables presented in Exhibits 4-6 and 4-8. The report provides a convenient summary of all of the process-costing calculations made under the weighted-average method.

Learning Objective **4-6**

Prepare a departmental production report under weighted-average process costing.

Why is this process-costing method called the *weighted-average* method? Because the cost per equivalent unit for March, for both direct material and conversion activity, is computed as a weighted average of the costs incurred during two different accounting periods, February and March. To demonstrate this fact, we will focus on direct material. Since direct material is placed into production at the beginning of the process, the 20,000 physical units in the March 1 work in process already have their direct material. The direct-material cost per equivalent unit in the March 1 work in process is $2.50 ($50,000 ÷ 20,000, from Exhibit 4–4). This cost was actually incurred in *February.*

In March, 30,000 physical units were entered into work in process and received their direct material. The direct-material cost incurred in March was $90,000. Thus, the direct-material cost per equivalent unit experienced in *March* was $3.00 ($90,000 ÷ 30,000).

Under the weighted-average method of process costing, the cost per equivalent unit for direct material was calculated in Exhibit 4–7 to be $2.80. *This $2.80 unit-cost figure is a weighted average* as the following calculation shows.

The point of this demonstration is that under weighted-average process costing, unit-cost figures are weighted averages of costs incurred over two or more accounting periods.

"The goal is for management to use the [cost] information daily. We want to . . . make sure that people have the information they need to make more informed decisions." (4c)

John Deere Health Care, Inc.

Weights

$$\left[\$2.50 \times \left(\frac{20{,}000}{20{,}000 + 30{,}000}\right)\right] + \left[\$3.00 \times \left(\frac{30{,}000}{20{,}000 + 30{,}000}\right)\right] = \$2.80$$

- $2.50: Direct-material cost per equivalent unit in February
- 20,000 / (20,000 + 30,000): Proportion of total equivalent units of direct material in the beginning work-in-process inventory
- $3.00: Direct-material cost per equivalent in March unit
- 30,000 / (20,000 + 30,000): Proportion of total equivalent units of direct material added during March
- $2.80: Weighted-average cost per equivalent unit of direct material

Exhibit 4–9
March Production Report: Cutting Department (weighted-average method)

MVP SPORTS EQUIPMENT COMPANY
March Production Report: Cutting Department

	Physical Units	Percentage of Completion with Respect to Conversion	Equivalent Units: Direct Material	Equivalent Units: Conversion
Work in process, March 1	20,000	10%		
Units started during March	30,000			
Total units to account for	50,000			
Units completed and transferred out during March	40,000	100%	40,000	40,000
Work in process, March 31	10,000	50%	10,000	5,000
Total units accounted for	50,000			
Total equivalent units			50,000	45,000

	Direct Material	Conversion	Total
Work in process, March 1 (from Exhibit 4–4)	$ 50,000	$ 7,200	$ 57,200
Costs incurred during March (from Exhibit 4–4)	90,000	193,500	283,500
Total costs to account for	$140,000	$200,700	$340,700
Equivalent units (from step 2, Exhibit 4–6)	50,000	45,000	
Costs per equivalent unit	$2.80	$4.46	$7.26
	$\frac{\$140{,}000}{50{,}000}$	$\frac{\$200{,}700}{45{,}000}$	$2.80 + $4.46

Cost of goods completed and transferred out of the Cutting Department during March:		
(Number of units transferred out) × (Total cost per equivalent unit)	40,000 × $7.26	$290,400
Cost remaining in March 31 work-in-process inventory in the Cutting Department:		
Direct material:		
(Number of equivalent units of direct material) × (Cost per equivalent unit of direct material)	10,000 × $2.80	$ 28,000
Conversion:		
(Number of equivalent units of conversion) × (Cost per equivalent unit of conversion)	5,000 × $4.46	22,300
Total cost of March 31 work in process		$ 50,300
Check: Cost of goods completed and transferred out		$290,400
Cost of March 31 work-in-process inventory		50,300
Total costs accounted for		$340,700

Other Issues in Process Costing

Several other issues related to process costing are worth discussion.

Actual versus Normal Costing

Our illustration of process costing assumed that *normal costing* was used. As explained in Chapter 3, in a normal-costing system, direct material and direct labor are applied to Work-in-Process Inventory at their *actual* amounts, but manufacturing overhead is applied to Work-in-Process Inventory using a predetermined overhead rate. In contrast, under an *actual-costing* system, the actual costs of direct material, direct labor, *and manufacturing overhead* are entered into Work-in-Process Inventory.

Either actual or normal costing may be used in conjunction with a process-costing system. Our illustration used normal costing since a predetermined overhead rate was used to compute applied manufacturing overhead in Exhibit 4–4. This resulted in applied overhead for March of $107,500 (125% × $86,000). If actual costing had been used, the manufacturing overhead cost for March would have been the actual overhead cost incurred instead of the applied overhead amount given in Exhibit 4–4. In all other ways, the process-costing procedures used under actual and normal costing are identical.

When normal costing is used, there may be overapplied or underapplied overhead at the end of the period. This amount is either closed into Cost of Goods Sold or prorated, as explained in Chapter 3.

Other Cost Drivers for Overhead Application

Our illustration used a predetermined overhead rate based on direct-labor cost. Since the application of manufacturing overhead was based on direct-labor cost, direct labor and manufacturing overhead were combined into the single cost element *conversion costs*. This procedure is quite common in practice. If some cost driver (or activity base) other than direct labor had been used to apply manufacturing overhead, then overhead costs would be accounted for separately from direct-labor costs in the process-costing calculations.

Suppose, for example, that manufacturing overhead is applied on the basis of machine hours. A group of 100 physical units is 100 percent complete as to direct material, 60 percent complete as to direct labor, and 40 percent complete as to machine time. This situation could arise in a production process that is labor-intensive in its early stages but more automated in its later stages. In this case, the 100 physical units represent the following quantities of equivalent units:

	Equivalent Units		
Physical Units	Direct Material	Direct Labor	Manufacturing Overhead
100	100	60	40
	↑	↑	↑
	100 × 100%	100 × 60%	100 × 40%

Throughout the entire process-costing procedure, there will now be three cost elements (direct material, direct labor, and manufacturing overhead) instead of only two (direct material and conversion). In all other respects, the process-costing calculations will be identical to those illustrated earlier in the chapter.

Subsequent Production Departments

In our illustration, production requires two sequential production operations: cutting and stitching. Although the process-costing procedures for the second department are similar to those illustrated for the first, there is one additional consideration. The cost of goods completed and transferred out of the Cutting Department must remain assigned to the partially completed product units as they undergo further processing in the Stitching Department. Process-costing procedures for subsequent production departments are covered in cost accounting texts.[3]

Hybrid Product-Costing Systems

Job-order and process costing represent the polar extremes of product-costing systems. However, some production processes exhibit characteristics of both job-order and process-costing environments. Examples of such production processes include some clothing and food-processing operations. In these production processes, the conversion activities may be very similar or identical across all of the firm's product lines, even though the direct materials may differ significantly. Different clothing lines require significantly different direct materials, such as cotton, silk, or wool. However, the conversion of these materials, involving direct labor and manufacturing overhead, may not differ much across product types. In the food industry, production of economy-grade or premium applesauce differs with regard to the quality and cost of the direct-material input, apples. However, the cooking, straining, and canning operations for these two product lines are nearly identical.

Operation Costing for Batch Manufacturing Processes

Learning Objective 4-7

Describe how an operation costing system accumulates and assigns the costs of direct-material and conversion activity in a batch manufacturing process.

The production processes described above often are referred to as **batch manufacturing** processes. Such processes are characterized by high-volume production of several product lines that differ in some important ways but are nearly identical in others. Since batch manufacturing operations have characteristics of both job-order costing and process-costing environments, a **hybrid product-costing system** is required. One common approach is called **operation costing.** This product-costing system is used when conversion activities are very similar across product lines, but the direct materials differ significantly. *Conversion costs* are accumulated by *department,* and process-costing methods are used to assign these costs to products. In contrast, *direct-material costs* are accumulated by *job order or batch,* and job-order costing is used to assign material costs to products.

The main features of operation costing are illustrated in Exhibit 4–10. Notice in the exhibit that products pass sequentially through production departments A and B. Direct-material costs are traced directly to each batch of goods, but conversion costs are applied on a departmental basis. Direct labor and manufacturing overhead are combined in a single cost category called conversion costs, rather than separately identifying direct labor. Moreover, under operation costing, conversion costs are applied to products using a *predetermined application rate.* This predetermined rate is based on *budgeted conversion costs,* as follows:[4]

$$\text{Predetermined application rate for conversion costs} = \frac{\text{Budgeted conversion costs (direct labor and manufacturing overhead)}}{\text{Budgeted cost driver (or activity base)}}$$

As an illustration of operation costing, we will focus on the Minnesota Division of MVP Sports Equipment Company. This division manufactures two different grades of basketballs: professional balls, which have genuine leather exteriors, and scholastic balls, which use imitation leather. The cutting and stitching operations for the two different products are identical. Scholastic balls are sold without special packaging, but professional balls are packaged in an attractive cardboard box.

[3]Sequential production operations are also covered in a supplement to this textbook titled *Process Costing in Sequential Production Departments.* This supplement is available to students and instructors in the Connect Library.

[4]The budgeted amount for the cost driver is based on the company's practical capacity for production.

Exhibit 4–10
Operation Costing

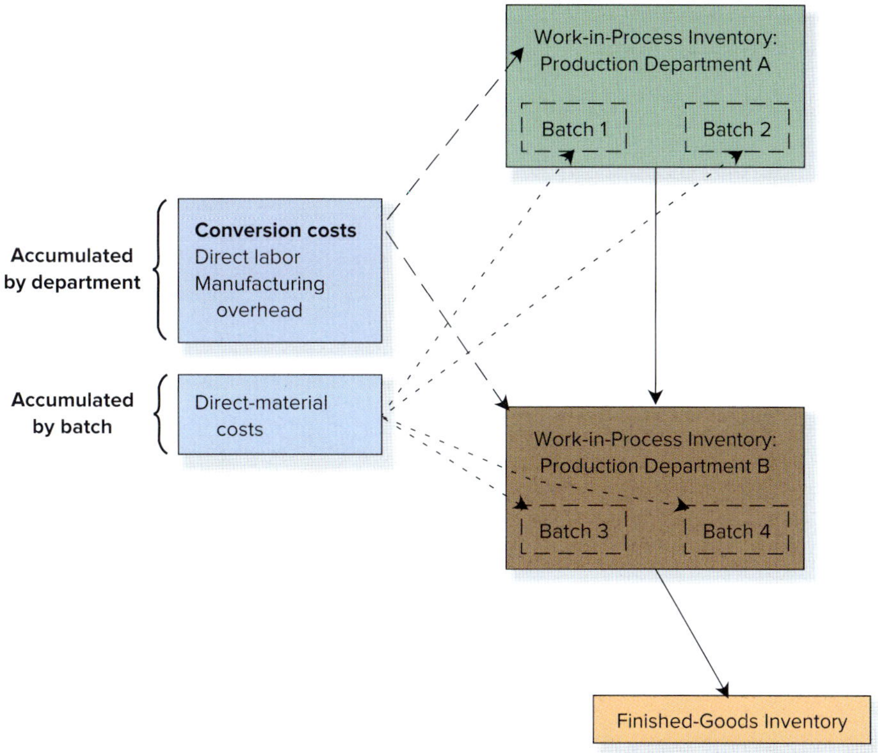

During October two batches were entered into production and finished. There was no beginning or ending inventory of work in process for October. Cost and production data are given in Exhibit 4–11. Notice in Exhibit 4–11 that the direct-material costs are identified by *batch.* The conversion costs, however, are associated with the two production departments and the Packaging Department.

The product cost for each of the basketballs is computed as follows:

	Professional	Scholastic
Direct material:		
Batch P19 ($20,000 ÷ 1,000)	$20.00	
Batch S28 ($30,000 ÷ 3,000)		$10.00
Conversion: Preparation Department		
(conversion costs of $30,000 ÷ 4,000 units produced)*	7.50	7.50
Conversion: Finishing Department		
(conversion costs of $24,000 ÷ 4,000 units produced)*	6.00	6.00
Conversion: Packaging Department		
(conversion costs of $500 ÷ 1,000 units packaged)*	.50	–0–
Total product cost	$34.00	$23.50

*The two production departments each worked on a total of 4,000 balls, but the Packaging Department handled only the 1,000 professional balls.

Notice in the preceding display that each ball receives the same conversion costs in the Preparation Department and the Finishing Department, since these operations are identical for the two products. Direct-material costs and packaging costs, though, differ for the products. The total costs of $104,500 (Exhibit 4–11) are accounted for in the product costs, as shown below.

Professional balls: 1,000 × $34.00	$ 34,000
Scholastic balls: 3,000 × $23.50	70,500
Total	$104,500

Exhibit 4–11
Basic Data for Illustration of Operation Costing

MVP Sports Equipment Company

Operation Costing Data

Direct-material costs:			
Batch P19 (1,000 professional balls)	$20,000	(includes $1,000 for packaging material)	
Batch S28 (3,000 scholastic balls)	30,000		
Total direct-material costs	$50,000		
Conversion costs (budgeted):			
Preparation Department			$ 30,000
Finishing Department			24,000
Packaging Department			500
Total			$ 54,500
Total costs:			
Direct material			50,000
Conversion: Preparation	$30,000		
Finishing	24,000		
Packaging	500		
Total conversion costs			54,500
Total			$104,500

Predetermined application rates for conversion costs:*

Preparation Department:

$$\frac{\text{Budgeted conversion costs}}{\text{Budgeted production}} = \frac{\$30{,}000}{4{,}000 \text{ units}} = \$7.50 \text{ per unit}$$

Finishing Department:

$$\frac{\text{Budgeted conversion costs}}{\text{Budgeted production}} = \frac{\$24{,}000}{4{,}000 \text{ units}} = \$6.00 \text{ per unit}$$

Packaging Department:

$$\frac{\text{Budgeted conversion costs}}{\text{Budgeted units packaged}} = \frac{\$500}{1{,}000 \text{ units}} = \$.50 \text{ per unit}$$

*The cost driver (or activity base) is the number of units processed.

The following journal entries are made to record the Minnesota Division's flow of costs. The first entry is made to record the requisition of raw material by the Preparation Department, when batch P19 is entered into production. (This amount excludes the $1,000 in packaging costs to be incurred subsequently for batch P19.)

Work-in-Process Inventory: Preparation Department	19,000	
Raw-Material Inventory		19,000

The following entry is made to record the requisition of raw material by the Preparation Department, when batch S28 is entered into production.

Work-in-Process Inventory: Preparation Department	30,000	
Raw-Material Inventory		30,000

Conversion costs are applied in the Preparation Department with the following journal entry.

Work-in-Process Inventory: Preparation Department	30,000	
Applied Conversion Costs		30,000

The following entry records the transfer of the partially completed professional and scholastic basketballs to the Finishing Department.

Work-in-Process Inventory: Finishing Department	79,000	
Work-in-Process Inventory: Preparation Department		79,000

The conversion costs applied in the Finishing Department are recorded as follows:

Work-in-Process Inventory: Finishing Department	24,000	
Applied Conversion Costs		24,000

Next, the professional balls are transferred to the Packaging Department, and the scholastic balls are transferred to finished goods.

Work-in-Process Inventory: Packaging Department	32,500	
Finished-Goods Inventory	70,500	
Work-in-Process Inventory: Finishing Department		103,000

Raw-material (packaging) costs and conversion costs are recorded in the Packaging Department as follows:

Work-in-Process Inventory: Packaging Department	1,500	
Raw-Material Inventory		1,000
Applied Conversion Costs		500

Finally, the professional basketballs are transferred to finished goods.

Finished-Goods Inventory	34,000	
Work-in-Process Inventory: Packaging Department		34,000

Suppose that at the end of an accounting period, applied conversion costs differ from the actual conversion costs incurred. Then the difference, called overapplied or underapplied conversion costs, would be closed into Cost of Goods Sold. This accounting treatment is similar to that described in Chapter 3 for overapplied or underapplied overhead.

Chapter Summary

LO4-1 List and explain the similarities and important differences between job-order and process costing. Process costing is used in production processes where relatively large numbers of nearly identical products are manufactured. The purpose of a process-costing system is the same as that of a job-order costing system—to accumulate costs and assign these costs to units of product. Job-order costing is used by firms that produce relatively small numbers of dissimilar products.

LO4-2 Prepare journal entries to record the flow of costs in a process-costing system with sequential production departments. Costs of direct material, direct labor, and manufacturing overhead are added to a Work-in-Process Inventory account. Direct labor and manufacturing overhead often are combined into a single cost category termed *conversion costs.* When products are completed, the costs assigned to them are transferred either to Finished-Goods Inventory or to the next production department's Work-in-Process Inventory account. Finally, when goods are sold, their costs are transferred to the expense account called Cost of Goods Sold.

LO4-3 Prepare a table of equivalent units under weighted-average process costing. The table of equivalent units, illustrated in the chapter, computes the equivalent units of activity for the period for both direct material and conversion costs.

LO4-4 Compute the cost per equivalent unit under the weighted-average method of process costing. The cost per equivalent unit, for both direct material and conversion, is calculated as shown in the chapter. For each factor input, direct material and conversion, the cost of that input is divided by the number of equivalent units for that input.

LO4-5 Analyze the total production costs for a department under the weighted-average method of process costing. The total production costs incurred during the period, for both direct material and conversion, are assigned to either ending work-in-process inventory or to the cost of goods completed and transferred out.

LO4-6 Prepare a departmental production report under weighted-average process costing. As illustrated in the chapter, there are four steps in preparing a departmental production report: (1) analyze the physical flow of units, (2) calculate the equivalent units, (3) compute the cost per equivalent unit, and (4) analyze the total costs of the department. In the weighted-average method of process costing, the cost per equivalent unit, for each cost category, is a weighted average of (1) the costs assigned to the beginning work-in-process inventory and (2) the costs incurred during the current period.

LO4-7 Describe how an operation costing system accumulates and assigns the costs of direct-material and conversion activity in a batch manufacturing process. Operation costing is a hybrid of job-order and process costing. It is designed for production processes in which the direct material differs significantly among product lines, but the conversion activities are essentially the same. Direct-material costs are accumulated by batches of products using job-order costing methods. Conversion costs are accumulated by production departments and are assigned to product units using process-costing methods.

Review Problem on Process Costing

The following data have been compiled for MVP's Cutting Department for the month of June. Conversion activity occurs uniformly throughout the production process.

Work in process, June 1—25,000 units:	
Direct material: 100% complete, cost of	$ 73,750
Conversion: 40% complete, cost of	46,000
Balance in work in process, June 1	$119,750
Units started during June	40,000
Units completed during June and transferred out	60,000
Work in process, June 30:	
Direct material: 100% complete	
Conversion: 60% complete	
Costs incurred during June:	
Direct material	$121,250
Conversion costs: direct labor and applied manufacturing overhead	237,500

Required: Prepare the Cutting Department's June production report using weighted-average process costing. (*Hint:* Follow the format of Exhibit 4–9.)

Solution to Review Problem

The Cutting Department's June production report is displayed in Exhibit 4–12.

Exhibit 4–12
June Production Report: Cutting Department (weighted-average method)

MVP SPORTS EQUIPMENT COMPANY
June Production Report: Cutting Department

	Physical Units	Percentage of Completion with Respect to Conversion	Equivalent Units: Direct Material	Equivalent Units: Conversion
Work in process, June 1	25,000	40%		
Units started during June	40,000			
Total units to account for	65,000			
Units completed and transferred out during June	60,000	100%	60,000	60,000
Work in process, June 30	5,000	60%	5,000	3,000
Total units accounted for	65,000			
Total equivalent units			65,000	63,000

	Direct Material	Conversion	Total
Work in process, June 1	$ 73,750	$ 46,000	$119,750
Costs incurred during June	121,250	237,500	358,750
Total costs to account for	$195,000	$283,500	$478,500
Equivalent units	65,000	63,000	
Costs per equivalent unit	$3.00	$4.50	$7.50
	↑ $\frac{\$195,000}{65,000}$	↑ $\frac{\$283,500}{63,000}$	↑ $3.00 + $4.50

(continued)

Cost of goods completed and transferred out of the Cutting Department during June:		
(Number of units transferred out) × (Total cost per equivalent unit)	60,000 × $7.50	$450,000
Cost remaining in June 30 work-in-process inventory in the Cutting Department:		
Direct material:		
(Number of equivalent units of direct material) × (Cost per equivalent unit of direct material)	5,000 × $3.00	$ 15,000
Conversion:		
(Number of equivalent units of conversion) × (Cost per equivalent unit of conversion)	3,000 × $4.50	13,500
Total cost of June 30 work in process		$ 28,500
Check: Cost of goods completed and transferred out		$450,000
Cost of June 30 work-in-process inventory		28,500
Total costs accounted for		$478,500

Key Terms

For each term's definition refer to the indicated page, or turn to the glossary at the end of the text.

batch manufacturing, 150
departmental production report, 142
equivalent unit, 141
hybrid product-costing system, 150
operation costing, 150
process-costing system, 138
transferred-in costs, 139
weighted-average method, 142

Review Questions

4-1. Explain the primary differences between job-order and process costing.

4-2. List five types of manufacturing in which process costing would be an appropriate product-costing system. What is the key characteristic of these products that makes process costing a good choice?

4-3. List three nonmanufacturing businesses in which process costing could be used. For example, a public accounting firm could use process costing to accumulate the costs of processing clients' tax returns.

4-4. What are the purposes of a product-costing system?

4-5. Define the term *equivalent unit* and explain how the concept is used in process costing.

4-6. List and briefly describe the purpose of each of the four process-costing steps.

4-7. Show how to prepare a journal entry to enter direct-material costs into the Work-in-Process Inventory account for the first department in a sequential production process. Show how to prepare the journal entry recording the transfer of goods from the first to the second department in the sequence.

4-8. What are *transferred-in costs?*

4-9. A food processing company has two sequential production departments: mixing and cooking. The cost of the January 1 work in process in the cooking department is detailed as follows:

Direct material	$ 79,000
Conversion	30,000
Transferred-in costs	182,000

During what time period and in what department were the $182,000 of costs listed above incurred? Explain your answer.

4-10. Explain the reasoning underlying the name of the weighted-average method.

4-11. How does process costing differ under normal or actual costing?

4-12. How would the process-costing computations differ from those illustrated in the chapter if overhead were applied on some activity base other than direct labor?

4-13. Explain the concept of *operation costing.* How does it differ from process or job-order costing? Why is operation costing well suited for batch manufacturing processes?

4-14. What is the purpose of a departmental production report prepared using process costing?

Exercises

All applicable Exercises are available in Connect. connect

Exercise 4-15
Physical Flow of Units
(LO 4-1, 4-3)

In each case below, fill in the missing amount.

1.	Work in Process, September 1	9,000 tons
	Units started during September	?
	Units completed during September	19,000 tons
	Work in process, September 30	2,000 tons

2.	Work in process, February 1	13,000 kilograms
	Units started during February	1,500 kilograms
	Units completed during February	9,200 kilograms
	Work in process, February 28	?
3.	Work in process, January 1	100,000 gallons
	Units started during the year	850,000 gallons
	Units completed during the year	?
	Work in process, December 31	200,000 gallons

Exercise 4–16
Process Costing; Use of Internet
(LO 4-1)

Use the Internet to access the website for Weyerhaeuser (www.weyerhaeuser.com), International Paper (www.internationalpaper.com), or Boise Cascade (www.boisecascade.com).

Required: Skim over the information presented on the website about the company's products and operations. Then discuss why process costing is an appropriate product-costing method for this company.

Exercise 4–17
Equivalent Units; Weighted-Average
(LO 4-1, 4-3)

Rainbow Glass Company manufactures decorative glass products. The firm employs a process-costing system for its manufacturing operations. All direct materials are added at the beginning of the process, and conversion costs are incurred uniformly throughout the process. The company's production schedule for October follows.

	Units
Work in process on October 1 (60% complete as to conversion)	1,000
Units started during October	5,000
Total units to account for	6,000
Units from beginning work in process, which were completed and transferred out during October	1,000
Units started and completed during October	3,000
Work in process on October 31 (20% complete as to conversion)	2,000
Total units accounted for	6,000

Required: Calculate each of the following amounts using weighted-average process costing.

1. Equivalent units of direct material during October.
2. Equivalent units of conversion activity during October.

(CMA, adapted)

Exercise 4–18
Equivalent Units; Weighted-Average
(LO 4-1, 4-3)

Terra Energy Company refines a variety of petrochemical products. The following data are from the firm's Lodi plant.

Work in process, November 1	2,000,000 gallons
Direct material	100% complete
Conversion	25% complete
Units started in process during November	950,000 gallons
Work in process, November 30	240,000 gallons
Direct material	100% complete
Conversion	80% complete

Required: Compute the equivalent units of direct material and conversion for the month of November. Use the weighted-average method of process costing.

Exercise 4–19
Physical Flow and Equivalent Units; Weighted-Average
(LO 4-1, 4-3)

The Evanston plant of Fit-for-Life Foods Corporation produces low-fat salad dressing. The following data pertain to the year just ended.

		Percentage of Completion	
	Units	**Direct Material**	**Conversion**
Work in process, January 1	20,000 lb.	80%	60%
Work in process, December 31	15,000 lb.	70%	30%

During the year, the company started 120,000 pounds of material in production.

Required: Prepare a schedule analyzing the physical flow of units and computing the equivalent units of both direct material and conversion for the year. Use weighted-average process costing.

Exercise 4–20
Cost per Equivalent Unit; Weighted-Average
(LO 4-1, 4-3, 4-4)

Idaho Lumber Company grows, harvests, and processes timber for use in construction. The following data pertain to the firm's sawmill during November.

Work in process, November 1:	
Direct material	$ 65,000
Conversion	180,000
Costs incurred during November:	
Direct material	$425,000
Conversion	690,000

The equivalent units of activity for November were as follows: 7,000 equivalent units of direct material and 1,740 equivalent units of conversion activity.

Required: Calculate the cost per equivalent unit, for both direct material and conversion, during November. Use weighted-average process costing.

Exercise 4–21
Cost per Equivalent Unit; Weighted-Average
(LO 4-1, 4-3, 4-4)

Otsego Glass Company manufactures window glass for automobiles. The following data pertain to the Plate Glass Department.

Work in process, June 1:	
Direct material	$ 37,000
Conversion	36,750
Costs incurred during June:	
Direct material	$150,000
Conversion	230,000

The equivalent units of activity for June were as follows: 17,000 equivalent units of direct material and 48,500 equivalent units of conversion activity.

Required: Calculate the cost per equivalent unit, for both direct material and conversion, during June. Use weighted-average process costing.

Exercise 4–22
Analysis of Total Costs; Weighted-Average
(LO 4-5)

Savannah Textiles Company manufactures a variety of natural fabrics for the clothing industry. The following data pertain to the Weaving Department for the month of September.

Equivalent units of direct material (weighted-average method)	60,000
Equivalent units of conversion (weighted-average method)	52,000
Units completed and transferred out during September	50,000

The cost data for September are as follows:

Work in process, September 1	
Direct material	$ 94,000
Conversion	44,400
Costs incurred during September	
Direct material	$164,000
Conversion	272,800

There were 20,000 units in process in the Weaving Department on September 1 (100% complete as to direct material and 40% complete as to conversion).

Required: Compute each of the following amounts using weighted-average process costing.

1. Cost of goods completed and transferred out of the Weaving Department.
2. Cost of the September 30 work-in-process inventory in the Weaving Department.
3. *Build a spreadsheet:* Construct an Excel spreadsheet to solve all of the preceding requirements. Show how the solution will change if the following data change: the costs incurred in September were $328,000 for direct material and $818,400 for conversion.

Exercise 4–23
Analysis of Total Costs; Weighted-Average
(LO 4-5)

The following data pertain to Tulsa Paperboard Company, a manufacturer of cardboard boxes.

Work in process, February 1		10,000 units*
Direct material	$ 5,500	
Conversion	17,000	
Costs incurred during February		
Direct material	$110,000	
Conversion	171,600	

*Complete as to direct material; 40% complete as to conversion.

The equivalent units of activity for February were as follows:

Direct material (weighted-average method)	110,000
Conversion (weighted-average method)	92,000
Completed and transferred out	90,000

Required: Compute the following amounts using weighted-average process costing.

1. Cost of goods completed and transferred out during February.
2. Cost of the February 28 work-in-process inventory.

Exercise 4–24
Operation Costing
(LO 4-7)

The November production of MVP's Minnesota Division consisted of batch P25 (2,000 professional basketballs) and batch S33 (4,000 scholastic basketballs). Each batch was started and finished during November, and there was no beginning or ending work in process. Costs incurred were as follows:

Direct Material:

Batch P25, $42,000, including $2,500 for packaging material; batch S33, $45,000.

Conversion Costs:

Preparation Department, predetermined rate of $7.50 per unit; Finishing Department, predetermined rate of $6.00 per unit; Packaging Department, predetermined rate of $.50 per unit. (Only the professional balls are packaged.)

Required:

1. Draw a diagram depicting the division's batch manufacturing process. Refer to Exhibit 4–10 for guidance.
2. Compute the November product cost for each type of basketball.
3. Prepare journal entries to record the cost flows during November.

Problems

All applicable Problems are available in Connect.

connect

■ **Problem 4–25**
Step-by-Step Weighted-Average Process Costing
(LO 4-3, 4-4, 4-5)

3. Cost per equivalent unit, total: $4.77

Timing Technology, Inc. manufactures timing devices. During 20x1, 900,000 units were completed and transferred to finished-goods inventory. On December 31, 20x1 there were 300,000 units in work in process. These units were 50 percent complete as to conversion and 100 percent complete as to direct material. Finished-goods inventory consisted of 200,000 units. Materials are added to production at the beginning of the manufacturing process, and overhead is applied to each product at the rate of 60 percent of direct-labor costs. There was no finished-goods inventory on January 1, 20x1. A review of the inventory cost records disclosed the following information:

		Costs	
	Units	**Materials**	**Labor**
Work in process, January 1, 20x1 (80% complete as to conversion)	200,000	$ 200,000	$ 315,000
Units started in production	1,000,000		
Direct-material costs		$1,300,000	
Direct-labor costs			$1,995,000

Required: Prepare schedules as of December 31, 20x1, to compute the following:

1. Physical flow of units.
2. Equivalent units of production using the weighted-average method.
3. Costs per equivalent unit for material and conversion.
3. Cost of the December 31, 20x1, finished-goods inventory and work-in-process inventory.

(CMA, adapted)

■ **Problem 4–26**
Straightforward Weighted-Average Process Costing, Step-by-Step Approach
(LO 4-3, 4-4, 4-5)

2. Total equivalent units, conversion: 226,000

Piscataway Plastics Company manufactures a highly specialized plastic that is used extensively in the automobile industry. The following data have been compiled for the month of June. Conversion activity occurs uniformly throughout the production process.

Work in process, June 1—50,000 units:	
Direct material: 100% complete, cost of	$120,000
Conversion: 40% complete, cost of	34,400
Balance in work in process, June 1	$154,400
Units started during June	200,000
Units completed during June and transferred out to finished-goods inventory	190,000
Work in process, June 30:	
Direct material: 100% complete	
Conversion: 60% complete	
Costs incurred during June:	
Direct material	$492,500
Conversion costs:	
Direct labor	$ 87,450
Applied manufacturing overhead	262,350
Total conversion costs	$349,800

Required: Prepare schedules to accomplish each of the following process-costing steps for the month of June. Use the weighted-average method of process costing.

1. Analysis of physical flow of units.
2. Calculation of equivalent units.
3. Computation of unit costs.
4. Analysis of total costs.

■ **Problem 4–27**
Missing Data; Production Report; Weighted-Average
(LO 4-4, 4-5, 4-6)

Cost remaining in ending work-in-process inventory, direct material: $123,750

Total cost of July 31 work in process: $202,950

The following data pertain to the Vesuvius Tile Company for July.

Work in process, July 1 (in units)	20,000
Units started during July	?
Total units to account for	65,000
Units completed and transferred out during July	?
Work in process, July 31 (in units)	15,000
Total equivalent units: direct material	65,000
Total equivalent units: conversion	?
Work in process, July 1: direct material	$164,400
Work in process, July 1: conversion	?
Costs incurred during July: direct material	?
Costs incurred during July: conversion	659,400
Work in process, July 1: total cost	244,200
Total costs incurred during July	1,031,250
Total costs to account for	1,275,450
Cost per equivalent unit: direct material	8.25
Cost per equivalent unit: conversion	?
Total cost per equivalent unit	21.45
Cost of goods completed and transferred out during July	?
Cost remaining in ending work-in-process inventory: direct material	?
Cost remaining in ending work-in-process inventory: conversion	79,200
Total cost of July 31 work in process	202,950

Additional Information:

a. Direct material is added at the beginning of the production process, and conversion activity occurs uniformly throughout the process.

b. The company uses weighted-average process costing.

c. The July 1 work in process was 30 percent complete as to conversion.

d. The July 31 work in process was 40 percent complete as to conversion.

Required: Compute the missing amounts, and prepare the firm's July production report.

■ **Problem 4–28**
Partial Production Report; Journal Entries; Weighted-Average Method
(LO 4-2, 4-3, 4-4, 4-5)

1(b). Cost per equivalent unit, direct material: $5.60

Triangle Fastener Corporation accumulates costs for its single product using process costing. Direct material is added at the beginning of the production process, and conversion activity occurs uniformly throughout the process. A partially completed production report for the month of May follows.

Production Report
For the Month of May

	Physical Units	Percentage of Completion with Respect to Conversion	Equivalent Units: Direct Material	Equivalent Units: Conversion
Work in process, May 1	25,000	40%		
Units started during May	30,000			
Total units to account for	55,000			
Units completed and transferred out during May	35,000		35,000	35,000
Work in process, May 31	20,000	80%	20,000	16,000
Total units accounted for	55,000			

	Direct Material	Conversion	Total
Work in process, May 1	$143,000	$ 474,700	$ 617,700
Costs incurred during May	165,000	2,009,000	2,174,000
Total costs to account for	$308,000	$2,483,700	$2,791,700

Required:

1. Complete each of the following process-costing steps using the weighted-average method:
   a. Calculation of equivalent units.
   b. Computation of unit costs.
   c. Analysis of total costs.
2. Prepare a journal entry to record the transfer of the cost of goods completed and transferred out during May.

Problem 4–29
Straightforward Weighted-Average Process Costing; Step-by-Step Approach
(LO 4-3, 4-4, 4-5)

2. Equivalent units, direct material: 110,000

Moravia Company processes and packages cream cheese. The following data have been compiled for the month of April. Conversion activity occurs uniformly throughout the production process.

Work in process, April 1—10,000 units:	
Direct material: 100% complete, cost of	$ 22,000
Conversion: 20% complete, cost of	4,500
Balance in work in process, April 1	$ 26,500
Units started during April	100,000
Units completed during April and transferred out to finished-goods inventory	80,000
Work in process, April 30:	
Direct material: 100% complete	
Conversion: 33⅓% complete	
Costs incurred during April:	
Direct material	$198,000
Conversion costs:	
Direct labor	$ 52,800
Applied manufacturing overhead	105,600
Total conversion costs	$158,400

Required: Prepare schedules to accomplish each of the following process-costing steps for the month of April. Use the weighted-average method of process costing.

1. Analysis of physical flow of units.
2. Calculation of equivalent units.
3. Computation of unit costs.
4. Analysis of total costs.
5. ***Build a spreadsheet:*** Construct an Excel spreadsheet to solve all of the preceding requirements. Show how the solution will change if the following data change: the April 1 work-in-process costs were $66,000 for direct material and $18,000 for conversion.

Problem 4–30
Partial Production Report; Journal Entries; Weighted-Average Method
(LO 4-2, 4-3, 4-4, 4-5)

2. Cost per equivalent unit, total: $11.43

5. Work-in-Process Inventory (credit): $1,143,000

Albany Company accumulates costs for its product using process costing. Direct material is added at the beginning of the production process, and conversion activity occurs uniformly throughout the process.

Production Report
For August 20x1

	Physical Units	Percentage of Completion with Respect to Conversion	Equivalent Units: Direct Material	Equivalent Units: Conversion
Work in process, August 1	40,000	80%		
Units started during August	80,000			
Total units to account for	120,000			
Units completed and transferred out during August	100,000		100,000	100,000
Work in process, August 31	20,000	30%	20,000	6,000
Total units accounted for	120,000			

(continued)

	Direct Material	Conversion	Total
Work in process, August 1	$ 42,000	$ 305,280	$ 347,280
Costs incurred during August	96,000	784,400	880,400
Total costs to account for	$138,000	$1,089,680	$1,227,680

Required: Use weighted-average process costing in completing the following requirements.

1. Prepare a schedule of equivalent units.
2. Compute the costs per equivalent unit.
3. Compute the cost of goods completed and transferred out during August.
4. Compute the cost remaining in the work-in-process inventory on August 31.
5. Prepare a journal entry to record the transfer of the cost of goods completed and transferred out during August.

Problem 4–31
Determination of Production Costs; Analysis of Equivalent Units
(LO 4-3, 4-4, 4-5)

1. Overhead applied: $379,500
3. Cost of ending work-in-process inventory: $324,000

Goodson Corporation assembles various components used in the telecommunications industry. The company's major product, a relay switch, is the result of assembling three parts: XY634, AA788, and GU321. The following information relates to activities of April:

- Beginning work-in-process inventory: 4,000 units, 75 percent complete as to conversion; cost, $286,000 (direct materials, $220,000; conversion cost, $66,000).
- Production started: 25,000 units.
- Production completed: 24,000 units.
- Ending work-in-process inventory: 5,000 units, 40 percent complete as to conversion.
- Direct materials used: XY634, $267,000; AA788, $689,000; GU321, $448,000.
- Hourly wage of direct laborers, $20; total direct-labor payroll, $126,500.
- Overhead application rate: $60 per direct-labor hour.

All parts are introduced at the beginning of Goodson's manufacturing process; conversion cost is incurred uniformly throughout production.

Required:

1. Calculate the total cost of direct material and conversion during April.
2. Determine the cost of goods completed during the month.
3. Determine the cost of the work-in-process inventory on April 30.
4. With regard to the ending work-in-process inventory:
   a. How much direct-material cost would be added to these units in May?
   b. What percentage of conversion would be performed on these units in May?
5. Assume that the relay switch required the addition of another part (HH887) at the 70 percent stage of completion. How many equivalent units with respect to part HH887 would be represented in April's ending work-in-process inventory?

Problem 4–32
Analysis of Work-in-Process Inventory Account
(LO 4-3, 4-4, 4-5)

3. Cost of June 30 work-in-process inventory: $34,600

A-1 Products manufactures wooden furniture using an assembly-line process. All direct materials are introduced at the start of the process, and conversion cost is incurred evenly throughout manufacturing. An examination of the company's Work-in-Process Inventory account for June revealed the following selected information.

Debit side:
June 1 balance: 300 units, 30% complete as to conversion, cost $21,300*
Production started: 900 units
Direct material used during June: $45,000
June conversion cost: $25,700
Credit side:
Production completed: 700 units

*Supplementary records revealed direct-material cost of $15,000 and conversion cost of $6,300.

Conversations with manufacturing personnel revealed that the ending work in process was 60 percent complete as to conversion.

Required:

1. Determine the number of units in the June 30 work-in-process inventory.
2. Calculate the cost of goods completed during June and prepare the appropriate journal entry to record completed production.
3. Determine the cost of the June 30 work-in-process inventory.
4. Briefly explain the meaning of equivalent units. Why are equivalent units needed to properly allocate costs between completed production and production in process?

Problem 4–33
Missing Data; Production Report; Weighted-Average
(LO 4-4, 4-5, 4-6)

Total equivalent units, conversion: 71,000

Total cost of May 31 work-in-process: $167,500

The following data pertain to the Hercules Tire and Rubber Company for the month of May.

Work in process, May 1 (in units)	?
Units started during May	60,000
Total units to account for	75,000
Units completed and transferred out during May	?
Work in process, May 31 (in units)	10,000
Total equivalent units: direct material	75,000
Total equivalent units: conversion	?
Work in process, May 1: direct material	$135,000
Work in process, May 1: conversion	?
Costs incurred during May: direct material	?
Costs incurred during May: conversion	832,250
Work in process, May 1: total cost	172,500
Total costs incurred during May	1,402,250
Total costs to account for	1,574,750
Cost per equivalent unit: direct material	9.40
Cost per equivalent unit: conversion	?
Total cost per equivalent unit	21.65
Cost of goods completed and transferred out during May	?
Cost remaining in ending work-in-process inventory: direct material	?
Cost remaining in ending work-in-process inventory: conversion	73,500
Total cost of May 31 work-in-process	167,500

Additional Information:

a. Direct material is added at the beginning of the production process, and conversion activity occurs uniformly throughout the process.
b. Hercules uses weighted-average process costing.
c. The May 1 work in process was 20 percent complete as to conversion.
d. The May 31 work in process was 60 percent complete as to conversion.

Required: Compute the missing amounts, and prepare the firm's May production report.

Problem 4–34
Process Costing in a Public Accounting Firm
(LO 4-3, 4-4, 4-5)

2. Total cost of returns in process, February 28: £14,250

Scrooge and Zilch, a public accounting firm in London, is engaged in the preparation of income tax returns for individuals. The firm uses the weighted-average method of process costing for internal reporting. The following information pertains to February. (£ denotes the British monetary unit, pounds sterling.)*

Returns in process, February 1:	
(25% complete)	200
Returns started in February	825
Returns in process, February 28:	
(80% complete)	125
Returns in process, February 1:	
Labor	£ 6,000
Overhead	2,500
Labor, February (4,000 hours)	89,000
Overhead, February	45,000

*Although the euro is used in most European markets, day-to-day business in the United Kingdom continues to be conducted in pounds sterling.

Required:

1. Compute the following amounts for labor and for overhead:
   a. Equivalent units of activity.
   b. Cost per equivalent unit. (Remember to express your answer in terms of the British pound sterling, denoted by £.)
2. Compute the cost of returns in process as of February 28.

(CMA, adapted)

Problem 4–35
Process Costing; Production Report; Journal Entries; Weighted-Average Method
(LO 4-2, 4-3, 4-4, 4-5, 4-6)

Cost of goods completed and transferred out, November: $306,300

GroFast Company manufactures a high-quality fertilizer, which is used primarily by commercial vegetable growers. Two departments are involved in the production process. In the Mixing Department, various chemicals are entered into production. After processing, the Mixing Department transfers a chemical called Chemgro to the Finishing Department. There the product is completed, packaged, and shipped under the brand name Vegegro.

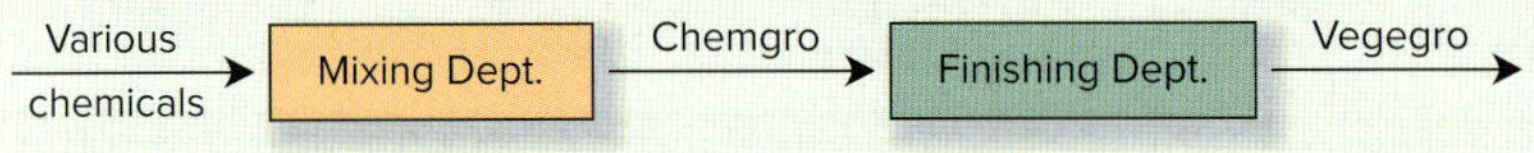

In the Mixing Department, the raw material is added at the beginning of the process. Labor and overhead are applied continuously throughout the process. All direct departmental overhead is traced to the departments, and plant overhead is allocated to the departments on the basis of direct-labor. The plant overhead rate for 20x2 is $.40 per direct-labor dollar.

The following information relates to production during November 20x2 in the Mixing Department.

a. Work in process, November 1 (4,000 pounds, 75 percent complete as to conversion):

Raw material	$22,800
Direct labor at $5.00 per hour	24,650
Departmental overhead	12,000
Allocated plant overhead	9,860

b. Raw material:

Inventory, November 1, 2,000 pounds	$10,000
Purchases, November 3, 10,000 pounds	51,000
Purchases, November 18, 10,000 pounds	51,500
Released to production during November, 16,000 pounds	

c. Direct-labor cost, $103,350
d. Direct departmental overhead costs, $52,000
e. Transferred to Finishing Department, 15,000 pounds
f. Work in process, November 30, 5,000 pounds, 20 percent complete

The company uses weighted-average process costing to accumulate product costs. However, for raw-material inventories, the firm uses the FIFO (i.e., first in, first out) inventory method.

Required:

1. Prepare a production report for the Mixing Department for November 20x2. The report should show:
   a. Equivalent units of production by cost factor (i.e., direct material and conversion).
   b. Cost per equivalent unit for each cost factor. (Round your answers to the nearest cent.)
   c. Cost of Chemgro transferred to the Finishing Department.
   d. Cost of the work-in-process inventory on November 30, 20x2, in the Mixing Department.
2. Prepare journal entries to record the following events:
   a. Release of direct material to production during November.
   b. Incurrence of direct-labor costs in November.
   c. Application of overhead costs for the Mixing Department (direct departmental and allocated plant overhead costs.)
   d. Transfer of Chemgro out of the Mixing Department.

(CMA, adapted)

Problem 4–36
Operation Costing; Unit Costs; Journal Entries
(LO 4-7)

1. Total product cost, deluxe model: $207,900

Plasto Corporation manufactures a variety of plastic products including a series of molded chairs. The three models of molded chairs, which are all variations of the same design, are Standard (can be stacked), Deluxe (with arms), and Executive (with arms and padding). The company uses batch manufacturing and has an operation-costing system. The production process includes an extrusion operation and subsequent operations to form, trim, and finish the chairs. Plastic sheets are produced by the extrusion operation, some of which are sold directly to other manufacturers. During the forming operation, the remaining plastic sheets are molded into chair seats and the legs are added; the Standard model is sold after this operation. During the trim operation, the arms are added to the Deluxe and Executive models and the chair edges are smoothed. Only the Executive model enters the finish operation where the padding is added. All of the units produced receive the same steps within each operation. The May production run had a total manufacturing cost of $898,000. The units of production and direct-material costs incurred were as follows:

	Units Produced	Extrusion Materials	Form Materials	Trim Materials	Finish Materials
Plastic sheets	5,000	$60,000			
Standard model	6,000	72,000	$24,000		
Deluxe model	3,000	36,000	12,000	$9,000	
Executive model	2,000	24,000	8,000	6,000	$12,000
Total	16,000	$192,000	$44,000	$15,000	$12,000

Manufacturing costs applied during the month of May were as follows:

	Extrusion Operation	Form Operation	Trim Operation	Finish Operation
Direct labor	$152,000	$60,000	$30,000	$18,000
Manufacturing overhead	240,000	72,000	39,000	24,000

Required:

1. For each product produced by Plasto Corporation during the month of May, determine the (*a*) unit cost and (*b*) total cost. Be sure to account for all costs incurred during the month.
2. Prepare journal entries to record the flow of production costs during May.

(CMA, adapted)

Problem 4–37
Operation Costing; Unit Costs
(LO 4-7)

2. Conversion cost per unit, department II: $10.00

5. Cost of etched, colored glass sheet: $76.25 per sheet

(Contributed by Roland Minch.) Glass Glow Company manufactures a variety of glass windows in its Egalton plant. In department I, clear glass sheets are produced, and some of these sheets are sold as finished goods. Other sheets made in department I have metallic oxides added in department II to form colored glass sheets. Some of these colored sheets are sold; others are moved to department III for etching and then are sold. The company uses operation costing.

Glass Glow Company's production costs applied to products in May are given in the following table. There was no beginning or ending inventory of work in process for May.

Cost Category	Dept. I	Dept. II	Dept. III
Direct material	$450,000	$72,000	–0–
Direct labor	38,000	22,000	$38,000
Manufacturing overhead	230,000	68,000	73,750

Products	Units	Dept. I Dir. Mat.	Dept. II Dir. Mat.
Clear glass, sold after dept. I	11,000	$247,500	–0–
Unetched colored glass, sold after dept. II	4,000	90,000	$32,000
Etched colored glass, sold after dept. III	5,000	112,500	40,000

Each sheet of glass requires the same steps within each operation.

Required: Compute each of the following amounts.

1. The conversion cost per unit in department I.
2. The conversion cost per unit in department II.
3. The cost of a clear glass sheet.

4. The cost of an unetched colored glass sheet.
5. The cost of an etched colored glass sheet.

Problem 4–38
Operation Costing; Unit Cost; Cost Flow; Journal Entries
(LO 4-7)

2. Unit cost, reflective Ceralam housing: $200.00

Orbital Industries of Canada, Inc. manufactures a variety of materials and equipment for the aerospace industry. A team of R & D engineers in the firm's Winnipeg plant has developed a new material that will be useful for a variety of purposes in orbiting satellites and spacecraft. Tradenamed Ceralam, the material combines some of the best properties of both ceramics and laminated plastics. Ceralam is already being used for a variety of housings in satellites produced in three different countries. Ceralam sheets are produced in an operation called rolling, in which the various materials are rolled together to form a multilayer laminate. Orbital Industries sells many of these Ceralam sheets just after the rolling operation to aerospace firms worldwide. However, Orbital also processes many of the Ceralam sheets further in the Winnipeg plant. After rolling, the sheets are sent to the molding operation, where they are formed into various shapes used to house a variety of instruments. After molding, the sheets are sent to the punching operation, where holes are punched in the molded sheets to accommodate protruding instruments, electrical conduits, and so forth. Some of the molded and punched sheets are then sold. The remaining units are sent to the dipping operation, in which the molded sheets are dipped in a special chemical mixture to give them a reflective surface.

During the month of March, the following products were manufactured at the Winnipeg plant. The direct-material costs also are shown.

	Units	Direct Materials Used in Ceralam Sheets	Direct Materials Used in Dipping
Ceralam sheets (sold after the rolling operation)	12,000	$480,000	
Nonreflective housings (sold after the punching operation)	5,000	200,000	
Reflective housings (sold after the dipping operation)	3,000	120,000	$30,000
Total	20,000	$800,000	$30,000

The costs incurred in producing the various Ceralam products in the Winnipeg plant during March are shown in the following table. Manufacturing overhead is applied on the basis of direct-labor dollars at the rate of 150 percent.

	Rolling	Molding	Punching	Dipping
Direct material	$ 800,000	–0–	–0–	$ 30,000
Direct labor	300,000	$112,000	$128,000	45,000
Manufacturing overhead	450,000	168,000	192,000	67,500
Total	$1,550,000	$280,000	$320,000	$142,500

Orbital Industries of Canada uses operation costing for its Ceralam operations in the Winnipeg plant.

Required:

1. Prepare a table that includes the following information *for each of the four operations.*
   - Total conversion costs.
   - Units manufactured.
   - Conversion cost per unit.
2. Prepare a second table that includes the following information *for each product* (i.e., rolled Ceralam sheets, nonreflective Ceralam housings, and reflective Ceralam housings).
   - Total manufacturing costs.
   - Units manufactured.
   - Total cost per unit.
3. Prepare journal entries to record the flow of all manufacturing costs through the Winnipeg plant's Ceralam operations during March. (Ignore the journal entries to record sales revenue.)
4. *Build a spreadsheet:* Construct an Excel spreadsheet to solve requirements 1 and 2 above. Show how the solution will change if the following data change: the cost of direct material used in dipping was $45,000 and the overhead application rate is 200% of direct-labor cost.

Case

Case 4–39
Weighted-Average Process Costing; Ethics
(LO 4-3, 4-4, 4-5, 4-6)

4. Weighted-average unit cost of completed leather belts: $6.10

Total cost of October 31 work in process: $4,700

Laredo Leather Company manufactures high-quality leather goods. The company's profits have declined during the past nine months. In an attempt to isolate the causes of poor profit performance, management is investigating the manufacturing operations of each of its products.

One of the company's main products is leather belts. The belts are produced in a single, continuous process in the Dallas Plant. During the process, leather strips are sewn, punched, and dyed. The belts then enter a final finishing stage to conclude the process. Labor and overhead are applied continuously during the manufacturing process. All materials, leather strips, and buckles are introduced at the beginning of the process. The firm uses the weighted-average method to calculate its unit costs.

The leather belts produced at the Dallas Plant are sold wholesale for $9.95 each. Management wants to compare the current manufacturing costs per unit with the market prices for leather belts. Top management has asked the Dallas plant controller to submit data on the cost of manufacturing the leather belts for the month of October. These cost data will be used to determine whether modifications in the production process should be initiated or whether an increase in the selling price of the belts is justified. The cost per belt used for planning and control is $5.35.

The work-in-process inventory consisted of 400 partially completed units on October 1. The belts were 25 percent complete as to conversion. The costs included in the inventory on October 1 were as follows:

Leather strips	$ 990
Buckles	260
Conversion costs	300
Total	$1,550

During October 7,600 leather strips were placed into production. A total of 7,000 leather belts were completed. The work-in-process inventory on October 31 consisted of 1,000 belts, which were 50 percent complete as to conversion.

The costs charged to production during October were as follows:

Leather strips	$19,900
Buckles	5,250
Conversion costs	20,700
Total	$45,850

Required:

In order to provide cost data regarding the manufacture of leather belts in the Dallas Plant to the top management of Laredo Leather Company, compute the following amounts for the month of October.

1. The equivalent units for material and conversion.
2. The cost per equivalent unit of material and conversion.
3. The assignment of production costs to the October 31 work-in-process inventory and to goods transferred out.
4. The weighted-average unit cost of leather belts completed and transferred to finished goods. Comment on the company's cost per belt used for planning and control.
5. Laredo Leather Company's production manager, Jack Murray, has been under pressure from the company president to reduce the cost of conversion. In spite of several attempts to reduce conversion costs, they have remained more or less constant. Now Murray is faced with an upcoming meeting with the company president, at which he will have to explain why he has failed to reduce conversion costs. Murray has approached his friend, Jeff Daley, who is the corporate controller, with the following request: "Jeff, I'm under pressure to reduce costs in the production process. There is no way to reduce material cost, so I've got to get the conversion costs down. If I can show just a little progress in next week's meeting with the president, then I can buy a little time to try some other cost-cutting measures I've been considering. I want you to do me a favor. If we raise the estimate of the percentage of completion of October's inventory to 60 percent, that will increase the number of equivalent units. Then the unit conversion cost will be a little lower." By how much would Murray's suggested manipulation lower the unit conversion cost? What should Daley do? Discuss this situation, citing specific ethical standards for managerial accountants.

(CMA, adapted)

5 Activity-Based Costing and Management

FOCUS COMPANY >>>

© Getty Images/Blend Images RF

THIS CHAPTER'S FOCUS COMPANY is the Patio Grill Company, which manufactures high-end gas barbeque grills in its Denver plant. The company has recently experienced intense competition in its two high-volume product lines, forcing management to drop these products' prices below their target levels. But then management implemented a new costing system, called activity-based costing, or ABC. ABC assigns product costs more accurately than traditional product-costing systems and, armed with the cost insights from the ABC system, management was able to change its pricing structure to compete more effectively in the gas-grill market.

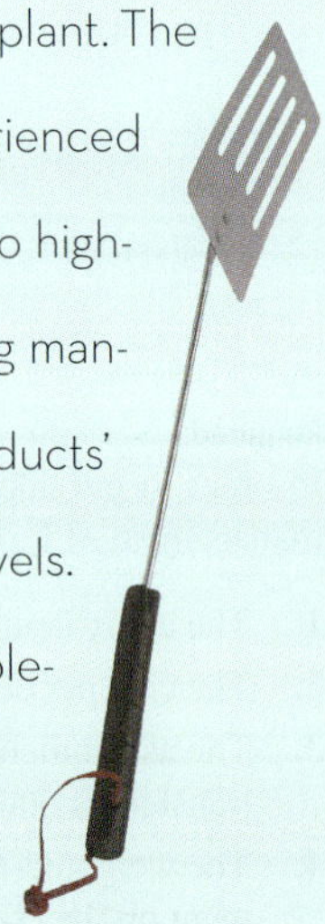

© Ingram Publishing/ SuperStock RF

<<< IN CONTRAST

Immunity Medical Center

In contrast to the manufacturing setting of the Patio Grill Company, we explore the use of activity-based costing by Immunity Medical Center in its Primary Care Unit. ABC is used in this health care services setting to assign treatment costs to categories of patient visits, such as routine, extended, and complex visits, as well as new and continuing patients. With a good understanding of how much it costs the Primary Care Unit to provide various types of patient care, the clinic's administration is in a much better position to make decisions about scheduling, services offered, and physician support.

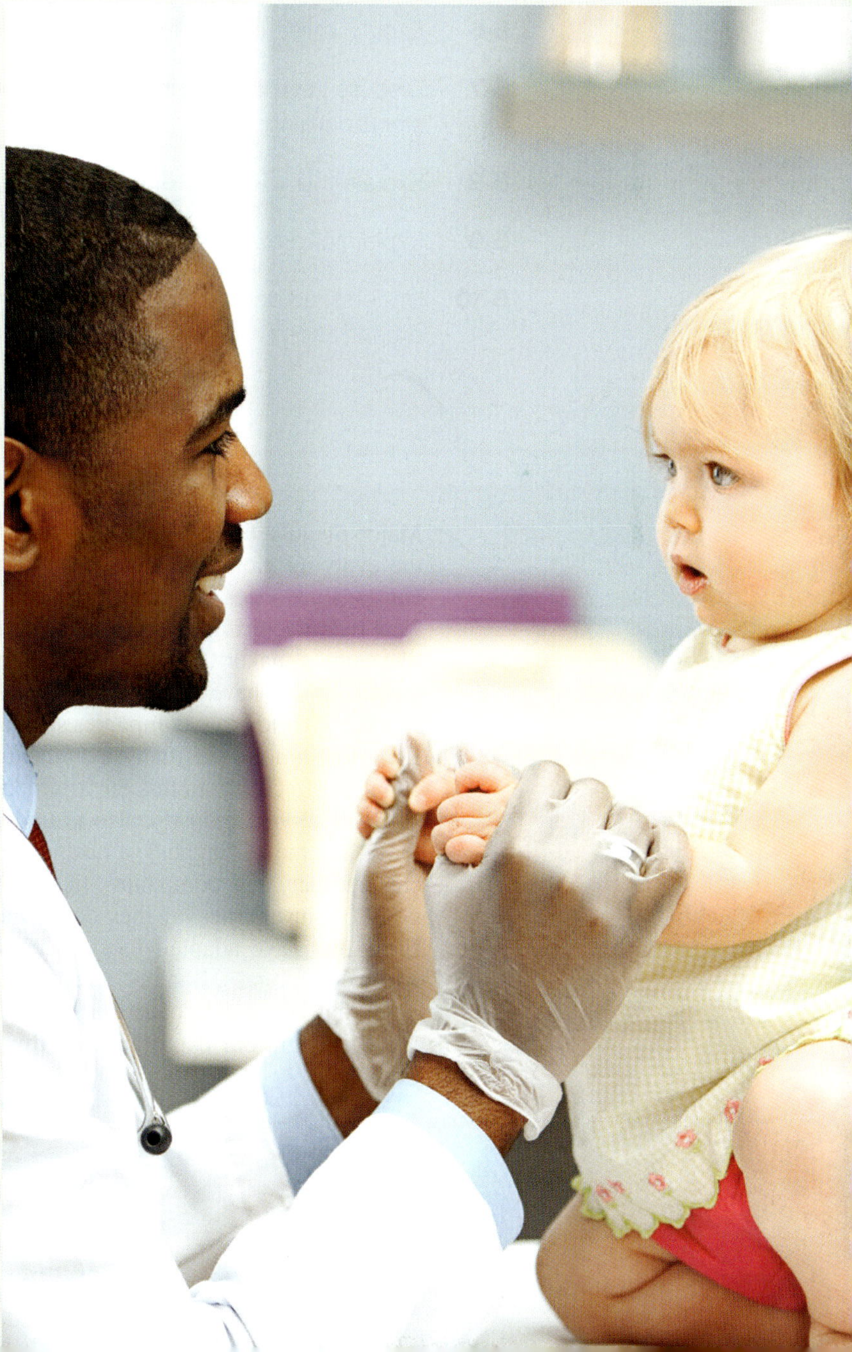

After completing this chapter, you should be able to:

5-1 Compute product costs under a traditional, volume-based product-costing system.

5-2 Explain how an activity-based costing system operates, including the use of a two-stage procedure for cost assignment, the identification of activity cost pools, and the selection of cost drivers.

5-3 Explain the concept of cost levels, including unit-level, batch-level, product-sustaining-level, and facility-level costs.

5-4 Compute product costs under an activity-based costing system.

5-5 Explain why traditional, volume-based costing systems tend to distort product costs.

5-6 Explain three criteria for selecting cost drivers.

5-7 Discuss several key issues in activity-based costing, including data collection and storyboarding.

5-8 Explain the concepts of activity-based management and two-dimensional ABC.

5-9 Explain and execute a customer-profitability analysis.

5-10 Understand and discuss how activity-based costing is used in service-industry organizations.

Major manufacturers worldwide must be nimble to respond to dynamic forces such as the evolving global marketplace, the breakneck pace of technological innovation, and constant advances in operational and business platforms like cloud-based computing. New manufacturing companies have emerged in response to this disruption, companies like camera maker GoPro and consumer drone producer DJI. And some long-established manufacturers have emerged as world-class producers, while others have fallen by the wayside. World-class companies such as Caterpillar, Coca-Cola, Johnson & Johnson, and Pfizer are among the many manufacturers that have changed key business processes to compete effectively in this environment.

The service industry also is undergoing dramatic transformation. App-based platforms and the willingness of businesses to outsource many critical service functions have created many new companies, like Uber and Airbnb, and caused many service organizations to reinvent the way they do business. Among the many established service-industry firms that have adapted most successfully to the changing business environment are American Express, Bank of America, UPS, Google, and Southwest Airlines.

What is the role of managerial accounting in this rapidly changing environment? We will begin our exploration of this issue by considering recent events at Patio Grill Company.

Traditional, Volume-Based Product-Costing System

Learning Objective 5-1

Compute product costs under a traditional, volume-based product-costing system.

Patio Grill Company's Denver plant manufactures three product lines, all high-end gas barbecue grills. The plant's three gas grill lines are the Patio Standard (STD), the Deluxe (DEL), and the Ultimate (ULT). Until recently, the Denver plant used a job-order product-costing system similar to the one described in Chapter 3: the cost of each product was the sum of its actual direct-material cost, actual direct-labor cost, and applied manufacturing overhead, which was applied using a predetermined overhead rate based on direct-labor hours. Exhibit 5–1 provides the basic data upon which the traditional costing system was based.

The Excel spreadsheet in Exhibit 5–2 shows the calculation of the product cost for each of three gas-grill lines (STD, DEL, and ULT). Overhead is applied to the products at the rate of $24 per direct-labor hour. Notice that all of the Denver plant's budgeted manufacturing overhead costs are lumped together in a single cost pool. This total budgeted overhead amount ($4,896,000) then is divided by the plant's total budgeted direct-labor hours (204,000 hours). The 204,000 direct labor hours is also equal to the plant's practical capacity for production, as expressed in terms of direct-labor hours.

Patio Grill Company's labor-hour-based product-costing system is typical of many manufacturing companies. Because labor hours are related closely to the volume of activity in the factory, these traditional product-costing systems often are said to be **volume-based (or throughput-based) costing systems.**

Exhibit 5–1

Basic Production and Cost Data: Patio Grill Company

	Patio Standard Grill STD	Deluxe Grill DEL	Ultimate Grill ULT
Planned annual production:			
Volume in units	10,000	8,000	2,000
Production runs	80 runs of 125 units each	80 runs of 100 units each	40 runs of 50 units each
Direct material	$100	$120	$180
Direct labor (not including setup time)	$180 (9 hours @ $20 per hour)	$220 (11 hours @ $20 per hour)	$260 (13 hours @ $20 per hour)
Machine hours (MH) per product unit	10 MH	12 MH	17 MH
Total machine hours consumed by product line	100,000 (10 MH × 10,000 units)	96,000 (12 MH × 8,000 units)	34,000 (17 MH × 2,000 units)

Exhibit 5–2

Product Costs from Traditional, Volume-Based Product-Costing System: Patio Grill Company

Patio Grill Company - Excel

F7 | fx =SUM(F3:F6)

	A	B	C	D	E	F	G
1		STD		DEL		ULT	
2							
3	Direct material	$ 100.00		$ 120.00		$ 180.00	
4	Direct labor						
5	(not including set-up time)	180.00	(9 hr. @ $20)	220.00	(11 hr. @ $20)	260.00	(13 hr. @ $20)
6	Manufacturing overhead*	216.00	(9 hr. @ $24)	264.00	(11 hr. @ $24)	312.00	(13 hr. @ $24)
7	Total cost	$ 496.00		$ 604.00		$ 752.00	
8							
9							
10	*Calculation of predetermined-overhead rate:						
11							
12	Budgeted manufacturing overhead	$ 4,896,000					
13							
14	Direct labor, budgeted hours:			Predetermined overhead rate			
15	STD: 10,000 units x 9 hours	90,000		= $4,896,000 / 204,000			
16	DEL: 8,000 units x 11 hours	88,000		= $24 per direct-labor hour			
17	ULT: 2,000 units x 13 hours	26,000					
18	Total direct-labor hours	204,000					
19							

Costs_Traditional

READY

Exhibit 5–3
Target and Actual Selling Prices: Patio Grill Company

	Patio Standard Grill STD	Deluxe Grill DEL	Ultimate Grill ULT
Production cost under traditional, volume-based system (Exhibit 5–2)	$496.00	$604.00	$752.00
Target selling price (cost × 120%)	595.20	724.80	902.40
Actual current selling price	585.00	705.00	940.00

Trouble in Denver

The profitability of Patio Grill Company's Denver operation has been faltering in recent years. The company's pricing policy has been to set a target price for each grill equal to 120 percent of the full product cost. Thus, the desired prices were determined as shown in Exhibit 5–3. Also shown are the actual prices that Patio Grill Company has been obtaining for its products.

Due to price competition from other grill manufacturers, the company's Standard (STD) grills were selling at $585, approximately $10 below their target price of $595.20. Moreover, Patio Grill Company's competition had forced management to reduce the price of the Deluxe grill (DEL) to $705, almost $20 below its target price of $724.80. Even at this lower price, the sales team was having difficulty getting orders for its planned volume of Deluxe grill production.

Fortunately, the disappointing profitability of the Patio Standard and Deluxe model grills was partially offset by greater-than expected profits on the Ultimate (ULT) line of grills. Patio Grill Company's sales personnel had discovered that the company was swamped with orders when the Ultimate grill's target price of $902.40 was charged. Consequently, in response to market demand management had raised the price on the Ultimate grills several times, and eventually the product was selling well for $940. Even at this price, Patio Grill Company's customers did not seem to hesitate to place orders.

Moreover, the company's competitors did not mount a challenge in the market for the Ultimate line of grills. Patio's management was pleased to have a niche for the Ultimate grill market, which appeared to be a highly profitable, low-volume specialty product. Nevertheless, concern continued to mount in Denver about the difficulty in the Patio Standard and Deluxe grill markets. After all, these were the Denver plant's bread-and-butter products, with projected annual sales of 10,000 Patio Standard grills and 8,000 Deluxe grills.

Activity-Based Costing System

Learning Objective 5-2

Explain how an activity-based costing system operates, including the use of a two-stage procedure for cost assignment, the identification of activity cost pools, and the selection of cost drivers.

Patio Grill Company's director of cost management, Hunter Burger, had been thinking for some time about a refinement in the Denver plant's product-costing system. He wondered if the traditional, volume-based system was providing management with accurate data about product costs. Burger had read about **activity-based costing (ABC) systems,** which follow a two-stage procedure to assign overhead costs to products. The first stage identifies significant activities in the production of the three products and assigns overhead costs to each activity in accordance with the cost of the organization's resources used by the activity. The overhead costs assigned to each activity comprise an **activity cost pool.**

After assigning overhead costs to activity cost pools in stage one, cost drivers appropriate for each cost pool are identified in stage two. Then the overhead costs are allocated from each activity cost pool to each product line in proportion to the amount of the cost driver consumed by the product line.

The two-stage cost-assignment process of activity-based costing is depicted in Exhibit 5–4.

Burger discussed activity-based costing with Esperanza Alvarez-Cook, the assistant director of cost management. Together they met with all of Patio Grill Company's department supervisors to discuss development of an ABC system. After initial discussion, an ABC proposal was made to the company's top management. Approval was obtained, and an

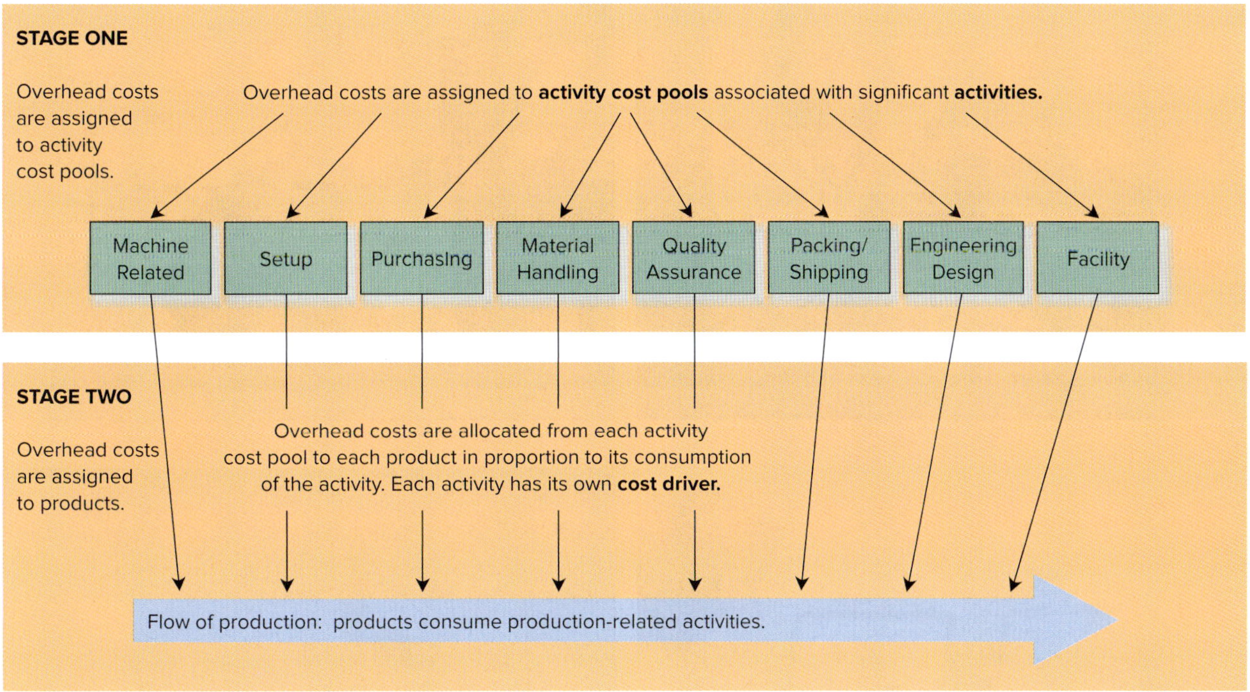

Exhibit 5–4
Activity-Based Costing System

ABC project team was formed, which included Burger, Alvarez-Cook, and representatives of various functional departments. Through several months of painstaking data collection and analysis, the project team was able to gather the data necessary to implement an ABC system.

ABC Stage One

Learning Objective 5-3

Explain the concept of cost levels, including unit-level, batch-level, product-sustaining-level, and facility-level costs.

Patio Grill Company's ABC project team identified eight activity cost pools, which fall into four broad categories.

1. *Unit level.* This type of activity must be done for each unit of production. The machine-related activity cost pool represents a **unit-level activity** since every product unit requires machine time.
2. *Batch level.* These activities must be performed for each batch of products, rather than each unit. Patio Grill Company's **batch-level activities** include the setup, purchasing, material handling, quality assurance, and packing/shipping activity cost pools.
3. *Product-sustaining level.* This category includes activities that are needed to support an entire product line but are not performed every time a new unit or batch of products is produced. Patio Grill Company's project team identified engineering design costs as a **product-sustaining-level activity** cost pool.
4. *Facility (or general operations) level.* **Facility-level activities** are required in order for the entire production process to occur. Examples of such activity costs include plant management salaries, plant depreciation, property taxes, plant maintenance, and insurance.

This classification of activities into unit-level, batch-level, product-sustaining-level, and facility-level activities is called a **cost hierarchy.**

Patio Grill Company's eight activity cost pools are depicted in Exhibit 5–5. Notice that the total overhead cost for all eight activity cost pools, $4,896,000, is shown at the top of the exhibit. This amount is the same as the total overhead cost shown in Exhibit 5–2, which shows the details of the product costs calculated under Patio Grill Company's traditional product-costing system.

© Culture Creative/Alamy RF

© Alistair Berg/Digital Vision/Getty Images RF

© Juice Images/Alamy RF

© Glow Images RF

The hierarchy of costs attempts to classify costs in a way that allows them to be applied to products or services more accurately. Here is an example from manufacturing. Upper left: When direct material is applied to products, the amount used is proportional to the number of units of product produced, so it is classified as a ***unit-level activity****. Upper right: This forklift operator is engaged in material handling, which is usually a* ***batch-level activity*** *in an ABC system because multiple units of varying amounts can be handled in one move. Lower left: When used by manufacturing engineers in a company, the depreciation of a computer-aided-design (CAD) system would be related to the* ***product-sustaining-level activity*** *of product support. Lower right: Once the commitment has been made to have a manufacturing facility, its related costs (insurance, taxes, depreciation, etc.) are incurred regardless of what happens inside, so it is usually classified as a* ***facility-level activity****.*

ABC Stage Two

Learning Objective 5-4

Compute product costs under an activity-based costing system.

In stage two of the activity-based costing project, Burger and Alvarez-Cook identified cost drivers for each activity cost pool. Then they used a three-step process to compute unit activity costs for each of Patio Grill Company's three product lines, and for each of the eight activity cost pools. In the following sections, we will discuss in detail how stage two of the ABC project was carried out for the various activity cost pools identified in stage one. Then we will complete the ABC project by developing new product costs for each of the company's gas-grill product lines.

Machine-Related Cost Pool Let's begin by focusing on only one of the eight activity cost pools. The machine-related cost pool, a unit-level activity, totals $1,242,000 and includes the costs of machine maintenance, depreciation, computer support, lubrication, electricity, and calibration. Burger and Alvarez-Cook selected machine hours for the cost driver, since a product that uses more machine hours should bear a larger share of machine-related costs. Exhibit 5–6 shows how machinery costs are assigned to products in stage two of the ABC analysis. Notice that the exhibit includes just a portion of a larger spreadsheet that we will examine in due course. The spreadsheet rows shown in Exhibit 5–6 focus just on the machine-related activity cost pool. Most of the columns in

Exhibit 5–5
Stage One of Activity-Based Costing: Identification of Activity Cost Pools

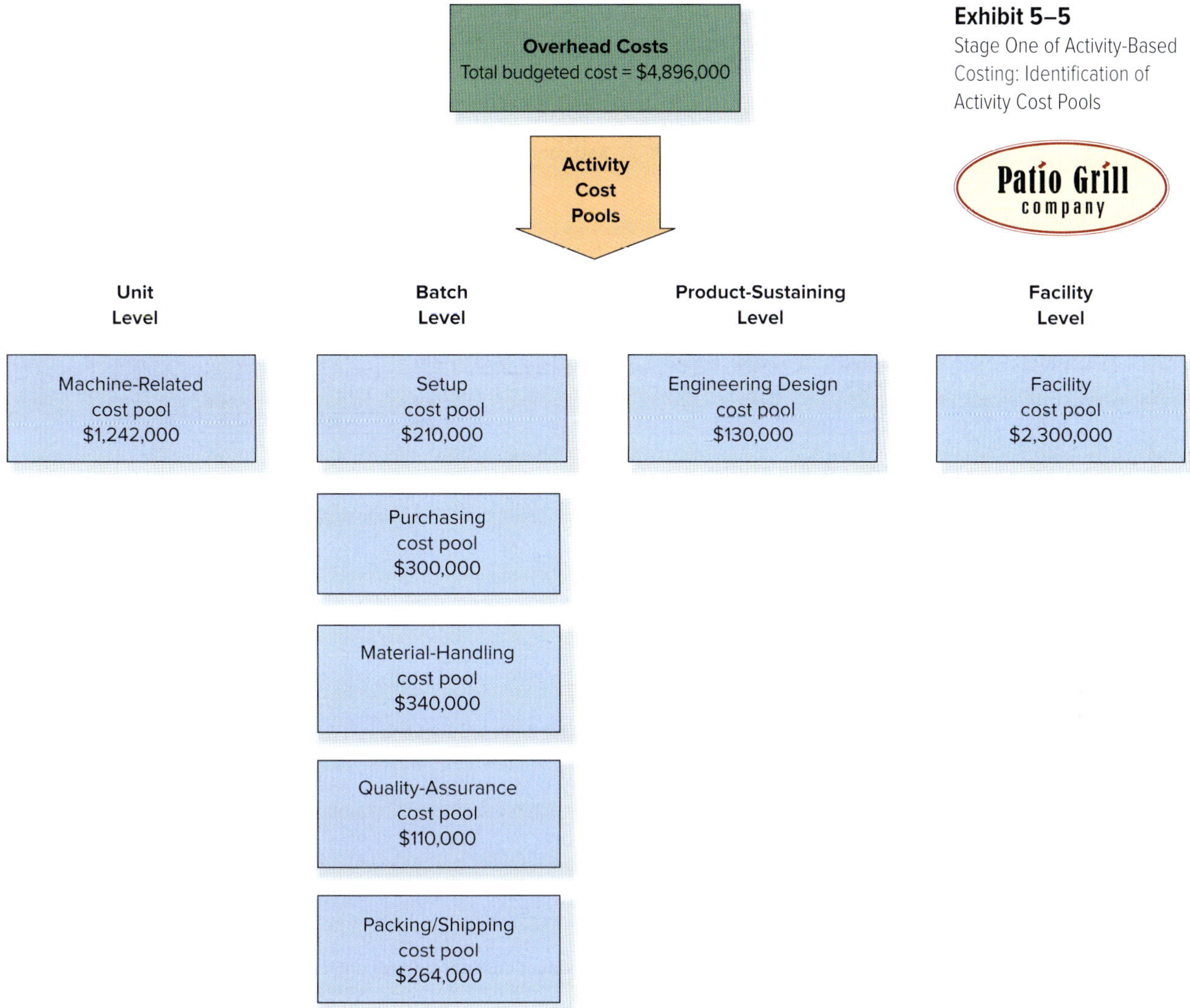

Exhibit 5–6 contains ABC data that were collected by the ABC project team. We will learn more later in this chapter about how that information is collected. For now, though, let's just take this ABC information as a given. As noted in Exhibit 5–6, the following columns contain *data collected by the ABC project team.*

Data Collected by ABC Project Team (Exhibit 5–6)

Column A	Activity: machine related
Column B	Activity cost pool: $1,242,000 (from Exhibit 5–5)
Column C	Cost driver: machine hours
Column D	Cost driver quantity: 230,000 machine hours (total of machine hours for the three product lines in column G)[1]
Column F	Product lines: STD, DEL, ULT
Column G	Cost driver quantity for each product line (from Exhibit 5–1): STD: 100,000 machine hours
	DEL: 96,000 machine hours
	ULT: 34,000 machine hours
Column I	Product line production volume (from Exhibit 5–1): STD: 10,000 units
	DEL: 8,000 units
	ULT: 2,000 units

[1]The 230,000 machine hours used to compute the pool rate for the machine-related cost pool is also equal to management's estimate of the company's practical capacity of production, as expressed in terms of machine hours.

Exhibit 5–6

ABC Data and Calculations for the Machine-Related Cost Pool: Patio Grill Company

INFORMATION SUPPLIED BY ABC PROJECT TEAM

Activity cost pools · **Cost drivers** · **Cost driver quantity for each product line; add column G to get total in column D** · **Product line production volume**

	A	B	C	D	E	F	G	H	I	J
1–4	Activity	Activity Cost Pool	Cost Driver	Cost Driver Quantity	Pool Rate	Product Line	Cost Driver Quantity for Product Line	Activity Cost for Product Line	Product Line Production Volume	Activity Cost per Unit of Product
5										
6	Machine	$ 1,242,000	Machine	230,000	$ 5.40	STD	100,000	$ 540,000	10,000	$ 54.00
7	Related		Hours			DEL	96,000	518,400	8,000	64.80
8						ULT	34,000	183,600	2,000	91.80
9						Total	230,000	$ 1,242,000		

ABC CALCULATIONS

1 Compute pool rate for machine-related activity

Activity cost pool ÷ Cost driver quantity = Pool rate

$1,242,000 ÷ 230,000 = $5.40

2 Compute total activity cost for each product line

Product line	Pool rate	×	Cost driver quantity for each product line	=	Activity cost for each product line
STD	$5.40	×	100,000	=	$540,000
DEL	5.40	×	96,000	=	518,400
ULT	5.40	×	34,000	=	183,600

3 Compute product cost per unit for each product line

Product line	Activity cost for each product line	÷	Product line production volume	=	Activity cost per unit of product
STD	$540,000	÷	10,000	=	$54.00
DEL	518,400	÷	8,000	=	64.80
ULT	183,600	÷	2,000	=	91.80

The remaining three columns in Exhibit 5–6, columns E, H, and J, contain the *amounts that are computed* during the ABC calculations, and they appear in red.

Amounts Computed During ABC Calculations (Exhibit 5–6)

Column E	Pool rate
Column H	Activity cost for each product line
Column J	Activity cost per unit of product for each product line

Exhibit 5–6 shows in detail how each of these amounts (shown in red) is computed. Take time now to examine Exhibit 5–6 carefully, in order to understand how these amounts are computed in the ABC calculations.

A key number computed in Exhibit 5–6 (column E) is the **pool rate,** which is defined as the cost per unit of the *cost driver* for a particular activity cost pool. The pool rate for the machine-related cost pool is $5.40, which means that Patio Grill Company's machine-related cost is $5.40 per machine hour. Each activity cost pool will have its own pool rate.

Now we have seen the type of data that the ABC project team must supply for the machine-related cost pool. In addition, we have studied how the ABC calculations are carried out in order to determine the machine-related activity cost per unit of each type of product (STD, DEL, and ULT). The final conclusion of the ABC analysis *for the machine-related cost pool only* is given in column J of Exhibit 5–6. Thus, under activity-based costing, the following machine-related costs per product unit should be assigned to each of the three product lines.

STD: $54.00 of machine-related cost per grill
DEL: $64.80 of machine-related cost per grill
ULT: $91.80 of machine-related cost per grill

Completing the ABC Calculations Now that we have studied the ABC data requirements and calculations for the machine-related cost pool (Exhibit 5–6), we can complete the ABC calculations by including all eight of the activity cost pools. These eight cost pools were given in Exhibit 5–5. The entire Excel spreadsheet for Patio Grill Company's activity-based costing project is displayed in Exhibit 5–7. As the cliché goes, there is good news and there is bad news.

The bad news is that the spreadsheet in Exhibit 5–7 contains eight times as many rows as the one we just examined in detail for the machine-related cost pool.

The good news, though, is that the ABC data requirements and calculations are conceptually *identical* for each of the eight activity cost pools. In other words, the same type of ABC data is supplied for each activity cost pool, and the three steps of ABC computations are performed for each activity cost pool in exactly the same manner as they were for the machine-related cost pool. So if we understand the computations in Exhibit 5–6 (for the machine-related costs), then we will understand the computations in Exhibit 5–7 for all eight activity cost pools. (The amounts that are *computed* in Exhibit 5–7 are shown in red.)

Pause here and take a few moments to examine Exhibit 5–7. Select an activity other than the machine-related activity we studied earlier. Try to verify the computations of the pool rate in column E, the activity cost for each product line in column H, and the ABC overhead cost per unit of product in column J.

Now that we have the activity cost per unit of product for each activity cost pool and each product line, it is straightforward to compute the total unit product cost for each type of grill. To do so, we need only add the direct-material and direct-labor costs for each grill type (given in Exhibit 5–1) to the ABC activity costs calculated in Exhibit 5–7. We do this in the Excel spreadsheet displayed as Exhibit 5–8.

Interpreting the ABC Product Costs

Hunter Burger was amazed to see the product costs reported under the activity-based costing system. Both the STD and DEL grills exhibited lower product costs under the ABC system than under the traditional system. This could explain the price competition Patio Grill Company faced on its STD and DEL grills. Patio Grill Company's competitors could sell their comparable standard and deluxe grills at a lower price because they realized it cost less to produce these grills than Patio Grill Company's traditional costing system had indicated. However, as Burger scanned the new product costs shown in Exhibit 5–8, he was alarmed by the substantial increase in the reported cost of an ULT grill. The cost of an ULT grill had risen by more than $100 above the company's original estimate. The complexity of the ULT grill, and its impact on costs, was hidden by the traditional, volume-based costing system. To compare the results of the two alternative costing systems, Burger prepared Exhibit 5–9.

As shown in Exhibit 5–9, the STD grills emerged as a profitable product, selling for approximately 120 percent of their reported cost under the activity-based costing system ($585 ÷ $487). The DEL grills also were selling at approximately 120 percent of their new reported product cost ($705 ÷ $586.30). "No wonder we couldn't sell the deluxe

Activity	Activity Cost Pool	Cost Driver	Cost Driver Quantity	Pool Rate	Product Line	Cost Driver Quantity for Product Line	Activity Cost for Product Line	Product Line Production Volume	Activity Cost per Unit of Product
Machine Related	$ 1,242,000	Machine Hours	230,000	$ 5.40	STD	100,000	$ 540,000	10,000	$ 54.00
					DEL	96,000	518,400	8,000	64.80
					ULT	34,000	183,600	2,000	91.80
					Total	230,000	$ 1,242,000		
Setup	210,000	Production Runs	200	1,050.00	STD	80	$ 84,000	10,000	8.40
					DEL	80	84,000	8,000	10.50
					ULT	40	42,000	2,000	21.00
					Total	200	$ 210,000		
Purchasing	300,000	Purchase Orders	600	500.00	STD	200	$ 100,000	10,000	10.00
					DEL	192	96,000	8,000	12.00
					ULT	208	104,000	2,000	52.00
					Total	600	$ 300,000		
Material Handling	340,000	Production Runs	200	1,700.00	STD	80	$ 136,000	10,000	13.60
					DEL	80	136,000	8,000	17.00
					ULT	40	68,000	2,000	34.00
					Total	200	$ 340,000		
Quality Assurance	110,000	Inspection Hours	2,200	50.00	STD	800	$ 40,000	10,000	4.00
					DEL	800	40,000	8,000	5.00
					ULT	600	30,000	2,000	15.00
					Total	2,200	$ 110,000		
Packing/ Shipping	264,000	Shipments	2,200	120.00	STD	1,000	$ 120,000	10,000	12.00
					DEL	800	96,000	8,000	12.00
					ULT	400	48,000	2,000	24.00
					Total	2,200	$ 264,000		
Engineering Design	130,000	Engineering Hours	1,300	100.00	STD	500	$ 50,000	10,000	5.00
					DEL	400	40,000	8,000	5.00
					ULT	400	40,000	2,000	20.00
					Total	1,300	$ 130,000		
Facility	2,300,000	Machine Hours	230,000	10.00	STD	100,000	$ 1,000,000	10,000	100.00
					DEL	96,000	960,000	8,000	120.00
					ULT	34,000	340,000	2,000	170.00
					Total	230,000	$ 2,300,000		
Grand Total	$ 4,896,000				Grand Total		$ 4,896,000	Total Overhead by Product	
								STD	$ 207.00
								DEL	246.30
								ULT	427.80

Exhibit 5–7
Activity-Based Costing Data and Calculations: Patio Grill Company

grills at the old target price of $724.80," said Burger to Alvarez-Cook, as they looked over the data. "Our competitors probably knew their deluxe grills cost around $586 to produce, and they priced them accordingly." When he got to the ULT column in Exhibit 5–9, Burger was appalled. "We thought those ultimate grills were a winner," lamented Burger, "but we've been selling them at a price that is only 8 percent over what it costs us to make them!" (Burger had made this calculation: actual current selling price of $940 ÷ ABC product cost of $867.80.) "And worse yet," Burger continued, "we've been selling the ultimate grills for more than one-hundred dollars below the new target price of $1,041.36." After looking over the data, Burger made a beeline for the president's office. "We've got to get this operation straightened out," he thought.

Burger also realized that the comparison of the two product-costing systems was even more striking when he focused on just the reported *overhead* costs. He commented

Exhibit 5–8
Product Costs from Activity-Based Costing System: Patio Grill Company

Patio Grill Company - Excel

G17 =SUM(G9:G16)

	A	B	C	D	E	F	G	H
1			STD		DEL		ULT	
2								
3	Direct material		$ 100.00		$ 120.00		$ 180.00	
4	Direct labor							
5	(not including set-up time)		180.00	(9 hr. @ $20)	220.00	(11 hr. @ $20)	260.00	(13 hr. @ $20)
6	Total direct costs per unit		$ 280.00		$ 340.00		$ 440.00	
7								
8	Manufacturing overhead (based on ABC):*							
9	Machine-related		$ 54.00		$ 64.80		$ 91.80	
10	Setup		8.40		10.50		21.00	
11	Purchasing		10.00		12.00		52.00	
12	Material handling		13.60		17.00		34.00	
13	Quality assurance		4.00		5.00		15.00	
14	Packing/shipping		12.00		12.00		24.00	
15	Engineering design		5.00		5.00		20.00	
16	Facility		100.00		120.00		170.00	
17	Total ABC overhead cost per unit		$ 207.00		$ 246.30		$ 427.80	
18	Total product cost per unit		$ 487.00		$ 586.30		$ 867.80	
19								
20	*ABC overhead costs from Exhibit 5-7							
21								

Costs_ABC

to Alvarez-Cook, "The direct-material and direct-labor costs for each product line don't change under ABC. They're the same under both costing systems. Since these are direct costs, it's straightforward to trace these costs to each product with considerable accuracy. It's the overhead costs that cause the problem." To see what Burger was getting at, look again at Exhibit 5–9 and focus on the top two rows. The overhead cost of a STD grill dropped from the old reported cost of $216 to $207 under ABC. Similarly, the overhead cost of a DEL grill dropped from the old reported cost of $264 to $246.30 under ABC. Now look at the ULT column, though. Here the overhead cost rose from the old reported cost of $312 to $427.80 under ABC! This represents an increase of more than a third. ($427.80 ÷ $312.00 is a little over 137 percent, which yields an *increase* of over 37 percent.)

The Punch Line

Learning Objective 5-5
Explain why traditional, volume-based costing systems tend to distort product costs.

What has happened at Patio Grill Company's Denver plant? The essence of the problem is that the traditional, volume-based costing system was overcosting the high-volume product lines (STD and DEL) and undercosting the complex, relatively low-volume product line (ULT). The high-volume products basically subsidized the low-volume line. The

Exhibit 5–9
Comparison of Product Costs and Target Prices from Alternative Product-Costing Systems: Patio Grill Company

	STD	DEL	ULT
Reported unit *overhead* cost:			
Traditional volume-based costing system (Exhibit 5–2)	$216.00	$264.00	$ 312.00
Activity-based costing system (Exhibit 5–8)	207.00	246.30	427.80
Reported unit *product* cost (direct material, direct labor, and overhead):			
Traditional volume-based costing system (Exhibit 5–2)	496.00	604.00	752.00
Activity-based costing system (Exhibit 5–8)	487.00	586.30	867.80
Sales price data:			
Original target price (120% of product cost based on traditional volume-based costing system (Exhibit 5–3)	595.20	724.80	902.40
New target price (120% of product cost based on activity-based costing system	584.40	703.56	$1,041.36
Actual current selling price (Exhibit 5–3)	585.00	705.00	940.00

	STD	DEL	ULT
Traditional volume-based costing system: reported product cost	$496.00	$604.00	$752.00
Activity-based costing system: reported product cost	487.00	586.30	867.80
Amount of cost distortion per unit	$ 9.00	$ 17.70	$ (115.80)
× Production volume	× 10,000	× 8,000	× 2,000
Total amount of cost distortion for entire product line	$90,000	$141,600	$(231,600)

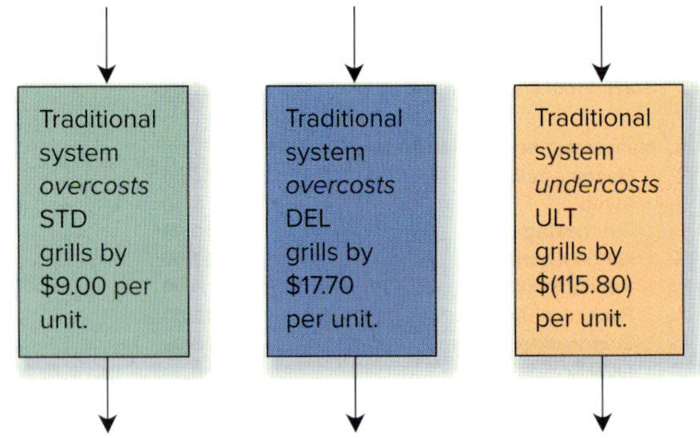

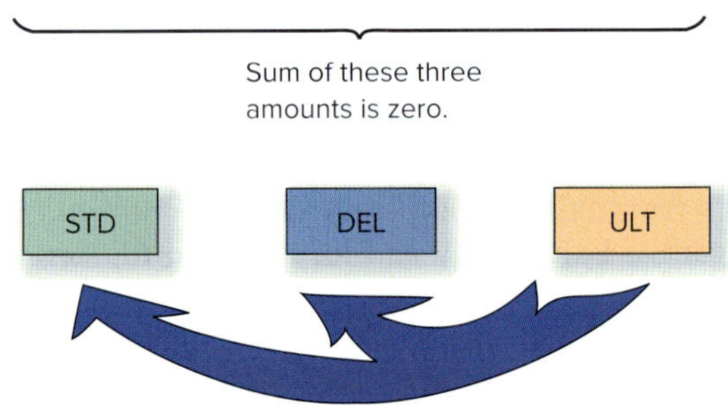

Traditional system shifts costs from ULT product line to STD and DEL product lines.

Exhibit 5–10
Cost Distortion under Patio Grill Company's Traditional Product-Costing System

activity-based costing system revealed this problem by more accurately assigning overhead costs to the three product lines.

Exhibit 5–10 summarizes the effects of the cost distortion under the traditional product-costing system. Patio Grill Company's traditional system *overcosted* each STD grill by $9.00, for a total of $90,000 for the STD product line on a volume of 10,000 units. Each DEL grill was *overcosted* by $17.70, for a total of $141,600 on a volume of 8,000 units for the DEL product line. These excess costs had to come from somewhere, and that place was the ULT product line. Each ULT grill was *undercosted* by $115.80, for a total of $231,600 for the ULT product line on a volume of 2,000 units. Notice that the *total* amount by which the STD and DEL grill lines were overcosted equals the *total* amount by which the ULT grill line was undercosted.

Why Traditional Volume-Based Systems Distort Product Costs

Why did Patio Grill Company's traditional product-costing system distort its product costs? The answer lies in the use of a single, volume-based cost driver. The company's old costing system assigned overhead to products on the basis of their relative usage of direct labor. Since the STD and DEL grill lines use substantially more direct labor than the ULT grill line, *in total,* the traditional system assigned them more overhead costs.

The problem with this result is that for every one of Patio Grill Company's overhead activities, the proportion of the activity actually consumed by the ULT grill line is far greater than its low volume would suggest. The ULT grill line has a budgeted production volume of just 2,000 units, which is only 10 percent of Patio Grill Company's total budgeted production volume of 20,000 units. (20,000 units = 10,000 STD units + 8,000 DEL units + 2,000 ULT units.) Now examine the ABC calculations in Exhibit 5–7. Focus on column G, which details the consumption of the cost driver by each product line for each activity cost pool. Notice that for every one of the overhead activities, the ULT grill line consumes much more than a 10 percent share of the activity, even though the ULT line represents only 10 percent of budgeted production volume. The relatively heavy consumption of overhead activities by the ULT product line is due to its greater complexity and small production runs. We must conclude, therefore, that direct labor is not a suitable cost driver for Patio Grill Company's overhead costs. Usage of direct labor does not drive most overhead costs in this company.

There are actually two factors working against Patio Grill Company's old product-costing system. First, many of the activities that result in the company's overhead costs are *not unit-level activities*. Second, the company manufactures a *diverse set of products*.

Non-Unit-Level Overhead Costs When Patio Grill Company's ABC project team designed the activity-based costing system, only the machine-related overhead cost pool was classified as a unit-level activity. All of the other activities were classified as batch-level, product-sustaining-level, or facility-level activities. This means that many of the company's overhead costs are not incurred every time a unit is produced. Instead, many of these overhead costs are related to starting new production batches, supporting an entire product line, or running the entire operation. Since direct labor is a unit-level cost driver, it fails to capture the forces that drive these other types of costs. In Patio Grill Company's new ABC system, cost drivers were chosen that were appropriate for each activity cost pool. For example, since setting up machinery for a new production run is a batch-level activity, the number of production runs is an appropriate batch-level cost driver.

Product Diversity Patio Grill Company manufactures three different products. Although all three are gas barbeque grills, the three grills are quite different. The STD and DEL grills are high-volume, relatively simple products. The ULT grills constitute a considerably more complex, and relatively low-volume, product line. As a result of this *product line diversity*, Patio Grill Company's three product lines consume overhead activities in different proportions. For example, compare the *consumption ratios* for the purchasing and material-handling activity cost pools shown below. The **consumption ratio** is the proportion of an activity consumed by a particular product.

	Consumption Ratios*		
Activity Cost Pool	**STD**	**DEL**	**ULT**
Purchasing activity (cost driver is purchase orders, or POs)	200 POs (33%)	192 POs (32%)	208 POs (35%)
Material-handling activity (cost driver is production runs)	80 runs (40%)	80 runs (40%)	40 runs (20%)

*The purchase order and production run data come from Exhibit 5-7.

These widely varying consumption ratios result from Patio Grill Company's product line diversity. A single cost driver will not capture the widely differing usage of these activities by the three products. The activity-based costing system uses two different cost drivers to assign these costs to the company's diverse products.

Management Accounting Practice

Rockwell International (now part of Meritor)

COST DISTORTION AT ROCKWELL INTERNATIONAL

When managers at Rockwell International noticed erratic sales in one of the company's lines of truck axles, they investigated. One of the company's best axle products was losing market share. A special cost study revealed that the firm's costing system, which applied costs to products in proportion to direct-labor costs, had resulted in major distortions. The reported product costs for high-volume axles were approximately 20 percent too high, and the low-volume axles were being undercosted by roughly 40 percent. The firm's practice of basing prices on reported product costs resulted in the overpricing of the high-volume axles. As a consequence, Rockwell's competitors entered the market for the high-volume axle business.[2]

Two Key Points To summarize, each of the following characteristics will undermine the ability of a volume-based product-costing system to assign overhead costs accurately.

- *A large proportion of non-unit-level activities.* A unit-level cost driver, such as direct labor, machine hours, or throughput, will not be able to assign the costs of non-unit-level activities accurately.
- *Product diversity.* When the consumption ratios differ widely between activities, no single cost driver will accurately assign the resulting overhead costs.

When either of these characteristics is present, a volume-based product-costing system is likely to distort product costs.

Activity-Based Costing: Some Key Issues

"Before the industry really became wide open in long distance competition [as the result of deregulation], you could get by with knowing less. You could get by with having price structures that were not based on the underlying activities and the costs associated with those activities, but were instead based on broad averages. It was okay. It worked. But it's not good enough anymore. We have to get more precise in our costs. We have to deliver the kinds of prices to our customers that they're willing to pay." (5a)

TELUS

Patio Grill Company's movement toward activity-based costing is typical of cost system enhancements made in many companies. Added domestic and foreign competition is forcing manufacturers to strive for a better understanding of their cost structures. Moreover, the cost structures of many manufacturers have changed significantly over the past decade. Years ago, a typical manufacturer produced a relatively small number of products that did not differ much in the amount and types of manufacturing support they required. Labor was the dominant element in such a firm's cost structure. Now, products are more numerous, tailored to more market segments, more complicated to produce, and vary more in their production requirements. Perhaps most important, labor has become a very small part of total production costs, less than five percent in many manufacturing companies. Just go to YouTube and look for one of the many manufacturing videos there: lots of machines and robots, not so many people.

All these factors mean manufacturers must take a close look at their traditional, volume-based costing systems and consider a move toward a more sophisticated approach to product costing. Among the many well-known manufacturers that have benefited from ABC are Boise Cascade, Caterpillar, Coca-Cola, Chrysler, Hewlett-Packard, John Deere, Johnson & Johnson, Pennzoil, and Pfizer, to name only a few.

The service sector also has undergone dynamic change in recent years. Increasing competition, outsourcing of key business processes, and the growth of the Internet have changed many service companies' business models. As their business environment changes, many service-industry firms have made use of activity-based costing. Service

[2]For up to date information about Meritor, see *The New York Times* (Business Day Section), March 1, 2013. The information about Meritor's Rockwell axles is from Ford S. Worthy, "Accounting Bores You? Wake Up," *Fortune* 116, no. 8, pp. 43–53. For another example of cost distortion, see S. L. Mintz, "Compaq's Secret Weapon," *CFO* 10, no. 10, pp. 93–97.

companies benefiting from ABC include American Airlines, American Express, AT&T, Blue Cross/Blue Shield, DHL Express, FedEx, Genworth, and Toronto Dominion Bank, among many others. Governmental units also have implemented activity-based costing. Among the governmental units that have benefited from ABC are such diverse organizations as the British Navy, the California Department of Taxation, the City of Indianapolis, and several agencies of the U.S. government, including the Citizenship and Immigration Services, the Internal Revenue Service, the Veterans Affairs Department, and the U.S. Postal Service.

An important factor in the move toward ABC systems is related to the information requirements of such systems. The data required for activity-based costing are more readily available than in the past. Increasing automation, coupled with sophisticated real-time information systems, provides the kind of data necessary to implement highly accurate product-costing systems. Some key issues related to activity-based costing systems are discussed in the following sections.

Cost Drivers

A **cost driver** is a characteristic of an event or activity that results in the incurrence of costs. In activity-based costing systems, an organization's most significant cost drivers are identified. Then a database is created, which shows how these cost drivers are distributed across products. Three factors are important in selecting appropriate cost drivers.

Learning Objective **5-6**

Explain three criteria for selecting cost drivers.

M anagement
A ccounting
P ractice

DHL Express (now a division of Deutsche Post AE)

"BIG DATA" AND ACTIVITY-BASED COSTING AT DHL EXPRESS

DHL Express, a division of the German logistics company Deutsche Post AE, provides international express mail services. DHL ships packages to 220 countries and territories throughout the world. Management at DHL found that it wasn't taking advantage of the masses of available data to gain insights about the company's operations and performance. Such masses of data, often called "big data," are challenging for companies like DHL to analyze, but they offer tantalizing opportunities for companies to outperform their competition - if they can work through the mass of data. (We discuss big data in greater depth in chapter 6.)

In order to access those insights, DHL "used data that already existed and then linked that to operational databases, billing systems to get revenue and customer information. We're in a very competitive industry. We have to distinguish ourselves from the competition, and one of the biggest advantages is data." But they found that some of the data that was needed wasn't collected, and the cost accounting system had distorted costs between the various types of express transport services the firm provided. "We couldn't produce a standard cost of shipment or pickup because we didn't have the data. We couldn't distinguish fixed and variable costs." For example, before implementation of a full activity-based costing system at DHL, express transport services provided to banks appeared to be unprofitable, whereas transport services provided to heavy manufacturers appeared to be highly profitable. "This was bad news because we [DHL] had a lot more banking customers than heavy manufacturing customers." After fully implementing ABC, however, management found that the previous costing system had used cost drivers that failed to account for costs and activities associated with package weights, thereby overcosting services to banks and undercosting those to heavy manufacturers. The ABC analysis revealed that express transport services to banks were actually quite profitable after all.[3]

[3]See Joanne Chiu, "DHL to Expand Asia Operations," *The Wall Street Journal Asia Business*, June 21, 2012, p. 1; Taylor Provost, "How DHL's Big Data Boosts Performance," *CFO.com*, January 30, 2013; and S. Player and C. Cobble, *Cornerstones of Decision Making: Profiles of Enterprise ABM* (Greensboro, NC: Oakhill Press, 1999), pp. 131–44.

1. *Degree of correlation.* The central concept of an activity-based costing system is to assign the costs of each activity to product lines on the basis of how each product line consumes the cost driver identified for that activity. The idea is to *infer* how each product line consumes the activity by *observing* how each product line consumes the cost driver. Therefore, the accuracy of the resulting cost assignments depends on the *degree of correlation* between consumption of the activity and consumption of the cost driver.

   Say that inspection cost is selected as an activity cost pool. The objective of the ABC system is to assign inspection costs to product lines on the basis of their consumption of the inspection activity. Two potential cost drivers come to mind: number of inspections and hours of inspection time. If every inspection requires the same amount of time for all products, then the number of inspections on a product line will be highly correlated with the consumption of inspection activity by that product line. On the other hand, if inspections vary significantly in the time required, then simply recording the number of inspections will not adequately portray the consumption of inspection activity. In this case, hours of inspection time would be more highly correlated with the actual consumption of the inspection activity.

> "ABC is not a magic bullet, but it is a tool to help you understand your business better." (5b)
> **Braas Company**

2. *Cost of measurement.* Designing any information system entails cost-benefit trade-offs. The more activity cost pools there are in an activity-based costing system, the greater will be the accuracy of the cost assignments. However, more activity cost pools also entail more cost drivers, which results in greater costs of implementing and maintaining the system.

   Similarly, the higher the correlation between a cost driver and the actual consumption of the associated activity, the greater the accuracy of the cost assignments. However, it also may be more costly to measure the more highly correlated cost driver. Returning to our example of the inspection activity, it may be that inspection hours make a more accurate cost driver than the number of inspections. It is likely, however, that inspection hours also will be more costly to measure and track over time.

3. *Behavioral effects.* Information systems have the potential not only to facilitate decisions but also to influence the behavior of decision makers. This can be good or bad, depending on the behavioral effects. In identifying cost drivers, an ABC analyst should consider the possible behavioral consequences. For example, in a just-in-time (JIT) production environment, a key goal is to reduce inventories and material-handling activities to the absolute minimum level possible. The number of material moves may be the most accurate measure of the consumption of the material-handling activity for cost assignment purposes. It also may have a desirable behavioral effect of inducing managers to reduce the number of times materials are moved, thereby reducing material-handling costs.

   Dysfunctional behavioral effects are also possible. For example, the number of vendor contacts may be a cost driver for the purchasing activity of vendor selection. This could induce purchasing managers to contact fewer vendors, which could result in the failure to identify the lowest-cost or highest-quality vendor.

> "After the initial run-through, we completed a separate analysis detailing how many times a [cost] driver was used. We performed a sort of cost-benefit analysis. We gave each [cost] driver a grade, such as how easy would the driver be to collect." (5c)
> **John Deere Health Care, Inc. (now part of UnitedHealthcare)**

Collecting ABC Data

Learning Objective 5-7

Discuss several key issues in activity-based costing including data collection and storyboarding.

The output of an organization's various departments consists of the activities performed by personnel or machines in those departments. Activities usually result in paperwork or the generation of computer documents. For example, engineering departments typically deal with documents such as specification sheets and engineering change orders. Purchasing departments handle requisitions and orders, which may be either hard-copy or computer documents. In an ABC system, analysis of documents such as these can be used to assign the costs of activities to product lines on the basis of the amount of activity generated by each product.

> "We were negotiating fees, and the customer was under the impression that they were paying more than they should . . . . To make this customer comfortable with the pricing, we needed a [more accurate] costing system." (5d)
>
> **Dana Commercial Credit Corporation**

Interviews and Paper Trails The information used in Patio Grill Company's ABC system came initially from extensive interviews with key employees in each of the organization's support departments and a careful review of each department's records. In the engineering area, for example, ABC project team members interviewed each engineer to determine the breakdown of time spent on each of the three products. They also examined every engineering change order completed in the past two years. The team concluded that engineering costs were driven largely by engineering hours and that the breakdown was 500 hours for the STD grill line, 400 hours for the DEL grill line, and 400 hours for the ULT grill line.

Storyboarding As Patio Grill Company's project team delved further into the ABC analysis, they made considerable use of another technique for collecting activity data. **Storyboarding** is a procedure used to develop a detailed process flowchart, which visually represents activities and the relationships among the activities. A storyboarding session involves all or most of the employees who participate in the activities oriented toward achieving a specific objective. A facilitator helps the employees identify the key activities involved in their jobs. These activities are written on small cards and placed on a large board in the order they are accomplished. Relationships among the activities are shown by the order and proximity of the cards. Other information about the activities is recorded on the cards, such as the amount of time and other resources that are expended on each activity and the events that trigger the activity. After several storyboarding sessions, a completed storyboard emerges, recording key activity information vital to the ABC project. Historically, storyboards have been used by Walt Disney and other film producers in the development of plots for animated films. More recently, storyboarding has been used by advertising agencies in developing event sequences for TV commercials.

Storyboarding provides a powerful tool for collecting and organizing the data needed in an ABC project. Patio Grill Company's ABC project team used storyboarding very effectively to study each of the firm's activity cost pools. The team concluded that purchasing costs were driven by the number of purchase orders. Material-handling costs were driven by the number of production runs. Quality-assurance costs were driven by the number of inspection hours devoted to each product line. Packaging and shipping costs were driven by the number of shipments made.

© ColorBlind Images/Getty Images RF

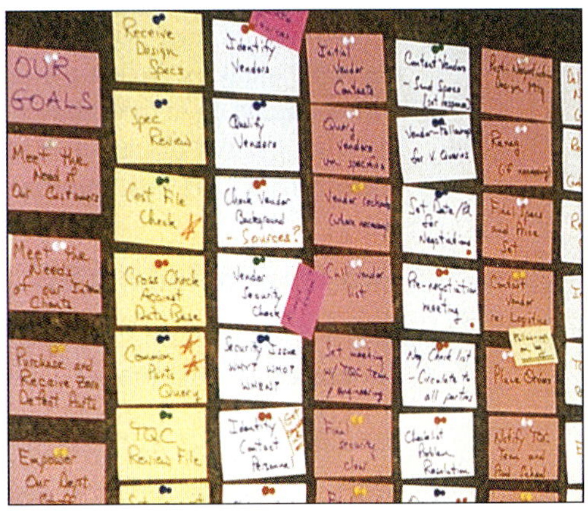

© Ronald W. Hilton

Interviews with department personnel and storyboarding sessions are often used by activity-based costing project teams to accumulate the data needed for an ABC study. In the interview sessions, an ABC project team member asks departmental employees to detail their activities, as well as the time and other resources consumed by the activities. Storyboards, like the one depicted here, visually show the relationships between the activities performed in an organization.

In summary, the ABC project team conducted a painstaking and lengthy analysis involving many employee interviews, the examination of hundreds of documents, and storyboarding sessions. The final result was the data used in the ABC calculations displayed in Exhibits 5-7 and 5-8.

Multidisciplinary ABC Project Teams In order to gather information from all facets of an organization's operations, it is essential to involve personnel from a variety of functional areas. A typical ABC project team includes accounting and finance people as well as engineers, marketing personnel, production and operations managers, and so forth. A multidisciplinary project team not only designs a better ABC system but also helps in gaining credibility for the new system throughout the organization.

Activity Dictionary and Bill of Activities

"Having a plant-level activity dictionary allows the plant to manage its activities locally and serves as a standard reference that employees can use to see which activities roll up into which processes." (5e)

Navistar International Corporation

Many organizations' ABC teams compile an **activity dictionary,** which is a complete listing of the activities identified and used in the ABC analysis. An activity dictionary helps in the implementation of activity-based costing across several divisions of an organization, because it provides for consistency in the ABC system terminology and the complexity of the ABC analyses in the various divisions.

A **bill of activities** is another commonly used element in an ABC analysis. A bill of activities for a product or service is a complete listing of the activities required for the product or service to be produced. As a familiar analogy, think about a recipe for chocolate chip cookies. The *bill of materials* for the cookies is the list of ingredients provided in the recipe. The *bill of activities* is the list of steps given in the recipe for making the cookies (e.g., combine ingredients in a bowl, stir in chocolate chips, place spoon-size globs of dough on greased cookie sheet, bake at 375° for 10 minutes or until done).

Activity-Based Management

Learning Objective 5-8

Explain the concepts of activity-based management and two-dimensional ABC.

Using activity-based costing (ABC) information to support organizational strategy, improve operations, and manage costs is called **activity-based management** or **ABM.** We have already caught a glimpse of activity-based management earlier in this chapter, where the management of Patio Grill Company used ABC information to better understand its product-pricing decisions. The company's management discovered through the ABC analysis that some products were overcosted and some products were undercosted by their traditional product-costing system. This important insight presented management with the opportunity to revise its product pricing in order to reflect the more accurate product costs provided by the ABC analysis. When management followed up on this product-pricing opportunity, it was engaging in activity-based management. However, ABM is a much broader concept than this. Activity-based management involves any use of ABC information to support the organization's strategy, improve operations, or manage activities and their resulting costs.

Two-Dimensional ABC

One way of picturing the relationship between ABC and ABM is in terms of the **two-dimensional ABC model** depicted in Exhibit 5–11.[4] The vertical dimension of the model depicts the cost assignment view of an ABC system. From the *cost assignment viewpoint,* the ABC system uses two-stage cost allocation to *assign* the costs of resources to the firm's cost objects. These cost objects could be products manufactured, services produced, or customers served.

---

[4]This section draws on Lewis J. Soloway, "Using Activity-Based Management in Aerospace and Defense Companies," *Journal of Cost Management* 6, no. 4 (Winter 1993), pp. 56–66; and Peter B. B. Turney, "What an Activity-Based Cost Model Looks Like," *Journal of Cost Management* 5, no. 4 (Winter 1992), pp. 54–60.

Exhibit 5–11
Two-Dimensional ABC Model

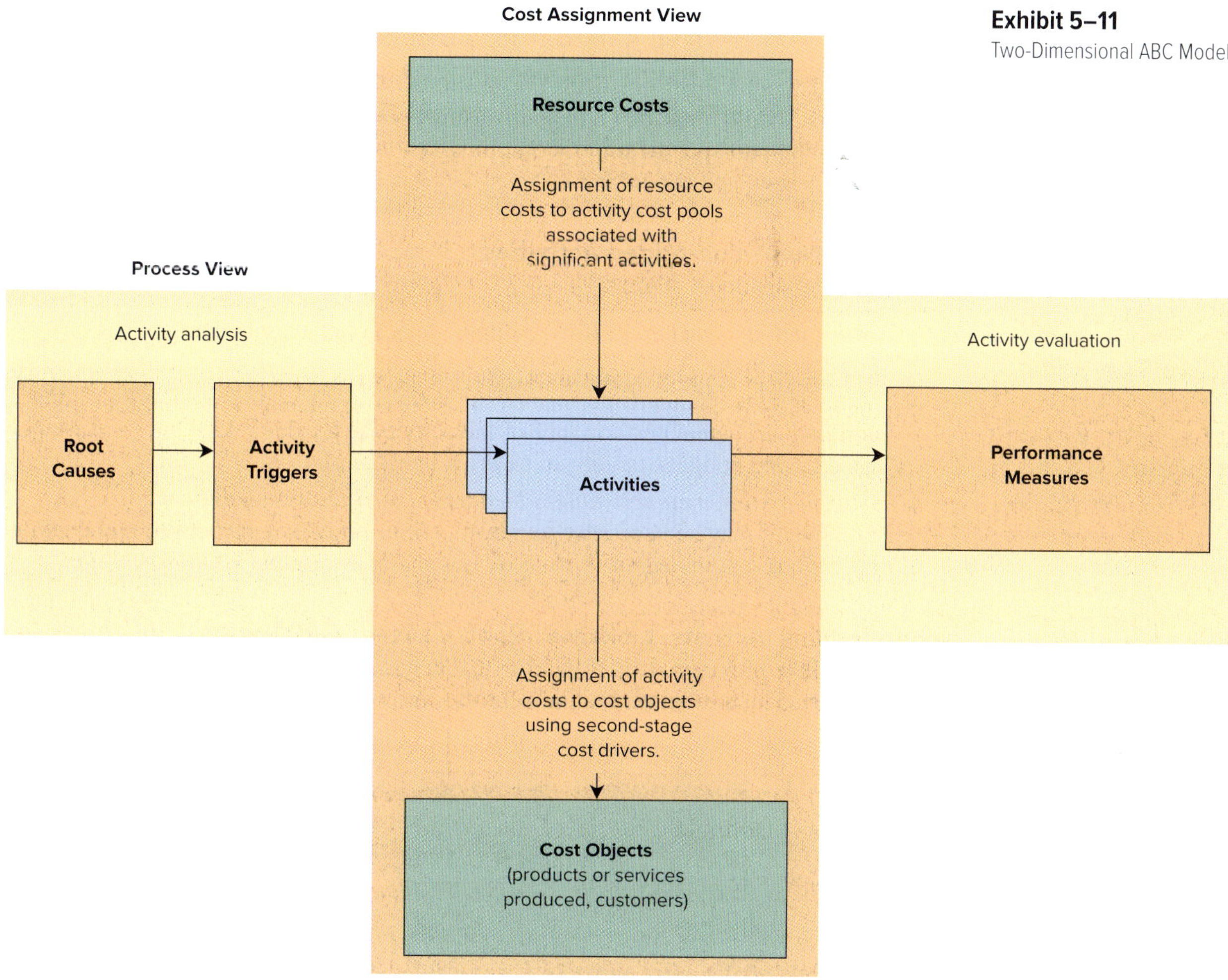

Now focus on the horizontal dimension of the model. Depicted here is the *process view* of an ABC system. The emphasis now is on the activities themselves, the various processes by which work is accomplished in the organization. The left-hand side of Exhibit 5–11 depicts **activity analysis,** which is the detailed identification and description of the activities conducted in the enterprise. Activity analysis entails identification not only of the activities but also of their *root causes,* the events that *trigger* activities, and the *linkages* among activities. The right-hand side of Exhibit 5–11 depicts the evaluation of activities through performance measures. It is these processes of *activity analysis and evaluation* that comprise activity-based management. Notice that the *activities,* which appear in the center of both dimensions in Exhibit 5–11, are the focal point of ABC and ABM.

Using ABM to Identify Non-Value-Added Activities and Costs

An important goal of activity-based management is to identify and eliminate non-value-added activities and costs. **Non-value-added activities** are operations that are either (1) unnecessary and dispensable or (2) necessary, but inefficient and improvable.[5] **Non-value-added costs,** which result from such activities, are the costs of activities that can be eliminated without deterioration of product quality, performance, or perceived value. The following five steps provide a strategy for eliminating non-value-added costs in both manufacturing and service industry firms.

[5]This definition, as well as other material in this section, is drawn from James A. Brimson, "Improvement and Elimination of Non-Value-Added Costs," *Journal of Cost Management* 2, no. 2 (Summer 1988), pp. 62–65.

Identifying Activities The first step is activity analysis, which identifies all of the organization's significant activities. The resulting activity list should be broken down to the most fundamental level practical. For example, rather than listing purchasing as an activity, the list should break down the purchasing operation into its component activities, such as obtaining part specifications, compiling vendor lists, selecting vendors, negotiating prices, ordering, and expediting.

> "You would be surprised. You put a bunch of people in a room to describe how a process works, and they don't all agree with each other - and they all work on the same process." (5f)
> **Dr Pepper Snapple Group**

Identifying Non-Value-Added Activities Three criteria for determining whether an activity adds value are as follows:

- *Is the activity necessary?* If it's a duplicate or nonessential operation, it is non-value-added.
- *Is the activity efficiently performed?* In answering this question, it is helpful to compare the actual performance of the activity to a value-added baseline established using budgets, targets, or external benchmarks.
- *Is an activity sometimes value-added and sometimes non-value-added?* For example, it may be necessary to move work-in-process units between production operations, but unnecessary to move raw materials around while in storage.

Understanding Activity Linkages, Root Causes, and Triggers In identifying non-value-added activities, it is critical to understand the ways in which activities are linked together. The following chain of activities provides an example:

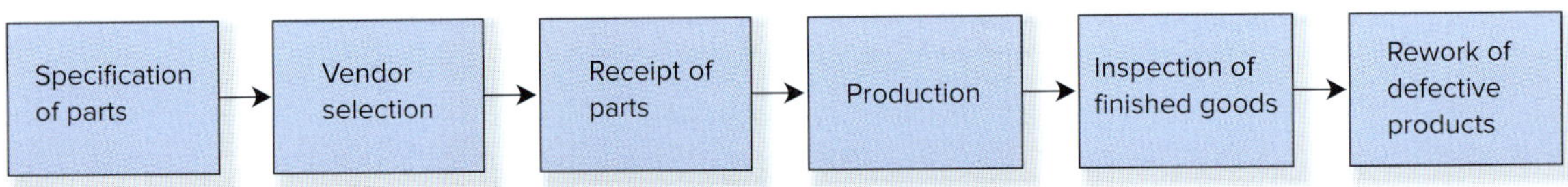

The rework of defective units is a non-value-added activity. The rework is *triggered* by the identification of defective products during inspection. The *root cause* of the rework, however, could lie in any one of a number of preceding activities. Perhaps the part specifications were in error. Possibly an unreliable vendor was selected. Maybe the wrong parts were received. Perhaps the production activity is to blame.

A set of linked activities (such as that depicted above) is called a **process.** Sometimes activity analysis is referred to as **process value analysis (PVA).**

Reporting Non-Value-Added Costs Non-value-added costs should be highlighted in activity center cost reports. By identifying non-value-added activities, and reporting their costs, management can strive toward the ongoing goals of process improvement and elimination of non-value-added costs.

One approach that cost-management analysts find helpful in identifying non-value-added activities is to categorize the ways in which time is spent in a production process. Let's return to our illustration of Patio Grill Company's Denver plant, where gas barbeque grills are manufactured. How is time spent in the plant from the time raw material arrives until a finished gas grill is shipped to a customer? As in most manufacturing operations, time is spent in the following five ways.

1. *Process time.* The time during which a product is undergoing conversion activity.
2. *Inspection time.* The amount of time spent ensuring that the product is of high quality.
3. *Move time.* The time spent moving raw materials, work in process, or finished goods between operations.

4. *Waiting time.* The amount of time that raw materials or work in process spend waiting for the next operation.
5. *Storage time.* The time during which materials, partially completed products, or finished goods are held in stock before further processing or shipment to customers.

Thinking about the production operation in these terms allows management to ask the questions, "Does the time spent in all of these activities add value to the product? Will the customer pay for it? Can the time spent on inspection be reduced without diminishing product quality? Can production efficiency be improved by reducing the number of times materials, work-in-process, or finished goods are moved from one place to another? Can production be scheduled so that partially completed products spend less time just waiting for the next operation? Can storage time be reduced by ordering raw material and producing products only as they are needed?" Many companies have implemented just-in-time (JIT) inventory and production management systems to reduce move, waiting, and storage time. JIT systems are covered in Appendix III at the end of this text.

If reductions can be made in any of these time-consuming activities, without diminishing product quality or functionality, management has a real opportunity to reduce non-value-added costs.

Some companies have begun making a distinction between *customer-value-added activities* and *business-value-added activities.* For example, the addition of a 24/7 customer-service hotline to assist customers in maximizing their benefits from the products or services they have purchased would likely be an activity that customers would value. In contrast, most customers would not value a company's expenditures on information technology (IT) or accounting, whereas these activities are likely to be critical to the success of the company's business model.

One widely used approach to cost reduction during a production process is **kaizen costing.** This Japanese word refers to continual and gradual cost reduction, rather than radical improvement through major innovation or investments in technology. The idea is simple. Improvement is the goal and responsibility of every worker, from the CEO to manual laborers, in every activity, every day, all the time!

Customer-Profitability Analysis

Learning Objective 5-9

Explain and execute a customer-profitability analysis.

It is quite possible for a company to have profitable products and, at the same time, incur customer-related costs that make certain customer relationships unprofitable. **Customer-profitability analysis** uses activity-based costing to determine the activities, costs, and profit associated with serving particular customers. Suppose, for example, that customer X frequently changes its orders after they are placed, but customer Y typically does not. Then the costs incurred in updating sales orders for changes should be recorded in a manner that reflects the fact that customer X is more responsible for those activities and costs than is customer Y. An effective cost management system should allow managers to derive such cost details.

Many factors can result in some customers being more profitable than others. Customers that order in small quantities, order frequently, often change their orders, require special packaging or handling, demand faster delivery, or need special parts or engineering design generally are less profitable than customers who demand less in terms of customized services. If managers have a good understanding of which customers are generating the greatest profit, they can make more-informed decisions about customer service. Moreover, this allows customers to be educated as to the costs they are causing when demanding special services. In many cases, customers' behavior can be changed in a way that reduces costs to the supplier. Then these cost savings can be shared by the supplier and the customer.

The task of assigning costs to customers is a challenge. A system must be in place that enables the company to identify which customers are using customer support services and how frequently they do so. How much time must the company spend on a customer to make the sale and to provide ongoing support services? These costs are in addition to the cost of manufacturing the product or initially providing a service for the customer.

Illustration of Customer-Profitability Analysis

To illustrate customer-profitability analysis, let's focus again on Patio Grill Company. Two more years have passed, and the company has successfully implemented its activity-based costing system in its Denver plant. At a recent strategy meeting with her senior management team, Patio Grill Company's president and CEO expressed interest in assessing the profitability of the entire company's various customer relationships. She found support for the idea from the director of cost management, who had been reading about customer-profitability analysis in some of his professional journals. The company's marketing manager also expressed interest in customer-profitability analysis, since he was concerned about the profitability of a couple of Patio Grill Company's customers in particular. "We have a few customers who seem to want the moon and the stars when it comes to customer service," he complained. "I know the customer is always right and all, but you really have to wonder if we're making any money from a couple of these customers, what with all the extra design and packaging they demand. And some of our other customers seem to require an awful lot of extra attention in sales calls, order processing, and billing. If we had a better idea of each customer's profitability, it would help our marketing and sales staffs to focus their efforts."

"An effective [pricing] strategy should rely on understanding economic profitability at the customer, product and segment level . . . and using that information to inform overall decision-making." (5g)
Deloitte Consulting

The controller soon had his cost management staff attacking the customer-profitability analysis that the president had requested. The first step required an activity-based costing analysis of certain *customer-related costs* that could seriously affect a customer's profitability. Recall that ABC analysis relies on a cost hierarchy with cost levels, such as unit-level, batch-level, product-line-level, customer-level, and facility- or general-operations-level costs. In this use of activity-based costing, the cost management team is focusing on the customer-related costs. After an extensive analysis and several interviews with personnel throughout Patio Grill Company, the cost management team came up with the ABC analysis in Exhibit 5–12.[6]

Based on the activity-based costing information, the cost management team assessed the profitability of each of Patio Grill Company's customer relationships. Detailed information from that analysis for five of these customers appears in the Excel spreadsheet in Exhibit 5–13. These five customers were singled out because three of them are key customers (i.e., customers 106, 112, and 113), and two of them (107 and 119) were suspected by the marketing manager to be at best marginally profitable. As it turned out, suspicions about customers 107 and 119 were well founded. Both customers were found to be unprofitable; in fact, customer 119 had caused a loss of almost $120,000 during the year.

A complete customer-profitability analysis for all of Patio Grill Company's customers appears in the spreadsheet in Exhibit 5–14. This exhibit reveals several interesting aspects of the company's customer-profitability profile. Seventeen of 20 customers are profitable.

Exhibit 5–12
ABC Analysis for Customer-Related Costs: Patio Grill Company

Customer-Related Activities	Cost Driver Base	Cost Driver Rate
Order processing	Purchase orders	$ 150
Sales contacts (phone calls, faxes, etc.)	Contacts	100
Sales visits	Visits	1,000
Shipment processing	Shipments	200
Billing and collection	Invoices	160
Design/engineering change orders	Engineering/design changes	4,000
Special packaging	Units packaged	40
Special handling	Units handled	60

[6]An important point that could be overlooked here is that activity-based costing analysis can be used in a very specific, targeted manner to address a particular management problem. In this case, the ABC focus is customer-profitability analysis. This is the essence of activity-based management, using the results of an ABC analysis to manage an enterprise more effectively.

Exhibit 5–13
Customer-Profitability Analysis for Five Designated Customers: Patio Grill Company

Patio Grill company

	Customer 106	Customer 107	Customer 112	Customer 113	Customer 119
	Designated Customers (by 3-Digit Customer Code)				
Sales revenue	$ 4,320,000	$ 3,480,000	$ 6,500,000	$ 4,490,000	$ 1,960,000
Cost of goods sold	3,220,000	2,810,000	4,890,000	3,380,000	1,480,000
Gross margin	$ 1,100,000	$ 670,000	$ 1,610,000	$ 1,110,000	$ 480,000
Selling and administrative costs:					
General selling costs	$ 362,000	$ 220,000	$ 530,000	$ 366,000	$ 160,000
General administrative costs	181,000	110,000	265,000	183,000	80,000
Customer-related costs:					
Order processing	11,100	80,250	16,050	22,200	38,400
Sales contacts	22,000	13,400	32,000	24,100	28,800
Sales visits	44,000	20,000	47,000	38,000	32,000
Shipment processing	33,000	27,800	64,200	44,600	19,200
Billing and collection	33,600	14,000	80,480	22,400	9,600
Design/engineering changes	93,000	96,000	84,000	112,000	68,000
Special packaging	88,000	27,200	64,440	44,480	76,800
Special handling	33,000	80,400	48,300	33,300	86,400
Total customer-related costs	357,700	359,050	436,470	341,080	359,200
Total selling and administrative costs	$ 900,700	$ 689,050	$ 1,231,470	$ 890,080	$ 599,200
Operating income	$ 199,300	$ (19,050)	$ 378,530	$ 219,920	$ (119,200)

CUSTOMER PROFITABILITY ANALYSIS AT BANK ONE CORP.

The Wall Street Journal described how Bank One Corp. (now part of JPMorgan Chase) has used customer-profitability analysis to guide decisions about customer service.

At Bank One Corp., at the time one of the largest banks, "the line in the sand between preferred and nonpreferred customers has become strikingly obvious." The bank redesigned its 218 branches in Louisiana so that its "Premier One" customers could be whisked away to a special teller window with no wait, or to the desk of an appropriate bank officer. "Customers qualify by keeping at least $2,500 in a checking account or a total of $25,000 in a combination of certain bank accounts," or by paying a $17 monthly fee. "Management estimates that the extra attention will go only to the top 20 percent of its customers."[7]

Management **A**ccounting **P**ractice

Bank One Corp. (now part of JPMorgan Chase)

The three unprofitable customers (107, 134, and 119) resulted in losses of over $240,000 in operating income for Patio Grill Company in a single year! Notice that over 25 percent of the company's profit is generated by its top three customers. Almost half the company's profit comes from its top six customers, and fully three-quarters of its profit is generated by half its customers. This sort of customer-profitability profile is quite typical for manufacturers. The lion's share of most companies' profits comes from a handful of their customers. Such an insight is important for management as it determines where to devote the company's resources in serving customers.[8]

A graphical portrayal of Patio Grill Company's complete customer-profitability analysis is given in Exhibit 5–15. This graph, formally called a **customer-profitability profile,** but more commonly referred to as a "whale chart" because of its characteristic shape, is a common and useful way of presenting the insights from customer-profitability analysis to management.

"Almost any person in any organization that implements ABM has some real surprises when they start seeing the data about customer profitability and product profitability." (5h)
Shiloh Industries, Inc.

[7]"Alienating Customers Isn't Always a Bad Idea Many Firms Discover," *The Wall Street Journal,* January 7, 1999.

[8]In a conversation with a vice president from a large consumer-products manufacturer, the author was struck by the executive's statement that, "You can bet we pay a lot of attention to the needs and desires of the 'Mart Brothers,' K and Wal."

Exhibit 5–14
Customer-Profitability Analysis with Customers Ranked by Operating Income: Patio Grill Company

Patio Grill company

3-Digit Customer Code	Customer Sales Revenue	Customer Gross Margin	Customer Operating Income	Cumulative Operating Income	Cumulative Operating Income as a % of Total Operating Income
112	$ 6,500,000	$ 1,610,000	$ 378,530	$ 378,530	8.8%
108	6,964,000	1,570,000	370,000	748,530	17.3%
114	6,694,000	1,484,300	351,000	1,099,530	25.5%
116	5,846,000	1,461,600	340,000	1,439,530	33.4%
110	5,602,000	1,430,000	336,070	1,775,600	41.1%
121	5,400,000	1,413,000	331,000	2,106,600	48.8%
124	5,601,000	1,405,520	330,000	2,436,600	56.5%
127	5,090,000	1,280,020	300,000	2,736,600	63.4%
128	4,760,000	1,160,200	281,400	3,018,000	69.9%
125	5,000,200	1,181,000	276,000	3,294,000	76.3%
135	4,431,000	1,150,000	270,000	3,564,000	82.6%
133	4,008,000	1,059,800	251,400	3,815,400	88.4%
113	4,490,000	1,110,000	219,920	4,035,320	93.5%
111	4,200,000	875,220	205,000	4,240,320	98.2%
106	4,320,000	1,100,000	199,300	4,439,620	102.9%
136	1,920,000	351,200	82,000	4,521,620	104.8%
137	1,641,000	139,400	35,600	4,557,220	105.6%
107	3,480,000	670,000	(19,050)	4,538,170	105.1%
134	2,820,000	582,000	(102,600)	4,435,570	102.8%
119	1,960,000	480,000	(119,200)	4,316,370	100.0%

Exhibit 5–15
Customer-Profitability Profile in Terms of Cumulative Operating Income as a Percentage of Total Operating Income: Patio Grill Company

Patio Grill company

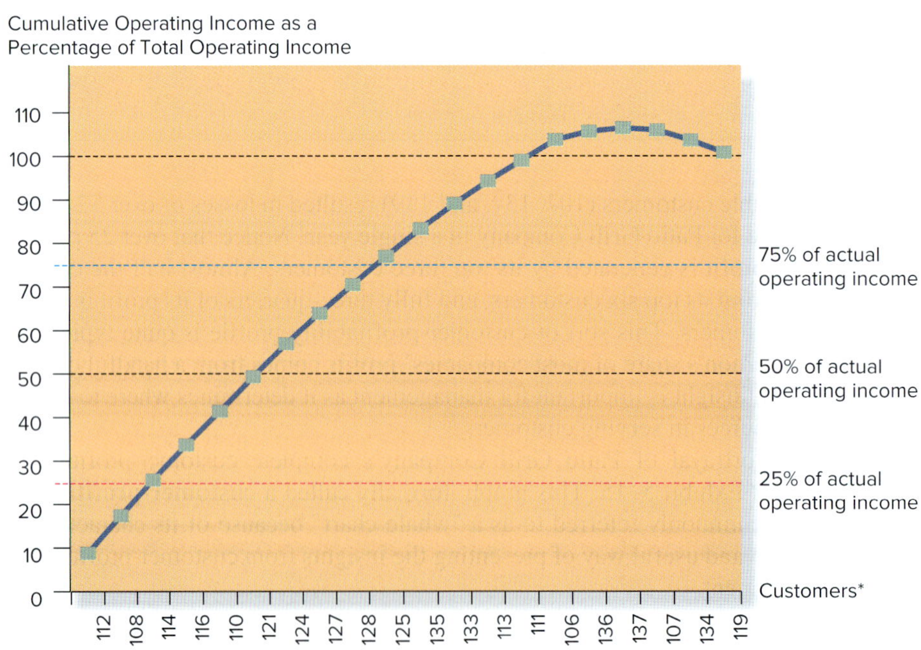

*Customers ranked by operating income.

Activity-Based Costing in the Service Industry

Learning Objective 5-10

Understand and discuss how activity-based costing is used in service-industry organizations.

We conclude this chapter with the important point that activity-based costing has found widespread usage in the service industry as well as in manufacturing. There have been many ABC success stories in such diverse organizations as airlines, insurance companies, banks, hospitals, financial services firms, hotels, railroads, and government agencies. Among the service organizations that have used activity-based costing are Air France, American Airlines, American Express, Bank of America, Cambridge Health Alliance, City of Indianapolis, FedEx, Owens & Minor, Telus, Union Pacific, U.S. Naval Supply Center, and the U.S. Postal Service.

The overall objectives of ABC in service firms are no different than they are in manufacturing companies. Managers want more accurate information about the cost of producing the services they are selling. Moreover, they want to use this information to improve operations and to better meet the needs of their customers in a more cost-effective manner. The general approach of identifying activities, activity cost pools, and cost drivers is used in the service industry as well as in manufacturing. The classification of activities into unit-level, batch-level, product-sustaining-level, and facility-level activities also applies in service industry settings. For example, a Blue Cross Blue Shield health insurance program in Pennsylvania used these activity classifications in its ABC system.[9] Examples from the Blue Cross Blue Shield system are as follows:

- *Unit level:* Entering initial claim data into the computer (for each claim received).
- *Batch level:* Moving a batch of claims from one processing step to the next.
- *Product-sustaining level:* Maintenance of the medical-services provider network (i.e., maintaining relationships with physicians and hospitals providing medical care to claimants).
- *Facility (general operations) level:* General administration of the claims business unit.

"If you know the true cost of providing care, you can ask yourself whether doing one thing is really more important than doing something else. Our mission statement is: the best medical result at the lowest necessary cost . . . But to do that, I've got to be able to measure and manage those costs." (5i)

Intermountain Healthcare

Time-Driven Activity-Based Costing

A version of ABC that has found wide acceptance in service-industry settings is called **time-driven activity-based costing (TDABC)**. In TDABC, costs are generally assumed to be driven by the time taken to perform various activities. As such, it is a simplified form of activity-based costing, and the time-driven element is well aligned with service industries where the resources deployed are often associated with labor and the amount of resources provided can be readily expressed in units of time. An overhead rate per time unit (typically cost per minute) can be calculated by dividing the cost of production overhead by the *practical capacity* of the company's resources expressed in time (minutes). The cost of an activity is simply the overhead cost per minute multiplied by the number of minutes the activity is expected to take.

The TDABC approach has two main advantages over conventional ABC:

- It is much easier to collect the time-based resource and activity data than it is to collect data on the variety of measures used in conventional ABC, many of which are not normally tracked by the company.
- Because the time-driven cost driver rate is calculated based on the practical capacity of the (often human) resources provided to perform the activities, the TDABC system will not assign costs to products or services for capacity that is (or should be) unused, instead leaving it unapplied as cost of excess capacity.

[9] Angela Norkiewicz, "Nine Steps to Implementing ABC," *Management Accounting* 75, no. 10 (April 1994), pp. 28–33.

The latter advantage has a dual benefit of assigning less cost to products or services, which makes the managers responsible for them happier, while also highlighting for management the cost associated with having capacity that is unused.[10]

Activity-Based Costing at Immunity Medical Center

Immunity Medical Center

To see how management can use activity-based costing in a service-industry setting, let's explore how TDABC is used at Immunity Medical Center's Primary Care Unit.[11] Immunity Medical Center serves patients in Raleigh, North Carolina, and several surrounding counties. The Primary Care Unit is the medical center's outpatient clinic and provides nearly 25,000 patient appointments in a typical year. The Primary Care Unit's administration implemented time-driven activity-based costing in order to determine how much it costs to serve patients in various categories. The most significant activities, representing almost 80 percent of spending, are time driven, although a few non-time cost drivers are included as well. Overall, it is reasonable to characterize this as a TDABC system. Notice that, consistent with TDABC, the Cost Driver Quantity for each cost driver associated with an activity cost pool is the practical capacity of that cost driver.

The Primary Care Unit classifies patient appointments as routine, extended, or complex, depending on the appointment length and complexity. In addition, each appointment is classified as either a new-patient appointment or a continuing-patient appointment. Thus, every patient appointment is one of the following six types.

	Routine	Extended	Complex
New patient	New patient; routine appointment	New patient; extended appointment	New patient; complex appointment
Continuing patient	Continuing patient; routine appointment	Continuing patient; extended appointment	Continuing patient; complex appointment

Every patient appointment involves a registered nurse (RN), who takes vital signs and prepares the patient for the primary health care professional. Then, every patient is seen by one primary health care professional, which can be a physician, a nurse practitioner, an intern, or a resident. No appointment involves more than one of these types of primary health care professionals.

The Primary Care Unit's TDABC project team designated the following activities and cost drivers.

Activity	Cost Driver
Physician time	Physician minutes with patient
Nurse practitioner time	Nurse practitioner minutes with patient
Intern or resident time	Intern or resident minutes with patient
Registered nurse time	Registered nurse minutes with patient
Clerical time: new patients	New patient visits
Clerical time: continuing patients	Continuing patient visits
Billing	Billing lines (i.e., number of line items on bill)
Facility	Patient visits (both new and continuing)

[10]TDABC is covered in greater detail in Cost Accounting texts. For a more detailed introduction to the technique, see Robert S. Kaplan and Steven R. Anderson, "Time-Driven Activity-Based Costing," *Harvard Business Review*, November 2004. For a discussion of the pros and cons of TDABC vs. conventional ABC, see Gary Cokins and Douglas Paul, "Time-Driven or Driver Rate-Based ABC: How Do You Choose?" *Strategic Finance*, February 2016.

[11]For a thorough discussion of costing in a medical context, including the application of time-driven activity-based costing (TDABC) in that setting, see Robert S. Kaplan and Michael E. Porter, "The Big Idea: How to Solve the Cost Crisis in Health Care," *Harvard Business Review*, September 2011. For a more elaborate example of activity-based costing in a hospital's primary care unit, see V. G. Narayanan, R. Moore, and L. Brem, "Cambridge Hospital Community Health Care Network—The Primary Care Unit" (Boston: The President and Fellows of Harvard College, 2000). In this case, minutes of time with a health care professional is a key cost driver.

Exhibit 5–16

Time-Driven Activity-Based Costing Analysis: Immunity Medical Center

Immunity Medical Center

Immunity Medical Center_Time-Driven Activity-Based Costing Analysis - Excel

FILE HOME INSERT PAGE LAYOUT FORMULAS DATA REVIEW VIEW David Platt

E7 =B7/D7

	A	B	C	D	E	F	G	H	I	J	K
1				Cost						Activity	
2				Driver			Cost Driver	Activity	Patient	Cost per	
3		Activity		Quantity		Patient	Quantity for	Cost for	Visit	Patient	
4		Cost	Cost	(Practical	Pool	Visit	Patient	Patient	Type	Visit of	
5	Activity	Pool	Driver	Capacity)	Rate	Type	Visit Type	Visit Type	Volume	Each Type	
6											
7	Physician	$ 960,000	Physician	240,000	$ 4.00	Routine	80,000	$ 320,000	8,000	$ 40.00	
8	Time		Minutes			Extended	100,000	400,000	5,000	80.00	
9			With Patient			Complex	60,000	240,000	2,000	120.00	
10						Total	240,000	$ 960,000			
11	Nurse	90,000	NP	30,000	3.00	Routine	12,000	$ 36,000	1,200	30.00	
12	Practitioner		Minutes			Extended	10,000	30,000	500	60.00	
13	(NP) Time		With Patient			Complex	8,000	24,000	320	75.00	
14						Total	30,000	$ 90,000			
15	Intern or	412,500	I/R	125,000	3.30	Routine	40,000	$ 132,000	4,000	33.00	
16	Resident		Minutes			Extended	50,000	165,000	2,500	66.00	
17	(I/R) Time		With Patient			Complex	35,000	115,500	1,000	115.50	
18						Total	125,000	$ 412,500			
19	Registered	281,980	RN	245,200	1.15	Routine	132,000	$ 151,800	13,200	11.50	
20	Nurse		Minutes			Extended	80,000	92,000	8,000	11.50	
21	(RN) Time		With Patient			Complex	33,200	38,180	3,320	11.50	
22						Total	245,200	$ 281,980			
23	Clerical Time:	135,300	New	12,300	11.00	Routine	7,200	$ 79,200	7,200	11.00	
24	New		Patient			Extended	3,000	33,000	3,000	11.00	
25	Patients		Visits			Complex	2,100	23,100	2,100	11.00	
26						Total	12,300	$ 135,300			
27	Clerical Time:	61,100	Continuing	12,220	5.00	Routine	6,000	$ 30,000	6,000	5.00	
28	Continuing		Patient			Extended	5,000	25,000	5,000	5.00	
29	Patients		Visits			Complex	1,220	6,100	1,220	5.00	
30						Total	12,220	$ 61,100			
31	Billing	38,480	Billing	76,960	0.50	Routine	26,400	$ 13,200	13,200	1.00	
32			Lines			Extended	24,000	12,000	8,000	1.50	
33						Complex	26,560	13,280	3,320	4.00	
34						Total	76,960	$ 38,480			
35	Facility	245,200	Patient	24,520	10.00	Routine	13,200	$ 132,000	13,200	10.00	
36			Visits			Extended	8,000	80,000	8,000	10.00	
37			(Both New &			Complex	3,320	33,200	3,320	10.00	
38			Continuing)			Total	24,520	$ 245,200			
39											
40	Grand Total	$2,224,560				Grand Total		$2,224,560			
41											

TDABC Pool Calculations

READY 100%

The time-driven activity-based costing analysis is displayed in the Excel spreadsheet in Exhibit 5–16. Notice that this TDABC spreadsheet for Immunity Medical Center's Primary Care Unit has a format that is identical to the ABC spreadsheet prepared for Patio Grill Company (Exhibit 5–7). The column headings are different, because the Primary Care Unit provides medical services to patients, whereas Patio Grill Company manufactures barbeque grills. Conceptually and computationally, however, the two Excel spreadsheets are identical.

The information supplied by the Primary Care Unit's TDABC project team is located in the following columns.

Column A: Activity
Column B: Activity cost pool
Column C: Cost driver
Column D: Cost driver quantity (practical capacity)
Column F: Patient visit type (routine, extended, or complex)
Column G: Cost driver quantity for each type of patient visit
Column I: Patient volume for each type of visit

The TDABC computations are in columns E, H, and J and are shown in red.

Column E: Pool rate

$$\text{Pool rate (column E)} = \text{Activity cost pool (column B)} \div \text{Cost driver quantity (column D)}$$

For example, the pool rate for physician time (cell E7) is calculated as follows:

$$\$4.00 \text{ per physician minute} = \$960{,}000 \div 240{,}000 \text{ minutes of physician time}$$

Column H: Activity cost for patient type

$$\text{Activity cost for patient visit type (column H)} = \text{Pool rate (column E)} \times \text{Cost driver quantity for patient visit type (column G)}$$

For example, the physician activity cost for a routine visit (cell H7) is calculated as follows:

$$\$320{,}000 = \$4.00 \text{ per physician minute} \times 80{,}000 \text{ physician minutes on routine visits}$$

Column J: Activity cost per patient visit of each type

$$\text{Activity cost per patient visit of each type (column J)} = \text{Activity cost for patient visit type (column H)} \div \text{Patient visit type volume (column I)}$$

For example, the physician activity cost per routine patient visit (cell J7) is calculated as follows:

$$\$40 \text{ per routine visit attended by a physician} = \$320{,}000 \div 8{,}000 \text{ routine visits attended by a physician}$$

Interpreting the Primary Care Unit's TDABC Information

The Immunity Medical Center Primary Care Unit's administration can use the TDABC information in Exhibit 5–16 to determine the cost of each of the six types of patient appointments discussed earlier. Notice, though, that there is an important conceptual difference in the interpretation of the Primary Care Unit's TDABC data in Exhibit 5–16 versus the interpretation of Patio Grill Company's ABC data in Exhibit 5–7.

In the Patio Grill Company manufacturing illustration, *all eight of the activities* identified in the ABC analysis were required by each line of barbeque grills manufactured. However, that is not true in the Primary Care Unit example. In this health care services setting, each patient sees *either* a physician, *or* a nurse practitioner, *or* an intern, *or* a resident—not all four. Moreover, each patient is *either* a new patient *or* a continuing patient—not both.

Therefore, to compute the cost of a particular type of appointment, we must *select only one of the primary health care professionals,* which are highlighted by the red bar on the right-hand side of Exhibit 5–16. Moreover, we select *just one of the two categories for clerical time,* new patient or continuing patient, which are highlighted by the green bar on the right-hand side of Exhibit 5–16. Finally, since every patient appointment involves a registered nurse, *and* billing, *and* use of the primary care unit facility, *all* of these activities must be included in the cost calculation. (These activities are highlighted by the yellow bars on the right-hand side of Exhibit 5–16.)

Let's compute the cost of an extended appointment in which a new patient sees a nurse practitioner.

Activity	Cost (spreadsheet cell)
Nurse practitioner time	$60.00 (cell J12 in Exhibit 5–16)
Registered nurse time	11.50 (cell J20)
Clerical time: new patients	11.00 (cell J24)
Billing	1.50 (cell J32)
Facility	10.00 (cell J36)
Total	$94.00

Now let's compute the cost of a routine appointment in which a continuing patient sees a physician.

Activity	Cost (spreadsheet cell)
Physician time	$40.00 (cell J7 in Exhibit 5–16)
Registered nurse time	11.50 (cell J19)
Clerical time: continuing patients	5.00 (cell J27)
Billing	1.00 (cell J31)
Facility	10.00 (cell J35)
Total	$67.50

With a good understanding of how much it costs the Primary Care Unit to provide various types of patient appointments, the clinic's administration is in a much better position to make decisions. Determining appropriate charges for appointments, justifying third-party reimbursements from insurance companies and government agencies, and adding or discontinuing services are among the types of decisions that will be enhanced by the ABC information.

Focus on Ethics

ETHICAL ISSUES SURROUNDING ACTIVITY-BASED COSTING

Xavier Auto Parts, Inc. manufactures a wide range of auto parts, which it sells to auto manufacturers, primarily in the United States and Canada.* The company's Engine Parts Division operated three plants in South Carolina and specialized in engine parts. The division's Charlotte plant manufactured some 6,500 different parts.

Trouble Brewing

Both the Engine Parts Division, as well as the Charlotte plant in particular, had shown satisfactory profitability for the past 20 years. In 2013, however, the Charlotte plant's profitability took a sharp downward turn, in spite of rising sales. The trend continued through the next several years. Management at both the division and plant levels took note of the plant's declining profits and held several strategy meetings as a result.

Division Strategy

The Engine Parts Division had always positioned itself as the industry's full-line producer. If a customer wanted a product, the division would make it. Although occasionally very-low-volume products were discontinued due to lack of consistent orders, the division's product line remained a full line of engine parts. As part of its strategy review, division management did two things. First, an activity-based costing study was initiated in the Charlotte plant in order to give management a better picture of each product line's profitability. Second, a high-level review was undertaken to determine whether the full-line-producer strategy continued to make sense.

Activity-based Costing

An ABC project team was formed, and a successful pilot study was conducted on two of the Charlotte plant's product lines. Then the ABC project was extended to the entire Charlotte operation. Management was astonished to find that fully a quarter of the plant's products were selling at a loss. Moreover, the ABC project highlighted the extent of the product-line proliferation at the Charlotte plant. It turned out that in many instances, unprofitable products had been dropped only to creep back into the product line-up after a customer requested it and a salesperson acquiesced. It became a joke around the plant that the only way to be sure a dropped product was really gone was to burn the engineering drawings and destroy the special tools required to make it.

ABC Team Recommendations

The ABC project team made sweeping recommendations to division management, which suggested that the Charlotte plant's product lines be pruned and that roughly 20 percent of its products be dropped. New emphasis would then be devoted to increasing the profitability of the remaining 80 percent of the Charlotte plant's products. Attention would be given to identifying inefficient processes, and process improvements would be evaluated.

Top Management Response

Top management balked at the recommendations of the ABC project team. Some top managers did not believe the ABC results. It just seemed impossible to them that so many of the Charlotte plant's products were losers. Other members of the management team largely accepted the validity of the ABC study, but they, too, hesitated to drop so many products. To do so would most likely have meant massive layoffs and even the possibility of closing the Charlotte plant altogether, while shifting its remaining production to the division's other two plants. Some members of the ABC project team quietly speculated that some of the division's managers were more concerned about their own pay and perks than they were about the well-being of the division. In the final analysis, only a handful of products were dropped, and then only if they were suspected to be unprofitable before the ABC study was undertaken.

Aftermath

The Charlotte plant's profits continued to deteriorate, as did the Engine Parts Division's profitability. Eventually, Xavier's corporate management cut its losses by selling off the Engine Parts Division to a competitor at bargain-basement prices. The division's new owners closed the Charlotte plant and changed the division's focus to be a boutique producer of high-quality engine parts, which was more in line with its own corporate strategy.

Ethical Issues

What ethical issues do you see in this scenario? How would you resolve them?

---

*The scenario described here, while fictitious, is based on several real-world events described in the ABC literature. Anecdotes in various ABC cases and other sources, as well as the author's research, form the basis for the events described. A key source is the well-known "Schrader-Bellows" case, by R. Cooper (Boston: President and Fellows of Harvard College), which remains a classic case describing issues surrounding activity-based costing.

Chapter Summary

LO5-1 Compute product costs under a traditional, volume-based product-costing system. Traditional product-costing systems are structured on single, volume-based cost drivers, such as direct labor or machine hours. Overhead is applied to production jobs using a predetermined overhead rate, which is based on estimates of manufacturing overhead (in the numerator) and the level of some cost driver (in the denominator).

LO5-2 Explain how an activity-based costing system operates, including the use of a two-stage procedure for cost assignment, the identification of activity cost pools, and the selection of cost drivers. In the first stage of ABC, resource costs are identified and divided into activity cost pools. In the second stage, a cost driver is selected for each activity cost pool, and the costs in each pool are assigned to cost objects, such as products, services, product lines, customers, and so forth.

LO5-3 Explain the concept of cost levels, including unit-level, batch-level, product-sustaining-level, and facility-level costs. Unit-level costs are incurred for each unit produced. Batch-level costs are incurred once for each batch of products (i.e., one production run). Product-sustaining-level costs are incurred once for each product line. Facility-level costs are incurred to keep the overall facility in operation.

LO5-4 Compute product costs under an activity-based costing system. A product's cost is the sum of its direct-material cost, its direct-labor cost, and its overhead cost, which is the accumulation of all the resource costs driven to the product by the various cost drivers selected for the ABC system.

LO5-5 Explain why traditional, volume-based costing systems tend to distort product costs. Traditional, volume-based costing systems tend to distort product costs because of two factors: (1) product-line diversity and (2) non-unit-level overhead costs. No single cost driver can capture the complex relationships between products and the myriad activities necessary to produce and sell them.

LO5-6 Explain three criteria for selecting cost drivers. Three criteria for selecting cost drivers are: (1) the degree of correlation between the cost driver and the incurrence of costs in the activity cost pool associated with the cost driver; (2) the cost of measurement of the cost driver; and (3) the behavioral effects that might result from the selection of a cost driver.

LO5-7 Discuss several key issues in activity-based costing, including data collection and storyboarding. Collecting ABC data is difficult and costly. Techniques for data collection include interviews, examination of work product and other documentation, and sometimes storyboarding, which is a detailed map of the processes used in the organization.

LO5-8 Explain the concepts of activity-based management and two-dimensional ABC. Activity-based management (ABM) is the use of activity-based costing information to improve operations and eliminate non-value-added costs. One way of depicting ABM is the two-dimensional ABC model. This model combines the cost assignment role of ABC with the process and activity evaluation view of an ABC system.

LO5-9 Explain and execute a customer-profitability analysis. Customer profitability analysis is an application of ABM in which management determines the cost drivers for customer-related costs. The resulting ABC information is then used to assess the profitability of key customer relationships.

LO5-10 Understand and discuss how activity-based costing is used in service-industry organizations. Activity-based costing has found widespread successful implementation in the service industry. While structurally similar to ABC in manufacturing, employing the same two-stage costing model, ABC in the service industry often takes the form of time-driven activity-based costing (TDABC). In TDABC, the practical capacity of activities and the quantity of the cost driver are both measured in units of time.

Review Problem on Cost Drivers and Product-Cost Distortion

Edgeworth Box Corporation manufactures a variety of special packaging boxes used in the pharmaceutical industry. The company's Dallas plant is semiautomated, but the special nature of the boxes requires some manual labor. The controller has chosen the following activity cost pools, cost drivers, and pool rates for the Dallas plant's product-costing system.

Activity Cost Pool	Overhead Cost	Cost Driver	Budgeted Level for Cost Driver	Pool Rate
Purchasing, storage, and material handling	$ 200,000	Raw-material costs	$ 1,000,000	20% of material cost
Engineering and product design	100,000	Hours in design department	5,000 hrs.	$20 per hour
Machine setup costs	70,000	Production runs	1,000 runs	$70 per run
Machine depreciation and maintenance	300,000	Machine hours	100,000 hrs.	$3 per hour
Factory depreciation, taxes, insurance, and utilities	200,000	Machine hours	100,000 hrs.	$2 per hour
Other manufacturing-overhead costs	150,000	Machine hours	100,000 hrs.	$1.50 per hour
Total	$1,020,000			

Two recent production orders had the following requirements.

	20,000 Units of Box C52	10,000 Units of Box W29
Direct-labor hours	42 hr.	21 hr.
Raw-material cost	$40,000	$35,000
Hours in design department	10	25
Production runs	2	4
Machine hours	24	20

Required:

1. Compute the total overhead that should be assigned to each of the two production orders, C52 and W29.
2. Compute the overhead cost per box in each order.
3. Suppose the Dallas plant were to use a single predetermined overhead rate based on direct-labor hours. The direct-labor budget calls for 4,000 hours.

   a. Compute the predetermined overhead rate per direct-labor hour.

   b. Compute the total overhead cost that would be assigned to the order for box C52 and the order for box W29.

   c. Compute the overhead cost per box in each order.
4. Why do the two product-costing systems yield such widely differing overhead costs per box?

Solution to Review Problem

1.

	Box C52	Box W29
Purchasing, storage, and material handling	$8,000 (20% × $40,000)	$7,000 (20% × $35,000)
Engineering and product design	200 (10 × $20/hr.)	500 (25 × $20/hr.)
Machine setup costs	140 (2 × $70/run)	280 (4 × $70/run)
Machine depreciation and maintenance	72 (24 × $3/hr.)	60 (20 × $3/hr.)
Factory depreciation, taxes, insurance, and utilities	48 (24 × $2/hr.)	40 (20 × $2/hr.)
Other manufacturing overhead costs	36 (24 × $1.50/hr.)	30 (20 × $1.50/hr.)
Total overhead assigned to production order	$8,496	$7,910

2. Overhead cost: Box C52 = $0.4248 per box $\left(\frac{\$8,496}{20,000}\right)$; Box W29 = $0.79 per box $\left(\frac{\$7,910}{10,000}\right)$

3. Computations based on a single predetermined overhead rate based on direct-labor hours:

   a. $\frac{\text{Total budgeted overhead}}{\text{Total budgeted direct-labor hours}} = \frac{\$1,020,000}{4,000} = \$255\text{/hr.}$

   b. Total overhead assigned to each order:

   Box C52 order: 42 direct-labor hours × $255/hr. = $10,710

   Box W29 order: 21 direct-labor hours × $255/hr. = $5,355

   c. Overhead cost per box:

   Box C52: $10,710 ÷ 20,000 = $.5355 per box

   Box W29: $5,355 ÷ 10,000 = $.5355 per box

4. The widely differing overhead costs are assigned as a result of the inherent inaccuracy of the single, volume-based overhead rate. The relative usage of direct labor by the two production orders does not reflect their relative usage of other manufacturing support services.

Key Terms

For each term's definition refer to the indicated page, or turn to the glossary at the end of the text.

activity analysis, 187
activity-based costing (ABC) system, 172
activity-based management (ABM), 186
activity cost pool, 172
activity dictionary, 186
batch-level activity, 173
bill of activities, 186
consumption ratio, 181
cost driver, 183
cost hierarchy, 173
customer-profitability analysis, 189
customer profitability profile, 191
facility-(or general-operations) level activity, 173
kaizen costing, 189
non-value-added activities, 187
non-value-added costs, 187
pool rate, 175
process, 188
process value analysis (PVA), 188
product-sustaining-level activity, 173
storyboarding, 185
two-dimensional ABC model, 186
unit-level activity, 173
volume-based (or through-put-based) costing system, 171

Review Questions

5–1. Briefly explain how a traditional, volume-based product-costing system operates.

5–2. Why was Patio Grill Company's management being misled by the traditional product-costing system? What mistakes were being made?

5–3. Explain how an activity-based costing system operates.

5–4. What are cost drivers? What is their role in an activity-based costing system?

5–5. List and briefly describe the four broad categories of activities identified in stage one of an activity-based costing system.

5–6. How can an activity-based costing system alleviate the problems Patio Grill Company's management was having under its traditional, volume-based product-costing system?

5–7. Why do product-costing systems based on a single, volume-based cost driver tend to overcost high-volume products? What undesirable strategic effects can such distortion of product costs have?

5–8. How is the distinction between direct and indirect costs handled differently under volume-based versus activity-based costing systems?

5–9. Explain the concept of a *pool rate* in activity-based costing. (Refer to Exhibit 5-6.)

5–10. Briefly explain two factors that tend to result in product cost distortion under traditional, volume-based product-costing systems.

5–11. List three factors that are important in selecting cost drivers for an ABC system.

5–12. What is the role of *activity dictionary* in an ABC project?

5–13. Explain why a new product-costing system may be needed when line managers suggest that an apparently profitable product be dropped.

5–14. Explain why a manufacturer with diverse product lines may benefit from an ABC system.

5–15. Are activity-based costing systems appropriate for the service industry? Explain.

5–16. Explain why maintaining their medical-services provider network is treated as a product-sustaining-level activity by Blue Cross Blue Shield.

5–17. How could the administration at Immunity Medical Center's Primary Care Unit use the information developed by the TDABC project team?

5–18. Explain a key difference in the interpretation of the ABC data in Exhibit 5-7 (Patio Grill Company) and the TDABC data in Exhibit 5-16 (Immunity Medical Center).

5–19. Explain the concept of *two-dimensional ABC.* Support your explanation with a diagram.

5–20. What is meant by the term *activity analysis?* Give three criteria for determining whether an activity adds value.

5–21. Distinguish between an activity's trigger and its root cause. Give an example of each.

5–22. What is meant by customer-profitability analysis? Give an example of an activity that might be performed more commonly for one customer than for another.

5–23. Explain the relationship between customer profitability analysis and activity-based costing.

5–24. What is a customer profitability profile?

5–25. Describe the use of practical capacity in a TDABC system.

Exercises

All applicable Exercises are available in Connect.

Exercise 5–26
Volume-Based Cost Driver versus ABC
(LO 5-1, 5-2, 5-4)

Tioga Company manufactures sophisticated lenses and mirrors used in large optical telescopes. The company is now preparing its annual profit plan. As part of its analysis of the profitability of individual products, the controller estimates the amount of overhead that should be allocated to the individual product lines from the following information.

	Lenses	Mirrors
Units produced	25	25
Material moves per product line	5	15
Direct-labor hours per unit	200	200

The total budgeted material-handling cost is $50,000.

Required:

1. Under a costing system that allocates overhead on the basis of direct-labor hours, the material-handling costs allocated to one lens would be what amount?
2. Answer the same question as in requirement (1), but for mirrors.
3. Under activity-based costing (ABC), the material-handling costs allocated to one lens would be what amount? The cost driver for the material-handling activity is the number of material moves.
4. Answer the same question as in requirement (3), but for mirrors.

(CMA, adapted)

Exercise 5–27
Activity-Based Costing; Quality Control Costs
(LO 5-1, 5-2, 5-4)

Urban Elite Cosmetics has used a traditional cost accounting system to apply quality-control costs uniformly to all products at a rate of 14.5 percent of direct-labor cost. Monthly direct-labor cost for Satin Sheen makeup is $27,500. In an attempt to more equitably distribute quality-control costs, management is considering activity-based costing. The monthly data shown in the following chart have been gathered for Satin Sheen makeup.

Activity Cost Pool	Cost Driver	Pool Rates	Quantity of Driver for Satin Sheen
Incoming material inspection	Type of material	$11.50 per type	12 types
In-process inspection	Number of units	.14 per unit	17,500 units
Product certification	Per order	77.00 per order	25 orders

Required:

1. Calculate the monthly quality-control cost to be assigned to the Satin Sheen product line under each of the following product-costing systems. (Round to the nearest dollar.)
   a. Traditional system, which assigns overhead on the basis of direct-labor cost.
   b. Activity-based costing.
2. Does the traditional product-costing system overcost or undercost the Satin Sheen product line with respect to quality-control costs? By what amount?

(CMA, adapted)

Exercise 5–28
Cost Drivers; Activity Cost Pools
(LO 5-2, 5-3, 5-6)

Kentaro Corporation manufactures Digital Video Recorders (DVRs) in its Tokyo plant. The following costs are budgeted for January. (Yen is the Japanese monetary unit.)

Raw materials and components	2,950,000 *yen*
Insurance, plant	600,000
Electricity, machinery	120,000
Electricity, light	60,000
Engineering design	610,000
Depreciation, plant	700,000
Depreciation, machinery	1,400,000
Custodial wages, plant	40,000
Equipment maintenance, wages	150,000
Equipment maintenance, parts	30,000
Setup wages	40,000
Inspection of finished goods	30,000
Property taxes	120,000
Natural gas, heating	30,000

Required: Divide these costs into activity cost pools, and identify a cost driver for assigning each pool of costs to products. Calculate the total cost in each activity cost pool.

Exercise 5–29
Categorizing Activity Cost Pools
(LO 5-2, 5-3)

Refer to the information given in the preceding exercise. For each of the activity cost pools identified, indicate whether it represents a unit-level, batch-level, product-sustaining-level, or facility-level activity.

Exercise 5–30
Activity-Based Costing in a Government Agency; Use of Internet
(LO 5-2, 5-7, 5-10)

Visit the website of a city, state, or Canadian province of your choosing (e.g., the City of Charlotte, N.C., www.charmeck.org).

Required: Read about the services offered to the public by this governmental unit. Then discuss how activity-based costing could be used effectively by the governmental unit to determine the cost of providing these services.

Exercise 5–31
Distortion of Product Costs
(LO 5-2, 5-5)

Wheelco, Inc. manufactures automobile and truck wheels. The company produces four basic, high-volume wheels used by each of the large automobile and pickup truck manufacturers. Wheelco also has two specialty wheel lines. These are fancy, complicated wheels used in expensive sports cars.

Lately, Wheelco's profits have been declining. Foreign competitors have been undercutting Wheelco's prices in three of its bread-and-butter product lines, and Wheelco's sales volume and market share have declined. In contrast, Wheelco's specialty wheels have been selling steadily, although in relatively small numbers, in spite of three recent price increases. At a recent staff meeting, Wheelco's president made the following remarks: "Our profits are going down the tubes, folks. It costs us 29 dollars to manufacture our A22 wheel. That's our best seller, with a volume last year of 17,000 units. But our chief competitor is selling basically the same wheel for 27 bucks. I don't see how they can do it. I think it's just one more example of foreign dumping. I'm going to write my senator about it! Thank goodness for our specialty wheels. I think we've got to get our salespeople to push those wheels more and more. Take the D52 model, for example. It's a complicated thing to make, and we don't sell many. But look at the profit margin. Those wheels cost us 49 dollars to make, and we're selling them for 105 bucks each."

Required: What do you think is behind the problems faced by Wheelco? Comment on the president's remarks. Do you think his strategy is a good one? What do you recommend, and why?

Exercise 5–32
Key Features of Activity-Based Costing
(LO 5-2, 5-5, 5-7)

Refer to the description given for Wheelco, Inc. in the preceding exercise. Suppose the firm's president has decided to implement an activity-based costing system.

Required:

1. List and briefly describe the key features that Wheelco's new product-costing system should have.
2. What impact will the new system be likely to have on the company's situation?
3. What strategic options would you expect to be suggested by the product-costing results from the new system?

Exercise 5–33
Winery; Classification of Activities
(LO 5-2, 5-3, 5-7)

Finger Lakes Winery is a small, family-run operation in upstate New York. The winery produces two varieties of wine: riesling and chardonnay. Among the activities engaged in by the winery are the following:

1. *Trimming:* At the end of a growing season, the vines are trimmed, which helps prepare them for the next harvest.
2. *Tying:* The vines are tied onto wires to help protect them from the cold. (This also occurs at the end of the season.)
3. *Hilling:* Dirt is piled up around the roots to help protect them from frost.
4. *Conditioning:* After the snow melts in the spring, dirt is leveled back from the roots.
5. *Untying:* The vines are untied from the wires to allow them freedom to grow during the spring and summer months.
6. *Chemical spraying:* The vines are sprayed in the spring to protect them from disease and insects.
7. *Harvesting:* All of the grapes of both varieties are picked by hand to minimize damage.
8. *Stemming and crushing:* Batches of grapes are hand-loaded into a machine, which gently removes the stems and mildly crushes them.
9. *Pressing:* After removal from the stemmer/crusher, the juice runs freely from the grapes.
10. *Filtering:* The grapes are crushed mechanically to render more juice from them.
11. *Fermentation:* The riesling grape juice is placed in stainless steel tanks for fermentation. The chardonnay grape juice undergoes a two-stage fermentation process in oak barrels.
12. *Aging:* The riesling wines are aged in the stainless steel tanks for approximately a year. The chardonnays are aged in the oak barrels for about two years.
13. *Bottling:* A machine bottles the wine and corks the bottles.
14. *Labeling:* Each bottle is manually labeled with the name of the vintner, vintage, and variety.
15. *Packing:* The bottles are manually packed in 12-bottle cases.
16. *Case labeling:* The cases are hand-stamped with the same information that the bottles received.
17. *Shipping:* The wine is shipped to wine distributors and retailers, mainly in central New York. Generally, about 100 cases are shipped at a time.
18. *Maintenance on buildings:* This is done during the slow winter months.
19. *Maintenance on equipment:* This is done when needed, and on a routine basis for preventive maintenance.

Required: Classify each of the activities listed as a unit-, batch-, product-sustaining-, or facility-level activity.

Exercise 5–34
United Technologies; Classification of Activities
(LO 5-2, 5-3, 5-7)

United Technologies Corporation implemented activity-based costing in two of its subsidiaries: Otis Elevator Company and Carrier Corporation. The following table shows 27 activities and eight accounts identified at Carrier, along with the classification determined by the ABC project team.[12]

Name of Activity or Account	Classification by Activity level
Acquiring material	Batch
Inspecting incoming materials	Batch
Moving materials	Batch
Planning production	Batch
Processing special orders	Batch
Processing supplier invoices	Batch
Receiving material	Batch
Scheduling production	Batch
Inspecting production processes	Batch
Processing purchase orders	Batch
Building occupancy	Facility
Depreciation	Facility
General management	Facility
Maintaining facilities	Facility
Managing the environment	Facility
Assuring quality	Product Sustaining
Expediting	Product Sustaining
Maintaining tools and dies	Product Sustaining
Maintaining/improving production processes	Product Sustaining
Managing human resources	Product Sustaining
Managing waste disposal	Product Sustaining
Processing payroll	Product Sustaining
Processing production information	Product Sustaining
Providing product cost	Product Sustaining
Setting manufacturing methods	Product Sustaining
Supervising production	Product Sustaining
Sustaining accounting	Product Sustaining
Maintaining production equipment	Product Sustaining
Direct-labor allowances	Unit
Direct-labor fringes	Unit
Utilities (equipment)	Unit
Overtime (hourly)	Unit
Rework	Unit
Shift differential	Unit
Spoilage	Unit

Required: Choose two activities or accounts from each of the four classifications and explain why you agree or disagree with the ABC project team's classification.

Exercise 5–35
ABC; Selling Costs
(LO 5-2, 5-4)

Redwood Company sells craft kits and supplies to retail outlets and through its catalog. Some of the items are manufactured by Redwood, while others are purchased for resale. For the products it manufactures, the company currently bases its selling prices on a product-costing system that accounts for direct material, direct labor, and the associated overhead costs. In addition to these product costs, Redwood incurs substantial selling costs, and Roger Jackson, controller, has suggested that these selling costs should be included in the product pricing structure.

[12]Robert Adams and Ray Carter, "United Technologies' Activity-Based Accounting Is a Catalyst for Success," *As Easy as ABC* 18, p 4. In the table, we have adjusted the nomenclature of United Technologies to match that used in this textbook. Specifically, United Technologies uses the term "*structural*-level activity" where we use "*facility*-level activity," and they shorten "*product-sustaining*-level activity to simply "*sustaining*-level activity."

After studying the costs incurred over the past two years for one of its products, skeins of knitting yarn, Jackson has selected four categories of selling costs and chosen cost drivers for each of these costs. The selling costs actually incurred during the past year and the cost drivers are as follows:

Cost Category	Amount	Cost Driver
Sales commissions	$ 675,000	Boxes of yarn sold to retail stores
Catalogs	295,400	Catalogs distributed
Cost of catalog sales	105,000	Skeins sold through catalog
Credit and collection	60,000	Number of retail orders
Total selling costs	$1,135,400	

The knitting yarn is sold to retail outlets in boxes, each containing 12 skeins of yarn. The sale of partial boxes is not permitted. Commissions are paid on sales to retail outlets but not on catalog sales. The cost of catalog sales includes telephone costs and the wages of personnel who take the catalog orders. Jackson believes that the selling costs vary significantly with the size of the order. Order sizes are divided into three categories as follows:

Order Size	Catalog Sales	Retail Sales
Small	1–10 skeins	1–10 boxes
Medium	11–20 skeins	11–20 boxes
Large	Over 20 skeins	Over 20 boxes

An analysis of the previous year's records produced the following statistics.

	Order Size			
	Small	Medium	Large	Total
Retail sales in boxes (12 skeins per box)	2,000	45,000	178,000	225,000
Catalog sales in skeins	79,000	52,000	44,000	175,000
Number of retail orders	485	2,415	3,100	6,000
Catalogs distributed	254,300	211,300	125,200	590,800

Required:

1. Prepare a schedule showing Redwood Company's total selling cost for each order size and the per-skein selling cost within each order size.
2. Explain how the analysis of the selling costs for skeins of knitting yarn is likely to impact future pricing and product decisions at Redwood Company.

(CMA, adapted)

Exercise 5–36
Classification of Activities in a University; Cost Drivers
(LO 5-2, 5-3, 5-6, 5-7, 5-10)

As a group, discuss the activities of your college or university (e.g., admission, registration, etc.). List as many activities as you can.

Required: Make a presentation to your class that includes the following:

1. Your list of activities.
2. The classification of each activity (e.g., unit level).
3. An appropriate cost driver for each activity.

Exercise 5–37
Non-Value-Added Costs
(LO 5-8)

Non-value-added costs occur in nonmanufacturing organizations, just as they do in manufacturing firms.

Required: Identify four potential non-value-added costs in (1) an airline, (2) a bank, and (3) a hotel.

Exercise 5–38
Design Your Own Production Process; Non-Value-Added Costs
(LO 5-8)

Since you have always wanted to be an entrepreneur, invent your own product and describe at least five steps used in its production.

Required: Explain how you would go about identifying non-value-added costs in the production process.

Exercise 5–39
Performance Measures in Two-Dimensional ABC; ABM
(LO 5-8, 5-10)

List five activities performed by the employees of an airline *on the ground.*

Required: For each of these activities, suggest a performance measure that could be used in activity-based management.

Exercise 5–40
Activity Analysis; Non-Value-Added Activities
(LO 5-8, 5-10)

Visit a restaurant for a meal or think carefully about a recent visit to a restaurant. List as many activities as you can think of that would be performed by the restaurant's employees for its customers.

Required: For each activity on your list, indicate the following:

1. Value-added or non-value-added.
2. The trigger of the activity.
3. The possible root causes of the activity.

Exercise 5–41
College Registration; Activity Analysis
(LO 5-8, 5-10)

As a group, think carefully about the various activities and steps involved in the course registration process at your college or university.

Required:

1. List the steps in the registration process in the sequence in which they occur.
2. Prepare an activity analysis of the registration process. Discuss the activity linkages, triggers, and root causes.
3. Redesign your institution's course registration process with these goals in mind:
   a. Improve the convenience and effectiveness of the process for a student registering.
   b. Improve the effectiveness and cost efficiency of the process from the standpoint of the institution.

Exercise 5–42
Customer Profitability Analysis; Customers Ranked by Sales Revenue
(LO 5-9)

The customer-profitability analysis for Patio Grill Company, which is displayed in Exhibit 5–14, ranks customers by operating income. An alternative, often-used approach is to rank customers by sales revenue.

Required:

1. List the customer numbers in the left-hand column of Exhibit 5–14 by sales revenue, from highest to lowest. Is the ranking different from that in Exhibit 5–14?
2. Patio Grill Company's smallest customers, in terms of sales revenue, are last in the listing prepared for requirement (1). Are these customers the company's least profitable?
3. Would the customer-profitability profile in Exhibit 5–15 be different if the customers were ranked by sales revenue instead of operating income? Explain.
4. What factors could cause a larger customer (in terms of sales revenue) to be less profitable than a smaller customer?

Exercise 5–43
Customer-Profitability Graph
(LO 5-9)

Big Apple Design Company specializes in designing commercial office space in Chicago. The firm's president recently reviewed the following income statement and noticed that operating profits were below her expectations. She had a hunch that certain customers were not profitable for the company and asked the controller to perform a customer-profitability analysis showing profitability by customer for the month of March.

BIG APPLE DESIGN COMPANY
Income Statement
For the Month Ended March 31

Sales revenue	$300,000
Cost of services billed	255,000
Gross margin	$ 45,000
Marketing and administrative costs	30,000
Operating profit	$ 15,000

The controller provided the following customer-profitability graph:

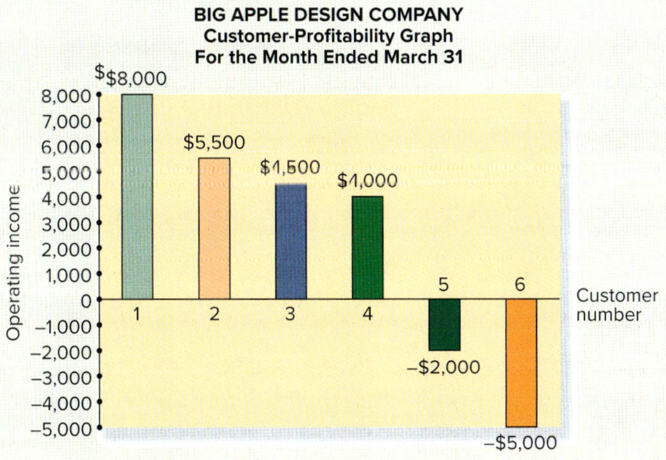

Required: Put yourself in the position of Big Apple's controller and write a memo to the president to accompany the customer-profitability graph. Comment on the implications of the customer-profitability analysis and raise four or more questions that should be addressed by the firm's management team.

Exercise 5–44
Activity-Based Costing
(LO 5-2, 5-3, 5-10)

Service-industry firms can make effective use of ABC systems as well as manufacturers. For each of the following businesses, list five key activities that are important in the provision of the firm's service. For each activity cost pool, suggest an appropriate cost driver to use in assigning costs from the activity cost pool to the services provided to customers.

1. Southwest Airlines
2. Burger King
3. Gold's Gym
4. Bank of America branch bank
5. Marriott Hotels
6. Massachusetts General Hospital

Problems

All applicable Problems are available in Connect.

connect

Problem 5–45
Overhead Application; Activity-Based Costing
(LO 5-1, 5-2, 5-7)

Borealis Manufacturing has just completed a major change in its quality control (QC) process. Previously, products had been reviewed by QC inspectors at the end of each major process, and the company's 10 QC inspectors were charged as direct labor to the operation or job. In an effort to improve efficiency and quality, a computerized video QC system was purchased for $250,000. The system consists of a minicomputer, 15 video cameras, other peripheral hardware, and software. The new system uses cameras stationed by QC engineers at key points in the production process. Each time an operation changes or there is a new operation, the cameras are moved, and a new master picture is loaded into the computer by a QC engineer. The camera takes pictures of the units in process, and the computer compares them to the picture of a "good" unit. Any differences are sent to a QC engineer, who removes the bad units and discusses the flaws with the production supervisors. The new system has replaced the 10 QC inspectors with two QC engineers.

The operating costs of the new QC system, including the salaries of the QC engineers, have been included as factory overhead in calculating the company's plantwide manufacturing-overhead rate, which is based on direct-labor dollars. The company's president is confused. His vice president of production has told him how efficient the new system is. Yet there is a large increase in the overhead rate. The computation of the rate before and after automation is as follows:

	Before	After
Budgeted manufacturing overhead	$1,900,000	$2,100,000
Budgeted direct-labor cost	1,000,000	700,000
Budgeted overhead rate	190%	300%

"Three hundred percent," lamented the president. "How can we compete with such a high overhead rate?"

Required:

1. *a.* Define "manufacturing overhead," and cite three examples of typical costs that would be included in manufacturing overhead.
   b. Explain why companies develop predetermined overhead rates.
2. Explain why the increase in the overhead rate should not have a negative financial impact on Borealis Manufacturing.
3. Explain how Borealis Manufacturing could change its overhead application system to eliminate confusion over product costs.
4. Discuss how an activity-based costing system might benefit Borealis Manufacturing.

(CMA, adapted)

Problem 5–46
Activity-Based Costing; Cost Analysis
(LO 5-1, 5-2, 5-4, 5-5, 5-7)

1. Total cost, standard: $157
2. Manufactured cost, standard unit: $181

Ontario, Inc. manufactures two products, Standard and Enhanced, and applies overhead on the basis of direct-labor hours. Anticipated overhead and direct-labor time for the upcoming accounting period are $800,000 and 25,000 hours, respectively. Information about the company's products follows.

Standard:

Estimated production volume, 3,000 units
Direct-material cost, $25 per unit
Direct labor per unit, 3 hours at $12 per hour

Enhanced:

Estimated production volume, 4,000 units
Direct-material cost, $40 per unit
Direct labor per unit, 4 hours at $12 per hour

Ontario's overhead of $800,000 can be identified with three major activities: order processing ($150,000), machine processing ($560,000), and product inspection ($90,000). These activities are driven by number of orders processed, machine hours worked, and inspection hours, respectively. Data relevant to these activities follow.

	Orders Processed	Machine Hours Worked	Inspection Hours
Standard	300	18,000	2,000
Enhanced	200	22,000	8,000
Total	500	40,000	10,000

Top management is very concerned about declining profitability despite a healthy increase in sales volume. The decrease in income is especially puzzling because the company recently undertook a massive plant renovation during which new, highly automated machinery was installed—machinery that was expected to produce significant operating efficiencies.

Required:

1. Assuming use of direct-labor hours to apply overhead to production, compute the unit manufacturing costs of the Standard and Enhanced products if the expected manufacturing volume is attained.

2. Assuming use of activity-based costing, compute the unit manufacturing costs of the Standard and Enhanced products if the expected manufacturing volume is attained.
3. Ontario's selling prices are based heavily on cost.
   a. By using direct-labor hours as an application base, which product is overcosted and which product is undercosted? Calculate the amount of the cost distortion for each product.
   b. Is it possible that overcosting and undercosting (i.e., cost distortion) and the subsequent determination of selling prices are contributing to the company's profit woes? Explain.
4. ***Build a spreadsheet:*** Construct an Excel spreadsheet to solve requirements 1, 2, and 3(*a*) above. Show how the solution will change if the following data change: the overhead associated with order processing is $300,000 and the overhead associated with product inspection is $270,000.

Problem 5–47
Straightforward ABC calculations
(LO 5-1, 5-2, 5-4, 5-5)

2. Machine-related cost, REG line: $135,000
3. Total cost per unit, under ABC, GMT line: $663.90
5. Cost distortion per unit, ADV line: overcosted by $8.85

Kitchen King's Toledo plant manufactures three product lines, all multi-burner, ceramic cook tops. The plant's three product models are the Regular (REG), the Advanced (ADV), and the Gourmet (GMT). Until recently, the plant used a job-order product-costing system, with manufacturing overhead applied on the basis of direct-labor hours. The following table displays the basic data upon which the traditional costing system was based.

	REG	ADV	GMT
Planned annual production:			
Volume in units	5,000	4,000	1,000
Production runs	40 runs of 125 units	40 runs of 100 units	20 runs of 50 units
Direct material	$129	$151	$203
Direct labor:			
(not including setup)	$171 (9 hrs. @ $19 per hr.)	$209 (11 hrs. @ $19 per hr.)	$247 (13 hrs. @ $19 per hr.)
Machine hours (MH)			
per product unit	10 MH	12 MH	17 MH
Total machine hours consumed			
by product line in a year	50,000 (10 MH × 5,000)	48,000 (12 MH × 4,000)	17,000 (17 MH × 1,000)

The annual budgeted overhead is $1,224,000, and the company's predetermined overhead rate is $12 per direct-labor hour. The product costs for the three product models, as reported under the plant's traditional costing system, are shown in the following table.

	REG	ADV	GMT
Direct material	$129.00	$151.00	$203.00
Direct labor (not including set-up time)	171.00 (9 hr. @ $19)	209.00 (11 hr. @ $19)	247.00 (13 hr. @ $19)
Manufacturing overhead	108.00 (9 hr. @ $12)	132.00 (11 hr. @ $12)	156.00 (13 hr. @ $12)
Total	$408.00	$492.00	$606.00

Kitchen King's pricing policy is to set a target price for each product equal to 130 percent of the full product cost. Due to price competition from other appliance manufacturers, REG units were selling at $525, and ADV units were selling for $628. These prices were somewhat below the firm's target prices. However, these results were partially offset by greater-than-expected profits on the GMT product line. Management had raised the price on the GMT model to $800, which was higher than the original target price. Even at this price, Kitchen King's customers did not seem to hesitate to place orders, Moreover, the company's competitors did not mount a challenge in the market for the GMT product line. Nevertheless, concern continued to mount in Toledo about the difficulty in the REG and ADV markets. After all, these were the plant's bread-and-butter products, with projected annual sales of 5,000 REG units and 4,000 ADV units.

Kitchen King's director of cost management, Angela Ramirez, had been thinking for some time about a refinement in the Toledo plant's product-costing system. Ramirez wondered if the traditional, volume-based system was providing management with accurate data about product costs. She had read about activity-based costing, and wondered if ABC would be an improvement to the plant's product-costing system. After some discussion, an ABC proposal was made to the company's top management, and approval was obtained. The data collected for the new ABC system is displayed in the following table.

Activity	Activity Cost Pool	Cost Driver	Product Line	Cost Driver Quantity for Product Line
Machine related	$310,500	Machine	REG	50,000
		Hours	ADV	48,000
			GMT	17,000
			Total	115,000
Material handling	52,500	Production	REG	40
		Runs	ADV	40
			GMT	20
			Total	100
Purchasing	75,000	Purchase	REG	100
		Orders	ADV	96
			GMT	104
			Total	300
Setup	85,000	Production	REG	40
		Runs	ADV	40
			GMT	20
			Total	100
Inspection	27,500	Inspection	REG	400
		Hours	ADV	400
			GMT	300
			Total	1,100
Shipping	66,000	Shipments	REG	500
			ADV	400
			GMT	200
			Total	1,100
Engineering	32,500	Engineering	REG	250
		Hours	ADV	200
			GMT	200
			Total	650
Facility	575,000	Machine	REG	50,000
		Hours	ADV	48,000
			GMT	17,000
			Total	115,000

Required:

1. Show how the company's overhead rate of $12 per direct-labor hour was calculated.
2. Complete an activity-based costing analysis for Kitchen King's three product lines. Display the results of your ABC analysis in a table similar to Exhibit 5–7 in the text.
3. Prepare a table similar to Exhibit 5–8, which computes the new product cost for each product line under ABC.
4. Prepare a table similar to Exhibit 5–9, which compares the overhead cost, total product cost, and target price for each product line under the two alternative costing systems.
5. Was each of Kitchen King's three product lines overcosted or undercosted? By how much per unit?
6. ***Build a spreadsheet:*** Construct an Excel spreadsheet to solve requirement (2) above. Show how the solution would change if the machine-related cost pool was $621,000, and the facility cost pool was $1,150,000.

Problem 5–48
Continuation of Preceding Problem; Explaining ABC
(LO 5-2, 5-4)

Refer to your solution to requirement (2) of the preceding problem.

Required: Prepare an exhibit similar to Exhibit 5–6 in the text to explain the ABC calculations for the material-handling activity. Use your exhibit to explain ABC to a friend who is not a business major.

Problem 5–49
Activity-Based Costing; Product Promotion
(LO 5-1, 5-2, 5-4, 5-5)

1. Type A manufacturing overhead cost: $160 per unit
2. Manufactured cost of type A cabinet: $243.50

Maxey & Sons manufactures two types of storage cabinets—Type A and Type B—and applies manufacturing overhead to all units at the rate of $80 per machine hour. Production information follows.

	Type A	Type B
Anticipated volume (units)	8,000	15,000
Direct-material cost per unit	$ 35	$60
Direct-labor cost per unit	20	20

The controller, who is studying the use of activity-based costing, has determined that the firm's overhead can be identified with three activities: manufacturing setups, machine processing, and product shipping. Data on the number of setups, machine hours, and outgoing shipments, which are the activities' three respective cost drivers, follow.

	Type A	Type B	Total
Setups	50	30	80
Machine hours	16,000	22,500	38,500
Outgoing shipments	100	75	175

The firm's total overhead of $3,080,000 is subdivided as follows: manufacturing setups, $672,000; machine processing, $1,848,000; and product shipping, $560,000.

Required:

1. Compute the unit manufacturing cost of Type A and Type B storage cabinets by using the company's current overhead costing procedures.
2. Compute the unit manufacturing cost of Type A and Type B storage cabinets by using activity-based costing.
3. Is the cost of the Type A storage cabinet overstated or understated (i.e., distorted) by the use of machine hours to allocate total manufacturing overhead to production? By how much?
4. Assume that the current selling price of a Type A storage cabinet is $260 and the marketing manager is contemplating a $30 discount to stimulate volume. Is this discount advisable? Briefly discuss.

Problem 5–50
Activity-Based Costing; Analysis of Operations
(LO 5-1, 5-2, 5-4, 5-5, 5-7, 5-10)

2. E-commerce consulting, income: $22,040
3. Activity-based application rate, staff support: $720 per client; Billings, information systems services: $387,500

Grady and Associates performs a variety of activities related to information systems and e-commerce consulting in Toronto, Canada. The firm, which bills $125 per hour for services performed, is in a very tight local labor market and is having difficulty finding quality help for its overworked professional staff. The cost per hour for professional staff time is $45. Selected information follows.

- Billable hours to clients for the year totaled 5,000, consisting of information systems services, 3,100; e-commerce consulting, 1,900.
- Administrative cost of $342,000 was (and continues to be) allocated to both services based on billable hours. These costs consist of staff support, $180,000; in-house computing, $136,400; and miscellaneous office charges, $25,600.

A recent analysis of staff support costs found a correlation with the number of clients served. In-house computing and miscellaneous office charges varied directly with the number of computer hours logged and number of client transactions, respectively. A tabulation revealed the following data:

	Information Systems Services	E-Commerce Consulting	Total
Number of clients	200	50	250
Number of computer hours	2,600	1,800	4,400
Number of client transactions	400	600	1,000

Required:

1. Activity-based costing (ABC) is said to result in improved costing accuracy when compared with traditional costing procedures. Briefly explain how this improved accuracy is attained.

2. Assume that the firm uses traditional costing procedures, allocating total costs on the basis of billable hours. Determine the profitability of the firm's information systems and e-commerce activities, expressing your answer both in dollars and as a percentage of activity revenue.
3. Repeat requirement (2), using activity-based costing.
4. Jeffrey Grady, one of the firm's partners, doesn't care where his professionals spend their time because, as he notes, "many clients have come to expect both services and we need both to stay in business. Also, information systems and e-commerce professionals are paid the same hourly rate." Should Grady's attitude change? Explain.
5. Is an aggressive expansion of either service currently desirable? Briefly discuss.

Problem 5–51
Automation; Robotics; Overhead Application; Activity-Based Costing
(LO 5-1, 5-2, 5-5, 5-8)

John Patrick has recently been hired as controller of Valdosta Vinyl Company (VVC), a manufacturer of vinyl siding used in residential construction. VVC has been in the vinyl siding business for many years and is currently investigating ways to modernize its manufacturing process. At the first staff meeting Patrick attended, Jack Kielshesky, chief engineer, presented a proposal for automating the Molding Department. Kielshesky recommended that the company purchase two robots that would have the capability of replacing the eight direct-labor employees in the department. The cost savings outlined in the proposal include the elimination of direct-labor cost in the Molding Department plus a reduction of manufacturing overhead cost in the department to zero, because VVC charges manufacturing overhead on the basis of direct-labor dollars using a plantwide rate. The president of VVC was puzzled by Kielshesky's explanation: "This just doesn't make any sense. How can a department's overhead rate drop to zero by adding expensive, high-tech manufacturing equipment? If anything, it seems like the rate ought to go up."

Kielshesky responded by saying "I'm an engineer, not an accountant. But if we're charging overhead on the basis of direct labor, and we eliminate the labor, then we eliminate the overhead."

Patrick agreed with the president. He explained that as firms become more automated, they should rethink their product-costing systems. The president then asked Patrick to look into the matter and prepare a report for the next staff meeting. Patrick gathered the following data on the manufacturing-overhead rates experienced by VVC over the years. Patrick also wanted to have some departmental data to present at the meeting and, by using VVC's accounting records, he was able to estimate the following annual averages for each manufacturing department over the five decades since VVC's formation.

Historical Plantwide Data

Decade	Average Annual Manufacturing-Overhead Cost	Average Annual Direct-Labor Cost	Average Manufacturing-Overhead Application Rate
1st	$ 2,200,000	$2,000,000	110%
2nd	6,240,000	2,400,000	260
3rd	13,600,000	4,000,000	340
4th	24,600,000	6,000,000	410
5th	38,710,000	7,900,000	490

Annual Averages during Recent Years

	Cutting Department	Finishing Department	Molding Department
Manufacturing overhead	$22,000,000	$14,000,000	$4,000,000
Direct labor	4,000,000	3,500,000	500,000

Required:

1. Disregarding the proposed use of robots in the Molding Department, describe the shortcomings of the system for applying overhead that is currently used by Valdosta Vinyl Company.
2. Explain the misconceptions underlying Kielshesky's statement that the manufacturing-overhead cost in the Molding Department will be reduced to zero if the automation proposal is implemented.

3. Recommend ways to improve VVC's method for applying overhead by describing how it should revise its product-costing system for each of the following departments:
   a. In the Cutting and Finishing Departments.
   b. To accommodate automation in the Molding Department.

(CMA, adapted)

■ **Problem 5–52**
Activity Cost Pools; Cost Drivers; Pool Rates
(LO 5-1, 5-2, 5-3, 5-4, 5-5, 5-7)

3. Predetermined overhead rate: $31.25 per machine hr.

The controller for Tulsa Medical Supply Company has established the following activity cost pools and cost drivers.

Activity Cost Pool	Budgeted Overhead Cost	Cost Driver	Budgeted Level for Cost Driver	Pool Rate
Machine setups	$250,000	Number of setups	125	$2,000 per setup
Material handling	75,000	Weight of raw material	37,500 lb.	$2 per pound
Hazardous waste control	25,000	Weight of hazardous chemicals used	5,000 lb.	$5 per pound
Quality control	75,000	Number of inspections	1,000	$75 per inspection
Other overhead costs	200,000	Machine hours	20,000	$10 per machine hour
Total	$625,000			

An order for 1,000 boxes of medical-testing agent has the following production requirements.

Machine setups	5 setups
Raw material	10,000 pounds
Hazardous materials	2,000 pounds
Inspections	10 inspections
Machine hours	500 machine hours

Required:

1. Compute the total overhead that should be assigned to the medical-testing agent order.
2. What is the overhead cost per box of testing agent?
3. Suppose Tulsa Medical Supply Company were to use a single predetermined overhead rate based on machine hours. Compute the rate per hour.
4. Under the approach in requirement (3), how much overhead would be assigned to the medical-testing agent order?
   a. In total.
   b. Per box of testing agent.
5. Explain why these two product-costing systems result in such widely differing costs. Which system do you recommend? Why?
6. ***Build a spreadsheet:*** Construct an Excel spreadsheet to solve requirements (1), (2), (3), and (4) above. Show how the solution will change if the following data change. The overhead associated with machine setups is $375,000, and there are 500 inspections budgeted.

■ **Problem 5–53**
Overhead Cost Drivers
(LO 5-2, 5-3, 5-4)

1. Unit cost per plate: $260.25

Refer to the original data given in the preceding problem for Tulsa Medical Supply Company.

Required:

1. Calculate the unit cost of a production order for 100 specially coated plates used in cancer testing. In addition to direct material costing $120 per plate and direct labor costing $40 per plate, the order requires the following:

Machine setups	3
Raw material	900 pounds
Hazardous materials	300 pounds
Inspections	3
Machine hours	50

2. *Build a spreadsheet:* Construct an Excel spreadsheet to solve the preceding requirement. (This will be an extension of the spreadsheet constructed for the preceding problem.) Show how the solution will change if the data given in the preceding problem change as follows: the overhead associated with machine setups is $375,000, and there are 500 inspections budgeted.

Problem 5–54
Activity-Based Costing; Activity-Based Management
(LO 5-2, 5-3, 5-4, 5-5, 5-7)

2. Total cost, royal: $4,431,900

Montreal Electronics Company manufactures two large-screen television models: the Nova, which has been produced for 10 years and sells for $900, and the Royal, a new model introduced in early 20x0, which sells for $1,140. Based on the following income statement for 20x1, a decision has been made to concentrate Montreal's marketing resources on the Royal model and to begin to phase out the Nova model.

MONTREAL ELECTRONICS COMPANY
Income Statement
For the Year Ended December 31, 20x1

	Royal	Nova	Total
Sales	$4,560,000	$19,800,000	$24,360,000
Cost of goods sold	3,192,000	12,540,000	15,732,000
Gross margin	$1,368,000	$ 7,260,000	$ 8,628,000
Selling and administrative expense	978,000	5,830,000	6,808,000
Net income	$ 390,000	$ 1,430,000	$ 1,820,000
Units produced and sold	4,000	22,000	
Net income per unit sold	$ 97.50	$ 65.00	

The standard unit costs for the Royal and Nova models are as follows:

	Royal	Nova
Direct material	$584	$208
Direct labor:		
Royal (3.5 hr. × $12)	42	
Nova (1.5 hr. × $12)		18
Machine usage:		
Royal (4 hr. × $18)	72	
Nova (8 hr. × $18)		144
Manufacturing overhead*	100	200
Standard cost	$798	$570

*Manufacturing overhead was applied on the basis of machine hours at a predetermined rate of $25 per hour.

Montreal Electronics Company's controller is advocating the use of activity-based costing and activity-based management and has gathered the following information about the company's manufacturing-overhead costs for 20x1.

		Number of Events		
Activity Center (cost driver)	**Traceable Costs**	**Royal**	**Nova**	**Total**
Soldering (number of solder joints)	$ 942,000	385,000	1,185,000	1,570,000
Shipments (number of shipments)	860,000	3,800	16,200	20,000
Quality control (number of inspections)	1,240,000	21,300	56,200	77,500
Purchase orders (number of orders)	950,400	109,980	80,100	190,080
Machine power (machine hours)	57,600	16,000	176,000	192,000
Machine setups (number of setups)	750,000	14,000	16,000	30,000
Total traceable costs	$4,800,000			

Required:

1. Briefly explain how an activity-based costing system operates.
2. Using activity-based costing, determine if Montreal Electronics should continue to emphasize the Royal model and phase out the Nova model.

(CMA, adapted)

Problem 5–55
Activity-Based Costing
(LO 5-1, 5-2, 5-4, 5-5)

2. Total contribution margin from PC board: $2,360,000
3. Using ABC, total contribution margin from TV board: $2,557,100

Manchester Technology, Inc. manufactures several different types of printed circuit boards; however, two of the boards account for the majority of the company's sales. The first of these boards, a television circuit board, has been a standard in the industry for several years. The market for this type of board is competitive and price-sensitive. Manchester plans to sell 65,000 of the TV boards in 20x1 at a price of $150 per unit. The second high-volume product, a personal computer circuit board, is a recent addition to Manchester's product line. Because the PC board incorporates the latest technology, it can be sold at a premium price. The 20x1 plans include the sale of 40,000 PC boards at $300 per unit.

Manchester's management group is meeting to discuss how to spend the sales and promotion dollars for 20x1. The sales manager believes that the market share for the TV board could be expanded by concentrating Manchester's promotional efforts in this area. In response to this suggestion, the production manager said, "Why don't you go after a bigger market for the PC board? The cost sheets that I get show that the contribution from a PC board is significantly larger than the contribution from a TV board. I know we get a premium price for the PC board. Selling it should help overall profitability."

The cost-accounting system shows that the following costs apply to the PC and TV boards.

	PC Board	TV Board
Direct material	$140	$80
Direct labor	4 hr.	1.5 hr.
Machine time	1.5 hr.	.5 hr.

Variable manufacturing overhead is applied on the basis of direct-labor hours. For 20x1, variable overhead is budgeted at $1,120,000, and direct-labor hours are estimated at 280,000. The hourly rates for machine time and direct labor are $10 and $14, respectively. The company applies a material-handling charge at 10 percent of material cost. This material-handling charge is not included in variable manufacturing overhead. Total 20x1 expenditures for direct material are budgeted at $10,800,000.

Andrew Fulton, Manchester's controller, believes that before the management group proceeds with the discussion about allocating sales and promotional dollars to individual products, it might be worthwhile to look at these products on the basis of the activities involved in their production. Fulton has prepared the following schedule to help the management group understand this concept.

"Using this information," Fulton explained, "we can calculate an activity-based cost for each TV board and each PC board and then compare it to the standard cost we have been using. The only cost that remains the same for both cost methods is the cost of direct material. The cost drivers will replace the direct labor, machine time, and overhead costs in the old standard cost figures."

Budgeted Cost		Cost Driver	Budgeted Annual Activity for Cost Driver
Procurement	$ 400,000	Number of parts	4,000,000 parts
Production scheduling	220,000	Number of boards	110,000 boards
Packaging and shipping	440,000	Number of boards	110,000 boards
Total	$1,060,000		
Machine setup	$ 446,000	Number of setups	278,750 setups
Hazardous waste disposal	48,000	Pounds of waste	16,000 pounds
Quality control	560,000	Number of inspections	160,000 inspections
General supplies	66,000	Number of boards	110,000 boards
Total	$1,120,000		
Machine insertion	$1,200,000	Number of parts	3,000,000 parts
Manual insertion	4,000,000	Number of parts	1,000,000 parts
Wave-soldering	132,000	Number of boards	110,000 boards
Total	$5,332,000		

Required per Unit	**PC Board**	**TV Board**
Parts:	55	25
Machine insertions	35	24
Manual insertions	20	1
Machine setups	3	2
Hazardous waste disposal, in lb	.35	.02
Inspections	2	1

Required:

1. Identify at least four general advantages associated with activity-based costing.
2. On the basis of Manchester's unit cost data given in the problem, calculate the total amount that each of the two product lines will contribute toward covering fixed costs and profit in 20x1. (In other words, for each product line, calculate the total sales revenue minus the total *variable* costs. This amount is often referred to as a product's total *contribution margin*.)
3. Repeat requirement (2) but now use the cost data from the activity-based costing system.
4. Explain how a comparison of the results of the two costing methods may impact the decisions made by Manchester's management group.

(CMA, adapted)

Problem 5–56
Activity-Based Costing
(LO 5-1, 5-2, 5-4, 5-5, 5-7)

2. New product cost, under ABC: $7.46 per pound of Kona

World Gourmet Coffee Company (WGCC) is a distributor and processor of different blends of coffee. The company buys coffee beans from around the world and roasts, blends, and packages them for resale. WGCC currently has 15 different coffees that it offers to gourmet shops in one-pound bags. The major cost is raw materials; however, there is a substantial amount of manufacturing overhead in the predominantly automated roasting and packing process. The company uses relatively little direct labor.

Some of the coffees are very popular and sell in large volumes, while a few of the newer blends have very low volumes. WGCC prices its coffee at full product cost, including allocated overhead, plus a markup of 30 percent. If prices for certain coffees are significantly higher than market, adjustments are made. The company competes primarily on the quality of its products, but customers are price-conscious as well.

Data for the 20x1 budget include manufacturing overhead of $3,000,000, which has been allocated on the basis of each product's direct-labor cost. The budgeted direct-labor cost for 20x1 totals $600,000. Based on the sales budget and raw-material budget, purchases and use of raw materials (mostly coffee beans) will total $6,000,000.

The expected prime costs for one-pound bags of two of the company's products are as follows:

	Kona	**Malaysian**
Direct material	$3.20	$4.20
Direct labor	.30	.30

WGCC's controller believes the traditional product-costing system may be providing misleading cost information. She has developed an analysis of the 20x1 budgeted manufacturing-overhead costs shown in the following chart.

Activity	**Cost Driver**	**Budgeted Activity**	**Budgeted Cost**
Purchasing	Purchase orders	1,158	$ 579,000
Material handling	Setups	1,800	720,000
Quality control	Batches	720	144,000
Roasting	Roasting hours	96,100	961,000
Blending	Blending hours	33,600	336,000
Packaging	Packaging hours	26,000	260,000
Total manufacturing-overhead cost			$3,000,000

Data regarding the 20x1 production of Kona and Malaysian coffee are shown in the following table. There will be no raw-material inventory for either of these coffees at the beginning of the year.

	Kona	Malaysian
Budgeted sales	2,000 lb.	100,000 lb.
Batch size	500 lb.	10,000 lb.
Setups	3 per batch	3 per batch
Purchase order size	500 lb.	25,000 lb.
Roasting time	1 hr. per 100 lb.	1 hr. per 100 lb.
Blending time	.5 hr. per 100 lb.	.5 hr. per 100 lb.
Packaging time	.1 hr. per 100 lb.	.1 hr. per 100 lb.

Required:

1. Using WGCC's current product-costing system:
   a. Determine the company's predetermined overhead rate using direct-labor cost as the single cost driver.
   b. Determine the full product costs and selling prices of one pound of Kona coffee and one pound of Malaysian coffee.
2. Develop a new product cost, using an activity-based costing approach, for one pound of Kona coffee and one pound of Malaysian coffee.
3. What are the implications of the activity-based costing system with respect to
   a. The use of direct labor as a basis for applying overhead to products?
   b. The use of the existing product-costing system as the basis for pricing?

(CMA, adapted)

Problem 5–57
Activity-Based Costing; Activity Cost Pools; Pool Rates; Calculation of Product Costs; Cost Distortion
(LO 5-1, 5-2, 5-3, 5-4, 5-5)

2. Pool rate, plant-related costs: $50 per sq. ft.
5. New target price, Odds: $605.16

Knickknack, Inc. manufactures two products: Odds and Ends. The firm uses a single, plantwide overhead rate based on direct-labor hours. Production and product-costing data are as follows:

	Odds	Ends
Production quantity	1,000 units	5,000 units
Direct material	$ 40	$ 60
Direct labor (not including setup time)	30 (2 hr. at $15)	45 (3 hr. at $15)
Manufacturing overhead	96 (2 hr. at $48)	144 (3 hr. at $48)
Total cost per unit	$ 166	$ 249

Calculation of predetermined overhead rate:
Manufacturing overhead budget:

Machine-related costs	$450,000
Setup and inspection	180,000
Engineering	90,000
Plant-related costs	96,000
Total	$816,000

Predetermined overhead rate:

$$\frac{\text{Budgeted manufacturing overhead}}{\text{Budgeted direct-labor hours}} = \frac{\$816{,}000}{(1{,}000)(2) + (5{,}000)(3)} = \$48 \text{ per direct-labor hour}$$

Knickknack, Inc. prices its products at 120 percent of cost, which yields target prices of $199.20 for Odds and $298.80 for Ends. Recently, however, Knickknack has been challenged in the market for Ends by a European competitor, Bricabrac Corporation. A new entrant in this market, Bricabrac has been selling Ends for $220 each. Knickknack's president is puzzled by Bricabrac's ability to sell Ends at such a low cost. She has asked you (the controller) to look into the matter. You have decided that Knickknack's traditional, volume-based product-costing system may be causing cost distortion between the firm's two products. Ends are a high-volume, relatively simple product. Odds, on the other hand, are quite complex and exhibit a much lower volume. As a result, you have begun work on an activity-based costing system.

Required:

1. Let each of the overhead categories in the budget represent an activity cost pool. Categorize each in terms of the type of activity (e.g., unit-level activity).
2. The following cost drivers have been identified for the four activity cost pools.

Activity Cost Pool	Cost Driver	Budgeted Level of Cost Driver
Machine-related costs	Machine hours	9,000 hr.
Setup and inspection	Number of production runs	40 runs
Engineering	Engineering change orders	100 change orders
Plant-related costs	Square footage of space	1,920 sq. ft.

You have gathered the following additional information:

- Each Odd requires 4 machine hours, whereas each End requires 1 machine hour.
- Odds are manufactured in production runs of 50 units each. Ends are manufactured in 250-unit batches.
- Three-quarters of the engineering activity, as measured in terms of change orders, is related to Odds.
- The plant has 1,920 square feet of space, 80 percent of which is used in the production of Odds.

For each activity cost pool, compute a pool rate. (Hint: Regarding the pool rate refer to Exhibit 5–6.)

3. Determine the unit cost, for each activity cost pool, for Odds and Ends.
4. Compute the new product cost per unit for Odds and Ends, using the ABC system.
5. Using the same pricing policy as in the past, compute prices for Odds and Ends. Use the product costs determined by the ABC system.
6. Show that the ABC system fully assigns the total budgeted manufacturing overhead costs of $816,000.
7. Show how Knickknack's traditional, volume-based costing system distorted its product costs. (Refer to Exhibit 5–10 for guidance.)

Problem 5–58
Activity-Based Costing; Forecasting; Ethics
(LO 5-1, 5-2, 5-4, 5-5)

1. Total Material-Handling Department costs: $288,000
3. Reduction in material-handling costs allocated to government contracts: $74,600
4. Cumulative impact of recommended change in allocating Material-Handling Department costs: $234,346

Northwest Aircraft Industries (NAI) was founded 45 years ago by Jay Preston as a small machine shop producing machined parts for the aircraft industry, which is prominent in the Seattle/Tacoma area of Washington. By the end of its first decade, NAI's annual sales had reached $15 million, almost exclusively under government contracts. The next 30 years brought slow but steady growth as cost-reimbursement government contracts continued to be the main source of revenue. Realizing that NAI could not depend on government contracts for long-term growth and stability, Drew Preston, son of the founder and now president of the company, began planning for diversified commercial growth. As a result of these efforts, three years ago NAI had succeeded in reducing the ratio of government contract sales to 50 percent of total sales.

Traditionally, the costs of the Material-Handling Department have been allocated to direct material as a percentage of direct-material dollar value. This was adequate when the majority of the manufacturing was homogeneous and related to government contracts. Recently, however, government auditors have rejected some proposals, stating that "the amount of Material-Handling Department costs allocated to these proposals is disproportionate to the total effort involved."

Kara Lindley, the newly hired cost-accounting manager, was asked by the manager of the Government Contracts Unit, Paul Anderson, to find a more equitable method of allocating Material-Handling Department costs to the user departments. Her review has revealed the following information.

- The majority of the direct-material purchases for government contracts are high-dollar, low-volume purchases, while commercial materials represent low-dollar, high-volume purchases.

- Administrative departments such as marketing, finance and administration, human resources, and maintenance also use the services of the Material-Handling Department on a limited basis but have never been charged in the past for material-handling costs.
- One purchasing agent with a direct phone line is assigned exclusively to purchasing high-dollar, low-volume material for government contracts at an annual salary of $36,000. Employee benefits are estimated to be 20 percent of the annual salary. The annual dedicated phone line costs are $2,800.

The components of the Material-Handling Department's budget for 20x1, as proposed by Lindley's predecessor, are as follows:

Payroll	$ 180,000
Employee benefits	36,000
Telephone	38,000
Other utilities	22,000
Materials and supplies	6,000
Depreciation	6,000
Total	$ 288,000
Direct-material budget:	
Government contracts	$2,006,000
Commercial products	874,000

Lindley has estimated the number of purchase orders to be processed in 20x1 to be as follows:

Government contracts*	80,000
Commercial products	156,000
Marketing	1,800
Finance and administration	2,700
Human resources	500
Maintenance	1,000
Total	242,000

*Exclusive of high-dollar, low-volume materials.

Lindley recommended to Anderson that material-handling costs be allocated on a per-purchase-order basis. Anderson realizes and accepts that the company has been allocating to government contracts more material-handling costs than can be justified. However, the implication of Lindley's analysis could be a decrease in his unit's earnings and, consequently, a cut in his annual bonus. Anderson told Lindley to "adjust" her numbers and modify her recommendation so that the results will be more favorable to the Government Contracts Unit.

Being new in her position, Lindley is not sure how to proceed. She feels ambivalent about Anderson's instructions and suspects his motivation. To complicate matters for Lindley, Preston has asked her to prepare a three-year forecast of the Government Contracts Unit's results, and she believes that the newly recommended allocation method would provide the most accurate data. However, this would put her in direct opposition to Anderson's directives.

Lindley has assembled the following data to project the material-handling costs.

- Total direct-material costs increase 2.5 percent per year.
- Material-handling costs remain the same percentage of direct-material costs.
- Direct government costs (payroll, employee benefits, and direct phone line) remain constant.
- The number of purchase orders increases 5 percent per year.
- The ratio of government purchase orders to total purchase orders remains at 33 percent.
- In addition, she has assumed that government material in the future will be 70 percent of total material.

Required:

1. Calculate the material-handling rate that would have been used by Kara Lindley's predecessor at Northwest Aircraft Industries.

2. *a.* Calculate the revised material-handling costs to be allocated on a per-purchase-order basis.
   b. Discuss why purchase orders might be a more reliable cost driver than the dollar amount of direct material.
3. Calculate the change in material-handling costs applied to government contracts by NAI as a result of the new cost assignment approach.
4. Prepare a forecast of the cumulative dollar impact over a three-year period from 20x1 through 20x3 of Kara Lindley's recommended change for allocating Material-Handling Department costs to the Government Contracts Unit. Round all calculations to the nearest whole number.
5. Referring to the standards of ethical conduct for management accountants:
   a. Discuss why Kara Lindley has an ethical conflict.
   b. Identify several steps that Lindley could take to resolve the ethical conflict.

(CMA, adapted)

Problem 5–59
Activity-Based Costing; Production and Pricing Decisions
(LO 5-1, 5-2, 5-3, 5-4, 5-5)

1(b). Tuff Stuff unit cost: $28.00
3. Fabricating cost per unit, Tuff Stuff: $4.93 per unit (rounded)

Marconi Manufacturing produces two items in its Trumbull Plant: Tuff Stuff and Ruff Stuff. Since inception, Marconi has used only one manufacturing-overhead cost pool to accumulate costs. Overhead has been allocated to products based on direct-labor hours. Until recently, Marconi was the sole producer of Ruff Stuff and was able to dictate the selling price. However, last year Marvella Products began marketing a comparable product at a price below the cost assigned by Marconi. Market share has declined rapidly, and Marconi must now decide whether to meet the competitive price or to discontinue the product line. Recognizing that discontinuing the product line would place an additional burden on its remaining product, Tuff Stuff, management is using activity-based costing to determine if it would show a different cost structure for the two products.

The two major indirect costs for manufacturing the products are power usage and setup costs. Most of the power is used in fabricating the products' components, while most of the setup costs are required in assembling them. The setup costs are predominantly related to the Tuff Stuff product line.

A decision was made to separate the Manufacturing Department costs into two activity cost pools as follows:

Fabrication: machine hours will be the cost driver.

Assembly: number of setups will be the cost driver.

The controller has gathered the following information.

MANUFACTURING DEPARTMENT
Annual Budget before Separation of Overhead

		Product Line	
	Total	**Tuff Stuff**	**Ruff Stuff**
Number of units		20,000	20,000
Direct-labor hours*		2 hours per unit	3 hours per unit
Total direct-labor cost	$800,000		
Direct material		$5.00 per unit	$3.00 per unit
Budgeted overhead:			
Indirect labor	$ 24,000		
Fringe benefits	5,000		
Indirect material	31,000		
Power	180,000		
Setup	75,000		
Quality assurance	10,000		
Other utilities	10,000		
Depreciation	15,000		

*Direct-labor hourly rate is the same in both departments.

MANUFACTURING DEPARTMENT
Cost Structure after Separation of Overhead into Activity Cost Pools

	Fabrication	Assembly
Direct-labor cost	75%	25%
Direct material (no change)	100%	0%
Indirect labor	75%	25%
Fringe benefits	80%	20%
Indirect material	$ 20,000	$11,000
Power	$160,000	$20,000
Setup	$ 5,000	$70,000
Quality assurance	80%	20%
Other utilities	50%	50%
Depreciation	80%	20%

	Product Line	
Cost driver:	**Tuff Stuff**	**Ruff Stuff**
Machine-hours per unit	4.4	6.0
Setups	1,000	272

Required:

1. Assigning overhead based on direct-labor hours, calculate the following:
   a. Total budgeted cost of the Manufacturing Department.
   b. Unit cost of Tuff Stuff and Ruff Stuff.
2. After separation of overhead into activity cost pools, compute the total budgeted cost of each activity: Fabrication and Assembly.
3. Using activity-based costing, calculate the unit costs for each product. (In computing the pool rates for the Fabrication and Assembly activity cost pools, round to the nearest cent. Then, in computing unit product costs, round to the nearest cent.)
4. Discuss how a decision regarding the production and pricing of Ruff Stuff will be affected by the results of your calculations in the preceding requirements.

(CMA, adapted)

Problem 5–60
Traditional versus Activity-Based Costing Systems
(LO 5-1, 5-2, 5-3, 5-4, 5-5)

5. Reported product costs with ABC, product G: $141.67
6. Reported product costs with ABC, product T: $163.74

Gigabyte, Inc. manufactures three products for the computer industry:

Gismos (product G): annual sales, 8,000 units
Thingamajigs (product T): annual sales, 15,000 units
Whatchamacallits (product W): annual sales, 4,000 units

The company uses a traditional, volume-based product-costing system with manufacturing overhead applied on the basis of direct-labor dollars. The product costs have been computed as follows:

	Product G		Product T		Product W	
Raw material	$ 35.00		$ 52.50		$17.50	
Direct labor	16.00	(.8 hr. at $20)	12.00	(.6 hr. at $20)	8.00	(.4 hr. at $20)
Manufacturing overhead*	140.00		105.00		70.00	
Total product cost	$191.00		$169.50		$95.50	

*Calculation of predetermined overhead rate:

Manufacturing overhead budget:	
Machine setup	$ 5,250
Machinery	1,225,000
Inspection	525,000
Material handling	875,000
Engineering	344,750
Total	$2,975,000

Direct-labor budget (based on budgeted annual sales):			
Product G:	8,000 × $16.00	=	$128,000
Product T:	15,000 × $12.00	=	180,000
Product W:	4,000 × $8.00	=	32,000
Total			$340,000

$$\text{Predetermined overhead rate} = \frac{\text{Budgeted overhead}}{\text{Budgeted direct labor}} = 875\%$$

Gigabyte's pricing method has been to set a target price equal to 150 percent of full product cost. However, only the thingamajigs have been selling at their target price. The target and actual current prices for all three products are the following:

	Product G	Product T	Product W
Product cost	$ 191.00	$169.50	$ 95.50
Target price	286.50	254.25	143.25
Actual current selling price	213.00	254.25	200.00

Gigabyte has been forced to lower the price of gismos in order to get orders. In contrast, Gigabyte has raised the price of whatchamacallits several times, but there has been no apparent loss of sales. Gigabyte, Inc. has been under increasing pressure to reduce the price even further on gismos. In contrast, Gigabyte's competitors do not seem to be interested in the market for whatchamacallits. Gigabyte apparently has this market to itself.

Required:

1. Is product G the company's least profitable product?
2. Is product W a profitable product for Gigabyte, Inc.?
3. Comment on the reactions of Gigabyte's competitors to the firm's pricing strategy. What dangers does Gigabyte, Inc. face?
4. Gigabyte's controller, Nan O'Second, recently attended a conference at which activity-based costing systems were discussed. She became convinced that such a system would help Gigabyte's management to understand its product costs better. She got top management's approval to design an activity-based costing system, and an ABC project team was formed. In stage one of the ABC project, each of the overhead items listed in the overhead budget was placed into its own activity cost pool. Then a cost driver was identified for each activity cost pool. Finally, the ABC project team compiled data showing the percentage of each cost driver that was consumed by each of Gigabyte's product lines. These data are summarized as follows:

Activity Cost Pool	Cost Driver	Product G	Product T	Product W
Machine setup	Number of setups	20%	30%	50%
Machinery	Machine hours	25%	50%	25%
Inspection	Number of inspections	15%	45%	40%
Material handling	Raw-material costs	25%	69%	6%
Engineering	Number of change orders	35%	10%	55%

Show how the controller determined the percentages given above for raw-material costs. (Round to the nearest whole percent.)

5. Develop product costs for the three products on the basis of an activity-based costing system. (Round to the nearest cent.)
6. Calculate a target price for each product, using Gigabyte's pricing formula. Compare the new target prices with the current actual selling prices and previously reported product costs.
7. ***Build a spreadsheet:*** Construct an Excel spreadsheet to solve requirements (5) and (6) above. Show how the solution will change if the inspection activity was divided among the three products in the following manner: product G, 20%; product T, 40%, and product W, 40%.

Problem 5–61
Strategic Cost Analysis; Continuation of Preceding Problem
(LO 5-2, 5-5, 5-7)

Refer to the new target prices for Gigabyte's three products, based on the new activity-based costing system calculated in the preceding problem.

Required: Write a memo to the company president commenting on the situation Gigabyte, Inc. has been facing regarding the market for its products and the actions of its competitors. Discuss the strategic options available to management. What do you recommend, and why?

Problem 5–62
Cost Distortion; Continuation of Problem 5–60
(LO 5-2, 5-5)

Traditional system undercosts product W by $120.25 per unit

Refer to the product costs developed in requirement (5) of Problem 5–60. Prepare a table showing how Gigabyte's traditional, volume-based product-costing system distorts the product costs of gismos, thingamajigs, and whatchamacallits. (You may wish to refer to Exhibit 5–10 for guidance. Because of rounding in the calculation of the product costs, there will be a small rounding error in this cost distortion analysis as well.)

Problem 5–63
Basic Elements of a Production Process; Non-Value-Added Costs
(LO 5-7, 5-8, 5-10)

Better Bagels, Inc. manufactures a variety of bagels, which are frozen and sold in grocery stores. The production process consists of the following steps.

1. Ingredients, such as flour and raisins, are received and inspected. Then they are stored until needed.
2. Ingredients are carried on hand carts to the mixing room.
3. Dough is mixed in 40-pound batches in four heavy-duty mixers.
4. Dough is stored on large boards in the mixing room until a bagel machine is free.
5. A board of dough is carried into the bagel room. The board is tipped, and the dough slides into the hopper of a bagel machine. This machine pulls off a small piece of dough, rolls it into a cylindrical shape, and then squeezes it into a doughnut shape. The bagel machines can be adjusted in a setup procedure to accommodate different sizes and styles of bagels. Workers remove the uncooked bagels and place them on a tray, where they are kept until a boiling vat is free.
6. Next the trays of uncooked bagels are carried into an adjoining room, which houses three 50-gallon vats of boiling water. The bagels are boiled for approximately one minute.
7. Bagels are removed from the vats with a long-handled strainer and placed on a wooden board. The boards full of bagels are carried to the oven room, where they are kept until an oven rack is free. The two ovens contain eight racks which rotate but remain upright, much like the seats on a Ferris wheel. A rack full of bagels is finished baking after one complete revolution in the oven. When a rack full of bagels is removed from the oven, a fresh rack replaces it. The oven door is opened and closed as each rack completes a revolution in the oven.
8. After the bagels are removed from the oven, they are placed in baskets for cooling.
9. While the bagels are cooling, they are inspected. Misshapen bagels are removed and set aside. (Most are eaten by the staff.)
10. After the bagels are cool, the wire baskets are carried to the packaging department. Here the bagels are dumped into the hopper on a bagging machine. This machine packages a half-dozen bagels in each bag and seals the bag with a twist tie.
11. Then the packaged bagels are placed in cardboard boxes, each holding 24 bags. The boxes are placed on a forklift and are driven to the freezer, where the bagels are frozen and stored for shipment.

Required:

1. Identify the steps in the bagel-production process that fall into each of the following categories: process time, inspection time, move time, waiting time, storage time.
2. List the steps in the production process that could be candidates for non-value-added activities.

Problem 5–64
Two-Dimensional Activity-Based Costing; Activity Analysis; ABM
(LO 5-8)

Midwest Home Furnishings Corporation (MHFC) manufactures a variety of housewares for the consumer market in the Midwest. The company's three major product lines are cooking utensils, tableware, and flatware. MHFC implemented activity-based costing four years ago and now has a well-developed ABC system in place for determining product costs. Only recently, however, has the ABC system been systematically used for the purposes of activity-based management. As a pilot project, MHFC's controller asked the ABC project team to do a detailed activity analysis of the purchasing activity. The following specific activities were identified.

1. Receipt of parts specifications from the Design Engineering Department.
2. Follow-up with design engineers to answer any questions.
3. Vendor (supplier) identification.
4. Vendor consultations (by phone or in person).
5. Price negotiation.
6. Vendor selection.
7. Ordering (by phone or mail).
8. Order follow-up.
9. Expediting (attempting to speed up delivery).
10. Order receiving.
11. Inspection of parts.
12. Return of parts not meeting specifications.
13. Consultation with design engineers and production personnel if parts do not satisfy intended purpose.
14. Further consultation and/or negotiation with vendor if necessary.
15. Ship parts back to vendor if necessary.
16. If satisfactory, move parts to storage.

Required:

1. Draw a diagram to depict MHFC's two-dimensional activity-based costing efforts. The diagram should include the following:
   a. The cost assignment role of ABC, with the cost pools, activities, and product lines represented.
   b. The process view of ABC, with the purchasing activities displayed. Also indicated here will be the linkages among the activities. (To save space, indicate the activities by their numbers.)
   c. The activity evaluation phase of two-dimensional ABC.
2. Identify the triggers for each of the following activities in MHFC's purchasing activity analysis:

   Follow-up with design engineers (activity 2)
   Expediting (activity 9)
   Inspection of parts (activity 11)
   Return of parts (activity 12)
   Consultation with design engineers and production personnel (activity 13)

3. For each of the activities listed in requirement (2), identify the possible root causes.
4. Choose four activities in MHFC's purchasing function, and suggest a performance measure for each of these activities.

Problem 5–65
Customer-Profitability Analysis; Activity-Based Costing
(LO 5-9)

1. Operating income, Trace Telecom: $7,000

Fresno Fiber Optics, Inc. manufactures fiber optic cables for the computer and telecommunications industries. At the request of the company vice president of marketing, the cost management staff has recently completed a customer-profitability study. The following activity-based costing information was the basis for the analysis.

Customer-Related Activities	Cost Driver Base	Cost Driver Rate
Sales activity	Sales visits	$1,000
Order taking	Purchase orders	200
Special handling	Units handled	50
Special shipping	Shipments	500

Cost-driver data for two of Fresno's customers for the most recent year are

Customer-Related Activities	Trace Telecom	Caltex Computer
Sales activity	8 visits	6 visits
Order taking	15 orders	20 orders
Special handling	800 units handled	600 units handled
Special shipping	18 shipments	20 shipments

The following additional information has been compiled for Fresno Fiber Optics for two of its customers, Trace Telecom and Caltex Computer, for the most recent year:

	Trace Telecom	Caltex Computer
Sales revenue	$190,000	$123,800
Cost of goods sold	80,000	62,000
General selling costs	24,000	18,000
General administrative costs	19,000	16,000

Required:

1. Prepare a customer profitability analysis for Trace Telecom and Caltex Computer. (*Hint:* Refer to Exhibit 5–13 for guidance.)
2. ***Build a spreadsheet:*** Construct an Excel spreadsheet to solve requirement (1) above. Show how the solution will change if the following information changes: Trace Telecom's sales revenue was $185,000 and Caltex Computer's cost of goods sold was $59,000.

Problem 5–66
Customer-Profitability Profile; Continuation of Preceding Problem (**LO 5-9**)

Tele-Install, operating profit: $(18,000)

Refer to the information given in the preceding problem for Fresno Fiber Optics and two of its customers, Trace Telecom and Caltex Computer. Additional information for six of Fresno's other customers for the most recent year follows:

Customer	Operating Income
Golden Gate Service Associates	$71,000
Tele-Install, Inc.	(18,000)
Graydon Computer Company	60,000
Mid-State Computing Company	42,000
Network-All, Inc .	93,000
The California Group	6,000

Required:

1. Prepare Fresno Fiber Optics' customer profitability profile for the most recent year.
2. As Fresno Fiber Optics' director of cost management, write a memo to the company's vice president of marketing that will accompany the customer profitability profile. Include a brief explanation of the methodology used and comment on the results.

Cases

■ **Case 5–67**
Activity-Based Costing; Budgeted Operating Margin
(LO 5-1, 5-2, 5-4, 5-5, 5-7)

3. Total cost, JR-14, estimated 20x2 product cost: $1,540,000
4. Gross margin, RM-13: $(113,000)

Whitestone Company produces two subassemblies, JR-14 and RM-13, used in manufacturing trucks. The company is currently using an absorption costing system that applies overhead based on direct-labor hours. The budget for the current year ending December 31, 20x1, is as follows:

WHITESTONE COMPANY
Budgeted Statement of Gross Margin for 20x1

	JR-14	RM-13	Total
Sales in units	5,000	5,000	10,000
Sales revenue	$1,700,000	$2,200,000	$3,900,000
Cost of goods manufactured and sold:			
Beginning finished-goods inventory	$ 240,000	$ 300,000	$ 540,000
Add: Direct material	1,000,000	1,750,000	2,750,000
Direct labor	185,185	92,593	277,778
Applied manufacturing overhead*	544,025	272,013	816,038
Cost of goods available for sale	$1,969,210	$2,414,606	$4,383,816
Less: Ending finished-goods inventory	240,000	300,000	540,000
Cost of goods sold	$1,729,210	$2,114,606	$3,843,816
Gross margin	$ (29,210)	$ 85,394	$ 56,184

*Total manufacturing overhead (applied on the basis of direct-labor hours:

Machining	$ 424,528
Assembly	216,981
Material handling	56,604
Inspection	117,925
Total	$ 816,038

Mark Ward, Whitestone's president, has been reading about a product-costing method called activity-based costing. Ward is convinced that activity-based costing will cast a new light on future profits. As a result, Brian Walters, Whitestone's director of cost management, has accumulated cost pool information for this year shown on the following chart. This information is based on a product mix of 5,000 units of JR-14 and 5,000 units of RM-13.

Cost Pool Information for 20x1

Cost Pool	Activity	JR-14	RM-13
Direct labor	Direct-labor hours	10,000	5,000
Machining	Machine hours	15,000	30,000
Assembly	Assembly hours	6,000	5,500
Material handling	Number of parts	5	10
Inspection	Inspection hours	5,000	7,500

In addition, the following information is projected for the next calendar year, 20x2.

	JR-14	RM-13
Beginning inventory, finished goods (in units)	800	600
Ending inventory, finished goods (in units)	700	700
Sales (in units)	5,100	4,900

On January 1, 20x2, Whitestone is planning to increase the prices of JR-14 to $355 and RM-13 to $455. Material costs are not expected to increase in 20x2, but direct labor will increase by 8 percent, and all manufacturing overhead costs will increase by 6 percent. Due to the nature of the manufacturing process, the company does not have any beginning or ending work-in-process inventories.

Whitestone uses a just-in-time inventory system and has materials delivered to the production facility directly from the vendors. The raw-material inventory at both the beginning and the end of the month is immaterial and can be ignored for the purposes of a budgeted income statement. The company uses the first-in, first-out (FIFO) inventory method.

Required:

1. Explain how activity-based costing differs from traditional product-costing methods.
2. Using activity-based costing, calculate the total cost for the following activity cost pools: machining, assembly, material handling, and inspection. (Round to the nearest dollar.) Then, calculate the pool rate per unit of the appropriate cost driver for each of the four activities. (Hint: Refer to Exhibit 5–6, regarding calculation of the pool rate.)
3. Prepare a table showing for each product line the estimated 20x2 cost for each of the following cost elements: direct material, direct labor, machining, assembly, material handling, and inspection. (Round to the nearest dollar.)
4. Prepare a budgeted statement showing the gross margin for Whitestone Company for 20x2, using activity-based costing. The statement should show each product and a total for the company. Be sure to include detailed calculations for the cost of goods manufactured and sold. (Round each amount in the statement to the nearest dollar.)

(CMA, adapted)

Case 5–68
Traditional versus Activity-Based Costing Systems
(LO 5-1, 5-2, 5-3, 5-4, 5-5)

2. Product costs with ABC, Standard Model: $437.75
3. New target price, Heavy-Duty Model: $248.73

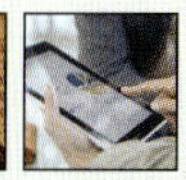

Morelli Electric Motor Corporation manufactures electric motors for commercial use. The company produces three models, designated as standard, deluxe, and heavy-duty. The company uses a job-order cost-accounting system with manufacturing overhead applied on the basis of direct-labor hours. The system has been in place with little change for 25 years. Product costs and annual sales data are as follows:

	Standard Model	Deluxe Model	Heavy-Duty Model
Annual sales (units)	20,000	1,000	10,000
Product costs:			
Raw material	$ 10	$ 25	$ 42
Direct labor	10 (.5 hr. at $20)	20 (1 hr. at $20)	20 (1 hr. at $20)
Manufacturing overhead	85	170	170
Total product cost	$105	$215	$232

Calculation of predetermined overhead rate:

Manufacturing-overhead budget:	
Depreciation, machinery	$1,480,000
Maintenance, machinery	120,000
Depreciation, taxes, and insurance for factory	300,000
Engineering	350,000
Purchasing, receiving and shipping	250,000
Inspection and repair of defects	375,000
Material handling	400,000
Miscellaneous manufacturing overhead costs	295,000
Total	$3,570,000

Direct-labor budget:	
Standard model:	10,000 hours
Deluxe model:	1,000 hours
Heavy-duty model:	10,000 hours
Total	21,000 hours

$$\text{Predetermined overhead rate: } \frac{\text{Budgeted overhead}}{\text{Budgeted direct-labor hours}} = \frac{\$3{,}570{,}000}{21{,}000 \text{ hours}} = \$170 \text{ per hour}$$

For the past 10 years, the company's pricing formula has been to set each product's target price at 110 percent of its full product cost. Recently, however, the standard-model motor has come under increasing price pressure from offshore competitors. The result was that the price on the standard model has been lowered to $110.

The company president recently asked the controller, "Why can't we compete with these other companies? They're selling motors just like our standard model for 106 dollars. That's only a buck more than our production cost. Are we really that inefficient? What gives?"

The controller responded by saying, "I think this is due to an outmoded product-costing system. As you may remember, I raised a red flag about our system when I came on board last year. But the decision was to keep our current system in place. In my judgment, our product-costing system is distorting our product costs. Let me run a few numbers to demonstrate what I mean."

Getting the president's go-ahead, the controller compiled the basic data needed to implement an activity-based costing system. These data are displayed in the following table. The percentages are the proportion of each cost driver consumed by each product line.

		Product Lines		
Activity Cost Pool	**Cost Driver**	**Standard Model**	**Deluxe Model**	**Heavy-Duty Model**
I. Depreciation, machinery Maintenance, machinery	Machine time	40%	13%	47%
II. Engineering Inspection and repair of defects	Engineering hours	47%	6%	47%
III. Purchasing, receiving, and shipping Material handling	Number of material orders	47%	8%	45%
IV. Depreciation, taxes, and insurance for factory Miscellaneous manufacturing overhead	Factory space usage	42%	15%	43%

Required:

1. Compute the target prices for the three models, based on the traditional, volume-based product-costing system.
2. Compute new product costs for the three products, based on the new data collected by the controller. Round to the nearest cent.
3. Calculate a new target price for the three products, based on the activity-based costing system. Compare the new target price with the current actual selling price for the standard-model electric motor.
4. Write a memo to the company president explaining what has been happening as a result of the firm's traditional, volume-based product-costing system.
5. What strategic options does Morelli Electric Motor Corporation have? What do you recommend, and why?

Case 5–69
Cost Distortion; Continuation of Preceding Case
(LO 5-2, 5-5)

Traditional system undercosts Deluxe Model by $222.75 per unit

Refer to the product costs developed in requirement (2) of the preceding case. Prepare a table showing how Morelli Electric Motor Corporation's traditional, volume-based product-costing system distorts the product costs of the standard, deluxe, and heavy-duty models. (You may wish to refer to Exhibit 5–10 for guidance. Because of rounding in the calculation of the product costs, there will be a small rounding error in this cost distortion analysis as well.)

Case 5–70
Ethical Issues Related to Product-Cost Distortion; Activity-Based Costing; Continuation of Case 5–69
(LO 5-2, 5-5, 5-7)

Morelli Electric Motor Corporation's controller, Erin Jackson, developed new product costs for the standard, deluxe, and heavy-duty models using activity-based costing. It was apparent that the firm's traditional product-costing system had been undercosting the deluxe-model electric motor by a significant amount. This was due largely to the low volume of the deluxe-model motor. Before she could report back to the president, Jackson received a phone call from her friend, Alan Tyler. He was the production manager for the deluxe-model electric motor. Tyler was upset, and he let Jackson know it. "Erin, I've gotten wind of your new product-cost analysis. There's no way the deluxe model costs anywhere near what your numbers say. For years and years, this line has been highly profitable, and its reported product cost was low. Now you're telling us it costs more than twice what we thought. I just don't buy it."

Jackson briefly explained to her friend about the principles of activity-based costing and why it resulted in more accurate product costs. "Alan, the deluxe model is really losing money. It simply has too low a volume to be manufactured efficiently."

Tyler was even more upset now. "Erin, if you report these new product costs to the president, he's going to discontinue the deluxe model. My job's on the line, Erin! How about massaging those numbers a little bit. Who's going to know?"

"I'll know, Alan. And you'll know," responded Jackson. "Look, I'll go over my analysis again, just to make sure I haven't made an error."

Required:

Discuss the ethical issues involved in this scenario.

1. Is the controller, Erin Jackson, acting ethically?
2. Is the production manager, Alan Tyler, acting ethically?
3. What are Jackson's ethical obligations? To the president? To her friend?

6 Activity Analysis, Cost Behavior, and Cost Estimation

FOCUS COMPANY >>>

© tanyaru/123RF.com

THIS CHAPTER'S FOCUS COMPANY is Donut Desire, Inc. a Canadian chain of 10 donut shops in Toronto, Ontario. Using the Donut Desire illustration, we explore cost behavior, cost estimation, and cost prediction. Cost behavior refers to the relationship between cost and activity. Variable and fixed costs, which we studied in Chapter 2, are two examples of the many types of cost behavior. Cost estimation is the process of determining how a particular cost behaves, often relying on historical cost data. Cost prediction means using our knowledge of cost behavior to forecast the cost to be incurred at a particular level of activity. Cost analysis helps Donut Desire's management plan for the costs to be incurred at various levels of donut sales activity.

© Photodisc/PunchStock RF

<<< IN CONTRAST

CONSTELLATION COMMUNICATIONS TECHNOLOGY

In contrast to the service-industry setting of Donut Desire, we turn to a manufacturing environment to explore the effect of the learning curve on cost behavior. In many production processes, production efficiency increases with experience. As cumulative production output increases, the average labor time required per unit declines. As the labor time declines, labor cost declines as well. This phenomenon is called the learning curve. To illustrate the learning-curve concept, we explore its use by Constellation Communications Technology (CCT), a Canadian manufacturer of sophisticated communications satellites in Vancouver, British Columbia. CCT's management has found that the learning curve applies to the labor-intensive assembly operation for each new satellite design.

© iLexx/Getty Images RF

After completing this chapter, you should be able to:

6-1 Explain the relationships between cost estimation, cost behavior, and cost prediction.

6-2 Define and describe the behavior of the following types of costs: variable, step-variable, fixed, step-fixed, semivariable (or mixed), and curvilinear.

6-3 Explain the importance of the relevant range in using a cost behavior pattern for cost prediction.

6-4 Define and give examples of engineered costs, committed costs, and discretionary costs.

6-5 Describe and use the following cost estimation methods: account classification, visual fit, high-low, and least-squares regression.

6-6 Describe the multiple regression, engineering, and learning-curve approaches to cost estimation.

6-7 Describe some problems often encountered in collecting data for cost estimation.

6-8 Perform and interpret a least-squares regression analysis with a single independent variable (appendix).

Managers in almost any organization want to know how costs will be affected by changes in the organization's activity. The relationship between cost and activity, called **cost behavior,** is relevant to the management functions of planning, control, and decision making. In order to *plan* operations and prepare a budget, managers at Nabisco need to predict the costs that will be incurred at different levels of production and sales. To *control* the costs of providing commercial-loan services at Wells Fargo, executives need to have a feel for the costs that the bank should incur at various levels of commercial-loan activity. In *deciding* whether to add a new intensive care unit, a hospital's administrators need to predict the cost of operating the new unit at various levels of patient demand. In each of these situations, knowledge of *cost behavior* will help the manager to make the desired cost prediction. A **cost prediction** is a forecast of cost at a particular level of activity. In the first half of this chapter, we will study cost behavior patterns and their use in making cost predictions.

Learning Objective 6-1

Explain the relationships between cost estimation, cost behavior, and cost prediction.

How does a managerial accountant determine the cost behavior pattern for a particular cost item? The determination of cost behavior, which is often called **cost estimation,** can be accomplished in a number of ways. One way is to analyze historical data concerning costs and activity levels. Cost estimation is covered in the second half of this chapter.

The following diagram summarizes the key points in the preceding discussion.

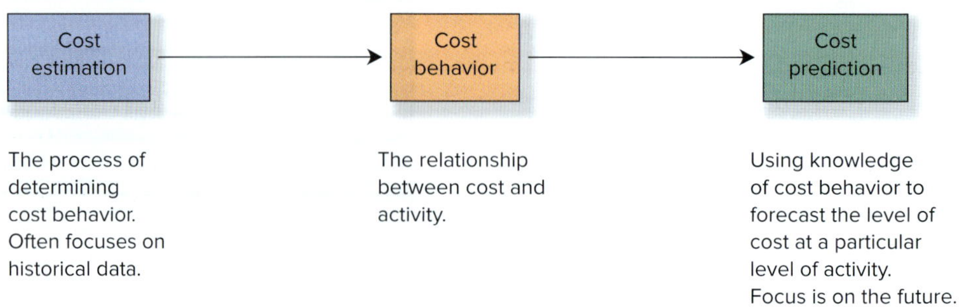

Cost Behavior Patterns

Our discussion of cost behavior patterns, also called *cost functions,* will be set in the context of a donut shop business. Donut Desire, Inc. operates a chain of 10 donut shops in the city of Toronto, Ontario. Each shop sells a variety of donuts, muffins, and sweet rolls as well as various beverages. Beverages, such as coffee and fruit juices, are prepared in each donut shop, but all of the company's donuts and baked products are made in a centrally located bakery. The company leases several small delivery trucks to transport the bakery items to its donut shops. Use of a central bakery is more cost-efficient. Moreover, this approach allows the firm to smooth out fluctuations in demand for each type of product. For example, the demand for glazed donuts may change from day to day in each donut shop, but these fluctuations tend to cancel each other out when the total demand is aggregated across all 10 shops.

The corporate controller for Donut Desire has recently completed a study of the company's cost behavior to use in preparing the firm's budget for the coming year. The controller studied the following costs.

> *Direct material:* ingredients for donuts, muffins, and sweet rolls; beverages; paper products, such as napkins and disposable cups.
>
> *Direct labor:* wages and fringe benefits of bakers, donut shop sales personnel, and delivery-truck drivers.
>
> *Overhead:*
>
> *Facilities costs:* property taxes; depreciation on bakery building, donut shops, and equipment; salaries and fringe benefits of maintenance personnel.
>
> *Indirect labor:* salaries and fringe benefits of managers and assistant managers for bakery and donut shops.
>
> *Delivery trucks:* rental payments under lease contract; costs of gasoline, oil, tires, and maintenance.
>
> *Utilities:* electricity, telephone, and trash collection.

In studying the behavior of each of these costs, the controller measured company *activity* in terms of *dozens of bakery items sold.* Thus, dozens of bakery items sold is the *cost driver* for each of the costs studied. A bakery item is one donut, muffin, or sweet roll. The costs to make each of these products are nearly identical. The number of bakery items sold each day is roughly the same as the number produced, since bakery goods are produced to keep pace with demand as reported by the company's donut shop managers.

> "Failure to understand costs would have left Portugal Telecom vulnerable to competition. Understanding the company's costs became essential to cost reduction efforts and to the company's long-term viability." (6a)
>
> **Accenture,** *(regarding its client, Portugal Telecom)*

Variable Costs

Learning Objective 6-2

Define and describe the behavior of the following types of costs: variable, step-variable, fixed, step-fixed, semivariable (or mixed), and curvilinear.

Variable costs were discussed briefly in Chapter 2. We will summarize that discussion here in the context of the Donut Desire illustration. A **variable cost** changes *in total* in direct proportion to a change in the activity level (or cost driver). Donut Desire's direct-material cost is a variable cost. As the company sells more donuts, muffins, and sweet rolls, the total cost of the ingredients for these goods increases in direct proportion to the number of items sold. Moreover, the quantities of beverages sold and paper products used by customers also increase in direct proportion to the number of bakery items sold. As a result, the costs of beverages and paper products are also variable costs.

Panel A of Exhibit 6–1 displays a graph of Donut Desire's direct-material cost. As the graph shows, *total* variable cost increases in proportion to the activity level (or cost driver). When activity triples, for example, from 50,000 dozen items to 150,000 dozen items, total direct-material costs triple, from $55,000 to $165,000. However, the variable cost *per unit* remains the same as activity changes. The total direct-material cost incurred *per dozen* items sold is constant at $1.10 per dozen. The table in panel B of Exhibit 6–1 illustrates this point. The variable cost per unit also is represented in the graph in panel A of Exhibit 6–1 as the slope of the cost line.

Exhibit 6–1
Variable Cost: Direct-Material Cost, Donut Desire, Inc.

A. Graph of Total Direct-Material Cost

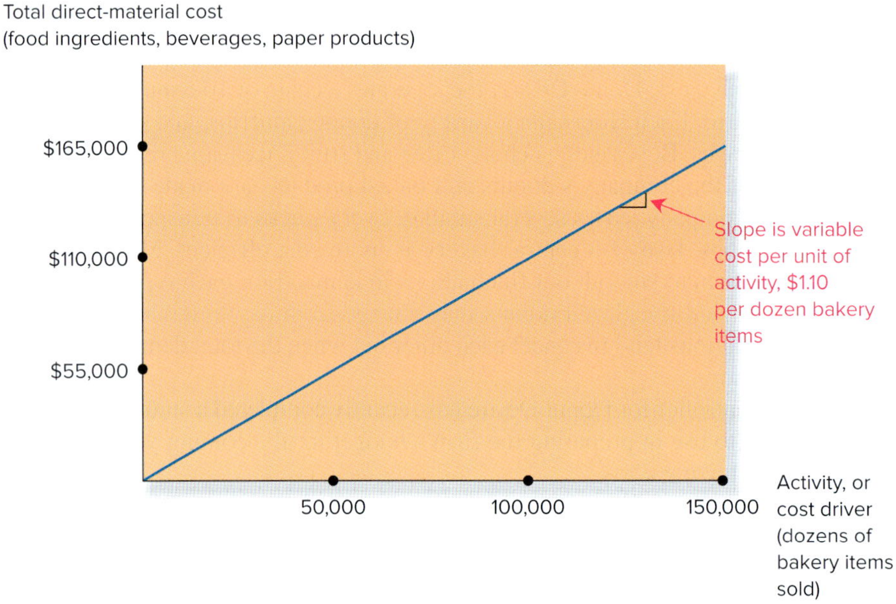

B. Tabulation of Direct-Material Cost

Activity (or cost driver)	Direct-Material Cost per Dozen Bakery Items Sold	Total Direct-Material Cost
50,000	$1.10	$ 55,000
100,000	1.10	110,000
150,000	1.10	165,000

To summarize, as activity changes, total variable cost increases in direct proportion to the change in activity level, but the variable cost per unit remains constant.

Step-Variable Costs

Some costs are nearly variable, but they increase in small steps instead of continuously. Such costs, called **step-variable costs,** usually include inputs that are purchased and used in relatively small increments. At Donut Desire, Inc. the direct-labor cost of bakers, counter-service personnel, and delivery-truck drivers is a step-variable cost. Many of these employees are part-time workers, called upon for relatively small increments of time, such as a few hours. On a typical day, for example, Donut Desire may have 35 employees at work in the bakery and the donut shops. If activity increases slightly, these employees can handle the extra work. However, if activity increases substantially, the bakery manager or various restaurant managers may call on additional help. Exhibit 6–2, a graph of Donut Desire's monthly direct-labor cost, shows that this cost remains constant within an activity range of about 5,000 dozen bakery items per month. When monthly activity increases beyond this narrow range, direct-labor costs increase.

Approximating a Step-Variable Cost If the steps in a step-variable cost behavior pattern are small, the step-variable cost function may be approximated by a variable cost function without much loss in accuracy. Exhibit 6–3 shows such an approximation for Donut Desire's direct-labor cost.

Fixed Costs

Fixed costs were covered briefly in Chapter 2. We will summarize that discussion here, using the Donut Desire illustration. A **fixed cost** remains unchanged *in total* as the

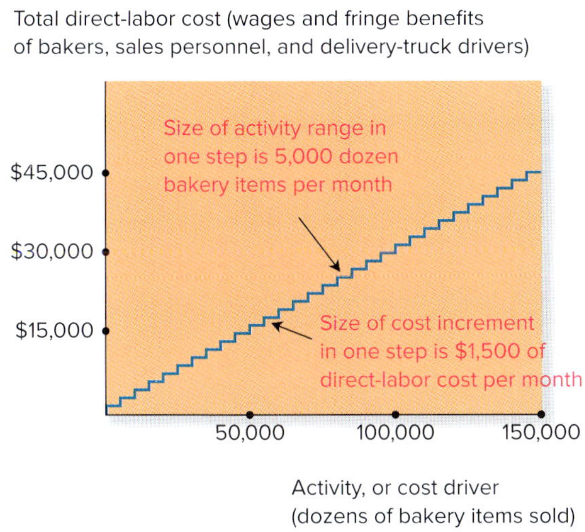

Exhibit 6–2
Step-Variable Cost: Direct-Labor Cost, Donut Desire, Inc.

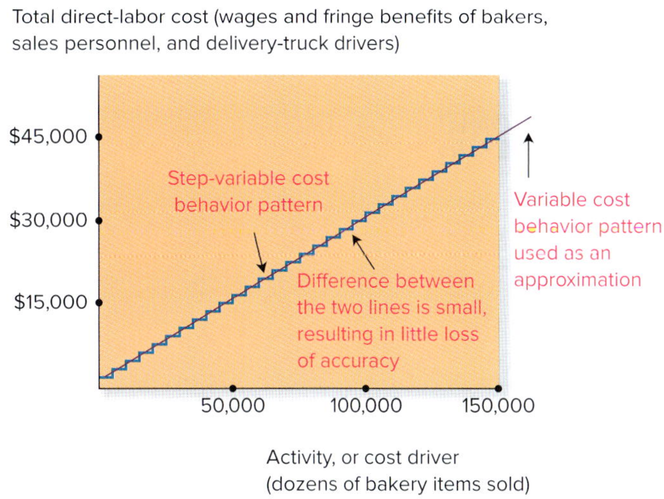

Exhibit 6–3
Approximating a Step-Variable Cost, Donut Desire, Inc.

activity level (or cost driver) varies. Facilities costs, which include property taxes, depreciation on buildings and equipment, and the salaries of maintenance personnel, are fixed costs for Donut Desire, Inc. These fixed costs are graphed in panel A of Exhibit 6–4. This graph shows that the *total* monthly cost of property taxes, depreciation, and maintenance personnel is $200,000 regardless of how many dozen bakery items are produced and sold during the month.

The fixed cost *per unit* does change as activity varies. Exhibit 6–4 (panel B) shows that the company's facilities cost per dozen bakery items is $4.00 when 50,000 dozen items are produced and sold. However, this unit cost declines to $2.00 when 100,000 dozen items are produced and sold. If activity increases to 150,000 dozen items, unit fixed cost will decline further, to about $1.33.

A graph provides another way of viewing the change in unit fixed cost as activity changes. Panel C of Exhibit 6–4 displays a graph of Donut Desire's cost of property taxes, depreciation, and maintenance personnel *per dozen bakery items.* As the graph shows, the fixed cost per dozen bakery items declines steadily as activity increases.

To summarize, as the activity level increases, total fixed cost does not change, but unit fixed cost declines. For this reason, it is preferable in any cost analysis to work with total fixed cost rather than fixed cost per unit.

Step-Fixed Costs

Some costs remain fixed over a wide range of activity but jump to a different amount for activity levels outside that range. Such costs are called **step-fixed costs.** Donut Desire's cost of indirect labor is a step-fixed cost. Indirect-labor cost consists of the salaries and fringe benefits for the managers and assistant managers of the company's bakery and donut shops. Donut Desire's monthly indirect-labor cost is graphed in Exhibit 6–5.

As Exhibit 6–5 shows, for activity in the range of 50,000 to 100,000 dozen bakery items per month, Donut Desire's monthly indirect-labor cost is $35,000. For this range of activity, the company employs a full-time manager and a full-time assistant manager in the bakery and in each donut shop. When monthly activity exceeds this range during the summer tourist season, the company employs additional part-time assistant managers in the bakery and in its busiest donut shops. The company hires college students who

"By understanding the costs and workload associated with the real business activities we undertake . . . we are better positioned to understand where value is created. . . . From this information, we can then make better decisions as to the management and direction of the business." (6b)
Transco

Exhibit 6–4
Fixed Cost: Facilities Costs, Donut Desire, Inc.

A. Graph of Total Monthly Fixed Costs: Facilities Costs

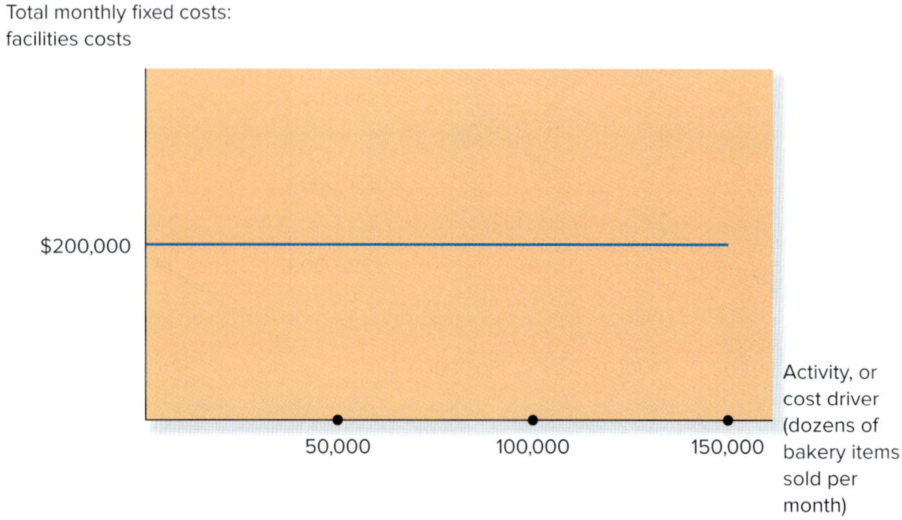

B. Tabulation of Monthly Fixed Costs: Facilities Costs

Activity (or cost driver)	Cost of Facilities per Dozen Bakery Items Sold	Total Monthly Cost of Facilities
50,000	$4.00	$200,000
100,000	2.00	200,000
150,000	1.33*	200,000

*Rounded.

C. Graph of Unit Fixed Costs: Cost of Facilities per Dozen Bakery Items Sold

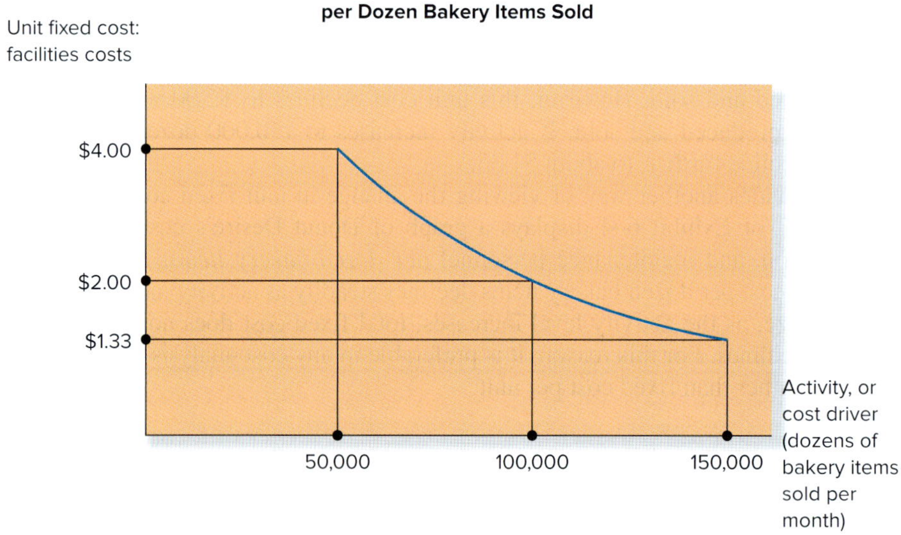

are majoring in restaurant management for these summer positions. Their salaries boost the monthly indirect-labor cost to $45,000. Donut Desire has not experienced demand of less than 50,000 dozen bakery items per month. However, the controller anticipates that if such a decrease in demand were to occur, the company would reduce the daily operating hours for its donut shops. This would allow the firm to operate each donut shop with only a full-time manager and no assistant manager. As the graph in Exhibit 6–5 indicates, such a decrease in managerial personnel would reduce monthly indirect-labor cost to $25,000.

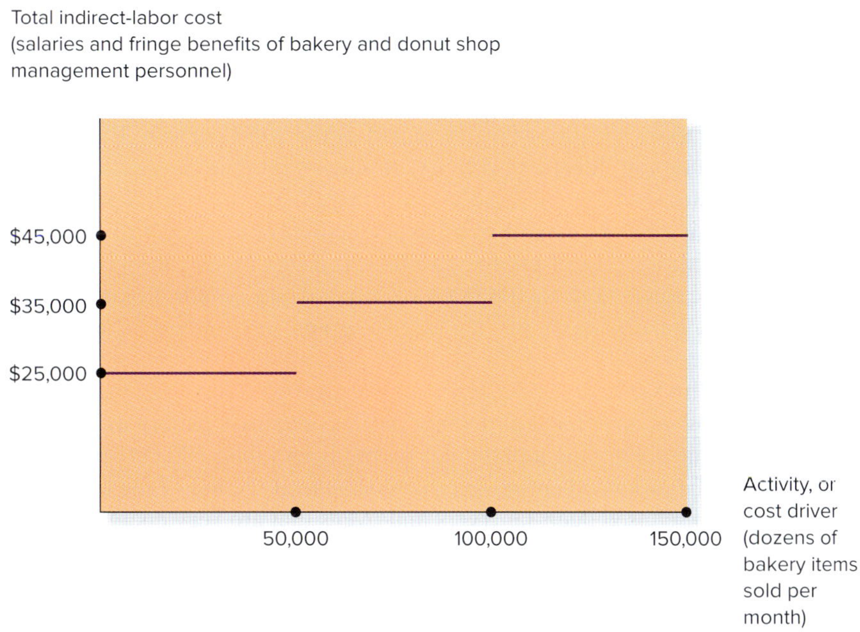

Exhibit 6–5
Step-Fixed Cost: Indirect-Labor Cost, Donut Desire, Inc.

Semivariable Cost

A **semivariable** (or **mixed**) **cost** has both a fixed and a variable component. The cost of operating delivery trucks is a semivariable cost for Donut Desire, Inc. These costs are graphed in Exhibit 6–6. As the graph shows, the company's delivery-truck costs have two components. The fixed-cost component is $3,000 per month, which is the monthly rental payment paid under the lease contract for the delivery trucks. The monthly rental payment is constant, regardless of the level of activity (or cost driver). The variable-cost component consists of the costs of gasoline, oil, routine maintenance, and tires. These costs vary with activity, since greater activity levels result in more deliveries. The distance between the fixed-cost line (dashed line) and the total-cost line in Exhibit 6–6 is the amount of variable cost. For example, at an activity level of 100,000 dozen bakery items, the total variable-cost component is $10,000.

The slope of the total-cost line is the variable cost per unit of activity. For Donut Desire, the variable cost of operating its delivery trucks is $.10 per dozen bakery items sold.

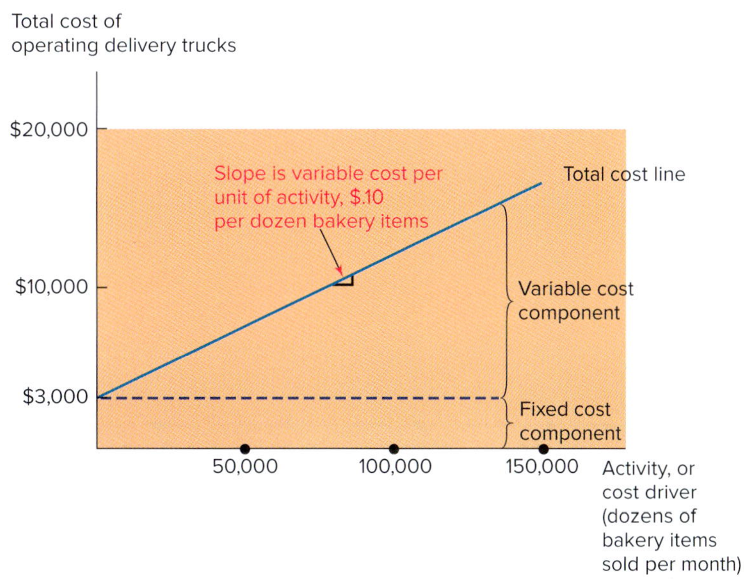

Exhibit 6–6
Semivariable Cost: Cost of Operating Delivery Trucks, Donut Desire, Inc.

Curvilinear Cost

The graphs of all of the cost behavior patterns examined so far consist of either straight lines or several straight-line sections. A **curvilinear cost** behavior pattern has a curved graph. Donut Desire's utilities cost, depicted as the *solid curve* in Exhibit 6–7, is a curvilinear cost. For low levels of activity, this cost exhibits *decreasing marginal costs.* As the discussion in Chapter 2 indicated, a marginal cost is the cost of producing the next unit, in this case the next dozen bakery items. As the graph in Exhibit 6–7 shows, the marginal utilities cost of producing the next dozen bakery items declines as activity increases in the range zero to 100,000 dozen items per month. For activity greater than 100,000 dozen bakery items per month, the graph in Exhibit 6–7 exhibits *increasing marginal costs.*

Donut Desire's utilities cost includes electricity, telephone, and trash-collection costs. The utilities cost is curvilinear as a result of the company's pattern of electricity usage in the bakery. If the demand in a particular month is less than 100,000 dozen bakery items, the goods can be produced entirely in the modernized section of the bakery. This section uses recently purchased deep-fat fryers and ovens that are very energy-efficient. As long as the bakery operates only the modernized section, the utilities cost per dozen items declines as production increases.

During the summer tourist months, when Donut Desire's sales exceed 100,000 dozen items per month, the older section of the bakery also must be used. This section uses

Exhibit 6–7

Curvilinear Cost: Utilities Cost, Donut Desire, Inc.

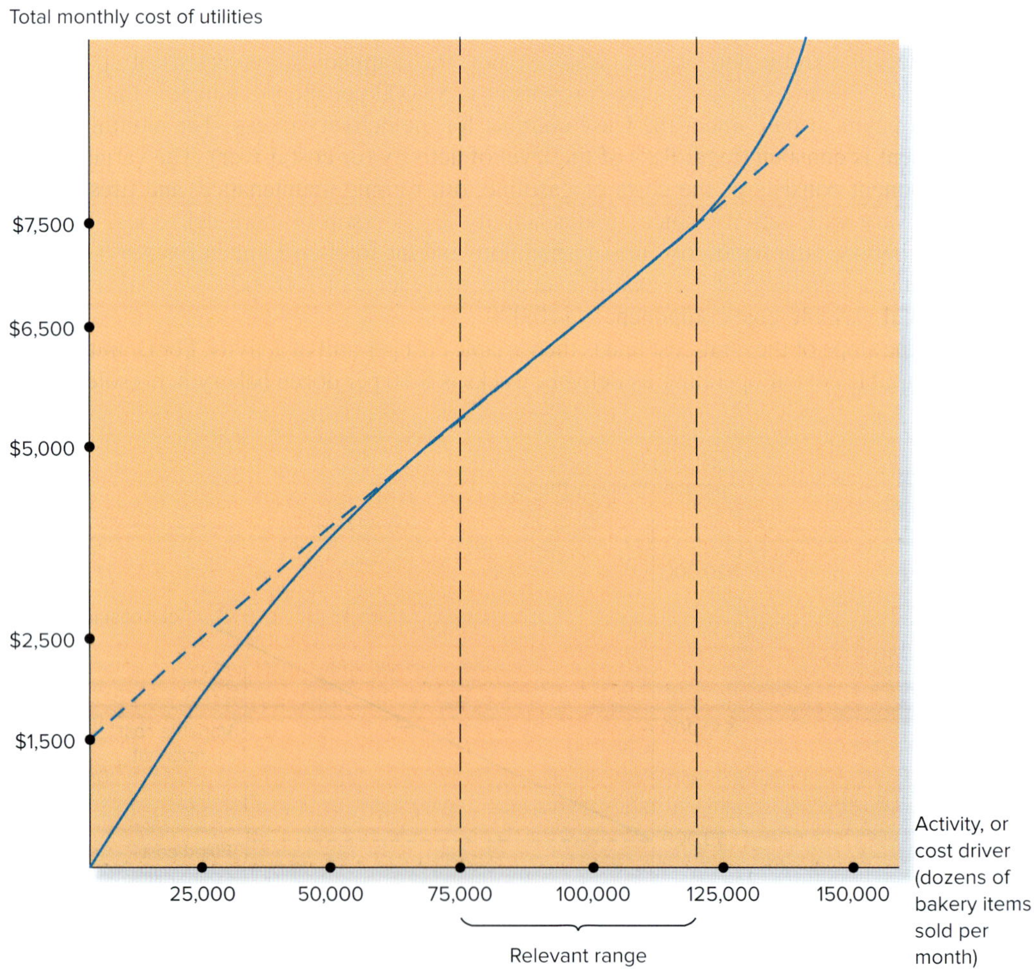

much older cooking equipment that is less energy-efficient. As a result, the marginal utilities cost per dozen bakery items rises as monthly activity increases in the range above 100,000 dozen items per month.

Relevant Range The cost behavior graphed in Exhibit 6–7 is very different at low activity levels (below 50,000) than it is at high activity levels (above 125,000). However, management need not concern itself with these extreme levels of activity if it is unlikely that Donut Desire, Inc. will operate at those activity levels. Management is interested in cost behavior within the company's **relevant range,** the range of activity within which management expects the company to operate. Donut Desire's management believes the firm's relevant range to be 75,000 to 120,000 dozen bakery items per month. Based on past experience and sales projections, management does not expect the firm to operate outside that range of monthly activity. Donut Desire's relevant range is shown in Exhibit 6–7 as the section of the graph between the dashed lines.

Learning Objective 6-3

Explain the importance of the relevant range in using a cost behavior pattern for cost prediction.

Approximating a Curvilinear Cost within the Relevant Range The straight, dashed line in Exhibit 6–7 may be used to approximate Donut Desire's utilities cost. Notice that the approximation is quite accurate for activity levels within the relevant range. However, as the activity level gets further away from the boundary of the relevant range, the approximation declines in accuracy. For monthly activity levels of 25,000 or 150,000, for example, the approximation is very poor.

"Cost estimation is a critical part of our job." (6c)
Ford Motor Company

The straight, dashed line used to approximate Donut Desire's utilities cost *within the relevant range* represents a semivariable cost behavior pattern. This straight-line graph has a slope of $.05, which represents a unit variable-cost component of $.05 per dozen bakery items. The line intersects the vertical axis of the graph at $1,500, which represents a fixed-cost component of $1,500 per month. Managerial accountants often use a semivariable-cost behavior pattern to approximate a curvilinear cost. However, it is important to limit this approximation to the range of activity in which its accuracy is acceptable.

Using Cost Behavior Patterns to Predict Costs

How can Donut Desire's corporate controller use the cost behavior patterns identified in the cost study to help in the budgeting process? First, a sales forecast is made for each month during the budget year. Suppose management expects Donut Desire's activity level to be 110,000 dozen bakery items during the month of June. Second, a *cost prediction* is made for each of the firm's cost items. The following cost predictions are based on the cost behavior patterns discussed earlier. (Try to verify these cost predictions by referring to the graphs in Exhibits 6–1 through 6–7.)

Cost Item	Cost Prediction for June (110,000 dozen bakery items per month)
Direct material	$121,000
Direct labor	33,000
Overhead:	
Facilities costs	200,000
Indirect labor	45,000
Delivery trucks	14,000
Utilities	7,000

Management Accounting Practice

Nestlé, Lincoln Electric, and Hilton Hotels

IS DIRECT LABOR A VARIABLE OR A FIXED COST?

A *BusinessWeek* article titled "The Disposable Worker," explained "how companies are making the era of the 'temp' more than temporary." This raises the question: Are direct-labor costs variable or fixed? The answer, as with many questions, is "it depends." What it depends on is the ability and willingness of a company's management to continually fine-tune the size of its workforce. If labor contracts make it difficult to lay off workers during an economic downturn, or if top management adopts a policy of maintaining a stable workforce, direct-labor costs will tend to be largely fixed (or step-fixed). However, if management can *and is willing to* reduce the labor force when activity declines, then labor cost will be a variable (or step-variable) cost.

The current trend in many companies seems to be toward adjusting the workforce to conform to current needs. Here are several cases in point.

Nestlé

"Nestlé's prepared foods unit has built an in-house roster of part-time workers in Cherokee County, South Carolina, who stick by the telephone to hear if they should report on a given day to assemble frozen chicken dinners. The county job-placement office sends Nestlé lists of 'call-ins', i.e., people available to work when Nestlé phones them. The workers usually get a day's notice. Some agree to stay by the phone in the morning, in case the company is short for the afternoon shift. They typically work two to six days a week and earn slightly more than $11 an hour, which is considered good part-time pay in the area."

The head of human resources for the prepared-foods division says demand for its Lean Cuisine glazed-chicken entrees and Stouffers creamed-spinach side dishes is fairly steady. The company still hires some people full time. But the Nestlé executive says it is still hard to predict labor needs, because schedules for producing certain meals vary, and each product requires a different number of people. "'We don't need the same number of people every day,' he says. 'They work as we need them.'"[1]

Lincoln Electric

"In Cleveland, Lincoln Electric Co. shifts salaried workers to hourly clerical jobs, paying them a different wage for each assignment. The Cleveland-based manufacturer of welding and cutting parts says that, for nearly 60 years, it has guaranteed long-term employment for all of its workers who have worked steadily for three years in its U.S. operations. The flip side is that employees have to be willing to change their job assignments, depending on the type and volume of orders Lincoln receives."[2]

Hilton Hotels

"Many employers, wary of losing valued workers altogether, are reducing the workweek rather than the workforce. Officials of Hilton Hotels Corp. in Beverly Hills, California, boast that they have laid off relatively few workers. However, Hilton says workweek reductions are widespread among its 77,000 workers."[3]

By relying more on part-time workers and daily call-ins, cross-training and frequently moving employees to new jobs, and shortening the workweek, Nestlé, Lincoln Electric, and Hilton Hotels are moving toward direct-labor costs that are much more variable than in the past. Other companies trending toward a "just-in-time workforce" are **Walmart**, **Taco Bell**, **Starbucks**, and **U-Haul**, among others. This is "all part of the larger development in corporate America of transforming labor from a fixed to a more flexible cost."[4]

[1]P. Coy, M. Conlin, and M. Herbst, "The Disposable Worker," *BusinessWeek,* January 18, 2010, pp. 33–45; and C. Ansberry, "In the New Workplace, Jobs Morph to Suit Rapid Change of Pace," *The Wall Street Journal,* March 3, 2002, pp. A1, A7. See also J. Jargon, L. Radnofsky, and A. Berzon, "Health-Care Law Spurs a Shift to Part-Time Workers," *The Wall Street Journal* (online), November 4, 2012, p. 1.

[2]Ibid., pp. A1, A7.

[3]J. Eig, "Do Part-Time Workers Hold Key to When the Recession Breaks?" *The Wall Street Journal,* January 3, 2002, p. A1.

[4]M. Conlin, "The Big Squeeze on Workers," *BusinessWeek,* May 13, 2002, pp. 96–98; and M. Conlin, "The Software Says You're Just Average," *BusinessWeek,* February 25, 2002, p. 126.

The preparation of a complete budget involves much more analysis and detailed planning than is shown here.[5] The point is that cost prediction is an important part of the planning process. The cost behavior patterns discussed in this chapter make those cost predictions possible.

Engineered, Committed, and Discretionary Costs

Learning Objective **6-4**

Define and give examples of engineered costs, committed costs, and discretionary costs.

In the process of budgeting costs, it is often useful for management to make a distinction between engineered, committed, and discretionary costs. An **engineered cost** bears a definitive physical relationship to the activity measure. Donut Desire's direct-material cost is an engineered cost. It is impossible to produce more donuts without incurring greater material cost for food ingredients.

A **committed cost** results from an organization's ownership or use of facilities and its basic organization structure. Property taxes, depreciation on buildings and equipment, costs of renting facilities or equipment, and the salaries of management personnel are examples of committed fixed costs. Donut Desire's facilities cost is a committed fixed cost.

A **discretionary cost** arises as a result of a *management decision* to spend a particular amount of money for some purpose. Examples of discretionary costs include amounts spent on research and development, advertising and promotion, management development programs, and contributions to charitable organizations. For example, suppose Donut Desire's management decided to spend $12,400 each month on promotion and advertising.

The distinction between committed and discretionary costs is an important one. Management can change committed costs only through relatively major decisions that have long-term implications. Decisions to build a new production facility, lease a fleet of vehicles, or add more management personnel to oversee a new division are examples of such decisions. These decisions will generally influence costs incurred over a long period of time. In contrast, discretionary costs can be changed in the short run much more easily. Management can be flexible about expenditures for advertising, promotion, employee training, or research and development. This does not imply that such programs are unimportant, but simply that management can alter them over time. For example, the

"Cost information about activities provides a benchmark to assess how we are doing against best-in-class and competitors." (6d)

BlueCross BlueShield of North Carolina

© CHAMUSSY/SIPA/Newscom

The raw material in these luxury shoes represents an engineered cost. The depreciation on the production equipment is a committed cost. Expenditures on advertising and promotion are discretionary costs. Pictured here is luxury shoe production by J. M. Weston in Limoges, France.

[5]The budgeting process is covered in Chapter 9.

management of a manufacturing firm may decide to spend $100,000 on research and development in the current year, but cut back to $60,000 in the next year because of an anticipated economic downturn.

Cost Behavior in Other Industries

"In the management of a university, just like any other organization, you have to know your cost structure. We think very carefully about how student enrollment will affect faculty salary costs, computing costs, and lots of other costs students don't necessarily tend to think about." (6e)

Cornell University

We have illustrated a variety of cost behavior patterns for Donut Desire's restaurant business. The same cost behavior patterns are used in other industries. The cost behavior pattern appropriate for a particular cost item depends on the organization and the activity base (or cost driver). In manufacturing firms, production quantity, direct-labor hours, and machine hours are common cost drivers. Direct-material and direct-labor costs are usually considered variable costs. Other variable costs include some manufacturing-overhead costs, such as indirect material and indirect labor. Fixed manufacturing costs are generally the costs of creating production capacity. Examples include depreciation on plant and equipment, property taxes, and the plant manager's salary. Such overhead costs as utilities and equipment maintenance are usually semivariable or curvilinear costs. A semivariable-cost behavior pattern is generally used to approximate a curvilinear cost within the relevant range. Supervisory salaries are usually step-fixed costs, since one person can supervise production over a range of activity. When activity increases beyond that range, such as when a new shift is added, an additional supervisor is added.

In merchandising firms, such as Home Depot, the activity base (or cost driver) usually is sales revenue. The cost of merchandise sold is a variable cost. Most labor costs are fixed or step-fixed costs, since a particular number of sales and stock personnel can generally handle sales activity over a fairly wide range of sales. Store facility costs, such as rent, depreciation on buildings and furnishings, and property taxes, are fixed costs.

In some industries, the choice of the cost driver is not obvious, and the cost behavior pattern can depend on the cost driver selected. At Southwest Airlines, for instance, the cost driver could be air miles flown, passengers flown, or passenger miles flown. A passenger mile is the transportation of one passenger for one mile. Fuel costs are variable with respect to air miles traveled, but are not necessarily variable with respect to passenger miles flown. An airplane uses more fuel in flying from New York to Los Angeles than from New York to Chicago. However, a plane does not require significantly more fuel to fly 200 people from one city to another than to fly 190 people the same distance. In contrast, an airport landing fee is a fixed cost for a particular number of aircraft arrivals, regardless of how far the planes have flown or how many people were transported. The point of this discussion is that both the organization and the cost driver are crucial determinants of the cost behavior for each cost item. Conclusions drawn about cost behavior in one industry are not necessarily transferable to another industry.

Cost Estimation

Learning Objective 6-5

Describe and use the following cost estimation methods: account classification, visual fit, high-low, and least-squares regression.

As the preceding discussion indicates, different costs exhibit a variety of cost behavior patterns. Cost estimation is the process of determining how a particular cost behaves. Several methods are commonly used to estimate the relationship between cost and activity. Some of these methods are simple, while some are quite sophisticated. In some firms, managers use more than one method of cost estimation. The results of the different methods are then combined by the cost analyst on the basis of experience and judgment. We will examine several methods of cost estimation in the context of the Donut Desire illustration.

Account-Classification Method

The **account-classification method** of cost estimation, also called **account analysis,** involves a careful examination of the organization's ledger accounts. The cost analyst classifies each cost item in the ledger as a variable, fixed, or semivariable cost. The classification is based on the analyst's knowledge of the organization's activities and experience with the organization's costs. For example, it may be obvious to the analyst going through the ledger that direct-material cost is variable, building depreciation is fixed, and utility costs are semivariable.

Once the costs have been classified, the cost analyst estimates cost amounts by examining job-cost records, paid bills, labor time cards, or other source documents. A property-tax bill, for example, will provide the cost analyst with the information needed to estimate this fixed cost. This examination of historical source documents is combined with other knowledge that may affect costs in the future. For example, the municipal government may have recently enacted a 10 percent property-tax increase, which takes effect the following year.

For some costs, particularly those classified as semivariable, the cost analyst may use one of several more systematic methods of incorporating historical data in the cost estimate. These methods are discussed next.

Visual-Fit Method

When a cost has been classified as semivariable, or when the analyst has no clear idea about the behavior of a cost item, it is helpful to use the **visual-fit method** to plot recent observations of the cost at various activity levels. The resulting **scatter diagram** helps the analyst visualize the relationship between cost and the level of activity (or cost driver). To illustrate, suppose Donut Desire's controller has compiled the following historical data for the company's utility costs.

Month	Utility Cost for Month	Activity or Cost Driver (dozens of bakery items sold per month)
January	$5,100	75,000
February	5,300	78,000
March	5,650	80,000
April	6,300	92,000
May	6,400	98,000
June	6,700	108,000
July	7,035	118,000
August	7,000	112,000
September	6,200	95,000
October	6,100	90,000
November	5,600	85,000
December	5,900	90,000

The scatter diagram of these data is shown in Exhibit 6–8. The cost analyst can *visually fit a line* to these data by laying a ruler on the plotted points. The line is positioned so that roughly equal numbers of plotted points lie above and below the line. Using this method, Donut Desire's controller visually fit the line shown in Exhibit 6–8.

Just a glance at the visually fit cost line reveals that Donut Desire's utilities cost is a semivariable cost *within the relevant range.* The scatter diagram provides little or no information about the cost relationship outside the relevant range. Recall from the discussion of Donut Desire's utilities cost (see Exhibit 6–7) that the controller believes the cost

Exhibit 6–8
Scatter Diagram of Cost Data with Visually Fit Cost Line, Donut Desire, Inc.

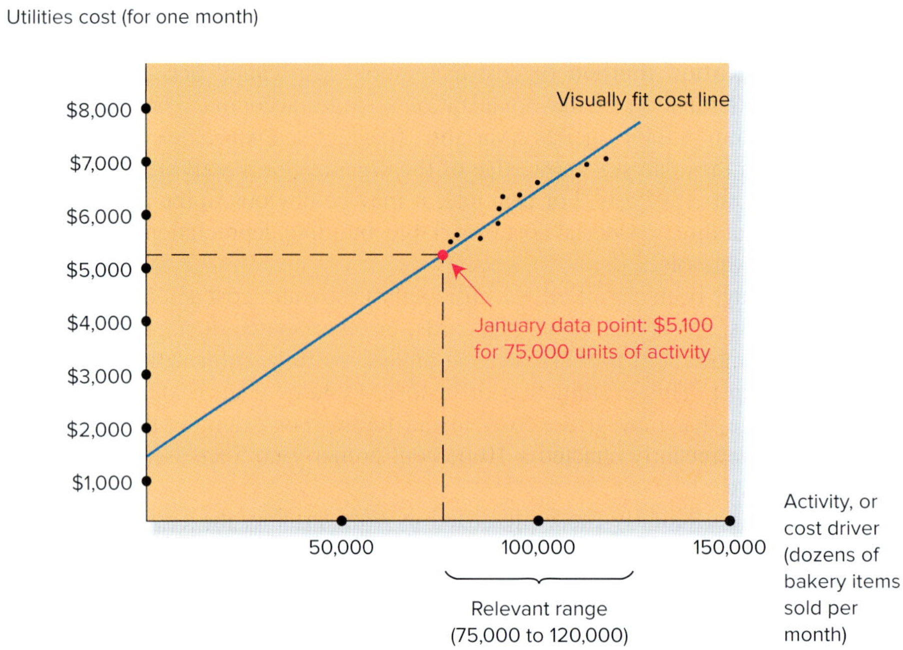

behavior pattern to be curvilinear over the *entire range* of activity. This judgment is based on the controller's knowledge of the firm's facilities and an understanding of electricity usage by the modern bakery equipment and the older bakery equipment. As Exhibit 6–7 shows, however, the curvilinear utilities cost can be approximated closely by a semivariable cost *within the relevant range.* The data plotted in the scatter diagram lie within the relevant range. Consequently, the data provide a sound basis for the semivariable approximation that the controller has chosen to use.

The visually fit cost line in Exhibit 6–8 intercepts the vertical axis at $1,500. Thus, $1,500 is the estimate of the fixed-cost component in the semivariable-cost approximation. To determine the variable cost per unit, subtract the fixed cost from the total cost at any activity level. The remainder is the total variable cost for that activity level. For example, the total variable cost for an activity level of 50,000 dozen items is $2,500 (total cost of $4,000 minus fixed cost of $1,500). This yields a variable cost of $.05 per dozen bakery items ($.05 = $2,500 ÷ 50,000).

These variable and fixed cost estimates were used for the semivariable-cost approximation discussed earlier in the chapter (Exhibit 6–7). These estimates are valid only *within the relevant range.*

Evaluation of Visual-Fit Method The scatter diagram and visually fit cost line provide a valuable first step in the analysis of any cost item suspected to be semivariable or curvilinear. The method is easy to use and to explain to others, and it provides a useful view of the overall cost behavior pattern.

The visual-fit method also enables an experienced cost analyst to spot *outliers* in the data. An **outlier** is a data point that falls far away from the other points in the scatter diagram and is not representative of the data. Suppose, for example, that the data point for January had been $6,000 for 75,000 units of activity. Exhibit 6–8 reveals that such a data point would be way out of line with the rest of the data. The cost analyst would follow up on such a cost observation to discover the reasons behind it. It could be that the data point is in error. Perhaps a utility bill was misread when the data were compiled, or possibly the billing itself was in error. Another possibility is that the cost observation is correct but due to unusual circumstances. Perhaps Toronto experienced a record cold wave during January that required the company's donut shops to use unusually high amounts of electric heat. Perhaps an oven in the bakery had a broken thermostat during January that caused the oven to overheat consistently until discovered and repaired. An outlier can result from many causes. If the outlier is due to an error or very unusual circumstances, the data point should be ignored in the cost analysis.

A significant drawback of the visual-fit method is its lack of objectivity. Two cost analysts may draw two different visually fit cost lines. This is not usually a serious problem, however, particularly if the visual-fit method is combined with other, more objective methods.

High-Low Method

In the **high-low method,** the semivariable-cost approximation is computed using exactly two data points. The high and low *activity levels* are chosen from the available data set. These activity levels, together with their associated cost levels, are used to compute the variable and fixed cost components as follows:

$$\text{Variable cost per dozen bakery items} = \frac{\text{Difference between the } costs \text{ corresponding to the highest and lowest activity levels}}{\text{Difference between the highest and lowest } activity \text{ levels}}$$

$$= \frac{\$7,035 - \$5,100}{118,000 - 75,000} = \frac{\$1,935}{43,000}$$

$$= \$.045 \text{ per dozen items}$$

Now we can compute the total variable cost at either the high or low activity level. At the low activity of 75,000 dozen items, the total variable cost is \$3,375 (\$.045 × 75,000). Subtracting the total variable cost from the total cost at the 75,000 dozen activity level, we obtain the fixed-cost estimate of \$1,725 (\$5,100 − \$3,375). Notice that the high and low *activity* levels are used to choose the two data points. In general, these two points need not necessarily coincide with the high and low cost levels in the data set.

Exhibit 6–9 presents a graph of Donut Desire's utilities cost, which is based on the high-low method of cost estimation. As in any cost estimation method, this estimate of the cost behavior pattern should be *restricted to the relevant range.*

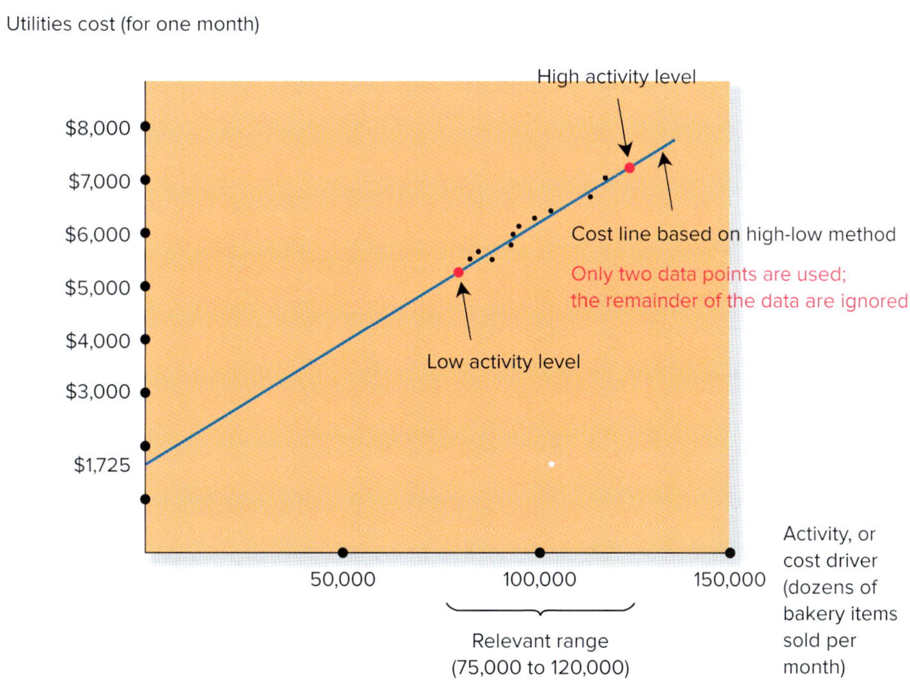

Exhibit 6–9
Graph of Utilities Cost Using High-Low Method, Donut Desire, Inc.

Evaluation of High-Low Method The high-low method is more objective than the visual-fit method, since it leaves no room for the cost analyst's judgment. However, the high-low method suffers from a major weakness. Only two data points are used to estimate the cost behavior pattern; the remainder of the data points are ignored. In this regard, the visual-fit method is superior to the high-low method, since the former approach uses all of the available data.

Least-Squares Regression Method

Statistical techniques may be used to estimate objectively a cost behavior pattern using all of the available data. The most common of these methods is called *least-squares regression.* To understand this method, examine Exhibit 6–10, which repeats the scatter diagram of Donut Desire's utilities cost data. The exhibit also includes a cost line that has been drawn through the plotted data points. Since the data points do not lie along a perfectly straight line, any cost line drawn through this scatter diagram will miss some or most of the data points. The objective is to draw the cost line so as to make the deviations between the cost line and the data points as small as possible.

In the **least-squares regression method,** the cost line is positioned so as to *minimize* the sum of the *squared deviations* between the cost line and the data points. The inset to Exhibit 6–10 depicts this technique graphically. Note that the deviations between the cost line and the data points are measured vertically on the graph rather than perpendicular

Exhibit 6–10
Graph of Utilities Cost Using Least-Squares Regression Method, Donut Desire, Inc.

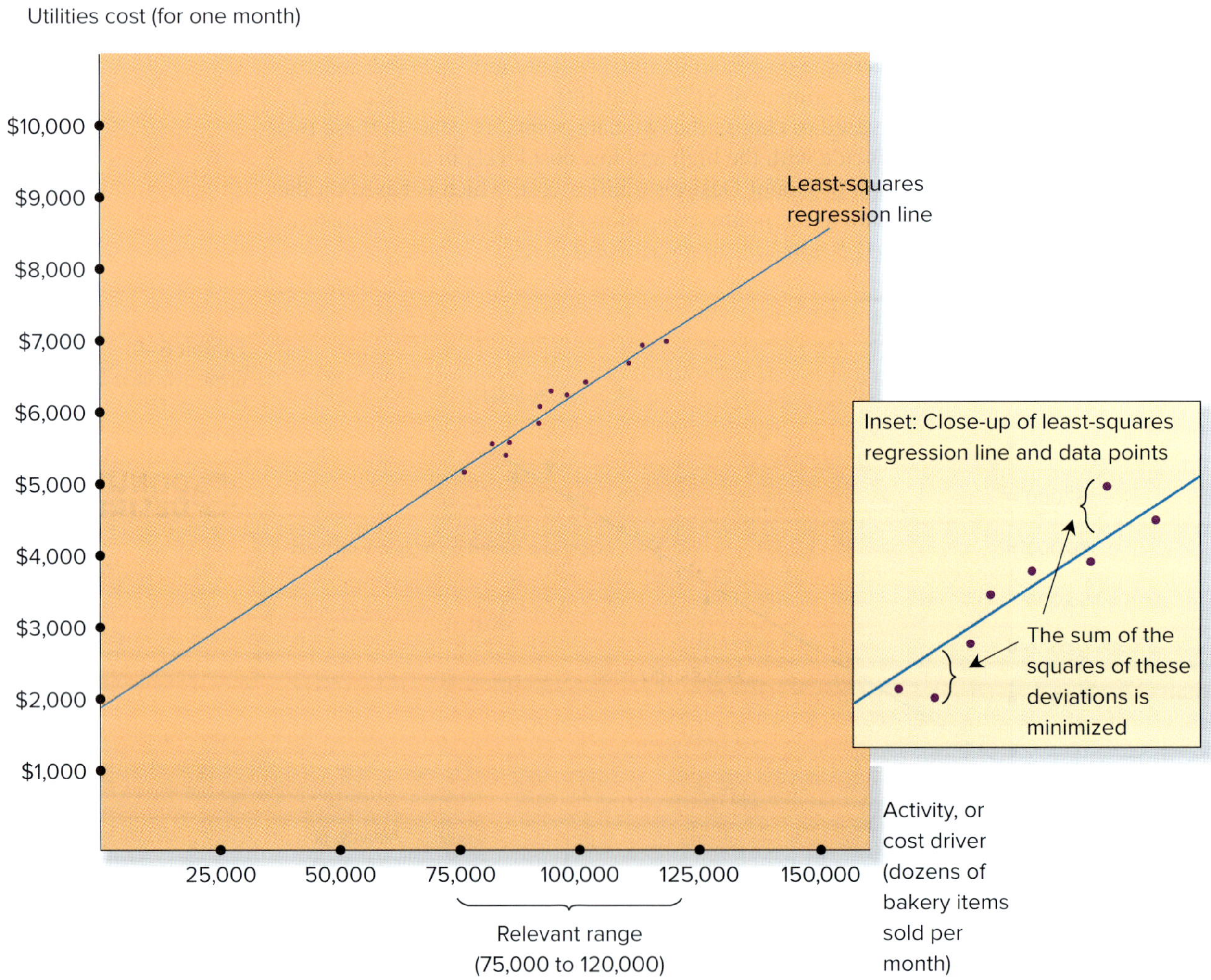

to the line. The cost line fit to the data using least-squares regression is called a *least-squares regression line* (or simply a **regression line**).

Why is the regression method based on minimizing the *squares* of the deviations between the cost line and the data points? A complete answer to this question lies in the theory of statistics. In short, statistical theorists have proved that a least-squares regression line possesses some very desirable properties for making cost predictions and drawing inferences about the estimated relationship between cost and activity. As always, the least-squares regression estimate of the cost behavior pattern should be restricted to the relevant range.

Equation Form of Least-Squares Regression Line The least-squares regression line shown in Exhibit 6–10 may be represented by the equation of a straight line. In the following equation, X denotes Donut Desire's activity level for a month, and Y denotes the estimated utilities cost for that level of activity. The intercept of the line on the vertical axis is denoted by a, and the slope of the line is denoted by b. *Within the relevant range,* a *is interpreted as an estimate of the fixed-cost component, and* b *is interpreted as an estimate of the variable cost per unit of activity.*

$$Y = a + bX \tag{1}$$

In regression analysis, X is referred to as the **independent variable,** since it is the variable upon which the estimate is based. Y is called the **dependent variable,** since its estimate depends on the independent variable.

The least-squares regression line for Donut Desire's utilities cost is shown below in equation form.

$$Y = 1{,}920 + .0448X$$

Y ↑ Estimated utilities cost for one month

X ↑ Activity level for one month

Within the relevant range of activity, the regression estimate of the fixed-cost component is \$1,920 per month, and the regression estimate of the variable-cost component is \$.0448 per dozen bakery items.

There are several statistical software packages available that do regression analysis. However, a common method of computing the least-squares regression estimates is to use a spreadsheet application such as Microsoft® Excel. This approach is covered in this chapter's appendix, which you may want to read now.

Evaluation of Least-Squares Regression Method We have seen that least-squares regression is an objective method of cost estimation that makes use of all available data. Moreover, the regression line has desirable statistical properties for making cost predictions and drawing inferences about the relationship between cost and activity. The method does require considerably more computation than either the visual-fit or high-low method. However, computer programs are readily available to perform least-squares regression.

Evaluating a Particular Least-Squares Regression Line We have seen the benefits of least-squares regression *in general.* How does a cost analyst evaluate a *particular* regression line based on a specific set of data? A number of criteria may be used, including *economic plausibility* and *goodness of fit.*

The cost analyst should always evaluate a regression line from the perspective of *economic plausibility.* Does the regression line make economic sense? Is it intuitively plausible to the cost analyst? If not, the analyst should reconsider using the regression line to make cost predictions. It may be that the chosen independent variable is not a good predictor of the cost behavior being analyzed. Perhaps another independent variable should be considered. Alternatively, there may be errors in the data upon which the regression is based. Rechecking the data will resolve this issue. It could be that fundamental assumptions that underlie the regression method have been violated. In this case, the analyst may have to resort to some other method of cost estimation.

Another criterion commonly used to evaluate a particular regression line is to assess its **goodness of fit.** Statistical methods can be used to determine objectively how well a regression line fits the data upon which it is based. If a regression line fits the data well, a large proportion of the variation in the dependent variable will be explained by the variation in the independent variable. One frequently used measure of goodness of fit is described in the appendix at the end of this chapter.[6]

Multiple Regression

Learning Objective 6-6

Describe the multiple regression, engineering, and learning-curve approaches to cost estimation.

In each of the cost estimation methods discussed so far, we have based the estimate on a single independent variable. Moreover, all of Donut Desire's cost behavior patterns were specified with respect to a single activity (or cost driver), dozens of bakery items produced and sold. However, there may be two or more independent variables that are important predictors of cost behavior.

To illustrate, we will continue our analysis of Donut Desire's utilities costs. The company uses electricity for two primary purposes: operating cooking equipment, such as deep-fat fryers and ovens, and heating the bakery and donut shops. The cost of electricity for food production is a function of the firm's activity, as measured in dozens of bakery items produced and sold. However, the cost of electricity for donut shop heating is related more closely to the number of customers than to the number of bakery items sold. A donut shop's heating costs go up each time the shop's door is opened, resulting in loss of heat. Two customers purchasing half a dozen donuts each result in greater heating cost than one customer buying a dozen donuts.

Suppose Donut Desire's controller wants to estimate a cost behavior pattern for utilities cost that is based on both units of sales and number of customers. The method of *multiple regression* may be used for this purpose. **Multiple regression** is a statistical method that estimates a linear (straight-line) relationship between one dependent variable and two or more independent variables. In Donut Desire's case, the following regression equation would be estimated.

$$Y = a + b_1X_1 + b_2X_2 \qquad (2)$$

where Y denotes the dependent variable, utilities cost

X_1 denotes the first independent variable, dozens of bakery items sold

X_2 denotes the second independent variable, number of customers served

In regression equation (2), a denotes the regression estimate of the fixed-cost component, b_1 denotes the regression estimate of the variable utilities cost per dozen bakery items, and b_2 denotes the regression estimate of the variable utilities cost per customer served. The multiple-regression equation will likely enable Donut Desire's controller to make more accurate cost predictions than could be made with the *simple regression* discussed previously. A **simple regression** is based on a single independent variable. Multiple regression is covered more extensively in cost accounting and statistics texts.

Data Collection Issues

Regardless of the method used, the resulting cost estimation will be only as good as the data upon which it is based. The collection of data appropriate for cost estimation

[6]We have only scratched the surface of regression analysis as a tool for cost estimation. For an expanded discussion of the least-squares regression method, see any statistics text.

requires a skilled and experienced cost analyst. Six problems frequently complicate the process of data collection:

Learning Objective 6-7

Describe some problems often encountered in collecting data for cost estimation.

1. *Missing data.* Misplaced source documents or failure to record a transaction can result in missing data.
2. *Outliers.* We have discussed these extreme observations of cost-activity relationships. If outliers are determined to represent errors or highly unusual circumstances, they should be eliminated from the data set.
3. *Mismatched time periods.* The units of time for which the dependent and independent variables are measured may not match. For example, production activity may be recorded daily, but costs may be recorded monthly. A common solution is to aggregate the production data to get monthly totals.
4. *Trade-offs in choosing the time period.* In choosing the length of the time period for which data are collected, there are conflicting objectives. One objective is to obtain as many data points as possible, which implies a short time period. Another objective is to choose a long enough time period to ensure that the accounting system has accurately associated costs with time periods. If, for example, a cost that resulted from production activity in one period is recorded in a later period, the cost and activity data will not be matched properly. Longer time periods result in fewer recording lags in the data.
5. *Allocated and discretionary costs.* Fixed costs are often *allocated* on a per-unit-of-activity basis. For example, fixed manufacturing-overhead costs such as depreciation are allocated to units of production. As a result, such costs may appear to be variable in the cost records. *Discretionary costs* often are budgeted in a manner that makes them appear variable. A cost such as advertising, for example, may be fixed once management decides on the level of advertising. If management's policy is to budget advertising on the basis of sales dollars, however, the cost will appear to be variable to the cost analyst. An experienced analyst will be wary of such costs and take steps to learn how their amounts are determined.
6. *Inflation.* During periods of inflation, historical cost data may not reflect future cost behavior. One solution is to choose historical data from a period of low inflation and then factor in the current inflation rate. Other, more sophisticated approaches are also available, and they are covered in cost accounting texts.

Big Data

The amount of information with which we all are confronted on a daily basis sometimes seems overwhelming. (How many social media contacts have you experienced today alone?) Yet the amount of data available to most large organizations is many billions of times as great as what we see as individuals. And beyond the scope of a single organization, "the amount of data that is being created and stored on a global level is almost inconceivable, and it just keeps growing."[7] This virtual explosion of data has given rise to the catch-phrase **big data,** which means a massive volume of both structured and unstructured data that is so large it is difficult to process using traditional methods.[8]

Imagine trying to understand cost behavior or make decisions using such a vast trove of data! Managers (and managerial accountants) are intrigued by the possibility that big data contains information that is important and relevant, and that may help them gain an advantage over their competitors or better achieve their goals. But they are also intimidated by the challenge of finding the proverbial needle in a haystack.

---

[7]"Big Data: What It Is and Why It Matters," http://www.sas.com/en_us/insights/big data/what-is-big-data.html, *SAS,* March 15, 2016.

[8]V. Beal, "Big Data," www.webopedia.com/TERM/B/big_data.html, *Webopedia,* March 14, 2016.

Characteristics of big data What is it about *big data* that presents such a challenge? Industry analyst Doug Laney was the first to articulate the defining characteristics of big data "as the *three Vs*."

1. *Volume*. Organizations collect data from a variety of sources, including business transactions, governmental records, social media, and many other sources. In the past, storing such a huge volume of data would have been impossible, but new storage technologies have eased the burden.
2. *Velocity*. Data streams in at an unprecedented speed and must be managed in a timely manner. New technologies are driving the need to deal with torrents of data in near-real time.
3. *Variety*. Data comes in all types of formats – from structured, numeric data in traditional databases to unstructured information, such as text documents, email, video, audio, and financial transactions.[9]

Potential uses of big data Storing and processing big data causes unprecedented challenges for most large organizations. Moreover, simply having access to huge volumes of data is useless unless it can be managed and analyzed effectively. So what are some of the benefits that can result from being able to analyze very large amounts of data? Among the uses for which various organizations are finding for their access to great amounts of data are the following: predicting customer needs and desires for new products and services; minimizing risk and fraud in banking; identifying at-risk students in education; managing governmental agencies, utilities and traffic patterns; increasing output and quality in manufacturing; managing transactions effectively in retail businesses; and managing routes in express delivery services.[10]

Addressing the management and analysis of big data is beyond the scope of this textbook. But as you think about decision making and the various uses of accounting data in companies that we discuss, remember that the information and insights they offer will often arrive as part of a tidal wave of bits and bytes. All managers, and perhaps especially managerial accountants, will need to learn skills for taking advantage of the potential of big data.

Engineering Method of Cost Estimation

Learning Objective 6-6

Describe the multiple regression, engineering, and learning-curve approaches to cost estimation.

All of the methods of cost estimation examined so far are based on historical data. Each method estimates the relationship between cost and activity by studying the relationship observed in the past. A completely different method of cost estimation is to study the process that results in cost incurrence. This approach is called the **engineering method** of cost estimation. In a manufacturing firm, for example, a detailed study is made of the production technology, materials, and labor used in the manufacturing process. Rather than asking what the cost of material was last period, the engineering approach is to ask how much material should be needed and how much it should cost. Industrial engineers sometimes perform *time and motion studies,* which determine the steps required for people to perform the manual tasks that are part of the production process. Cost behavior patterns for various types of costs are then estimated on the basis of the engineering analysis. Engineering cost studies are time-consuming and expensive, but they often provide highly accurate estimates of cost behavior. Moreover, in rapidly evolving, high-technology industries, there may not be any historical data on which to base cost estimates. Such industries as genetic engineering, superconductivity, and electronics are evolving so rapidly that historical data are often irrelevant in estimating costs.

---

[9]"Big Data: What It Is and Why It Matters," http://www.sas.com/en_us/insights/big-data/what-is-big-data.html, *SAS,* March 15, 2016.

[10]Ibid.

Effect of Learning on Cost Behavior

In many production processes, production efficiency increases with experience. As cumulative production output increases, the average labor time required per unit declines. As the labor time declines, labor cost declines as well. This phenomenon is called the **learning curve.** First documented by aeronautical engineer P. T. Wright in the 1930s, the learning curve concept was popularized by the Boston Consulting Group (BCG) in the 1970s. BCG broadened the learning curve idea to include costs other than direct labor and named this phenomenon the **experience curve.** The learning-curve and experience-curve concepts have been applied primarily to complex, labor-intensive manufacturing operations, such as aircraft assembly and shipbuilding. Boeing and Airbus, for example, make extensive use of the learning and experience curve concepts when budgeting the cost for a new aircraft design. However, the learning curve also has seen limited application in the health care services industry, mainly focusing on complex surgical procedures.

To illustrate the learning curve concept, let's explore its use by Constellation Communications Technology (CCT), a Canadian manufacturer of sophisticated communications satellites in Vancouver, British Columbia. The company's satellites transmit voice and data communications around the world. CCT's management has found that the learning curve applies to the labor-intensive assembly operation for each new satellite design. A graphical portrayal of CCT's learning curve is shown in panel A of Exhibit 6–11. On this learning curve, when cumulative output doubles, the average labor time per unit declines by 20 percent. Panel B of Exhibit 6–11 displays the total labor time and average labor time per unit for various levels of cumulative output. As cumulative output doubles from 5 to 10 units, for example, the average labor time per unit declines by 20 percent, from 100 hours per unit to 80 hours per unit. As CCT gains experience with a new satellite design, estimates of the cost of direct labor should be adjusted downward to take this learning effect into account.

Exhibit 6–11
Learning Curve

A. Graphical Presentation of Learning Curve

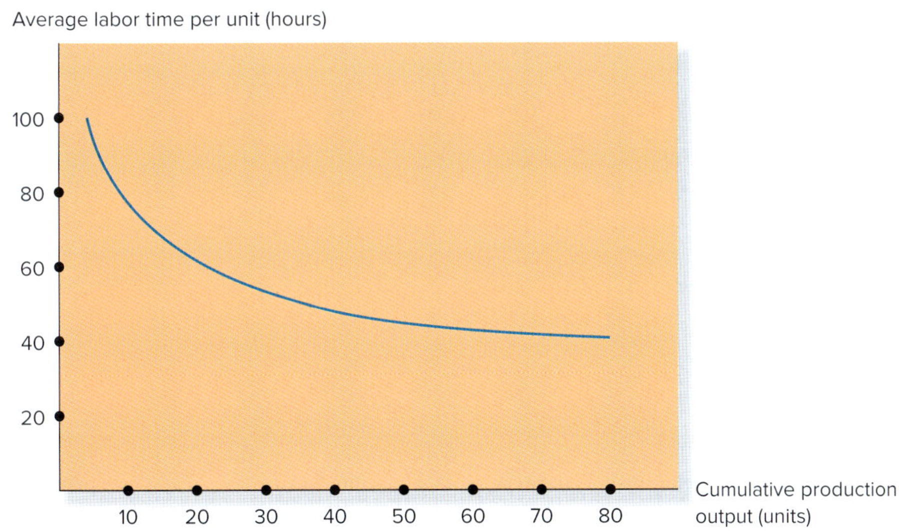

B. Tabular Presentation of Learning Curve

Cumulative Output (In units)	Average Labor Time per Unit (hours)	Total Labor Time (hours)
5	100.0	500.0
10	80.0	800.0
20	64.0	1,280.0
40	51.2	2,048.0

When the learning-curve concept is applied to a broader set of costs than just labor costs, it is referred to as an *experience curve*. Suppose, for example, that all labor and variable overhead costs are observed to decline by 20 percent every time cumulative output doubles. Then we would change the vertical axis of Exhibit 6–11 to *labor and variable overhead costs*. The graph would then be called an *experience curve*.

Learning curves have been used extensively in such industries as aircraft production, shipbuilding, and electronics to assist cost analysts in predicting labor costs. These cost predictions are then used in scheduling production, budgeting, setting product prices, and other managerial decisions.

Focus on Ethics

CISCO SYSTEMS, WALMART, TACO BELL, STARBUCKS, U-HAUL, GENERAL DYNAMICS, AND FARMER'S INSURANCE: IS DIRECT LABOR A VARIABLE COST?

The question as to whether direct labor is a variable cost is interesting from a cost estimation perspective, but it also presents an interesting ethical issue.

Direct material is always a variable cost. At the other extreme, depreciation on fixed facilities and infrastructure typically is not. What about direct labor? Here it depends on the ability and willingness of management to adjust the labor force to current needs. If management is able *and willing* to hire workers as needed and lay them off when activity declines, direct labor would be a variable cost. The contemporary trend at many companies seems to be in this direction. "Companies are looking first to bring in contract workers that they can quickly *tap and zap* without paying any benefits or severance."* In fact, the temps have recently been the fastest-growing sector of employment. "And they aren't accounted for as regular employees. This helps companies that use a lot of them, like **Cisco Systems Inc.**, to drive up revenue per employee."

"The growing use of the *just-in-time workforce* is not the only means by which companies are priming the productivity pump. Workers complain that many employers are taking advantage of outdated labor laws by misclassifying them as salaried-exempt so they can skirt overtime pay. **Walmart**, **Taco Bell**, **Starbucks**, and **U-Haul**, among others, have been slapped with class actions. In the case of **General Dynamics Corp.**, this resulted in a $100 million award that is now on appeal. At **Farmer's Insurance**, employees got $90 million. Some employers are so worried about the issue that they are now doing wage-and-hour audits."

Is it ethical to "tap and zap" employees? What do you think? (For more on this issue, see Management Accounting Practice: *Is Direct Labor a Variable or a Fixed Cost?*, page 240.)

*The information and quotations in this box are from Michelle Conlin, "The Big Squeeze on Workers," *BusinessWeek*, May 13, 2002, pp. 96, 97. See also P. Coy, M. Conlin, and M. Herbst, "The Disposable Worker," *BusinessWeek*, January 18, 2010, pp. 33–39.

Chapter Summary

LO6-1 Explain the relationships between cost estimation, cost behavior, and cost prediction. Cost behavior is the relationship between cost and activity. Cost estimation refers to the determination of a cost's behavior. A cost prediction is a forecast of a cost at a particular level of activity.

LO6-2 Define and describe the behavior of the following types of costs: variable, step-variable, fixed, step-fixed, semivariable (or mixed), and curvilinear. A variable cost changes in total in direct proportion to a change in the activity level (or cost driver). A step-variable cost is nearly variable, but increases in small steps instead of continuously. A fixed cost remains unchanged in total as the activity level (or cost driver) varies. A step-fixed cost remains constant over a wide range of activity but jumps to a different amount for activity levels outside that range. A semivariable (or mixed) cost has both a variable and a semivariable component. A curvilinear cost behavior pattern has a curved graph.

LO6-3 Explain the importance of the relevant range in using a cost behavior pattern for cost prediction. Cost predictions should be confined to the relevant range, which is the range of activity expected for the organization. If the organization operates at an activity level outside the relevant range, any cost predictions based on data from the relevant range may not be very accurate.

LO6-4 Define and give examples of engineered costs, committed costs, and discretionary costs. An engineered cost bears a definitive physical relationship to the activity measure. Direct material cost is an example. A committed cost results from an organization's ownership or use of facilities and its basic organization structure. Examples include property taxes and depreciation on buildings and equipment. A discretionary cost arises as a result of a management decision to spend a particular amount of money for some purpose. Examples include research and development, advertising, and promotion.

LO6-5 Describe and use the following cost-estimation methods: account classification, visual fit, high-low, and least-squares regression. The account-classification, visual-fit, high-low, and least-squares regression methods of cost estimation are all based on an analysis of historical cost data observed at a variety of activity levels. The account-classification method involves a careful examination of an organization's ledger accounts. In the visual-fit method, a cost analyst plots recent observations of cost at various activity levels. In the high-low method, a semivariable cost is estimated using only two data points: the high and the low activity levels. In the least-squares regression method, the cost line is estimated so as to minimize the sum of the squared deviations between the cost line and the data points.

LO6-6 Describe the multiple regression, engineering, and learning-curve approaches to cost estimation. Multiple regression is a statistical method that estimates a linear (straight-line) relationship between one dependent variable and two or more independent variables. The engineering method of cost estimation is based on a detailed analysis of the process that results in cost incurrence. Under the learning-curve approach, the labor cost is estimated by studying the relationship between the cumulative production quantity and the average labor time required per unit. When this approach is applied to costs other than labor, it is referred to as the experience-curve approach.

LO6-7 Describe some problems often encountered in collecting data for cost estimation. Some common data collection problems include missing data, outliers (highly unusual observations), mismatched time periods, and cost inflation. Allocated and discretionary costs create other challenges in data collection and cost estimation.

LO6-8 Perform and interpret a least-squares regression analysis with a single independent variable (appendix). In the least-squares regression method, the cost line is estimated so as to minimize the sum of the squared deviations between the cost line and the data points. The resulting regression line has an intercept on the vertical (cost) axis and a slope, which measures how steeply the cost line rises as activity increases.

Review Problems on Cost Behavior and Estimation

Problem 1

Erie Hardware, Inc. operates a chain of four retail stores. Data on the company's maintenance costs for its store buildings and furnishings are as follows:

Month	Maintenance Cost	Sales
January	$53,000	$600,000
February	55,000	700,000
March	47,000	550,000
April	51,000	650,000
May	45,000	500,000
June	49,000	610,000

Using the high-low method, estimate and graph the cost behavior for the firm's maintenance costs.

Problem 2

The *Keystone Sentinel* is a weekly newspaper sold throughout Pennsylvania. The following costs were incurred by its publisher during a week when circulation was 100,000 newspapers: total variable costs, $40,000; total fixed costs, $66,000. Fill in your predictions for the following cost amounts.

Circulation		
	110,000 Newspapers	**120,000 Newspapers**
Total variable cost	______	______
Variable cost per unit	______	______
Total fixed cost	______	______
Fixed cost per unit	______	______

Solutions to Review Problems

Problem 1

	Sales	Cost
At high activity level, February	$700,000	$55,000
At low activity level, May	500,000	45,000
Difference	$200,000	$10,000

$$\text{Variable cost per sales dollar} = \frac{\$10{,}000}{200{,}000} = \$.05 \text{ per sales dollar}$$

Total cost at $700,000 of sales	$55,000
Total variable cost at $700,000 of sales (700,000 × $.05)	35,000
Difference is total fixed cost	$20,000

The company's maintenance cost may be expressed by the following equation.

$$\text{Total maintenance cost} = \$20{,}000 + \$.05 \text{ (sales dollars)}$$

Alternatively, the maintenance cost can be expressed in the following graph.

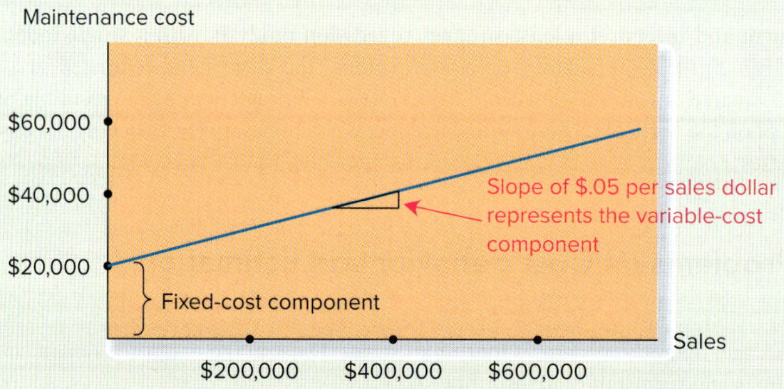

Problem 2

Circulation		
	110,000 Newspapers	**120,000 Newspapers**
Total variable cost	$\$40{,}000 \times \left(\frac{110{,}000}{100{,}000}\right) = \$44{,}000$	$\$40{,}000 \times \left(\frac{120{,}000}{100{,}000}\right) = \$48{,}000$
Variable cost per unit	$44,000 ÷ 110,000 = $.40	$48,000 ÷ 120,000 = $.40
Total fixed cost	$66,000	$66,000
Fixed cost per unit	$66,000 ÷ 110,000 = $.60	$66,000 ÷ 120,000 = $.55

Key Terms

For each term's definition refer to the indicated page, or turn to the glossary at the end of the text.

account-classification method (also called account analysis), 243
big data, 249
coefficient of determination*, 257
committed cost, 241
cost behavior, 232
cost estimation, 232
cost prediction, 232
curvilinear cost, 238
dependent variable, 247
discretionary cost, 241
engineered cost, 241
engineering method, 250
experience curve, 251
fixed cost, 234
goodness of fit, 248
high-low method, 245
independent variable, 247
learning curve, 251
least-squares regression method, 246
multiple regression, 248
outlier, 244
regression line, 247
relevant range, 239
scatter diagram, 243
semivariable (or mixed) cost, 237
simple regression, 248
step-fixed costs, 235
step-variable costs, 234
variable cost, 233
visual-fit method, 243

*Term appears in the appendix.

APPENDIX TO CHAPTER 6

Least-Squares Regression Using Microsoft® Excel

The least-squares regression line, which is shown below in equation form, includes two estimates. These estimates, which are called *parameters,* are the *intercept* (denoted by a) and the *slope coefficient* (denoted by b).

$$Y = a + bX \qquad (3)$$

where X denotes the independent variable (activity level for one month)

Y denotes the dependent variable (cost for one month)

Learning Objective **6-8**

Perform and interpret a least-squares regression analysis with a single independent variable.

Statistical theorists have shown that these parameters are defined by the following two equations.[11]

$$a = \frac{(\Sigma Y)(\Sigma X^2) - (\Sigma X)(\Sigma XY)}{n(\Sigma X^2) - (\Sigma X)(\Sigma X)} \qquad (4)$$

$$b = \frac{n(\Sigma XY) - (\Sigma X)(\Sigma Y)}{n(\Sigma X^2) - (\Sigma X)(\Sigma X)} \qquad (5)$$

where n denotes the number of data points

Σ denotes summation; for example, ΣY denotes the sum of the Y (cost) values in the data

Calculating the intercept (a) and the slope coefficient (b) would be very laborious to do manually. Fortunately, there are many statistical software programs available to do the regression calculations. Alternatively, Microsoft Excel can calculate the regression estimates, as the next section demonstrates.

Using Microsoft Excel to Calculate the Regression Parameters

A cost analyst can use commands in Microsoft Excel to easily calculate the regression estimate for the intercept (a) and the slope (b). All the analyst needs to do is input the data in a spreadsheet. The spreadsheet in Exhibit 6–12 displays the data used to compute Donut Desire's utilities cost. The dependent variable (utilities cost) is in column B, and the independent variable (activity) is in column C. Then the Excel functions INTERCEPT and SLOPE are used to compute the parameters. To use each command, the analyst specifies the range of cells in the spreadsheet in which the values of the dependent variable

[11]The derivation of these equations, which requires calculus, is covered in any introductory statistics text.

Exhibit 6–12
Using Microsoft Excel to Compute the Least-Squares Regression Estimates

DONUT DESIRE

Donut Desire - Excel

FILE HOME INSERT PAGE LAYOUT FORMULAS DATA REVIEW VIEW

B24 =INTERCEPT(B7:B18,C7:C18)

	A	B	C
1	Prior Year Utility Cost at Donut Desire		
2		Utility	
3	Month	Cost	Activity
4	of	for	during
5	Preceding	Month	Month
6	Year	Y	X
7	January	5,100	75,000
8	February	5,300	78,000
9	March	5,650	80,000
10	April	6,300	92,000
11	May	6,400	98,000
12	June	6,700	108,000
13	July	7,035	118,000
14	August	7,000	112,000
15	September	6,200	95,000
16	October	6,100	90,000
17	November	5,600	85,000
18	December	5,900	90,000
19	Total	73,285	1,121,000
20			
21	Computation of Regression Parameters		
22	Using Spreadsheet Functions		
23			
24	Intercept	1,920	
25	Slope	0.0448	
26	R^2	0.949	

Regression Calculations

READY 145%

reside and the range of cells in which the values of the independent variable reside. This is illustrated in the Excel worksheet in Exhibit 6–12 as follows:

Cell B24 contains the following formula: =INTERCEPT(B7:B18,C7:C18)

Cell B25 contains the following formula: =SLOPE(B7:B18,C7:C18)

In these formulas, B7:B18 specifies the range of cells where the values of the dependent variable reside, and C7:C18 specifies the range of cells where the values of the independent variable reside.

As the Excel calculations show in Exhibit 6–12, the regression estimates are as follows:

Intercept: $a = 1{,}920$
Slope: $b = .0448$

So the regression equation is the following:

$$Y = 1{,}920 + .0448X$$

Y: Estimated utilities cost for one month
X: Activity level for one month

Goodness of Fit

The goodness of fit for Donut Desire's regression line may be measured by the **coefficient of determination**, commonly denoted by R^2. This measure is defined as the percentage of the variability of the dependent variable about its mean that is explained by the variability of the independent variable about its mean. The higher the R^2, the better the regression line fits the data. The interpretation for a high R^2 is that the independent variable is a good predictor of the behavior of the dependent variable. In cost estimation, a high R^2 means that the cost analyst can be relatively confident in the cost predictions based on the estimated cost behavior pattern.

Statistical theorists have shown that R^2 can be computed using the following formula:

$$R^2 = 1 - \frac{\Sigma(Y - Y')^2}{\Sigma(Y - \bar{Y})^2} \qquad (6)$$

where Y denotes the observed value of the dependent variable (cost) at a particular activity level

Y' denotes the predicted value of the dependent variable (cost), based on the regression line, at a particular activity level

$\bar{Y}$ denotes the mean (average) observation of the dependent variable (cost)

Excel can be used once again to calculate the R^2. The analyst simply uses the RSQ command in Excel. As shown in cell B26 of the Excel worksheet in Exhibit 6–12, the R^2 is .949.

Cell B26 contains the following formula: = RSQ(B7:B18,C7:C18)

This is a high value for R^2, and Donut Desire's controller may be quite confident in the resulting cost predictions. As always, these predictions should be confined to the relevant range.

Review Questions

6–1. Describe the importance of cost behavior patterns in planning, control, and decision making.

6–2. Define the following terms, and explain the relationship between them: (*a*) cost estimation, (*b*) cost behavior, and (*c*) cost prediction.

6–3. Suggest an appropriate activity base (or cost driver) for each of the following organizations: (*a*) hotel, (*b*) hospital, (*c*) computer manufacturer, (*d*) computer sales store, (*e*) computer repair service, and (*f*) public accounting firm.

6–4. Draw a simple graph of each of the following types of cost behavior patterns: (*a*) variable, (*b*) step-variable, (*c*) fixed, (*d*) step-fixed, (*e*) semivariable, and (*f*) curvilinear.

6–5. Explain the impact of an increase in the level of activity (or cost driver) on (*a*) total fixed cost and (*b*) fixed cost per unit of activity.

6–6. Explain why a manufacturer's cost of supervising production might be a step-fixed cost.

6–7. Explain the impact of an increase in the level of activity (or cost driver) on (*a*) total variable cost and (*b*) variable cost per unit.

6–8. Using graphs, show how a semivariable (or mixed) cost behavior pattern can be used to approximate (*a*) a step-variable cost and (*b*) a curvilinear cost.

6–9. Indicate which of the following descriptions is most likely to describe each cost listed below.

Description	Costs
Engineered cost	Annual cost of maintaining an highway
Committed cost	Cost of ingredients in a breakfast cereal
Discretionary cost	Cost of advertising for a credit card company
	Depreciation on an insurance company's computer
	Cost of charitable donations that are budgeted as 1 percent of sales revenue
	Research and development costs, which have been budgeted at $45,000 per year

6–10. A cost analyst showed the company president a graph that portrayed the firm's utility cost as semivariable. The president criticized the graph by saying, "This fixed-cost component doesn't look right to me. If we shut down the plant for six months, we wouldn't incur half of these costs." How should the cost analyst respond?

6–11. What is meant by a *learning curve?* Explain its role in cost estimation.

6–12. Suggest an appropriate independent variable to use in predicting the costs of the following tasks.

a. Handling materials at a loading dock.

b. Registering vehicles at a county motor vehicle office.

c. Picking oranges.

d. Inspecting computer components in an electronics firm.

6–13. What is an *outlier?* List some possible causes of outliers. How should outliers be handled in cost estimation?

6–14. Explain the cost estimation problem caused by allocated and discretionary costs.

6–15. Describe the visual-fit method of cost estimation. What are the main strengths and weaknesses of this method?

6–16. What is the chief drawback of the high-low method of cost estimation? What problem could an outlier cause if the high-low method were used?

6–17. Explain the meaning of the term *least squares* in the least-squares regression method of cost estimation.

6–18. Use an equation to express a least-squares regression line. Interpret each term in the equation.

6–19. Distinguish between *simple regression* and *multiple regression.*

6–20. List several possible cost drivers that could be used by a cruise line such as Carnival.

6–21. Briefly describe two methods that can be used to evaluate a particular least-squares regression line.

Exercises

All applicable Exercises are available in Connect.

Exercise 6–22
Graphing Cost Behavior Patterns; Hospital
(LO 6-1, 6-2)

Draw a graph of the cost behavior for each of the following costs incurred by the Mountain Summit Hospital. The hospital measures monthly activity in patient days. Label both axes and the cost line in each graph.

1. The cost of food varies in proportion to the number of patient days of activity. In January, the hospital provided 3,000 patient days of care, and food costs amounted to $24,000.
2. The cost of salaries and fringe benefits for the administrative staff totals $12,000 per month.
3. The hospital's laboratory costs include two components: (*a*) $40,000 per month for compensation of personnel and depreciation on equipment and (*b*) $10 per patient day for chemicals and other materials used in performing the tests.
4. The cost of utilities depends on how many wards the hospital needs to use during a particular month. During months with activity under 2,000 patient days of care, two wards are used, resulting in utility costs of $10,000. During months with greater than 2,000 patient days of care, three wards are used, and utility costs total $15,000.
5. Many of the hospital's nurses are part-time employees. As a result, the hours of nursing care provided can be easily adjusted to the amount required at any particular time. The cost of wages and fringe benefits for nurses is approximately $2,500 for each block of 200 patient days of care provided during a month. For example, nursing costs total $2,500 for 1 to 200 patient days, $5,000 for 201 to 400 patient days, $7,500 for 401 to 600 patient days, and so forth.

Exercise 6–23
Approximating a Curvilinear Cost; Public School District
(LO 6-1, 6-2, 6-3)

The behavior of the annual maintenance and repair cost in the Bus Transportation Department of the Summerset Public School District is shown by the solid line in the following graph. The dashed line depicts a semivariable-cost approximation of the department's repair and maintenance cost.

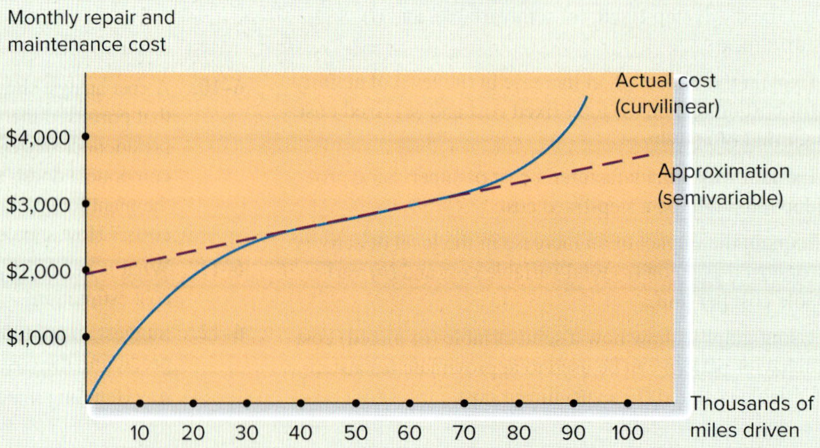

Required:

1. What is the actual (curvilinear) and estimated (semivariable) cost shown by the graph for each of the following activity levels?

	Actual	Estimated
a. 20,000 miles		
b. 40,000 miles		
c. 60,000 miles		
d. 90,000 miles		

2. How good an approximation does the semivariable-cost pattern provide if the department's relevant range is 40,000 to 60,000 miles per month? What if the relevant range is 20,000 to 90,000 miles per month?

Exercise 6–24
Behavior of Fixed and Variable Costs; Television Station
(LO 6-1, 6-2)

WMEJ is an independent television station run by a major state university. The station's broadcast hours vary during the year depending on whether the university is in session. The station's production-crew and supervisory costs are as follows for July and September.

Cost Item	Cost Behavior	Cost Amount	Broadcast Hours during Month
Production crew	Variable		
July		$4,875	390
September		8,000	640
Supervisory employees	Fixed		
July		5,000	390
September		5,000	640

Required:

1. Compute the cost per broadcast hour during July and September for each of these cost items.
2. What will be the total amount incurred for each of these costs during December, when the station's activity will be 420 broadcast hours?
3. What will be the cost per broadcast hour in December for each of the cost items?

Exercise 6–25
Estimating Cost Behavior; High-Low Method
(LO 6-1, 6-2, 6-5)

Jonathan Macintosh is a highly successful Pennsylvania orchardman who has formed his own company to produce and package applesauce. Apples can be stored for several months in cold storage, so applesauce production is relatively uniform throughout the year. The recently hired controller for the firm is about to apply the high-low method in estimating the company's energy cost behavior. The following costs were incurred during the past 12 months:

Month	Pints of Applesauce Produced	Energy Cost
January	35, 000	$23,400
February	21,000	22,100
March	22,000	22,000
April	24,000	22,450
May	30,000	22,900
June	32,000	23,350
July	40,000	28,000
August	30,000	22,800
September	30,000	23,000
October	28,000	22,700
November	41,000	24,100
December	39,000	24,950

Required:

1. Use the high-low method to estimate the company's energy cost behavior and express it in equation form.
2. Predict the energy cost for a month in which 26,000 pints of applesauce are produced.

Exercise 6–26
Estimating Cost Behavior; Visual-Fit Method
(LO 6-1, 6-2, 6-5)

Refer to the data in the preceding exercise.

Required:

1. Draw a scatter diagram and graph the company's energy cost behavior using the visual-fit method.
2. Predict the energy cost for a month in which 26,000 pints of applesauce are produced.
3. What peculiarity is apparent from the scatter diagram? What should the cost analyst do?

Exercise 6–27
Cost Behavior; Use of Internet
(LO 6-2)

Visit the website of one of the following companies, or a different company of your choosing.

Boeing	www.boeing.com
Ford	www.ford.com/us
Honeywell	www.honeywell.com
Levi Strauss	www.levi.com
Dell Inc.	www.dell.com
General Electric	www.ge.com
AOL	www.aol.com
Hertz	www.hertz.com
Lands' End	www.landsend.com
McDonald's	www.mcdonalds.com
Pizza Hut	www.pizzahut.com
U-Haul	www.uhaul.com

Required: Read about the company's products and operations. Then list five costs that the company would incur and explain what type of cost behavior you believe would be appropriate for each of these cost items.

Exercise 6–28
Visual-Fit Method; Veterinary Laboratory
(LO 6-1, 6-2, 6-5)

The Iowa City Veterinary Laboratory performs a variety of diagnostic tests on commercial and domestic animals. The lab has incurred the following costs over the past year.

Month	Diagnostic Tests Completed	Cost
January	3,050	$61,000
February	4,500	74,500
March	7,100	99,000
April	6,200	95,600
May	4,700	74,800
June	5,900	89,000
July	6,000	91,000
August	6,100	90,000
September	5,300	87,000
October	4,900	76,200
November	4,800	78,100
December	5,050	80,700

Required:

1. Plot the data above in a scatter diagram. Assign cost to the vertical axis and the number of diagnostic tests to the horizontal axis. Visually fit a line to the plotted data.
2. Using the visually fit line, estimate the monthly fixed cost and the variable cost per diagnostic test.

Exercise 6–29
Account-Classification Method; Food Processing
(LO 6-1, 6-2, 6-5)

Chillicothe Meat Company produces one of the best sausage products in southern Ohio. The company's controller used the account-classification method to compile the following information.

a. Depreciation schedules revealed that monthly depreciation on buildings and equipment is $19,000.
b. Inspection of several invoices from meat packers indicated that meat costs the company $1.10 per pound of sausage produced.
c. Wage records showed that compensation for production employees costs $.70 per pound of sausage produced.
d. Payroll records showed that supervisory salaries total $10,000 per month.
e. Utility bills revealed that the company incurs utility costs of $4,000 per month plus $.20 per pound of sausage produced.

Required:

1. Classify each cost item as variable, fixed, or semivariable.
2. Write a cost formula to express the cost behavior of the firm's production costs. (Use the formula $Y = a + bX$, where Y denotes production cost and X denotes quantity of sausage produced.)

Exercise 6–30
High-Low Method; Tour Company
(LO 6-1, 6-2, 6-5)

Rio Bus Tours has incurred the following bus maintenance costs during the recent tourist season. (The *real* is Brazil's national monetary unit. On the day this exercise was written, the *real* was equivalent in value to .269 U.S. dollar.)

Month	Miles Traveled by Tour Buses	Cost
November	8,500	11,400 *real*
December	10,600	11,600
January	12,700	11,700
February	15,000	12,000
March	20,000	12,500
April	8,000	11,000

Required:

1. Use the high-low method to estimate the variable cost per tour mile traveled and the fixed cost per month.
2. Develop a formula to express the cost behavior exhibited by the company's maintenance cost.
3. Predict the level of maintenance cost that would be incurred during a month when 22,000 tour miles are driven. (Remember to express your answer in terms of the *real.*)
4. ***Build a spreadsheet:*** Construct an Excel spreadsheet to solve all of the preceding requirements. Show how the solution will change if the following information changes: in March there were 21,000 miles traveled and the cost was 12,430 *real.*

Exercise 6–31
Work Measurement; Government Agency
(LO 6-2, 6-6)

The State Department of Taxation processes and audits income-tax returns for state residents. The state tax commissioner has recently begun a program of work measurement to help in estimating the costs of running the department. The independent variable used in the program is the number of returns processed. The analysis revealed that the following variable costs are incurred in auditing a typical tax return.

Time spent by clerical employees, 10 hours at $12 per hour
Time spent by tax professional, 20 hours at $25 per hour
Computer time, $50 per audit
Telephone charges, $10 per audit
Postage, $2 per audit

In addition, the department incurs $10,000 of fixed costs each month that are associated with the process of auditing returns.

Required: Draw a graph depicting the monthly costs of auditing state tax returns. Label the horizontal axis "Tax returns audited."

Exercise 6–32
Learning Curve; High Technology
(LO 6-1, 6-6)

Weathereye, Inc. manufactures weather satellites. The final assembly and testing of the satellites is a largely manual operation involving dozens of highly trained electronics technicians. The following learning curve has been estimated for the firm's newest satellite model, which is about to enter production.

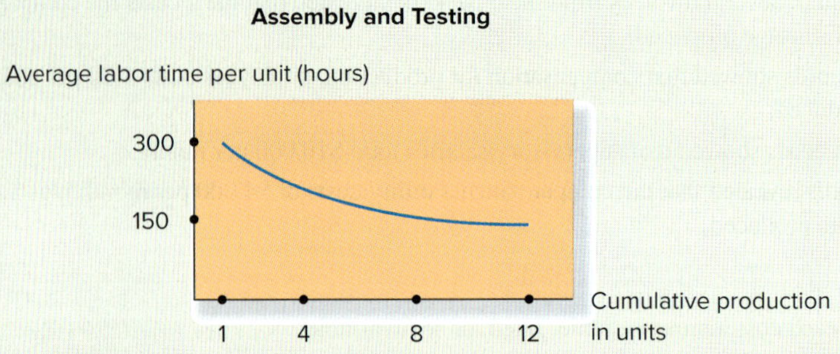

Required:

1. What will be the average labor time required to assemble and test each satellite when the company has produced four satellites? Eight satellites?
2. What will be the total labor time required to assemble and test all satellites produced if the firm manufactures only four satellites? Eight satellites?
3. How can the learning curve be used in the company's budgeting process? In setting cost standards?

Exercise 6–33
Airline; Least-Squares Regression (Appendix)
(LO 6-1, 6-2, 6-5, 6-8)

Recent monthly costs of providing on-board flight service incurred by Great Plains Airlines are shown in the following table.

Month	Number of Passengers	Cost of On-Board Flight Service
January	16,000	$18,000
February	17,000	18,000
March	16,000	19,000
April	18,000	20,000
May	15,000	18,000
June	17,000	19,000

Required:

1. *Build a spreadsheet:* Construct an Excel spreadsheet and use the Excel commands to perform a least-squares regression. Estimate the cost behavior of the airline's on-board flight service. Express the cost behavior in equation form.
2. Use Excel to calculate and interpret the R^2 value for the regression.

Exercise 6–34
Estimating Cost Behavior by Multiple Methods (Appendix)
(LO 6-1, 6-2, 6-5, 6-8)

Gator Beach Marts, a chain of convenience grocery stores in the Fort Lauderdale area, has store hours that fluctuate from month to month as the tourist trade in the community varies. The utility costs for one of the company's stores are listed below for the past six months.

Month	Total Hours of Operation	Total Utility Cost
January	550	$1,620
February	600	1,700
March	700	1,900
April	500	1,600
May	450	1,350
June	400	1,300

Required:

1. Use the high-low method to estimate the cost behavior for the store's utility costs. Express the cost behavior in formula form ($Y = a + bX$). What is the variable utility cost per hour of operation?
2. Draw a scatter diagram of the store's utility costs. Visually fit a cost line to the plotted data. Estimate the variable utility cost per hour of operation.
3. *Build a spreadsheet:* Construct an Excel spreadsheet and use the Excel commands to perform a least-squares regression. Estimate the cost behavior for the store's utility cost. Express the cost behavior in formula form. What is the variable utility cost per hour of operation?
4. During July, the store will be open 300 hours. Predict the store's total utility cost for July using each of the cost-estimation methods employed in requirements (1), (2), and (3).
5. Use your Excel sheet from requirement (3) to calculate and interpret the R^2 value for the regression.

Problems

All applicable Problems are available in Connect.

connect

Problem 6–35
Cost Behavior Patterns in a Variety of Settings; International Issues
(LO 6-1, 6-2)

For each of the cost items described below, choose the graph (see below) that best represents it.

1. The salary costs of the shift supervisors at a truck depot. Each shift is eight hours. The depot operates with one, two, or three shifts at various times of the year.
2. The salaries of the security personnel at a factory. The security guards are on duty around the clock.
3. The wages of table-service personnel in a restaurant. The employees are part-time workers, who can be called upon for as little as two hours at a time.
4. The cost of electricity during peak-demand periods is based on the following schedule.

Up to 9,500 kilowatt-hours (kwh)	$.10 per kwh
Above 9,500 kilowatt-hours	$.13 per kwh

   The price schedule is designed to discourage overuse of electricity during periods of peak demand.
5. The cost of sheet metal used to manufacture automobiles.
6. The cost of utilities at a university. For low student enrollments, utility costs increase with enrollment, but at a decreasing rate. For large student enrollments, utility costs increase at an increasing rate.
7. The cost of online back-up storage at a rate of $2.50 per gigabyte, up to 50 gigabytes, beyond which storage is unlimited, at no additional cost.
8. The cost of the nursing staff in a hospital. The staff always has a minimum of nine nurses on duty. Additional nurses are used depending on the number of patients in the hospital. The hospital administrator estimates that this additional nursing staff costs approximately $195 per patient per day.
9. The cost of chartering a private airplane. The cost is $390 per hour for the first three hours of a flight. Then the charge drops to $280 per hour.
10. Under a licensing agreement with a South American import/export company, your firm has begun shipping machine tools to several countries. The terms of the agreement call for an annual licensing fee of $100,000 to be paid to the South American import company if total exports are under $5,000,000. For sales in excess of $5,000,000, an additional licensing fee of 10 percent of sales is due.
11. Your winery exports wine to several Pacific Rim countries. In one nation, you must pay a tariff for every case of wine brought into the country. The tariff schedule is the following:

0 to 5,500 cases per year	$12 per case
5,501 to 11,000 cases per year	$15 per case
Above 11,000 cases per year	$20 per case

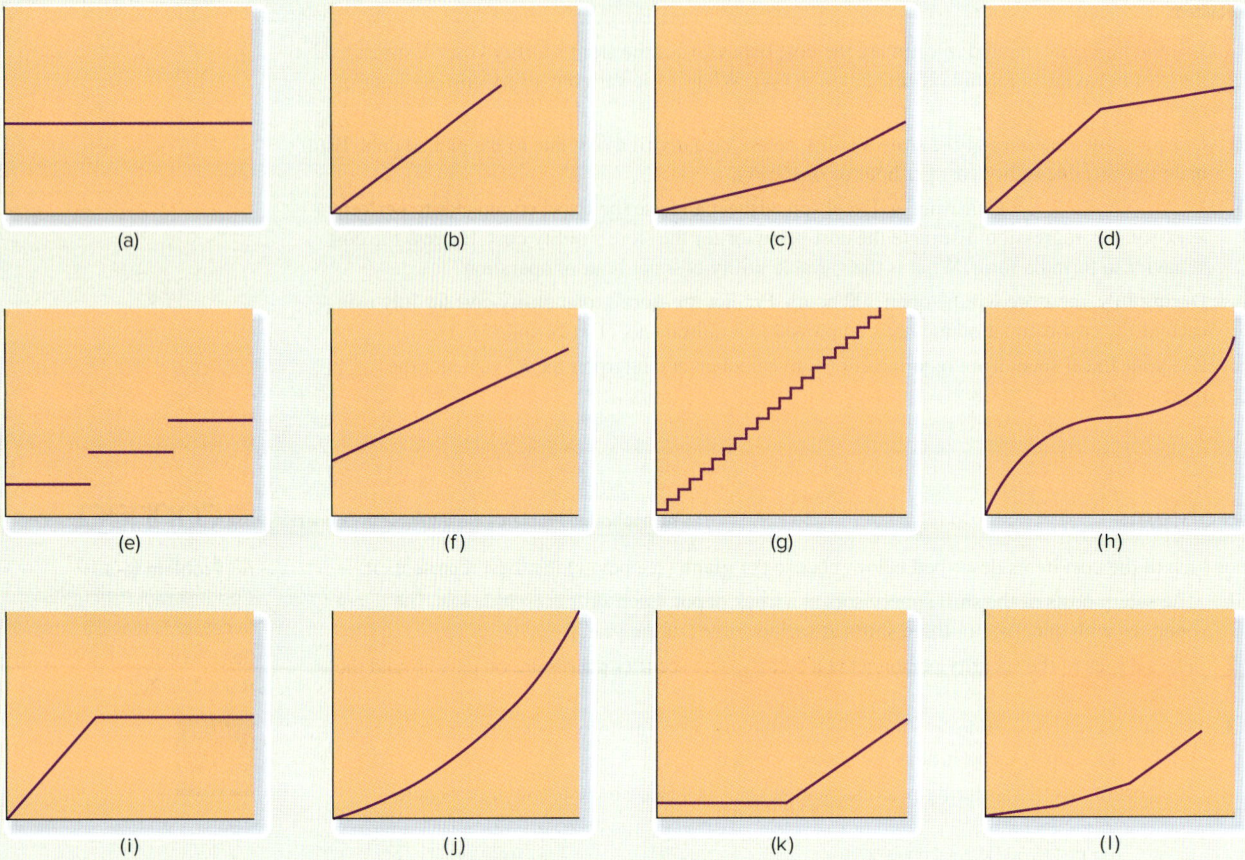

Problem 6–36
Cost Behavior and Analysis; High-Low Method
(LO 6-2, 6-5)

2. Variable maintenance cost: $9 per hour

The following selected data were taken from the accounting records of Metcalf Manufacturing. The company uses direct-labor hours as its cost driver for overhead costs.

Month	Direct-Labor Hours	Manufacturing Overhead
January	23,000	$454,000
February	30,000	517,000
March	34,000	586,000
April	26,000	499,500
May	25,000	480,000
June	28,000	515,000

March's costs consisted of machine supplies ($102,000), depreciation ($15,000), and plant maintenance ($469,000). These costs exhibit the following respective behavior: variable, fixed, and semivariable.

The manufacturing overhead figures presented in the preceding table do not include Metcalf's supervisory labor cost, which is step-fixed in nature. For volume levels of less than 15,000 hours, supervisory labor amounts to $45,000. The cost is $90,000 from 15,000–29,999 hours and $135,000 when activity reaches 30,000 hours or more.

Required:

1. Determine the machine supplies cost and depreciation for January.
2. Using the high-low method, analyze Metcalf's plant maintenance cost and calculate the monthly fixed portion and the variable cost per direct-labor hour.
3. Assume that present cost behavior patterns continue into the latter half of the year. Estimate the *total* amount of manufacturing overhead the company can expect in November if 29,500 direct-labor hours are worked.

4. Briefly explain the difference between a fixed cost and a step-fixed cost.
5. Assume that a company has a step-fixed cost. Generally speaking, where on a step should the firm attempt to operate if it desires to achieve a maximum return on its investment?

Problem 6–37
Cost Behavior and Analysis; High-Low Method
(LO 6-2, 6-4, 6-5)

2. Total cost for 1,650 tons: $823,500

Antioch Extraction, which mines ore in Montana, uses a calendar year for both financial-reporting and tax purposes. The following selected costs were incurred in December, the low point of activity, when 1,500 tons of ore were extracted:

Straight-line depreciation	$ 25,000	Royalties	$135,000
Charitable contributions*	11,000	Trucking and hauling	275,000
Mining labor/fringe benefits	345,000		

*Incurred only in December.

Peak activity of 2,600 tons occurred in June, resulting in mining labor/fringe benefit costs of $598,000, royalties of $201,000, and trucking and hauling outlays of $325,000. The trucking and hauling outlays exhibit the following behavior:

Less than 1,500 tons	$250,000
From 1,500–1,899 tons	275,000
From 1,900–2,299 tons	300,000
From 2,300–2,699 tons	325,000

Antioch uses the high-low method to analyze costs.

Required:

1. Classify the five costs listed in terms of their behavior: variable, step-variable, committed fixed, discretionary fixed, step-fixed, or semivariable. Show calculations to support your answers for mining labor/fringe benefits and royalties.
2. Calculate the total cost for next February when 1,650 tons are expected to be extracted.
3. Comment on the cost-effectiveness of hauling 1,500 tons with respect to Antioch's trucking/hauling cost behavior. Can the company's effectiveness be improved? How?
4. Distinguish between committed and discretionary fixed costs. If Antioch were to experience severe economic difficulties, which of the two types of fixed costs should management try to cut? Why?
5. Speculate as to why the company's charitable contribution cost arises only in December.

Problem 6–38
High-Low Method; Fitness Centers
(LO 6-1, 6-2, 6-5)

3. Cost prediction at 590 hours of activity, maintenance cost: $4,995

Nation's Capital Fitness, Inc. operates a chain of fitness centers in the Washington, D.C., area. The firm's controller is accumulating data to be used in preparing its annual profit plan for the coming year. The cost behavior pattern of the firm's equipment maintenance costs must be determined. The accounting staff has suggested the use of an equation, in the form of $Y = a + bX$, for maintenance costs. Data regarding the maintenance hours and costs for last year are as follows:

Month	Hours of Maintenance Service	Maintenance Costs
January	520	$ 4,470
February	490	4,260
March	300	2,820
April	500	4,350
May	310	2,960
June	480	4,200
July	320	3,000
August	400	3,600
September	470	4,050
October	350	3,300
November	340	3,160
December	320	3,030
Total	4,800	$43,200
Average	400	$ 3,600

Required:

1. Using the high-low method of cost estimation, estimate the behavior of the maintenance costs incurred by Nation's Capital Fitness, Inc. Express the cost behavior pattern in equation form.
2. Using your answer to requirement (1), what is the variable component of the maintenance cost?
3. Compute the predicted maintenance cost at 590 hours of activity.
4. Compute the variable cost per hour and the fixed cost per hour at 600 hours of activity. Explain why the fixed cost per hour could be misleading.

(CMA, adapted)

Problem 6–39
Account-Classification Method; Private School
(LO 6-1, 6-2, 6-5)

The Allegheny School of Music has hired you as a consultant to help in analyzing the behavior of the school's costs. Use the account-classification method of cost estimation to classify each of the following costs as variable, fixed, or semivariable. Before classifying the costs, choose an appropriate measure for the school's activity.

1. Salaries and fringe benefits of the school's full-time teachers.
2. Salaries and fringe benefits of the school's full-time administrative staff.
3. Cost of buying books, sheet music, and other academic materials that are supplied to the students by the school.
4. Repairs on musical instruments. The school employs a full-time repair technician. Repair jobs that are beyond the technician's capability are taken to a local musical-instrument dealer for repairs.
5. Fee charged by a local public accounting firm to audit the school's accounting records.
6. Wages of the school's part-time assistant recital instructors. These employees are hired on a temporary basis. For each student enrolled in the school's music programs, four hours of assistant instructor time are needed per week.
7. Depreciation on the school's musical instruments.
8. Rent for the building in which the school operates.
9. Electricity for the school. The school pays a fixed monthly charge plus $.11 per kilowatt-hour of electricity.

Problem 6–40
Approximating a Step-Variable Cost; Visual-Fit Method; Golf Course
(LO 6-1, 6-2, 6-5)

3. Fixed-cost component: $12,010

Rolling Hills Golf Association is a nonprofit, private organization that operates three 18-hole golf courses north of Philadelphia. The organization's financial director has just analyzed the course maintenance costs incurred by the golf association during recent summers. The courses are maintained by a full-time crew of four people, who are assisted by part-time employees. These employees are typically college students on their summer vacations. The course maintenance costs vary with the number of people using the course. Since a large part of the maintenance work is done by part-time employees, the maintenance crew size can easily be adjusted to reflect current needs. The financial director's analysis revealed that the course maintenance cost includes two components:

1. A fixed component of $12,000 per month (when the courses are open).
2. A step-variable cost component. For each additional 1 to 10 people teeing off in one day, $20 in costs are incurred. Thus, if 101 to 110 people tee off, $220 of additional cost will be incurred. If 111 to 120 people tee off, $240 of additional cost will be incurred.

Required:

1. Draw a graph of Rolling Hills Golf Association's course maintenance costs. Show on the graph the fixed-cost component and the step-variable cost component. Label each clearly.
2. Use a semivariable-cost behavior pattern to approximate the golf association's course maintenance cost behavior. Visually fit the semivariable cost line to your graph.
3. Using your graph, estimate the variable- and fixed-cost components included in your semivariable approximation. Express this approximate cost behavior pattern in equation form.
4. Fill in the following table of cost predictions.

	Predicted Course Maintenance Costs	
	Using Fixed Cost Coupled with Step-Variable Cost Behavior Pattern	**Using Semivariable Cost Approximation**
150 people tee off	?	?
158 people tee off	?	?

Problem 6–41
Work Measurement; Cost Estimation with Different Methods; Wholesaler
(LO 6-1, 6-2, 6-5, 6-6)

3. Variable cost per unit of activity: $1.00

(*Note:* Instructors who wish to cover all three cost-estimation methods with the same data set may assign this problem in conjunction with the next one.) Martha's Vineyard Marine Supply is a wholesaler for a large variety of boating and fishing equipment. The company's controller, Mathew Knight, has recently completed a cost study of the firm's material-handling department in which he used work measurement to quantify the department's activity. The control factor unit used in the work-measurement study was hundreds of pounds of equipment unloaded or loaded at the company's loading dock. Knight compiled the following data.

Month	Units of Activity (hundreds of pounds of equipment loaded or unloaded)	Material-Handling Department Costs
January	1,400	$11,350
February	1,200	11,350
March	1,100	11,050
April	2,600	12,120
May	1,800	11,400
June	2,000	12,000
July	2,400	12,550
August	2,200	11,100
September	1,000	10,200
October	1,300	11,250
November	1,600	11,300
December	1,800	11,700

Required:

1. Draw a scatter diagram of the cost data for the material-handling department.
2. Visually fit a cost line to the scatter diagram.
3. Estimate the variable and fixed components of the department's cost behavior pattern using the visually fit cost line.
4. Using your estimate from requirement (3), specify an equation to express the department's cost behavior.
5. Estimate the material-handling department's cost behavior using the high-low method. Use an equation to express the results of this estimation method.
6. Write a brief memo to the company's president explaining why the cost estimates developed in requirements (4) and (5) differ.
7. Predict the company's material-handling costs for a month when 2,300 units of activity are recorded. Use each of your cost equations to make the prediction. Which prediction would you prefer to use? Why?

Problem 6–42
Continuation of Preceding Problem; Computing Least-Squares Regression Estimates; Comparing Multiple Methods (Appendix)
(LO 6-1, 6-2, 6-5, 6-6, 6-8)

2. Total monthly cost: $9,943 + $.89 per unit of activity

Refer to the original data in the preceding problem for Martha's Vineyard Marine Supply.

Required:

1. ***Build a spreadsheet:*** Construct an Excel spreadsheet and use the Excel commands to perform a least-squares regression. Estimate the variable- and fixed-cost components in the company's material-handling department costs.
2. Write the least-squares regression equation for the department's costs.

3. Predict the firm's material-handling department's costs for a month when 2,300 units of activity are recorded.
4. Why do the three cost predictions computed in this and the preceding problem differ? Which method do you recommend? Why?
5. ***Build a spreadsheet:*** Use your Excel spreadsheet from requirement (1) to compute the R^2 value for the regression. Interpret the R^2 value.

Problem 6–43
Cost Estimation Methods; Cost Analysis; E-Commerce
(LO 6-2, 6-5)

4. C: $1,567,000

Shortly after being hired as an analyst with Global American Airlines, Kim Williams was asked to prepare a report that focused on passenger ticketing cost. The airline writes most of its own tickets (largely through reservations personnel), makes little use of travel agents, and has seen an ever-increasing passenger interest in e-ticketing (i.e., electronic reservations and tickets handled over the Internet).

After some discussion, Williams thought it would be beneficial to begin her report with an overview of three different cost estimation tools: scatter diagrams, least-squares regression, and the high-low method. She would then present the results of her analysis of the past year's monthly ticketing cost, which was driven largely by the number of tickets written. These results would be presented in the form of algebraic equations that were derived by the three tools just cited. The equations follow. (C denotes ticketing cost, and PT denotes number of passenger tickets written.)

Scatter diagram: C = $320,000 + $2.15PT
Least-squares regression: C = $312,000 + $2.30PT
High-low method: C = $295,000 + $2.55PT

Williams had analyzed data over the past 12 months and built equations on these data, purposely including the slowest month of the year (February) and the busiest month (November) so that things would ". . . tend to average out." She observed that November was especially busy because of Thanksgiving, passengers purchasing tickets for upcoming holiday travel in December, and the effects of a strike by Delta Western Airlines, Global American's chief competitor. The lengthy strike resulted in many of Delta Western's passengers being rerouted on Global American flights.

Required:

1. Prepare a bullet-point list suitable for use in Williams's report that describes the features of scatter diagrams, least-squares regression, and the high-low method. Determine which of the three tools will typically produce the most accurate results.
2. Will the three cost estimation tools normally result in different equations? Why?
3. Assuming the use of least-squares regression, explain what the $312,000 and $2.30 figures represent.
4. Assuming the use of a scatter diagram, predict the cost of an upcoming month when Global American expects to write 580,000 tickets.
5. Did Williams err in constructing the equations on data of the past 12 months? Briefly explain.
6. Assume that over the next few years, more of Global American's passengers will take advantage of e-ticketing over the Internet. What will likely happen to the airline's cost structure in terms of variable and fixed cost incurred?

Problem 6–44
Comparing Regression and High-Low Estimates; Manufacturer
(LO 6-1, 6-2, 6-5, 6-7)

5. Fixed cost: $150

The controller of Chittenango Chain Company believes that the identification of the variable and fixed components of the firm's costs will enable the firm to make better planning and control decisions. Among the costs the controller is concerned about is the behavior of indirect-materials cost. She believes there is a correlation between machine hours and the amount of indirect materials used.

A member of the controller's staff has suggested that least-squares regression be used to determine the cost behavior of indirect materials. The regression equation shown below was developed from 40 pairs of observations.

S = $200 + $4H
where S = Total monthly cost of indirect materials
H = Machine hours per month

Required:

1. Explain the meaning of "200" and "4" in the regression equation $S = \$200 + \$4H$.
2. Calculate the estimated cost of indirect materials if 900 machine hours are to be used during a month.

3. To determine the validity of the cost estimate computed in requirement (2), what question would you ask the controller about the data used for the regression?
4. The high and low activity levels during the past four years, as measured by machine hours, occurred during April and August, respectively. Data concerning machine hours and indirect-material usage follow.

	April	August
Machine hours	1,100	800
Indirect supplies:		
Beginning inventory	$1,200	$ 950
Ending inventory	1,550	2,900
Purchases	6,000	6,100

Determine the cost of indirect materials used during April and August.

5. Use the high-low method to estimate the behavior of the company's indirect-material cost. Express the cost behavior pattern in equation form.
6. Which cost estimate would you recommend to the controller, the regression estimate or the high-low estimate? Why?

(CMA, adapted)

Problem 6–45
Interpreting Regression Analysis in Cost Estimation
(LO 6-1, 6-2, 6-5)

3. Minimum bid for 200-person cocktail party: $4,400

Dana Rand owns a catering company that prepares banquets and parties for both individual and business functions throughout the year. Rand's business is seasonal, with a heavy schedule during the summer months and the year-end holidays and a light schedule at other times. During peak periods, there are extra costs; however, even during nonpeak periods Rand must work more to cover her expenses.

One of the major events Rand's customers request is a cocktail party. She offers a standard cocktail party and has developed the following cost structure on a per-person basis.

Food and beverages	$15
Labor (.5 hr. @ $10 per hour)	5
Overhead (.5 hr. @ $14 per hour)	7
Total cost per person	$27

When bidding on cocktail parties, Rand adds a 15 percent markup to this cost structure as a profit margin. Rand is quite certain about her estimates of the prime costs but is not as comfortable with the overhead estimate. This estimate was based on the actual data for the past 12 months presented in the following table. These data indicate that overhead expenses vary with the direct-labor hours expended. The $14 estimate was determined by dividing total overhead expended for the 12 months ($805,000) by total labor hours (57,600) and rounding to the nearest dollar.

Month	Labor Hours	Overhead Expenses
January	2,500	$55,000
February	2,800	59,000
March	3,000	60,000
April	4,200	64,000
May	4,500	67,000
June	5,500	71,000
July	6,500	74,000
August	7,500	77,000
September	7,000	75,000
October	4,500	68,000
November	3,100	62,000
December	6,500	73,000
Total	57,600	$805,000

Rand recently attended a meeting of the local chamber of commerce and heard a business consultant discuss regression analysis and its business applications. After the meeting, Rand decided to do a regression analysis of the overhead data she had collected. The following results were obtained.

Intercept (*a*)	48,000
Coefficient (*b*)	4

Required:

1. Explain the difference between the overhead rate originally estimated by Dana Rand and the overhead rate developed from the regression method.
2. Using data from the regression analysis, develop the following cost estimates per person for a cocktail party.
   a. Variable cost per person
   b. Absorption cost per person
   Assume that the level of activity remains within the relevant range.
3. Dana Rand has been asked to prepare a bid for a 200-person cocktail party to be given next month. Determine the minimum bid price that Rand should be willing to submit.
4. What other factors should Dana Rand consider in developing the bid price for the cocktail party?

(CMA, adapted)

Problem 6–46
Computing Least-Squares Regression Estimates; Airport Costs (Appendix)
(LO 6-1, 6-2, 6-5, 6-8)

2. Variable: $6.77 per flight
2. Fixed: $11,796 per month
4. Cost prediction, 1,600 flights: $22,628

Madison County Airport handles several daily commuter flights and many private flights. The county budget officer has compiled the following data regarding airport costs and activity over the past year.

Month	Flights Originating at Madison County Airport	Airport Costs
January	1,100	$20,000
February	800	17,000
March	1,400	19,000
April	900	18,000
May	1,000	19,000
June	1,200	20,000
July	1,100	18,000
August	1,400	24,000
September	1,000	19,000
October	1,200	21,000
November	900	17,000
December	1,500	21,000

Required:

1. Draw a scatter diagram of the airport costs shown above.
2. ***Build a spreadsheet:*** Construct an Excel spreadsheet and use the Excel commands to perform a least-squares regression. Estimate the variable- and fixed-cost components in the airport's cost behavior pattern.
3. Write the least-squares regression equation for the airport's costs.
4. Predict the airport's costs during a month when 1,600 flights originate at the airport.
5. Using the Excel spreadsheet prepared for requirement (2), compute the coefficient of determination (R^2) for the regression equation. Briefly interpret R^2.

Cases

■ **Case 6–47**

Interpreting Least-Squares Regression; Landscaping Service; Activity-Based Costing **(LO 6-1, 6-2, 6-5)**

2. Total variable cost per 1,000 square feet: $496.25
5(b). Total incremental variable overhead: $3,285

Earth and Artistry, Inc. provides commercial landscaping services. Sasha Cairns, the firm's owner, wants to develop cost estimates that she can use to prepare bids on jobs. After analyzing the firm's costs, Cairns has developed the following preliminary cost estimates for each 1,000 square feet of landscaping.

Direct material	$400
Direct labor (5 direct-labor hours at $10 per hour)	50
Overhead (at $18 per direct-labor hour)	90
Total cost per 1,000 square feet	$540

Cairns is quite certain about the estimates for direct material and direct labor. However, she is not as comfortable with the overhead estimate. The estimate for overhead is based on the overhead costs that were incurred during the past 12 months as presented in the following schedule. The estimate of $18 per direct-labor hour was determined by dividing the total overhead costs for the 12-month period ($648,000) by the total direct-labor hours (36,000).

	Total Overhead	Regular Direct-Labor Hours	Overtime Direct-Labor Hours*	Total Direct-Labor Hours
January	$ 54,000	2,910	190	3,100
February	47,000	2,380	20	2,400
March	48,000	2,210	40	2,250
April	56,000	2,590	210	2,800
May	57,000	3,030	470	3,500
June	65,000	3,240	760	4,000
July	64,000	3,380	620	4,000
August	56,000	3,050	350	3,400
September	53,000	2,760	40	2,800
October	47,000	2,770	30	2,800
November	47,000	2,120	30	2,150
December	54,000	2,560	240	2,800
Total	$648,000	33,000	3,000	36,000

*The overtime premium is 50 percent of the direct-labor wage rate.

Cairns believes that overhead is affected by total monthly direct-labor hours. Cairns decided to perform a least-squares regression of overhead (OH) on total direct-labor hours (DLH). The following regression formula was obtained.

$$OH = 26{,}200 + 9.25DLH$$

Required:

1. The overhead rate developed from the least-squares regression is different from Cairns' preliminary estimate of $18 per direct-labor hour. Explain the difference in the two overhead rates.
2. Using the overhead formula that was derived from the least-squares regression, determine a total variable-cost estimate for each 1,000 square feet of landscaping.
3. Cairns has been asked to submit a bid on a landscaping project for the city government consisting of 60,000 square feet. Cairns estimates that 40 percent of the direct-labor hours required for the project will be on overtime. Calculate the incremental costs that should be included in any bid that Cairns would submit on this project. Use the overhead formula derived from the least-squares regression.
4. Should management rely on the overhead formula derived from the least-squares regression as the basis for the variable overhead component of its cost estimate? Explain your answer.
5. After attending a seminar on activity-based costing, Cairns decided to further analyze the company's activities and costs. She discovered that a more accurate portrayal of the firm's cost behavior

could be achieved by dividing overhead into three separate pools, each with its own cost driver. Separate regression equations were estimated for each of the cost pools, with the following results.

$OH_1 = 10{,}000 + 4.10DLH$,

where DLH denotes direct-labor hours

$OH_2 = 9{,}100 + 13.50SFS$,

where SFS denotes the number of square feet of turf seeded (in thousands)

$OH_3 = 8{,}000 + 6.60PL$,

where PL denotes the number of individual plantings (e.g., trees and shrubs)

Assume that 5 direct-labor hours will be needed to landscape each 1,000 square feet, regardless of the specific planting material used.

a. Suppose the landscaping project for the city will involve seeding all 60,000 square feet of turf and planting 80 trees and shrubs. Calculate the incremental *variable overhead* cost that Cairns should include in the bid.

b. Recompute the incremental variable overhead cost for the city's landscaping project assuming half of the 60,000-square-foot landscaping area will be seeded and there will be 250 individual plantings. The plantings will cover the entire 60,000-square-foot area.

c. Briefly explain, using concepts from activity-based costing, why the incremental costs differ in requirements (*a*) and (*b*).

(CMA, adapted)

Case 6–48

Approximating a Curvilinear Cost; Visual-Fit Method; Pediatrics Clinic

(LO 6-1, 6-2, 6-5)

6. Administrative cost = \$7,000 + \$3.00X, where X denotes number of patients

(*Note:* Instructors who wish to cover all three cost-estimation methods with the same data set may assign this case in conjunction with the following case.)

"I don't understand this cost report at all," exclaimed Jeff Mahoney, the newly appointed administrator of Mountainview General Hospital. "Our administrative costs in the new pediatrics clinic are all over the map. One month the report shows \$8,300, and the next month it's \$16,100. What's going on?"

Mahoney's question was posed to Megan McDonough, the hospital's director of Cost Management. "The main problem is that the clinic has experienced some widely varying patient loads in its first year of operation. There seems to be some confusion in the public's mind about what services we offer in the clinic. When do they come to the clinic? When do they go to the emergency room? That sort of thing. As the patient load has varied, we've frequently changed our clinic administrative staffing."

Mahoney continued to puzzle over the report. "Could you pull some data together, Megan, so we can see how this cost behaves over a range of patient loads?"

"You'll have it this afternoon," McDonough responded. Later that morning, she gathered the following data:

Month	Patient Load	Administrative Cost
January	1,400	\$13,900
February	500	7,000
March	400	6,000
April	1,000	10,000
May	1,300	11,900
June	900	9,200
July	1,100	10,200
August	300	4,100
September	700	9,400
October	1,200	11,100
November	600	8,300
December	1,500	16,100

McDonough does not believe the first year's widely fluctuating patient load will be experienced again in the future. She has estimated that the clinic's relevant range of monthly activity in the future will be 600 to 1,200 patients.

Required:

1. Draw a scatter diagram of the clinic's administrative costs during its first year of operation.
2. Visually fit a curvilinear cost line to the plotted data.
3. Mark the clinic's relevant range of activity on the scatter diagram.
4. Visually fit a semivariable-cost line to approximate the curvilinear cost behavior pattern within the clinic's relevant range.
5. Estimate the fixed- and variable-cost components of the visually fit semivariable-cost line.
6. Use an equation to express the semivariable-cost approximation of the clinic's administrative costs.
7. What is your prediction of the clinic's administrative cost during a month when 800 patients visit the clinic? When 300 patients visit? Which one of your visually fit cost lines did you use to make each of these predictions? Why?

Case 6–49
Comparing Multiple Cost Estimation Methods; Ethics (Appendix)
(LO 6-1, 6-2, 6-3, 6-5, 6-8)

1. High-low method, variable administrative cost per patient: $10
2. Total monthly administrative cost = $2,671 + $7.81X, where X denotes number of patients per month

Refer to the data and accompanying information in the preceding case.

Required:

1. Use the high-low method to estimate the cost behavior for the clinic's administrative costs. Express the cost behavior in formula form ($Y = a + bX$). What is the variable cost per patient?
2. ***Build a spreadsheet:*** Construct an Excel spreadsheet and use the Excel commands to perform a least-squares regression and estimate the administrative cost behavior. Express the cost behavior in formula form. What is the variable cost per patient? Compute and interpret the R^2 value for the regression.
3. Write a memo to the hospital administrator comparing the cost estimates using (*a*) least-squares regression, (*b*) the high-low method, and (*c*) the scatter diagram and visually fit semivariable-cost line from the preceding case (requirement (4). Make a recommendation as to which estimate should be used, and support your recommendation. Make any other suggestions you feel are appropriate.
4. After receiving the memo comparing the three cost estimates, Mahoney called McDonough to discuss the matter. The following exchange occurred.

Mahoney: "As you know, Megan, I was never in favor of this clinic. It's going to be a drag on our administrative staff, and we'd have been far better off keeping the pediatrics operation here in the hospital."

McDonough: "I was aware that you felt the clinic was a mistake. Of course, the board of trustees had other issues to consider. I believe the board felt the clinic should be built to make pediatric care more accessible to the economically depressed area on the other side of the city."

Mahoney: "That's true, but the board doesn't realize how difficult it's going to make life for us here in the hospital. In any case, I called to tell you that when you and I report to the board next week, I'm going to recommend that the clinic be shut down. I want you to support my recommendation with one of your cost estimates showing that administrative costs will soar at high activity levels."

McDonough: "But that estimate was based on the high-low method. It's not an appropriate method for this situation."

Mahoney: "It *is* an estimate, Megan, and it's based on a well-known estimation method. This is just the ammunition I need to make the board see things my way."

McDonough: "I don't know, Jeff. I just don't think I can go along with that."

Mahoney: "Be a team player, Megan. I've got a meeting now. Got to run."

That night McDonough called to discuss the matter with her best friend, you. What would you advise her?

7 Cost-Volume-Profit Analysis

FOCUS COMPANY >>>

© Kirk McKoy/Los Angeles Times/Getty Images

THIS CHAPTER'S FOCUS is on the Seattle Contemporary Theater. This non-profit enterprise was formed to bring contemporary drama to the Seattle area. The theater operates in a historic theater building owned by the city, for which Seattle Contemporary Theater pays the city a fixed monthly rental charge and a portion of the price of each ticket sold. The theater must cover its operating expenses with ticket revenue in order to break even. Using the Seattle Contemporary Theater as an illustration, we will explore a technique called cost-volume-profit (or CVP) analysis, which the theater's managing director and business manager use to better understand the relationships between the theater's costs, ticket sales volume, and revenue.

© Ingram Publishing/Alamy RF

<<< IN CONTRAST

In contrast to the non-profit, entertainment-service setting of the Seattle Contemporary Theater, we explore the use of cost-volume-profit analysis by Digital Time Company. The management of this manufacturer of digital clocks uses CVP analysis to better understand the relationships between the company's costs, sales volume, and profit. The company's management also analyzes the firm's cost structure, which refers to the relative proportion of fixed and variable costs.

After completing this chapter, you should be able to:

7-1 Compute a break-even point using the contribution-margin approach and the equation approach.

7-2 Compute the contribution-margin ratio and use it to find the break-even point in sales dollars.

7-3 Prepare a cost-volume-profit (CVP) graph and explain how it is used.

7-4 Apply CVP analysis to determine the effect on profit of changes in fixed expenses, variable expenses, sales prices, and sales volume.

7-5 Compute the break-even point and prepare a profit-volume graph for a multiproduct enterprise.

7-6 List and discuss the key assumptions of CVP analysis.

7-7 Prepare and interpret a contribution income statement.

7-8 Explain the role of cost structure and operating leverage in CVP relationships.

7-9 Understand the implications of activity-based costing for CVP analysis.

7-10 Be aware of the effects of advanced manufacturing technology on CVP relationships.

7-11 Understand the effect of income taxes on CVP analysis (appendix).

What effect on profit can United Airlines expect if it adds a flight on the Chicago to New York route? How will NBC's profit change if the ratings increase for its evening news program? How many patient days of care must Massachusetts General Hospital provide to break even for the year? What happens to this break-even patient load if the hospital leases a new computerized system for patient records?

Each of these questions concerns the effects on costs and revenues when the organization's activity changes. The analytical technique used by managerial accountants to address these questions is called **cost-volume-profit analysis.** Often called **CVP analysis** for short, this technique summarizes the effects of changes in an organization's *volume* of activity on its *costs,* revenue, and *profit.* Cost-volume-profit analysis can be extended to cover the effects on profit of changes in selling prices, service fees, costs, income-tax rates, and the organization's mix of products or services. What will happen to profit, for example, if the New York Yankees raise ticket prices for stadium seats? In short, CVP analysis provides management with a comprehensive overview of the effects on revenue and costs of all kinds of short-run financial changes.

Although the word *profit* appears in the term, cost-volume-profit analysis is not confined to profit-seeking enterprises. Managers in nonprofit organizations also routinely use CVP analysis to examine the effects of activity and other short-run changes on revenue and costs. For example, as the State of Florida gains approximately 1,000 people a day in population, the state's political leaders must analyze the effects of this change on sales-tax revenues and the cost of providing services, such as education, transportation, and police protection. Managers at such diverse nonprofit institutions as Massachusetts General Hospital, Stanford University, and the United Way all use CVP analysis as a routine operational tool.

Illustration of Cost-Volume-Profit Analysis

To illustrate the various analytical techniques used in cost-volume-profit analysis, we will focus on a performing arts organization. The Seattle Contemporary Theater was recently formed as a nonprofit enterprise to bring contemporary drama to the Seattle area. The organization has a part-time, unpaid board of trustees comprised of local professional people who are avid theater fans. The board has hired the following full-time employees.

Managing director: Responsibilities include overall management of the organization; direction of six plays per year.

Artistic director: Responsibilities include hiring of actors and production crews for each play; direction of six plays per year.

Business manager and producer: Responsibilities include managing the organization's business functions and ticket sales; direction of the production crews, who handle staging, lighting, costuming, and makeup.

The board of trustees has negotiated an agreement with the city of Seattle to hold performances in a historic theater owned by the city. The theater has not been used for 30 years, but the city has agreed to refurbish it and to provide lighting and sound equipment. In return, the city will receive a rental charge of $10,000 per month plus $8 for each theater ticket sold.

> "Accounting is changing. You're no longer sitting behind a desk just working on a computer, just crunching the numbers. You're actually getting to be a part of the day-to-day functions of the business." (7a)
>
> **Abbott Laboratories**

Projected Expenses and Revenue

The theater's business manager and producer, Andrew Lloyd, has made the following projections for the first few years of operation.

Fixed expenses per month:	
Theater rental	$10,000
Employees' salaries and fringe benefits	8,000
Actors' wages	15,000
(to be supplemented with local volunteer talent)	
Production crew's wages	5,600
(to be supplemented with local volunteers)	
Playwrights' royalties for use of plays	5,000
Insurance	1,000
Utilities—fixed portion	1,400
Advertising and promotion	800
Administrative expenses	1,200
Total fixed expenses per month	$48,000
Variable expenses per ticket sold:	
City's charge per ticket for use of theater	$ 8
Other miscellaneous expenses (for example, printing of playbills and tickets, variable portion of utilities)	2
Total variable cost per ticket sold	$10
Revenue:	
Price per ticket	$16

Importance of Cost Behavior Notice that the theater's expenses have been categorized according to their cost behavior: fixed or variable. Analyzing an organization's cost behavior, the topic of Chapter 6, is a necessary first step in any cost-volume-profit analysis. As we proceed through this chapter, the data pertaining to Seattle Contemporary Theater will be an important part of our cost-volume-profit analysis.

The Break-Even Point

Learning Objective 7-1

Compute a break-even point using the contribution-margin approach and the equation approach.

As the first step in the CVP analysis for Seattle Contemporary Theater, we will find the **break-even point.** The break-even point is the volume of activity where the organization's revenues and expenses are equal. At this amount of sales, the organization has no profit or loss; it *breaks even.*

Suppose Seattle Contemporary Theater sells 8,000 tickets during a play's one-month run. The following income statement shows that the profit for the month will be zero; thus, the theater will break even.

Sales revenue (8,000 × $16)	$128,000
Less variable expenses (8,000 × $10)	80,000
Total contribution margin	$ 48,000
Less fixed expenses	48,000
Profit	$ 0

"Break-even analyses figure prominently in any discussion of new programs. Although we have programs that operate at a loss because of their importance educationally, overall our cash inflows have to be sufficient to support our total program." (7b)
Cornell University

Notice that this income statement highlights the distinction between variable and fixed expenses. The statement also shows the **total contribution margin,** which is defined as total sales revenue minus total variable expenses. This is the amount of revenue that is available to *contribute* to covering fixed expenses after all variable expenses have been covered. The contribution income statement will be covered in more depth later in the chapter. At this juncture, it provides a useful way to think about the meaning of breaking even.

How could we compute Seattle Contemporary Theater's break-even point if we did not already know it is 8,000 tickets per month? This is the question to which we turn our attention next.

Contribution-Margin Approach

Seattle Contemporary Theater will break even when the organization's revenue from ticket sales is equal to its expenses. How many tickets must be sold during one month (one play's run) for the organization to break even?

© Jack Hollingsworth/Getty Images RF

© Ken James/Bloomberg/Getty Images

Whether running a small business or a worldwide enterprise, understanding cost-volume-profit relationships is crucial in managing any organization.

Each ticket sells for \$16, but \$10 of this is used to cover the variable expense per ticket. This leaves \$6 per ticket to *contribute* to covering the fixed expenses of \$48,000. When enough tickets have been sold in one month so that these \$6 contributions per ticket add up to \$48,000, the organization will break even for the month. Thus, we may compute the break-even volume of tickets as follows:

$$\frac{\text{Fixed expenses}}{\text{Contribution of each ticket toward covering fixed expenses}} = \frac{\$48{,}000}{\$6} = 8{,}000$$

Seattle Contemporary Theater must sell 8,000 tickets during a play's one-month run to break even for the month.

The \$6 amount that remains of each ticket's price, after the variable expenses are covered, is called the **unit contribution margin.** The general formula for computing the break-even sales volume in units is given below.

$$\frac{\text{Fixed expenses}}{\text{Unit contribution margin}} = \text{Break-even point (in units)} \qquad (1)$$

Contribution-Margin Ratio Sometimes management prefers that the break-even point be expressed in sales *dollars* rather than *units.* Seattle Contemporary Theater's break-even point in sales dollars is computed as follows.

Learning Objective 7-2

Compute the contribution-margin ratio and use it to find the break-even point in sales dollars.

Break-even point in units (tickets)	8,000
Sales price per unit	× \$16
Break-even point in sales dollars	\$128,000

The following computation provides an alternative way to determine the break-even point in sales dollars.

$$\frac{\text{Fixed expenses}}{\dfrac{\text{Unit contribution margin}}{\text{Unit sales price}}} = \frac{\$48{,}000}{\dfrac{\$6}{\$16}} = \frac{\$48{,}000}{.375} = \$128{,}000$$

"Delta Air Lines computes a break-even load factor, which is the average percentage of available passenger seats that need to be occupied on our flights in order for the company to break even." (7c)

Delta Air Lines

The unit contribution margin divided by the unit sales price is called the **contribution-margin ratio.** This ratio also can be expressed as a percentage, in which case it is called the *contribution-margin percentage.* Seattle Contemporary Theater's contribution-margin ratio is .375 (in percentage form, 37.5%). Thus, the organization's break-even point in sales dollars may be found by dividing its fixed expenses by its contribution-margin ratio. The logic behind this approach is that 37.5 percent of each sales dollar is available to make a contribution toward covering fixed expenses. The general formula is given below.

$$\frac{\text{Fixed expenses}}{\text{Contribution-margin ratio}} = \text{Break-even point in sales dollars} \qquad (2)$$

Equation Approach An alternative approach to finding the break-even point is based on the profit equation. Income (or profit) is equal to sales revenue minus expenses. If expenses are separated into variable and fixed expenses, the essence of the income (profit) statement is captured by the following equation.

$$\text{Sales revenue} - \text{Variable expenses} - \text{Fixed expenses} = \text{Profit}$$

This equation can be restated as follows:

$$\left[\begin{pmatrix}\text{Unit}\\\text{sales}\\\text{price}\end{pmatrix} \times \begin{pmatrix}\text{Sales}\\\text{volume}\\\text{in units}\end{pmatrix}\right] - \left[\begin{pmatrix}\text{Unit}\\\text{variable}\\\text{expense}\end{pmatrix} \times \begin{pmatrix}\text{Sales}\\\text{volume}\\\text{in units}\end{pmatrix}\right] - \begin{pmatrix}\text{Fixed}\\\text{expenses}\end{pmatrix} = \text{Profit} \qquad (3)$$

To find Seattle Contemporary Theater's break-even volume of ticket sales per month, we define profit in equation (3) to be zero.

$$(\$16 \times X) - (\$10 \times X) - \$48{,}000 = 0$$

$$\left[\begin{pmatrix}\text{Unit}\\\text{sales}\\\text{price}\end{pmatrix} \times \begin{pmatrix}\text{Sales}\\\text{volume}\\\text{in units}\end{pmatrix}\right] - \left[\begin{pmatrix}\text{Unit}\\\text{variablle}\\\text{expense}\end{pmatrix} \times \begin{pmatrix}\text{Sales}\\\text{volume}\\\text{in units}\end{pmatrix}\right] - \begin{pmatrix}\text{Fixed}\\\text{expenses}\end{pmatrix} = \begin{matrix}\text{Break-even}\\\text{profit (zero)}\end{matrix} \quad (4)$$

where

X denotes the number of sales units (tickets) required to break even.

Equation (4) can be solved for X as shown below.

$$\$16X - \$10X - \$48{,}000 = 0$$
$$\$6X = \$48{,}000$$
$$X = \frac{\$48{,}000}{\$6} = 8{,}000$$

Using the equation approach, we have arrived at the same general formula for computing the break-even sales volume (formula (1).

The contribution-margin and equation approaches are two equivalent techniques for finding the break-even point. Both methods reach the same conclusion, and so personal preference dictates which approach should be used.

Graphing Cost-Volume-Profit Relationships

Learning Objective 7-3

Prepare a cost-volume-profit (CVP) graph and explain how it is used.

While the break-even point conveys useful information to management, it does not show how profit changes as activity changes. To capture the relationship between profit and volume of activity, a **cost-volume-profit (CVP) graph** is commonly used. The following steps are used to prepare a CVP graph for Seattle Contemporary Theater. The graph is displayed in Exhibit 7–1. Notice that the graph shows the *relevant range,* which is the range of activity within which management expects the theater to operate.

Step 1: Draw the axes of the graph. Label the vertical axis in dollars and the horizontal axis in units of sales (tickets).

Step 2: Draw the fixed-expense line. It is parallel to the horizontal axis, since fixed expenses do not change with activity.

Step 3: Compute *total* expense at any convenient volume. For example, select a volume of 6,000 tickets.

Variable expenses (6,000 × $10 per ticket)	$ 60,000
Fixed expenses	48,000
Total expenses (at 6,000 tickets)	$108,000

Plot this point ($108,000 at 6,000 tickets) on the graph. See point *A* on the graph in Exhibit 7–1.

Step 4: Draw the total-expense line. This line passes through the point plotted in step 3 (point *A*) and the intercept of the fixed-expense line on the vertical axis ($48,000).

Step 5: Compute total sales revenue at any convenient volume. We will choose 6,000 tickets again. Total revenue is $96,000 (6,000 × $16 per ticket). Plot this point ($96,000 at 6,000 tickets) on the graph. See point *B* on the graph in Exhibit 7–1.

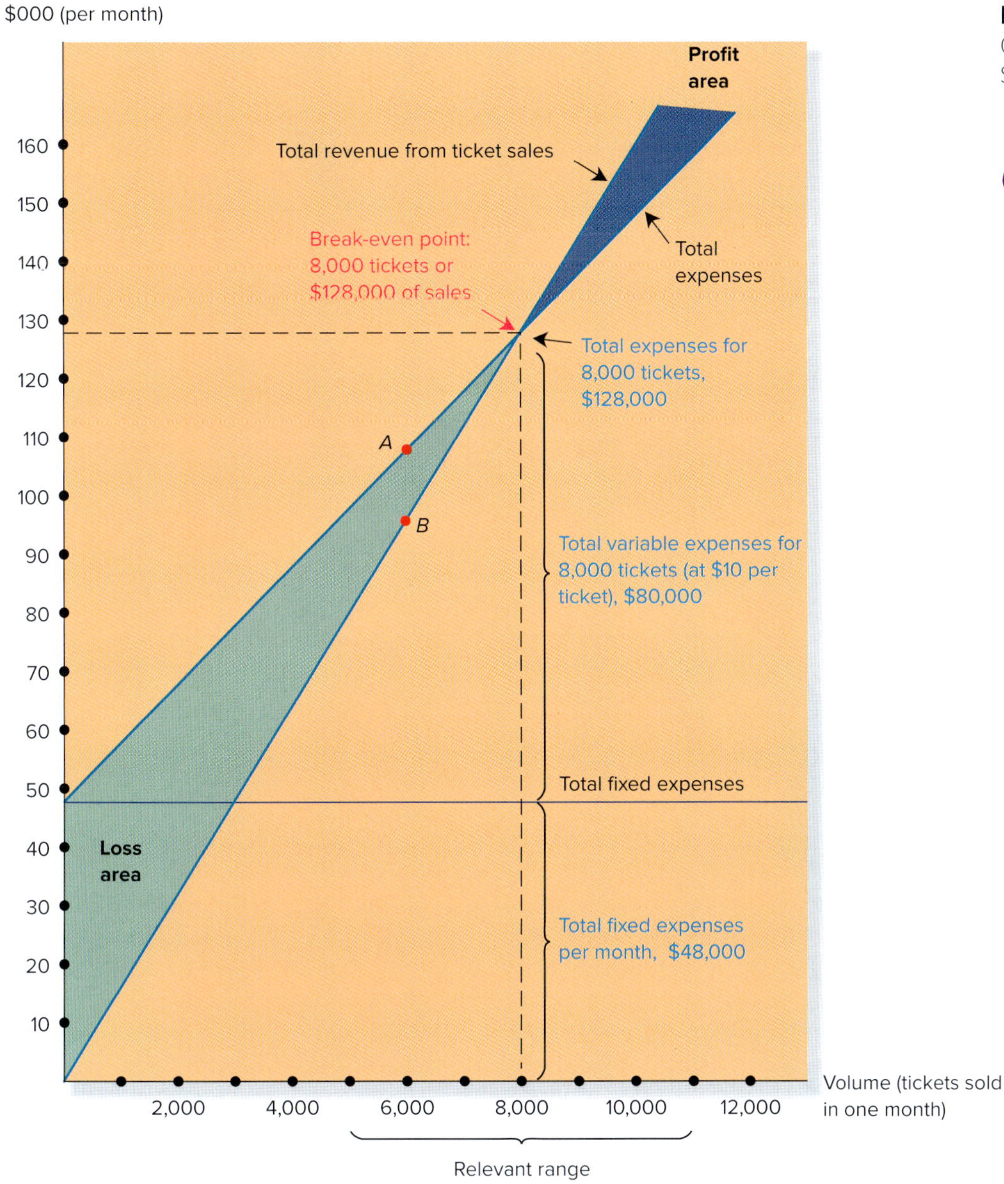

Exhibit 7–1
Cost-Volume-Profit Graph: Seattle Contemporary Theater

Step 6: Draw the total revenue line. This line passes through the point plotted in step 5 (point *B*) and the origin.

Step 7: Label the graph as shown in Exhibit 7–1.

Interpreting the CVP Graph

Several conclusions can be drawn from the CVP graph in Exhibit 7–1.

Learning Objective 7-3

Prepare a cost-volume-profit (CVP) graph and explain how it is used.

Break-Even Point The break-even point is determined by the intersection of the total-revenue line and the total-expense line. Seattle Contemporary Theater breaks even for the month at 8,000 tickets, or $128,000 of ticket sales. This agrees with our calculations in the preceding section.

Profit and Loss Areas The CVP graph discloses more information than the break-even calculation. From the graph, a manager can see the effects on profit of changes

Exhibit 7–2
Alternative Format for CVP Graph: Seattle Contemporary Theater

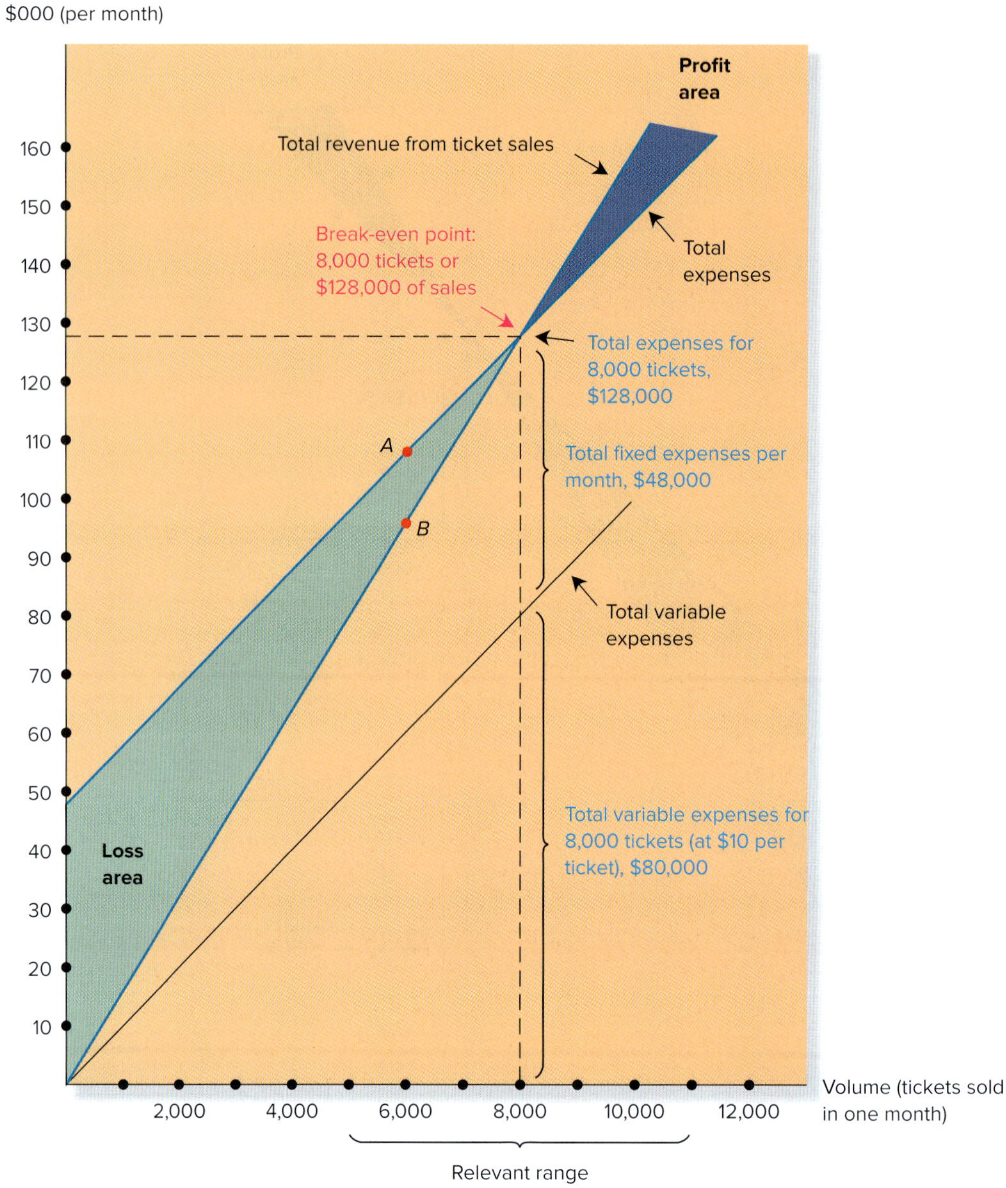

in volume. The vertical distance between the lines on the graph represents the profit or loss at a particular sales volume. If Seattle Contemporary Theater sells fewer than 8,000 tickets in a month, the organization will suffer a loss. The magnitude of the loss increases as ticket sales decline. The theater organization will have a profit if sales exceed 8,000 tickets in a month.

Implications of the Break-Even Point The position of the break-even point within an organization's relevant range of activity provides important information to management. The Seattle Contemporary Theater building seats 450 people. The agreement with the city of Seattle calls for 20 performances during each play's one-month run. Thus, the maximum number of tickets that can be sold each month is 9,000 (450 seats × 20 performances). The organization's break-even point is quite close to the maximum possible sales volume. This could be cause for concern in a nonprofit organization operating on limited resources.

What could management do to improve this situation? One possibility is to renegotiate with the city to schedule additional performances. However, this might not be feasible, because the actors need some rest each week. Also, additional performances would likely entail additional costs, such as increased theater-rental expenses and increased compensation for the actors and production crew. Other possible solutions are to raise ticket prices or reduce costs. These kinds of issues will be explored later in the chapter.

The CVP graph will not resolve this potential problem for the management of Seattle Contemporary Theater. However, the graph will *direct management's attention* to the situation.

Alternative Format for the CVP Graph

An alternative format for the CVP graph, preferred by some managers, is displayed in Exhibit 7-2 . The key difference is that fixed expenses are graphed above variable expenses, instead of the reverse as they were in Exhibit 7–1.

Profit-Volume Graph

Yet another approach to graphing cost-volume-profit relationships is displayed in Exhibit 7–3. This format is called a **profit-volume graph,** since it highlights the amount of profit or loss. Notice that the graph intercepts the vertical axis at the amount equal to fixed expenses at the zero activity level. The graph crosses the horizontal axis at the break-even point. The vertical distance between the horizontal axis and the profit line, at a particular level of sales volume, is the profit or loss at that volume.

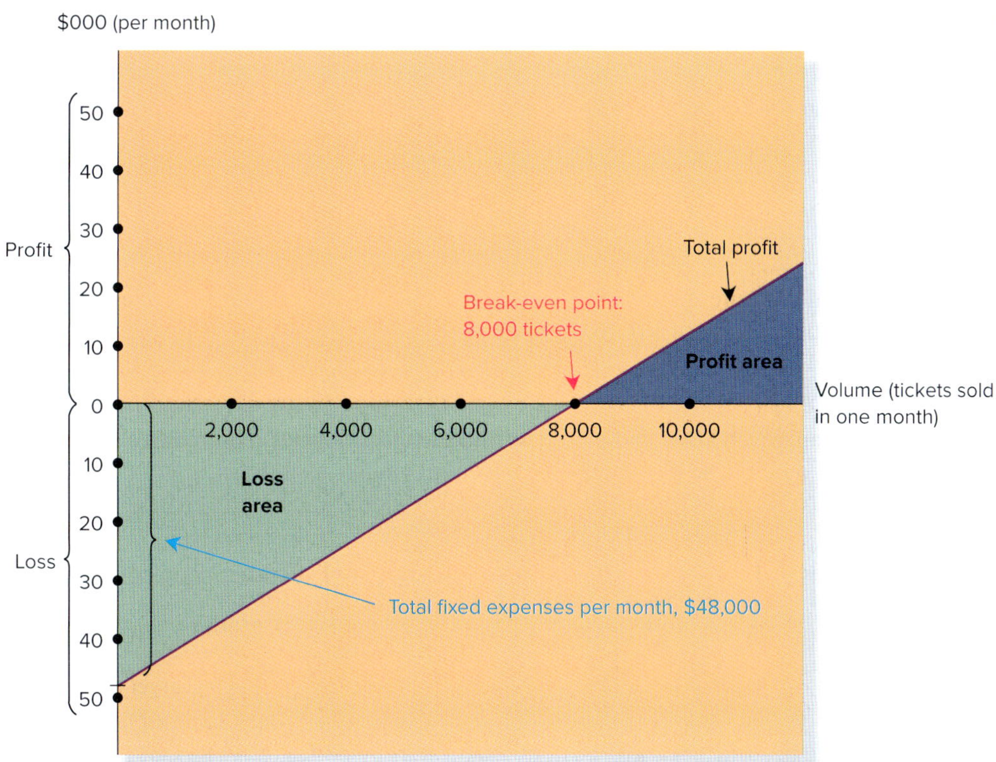

Exhibit 7–3
Profit-Volume Graph: Seattle Contemporary Theater

Target Profit

Learning Objective 7-4

Apply CVP analysis to determine the effect on profit of changes in fixed expenses, variable expenses, sales prices, and sales volume.

The board of trustees for Seattle Contemporary Theater would like to run free workshops and classes for young actors and aspiring playwrights. This program would cost \$3,600 per month in fixed expenses, including teachers' salaries and rental of space at a local college. No variable expenses would be incurred. If Seattle Contemporary Theater could make a profit of \$3,600 per month on its performances, the Seattle Drama Workshop could be opened. The board has asked Andrew Lloyd, the organization's business manager and producer, to determine how many theater tickets must be sold during each play's one-month run to make a profit of \$3,600.

The desired profit level of \$3,600 is called a **target profit (or income).** The problem of computing the volume of sales required to earn a particular target profit is very similar to the problem of finding the break-even point. After all, the break-even point is the number of units of sales required to earn a target profit of zero.[1]

Contribution-Margin Approach

Each ticket sold by Seattle Contemporary Theater has a unit contribution margin of \$6 (sales price of \$16 minus unit variable expense of \$10). Eight thousand of these \$6 contributions will contribute just enough to cover fixed expenses of \$48,000. *Each additional ticket sold will contribute \$6 toward profit.* Thus, we can modify formula (1) given earlier in the chapter as follows:

$$\frac{\text{Fixed expenses} + \text{Target profit}}{\text{Unit contribution margin}} = \begin{array}{c}\text{Number of sales units required}\\ \text{to earn target profit}\end{array} \qquad (5)$$

$$\frac{\$48{,}000 + \$3{,}600}{\$6} = 8{,}600 \text{ tickets}$$

If Seattle Contemporary Theater sells 8,600 tickets during each play's one-month run, the organization will make a monthly profit of \$3,600 on its performances. This profit can be used to fund the Seattle Drama Workshop. The total dollar sales required to earn a target profit is found by modifying formula (2) given previously.

$$\frac{\text{Fixed expenses} + \text{Target profit}}{\text{Contribution-margin ratio}} = \begin{array}{c}\text{Dollar sales required to earn}\\ \text{target profit}\end{array} \qquad (6)$$

$$\frac{\$48{,}000 + \$3{,}600}{.375} = \$137{,}600$$

$$\text{where the contribution margin ratio} = \frac{\$6}{\$16} = .375$$

This dollar sales figure also can be found by multiplying the required sales of 8,600 tickets by the ticket price of \$16 (8,600 × \$16 = \$137,600).

Equation Approach

The equation approach also can be used to find the units of sales required to earn a target profit. We can modify the profit equation given previously as follows:

$$\left[\begin{pmatrix}\text{Unit}\\ \text{sales}\\ \text{price}\end{pmatrix} \times \begin{pmatrix}\text{Sales volume}\\ \text{required to}\\ \text{earn target}\\ \text{profit}\end{pmatrix}\right] - \left[\begin{pmatrix}\text{Unit}\\ \text{variable}\\ \text{expense}\end{pmatrix} \times \begin{pmatrix}\text{Sales volume}\\ \text{required to}\\ \text{earn target}\\ \text{profit}\end{pmatrix}\right] - \begin{pmatrix}\text{Fixed}\\ \text{expenses}\end{pmatrix} = \text{Target profit}$$

[1]Remember that Seattle Contemporary Theater is a nonprofit enterprise. CVP analysis in a for-profit enterprise, including the effect of income taxes, is covered in the appendix to this chapter.

Filling in the values for Seattle Contemporary Theater, we have the following equation.

$$(\$16 \times X) - (\$10 \times X) - \$48{,}000 = \$3{,}600 \qquad (7)$$

where X denotes the sales volume required to earn the target profit

Equation (7) can be solved for X as follows:

$$\$16X - \$10X - \$48{,}000 = \$3{,}600$$
$$\$6X = \$51{,}600$$
$$X = \frac{\$51{,}600}{\$6} = 8{,}600$$

Graphical Approach

The profit-volume graph in Exhibit 7–3 also can be used to find the sales volume required to earn a target profit. First, locate Seattle Contemporary Theater's target profit of \$3,600 on the vertical axis. Then move horizontally until the profit line is reached. Finally, move down from the profit line to the horizontal axis to determine the required sales volume.

Applying CVP Analysis

The cost-volume-profit relationships that underlie break-even calculations and CVP graphs have wide-ranging applications in management. We will look at several common applications illustrated by Seattle Contemporary Theater.

Learning Objective 7-4

Apply CVP analysis to determine the effect on profit of changes in fixed expenses, variable expenses, sales prices, and sales volume.

Safety Margin

The **safety margin** of an enterprise is the difference between the budgeted sales revenue and the break-even sales revenue. Suppose Seattle Contemporary Theater's business manager expects every performance of each play to be sold out. Then budgeted monthly sales revenue is \$144,000 (450 seats × 20 performances of each play × \$16 per ticket). Since break-even sales revenue is \$128,000, the organization's safety margin is \$16,000 (\$144,000 − \$128,000). The safety margin gives management a feel for how close projected operations are to the organization's break-even point. We will further discuss the safety margin concept later in the chapter.

"Basically the role of the [accountant] on the team [is] analyzing the financial impact of the business decision and providing advice. Does this make sense financially or not?" (7d)
Abbott Laboratories

Changes in Fixed Expenses

What would happen to Seattle Contemporary Theater's break-even point if fixed expenses change? Suppose the business manager is concerned that the estimate for fixed utilities expenses, \$1,400 per month, is too low. What would happen to the break-even point if fixed utilities expenses prove to be \$2,600 instead? The break-even calculations for both the original and the new estimate of fixed utilities expenses are as follows:

	Original Estimate	New Estimate
Fixed utilities expenses	\$ 1,400	\$ 2,600
Total fixed expenses	\$48,000	\$49,200
Break-even calculation	\$48,000 ÷ \$6	\$49,200 ÷ \$6
(Fixed expenses ÷ unit contribution margin)		
Break-even point (units)	8,000 tickets	8,200 tickets
Break-even point (dollars)	\$128,000	\$131,200

The estimate of fixed expenses has increased by 2.5 percent, since \$1,200 is 2.5 percent of \$48,000. Notice that the break-even point also increased by 2.5 percent (200 tickets is 2.5 percent of 8,000 tickets). This relationship will always exist.

$$\frac{\text{Fixed expenses}}{\text{Unit contribution margin}} = \text{Break-even point (in units)}$$

$$\frac{\text{Fixed expenses} \times 1.025}{\text{Unit contribution margin}} = (\text{Break-even point in units}) \times 1.025$$

Donations to Offset Fixed Expenses Nonprofit organizations often receive cash donations from people or organizations desiring to support a worthy cause. A donation is equivalent to a reduction in fixed expenses, and it reduces the organization's break-even point. In our original set of data, Seattle Contemporary Theater's monthly fixed expenses total \$48,000. Suppose that various people pledge donations amounting to \$6,000 per month. The new break-even point is computed as follows:

$$\frac{\text{Fixed expenses} - \text{Donations}}{\text{Unit contribution margin}} = \text{Break-even point (in units)}$$

$$\frac{\$48,000 - \$6,000}{\$6} = 7,000 \text{ tickets}$$

Changes in the Unit Contribution Margin

What would happen to Seattle Contemporary Theater's break-even point if miscellaneous variable expenses were \$3 per ticket instead of \$2? Alternatively, what would be the effect of raising the ticket price to \$18?

Change in Unit Variable Expenses If the theater organization's miscellaneous variable expenses increase from \$2 to \$3 per ticket, the unit contribution margin will fall from \$6 to \$5. The original and new break-even points are computed as follows:

	Original Estimate	New Estimate
Miscellaneous variable expenses	\$2 per ticket	\$3 per ticket
Unit contribution margin	\$6	\$5
Break-even calculation	\$48,000 ÷ \$6	\$48,000 ÷ \$5
(Fixed expenses ÷ unit contribution margin)		
Break-even point (units)	8,000 tickets	9,600 tickets
Break-even point (dollars)	\$128,000	\$153,600

If this change in unit variable expenses actually occurs, it will no longer be possible for the organization to break even. Only 9,000 tickets are available for each play's one-month run (450 seats × 20 performances), but 9,600 tickets would have to be sold to break even. Once again, CVP analysis will not solve this problem for management, but it will direct management's attention to potentially serious difficulties.

Change in Sales Price Changing the unit sales price will also alter the unit contribution margin. Suppose the ticket price is raised from \$16 to \$18. This change will raise the unit contribution margin from \$6 to \$8. The new break-even point will be 6,000 tickets (\$48,000 ÷ \$8).

A \$2 increase in the ticket price will lower the break-even point from 8,000 tickets to 6,000 tickets. Is this change desirable? A lower break-even point decreases the risk of operating with a loss if sales are sluggish. However, the organization may be more likely to at least break even with a \$16 ticket price than with an \$18 ticket price. The reason is that the lower ticket price encourages more people to attend the theater's performances.

It could be that break-even sales of 8,000 tickets at $16 are more likely than break-even sales of 6,000 tickets at $18. Ultimately, the desirability of the ticket-price increase depends on management's assessment of the likely reaction by theater patrons.

Management's decision about the ticket price increase also will reflect the fundamental goals of Seattle Contemporary Theater. This nonprofit drama organization was formed to bring contemporary drama to the people of Seattle. The lower the ticket price, the more accessible the theater's productions will be to people of all income levels.

The point of this discussion is that CVP analysis provides valuable information, but it is only one of several elements that influence management's decisions.

Predicting Profit Given Expected Volume

So far, we have focused on finding the required sales volume to break even or achieve a particular target profit. Thus, we have asked the following question.

$$\text{Given: } \left\{ \begin{array}{l} \text{Fixed expenses} \\ \text{Unit contribution margin} \\ \text{Target profit} \end{array} \right\}, \text{ Find: } \{\text{required sales volume}\}$$

We also can use CVP analysis to turn this question around and make the following query.

$$\text{Given: } \left\{ \begin{array}{l} \text{Fixed expenses} \\ \text{Unit contribution margin} \\ \text{Expected sales volume} \end{array} \right\}, \text{ Find: } \{\text{expected profit}\}$$

Suppose the management of Seattle Contemporary Theater expects fixed monthly expenses of $48,000 and unit variable expenses of $10 per ticket. The organization's board of trustees is considering two different ticket prices, and the business manager has forecast monthly demand at each price.

Ticket Price	Forecast Monthly Demand
$16	9,000
$20	6,000

Expected profit may be calculated at each price as shown in the following table. In these profit calculations, the **total contribution margin** is the difference between *total* sales revenue and *total* variable expenses. This use of the term *contribution margin* is a "total" concept rather than the "per unit" concept used earlier in the chapter. The *total contribution margin* is the *total* amount left to contribute to covering fixed expenses after *total* variable expenses have been covered.

	Ticket Price	
	$16	**$20**
Sales revenue:		
9,000 × $16	$144,000	
6,000 × $20		$120,000
Less variable expenses:		
9,000 × $10	90,000	
6,000 × $10		60,000
Total contribution margin	$ 54,000	$ 60,000
Less fixed expenses	48,000	48,000
Profit	$ 6,000	$ 12,000

The difference in expected profit at the two ticket prices is due to two factors:

1. A different *unit* contribution margin, defined previously as *unit* sales price minus *unit* variable expenses.
2. A different sales volume.

Incremental Approach Rather than presenting the entire income statement under each ticket price alternative, we can use a simpler incremental approach. This analysis focuses only on the difference in the total contribution margin under the two prices. Thus, the combined effect of the change in unit contribution margin and the change in sales volume is as follows:

Expected *total* contribution margin at $20 ticket price:	
6,000 × ($20 − $10)	$60,000
Expected *total* contribution margin at $16 ticket price:	
9,000 × ($16 − $10)	54,000
Difference in *total* contribution margin	$ 6,000

The $6,000 difference in expected profit, at the two ticket prices, is due to a $6,000 difference in the total contribution margin. The board of trustees will consider these projected profits as it decides which ticket price is best. Even though Seattle Contemporary Theater is a nonprofit organization, it may still have legitimate reasons for attempting to make a profit on its theater performances. For example, the board might use these profits to fund a free drama workshop, provide scholarships for local young people to study drama in college, or produce a free outdoor play for Seattle's residents.

Interdependent Changes in Key Variables

Sometimes a change in one key variable will cause a change in another key variable. Suppose the board of trustees is choosing between ticket prices of $16 and $20, and the business manager has projected demand as shown in the preceding section. A famous retired actress who lives in Seattle has offered to donate $10,000 per month to Seattle Contemporary Theater if the board will set the ticket price at $16. The actress is interested in making the theater's performances affordable for as many people as possible. The facts are now as follows:

Ticket Price	Unit Contribution Margin	Forecast Monthly Demand	Net Fixed Expenses (after subtracting donation)
$16	$ 6	9,000	$38,000 ($48,000 − $10,000)
20	10	6,000	48,000

The organization's expected profit at each price is computed as follows:

	Ticket Price	
	$16	**$20**
Sales revenue:		
9,000 × $16	$144,000	
6,000 × $20		$120,000
Less variable expenses:		
9,000 × $10	90,000	
6,000 × $10		60,000
Total contribution margin	$ 54,000	$ 60,000
Less net fixed expenses (net of donation)	38,000	48,000
Profit	$ 16,000	$ 12,000

Now the difference in expected profit at the two ticket prices is due to three factors:

1. A different *unit* contribution margin.
2. A different sales volume.
3. A difference in the *net* fixed expenses, after deducting the donation.

Incremental Approach The combined effect of these factors is shown in the following analysis, which focuses on the effects of the price alternatives on the total contribution margin and the net fixed expenses.

Expected *total* contribution margin at $20 ticket price:	
6,000 × ($20 − $10)	$60,000
Expected *total* contribution margin at $16 ticket price:	
9,000 × ($16 − $10)	54,000
Difference in *total* contribution margin (higher with $20 ticket price)	$ 6,000
Net fixed expenses at $20 ticket price	$48,000
Net fixed expenses at $16 ticket price	38,000
Difference in net fixed expenses (higher with $20 ticket price)	$10,000

The expected total contribution margin is $6,000 higher with the $20 ticket price, but net fixed expenses are $10,000 higher. Thus, Seattle Contemporary Theater will make $4,000 more in profit at the $16 price ($10,000 − $6,000).

CVP Information in Published Annual Reports

Cost-volume-profit relationships are so important to understanding an organization's operations that some companies disclose CVP information in their published annual reports. The following illustration is from the airline industry.

AIRLINES KEEP A CLOSE EYE ON BREAK-EVEN LOAD FACTORS

Management **A**ccounting **P**ractice

American Airlines, JetBlue Airways, Southwest Airlines, and United Airlines

An airline's *break-even load factor* is the percentage of available seats that must be filled in order for the airline's revenues to equal its expenses. This is the point where the airline breaks even on its flight operations. Airlines pay close attention to their system-wide break-even load factors and often disclose them in their annual reports.

JetBlue, a successful discount airline founded in 1998, now serves over 70 cities in the USA in addition to a number of destinations in the Caribbean, Latin America, and South America. A recent airline industry analysis listed JetBlue's break-even load factor as 81.79 percent. By comparison, the break-even load factors for a few other well-known airlines were reported as follows: **American**, 83.14 percent; **United**, 88.6 percent; and **Southwest**, 79.6 percent.[2]

It is not necessarily valid, however, to compare operating statistics, such as break-even load factors, across airlines. According to industry analysts, the definition of operating expenses used in calculating the break-even load factor differs across airlines. For example, some airlines exclude fuel costs from the calculation of operating expenses, because oil prices fluctuate widely and are not under an airline management's control. Given the disparity in the definition of the expenses used to calculate the break-even load factor, comparisons across airlines are suspect. However, it is worthwhile to track a particular airline's break-even load factor across time periods.[3]

[2] "4Q 2012 Scorecard" www.theairlinewebsite.com.
[3] Based on the authors' research.

CVP Analysis with Multiple Products

Major airlines keep a close watch on the break-even passenger load factor.

© Royalty-Free/Corbis

Learning Objective 7-5

Compute the break-even point and prepare a profit-volume graph for a multiproduct enterprise.

Our CVP illustration for Seattle Contemporary Theater has assumed that the organization has only one product, a theater seat at a dramatic performance. Most firms have a *sales mix* consisting of more than one product, and this adds some complexity to their CVP analyses.

As we have seen, Seattle Contemporary Theater's monthly fixed expenses total $48,000, and the unit variable expense per ticket is $10. Now suppose that the city of Seattle has agreed to refurbish 10 theater boxes in the historic theater building. Each box has five seats, which are more comfortable and afford a better view of the stage than the theater's general seating. The board of trustees has decided to charge $16 per ticket for general seating and $20 per ticket for box seats. These facts are summarized as follows:

Seat Type	Ticket Price	Unit Variable Expense	Unit Contribution Margin	Seats in Theater	Seats Available per Month (20 performances)
Regular	$16	$10	$ 6	450	9,000
Box	20	10	10	50	1,000

Notice that 90 percent of the available seats are regular seats, and 10 percent are box seats. The business manager estimates that tickets for each type of seat will be sold in the same proportion as the number of seats available. If, for example, 5,000 tickets are sold during a month, sales will be as follows:

Regular seats: 90% × 5,000	4,500
Box seats: 10% × 5,000	500
Total	5,000

For any organization selling multiple products, the relative proportion of each type of product *sold* is called the **sales mix.** The business manager's estimate of Seattle Contemporary Theater's *sales mix* is 90 percent regular seats and 10 percent box seats.

The sales mix is an important assumption in multiproduct CVP analysis. The sales mix is used to compute a **weighted-average unit contribution margin.** This is the *average* of the several products' *unit contribution margins, weighted* by the relative sales proportion of each product. Seattle Contemporary Theater's weighted-average unit contribution margin is computed below.

$$\text{Weighted-average unit contribution margin} = (\$6 \times 90\%) + (\$10 \times 10\%) = \$6.40$$

The organization's break-even point in units is computed using the following formula.

$$\text{Break-even point} = \frac{\text{Fixed expenses}}{\text{Weighted-average unit contribution margin}} \tag{8}$$

$$= \frac{\$48{,}000}{\$6.40} = 7{,}500 \text{ tickets}$$

The break-even point of 7,500 tickets must be interpreted in light of the sales mix. Seattle Contemporary Theater will break even for the month if it sells 7,500 tickets as follows:

Break-even sales in units:	Regular seats: 7,500 × 90%	6,750 tickets
	Box seats: 7,500 × 10%	750 tickets
	Total	7,500 tickets

The following income calculation verifies the break-even point.

Sales revenue:	
Regular seats: 6,750 × $16	$108,000
Box seats: 750 × $20	15,000
Total revenue: 7,500 seats in total	$123,000
Less variable expenses: 7,500 × $10	75,000
Total contribution margin	$ 48,000
Less fixed expenses	48,000
Profit	$ 0

The break-even point of 7,500 tickets per month is *valid only for the sales mix assumed* in computing the weighted-average unit contribution margin. If 7,500 tickets are sold in any other mix of regular and box seats, the organization will not break even.

Notice that break-even formula (8) is a modification of formula (1) given earlier in the chapter. The only difference is that formula (8) uses the *weighted-average* unit contribution margin.

Seattle Contemporary Theater's business manager has constructed the profit-volume graph in Exhibit 7–4. The PV graph shows the organization's profit at any level of total monthly sales, assuming the sales mix of 90 percent regular seats and 10 percent box seats. For example, if 9,000 tickets are sold in total, at the assumed sales mix, the PV graph indicates that profit will be $9,600.

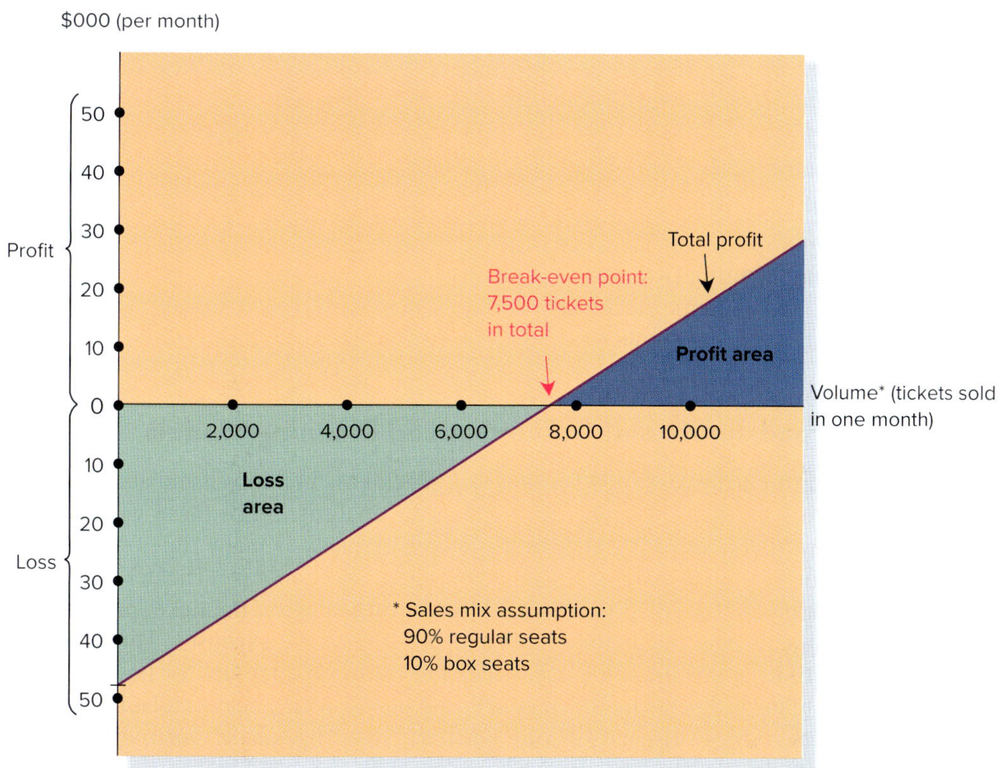

Exhibit 7–4
Profit-Volume Graph with Multiple Products: Seattle Contemporary Theater

With multiproduct CVP analysis, a managerial accountant can investigate the impact on profit of changes in sales volume, prices, variable costs, fixed costs, or the sales mix itself. For example, what would be the effect on Seattle Contemporary Theater's break-even point if the sales mix were 95 percent regular seats and 5 percent box seats? With this sales mix, the weighted-average unit contribution margin is computed as follows:

$$\text{Weighted-average unit contribution margin} = (\$6 \times 95\%) + (\$10 \times 5\%) = \$6.20$$

The break-even point increases from 7,500 tickets to approximately 7,742 tickets as a result of the lower proportion of expensive seats in the sales mix.

$$\text{Break-even point} = \frac{\text{Fixed expenses}}{\text{Weighted-average unit contribution margin}}$$

$$= \frac{\$48,000}{\$6.20} = 7,742 \text{ tickets*}$$

*Rounded

Assumptions Underlying CVP Analysis

Learning Objective 7-6

List and discuss the key assumptions of CVP analysis.

For any cost-volume-profit analysis to be valid, the following important assumptions must be reasonably satisfied *within the relevant range.*

1. The behavior of total revenue is linear (straight-line). This implies that the price of the product or service will not change as sales volume varies within the relevant range.
2. The behavior of total expenses is linear (straight-line) over the relevant range. This implies the following more specific assumptions.
   a. Expenses can be categorized as fixed, variable, or semivariable. *Total* fixed expenses remain constant as activity changes, and the *unit* variable expense remains unchanged as activity varies.
   b. The efficiency and productivity of the production process and workers remain constant.
3. In multiproduct organizations, the sales mix remains constant over the relevant range.
4. In manufacturing firms, the inventory levels at the beginning and end of the period are the same. This implies that the number of units produced during the period equals the number of units sold.

Role of Spreadsheets and Computerized Planning Models

Cost-volume-profit analysis is based on the four general assumptions listed above as well as specific estimates of all the variables used in the analysis. Since these variables are rarely known with certainty, it is helpful to run a CVP analysis many times with different combinations of estimates. For example, Seattle Contemporary Theater's business manager might do the CVP analysis using different estimates for the ticket prices, sales mix for regular and box seats, unit variable expenses, and fixed expenses. This approach is called **sensitivity analysis,** since it provides the analyst with a feel for how sensitive the analysis is to the estimates upon which it is based. The widespread availability of personal computers and spreadsheet software (such as Excel) has made sensitivity analysis relatively easy to do.

CVP Relationships and the Income Statement

The management functions of planning, control, and decision making all are facilitated by an understanding of cost-volume-profit relationships. These relationships are important enough to operating managers that some businesses prepare income statements in a way that highlights CVP issues. Before we examine this new income-statement format, we will review the more traditional income statement used in the preceding chapters.

Traditional Income Statement

An income statement for Digital Time Company, a manufacturer of digital clocks, is shown in Exhibit 7–5 (panel A). During 20x1 the firm manufactured and sold 20,000 clocks at a price of $25 each. This income statement is prepared in the traditional manner. *Cost of goods sold* includes both variable and fixed manufacturing costs, as measured by the firm's product-costing system. The **gross margin** is computed by subtracting cost of goods sold from sales. Selling and administrative expenses are then subtracted; each expense includes both variable and fixed costs. *The traditional income statement does not disclose the breakdown of each expense into its variable and fixed components.*

Digital:Time

Contribution Income Statement

Learning Objective 7-7

Prepare and interpret a contribution income statement.

Many operating managers find the traditional income-statement format difficult to use, because it does not separate variable and fixed expenses. Instead they prefer the **contribution income statement.** A contribution income statement for Digital Time is shown in Exhibit 7–5 (panel B). *The contribution format highlights the distinction*

Exhibit 7–5

Income Statement: Traditional and Contribution Formats

Digital:Time

A. Traditional Format

DIGITAL TIME COMPANY
Income Statement
For the Year Ended December 31, 20x1

Sales		$500,000
Less: Cost of goods sold		380,000
Gross margin		$120,000
Less: Operating expenses:		
Selling expenses	$ 35,000	
Administrative expenses	35,000	70,000
Net income		$ 50,000

B. Contribution Format

DIGITAL TIME COMPANY
Income Statement
For the Year Ended December 31, 20x1

Sales		$500,000
Less: Variable expenses:		
Variable manufacturing	$280,000	
Variable selling	15,000	
Variable administrative	5,000	300,000
Contribution margin		$200,000
Less: Fixed expenses:		
Fixed manufacturing	$100,000	
Fixed selling	20,000	
Fixed administrative	30,000	150,000
Net income		$ 50,000

between variable and fixed expenses. The variable manufacturing cost of each clock is \$14, and the total fixed manufacturing cost is \$100,000. On the contribution income statement, all variable expenses are subtracted from sales to obtain the *contribution margin.* For Digital Time, \$200,000 remains from total sales revenue, after all variable costs have been covered, to contribute to covering fixed costs and making a profit. All fixed costs are then subtracted from the contribution margin to obtain net income.

Comparison of Traditional and Contribution Income Statements

Operating managers frequently prefer the contribution income statement, because its separation of fixed and variable expenses highlights cost-volume-profit relationships. It is readily apparent from the contribution format statement how income will be affected when sales volume changes by a given percentage. Suppose management projects that sales volume in 20x2 will be 20 percent greater than in 20x1. No changes are anticipated in the sales price, variable cost per unit, or fixed costs. Examination of the contribution income statement shows that if sales volume increases by 20 percent, the following changes will occur. (Our discussion ignores income taxes, which are covered in the appendix at the end of this chapter.)

Income Statement Item	20x1 Amount	Change	20x2 Amount
Sales	\$500,000	\$100,000 (20% × \$500,000)	\$600,000
Total variable expenses	\$300,000	\$60,000 (20% × \$300,000)	\$360,000
Contribution margin	\$200,000	\$40,000 (20% × \$200,000)	\$240,000
Total fixed expenses	\$ 150,000	–0– (no change in fixed expenses when volume changes)	\$ 150,000
Net income	\$ 50,000	\$40,000 (income changes by the amount of the contribution-margin change)	\$ 90,000

Notice that net income increases by the same amount as the increase in the contribution margin. Moreover, the contribution margin changes in direct proportion to the change in sales volume. These two facts enable us to calculate the increase in net income using the following shortcut. Recall that the *contribution-margin ratio* is the percentage of contribution margin to sales.

$$\begin{pmatrix}\text{Increase in}\\\text{sales revenue}\end{pmatrix} \times \begin{pmatrix}\text{Contribution-margin}\\\text{ratio}\end{pmatrix} = \begin{pmatrix}\text{Increase in}\\\text{net income}\end{pmatrix}$$

$$\$100{,}000 \times .40 = \$40{,}000$$

$$\text{where} \quad \begin{pmatrix}\text{Contribution-margin}\\\text{ratio}\end{pmatrix} = \frac{\text{Contribution margin}}{\text{Sales revenue}}$$

$$.40 = \frac{\$200{,}000}{\$500{,}000}$$

The preceding analysis makes use of cost-volume-profit relationships that are disclosed in the contribution income statement. Such an analysis cannot be made with the information presented in the traditional income statement.

Exhibit 7–6
Comparison of Cost Structures

	A	B	C	D	E	F	G
1		Contribution Format Income Statements					
2		Company A		Company B		Company C	
3		(Digital Time Company)		(Manual System)		(Automated System)	
4							
5		Amount	%	Amount	%	Amount	%
6							
7	Sales	$ 500,000	100	$ 500,000	100	$ 500,000	100
8	Variable expenses	300,000	60	400,000	80	50,000	10
9	Contribution margin	$ 200,000	40	$ 100,000	20	$ 450,000	90
10	Fixed expenses	150,000	30	50,000	10	400,000	80
11	Net income	$ 50,000	10	$ 50,000	10	$ 50,000	10

Cost Structure and Operating Leverage

Learning Objective 7-8
Explain the role of cost structure and operating leverage in CVP relationships.

The **cost structure** of an organization is the relative proportion of its fixed and variable costs. Cost structures differ widely among industries and among firms within an industry. A company using a computer-integrated manufacturing system has a large investment in plant and equipment, which results in a cost structure dominated by fixed costs. In contrast, a home building contractor's cost structure has a much higher proportion of variable costs. The highly automated manufacturing firm is capital-intensive, whereas the home building contractor is labor-intensive.

An organization's cost structure has a significant effect on the sensitivity of its profit to changes in volume. A convenient way to portray a firm's cost structure is shown in the Excel spreadsheet in Exhibit 7–6.[4] The data for Digital Time Company (company A) comes from the firm's 20x1 contribution income statement in Exhibit 7–5. For comparison purposes, two other firms' cost structures also are shown. Although these three firms have the same sales revenue ($500,000) and net income ($50,000), they have very different cost structures. Company B's production process is largely manual, and its cost structure is dominated by variable costs. It has a low contribution-margin ratio of only 20 percent. In contrast, company C employs a highly automated production process, and its cost structure is dominated by fixed costs. The firm's contribution-margin ratio is 90 percent. Company A falls between these two extremes with a contribution-margin ratio of 40 percent.

Suppose sales revenue increases by 10 percent, or $50,000, in each company. The resulting increase in each company's profit is calculated in Exhibit 7–7.

Notice that company B, with its high variable expenses and low contribution-margin ratio, shows a relatively low *percentage* increase in profit. In contrast, the high fixed expenses and large contribution-margin ratio of company C result in a relatively high *percentage* increase in profit. Company A falls in between these two extremes.

Exhibit 7–7
Effect on Profit of Increase in Sales Revenue

	(Increase In Sales Revenue)	×	(Contribution Margin Ratio)	=	(Increase In Net Income)	Percentage Increase in Net Income
Company A (Digital Time)	$50,000	×	40%	=	$20,000	40% ($20,000 ÷ $50,000)
Company B (high variable expenses)	$50,000	×	20%	=	$10,000	20% ($10,000 ÷ $50,000)
Company C (high fixed expenses)	$50,000	×	90%	=	$45,000	90% ($45,000 ÷ $50,000)

[4] This form of income statement, in which each item on the statement is expressed as a percentage of sales revenue, is often called a *common-size income statement*.

To summarize, the greater the proportion of fixed costs in a firm's cost structure, the greater the impact on profit will be from a given percentage change in sales revenue.

Operating Leverage

The extent to which an organization uses fixed costs in its cost structure is called **operating leverage.** The operating leverage is greatest in firms with a large proportion of fixed costs, low proportion of variable costs, and the resulting high contribution-margin ratio. Exhibit 7–6 shows that company B has low operating leverage, company C has high operating leverage, and company A falls in between. To a physical scientist, *leverage* refers to the ability of a small force to move a heavy weight. To the managerial accountant, *operating leverage* refers to the ability of the firm to generate an increase in net income when sales revenue increases.

Measuring Operating Leverage The managerial accountant can measure a firm's operating leverage, *at a particular sales volume,* using the **operating leverage factor:**

$$\text{Operating leverage factor} = \frac{\text{Contribution margin}}{\text{Net income}}$$

Using the data in Exhibit 7–6, the operating leverage factors of companies A, B, and C are computed as follows:

	(Contribution Margin)	÷	(Net Income)	=	(Operating Leverage Factor)
Company A (Digital Time)	$200,000	÷	$50,000	=	4
Company B (high variable expenses)	$100,000	÷	$50,000	=	2
Company C (high fixed expenses)	$450,000	÷	$50,000	=	9

The operating leverage factor is a measure, at a particular level of sales, of the *percentage* impact on net income of a given *percentage* change in sales revenue. Multiplying the *percentage* change in sales revenue by the operating leverage factor yields the *percentage* change in net income.

	(Percentage Increase in Sales Revenue)	×	(Operating Leverage Factor)	=	(Percentage Change in Net Income)
Company A (Digital Time)	10%	×	4	=	40%
Company B (high variable expenses)	10%	×	2	=	20%
Company C (high fixed expenses)	10%	×	9	=	90%

The percentage change in net income shown above for each company may be verified by re-examining Exhibit 7–7.

Break-Even Point and Safety Margin A firm's operating leverage also affects its break-even point. Since a firm with relatively high operating leverage has proportionally high fixed expenses, the firm's break-even point will be relatively high. This fact is illustrated using the data from Exhibit 7–6.

	(Fixed Expenses)	÷	(Contribution Margin Ratio)	=	(Break-Even Sales Revenue)
Company A (Digital Time)	$150,000	÷	40%	=	$375,000
Company B (high variable expenses)	$ 50,000	÷	20%	=	$250,000
Company C (high fixed expenses)	$400,000	÷	90%	=	$444,444*

*Rounded

The safety margin also is affected by a firm's operating leverage. Suppose the budgeted sales revenue for each of the three companies is $500,000. Then the safety margin, defined as budgeted sales revenue minus break-even sales revenue, is calculated as shown next.

	Budgeted Sales Revenue	Break-Even Sales Revenue	Safety Margin
Company A (Digital Time)	$500,000	$375,000	$125,000
Company B (high variable expenses)	500,000	250,000	250,000
Company C (high fixed expenses)	500,000	444,444	55,556

To summarize, company C's high fixed expenses result in a high break-even point and low safety margin. Company B displays the opposite characteristics, and company A falls in between the two extremes.

Labor-Intensive Production Processes versus Advanced Manufacturing Systems The effects of labor-intensive (manual) production processes and highly automated, advanced manufacturing systems illustrated by companies A, B, and C are typical. As Exhibit 7–8 shows, a movement toward an advanced manufacturing environment often results in a higher break-even point, lower safety margin, and higher operating leverage. However, high-technology manufacturing systems generally have greater throughput, thus allowing greater potential for profitability. Along with the increased potential for profitability comes increased risk. In an economic recession, for example, a highly automated company with high fixed costs will be less able to adapt to lower consumer demand than will a firm with a more labor-intensive production process.

Management Accounting Practice

Expedia and Amazon

OPERATING LEVERAGE HELPS WEB COMPANIES TO BE PROFITABLE

© Design Pics/Don Hammond RF

Some Web-based companies are demonstrating that "once they turn profitable, they can become big moneymakers. The reason is operating leverage. That's accounting-speak for a simple concept: Once you invest enough to build a website and your basic operations, you don't need to spend much money as sales rise. After you cover your fixed costs, the expense of processing each sale is so little that profits grow faster than revenues."

Expedia, the online travel agency, is an example of a successful Web-based company benefiting from the operating leverage concept. In one quarter alone, Expedia doubled its sales. Yet its overhead, including administrative and marketing costs, rose less than ten percent. "One big reason is that the company had already paid for the computer gear it needed to handle the higher volume of ticket sales."[5]

Expedia's high operating leverage factor enables it to have a high contribution-margin ratio and also a high gross margin percentage. In 2012, Expedia's annual gross margin percentage was 81.8 percent. This means that over 81 cents of every sales dollar at Expedia went to the firm's gross margin. In comparison, Amazon's annual gross margin percentage for the same year was 28.3 percent.

[5]R. Crum, "Expedia Reports Ten Percent Earnings Increase," www.marketwatch.com, by *The Wall Street Journal,* February 5, 2013; T. J. Mullaney and R. D. Hof, "Finally, the Pot of Gold," *Business Week,* June 24, 2002, p. 106.

Exhibit 7–8
Labor-Intensive Production Processes versus Advanced Manufacturing Systems

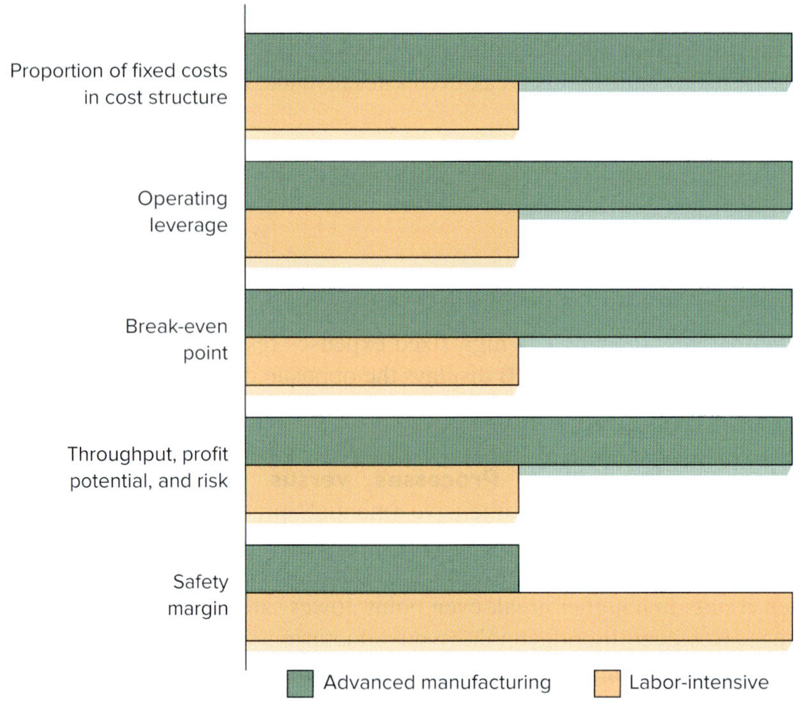

Cost Structure and Operating Leverage: A Cost-Benefit Issue

A firm's cost structure plays an important role in determining its cost-volume-profit relationships. A company with proportionately high fixed costs has relatively high operating leverage. The result of high operating leverage is that the firm can generate a large percentage increase in net income from a relatively small percentage increase in sales revenue. On the other hand, a firm with high operating leverage has a relatively high break-even point. This entails some risk to the firm.

The optimal cost structure for an organization involves a trade-off. Management must weigh the benefits of high operating leverage against the risks of large committed fixed costs and the associated high break-even point.

Management Accounting Practice
Kaiser Permanente

HEALTH CARE COSTS AND OPERATING LEVERAGE

Kaiser Permanente was founded in 1945 to provide health care for workers at Henry F. Kaiser's West Coast shipyards and steel mills. It led the U.S. HMOs by building its own hospitals, marketing its own health insurance, and working with doctors in the Permanente Medical Group, who practice exclusively for Kaiser. Such a vertical integration allows Kaiser to control costs better than HMOs that contract with independent doctors and hospitals. This strategy results in Kaiser's cost structure being dominated by fixed costs. Kaiser has to focus on maintaining membership growth because of its high operating leverage.[6] As a result of the Affordable Care Act, Kaiser Permante expects its membership roles of individual subscribers to rise substantially in the next few years.

[6]Based on the authors' research; and Geoff Colvin, "Kaiser Permanente Prepares for Obamacare," money.cnn.com, October 3, 2012.

CVP Analysis, Activity-Based Costing, and Advanced Manufacturing Systems

Learning Objective 7-9

Understand the implications of activity-based costing for CVP analysis.

Traditional cost-volume-profit analysis focuses on the number of units sold as the only cost and revenue driver. Sales revenue is assumed to be linear in units sold. Moreover, costs are categorized as fixed or variable, with respect to the number of units sold, within the relevant range. This approach is consistent with traditional product-costing systems, in which cost assignment is based on a single, volume-related cost driver. In CVP analysis, as in product costing, the traditional approach can be misleading or provide less than adequate information for various management purposes. An activity-based costing system can provide a much more complete picture of cost-volume-profit relationships and thus provide better information to managers.

To illustrate the potential impact of activity-based costing on CVP analysis, we will continue our discussion of Digital Time Company. The basic data underlying the contribution income statement shown in Exhibit 7–5 are as follows:

Sales volume	20,000 units
Sales price	$25
Unit variable costs:	
Variable manufacturing	$14
Variable selling and administrative	1
Total unit variable cost	$15
Unit contribution margin	$10
Fixed costs:	
Fixed manufacturing	$100,000
Fixed selling and administrative	50,000
Total fixed costs	$150,000

"ABC was critical to the organization in helping us gain a better understanding of our costs. . . . It provided us with a foundation for managing expenses better." (7e)

BlueCross BlueShield of North Carolina

These data are adequate for a traditional CVP analysis of various questions management may ask. For example, the break-even point is easily calculated as 15,000 units, as the following analysis shows:

$$\text{Break-even point} = \frac{\text{Fixed costs}}{\text{Unit contribution margin}} = \frac{\$150{,}000}{\$10} = 15{,}000 \text{ units}$$

Alternatively, management may determine how many clocks must be sold to earn a target profit of $200,000, as the following calculation demonstrates:

$$\begin{aligned}\text{Sales volume required to earn target profit of \$200,000} &= \frac{\text{Fixed costs} + \text{Target profit}}{\text{Unit contribution margin}} \\ &= \frac{\$150{,}000 + \$200{,}000}{\$10} = 35{,}000 \text{ units}\end{aligned}$$

What do these questions have in common? They both focus on *sales volume* as the sole revenue and cost driver. The CVP analysis depends on a distinction between costs that are fixed and costs that are variable *with respect to sales volume.*

A Move Toward JIT and Flexible Manufacturing

Learning Objective 7-10

Be aware of the effects of advanced manufacturing technology on CVP relationships.

Now let's examine another question Digital Time's management could face. Suppose management is considering the installation of a *flexible manufacturing system* and a move toward just-in-time (JIT) production. A flexible manufacturing system uses highly automated material-handling and production equipment to manufacture a variety of similar products. In the new production process, setups would be quicker and more frequent and production runs would be smaller. Fewer inspections would be required, due to the

Pictured here is a production cell in a flexible manufacturing system engaged in the production of disks for computer hard disk drives. In such a high-tech manufacturing environment, setups are quicker and more frequent, and production runs are smaller. An activity-based costing CVP analysis will give management a better understanding of cost-volume-profit relationships.

© Lonnie Duka/Getty Images

total quality control (TQC) philosophy that often accompanies JIT. Variable manufacturing costs would be lower, due to savings in direct labor. Finally, general factory overhead costs would increase, due to the greater depreciation charges on the new production equipment.

Suppose management wants to answer the same two questions addressed previously, under the assumption that the production process changes are adopted. To properly address this issue, we need a much more detailed understanding of the impact of other, *non-volume-based cost drivers* on Digital Time's costs. This type of detail is the hallmark of an activity-based costing system. Suppose Digital Time's controller completes an ABC analysis of the company's 20x1 activity before the new equipment is installed. The results are shown in Exhibit 7–9.

There is a subtle but important point to realize about the cost behavior depicted in Exhibit 7–9. Setup, inspection, and material handling are listed as fixed costs. *They are*

Exhibit 7–9

Activity-Based Costing Data under Current Production Process (20x1)

Digital:Time

Sales price	$25
Unit variable costs:	
Variable manufacturing	$14
Variable selling and administrative	1
Total unit variable costs	$15
Unit contribution margin	$10
Fixed costs (fixed with respect to sales volume):	
General factory overhead (including depreciation on plant and equipment)	$ 60,000
Setup (52 setups at $100 per setup)*	5,200
Inspection [(52)(21) inspections at $20 per inspection]†	21,840
Material handling (1,080 hours at $12 per hour)	12,960
Total fixed manufacturing costs	$100,000
Fixed selling and administrative costs	50,000
Total fixed costs	$150,000

*One setup per week.

†Three inspections per day, seven days a week (52 weeks per year).

largely fixed with respect to sales volume. However, they are *not* fixed with respect to *other cost drivers,* such as the number of setups, inspections, and hours of material handling. This is the fundamental distinction between a traditional CVP analysis and an activity-based costing CVP analysis. The traditional CVP analysis recognizes a single, volume-based cost driver, namely, sales volume. The activity-based costing CVP analysis recognizes multiple cost drivers. As a result, some costs viewed as fixed under the traditional analysis are considered variable (with respect to the appropriate cost drivers) under the ABC approach.

Now let's return to management's decision regarding the installation of a flexible manufacturing system and the adoption of the JIT and TQC philosophies. The activity-based costing analysis of the proposed production technology is displayed in Exhibit 7–10. Due to the decreased use of direct labor, the unit variable manufacturing cost has declined from \$14 to \$9, thus bringing the total unit variable cost down to \$10. This results in an increase in the unit contribution margin to \$15. The installation of sophisticated new manufacturing equipment has more than tripled general factory overhead, from \$60,000 to \$184,000. Under the proposed JIT approach, setups will be daily instead of weekly; each setup will be quicker and less expensive. As a result of the emphasis on total quality control, only one inspection per day will be necessary, instead of three as before. Moreover, each inspection will be less expensive. Finally, the amount of material-handling activity will decline dramatically, although there will be a slight increase in the cost per hour. This is due to the higher skill grade of labor required to operate the new automated material-handling system.

Using the ABC data in Exhibit 7–10, we can answer the two CVP questions posed by management. If the new production technology is adopted, the following CVP computations will be appropriate.

$$\text{Break-even point} = \frac{\text{Fixed costs}}{\text{Unit contribution margin}} = \frac{\$250{,}000}{\$15} = \begin{matrix}\text{16,667 units}\\ \text{(rounded)}\end{matrix}$$

$$\begin{matrix}\text{Sales volume required to earn}\\ \text{target profit of \$200,000}\end{matrix} = \frac{\text{Fixed costs} + \text{Target profit}}{\text{Unit contribution margin}}$$

$$= \frac{\$250{,}000 + \$200{,}000}{\$15} = 30{,}000 \text{ units}$$

Notice that Digital Time's break-even point increased with the introduction of the advanced manufacturing system (from 15,000 to 16,667 units). However, the number of sales units required to earn a target profit of \$200,000 declined (from 35,000 to 30,000 units). These kinds of CVP changes are typical when firms install an advanced manufacturing

Exhibit 7–10
Activity-Based Costing Data under Proposed Production Technology

Digital:Time

Sales price		\$25
Unit variable costs:		
Variable manufacturing		\$ 9
Variable selling and administrative		1
Total unit variable costs		\$10
Unit contribution margin		\$15
Fixed costs (fixed with respect to sales volume):		
General factory overhead (including depreciation on plant and equipment)		\$184,000
Setup (365 setups at \$30 per setup)		10,950
Inspection (365 inspections at \$10 per inspection)		3,650
Material handling (100 hours at \$14 per hour)		1,400
Total fixed manufacturing costs		\$200,000
Fixed selling and administrative costs		50,000
Total fixed costs		\$250,000

system. Typically, the cost structure of an advanced manufacturing environment is characterized by a lower proportion of variable costs and a larger proportion of costs that are fixed (with respect to sales volume).

ABC Provides a Richer Understanding of Cost Behavior and CVP Relationships

The point of this section is that activity-based costing provides a richer description of a company's cost behavior. Digital Time's traditional costing system treated setup, inspection, and material handling as fixed costs. However, the ABC analysis showed that while these costs are largely fixed with respect to sales volume, they are not fixed with respect to other appropriate cost drivers. In analyzing the cost-volume-profit implications of the proposed changes in manufacturing technology, it was crucial to have an understanding of how these costs would change with respect to such cost drivers as the number of setups, number of quality-assurance inspections, and amount of material-handling activity.

Just as ABC can improve an organization's product-costing system, it also can facilitate a deeper understanding of cost behavior and CVP relationships.

Chapter Summary

LO7-1 Compute a break-even point using the contribution-margin approach and the equation approach. These two approaches result in the same general formula for computing the break-even point (in units). Under the equation approach, the profit equation is specified as follows: Sales revenue − Variable expenses − Fixed expenses = Profit. When this equation is manipulated, the contribution-margin approach to the break-even point results, as follows: Break-even point (in units) = Fixed expenses ÷ Unit contribution margin.

LO7-2 Compute the contribution-margin ratio and use it to find the break-even point in sales dollars. The contribution-margin ratio is defined as follows: Unit contribution margin ÷ Unit sales price. The break-even point (in sales dollars) can be computed as follows: Fixed expenses ÷ Contribution-margin ratio.

LO7-3 Prepare a cost-volume-profit (CVP) graph and explain how it is used. A cost-volume-profit graph shows the break-even point (in sales dollars) as the intersection of the total revenue line and the total expense line. The graph can be used to help management understand how changes in the volume of activity affect cost and profit.

LO7-4 Apply CVP analysis to determine the effect on profit of changes in fixed expenses, variable expenses, sales prices, and sales volume. Management can use the break-even equation to predict the effects on the break-even point of changes in any component of the equation, e.g., sales price, unit variable cost, fixed cost, and so forth. Such prediction can help management in making a variety of operational decisions.

LO7-5 Compute the break-even point and prepare a profit-volume graph for a multiproduct enterprise. Break-even analysis in a multiproduct firm is accomplished by computing a weighted-average contribution margin, which is based on the expected sales mix. The same break-even formulas are used as in a single-product analysis, except that the unit contribution margin is replaced by the weighted-average contribution margin. This analysis is limited by the assumption of a constant sales mix across the range of total sales volume.

LO7-6 List and discuss the key assumptions of CVP analysis. CVP analysis involves several key assumptions, which follow: (1) Total revenue is linear (i.e., a straight line) with respect to changes in the volume of activity. (2) Total expense is linear (i.e., a straight line) with respect to changes in the volume of activity. An implication of this assumption is that the efficiency and productivity of the production process remains constant. (3) The sales mix remains constant over the relevant range. (4) The beginning and ending inventory levels are the same in a manufacturing firm.

LO7-7 Prepare and interpret a contribution income statement. Cost-volume-profit relationships are important enough to operating managers that some firms prepare a contribution income statement. This income-statement format separates fixed and variable expenses and computes the aggregate contribution margin. This statement format helps managers discern the effects on profit from changes in volume. The contribution income statement also discloses an organization's cost structure, which is the relative proportion of its fixed and variable costs.

LO7-8 Explain the role of cost structure and operating leverage in CVP relationships. An organization's cost structure is the relative proportions of its fixed and variable costs. The extent to which an organization uses fixed costs in its cost structure is called operating leverage. Firms with high operating leverage tend to have higher break-even points, other things being equal.

LO7-9 Understand the implications of activity-based costing for CVP analysis. Activity-based costing (ABC) provides a richer description of an organization's cost behavior and CVP relationships than is provided by a traditional costing system. An ABC cost-volume-profit analysis recognizes that some costs that are fixed with respect to sales volume may not be fixed with respect to other important cost drivers. In many cases, management can benefit substantially from such an improved understanding of cost behavior and CVP relationships.

LO7-10 Be aware of the effects of advanced manufacturing technology on CVP relationships. Companies with advanced manufacturing technology tend to have higher fixed costs, lower variable costs, and higher break-even points.

LO7-11 Understand the effect of income taxes on CVP analysis (appendix). When a firm is required to pay taxes on income, it is important to distinguish between after-tax (AT) income and before-tax (BT) income. AT income is equal to BT income minus income tax expense. Therefore, BT income is equal to AT income ÷ (1 − tax rate). The number of units of sales required to earn a specified AT income is equal to (BT income + fixed expenses) ÷ unit contribution margin.

Review Problem on Cost-Volume-Profit Analysis

Overlook Inn is a small bed-and-breakfast inn located in the Great Smoky Mountains of Tennessee. The charge is $50 per person for one night's lodging and a full breakfast in the morning. The retired couple who own and manage the inn estimate that the variable expense per person is $20. This includes such expenses as food, maid service, and utilities. The inn's fixed expenses total $42,000 per year. The inn can accommodate 10 guests each night.

Required: Compute the following:

1. Contribution margin per unit of service. (A unit of service is one night's lodging for one guest.)
2. Contribution-margin ratio.
3. Annual break-even point in units of service and in dollars of service revenue.
4. The number of units of service required to earn a target profit of $60,000 for the year. (Ignore income taxes.)

Solution to Review Problem

1. Contribution margin per unit of service = Nightly room charge − Variable expense per person

$$\$30 = \$50 - \$20$$

2. $$\text{Contribution-margin ratio} = \frac{\text{Contribution margin per unit}}{\text{Nightly room charge}}$$

$$.60 = \frac{\$30}{\$50}$$

3. $$\text{Break-even point in units of service} = \frac{\text{Fixed expenses}}{\text{Contribution margin per unit}}$$

$$1{,}400 = \frac{\$42{,}000}{\$30}$$

$$\text{Break-even point in dollars of revenue} = \frac{\text{Fixed expenses}}{\text{Contribution-margin ratio}}$$

$$\$70{,}000 = \frac{\$42{,}000}{.60}$$

4. $$\text{Number of units of service required to earn target profit} = \frac{\text{Fixed expenses} + \text{Target profit}}{\text{Contribution margin per unit of service}}$$

$$3{,}400 = \frac{\$42{,}000 + \$60{,}000}{\$30}$$

Key Terms

For each term's definition refer to the indicated page, or turn to the glossary at the end of the text.

after-tax net income,* 304
before-tax income,* 304
break-even point, 278
contribution income statement, 293
contribution-margin ratio, 279
cost structure, 295
cost-volume-profit (CVP) analysis, 276
cost-volume-profit (CVP) graph, 280
gross margin, 293
operating leverage, 296
operating leverage factor, 296
profit-volume graph, 283
safety margin, 285
sales mix, 290
sensitivity analysis, 292
target profit (or income), 284
total contribution margin, 278
unit contribution margin, 279
weighted-average unit contribution margin, 290

*Term appears in the appendix.

APPENDIX TO CHAPTER 7

Learning Objective 7-11

Understand the effect of income taxes on CVP analysis.

Effect of Income Taxes

Profit-seeking enterprises must pay income taxes on their profits. A firm's **after-tax net income**, the amount of income remaining after subtracting the firm's income tax expense, is less than its **before-tax income**. This fact is expressed in the following formula.

$$\text{(After-tax net income)} = \text{(Before-tax income)} - t\text{(Before-tax income)}$$

where t denotes the income tax rate.

Rearranging this equation yields the following formula.

$$\text{After-tax net income} = \text{(Before-tax income)}(1 - t) \qquad (9)$$

Digital:Time

To illustrate this formula, suppose Digital Time Company must pay income taxes of 40 percent of its before-tax income. The company's contribution income statement for 20x1 follows.

Sales, 20,000 units at $25 each	$500,000
Variable expenses, 20,000 units at $15 each*	300,000
Contribution margin	$200,000
Fixed expenses	150,000
Income before taxes	$ 50,000
Income tax expense, .40 × $50,000	20,000
Net income, $50,000 × (1 − .40)	$ 30,000

*Variable cost per unit is $15: variable manufacturing cost of $14 plus variable selling and administrative costs of $1.

The requirement that companies pay income taxes affects their cost-volume-profit relationships. To earn a particular after-tax net income will require greater before-tax income than if there were no tax. For example, if Digital Time's target after-tax net income were $30,000, the company would have to earn before-tax income of $50,000. Digital Time's income statement shows this relationship.

How much before-tax income must be earned in order to achieve a particular target after-tax net income? Rearranging equation (9) above yields the following formula.

$$\text{Target after-tax net income} = \left(\text{Target before-tax income}\right)(1 - t)$$

Divide both sides by $(1 - t)$

$$\frac{\text{Target after-tax net income}}{1 - t} = \left(\text{Target before-tax income}\right)\frac{1 - t}{1 - t}$$

$$\frac{\text{Target after-tax net income}}{1 - t} = \text{Target before-tax income}$$

If Digital Time Company's target after-tax net income is \$30,000, its target before-tax income is calculated as follows:

$$\frac{\text{Target after-tax net income}}{1-t} = \frac{\$30{,}000}{1-.40} = \$50{,}000 = \text{Target before-tax income}$$

Now we are in a position to compute the number of digital clocks that Digital Time must sell in order to achieve a particular after-tax net income. We begin with the following before-tax income equation.

$$\text{Sales} - \text{Variable expenses} - \text{Fixed expenses} = \text{Before-tax income}$$

Now we use our formula for before-tax income.

$$\text{Sales} - \text{Variable expenses} - \text{Fixed expenses} = \frac{\text{After-tax income}}{1-t}$$

$$\left[\begin{pmatrix}\text{Unit}\\\text{sales}\\\text{price}\end{pmatrix} \times \begin{pmatrix}\text{Sales}\\\text{volume}\\\text{in units}\end{pmatrix}\right] - \left[\begin{pmatrix}\text{Unit}\\\text{variable}\\\text{expense}\end{pmatrix} \times \begin{pmatrix}\text{Sales}\\\text{volume}\\\text{in units}\end{pmatrix}\right] - \begin{pmatrix}\text{Fixed}\\\text{expenses}\end{pmatrix} = \frac{\text{After-tax net income}}{1-t}$$

Using the data for Digital Time Company, and assuming target after-tax net income of \$30,000:

$$(\$25 \times X) - (\$15 \times X) - \$150{,}000 = \frac{\$30{,}000}{1-.40}$$

where X denotes the number of units that must be sold to achieve the target after-tax net income.

Now we solve for X as follows:

$$\underbrace{(\$25 - \$15)} \times X = \$150{,}000 + \frac{\$30{,}000}{1-.40}$$

$$\$10 \quad \times X = \$150{,}000 + \frac{\$30{,}000}{1-.40}$$

$$X = \frac{\$150{,}000 + \dfrac{\$30{,}000}{1-.40}}{\$10}$$

$$= 20{,}000 \text{ units}$$

In terms of sales revenue, Digital Time must achieve a sales volume of \$500,000 (20,000 units × \$25 sales price). We can verify these calculations by examining Digital Time's income statement given previously.

Notice in the preceding calculations that \$10 is the unit contribution margin (\$25 sales price minus \$15 variable expense). Thus, the general formula illustrated for Digital Time is the following:

$$\text{Number of units of sales required to earn target after-tax net income} = \frac{\text{Fixed expenses} + \dfrac{\text{Target after-tax net income}}{1-t}}{\text{Unit contribution margin}}$$

where t denotes the income tax rate.

A cost-volume-profit graph for Digital Time Company is displayed in Exhibit 7–11. As the graph shows, 20,000 units must be sold to achieve \$30,000 in after-tax net income. The company's break-even point is 15,000 units. The break-even point is not affected by income taxes, because at the break-even point, there is no income.

Notice that Digital Time Company must sell 5,000 units *beyond the break-even point* in order to achieve after-tax net income of \$30,000. Each unit sold beyond the break-even point contributes \$10 toward *before-tax* income. However, of that \$10 contribution margin, \$4 will have to be paid in income taxes. This leaves an *after-tax contribution* of \$6 toward after-tax net income. Thus, selling 5,000 units beyond the break-even point results in after-tax net income of \$30,000 (5,000 units × \$6 after-tax contribution per unit).

Exhibit 7–11
Cost-Volume-Profit Graph (with income taxes)

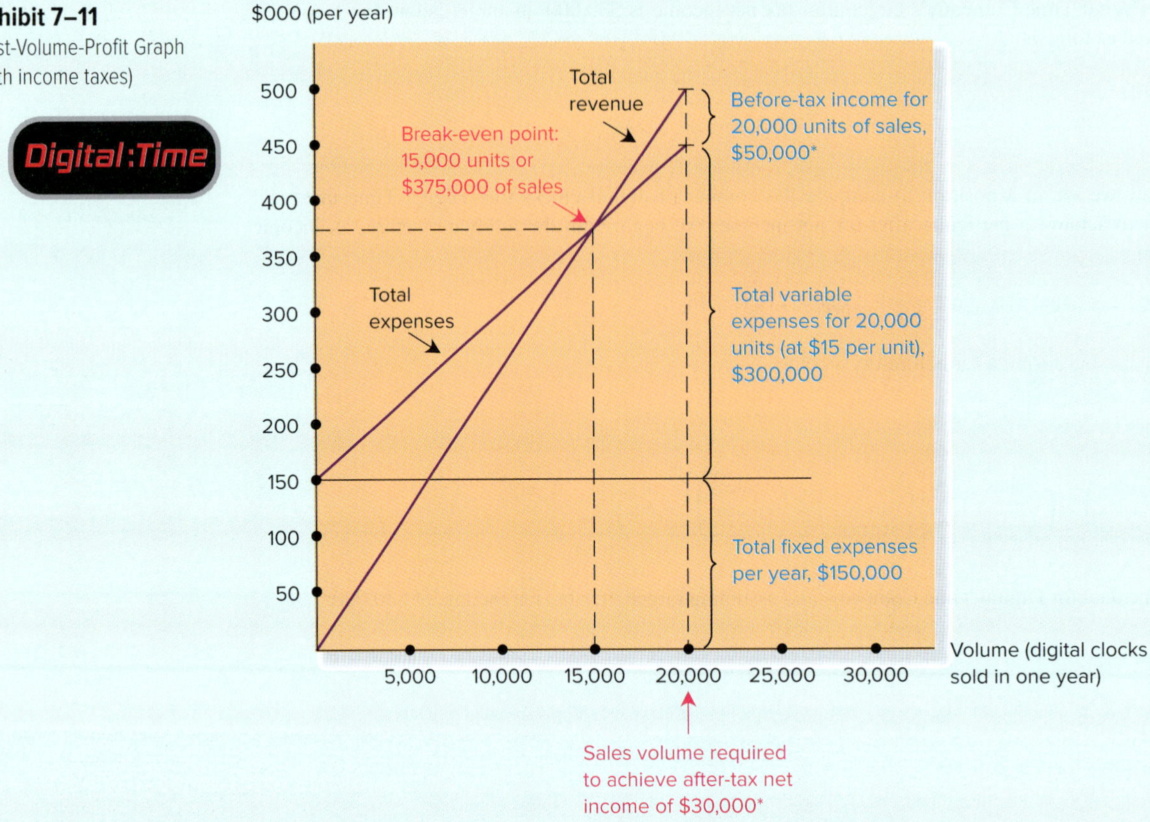

*(Before-tax income) × (1 – Tax rate) = After-tax income
$50,000 × (1 – .40) = $30,000

Review Questions

7–1. Briefly explain each of the following methods of computing a break-even point in units: (*a*) contribution-margin approach, (*b*) equation approach, and (*c*) graphical approach.

7–2. What is the meaning of the term *unit contribution margin?* Contribution to what?

7–3. What information is conveyed by a cost-volume-profit graph in addition to a company's break-even point?

7–4. What does the term *safety margin* mean?

7–5. Suppose the fixed expenses of a travel agency increase. What will happen to its break-even point, measured in number of clients served? Why?

7–6. Delmarva Oyster Company has been able to decrease its variable expenses per pound of oysters harvested. How will this affect the firm's break-even sales volume?

7–7. In a strategy meeting, a manufacturing company's president said, "If we raise the price of our product, the company's break-even point will be lower." The financial vice president responded by saying, "Then we should raise our price. The company will be less likely to incur a loss." Do you agree with the president? Why? Do you agree with the financial vice president? Why?

7–8. What will happen to a company's break-even point if the sales price and unit variable cost of its only product increase by the same dollar amount?

7–9. An art museum covers its operating expenses by charging a small admission fee. The objective of the nonprofit organization is to break even. A local arts enthusiast has just pledged an annual donation of $10,000 to the museum. How will the donation affect the museum's break-even attendance level?

7–10. How can a profit-volume graph be used to predict a company's profit for a particular sales volume?

7–11. List the most important assumptions of cost-volume-profit analysis.

7–12. Why do many operating managers prefer a contribution income statement instead of a traditional income statement?

7–13. What is the difference between a manufacturing company's *gross margin* and its total *contribution margin?*

7–14. East Company manufactures VCRs using a completely automated production process. West Company also manufactures VCRs, but its products are assembled manually. How will these two firms' cost structures differ? Which company will have a higher operating leverage factor?

7–15. When sales volume increases, which company will experience a larger percentage increase in profit: company X, which has mostly fixed expenses, or company Y, which has mostly variable expenses?

7–16. What does the term *sales mix* mean? How is a *weighted-average unit contribution margin* computed?

7–17. A car rental agency rents subcompact, compact, and full-size automobiles. What assumptions would be made about the agency's sales mix for the purpose of a cost-volume-profit analysis?

7–18. How can a hotel's management use cost-volume-profit analysis to help in deciding on room rates?

7–19. How could cost-volume-profit analysis be used in budgeting? In making a decision about advertising?

7–20. Two companies have identical fixed expenses, unit variable expenses, and profits. Yet one company has set a much lower price for its product. Explain how this can happen.

7–21. A company with an advanced manufacturing environment typically will have a higher break-even point, greater operating leverage, and larger safety margin than a labor-intensive firm. True or false? Explain.

7–22. Explain briefly how activity-based costing (ABC) affects cost-volume-profit analysis.

Exercises

All applicable Exercises are available in Connect.

connect

Exercise 7–23
Fill in Blanks; Basic CVP Relationships
(LO 7-1, 7-2)

Fill in the missing data for each of the following independent cases. (Ignore income taxes.)

	Sales Revenue	Variable Expenses	Total Contribution Margin	Fixed Expenses	Net Income	Break-Even Sales Revenue
1.	?	$40,000	?	$30,000	?	$40,000
2.	$ 80,000	?	$15,000	?	?	80,000
3.	?	40,000	80,000	?	$50,000	?
4.	110,000	22,000	?	?	38,000	?

Exercise 7–24
Pizza Delivery Business; Basic CVP Analysis
(LO 7-1, 7-2, 7-4)

College Pizza delivers pizzas to the dormitories and apartments near a major state university. The company's annual fixed expenses are $40,000. The sales price of a pizza is $10, and it costs the company $5 to make and deliver each pizza. (In the following requirements, ignore income taxes.)

Required:

1. Using the contribution-margin approach, compute the company's break-even point in units (pizzas).
2. What is the contribution-margin ratio?
3. Compute the break-even sales revenue. Use the contribution-margin ratio in your calculation.
4. How many pizzas must the company sell to earn a target profit of $65,000? Use the equation method.

Exercise 7–25
Manufacturing; Using CVP Analysis
(LO 7-1, 7-4)

Rosario Company, which is located in Buenos Aires, Argentina, manufactures a component used in farm machinery. The firm's fixed costs are 4,000,000 *p* per year. The variable cost of each component is 2,000 *p*, and the components are sold for 3,000 *p* each. The company sold 5,000 components during the prior year. (*p* denotes the peso, Argentina's national currency. Several countries use the peso as their monetary unit. On the day this exercise was written, Argentina's peso was worth .104 U.S. dollar. In the following requirements, ignore income taxes.)

Required: Answer requirements (1) through (4) independently.

1. Compute the break-even point in units.
2. What will the new break-even point be if fixed costs increase by 10 percent?
3. What was the company's net income for the prior year?
4. The sales manager believes that a reduction in the sales price to 2,500 *p* will result in orders for 1,200 more components each year. What will the break-even point be if the price is changed?
5. Should the price change discussed in requirement (4) be made?

Exercise 7–26
Sports Franchise; CVP Graph
(LO 7-3, 7-4)

The Houston Armadillos, a minor-league baseball team, play their weekly games in a small stadium just outside Houston. The stadium holds 10,000 people and tickets sell for $10 each. The franchise owner estimates that the team's annual fixed expenses are $180,000, and the variable expense per ticket sold is $1. (In the following requirements, ignore income taxes.)

Required:

1. Draw a cost-volume-profit graph for the sports franchise. Label the axes, break-even point, profit and loss areas, fixed expenses, variable expenses, total-expense line, and total-revenue line.
2. If the stadium is half full for each game, how many games must the team play to break even?

Exercise 7–27
Continuation of Preceding Exercise; Profit-Volume Graph; Safety Margin
(LO 7-3, 7-4)

Refer to the data given in the preceding exercise. (Ignore income taxes.)

Required:

1. Prepare a fully labeled profit-volume graph for the Houston Armadillos.
2. What is the safety margin for the baseball franchise if the team plays a 12-game season and the team owner expects the stadium to be 30 percent full for each game?
3. If the stadium is half full for each game, what ticket price would the team have to charge in order to break even?

Exercise 7–28
Publishing; Contribution Income Statement
(LO 7-7, 7-8)

Europa Publications, Inc. specializes in reference books that keep abreast of the rapidly changing political and economic issues in Europe. The results of the company's operations during the prior year are given in the following table. All units produced during the year were sold. (Ignore income taxes.)

Sales revenue	$2,000,000
Manufacturing costs:	
Fixed	500,000
Variable	1,000,000
Selling costs:	
Fixed	50,000
Variable	100,000
Administrative costs:	
Fixed	120,000
Variable	30,000

Required:

1. Prepare a traditional income statement and a contribution income statement for the company.
2. What is the firm's operating leverage for the sales volume generated during the prior year?
3. Suppose sales revenue increases by 10 percent. What will be the percentage increase in net income?
4. Which income statement would an operating manager use to answer requirement (3)? Why?

Exercise 7–29
Retail; CVP Analysis with Multiple Products
(LO 7-1, 7-2, 7-5)

Tim's Bicycle Shop sells 21-speed bicycles. For purposes of a cost-volume-profit analysis, the shop owner has divided sales into two categories, as follows:

Product Type	Sales Price	Invoice Cost	Sales Commission
High-quality	$500	$275	$25
Medium-quality	300	135	15

Three-quarters of the shop's sales are medium-quality bikes. The shop's annual fixed expenses are $65,000. (In the following requirements, ignore income taxes.)

Required:

1. Compute the unit contribution margin for each product type.
2. What is the shop's sales mix?
3. Compute the weighted-average unit contribution margin, assuming a constant sales mix.
4. What is the shop's break-even sales volume in dollars? Assume a constant sales mix.
5. How many bicycles of each type must be sold to earn a target net income of $48,750? Assume a constant sales mix.

Exercise 7–30
Cost-Volume-Profit Analysis in an Airline; Use of Internet
(LO 7-4)

Use the Internet to access the website of one of these airlines, or a different airline of your choosing.

American Airlines	www.aa.com
British Airways	www.britishairways.com
Delta Air Lines	www.delta.com
Southwest Airlines	www.southwest.com

Required: Find the company's most recent annual report. Does the management discussion in the report disclose the airline's break-even load factor? If so, what is it for the most recent year reported?

Exercise 7–31
Hotel and Restaurant; Cost Structure and Operating Leverage
(LO 7-2, 7-4, 7-8)

A contribution income statement for the Nantucket Inn is shown below. (Ignore income taxes.)

Revenue	$500,000
Less: Variable expenses	300,000
Contribution margin	$200,000
Less: Fixed expenses	150,000
Net income	$ 50,000

Required:

1. Show the hotel's cost structure by indicating the percentage of the hotel's revenue represented by each item on the income statement.
2. Suppose the hotel's revenue declines by 15 percent. Use the contribution-margin percentage to calculate the resulting decrease in net income.
3. What is the hotel's operating leverage factor when revenue is $500,000?
4. Use the operating leverage factor to calculate the increase in net income resulting from a 20 percent increase in sales revenue.

Exercise 7–32
Continuation of Preceding Exercise
(LO 7-4, 7-7)

Refer to the income statement given in the preceding exercise. Prepare a new contribution income statement for the Nantucket Inn in each of the following independent situations. (Ignore income taxes.)

1. The hotel's volume of activity increases by 20 percent, and fixed expenses increase by 40 percent.
2. The ratio of variable expenses to revenue doubles. There is no change in the hotel's volume of activity. Fixed expenses decline by $25,000.

Exercise 7–33
Consulting Firm; CVP Analysis with Income Taxes (Appendix)
(LO 7-1, 7-4, 7-11)

Hydro Systems Engineering Associates, Inc. provides consulting services to city water authorities. The consulting firm's contribution-margin ratio is 20 percent, and its annual fixed expenses are $120,000. The firm's income-tax rate is 40 percent.

Required:

1. Calculate the firm's break-even volume of service revenue.
2. How much before-tax income must the firm earn to make an after-tax net income of $48,000?
3. What level of revenue for consulting services must the firm generate to earn an after-tax net income of $48,000?
4. Suppose the firm's income-tax rate rises to 45 percent. Explain what will happen to the break-even level of consulting service revenue.

Problems

All applicable Problems are available in Connect.

Problem 7–34
Basic CVP Relationships; Retailer
(LO 7-1, 7-2, 7-4)

2. Net income: $280,000

Disk City, Inc. is a retailer for digital video disks. The projected net income for the current year is $200,000 based on a sales volume of 200,000 video disks. Disk City has been selling the disks for $16 each. The variable costs consist of the $10 unit purchase price of the disks and a handling cost of $2 per disk. Disk City's annual fixed costs are $600,000.

Management is planning for the coming year, when it expects that the unit purchase price of the video disks will increase 30 percent. (Ignore income taxes.)

Required:

1. Calculate Disk City's break-even point for the current year in number of video disks.
2. What will be the company's net income for the current year if there is a 10 percent increase in projected unit sales volume?
3. What volume of sales (in dollars) must Disk City achieve in the coming year to maintain the same net income as projected for the current year if the unit selling price remains at $16?
4. In order to cover a 30 percent increase in the disk's purchase price for the coming year and still maintain the current contribution-margin ratio, what selling price per disk must Disk City establish for the coming year?
5. ***Build a spreadsheet:*** Construct an Excel spreadsheet to solve requirements (1), (2), and (3) above. Show how the solution will change if the following information changes: the selling price is $17 and the annual fixed costs are $640,000.

(CMA, adapted)

Problem 7–35
Basic CVP Computations
(LO 7-1, 7-2, 7-4)

2. Sales units required for $180,000 income: 54,000 units

CollegePak Company produced and sold 60,000 backpacks during the year just ended at an average price of $20 per unit. Variable manufacturing costs were $8 per unit, and variable marketing costs were $4 per unit sold. Fixed costs amounted to $180,000 for manufacturing and $72,000 for marketing. There was no year-end work-in-process inventory. (Ignore income taxes.)

Required:

1. Compute CollegePak's break-even point in sales dollars for the year.
2. Compute the number of sales units required to earn a net income of $180,000 during the year.
3. CollegePak's variable manufacturing costs are expected to increase by 10 percent in the coming year. Compute the firm's break-even point in sales dollars for the coming year.
4. If CollegePak's variable manufacturing costs do increase by 10 percent, compute the selling price that would yield the same contribution-margin ratio in the coming year.

(CMA, adapted)

Problem 7–36
CVP Relationships; Indifference Point
(LO 7-1, 7-4)

2. Net income, model no. 4399: $1,094,400

Corrigan Enterprises is studying the acquisition of two electrical component insertion systems for producing its sole product, the universal gismo. Data relevant to the systems follow.

Model no. 6754:
Variable costs, $16.00 per unit
Annual fixed costs, $985,600

Model no. 4399:
Variable costs, $12.80 per unit
Annual fixed costs, $1,113,600

Corrigan's selling price is $64 per unit for the universal gismo, which is subject to a 5 percent sales commission. (In the following requirements, ignore income taxes.)

Required:

1. How many units must the company sell to break even if Model 6754 is selected?
2. Which of the two systems would be more profitable if sales and production are expected to average 46,000 units per year?
3. Assume Model 4399 requires the purchase of additional equipment that is not reflected in the preceding figures. The equipment will cost $450,000 and will be depreciated over a five-year life by the straight-line method. How many units must Corrigan sell to earn $956,400 of income if Model 4399 is selected? As in requirement (2), sales and production are expected to average 46,000 units per year.
4. Ignoring the information presented in requirement (3), at what volume level will management be indifferent between the acquisition of Model 6754 and Model 4399? In other words, at what volume level will the annual total cost of each system be equal? (*Hint:* At any given sales volume, sales commissions will be the same amount regardless of which model is selected.)

Problem 7–37
CVP Analysis; Impact of Operating Changes
(LO 7-1, 7-4)

2. Break-even point: 32,000 units

Houston-based Advanced Electronics manufactures audio speakers for desktop computers. The following data relate to the period just ended when the company produced and sold 42,000 speaker sets:

Sales	$3,360,000
Variable costs	840,000
Fixed costs	2,280,000

Management is considering relocating its manufacturing facilities to northern Mexico to reduce costs. Variable costs are expected to average $18 per set; annual fixed costs are anticipated to be $1,984,000. (In the following requirements, ignore income taxes.)

Required:

1. Calculate the company's current income and determine the level of dollar sales needed to double that figure, assuming that manufacturing operations remain in the United States.
2. Determine the break-even point in speaker sets if operations are shifted to Mexico.
3. Assume that management desires to achieve the Mexican break-even point; however, operations will remain in the United States.
   a. If variable costs remain constant, what must management do to fixed costs? By how much must fixed costs change?
   b. If fixed costs remain constant, what must management do to the variable cost per unit? By how much must unit variable cost change?
4. Determine the impact (increase, decrease, or no effect) of the following operating changes.
   a. Effect of an increase in direct material costs on the break-even point.
   b. Effect of an increase in fixed administrative costs on the unit contribution margin.
   c. Effect of an increase in the unit contribution margin on net income.
   d. Effect of a decrease in the number of units sold on the break-even point.

Problem 7–38
Sales Mix and Employee Compensation; Operating Changes
(LO 7-4, 7-5)

2(c). Commissions, total: $535,600

Lawrence Corporation sells two ceiling fans, Deluxe and Basic. Current sales total 60,000 units, consisting of 39,000 Deluxe units and 21,000 Basic units. Selling price and variable cost information follow.

	Deluxe	Basic
Selling price	$86	$74
Variable cost	65	41

Salespeople currently receive flat salaries that total $400,000. Management is contemplating a change to a compensation plan that is based on commissions in an effort to boost the company's presence in the marketplace. Two plans are under consideration:

Plan A: 10% commission computed on gross dollar sales. Deluxe sales are expected to total 45,500 units; Basic sales are anticipated to be 19,500 units.

Plan B: 30% commission computed on the basis of production contribution margins. Deluxe sales are anticipated to be 26,000 units; Basic sales are expected to total 39,000 units.

Required:

1. Define the term *sales mix.*
2. Comparing Plan A to the current compensation arrangement:
   a. Will Plan A achieve management's objective of an increased presence in the marketplace? Briefly explain.
   b. From a sales-mix perspective, will the salespeople be promoting the product that one would logically expect? Briefly discuss.
   c. Will the sales force likely be satisfied with the results of Plan A? Why?
   d. Will Lawrence likely be satisfied with the resulting impact of Plan A on company profitability? Why?

3. Assume that Plan B is under consideration.
    a. Compare Plan A and Plan B with respect to total units sold and the sales mix. Comment on the results.
    b. In comparison with flat salaries, is Plan B more attractive to the sales force? To the company? Show calculations to support your answers.

Problem 7–39
Leverage; Analysis of Operating Change
(LO 7-1, 7-4, 7-8)

1. Plan B break-even point: 2,200 units
3. Operating leverage factor, plan A: 1.2

Consolidated Industries is studying the addition of a new valve to its product line. The valve would be used by manufacturers of irrigation equipment. The company anticipates starting with a relatively low sales volume and then boosting demand over the next several years. A new salesperson must be hired because Consolidated's current sales force is working at capacity. Two compensation plans are under consideration:

Plan A: An annual salary of $22,000 plus a 10% commission based on gross dollar sales.
Plan B: An annual salary of $66,000 and no commission.

Consolidated Industries will purchase the valve for $50 and sell it for $80. Anticipated demand during the first year is 6,000 units. (In the following requirements, ignore income taxes.)

Required:

1. Compute the break-even point in units for Plan A and Plan B.
2. What is meant by the term *operating leverage*?
3. Analyze the cost structures of both plans at the anticipated demand of 6,000 units. Which of the two plans has a higher operating leverage factor?
4. Assume that a general economic downturn occurred during year 2, with product demand falling from 6,000 to 5,000 units. Determine the percentage decrease in company net income if Consolidated had adopted Plan A.
5. Repeat requirement (4) for Plan B. Compare Plan A and Plan B, and explain a major factor that underlies any resulting differences.
6. Briefly discuss the likely profitability impact of an economic recession for highly automated manufacturers. What can you say about the risk associated with these firms?

Problem 7–40
Basic CVP Relationships
(LO 7-1, 7-2, 7-4)

3. Sales units required for target net profit: 140,000 units
6. Old contribution-margin ratio: .208

Serendipity Sound, Inc. manufactures and sells compact discs. Price and cost data are as follows:

Selling price per unit (package of two CDs)		$ 25.00
Variable costs per unit:		
Direct material	$ 10.50	
Direct labor	5.00	
Manufacturing overhead	3.00	
Selling expenses	1.30	
Total variable costs per unit		$ 19.80
Annual fixed costs:		
Manufacturing overhead	$ 192,000	
Selling and administrative	276,000	
Total fixed costs		$ 468,000
Forecasted annual sales volume (120,000 units)		$3,000,000

In the following requirements, ignore income taxes.

Required:

1. What is Serendipity Sound's break-even point in units?
2. What is the company's break-even point in sales dollars?
3. How many units would Serendipity Sound have to sell in order to earn $260,000?
4. What is the firm's margin of safety?

5. Management estimates that direct-labor costs will increase by 8 percent next year. How many units will the company have to sell next year to reach its break-even point?
6. If the company's direct-labor costs do increase by 8 percent, what selling price per unit of product must it charge to maintain the same contribution-margin ratio?

(CMA, adapted)

Problem 7–41
CVP Graph; Cost Structure; Operating Leverage
(LO 7-2, 7-3, 7-4, 7-8)

3. Margin of safety: $4,000,000

Athletico, Inc. manufactures warm-up suits. The company's projected income for the coming year, based on sales of 160,000 units, is as follows:

Sales		$8,000,000
Operating expenses:		
Variable expenses	$2,000,000	
Fixed expenses	3,000,000	
Total expenses		5,000,000
Net income		$3,000,000

Required: In completing the following requirements, ignore income taxes.

1. Prepare a CVP graph for Athletico, Inc. for the coming year.
2. Calculate the firm's break-even point for the year in sales dollars.
3. What is the company's margin of safety for the year?
4. Compute Athletico's operating leverage factor, based on the budgeted sales volume for the year.
5. Compute Athletico's required sales in dollars in order to earn income of $4,500,000 in the coming year.
6. Describe the firm's cost structure. Calculate the percentage relationships between variable and fixed expenses and sales revenue.

(CMA, adapted)

Problem 7–42
Break-Even Point; After-Tax Net Income; Profit-Volume Graph; International Issues (Appendix)
(LO 7-1, 7-2, 7-3, 7-4, 7-11)

3. Break-even point (units): 80,500 units

The European Division of Worldwide Reference Corporation produces a pocket dictionary containing popular phrases in six European languages. Annual budget data for the coming year follow. Projected sales are 100,000 books.

	Fixed	Variable	
Sales			$1,000,000
Costs:			
Direct material	$ -0-	$300,000	
Direct labor	-0-	200,000	
Manufacturing overhead	100,000	150,000	
Selling and administrative	110,000	50,000	
Total costs	$210,000	$700,000	910,000
Budgeted operating income			$ 90,000

Required:

1. Calculate the break-even point in units and in sales dollars.
2. If the European Division is subject to an income-tax rate of 40 percent, compute the number of units the company would have to sell to earn an after-tax profit of $90,000.
3. If fixed costs increased $31,500 with no other cost or revenue factor changing, compute the firm's break-even sales in units.
4. Prepare a profit-volume graph for the European Division.
5. Due to an unstable political situation in the country in which the European Division is located, management believes the country may split into two independent nations. If this happens, the tax rate could rise to 50 percent. Assuming all other data as in the original problem, how many pocket dictionaries must be sold to earn $90,000 after taxes?

6. ***Build a spreadsheet:*** Construct an Excel spreadsheet to solve requirements (1), (2), (3), and (5) above. Show how the solution will change if the following information changes: sales amounted to $1,100,000 and fixed manufacturing overhead was $110,000.

(CMA, adapted)

Problem 7–43
Break-Even Point; Safety Margin; Law Firm
(LO 7-1, 7-4)

1. Total fixed expenses: $1,491,980
2. Safety margin: $1,167,000

Terry Smith and two of his colleagues are considering opening a law office in a large metropolitan area that would make inexpensive legal services available to those who could not otherwise afford services. The intent is to provide easy access for their clients by having the office open 360 days per year, 16 hours each day from 7:00 a.m. to 11:00 p.m. The office would be staffed by a lawyer, paralegal, legal secretary, and clerk-receptionist for each of the two eight-hour shifts.

In order to determine the feasibility of the project, Smith hired a marketing consultant to assist with market projections. The results of this study show that if the firm spends $490,000 on advertising the first year, the number of new clients expected each day will be 50. Smith and his associates believe this number is reasonable and are prepared to spend the $490,000 on advertising. Other pertinent information about the operation of the office follows:

- The only charge to each new client would be $30 for the initial consultation. All cases that warrant further legal work will be accepted on a contingency basis with the firm earning 30 percent of any favorable settlements or judgments. Smith estimates that 20 percent of new client consultations will result in favorable settlements or judgments averaging $2,000 each. It is not expected that there will be repeat clients during the first year of operations.
- The hourly wages of the staff are projected to be $25 for the lawyer, $20 for the paralegal, $15 for the legal secretary, and $10 for the clerk-receptionist. Fringe benefit expense will be 40 percent of the wages paid. A total of 400 hours of overtime is expected for the year; this will be divided equally between the legal secretary and the clerk-receptionist positions. Overtime will be paid at one and one-half times the regular wage, and the fringe benefit expense will apply to the full wage.
- Smith has located 6,000 square feet of suitable office space that rents for $28 per square foot annually. Associated expenses will be $27,000 for property insurance and $37,000 for utilities.
- It will be necessary for the group to purchase malpractice insurance, which is expected to cost $180,000 annually.
- The initial investment in the office equipment will be $60,000. This equipment has an estimated useful life of four years.
- The cost of office supplies has been estimated to be $4 per expected new client consultation.

Required:

1. Determine how many new clients must visit the law office being considered by Terry Smith and his colleagues in order for the venture to break even during its first year of operations.
2. Compute the law firm's safety margin.

(CMA, adapted)

Problem 7–44
Break-Even Analysis; Operating Leverage; New Manufacturing Environment
(LO 7-1, 7-8, 7-10)

1(a). Computer-assisted manufacturing system, break-even point: 210,000 units

Celestial Products, Inc. has decided to introduce a new product, which can be manufactured by either a computer-assisted manufacturing system or a labor-intensive production system. The manufacturing method will not affect the quality of the product. The estimated manufacturing costs by the two methods are as follows:

	Computer-Assisted Manufacturing System		Labor-Intensive Production System	
Direct material		$5.00		$5.60
Direct labor (DLH denotes direct-labor hours)	.5DLH @ $12	6.00	.8DLH @ $9	7.20
Variable overhead	.5DLH @ $6	3.00	.8DLH @ $6	4.80
Fixed overhead*		$2,440,000		$1,320,000

*These costs are directly traceable to the new product line. They would not be incurred if the new product were not produced.

The company's marketing research department has recommended an introductory unit sales price of $30. Selling expenses are estimated to be $500,000 annually plus $2 for each unit sold. (Ignore income taxes.)

Required:

1. Calculate the estimated break-even point in annual unit sales of the new product if the company uses the (*a*) computer-assisted manufacturing system; (*b*) labor-intensive production system.
2. Determine the annual unit sales volume at which the firm would be indifferent between the two manufacturing methods.
3. Management must decide which manufacturing method to employ. One factor it should consider is operating leverage. Explain the concept of operating leverage. How is this concept related to Celestial Products' decision?
4. Describe the circumstances under which the firm should employ each of the two manufacturing methods.
5. Identify some business factors other than operating leverage that management should consider before selecting the manufacturing method.

(CMA, adapted)

Problem 7–45
Break-Even Analysis; Profit-Volume Graph; Movie Theaters
(LO 7-1, 7-3, 7-4)

1. Break-even sales volume, regular model: 27,500 tubs
3. Volume at which both machines produce same profit: 37,500 tubs

Silver Screen, Inc. owns and operates a nationwide chain of movie theaters. The 500 properties in the Silver Screen chain vary from low-volume, small-town, single-screen theaters to high-volume, urban, multiscreen theaters. The firm's management is considering installing popcorn machines, which would allow the theaters to sell freshly popped corn rather than prepopped corn. This new feature would be advertised to increase patronage at the company's theaters. The fresh popcorn will be sold for $1.75 per tub. The annual rental costs and the operating costs vary with the size of the popcorn machines. The machine capacities and costs are shown below. (Ignore income taxes.)

	Popper Model		
	Economy	Regular	Super
Annual capacity	45,000 tubs	90,000 tubs	140,000 tubs
Costs:			
Annual machine rental	$8,000	$11,000	$20,000
Popcorn cost per tub	.13	.13	.13
Other costs per tub	1.22	1.14	1.05
Cost of each tub	.08	.08	.08

Required:

1. Calculate each theater's break-even sales volume (measured in tubs of popcorn) for each model of popcorn popper.
2. Prepare a profit-volume graph for one theater, assuming that the Super Popper is purchased.
3. Calculate the volume (in tubs) at which the Economy Popper and the Regular Popper earn the same profit or loss in each movie theater.

(CMA, adapted)

Problem 7–46
CVP Analysis of Changes in Sales Prices and Costs
(LO 7-1, 7-4)

3. New break-even point: 19,125 units
5. New contribution-margin ratio: .40 (rounded)

Jupiter Game Company manufactures pocket electronic games. Last year Jupiter sold 25,000 games at $25 each. Total costs amounted to $525,000, of which $150,000 were considered fixed.

In an attempt to improve its product, the company is considering replacing a component part that has a cost of $2.50 with a new and better part costing $4.50 per unit in the coming year. A new machine also would be needed to increase plant capacity. The machine would cost $18,000 with a useful life of six years and no salvage value. The company uses straight-line depreciation on all plant assets. (Ignore income taxes.)

Required:

1. What was Jupiter's break-even point in number of units last year?
2. How many units of product would the company have had to sell in the last year to earn $140,000?

3. If management holds the sales price constant and makes the suggested changes, how many units of product must be sold in the coming year to break even?
4. If the firm holds the sales price constant and makes the suggested changes, how many units of product will the company have to sell to make the same net income as last year?
5. If Jupiter wishes to maintain the same contribution-margin ratio, what selling price per unit of product must it charge next year to cover the increased direct-material cost?

(CMA, adapted)

Problem 7–47
Continuation of Preceding Problem; Activity-Based Costing; Advanced Manufacturing Systems; Ethical Issues
(LO 7-4, 7-9, 7-10)

2. Break-even point: 17,000 units

Refer to the original data given for Jupiter Game Company in the preceding problem. An activity-based costing study has revealed that Jupiter's $150,000 of fixed costs include the following components:

Setup (40 setups at $400 per setup)	$ 16,000
Engineering (500 hours at $25 per hour)	12,500
Inspection (1,000 inspections at $30 per inspection)	30,000
General factory overhead	61,500
Total	$120,000
Fixed selling and administrative costs	30,000
Total fixed costs	$150,000

Management is considering the installation of new, highly automated manufacturing equipment that would significantly alter the production process. In addition, management plans a move toward just-in-time inventory and production management. If the new equipment is installed, setups will be quicker and less expensive. Under the proposed JIT approach, there would be 300 setups per year at $50 per setup. Since a total quality control program would accompany the move toward JIT, only 100 inspections would be anticipated annually, at a cost of $45 each. After the installation of the new production system, 800 hours of engineering would be required at a cost of $28 per hour. General factory overhead would increase to $166,100. However, the automated equipment would allow Jupiter to cut its unit variable cost by 20 percent. Moreover, the more consistent product quality anticipated would allow management to raise the price of electronic games to $26 per unit. (Ignore income taxes.)

Required:

1. Upon seeing the ABC analysis given in the problem, Jupiter's vice president for manufacturing exclaimed to the controller, "I thought you told me this $150,000 cost was fixed. These don't look like fixed costs at all. What you're telling me now is that setup costs us $400 every time we set up a production run. What gives?"

   As Jupiter's controller, write a short memo explaining to the vice president what is going on.
2. Compute Jupiter's new break-even point if the proposed automated equipment is installed.
3. Determine how many units Jupiter will have to sell to show a profit of $140,000, assuming the new technology is adopted.
4. If Jupiter adopts the new manufacturing technology, will its break-even point be higher or lower? Will the number of sales units required to earn a profit of $140,000 be higher or lower? (Refer to your answers for the first two requirements of the preceding problem.) Are the results in this case consistent with what you would typically expect to find? Explain.
5. The decision as to whether to purchase the automated manufacturing equipment will be made by Jupiter's board of directors. In order to support the proposed acquisition, the vice president for manufacturing asked the controller to prepare a report on the financial implications of the decision. As part of the report, the vice president asked the controller to compute the new break-even point, assuming the installation of the equipment. The controller complied, as in requirement (2) of this problem.

   When the vice president for manufacturing saw that the break-even point would increase, he asked the controller to delete the break-even analysis from the report. What should the controller do? Which ethical standards for managerial accountants are involved here?

■ **Problem 7–48**
CVP Relationships; Retail
(LO 7-1, 7-4)

2. Decrease in operating income: $(1,400)

Condensed monthly income data for Thurber Book Stores are presented in the following table for November 20x1. (Ignore income taxes.)

	Mall Store	Downtown Store	Total
Sales	$80,000	$120,000	$200,000
Less: Variable expenses	32,000	84,000	116,000
Contribution margin	$48,000	$ 36,000	$ 84,000
Less: Fixed expenses	20,000	40,000	60,000
Operating income	$28,000	$ (4,000)	$ 24,000

Additional Information:

- Management estimates that closing the downtown store would result in a 10 percent decrease in mall store sales, while closing the mall store would not affect downtown store sales.
- One-fourth of each store's fixed expenses would continue through December 31, 20x2, if either store were closed.
- The operating results for November 20x1 are representative of all months.

Required:

1. Calculate the increase or decrease in Thurber's monthly operating income during 20x2 if the downtown store is closed.
2. The management of Thurber Book Stores is considering a promotional campaign at the downtown store that would not affect the mall store. Annual promotional expenses at the downtown store would be increased by $60,000 in order to increase downtown store sales by 10 percent. What would be the effect of this promotional campaign on the company's monthly operating income during 20x2?
3. One-half of the downtown store's dollar sales are from items sold at their variable cost to attract customers to the store. Thurber's management is considering the deletion of these items, a move that would reduce the downtown store's direct fixed expenses by 15 percent and result in the loss of 20 percent of the remaining downtown store's sales volume. This change would not affect the mall store. What would be the effect on Thurber's monthly operating income if the items sold at their variable cost are eliminated?
4. ***Build a spreadsheet:*** Construct an Excel spreadsheet to solve all of the preceding requirements. Show how the solution will change if the following information changes: the downtown store's sales amounted to $126,000 and its variable expenses were $86,000.

(CMA, adapted)

■ **Problem 7–49**
CVP; Multiple Products; Changes in Costs and Sales Mix
(LO 7-4, 7-5)

2. Total sales to break even: 162,500 units
3. Weighted-average unit contribution margin: $13.00

Cincinnati Tool Company (CTC) manufactures a line of electric garden tools that are sold in general hardware stores. The company's controller, Will Fulton, has just received the sales forecast for the coming year for CTC's three products: hedge clippers, weeders, and leaf blowers. CTC has experienced considerable variations in sales volumes and variable costs over the past two years, and Fulton believes the forecast should be carefully evaluated from a cost-volume-profit viewpoint. The preliminary budget information for 20x2 follows:

	Weeders	Hedge Clippers	Leaf Blowers
Unit sales	50,000	50,000	100,000
Unit selling price	$28	$36	$48
Variable manufacturing cost per unit	13	12	25
Variable selling cost per unit	5	4	6

For 20x2, CTC's fixed manufacturing overhead is budgeted at $2,000,000, and the company's fixed selling and administrative expenses are forecasted to be $600,000. CTC has a tax rate of 40 percent.

Required:

1. Determine CTC's budgeted net income for 20x2.
2. Assuming the sales mix remains as budgeted, determine how many units of each product CTC must sell in order to break even in 20x2.

3. After preparing the original estimates, management determined that its variable manufacturing cost of leaf blowers would increase by 20 percent, and the variable selling cost of hedge clippers could be expected to increase by $1.00 per unit. However, management has decided not to change the selling price of either product. In addition, management has learned that its leaf blower has been perceived as the best value on the market, and it can expect to sell three times as many leaf blowers as each of its other products. Under these circumstances, determine how many units of each product CTC would have to sell in order to break even in 20x2.

(CMA, adapted)

Problem 7–50
CVP Relationships; International Business; Automation
(LO 7-1, 7-4, 7-10)

3. Variable cost per ton: $275 per ton
6. Dollar sales required for target net profit: $1,140,000

Ohio Limestone Company produces thin limestone sheets used for cosmetic facing on buildings. The following income statement represents the operating results for the year just ended. The company had sales of 1,800 tons during the year. The manufacturing capacity of the firm's facilities is 3,000 tons per year. (Ignore income taxes.)

OHIO LIMESTONE COMPANY
Income Statement
For the Year Ended December 31, 20x1

Sales		$900,000
Variable costs:		
Manufacturing	$315,000	
Selling costs	180,000	
Total variable costs		$495,000
Contribution margin		$405,000
Fixed costs:		
Manufacturing	$100,000	
Selling	107,500	
Administrative	40,000	
Total fixed costs		$247,500
Net income		$157,500

Required:

1. Calculate the company's break-even volume in tons for 20x1.
2. If the sales volume is estimated to be 2,100 tons in the next year, and if the prices and costs stay at the same levels and amounts, what is the net income that management can expect for 20x2?
3. Ohio Limestone has been trying for years to get a foothold in the European market. The company has a potential German customer that has offered to buy 1,500 tons at $450 per ton. Assume that all of the firm's costs would be at the same levels and rates as in 20x1. What net income would the firm earn if it took this order and rejected some business from regular customers so as not to exceed capacity?
4. Ohio Limestone plans to market its product in a new territory. Management estimates that an advertising and promotion program costing $61,500 annually would be needed for the next two or three years. In addition, a $25 per ton sales commission to the sales force in the new territory, over and above the current commission, would be required. How many tons would have to be sold in the new territory to maintain the firm's current net income? Assume that sales and costs will continue as in 20x1 in the firm's established territories.
5. Management is considering replacing its labor-intensive process with an automated production system. This would result in an increase of $58,500 annually in fixed manufacturing costs. The variable manufacturing costs would decrease by $25 per ton. Compute the new break-even volume in tons and in sales dollars.
6. Ignore the facts presented in requirement (5). Assume that management estimates that the selling price per ton would decline by 10 percent next year. Variable costs would increase by $40 per ton, and fixed costs would not change. What sales volume in dollars would be required to earn a net income of $94,500 next year?

(CMA, adapted)

Problem 7–51
Cost-Volume-Profit Analysis with Income Taxes and Multiple Products (Appendix)
(LO 7-1, 7-2, 7-4, 7-5, 7-11)

3. Break-even point, mountaineering model: 10,500 units

Alpine Thrills Ski Company recently expanded its manufacturing capacity. The firm will now be able to produce up to 15,000 pairs of cross-country skis of either the mountaineering model or the touring model. The sales department assures management that it can sell between 9,000 and 13,000 units of either product this year. Because the models are very similar, the company will produce only one of the two models.

The following information was compiled by the accounting department.

	Model	
	Mountaineering	**Touring**
Selling price per unit	$88.00	$80.00
Variable costs per unit	52.80	52.80

Fixed costs will total $369,600 if the mountaineering model is produced but will be only $316,800 if the touring model is produced. Alpine Thrills Ski Company is subject to a 40 percent income tax rate. (Round each answer to the nearest whole number.)

Required:

1. Compute the contribution-margin ratio for the touring model.
2. If Alpine Thrills Ski Company desires an after-tax net income of $22,080, how many pairs of touring skis will the company have to sell?
3. How much would the variable cost per unit of the touring model have to change before it had the same break-even point in units as the mountaineering model?
4. Suppose the variable cost per unit of touring skis decreases by 10 percent, and the total fixed cost of touring skis increases by 10 percent. Compute the new break-even point.
5. Suppose management decided to produce both products. If the two models are sold in equal proportions, and total fixed costs amount to $343,200, what is the firm's break-even point in units?

(CMA, adapted)

Problem 7–52
CVP Analysis; Marketing Decisions; Income Taxes (Appendix)
(LO 7-1, 7-4, 7-11)

2. Required sales dollars to break even: $19,692,308 (rounded)

Colorado Telecom, Inc. manufactures telecommunications equipment. The company has always been production oriented and sells its products through agents. Agents are paid a commission of 15 percent of the selling price. Colorado Telecom's budgeted income statement for 20x2 follows:

COLORADO TELECOM, INC.
Budgeted Income Statement
For the Year Ended December 31, 20x2
(in thousands)

Sales		$16,000
Manufacturing costs:		
Variable	$ 7,200	
Fixed overhead	2,340	9,540
Gross margin		$ 6,460
Selling and administrative expenses:		
Commissions	$ 2,400	
Fixed marketing expenses	140	
Fixed administrative expenses	1,780	4,320
Net operating income		$ 2,140
Less fixed interest expense		540
Income before income taxes		$ 1,600
Less income taxes (30%)		480
Net income		$ 1,120

After the profit plan was completed for the coming year, Colorado Telecom's sales agents demanded that the commissions be increased to 22½ percent of the selling price. This demand was the latest in a series of actions that Liliana Richmond, the company's president, believed had gone too far. She asked

Molly Rosewood, the most sales-oriented officer in her production-oriented company, to estimate the cost to the company of employing its own sales force. Rosewood's estimate of the additional annual cost of employing its own sales force, exclusive of commissions, follows. Sales personnel would receive a commission of 10 percent of the selling price in addition to their salary.

Estimated Annual Cost of Employing a Company Sales Force (in thousands)

Salaries:	
Sales manager	$ 100
Sales personnel	1,000
Travel and entertainment	400
Fixed marketing costs	900
Total	$2,400

Required:

1. Calculate Colorado Telecom's estimated break-even point in sales dollars for 20x2.
   a. If the events that are represented in the budgeted income statement take place.
   b. If the company employs its own sales force.
2. If Colorado Telecom continues to sell through agents and pays the increased commission of 22½ percent of the selling price, determine the estimated volume in sales dollars for 20x2 that would be required to generate the same net income as projected in the budgeted income statement.
3. Determine the estimated volume in sales dollars that would result in equal net income for 20x2 regardless of whether the company continues to sell through agents and pays a commission of 22½ percent of the selling price or employs its own sales force.

(CMA, adapted)

Cases

Case 7–53
Break-Even Analysis; Hospital CVP Relationships
(LO 7-1, 7-4)
1. Contribution margin per patient day: $200
2. Increase in revenue: $540,000

Delaware Medical Center operates a general hospital. The medical center also rents space and beds to separately owned entities rendering specialized services, such as Pediatrics and Psychiatric Care. Delaware charges each separate entity for common services, such as patients' meals and laundry, and for administrative services, such as billings and collections. Space and bed rentals are fixed charges for the year, based on bed capacity rented to each entity. Delaware Medical Center charged the following costs to Pediatrics for the year ended June 30, 20x1:

	Patient Days (variable)	Bed Capacity (fixed)
Dietary	$ 600,000	—
Janitorial	—	$ 70,000
Laundry	300,000	—
Laboratory	450,000	—
Pharmacy	350,000	—
Repairs and maintenance	—	30,000
General and administrative	—	1,300,000
Rent	—	1,500,000
Billings and collections	300,000	—
Total	$2,000,000	$2,900,000

During the year ended June 30, 20x1, Pediatrics charged each patient an average of $300 per day, had a capacity of 60 beds, and had revenue of $6 million for 365 days. In addition, Pediatrics directly employed personnel with the following annual salary costs per employee: supervising nurses, $25,000; nurses, $20,000; and aides, $9,000.

Delaware Medical Center has the following minimum departmental personnel requirements, based on total annual patient days:

Annual Patient Days	Aides	Nurses	Supervising Nurses
Up to 22,000	20	10	4
22,001 to 26,000	25	14	5
26,001 to 29,200	31	16	5

Pediatrics always employs only the minimum number of required personnel. Salaries of supervising nurses, nurses, and aides are therefore fixed within ranges of annual patient days.

Pediatrics operated at 100 percent capacity on 90 days during the year ended June 30, 20x1. Administrators estimate that on these 90 days, Pediatrics could have filled another 20 beds above capacity. Delaware Medical Center has an additional 20 beds available for rent for the year ending June 30, 20x2. Such additional rental would increase Pediatrics' fixed charges based on bed capacity. (In the following requirements, ignore income taxes.)

Required:

1. Calculate the minimum number of patient days required for Pediatrics to break even for the year ending June 30, 20x2, if the additional 20 beds are not rented. Patient demand is unknown, but assume that revenue per patient day, cost per patient day, cost per bed, and salary rates will remain the same as for the year ended June 30, 20x1.
2. Assume that patient demand, revenue per patient day, cost per patient day, cost per bed, and salary rates for the year ending June 30, 20x2, remain the same as for the year ended June 30, 20x1. Prepare a schedule of Pediatrics' increase in revenue and increase in costs for the year ending June 30, 20x2. Determine the net increase or decrease in Pediatrics' earnings from the additional 20 beds if Pediatrics rents this extra capacity from Delaware Medical Center.

(CPA, adapted)

Case 7–54
CVP Analysis with Production and Marketing Decisions; Taxes (Appendix)
(LO 7-1, 7-4, 7-11)

1(b). To achieve after-tax profit objective, Oakley must sell 2,500 units
2. Alternative (3), after-tax profit: $204,000

Oakley Company manufactures and sells adjustable canopies that attach to motor homes and trailers. The market covers both new units as well as replacement canopies. Oakley developed its 20x2 business plan based on the assumption that canopies would sell at a price of $400 each. The variable cost of each canopy is projected at $200, and the annual fixed costs are budgeted at $100,000. Oakley's after-tax profit objective is $240,000; the company's tax rate is 40 percent.

While Oakley's sales usually rise during the second quarter, the May financial statements reported that sales were not meeting expectations. For the first five months of the year, only 350 units had been sold at the established price, with variable costs as planned. It was clear the 20x2 after-tax profit projection would not be reached unless some actions were taken. Oakley's president, Melanie Grand, assigned a management committee to analyze the situation and develop several alternative courses of action. The following mutually exclusive alternatives were presented to the president.

- Reduce the sales price by $40. The sales organization forecasts that with the significantly reduced sales price, 2,700 units can be sold during the remainder of the year. Total fixed and variable unit costs will stay as budgeted.
- Lower variable costs per unit by $25 through the use of less expensive raw materials and slightly modified manufacturing techniques. The sales price also would be reduced by $30, and sales of 2,200 units for the remainder of the year are forecast.
- Cut fixed costs by $10,000 and lower the sales price by 5 percent. Variable costs per unit will be unchanged. Sales of 2,000 units are expected for the remainder of the year.

Required:

1. If no changes are made to the selling price or cost structure, determine the number of units that Oakley Company must sell
   a. In order to break even.
   b. To achieve its after-tax profit objective.
2. Determine which one of the alternatives Oakley Company should select to achieve its annual after-tax profit objective.

(CMA, adapted)

Case 7–55
Sales Commissions in a Wholesale Firm; Income Taxes (Appendix)
(LO 7-1, 7-2, 7-4, 7-11)

1. Break-even point: $500,000
3. New contribution-margin ratio: .15

Niagra Falls Sporting Goods Company, a wholesale supply company, engages independent sales agents to market the company's products throughout New York and Ontario. These agents currently receive a commission of 20 percent of sales, but they are demanding an increase to 25 percent of sales made during the year ending December 31, 20x2. The controller already prepared the 20x2 budget before learning of the agents' demand for an increase in commissions. The budgeted 20x2 income statement is shown below. Assume that cost of goods sold is 100 percent variable cost.

NIAGRA FALLS SPORTING GOODS COMPANY
Budgeted Income Statement
For the Year Ended December 31, 20x2

Sales		$10,000,000
Cost of goods sold		6,000,000
Gross margin		$ 4,000,000
Selling and administrative expenses:		
Commissions	$2,000,000	
All other expenses (fixed)	100,000	2,100,000
Income before taxes		$ 1,900,000
Income tax (30%)		570,000
Net income		$ 1,330,000

The company's sales manager, Joey Dulwich, is considering the possibility of employing full-time sales personnel. Three individuals would be required, at an estimated annual salary of $30,000 each, plus commissions of 5 percent of sales. In addition, a sales manager would be employed at a fixed annual salary of $160,000. All other fixed costs, as well as the variable cost percentages, would remain the same as the estimates in the 20x2 budgeted income statement.

Required:

1. Compute Niagra Falls Sporting Goods' estimated break-even point in sales dollars for the year ending December 31, 20x2, based on the budgeted income statement prepared by the controller.
2. Compute the estimated break-even point in sales dollars for the year ending December 31, 20x2, if the company employs its own sales personnel.
3. Compute the estimated volume in sales dollars that would be required for the year ending December 31, 20x2, to yield the same net income as projected in the budgeted income statement, if management continues to use the independent sales agents and agrees to their demand for a 25 percent sales commission.
4. Compute the estimated volume in sales dollars that would generate an identical net income for the year ending December 31, 20x2, regardless of whether Niagra Falls Sporting Goods Company employs its own sales personnel or continues to use the independent sales agents and pays them a 25 percent commission.

(CPA, adapted)

8 Variable Costing and the Costs of Quality and Sustainability

FOCUS COMPANY >>>

© Blend Images/Michael DeYoung/Getty Images RF

THIS CHAPTER'S FOCUS COMPANY is FitDat.com, a designer and manufacturer of fitness monitors that operate by sending data to a smartphone during exercise. FitDat.com promotes its product in fitness magazines and online, and virtually all of its sales are Web-based. In the first half of this chapter, we explore two product-costing methods, called absorption costing and variable costing. Under absorption costing, all manufacturing costs, including fixed manufacturing overhead, are assigned as product costs and stored in inventory until the products are sold. Under variable costing, fixed manufacturing overhead is not included in inventory as a product cost. Instead, fixed manufacturing overhead is treated as a period cost, and it is expensed during the period in which it is incurred. The choice between absorption and variable costing arises only in manufacturing firms.

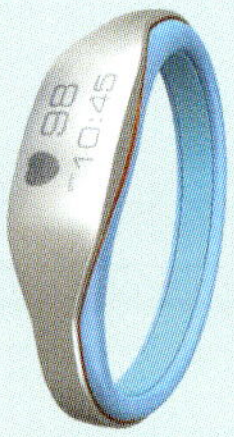

© Haiyin Wang/ Alamy RF

<<< IN CONTRAST

In contrast to the absorption and variable costing systems discussed in the first part of the chapter, we turn our attention in the remainder of the chapter to two important topics related to costing and production. Again using the illustration of FitDat.com, we explore the measurement of quality costs in the production of products and services. The chapter concludes with a discussion of the costs of environmental sustainability. As a company that markets to health-conscious consumers, FitDat.com needs to be especially aware of the environmental impact of its operations and to incorporate the costs of sustainability in its decision making.

© Ariel Skelley/Blend Images/Corbis RF

After completing this chapter, you should be able to:

8-1 Explain the accounting treatment of fixed manufacturing overhead under absorption and variable costing.

8-2 Prepare an income statement under absorption costing.

8-3 Prepare an income statement under variable costing.

8-4 Reconcile reported income under absorption and variable costing.

8-5 Explain the implications of absorption and variable costing for cost-volume-profit analysis.

8-6 Evaluate absorption and variable costing.

8-7 Prepare a quality-cost report.

8-8 Discuss two contrasting views of the optimal level of product quality.

8-9 Understand the different types of environmental costs, and discuss the management of these costs.

Income is one of many important measures used by managers to make decisions and evaluate operational performance. In a manufacturing firm, two alternative accounting treatments of fixed manufacturing overhead can result in different reported income amounts for the company. The difference in reported income can alter management's view of the profitability of a particular decision or segment of the company. In Section 1 of this chapter, we will examine these alternative accounting methods, called *absorption costing* and *variable costing.*[1]

In Sections 2 and 3 of the chapter, we will cover two additional costing issues that are taking on ever greater importance in managing any enterprise. Assessing and reporting the *costs of assuring quality* in a company's products or services is important as companies increasingly compete in a global market to sell their goods and services. And measuring and managing the *costs of environmental sustainability* has become one of the most important and challenging objectives for organizations of all types.[2]

Section 1: Absorption and Variable Costing

In the product-costing systems we have studied so far, manufacturing overhead is applied to Work-in-Process Inventory as a product cost along with direct material and direct labor. When the manufactured goods are finished, these product costs flow from Work-in-Process Inventory into Finished-Goods Inventory. Finally, during the accounting period

---

[1]Section 1, which covers absorption and variable costing, is written as a module, and it can be studied separately from the rest of the chapter. This material may be studied after the completion of Chapter 3.

[2]Sections 2 and 3, which cover the costs of quality assurance and environmental sustainability, respectively, are written as modules, and each can be studied separately from the rest of the chapter. The material in these two sections can be studied after the completion of Chapter 2.

when the goods are sold, the product costs flow from Finished-Goods Inventory into Cost of Goods Sold, an expense account. The following diagram summarizes this flow of costs.

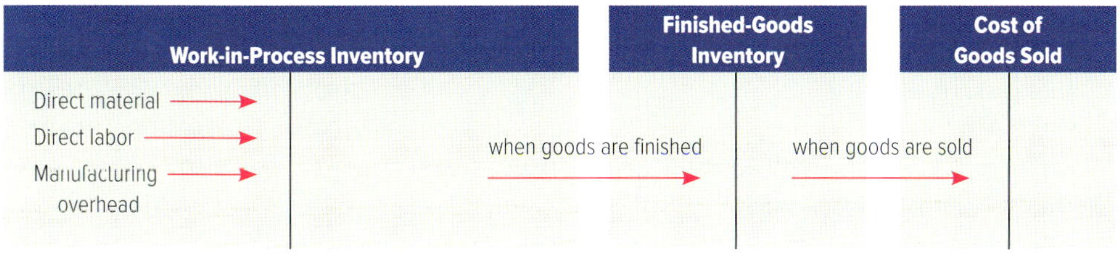

Since the costs of production are stored in inventory accounts until the goods are sold, these costs are called *inventoriable costs* and, when assigned to an inventory account, are described as *inventoried costs.*

Fixed Manufacturing Overhead: The Key

In our study of product-costing systems, we have included both variable and fixed manufacturing overhead in the product costs that flow through the manufacturing accounts. This approach to product costing is called **absorption costing (or full costing),** because *all* manufacturing-overhead costs are applied to (or absorbed by) manufactured goods.

Learning Objective 8-1

Explain the accounting treatment of fixed manufacturing overhead under absorption and variable costing.

We now introduce an alternative approach to product costing called **variable costing (or direct costing),** in which *only variable* manufacturing overhead is applied to Work-in-Process Inventory as a product cost.

The distinction between absorption and variable costing is summarized in Exhibit 8–1. Notice that the distinction involves the *timing* with which fixed manufacturing overhead becomes an expense. Under variable costing, fixed overhead is expensed *immediately,* as it is incurred. Under absorption costing, fixed overhead is *inventoried* until the accounting period during which the manufactured goods are sold. But under both approaches, fixed overhead is eventually expensed.

Exhibit 8–1

Absorption versus Variable Costing

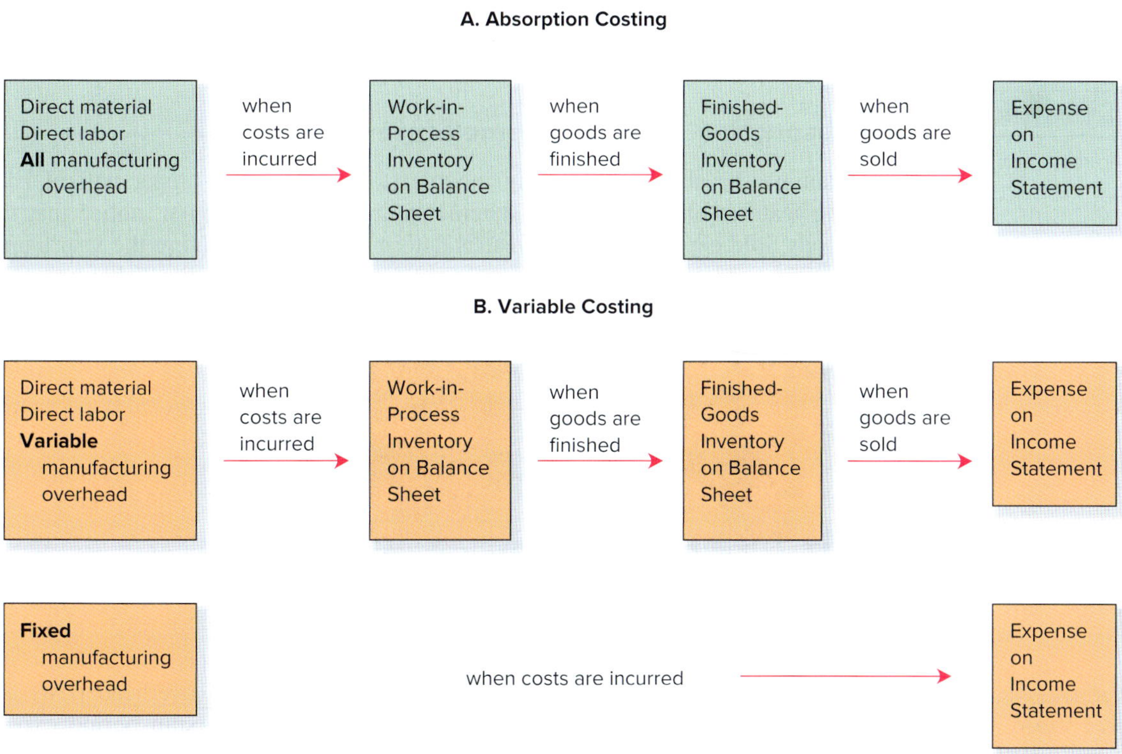

Exhibit 8–2
Data for Illustration: FitDat.com

		20x0	20x1	20x2
Production and inventory data:				
Planned production (in units)		50,000	50,000	50,000
Finished-goods inventory (in units), January 1		–0–	–0–	15,000
Actual production (in units)		50,000	50,000	50,000
Sales (in units)		50,000	35,000	65,000
Finished-goods inventory (in units), December 31		–0–	15,000	–0–
Revenue and cost data, all three years:				
Sales price per unit				$48
Manufacturing costs per unit:				
Direct material				$12
Direct labor				8
Variable manufacturing overhead				4
Total variable cost per unit				$24
Used only under absorption costing: Fixed manufacturing overhead:				
Budgeted annual fixed overhead / Planned annual production*	$600,000 / 50,000			12
Total absorption cost per unit				$36
Variable selling and administrative cost per unit				$ 4
Fixed selling and administrative cost per year				$100,000

*Planned annual production of 50,000 units is management's estimate of the company's practical capacity for production.

Illustration of Absorption and Variable Costing

FitDat.com began operations on January 1, 20x0, to manufacture its electronic personal fitness monitors. Cost, production, and sales data for the first three years of FitDat.com's operations are given in Exhibit 8–2. Comparative income statements for 20x0, 20x1, and 20x2 are presented in Exhibit 8–3, using both absorption and variable costing.

Learning Objective 8-2

Prepare an income statement under absorption costing.

Absorption-Costing Income Statements

Examine the absorption-costing income statements in the upper half of Exhibit 8–3. Two features of these income statements are highlighted. First, notice that the Cost of Goods Sold expense for each year is determined by multiplying the year's unit sales by the absorption manufacturing cost per unit, $36. Included in the $36 cost per unit is the predetermined fixed manufacturing-overhead cost of $12 per unit. Second, notice that on FitDat.com's absorption-costing income statements, the only period expenses are the selling and administrative expenses. There is no deduction of fixed-overhead costs as a lump-sum period expense at the bottom of each income

Pictured here is a robotic automobile assembly operation. General Motors and other companies spend well over $1 billion for each such plant. The fixed costs of operating the plant include the depreciation on plant and equipment, property taxes, insurance, and the salary of the plant manager. Under absorption costing, these costs are treated as product costs and included in the cost of inventory. But under variable costing, these costs are expensed during the period incurred.

Exhibit 8–3
Income Statements under Absorption and Variable Costing

FITDAT.COM
Absorption-Costing Income Statement

		20x0	20x1	20x2
	Sales revenue (at $48 per unit)	$2,400,000	$1,680,000	$3,120,000
1	Less: Cost of goods sold (at absorption cost of $36 per unit)	1,800,000	1,260,000	2,340,000
	Gross margin	$ 600,000	$ 420,000	$ 780,000
	Less: Selling and administrative expenses:			
2 No fixed overhead	Variable (at $4 per unit)	200,000	140,000	260,000
	Fixed	100,000	100,000	100,000
	Operating income	$ 300,000	$ 180,000	$ 420,000

FITDAT.COM
Variable-Costing Income Statement

		20x0	20x1	20x2
	Sales revenue (at $48 per unit)	$2,400,000	$1,680,000	$3,120,000
	Less: Variable expenses:			
1	Variable manufacturing costs (at variable cost of $24 per unit)	1,200,000	840,000	1,560,000
	Variable selling and administrative costs (at $4 per unit)	200,000	140,000	260,000
	Contribution margin	$1,000,000	$ 700,000	$1,300,000
	Less: Fixed expenses:			
2	Fixed manufacturing overhead	600,000	600,000	600,000
	Fixed selling and administrative expenses	100,000	100,000	100,000
	Operating income	$ 300,000	$ 0	$ 600,000

statement. As mentioned above, fixed manufacturing-overhead costs are included in Cost of Goods Sold on these absorption-costing income statements.

Variable-Costing Income Statements

Learning Objective 8-3
Prepare an income statement under variable costing

Now examine the income statements based on variable costing in the lower half of Exhibit 8–3. Notice that the format of the statements is different from the format used in the absorption-costing statements. In the variable-costing statements, the contribution format introduced in Chapter 7 is used to highlight the separation of variable and fixed costs. Let's focus on the same two aspects of the variable-costing statements that we discussed for the absorption-costing statements. First, the manufacturing expenses subtracted from sales revenue each year include only the variable manufacturing costs, which amount to $24 per unit. Second, fixed manufacturing overhead is subtracted as a lump-sum period expense at the bottom of each year's income statement.

Reconciling Income under Absorption and Variable Costing

Learning Objective 8-4
Reconcile reported income under absorption and variable costing.

Examination of Exhibit 8–3 reveals that the income reported under absorption and variable costing is sometimes different. Although income is the same for the two product-costing methods in 20x0, it is different in 20x1 and 20x2. Let's figure out why these results occur.

No Change in Inventory In 20x0 there is no change in inventory over the course of the year. Beginning and ending inventory are the same, because actual production and sales are the same. Think about the implications of the stable inventory level for the treatment of fixed manufacturing overhead. On FitDat.com's variable-costing statement, the $600,000 of fixed

Exhibit 8–4
Reconciliation of Income under Absorption and Variable Costing: FitDat.com

		20x0	20x1	20x2
1	Cost of goods sold under absorption costing	$1,800,000	$1,260,000	$2,340,000
1	Variable manufacturing costs under variable costing	1,200,000	840,000	1,560,000
	Subtotal	$ 600,000	$ 420,000	$ 780,000
2	Fixed manufacturing overhead as period expense under variable costing	600,000	600,000	600,000
	Total	$ 0	$ (180,000)	$ 180,000
	Operating income under variable costing	$ 300,000	$ 0	$ 600,000
	Operating income under absorption costing	300,000	180,000	420,000
	Difference in operating income	$ 0	$ (180,000)	$ 180,000

manufacturing overhead incurred during 20x0 is an expense in 20x0. Under absorption costing, however, fixed manufacturing overhead was applied to production at the predetermined rate of $12 per unit. Since all of the units produced in 20x0 also were sold in 20x0, all of the fixed manufacturing-overhead cost flowed through into Cost of Goods Sold. Thus, $600,000 of fixed manufacturing overhead was expensed in 20x0 under absorption costing also.

The 20x0 column of Exhibit 8–4 reconciles the 20x0 operating income reported under absorption and variable costing. The reconciliation focuses on the two places in the income statements where differences occur between absorption and variable costing. The numbers in the left-hand margin of Exhibit 8–4 correspond to the numbers in the left-hand margin of the income statements in Exhibit 8–3.

"Another factor making inventory management more difficult has been growing globalization. . . . Corning Inc. last month said that it slashed production and cut wholesale prices on the big sheets of glass it makes for flat-panel televisions because of bloated inventories—not at Corning, but at companies further up the supply chain." (8a)

Corning Inc.

Increase in Inventory In 20x1, inventory increased from zero on January 1 to 15,000 units on December 31. The increase in inventory was the result of production exceeding sales. Under variable costing, the $600,000 of fixed overhead cost incurred in 20x1 is expensed, just as it was in 20x0. Under absorption costing, however, only a portion of the 20x1 fixed manufacturing overhead is expensed in 20x1. Since the fixed overhead is inventoried under absorption costing, some of this cost *remains in inventory* at the end of 20x1.

The 20x1 column of Exhibit 8–4 reconciles the 20x1 operating income reported under absorption and variable costing. As before, the reconciliation focuses on the two places in the income statements where differences occur between absorption and variable costing.

Decrease in Inventory In 20x2, inventory decreased from 15,000 units to zero. Sales during the year exceeded production. As in 20x0 and 20x1, under variable costing, the $600,000 of fixed manufacturing overhead incurred in 20x2 is expensed in 20x2. Under absorption costing, however, *more than* $600,000 of fixed overhead is expensed in 20x2. Why? Because some of the fixed overhead incurred during the prior year, which was inventoried then, is now expensed in 20x2 as the goods are sold.

The 20x2 column of Exhibit 8–4 reconciles the 20x2 income under absorption and variable costing. Once again, the numbers on the left-hand side of Exhibit 8–4 correspond to those on the left-hand side of the income statements in Exhibit 8–3.

A Shortcut to Reconciling Income When inventory increases or decreases during the year, reported income differs under absorption and variable costing. This results from the fixed overhead that is inventoried under absorption costing but expensed immediately under variable costing. The following formula may be used to compute the difference in the amount of fixed overhead expensed in a given time period under the two product-costing methods.[3]

$$\begin{array}{c}\text{Difference in fixed overhead}\\ \text{expensed under absorption}\\ \text{and variable costing}\end{array} = \begin{pmatrix}\text{Change in}\\ \text{inventory,}\\ \text{in units}\end{pmatrix} \times \begin{pmatrix}\text{Predetermined}\\ \text{fixed-overhead}\\ \text{rate per unit}\end{pmatrix}$$

[3]This approach assumes that the predetermined fixed-overhead rate per unit does not change across time periods.

As the following table shows, this difference in the amount of fixed overhead expensed explains the difference in reported income under absorption and variable costing.

Year	Change in Inventory (in units)		Predetermined Fixed-Overhead Rate		Difference in Fixed Overhead Expensed		Absorption-Costing Income Minus Variable-Costing Income
20x0	–0–	×	$12	=	–0–	=	–0–
20x1	15,000 increase	×	$12	=	$ 180,000	=	$ 180,000
20x2	15,000 decrease	×	$12	=	$(180,000)	=	$(180,000)

Length of Time Period The discrepancies between absorption-costing and variable-costing income in Exhibit 8–3 occur because of the changes in inventory levels during 20x1 and 20x2. It is common for production and sales to differ over the course of a week, month, or year. Therefore, the income measured for those time periods often will differ between absorption and variable costing. This discrepancy is likely to be smaller over longer time periods. Over the course of a decade, for example, FitDat.com cannot sell much more or less than it produces. Thus, the income amounts under the two product-costing methods, when added together over a lengthy time period, will be approximately equal under absorption and variable costing.

Notice in Exhibit 8–3 that FitDat.com total income over the three-year period is $900,000 under *both* absorption and variable costing. This results from the fact that the company produced and sold the same total amount over the three-year period.

Cost-Volume-Profit Analysis

Learning Objective **8-5**

Explain the implications of absorption and variable costing for cost-volume-profit analysis.

One of the tools used by managers to plan and control business operations is cost-volume-profit analysis, which we studied in Chapter 7. FitDat.com's break-even point in units can be computed as follows:

$$\text{Break–even point} = \frac{\text{Fixed costs}}{\text{Unit contribution margin}} = \frac{\$600,000 + \$100,000}{\$48 - \$24 - \$4}$$

$$= \frac{\$700,000}{\$20} = 35,000 \text{ units}$$

If FitDat.com sells 35,000 fitness monitors, income should be zero, as Exhibit 8–5 confirms. Notice that at the break-even point, $1,680,000 is both the total revenue (35,000 units × $48 price/unit) and total cost ($700,000 fixed cost plus variable cost of 35,000 units × $28 per unit).

Now return to Exhibit 8–3 and examine the 20x1 income statements under absorption and variable costing. In 20x1, FitDat.com sold 35,000 units, the break-even volume. This fact is confirmed on the variable-costing income statement, since operating income is zero. On the absorption-costing income statement, however, the 20x1 operating income is $180,000. What has happened here?

The answer to this inconsistency lies in the different treatment of fixed manufacturing overhead under absorption and variable costing. Variable costing highlights the separation between fixed and variable costs, as do cost-volume-profit analysis and break-even calculations. Both of these techniques account for fixed manufacturing overhead as a lump sum. In contrast, *absorption costing is inconsistent with CVP analysis,* because fixed overhead is applied to goods as a product cost on a per-unit basis.

Evaluation of Absorption and Variable Costing

Learning Objective **8-6**

Evaluate absorption and variable costing.

Some managers find the inconsistency between absorption costing and CVP analysis troubling enough to warrant using variable costing for internal income reporting. Variable costing dovetails much more closely than absorption costing with any operational analyses that require a separation between fixed and variable costs.

Exhibit 8–5
Break-Even Graph: FitDat.com

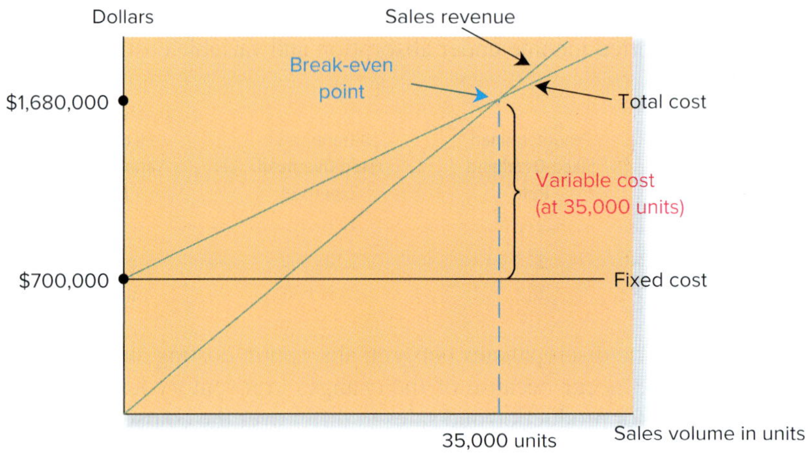

Pricing Decisions Many managers prefer to use absorption-costing data in cost-based pricing decisions. They argue that fixed manufacturing overhead is a necessary cost incurred in the production process. To exclude this fixed cost from the inventoried cost of a product, as is done under variable costing, is to understate the cost of the product. For this reason, most companies that use cost-based pricing base their prices on absorption-costing data.

Proponents of variable costing argue that a product's variable cost provides a better basis for the pricing decision. They point out that any price above a product's variable cost makes a positive contribution to covering fixed cost and profit.

Definition of an Asset Another controversy about absorption and variable costing hinges on the definition of an asset. An *asset* is a thing of value owned by the organization with future service potential. By accounting convention, assets are valued at their cost. Since fixed costs comprise part of the cost of production, advocates of absorption costing argue that inventory (an asset) should be valued at its full (absorption) cost of production. Moreover, they argue that these costs have future service potential since the inventory can be sold in the future to generate sales revenue.

Proponents of variable costing argue that the fixed-cost component of a product's absorption-costing value has no future service potential. Their reasoning is that the fixed manufacturing-overhead costs during the current period will not prevent these costs from having to be incurred again next period. Fixed-overhead costs will be incurred every period, regardless of production levels. In contrast, variable costs incurred to manufacture a product will not be repeated.

To illustrate, FitDat.com produced 15,000 more fitness monitors in 20x1 than it sold. These units will be carried in inventory until they are sold in some future year. FitDat.com will never again have to incur the costs of direct material, direct labor, and variable overhead incurred in 20x1 to produce those fitness monitors. Yet FitDat.com will have to incur approximately $600,000 of fixed-overhead costs every year, even though the firm has the 15,000 units from 20x1 in inventory.

External Reporting For external reporting purposes, generally accepted accounting principles require that income reporting be based on absorption costing. Federal tax laws also require the use of absorption costing in reporting income for tax purposes.

Why Not Both? Using computerized accounting systems, it is straightforward for a company to prepare income statements under both absorption and variable costing. Since absorption-costing statements are required for external reporting, managers will want to keep an eye on the effects of their decisions on financial reports to outsiders. Yet the superiority of variable-costing income reporting as a method for dovetailing with operational analysis and short-term decision making cannot be denied. Preparation of both absorption-costing and variable-costing data is perhaps the best solution to the controversy.

IRS: UNIQUE PRODUCT PACKAGING IS AN INVENTORIABLE COST

Most national tax authorities require the use of absorption costing for tax purposes. Thus, absorption costing must be used in valuing inventory and in determining cost-of-goods-sold expense, which in turn affects taxable income. In the United States, the Internal Revenue Service (IRS) defines inventoriable costs (i.e., product costs) that must be included in valuing inventory and cost-of-goods-sold expense to include the following: (1) direct material consumed in the production of the product, (2) direct labor, and (3) all indirect costs deemed to be necessary for the production of the company's product. These necessary indirect costs include fixed-overhead costs. Thus, absorption costing is mandated by the IRS.

One interesting nuance in the IRS interpretation of what constitutes inventoriable costs concerns a company's expenditures on the design of the packaging for the company's products. Packaging design costs can run into hundreds of thousands of dollars for large consumer products companies such as Procter & Gamble. The IRS has specified that packaging design costs must be inventoried as product costs if the resulting design is successful—that is, it remains in use for several years. If, however, a package design fails in the marketplace, the company can deduct the package design costs early as an expense. Examples of unique and successful packaging designs that would be affected by this ruling include Pringles potato chip cans, Yoplait yogurt containers, and Perrier sparkling water bottles.

Management
Accounting
Practice

IRS, Procter & Gamble, Pringles, Yoplait, and Perrier

JIT Manufacturing Environment In a just-in-time inventory and production management system, all inventories are kept very low. Since finished-goods inventories are minimal, there is little change in inventory from period to period. Thus, in a low-inventory JIT environment, the income differences under absorption and variable costing generally will be insignificant.

Section 2: Costs of Assuring Quality

In the manufacturing industry, product quality has become a key factor in determining a firm's success or failure in the global marketplace. Advanced, highly reliable manufacturing methods have made it possible to achieve very high standards of product quality. And in service firms, the quality of service can spell the difference between a profitable future and one of struggle and even failure. Hotel guests, for instance, are ever more discriminating as they assess the overall quality of service and then select their accommodations accordingly. Similar comments apply to the airlines, cellphone service providers, banks, car rental firms, and financial investment firms. As a result, more and more firms are making product quality a keystone of their competitive strategy.

Measuring and Reporting Quality Costs

Learning Objective **8-7**

Prepare a quality-cost report.

Recognizing the importance of maintaining high product quality, companies often measure and report the costs of doing so. Before we examine the costs that companies incur to maintain high product quality, let's consider what product quality means.

Product Quality Be careful not to confuse a product's *grade* with its *quality*. A product's **grade** refers to the extent of its capabilities in performing an intended purpose, in relation to other products with the same functional use. For example, a laser printer that prints in color is of a higher grade than a laser printer that only prints in black-and-white.

So what is meant by a high-*quality* product? There are two concepts of quality that determine a product's degree of excellence or the product's ultimate fitness for its intended use. A product's **quality of design** refers to how well it is conceived or designed for its intended use. For example, a color laser printer intended for business use that has to be refilled three times a day because its paper tray is too small is a low-quality color laser printer with respect to its quality of design. The **quality of conformance** refers to the extent to which a product meets the specifications of its design. A color laser printer with an appropriately sized paper tray may be well designed, but if the paper jams due to shoddy manufacturing, it will be useless. This printer is a low-quality product with respect to its quality of conformance: it fails to conform to its design specifications. Both quality of design and quality of conformance are required in order to achieve a high-quality finished product.

> "The 'cost of quality' isn't the price of creating a quality product or service. It's the cost of NOT creating a quality product or service." (8b)
>
> ASQ

Costs of Quality Due to the increasing importance of maintaining high product quality, many companies routinely measure and report the costs of ensuring high quality. Four types of costs are monitored:

1. **prevention costs,** the costs of preventing defects;
2. **appraisal costs,** the costs of determining whether defects exist;
3. **internal failure costs,** the costs of repairing defects found prior to product delivery; and
4. **external failure costs,** costs incurred after defective products have been delivered.

Exhibit 8–6 shows a production quality-cost report prepared by FitDat.com for the month of May 20x2. As a manufacturer of smartphone-linked personal fitness monitors that are sold online, FitDat.com must identify quality costs in several different areas of operations, including production quality, service quality, and shipping quality.[4] As is always true in cost monitoring, quality-cost reporting is most useful when cost trends are examined over a period of time. Through trend analysis, management can see where improvement is occurring and where difficulties exist.

Goals can be set to achieve a particular cost target in an area of concern. For example, FitDat.com management might strive to reduce annual external failure costs to less than 0.5 percent of sales by a certain date. If May 20x2 is a typical month for FitDat.com, then the external failure costs in 20x2 are about \$45,600 (\$3,800 from Exhibit 8–6 × 12 mo.). Sales in 20x2 are \$3,120,000 (Exhibit 8–3), so external failure costs are running at 1.46 percent of sales and reaching the 0.5 percent target will require a substantial effort.

Observable versus Hidden Quality Costs The quality costs discussed in the preceding section are *observable.* They can be measured and reported, often on the basis of information in the accounting records. In addition to these observable quality costs, however, companies incur *hidden* quality costs. When products of inferior quality make it to market, customers are dissatisfied. Their dissatisfaction can result in decreased sales and a tarnished reputation for the company. Not only does the company experience lost sales for the inferior products but it will also likely experience lost sales in its other product lines. The opportunity cost of these lost sales and decreased market share can represent a significant hidden cost. Such hidden costs are difficult to estimate or report.

Learning Objective 8-8

Discuss two contrasting views of the optimal level of product quality.

Changing Views of Optimal Product Quality

One way to express product quality is in the percentage of products that fail to conform to their specifications, that is, the percentage of defects. Given this perspective, what is the optimal level of product quality?[5]

[4]For further information on cost of quality, see Zafar U. Khan, "Cost of Quality," in Barry J. Brinker, ed., *Guide to Cost Management* (New York: John Wiley & Sons, 2000), pp. 319–44; and Steve Ball, "Making the Cost of Quality Practical," *Strategic Finance* (July 2006), pp. 34–41.

[5]This discussion is based on the following sources: American Productivity and Quality Center, *Using Enterprise Quality Measurement to Drive Business Value (Best Practices Report),* 2012; Gary Cokins, "Measuring the Costs of Quality for Management," *Quality Progress,* September 2006, pp. 45–51; and Jack Campanella, ed., *Principles of Quality Costs,* 3rd ed. (Milwaukee, WI: ASQC Quality Press, 1999).

Exhibit 8–6
Quality-Cost Report: FitDat.com

	May 20x2 Quality Costs	Percent of Total
Prevention costs		
Quality training	$ 200	1.3
Reliability engineering	1,000	6.5
Pilot studies	500	3.3
Systems development	800	5.2
Total prevention costs	$ 2,500	16.3
Appraisal costs		
Materials inspection	$ 600	3.9
Supplies inspection	300	2.0
Reliability testing	500	3.3
Testing laboratory	2,500	16.3
Total appraisal costs	$ 3,900	25.5
Internal failure costs		
Scrap	$ 1,500	9.8
Repair	1,800	11.8
Rework	1,200	7.8
Downtime	600	3.9
Total internal failure costs	$ 5,100	33.3
External failure costs		
Warranty costs	$ 1,400	9.2
Out-of-warranty repairs and replacement	600	3.9
Customer complaints	300	2.0
Product liability	1,000	6.5
Transportation losses	500	3.3
Total external failure costs	$ 3,800	24.9
Total quality costs	$15,300	100.00

Observable-Cost Perspective The traditional view of quality costs holds that finding the optimal level of product quality is a balancing act between incurring costs of prevention and appraisal on one hand and incurring costs of failure on the other. These are *observable costs,* as discussed in the previous section. Panel A of Exhibit 8–7 depicts this trade-off. As the percentage of defective products decreases, the costs of prevention and appraisal increase. However, the costs of internal and external failure decrease. Adding the costs of prevention, appraisal, and internal and external failure yields total quality costs. The optimal product quality level is the point that minimizes total quality costs.

Zero-Defect Perspective Due largely to the influence of Japanese product quality expert Genichi Taguchi, most companies now assess the optimal cost of quality from a different perspective. The contemporary view is that if both observable *and hidden* costs of quality are considered, *any*

Costs of external failure are considered to be the most damaging for a company. In addition to the added costs of receiving and processing returned goods, external failure causes hard-to-measure costs of customer dissatisfaction and possibly loss of future business.

Exhibit 8–7
Quality Costs and the Optimal Level of Product Quality

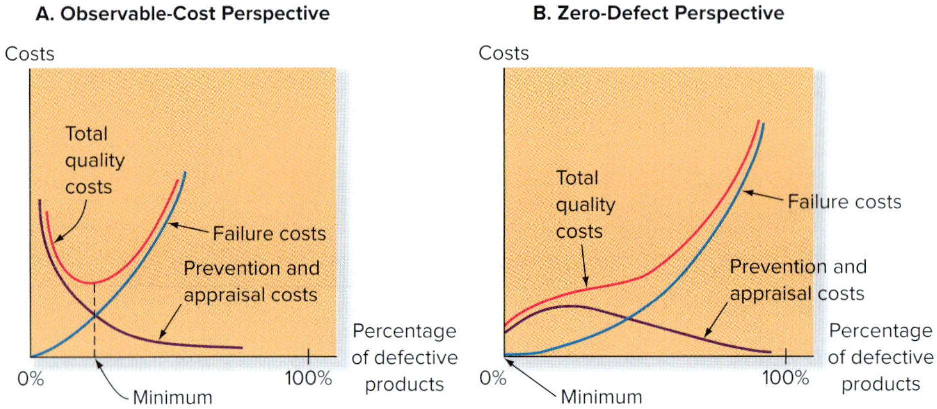

deviation from a product's target specifications results in increased quality costs. Under this zero-defect viewpoint, as depicted in Panel B of Exhibit 8–7, the optimal level of product quality occurs at the *zero defect level.* As Panel B shows, the observable and hidden costs of internal and external failure increase as the percentage of defective products increases. The observable and hidden costs of prevention and appraisal increase slightly and then decrease as the percentage of defects increases. The most important point, though, is that the total costs of quality are minimized at the zero defect level.

The relative merits of these two views of optimal product quality are still being debated by quality control experts. Moreover, the exact shape of the cost functions in Exhibit 8–7 probably differs among industries and product types. One thing is certain, though. To compete successfully in today's global market, any company must pay very close attention to achieving a very high level of product quality.

Total Quality Management Monitoring product quality coupled with measuring and reporting quality costs helps companies maintain programs of **total quality management,** or **TQM**. This refers to the broad set of management and control processes designed to focus the entire organization and all of its employees on providing products or services that do the best possible job of satisfying the customer. Among the tools used in total quality management is the **Six Sigma** program, an analytical method that aims at achieving near-perfect results in a production process. More information about Six Sigma is included in the Management Accounting Practice box below.

> "Six Sigma might be the maturation of everything we've learned over the past 100 years about quality." (8c)
>
> **ASQ**

Identifying Quality Control Problems An effective TQM program includes methods for identifying quality control problems. One method of identifying quality problems is the cause-and-effect diagram (also called an Ishikawa or fishbone diagram). Exhibit 8–8 displays a cause-and-effect diagram used by Xerox Corporation to identify the causes of errors in its customer billing process. As the diagram shows, the quality improvement team has identified a wide range of possible causes for billing errors. After identifying possible causes for billing errors, the Xerox team, nicknamed the Billing Bloopers Team, could take systematic steps to eliminate the root causes of the errors.

Another helpful tool in quality improvement programs is the Pareto diagram. Depicted in Exhibit 8–9, the Pareto diagram shows graphically the frequency with which various quality control problems are observed for FitDat.com's fitness monitors. The Pareto diagram helps the TQM team visualize and communicate to others what the most serious types of defects are. Steps can be taken then to attack the most serious and most frequent problems first.

Exhibit 8–8
Cause-and-Effect Diagram: Billing Quality at Xerox Corporation

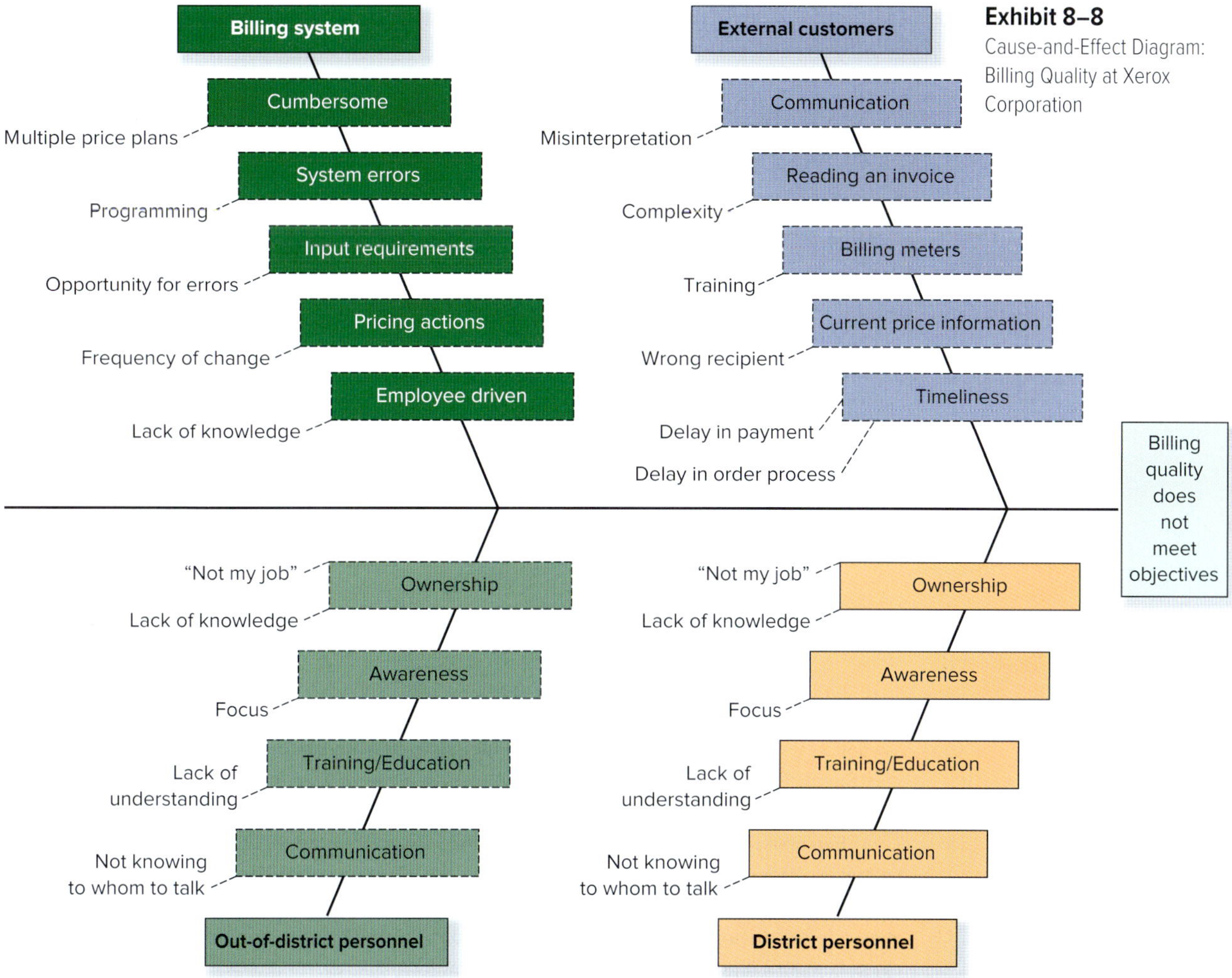

Source: David M. Buehlman and Donald Stover, "How Xerox Solves Quality Problems," *Management Accounting* 75, no. 3 (September 1993), pp. 33–36.

Exhibit 8–9
Pareto Diagram: Frequency of Defect Types for FitDat.com's Fitness Monitors

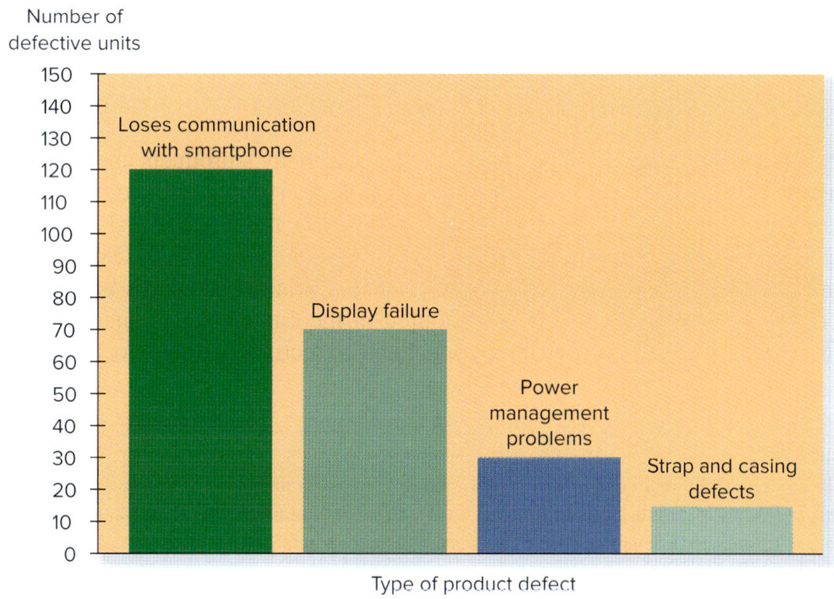

Management
Accounting
Practice

Motorola, General Electric, Caterpillar, and National City Bank

SIX SIGMA FOR QUALITY MANAGEMENT AND COST REDUCTION

"Originally conceived by Motorola Inc. as a quality-improvement device" two decades ago, "Six Sigma soon morphed into a cost-cutting utensil for manufacturers of all stripes. Now, it's fast becoming the Swiss army knife of the business world."

Six Sigma is "an analytical method aimed at achieving *near-perfect results* in a production process. In statistics, the Greek letter *sigma* denotes variation in a standard bell curve. One sigma equals 690,000 defects per 1 million. Most companies do no better than three sigma, or 66,000 errors per million. Six Sigma reduces that count to *3.4 defects per million.* That saves money by preventing waste."

Six Sigma "achieves results by reducing subjective errors in the assessment of problems. First, auditors *define* a process where results are subpar. Then they *measure* the process to determine current performance, *analyze* this information to pinpoint where things are going wrong, and *improve* the process and eliminate the error. Last, *controls* are set up to prevent future bugs."

"In the world of manufacturing, Six Sigma has become something akin to a religion." When General Electric's former chairman Jack Welch embraced Six Sigma, for example, "he quickly assembled an unprecedented army of employees to pinpoint and fix problems throughout GE" using their Six Sigma training. "The results were awesome: In three years alone, these troops saved the company $8 billion, according to GE."[6]

More recently, Six Sigma has been applied well beyond manufacturing. At Caterpillar, "anywhere there was an outcome, there was a process. If there was a process, there was variation in performance. If there was variation in performance, the process was subject to Six Sigma. No area of the company was excluded, from production to revenue recognition to client services."[7]

Examples of Six Sigma in a service setting include insurance, consulting, and financial services. National City Bank in Cleveland used Six Sigma to improve the quality of its new customer process. "The bank wanted to eliminate unnecessary steps that didn't provide value to the customer and to reduce the number of defects that flowed from the process, [resulting in] a dramatic improvement in customer satisfaction [and] a significant decrease in cycle time and operational defects."[8]

ISO 9000 Standards

A key factor in determining the quality of a company's products and services is its quality control system. The organizational structure, personnel, procedures, and policies that are in place to monitor product quality will greatly affect a firm's ability to achieve high-quality standards. In 1987, ISO, the International Organization for Standardization, based in Geneva, Switzerland, issued a set of quality control standards for companies selling products in Europe. Now widely adopted in the United States and other countries, the ISO 9000 standards, as they have come to be collectively known, focus on the processes a

---

[6]R. Crockett, C. Edwards, and S. Anté, "How Motorola Got Its Groove Back," *BusinessWeek,* August 8, 2005, pp. 68–70; and M. Arndt, "Quality Isn't Just for Widgets," *BusinessWeek,* July 22, 2002, pp. 72, 73.

[7]Keith T. Jones and Clement C. Chen, "The Pervasive Success of 6 Sigma at Caterpillar," *Strategic Finance,* April 2010, pp. 29–33.

[8]Peter Carlivati, "Six Sigma: A New Path to Perfection," *ABA Bank Marketing,* April 2007, pp. 24–29.

Exhibit 8–10
ISO 9000 Quality Management Principles

Customer focus	Organizations depend on their customers and therefore should understand current and future customer needs, should meet customer requirements and strive to exceed customer expectations.
Leadership	Leaders establish unity of purpose and direction of the organization. They should create and maintain the internal environment in which people can become fully involved in achieving the organization's objectives.
Involvement of people	People at all levels are the essence of an organization and their full involvement enables their abilities to be used for the organization's benefit.
Process approach	A desired result is achieved more efficiently when activities and related resources are managed as a process.
System approach to management	Identifying, understanding and managing interrelated processes as a system contributes to the organization's effectiveness and efficiency in achieving its objectives.
Continual improvement	Continual improvement of the organization's overall performance should be a permanent objective of the organization.
Factual approach to decision making	Effective decisions are based on the analysis of data and information.
Mutually beneficial supplier relationships	An organization and its suppliers are interdependent and a mutually beneficial relationship enhances the ability of both to create value.

Source: ISO, *Quality Management Principles,* 2012, www.iso.org/iso/qmp_2012.pdf.

company uses to match the quality of design and quality of conformance that its products and services offer with the expectations of its customers. The ISO 9000 standards basically require that a company have a well-defined quality control system in place, and that the target level of product quality be maintained consistently. Moreover, the ISO 9000 standards require a company to prepare extensive documentation of all aspects of the quality control system. The first standard, ISO 9000, identifies the eight quality management principles shown in Exhibit 8–10.

The ISO 9000 standards consist of three major parts. ISO 9000 states the scope of the standard, defines and describes a quality management system, and establishes a quality-related vocabulary. ISO 9001 provides a model for quality assurance in design, development, production, installation, and servicing. And ISO 9004 provides guidelines for the design of a quality assurance system.[9]

Implications for Managerial Accounting The ISO 9000 standards have several implications for managers and managerial accountants. First, the standards require extensive documentation of the quality control system. This task often falls to the finance department or controller's office. In fact, several of the largest public accounting firms offer assurance services to help companies meet the ISO documentation requirements for certification. Second, the ISO standards require that the costs and benefits of the quality control system be measured and documented. Managerial accountants are responsible for measuring and reporting product life-cycle costs, quality costs, and the effectiveness of efforts at continuous improvement.

To summarize, the ISO 9000 standards have a global impact on the way companies approach their quality assurance objectives. The standards affect virtually every area within a firm subject to their guidelines. Managerial accountants are integrally involved in the informational and documentation aspects of the ISO 9000 program.[10]

---

[9]The standards originally issued as ISO 9002 and 9003 were subsequently absorbed into ISO 9001.

[10]More information on the ISO 9000 standards can be found at www.iso.org/iso/iso_9000_selection_and_use-2009.pdf.

Section 3: Costs of Environmental Sustainability

Learning Objective **8-9**

Understand the different types of environmental costs, and discuss the management of these costs.

As the world's population grows and business activity expands, concerned citizens the world over have become increasingly vocal about the critical need to preserve our environment for ourselves and for future generations. Issues like air and water quality, hidden carcinogens, global warming, and the overconsumption of nonrenewable energy sources are in the headlines every day. Business leaders have come to talk of the desirability of **sustainable development,** which means business activity that produces the goods and services needed in the present without limiting the ability of future generations to meet their needs. Many companies are striving for greater *ecoefficiency,* which means increasing their production of goods and services while at the same time decreasing the deleterious effects on the environment of that production. Unfortunately, not all companies are striving equally hard toward these desirable goals.

To force companies to pay attention to environmental issues, the U.S. has environmental laws, such as the *Clean Air Act* and the *Comprehensive Environmental Response, Compensation and Liability* ("Superfund") *Act.* These and other environmental laws are monitored and enforced by a federal watchdog agency, the Environmental Protection Agency (EPA). On a global scale, there are literally dozens of environmental agreements addressing the atmosphere, hazardous substances, the marine environment, nature conservation, and nuclear power issues.

So, besides being a very important issue to all of us because of its health and quality-of-life implications, what does any of this have to do with managerial accounting? The answer is that the *costs* of dealing with environmental issues in one way or another are enormous. These **environmental costs** take many forms, such as installing scrubbers on a smokestack to comply with EPA regulations, improving a production process to reduce or eliminate certain pollutants, or cleaning up a contaminated river. For many large companies, simply understanding the many environmental agreements and regulations that apply, or may apply, to their operations, is a complex and costly process. In this section, we will systematically explore these costs with the goal of having a better understanding of how to manage them.

Classifying Environmental Costs

There are many types of environmental costs. By organizing them into groups of similar costs, we can begin to organize our ideas about how to manage them.

"When there's heightened attention [to corporate responsibility] . . . we have a huge opportunity to effect meaningful change, given our size, scope, and number of customers." (8d)
Procter & Gamble

Private versus Social Environmental Costs One important distinction is between private costs and social (or public) costs. *Private environmental costs* are those borne by a company or individual. Examples would be costs incurred by a company to understand global environmental agreements, to comply with EPA regulations, or to clean up a polluted lake. *Social environmental costs* are those borne by the public at large. Examples of these include costs borne by the taxpayers to staff the EPA; costs borne by the taxpayers to clean up a polluted lake or river; costs borne by individuals, insurance companies, and Medicare due to health problems caused by pollutants; and the unquantifiable quality-of-life costs we all bear from a degraded environment.

The tragic 2010 oil spill in the Gulf of Mexico stemming from an explosion on the Deepwater Horizon oil rig provides an unfortunate example of both social and private environmental costs. Huge private environmental costs were borne by the companies involved in the Deepwater Horizon's drilling operations, such as BP and its partners.[11] The social environmental costs associated with this disaster included costs such as cleaning up fouled beaches and fragile wetlands, lost profits of the Gulf states' recreational and

[11] BP alone estimates its costs at over $50 billion. See Campbell Robertson, John Schwartz, and Richard Perez-Pena, "$18.7 Billion Deal Reached with BP on Gulf Oil Spill," New York Times, July 3, 2015, p. A1, *New York Times*.

fishing industries, and possible human health hazards from the hydrocarbons contaminating the Gulf's waters, marshes, and beaches. Through the legal process, some of the social environmental costs have been converted to private environmental costs as costs of cleanup or lost business are reimbursed by BP and the other companies involved in the disaster. But no one would dispute, despite the billions of dollars paid by BP and others, that the social environmental costs are enormous.

We will focus our attention here on **environmental cost management,** which is the strategic implementation of systems for identifying, measuring, controlling and reducing the private environmental costs borne by a company or other organization.[12]

© Creatas Images/Jupiterimages RF

Many companies invest in significant private environmental costs to monitor and maintain the environment. In this photo, a company inspector tests wastewater for compliance with its own standards and government requirements.

Visible versus Hidden Environmental Costs Both social and private environmental costs can be *visible* or *hidden. Visible social environmental costs* are those that are known and clearly identified as tied to environmental issues, such as the taxpayers' costs of staffing the EPA or cleaning up a polluted lake. *Hidden social environmental costs* include those that are caused by environmental issues but have not been so identified, such as the costs borne by individuals, insurance companies, or Medicare due to cancers caused by pollutants but not clearly identified as such. For example, is a melanoma (a serious type of skin cancer) caused by an inherited genetic tendency, failure to use sunscreen, or a thinning of the ozone layer resulting from industrial emissions of chlorofluorocarbons? All three are generally considered to play a role, but no one knows their relative importance so no one knows how to apportion the costs. The extent of costs with an industrial origin remains hidden.

Managing Private Environmental Costs

Let's focus our attention now on environmental cost management, or the measuring and control or reduction of private environmental costs.

Visible versus Hidden Private Environmental Costs Once again, we need to distinguish between visible and hidden costs. *Visible private environmental costs* are those that are measurable and have been clearly identified as tied to environmental issues. *Hidden private environmental costs* are those that are caused by environmental issues but have not been so identified by the accounting system.[13]

For example, a company engaged in the controversial practice of natural gas "fracking" (drilling oil and gas wells using a process that injects water, sand, and chemicals under high pressure to fracture the rock trapping the hydrocarbons) has visible private environmental costs including restoration of drilling sites after the well has been bored and extensive public relations efforts. But it also may have hidden private environmental costs associated with loss in market value of the company due to added uncertainty over future environmental liabilities.

---

[12]Based on the discussion in German Böer, Margaret Curtin, and Louis Hoyt, "Environmental Cost Management," *Management Accounting* 80, no. 3 (September 1998), pp. 28–38. See also Ramona Dzinkowski, "Saving the Environment," *Strategic Finance* 89, no. 1 (July 2007), pp. 51–53.

[13]Based on Satish Joshi, Ranjani Krishnan, and Lester Lave, "Estimating the Hidden Costs of Environmental Regulation," *The Accounting Review* 76, no. 2 (April 2001), pp. 171–98. See also Kathryn Kranhold, "GE's Environmental Push Hits Business Realities," *The Wall Street Journal*, September 14, 2007, p. A1.

Exhibit 8–11
Private Environmental Costs

	Visible Costs	Hidden Costs*
Monitoring	Inspecting products for contamination Measuring contamination of processes or machinery Verifying vendor compliance with environmental standards	Inspection of products Incremental costs of procurement staff to ensure vendor compliance with environmental standards
Abatement	Qualifying vendors for environmental compliance Recycling materials, containers, or water Designing products and processes to reduce or eliminate negative environmental impacts Doing environmental impact analyses	Incremental material costs incurred to use less-polluting materials Incremental direct-labor costs incurred to perform duties related to reducing pollution Incremental costs of more expensive processes installed all or in part to reduce pollution Incremental costs of purchasing hybrid (electric and gasoline powered) vehicles to reduce air pollution
Remediation		
On-site	Installing pollution reduction or elimination devices Disposing of toxic waste in an environmentally sound manner Treating toxic waste	Incremental direct-labor costs incurred to maintain remediation equipment Incremental energy or other overhead costs incurred to operate remediation equipment
Off-site	Cleaning up polluted sites (e.g., water, soil, or buildings) Defending or settling environmental lawsuits Paying EPA fines	Incremental direct-labor costs for workers used to perform environmental cleanup tasks Forgone contribution margins on lost sales due to an unfavorable environmental record or reputation

*Each of the costs listed in the hidden costs column is included under the assumption that although these costs are caused by environmental concerns, the accounting system has not identified them as such. A study by Joshi et al. provides evidence for the plausibility of this assumption. See Satish Joshi, Ranjani Krishnan, and Lester Lave, "Estimating the Hidden Costs of Environmental Regulation," *The Accounting Review 76*, no. 2 (April 2001), pp. 171–98.

Exhibit 8–11 provides examples of both visible and hidden private environmental costs.[14] Notice that the visible and the hidden costs listed in Exhibit 8–11 are further classified as follows:

- *Monitoring costs.* Costs of monitoring the regulatory environment as well as monitoring the production process to determine if pollution is being generated (e.g., costs of testing wastewater for contaminants).
- *Abatement costs.* Costs incurred to reduce or eliminate pollution (e.g., changing a product's design to use more expensive materials that do not result in environmental contamination).
- *Remediation costs* (i.e., cleanup costs), including:

  On-site remediation. Costs of reducing or preventing the discharge into the environment of pollutants that have been generated in the production process (e.g., cost of installing scrubbers on a smokestack to remove certain air pollutants in the smoke).

  Off-site remediation. Costs of reducing or eliminating pollutants from the environment after they have been discharged (e.g., cost of cleaning up a river polluted by a company's operations).

The distinction between the visible and hidden costs listed in Exhibit 8–11 is an important but subtle one. Consider, for example, the incremental cost of using a more expensive material because it provides a smaller environmental impact. Is this a visible or a hidden cost? The answer is *it depends* on whether the accounting system has measured

[14]Ibid.

this cost and identified it as an environmental cost. Studies show that many environmental costs are hidden, because the accounting system does not measure and identify them as environmental costs. "Most accounting systems accumulate visible costs into environmental cost pools, separate from other overhead cost pools. . . . For example, many steel mills compile separate cost pools for wastewater treatment, remediation, hazardous waste disposal, pollution-abatement capital expenditures, and depreciation on pollution abatement equipment."[15] However, a steel mill's incremental material costs caused by changing from sinters to less-polluting pellets in response to more stringent environmental regulations is typically not separately reported by the accounting system as an environmental cost.[16] Hence, it remains a *hidden* environmental cost.

Why is this point about visible versus hidden costs so important? Because many observers believe that the visible costs reported by most accounting systems may be only a small proportion of the hidden costs. A steel-industry study, for example, concluded that the hidden costs were nearly 10 times the visible costs!

ISO 14000 Standards and the GRI Sustainability Reporting Framework

In 1996, the International Organization for Standardization (ISO), based in Geneva, Switzerland, introduced standards on environmental sustainability and management. Although not as widely implemented as the ISO 9000 standards,[17] they have still enjoyed a large influence on the discussion of environmental reporting and management and the implementation of ISO 14000 is often cited proudly by companies whose efforts have been certified.

> "Sustainability is essential to the health and future of our business. . . . [S]ince ecosystem services are vital to the performance of most companies, integrating the true cost for these services in the future could have significant impacts on corporate bottom lines." (8e)
>
> **Puma**

ISO 14000 is a family of standards, of which ISO 14001 and 14004 include guidelines for establishing and operating an *Environmental Management System (EMS),* and the other standards in the series further develop specific applications of the EMS concepts. The EMS defines the processes the company will follow in achieving its environmental objectives and targets. However, the standard does not specify the elements of environmental performance that are appropriate for a given company, nor does it address the costs of environmental sustainability. Rather, it relies on the EMS and related processes to help each company define and tailor performance metrics, outcomes, and investments that are appropriate for it. In this way, the ISO 14000 standards provide a structured approach to environmental management that is broadly applicable to many kinds of companies.

For more specific guidance on environmental reporting and management, many companies turn to another source that is compatible with ISO 14000 but more prescriptive. The Global Reporting Initiative (GRI), based in Boston, was founded to define and promote a concrete framework for environmental reporting. GRI's *Sustainability Reporting Framework,* which has evolved to address many aspects of social impact reporting, requires companies to define specific goals and measure performance relating to their environmental performance. Measurement categories include energy, water, and biodiversity, and many specific *Environmental Performance Indicators* are prescribed. These include, for example, the following indicators:

- Percentage of materials used that are recycled input materials.
- Energy saved due to conservation and efficiency improvements.
- Total direct and indirect greenhouse gas emissions by weight.
- Percentage of products sold and their packaging materials that are reclaimed by category.
- Total environmental protection expenditures by type.[18]

---

[15]Ibid.

[16]Ibid.

[17]The ISO 9000 Standards are discussed in Chapter 8, "Section 2: Costs of Assuring Quality."

[18]GRI, *Sustainability Reporting Guidelines v.3.1,* 2011, www.globalreporting.org/resourcelibrary/G3.1-Guidelines-Incl-Technical-Protocol.pdf.

A report by the global accounting and consulting firm KPMG found that all forms of corporate responsibility reporting are gaining in importance. The findings conclude that, "Where [corporate responsibility] reporting was once seen as fulfilling a moral obligation to society, many companies are now recognizing it as a business imperative . . . [and] are increasingly demonstrating that [it] provides financial value and drives innovation."[19, 20]

Implications for Managerial Accounting Programs such as the ones needed to track ISO 14000 and the GRI Sustainability Reporting Initiative require a substantial investment in systems and people to document and track performance. This responsibility is usually trusted to those individuals in companies who are experienced in process design and in the challenges of measurement, individuals who are often found in the CFO's and controller's organizations. The skills needed for measurement and decision making in an environmental context are no different from those needed in other operational contexts, and professionals trained in managerial accounting bring the ideal skills and perspectives to an area whose importance is on the rise.[21]

[19]KPMG, *International Survey of Corporate Responsibility Reporting,* 2011, www.kpmg.com/PT/pt/IssuesAnd Insights/Documents/corporate-responsibility2011.pdf.

[20]For some examples of how leading companies are responding to the challenges of sustainability, refer to the following articles published by the IMA: Susan C. Borkowski, Mary Jeanne Welsh, and Kristin Wentzel, "Johnson & Johnson: A Model for Sustainability Reporting," *Strategic Finance,* September 2010, pp. 29–37; Cristiano Busco, Mark. L. Frigo, Emilia L. Leone, and Angelo Riccaboni, "Cleaning Up," *Strategic Finance,* July 2010, pp. 29–37; and Jon Bartley et al., "Flexible Budgeting Meets Sustainability at Bacardi Limited," *Strategic Finance,* December 2012, pp. 29–34.

[21]A thorough discussion of sustainability reporting and its implications for managerial accounting can be found in the following resource: Institute of Management Accounting, *Statements on Management Accounting 67: The Evolution of Accountability—Sustainability Reporting for Accountants,* 2008, www.imanet.org/PDFs/Public/Research/SMA/The Evolution of Accountability.pdf.

Focus on Ethics

INCENTIVE TO OVERPRODUCE INVENTORY

The absorption of fixed overhead costs as part of the cost of inventory on the balance sheet presents ethical challenges because it provides the opportunity to manipulate reported income. This classic case is based on an actual company's experience.*

Brandolino Company uses an actual-cost system to apply all production costs to units produced. The plant has a maximum production capacity of 40 million units but during year 1 it produced and sold only 10 million units. There were no beginning or ending inventories. The company's absorption-costing income statement for year 1 follows:

BRANDOLINO COMPANY
Income Statement
For Year 1

Sales (10,000,000 units at $6)		$ 60,000,000
Cost of goods sold:		
Direct costs (material and labor) (10,000,000 at $2)	$20,000,000	
Manufacturing overhead	48,000,000	68,000,000
Gross margin		$ (8,000,000)
Less: Selling and administrative expenses		10,000,000
Operating income (loss)		$(18,000,000)

The board of directors is upset about the $18 million loss. A consultant approached the board with the following

*This scenario is based on the case "I Enjoy Challenges," originally written by Michael W. Maher. It is used here with permission.

offer: "I agree to become president for no fixed salary. But I insist on a year-end bonus of 10 percent of operating income (before considering the bonus)." The board of directors agreed to these terms and hired the consultant as Brandolino's new president. The new president promptly stepped up production to an annual rate of 30 million units. Sales for year 2 remained at 10 million units. Here is the resulting absorption-costing income statement for year 2:

The day after the year 2 statement was verified, the president took his check for $1,400,000 and resigned to take a job with another corporation. He remarked, "I enjoy challenges. Now that Brandolino Company is in the black, I'd prefer tackling another challenging situation." (His contract with his new employer is similar to the one he had with Brandolino Company.)

What do you think is going on here?

- How would you evaluate the company's year 2 performance?
- Using variable costing, what would operating income be for year 1? For year 2? (Assume that all selling and administrative costs are committed and unchanged.)
- Compare those results with the absorption-costing statements.

Comment on the ethical issues in this scenario.

BRANDOLINO COMPANY
Income Statement
For Year 2

Sales (10,000,000 units at $6)		$60,000,000
Cost of goods sold:		
Costs of goods manufactured:		
Direct costs (material and labor) (30,000,000 at $2)	$ 60,000,000	
Manufacturing overhead	48,000,000	
Total cost of goods manufactured	$108,000,000	
Less: Ending inventory:		
Direct costs (material and labor) (20,000,000 at $2)	$ 40,000,000	
Manufacturing overhead (20/30 × $48,000,000)	32,000,000	
Total ending inventory costs	$ 72,000,000	
Cost of goods sold		36,000,000
Gross margin		$24,000,000
Less: Selling and administrative expenses		10,000,000
Operating income before bonus		$14,000,000
Bonus		1,400,000
Operating income after bonus		$12,600,000

Chapter Summary

LO8-1 Explain the accounting treatment of fixed manufacturing overhead under absorption and variable costing. Under absorption (or full) costing, fixed overhead is applied to manufactured goods as a product cost. The fixed-overhead cost remains in inventory until the goods are sold. Under variable (or direct) costing, fixed overhead is a period cost expensed during the period when it is incurred.

LO8-2 Prepare an income statement under absorption costing. On an absorption-costing income statement, the cost of goods sold is measured at absorption cost (i.e., includes direct material, direct labor, and both variable and fixed manufacturing overhead) and, therefore, fixed overhead is not a period cost.

LO8-3 Prepare an income statement under variable costing. On a variable-costing income statement, the cost of goods sold is measured at variable cost (i.e., includes direct material, direct labor, and only variable manufacturing overhead), and fixed overhead is treated as a period cost.

LO8-4 Reconcile reported income under absorption and variable costing. Income reported under absorption and variable costing can be reconciled by focusing on the effects of the two places where the two statements differ: (1) calculation of cost of goods sold and (2) period costs.

LO8-5 Explain the implications of absorption and variable costing for cost-volume-profit analysis. Variable costing highlights the separation between fixed and variable costs, as do cost-volume-profit analysis and break-even calculations. Both of these techniques account for fixed manufacturing overhead as a lump-sum period cost. In contrast, absorption costing is inconsistent with CVP analysis, because fixed overhead is applied to goods as a product cost on a per-unit basis.

LO8-6 Evaluate absorption and variable costing. There are pros and cons to both costing methods. Variable costing dovetails much more closely than absorption costing with any operational analysis that requires a separation between fixed and variable costs (e.g., CVP analysis). On the other hand, variable costing understates a product's cost, because it excludes fixed manufacturing overhead from the unit cost calculation. In contrast, absorption costing alleviates that objection by including fixed overhead on a per-unit basis in a product's cost. However, this distorts the cost behavior of fixed costs, which do not in fact vary with production activity.

LO8-7 Prepare a quality-cost report. Most firms carefully monitor the costs of maintaining product quality. Quality costs often are categorized as follows: prevention costs, appraisal costs, internal failure costs, and external failure costs. These quality costs are periodically listed on a quality-cost report, which is used by management as it seeks to ensure quality products and services and manage the costs of providing them.

LO8-8 Discuss two contrasting views of the optimal level of product quality. In addition to observable quality costs, companies experience hidden quality costs, such as the opportunity cost associated with lost market share. The predominant zero-defects perspective on product quality holds that if both observable and hidden costs of product quality are considered, the optimal level of product quality occurs at the zero-defect level. In contrast, the more traditional observable-cost perspective holds that the optimal level of product quality occurs at the minimum point on the total quality cost curve, which typically is above the zero-defect level.

LO8-9 Understand the different types of environmental costs, and discuss the management of these costs. Companies incur a variety of environmental costs. These costs include private versus social environmental costs, and the private environmental costs include some visible and some hidden costs. These visible and hidden environmental costs include the costs of monitoring, abatement, and both on-site and off-site remediation.

Review Problem on Absorption and Variable Costing

ScholasticPak Company manufactures backpacks used by students. A typical backpack has the following price and variable costs.

Sales price	$45
Direct material	15
Direct labor	6
Variable overhead	9

Budgeted fixed overhead in the company's first year of operations, was $900,000. Actual and planned production was 150,000 units, of which 125,000 were sold. ScholasticPak incurred the following selling and administrative expenses.

Fixed	$150,000 for the year
Variable	$3 per unit sold

Required:

1. Compute the product cost per backpack under (*a*) variable costing and (*b*) absorption costing.
2. Prepare income statements for the year using (*a*) variable costing and (*b*) absorption costing.
3. Reconcile the income reported under the two methods by analyzing the two key places where the income statements differ.

Solution to Review Problem

1. $$\text{Predetermined fixed overhead rate} = \frac{\text{Budgeted fixed overhead}}{\text{Budgeted production}}$$

$$= \frac{\$900,000}{150,000} = \$6 \text{ per unit}$$

Product Cost per Unit

Direct material	$15
Direct labor	6
Variable overhead	9
a. Cost per unit under variable costing	$30
Fixed overhead per unit under absorption costing	6
b. Cost per unit under absorption costing	$36

2. *a.* **Variable-Costing Income Statement**

Sales revenue (125,000 units sold at $45 per unit)	$5,625,000
Less: Variable expenses:	
Variable manufacturing costs (at variable cost of $30 per unit)	3,750,000
Variable selling and administrative costs (at $3 per unit × 125,000 units sold)	375,000
Contribution margin	$1,500,000
Less: Fixed expenses:	
Fixed manufacturing overhead	900,000
Fixed selling and administrative expenses	150,000
Operating income	$ 450,000

b. **Absorption-Costing Income Statement**

Sales revenue (125,000 units sold at $45 per unit)	$5,625,000
Less: Cost of goods sold (at absorption cost of $36 per unit)	4,500,000
Gross margin	$1,125,000
Less: Selling and administrative expenses:	
Variable (at $3 per unit × 125,000 units sold)	375,000
Fixed	150,000
Operating income	$ 600,000

3.

Cost of goods sold under absorption costing	$4,500,000
Less: Variable manufacturing costs under variable costing	3,750,000
Subtotal	$ 750,000
Less: Fixed manufacturing overhead as period expense under variable costing	900,000
Total	$ (150,000)
Operating income under variable costing	$ 450,000
Less: Operating income under absorption costing	600,000
Difference in operating income	$ (150,000)

Key Terms

For each term's definition refer to the indicated page, or turn to the glossary at the end of the text.

absorption (or full) costing, 327
appraisal costs, 334
environmental cost management, 341
environmental costs, 340
external failure costs, 334
grade, 333
internal failure costs, 334
prevention costs, 334
quality of conformance, 334
quality of design, 333
Six Sigma, 336
sustainable development, 340
total quality management (TQM), 336
variable (or **direct**) **costing, 327**

Review Questions

8–1. Briefly explain the difference between absorption costing and variable costing.

8–2. Timing is the key in distinguishing between absorption and variable costing. Explain this statement.

8–3. The term *direct costing* is a misnomer. *Variable costing* is a better term for the product-costing method. Do you agree or disagree? Why?

8–4. When inventory increases, will absorption-costing or variable-costing income be greater? Why?

8–5. Why do many managers prefer variable costing over absorption costing?

8–6. Explain why some management accountants believe that absorption costing may provide an incentive for managers to overproduce inventory.

8–7. Will variable and absorption costing result in significantly different income measures in a JIT setting? Why?

8–8. Why do proponents of absorption costing argue that absorption costing is preferable as the basis for pricing decisions?

8–9. Why do proponents of variable costing prefer variable costing when making pricing decisions?

8–10. Which is more consistent with cost-volume-profit analysis, variable costing or absorption costing? Why?

8–11. Explain how the accounting definition of an asset is related to the choice between absorption and variable costing.

8–12. List and define four types of product quality costs.

8–13. Explain the difference between observable and hidden quality costs.

8–14. Distinguish between a product's quality of design and its quality of conformance.

8–15. What is meant by a product's *grade,* as a characteristic of quality? Give an example in the service industry.

8–16. "An ounce of prevention is worth a pound of cure." Interpret this old adage in light of Exhibit 8–6.

8–17. Briefly explain the purpose of a cause-and-effect (or fishbone) diagram.

8–18. Define the following types of environmental costs: private, social, visible, hidden, monitoring, abatement, and both on-site and off-site remediation.

8–19. Explain three strategies of environmental cost management.

Exercises

All applicable Exercises are available in Connect. connect

Exercise 8–20
Difference in Operating Income under Absorption and Variable Costing
(LO 8-1, 8-4)

Manta Ray Company manufactures diving masks with a variable cost of $25. The masks sell for $34. Budgeted fixed manufacturing overhead for the most recent year was $792,000. Actual production was equal to planned production.

Required: Under each of the following conditions, state (*a*) whether operating income is higher under variable or absorption costing and (*b*) the amount of the difference in reported operating income under the two methods. Treat each condition as an independent case.

1.	Production	110,000 units
	Sales	108,000 units
2.	Production	90,000 units
	Sales	95,000 units
3.	Production	79,200 units
	Sales	79,200 units

Exercise 8–21
Absorption and Variable Costing
(LO 8-1)

Information taken from Tuscarora Paper Company's records for the most recent year is as follows:

Direct material used	$290,000
Direct labor	100,000
Variable manufacturing overhead	50,000
Fixed manufacturing overhead	80,000
Variable selling and administrative costs	40,000
Fixed selling and administrative costs	20,000

Required:

1. Assuming Tuscarora Paper Company uses variable costing, compute the inventoriable costs for the year.
2. Compute the year's inventoriable costs using absorption costing.

(CMA, adapted)

Exercise 8–22
Absorption and Variable Costing
(LO 8-1, 8-4)

Easton Pump Company's planned production for the year just ended was 20,000 units. This production level was achieved, and 21,000 units were sold. Other data follow:

Direct material used	$600,000
Direct labor incurred	300,000
Fixed manufacturing overhead	420,000
Variable manufacturing overhead	200,000
Fixed selling and administrative expenses	350,000
Variable selling and administrative expenses	105,000
Finished-goods inventory, January 1	2,000 units

The cost per unit remained the same in the current year as in the previous year. There were no work-in-process inventories at the beginning or end of the year.

Required:

1. What would be Easton Pump Company's finished-goods inventory cost on December 31 under the variable-costing method?
2. Which costing method, absorption or variable costing, would show a higher operating income for the year? By what amount?

(CMA, adapted)

Exercise 8–23
Absorption and Variable Costing
(LO 8-1, 8-4)

Pandora Pillow Company's planned production for the year just ended was 10,000 units. This production level was achieved, but only 9,000 units were sold. Other data follow:

Direct material used	$40,000
Direct labor incurred	20,000
Fixed manufacturing overhead	25,000
Variable manufacturing overhead	12,000
Fixed selling and administrative expenses	30,000
Variable selling and administrative expenses	4,500
Finished-goods inventory, January 1	None

The cost per unit remained the same in the current year as in the previous year. There were no work-in-process inventories at the beginning or end of the year.

Required:

1. What would be Pandora Pillow Company's finished-goods inventory cost on December 31 under the variable-costing method?
2. Which costing method, absorption or variable costing, would show a higher operating income for the year? By what amount?

Exercise 8–24
Difference in Operating Income under Absorption and Variable Costing
(LO 8-1, 8-4)

Bianca Bicycle Company manufactures mountain bikes with a variable cost of $200. The bicycles sell for $350 each. Budgeted fixed manufacturing overhead for the most recent year was $2,200,000. Planned and actual production for the year were the same.

Required: Under each of the following conditions, state (*a*) whether operating income is higher under variable or absorption costing and (*b*) the amount of the difference in reported operating income under the two methods. Treat each condition as an independent case.

1.	Production	20,000 units
	Sales	23,000 units
2.	Production	10,000 units
	Sales	10,000 units
3.	Production	11,000 units
	Sales	9,000 units

■ **Exercise 8–25**
Variable Costing and Cost-Volume-Profit Analysis
(LO 8-5)

Refer to the data given in the preceding exercise for Bianca Bicycle Company.

Required:

1. Prepare a cost-volume-profit graph for the company. (Scale the vertical axis in millions of dollars.)
2. Calculate Bianca Bicycle Company's break-even point in units, and show the break-even point on the CVP graph.
3. Explain why variable costing is more compatible with your CVP graph than absorption costing would be.

■ **Exercise 8–26**
Absorption versus Variable Costing
(LO 8-1)

Information taken from Allied Pipe Company's records for the most recent year is as follows:

Direct material used	$340,000
Direct labor	160,000
Variable manufacturing overhead	75,000
Fixed manufacturing overhead	125,000
Variable selling and administrative costs	70,000
Fixed selling and administrative costs	37,000

Required:

1. Assuming Allied Pipe Company uses absorption costing, compute the inventoriable costs for the year.
2. Compute the year's inventoriable costs using variable costing.

(CMA, adapted)

■ **Exercise 8–27**
Absorption and Variable Costing; Use of Internet
(LO 8-1, 8-6)

Visit the website for one of the following companies, or a different company of your choosing.

Coca-Cola	www.coca-cola.com
Bridgestone	www.bridgestone.com
Motorola	www.motorola.com
Casio	www.casio.com
Toyota	www.toyota.com
Xerox	www.xerox.com

Required: Read about the company's products and operations. Discuss the pros and cons of absorption and variable costing as the basis for product costing if the firm uses cost-based pricing.

■ **Exercise 8–28**
Quality Costs
(LO 8-7)

The following costs were incurred by Osaka Metals Company to maintain the quality of its products. (The *yen* is the national currency of Japan.)

1. Operating an X-ray machine to detect faulty welds, 110,000 *yen*
2. Repairs of products sold last year, 116,000 *yen*
3. Cost of rewelding faulty joints, 17,000 *yen*
4. Cost of sending machine operators to a three-week training program so they could learn to use new production equipment with a lower defect rate, 18,100 *yen*

Required: Classify each of these costs as a prevention, appraisal, internal failure, or external failure cost.

■ **Exercise 8–29**
Quality-Cost Report
(LO 8-7)

San Mateo Circuitry manufactures electrical instruments for a variety of purposes. The following costs related to maintaining product quality were incurred in May.

Training of quality-control inspectors	$21,000
Tests of instruments before sale	30,000
Inspection of electrical components purchased from outside suppliers	12,000
Costs of rework on faulty instruments	9,000
Replacement of instruments already sold, which were still covered by warranty	16,500
Costs of defective parts that cannot be salvaged	6,100

Required: Prepare a quality-cost report similar to the report shown in Exhibit 8–6.

■ **Exercise 8–30**
Costs of Quality; Airline
(LO 8-7)

List three observable and three hidden quality costs that could occur in the airline industry related to the quality of service provided.

■ **Exercise 8–31**
Environmental Cost Management; Internet
(LO 8-9)

Visit the website of **Interface, Inc.** at http://www.interfaceglobal.com. Read about its efforts toward sustainable development by clicking on the "Sustainability" link.

Required:

What is Interface's product? Describe the company's efforts toward sustainable development.

Problems

All applicable Problems are available in Connect.

connect

■ **Problem 8–32**
Straightforward Problem on Absorption versus Variable Costing
(LO 8-2, 8-3, 8-4)

2(a). Operating income: $200,000
3. Cost of goods sold under absorption costing: $1,500,000

Skinny Dippers, Inc. produces nonfat frozen yogurt. The product is sold in five-gallon containers, which have the following price and variable costs.

Sales price	$15
Direct material	5
Direct labor	2
Variable overhead	3

Budgeted fixed overhead in 20x1, the company's first year of operations, was $300,000. Actual production was 150,000 five-gallon containers, of which 125,000 were sold. Skinny Dippers, Inc. incurred the following selling and administrative expenses.

Fixed	$50,000 for the year
Variable	$1 per container sold

Required:

1. Compute the product cost per container of frozen yogurt under (*a*) variable costing and (*b*) absorption costing.
2. Prepare operating income statements for 20x1 using (*a*) absorption costing and (*b*) variable costing.
3. Reconcile the operating income reported under the two methods by listing the two key places where the income statements differ.
4. Reconcile the operating income reported under the two methods using the shortcut method.
5. ***Build a spreadsheet:*** Construct an Excel spreadsheet to solve all of the preceding requirements. Show how the solution will change if the following information changes: the selling price and direct-material cost per unit are $16.00 and $4.50, respectively.

■ **Problem 8–33**
Absorption and Variable Costing; CVP Analysis
(LO 8-2, 8-3, 8-4, 8-5)

1. Total contribution margin: $320,000
2. Break-even point: 25,000 units

Yellowstone Company began operations on January 1 to produce a single product. It used an absorption costing system with a planned production volume of 100,000 units. During its first year of operations, the planned production volume was achieved, and there were no fixed selling or administrative expenses. Inventory on December 31 was 20,000 units, and operating income for the year was $240,000.

Required:

1. If Yellowstone Company had used variable costing, its operating income would have been $220,000. Compute the break-even point in units under variable costing.
2. Draw a profit-volume graph for Yellowstone Company. (Use variable costing.)

■ **Problem 8–34**
Variable versus Absorption Costing
(LO 8-1, 8-4)

2. Budgeted variable manufacturing costs: $3,500,000
3. Increase in inventory (in units): 5,000 units

Outback Corporation manufactures tactical LED flashlights in Brisbane, Australia. The firm uses an absorption costing system for internal reporting purposes; however, the company is considering using variable costing. Data regarding Outback's planned and actual operations for 20x1 follow:

	Budgeted Costs		
	Per Unit	**Total**	**Actual Costs**
Direct material	$12.00	$1,680,000	$1,560,000
Direct labor	9.00	1,260,000	1,170,000
Variable manufacturing overhead	4.00	560,000	520,000
Fixed manufacturing overhead	5.00	700,000	715,000
Variable selling expenses	8.00	1,120,000	1,000,000
Fixed selling expenses	7.00	980,000	980,000
Variable administrative expenses	2.00	280,000	250,000
Fixed administrative expenses	3.00	420,000	425,000
Total	$50.00	$7,000,000	$6,620,000

	Planned Activity	Actual Activity
Beginning finished-goods inventory in units	35,000	35,000
Sales in units	140,000	125,000
Production in units	140,000	130,000

The budgeted per-unit cost figures were based on Outback producing and selling 140,000 units in 20x1. Outback uses a predetermined overhead rate for applying manufacturing overhead to its product. A total manufacturing overhead rate of $9.00 per unit was employed for absorption costing purposes in 20x1. Any overapplied or underapplied manufacturing overhead is closed to the Cost of Goods Sold account at the end of the year. The 20x1 beginning finished-goods inventory for absorption costing purposes was valued at the 20x0 budgeted unit manufacturing cost, which was the same as the 20x1 budgeted unit manufacturing cost. There are no work-in-process inventories at either the beginning or the end of the year. The planned and actual unit selling price for 20x1 was $70 per unit.

Required: Was Outback's 20x1 operating income higher under absorption costing or variable costing? Why? Compute the following amounts.

1. The value of Outback Corporation's 20x1 ending finished-goods inventory under absorption costing.
2. The value of Outback Corporation's 20x1 ending finished-goods inventory under variable costing.
3. The difference between Outback Corporation's 20x1 reported operating income calculated under absorption costing and calculated under variable costing.

(CMA, adapted)

■ **Problem 8–35**
Variable-Costing and Absorption-Costing Income Statements
(LO 8-2, 8-3, 8-4, 8-6)

1. Total variable cost: $39
2(b). Operating income: $320,000

Great Outdoze Company manufactures sleeping bags, which sell for $65 each. The variable costs of production are as follows:

Direct material	$20
Direct labor	11
Variable manufacturing overhead	8

Budgeted fixed overhead in 20x1 was $200,000 and budgeted production was 25,000 sleeping bags. The year's actual production was 25,000 units, of which 22,000 were sold. Variable selling and administrative costs were $1 per unit sold; fixed selling and administrative costs were $30,000.

Required:

1. Calculate the product cost per sleeping bag under (*a*) absorption costing and (*b*) variable costing.
2. Prepare operating income statements for the year using (*a*) absorption costing and (*b*) variable costing.
3. Reconcile reported operating income under the two methods using the shortcut method.

Problem 8–36
Variable and Absorption Costing
(LO 8-1, 8-4)

2(a). Contribution margin per unit: $22
2(b). Projected operating income for the year under absorption costing: $238,000

Dayton Lighting Company had operating income for the first 10 months of the current year of $200,000. One hundred thousand units were manufactured during this period (the same as the planned production), and 100,000 units were sold. Fixed manufacturing overhead was $2,000,000 over the 10-month period (i.e., $200,000 per month). There are no selling and administrative expenses for Dayton Lighting Company. Both variable and fixed costs are expected to continue at the same rates for the balance of the year (i.e., fixed costs at $200,000 per month and variable costs at the same variable cost per unit). There were 10,000 units in inventory on October 31. Twenty thousand units are to be produced and 19,000 units are to be sold in total over the last two months of the current year. Assume the unit variable cost is the same in the current year as in the previous year. (*Hint:* You cannot calculate revenue or cost of goods sold; you must work directly with contribution margin or gross margin.)

Required:

1. If operations proceed as described, will operating income be higher under variable or absorption costing for the current year in total? Why?
2. If operations proceed as described, what will operating income for the year *in total* be under (*a*) variable costing and (*b*) absorption costing?
3. Discuss the advantages and disadvantages of absorption and variable costing.

Problem 8–37
Absorption Costing, and Variable Costing
(LO 8-1, 8-2, 8-3)

1. Total cost: $644,800

Emerson Corporation just completed its first year of operations. Planned and actual production equaled 10,000 units, and sales totaled 9,600 units at $72 per unit. Cost data for the year are as follows:

Direct material (per unit)	$12
Conversion cost:	
Direct labor	45,000
Variable manufacturing overhead	65,000
Fixed manufacturing overhead	220,000
Selling and administrative costs:	
Variable (per unit)	8
Fixed	118,000

Required:

1. Compute the company's total cost for the year assuming that variable manufacturing costs are driven by the number of units produced, and variable selling and administrative costs are driven by the number of units sold.
2. How much of this cost would be held in year-end inventory under (*a*) absorption costing and (*b*) variable costing?
3. How much of the company's total cost for the year would be included as an expense on the period's income statement under (*a*) absorption costing and (*b*) variable costing?
4. ***Build a spreadsheet:*** Construct an Excel spreadsheet to solve requirements (1) and (2) above. Show how the solution will change if the following information changes: the direct-material cost is $11 per unit, and the total direct-labor cost is $46,000.

Problem 8–38
Variable Costing and Absorption Costing Income Statements; Reconciling Reported Operating Income
(LO 8-2, 8-3, 8-4)

1(a). Absorption cost per case is $42
1(b). Variable costing, operating income, year 2: $145,000

Chataqua Can Company manufactures metal cans used in the food-processing industry. A case of cans sells for $50. The variable costs of production for one case of cans are as follows:

Direct material	$15
Direct labor	5
Variable manufacturing overhead	12
Total variable manufacturing cost per case	$32

Variable selling and administrative costs amount to $1 per case. Budgeted fixed manufacturing overhead is $800,000 per year, and fixed selling and administrative cost is $75,000 per year. The following data pertain to the company's first three years of operation.

	Year 1	Year 2	Year 3
Planned production (in units)	80,000	80,000	80,000
Finished-goods inventory (in units), January 1	0	0	20,000
Actual production (in units)	80,000	80,000	80,000
Sales (in units)	80,000	60,000	90,000
Finished-goods inventory (in units), December 31	0	20,000	10,000

Actual costs were the same as the budgeted costs.

Required:

1. Prepare operating income statements for Chataqua Can Company for its first three years of operations using:
   a. Absorption costing.
   b. Variable costing.
2. Reconcile Chataqua Can Company's operating income reported under absorption and variable costing for each of its first three years of operation. Use the shortcut method.
3. Suppose that during Chataqua's fourth year of operation actual production equals planned production, actual costs are as expected, and the company ends the year with no inventory on hand.
   a. What will be the difference between absorption-costing income and variable-costing income in year 4?
   b. What will be the relationship between total operating income for the four-year period as reported under absorption and variable costing? Explain.

Problem 8–39
Quality Costs: Identification and Analysis
(LO 8-7)

2. Total quality costs, no. 165: $439,900

Advanced Technologies (AT) produces two compression machines that are popular with manufacturers of plastics: no. 165 and no. 172. Machine no. 165 has an average selling price of $60,000, whereas no. 172 typically sells for approximately $55,000. The company is very concerned about quality and has provided the following information:

	No. 165	No. 172
Number of machines produced and sold	80	100
Warranty costs:		
Average repair cost per unit	$1,200	$400
Percentage of units needing repair	70%	10%
Reliability engineering at $150 per hour	1,600 hours	2,000 hours
Rework at AT's manufacturing plant:		
Average rework cost per unit	$1,900	$1,600
Percentage of units needing rework	35%	25%
Manufacturing inspection at $50 per hour	300 hours	500 hours
Transportation costs to customer sites to fix problems	$29,500	$15,000
Quality training for employees	$35,000	$50,000

Required:

1. Classify the preceding costs as prevention, appraisal, internal failure, or external failure.
2. Using the classifications in requirement (1), compute AT's quality costs for machine no. 165 in dollars and as a percentage of sales revenues. Also calculate prevention, appraisal, internal failure, and external failure costs as a percentage of total quality costs.
3. Repeat requirement (2) for machine no. 172.
4. Comment on your findings, noting whether the company is "investing" its quality expenditures differently for the two machines.
5. Quality costs can be classified as observable or hidden. What are hidden quality costs, and how do these costs differ from observable costs?

Problem 8–40
Quality-Improvement Programs and Quality Costs
(LO 8-7, 8-8)

Laser News Technology, Inc. manufactures computerized laser printing equipment used by newspaper publishers throughout North America. In recent years, the company's market share has been eroded by stiff competition from Asian and European competitors. Price and product quality are the two key areas in which companies compete in this market.

Ben McDonough, Laser News Technology's president, decided to devote more resources to the improvement of product quality after learning that his company's products had been ranked fourth in product quality in a recent survey of newspaper publishers. He believed that the company could no longer afford to ignore the importance of product quality. McDonough set up a task force that he headed to implement a formal quality-improvement program. Included on the task force were representatives from engineering, sales, customer service, production, and accounting, as McDonough believed this was a companywide program and all employees should share the responsibility for its success.

After the first meeting of the task force, Sheila Hayes, manager of sales, asked Tony Reese, the production manager, what he thought of the proposed program. Reese replied, "I have reservations. Quality is too abstract to be attaching costs to it and then to be holding you and me responsible for cost improvements. I like to work with goals that I can see and count! I don't like my annual income to be based on a decrease in quality costs; there are too many variables that we have no control over!"

Laser News Technology's quality-improvement program has now been in operation for 18 months, and the following quality cost report has recently been issued. As they were reviewing the report, Hayes asked Reese what he thought of the quality program now. "The work is really moving through the Production Department," replied Reese. "We used to spend time helping the Customer Service Department solve their problems, but they are leaving us alone these days. I have no complaints so far. I'll be anxious to see how much the program increases our bonuses."

LASER NEWS TECHNOLOGY, INC.
Cost of Quality Report
(in thousands)

	Quarter Ended					
	6/30/x0	**9/30/x0**	**12/31/x0**	**3/31/x1**	**6/30/x1**	**9/30/x1**
Prevention costs:						
Design review	$ 20	$ 102	$ 111	$ 100	$ 104	$ 95
Machine maintenance	215	215	202	190	170	160
Training suppliers	5	45	25	20	20	15
Total	$ 240	$ 362	$ 338	$ 310	$ 294	$ 270
Appraisal costs:						
Incoming inspection	$ 45	$ 53	$ 57	$ 36	$ 34	$ 22
Final testing	160	160	154	140	115	94
Total	$ 205	$ 213	$ 211	$ 176	$ 149	$ 116
Internal failure costs:						
Rework	$ 120	$ 106	$ 114	$ 88	$ 78	$ 62
Scrap	68	64	53	42	40	40
Total	$ 188	$ 170	$ 167	$ 130	$ 118	$ 102
External failure costs:						
Warranty repairs	$ 69	$ 31	$ 24	$ 25	$ 23	$ 23
Customer returns	262	251	122	116	87	80
Total	$ 331	$ 282	$ 146	$ 141	$ 110	$ 103
Total quality cost	$ 964	$1,027	$ 862	$ 757	$ 671	$ 591
Total production cost	$4,120	$4,540	$4,380	$4,650	$4,580	$4,510

Required:

1. Identify at least three factors that should be present for an organization to successfully implement a quality improvement program.
2. By analyzing the cost of quality report presented, determine if Laser News Technology's quality improvement program has been successful. List specific evidence to support your answer.
3. Discuss why Tony Reese's current reaction to the quality improvement program is more favorable than his initial reaction.

4. Laser News Technology's president believed that the quality improvement program was essential and that the firm could no longer afford to ignore the importance of product quality. Discuss how the company could measure the opportunity cost of not implementing the quality-improvement program.

(CMA, adapted)

Problem 8–41
Environmental Cost Management
(LO 8-9)

As a group, take a walking tour of your campus and the surrounding community. Make a list of all of the environmental costs of which you see evidence.

Required: Make a presentation to the class about your findings. List and categorize the environmental costs you noted either for your college or for businesses in the community. (You might consider writing a letter to your campus newspaper regarding these environmental issues and their costs.)

Cases

Case 8–42
Comparison of Absorption and Variable Costing; Actual Costing
(LO 8-2, 8-3, 8-4)

1. Operating income, year 1: $27,500
2. Operating income, year 2: $20,500

Lehighton Chalk Company manufactures sidewalk chalk, which it sells online by the box at $50 per unit. Lehighton uses an actual costing system, which means that the actual costs of direct material, direct labor, and manufacturing overhead are entered into work-in-process inventory. The actual application rate for manufacturing overhead is computed each year; actual manufacturing overhead is divided by actual production (in units) to compute the application rate. Information for Lehighton's first two years of operation is as follows:

	Year 1	Year 2
Sales (in units)	2,500	2,500
Production (in units)	3,000	2,000
Production costs:		
Variable manufacturing costs	$21,000	$14,000
Fixed manufacturing overhead	42,000	42,000
Selling and administrative costs:		
Variable	25,000	25,000
Fixed	20,000	20,000

Required: Lehighton Chalk Company had no beginning or ending work-in-process inventories for either year.

1. Prepare operating income statements for both years based on absorption costing.
2. Prepare operating income statements for both years based on variable costing.
3. Prepare a numerical reconciliation of the difference in income reported under the two costing methods used in requirements (1) and (2).

Case 8–43
Analysis of Differences in Absorption-Costing and Variable-Costing Income Statements; Continuation of Preceding Case
(LO 8-1, 8-6)

1. Cost of goods sold, year 1, absorption costing income statement: $52,500
Cost of goods sold, year 2, variable costing income statement: $17,500
5(a). Total sales revenue minus total costs expensed across both years, absorption costing: $41,000

Refer to the information given in the preceding case for Lehighton Chalk Company.

Required:

1. Reconcile Lehighton's operating income reported under absorption and variable costing, during each year, by comparing the following two amounts on each income statement:
   - Cost of goods sold
   - Fixed cost (expensed as a period expense)
2. What was Lehighton's total operating income across both years under absorption costing and under variable costing?
3. What was the total sales revenue across both years under absorption costing and under variable costing?
4. What was the total of all costs expensed on the operating income statements across both years under absorption costing and under variable costing?

5. Subtract the total costs expensed across both years [requirement (4)] from the total sales revenue across both years [requirement (3)]: (*a*) under absorption costing and (*b*) under variable costing.
6. Comment on the results obtained in requirements (1), (2), (3), and (4) in light of the following assertion: *Timing is the key in distinguishing between absorption and variable costing.*

Case 8–44
Absorption and Variable Costing; Effect on the Balance Sheet; Continuation of Preceding Case
(LO 8-1, 8-4)

4. Absorption costing, finished-goods inventory, end of year 1: $10,500
5. Variable costing, reported operating income for year 2, $20,500

Refer to the information given in Case 8–42 for Lehighton Chalk Company. Selected information from Lehighton's year-end balance sheets for its first two years of operation is as follows:

LEHIGHTON CHALK COMPANY
Selected Balance Sheet Information

Based on absorption costing	**End of Year 1**	**End of Year 2**
Finished-goods inventory	$10,500	$ 0
Retained earnings	16,500	24,600
Based on variable costing	**End of Year 1**	**End of Year 2**
Finished-goods inventory	$ 3,500	$ 0
Retained earnings	9,500	24,600

Required:

1. Why is the year 1 ending balance in finished-goods inventory higher if absorption costing is used than if variable costing is used?
2. Why is the year 2 ending balance in finished-goods inventory the same under absorption and variable costing?
3. Notice that the ending balance of finished-goods inventory under absorption costing is greater than or equal to the ending finished-goods inventory balance under variable costing *for both years 1 and 2.* Will this relationship always hold true at any balance sheet date? Explain.
4. Compute the amount by which the year-end balance in finished-goods inventory declined during year 2 (i.e., between December 31 of year 1 and December 31 of year 2):
    - Using the data from the balance sheet prepared under absorption costing.
    - Using the data from the balance sheet prepared under variable costing.
5. Refer to your calculations from requirement (4). Compute the difference in the amount by which the year-end balances in finished-goods inventory declined under absorption versus variable costing. Then compare the amount of this difference with the difference in the company's reported operating income for year 2 under absorption versus variable costing. (Refer to the operating income statements prepared in Case 8–42.)
6. Notice that the retained earnings balance at the end of both years 1 and 2 on the balance sheet prepared under absorption costing is greater than or equal to the corresponding retained earnings balance on the statement prepared under variable costing. Will this relationship hold true at any balance sheet date? Explain.

9 Financial Planning and Analysis: The Master Budget

FOCUS COMPANY >>>

© Tony Tallec/Alamy RF

Snowcap Music Festivals

THIS CHAPTER'S FOCUS COMPANY is Snowcap Music Festivals, a producer and event manager of destination music events worldwide. Snowcap Music Festivals prides itself on attracting leading musical talent to its events while also exposing festival guests to the "next big thing" by featuring new talent. The fun festival scene is made possible by a modern business organization that keeps operations running smoothly while ensuring that Snowcap Music Festivals stays profitable.

© phaitoons/ Getty Images RF

One of the core elements of this business organization is a Financial Planning and Analysis (FP&A) system, and a key element of this system is the master budget. In this chapter, we will explore how Snowcap Music Festivals develops its master budget and uses it for planning individual events and overall company performance, communicating within the company, allocating resources to different festivals, controlling operations, evaluating performance, and providing incentives.

How can one accounting process do all of that? Read on!

<<< IN CONTRAST

In contrast to the service and merchandising setting of Snowcap Music Festivals, we explore the manufacturing budgets for FestiChair.com, a manufacturer of outdoor chairs based in Denver, Colorado.

Manufacturing adds complexity to the budgeting process because of the variety of resources needed and because manufacturers hold inventory. The budget provides a means for planning and managing the various resources in manufacturing. And inventory presents some special challenges. As we explore how FestiChair.com goes about developing its annual budget, differences in the manufacturing setting will be emphasized.

© Image Source RF

After completing this chapter, you should be able to:

- **9-1** Explain the relationship between financial planning and analysis and the master budget.
- **9-2** List and explain five purposes of budgeting.
- **9-3** Describe the similarities and differences in the operational budgets prepared by manufacturers, service-industry firms, merchandisers, and nonprofit organizations.
- **9-4** Explain the concept of activity-based budgeting and the logic it brings to the budgeting process.
- **9-5** Prepare each of the budget schedules that make up the master budget in a nonmanufacturing firm, and that exist in manufacturing budgets as well.
- **9-6** Prepare the additional master budget schedules required by a manufacturing firm.
- **9-7** Discuss the role of assumptions and predictions in budgeting.
- **9-8** Describe a typical organization's process of budget administration.
- **9-9** Discuss the behavioral issues in budgeting.

Financial Planning and Analysis (FP&A) Systems

Learning Objective 9-1

Explain the relationship between financial planning and analysis and the master budget.

As a company grows and its founder can no longer keep all of the company details in her head, it will need to create systems to track that data and provide it when and where needed, and in a format that managers find useful. One of those systems, the one that helps managers assess the company's future and know if they are reaching their performance goals, is called a **financial planning and analysis (FP&A) system.**

A complete FP&A system includes subsystems for (1) planning, (2) measuring and recording results, and (3) evaluating performance. If you were to design an FP&A system for an organization that you are part of, you might concentrate mostly on measuring and recording results. But if you did that, you would be missing out on one of the most important benefits of an FP&A system: forcing different parts of the organization to communicate with one another to create performance targets and set expectations about the financial and nonfinancial results of operations.

Snowcap Music Festivals

For example, suppose that the senior management of our focus company, Snowcap Music Festivals, decides to increase by 10 percent the number of tickets available for each of its three largest festivals. But they neglect to tell the merchandise ("merch") department about the change. Unaware of the increased traffic that will be coming to the merchandise tent, the merch department orders the same number of T-shirts as the prior year. When T-shirts begin running out on the second day of the first big festival, it is too late to order more. Sales and profits are lost and there are a lot of unhappy guests. Then the merch group, now aware of the mistake, orders additional shirts for the next festival. But with the event only three weeks away, the T-shirt printer has already committed all of its production capacity. So now Snowcap has an unpleasant choice: either pay for costly overtime production by the T-shirt printer or try to find another printer of equal quality that has not already committed all of its capacity. Even if they succeed, it will have been a frustrating and costly way to start the festival season!

The planning component of the FP&A system is called the master budget and it is intended to help prevent these kinds of problems. By formalizing the communication and coordination of operating and financial plans, the master budget makes sure that everyone's plans are consistent and that the total output of all those plans yields a result that makes sense for the organization. The master budget collects all of the operating plans and translates them into a financial picture of the results of the planned operations, along the way identifying the resources required to accomplish those plans and the costs of those resources.

Developing a budget is a critical step in planning any economic activity. This is true for businesses, for governmental agencies, and for individuals. We all must budget our money to meet day-to-day expenses and to plan for major expenditures, such as buying a car or paying for college tuition. Similarly, businesses of all types and governmental units at every level must make financial plans to carry out routine operations, to plan for major expenditures, and to help in making financial decisions.

"We view the role of finance as the trusted adviser to the business . . . providing a single version of data, but also business judgment and business insight. That requires a different set of skills like analytics and consultative abilities." (9a)

IBM

Purposes of Budgeting

Learning Objective **9-2**

List and explain five purposes of budgeting.

A **budget** is a detailed plan, expressed in quantitative terms, that specifies how resources will be acquired and used during a specified period of time. As one of the key tools of an FP&A system, the budget has five primary purposes: planning; facilitating communication and coordination; allocating resources; controlling profit and operations; and evaluating performance and providing incentives.

Planning The most obvious purpose of a budget is to quantify a plan of action. The process of creating a budget forces the individuals who make up an organization to plan ahead. The development of a quarterly budget for a Sheraton Hotel, for example, forces the hotel manager, the reservation manager, and the food and beverage manager to plan for the staffing and supplies needed to meet anticipated demand for the hotel's services.

Facilitating Communication and Coordination For any organization to be effective, each manager throughout the organization must be aware of the plans made by other managers. In order to plan reservations and ticket sales effectively, the reservations manager for Delta Air Lines must know the flight schedules developed by the airline's route manager. The budgeting process pulls together the plans of each manager in an organization.

Allocating Resources As we discussed in earlier chapters, an organization's resources have limited capacity, and budgets provide one means of allocating resources among competing uses. The City of Chicago, for example, must allocate its revenue among basic life services (such as police and fire protection), maintenance of property and equipment (such as city streets, parks, and vehicles), and other community services (such as child-care services and programs to prevent alcohol and drug abuse).

Controlling Profit and Operations A budget is a plan, and plans are subject to change. Nevertheless, a budget serves as a useful benchmark with which actual results can be compared. For example, Prudential Insurance Company can compare its actual sales of insurance policies for a year against its budgeted sales. Such a comparison can help managers evaluate the firm's effectiveness in selling insurance. The next two chapters examine the control purpose of budgets in more depth.

Evaluating Performance and Providing Incentives Comparing actual results with budgeted results also helps managers evaluate the performance of individuals, departments, divisions, or entire companies. Since budgets are used to evaluate performance, they also can be used to provide incentives for people to perform well. For example, General Motors Company, like many other companies, provides incentives for managers to improve profits by awarding bonuses to managers who meet or exceed their budgeted profit goals.

"Budgeting is used extensively for cost control. Each plant manager develops a plant budget, and then each department supervisor is responsible for his or her own cost center. . . . There are budgets for every department in the company." (9b)

Best Foods (a subsidiary of **Unilever**)

Diverse organizations use budgets for a variety of reasons. A resort hotel, such as this one on Mexico's Caribbean coast, uses budgets to plan for meeting the payroll and operating expenses and to coordinate operations by matching staffing with projected seasonal demand. The resort also uses its budgeting process to allocate capital improvement funds among competing projects, such as expanding the resort by acquiring a neighboring property or improving existing facilities.

Types of Budgets

Different types of budgets serve different purposes. A **master budget** or **profit plan,** discussed below, is a comprehensive set of budgets covering all phases of an organization's operations for a specified period of time.

Budgeted financial statements, often called **pro forma financial statements,** show how the organization's financial statements will appear at a specified time if operations proceed according to plan. Budgeted financial statements include a *budgeted income statement, a budgeted balance sheet,* and a *budgeted statement of cash flows.*

A **capital budget** is a plan for the acquisition of capital assets, such as buildings and equipment. (Capital budgeting is covered in depth in a future chapter.) A **financing budget** is a plan that shows how the organization will acquire its financial resources, such as through the issuance of stock or incurrence of debt.

Budgets are developed for specific time periods. *Short-range budgets* cover a year, a quarter, or a month, whereas *long-range budgets* cover periods longer than a year. **Rolling budgets** are continually updated by periodically adding a new incremental time period, such as a quarter, and dropping the period just completed. Rolling budgets are also called **revolving budgets** or **continuous budgets.**

The Master Budget: A Planning Tool

When developing a budget, it is helpful to think of the production process for goods or services as a big machine: certain inputs are fed into the machine, various resources are then applied to convert those inputs into something different, and the output from the machine is what people are willing to buy. These are exactly the things that a company needs to plan for in its budget: the quantity and cost of inputs, the quantity and cost of resources needed for conversion, and the units and revenues of outputs that can be sold.

However, it is important to notice that in budgeting, the order of these plans is reversed. The sales planning process and sales budget are created first, because the need for products and services to fill sales orders is what drives the company's production plans and the related production budget. The production budget, in turn, tells the company how much of each input and conversion resource is needed. Combining this information with the company's input and resource cost estimates yields the appropriate budgets.

This logic, and the main types of budgets, are shown in Exhibit 9–1. Collectively, these interdependent budgets comprise the master budget, a comprehensive profit plan that ties together all phases of an organization's operations. It is a complicated process, but if you will devote some time to understanding Exhibit 9–1, you will be well on your way to understanding budgeting. Later in the chapter, we provide a comprehensive example that shows how all the parts fit together.

Sales of Services or Goods

The market demand for a service or product drives the production process. For this reason, as we can see in Exhibit 9–1, the starting point for any master budget is a sales revenue budget based on a sales forecast for services or goods. Airlines forecast the number of passengers on each of their routes. Banks forecast the number and dollar amount of consumer loans and home mortgages to be provided. E-commerce companies forecast the number of customers visiting their sites and the percentage who will make purchases. Manufacturing and merchandising companies forecast sales of their goods.

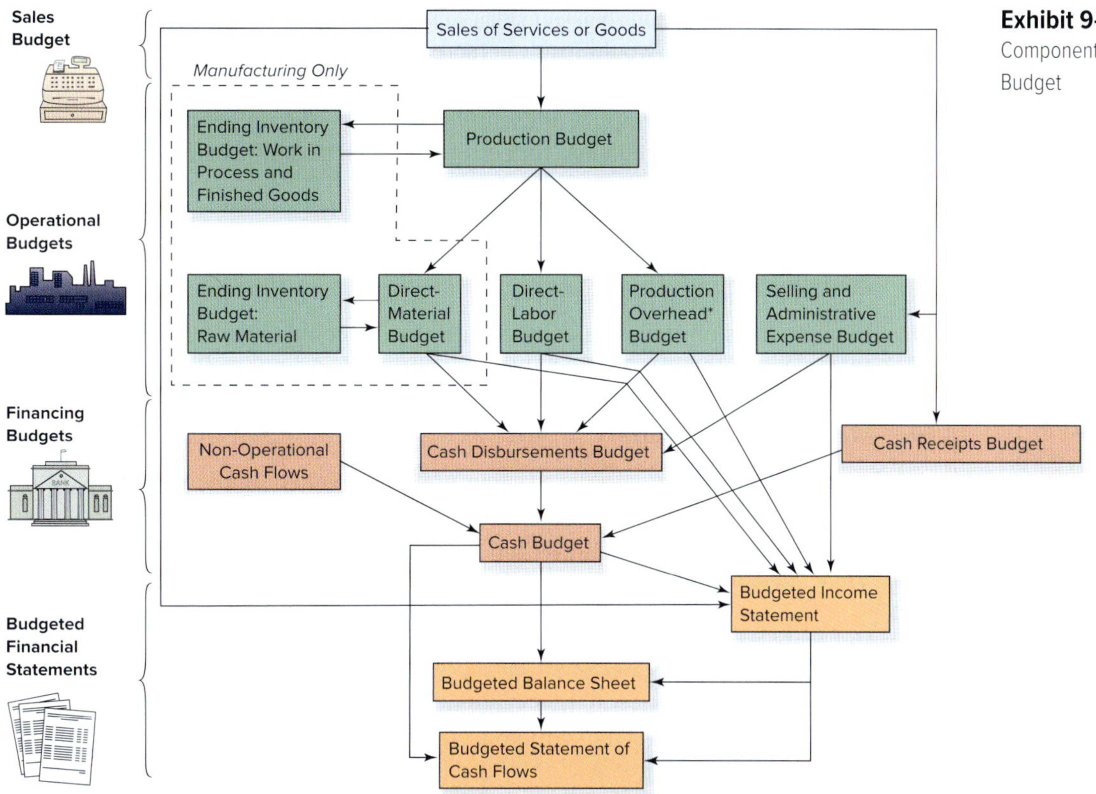

Exhibit 9–1
Components of a Master Budget

*In previous chapters, *production overhead* was referred to as *manufacturing overhead*. However, we now employ the more general term to move beyond manufacturing and include service and merchandising operations.

Some companies sell both goods and services, and these companies must forecast both to drive the budgeting process. For example, IBM makes a significant portion of its revenues from the sale of computing equipment and software, but it makes even more from the sale of consulting and technology services. Its planning and budgeting process includes five different business segments: business services, technology services, software, systems and technology, and financing.

Sales Forecasting

As we will demonstrate shortly, the accuracy of the entire budgeting process depends on first getting the sales budget right. **Sales forecasting** is a critical step in the budgeting process. But as baseball legend and folksy philosopher Yogi Berra is reported to have said, "It's tough to make predictions, especially about the future."

Various procedures are used in sales forecasting, and the final forecast usually combines information from many different sources. Many firms have a top-management-level market research staff whose job is to coordinate the company's sales forecasting efforts. Typically, everyone from key executives to the firm's sales personnel will be asked to contribute sales projections.

Major factors considered when forecasting sales include the following:

1. Past sales levels and trends:
   a. For the firm developing the forecast (for example, Exxon).
   b. For the entire industry (for example, the petroleum industry).
2. General economic trends. (Is the economy growing? How fast? Is a recession or economic slowdown expected?)
3. Economic trends in the company's industry. (In the petroleum industry, for example, will sales of hybrid and electric vehicles continue to grow rapidly, thereby implying decreased demand for gasoline?)

"I may be able to tell you how many toothbrushes we sold in Europe yesterday. But we want to get to the point where I can tell you today how many toothbrushes we will sell 45 to 60 days from now. If I figure that out, we can't get beat." (9c)

Walmart

"Historically, the personality types that drive sales and those that drive finance and operations are very different. They tend not to spend time with each other. And that's a mistake. . . . The whole point of a forecast is that it's supposed to give you guideposts for what your actions are, how you allocate your resources, what you spend your time focusing on. At the very base of that, you need to involve the person who is out there actually driving the sale." (9d)

ePartners Solutions, Inc.

4. Other factors expected to affect sales in the industry. (Is an unusually cold winter expected, which would result in increased demand for home heating oil and natural gas in northern climates?)
5. Political and legal events. (For example, is any legislation pending in Congress that would affect the demand for petroleum, such as tax incentives to use alternative energy sources?)
6. The intended pricing policy of the company.
7. Planned advertising and product promotion.
8. Expected actions of competitors.
9. New products or processes contemplated by the company or other firms. (For example, will the use of "fracking" [hydraulic fracturing] well-drilling techniques continue to expand domestic natural gas supplies?)
10. Market research studies.

The starting point in the sales forecasting process is generally the sales level of the prior year. Then the market research staff considers the information discussed above along with input from key executives and sales personnel. In many firms, elaborate *econometric models* are built to incorporate all the available information systematically. (*Econometric* means economic measurement.) Statistical methods, such as regression analysis and probability distributions for sales, are often used. All in all, a great deal of effort generally goes into the sales forecast, since it is such a critical step in the budgeting process. Making a sales forecast is like shooting an arrow. If the archer's aim is off by only a fraction of an inch, the arrow will go further and further astray and miss the bull's eye by a wide margin. Similarly, a slightly inaccurate sales forecast, coming at the very beginning of the budgeting process, will throw off all of the other schedules comprising the master budget.

Learning Objective **9-3**

Describe the similarities and differences in the operational budgets prepared by manufacturers, service-industry firms, merchandisers, and nonprofit organizations.

Operational Budgets

Based on the sales budget, a company develops a set of **operational budgets** that specify how its operations will be carried out to meet the demand for its goods or services. The budgets constituting this operational portion of the master budget are depicted in the upper half of Exhibit 9–1.

Manufacturing Firms A manufacturing company develops a production budget that shows the number of units of each product to be manufactured. Coupled with the production budget are ending-inventory budgets for raw material, work in process, and finished goods. The ending-inventory budgets reflect the manufacturer's plan to have some level of inventory on hand at all times, to meet peak demand while keeping production at a stable level. From the production budget, a manufacturer develops budgets for the direct materials, direct labor, and overhead that will be required in the production process. A budget for selling and administrative expenses also is prepared.

© Jack Kurtz/The Image Works

One advantage that "etailers," such as Amazon, have in the sales-forecasting process is the large amount of information collected online about their customers' buying patterns. This data, in theory at least, helps these firms in forecasting future sales. Pictured here is the Amazon distribution center in Fernley, Nevada.

Merchandising Firms A merchandising firm does not manufacture products. Instead, it purchases products manufactured by others and sells them to the end users, adding value through a combination of distribution and retail operations. The operational portion of the master budget of a merchandising firm is similar to that of a manufacturing firm, but instead of a production budget for goods, a merchandiser develops a budget for merchandise purchases. A merchandising firm will not have a budget for direct material, because it does not engage in production.

However, the merchandiser will develop budgets for labor (or personnel), overhead, and selling and administrative expenses.

Service-Industry Firms Based on the sales budget for its services, a service-industry firm develops a set of budgets that show how the demand for those services will be met. A service firm prepares a production budget (for the production of its services) and the related operational budgets, but the precise nature of these budgets depends on the industry. An airline, for example, prepares the following operational budgets: a budget of planned air miles to be flown; material budgets for spare aircraft parts, aircraft fuel, and in-flight food; labor budgets for flight crews and maintenance personnel; and an overhead budget.

Nonprofit Organizations The master budget for a nonprofit organization includes many of the components shown in Exhibit 9–1. However, there are some important differences. The fundamental goal of a nonprofit organization is not to sell products or services (although some do that as a way of raising funds) but rather to complete programs in support of their mission. So instead of a sales budget, nonprofits generally begin the budgeting process with a programs budget that shows the level of services to be provided. From that beginning, operational budgets can be developed to identify the resources necessary for producing the programs.

Consider Goodwill Industries International, Inc. Their mission is "helping people in need reach their fullest potential through the power of work." They plan programs to support that mission. For each program planned, Goodwill must budget the level of service to be provided, such as number of people served and hours of operation. Each program requires resources to operate, and those resources are documented in the operational budgets of the organization.

Nonprofit organizations also prepare budgets showing their anticipated funding. Goodwill budgets for revenues from thrift-store sales, government grants, and cash contributions.

In summary, all organizations begin the budgeting process with plans for (1) the goods or services to be provided and (2) the revenue to be available, whether from sales or from other funding sources.

Summary of Operational Budgets Operational budgets differ since they are adapted to the operations of individual companies in various industries. However, operational budgets are also similar in important ways. In each firm, they encompass a detailed plan for using the basic factors of production—material, labor, and overhead—to produce a product or provide a service.

Financing Budgets

After developing its sales and operational budgets, a company knows where its money will be coming from and where it will go. But several timing issues affect when they can collect the cash. To plan for this, companies develop a set of **financing budgets,** shown in the lower half of Exhibit 9–1, that project their cash flow and identify likely cash shortfalls and surpluses.

Cash Receipts Budget The cash receipts budget provides information about the cash flows into the company based on sales of its services or products (or from cash contributions and grants, in the case of nonprofits). These inflows often will not precisely match budgeted sales. Reasons can include:

- The timing of sales and collections can differ customer-to-customer. Between businesses, it is common to have payment terms specifying that cash will not change hands until 30 days or more after the sale date.
- Different payment methods convert to cash at different speeds. Cash payments can usually be deposited to the bank the same day as the sale. Proceeds from credit cards can take several days to be received, and check payments may take even longer.
- Some sales are never collected. Uncollectible accounts receivable due to bounced checks, counterfeit money, credit and debit card fraud, and customers who default on their obligations are all challenges that companies confront.

Cash Disbursements Budget As shown in Exhibit 9–1, the cash disbursements budget depends on the spending plans reflected in several operational budgets, making it quite a complex budget. To further complicate matters, the timing of cash flows out of the company does not precisely align with the expenditures reflected in the operational budgets. The company will not pay cash immediately for most of its expenditures. Rather, it will pay its suppliers according to standard commercial arrangements, often delaying payment 30 days or more past the delivery date.

Cash Budget The cash budget plays a critical role in planning the firm's cash needs. Not only does it summarize the various cash inflows and outflows from operations, as represented in the cash receipts and cash disbursements budgets discussed above, but it also incorporates nonoperational cash flows and addresses financing issues. Non-operational cash flows may include, for example, the purchase and sale of fixed assets from the capital budget, payments

Management Accounting Practice

GE, Statoil, Elkay Manufacturing, and Northern Quest Resort & Casino

THE BUDGET: VALUABLE PLANNING TOOL OR COSTLY WASTE OF TIME?

In Learning Objective 9-2, we discussed five very important purposes of budgeting. But as we will see in this chapter, budgeting is also an intricate process that is often time-consuming and costly. In the words of **GE**'s legendary ex-CEO Jack Welch, "The budgeting process at most companies has to be the most ineffective practice in management. It sucks the energy, time, fun, and big dreams out of an organization . . . [and] brings out the most unproductive behaviors."[1] Strong words!

Some argue that the purposes of budgeting can be achieved without the conventional budgeting process. These companies espouse an idea called "Beyond Budgeting" that proposes to replace annual budgets with rolling forecasts of key performance indicators. One convert is **Statoil**, a leading energy company based in Norway. Statoil split the budgeting process into separate forecasting, goal setting, and resource allocation processes. It updates these plans often in order to maintain a long view of expected performance. "The goal is to set targets that motivate and inspire people without all the gaming and pay negotiations."[2]

Kitchen products company **Elkay Manufacturing** calls its implementation of this idea "Continuous Planning." In Elkay's case, their motivation is to make the planning process more responsive to strategic planning and to adapt to the changing business environment. "There are no crystal balls. . . . [Our] process allows us to respond to changes in our business on a real-time basis, thereby negating the need for a budget.[3]

Northern Quest Resort & Casino, a tribal casino located in Washington, converted to a rolling 15-month forecast model based around quarterly financial results when they decided the annual budget was "a roadblock for progress." As their vice president of finance notes about the budget, "Once you've got it all approved, it's irrelevant . . . things change, and what you thought was going to happen doesn't happen." With a rolling forecast, he believes that there is less incentive to distort projections because they are not locked in for a year, and the improved "accuracy will ultimately help drive up revenue and reduce costs."[4]

Others disagree, pointing out that the work of continuous planning is more costly than budgeting and that doing something continuously tends to make the process superficial.

The jury is still out. But so far, GE still prepares budgets!

---

[1]Jack Welch and Suzy Welch, *Winning* (HarperBusiness, 2005), p. 189.

[2]Russ Banham, "Freed from the Budget," *CFO Magazine,* September 1, 2012, http://www3.cfo.com/article/2012/9/budgeting_budgets-rolling-forecasts-continuous-planning-beyond-budgeting-round-table-statoil-elkay-group-health-holt-cat.

[3]Steve Player, "The Remodel: A Talk with Elkay's VP of Finance," *BusinessFinance,* January 27, 2010, http://businessfinancemag.com/article/total-remodel-0127.

[4]Neil Amato, "Forward Roll: How Companies Can Move Beyond Traditional Budgeting," *Journal of Accountancy*, October 2013.

to or from investors, plans to purchase other companies, and short-term borrowings. By predicting the company's net cash position at frequent points during the planning period, the firm can plan ahead. It can arrange sources of short-term borrowing for times when cash outflows exceed inflows, and it can plan to pay off those borrowings and make short-term investments when the cash flow reverses. It can also signal cash flow trends and events that will require long-term capital acquisition via debt or equity financing. This ability to foresee and avoid cash emergencies makes the cash budget a very important and powerful tool.

Budgeted Financial Statements

The final portion of the master budget, depicted in Exhibit 9–1, includes a budgeted income statement, a budgeted balance sheet, and a budgeted statement of cash flows. These budgeted financial statements show the overall financial results of the organization's planned operations for the budget period. Notice that they are not the beginning of the master budgeting process, they are the end result!

Activity-Based Budgeting

Learning Objective 9-4

Explain the concept of activity-based budgeting and the logic it brings to the budgeting process.

The concepts that underlie activity-based costing (ABC) can be used to better understand the budgeting process.[5] Activity-based costing uses a two-stage cost-assignment process. In Stage I, overhead costs are assigned to cost pools that represent the most significant *activities* constituting the production process. The activities identified vary across companies, but such activities as order processing, material handling, machine setup, labor scheduling, quality control, and purchasing provide examples.

After assigning costs to the activity cost pools in Stage I, cost drivers appropriate for each cost pool are identified. Then, in Stage II, the overhead costs are allocated from each activity cost pool to cost objects (e.g., products, services, and customers) in proportion to the amount of activity consumed.

Exhibit 9–2 portrays the two-stage allocation process used in activity-based costing systems.

Exhibit 9–2
Activity-Based Costing System

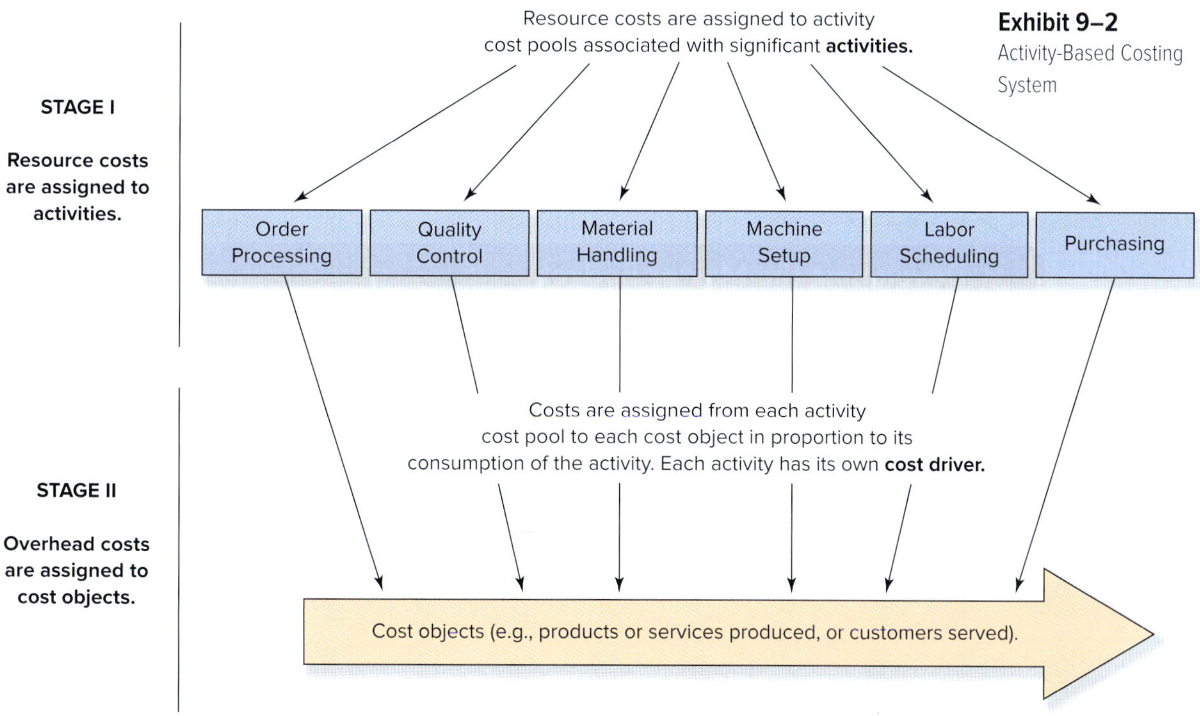

[5] Activity-based costing (ABC) is covered in Chapter 5.

Exhibit 9–3
Activity-Based Budgeting Reverses Activity-Based Costing

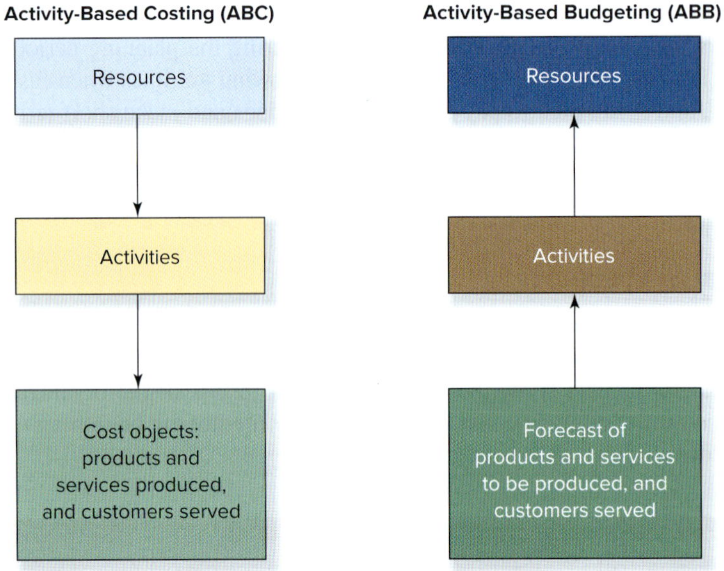

Source: Robert S. Kaplan and Robin Cooper, *Cost and Effect* (Boston: Harvard Business School Press, 1998), p. 303.

> *Commenting on how the company's ABC and ABM initiatives led to activity-based budgeting:* "We are using ABM as a means to execute our strategic management process." (9e)
> **AT&T Paradyne Corporation**

Applying ABC concepts to the budgeting process helps to explain the logic of budgeting. Sometimes the process is even referred to as **activity-based budgeting (ABB).**[6] Conceptually, ABB takes the ABC model and reverses the flow of the analysis, as depicted in Exhibit 9–3. The first step is to specify the products or services to be produced and the customers to be served. Then the activities that are necessary to produce these products and services are determined. Finally, the resources necessary to perform the specified activities are quantified. As portrayed in the diagram, ABC assigns resource costs to activities, and then it assigns activity costs to products and services produced and customers served. ABB, on the other hand, begins by forecasting the demand for products and services as well as the customers to be served. These forecasts then are used to plan the activities for the budget period and budget the resources necessary to carry out the activities.

In the next section of the chapter, we will illustrate the process of constructing a master budget. As we do so, notice how the conceptual activity-based budgeting model helps explain the steps in the budgeting process.

Developing the Master Budget

Learning Objective 9-5
Prepare each of the budget schedules that make up the master budget in a nonmanufacturing firm, and that exist in manufacturing budgets as well.

To illustrate the steps in developing a master budget, we begin with this chapter's focus company, Snowcap Music Festivals. Snowcap is a producer and event manager of destination music events worldwide. The company prides itself on attracting leading musical talent to its events, known as SMurFests, while also exposing festival guests to the "next big thing" by identifying and promoting new talent. The Snowcap brand enjoys exceptional consumer loyalty: frequent festivalgoers call themselves, naturally, SMurFs and SMurFettes. This translates into profits through repeat business, strong festival attendance,

[6]This section is based on the following references: James A. Brimson and John Antos, *Driving Value Using Activity-Based Budgeting* (New York: John Wiley & Sons, 1999); Sofia Börjesson, "A Case Study on Activity-Based Budgeting," *Journal of Cost Management* 10, no. 4 (Winter 1997), pp. 7–18; and Robert S. Kaplan and Robin Cooper, *Cost and Effect* (Boston: Harvard Business School Press, 1998), pp. 301–15.

and significant merchandise sales. The company works hard to create a stimulating and creative but safe environment.

Snowcap Music Festivals is based in Boulder, Colorado, with European operations managed from a satellite office in Salzburg, Austria. The company is wholly owned by founder Wendee Redhawk and two partners. Redhawk started the company from her apartment in Boulder almost 20 years ago. Initially it wasn't so much a company as a project to host a really big party for her college friends, their friends, and the community. But she managed to attract some talented bands to that first festival. After one of them subsequently became an international phenomenon, word of the festival spread quickly. Redhawk decided to make it a business venture and "We heard them first at Snowcap" became the company's slogan.

Snowcap Music Festivals

Unfortunately, Wendee Redhawk proved to be better at picking bands than she was at running a business. After three difficult years she brought in a partner with business training. The new partner, Doug Wing, realized that the fun festival scene would only be sustainable if supported by a modern business organization, keeping operations running smoothly while ensuring that Snowcap Music Festivals stayed profitable. Wing's business skill and Redhawk's ear for music were a winning combination: Snowcap became a big success and the SMurFest phenomenon was born. After expanding to multiple festivals in the United States, Snowcap took on a European partner to expand the company into festivals abroad, beginning in Europe.

As explained by Doug Wing, the core element of this business organization is the company's Financial Planning and Analysis (FP&A) system. The FP&A system includes preparation of a master budget for each of the festivals. These festival budgets are combined with the headquarters budget to create an overall master budget for Snowcap Music Festivals. "When we run a festival, we have to commit to everything in advance: how many bands, what we'll pay them, how many T-shirts to order, how much cash we'll need to borrow or invest, and so on. The master budget is our formal plan for each event and the overall company. It helps us to achieve our FP&A goals." When pressed for specific examples of these, Wing listed the following:

1. Documenting our plan for operations and financial results. *Which festivals are most and least profitable? How profitable is the company overall? How will we manage cash flow?*
2. Communicating our plans for, and assumptions about, the various festivals. *Which festivals are planned for this year? When does each start and end? How many people should we plan for at each one?*
3. Deciding how to share resources. *How many people are needed for marketing? For operations? At each festival? At headquarters?*
4. Controlling operations by developing benchmarks for the financial and operational results of the festival. *How much profit is each festival expected to generate? What is the goal for T-shirt sales? What is our carbon footprint goal?*
5. Evaluating performance of festival managers against those benchmarks, providing a baseline for incentive compensation. *Who is responsible for achieving attendance goals? What is the reward for meeting and exceeding attendance goals?*

In conclusion, Wing noted that, "Planning a festival without a master budget would be like driving to the festival without a map: you would have a rough idea of where you wanted to go but no idea of the best way to get there. And by the time you found your way the party might be over!" Wendee Redhawk added, "Is budgeting a pain? Sure it is. But so is practicing guitar: you can't be any good without it, and at least in budgeting your fingers don't bleed!"

We will trace Snowcap Music Festival's 20x2 master budget for its three-day Rocky Mountain SMurFest, which will be held on the second weekend of July 20x2.

The festival's master budget contains the following schedules, which are displayed and explained in the following pages.

Schedule	Sequence of Budgets	Budget Category (from Exhibit 9–1)
1	Sales Budget	Sales Budget
2	Purchases Budget	Operational Budget
3	Direct Labor Budget	Operational Budget
4	Production Overhead Budget	Operational Budget
5	Selling, General and Administrative Expense Budget	Operational Budget
6	Cash Receipts Budget	Financing Budget
7	Cash Disbursements Budget	Financing Budget
8	Cash Budget	Financing Budget
9	Budgeted Income Statement	Budgeted Financial Statement
10	Budgeted Statement of Cash Flows	Budgeted Financial Statement

Notice that this is a nonmanufacturing budget. It will demonstrate the basic operations of a budget without all of the complexities added by the need to produce and maintain inventories. Later in the chapter, we will look at the additional schedules needed in a manufacturing company's budget to incorporate those complexities, so make sure you understand this basic budget first.

Sales Budget

As discussed earlier in the chapter, the *first step in developing a master budget is always the creation of a sales budget.* The **sales budget** for the 20x2 Rocky Mountain SMurFest is displayed as Schedule 1. This budget shows the projected sales in units for the event and then multiplies the unit sales by the sales price to determine sales revenue. Tickets, which are sold only as a three-day pass for the entire festival, go on sale in January. Quarterly budgets show the timing of sales through the year, with significant ticket presales in the first quarter but also significant sales of tickets during the event in July. Also, ticket prices are discounted for early purchasers. All T-shirt sales occur during the event and this is also reflected in the sales budget.

Schedule 1

Rocky Mountain SMurFest is held the second weekend in July.

Snowcap Music Festivals

SNOWCAP MUSIC FESTIVALS: Rocky Mountain SMurFest
Sales Budget
For the Year Ending December 31, 20x2

	Quarter 1st	2nd	3rd	4th	Year
Ticket sales revenue:					
Ticket sales, in units*	10,000	10,000	5,000	0	25,000
Sales price per ticket	× $100	× $100	× $150	—	
Ticket sales revenue	$1,000,000	$1,000,000	$750,000	$0	$2,750,000
T-shirt sales revenue:					
Festival attendance, based on total ticket sales			25,000		
Percent of guests buying T-shirt during festival			× 20%		
T-shirts sold, in units	0	0	5,000	0	
Unit sales price			× $35	—	
T-shirt sales revenue	$ 0	$ 0	$175,000	$0	$ 175,000
Total sales revenue	$1,000,000	$1,000,000	$925,000	$0	$2,925,000

*Tickets are sold only as a three-day pass for the entire festival. One ticket = one three-day pass.

Now that we know the sales forecast and the plan for revenues, we can begin to budget for the costs of the purchases needed to make the revenues possible. For Snowcap Music Festivals, there are two main inputs (music and T-shirts) and two main conversion resources (direct labor and production overhead).

Purchases Budget

A company like Snowcap Music Festivals buys a lot of goods and services from outside the organization in order to create its product (a music festival). It documents its plans for acquiring these goods and services in a **purchases budget.** The purchases budget, in turn, is based on the goods and services that Snowcap Music Festivals plans to sell, as documented in the sales budget discussed in the preceding section. For the 20x2 Rocky Mountain SMurFest, the purchases to be budgeted are the music that will be played and the merchandise that will be sold. The purchases budget is displayed in Schedule 2.

Other common purchases budgets are for the direct materials needed in manufacturing and the goods needed for retail and distribution. Both of these bring added complexities relating to inventory planning and will be introduced later in the chapter. For the music festival, there are no inventory issues. All merchandise is assumed to be sold or returned.

Notice that, as in the sales budget, this budget brings together operational assumptions and financial data to create a plan. For example, the cost of two different types of performers is considered. Although the cost of groups may differ, use of an average cost per band within performer category simplifies planning.

We also begin to see the effect of budget interactions. The number of T-shirts sold depends upon the number of festival attendees, so the purchases budget is constructed using the ticket sales information built into the sales budget. In this, and in subsequent budget schedules, we see the activity-based budgeting logic that was discussed earlier.

Schedule 2

SNOWCAP MUSIC FESTIVALS: Rocky Mountain SMurFest
Purchases Budget
For the Year Ending December 31, 20x2

Snowcap Music Festivals

	Quarter				
	1st	2nd	3rd	4th	Year
Music purchases:					
Number of headliner bands booked	0	0	3	0	
Average cost per headliner band	—	—	× $250,000	—	
Total cost for headliner bands	$0	$0	$ 750,000	$0	$ 750,000
Number of undiscovered bands booked	0	0	24	0	
Average cost per undiscovered band	—	—	× $40,000	—	
Total cost for undiscovered bands	$0	$0	$ 960,000	$0	960,000
Total music cost	$0	$0	$ 1,710,000	$0	$1,710,000
T-shirt purchases:					
Number of attendees *(from Schedule 1)*	0	0	25,000	0	
Percent of guests buying T-shirt during festival	—	—	× 20%	—	
T-shirts needed, in units	0	0	5,000	0	
Cost per T-shirt	—	—	× $15	—	
Total T-shirt cost	$0	$0	$ 75,000	$0	75,000
Total music and merchandise costs	$0	$0	$ 1,785,000	$0	$1,785,000

Direct Labor Budget

While the musicians are the critical element of a music festival, without a stage and a sound system it wouldn't be much of a festival. Many other resources are needed to pull off an enjoyable, safe, and professional event, and many music festivals have failed because they didn't pay attention to sound quality, security, or parking.

We introduced conversion costs in Chapter 2 as the direct labor and overhead needed to convert raw materials into a finished product, and here we put them in their broader context: **conversion costs** are the costs of the resources needed to convert purchased inputs into a marketable product or service. These conversion resources are usually direct labor and various kinds of production overhead, and companies must plan for their availability, use, and cost.

Recall that direct labor is labor that is traceable to a particular cost object and whose quantity varies systematically with some aspect of the production. In this case the cost object is the Rocky Mountain SMurFest, and the **direct-labor budget** captures the costs of labor that are directly traceable to the event.

Ask yourself, "How would I create a labor budget for this event?" You might be tempted to just look at last year's festival to see how many people were needed to work. However, last year's employee numbers don't include the effects of changes planned for this year's Rocky Mountain SMurFest (different number of attendees, different number of bands, different hours of operation) and may not be appropriate for the current plan. A better way to answer the question is to understand what drives the need for different kinds of labor and build the budget on that basis. Again, this reflects the activity-based budgeting logic.

For a music festival, direct labor would comprise the operating personnel such as technicians (electricians and sound crew), guest-logistics staff (ticket takers, parking attendants, security), and musician-support staff (stage crew, backstage hosts). Festival hours, defined as the hours that musicians are performing, is the cost driver for technical labor. Attendee hours, based on the festival hours and the number of tickets sold, is the cost driver for guest-logistics labor. And the number of bands scheduled to perform is the cost driver for musician-support labor. These costs and relationships are budgeted in Schedule 3.

Schedule 3

Snowcap Music Festivals

SNOWCAP MUSIC FESTIVALS: Rocky Mountain SMurFest
Direct-Labor Budget
For the Year Ending December 31, 20x2

	Quarter				
	1st	**2nd**	**3rd**	**4th**	**Year**
Technician Labor:					
Festival hours*	0	0	48	0	
Technician labor hours needed per festival hour	—	—	× 17.5	—	
Total technician labor hours needed	0	0	840	0	
Average technician rate per hour	—	—	× $45	—	
Total cost for technician labor	$0	$0	$ 37,800	$0	$37,800
Guest-Logistics Staff Labor:					
Number of attendees *(from Schedule 1)*	0	0	25,000	0	
Festival hours	—	—	× 48	—	
Total attendee hours	0	0	1,200,000	0	
Staffing ratio (attendee hours per staff hour)	—	—	÷ 1,000	—	
Total guest-logistics staff hours needed	0	0	1,200	0	
Average guest-logistics staff rate per hour	—	—	× $20	—	
Total cost for guest-logistics staff labor	$0	$0	$ 24,000	$0	24,000
Musician-Support Staff Labor:					
Number of bands	0	0	27	0	
Musician-support staff hours per band	—	—	× 15	—	
Total musician-support staff hours needed	0	0	405	0	
Average musician-support staff rate per hour	—	—	× $25	—	
Total cost for musician-support staff labor	$0	$0	$ 10,125	$0	10,125
Total direct-labor costs	$0	$0	$ 71,925	$0	$71,925

*Musicians perform at the festival from 10:00 a.m. until 2:00 a.m., for three days. Although technicians and guest-support staff also work before and after the musicians perform, the average number of these staff needed is driven by the festival's music hours and attendee hours, respectively.

Production Overhead and SG&A Budgets

In addition to direct labor, other resources required to put on the festival include supervision, facilities costs, marketing, and costs incurred centrally by Snowcap Music Festivals in support of all of their festivals. These costs are divided into two different budgets. The production overhead budget includes conversion costs that relate to operating the festival. And the selling, general and administrative expense (SG&A) budget comprises costs relating to sales and marketing and to general company administration.

In Schedule 4, the **production overhead budget** summarizes the costs of production other than purchases and direct labor. We can subdivide the production overhead costs into direct costs, which are traceable to the Rocky Mountain SMurFest, and indirect costs, which are incurred centrally within the Snowcap Music Festivals organization and then allocated among the various festivals.

Each production overhead cost is budgeted according to the planned need for that resource. For example, the two guest-logistics supervisors begin work well in advance of the festival, working the entire months of May and June at a cost of $5,000 per month per supervisor. During July, the month of the festival, the guest-logistics supervisors continue to work the entire month. In addition, one technician supervisor ($8,000 per month) and one musician-support supervisor ($4,000 per month) are added for the entire month of July. At the end of July, all supervisors move on to other festivals. Accordingly, $20,000 is budgeted for the second quarter of 20x2 (two guest-logistics supervisors in both May and June at $5,000 per month per supervisor) and $22,000 is budgeted for the third quarter ($10,000 for two guest-logistics supervisors in July plus the cost of the other two supervisors in July).

Schedule 4

SNOWCAP MUSIC FESTIVALS: Rocky Mountain SMurFest
Production Overhead Budget
For the Year Ending December 31, 20x2

	Quarter				
	1st	2nd	3rd	4th	Year
Direct Production Overhead Costs:	$ 0			$ 0	
Supervisory labor*	0	$20,000	$ 22,000	0	$ 42,000
Utilities (electricity, portable toilets)	0	5,000	80,000	0	85,000
Security, maintenance, and custodial	0	0	30,000	0	30,000
Catering	0	0	50,000	0	50,000
Rental: Audio equipment	0	0	100,000	0	100,000
Rental: Festival grounds	0	0	50,000	0	50,000
Rental: Other	0	1,000	40,000	0	41,000
Total direct production overhead costs	$ 0	$26,000	$372,000	$ 0	$398,000
Allocated Production Overhead Costs:					
Tickets sold *(from Schedule 1)*	10,000	10,000	5,000	0	25,000
Cost per ticket sold (rate set by headquarters)	× $2.50	× $2.50	× $2.50	× $2.50	× $2.50
Allocated ticketing costs	$25,000	$25,000	$ 12,500	$ 0	$ 62,500
Purchasing and general supplies	10,000	25,000	35,000	10,000	80,000
Liability insurance	10,000	10,000	10,000	10,000	40,000
Total allocated production overhead costs	$45,000	$60,000	$ 57,500	$20,000	$182,500
Total production overhead costs	$45,000	$86,000	$429,500	$20,000	$580,500

*2nd Quarter: 4 supervisor-months of guest-services supervisors at $5,000 per supervisor-month.
3rd Quarter: 2 supervisor-months for guest-services at $5,000 per supervisor-month, plus 1 supervisor-month of a technician supervisor at $8,000 per supervisor-month, plus 1 supervisor-month of a musician-support supervisor at $4,000 per supervisor-month.

Snowcap Music Festivals

The method for allocating indirect production costs is determined by the central administration of Snowcap Music Festivals. For example, ticketing for all festivals is handled at the company's headquarters. The accountants there consider number of tickets sold to be the cost driver for ticketing, and they estimate the cost driver rate to be $2.50 per ticket handled. Each festival is therefore allocated an overhead cost related to ticketing of $2.50 per ticket. (Allocation of centralized costs will be discussed more extensively in Chapter 12.)

The **selling, general and administrative expense (SG&A) budget,** shown in Schedule 5, includes the sales and marketing costs of the company. As in the previous budget, these overhead costs can be divided between direct costs, such as advertising that is specifically for the Rocky Mountain SMurFest, and shared marketing costs that are allocated from headquarters to all of the festivals. Similarly, the general and administrative support provided by headquarters is allocated among the various festivals.

The general and administrative costs allocated by Snowcap Music Festivals include depreciation costs of the headquarters building and various other fixed assets owned by Snowcap. The depreciation cost is included in the "Total SG&A expenses" line that will soon become part of the budgeted income statement. However, at the bottom of the SG&A budget, the depreciation is deducted as a *noncash cost.* This is done so that the cash portion of SG&A spending can be separated out for inclusion in the cash disbursements budget. A similar adjustment would be made for noncash costs included in any other budget schedule.

Schedule 5

Snowcap Music Festivals

SNOWCAP MUSIC FESTIVALS: Rocky Mountain SMurFest
Selling, General and Administrative Expense (SG&A) Budget
For the Year Ending December 31, 20x2

	Quarter				
	1st	**2nd**	**3rd**	**4th**	**Year**
Direct SG&A expenses:					
Event advertising	$25,000	$25,000	$15,000	$ 5,000	$ 70,000
Allocated SG&A expenses:					
Sales and marketing support	20,000	20,000	20,000	20,000	80,000
General and administrative support	25,000	25,000	25,000	25,000	100,000
Total SG&A expenses	$70,000	$70,000	$60,000	$50,000	$250,000
Less: Noncash SG&A expenses (depreciation)	(7,500)	(7,500)	(7,500)	(7,500)	(30,000)
Total cash disbursements for SG&A	$62,500	$62,500	$52,500	$42,500	$220,000

Financing Budgets

The three financing budgets collectively show how a company manages the cash it needs to finance its operations. The cash receipts and cash disbursements budgets show the estimated inflows and outflows of cash relating to revenues and expenses, respectively. In these budgets, the revenue and expense numbers must be adjusted for any issues that affect the timing of cash flows. After the expected cash inflows and outflows have been determined, the overall cash budget combines this information to predict expected cash shortfalls and surpluses. Once they have been identified, plans can be made for financing the shortfalls and investing the surpluses.

The **cash receipts budget** in Schedule 6 details Snowcap Music Festivals' expected cash collections for the Rocky Mountain SMurFest during the budget period. Most ticket sales for the event are paid by debit or credit card, with funds available to the company in the same quarter as the sale. However, to promote early sales and cash inflow, Snowcap allows early ticket purchasers to pay 25 percent by credit card at the time of sale, with the other 75 percent automatically charged to the same card 90 days later. For the Rocky Mountain SMurFest, all tickets purchased during the first quarter of the year, between early January (when they go on sale) and the end of March, are sold this way. Beginning in April, all tickets must be paid for in full at the time of purchase.

Festival T-shirts are very popular and are purchased by festival guests using credit cards, debit cards, and cash. Historically, a small number of purchases turn out to be fraudulent (using forged or stolen cards or counterfeit cash), and Snowcap Music Festival budgets this uncollectible portion at 2.5 percent of sales.

Schedule 6

SNOWCAP MUSIC FESTIVALS: Rocky Mountain SMurFest
Cash Receipts Budget
For the Year Ending December 31, 20x2

	Quarter				
	1st	2nd	3rd	4th	Year
Ticket revenue *(from Schedule 1)*:	$1,000,000	$1,000,000	$750,000	$0	$2,750,000
Collections in quarter of sale*	$ 250,000	$1,000,000	$750,000		$2,000,000
Collections in quarter after sale†	0	750,000	0		750,000
Total cash receipts from ticket sales	$ 250,000	$1,750,000	$750,000	$0	$2,750,000
T-shirt revenue *(from Schedule 1)*:	$ 0	$ 0	$175,000	$0	$ 175,000
Less: Uncollectible accounts expense‡	(0)	(0)	(4,375)	(0)	(4,375)
Total cash receipts from T-shirt sales	$ 0	$ 0	$170,625	$0	$ 170,625
Total cash receipts	$ 250,000	$1,750,000	$920,625	$0	$2,920,625

*25% of 1st quarter ticket sales; 100% of ticket sales in all other quarters.
†75% of 1st quarter ticket sales.
‡2.5% of T-shirt sales are expected to be uncollectible: $175,000 (T-shirt sales, from Schedule 1) × 2.5% = $4,375.

How to Budget Cash Flows To understand how the cash receipts and cash disbursements budgets are prepared, we focus on the timing of cash flows. Consider the second quarter column of Schedule 6. The ticket revenue estimate comes directly from Schedule 1, the sales budget. Since Snowcap Music Festival entices early purchasers by allowing them to pay in two installments if they buy during the first quarter (25 percent at time of purchase, 75 percent 90 days later), some of the first quarter's revenue will be collected during the second quarter. Therefore, the cash that the firm will collect during the second quarter comprises two components, as depicted in the following diagram.

The second quarter's total cash receipts from ticket sales are the sum of $1,000,000 (100 percent of second quarter ticket sales) and $750,000 (75 percent of first quarter ticket sales).

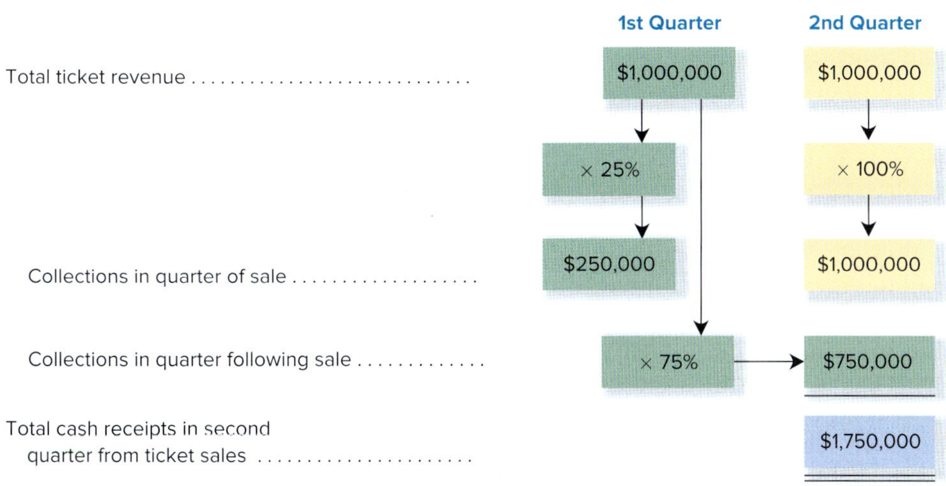

One final point to notice is that 2.5 percent of T-shirt sales are not expected to be collected. Thus, the $4,375 of third quarter uncollectible accounts amounts to 2.5 percent of Rocky Mountain SMurFest T-shirt sales ($4,375 = $175,000 × 2.5 percent), and cash receipts from T-shirt sales are only 97.5 percent of T-shirt sales revenue.

In Schedule 7, the **cash disbursements budget** shows the timing of the cash flowing out of the company. Just as we saw that cash from sales does not always flow into the company exactly when the sale is made, cash for purchases does not necessarily flow out of the company at the exact time the purchase is made. Payment policies will differ between vendors and types of payments, and any significant differences need to be anticipated in the budget. Often purchases are made *on account,* which means that payment is not made in cash at the time of the purchase. Instead, payment is made later under terms that are negotiated, often 30–60 days after delivery of the product or service.

For band payments at Snowcap Music Festivals, the payment schedule for "headliner" bands is typically 50 percent in advance and 50 percent after the show. However the "undiscovered" bands, which do not have the market power to demand advance payment, are paid after they perform. In another type of arrangement, Snowcap's contract with its T-shirt vendor for the Rocky Mountain SMurFest specifies that they will be paid 25 percent one month before the festival to help cover up-front costs for the unprinted shirts needed for this very large order, with the balance paid within 30 days after the festival ends. All other vendors for the Rocky Mountain SMurFest are paid in the same month that the expense is recorded.

Schedule 7

Snowcap Music Festivals

SNOWCAP MUSIC FESTIVALS: Rocky Mountain SMurFest
Cash Disbursements Budget
For the Year Ending December 31, 20x2

	Quarter				
	1st	2nd	3rd	4th	Year
Payments for purchases *(from Schedule 2)*:					
Headliner bands (50% paid in prior quarter)	$ 0	$375,000	$ 375,000	$ 0	$ 750,000
Undiscovered bands	0	0	960,000	0	960,000
T-shirts (25% paid in prior quarter)	0	18,750	56,250	0	75,000
Total cash disbursements for purchases	$ 0	$393,750	$1,391,250	$ 0	$1,785,000
Other cash disbursements:					
Direct labor *(from Schedule 3)*	$ 0	$ 0	$ 71,925	$ 0	$ 71,925
Production overhead costs *(from Schedule 4)*	45,000	86,000	429,500	20,000	580,500
SG&A expenses *(from Schedule 5, cash part only)*	62,500	62,500	52,500	42,500	220,000
Total other cash disbursements	$107,500	$148,500	$ 553,925	$62,500	$ 872,425
Total cash disbursements	$107,500	$542,250	$1,945,175	$62,500	$2,657,425

Finally, in Schedule 8, the **cash budget** summarizes the company's cash position. It shows that the Rocky Mountain SMurFest spends more cash than it takes in during the festival (which falls in the third quarter), but ticket presales are expected to have built a cash balance large enough to offset the shortfall. As a result, no outside sources of funding are needed.

However, the excess cash generated before the festival is not just hidden in a bass drum! It is invested until it is needed, and while invested it earns interest for the company. This interest earned is shown near the bottom of the cash budget. Snowcap Music Festivals earns an annual interest rate of 5 percent on its invested cash. For simplicity, we will assume that the net cash generated or used during a quarter occurs evenly throughout the quarter being budgeted, and that the interest rate is applied to the average cash balance for the quarter. While not precisely accurate, this is close enough for a planning estimate. See the footnotes to Schedule 8 for an example of how interest income is calculated.

Schedule 8

SNOWCAP MUSIC FESTIVALS: Rocky Mountain SMurFest
Cash Budget
For the Year Ending December 31, 20x2

	Quarter				
	1st	2nd	3rd	4th	Year
Beginning cash balance	$ 0	$ 143,391	$ 1,360,482	$346,535	$ 0
Cash receipts *(from Schedule 6)*	$250,000	$1,750,000	$ 920,625	$ 0	$2,920,625
Less: Cash disbursements *(from Schedule 7)*	(107,500)	(542,250)	(1,945,175)	(62,500)	(2,657,425)
Change in cash balance due to operations	$142,500	$1,207,750	$(1,024,550)	$ (62,500)	$ 263,200
Interest earned on investment of cash balance*	891	9,341	10,603	3,941	24,776
Total change in cash balance	$143,391	$1,217,091	$(1,013,947)	$ (58,559)	$ 287,976
Ending cash balance	$143,391	$1,360,482	$ 346,535	$287,976	$ 287,976

*The change in cash balance is assumed to occur evenly throughout the quarter and the 5% annual rate of return is applied to the average cash balance for the quarter.

Example computation for the 2nd quarter:

Average cash balance for the quarter = balance beginning of quarter + 1/2 of the change in cash balance for quarter

= $143,391 + ($1,207,750 / 2) = $747,266

Rate of return for quarter = 5% annual rate / 4 quarters = 1.25%

Quarterly interest earned = $747,266 × 1.25% = $9,341 (rounded).

Budgeted Financial Statements

The **budgeted income statement** in Schedule 9, showing the expected revenues and expenses in 20x2 for the Rocky Mountain SMurFest, assumes that the built-in expectations about the festival are met. Arriving at net income requires an estimate of the appropriate tax rate, and Snowcap Music Festivals instructs its festivals to use their corporate rate of 35 percent in the festival budgets.

Schedule 9

SNOWCAP MUSIC FESTIVALS: Rocky Mountain SMurFest
Budgeted Income Statement
For the Year Ending December 31, 20x2

Sales revenue *(from Schedule 1)*		$2,925,000
Cost of goods sold:		
Cost of purchases *(from Schedule 2)*	$1,785,000	
Direct labor costs *(from Schedule 3)*	71,925	
Production overhead costs *(from Schedule 4)*	580,500	
Total cost of goods sold		2,437,425
Gross margin		$ 487,575
Other income and expenses:		
SG&A expenses *(from Schedule 5)*		(250,000)
Uncollectible accounts expense *(from Schedule 6)*		(4,375)
Interest income *(from Schedule 8)*		24,776
Pretax income		$ 257,976
Income tax (35%, rounded)		(90,292)
Net income		$ 167,684

Lastly, Schedule 10 displays the **budgeted statement of cash flows.** Notice that the format used in the budgeted statement of cash flows follows that specified under the *direct method* of preparing the statement, which is recommended by the Financial

Accounting Standards Board (FASB).[7] The format used in the statement of cash flows, which is a statement prepared by companies for external reporting purposes, generally differs from the format used in the financing budgets, which are prepared for internal use by management. Notice the differences in the format of Schedule 10 when compared with the financing budgets in Schedules 6, 7, and 8. The greater detail in the internal schedules provides information that is useful to management.

Schedule 10

SNOWCAP MUSIC FESTIVALS: Rocky Mountain SMurFest
Budgeted Statement of Cash Flows
For the Year Ending December 31, 20x2

Cash flows from operating activities:		
Cash receipts:		
From customers *(from Schedule 6)*	$2,920,625	
From interest *(from Schedule 8)*	24,776	
Total cash receipts from operating activities		$2,945,401
Cash disbursements *(from Schedule 7):*		
To suppliers of purchases	$1,785,000	
For direct labor	71,925	
For production overhead	580,500	
For SG&A expenses	220,000	
Total cash disbursements for operating activities		2,657,425
Net cash flow from operating activities		$ 287,976
Cash flows from investing activities (none)		0
Cash flows from financing activities (none)		0
Net increase in cash and cash equivalents		$ 287,976
Balance in cash and cash equivalents, beginning of year		0
Balance in cash and cash equivalents, end of year		$ 287,976

Normally, the budgeted financial statements of an organization would include a **budgeted balance sheet.** However, this budget is only for the 20x2 Rocky Mountain SMurFest. Most of the assets and liabilities, and all of the equity, are found only on the consolidated (overall) Snowcap Music Festivals budget. For this reason, the balance sheet is omitted from this festival budget. The only asset of the festival is its cash position, which is presented in both the cash budget (Schedule 8) and the budgeted statement of cash flows (Schedule 10), and its primary contribution to the company is its generation of profits, as presented in the budgeted income statement (Schedule 9).

Summary: Key Features of a Master Budget

The event budget for the 20x2 Rocky Mountain SMurFest includes many of the key features of a master budget.

- It consists of a series of budget schedules.
- Operational assumptions are specifically identified and incorporated into the budget.
- The budget schedules are heavily interdependent, with outputs of one schedule serving as inputs to another.

[7]The direct and indirect methods of preparing the statement of cash flows are covered in financial accounting texts. They also are covered in the supplement to this text entitled *The Statement of Cash Flows and Financial Statement Analysis,* which is available from the publisher. This supplement is not required in order to understand the preparation of the budget, as explained in this chapter.

- The budget schedules follow a logical sequence, beginning with the sales budget and building to the budgeted financial statements.
- Activity-based budgeting logic is incorporated.
- All of the key types of master budget schedules are present: sales, operational, financing, and financial statements.

Just as every company is different, every master budget will be different. But these elements are present in all master budgets and if you understand the logic and flow presented above you will know how to approach budgeting in any context.[8]

However, this is not the end of the budgeting story. Manufacturing products and maintaining inventories introduce complexities to the budgeting process that we address in the next section.

Extending the Master Budget for a Manufacturing Firm

Learning Objective 9-6

Prepare the additional master budget schedules required by a manufacturing firm.

Manufacturing firms have several characteristics that complicate the budgeting process. Foremost among these are inventories, which add several additional steps in order to adjust for planned changes in inventory levels. Both inventories of finished products and inventories of raw materials and components require additional budgeting steps.

In many cases, manufacturing firms also have more complex cash flows because of the many transactions involved in their conversion processes and because of the many different ways they sell their products. Frequently, manufacturers also have large investments in property, plant, and equipment that require periodic reinvestment.

FestiChair

To help illustrate how these complexities are handled in budgeting, we will investigate the master budget of FestiChair.com, a manufacturer of outdoor chairs based in Denver, Colorado. The company is wholly owned by Mary Edwards, who started the company in her basement 15 years ago. Success came quickly for the company, and Edwards eventually built a production facility outside Denver. The company's manufacturing process is highly automated, using several machines to cut out pieces of chair fabric and sew them together to form a variety of lightweight but durable seating products. Production of the metal chair frame is outsourced to a company in Monterrey, Mexico, and the frames are scheduled to arrive at FestiChair.com just before they are needed in production.

Initially, Edwards called her firm FestiChair Company, and its chairs were sold wholesale to event producers such as Snowcap Music Festivals using a traditional sales approach. Three years ago, however, Edwards changed the company's name to FestiChair.com and made a major foray into the world of Internet sales, marketing its strong, light chairs to the active outdoor consumer segment. Now almost 75 percent of FestiChair.com's sales are made through the company's website. Although FestiChair.com retained several of its sales personnel to handle the traditional sales to event producers, new personnel had to be hired to handle the company's Internet sales. Chairs are shipped to Internet customers via UPS, FedEx, and other express delivery services.

In order to manufacture the appropriate quantity of chairs and get them to consumers when and where they are needed, FestiChair.com needs to predict seasonality, anticipate raw material needs, and plan production resources such as workers and machines. The company's master budget is a crucial part of that process. Some of the budget schedules

---

[8]There are some structural differences in the budgets of nonprofit organizations. As discussed earlier in the chapter, the master budget of a nonprofit begins with the quantified program goals rather than a sales budget. And their financial statements are sometimes prepared according to different accounting standards. However, other than these structural differences, the logic and flow of the master budget is identical in the nonprofit and for-profit settings.

listed below were discussed earlier in conjunction with the Snowcap Music Festivals master budget, but the ones that are highlighted were not. The first three new schedules are specific to the manufacturing setting, and a *budgeted balance sheet* is also included in this example. We will consider only these additional schedules in this section. (The schedules added for FestiChair.com are labelled A, B, C, and D to distinguish them from the Snowcap Music Festival schedules.)

Schedule	Sequence of Budgets	Budget Category (from Exhibit 9–1)
	Sales Budget	
A	Production Budget	Operational Budget
B	Direct-Material Budget	Operational Budget
	Direct-Labor Budget	
	Production Overhead Budget	
	Selling, General and Administrative Expense Budget	
	Cash Receipts Budget	
	Cash Disbursements Budget	
	Cash Budget	
C	Budgeted Schedule of Cost of Goods Manufactured and Sold	Budgeted Financial Statements
	Budgeted Income Statement	
	Budgeted Statement of Cash Flows	
D	Budgeted Balance Sheet	Budgeted Financial Statements

Production Budget

Resources for manufacturing, such as raw materials, production workers, and machines, are needed when the products are produced, not when they are sold. Why is there a difference in timing between units sold and units produced?

- Sales are sometimes hard to predict.
- Often a logistical lag exists between when a product is made and when it can be sold. (Think of the China-to-U.S. supply chain.)
- Companies build products for inventory as a way to smooth production levels so they don't have to lay off workers or buy as many machines.

The **production budget** shows the number of units that are to be produced during a budget period. As we saw in Exhibit 9–1, it serves as the bridge between the sales budget and the operational budgets that plan for spending on production.

FestiChair.com's production budget, displayed as Schedule A, determines the number of chairs to be produced each quarter based on the quarterly sales projections in the sales budget. Schedule A is based on the following formula.

$$\text{Sales in units} + \text{Desired ending inventory of finished goods} = \text{Total units required}$$

$$\text{Total units required} - \text{Expected beginning inventory of finished goods} = \text{Units to be produced}$$

Focus on the second-quarter column in Schedule A, which is shaded. Expected second-quarter sales are 15,000 chairs. FestiChair.com also wants to have enough finished chairs on hand at the end of the second quarter to provide 10 percent of the expected sales for the third quarter. Since 1,500 chairs are expected to be in inventory at the beginning of the second quarter and (20,000 chairs × 10%) = 2,000 chairs are needed in inventory at the end of the second quarter, 500 additional chairs need to be produced for inventory. Therefore, in total, (15,000 + 500) = 15,500 chairs need to be produced during the quarter.

Schedule A

FestiChair

FestiChair.com
Production Budget
For the Year Ending December 31, 20x2

	Quarter				
	1st	**2nd**	**3rd**	**4th**	**Year**
Sales in units *(from sales budget - not shown)*	5,000	15,000	20,000	10,000	50,000
Add: Desired ending inventory of finished goods*	1,500	2,000	1,000	500†	500
Total units required	6,500	17,000	21,000	10,500	50,500
Less: Expected beginning inventory of finished goods	(500)	(1,500)	(2,000)	(1,000)	(500)
Units to be produced	6,000	15,500	19,000	9,500	50,000

*Ten percent of the next quarter's expected sales.

†Ten percent of the expected sales for the 1st quarter of the next year, 20x3, which is predicted to be 5,000 units.

Direct-Material Budget

In the master budget of a manufacturing company, the **direct-material budget** shows the number of units and the cost of material to be purchased and used during a budget period. FestiChair.com's direct-material budget, which is displayed as Schedule B, has two sections: one for chair fabric and one for chair frames. As is true for almost all manufacturers, FestiChair.com's direct-material cost is a unit-level cost.[9] Each chair requires 12 sq. ft. of fabric and one chair frame. The frames required for chair production are prepackaged in small batches by the vendor in Monterrey and delivered to FestiChair.com on a just-in-time basis.[10] The top section of FestiChair.com's direct-material budget shows the total amount of fabric needed to make chairs during each quarter. The darker-shaded portion of Schedule B computes the amount of fabric to be purchased each quarter. This part of the schedule is based on the following formula.

$$\text{Raw material required for production} + \text{Desired ending inventory of raw material} = \text{Total raw material required}$$

$$\text{Total raw material required} - \text{Expected beginning inventory of raw material} = \text{Raw material to be purchased}$$

This section of Schedule B also computes the cost of each quarter's chair fabric purchases. The lower, lighter-shaded portion of Schedule B calculates the quantity and cost of chair frames to be purchased each quarter. Finally, the last row of Schedule B totals the cost of chair fabric and chair frames to yield the total cost of raw material to be purchased each quarter.

[9] A unit-level cost is one that must be incurred each time a unit is produced.

[10] Just-in-time production and inventory control systems are covered in Appendix III at the end of the text.

Schedule B

FestiChair.com
Direct-Material Budget
For the Year Ending December 31, 20x2

	Quarter 1st	2nd	3rd	4th	Year
Chair fabric:					
Chairs to be produced *(from Schedule A)*	6,000	15,500	19,000	9,500	50,000
Raw material required per unit (sq. ft of fabric)	× 12	× 12	× 12	× 12	× 12
Raw material required for production (sq. ft.)	72,000	186,000	228,000	114,000	600,000
Add: Desired ending inventory of raw material (sq. ft.)*	18,600	22,800	11,400	7,200†	7,200
Total raw material required	90,600	208,800	239,400	121,200	607,200
Less: Expected beginning inventory of raw material (sq. ft.)	(7,200)	(18,600)	(22,800)	(11,400)	(7,200)
Raw material to be purchased (sq. ft.)	83,400	190,200	216,600	109,800	600,000
Cost per sq. ft.	× $9	× $9	× $9	× $9	× $9
Total cost of chair fabric purchases	$750,600	$1,711,800	$1,949,400	$ 988,200	$5,400,000
Chair frames:					
Chairs to be produced *(from Schedule A)*	6,000	15,500	19,000	9,500	50,000
Chair frames required per chair	× 1	× 1	× 1	× 1	× 1
Chair frames to be purchased‡	6,000	15,500	19,000	9,500	50,000
Cost per chair frame	× $20	× $20	× $20	× $20	× $20
Total cost of chair frame purchases	$120,000	$ 310,000	$ 380,000	$ 190,000	$1,000,000
Total cost of raw material purchases (fabric and frames)	$870,600	$2,021,800	$2,329,400	$1,178,200	$6,400,000

*Ten percent of the next quarter's expected raw material requirements.

†Ten percent of the expected raw material requirements for the 1st quarter of the next year, 20x3, which is assumed to be 72,000 sq. ft. (Sales, and therefore production, is predicted to be the same in each quarter of 20x3 as in the corresponding quarter of 20x2.)

‡Since the chair frames are delivered on a just-in-time basis, there is no need for buffer inventory stocks. Thus, the number of frames purchased each quarter is the same as the number needed each quarter.

Production and Purchasing: An Important Link Notice the important link between planned production and purchases of raw material. This link is apparent in Schedule B, and it is also emphasized in the formula preceding the schedule. Let's focus on the second quarter. Since 15,500 chairs are to be produced, 186,000 sq. ft. of material will be needed (15,500 chairs × 12 sq. ft. per unit). In addition, FestiChair.com wants to have 22,800 sq. ft. of material in inventory at the end of the quarter.[11] Thus, total needs are 208,800 sq. ft. Does FestiChair.com need to purchase this much raw material? No it does not, because 18,600 sq. ft. will be in inventory at the beginning of the quarter. Therefore, the firm needs to purchase only 190,200 sq. ft. of material during the quarter (208,800 sq. ft. less 18,600 sq. ft. in the beginning inventory).

Inventory Management The linkage between planned production and raw material purchases is a particularly critical linkage in manufacturing firms. Thus, considerable effort is devoted to careful inventory planning and management. How did FestiChair.com decide how much raw material to have in inventory at the end of each quarter? Examination of Schedule B reveals that each quarter's desired ending inventory of raw material is 10 percent of the

[11]It often is desirable to have a buffer inventory just before a bottleneck manufacturing operation.

material needed for production in the next quarter. For example, 22,800 sq. ft. of raw material will be in inventory at the end of the second quarter, because 228,000 sq. ft. will be needed for production in the third quarter (22,800 = 10% × 228,000). The effect of this approach is to have a larger ending inventory when the next quarter's planned production is greater. Inventories are drawn down when the subsequent quarter's planned production is lower.

Further discussion of inventory management can be found in Appendix III at the end of the text.

Budgeted Schedule of Cost of Goods Manufactured and Sold

During our discussion of Snowcap Music Festivals, we introduced two of the budgeted financial statements: the budgeted income statement and the budgeted statement of cash flows. We now turn to the remaining budget schedule that is needed before manufacturer FestiChair.com can complete its budgeted financial statements.

The **budgeted schedule of cost of goods manufactured and sold** shows the production costs that are expected to flow through the inventory accounts, and identifies the portion of production costs expected to be in work-in-process inventory, finished-goods inventory and cost of goods sold at the end of the period.

- This budget schedule first summarizes the various costs of production from other budget schedules to compute the period's total manufacturing costs.
- It then adjusts for the beginning and ending cost of work-in-process inventory to compute the cost of goods manufactured. (Recall from Chapter 2 that cost of goods manufactured represents the total cost of products completed and transferred to finished-goods inventory.)
- Finally, the cost of goods manufactured is adjusted by the beginning and ending balances in finished-goods inventory to compute cost of goods sold.

Schedule C shows FestiChair.com's budgeted schedule of cost of goods manufactured and sold.

Schedule C

FestiChair

FestiChair.com
Budgeted Schedule of Cost of Goods Manufactured and Sold
For the Year Ending December 31, 20x2

Direct material (*see Schedule B for details*):		
Raw-material inventory, January 1	$ 64,800[a]	
Add: Purchases of raw material	6,400,000[b]	
Raw material available for use	$6,464,800	
Deduct: Raw-material inventory, December 31	64,800[a]	
Direct material used		$6,400,000[b]
Direct labor (from direct-labor budget*)		375,000
Production overhead (from production overhead budget*)		1,400,000
Total manufacturing costs		$8,175,000
Add: Work-in-process inventory, January 1		0[c]
Subtotal		$8,175,000
Deduct: Work-in-process inventory, December 31		0[c]
Cost of goods manufactured		$8,175,000
Add: Finished-goods inventory, January 1		81,750[d]
Cost of goods available for sale		$8,256,750
Deduct: Finished-goods inventory, December 31		81,750[d]
Cost of goods sold		$8,175,000

[a]From Schedule B: 7,200 sq. ft. of chair fabric × $9 per sq. ft., and zero inventory of chair frames.

[b]From Schedule B: $5,400,000 for chair fabric + $1,000,000 for chair frames.

[c]The company's production cycle is short enough that there is no work-in-process inventory at any time.

[d]From Schedule A: 500 units × $163.50 per unit, which is the absorption manufacturing cost per unit ($8,175,000 cost of goods manufactured ÷ 50,000 units from Schedule A).

Budgeted Balance Sheet

After completing the budgeted income statement and budgeted statement of cash flows (discussed earlier in the chapter and so omitted from the FestiChair.com example), we turn last to the budgeted balance sheet. The **budgeted balance sheet** shows the expected end-of-period balances for the company's assets, liabilities, and owner's equity, assuming that planned operations are carried out. FestiChair.com's budgeted balance sheet for December 31, 20x2, is displayed as Schedule D. To construct this budgeted balance sheet, we start with the firm's balance sheet projected for the *beginning* of the budget year (Exhibit 9–4) and then adjust each account balance for the changes expected during 20x2. These expected changes are reflected in the various 20x2 budget schedules.

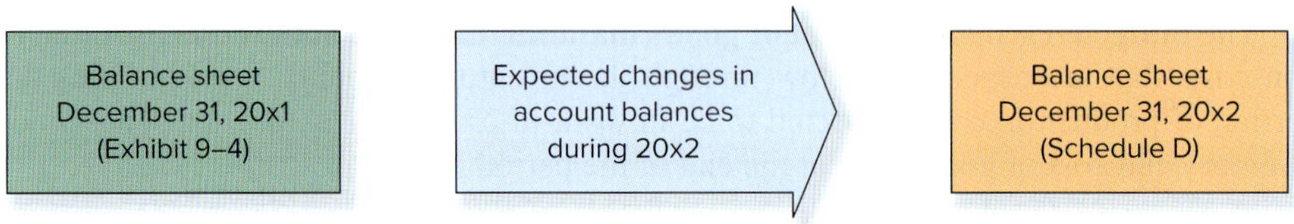

Explanations for the account balances on the budgeted balance sheet for December 31, 20x2, are given in the second half of Schedule D. Examine these explanations carefully. Notice how the budgeted balance sheet pulls together information from most of the schedules constituting the master budget.

Exhibit 9–4
Prior-Year-End Balance Sheet

FestiChair

F30 =SUM(F28:F29)

	A	B	C	D	E	F
1				FESTICHAIR.COM		
2				Balance Sheet		
3				For the Year Ended December 31, 20x1		
4						
5	Assets:					
6		Current assets:				
7			Cash			$ 10,000
8			Accounts receivable (net of allowance for doubtful accounts)			405,000
9			Inventory:			
10				Raw material	$ 64,800	
11				Finished goods	81,750	
12				Supplies	42,000	
13			Total inventory			188,550
14		Total current assets				$ 603,550
15		Long-term assets:				
16			Building		$ 8,200,000	
17			Equipment		2,280,000	
18				Less accumulated depreciation on building and equipmeny	(1,883,550)	
19		Total long-term assets				8,596,450
20	Total assets					$ 9,200,000
21						
22	Liabilities and Owners' Equity					
23		Current liabilities:				
24			Accounts payable			$ 471,280
25		Total current liabilities				$ 471,280
26		Long-term liabilities:				
27			Note payable (non-interest bearing; due December 31, 20x4)			4,100,000
28		Total liabilities				$ 4,571,280
29		Owners' equity				4,628,720
30	Total liabilities and owners' equity					$ 9,200,000

Balance Sheet

Schedule D

FestiChair

FestiChair.com
Budgeted Balance Sheet
December 31, 20x2

Assets		
Current assets:		
Cash (from cash budget*)		$ 831,000
Accounts receivable (net of allowance for uncollectible accounts)		405,000[a]
Inventory:		
Raw material (*from Schedule C*)	$ 64,800	
Finished goods (*from Schedule C*)	81,750	
Supplies	42,000	
Total inventory		188,550
Total current assets		$1,424,550
Long-lived assets:		
Building	$ 9,200,000[b]	
Equipment	2,280,000	
Less accumulated depreciation on building and equipment	(2,323,550)[c]	
Building and equipment, net of accumulated depreciation		9,156,450
Total assets		$10,581,000
Liabilities and Owner's Equity		
Current liabilities:		
Accounts payable		$ 471,280[d]
Total current liabilities		$ 471,280
Long-term liabilities:		
Note payable (non-interest-bearing; due on December 31, 20X4)		4,100,000
Total liabilities		4,571,280
Owner's equity		6,009,720[e]
Total liabilities and owner's equity		$10,581,000

[a]From cash receipts budget*: uncollected portion of 4th quarter sales.
[b]Balance in the Building account on the December 31, 20x1, balance sheet, plus a $1,000,000 building construction project in 20x2 (from capital budget and cash budget*).
[c]Balance in the Accumulated Depreciation account on the December 31, 20x1, balance sheet, plus $440,000 in depreciation during 20x2 (from production overhead budget*).
[d]From cash disbursements budget*: unpaid portion of 4th quarter purchases.
[e]Balance in Owner's Equity on the December 31, 20x1, balance sheet, plus the 20x2 budgeted net income of $1,381,000 from budgeted income statement.*
*This budget schedule was discussed earlier in this chapter and is not included in the FestiChair.com example.

Assumptions and Predictions Underlying the Master Budget

Learning Objective 9-7

Discuss the role of assumptions and predictions in budgeting.

A master budget is based on many assumptions and estimates of unknown parameters. Some estimates tend to be quite accurate, while other predictions are much more difficult to make accurately.

What are some of the assumptions and predictions that are reflected in FestiChair.com's budget? Consider Schedules A and B. First, the company's managers have assumed that people will continue to purchase more chairs in the spring and summer than in the cooler months of the year, as they have in the past. Second, they have assumed that production capacity is sufficient to meet the peak production requirement of 19,000 chairs in the third quarter. And third, the managers have assumed that the quantity of chair material needed for production will be available, when needed, at a price of $9 per sq. ft. for the entire year. Based on these assumptions, the managers have predicted direct-material costs for each quarter.

FestiChair.com's master budget reflects many other predictions, such as salaries, wage rates, electric and other utility rates, insurance and property tax rates, and so forth.

Some of these predictions—property tax rates, for example—would likely be quite accurate. Other predictions would be more difficult. For example, the cost of natural gas for heating purposes is hard to predict because it depends on the weather.

Making predictions and agreeing on assumptions are valuable parts of the budgeting process. Managers are forced to identify and agree on the assumptions that will be part of the year's financial plan. And after making the predictions, the risk of being wrong can sometimes be mitigated by managers' actions. For example, if the company is going to assume that chair fabric will be available all year at $9 per sq. ft., then the company will consider entering into purchasing contracts that will guarantee that availability. But these contracts also bring risk: if the sales volume predictions are too high, they could be stuck with a lot of extra fabric; and if market prices for fabric drop, their chair production costs might be higher than their competitors' costs. Managers get paid to make decisions like these, and building them into the budgeting process helps.

Financial Planning Models

"Implementing a Web-based, enterprise-wide budgeting solution will help us develop business plans and allow our analysts to be proactive in monitoring quarterly results." (9f)
TD Bank Financial Group

Managers must make assumptions and predictions in preparing budgets because organizations operate in a world of uncertainty. That is why the master budget is just one part of the financial planning and analysis (FP&A) system. Another part of that system is the *financial planning model.* A **financial planning model** is a set of mathematical relationships that express the interactions among the various operational, financial, and environmental events that determine the overall results of an organization's activities. A financial planning model is a mathematical expression of all the relationships expressed in the flowchart of Exhibit 9–1.

To illustrate this concept, focus on the following equation, which is used to budget FestiChair.com's employee fringe benefits.

$$\text{Employee fringe benefits} = .30 \times (\text{Total salaries and wages})$$

However, suppose the company's managers are uncertain about this 30 percent estimate. A financial planning model might include the following equation instead.

$$\text{Employee fringe benefits} = p \times (\text{Total salaries and wages})$$

where $0 \leq p \leq 1.0$.

The budget staff can run the financial planning model as many times as desired on a computer, using a different value for p each time. Perhaps the following values would be tried: .29, .295, .30, .305, and .31. Now management can answer the question, What would be the effect on budgeted net income if employee fringe benefit costs increase to 30.5 percent of salaries and wages instead of 30 percent? In a fully developed financial planning model, all of the key estimates and assumptions are expressed as general mathematical relationships. Then the model is run on a computer many times to determine the impact of different combinations of these unknown variables. "What if" questions can be answered about such unknown variables as inflation, interest rates, the value of the dollar, demand, competitors' actions, union demands in forthcoming wage negotiations, and a host of other factors. The widespread availability of economical spreadsheet tools and cloud-based FP&A solutions has made financial planning models a more and more common management tool.

Budget Administration

Learning Objective 9-8

Describe a typical organization's process of budget administration.

In small organizations, the procedures used to gather information and construct a master budget are usually informal. In contrast, larger organizations use a formal process to collect data and prepare the master budget. Such organizations usually designate a **budget director** or **chief budget officer.** This is often the organization's controller. The budget director specifies the process by which budget data will be gathered, collects the information, and prepares the master budget. To communicate budget procedures and deadlines to employees throughout the organization, the budget director often develops and disseminates a **budget manual.** The budget manual states who is responsible for providing various types of information, when the information is required, and what form the information is to take. For example, the budget manual for a manufacturing firm might specify that each regional sales director is to send an estimate of the following year's sales, by product line, to the budget director by September 1. The budget manual also states who should receive each schedule when the master budget is complete.

A **budget committee,** consisting of key senior executives, often is appointed to advise the budget director during the preparation of the budget. The authority to give final approval to the master budget usually belongs to the board of directors, or a board of trustees in many nonprofit organizations. Usually the board has a subcommittee whose task is to examine the proposed budget carefully and recommend approval or any changes deemed necessary. By exercising its authority to make changes in the budget and grant final approval, the board of directors, or trustees, can wield considerable influence on the overall direction the organization takes.

As more and more companies operate globally, the Internet is playing an ever-greater role in the budgeting process. E-budgeting is an increasingly popular, Internet-based budgeting tool that can help streamline and speed up an organization's budgeting process. The *e* in **e-budgeting** stands for both *electronic* and *enterprisewide;* employees throughout an organization, at all levels and around the globe, can submit and retrieve budget information electronically via the Internet. Often part of a larger FP&A system, e-budgeting can occur in two different ways. In the first, a company runs a central FP&A application (software) on the company's computers, and employees companywide use the Internet to access that centralized application (the *enterprise-hosted* model).

"The rise of the cloud is more than just another platform shift that gets geeks excited. It will profoundly change the way people work and companies operate." (9g)
***The Economist* magazine**

In an increasingly popular alternative approach, an FP&A software provider hosts the application on its website and the company's employees use the Internet to access the application and record data there. Unlike the enterprise-hosted model, this *provider-hosted* approach, often called a *cloud* or *SaaS* (software-as-a-service) solution, has the advantages of frequent, centralized updating of the e-budgeting software by the software vendor combined with the outsourcing of the technology issues associated with hosting and running

Management Accounting Practice
Cornell University

BUDGET ADMINISTRATION AT CORNELL UNIVERSITY

Cornell University's annual budget covers the period from July 1 through the following June 30. The budgeting process begins in October, when the deans and senior vice presidents have meetings to discuss the programs the university will conduct during the following budget year. The university's priorities in educational, research, and public service programs are established during these meetings. In early January, the university's budget director, together with other members of the Operating Plans Committee, settles on a set of assumptions to be used during the remainder of the budgeting process. These assumptions include such key forecasts as the next year's inflation rate, interest rates, and tuition levels. Based on these assumptions, the dean of each of Cornell's colleges or professional schools must develop a detailed budget for salaries and general expenses. These detailed budgets are prepared during January and February by the financial staff in each college or professional school. In March, the university president and provost review these budgets with the deans. After any needed revisions have been made, the budgets for the various colleges and professional schools are consolidated by the university controller's staff into a master budget. This budget is presented to the university's board of trustees in May for final approval.

the software. However, it also has one very important disadvantage: the company's proprietary financial data resides outside of the company's walls. This is a serious data security risk, but one that FP&A software providers are increasingly mitigating to the satisfaction of their clients via extensive security procedures.

Managers in organizations using e-budgeting have found that it greatly streamlines the entire budgeting process. In the past, these organizations have compiled their master budgets on hundreds of spreadsheets, which had to be collected and integrated by the corporate controller's office. One result of this cumbersome approach was that a disproportionate amount of time was spent compiling and verifying data from multiple sources. Under e-budgeting, both the submission of budget information and its compilation are accomplished electronically. Thus, e-budgeting is just one more area where the Internet has transformed how the workplace operates in the era of e-business.

International Aspects of Budgeting

As this photo from Japan shows, McDonald's operates throughout the world. Multinational companies face special challenges in preparing their budgets.

© McGraw-Hill Education/Christopher Kerrigan, photographer

As the economies and cultures of countries throughout the world become intertwined, more and more companies are becoming multinational in their operations. Firms with international operations face a variety of additional challenges in preparing their budgets. First, a multinational firm's budget must reflect the translation of foreign currencies into the company's official corporate currency, which is usually determined by the location of the corporate headquaters or the stock exchange on which the company has its primary listing. A U.S.-based company like McDonald's converts the results of worldwide operations into U.S. dollars. Since almost all the world's currencies fluctuate in their values relative to the dollar, this makes budgeting for those translations difficult. Although multinationals have sophisticated financial ways of hedging against such currency fluctuations, the budgeting task is still more challenging.

Second, it is difficult to prepare budgets when inflation is high or unpredictable. Most countries occasionally experience periods of high inflation, and some countries have experienced hyperinflation, sometimes with annual inflation rates well over 100 percent. Predicting such high inflation rates is difficult and further complicates a multinational's budgeting process.

Finally, the economies of all countries fluctuate in terms of consumer demand, availability of skilled labor, laws affecting commerce, and so forth. Companies with offshore operations face the task of anticipating such changing conditions in their budgeting processes.

Behavioral Impact of Budgets

Learning Objective 9-9

Discuss the behavioral issues in budgeting.

One of the underlying themes stressed in this text is the behavioral impact of managerial accounting practices. There is no other area where the behavioral implications are more important than in the budgeting area. A budget affects virtually everyone in an organization: those who prepare the budget, those who use the budget to facilitate decision making, and those who are evaluated using the budget. The human reactions to the budgeting process can have considerable influence on an organization's overall effectiveness.

A great deal of study has been devoted to the behavioral effects of budgets. Here we will barely scratch the surface by briefly considering two issues: budgetary slack and participative budgeting.

Budgetary Slack: Padding the Budget

The information upon which a budget is based comes largely from people throughout an organization. For example, the sales forecast relies on market research and analysis by market research staff but also incorporates the projections of sales personnel. If a territorial sales manager's performance is evaluated on the basis of whether the sales budget for the territory is exceeded, what is the incentive for the sales manager in projecting sales? The incentive is to give a conservative, or cautiously low, sales estimate. The sales manager's performance will look much better in the eyes of top management when a conservative estimate is exceeded than when an ambitious estimate is not met. At least that is the *perception* of many sales managers, and, in the behavioral area, perceptions are what count most.

When a supervisor provides a departmental cost projection for budgetary purposes, there is an incentive to overestimate costs. That way, throughout the year there is always enough money left in the budget to pay for what the department needs. And when the actual cost incurred in the department proves to be less than the inflated cost projection, the supervisor appears to have managed in a cost-effective way.

These illustrations are examples of **padding the budget.** Padding the budget means intentionally underestimating revenue or overestimating costs. The difference between the revenue or cost projection that a person provides and a realistic estimate of the revenue or cost is called **budgetary slack.** For example, if a manager believes the annual utilities cost will be $18,000, but gives a budgetary projection of $20,000, the manager has built $2,000 of slack into the budget.

Why do people pad budgets with budgetary slack? There are three primary reasons. First, people often *perceive* that their performance will look better in their superiors' eyes if they can "beat the budget." Second, budgetary slack often is used to cope with uncertainty. A departmental supervisor may feel confident in her cost projections. However, the supervisor also may feel that some unforeseen event during the budgetary period could result in unanticipated costs. For example, an unexpected machine breakdown could occur. One way of dealing with that unforeseen event is to pad the budget. If nothing goes wrong, the supervisor can beat the cost budget. If some negative event does occur, the supervisor can use the budgetary slack to absorb the impact of the event and still meet the cost budget.

The third reason why cost budgets are padded is that budget cuts are often required when early drafts of the budget show that resources are not adequate to cover all planned spending. Thus, we have a vicious circle. Budgetary projections are padded because they will likely be cut, and they are cut because they are likely to have been padded.

How does an organization solve the problem of budgetary slack? First, it can avoid relying on the budget as a negative evaluation tool. If a departmental supervisor is harassed by the budget director or some other top manager every time a budgetary cost projection is exceeded, the likely behavioral response will be to pad the budget. In contrast, if the supervisor is allowed some managerial discretion to exceed the budget when necessary, there will be less tendency toward budgetary padding. Second, managers can be given incentives not only to achieve budgetary projections but also to *provide accurate projections.* This can be accomplished by asking managers to justify all or some of their projections and by rewarding managers who consistently provide accurate estimates. And finally, across-the-board budget cuts during the budgeting process should be avoided in favor of more targeted approaches that are based on spending justifications.

Participative Budgeting

Most people will perform better and make greater attempts to achieve a goal if they have been consulted in setting the goal. The idea of **participative budgeting** is to involve employees throughout an organization in the budgetary process. Such participation can give employees the feeling that "this is our budget," rather than the all-too-common feeling that "this is the budget you imposed on us."

While participative budgeting can be very effective, it also can have shortcomings. Too much participation and discussion can lead to vacillation and delay. Also, when those involved in the budgeting process disagree in significant and irreconcilable ways, the process of participation can accentuate those differences. Finally, the problem of budget padding can be severe unless incentives for accurate projections are provided.

Focus on Ethics

IS PADDING THE BUDGET UNETHICAL?

A departmental or divisional budget often is used as the basis for evaluating a manager's performance. Actual results are compared with budgeted performance levels, and those who outperform the budget often are rewarded with promotions or salary increases. In many cases, bonuses are tied explicitly to performance relative to a budget. For example, the top-management personnel of a division may receive a bonus if divisional profit exceeds budgeted profit by a certain percentage.

Serious ethical issues can arise in situations where a budget is the basis for rewarding managers. For example, suppose a division's top-management personnel will split a bonus equal to 10 percent of the amount by which actual divisional profit exceeds the budget. This may create an incentive for the divisional budget officer, or other managers supplying data, to pad the divisional profit budget. Such padding would make the budget easier to achieve, thus increasing the chance of a bonus. Alternatively, there may be an incentive to manipulate the actual divisional results in order to maximize management's bonus. For example, year-end sales could be shifted between years to increase reported revenue in a particular year. Budget personnel could have such incentives for either of two reasons: (1) they might share in the bonus or (2) they might feel pressure from the managers who would share in the bonus.

Put yourself in the position of the division controller. Your bonus, and that of your boss, the division vice president, will be determined in part by the division's income in comparison to the budget. When your division has submitted budgets in the past, the corporate management has usually cut your budgeted expenses, thereby increasing the division's budgeted profit. This, of course, makes it more difficult for your division to achieve the budgeted profit. Moreover, it makes it less likely that you and your divisional colleagues will earn a bonus.

Now your boss is pressuring you to pad the expense budget, because "the budgeted expenses will just be cut anyway at the corporate level." Is padding the budget ethical under these circumstances? What do you think? And how could you resolve the situation?

Chapter Summary

LO9-1 Explain the relationship between financial planning and analysis and the master budget. The master budget is not created in isolation but is a key element of a larger system of financial planning and analysis. Use of an integrated system forces communication of operational and financial goals across the organization.

LO9-2 List and explain five purposes of budgeting. The budget is a key tool for planning, control, and decision making in virtually every organization. The five purposes of budgeting systems are: to force planning, to facilitate communication and coordination, to allocate resources, to control profit and operations, and to evaluate performance and provide incentives.

LO9-3 Describe the similarities and differences in the operational budgets prepared by manufacturers, service-industry firms, merchandisers, and nonprofit organizations. The key difference in the operational budgets of manufacturers and merchandisers versus service-industry and nonprofit organizations is that the operational budgets of manufacturers and merchandisers must account for the production or purchase and holding of inventory. In contrast, the budgets of service-industry and nonprofit organizations generally do not have inventories of manufactured or purchased inventories.

LO9-4 Explain the concept of activity-based budgeting and the logic it brings to the budgeting process. Activity-based budgeting (ABB) applies the concepts of activity-based costing (ABC) to the budgeting process. Utilizing ABC information in the budgeting process through ABB provides sound information for budgeting costs, because the underlying ABC information is based explicitly on the relationships among cost drivers, activities, and resources consumed.

LO9-5 Prepare each of the budget schedules that make up the master budget in a nonmanufacturing firm, and that exist in manufacturing budgets as well. As shown in the chapter, the master budget of all firms includes the following key budget schedules: sales; purchases; direct-labor; production overhead; selling, general and administrative expense; cash receipts; cash disbursements; and cash. Also included are the budgeted income statement and the budgeted statement of cash flows.

LO9-6 Prepare the additional master budget schedules required by a manufacturing firm. Several additional budget schedules are needed in a manufacturing firm, primarily due to changing inventory levels. These include budget schedules for production; direct materials; and cost of goods manufactured and sold. Also included is the budgeted balance sheet, which is needed in a nonmanufacturing firm as well.

LO9-7 Discuss the role of assumptions and predictions in budgeting. A master budget is based on many assumptions and predictions of unknown parameters. Some estimates tend to be quite accurate, while other predictions are much more difficult. Financial planning models provide insight into the impact of alternate predictions.

LO9-8 Describe a typical organization's process of budget administration. Most organizations have a well-defined process by which budget data is collected and the budget is prepared. This administrative process often includes a budget director or chief budget officer, a budget manual, and a budgeting committee.

LO9-9 Discuss the behavioral issues in budgeting. A common problem in budgeting is the tendency of people to pad budgets. The resulting budgetary slack makes the budget less useful because the padded budget does not present an accurate picture of expected revenue and expenses. Participative budgeting is the process of allowing employees throughout the organization to have a significant role in developing the budget. Participative budgeting can result in greater commitment to meet the budget by those who participated in the process.

Review Problem on Preparing Master Budget Schedules

SolarTech, Inc., manufactures a special ceramic tile used as a component in residential solar energy systems. Sales are seasonal due to the seasonality in the home-building industry.

- The expected pattern of sales for the next year (20x8) is as follows:

	Quarter				
	1st	2nd	3rd	4th	Year
Sales in units	2,000	6,000	8,000	4,000	20,000

- Each tile sells for $25. All sales are on account, and SolarTech's experience with cash collections is that 60 percent of each quarter's sales are collected during the same quarter as the sale. The remaining 40 percent of sales is collected in the quarter after the sale. SolarTech experiences negligible bad debts, and so this is ignored in the budgeting process. Sales in the fourth quarter of 20x7 are expected to be $100,000 (4,000 units).
- SolarTech desires to have 10 percent of the following quarter's sales needs in finished-goods inventory at the end of each quarter. (On December 31, 20x7, SolarTech expects to have 200 units in inventory.)
- Each tile requires two pounds of raw material. SolarTech desires to have 10 percent of the next quarter's raw material in inventory at the end of each quarter. (On December 31, 20x7, SolarTech expects to have 480 pounds of raw material in inventory.)
- The raw material price is $5 per pound. The company buys its raw material on account and pays 70 percent of the resulting accounts payable during the quarter of the purchase. The remaining 30 percent is paid during the following quarter. (The raw-material purchases in the fourth quarter of 20x7 are expected to be $36,600.)

Required:
Prepare the following budget schedules for 20x8. Include a column for each quarter and for the year.

1. Sales budget (in units and dollars).
2. Cash receipts budget.
3. Production budget.
4. Direct material budget. (*Hint:* The desired ending inventory in the fourth quarter is 480 pounds.)
5. Cash disbursements budget for raw material purchases.

Solution to Review Problem

1. Sales budget for 20x8:

	Quarter				
	1st	**2nd**	**3rd**	**4th**	**Year**
Sales in units	2,000	6,000	8,000	4,000	20,000
Unit sales price	$ 25	$ 25	$ 25	$ 25	$ 25
Total sales revenue	$50,000	$150,000	$200,000	$100,000	$500,000

2. Cash receipts budget for 20x8:

	Quarter				
	1st	**2nd**	**3rd**	**4th**	**Year**
Sales revenue (from sales budget)	$50,000	$150,000	$200,000	$100,000	$500,000
Collections in quarter of sale (60% of revenue)	$30,000	$ 90,000	$120,000	$ 60,000	$300,000
Collections in quarter after sale (40% of prior quarter's revenue)*	40,000*	20,000	60,000	80,000	200,000
Total cash receipts	$70,000	$110,000	$180,000	$140,000	$500,000

*Forty percent of sales revenue from the 4th quarter of 20x7, which was given at $100,000.

3. Production budget for 20x8:

	Quarter				
	1st	**2nd**	**3rd**	**4th**	**Year**
Sales in units (from sales budget)	2,000	6,000	8,000	4,000	20,000
Add desired ending inventory of finished goods*	600	800	400	200†	200
Total units required	2,600	6,800	8,400	4,200	20,200
Less expected beginning inventory of finished goods	200	600	800	400	200
Units to be produced	2,400	6,200	7,600	3,800	20,000

*Ten percent of the next quarter's expected sales.

†Ten percent of the expected sales for the 1st quarter of the next year, 20x9, which is predicted to be 5,000 units.

4. Direct-material budget for 20x8:

	Quarter				
	1st	**2nd**	**3rd**	**4th**	**Year**
Units to be produced (from production budget)	2,400	6,200	7,600	3,800	20,000
Raw material required per unit (pounds)	x 2	x 2	x 2	x 2	x 2
Raw material required for production (pounds)	4,800	12,400	15,200	7,600	40,000
Add desired ending inventory of raw material (pounds)*	1,240	1,520	760	480†	480
Total raw material required	6,040	13,920	15,960	8,080	40,480
Less expected beginning inventory of raw material (pounds)	480‡	1,240	1,520	760	480
Raw material to be purchased (pounds)	5,560	12,680	14,440	7,320	40,000
Cost per pound	x $5	x $5	x $5	x $5	x $5
Total cost of raw material purchases	$27,800	$63,400	$72,200	$36,600	$200,000

*Ten percent of the next quarter's raw material requirements.

†The desired ending raw material inventory for the fourth quarter of 20x8 is given at 480 pounds. However, it can also be computed independently by noting that the expected sales pattern for 20x9 is the same as that for 20x8. Therefore, the first quarter budgets for 20x9 will be the same as those for the first quarter of 20x8. So the desired ending raw-material inventory for the fourth quarter of 20x8 is 480 pounds (10% × 4,800 pounds required for production in the first quarter of 20x9.)

‡Given in problem.

5. Cash disbursements budget for raw material purchases for 20x8:

	Quarter				
	1st	**2nd**	**3rd**	**4th**	**Year**
Cost of raw material purchases (from direct-material budget)	$27,800	$63,400	$72,200	$36,600	$200,000
Cash payments for purchases made during the quarter (70% of current quarter's purchases)	$19,460	$44,380	$50,540	$25,620	$140,000
Cash payments for prior quarter's purchases (30% of prior quarter's purchases)	10,980*	8,340	19,020	21,660	60,000
Total cash payments for raw material purchases	$30,440	$52,720	$69,560	$47,280	$200,000

*Purchases in the fourth quarter of 20x7 were given at $36,600.

Key Terms

For each term's definition refer to the indicated page, or turn to the glossary at the end of the text.

activity-based budgeting (ABB), 368
budget, 361
budget committee, 387
budget director (or chief budget officer), 386
budget manual, 387
budgetary slack, 389
budgeted balance sheet, 378
budgeted financial statements (or pro forma financial statements), 362
budgeted income statement, 377
budgeted schedule of cost of goods manufactured and sold, 383
budgeted statement of cash flows, 377
capital budget, 362
cash budget, 376
cash disbursements budget, 376
cash receipts budget, 374
conversion costs, 372
direct-labor budget, 372
direct-material budget, 381
e-budgeting, 387
financial planning and analysis (FP&A) system, 360
financial planning model, 386
financing budget, 362
master budget (or profit plan), 362
operational budgets, 364
padding the budget, 389
participative budgeting, 389
production budget, 380
production overhead budget, 373
profit plan (or master budget), 362
purchases budget, 371
rolling budget (also revolving or continuous budget), 362
sales budget, 370
sales forecasting, 363
selling, general and administrative expense (SG&A) budget, 374

Review Questions

9–1. Explain how a budget facilitates communication and coordination.

9–2. Use an example to explain how a budget could be used to allocate resources in a university.

9–3. Explain what a *master budget* is, and list five of its parts.

9–4. Draw a flowchart similar to the one in Exhibit 9–1 for a service station. The service station provides automotive maintenance services in addition to selling gasoline and related products.

9–5. Give an example of how general economic trends would affect sales forecasting in the airline industry.

9–6. What is meant by the term *operational budgets?* List three operational budgets that would be prepared by Memorial Sloan Kettering Cancer Center in New York.

9–7. How does activity-based budgeting explain the logic of budgeting?

9–8. How does e-budgeting make use of the Internet?

9–9. Give three examples of how the City of Boston could use a budget for planning purposes.

9–10. Describe the role of a *budget director.*

9–11. What is the purpose of a *budget manual?*

9–12. How can a company's board of directors use the budget to influence the future direction of the firm?

9–13. Discuss the importance of predictions and assumptions in the budgeting process.

9–14. Define the term *budgetary slack,* and briefly describe a problem it can cause.

9–15. How can an organization help to reduce the problems caused by budgetary slack?

9–16. Why is participative budgeting often an effective management tool?

9–17. Discuss this comment by a small-town bank president: "Budgeting is a waste of time. I've been running this business for 40 years. I don't need to plan."

9–18. List the steps you would go through in developing a budget to meet your college expenses.

9–19. Briefly describe three issues that create special challenges for multinational firms in preparing their budgets.

9–20. What are the primary differences in budgeting between manufacturing and nonmanufacturing firms?

Exercises

All applicable Exercises are available in Connect. connect

Exercise 9–21
Missing Amounts; Various Types of Budgets
(LO 9-3, 9-5, 9-6)

Fill in the missing amounts in the following schedules.

	April	May	June
1. Sales*	$80,000	$60,000	$?
Cash receipts:			
From cash sales	$?	$?	$45,000
From sales on account†	?	34,000	?
Total cash receipts	$?	$?	$?

2. Accounts payable, 12/31/x0	300,000 *euros*
Purchase of goods and services on account during 20x1	1,200,000
Payments of accounts payable during 20x1	?
Accounts payable, 12/31/x1	400,000
3. Accounts receivable, 12/31/x0	340,000 *yen*‡
Sales on account during 20x1	900,000
Collections of accounts receivable during 20x1	780,000
Accounts receivable, 12/31/x1	?
4. Accumulated depreciation, 12/31/x0	$ 810,000
Depreciation expense during 20x1	150,000
Accumulated depreciation, 12/31/x1	?
5. Retained earnings, 12/31/x0	$2,050,000
Net income for 20x1	400,000
Dividends paid in 20x1	–0–
Retained earnings, 12/31/x1	?

*Half of each month's sales are on account. March sales amounted to $60,000.
†60% of credit sales is collected in the month of sale; 40% is collected in the following month.
‡Yen is the Japanese national currency.

Exercise 9–22
City or State Budget; Use of Internet
(LO 9-2, 9-3)

Choose a city or state in the United States (or a Canadian city or province), and use the Internet to explore the annual budget of the governmental unit you selected. For example, you could check out the budget for Houston, Texas, at www.houstontx.gov/budget.

Required: List three items in the budget that you found surprising or particularly interesting, and explain why.

Exercise 9–23
Budgeting Production and Direct-Material Purchases
(LO 9-3, 9-6)

Bodin Company budgets on an annual basis. The following beginning and ending inventory levels (in units) are plannned for the year 20x1. Two units of raw material are required to produce each unit of finished product.

	January 1	December 31
Raw material	35,000	45,000
Work in process	12,000	12,000
Finished goods	80,000	50,000

Required:

1. If Bodin Company plans to sell 480,000 units during the year, compute the number of units the firm would have to manufacture during the year.
2. If 500,000 finished units were to be manufactured by Bodin Company during the year, determine the amount of raw material to be purchased.

(CMA, adapted)

Exercise 9–24
Cash Collections
(LO 9-3, 9-5)

Coyote Loco, Inc., a distributor of salsa, has the following historical collection pattern for its credit sales.

70 percent collected in the month of sale.
15 percent collected in the first month after sale.
10 percent collected in the second month after sale.
4 percent collected in the third month after sale.
1 percent uncollectible.

The sales on account have been budgeted for the last seven months as follows:

June	$ 49,000
July	60,000
August	70,000
September	80,000
October	90,000
November	100,000
December	85,000

Required:

1. Compute the estimated total cash collections during October from credit sales.
2. Compute the estimated total cash collections during the fourth quarter from sales made on account during the fourth quarter.
3. ***Build a spreadsheet:*** Construct an Excel spreadsheet to solve both of the preceding requirements. Show how the solution will change if the following information changes: sales in June and July were $50,000 and $65,000, respectively.

(CMA, adapted)

Exercise 9–25
Budgeting Production and Raw-Material Purchases
(LO 9-3, 9-6)

Greener Grass Fertilizer Company plans to sell 200,000 units of finished product in July and anticipates a growth rate in sales of 5 percent per month. The desired monthly ending inventory in units of finished product is 80 percent of the next month's estimated sales. There are 160,000 finished units in inventory on June 30. Each unit of finished product requires four pounds of raw material at a cost of $1.15 per pound. There are 700,000 pounds of raw material in inventory on June 30.

Required:

1. Compute the company's total required production in units of finished product for the entire three-month period ending September 30.
2. Independent of your answer to requirement (1), assume the company plans to produce 600,000 units of finished product in the three-month period ending September 30, and to have raw-material inventory on hand at the end of the three-month period equal to 25 percent of the use in that period. Compute the total estimated cost of raw-material purchases for the entire three-month period ending September 30.

(CMA, adapted)

Exercise 9–26
Cash Budgeting
(LO 9-3, 9-5)

The following information is from Tejas WindowTint's financial records.

Month	Sales	Purchases
April	$72,000	$42,000
May	66,000	48,000
June	60,000	36,000
July	78,000	54,000

Collections from customers are normally 70 percent in the month of sale, 20 percent in the month following the sale, and 9 percent in the second month following the sale. The balance is expected to be uncollectible. All purchases are on account. Management takes full advantage of the 2 percent discount allowed on purchases paid for by the tenth of the following month. Purchases for August are budgeted at $60,000, and sales for August are forecasted at $66,000. Cash disbursements for expenses are expected to be $14,400 for the month of August. The company's cash balance on August 1 was $22,000.

Required: Prepare the following schedules.

1. Expected cash collections during August.
2. Expected cash disbursements during August.
3. Expected cash balance on August 31.

Exercise 9–27
Budgetary Slack; Bank
(LO 9-9)

Tanya Williams is the new accounts manager at East Bank of Mississippi. She has just been asked to project how many new bank accounts she will generate during 20x2. The economy of the county in which the bank operates has been growing, and the bank has experienced a 10 percent increase in its number of bank accounts over each of the past five years. In 20x1, the bank had 10,000 accounts.

The new accounts manager is paid a salary plus a bonus of $15 for every new account she generates above the budgeted amount. Thus, if the annual budget calls for 500 new accounts, and 540 new accounts are obtained, Williams's bonus will be $600 (40 × $15).

Williams believes the economy of the county will continue to grow at the same rate in 20x2 as it has in recent years. She has decided to submit a budgetary projection of 700 new accounts for 20x2.

Required: Your consulting firm has been hired by the bank president to make recommendations for improving its operations. Write a memorandum to the president defining and explaining the negative consequences of budgetary slack. Also discuss the bank's bonus system for the new accounts manager and how the bonus program tends to encourage budgetary slack.

Exercise 9–28
Using Budgets for Financial Planning
(LO 9-2, 9-5, 9-7)

Sound Investments, Inc. is a large retailer of stereo equipment. The controller is about to prepare the budget for the first quarter of 20x2. Past experience has indicated that 75 percent of the store's sales are cash sales. The collection experience for the sales on account is as follows:

80 percent during month of sale
15 percent during month following sale
5 percent uncollectible

The total sales for December 20x1 are expected to be $190,000. The controller feels that sales in January 20x2 could range from $100,000 to $160,000.

Required:

1. Demonstrate how financial planning can be used to project cash receipts in January of 20x2 for three different levels of January sales. Use the following columnar format.

	Total Sales in January 20x2		
	$100,000	**$130,000**	**$160,000**
Cash receipts in January 20x2:			
From December sales on account	$	$	$
From January cash sales			
From January sales on account			
Total cash receipts	$	$	$

2. How could the controller of Sound Investments, Inc. use this financial planning approach to help in planning operations for January?

Exercise 9–29
Budgeted Financial Statements; Retailer
(LO 9-3, 9-5)

Handy Hardware is a retail hardware store. Information about the store's operations follows.

- November 20x1 sales amounted to $200,000.
- Sales are budgeted at $220,000 for December 20x1 and $200,000 for January 20x2.
- Collections are expected to be 60 percent in the month of sale and 38 percent in the month following the sale. Two percent of sales are expected to be uncollectible. Bad debts expense is recognized monthly.
- The store's gross margin is 25 percent of its sales revenue.

- A total of 80 percent of the merchandise for resale is purchased in the month prior to the month of sale, and 20 percent is purchased in the month of sale. Payment for merchandise is made in the month following the purchase.
- Other monthly expenses paid in cash amount to $22,600.
- Annual depreciation is $216,000.

The company's balance sheet as of November 30, 20x1, is as follows:

HANDY HARDWARE, INC.
Balance Sheet
November 30, 20x1

Assets	
Cash	$ 22,000
Accounts receivable (net of $3,500 allowance for uncollectible accounts)	76,000
Inventory	140,000
Property, plant, and equipment (net of $590,000 accumulated depreciation)	862,000
Total assets	$1,100,000
Liabilities and Stockholders' Equity	
Accounts payable	$ 162,000
Common stock	795,000
Retained earnings	143,000
Total liabilities and stockholders' equity	$1,100,000

Required: Compute the following amounts.

1. The budgeted cash collections for December 20x1.
2. The budgeted income (loss) before income taxes for December 20x1.
3. The projected balance in accounts payable on December 31, 20x1.

(CMA, adapted)

Exercise 9–30
Professional Services Budget; Dental Practice; Activity-Based Budgeting
(LO 9-3, 9-4, 9-5)

Metropolitan Dental Associates is a large dental practice in Chicago. The firm's controller is preparing the budget for the next year. The controller projects a total of 48,000 office visits, to be evenly distributed throughout the year. Eighty percent of the visits will be half-hour appointments, and the remainder will be one-hour visits. The average rates for professional dental services are $40 for half-hour appointments and $70 for one-hour office visits. Ninety percent of each month's professional service revenue is collected during the month when services are rendered, and the remainder is collected the month following service. Uncollectible billings are negligible. Metropolitan's dental associates earn $60 per hour.

Metropolitan uses activity-based budgeting to budget office overhead and administrative expenses. Two cost drivers are used: office visits and direct professional labor. The cost-driver rates are as follows:

Patient registration and records	$2.00 per office visit (of any length)
All other overhead and administrative expenses	$5.00 per direct professional labor hour

Required: Prepare the following budget schedules.

1. Direct-professional-labor budget for the month of June.
2. Cash collections during June for professional services rendered during May and June.
3. Overhead and administrative expense budget for the month of June.
4. *Build a spreadsheet:* Construct an Excel spreadsheet to solve all of the preceding requirements. Show how the solution will change if the following information changes: a total of 54,000 office visits are expected for the year and 70 percent of the office visits are half-hour appointments.

Problems

Problem 9–31
Production and Direct-Labor Budgets; Activity-Based Overhead Budget
(LO 9-3, 9-4, 9-5, 9-6)

1. Total direct-labor cost for the quarter: $470,155

Spiffy Shades Corporation manufactures artistic frames for sunglasses. Talia Demarest, controller, is responsible for preparing the company's master budget. In compiling the budget data for 20x1, Demarest has learned that new automated production equipment will be installed on March 1. This will reduce the direct labor per frame from 1 hour to .75 hour.

Labor-related costs include pension contributions of $.50 per hour, workers' compensation insurance of $.20 per hour, employee medical insurance of $.80 per hour, and employer contributions to Social Security equal to 7 percent of direct-labor wages. The cost of employee benefits paid by the company on its employees is treated as a direct-labor cost. Spiffy Shades Corporation has a labor contract that calls for a wage increase to $18.00 per hour on April 1, 20x1. Management expects to have 16,000 frames on hand at December 31, 20x0, and has a policy of carrying an end-of-month inventory of 100 percent of the following month's sales plus 50 percent of the second following month's sales.

These and other data compiled by Demarest are summarized in the following table.

	January	February	March	April	May
Direct-labor hours per unit	1.0	1.0	.75	.75	.75
Wage per direct-labor hour	$16.00	$16.00	$16.00	$18.00	$18.00
Estimated unit sales	10,000	12,000	8,000	9,000	9,000
Sales price per unit	$50.00	$47.50	$47.50	$47.50	$47.50
Production overhead:					
Shipping and handling (per unit sold)	$2.00	$2.00	$2.00	$2.00	$2.00
Purchasing, material handling, and inspection (per unit produced)	$3.00	$3.00	$3.00	$3.00	$3.00
Other production overhead (per direct-labor hour)	$7.00	$7.00	$7.00	$7.00	$7.00

Required:

1. Prepare a production budget and a direct-labor budget for Spiffy Shades Corporation by month and for the first quarter of 20x1. Both budgets may be combined in one schedule. The direct-labor budget should include direct-labor hours and show the detail for each direct-labor cost category.
2. For each item used in the firm's production budget and direct-labor budget, identify the other components of the master budget (except for financial statement budgets) that also would, directly or indirectly, use these data.
3. Prepare a production overhead budget for each month and for the first quarter.

(CMA, adapted)

Problem 9–32
Revenue and Labor Budgeting for a University; Budget Linkages
(LO 9-3, 9-5, 9-7, 9-8)

2. Faculty needed: 672

Western State University (WSU) is preparing its master budget for the upcoming academic year. Currently, 8,000 students are enrolled on campus; however, the admissions office is forecasting a 5 percent growth in the student body despite a tuition hike to $75 per credit hour. The following additional information has been gathered from an examination of university records and conversations with university officials:

- WSU is planning to award 120 tuition-free scholarships.
- The average class has 25 students, and the typical student takes 15 credit hours each semester. Each class is three credit hours.
- WSU's faculty members are evaluated on the basis of teaching, research, and university and community service. Each faculty member teaches five classes during the academic year.

Required:

1. Prepare a tuition revenue budget for the upcoming academic year.
2. Determine the number of faculty members needed to cover classes.
3. Assume there is a shortage of full-time faculty members. List at least five actions that WSU might take to accommodate the growing student body.

4. You have been requested by the university's administrative vice president (AVP) to construct budgets for other areas of operation (e.g., the library, grounds, dormitories, and maintenance). The AVP noted: "The most important resource of the university is its faculty. Now that you know the number of faculty needed, you can prepare the other budgets. Faculty members are indeed the key driver—without them we don't operate." Does the administrative vice president really understand the linkages within the budgeting process? Explain.

Problem 9–33
Cash budgeting
(LO 9-3, 9-5)

2. Total cash disbursements, February: $121,000

Mary and Kay, Inc., a distributor of cosmetics throughout Florida, is in the process of assembling a cash budget for the first quarter of 20x1. The following information has been extracted from the company's accounting records:

- All sales are on account. Sixty percent of customer accounts are collected in the month of sale; 35 percent are collected in the following month. Uncollectibles amounting to 5 percent of sales are anticipated, and management believes that only 20 percent of the accounts outstanding on December 31, 20x0, will be recovered and that the recovery will be in January 20x1.
- Seventy percent of the merchandise purchases are paid for in the month of purchase; the remaining 30 percent are paid for in the month after acquisition.
- The December 31, 20x0, balance sheet disclosed the following selected figures: cash, $20,000; accounts receivable, $55,000; and accounts payable, $22,000.
- Mary and Kay, Inc. maintains a $20,000 minimum cash balance at all times. Financing is available (and retired) in $1,000 multiples at an 8 percent interest rate, with borrowings taking place at the beginning of the month and repayments occurring at the end of the month. Interest is paid at the time of repaying principal and computed on the portion of principal repaid at that time.
- Additional data:

	January	February	March
Sales revenue	$150,000	$180,000	$185,000
Merchandise purchases	90,000	100,000	140,000
Cash operating costs	31,000	24,000	45,000
Proceeds from sale of equipment	—	—	5,000

Required:

1. Prepare a schedule that discloses the firm's total cash collections for January through March.
2. Prepare a schedule that discloses the firm's total cash disbursements for January through March.
3. Prepare a schedule that summarizes the firm's financing cash flows for January through March. The schedule should present the following information in the order cited: Beginning cash balance, total receipts (from requirement (1)), total payments (from requirement (2)), the cash excess (deficiency) before financing, borrowing needed to maintain minimum balance, loan principal repaid, loan interest paid, and ending cash balance.

Problem 9–34
Relationships of the Master-Budget Components
(LO 9-3, 9-5, 9-6)

5. December 31 inventory: 1,900 units

Badlands, Inc. manufactures a household fan that sells for $40 per unit. All sales are on account, with 40 percent of sales collected in the month of sale and 60 percent collected in the following month. The data that follow were extracted from the company's accounting records.

- Badlands maintains a minimum cash balance of $30,000. Total payments in January 20x1 are budgeted at $390,000.
- A schedule of cash collections for January and February of 20x1 revealed the following receipts for the period:

	Cash Receipts	
	January	February
From December 31 accounts receivable	$216,000	
From January sales	152,000	$228,000
From February sales		156,800

- March 20x1 sales are expected to total 10,000 units.
- Finished-goods inventories are maintained at 20 percent of the following month's sales.
- The December 31, 20x0, balance sheet revealed the following selected figures: cash, $45,000; accounts receivable, $216,000; and finished goods, $44,700.

Required:

1. Determine the number of units that Badlands sold in December 20x0.
2. Compute the sales revenue for March 20x1.
3. Compute the total sales revenue to be reported on Badlands' budgeted income statement for the first quarter of 20x1.
4. Determine the accounts receivable balance to be reported on the March 31, 20x1, budgeted balance sheet.
5. Calculate the number of units in the December 31, 20x0, finished-goods inventory.
6. Calculate the number of units of finished goods to be manufactured in January 20x1.
7. Calculate the financing required in January, if any, to maintain the firm's minimum cash balance.

Problem 9–35
Cash Budget; Wholesaler
(LO 9-2, 9-3, 9-5)

1. Total cash disbursements, April: $9,785,000

Ending cash balance, June: $2,605,000

Alpha-Tech, a rapidly growing distributor of electronic components, is formulating its plans for 20x5. Carol Jones, the firm's marketing director, has completed the following sales forecast.

ALPHA-TECH
20x5 Forecasted Sales
(in thousands)

Month	Sales	Month	Sales
January	$ 9,000	July	$15,000
February	10,000	August	15,000
March	9,000	September	16,000
April	11,500	October	16,000
May	12,500	November	15,000
June	14,000	December	17,000

Phillip Smith, an accountant in the Planning and Budgeting Department, is responsible for preparing the cash flow projection. The following information will be used in preparing the cash flow projection.

- Alpha-Tech's excellent record in accounts receivable collection is expected to continue. Sixty percent of billings are collected the month after the sale, and the remaining 40 percent two months after.
- The purchase of electronic components is Alpha-Tech's largest expenditure, and each month's cost of goods sold is estimated to be 40 percent of sales. Seventy percent of the parts are received by Alpha-Tech one month prior to sale, and 30 percent are received during the month of sale.
- Historically, 75 percent of accounts payable has been paid one month after receipt of the purchased components, and the remaining 25 percent has been paid two months after receipt.
- Hourly wages and fringe benefits, estimated to be 30 percent of the current month's sales, are paid in the month incurred.
- General and administrative expenses are projected to be $15,620,000 for the year. The breakdown of these expenses is presented in the following schedule. All cash expenditures are paid uniformly throughout the year, except the property taxes, which are paid in four equal installments at the end of each quarter.

20x5 Forecasted General and Administrative Costs
(in thousands)

Salaries and fringe benefits	$ 3,200
Promotion	3,800
Property taxes	1,360
Insurance	2,000
Utilities	1,800
Depreciation	3,460
Total	$15,620

- Income-tax payments are made at the beginning of each calendar quarter based on the income of the prior quarter. Alpha-Tech is subject to an income-tax rate of 40 percent. Alpha-Tech's operating income for the first quarter of 20x5 is projected to be $3,200,000. The company pays 100 percent of the estimated tax payment.
- Alpha-Tech maintains a minimum cash balance of $500,000. If the cash balance is less than $500,000 at the end of each month, the company borrows amounts necessary to maintain this balance. All amounts borrowed are repaid out of the subsequent positive cash flow. The projected April 1, 20x5, opening balance is $500,000.
- Alpha-Tech has no short-term debt as of April 1, 20x5.
- Alpha-Tech uses a calendar year for both financial reporting and tax purposes.

Required:

1. Prepare a cash budget for Alpha-Tech by month for the second quarter of 20x5. For simplicity, ignore any interest expense associated with borrowing.
2. Discuss why cash budgeting is important for Alpha-Tech.

(CMA, adapted)

Problem 9–36
Ethics; Budgetary Pressure; Management Bonuses; Budgetary Constraints
(LO 9-1, 9-7, 9-8, 9-9)

Tulsa Chemical Company (TCC) produces and distributes industrial chemicals, TCC's earnings increased sharply in 20x1, and bonuses were paid to the management staff for the first time in several years. Bonuses are based in part on the amount by which reported income exceeds budgeted income.

Jim Kern, vice president of finance, was pleased with TCC's 20x1 earnings and thought that the pressure to show financial results would ease. However, Ellen North, TCC's president, told Kern that she saw no reason why the 20x2 bonuses should not be double those of 20x1. As a result, Kern felt pressure to increase reported income in order to exceed budgeted income by an even greater amount. This would assure increased bonuses.

Kern met with Bill Keller of Pristeel, Inc., a primary vendor of TCC's manufacturing supplies and equipment. Kern and Keller have been close business contacts for many years. Kern asked Keller to identify all of TCC's purchases of perishable supplies as equipment on Pristeel's sales invoices. The reason Kern gave for his request was that TCC's president had imposed stringent budget constraints on operating expenses but not on capital expenditures. Kern planned to capitalize the purchase of perishable supplies, and include them with the Equipment account on the balance sheet. In this way Kern could defer the expense recognition for these items to a later year. This procedure would increase reported earnings, leading to increased bonuses. Keller agreed to do as Kern had asked.

While analyzing the second quarter financial statements, Gary Wood, TCC's controller, noticed a large decrease in supplies expense from one year ago. Wood reviewed the Supplies Expense account and noticed that only equipment and no supplies had been purchased from Pristeel, a major source for supplies. Wood, who reports to Kern, immediately brought this to Kern's attention.

Kern told Wood of North's high expectations and of the arrangement made with Keller of Pristeel. Wood told Kern that his action was an improper accounting treatment for the supplies purchased from Pristeel. Wood requested that he be allowed to correct the accounts and urged that the arrangement with Pristeel be discontinued. Kern refused the request and told Wood not to become involved in the arrangement with Pristeel.

After clarifying the situation in a confidential discussion with an objective and qualified peer within TCC, Wood arranged to meet with North, TCC's president. At the meeting, Wood disclosed the arrangement Kern had made with Pristeel.

Required:

1. Explain why the use of alternative accounting methods to manipulate reported earnings is unethical.
2. Is Gary Wood, TCC's controller, correct in saying that the supplies purchased from Pristeel, Inc. were accounted for improperly? Explain your answer.
3. Assuming that Jim Kern's arrangement with Pristeel, Inc. was in violation of the standards of ethical professional practice for managerial accountants, discuss whether the actions of Wood were appropriate or inappropriate. (The guidelines for Resolution of Ethical Conflict are given in Chapter 1.)

(CMA, adapted)

Problem 9–37
Completion of Budget Schedules
(LO 9-3, 9-5, 9-6)

2. Planned production, June: 15,000 sets
4. Planned direct-labor cost, May: $378,000

Scholastic Furniture, Inc. manufactures a variety of desks, chairs, tables, and shelf units that are sold to public school systems throughout the Midwest. The controller of the company's Desk Division is currently preparing a budget for the second quarter of the year. The following sales forecast has been made by the division's sales manager.

April	10,000 desk-and-chair sets
May	12,000 desk-and-chair sets
June	15,000 desk-and-chair sets

Each desk-and-chair set requires 10 board feet of pine planks and 1.5 hours of direct labor. Each set sells for $50. Pine planks cost $.50 per board foot, and the division ends each month with enough wood to cover 10 percent of the next month's production requirements. The division incurs a cost of $20 per hour for direct-labor wages and fringe benefits. The division ends each month with enough finished-goods inventory to cover 20 percent of the next month's sales.

Required: Complete the following budget schedules.

1. Sales budget:

	April	May	June
Sales (in sets)	10,000		
Sales price per set	×$50		
Sales revenue	$500,000		

2. Production budget (in sets):

	April	May	June
Sales	10,000		
Add: Desired ending inventory	2,400		3,000
Total requirements	12,400		
Less: Projected beginning inventory	2,000		
Planned production	10,400		

3. Raw-material purchases:

	April	May	June
Planned production (sets)	10,400		
Raw material required per set (board feet)	×10		
Raw material required for production (board feet)	104,000		
Add: Desired ending inventory of raw material, in board feet (10% of next month's requirement)	12,600		16,000
Total requirements	116,600		
Less: Projected beginning inventory of raw material, in board feet (10% of current month's requirement)	10,400		
Planned purchases of raw material (board feet)	106,200		
Cost per board foot	×$.50		
Planned purchases of raw material (dollars)	$53,100		

4. Direct-labor budget:

	April	May	June
Planned production (sets)	10,400		
Direct-labor hours per set	×1.5		
Direct-labor hours required	15,600		
Cost per hour	×$20		
Planned direct-labor cost	$312,000		

5. *Build a spreadsheet:* Construct an Excel spreadsheet to solve all of the preceding requirements. Show how the solution will change if the following information changes: each set sells for $55 and the direct-labor cost per hour is $21.

Problem 9–38
Production and Materials Budgets
(LO 9-3, 9-6, 9-7)

2. Conversion cost budget: $245,040
4. Increase in cost of raw material: $100,820

Empire Chemical Company produces three products using three different continuous processes. The products are Yarex, Darol, and Norex. Projected sales in gallons for the three products for the years 20x2 and 20x3 are as follows:

	20x2	20x3
Yarex	60,000	65,000
Darol	40,000	35,000
Norex	25,000	30,000

- Inventories are planned for each product so that the projected finished-goods inventory at the beginning of each year is equal to 8 percent of that year's projected sales.
- Because of the continuous nature of Empire's processes, work-in-process inventory for each of the products remains constant throughout the year.
- The raw-material requirements of the three products are shown in the following chart.

Raw Material	Units	Unit Price	Yarex	Darol	Norex
Gamma	pounds	$ 8.00	.2	.4	0
Murad	pounds	6.00	.4	0	.5
Islin	gallons	5.00	1.0	.7	.5
Tarden	gallons	10.00	0	.3	.5

- Raw-material inventories are planned so that each raw material's projected inventory at the beginning of a year is equal to 10 percent of the previous year's usage of that raw material.

The conversion requirements in hours per gallon for the three products are Yarex, .07 hour; Darol, .10 hour; and Norex, .16 hour. The conversion cost of $20 per hour is considered 100 percent variable.

Required:

1. Determine Empire Chemical Company's production budget (in gallons) for the three products for 20x2.
2. Determine Empire Chemical Company's conversion cost budget for 20x2.
3. Assuming the 20x1 usage of Islin is 100,000 gallons, determine the company's raw-material purchases budget (in dollars) for Islin for 20x2.
4. Assume that for 20x2 production, Empire Chemical Company could replace the raw material Islin with the raw material Philin. The usage of Philin would be the same as the usage of Islin. However, Philin would cost 20 percent more than Islin and would cut production times on all three products by 10 percent. Determine whether management should use Philin or Islin for the 20x2 production, supporting your decision with appropriate calculations. For this requirement, ignore any impact of beginning and ending inventory balances.

(CMA, adapted)

Problem 9–39
Sales, Production, and Purchases Budgets; Activity-Based Overhead Budget
(LO 9-3, 9-4, 9-5, 9-6)

2. Production required (units), heavy coils: 41,000
6. Production overhead budget for 20x0, total production overhead: $1,464,250

Vista Electronics, Inc. manufactures two different types of coils used in electric motors. In the fall of the current year, Erica Becker, the controller, compiled the following data.

- Sales forecast for 20x0 (all units to be shipped in 20x0):

Product	Units	Price
Light coil	60,000	$120
Heavy coil	40,000	170

- Raw-material prices and inventory levels:

Raw Material	Expected Inventories, January 1, 20x0	Desired Inventories, December 31, 20x0	Anticipated Purchase Price
Sheet metal	32,000 lb.	36,000 lb.	$8
Copper wire	29,000 lb.	32,000 lb.	5
Platforms	6,000 units	7,000 units	3

- Use of raw material:

Raw Material	Amount Used per Unit	
	Light Coil	Heavy Coil
Sheet metal	4 lb.	5 lb.
Copper wire	2 lb.	3 lb.
Platforms		1 unit

- Direct-labor requirements and rates:

Product	Hours per Unit	Rate per Hour
Light coil	2	$15
Heavy coil	3	20

- Finished-goods inventories (in units):

Product	Expected January 1, 20x0	Desired December 31, 20x0
Light coil	20,000	25,000
Heavy coil	8,000	9,000

- Production overhead:

Overhead Cost Item	Activity-Based Budget Rate
Purchasing and material handling	$.25 per pound of sheet metal and copper wire purchased
Depreciation, utilities, and inspection	$4.00 per coil produced (either type)
Shipping	$1.00 per coil shipped (either type)
General production overhead	$3.00 per direct-labor hour

Required: Prepare the following budgets for 20x0.

1. Sales budget (in dollars).
2. Production budget (in units).
3. Raw-material purchases budget (in quantities).
4. Raw-material purchases budget (in dollars).
5. Direct-labor budget (in dollars).
6. Production-overhead budget (in dollars).

(CPA, adapted)

Problem 9–40
Interrelationships Between Components of Master Budget
(LO 9-5, 9-6, 9-8)

United Security Systems, Inc. (USSI) manufactures and sells security systems. The company started by installing photoelectric security systems in offices and has expanded into the private-home market. USSI has a basic security system that has been developed into three standard products, each of which can be adapted to meet the specific needs of customers. The manufacturing operation is moderate in size, as the bulk of the component manufacturing is completed by independent contractors. The security systems are approximately 85 percent complete when received from contractors and require only final assembly in the USSI plant. Each product passes through at least one of three assembly operations.

USSI operates in a rapidly growing community. There is evidence that a great deal of new commercial construction will take place in the near future, and management has decided to pursue this new market. In order to be competitive, the firm will have to expand its operations.

In view of the expected increase in business, Sandra Feldman, the controller, believes that USSI should implement a complete budgeting system. Feldman has decided to make a formal presentation to the company's president explaining the benefits of a budgeting system and outlining the budget schedules and reports that would be necessary.

Required:

1. Explain the benefits that USSI would gain from implementing a budgeting system.
2. If Sandra Feldman develops a master budget:
   a. Identify, in order, the schedules that will have to be prepared.
   b. Identify the subsequent schedules that would be based on the schedules identified above. Use the following format for your answer.

Schedule	Subsequent Schedule

(CMA, adapted)

Problem 9–41
Revised Operating Budget; Consulting Firm
(LO 9-2, 9-5, 9-7)

1. Operating income: $179,600
Total compensation, management consulting: $245,000

Toronto Business Associates, a division of Maple Leaf Services Corporation, offers management and computer consulting services to clients throughout Canada and the northwestern United States. The division specializes in website development and other Internet applications. The corporate management at Maple Leaf Services is pleased with the performance of Toronto Business Associates for the first nine months of the current year and has recommended that the division manager, Richard Howell, submit a revised forecast for the remaining quarter, as the division has exceeded the annual plan year-to-date by 20 percent of operating income. An unexpected increase in billed hour volume over the original plan is the main reason for this increase in income. The original operating budget for the first three quarters for Toronto Business Associates follows.

TORONTO BUSINESS ASSOCIATES
20x1 Operating Budget

	1st Quarter	2nd Quarter	3rd Quarter	Total for First Three Quarters
Revenue:				
Consulting fees:				
Computer system consulting	$421,875	$421,875	$421,875	$1,265,625
Management consulting	315,000	315,000	315,000	945,000
Total consulting fees	$736,875	$736,875	$736,875	$2,210,625
Other revenue	10,000	10,000	10,000	30,000
Total revenue	$746,875	$746,875	$746,875	$2,240,625
Expenses:				
Consultant salary expenses	$386,750	$386,750	$386,750	$1,160,250
Travel and related expenses	45,625	45,625	45,625	136,875
General and administrative expenses	100,000	100,000	100,000	300,000
Depreciation expense	40,000	40,000	40,000	120,000
Corporate expense allocation	50,000	50,000	50,000	150,000
Total expenses	$622,375	$622,375	$622,375	$1,867,125
Operating income	$124,500	$124,500	$124,500	$ 373,500

Howell will reflect the following information in his revised forecast for the fourth quarter.

- Toronto Business Associates currently has 25 consultants on staff: 10 for management consulting and 15 for computer systems consulting. Three additional management consultants have been hired to start work at the beginning of the fourth quarter in order to meet the increased client demand.
- The hourly billing rate for consulting revenue will remain at $90 per hour for each management consultant and $75 per hour for each computer consultant. However, due to the favorable increase in billing hour volume when compared to the plan, the hours for each consultant will be increased by 50 hours per quarter.

- The budgeted annual salaries and actual annual salaries, paid monthly, are the same: $50,000 for a management consultant and $46,000 for a computer consultant. Corporate management has approved a merit increase of 10 percent at the beginning of the fourth quarter for all 25 existing consultants, while the new consultants will be compensated at the planned rate.
- The planned salary expense includes a provision for employee fringe benefits amounting to 30 percent of the annual salaries. However, the improvement of some corporatewide employee programs will increase the fringe benefits to 40 percent.
- The original plan assumes a fixed hourly rate for travel and other related expenses for each billing hour of consulting. These are expenses that are not reimbursed by the client, and the previously determined hourly rate has proven to be adequate to cover these costs.
- Other revenue is derived from temporary rentals and interest income and remains unchanged for the fourth quarter.
- General and administrative expenses have been favorable at 7 percent below the plan; this 7 percent savings on fourth quarter expenses will be reflected in the revised plan.
- Depreciation of office equipment and personal computers will stay constant at the projected straight-line rate.
- Due to the favorable experience for the first three quarters and the division's increased ability to absorb costs, the corporate management at Maple Leaf Services has increased the corporate expense allocation by 50 percent.

Required:

1. Prepare a revised operating budget for the fourth quarter for Toronto Business Associates that Richard Howell will present to corporate management.
2. Discuss the reasons why an organization would prepare a revised operating budget.

(CMA, adapted)

Problem 9–42
Preparation of Master Budget
(LO 9-3, 9-4, 9-5)

1. Total sales revenue: $1,100,000
3. Cost of purchases (paperboard): $97,000
5. Total overhead: $148,500
7. Predetermined overhead rate: $40 per hour

FreshPak Corporation manufactures two types of cardboard boxes used in shipping canned food, fruit, and vegetables. The canned food box (type C) and the perishable food box (type P) have the following material and labor requirements.

	Type of Box	
	C	P
Direct material required per 100 boxes:		
Paperboard ($.20 per pound)	30 pounds	70 pounds
Corrugating medium ($.10 per pound)	20 pounds	30 pounds
Direct labor required per 100 boxes ($12.00 per hour)	.25 hour	.50 hour

The following production-overhead costs are anticipated for the next year. The predetermined overhead rate is based on a production volume of 495,000 units for each type of box. Production overhead is applied on the basis of direct-labor hours.

Indirect material	$10,500
Indirect labor	50,000
Utilities	25,000
Property taxes	18,000
Insurance	16,000
Depreciation	29,000
Total	$148,500

The following selling and administrative expenses are anticipated for the next year.

Salaries and fringe benefits of sales personnel	$ 75,000
Advertising	15,000
Management salaries and fringe benefits	90,000
Clerical wages and fringe benefits	26,000
Miscellaneous administrative expenses	4,000
Total	$210,000

The sales forecast for the next year is as follows:

	Sales Volume	Sales Price
Box type C	500,000 boxes	$ 90.00 per hundred boxes
Box type P	500,000 boxes	130.00 per hundred boxes

The following inventory information is available for the next year. The unit production costs for each product are expected to be the same this year and next year.

	Expected Inventory January 1	Desired Ending Inventory December 31
Finished goods:		
Box type C	10,000 boxes	5,000 boxes
Box type P	20,000 boxes	15,000 boxes
Raw material:		
Paperboard	15,000 pounds	5,000 pounds
Corrugating medium	5,000 pounds	10,000 pounds

Required: Prepare a master budget for FreshPak Corporation for the next year. Assume an income tax rate of 40 percent. Include the following schedules.

1. Sales budget.
2. Production budget.
3. Direct-material budget.
4. Direct-labor budget.
5. Production-overhead budget.
6. Selling and administrative expense budget.
7. Budgeted income statement. (*Hint:* To determine cost of goods sold, first compute the production cost per unit for each type of box. Include applied production overhead in the cost.)

Problem 9–43
Budgeting; Financial Objectives; Ethics
(LO 9-1, 9-5, 9-6, 9-7)

2. Increase in sales: 11.5%

Healthful Foods Inc., a manufacturer of breakfast cereals and snack bars, has experienced several years of steady growth in sales, profits, and dividends while maintaining a relatively low level of debt. The board of directors has adopted a long-run strategy to maximize the value of the shareholders' investment. In order to achieve this goal, the board of directors established the following five-year financial objectives.

- Increase sales by 12 percent per year.
- Increase income before taxes by 15 percent per year.
- Maintain long-term debt at a maximum of 16 percent of assets.

These financial objectives have been attained for the past three years. At the beginning of last year, the president of Healthful Foods, Andrea Donis, added a fourth financial objective of maintaining cost of goods sold at a maximum of 70 percent of sales. This goal also was attained last year.

The budgeting process at Healthful Foods is to be directed toward attaining these goals for the forthcoming year, a difficult task with the economy in a prolonged recession. In addition, the increased emphasis on eating healthful foods has driven up the price of ingredients used by the company significantly faster than the expected rate of inflation. John Winslow, cost accountant at Healthful Foods, has responsibility for preparation of the profit plan for next year. Winslow assured Donis that he could present a budget that achieved all of the financial objectives. Winslow believed that he could overestimate the ending inventory and reclassify fruit and grain inspection costs as administrative rather than production costs to attain the desired objective. The actual statements for 20x1 and the budgeted statements for 20x2 that Winslow prepared are as follows:

HEALTHFUL FOODS INC.
Income Statement

	20x1 Actual	20x2 Budgeted
Sales	$850,000	$947,750
Less: Variable costs:		
Cost of goods sold	510,000	574,725
Selling and administrative	90,000	87,500
Contribution margin	$250,000	$285,525
Less: Fixed costs:		
Production	85,000	94,775
Selling and administrative	60,000	70,000
Income before taxes	$105,000	$120,750

HEALTHFUL FOODS INC.
Balance Sheet

	20x1 Actual	20x2 Budgeted
Assets:		
Cash	$ 10,000	$ 17,000
Accounts receivable	60,000	68,000
Inventory	300,000	365,000
Plant and equipment (net of accumulated depreciation)	1,630,000	1,600,000
Total	$2,000,000	$2,050,000
Liabilities:		
Accounts payable	$ 110,000	$ 122,000
Long-term debt	320,000	308,000
Stockholders' equity:		
Common stock	400,000	400,000
Retained earnings	1,170,000	1,220,000
Total	$2,000,000	$2,050,000

The company paid dividends of $27,720 in 20x1, and the expected tax rate for 20x2 is 34 percent.

Required:

1. Describe the role of budgeting in a firm's strategic planning.
2. For each of the financial objectives established by the board of directors and the president of Healthful Foods Inc., determine whether John Winslow's budget attains these objectives. Support your conclusion in each case by presenting appropriate calculations, and use the following format for your answer.

Objective	Attained/Not Attained	Calculations

3. Explain why the adjustments contemplated by John Winslow are unethical, citing specific standards of ethical professional practice for management accountants.

(CMA, adapted)

Problem 9–44
Comprehensive Master Budget; Borrowing; Acquisition of Automated Material-Handling System
(LO 9-2, 9-3, 9-5, 9-6)

2. Total cash receipts, first quarter: $1,367,030
4. Total cash disbursements, first quarter: $1,213,576
6. Required short-term borrowing: $(100,000)
7. Net income: $160,656

"We really need to get this new material-handling equipment in operation just after the new year begins. I hope we can finance it largely with cash and marketable securities, but if necessary we can get a short-term loan down at MetroBank." This statement by Beth Davies-Lowry, president of Intercoastal Electronics Company, concluded a meeting she had called with the firm's top management. Intercoastal is a small, rapidly growing wholesaler of consumer electronic products. The firm's main product lines are small kitchen appliances and power tools. Marcia Wilcox, Intercoastal's General Manager of Marketing, has recently completed a sales forecast. She believes the company's sales during the first quarter of 20x1 will increase by 10 percent each month over the previous month's sales. Then Wilcox expects sales to remain constant for several months. Intercoastal's projected balance sheet as of December 31, 20x0, is as follows:

Cash	$ 35,000
Accounts receivable	270,000
Marketable securities	15,000
Inventory	154,000
Buildings and equipment (net of accumulated depreciation)	626,000
Total assets	$1,100,000
Accounts payable	$ 176,400
Bond interest payable	12,500
Property taxes payable	3,600
Bonds payable (10%; due in 20x6)	300,000
Common stock	500,000
Retained earnings	107,500
Total liabilities and stockholders' equity	$1,100,000

Jack Hanson, the assistant controller, is now preparing a monthly budget for the first quarter of 20x1. In the process, the following information has been accumulated:

1. Projected sales for December of 20x0 are $400,000. Credit sales typically are 75 percent of total sales. Intercoastal's credit experience indicates that 10 percent of the credit sales are collected during the month of sale, and the remainder are collected during the following month.
2. Intercoastal's cost of goods sold generally runs at 70 percent of sales. Inventory is purchased on account, and 40 percent of each month's purchases are paid during the month of purchase. The remainder is paid during the following month. In order to have adequate stocks of inventory on hand, the firm attempts to have inventory at the end of each month equal to half of the next month's projected cost of goods sold.
3. Hanson has estimated that Intercoastal's other monthly expenses will be as follows:

Sales salaries	$21,000
Advertising and promotion	16,000
Administrative salaries	21,000
Depreciation	25,000
Interest on bonds	2,500
Property taxes	900

In addition, sales commissions run at the rate of 1 percent of sales.

4. Intercoastal's president, Davies-Lowry, has indicated that the firm should invest $125,000 in an automated inventory-handling system to control the movement of inventory in the firm's warehouse just after the new year begins. These equipment purchases will be financed primarily from the firm's cash and marketable securities. However, Davies-Lowry believes that Intercoastal needs to keep a minimum cash balance of $25,000. If necessary, the remainder of the equipment purchases will be financed using short-term credit from a local bank. The minimum period for such a loan is three months. Hanson believes short-term interest rates will be 10 percent per year at the time of the equipment purchases. If a loan is necessary, Davies-Lowry has decided it should be paid off by the end of the first quarter if possible.
5. Intercoastal's board of directors has indicated an intention to declare and pay dividends of $50,000 on the last day of each quarter.
6. The interest on any short-term borrowing will be paid when the loan is repaid. Interest on Intercoastal's bonds is paid semiannually on January 31 and July 31 for the preceding six-month period.
7. Property taxes are paid semiannually on February 28 and August 31 for the preceding six-month period.

Required: Prepare Intercoastal Electronics Company's master budget for the first quarter of 20x1 by completing the following schedules and statements.

1. Sales budget:

	20x0	20x1			
	December	January	February	March	1st Quarter
Total sales					
Cash sales					
Sales on account					

2. Cash receipts budget:

	20x1			
	January	February	March	1st Quarter
Cash sales				
Cash collections from credit sales made during current month				
Cash collections from credit sales made during preceding month				
Total cash receipts				

3. Purchases budget:

	20x0	20x1			
	December	January	February	March	1st Quarter
Budgeted cost of goods sold					
Add: Desired ending inventory					
Total goods needed					
Less: Expected beginning inventory					
Purchases					

4. Cash disbursements budget:

	20x1			
	January	February	March	1st Quarter
Inventory purchases:				
Cash payments for purchases during the current month*				
Cash payments for purchases during the preceding month†				
Total cash payments for inventory purchases				
Other expenses:				
Sales salaries				
Advertising and promotion				
Administrative salaries				
Interest on bonds‡				
Property taxes‡				
Sales commissions				
Total cash payments for other expenses				
Total cash disbursements				

*40% of the current month's purchases (schedule 3).

†60% of the prior month's purchases (schedule 3).

‡Bond interest is paid every six months, on January 31 and July 31. Property taxes also are paid every six months, on February 28 and August 31.

5. Complete the first three lines of the summary cash budget. Then do the analysis of short-term financing needs in requirement (6). Then finish requirement (5).

Summary cash budget:

	20x1			
	January	**February**	**March**	**1st Quarter**
Cash receipts (from schedule 2)				
Less: Cash disbursements (from schedule 4)				
Change in cash balance during period due to operations				
Sale of marketable securities (1/2/x1)				
Proceeds from bank loan (1/2/x1)				
Purchase of equipment				
Repayment of bank loan (3/31/x1)				
Interest on bank loan				
Payment of dividends				
Change in cash balance during first quarter				
Cash balance, 1/1/x1				
Cash balance, 3/31/x1				

6. Analysis of short-term financing needs:

Projected cash balance as of December 31, 20x0	$
Less: Minimum cash balance	
Cash available for equipment purchases	$
Projected proceeds from sale of marketable securities	
Cash available	$
Less: Cost of investment in equipment	
Required short-term borrowing	

7. Prepare Intercoastal Electronics' budgeted income statement for the first quarter of 20x1. (Ignore income taxes.)

8. Prepare Intercoastal Electronics' budgeted statement of retained earnings for the first quarter of 20x1.

9. Prepare Intercoastal Electronics' budgeted balance sheet as of March 31, 20x1. (*Hint:* On March 31, 20x1, Bond Interest Payable is $5,000 and Property Taxes Payable is $900.)

Cases

Case 9–45
Using Budgets to Evaluate Business Decisions
(LO 9-2, 9-3, 9-7)

City Racquetball Club (CRC) offers racquetball and other physical fitness facilities to its members. There are four of these clubs in the metropolitan area. Each club has between 1,800 and 2,500 members. Revenue is derived from annual membership fees and hourly court fees. The annual membership fees are as follows:

Individual	$ 40
Student	25
Family	95

The hourly court fees vary from $6 to $10 depending upon the season and the time of day (prime versus nonprime time).

The peak racquetball season is considered to run from September through April. During this period, court usage averages 90 to 100 percent of capacity during prime time (5:00–9:00 p.m.) and 50 to 60 percent of capacity during the remaining hours. Daily court usage during the off-season (i.e., summer) averages only 20 to 40 percent of capacity.

Most of CRC's memberships have September expirations. A substantial amount of the cash receipts are collected during the early part of the racquetball season due to the renewal of the annual membership fees and heavy court usage. However, cash receipts are not as large in the spring and drop significantly in the summer months.

CRC is considering changing its membership and fee structure in an attempt to change its cash receipts. Under the new membership plan, only an annual membership fee would be charged, rather than a membership fee plus hourly court fees. There would be two classes of membership as follows:

Individual	$250
Family	400

The annual fee would be collected in advance at the time the membership application is completed. Members would be allowed to use the racquetball courts as often as they wish during the year under the new plan.

All future memberships would be sold under these new terms. Current memberships would be honored on the old basis until they expire. However, a special promotional campaign would be instituted to attract new members and to encourage current members to convert to the new membership plan immediately.

The annual fees for individual and family memberships would be reduced to $200 and $300, respectively, during the two-month promotional campaign. In addition, all memberships sold or renewed during this period would be for 15 months rather than the normal one-year period. Current members also would be given a credit toward the annual fee for the unexpired portion of their membership fee, and for all prepaid hourly court fees for league play that have not yet been used.

CRC's management estimates that 60 to 70 percent of the present membership would continue with the club. The most active members (45 percent of the present membership) would convert immediately to the new plan, while the remaining members who continue would wait until their current memberships expire. Those members who would not continue are not considered active (i.e., they play five or less times during the year). Management estimates that the loss of members would be offset fully by new members within six months of instituting the new plan. Furthermore, many of the new members would be individuals who would play during nonprime time. Management estimates that adequate court time will be available for all members under the new plan.

If the new membership plan is adopted, it would be instituted on February 1, well before the summer season. The special promotional campaign would be conducted during March and April. Once the plan is implemented, annual renewal of memberships and payment of fees would take place as each individual or family membership expires.

Required: Your consulting firm has been hired to help CRC evaluate its new fee structure. Write a letter to the club's president answering the following questions.

1. Will City Racquetball Club's new membership plan and fee structure improve its ability to plan its cash receipts? Explain your answer.
2. City Racquetball Club should evaluate the new membership plan and fee structure completely before it decides to adopt or reject it.
   a. Identify the key factors that CRC should consider in its evaluation.
   b. Explain what type of financial analyses CRC should prepare in order to make a complete evaluation.
3. Explain how City Racquetball Club's cash management would differ from the present if the new membership plan and fee structure were adopted.

(CMA, adapted)

Case 9–46
Participative Budgeting
(LO 9-2, 9-3, 9-9)

Patricia Eklund, controller in the division of social services for the state, recognizes the importance of the budgetary process for planning, control, and motivational purposes. She believes that a properly implemented participative budgetary process for planning purposes and an evaluation procedure will motivate the managers to improve productivity within their particular departments. Based upon this philosophy, Eklund has implemented the following budgetary procedures.

- An appropriation target figure is given to each department manager. This amount is the maximum funding that each department can expect to receive in the next year.
- Department managers develop their individual budgets within the following spending constraints as directed by the controller's staff.

 - Expenditure requests cannot exceed the appropriation target.
 - All fixed expenditures should be included in the budget. Fixed expenditures would include such items as contracts and salaries at current levels.
 - All government projects directed by higher authority should be included in the budget in their entirety.
- The controller's staff consolidates the budget requests from the various departments into a master budget submission for the entire division.
- Upon final budget approval by the legislature, the controller's staff allocates the appropriation to the various departments on instructions from the division manager. However, a specified percentage of each department's appropriation is held back in anticipation of potential budget cuts and special funding needs. The amount and use of this contingency fund is left to the discretion of the division manager.
- Each department is allowed to adjust its budget when necessary to operate within the reduced appropriation level. However, as stated in the original directive, specific projects authorized by higher authority must remain intact.
- The final budget is used as the basis of control. Excessive expenditures by account for each department are highlighted on a monthly basis. Department managers are expected to account for all expenditures over budget. Fiscal responsibility is an important factor in the overall performance evaluation of department managers.

Eklund believes her policy of allowing the department managers to participate in the budgetary process and then holding them accountable for their performance is essential, especially during times of limited resources. She further believes that the department managers will be positively motivated to increase the efficiency and effectiveness of their departments because they have provided input into the initial budgetary process and are required to justify any unfavorable performances.

Required:

1. Describe several operational and behavioral benefits that are generally attributed to a participative budgetary process.
2. Identify at least four deficiencies in Patricia Eklund's participative policy for planning and performance evaluation purposes. For each deficiency identified, recommend how it can be corrected.

(CMA, adapted)

Case 9–47

Comprehensive Master Budget; Short-Term Financing; Acquisition of Robotic Equipment

(LO 9-2, 9-3, 9-5, 9-6)

1. Total sales revenue, entire year: $5,650,000
3. Production budget, S frames, units to be produced, entire year: 254,000
7. Cost of goods sold: $3,850,000
10. Total assets: $9,634,700

Jeffrey Vaughn, president of Frame-It Company, was just concluding a budget meeting with his senior staff. It was November of 20x0, and the group was discussing preparation of the firm's master budget for 20x1. "I've decided to go ahead and purchase the industrial robot we've been talking about. We'll make the acquisition on January 2 of next year, and I expect it will take most of the year to train the personnel and reorganize the production process to take full advantage of the new equipment."

In response to a question about financing the acquisition, Vaughn replied as follows: "The robot will cost $1,000,000. We'll finance it with a one-year $1,000,000 loan from Shark Bank and Trust Company. I've negotiated a repayment schedule of four equal installments on the last day of each quarter. The interest rate will be 10 percent, and interest payments will be quarterly as well." With that the meeting broke up, and the budget process was on.

Frame-It Company is a manufacturer of metal picture frames. The firm's two product lines are designated as S (small frames, 5×7 inches) and L (large frames, 8×10 inches). The primary raw materials are flexible metal strips and 9-inch by 24-inch glass sheets. Each S frame requires a 2-foot metal strip; an L frame requires a 3-foot strip. Allowing for normal breakage and scrap glass, Frame-It can get either four S frames or two L frames out of a glass sheet. Other raw materials, such as cardboard backing, are insignificant in cost and are treated as indirect materials. Emily Jackson, Frame-It's controller, is in charge of preparing the master budget for 20x1. She has gathered the following information:

1. Sales in the fourth quarter of 20x0 are expected to be 50,000 S frames and 40,000 L frames. The sales manager predicts that over the next two years, sales in each product line will grow by 5,000 units each quarter over the previous quarter. For example, S frame sales in the first quarter of 20x1 are expected to be 55,000 units.
2. Frame-It's sales history indicates that 60 percent of all sales are on credit, with the remainder of the sales in cash. The company's collection experience shows that 80 percent of the credit sales are collected during the quarter in which the sale is made, while the remaining 20 percent is collected in the following quarter. (For simplicity, assume the company is able to collect 100 percent of its accounts receivable.)

3. The S frame sells for $10, and the L frame sells for $15. These prices are expected to hold constant throughout 20x1.
4. Frame-It's production manager attempts to end each quarter with enough finished-goods inventory in each product line to cover 20 percent of the following quarter's sales. Moreover, an attempt is made to end each quarter with 20 percent of the glass sheets needed for the following quarter's production. Since metal strips are purchased locally, Frame-It buys them on a just-in-time basis; inventory is negligible.
5. All of Frame-It's direct-material purchases are made on account, and 80 percent of each quarter's purchases are paid in cash during the same quarter as the purchase. The other 20 percent is paid in the next quarter.
6. Indirect materials are purchased as needed and paid for in cash. Work-in-process inventory is negligible.
7. Projected production costs in 20x1 are as follows:

	S Frame	L Frame
Direct material:		
Metal strips:		
S: 2 ft. @ $1 per foot	$2	
L: 3 ft. @ $1 per foot		$ 3
Glass sheets:		
S: ¼ sheet @ $8 per sheet	2	
L: ½ sheet @ $8 per sheet		4
Direct labor:		
.1 hour @ $20 per hour	2	2
Production overhead:		
.1 direct-labor hour × $10 per hour	1	1
Total production cost per unit	$7	$10

8. The predetermined overhead rate is $10 per direct-labor hour. The following production overhead costs are budgeted for 20x1.

	1st Quarter	2nd Quarter	3rd Quarter	4th Quarter	Entire Year
Indirect material	$ 10,200	$ 11,200	$ 12,200	$ 13,200	$ 46,800
Indirect labor	40,800	44,800	48,800	52,800	187,200
Other overhead	31,000	36,000	41,000	46,000	154,000
Depreciation	20,000	20,000	20,000	20,000	80,000
Total overhead	$102,000	$112,000	$122,000	$132,000	$468,000

All of these costs will be paid in cash during the quarter incurred except for the depreciation charges.

9. Frame-It's quarterly selling and administrative expenses are $100,000, paid in cash.
10. Jackson anticipates that dividends of $50,000 will be declared and paid in cash each quarter.
11. Frame-It's projected balance sheet as of December 31, 20x0, follows:

Cash	$ 95,000
Accounts receivable	132,000
Inventory:	
Raw material	59,200
Finished goods	167,000
Plant and equipment (net of accumulated depreciation)	8,000,000
Total assets	$8,453,200
Accounts payable	$ 99,400
Common stock	5,000,000
Retained earnings	3,353,800
Total liabilities and stockholders' equity	$8,453,200

Required: Prepare Frame-It Company's master budget for 20x1 by completing the following schedules and statements.

1. Sales budget:

	20x0	20x1				
	4th Quarter	1st Quarter	2nd Quarter	3rdQuarter	4th Quarter	EntireYear
S frame unit sales						
× S sales price						
S frame sales revenue						
L frame unit sales						
× L sales price						
L frame sales revenue						
Total sales revenue						
Cash sales*						
Sales on account†						

*40% of total sales.

†60% of total sales.

2. Cash receipts budget:

	20x1				
	1st Quarter	2nd Quarter	3rd Quarter	4th Quarter	Entire Year
Cash sales					
Cash collections from credit sales made during current quarter*					
Cash collections from credit sales made during previous quarter†					
Total cash receipts					

*80% of current quarter's credit sales.

†20% of previous quarter's credit sales.

3. Production budget:

	20x0	20x1				
	4th Quarter	1st Quarter	2nd Quarter	3rd Quarter	4th Quarter	Entire Year
S frames:						
Sales (in units)						
Add: Desired ending inventory						
Total units needed						
Less: Expected beginning inventory						
Units to be produced						
L frames:						
Sales (in units)						
Add: Desired ending inventory						
Total units needed						
Less: Expected beginning inventory						
Units to be produced						

4. Direct-material budget:

	20x0	20x1				
	4th Quarter	**1st Quarter**	**2nd Quarter**	**3rd Quarter**	**4th Quarter**	**Entire Year**
Metal strips:						
S frames to be produced						
× Metal quantity per S unit (ft.)						
Needed for S frame production						
L frames to be produced						
× Metal quantity per L unit (ft.)						
Needed for L frame production						
Total metal needed for production; to be purchased (ft.)						
× Price per foot						
Cost of metal strips to be purchased						
Glass sheets:						
S frames to be produced						
× Glass quantity per S unit (sheets)						
Needed for S frame production						
L frames to be produced						
× Glass quantity per L unit (sheets)						
Needed for L frame production						
Total glass needed for production (sheets)						
Add: Desired ending inventory					10,400	10,400
Total glass needs						
Less: Expected beginning inventory						
Glass to be purchased						
× Price per glass sheet						
Cost of glass to be purchased						
Total raw-material purchases (metal and glass)						

5. Cash disbursements budget:

	20x1				
	1st Quarter	**2nd Quarter**	**3rd Quarter**	**4th Quarter**	**Entire Year**
Raw-material purchases:					
Cash payments for purchases during the current quarter					
Cash payments for purchases during the preceding quarter					
Total cash payments for raw-material purchases					
Direct labor:					
Frames produced (S and L)					
× Direct-labor hours per frame					
Direct-labor hours to be used					
× Rate per direct-labor hour					
Total cash payments for direct labor					
Production overhead:					
Indirect material					
Indirect labor					
Other					
Total cash payments for production overhead					
Cash payments for selling and administrative expenses					
Total cash disbursements					

6. Summary cash budget:

	20x1				
	1st Quarter	**2nd Quarter**	**3rd Quarter**	**4th Quarter**	**Entire Year**
Cash receipts (from schedule 2)					
Less: Cash disbursements (from schedule 5)					
Change in cash balance due to operations					
Payment of dividends					
Proceeds from bank loan (1/2/x1)					
Purchase of equipment					
Quarterly installment on loan principal					
Quarterly interest payment					
Change in cash balance during the period					
Cash balance, beginning of period					
Cash balance, end of period					

7. Prepare a budgeted schedule of cost of goods manufactured and sold for the year 20x1. (*Hint:* In the budget, actual and applied overhead will be equal.)

8. Prepare Frame-It's budgeted income statement for 20x1. (Ignore income taxes.)

9. Prepare Frame-It's budgeted statement of retained earnings for 20x1.

10. Prepare Frame-It's budgeted balance sheet as of December 31, 20x1.

10 Standard Costing and Analysis of Direct Costs

FOCUS COMPANY >>>

© John A. Rizzo/Photodisc/Getty Images RF

THIS CHAPTER'S FOCUS COMPANY is DCdesserts.com, which supplies fancy desserts to a variety of restaurants, caterers, and upscale food stores in Washington, D.C. The company's order-taking system is entirely Web-based. Each day, DCdesserts.com posts its dessert menu on its website, and orders are accepted via the Internet. In this chapter, we explore DCdesserts.com's use of standard costing. A standard-costing system sets predetermined (or standard) costs for each of a product's inputs, such as direct material and direct labor. Then the actual costs to produce the product are compared with the standard costs that should have been incurred. DCdesserts.com's management uses the standard-costing system to help control the company's production costs.

© Iconotec/Glow Images RF

<<< IN CONTRAST

Forest Home
National Bank

In contrast to the food-processing setting of DCdesserts.com, we will turn our attention to the financial-services industry. Here we will explore Forest Home National Bank's (FHNB) implementation of a standard costing system to better manage its business. FHNB uses direct-labor standards to understand and manage its performance of the various service tasks that are required in a modern bank, and variance analysis helps the company to pinpoint opportunities for improvement.

After completing this chapter, you should be able to:

10-1 Describe the elements of a cost control system.

10-2 Describe two ways to set cost standards and distinguish between perfection and practical standards.

10-3 Compute and interpret the direct-material price and quantity variances and the direct-labor rate and efficiency variances.

10-4 Explain several methods for determining the significance of cost variances.

10-5 Describe some behavioral effects of standard costing.

10-6 Explain how standard costs are used in product costing.

10-7 Summarize some advantages of standard costing.

10-8 Explain several common criticisms of standard costing.

10-9 Prepare journal entries to record and close out cost variances (appendix).

The Financial Planning and Analysis (FP&A) process, introduced in Chapter 9, includes steps prior to operations (*planning*) and after operations (*analysis*). A budget provides a plan for managers to follow in making decisions and directing an organization's activities. As a company subsequently operates during the period that was budgeted, the budget serves another useful purpose: managers use the budget as a benchmark against which to compare the results of actual operations. Did the company make as much profit as anticipated in the budget? Were costs greater or less than expected? Why? In this chapter, we will study *standard costing* and *variance analysis,* tools used by accountants and managers for analyzing and controlling an organization's operations and costs.

Managing Costs

Learning Objective **10-1**

Describe the elements of a cost control system.

Any control system has three basic parts: a predetermined or *standard* performance level, a measure of *actual* performance, and a *comparison* between standard and actual performance. A thermostat is a control system with which we are all familiar. First, a thermostat has a predetermined or standard temperature that can be set at any desired level. If you want the temperature in a room to be 68 degrees, you set the thermostat at the *standard* of 68 degrees. Second, the thermostat contains a thermometer that measures the *actual* temperature in the room. Third, the thermostat *compares* the preset or standard temperature with the actual room temperature. If the actual temperature deviates by more than a small amount from the preset or standard temperature, the thermostat triggers a response, activating a heating or cooling device. The three features of a control system are depicted in Exhibit 10–1.

A financial planning and analysis system includes a cost-control system that works like a thermostat. First, a predetermined or **standard cost** is set. In essence, a standard cost is the company's best estimate of the average cost to produce a single unit of product or service. This cost estimate serves as the starting point for creating the relevant budgets. When the firm plans to produce multiple units, managers use the standard unit cost

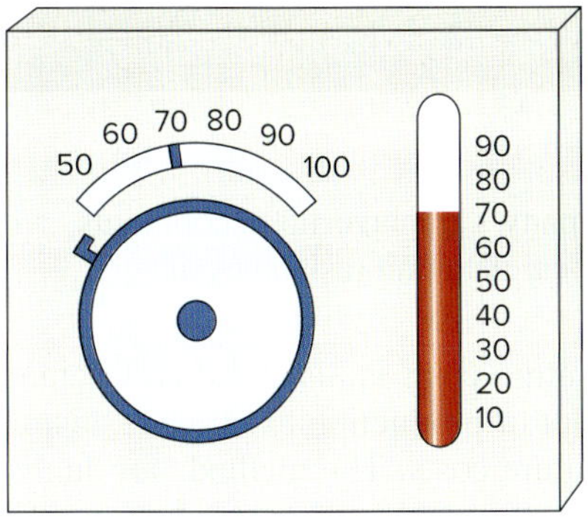

Exhibit 10–1

Control System: A Thermostat.

to determine the total standard or budgeted cost of production. For example, suppose the standard cost of the cream (a direct material) used to make one gallon of ice cream at Blue Bell Creameries is $1, and the company expects to manufacture 100,000 gallons. The total standard or budgeted direct-material cost of cream for 100,000 gallons is $100,000 ($1 × 100,000).

Second, the cost-control system measures the actual cost incurred in the production process. For our example, suppose Blue Bell does produce 100,000 gallons of ice cream, as planned, and the actual cost of cream used in production is measured by the cost-control system at $120,000.

Third, the manager compares the actual cost of cream with the budgeted or standard cost. Any difference between the two is called a **cost variance.** Cost variances then are used in controlling costs. The $20,000 cost variance in this example ($120,000 – $100,000) tells Blue Bell that their planning figures were incorrect and that they were unable to produce the quantity of product anticipated at the cost for materials anticipated. This information may well lead the company to look for an explanation for the incorrect prediction.

Notice that because the variance in the example above was measured specifically for a direct material, we can imagine specific reasons for the cost variance. For example, maybe the market price for cream had risen unexpectedly after the budget was finalized. Or maybe the cream purchased had a lower milkfat level than expected, causing more cream to be used for the same quantity and quality of ice cream. By setting standard costs and measuring cost variances for specific types of costs, we can find meaningful explanations for the variances.

For that reason, standards are set and variances are measured for many different direct materials, many classes of direct labor, and sometimes many different categories of overhead. We will discuss these in more detail later in this chapter and the next.

> "I have been struck by how important measurement is to improving the human condition. You can achieve incredible progress if you set a clear goal and find a measure that will drive progress toward that goal." (10a)
>
> **Bill and Melinda Gates Foundation**

Management by Exception

Although many different cost variances are measured, they are not all investigated. Managers are busy people. They do not have time to look into the causes of every variance between actual and standard costs. However, they do take the time to investigate the causes of *significant* cost variances. This process of following up on only significant cost variances is called **management by exception.** When operations are going along as planned, actual costs and profit will typically be close to the budgeted amounts. However, if there are significant departures from planned operations, such effects will show up as significant cost variances. Managers investigate these variances to determine their causes, if possible, and take corrective action when indicated.

What constitutes a significant variance? No precise answer can be given to this question, since it depends on the size and type of the organization, its production process, and what is being measured. We will consider this issue later in the chapter when we discuss common methods for determining the significance of cost variances. First, however, we will turn our attention to the process of setting standards.

Setting Standards

Methods for Setting Standards

Learning Objective **10-2**

Describe two ways to set cost standards and distinguish between perfection and practical standards.

Cost standards generally are established by a company's managerial accountants, who use two methods for setting them: analysis of historical data and task analysis.

Analysis of Historical Data One indicator of future costs is historical cost data. In a mature production process, where the firm has a lot of production experience, historical costs can provide a good basis for predicting future costs. The methods for analyzing cost behavior that we studied in Chapter 6 are used in making cost predictions. The company often will need to adjust these predictions to reflect movements in price levels or technological changes in the production process. For example, the amount of rubber required to manufacture a particular type of tire will likely be the same this year as last year, unless there has been a significant change in the process used to manufacture tires. However, the price of rubber is likely to be different this year than last, and this fact must be reflected in the new standard cost of a tire.

Despite the relevance of historical cost data in setting cost standards, managers must guard against relying on them blindly. Understanding how standards were derived can provide important insights into their reliability. For example, even a seemingly minor change in the way a product is manufactured may make historical data almost totally irrelevant. Moreover, new products also require new cost standards. For new products, such as genetically engineered medicines, there are no historical cost data upon which to base standards. In such cases, the manager should turn to another approach.

Task Analysis Another way to set cost standards is to analyze the process of manufacturing a product to determine what it *should* cost. The emphasis shifts from what the product *did* cost in the past to what it *should* cost in the future. In using **task analysis,** the manager or accountant typically works with engineers who are intimately familiar with the production process. Together they conduct studies to determine exactly how much direct material should be required and how machinery should be used in the production process. Time and motion studies are conducted to determine how long each step performed by direct-labor production workers should take.

A Combined Approach Managerial accountants often apply both historical cost analysis and task analysis in setting cost standards. It may be, for example, that the technology has changed for only one step in the production process. In such a case, the managerial accountant would work with engineers to set cost standards for the technologically changed part of the production process. However, the accountant would likely rely on the less time-consuming method of analyzing historical cost data to update the cost standards for the remainder of the production process.

Participation in Setting Standards

Standards should not be determined by the managerial accountant alone. Besides needing to assess the standard's reliability, as discussed above, managers generally will be more committed to meeting standards if they participate in setting them. For example, production supervisors should have a role in setting production cost standards, and sales managers should be involved in setting targets for sales prices and volume. In addition, knowledgeable staff personnel should participate in the standard-setting process. For example, task analysis should be carried out by a team consisting of production engineers, production supervisors, and managerial accountants.

Perfection versus Practical Standards: A Behavioral Issue

How difficult should it be to attain standard costs? Should standards be set so that actual costs rarely exceed standard costs? Or should it be so hard to attain standards that actual costs frequently exceed them? The answers to these questions depend on the purpose for which standards will be used and how standards affect behavior.

Perfection Standards A **perfection (or ideal) standard** is one that can be attained only under nearly perfect operating conditions. Such standards assume peak efficiency, the lowest possible input prices, the best-quality materials obtainable, and no disruptions in production due to such causes as machine breakdowns or power failures. Some managers believe that perfection standards help achieve the lowest production cost by motivating employees to achieve the lowest cost possible. They claim that since the standard is theoretically attainable, employees will have an incentive to come as close as possible to achieving it.

Other managers and many behavioral scientists disagree. They feel that perfection standards discourage employees, since they are so unlikely to be attained. Moreover, setting unrealistically difficult standards may encourage employees to sacrifice product quality to achieve lower costs. By skimping on raw-material quality or the attention given to manual production tasks, employees may be able to lower the production cost. However, this lower cost may come at the expense of a higher rate of defective units. Thus, the firm ultimately may incur higher costs than necessary as defective products are returned by customers or scrapped upon inspection.

Practical Standards Standards that are perhaps challenging but still able to be regularly attained, are called **practical (or attainable) standards.** Such standards assume a production process that is as efficient as practical under normal operating conditions. Practical standards allow for such occurrences as occasional machine breakdowns and normal amounts of raw-material waste. Attaining a practical standard keeps employees on their toes without demanding miracles. Most behavioral theorists believe that practical standards encourage more positive and productive employee attitudes than do perfection standards.

"At Best Foods, standard costs are set at attainable levels." (10b)
Best Foods
(a subsidiary of **Unilever**)

Use of Standards by Service Organizations

Many service industry firms, nonprofit organizations, and governmental units make use of standards. For example, Boeing has established that it should take 12 minutes to unload the cargo hold of its 757-300 airplane, a statistic that can be used by airlines flying that plane to set performance standards for their ground crews. Five Guys sets a standard for the amount of meat in a hamburger. Insurance companies such as Allstate or State Farm set standards for the amount of time to process an insurance application. Even a county motor vehicle office may have a standard for the number of days required to process an application for vehicle registration. These and similar organizations use standards in budgeting and cost control in much the same way that manufacturers use standards.

© Chris Ryan/agefotostock RF

Insurance companies use standards to manage how long it takes to underwrite a new policy or settle a claim.

Cost Variance Analysis

Learning Objective 10-3

Compute and interpret the direct-material price and quantity variances and the direct-labor rate and efficiency variances.

To illustrate the use of standards in managing costs, we will focus on a producer of fancy desserts located in the Washington, D.C., area. You might be surprised to learn that the fancy desserts available in a lot of restaurants are not actually made there. A pastry chef is a luxury that not all restaurants can afford. That is where DCdesserts.com comes in.

DCdesserts.com supplies fresh and frozen desserts to a variety of restaurants, caterers, and upscale food stores. The company's order-taking system is entirely Web-based. DCdesserts.com posts its menu of fresh fancy dessert products for each day on its website four days in advance of the delivery date. Orders are accepted via the Internet three days in advance of delivery. For example, the menu of desserts to be available for delivery on Friday afternoon is posted to DCdesserts.com's website on Monday, and orders are accepted up to midnight on Tuesday. The company places orders for ingredients on Wednesday and accepts delivery on Thursday. DCdesserts.com's ordering is also done largely via the Internet. Production then takes place throughout the day on Friday, and the desserts are delivered Friday afternoon. DCdesserts.com uses three independent delivery services to deliver its dessert products: Capital Couriers, Potomac Door-to-Door, and Washington Delivery Service.

DCdesserts.com also produces frozen dessert products for upscale grocery stores. Unlike the fresh desserts, which vary daily, the frozen desserts are stock items that are varied less frequently. Like the fresh desserts, however, the frozen dessert menu is posted to DCdesserts.com's website, and orders are accepted entirely via the Internet. The company produces its fresh fancy desserts and frozen desserts in two different production facilities, both located on the outskirts of central Washington, D.C.

The production process for the fresh fancy desserts involves a combination of semi-automated equipment and manual labor. Even in this era of widespread automation, making fancy desserts still involves considerable direct labor. In the words of DCdesserts.com's founder and owner, "Making a Black Forest cake or a Linzer torte to be served in the U.S. Senate dining room is not the same as making your basic pumpkin pie. There's a lot of touch labor by skilled people in doing these fancy desserts." The basic steps in the production process are much as you might expect. These steps include selecting ingredients, mixing, baking, cooling, and finishing. The finishing work, of course, involves the most skilled direct labor. In making a six-layer chocolate raspberry cake, for example, each individual cake layer must be sliced into two pieces, and then fillings and icings are spread on each layer. The cake's top is finished artistically, and any additional toppings are carefully applied.

DCdesserts.com's director of cost management has set standards for direct material and direct labor as follows for a category of dessert products generically referred to as multilayer fancy cakes.

Direct-Material Standards

The standard quantity and price of ingredients for one multilayer fancy cake, such as a Black Forest cake, are shown in the following table:

Standard quantity:	
Ingredients in finished product	4.75 pounds
Allowance for normal waste	.25 pound
Total standard quantity required per multilayer fancy cake	5.00 pounds
Standard price:	
Purchase price per pound of ingredients (net of purchase discounts)	$1.30
Transportation cost per pound	.10
Total standard price per pound of ingredients	$1.40

The standard quantity of ingredients needed to produce one cake is 5 pounds, even though only 4.75 pounds actually remain in the finished product. One-quarter pound of ingredients is wasted as a normal result of the production process. Therefore, the entire amount of ingredients needed to produce a fancy cake is included in the standard quantity of material.

The standard price of ingredients reflects all of the costs incurred to acquire the material and transport it to the plant. Notice that the cost of transportation is added to the purchase price. Any purchase discounts would be subtracted out from the purchase price to obtain a net price.

To summarize, the **standard direct-material quantity** is the total amount of direct material normally required to produce one unit of finished product, including allowances for normal waste or inefficiency. The **standard direct-material price** is the total delivered cost, after subtracting any purchase discounts, of one direct-material unit. Notice that the standard price is expressed in the same units that are used to describe the standard quantity. At DCdesserts.com, standard direct-material quantity is expressed in *pounds* per unit, so standard direct-material price is expressed *per pound.* If a similar company were based in Paris, the quantity would be measured in *kilograms* per unit and the price would be expressed *per kilogram* (and in euros per kilogram, not dollars).

Direct-Labor Standards

The standard quantity and rate for direct labor for the production of one multilayer fancy cake are as follows:

Standard quantity:		
Direct labor required per multilayer fancy cake		.5 hour
Standard rate:		
Hourly wage rate	$16	
Fringe benefits (25% of wages)	4	
Total standard rate per hour	$20	

The **standard direct-labor quantity** is the number of direct-labor hours normally needed to manufacture one unit of product. The **standard direct-labor rate** is the total hourly cost of compensation, including fringe benefits.

Standard Costs Given Actual Output

During September, DCdesserts.com produced 2,000 multilayer fancy cakes. The total standard or budgeted costs for direct material and direct labor are computed as follows:

Direct material:	
Standard direct-material cost per cake (5 pounds × $1.40 per pound)	$ 7
Actual output	× 2,000
Total standard direct-material cost	$14,000
Direct labor:	
Direct-labor cost per cake (.5 hour × $20 per hour)	$ 10
Actual output	× 2,000
Total standard direct-labor cost	$20,000

Notice that the total standard cost for the direct-material and direct-labor inputs is based on DCdesserts.com's *actual output.* The company should incur costs of $34,000 for direct material and direct labor, *given that it produced 2,000 multilayer fancy cakes.* The total standard costs for direct material and direct labor serve as the manager's benchmarks against which to compare actual costs. This comparison then serves as the basis for controlling direct-material and direct-labor costs.

Actual versus Budgeted Output: A Key Point The use of actual output in variance calculations is a common point of confusion for students. When DCdesserts.com prepared its budget, it estimated its costs of production based on its standard costs per unit and a forecast of the demand for its products. Suppose that DCdesserts.com's demand forecast resulted in a budgeted production output of 2,200 multilayer fancy cakes in September. Based on that level of output, the September budget would have included the following costs:

Direct material:	
Standard direct-material cost per cake (5 pounds × $1.40 per pound)	$ 7
Forecast output	× 2,200
Total budgeted direct-material cost	$ 15,400
Direct labor:	
Direct-labor cost per cake (.5 hour × $20 per hour)	$ 10
Forecast output	× 2,200
Total budgeted direct-labor cost	$22,000

But we know, from the prior section, that DCdesserts.com only produced 2,000 multilayer fancy cakes in September. Is it surprising that the budgeted output would differ from the actual output? Not really. After all, the current year's budget was finalized almost a year earlier, late in the prior year! But while the costs in the budget were useful for planning, they are outdated for analyzing performance. DCdesserts.com should now compare actual costs to the standard cost for the actual output.

For example, if DCdesserts.com compares its actual direct-material cost, reported by the accounting system to be $14,555 in September, against its budgeted direct-material cost, they will observe that the cost was $845 less than expected ($15,400 – $14,555). Should DCdesserts.com conclude from this comparison that costs were effectively controlled? Of course not! It should not have cost as much to make 2,000 cakes as it would have cost to make 2,200 cakes. So, during cost variance analysis, we will update our expectation about the cost of production inputs to what it *should have cost to make the actual output.* We conclude that, because DCdesserts.com would have expected production of 2,000 cakes to cost $14,000 for direct material (not the $15,400 originally budgeted), direct-material costs were actually $555 *more* than expected in September ($14,555 – $14,000).

Analysis of Cost Variances

During September, DCdesserts.com incurred the following actual costs for direct material and direct labor in the production of multilayer fancy cakes.

Direct material used: actual cost 10,250 pounds at $1.42 per pound	$14,555
Direct labor: actual cost 980 hours at $21 per hour	$20,580

Compare these actual expenditures with the total standard costs for the production of 2,000 multilayer fancy cakes. DCdesserts.com spent more than the expected amount for both direct material and direct labor. When spending is higher than expected, the excess spending is called an **unfavorable variance,** abbreviated U. And when spending is lower than expected, the amount by which spending is less than planned is called a **favorable variance** (F). For DCdesserts.com, the overall direct-material variance is unfavorable ($14,555 – $14,000 = $555 U) and so is the overall direct-labor variance ($20,580 – $20,000 = $580 U).

But why were these excess costs incurred? A manager would need to do additional analysis in order to answer this question. **Cost variance analysis** is the process of systematically comparing expected costs (standards) against actual costs, analyzing the

Exhibit 10–2
Direct-Material Price and Quantity Variances

DC desserts

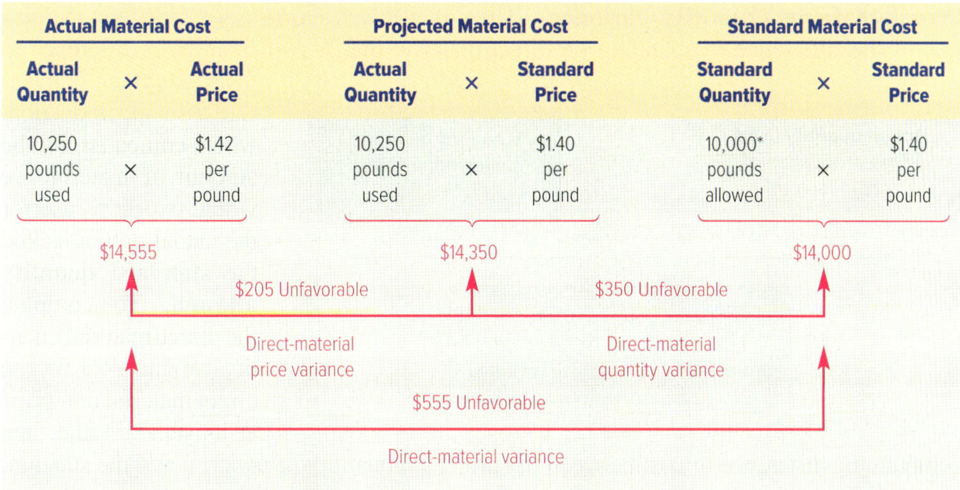

*Actual output × Standard quantity per unit = 2,000 units × 5 pounds per unit = 10,000 pounds allowed.

differences, and explaining significant deviations. We begin our systematic comparison by analyzing the variance in spending on direct material.

Direct-Material Variances

What caused DCdesserts.com to spend more than the anticipated amount on direct material? First, the company purchased ingredients at a higher price ($1.42 per pound) than the standard price ($1.40 per pound). Second, the company used more ingredients than the standard amount. The amount actually used was 10,250 pounds instead of the standard amount of 10,000 pounds, which is based on actual output of 2,000 multilayer fancy cakes. The financial planning and analysis system can identify both of these deviations from standards by computing a **direct-material price variance** and a **direct-material quantity variance.** The computation of these variances is depicted in Exhibit 10–2.

Direct-Material Price Variance As illustrated in Exhibit 10–2, we compute the portion of the spending difference that is caused by a difference in the price of direct material by establishing a benchmark cost for the actual amount of material used, which we label the *projected material cost.* The deviation between the actual and projected material costs is caused by a difference in the price of material, and it is called the *direct-material price variance.*

This can be seen in the formula for the direct-material price variance as follows:

$$\text{Direct-material price variance} = (AQ \times AP) - (AQ \times SP) = AQ(AP - SP)$$

where

AQ = Actual quantity used

AP = Actual price

SP = Standard price

DCdesserts.com's direct-material price variance for September's production of multilayer fancy cakes is computed as follows:

$$\begin{aligned}\text{Direct-material price variance} &= AQ(AP - SP)\\ &= 10{,}250(\$1.42 - \$1.40)\\ &= \$205 \text{ Unfavorable}\end{aligned}$$

This variance is unfavorable, because the actual purchase price exceeded the standard price.

Direct-Material Quantity Variance The direct-material quantity variance is the portion of the difference in spending on direct material that is explained by a difference in the quantity of material used in production, when compared to the amount of material we would expect to use for the actual output, called the **standard quantity allowed**. To compute the direct-material quantity variance, we fix the direct material unit price at its standard and then compute the difference in cost between the projected quantity of material and the standard quantity of material.

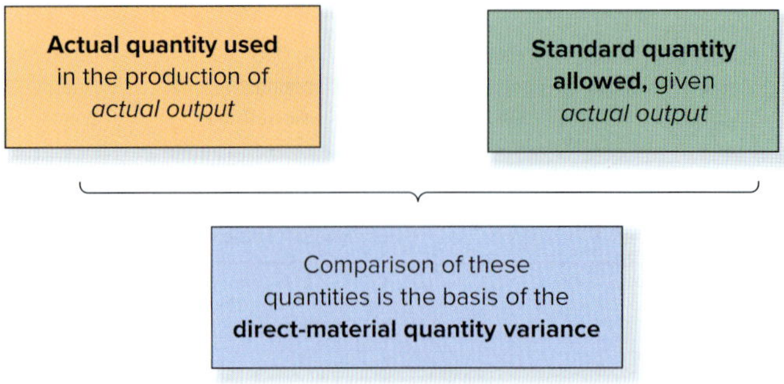

As Exhibit 10–2 shows, the following formula defines the direct-material quantity variance.

$$\text{Direct-material quantity variance} = (AQ \times SP) - (SQ \times SP) = SP(AQ - SQ)$$

where

$$SQ = \text{Standard quantity allowed}$$

DCdesserts.com's direct-material quantity variance for September's production of multilayer fancy cakes is computed as follows:

$$\begin{aligned}\text{Direct-material quantity variance} &= SP(AQ - SQ)\\ &= \$1.40(10{,}250 - 10{,}000)\\ &= \$350 \text{ Unfavorable}\end{aligned}$$

This variance is unfavorable, because the actual quantity of direct material used in September exceeded the standard quantity allowed for actual September output of 2,000 multilayer fancy cakes.

Notice that the direct-material price variance ($205 U) and direct-material quantity variance ($350 U) together explain the overall direct-material variance of $555 U. This is the purpose of cost variance analysis, to help managers analyze and understand the reasons for the difference in spending between actual costs and the costs expected based on standards.

> "In most cases, purchases account for one of the largest if not the largest part of the total cost. . . . Deciding what to purchase from which supplier is a key purchasing decision, and one of the key factors in this decision is the net cost of goods." (10c)
>
> **Vereeniging Refractories** (South African manufacturer of heat-resistant products)

Alternate Version of the Direct-Material Price Variance As discussed above, the direct-material price variance is based on the actual quantity of material used in production (AQ), and it helps explain why spending on direct material for production differs from what we would have expected. However, deviations between the actual and standard price of direct material originate in the *purchasing* function of the firm, not the production function. The purchasing department is charged with the responsibility for acquiring the materials needed in production. The standard direct-material price represents the price at which the purchasing department is expected to be able to buy them.

To help control this function, some companies compute a second version of the direct-material price variance, called the **direct-material *purchase* price variance.** The purpose of this alternate version is to determine if the company was able to acquire direct materials at the planned price and to analyze the performance of the purchasing department in meeting the price standards.

As shown in Exhibit 10-3, consistent with its goal of measuring purchasing performance the quantity used in computing the direct-material purchase price variance is the actual quantity of direct material *purchased.* This calculation stands in contrast to the computation of the direct-material price variance earlier in the chapter, which was based

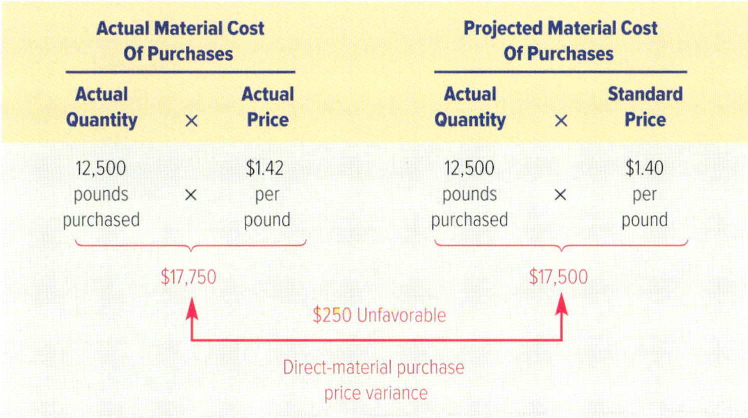

Exhibit 10–3
Direct-Material Purchase Price Variance

on the actual quantity *used* in production. (When all material purchased is used in production, there is no difference between the two versions of the direct-material price variance.)

Suppose that during September DCdesserts.com made the following purchases of direct material:

Direct material purchased: actual cost 12,500 pounds at $1.42 per pound	$17,750

As Exhibit 10-3 demonstrates, the formula for the direct-material purchase price variance is as follows:

$$\text{Direct-material purchase price variance} = (PQ \times AP) - (PQ \times SP) = PQ(AP - SP)$$

where

PQ = Quantity purchased

DCdesserts.com's direct-material purchase price variance for September is computed as follows:

$$\begin{aligned}\text{Direct-material purchase price variance} &= PQ(AP - SP)\\ &= 12{,}500(\$1.42 - \$1.40)\\ &= \$250 \text{ Unfavorable}\end{aligned}$$

This variance is unfavorable, because the actual purchase price for materials purchased during the month exceeded the standard price, causing spending on purchases during the month to be higher than planned.[1] Timely action to follow up a significant purchase price variance will be facilitated by calculating this variance as soon as possible after the material is *purchased.*

Direct-Labor Variances

Why did DCdesserts.com spend more than the anticipated amount on direct labor during September? First, the division incurred a cost of $21 per hour for direct labor instead of the standard amount of $20 per hour. Second, the division used only 980 hours of direct labor, which is less than the standard quantity allowed of 1,000 hours for the actual output of 2,000 multilayer fancy cakes. We analyze direct-labor costs by computing a **direct-labor rate variance** and a **direct-labor efficiency variance.** Exhibit 10–4 depicts the computation of these variances.

[1]In the DCdesserts.com example, the price paid for materials purchased is the same as the price paid for materials used in production. Often the price paid for materials purchased during the month will differ from the price that was paid for materials in a prior month and that are now being used in production. In that case, the price used in calculating the two different direct-material price variances would be different.

Exhibit 10–4
Direct-Labor Rate and Efficiency Variances

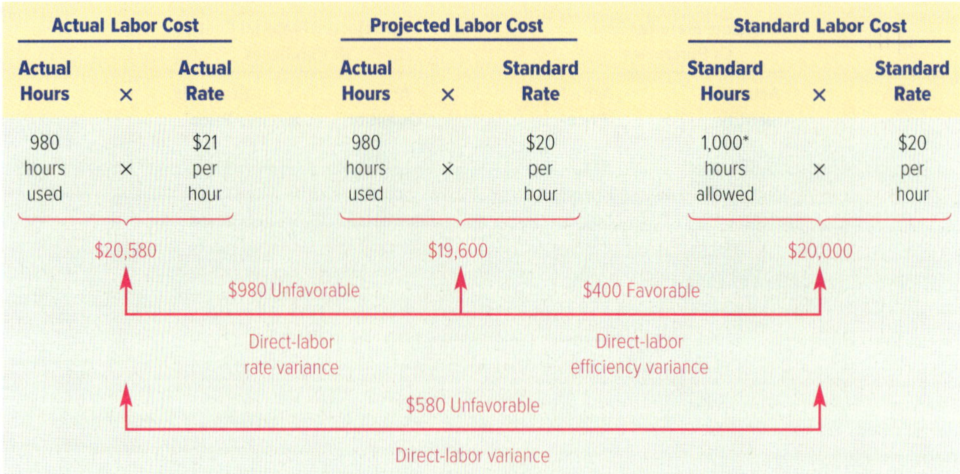

*Actual output × Standard hours per unit = 2,000 units × .5 hour per unit = 1,000 hours allowed.

Notice that the direct-labor rate variance and the direct-material price variance that we discussed earlier are related: both measure the difference in spending that is caused by the *price* of an input into production. The "price" paid for labor is generally called the "labor rate," so the name of that variance is changed to match. Similarly, the direct-labor efficiency variance corresponds to the direct-material quantity variance: both refer to the difference in spending caused by the *amount* of an input needed to produce the production output.

Direct-Labor Rate Variance Similar to the process we used for materials, we compute the portion of the spending difference that is caused by a difference in the direct-labor rate by establishing a benchmark cost for the actual amount of direct labor used, which we label the *projected direct-labor cost.* The deviation between the actual and projected direct-labor cost is caused by a difference in the direct-labor rate, and it is called the *direct-labor rate variance*.

The formula for the direct-labor rate variance is shown below.

$$\text{Direct-labor rate variance} = (AH \times AR) - (AH \times SR) = AH(AR - SR)$$

where

AH = Actual hours used
AR = Actual rate per hour
SR = Standard rate per hour

DCdesserts.com's direct-labor rate variance for September's production of multilayer fancy cakes is computed as follows:

$$\begin{aligned}\text{Direct-labor rate variance} &= AH(AR - SR)\\ &= 980(\$21 - \$20)\\ &= \$980 \text{ Unfavorable}\end{aligned}$$

This variance is unfavorable because the actual rate exceeded the standard rate during September, causing spending to be higher than projected.

Direct-Labor Efficiency Variance As Exhibit 10–4 shows, the formula for the direct-labor efficiency variance is as follows:

$$\text{Direct-labor efficiency variance} = (AH \times SR) - (SH \times SR) = SR(AH - SH)$$

where

SH = Standard hours allowed

DCdesserts.com's direct-labor efficiency variance for September is computed as follows:

$$\begin{aligned}\text{Direct-labor efficiency variance} &= SR(AH - SH)\\ &= \$20(980 - 1{,}000)\\ &= \$400 \text{ Favorable}\end{aligned}$$

This variance is favorable, because the actual direct-labor hours used in September were less than the standard hours allowed for actual September output of 2,000 multilayer fancy cakes.

Notice that the direct-labor rate and efficiency variances add up to the total direct-labor variance. However, the rate and efficiency variances have opposite signs, since one variance is unfavorable and the other is favorable.

Direct-labor rate variance	$980 Unfavorable	Different signs of variances cancel just as plus
Direct-labor efficiency variance	400 Favorable	and minus signs cancel in arithmetic.
Direct-labor variance	$580 Unfavorable	

PARKER HANNIFIN CORPORATION'S BRASS PRODUCTS DIVISION

Management Accounting Practice

Parker Hannifin

Parker Hannifin's Brass Products Division, a world-class manufacturer of brass fittings, valves, and tubing, is a standard-costing success story.[2] "Parker Brass uses its standard-costing system and variance analyses as important business tools to target problem areas so it can develop solutions for continuous improvement. Variances are reported for each product line, and if any production variance exceeds 5 percent of product-line sales, the product-line manager is required to provide an explanation. Also required is a plan to correct the problems underlying any unfavorable variances. Variance reports, which are generated within one day of the completion of a job order, are distributed to managers and production schedulers. A variance database is kept, which can be accessed by product-line managers, to provide variance data by part number, by job-order number, or by dollar amount."

From the perspective of Parker Brass's management, the division has modified its standard-costing system to provide disaggregated and timely cost information to enable quick corrective action in a rapidly changing business environment.

Multiple Types of Direct Material or Direct Labor

Manufacturing processes usually involve several types of direct material. In such cases, direct-material price and quantity variances are computed for each type of material. Then these variances are added to obtain a total price variance and a total quantity variance. For example, a more detailed analysis of direct-material costs at DCdesserts.com might reveal the following:

	Price Variance	Quantity Variance
Flour	$105 F	$225 U
Eggs	265 U	140 U
Sugar	50 U	25 F
Flavorings and other	5 F	10 U
Overall direct material variance	$205 U	$350 U

[2]David Johnsen and Parvez Sopariwala, "Standard Costing Is Alive and Well at Parker Brass," *Management Accounting Quarterly* 1, no. 2 (Winter 2000), pp. 12–20.

This level of detail can provide greater insight into the reasons that costs were not incurred as expected.

Similarly, if a production process involves several types of direct labor, rate and efficiency variances are computed for each labor type. Then they are added to obtain a total rate variance and a total efficiency variance.

Allowing for Production Loss

In many production processes, a certain amount of production loss is normal. This can be inherent in the production process (evaporation, chemical reaction) or it can be due to unavoidable spoilage or defective production. Whatever the reason, the loss must be taken into account when the standard quantity of material is computed. To illustrate, suppose that 100 quarts of cream are normally required to obtain 80 quarts of pastry filling, due to evaporation during the cooking process. If DCdesserts.com's September production output of 2,000 multilayer fancy cakes is expected to require 500 quarts of pastry filling, what is the standard allowed quantity of input (cream)?

$$\text{Good output quantity} = 80\% \times \text{Input quantity allowed}$$

Dividing both sides of the equation by 80%

$$\frac{\text{Good output quantity}}{80\%} = \text{Input quantity allowed}$$

Using the numbers in the illustration

$$\frac{\text{500 quarts of good output}}{80\%} = \text{625 quarts of input allowed}$$

The total standard allowed input is 625 quarts of cream, which should yield 500 quarts of good output of pastry filling.

Significance of Cost Variances

Learning Objective 10-4

Explain several methods for determining the significance of cost variances.

Managers do not have time to investigate the causes of every cost variance. Management by exception enables managers to look into the causes of only significant variances. But what constitutes an exception that is worth investigating? How does the manager know when to follow up on a cost variance and when to ignore it?

These questions are difficult to answer, because to some extent the answers are part of the art of management. A manager applies judgment and experience in making guesses, pursuing hunches, and relying on intuition to determine when a variance should be investigated. Nevertheless, there are guidelines and rules of thumb that managers often apply.

Forest Home National Bank

We will explore these and other issues relating to the implementation of a standard costing system by considering the operations of Forest Home National Bank (FHNB). FHNB is a regional financial services firm based in Boise, Idaho. The firm develops standards relating to the provision of services in its five branch offices and its central loan processing facility. In a bank, most direct-cost standards relate to the direct labor associated with providing financial services. This may include handling customer deposits, filling ATM machines, processing loan applications, and many other financial-transaction services.

Size of Variances When deciding which variances to investigate, the *absolute size* of a variance is an important consideration. Managers are more likely to follow up on large variances than on small ones. But the *relative size* of the variance is probably even more important. A manager is more likely to investigate a $20,000 material quantity variance that is 20 percent of the standard direct-material cost of $100,000 than a $50,000 labor efficiency variance that is only 2 percent of the standard direct-labor cost of $2,500,000. The *relative* magnitude of the $20,000 material quantity variance (20 percent) is greater than the *relative* magnitude of the $50,000 labor efficiency variance (2 percent). For this

Exhibit 10–5
Cost Variance Report for April: FHNB, All Branches

Forest Home
National Bank

	Amount	Percentage of Standard Cost	Investigate*
Teller operations			
Standard cost allowed (for 15,800 actual transactions)	$31,600		
Direct-labor rate variance	$ 1,060 U	3.4%	Yes
Direct-labor efficiency variance	$ 3,400 F	10.8%	Yes
Consumer-loan processing			
Standard cost allowed (for 190 actual loan applications)	$ 7,600		
Direct-labor rate variance	$ 680 U	8.9%	No
Direct-labor efficiency variance	$ 840 U	11.1%	Yes

*Investigate variances greater than $1,000 or 10% of standard cost.

reason, cost variance reports often show the relative magnitude of variances. For example, the April cost variance report for FHNB's financial services includes the items shown in Exhibit 10–5.

Managers often apply a rule of thumb that takes into account both the absolute and the relative magnitudes of a variance. As indicated in Exhibit 10–5, the rule at FHNB is the following: Investigate variances that are either greater than $1,000 or greater than 10 percent of standard cost.

Recurring Variances Another consideration in deciding when to investigate a variance is whether the variance occurs repeatedly or only infrequently. Suppose FHNB managers use the rule of thumb stated above and direct-labor rate variances for consumer-loan processing occur as shown in the following Excel spreadsheet.

FOREST HOME NATIONAL BANK - Consumer Loans

Month	Standard Allowed Direct-Labor Cost	Direct-Labor Rate Variance		Percentage of Standard Cost
January	$ 8,800	$ 720	U*	8.2%
February	6,400	590	U	9.2%
March	7,200	640	U	8.9%
April	7,600	680	U	8.9%

*U denotes an unfavorable variance.

In this case, a strict adherence to the rule of thumb indicates no investigation, since none of the monthly variances is greater than $1,000 or 10 percent of standard cost. Nevertheless, the FHNB loan office manager might investigate this variance in April, since it has *recurred* at a reasonably high level for several consecutive months. In this case, the consistency of the variance is what triggers an investigation, not its absolute or relative magnitude.

Trends A trend in a variance also may call for investigation. Suppose the FHNB loan office manager observes the consumer-loan direct-labor efficiency variances shown in the following Excel spreadsheet.

None of these variances is large enough to trigger an investigation if the manager uses the "$1,000 or 10 percent" rule of thumb. However, the three-month *trend* is worrisome. An alert manager will likely follow up on this unfavorable trend to determine its causes before costs get out of hand. Indeed, as we saw in Exhibit 10–5, left uncorrected

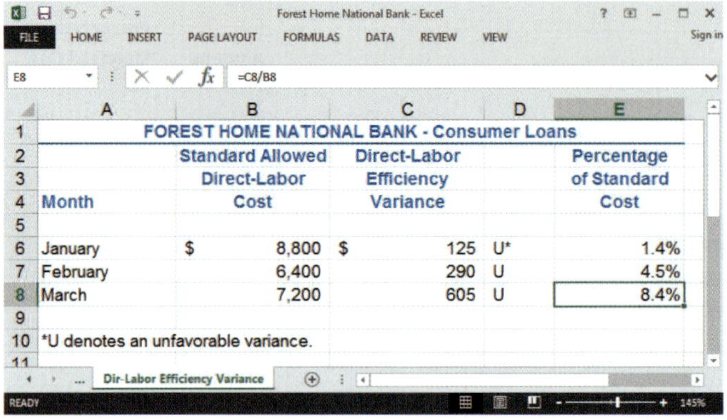

	A	B		C		D	E
1	FOREST HOME NATIONAL BANK - Consumer Loans						
2		Standard Allowed		Direct-Labor			Percentage
3		Direct-Labor		Efficiency			of Standard
4	Month	Cost		Variance			Cost
5							
6	January	$	8,800	$	125	U*	1.4%
7	February		6,400		290	U	4.5%
8	March		7,200		605	U	8.4%
9							
10	*U denotes an unfavorable variance.						

the direct-labor efficiency variance for consumer loans triggers an investigation in April. However, investigating the trend in March might have avoided the continued deterioration in performance.

Controllability Another important consideration in deciding when to look into the causes of a variance is the manager's view of the **controllability** of the cost item. A manager is more likely to investigate the variance for a cost that is controllable by someone in the organization than one that is not. For example, there may be little point in investigating a labor rate variance if the organization has no control over the staffing decisions. This could happen, for example, if FHNB's tellers operate under a union contract that specifies who does what work according to seniority and how much they will be paid. In contrast, the manager responsible for tellers is likely to follow up on a variance that should be controllable, such as a direct-labor efficiency variance.

Favorable Variances It is just as important to investigate significant favorable variances as significant unfavorable variances. The fact that a significant variance has occurred indicates that something has not gone as planned, which warrants attention even if it is favorable. For example, the significant and favorable direct-labor efficiency variance for teller operations at FHNB may indicate that tellers at one branch have developed a more efficient way of performing their transactions. By investigating the variance, management will become aware of the improved method and may be able to implement it in other FHNB branches.

On the other hand, favorable variances can sometimes indicate a problem. For example, an alternative explanation for the significant and favorable direct-labor efficiency variance for teller operations might be that tellers are being pressured to perform faster and to do so they are taking shortcuts that result in more errors. These errors could lead to higher customer dissatisfaction and additional cost and effort by FHNB to correct them after the fact. Remember, "favorable" is not necessarily equivalent to "good"!

Costs and Benefits of Investigation The decision whether to investigate a cost variance is a cost-benefit decision. The costs of investigation include the time spent by the investigating manager and the employees in the department where the investigation occurs. Other potential costs include disruption of the production process as the investigation is conducted, and corrective actions taken to eliminate the cause of a variance. The benefits of a variance investigation include reduced future production costs if the cause of an unfavorable variance is eliminated. Another potential benefit is the cost saving associated with the lowering of cost standards or avoiding problems in other areas when the cause of a favorable variance is discovered.

Weighing these considerations takes the judgment of skillful and experienced managers. Key to this judgment is an intimate understanding of the organization's production process and day-to-day contact with its operations.

Exhibit 10–6
Statistical Control Chart

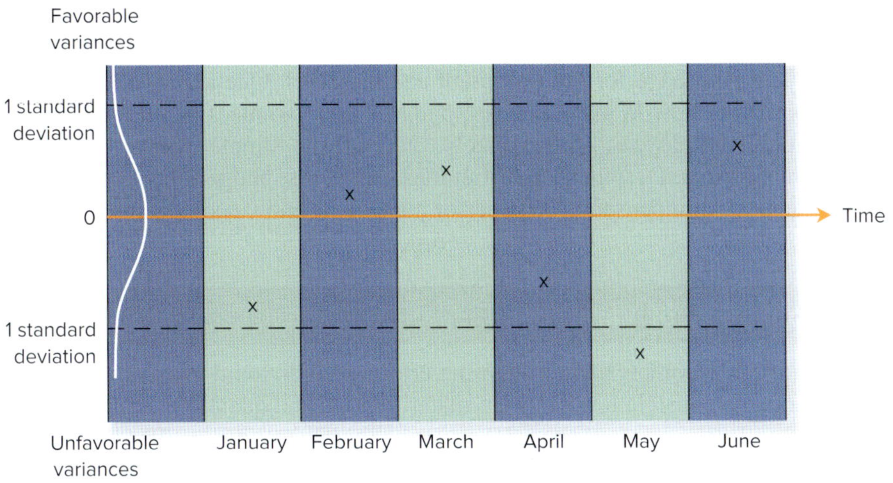

A Statistical Approach

There are many reasons for cost variances. For example, a direct-labor efficiency variance could be caused by inexperienced employees, employee inefficiency, poor-quality raw materials, poorly maintained machinery, an intentional work slowdown due to employee grievances, or many other factors. In addition to these substantive reasons, there are purely random causes of variances. People are not robots, and they are not perfectly consistent in their work habits. Random fluctuations in direct-labor efficiency variances can be caused by such factors as employee illnesses, workers experimenting with different production methods, or simply random fatigue. Ideally, managers would be able to sort out the randomly caused variances from those with substantive and controllable underlying causes. It is impossible to accomplish this with 100 percent accuracy, but a **statistical control chart** can help.

A statistical control chart plots cost variances across time and compares them with a statistically determined *critical value* that triggers an investigation. This critical value is usually determined by assuming that cost variances have a normal probability distribution with a mean of zero. The critical value is set at some multiple of the distribution's standard deviation. Variances greater than the critical value are investigated.

Exhibit 10–6 shows a statistical control chart with a critical value of 1 standard deviation. The manager would investigate the variance observed in May, since it falls further than 1 standard deviation from the mean (zero). The variances for the remaining five months would not be investigated. The presumption is that these minor variances are due to random causes and are not worth investigating.

Behavioral Impact of Standard Costing

Learning Objective 10-5

Describe some behavioral effects of standard costing.

Standard costs and variance analysis are useful in diagnosing organizational performance. These tools help managers discern "the story behind the story"—the details of operations that underlie reported cost and profit numbers. Standard costs, budgets, and variances also are used to evaluate the performance of individuals and departments. The performance of individuals, relative to standards or budgets, often is used to help determine salary increases, bonuses, and promotions. When standards and variances affect employee reward structures, they can profoundly influence behavior.

For example, suppose a hotel's food and beverage department manager earns a bonus when food and beverage costs are below the budgeted amount. This reward structure will provide a concrete incentive for the manager to keep food and beverage costs under control. But such an incentive can have either positive or negative effects. The bonus may induce the manager to seek the most economical food suppliers and to watch more carefully for employee theft and waste. However, the bonus also could persuade the manager to buy cheaper but less tender cuts of meat for the restaurant. This could ultimately result in lost patronage for the restaurant and the hotel. One aspect of skillful management is knowing how to use standards, budgets, and variances to get the most out of an organization's employees. Unfortunately, there are no simple answers or formulas for success in this area. Despite such difficulties, standards, budgets, and variances are used in the executive compensation schemes of many well-known companies.

Controllability of Variances

> "Effective performance management focuses on controllable costs . . . variance analysis and remediation activity should focus on the controllable elements of performance." (10d)
>
> **KPMG**

Cost control is accomplished through the efforts of individual managers in an organization. Who is responsible for the direct-material price and quantity variances? The direct-labor rate and efficiency variances? Answering these questions is often difficult, because it is rare that any one person completely controls any event. Nevertheless, it is often possible to identify the manager who is *most able to influence* a particular variance, even if he or she does not exercise complete control over the outcome.

Direct-Material Price Variance The purchasing manager is generally in the best position to influence material price variances. Through skillful purchasing practices, an expert purchasing manager can get the best prices available for purchased goods and services. To achieve this goal, the purchasing manager uses such practices as buying in quantity, negotiating purchase contracts, comparing prices among vendors, and global sourcing.

Despite these purchasing skills, the purchasing manager is not in complete control of prices. The need to purchase component parts with precise engineering specifications, the all-too-frequent rush requests from the production department, and worldwide shortages of critical materials all contribute to the challenges faced by the purchasing manager.

The material prices negotiated by the purchasing manager affect the reported cost of production, so to identify the variance in production cost that is attributable to purchasing, we compute the direct-material price variance based on *usage* of materials. However, to get a more timely report of the purchasing manager's success or failure, we also compute and report the alternate version of the direct-material price variance, the direct-material *purchase* price variance, that was discussed earlier in the chapter.

Direct-Material Quantity Variance The production supervisor is usually in the best position to influence material quantity variances. Skillful supervision and motivation of production employees, coupled with the careful use and handling of materials, contribute to minimal waste. Production engineers are also partially responsible for material quantity variances, since they determine the grade and technical specifications of materials and component parts. In some cases, using a low-grade material may result in greater waste than using a high-grade material.

Direct-Labor Rate Variance Direct-labor rate variances generally result from using a different mix of employees than that anticipated when the standards were set. Wage rates differ among employees due to their skill levels and their seniority with the organization. Using a higher proportion of more senior or more highly skilled employees than a task requires can result in unfavorable direct-labor rate variances. The production supervisor is generally in the best position to influence the work schedules of employees.

Direct-Labor Efficiency Variance Once again, the production supervisor is usually most responsible for the efficient use of employee time. Through motivation toward production goals and effective work schedules, the efficiency of employees can be maximized.

Interaction among Variances

Interactions among variances often occur, making it even more difficult to determine the responsibility for a particular variance. To illustrate, consider the following anecdote from a manufacturer of brass musical instruments. The purchasing manager obtained a special price on brass alloy from a new supplier. When the material was placed into production, it turned out to be a lower grade of material than the production employees were used to. The alloy was of a slightly different composition, which made the material bend less easily during the formation of brass instruments. The company could have returned the material to the supplier, but that would have interrupted production and kept the division from filling its orders on time. Since using the off-standard material would not affect the quality of the company's finished products, the division manager decided to keep the material and make the best of the situation.

The ultimate result was that the company incurred four interrelated variances during May. The material was less expensive than normal, so the direct-material price variance was favorable. However, the employees had difficulty using the material, which resulted in more waste than expected. Hence, the division incurred an unfavorable direct-material quantity variance.

What were the labor implications of the off-standard material? Due to the difficulty in working with the metal alloy, the employees required more than the standard amount of time to form the instruments. This resulted in an unfavorable direct-labor efficiency variance. Finally, the production supervisor had to use his most senior employees to work with the off-standard material. Since these people earned relatively high wages, the direct-labor rate variance was also unfavorable.

To summarize, the purchase of off-standard material resulted in the following interrelated variances.

Purchase of off-standard material →
- Favorable direct-material price variance
- Unfavorable direct-material quantity variance
- Unfavorable direct-labor rate variance
- Unfavorable direct-labor efficiency variance

Such interactions of variances make it more difficult to assign responsibility for any particular variance.

Trade-Offs among Variances Does the incident described above mean that the decision to buy and use the off-standard material was a poor one? Not necessarily. Perhaps these variances were anticipated, and a conscious decision was made to buy the material anyway. How could this be a wise decision? Suppose the amounts of the variances attributable to buying the cheaper brass were as follows:

$(8,500)	Favorable direct-material price variance
1,000	Unfavorable direct-material quantity variance
2,000	Unfavorable direct-labor rate variance
1,500	Unfavorable direct-labor efficiency variance
$(4,000)	Favorable net overall variance

The company saved money overall on the decision to use a different grade of brass alloy. Given that the quality of the final product was not affected, the company's management acted wisely.

Standard Costs and Product Costing

Learning Objective 10-6

Explain how standard costs are used in product costing.

Our discussion of standard costing has focused on its use in controlling costs. But firms that use standard costs for control also use them for product costing. Recall from Chapter 3 that *product costing* is the process of accumulating the costs of a production process and assigning them to the completed products. Product costs are used for various purposes in both financial and managerial accounting.

Exhibit 10–7
Flow of Product Costs through Production Accounts

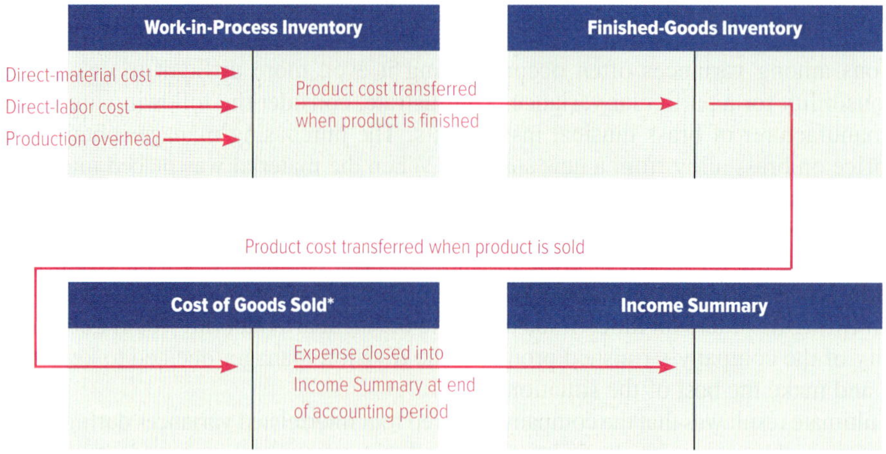

*Cost of Goods Sold is an expense. Although it is more descriptive, the term cost-of-goods-sold expense is not used as much in practice as the simpler term *cost of goods sold.*

> "[I]nnovation and knowledge of the technology led to . . . a significant reduction in standard costs, enabling new business opportunities in the government transport market." (10e)
> **Rockwell Collins**

As production takes place, product costs are added to the Work-in-Process Inventory account. The flow of product costs through a firm's production accounts is depicted in Exhibit 10–7.

Different types of product-costing systems are distinguished by the type of costs that are entered into Work-in-Process Inventory. In Chapter 3, we studied *actual-* and *normal-*costing systems. In these product-costing systems, the *actual* costs of direct material and direct labor are charged to Work-in-Process Inventory. In a **standard-costing system,** the *standard* costs of direct material and direct labor are entered into Work-in-Process Inventory.

Further explanation of the use of standard costs for product-costing purposes is provided in the appendix at the end of this chapter, which can be studied now if desired.

Evaluation of Standard Costing Systems

Learning Objective 10-7

Summarize some advantages of standard costing.

Standard costing has been the predominant accounting system in manufacturing companies, for both cost control and product-costing purposes, for several decades. This remains true today, and the use of standard costing is spreading to nonmanufacturing firms such as Forest Home National Bank as well. The widespread use of standard costing over such a long time period suggests that it has traditionally been perceived as offering several advantages. However, today's production environment for both goods and services is changing dramatically. Some managers are calling into question the usefulness of the traditional standard-costing approach. After performing a survey on UK companys' standard costing practices, accounting firm KPMG concluded: "All companies surveyed use standard costs and variances to value inventory for statutory purposes, for management reporting purposes and for performance measurement and management. Despite its prevalence no respondents are finding it easy to obtain the information and insight required to satisfy all three of these areas."[3]

Advantages of Standard Costing

In this section, we will list some of the advantages traditionally attributed to standard-costing systems. In the next section, we will discuss some of the criticisms of the standard-costing approach, and suggest several ways in which the role of standard costing is beginning to change.

Some advantages traditionally attributed to standard costing include the following:

1. Standard costs provide a basis for *sensible cost comparisons.* As we discussed earlier, it would make no sense to compare budgeted costs at one (planned)

[3]KPMG, "Standard Costing: Insights from Leading Companies," February 2010. http://www.cimaglobal.com/Documents/Thought_leadership_docs/StandardCosting2010Insightsfromcompanies.pdf

activity level with actual costs incurred at a different (actual) activity level. Standard costs enable the manager to see the standard allowed cost, given actual output, which then serves as a sensible benchmark to compare with the actual cost.

2. Computation of standard costs and cost variances enables managers to employ *management by exception.* This approach conserves valuable management time.
3. Variances provide a means of *performance evaluation* and rewards for employees.
4. Since the variances are used in performance evaluation, they provide *motivation* for employees to adhere to standards.
5. Use of standard costs in product costing results in *more stable product costs* than if actual production costs are used. Actual costs often fluctuate erratically, whereas standard costs are changed only periodically.

Like any tool, a standard-costing system can be misused. When employees are criticized for every cost variance, the positive motivational effects will quickly vanish. Moreover, if standards are not revised often enough, they will become outdated. Then the benefits of cost benchmarks and product costing will disappear.

"Many people have condemned standard costing, saying it is irrelevant to the current just-in-time, fast-paced business environment. Yet surveys consistently show that most industrial companies in the U.S. and abroad still use it. Apparently, these companies have successfully adapted their standard-costing system to their particular business environments." (10f)

Brass Products Division, Parker Hannifin Corporation

Criticisms of Standard Costing in Today's Manufacturing Environment

Learning Objective 10-8

Explain several common criticisms of standard costing.

Listed below are several drawbacks attributed to standard costing in an advanced manufacturing setting.[4]

1. The variances calculated under standard costing are at too aggregate a level and come too late to be useful. A production process comprises many activities that result in costs. By focusing on the activities that cause costs to be incurred, by eliminating non-value-added activities, and by continually improving performance in value-added activities, costs will be minimized and profit maximized.[5] What is needed are performance measures that focus directly on performance in the activities that management wants to improve. For example, such activities could include product quality, processing time, and delivery performance. (We will explore such measures in Chapter 12.)
2. Traditional cost variances are also too aggregate in the sense that they are not tied to specific product lines or production batches. The aggregate nature of the variances makes it difficult for managers to determine their cause.

© Bloomberg/Getty Images

This Texas Instruments manufacturing facility relies on its suppliers for high-quality raw materials delivered on a timely basis. Texas Instruments, like many other companies, employs a sophisticated supplier rating system to measure the performance of its vendors.

[4]The sources for this material are Robert S. Kaplan, "Limitations of Cost Accounting in Advanced Manufacturing Environments," in *Measures for Manufacturing Excellence,* ed. Robert S. Kaplan (Boston: Harvard Business School Press, 1990), pp. 1–14; H. Thomas Johnson, "Performance Measurement for Competitive Excellence," in *Measures for Manufacturing Excellence,* ed. Robert S. Kaplan (Boston: Harvard Business School Press, 1990), pp. 63–90; Robert A. Bonsack, "Does Activity-Based Costing Replace Standard Costing?" *Journal of Cost Management* 4, no. 4 (Winter 1991), pp. 46, 47; and Michiharu Sukurai, "The Influence of Factory Automation on Management Accounting Practices: A Study of Japanese Companies," in *Measures for Manufacturing Excellence,* ed. Robert S. Kaplan (Boston: Harvard Business School Press, 1990), pp. 39–62.

[5]Cost management systems and activity-based management are covered in Chapter 5. Elimination of non-value-added costs also is covered in Chapter 5.

3. Traditional standard-costing systems focus too much on the cost and efficiency of direct labor, which is rapidly becoming a relatively unimportant factor of production in manufacturing.
4. One of the most important conditions for the successful use of standard costing is a stable production process. Yet the introduction of flexible manufacturing systems has reduced this stability, with frequent switching among a variety of products on the same production line.
5. Shorter product life cycles mean that standards are relevant for only a short time. When new products are introduced, new standards must be developed.
6. Traditional standard costs are not defined broadly enough to capture various important aspects of performance. For example, the standard direct-material price does not capture all of the *costs of ownership.* In addition to the purchase price and transportation costs, the *cost of ownership* includes the costs of ordering, paying bills, scheduling delivery, receiving, inspecting, handling and storing, and any production-line disruptions resulting from untimely or incorrect delivery.
7. Traditional standard-costing systems tend to focus too much on cost minimization, rather than increasing product quality or customer service. For example, buying the least expensive materials of a given quality, in order to avoid a material price variance, may result in using a vendor whose delivery capabilities are not consistent with supply-chain requirements.

Management Accounting Practice

ABB, Bosch Chassis Systems, and Hewlett-Packard

WORKING WITH SUPPLIERS TO MANAGE COSTS

Many companies have developed supplier rating systems that contribute to cost competitiveness by identifying the various costs of ownership. Standard costs often serve as a reference point in such systems. By targeting aspects of performance that affect the standard cost of production, these rating systems help companies achieve cost control and even reductions in standard costs.

ABB has developed a supplier rating system that is designed to minimize the costs of direct materials by focusing on costly defects and shipping errors. "The process consists of a data-driven approach to regularly measure and provide feedback to suppliers. This feedback enables ongoing communication, continuous process improvement, and supplier development."[6]

Bosch Chassis Systems tracks various elements of supplier performance through its Monthly Supplier Performance Rating System. Bosch's model provides for an annual "Supplier of the Year Award," which includes criteria relating to cost reduction, achieving cost targets, and the supplier's role in "value management activities which bring about incremental improvement."[7]

Cost of quality is a significant component of standard cost but one that is difficult to measure. **Hewlett-Packard** uses a supplier measurement system to engage suppliers in the effort to identify and reduce these costs. "By forming a concrete set of standards regarding product technology, quality, responsiveness, delivery, cost, and environmental impact, HP has been able to weed out noncompliant suppliers, and drive performance higher in others. . . . Several quality metrics are measured weekly for cost of quality impact, including annualized failure rate (AFR), annualized return rate (ARR), defects parts per million (PPM), and component failure rate."[8]

---

[6]ABB website, "Supplier Performance Assessment," March 15, 2006, http://www02.abb.com/global/abbzh/abbzh251.nsf!OpenDatabase&db=/global/seitp/seitp161.nsf&v=17EBE&e=us&m=2A46&c=E4D128636CAEFA9EC12569AC0032F1C2.

[7]Bosch Chassis Systems Work Instruction WIG 11-005, "Monthly Supplier Performance Rating System," May 8, 2008, www.pbr.com.au/supplier/documents/WIG11-005.pdf.

[8]Maria Varmazis, "How HP Measures Supplier Performance and Compliance," *Purchasing* 135, issue 13 (September 21, 2006), pp. 47–49.

Focus on Ethics

SACRIFICING QUALITY TO CUT STANDARD COSTS

Pressures to control costs, coupled with bonus systems based on adherence to standards, can present a temptation to engage in ethical lapses. The following hypothetical scenario describes such a situation.

Keystone Company manufactures small wooden household items such as cutting boards and knife racks. Keystone's controller, Marc Rigas, recently completed the installation of a new standard-costing system, which has been in place now for six months. Jack Smith, the purchasing manager, is about to place an order for wood to be used in Keystone's cutting boards. Smith has found a supplier that will furnish the necessary wood at $2.00 per board foot, rather than the standard cost of $3.00. This is very appealing to Smith, since his annual bonus is influenced by any favorable price variances he is able to obtain. Smith is due to be transferred at the end of the year to Keystone's Allentown Division, which manufactures metal kitchen utensils. The transfer is a promotion for Smith.

After further discussions with the potential supplier, Smith realized that the wood being offered would not be well-suited for use in cutting boards. Although the wood would seem fine in the manufacturing process, and it would result in an attractive product, it would not hold up well over time. This particular type of wood, after repeated cycles of getting wet and then drying out, would tend to crack. Smith figured that it would take about a year for the cutting boards to deteriorate, and then Keystone Company would be beset with customer complaints.

Smith mulled over the situation for a while and then decided to accept the new supplier's offer. The $2.00 price would help him get a nice annual bonus, which he could use to help with the down payment on a new home. By the time the cutting boards cracked and customers started to complain, he would be long gone. Someone else could worry about the problem then, he reasoned. After all, he thought, people shouldn't expect a cutting board to last forever.

Several weeks later, when the invoice for the first shipment of wood came through, Rigas noticed the large, favorable price variance. When he ran into Smith on the golf course, Rigas congratulated Smith on the purchase. The following conversation resulted.

Rigas (C): "That was quite a price break on that wood, Jack. How'd you swing it?"

Smith (PM): "Hard-ball negotiating, Marc. It's as simple as that."

Rigas (C): "Is it good wood? And how about the supplier, Jack? Will they deliver on time?"

Smith (PM): "This supplier is very timely in their deliveries. I made sure of that."

Rigas (C): "How about the quality, Jack? Did you check into that?"

Smith (PM): "Sure I did, Marc. Hey, what is this? An interrogation? I thought we were here to play golf."

Rigas was left feeling puzzled and disconcerted by Smith's evasiveness. The next day, Rigas talked to the production manager, Amy Wilcox, about his concerns. Later that day, Wilcox raised the issue with Smith. After a lengthy and sometimes heated exchange, the story came out.

Discuss the ethical issues involved in this scenario. Did the purchasing manager, Jack Smith, act ethically? Did the controller, Marc Rigas, act ethically when he asked Smith about the quality of the wood? Did Rigas act ethically when he went to the production manager with his concerns? What should the controller do now?

Chapter Summary

LO10-1 Describe the elements of a cost control system. Managers and managerial accountants set standard costs for direct material, direct labor, and production overhead through either historical cost analysis or task analysis. They use the standard cost as a benchmark against which to compare actual costs incurred. Managers use management by exception to determine the causes of significant cost variances.

LO10-2 Describe two ways to set cost standards and distinguish between perfection and practical standards. One way to set standards is to analyze historical data, which will show how much it has cost in the past to produce a product or service. Another way to set standards is to perform task analysis, in which the production process is analyzed to determine what it should cost to produce. A perfection (or ideal) standard is one that can be attained only under nearly perfect operating conditions. A practical (or attainable) standard can be achieved with a production process that is as efficient as practical under normal operating conditions.

LO10-3 Compute and interpret the direct-material price and quantity variances and the direct-labor rate and efficiency variances. The direct-material price variance calculates the effect on production cost of deviations between actual and standard direct-material prices. The direct-material quantity variance calculates the effect on production cost of deviations between actual and standard direct-material quantities allowed, given actual production output. The direct-labor rate variance calculates the effect on production cost of deviations between actual and standard direct-labor rates. The direct-labor efficiency variance calculates the effect on production cost of deviations between actual and standard direct-labor hours allowed, given actual production output. In addition, the direct-material purchase price variance calculates the effect on spending for material purchases that is caused by deviations between actual and standard direct-material prices.

LO10-4 Explain several methods for determining the significance of cost variances. Managers determine the significance of cost variances through judgment and rules of thumb. The absolute and relative sizes of variances, recurrence of variances, variance trends, and controllability of variances are all considered in deciding whether variances warrant investigation. In some cases a statistical control chart can help determine the significance of cost variances.

LO10-5 Describe some behavioral effects of standard costing. When variances can affect employees' reward structures, such as pay increases or promotions, they can significantly affect employee behavior. For example, an unfavorable direct-material price variance may cause a purchasing manager to purchase a lower quality of material than what is specified or needed.

LO10-6 Explain how standard costs are used in product costing. The standard-costing system achieves its product-costing purpose by recording the standard cost of production into Work-in-Process Inventory as a product cost. This standard cost then flows through the Finished-Goods Inventory account and into the Cost of Goods Sold account.

LO10-7 Summarize some advantages of standard costing. Standard-costing systems offer an organization many advantages. Among these are: sensible cost comparisons; management by exception; performance evaluation; employee motivation; and more stable product costs.

LO10-8 Explain several common criticisms of standard costing. Some common criticisms of standard costing include: too high a level of aggregation exhibited by variances; untimely reporting of variances; excessive focus on direct labor; inconsistency with flexible manufacturing systems; quick outdating of standards; narrow focus of standard costs, such as ignoring the total cost of ownership; and an excessive focus on cost minimization.

LO10-9 Prepare journal entries to record and close out cost variances (appendix). The managerial accountant prepares journal entries: to enter the standard cost of production into Work-in-Process Inventory as a product cost; to transfer the standard production cost to Finished-Goods Inventory; and to close the standard production cost into Cost of Goods Sold.

Review Problem on Standard Costing and Analysis of Direct Costs

In November, DCdesserts.com produced 3,000 multilayer fancy cakes and incurred the following actual costs for direct material and direct labor.

Purchased 16,500 pounds of ingredients at $1.44 per pound.

Used 15,500 pounds of ingredients at $1.44 per pound.

Used 1,520 hours of direct labor at $22 per hour.

The standard costs for production of multilayer fancy cakes were the same in November as those given earlier in the chapter for September.

Compute DCdesserts.com's direct-material variances (price, quantity, and purchase price) and direct-labor variances (rate and efficiency) for November using the format shown in Exhibits 10–2, 10–3, and 10–4.

Solution to Review Problem

Direct-Material Price and Quantity Variances

Actual Material Cost			**Projected Material Cost**			**Standard Material Cost**		
Actual Quantity	×	**Actual Price**	**Actual Quantity**	×	**Standard Price**	**Standard Quantity**	×	**Standard Price**
15,500 pounds used	×	$1.44 per pound	15,500 pounds used	×	$1.40 per pound	15,000* pounds allowed	×	$1.40 per pound
$22,320			$21,700			$21,000		

$22,320 − $21,700: $620 Unfavorable — Direct-material price variance

$21,700 − $21,000: $700 Unfavorable — Direct-material quantity variance

$22,320 − $21,000: $1,320 Unfavorable — Direct-material variance

*Actual output × Standard quantity per unit = 3,000 units × 5 pounds per unit = 15,000 pounds allowed.

Using Formulas

Direct-material variance = Actual cost − Standard cost = (AQ × AP) − (SQ × SP)
= (15,500 × $1.44) − (15,000 × $1.40)
= $22,320 − $21,000
= $1,320 Unfavorable

Direct-material price variance = AQ(AP − SP)
= 15,500($1.44 − $1.40)
= $620 Unfavorable

Direct-material quantity variance = SP(AQ − SQ)
= $1.40(15,500 − 15,000)
= $700 Unfavorable

Check:
Price variance + Quantity variance =
$620 U + $700 U = $1,320 U

Direct-Material Purchase Price Variance

Actual Material Cost of Purchases			**Projected Material Cost of Purchases**		
Actual Quantity	×	**Actual Price**	**Actual Quantity**	×	**Standard Price**
16,500 pounds purchased	×	$1.44 per pound	16,500 pounds purchased	×	$1.40 per pound
$23,760			$23,100		

$23,760 − $23,100: $660 Unfavorable — Direct-material purchase price variance

Using Formula

Direct-material purchase price variance = PQ(AP − SP)
= 16,500($1.44 − $1.40)
= $660 Unfavorable

Direct-Labor Rate and Efficiency Variances

Actual Labor Cost			Projected Labor Cost			Standard Labor Cost		
Actual Hours	×	**Actual Rate**	**Actual Hours**	×	**Standard Rate**	**Standard Hours**	×	**Standard Rate**
1,520 hours used	×	$22 per hour	1,520 hours used	×	$20 per hour	1,500* hours allowed	×	$20 per hour
$33,440			$30,400			$30,000		

$3,040 Unfavorable — Direct-labor rate variance

$400 Unfavorable — Direct-labor efficiency variance

$3,440 Unfavorable — Direct-labor variance

*Actual output × Standard hours per unit = 3,000 units × .5 hour per unit = 1,500 hours allowed.

Using Formulas

Direct-labor variance = Actual cost − Allowed cost
= (AQ × AR) − (SQ × SR)
= (1,520 × $22) − (1,500 × $20)
= $33,440 − $30,000
= $3,440 Unfavorable

Direct-labor rate variance = AH(AR − SR)
= 1,520($22 − $20)
= $3,040 Unfavorable

Direct-labor efficiency variance = SR(AH − SH)
= $20(1,520 − 1,500)
= $400 Unfavorable

Check:
Price variance + Quantity variance = $3,040 U + $400 U = $3,440 U

Key Terms

For each term's definition refer to the indicated page, or turn to the glossary at the end of the text.

APPENDIX TO CHAPTER 10

Use of Standard Costs for Product Costing

Learning Objective 10-9

Prepare journal entries to record and close out cost variances.

In addition to providing a tool for *cost management,* standard-costing systems also provide the necessary information to be used in *product costing.* As shown in Exhibit 10–7, under standard costing it is the *standard costs* that are entered into Work-in-Process Inventory as a product cost.

Journal Entries under Standard Costing To illustrate the use of standard costs in product costing, we will continue our illustration of DCdesserts.com. For September's production of multilayer fancy cakes, the company purchased 12,500 pounds of direct material for \$17,750. The actual quantity of material used in production was 10,250 pounds. However, the standard cost of direct material, given September's actual output of 2,000 multilayer fancy cakes, was only \$14,000. The following journal entries record these facts and isolate the direct-material price and quantity variances.

Raw-Material Inventory	17,500	
Direct-Material Purchase Price Variance	250	
Accounts Payable		17,750
To record the purchase of raw material and the incurrence of an unfavorable purchase price variance.		

Work-in-Process Inventory	14,000	
Direct-Material Quantity Variance	350	
Raw-Material Inventory		14,350
To record the use of direct material in production and the incurrence of an unfavorable quantity variance.		

Notice that the material purchase is recorded in the Raw-Material Inventory account at its standard price for the actual amount purchased (\$17,500 = 12,500 pounds purchased × \$1.40 per pound) which we referred to earlier as the *projected material cost of purchases.* The difference of \$250 between that amount and the \$17,750 actually paid for the materials is the *direct-material purchase price variance* that we discussed in this chapter.

The \$14,000 debit entry to Work-in-Process Inventory adds only the standard cost of the material allowed to Work-in-Process Inventory as a product cost (\$14,000 = 10,000 pounds allowed × \$1.40 per pound). But the actual quantity of material used in production is removed from the Raw-Material Inventory account at its standard cost (\$14,350 = 10,250 pounds × \$1.40 per pound).

The two variances are isolated in their own variance accounts. Since they are both unfavorable, they are represented by debit entries.

You might be wondering about the direct-material price variance that was calculated based on material used, not material purchased. That variance is used for control purposes only and not for recording cost of inventory. The reason is that it simply represents a portion of the total materials purchased, some of which was used in production and some of which remains in inventory. As such it is already a part of the first journal entry above.

The following journal entry records the actual September cost of direct labor, as an addition to Wages and Benefits Payable (the actual wages that will be paid to employees and the benefit costs to be paid to benefit providers). The entry also adds the standard cost of direct labor to Work-in-Process Inventory.

Work-in-Process Inventory	20,000	
Direct-Labor Rate Variance	980	
Direct-Labor Efficiency Variance		400
Wages and Benefits Payable		20,580
To record the usage of direct labor and the direct-labor variances for September.		

Notice that the direct-labor cost added (debited) to Work-in-Process Inventory is the standard cost based on the labor quantity allowed for the actual number of multilayer fancy cakes produced ($20,000 = 1,000 direct-labor hours allowed × $20 per direct-labor hour). The journal entry also accounts for the difference between the amount actually payable and the amount added to inventory by isolating the direct-labor variances. Since the direct-labor efficiency variance is favorable, it is recorded as a credit entry.

The variances and other numbers in this and the preceding journal entries were calculated in Exhibits 10–2, 10–3, and 10–4.

Disposition of Variances Variances are temporary accounts, like revenue and expense accounts, and they are closed out at the end of each accounting period. Most companies close their variance accounts directly into Cost of Goods Sold. The journal entry required to close out the September variances incurred in the production of multilayer fancy cakes is as follows:

Cost of Goods Sold	1,180	
Direct-Labor Efficiency Variance	400	
Direct-Labor Rate Variance		980
Direct-Material Purchase Price Variance		250
Direct-Material Quantity Variance		350

The increase of $1,180 in Cost of Goods Sold is explained as follows:

	Unfavorable Variances Increase Cost of Goods Sold		Favorable Variance Decreases Cost of Goods Sold		Net Increase in Cost of Goods Sold
Direct-labor efficiency variance			$400		
Direct-labor rate variance	$ 980				
Direct-material purchase price variance	250				
Direct-material quantity variance	350				
Total	$1,580	−	$400	=	$1,180

The unfavorable variances represent costs of operating inefficiently, relative to the standards, and thus cause Cost of Goods Sold to be higher. The opposite is true for favorable variances.

An alternative method of variance disposition is to apportion all variances among Work-in-Process Inventory, Finished-Goods Inventory, and Cost of Goods Sold. This accounting treatment reflects the effects of unusual inefficiency or efficiency in all of the accounts through which the production costs flow. This method, called *variance proration,* is covered more fully in cost accounting texts.

Cost Flow Under Standard Costing In a standard-costing system, since standard costs are entered into Work-in-Process Inventory, standard costs flow through all of the production accounts. Thus, as depicted in Exhibit 10–7, all of the product costs flowing through the accounts are standard costs. To illustrate, suppose DCdesserts.com produced 2,000 multilayer fancy cakes in September and sold all 2,000 of them. The journal entries to record the flow of standard direct-material and direct-labor costs are shown below.

Finished-Goods Inventory	34,000*	
Work-in-Process Inventory		34,000

*Total standard cost of direct material and direct labor: $34,000 = $14,000 + $20,000.

Cost of Goods Sold	34,000*	
Finished-Goods Inventory		34,000

*All 2,000 multilayer fancy cakes were sold.

Our illustration is not really complete yet, because we have not discussed production-overhead costs. This topic is covered in the next chapter. The important point at this juncture is that in a standard-costing system, *standard costs rather than actual costs flow through the production accounts.*

A Note on Perishable Products and JIT Production Management Systems Traditional manufacturing systems typically exhibit the cost flows explained in this section. Direct-material, direct-labor, and production-overhead costs are entered in Work-in-Process Inventory, from which they flow into Finished-Goods Inventory when the goods are finished, and then on into Cost of Goods Sold. Since DCdesserts.com produces perishable goods, which are produced and sold on the same day, a simpler procedure could be used. In DCdesserts.com's case, the *standard* costs of direct material, direct labor, and production overhead could be entered directly into Cost of Goods Sold as they are incurred. This simplified procedure could be used, because the production process is very short and the goods are sold immediately. Thus, there is never any work-in-process inventory or finished-goods inventory on hand. Such situations are common with producers of perishable goods.

An analogous situation occurs in manufacturers that employ a just-in-time (JIT) production and inventory control system. In a JIT environment, raw materials are delivered just in time to be entered into production, and parts or components are manufactured in each stage of the production process just in time for the next production stage. Thus, like the case of perishable goods, there is little or no work-in-process or finished-goods inventory at any given time in a JIT environment. For this reason, many manufacturers that employ the JIT approach make use of highly simplified cost accounting procedures similar to those explained in the preceding paragraph for DCdesserts.com.

Review Questions

10–1. List the three parts of a control system, and explain how such a system works.

10–2. What is meant by the phrase *management by exception?*

10–3. Describe two methods of setting standards.

10–4. Distinguish between *perfection* and *practical* standards. Which type of standard is likely to produce the best motivational effects?

10–5. Describe how a bank might use standards.

10–6. Explain how standard material prices and quantities are set.

10–7. What is the interpretation of the *direct-material price variance* and the *direct-material purchase price variance?*

10–8. What manager is usually in the best position to influence the direct-material price variance?

10–9. What is the interpretation of the *direct-material quantity variance?*

10–10. What manager is usually in the best position to influence the direct-material quantity variance?

10–11. Explain why the quantity purchased (PQ) is used in computing the direct-material *purchase* price variance, but the actual quantity consumed (AQ) is used in computing the direct-material price and quantity variances.

10–12. What is the interpretation of the *direct-labor rate variance?* What are some possible causes?

10–13. What manager is generally in the best position to influence the direct-labor rate variance?

10–14. What is the interpretation of the *direct-labor efficiency variance?*

10–15. What manager is generally in the best position to influence the direct-labor efficiency variance?

10–16. Refer to Review Question 10–11. Why does an analogous question *not* arise in the context of the direct-labor variances?

10–17. Describe five factors that managers often consider when determining the significance of a variance.

10–18. Discuss several ways in which standard-costing systems should be adapted in today's manufacturing environment.

10–19. Describe how standard costs are used for product costing.

10–20. List six advantages of a standard-costing system.

10–21. List seven criticisms of standard costing in an advanced manufacturing environment.

Exercises

All applicable Exercises are available in Connect. connect

Exercise 10–22
Straightforward Computation of Variances
(LO 10-1, 10-3)

Saskatewan Can Company manufactures recyclable soft-drink cans. A unit of production is a case of 12 dozen cans. The following standards have been set by the production-engineering staff and the controller.

Direct labor:	Direct material:
Quantity, .25 hour	Quantity, 4 kilograms
Rate, $16 per hour	Price, $.80 per kilogram

Actual material purchases amounted to 240,000 kilograms at $.81 per kilogram. Actual costs incurred in the production of 50,000 units were as follows:

Direct labor:	$211,900 for 13,000 hours
Direct material:	$170,100 for 210,000 kilograms

Required:

1. Use the variance formulas to compute the direct-material price and quantity variances, the direct-material purchase price variance, and the direct-labor rate and efficiency variances. Indicate whether each variance is favorable or unfavorable.
2. *Build a spreadsheet:* Construct an Excel spreadsheet to solve the preceding requirement. Show how the solution will change if the following information changes: the standard direct-labor rate is $15 per hour, and the standard direct-material price is $.79 per kilogram.

Exercise 10–23
Determination of Variances Using Diagrams
(LO 10-3)

Refer to the data in the preceding exercise. Use diagrams similar to those in Exhibits 10-2, 10–3, and 10–4 to determine the direct-material and direct-labor variances. Indicate whether each variance is favorable or unfavorable.

Exercise 10–24
Developing Standards for New Products; Use of Internet
(LO 10-2)

Choose one of the following manufacturers (or any manufacturer of your choosing), and use the Internet to gather information about any new products the company has recently introduced or plans to introduce.

Boeing	www.boeing.com	Yakima	www.yakima.com
Caterpillar	www.caterpillar.com	Pfizer	www.pfizer.com
Tesla	www.teslamotors.com	Yoplait	www.Yoplait.com

Required: Discuss the steps you think the company would go through in establishing standard costs for its new product.

Exercise 10–25
Computing Standard Direct-Material Cost
(LO 10-2)

Cayuga Hardwoods produces handcrafted jewelry boxes. A standard-size box requires 8 board feet of hardwood in the finished product. In addition, 2 board feet of scrap lumber are normally left from the production of one box. Hardwood costs $4.00 per board foot, plus $1.50 in transportation charges per board foot.

Required: Compute the standard direct-material cost of a jewelry box.

Exercise 10–26
Straightforward Calculation of Variances
(LO 10-1, 10-3)

During June, Danby Company's material purchases amounted to 6,000 pounds at a price of $7.30 per pound. Actual costs incurred in the production of 2,000 units were as follows:

Direct labor:	$116,745 ($18.10 per hour)
Direct material:	$30,660 ($7.30 per pound)

The standards for one unit of Danby Company's product are as follows:

Direct labor:	Direct material:
Quantity, 3 hours per unit	Quantity, 2 pounds per unit
Rate, $18 per hour	Price, $7 per pound

Required: Compute the direct-material price and quantity variances, the direct-material purchase price variance, and the direct-labor rate and efficiency variances. Indicate whether each variance is favorable or unfavorable.

Exercise 10–27
Diagramming Direct-Material and Direct-Labor Variances
(LO 10-3)

Refer to the data in the preceding exercise. Draw diagrams depicting the direct-material and direct-labor variances similar to the diagrams in Exhibits 10–2, 10–3, and 10–4.

Exercise 10–28
Cost Variance Investigation
(LO 10-4)

The director of cost management for Odessa Company uses a statistical control chart to help management determine when to investigate variances. The critical value is 1 standard deviation. The company incurred the following direct-labor efficiency variances during the first six months of the current year.

January	$250 F	April	$ 900 U
February	800 U	May	1,050 U
March	700 U	June	1,200 U

The standard direct-labor cost during each of these months was $19,000. The controller has estimated that the firm's monthly direct-labor variances have a standard deviation of $950.

Required:

1. Draw a statistical control chart and plot the variance data given above. Which variances will be investigated?
2. Suppose the controller's rule of thumb is to investigate all variances equal to or greater than 6 percent of standard cost. Then which variances will be investigated?
3. Would you investigate any of the variances listed above other than those indicated by the rules discussed in requirements (1) and (2)? Why?

Exercise 10–29
Standard Allowed Input
(LO 10-2)

Due to evaporation during production, Plano Plastics Company requires 8 pounds of material input for every 7 pounds of good plastic sheets manufactured. During May, the company produced 4,200 pounds of good sheets.

Required: Compute the total standard allowed input quantity, given the good output produced.

Exercise 10–30
Reconstructing Standard-Cost Information from Partial Data
(LO 10-1, 10-3)

Part of your company's accounting database was destroyed when Godzilla attacked the city. You have been able to gather the following data from your files. Reconstruct the remaining information using the available data. All of the raw material purchased during the period was used in production. (*Hint:* It is helpful to solve for the unknowns in the order indicated by the letters in the following table.)

	Direct Labor	Direct Material
Standard price or rate per unit of input	e	$8 per pound
Standard quantity per unit of output	f	c
Actual quantity used per unit of output	3.5 hours	a
Actual price or rate per unit of input	$21 per hour	$7 per pound
Actual output	10,000 units	10,000 units
Direct-material price variance	—	$30,000 F
Direct-material quantity variance	—	b
Total direct-material variance	—	$10,000 F
Direct-labor rate variance	d	—
Direct-labor efficiency variance	$100,000 F	—
Total direct-labor variance	$ 65,000 F	—

Exercise 10–31
Journal Entries under Standard Costing (Appendix)
(LO 10-6, 10-9)

Refer to the data in Exercise 10–22, regarding Saskatewan Can Company. Prepare journal entries to:

1. Record the purchase of direct material on account.
2. Add direct-material and direct-labor cost to Work-in-Process Inventory.
3. Record the direct-material and direct-labor variances.
4. Close these variances into Cost of Goods Sold.

Exercise 10–32
Posting Journal Entries for Variances (Appendix)
(LO 10-6, 10-9)

Refer to your answer for Exercise 10–31. Set up T-accounts, and post the journal entries to the general ledger.

Problems

All applicable Problems are available in Connect.

Problem 10–33
Direct-Material and Direct-Labor Variances
(LO 10-1, 10-3)

2. Direct-material quantity variance: $750 F

New Jersey Valve Company manufactured 7,800 units during January of a control valve used by milk processors in its Camden plant. Records indicated the following:

Direct labor	40,100 hr. at $14.60 per hr.
Direct material purchased	25,000 lb. at $2.60 per lb.
Direct material used	23,100 lb.

The control valve has the following standard prime costs:

Direct material:	3 lb. at $2.50 per lb	$ 7.50
Direct labor:	5 hr. at $15.00 per hr	75.00
Standard prime cost per unit		$82.50

Required:

1. Prepare a schedule of standard production costs for January, based on actual production of 7,800 units.
2. For the month of January, compute the following variances, indicating whether each is favorable or unfavorable.
   a. Direct-material price variance.
   b. Direct-material quantity variance.
   c. Direct-material purchase price variance.
   d. Direct-labor rate variance.
   e. Direct-labor efficiency variance.
3. ***Build a spreadsheet:*** Construct an Excel spreadsheet to solve all of the preceding requirements. Show how the solution will change if the following information changes: the standard direct-labor rate is $16 per hour, and the standard direct-material price is $2.60 per pound.

Problem 10–34
Determining Standard Material Cost
(LO 10-2)

South Atlantic Chemical Company manufactures industrial chemicals in Rio de Janeiro, Brazil. The company plans to introduce a new chemical solution and needs to develop a standard product cost. The new chemical solution is made by combining a chemical compound (nyclyn) and a solution (salex), heating the mixture, adding a second compound (protet), and bottling the resulting solution in 10-liter containers. The initial mix, which is 11 liters in volume, consists of 12 kilograms of nyclyn and 9.6 liters of salex. A 1-liter reduction in volume occurs during the boiling process. The solution is cooled slightly before 5 kilograms of protet are added. The addition of protet does not affect the total liquid volume.

The purchase price of the direct materials used in the manufacture of this new chemical solution are given below. (The *real,* abbreviated R$, is Brazil's national currency. On the day this problem was written, one *real* was equivalent to 0.320 U.S. dollar.)

Nyclyn	R$ 1.45 per kilogram
Salex	R$ 1.80 per liter
Protet	R$ 2.40 per kilogram

Required: Determine the standard material cost of a 10-liter container of the new product. (Remember to express your answer in R$.)

(CMA, adapted)

Problem 10–35
Direct-Material and Direct-Labor Variances
(LO 10-1, 10-3)

3. Direct-material purchase price variance: $540 U

During May, Joliet Fabrics Corporation manufactured 500 units of a special multilayer fabric with the trade name Stylex. The following information from the Stylex production department also pertains to May.

Direct material purchased: 18,000 yards at $1.38 per yard	$24,840
Direct material used: 9,500 yards at $1.38 per yard	13,110
Direct labor: 2,100 hours at $9.15 per hour	19,215

The standard prime costs for one unit of Stylex are as follows:

Direct material: 20 yards at $1.35 per yard	$27
Direct labor: 4 hours at $9.00 per hour	36
Total standard prime cost per unit of output	$63

Required: Compute the following variances for the month of May, indicating whether each variance is favorable or unfavorable.

1. Direct-material price variance.
2. Direct-material quantity variance.

3. Direct-material purchase price variance.
4. Direct-labor rate variance.
5. Direct-labor efficiency variance.

(CPA, adapted)

Problem 10–36
Variance Calculation; Analysis; Service Business
(LO 10-1, 10-3)

2. Direct-labor efficiency variance: $495.00 F
4. Total material and labor variances: $897.50 F

Sal Amato operates a residential landscaping business in an affluent suburb of St. Louis. In an effort to provide quality service, he has concentrated solely on the design and installation of upscale landscaping plans (e.g., trees, shrubs, fountains, and lighting). With his clients continually requesting additional services, Sal recently expanded into lawn maintenance, including fertilization.

The following data relate to his first year's experience with 55 fertilization clients:

- Each client required six applications throughout the year and was billed $40 per application.
- Two applications involved Type I fertilizer, which contains a special ingredient for weed control. The remaining four applications involved Type II fertilizer.
- Sal purchased 5,000 pounds of Type I fertilizer at $.53 per pound and 10,000 pounds of Type II fertilizer at $.40 per pound. Actual usage amounted to 3,700 pounds of Type I and 7,800 pounds of Type II.
- A new, part-time employee was hired to spread the fertilizer. Sal had to pay premium wages of $11.50 per hour because of a very tight labor market; the employee logged a total of 165 hours at client residences.
- Based on previous knowledge of the operation, articles in trade journals, and conversations with other landscapers, Sal established the following standards:

  Fertilizer purchase price per pound: Type I, $.50; Type II, $.42
  Fertilizer usage: 40 pounds per application
  Typical hourly wage rate of landscape personnel: $9
  Labor time per application: 40 minutes

- The operation did not go as smoothly as planned, with customer complaints actually much higher than expected.

Required:

1. Compute Sal's direct-material variances of each type of fertilizer.
2. Compute the direct-labor variances.
3. Compute the actual cost of the client applications. (*Note:* Exclude any fertilizer in inventory, as remaining fertilizer can be used next year.) Was the new service a financial success? Explain.
4. Analyze the variances that you computed in requirements (1) and (2).
   a. Was the new service a success from an overall cost-control perspective? Briefly discuss.
   b. What seems to have happened that would give rise to customer complaints?
5. In view of the complaints, should the fertilizer service be continued next year? Why?

Problem 10–37
Variance Computation; Analysis of Performance and Responsibility
(LO 10-1, 10-3)

2. Direct-labor rate variance: $47,025 U

Santa Rosa Industries uses a standard-costing system to assist in the evaluation of operations. The company has had considerable trouble in recent months with suppliers and employees, so much so that management hired a new production supervisor, Frank Schmidt. The new supervisor has been on the job for five months and has seemingly brought order to an otherwise chaotic situation.

The vice president of manufacturing recently commented that ". . . Schmidt has really done the trick. The change to a new direct-material supplier and Schmidt's team-building/morale-boosting training exercises have truly brought things under control." The VP's comments were based on both a plant tour, where he observed a contented workforce, and a review of the following data, which was excerpted from a performance report:

Direct-material variances	$4,620 Favorable
Direct-labor variances	6,175 Favorable

These variances are especially outstanding, given that the amounts are favorable and small. (Santa Rosa's budgeted material and labor costs generally each average about $350,000 for similar periods.) Additional data follow.

- The company purchased and consumed 45,000 pounds of direct materials at $7.70 per pound, and paid $16.25 per hour for 20,900 direct-labor hours of activity. Total completed production amounted to 9,500 units.
- A review of the firm's standard cost records found that each completed unit requires 4.2 pounds of direct material at $8.80 per pound and 2.6 direct-labor hours at $14 per hour.

Required:

1. On the basis of the information contained in the performance report, should Santa Rosa be concerned about its variances? Why?
2. Calculate the company's direct-material variances and direct-labor variances.
3. On the basis of your answers to requirement (2), should Santa Rosa be concerned about its variances? Why?
4. Are things going as smoothly as the vice president believes? Evaluate the company's variances and determine whether the change to a new supplier and Schmidt's team-building/morale-boosting training exercises appear to be working. Explain.
5. Is it possible that some of the company's current problems lie outside Schmidt's area of responsibility? Explain.

Problem 10–38
Direct-Labor Variances at Colgate-Palmolive Company; Cost Variance Investigation
(LO 10-3, 10-4)

2(a). Standard direct-labor cost, January: $9,983 (rounded)

The following data pertain to Colgate-Palmolive's liquid filling line during the first 10 months of a particular year. The standard ratio of direct-labor hours to machine hours is 4:1. The standard direct-labor rate is $15.08.

Colgate-Palmolive: Direct-Labor Efficiency Variance Data*

	Units Produced	Machine Hours	Standard Direct-Labor Hours	Actual Direct-Labor Hours	Direct-Labor Efficiency Variance
January	50,478	165.5	662.00	374.00	$ 4,343
February	31,943	100.3	401.20	214.00	2,823
March	185,179	552.0	2,208.00	1,068.00	17,191
April	212,274	713.8	2,855.20	1,495.75	20,501
May	48,390	160.0	640.00	364.00	4,162
June	82,436	232.0	928.00	536.50	5,904
July	36,208	104.0	416.00	283.00	2,006
August	33,483	96.0	384.00	317.50	1,003
September	31,560	96.0	384.00	328.50	837
October	28,191	72.0	288.00	158.00	1,960

*Source of data: Alan S. Levitan and Sidney J. Baxendale, "Analyzing the Labor Efficiency Variance to Signal Process Engineering Problems," *Journal of Cost Management* 6, no. 2, p. 70.

Required:

1. Show how the following amounts were calculated for the month of January:
   a. Standard direct-labor hours.
   b. Direct-labor efficiency variance.
2. Calculate the following amounts.
   a. The standard direct-labor cost for each of the 10 months.
   b. For each month, 20 percent of the standard direct-labor cost.
3. Suppose management investigates all variances in excess of 20 percent of standard cost. Which variances will be investigated?
4. Suppose the standard deviation for the direct-labor efficiency variance is $5,000. Draw a statistical control chart, and plot the variance data.
5. Using the chart developed in requirement (4), which variances will be investigated?
6. The variances for March, April, and June are much larger than the others. Suggest at least one reason for this.

Problem 10–39
Direct-Material and Direct-Labor Variances
(LO 10-1, 10-3)

2. Direct-material quantity variance: $16,625 F

Orion Corporation has established the following standards for the prime costs of one unit of its chief product, dartboards.

	Standard Quantity	Standard Price or Rate	Standard Cost
Direct material	8 pounds	$1.75 per pound	$14.00
Direct labor	.25 hour	$8.00 per hour	2.00
Total			$16.00

During June, Orion purchased 160,000 pounds of direct material at a total cost of $304,000. The total wages for June were $42,000, 90 percent of which were for direct labor. Orion manufactured 19,000 dartboards during June, using 142,500 pounds of the direct material purchased in June and 5,000 direct-labor hours.

Required:
Compute the following variances for June, and indicate whether each is favorable or unfavorable.

1. The direct-material price variance.
2. The direct-material quantity variance.
3. Direct-material purchase price variance.
4. The direct-labor rate variance.
5. The direct-labor efficiency variance.

(CMA, adapted)

Problem 10–40
Setting Standards; Responsibility for Variances
(LO 10-2)

Associated Media Graphics (AMG) is a rapidly expanding company involved in the mass reproduction of instructional materials. Ralph Boston, owner and manager of AMG, has made a concentrated effort to provide a quality product at a fair price, with delivery on the promised date. Boston is finding it increasingly difficult to personally supervise the operations of AMG, and he is beginning to institute an organizational structure that would facilitate management control.

One change recently made was the transfer of control over departmental operations from Boston to each departmental manager. However, the Quality Control Department still reports directly to Boston, as do the Finance and Accounting Departments. A materials manager was hired to purchase all raw materials and to oversee the material-handling (receiving, storage, etc.) and recordkeeping functions. The materials manager also is responsible for maintaining an adequate inventory based on planned production levels.

The loss of personal control over the operations of AMG caused Boston to look for a method of efficiently evaluating performance. Dave Cress, a new managerial accountant, proposed the use of a standard-costing system. Variances for material and labor could then be calculated and reported directly to Boston.

Required:

1. Assume that Associated Media Graphics is going to implement a standard-costing system and establish standards for materials and labor. Identify and discuss for each of these cost components:
   a. Who should be involved in setting the standards?
   b. What factors should be considered in establishing the standards?
2. Describe the basis for assignment of responsibility for variances under a standard-costing system.

(CMA, adapted)

Problem 10–41
Direct-Labor Variances
(LO 10-1, 10-3)

1(b). Direct-labor efficiency variance, labor class III: $800 U

The director of cost management for Portland Instrument Corporation compares each month's actual results with a monthly plan. The standard direct-labor rates for the year just ended and the standard hours allowed, given the actual output in April, are shown in the following schedule.

	Standard Direct-Labor Rate per Hour	Standard Direct-Labor Hours Allowed, Given April Output
Labor class III	$16.00	500
Labor class II	14.00	500
Labor class I	10.00	500

A new union contract negotiated in March resulted in actual wage rates that differed from the standard rates. The actual direct-labor hours worked and the actual direct-labor rates per hour experienced for the month of April were as follows:

	Actual Direct-Labor Rate per Hour	Actual Direct-Labor Hours
Labor class III	$17.20	550
Labor class II	15.00	650
Labor class I	10.80	375

Required:

1. Compute the following variances for April. Indicate whether each is favorable or unfavorable.
   a. Direct-labor rate variance for *each* labor class.
   b. Direct-labor efficiency variance for *each* labor class.
2. Discuss the advantages and disadvantages of a standard-costing system in which the standard direct-labor rates are not changed during the year to reflect such events as a new labor contract.
3. ***Build a spreadsheet:*** Construct an Excel spreadsheet to solve requirements (1) above. Show how the solution will change if the following information changes: the actual labor rates were $16.95, $15.10, and $10.60 for labor classes III, II, and I, respectively.

(CMA, adapted)

Problem 10–42
Development of Standard Costs
(LO 10-1, 10-2, 10-5)

1. Total standard unit cost: $8.62

Ogwood Company's Johnstown Division is a small manufacturer of wooden household items. Al Rivkin, division controller, plans to implement a standard-costing system. Rivkin has collected information from several co-workers that will assist him in developing standards. One of the Johnstown Division's products is a wooden cutting board. Each cutting board requires 1.25 board feet of lumber and 12 minutes of direct-labor time to prepare and cut the lumber. The cutting boards are inspected after they are cut. Because the cutting boards are made of a natural material that has imperfections, one board is normally rejected for each five that are accepted. Four rubber foot pads are attached to each good cutting board. A total of 15 minutes of direct-labor time is required to attach all four foot pads and finish each cutting board. The lumber for the cutting boards cost $3.00 per board foot, and each foot pad costs $.05. Direct labor is paid at the rate of $8.00 per hour.

Required:

1. Develop the standard cost for direct material and direct labor of a cutting board.
2. Explain the role of each of the following people in developing standards.
   a. Purchasing manager.
   b. Industrial engineer.
   c. Managerial accountant.
3. The production manager complained that the standards are unrealistic, stifle motivation by concentrating only on unfavorable variances, and are out of date too quickly. He noted that his recent switch to cherry for the cutting boards has resulted in higher material costs but decreased labor hours. The net result was no increase in the total cost to produce the product. The monthly reports continue to show an unfavorable material variance and a favorable labor variance despite indications that the workers are slowing down.
   a. Explain why a standard-costing system can strengthen cost management.
   b. Give at least two reasons to explain why a standard-costing system could negatively impact the motivation of production employees.

Problem 10–43
Determining Standard Costs; Ethics
(LO 10-1, 10-2)

1. Total standard cost per 10-gallon batch: $30.20

Quincy Farms produces items made from local farm products that are distributed to supermarkets. For many years, Quincy's products have had strong regional sales on the basis of brand recognition: however, other companies have begun marketing similar products in the area, and price competition has become increasingly important. Doug Gilbert, the company's controller, is planning to implement a standard cost system for Quincy and has gathered considerable information from his co-workers on production and material requirements for Quincy's products. Gilbert believes that the use of standard costing will allow Quincy to improve cost control and make better pricing decisions.

Quincy's most popular product is strawberry jam. The jam is produced in 10-gallon batches, and each batch requires six quarts of good strawberries. The fresh strawberries are sorted by hand before entering the production process. Because of imperfections in the strawberries and normal spoilage, one quart of berries is discarded for every four quarts of acceptable berries. Three minutes is the standard direct-labor time for sorting required to obtain one quart of acceptable strawberries. The acceptable strawberries are then blended with the other ingredients. Blending requires 12 minutes of direct-labor time per batch. After blending, the jam is packaged in quart containers. Gilbert has gathered the following information from Joe Adams, Quincy's cost accountant.

- Quincy purchases strawberries at a cost of $.80 per quart. All other ingredients cost a total of $.45 per gallon.
- Direct labor is paid at the rate of $9.00 per hour.
- The total cost of material and labor required to package the jam is $.38 per quart.

Adams has a friend who owns a strawberry farm that has been losing money in recent years. Because of good crops, there has been an oversupply of strawberries, and prices have dropped to $.50 per quart. Adams has arranged for Quincy to purchase strawberries from his friend and hopes that $.80 per quart will help his friend's farm become profitable again.

Required:

1. Develop the standard cost for the direct-cost components of a 10-gallon batch of strawberry jam. The standard cost should identify the following amounts for each direct-cost component of a batch of strawberry jam: (*a*) standard quantity, (*b*) standard price or rate, and (*c*) standard cost per batch.
2. Citing the specific ethical standards of competence, confidentiality, integrity, and credibility for management accountants (*see* "IMA Statement of Ethical Professional Practice" in Chapter 1), explain why Joe Adams's behavior regarding the cost information provided to Doug Gilbert is unethical.
3. As part of the implementation of a standard-costing system at Quincy Farms, Doug Gilbert plans to train those responsible for maintaining the standards in the use of variance analysis. Gilbert is particularly concerned with the causes of unfavorable variances. Discuss the possible causes of the following unfavorable variances and identify the individual(s) who should be held responsible: (*a*) direct-material purchase price variance and (*b*) direct-labor efficiency variance.

(CMA, adapted)

Problem 10–44
Investigating Cost Variances
(LO 10-4)

Schiffer Corporation manufactures agricultural machinery. At a recent staff meeting, the following direct-labor variance report for the year just ended was presented by the controller.

SCHIFFER CORPORATION
Direct-Labor Variance Report

	Direct-Labor Rate Variance		Direct-Labor Efficiency Variance	
	Amount	**Standard Cost, %**	**Amount**	**Standard Cost, %**
January	$ 800 F	.16%	$ 5,000 U	1.00%
February	4,900 F	.98%	7,500 U	1.50%
March	100 U	.02%	9,700 U	1.94%
April	2,000 U	.40%	12,800 U	2.56%
May	3,800 F	.76%	20,100 U	4.02%
June	3,900 F	.78%	17,000 U	3.40%
July	4,200 F	.84%	28,500 U	5.70%
August	5,100 F	1.02%	38,000 U	7.60%
September	4,800 F	.96%	37,000 U	7.40%
October	5,700 F	1.14%	42,000 U	8.40%
November	4,200 F	.84%	60,000 U	12.00%
December	4,300 F	.86%	52,000 U	10.40%

Schiffer's controller uses the following rule of thumb: Investigate all variances equal to or greater than $30,000, which is 6 percent of standard cost.

Required:

1. Which variances would have been investigated during the year? (Indicate month and type of variance.)
2. What characteristics of the variance pattern shown in the report should draw the controller's attention, regardless of the usual investigation rule? Explain. Given these considerations, which variances would you have investigated? Why?
3. Is it important to follow up on favorable variances, such as those shown in the report? Why?
4. The controller believes that the firm's direct-labor rate variance has a normal probability distribution with a mean of zero and a standard deviation of $5,000. Prepare a statistical control chart, and plot the company's direct-labor rate variances for each month. The critical value is one standard deviation. Which variances would have been investigated under this approach?

Problem 10–45
Variances; Journal Entries; Missing Data (Appendix)
(LO 10-3, 10-6, 10-9)

1(b). Total standard hours allowed: 37,200 hours
2. Direct-material purchase price variance: $750 F

Aquafloat Corporation manufactures rafts for use in swimming pools. The standard cost for material and labor is $89.20 per raft. This includes 8 kilograms of direct material at a standard cost of $5.00 per kilogram, and 6 hours of direct labor at $8.20 per hour. The following data pertain to November:

- Work-in-process inventory on November 1: none.
- Work-in-process inventory on November 30: 800 units (75 percent complete as to labor; material is issued at the beginning of processing).
- Units completed: 5,600 units.
- Purchases of materials: 50,000 kilograms for $249,250.
- Total actual labor costs: $300,760.
- Actual hours of labor: 36,500 hours.
- Direct-material quantity variance: $ 1,500 unfavorable.

Required:

1. Compute the following amounts. Indicate whether each variance is favorable or unfavorable.
   a. Direct-labor rate variance for November.
   b. Direct-labor efficiency variance for November.
   c. Actual kilograms of material used in the production process during November.
   d. Actual price paid per kilogram of direct material in November.
   e. Total amounts of direct-material and direct-labor cost transferred to Finished-Goods Inventory during November.
   f. The total amount of direct-material and direct-labor cost in the ending balance of Work-in-Process Inventory at the end of November.
2. Prepare journal entries to record the following:
   - Purchase of raw material.
   - Adding direct material to Work-in-Process Inventory.
   - Adding direct labor to Work-in-Process Inventory.
   - Recording of variances.

(CMA, adapted)

Problem 10–46
Direct-Material Variances; Journal Entries (Appendix)
(LO 10-1, 10-3, 10-9)

1. Direct-material quantity variance: $300 U

Rocky Mountain Camping Equipment, Inc. has established the following direct-material standards for its two products.

	Standard Quantity	Standard Price
Standard camping tent	12 yards	$6 per yard
Deluxe backpacking tent	6 yards	$8 per yard

During March, the company purchased 2,100 yards of tent fabric for its standard model at a cost of $13,440. The actual March production of the standard tent was 100 tents, and 1,250 yards of fabric were used. Also during March, the company purchased 800 yards of the same tent fabric for its deluxe backpacking tent at a cost of $6,320. The firm used 720 yards of the fabric during March in the production of 120 deluxe tents.

Required:

1. Compute the direct-material purchase price variance and quantity variance for March.
2. Prepare journal entries to record the purchase of material, use of material, and incurrence of variances in March.

Problem 10–47
Comprehensive Problem on Variance Analysis
(LO 10-1, 10-3, 10-6)

1. Total standard cost of direct material in July, Finishing Dept: $7,500
2. Construction Dept, standard material cost: $48,000
3. Direct-material quantity variance, Construction Dept: $6,000 U

Springsteen Company manufactures guitars. The company uses a standard, job-order cost-accounting system in two production departments. In the Construction Department, the wooden guitars are built by highly skilled craftsmen and coated with several layers of lacquer. Then the units are transferred to the Finishing Department, where the bridge of the guitar is attached and the strings are installed. The guitars also are tuned and inspected in the Finishing Department. The diagram below depicts the production process.

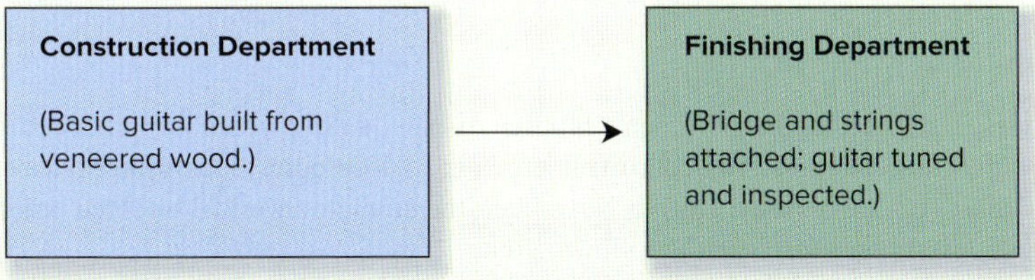

Each finished guitar contains seven pounds of veneered wood. In addition, one pound of wood is typically wasted in the production process. The veneered wood used in the guitars has a standard price of $12 per pound. The other parts needed to complete each guitar, such as the bridge and strings, cost $15 per guitar. The labor standards for Springsteen's two production departments are as follows:

Construction Department: 6 hours of direct labor at $20 per hour
Finishing Department: 3 hours of direct labor at $15 per hour

The following pertains to the month of July.

1. There were no beginning or ending work-in-process inventories in either production department.
2. There was no beginning finished-goods inventory.
3. Actual production was 500 guitars, and 300 guitars were sold on account for $400 each.
4. The company purchased 6,000 pounds of veneered wood at a price of $12.50 per pound.
5. Actual usage of veneered wood was 4,500 pounds of the wood purchased during July.
6. Enough parts (bridges and strings) to finish 600 guitars were purchased at a cost of $9,000.
7. The Construction Department used 2,850 direct-labor hours. The total direct-labor cost in the Construction Department was $54,150.
8. The Finishing Department used 1,570 direct-labor hours. The total direct-labor cost in that department was $25,120.
9. There were no direct-material variances in the Finishing Department.

Required:

1. Prepare a schedule that computes the standard costs of direct material and direct labor in each production department.
2. Prepare three exhibits that compute the July direct-material and direct-labor variances in the Construction Department and the July direct-labor variances in the Finishing Department. (Refer to Exhibits 10–2, 10–3, and 10–4 for guidance.)
3. Prepare a cost variance report for July similar to that shown in Exhibit 10–5. Springsteen Company investigates all variances greater than $5,000 or 5%.

Problem 10–48
Journal Entries under Standard Costing; Continuation of Preceding Problem (Appendix)
(LO 10-7, 10-9)

To close variances into Cost of Goods Sold (CGS): $5,770 (debit to CGS)

Refer to your solution for the preceding problem regarding Springsteen Company.

Required:

1. Prepare journal entries to record all of the events listed for Springsteen Company during July. Specifically, these journal entries should reflect the following events.
   a. Purchase of direct material.
   b. Use of direct material.
   c. Incurrence of direct-labor costs.
   d. Addition of production costs to the Work-in-Process Inventory account for each department.
   e. Incurrence of all variances.
   f. Completion of 500 guitars.
   g. Sale of 300 guitars.
   h. Closing of all variance accounts into Cost of Goods Sold.
2. Draw T-accounts, and post the journal entries prepared in requirement (1). Assume the beginning balance in all accounts is zero.

Cases

Case 10–49
Direct-Material and Direct-Labor Variances; Job-Order Costing; Journal Entries (Appendix)
(LO 10-1, 10-3, 10-6, 10-9)

2. Direct-material purchase price variance: $1,900 U
3. Direct-material purchase price variance (debit): $1,900

European Styles, Inc. manufactures women's blouses of one quality, which are produced in lots to fill each special order. Its customers are department stores in various cities. European Styles sews the particular stores' labels on the blouses. During November, the company worked on three orders, for which the month's job-cost records disclose the following data.

Lot Number	Boxes in Lot	Material Used (yards)	Hours Worked
22	1,000	24,100	2,980
23	1,700	40,440	5,130
24	1,200	28,825	2,890

The following additional information is available:

1. The firm purchased 95,000 yards of material during November at a cost of $106,400.
2. Direct labor during November amounted to $165,000. According to payroll records, production employees were paid $15.00 per hour.
3. There was no work in process on November 1. During November, lots 22 and 23 were completed. All material was issued for lot 24, which was 80 percent completed as to direct labor.
4. The standard costs for a box of six blouses are as follows:

Direct material	24 yards at $1.10 per yard	$ 26.40
Direct labor	3 hours at $14.70 per hr.	44.10
Production overhead	3 hours at $12.00 per hr.	36.00
Standard cost per box		$106.50

Required:

1. Prepare a schedule computing the standard cost of lots 22, 23, and 24 for November.
2. Prepare a schedule showing, for each lot produced during November:
   a. Direct-material purchase price variance.
   b. Direct-material quantity variance.
   c. Direct-labor efficiency variance.
   d. Direct-labor rate variance.
   Indicate whether each variance is favorable or unfavorable.
3. Prepare journal entries to record each of the following events.
   - Purchase of material.
   - Incurrence of direct-labor cost.

- Addition of direct-material and direct-labor cost to Work-in-Process Inventory.
- Recording of direct-material and direct-labor variances.

(CPA, adapted)

Case 10–50
Missing Data; Variances, Ledger Accounts (Appendix)
(LO 10-1, 10-3, 10-9)

1. Actual output (in drums): 1,000 drums
2. Direct material, quantity variance, A: $2,500 U
3. Direct labor, actual hours (mixers): 2,000 hr
4. Total of all variances for the month: $1,510 F

MacGyver Corporation manufactures a product called Miracle Goo, which comes in handy for just about anything. The thick tarry substance is sold in six-gallon drums. Two raw materials are used; these are referred to by people in the business as A and B. Two types of labor are required also. These are mixers (labor class I) and packers (labor class II). You were recently hired by the company president, Pete Thorn, to be the controller. You soon learned that MacGyver uses a standard-costing system. Variances are computed and closed into Cost of Goods Sold monthly. After your first month on the job, you gathered the necessary data to compute the month's variances for direct material and direct labor. You finished everything up by 5:00 p.m. on the 31st, including the credit to Cost of Goods Sold for the sum of the variances. You decided to take all your notes home to review them prior to your formal presentation to Thorn first thing in the morning. As an afterthought, you grabbed a drum of Miracle Goo as well, thinking it could prove useful in some unanticipated way.

You spent the evening boning up on the data for your report and were ready to call it a night. As luck would have it though, you knocked over the Miracle Goo as you rose from the kitchen table. The stuff splattered everywhere, and, most unfortunately, obliterated most of your notes. All that remained legible is the following information.

Direct Material A: Quantity Variance

2,500	

Direct Material B: Purchase Price Variance

1,200	

Direct Labor I: Rate Variance

600	

Direct Labor II: Efficiency Variance

1,200	

Cost of Goods Sold

143,000	
	1,510

Accounts Payable

	1,500 Beg. bal.
70,000	73,200
	4,700 End. bal.

Other assorted data gleaned from your notes:

- The standards for each drum of Miracle Goo include 10 pounds of material A at a standard price of $5 per pound.
- The standard cost of material B is $15 for each drum of Miracle Goo.
- Purchases of material A were 12,000 pounds at $4.50 per pound.
- Given the actual output for the month, the standard allowed quantity of material A was 10,000 pounds. The standard allowed quantity of material B was 5,000 gallons.
- Although 6,000 gallons of B were purchased, only 4,800 gallons were used.
- The standard wage rate for mixers is $15 per hour. The standard labor cost per drum of product for mixers is $30 per drum.
- The standards allow 4 hours of direct labor II (packers) per drum of Miracle Goo. The standard labor cost per drum of product for packers is $48 per drum.
- Packers were paid $11.90 per hour during the month.

You happened to remember two additional facts. There were no beginning or ending inventories of either work in process or finished goods for the month. The increase in accounts payable relates to direct-material purchases only.

Required: Now you've got a major problem. Somehow you've got to reconstruct all the missing data in order to be ready for your meeting with the president. You start by making the following list of the facts you want to use in your presentation. Before getting down to business, you need a brief walk to clear your head. Out to the trash you go, and toss the remaining Miracle Goo.

Fill in the missing amounts in the list, using the available facts.

1. Actual output (in drums): ______

2. Direct material:

	A	B
a. Standard quantity per drum:	______	______
b. Standard price:	______	______
c. Standard cost per drum:	______	______
d. Standard quantity allowed, given actual output:	______	______
e. Actual quantity purchased:	______	______
f. Actual price:	______	______
g. Actual quantity used:	______	______
h. Purchase price variance:	______	______
i. Quantity variance:	______	______

3. Direct labor:

	I (mixers)	II (packers)
a. Standard hours per drum:	______	______
b. Standard rate per hour:	______	______
c. Standard cost per drum:	______	______
d. Standard quantity allowed, given actual output:	______	______
e. Actual rate per hour:	______	______
f. Actual hours:	______	______
g. Rate variance:	______	______
h. Efficiency variance:	______	______

4. Total of all variances for the month: ______

11 Flexible Budgeting and Analysis of Overhead Costs

FOCUS COMPANY >>>

© Eileen Bach/Getty Images RF

THIS CHAPTER'S FOCUS COMPANY is DCdesserts.com, and continues our discussion from the previous chapter. DCdesserts.com supplies fancy desserts to a variety of restaurants, caterers, and upscale food stores in Washington, D.C. In this chapter, we explore DCdesserts.com's use of flexible budgeting to plan for and control overhead costs. A flexible budget allows for a variety of levels of activity. As activity increases, the costs in the flexible budget rise as well. This tool enables management to compare the actual overhead costs incurred with the costs that should have been incurred, given the actual level of production activity.

© Yvonne Duivenvoorden/Getty Images RF

<<< IN CONTRAST

In contrast to the food-processing setting of DCdesserts.com, we turn our attention to flexible budgeting in the service industry. Upstate Auto Rentals is a small automobile rental company in upstate New York. The company has four rental locations in and around Syracuse and specializes in short-term car rentals, primarily for local use when a customer's car is in the repair shop. Upstate's flexible budget uses two cost drivers: the number of miles driven by its rental cars and the number of customer contracts.

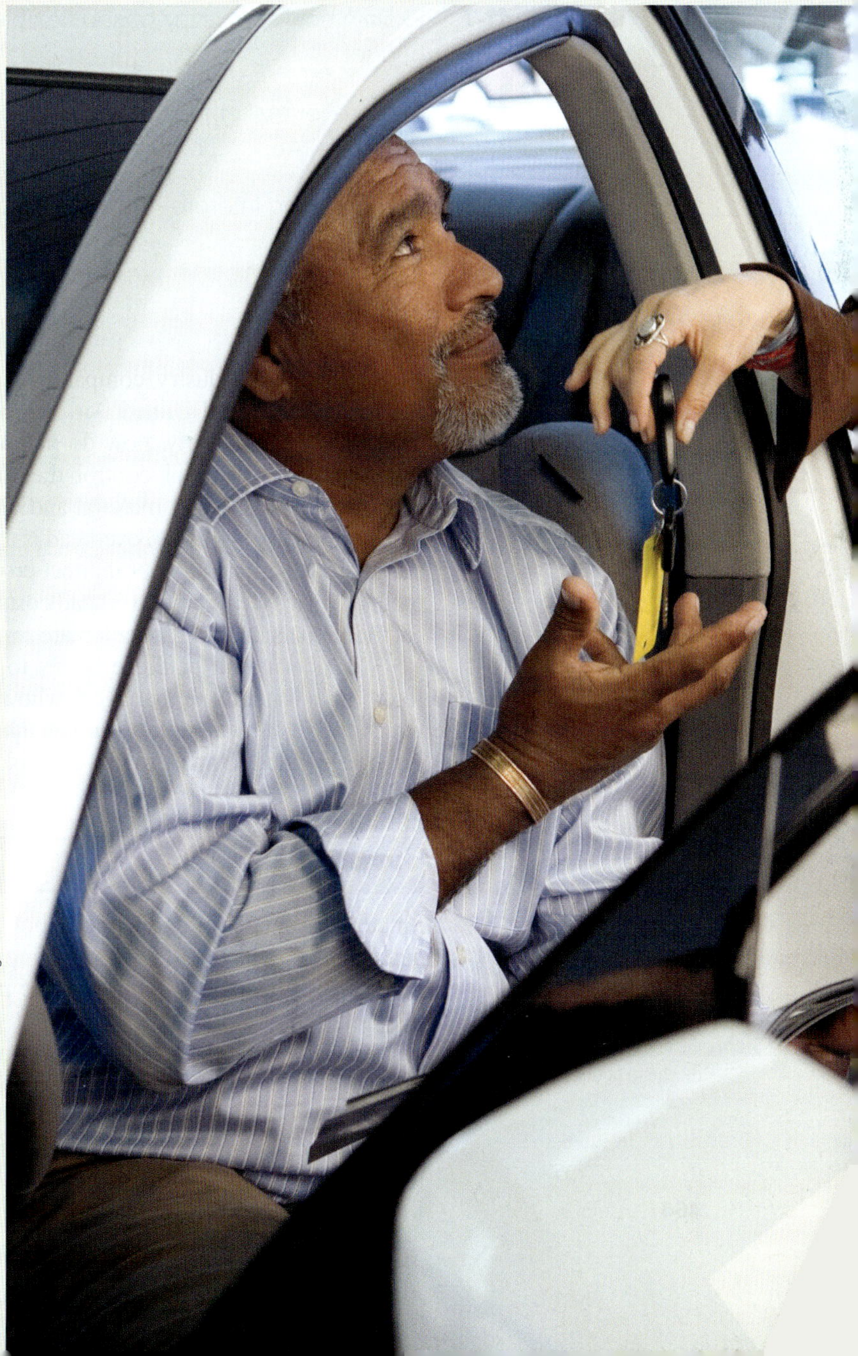

After completing this chapter, you should be able to:

11-1 Distinguish between static and flexible budgets and explain the advantages of a flexible overhead budget.

11-2 Prepare a flexible overhead budget, using both a formula and a columnar format.

11-3 Explain how overhead is applied to Work-in-Process Inventory under standard costing.

11-4 Explain the important issues in choosing an activity measure for overhead budgeting and application.

11-5 Compute and interpret the variable-overhead spending and efficiency variances and the fixed-overhead budget and volume variances.

11-6 Prepare an overhead cost performance report.

11-7 Explain how an activity-based flexible budget differs from a conventional flexible budget.

11-8 Prepare journal entries to record production overhead under standard costing (appendix A).

11-9 Compute and interpret the sales-price and sales-volume variances (appendix B).

How do service industry companies, such as Ben & Jerry's, Budget Rent-a-Car, Chase Bank, Days Inn, and United Airlines control the overhead costs they incur in producing their services? Similarly, how do manufacturing firms such as General Motors, Hewlett-Packard, and Whirlpool control the many overhead costs incurred in their production processes? Unlike direct material and direct labor, overhead costs are not traceable to individual products. Moreover, overhead is a pool of many different kinds of costs. Indirect material, indirect labor, and other indirect production costs often exhibit different relationships to productive activity. Some overhead costs are variable, and some are fixed. Moreover, different individuals in an organization are responsible for different types of overhead costs.

Considering all of these issues together, controlling overhead presents a challenge for companies and the managers who run them. In this chapter, we will explore ways in which the financial planning and analysis (FP&A) system discussed in Chapters 9 and 10 can be extended to analyze and control overhead costs.

Overhead Budgets

Learning Objective 11–1

Distinguish between static and flexible budgets and explain the advantages of a flexible overhead budget.

Since direct material and direct labor are traceable to products, it is straightforward to determine standard costs for these inputs. If the top of a conference table requires 220 board feet of mahogany lumber at $15 per board foot, the standard direct-material cost for the tabletop is $3,300.

But how much electricity does it take to produce a tabletop? How much supervisory time, equipment depreciation, or machinery repair services does the table require? Since all of these overhead costs are indirect costs of production, we cannot set overhead cost standards for the mahogany tabletop. If standard costs do not provide the answer to controlling overhead, what does?

Flexible Budgets

The tool used by most companies to control overhead costs is called a **flexible budget.** A flexible budget resembles the budgets we studied in Chapter 9, with one important difference: *A flexible budget is not based on only one level of activity.* Instead, when used as a planning tool, the flexible budget covers a range of activity within which the firm may operate. A *flexible overhead budget* is defined as a detailed plan for controlling overhead costs that is valid in the firm's relevant range of activity. In contrast, a **static budget** is based on a particular planned level of activity.

Moreover, a flexible budget can tell us, after the fact, what it *should have cost* to produce a particular level of output. This turns out to be a key control concept for analyzing cost variances, because it allows us to split the variance in spending into different, more easily explained pieces. In this chapter, we will apply this concept to overhead costs. But remember the *standard quantity allowed* for direct material in the prior chapter? That was the basis for calculating the flexible budget amount, after the fact, for controlling direct material (what it *should have cost for direct material to make the actual output).* The *standard hours allowed* filled the same role for direct labor. So the concept is not entirely new to us.

At DCdesserts.com, the measure of activity used for planning the overhead costs is *process time.* The process time for a dessert is the total amount of time the product is in production including selecting ingredients, mixing, baking, cooling, assembly and finishing, and packaging. DCdesserts.com's director of cost management estimates that the average process time required for fancy desserts is three hours.

To illustrate the flexible budgeting concept, suppose DCdesserts.com's director of cost management has determined that electricity is a variable cost, incurred at the rate of $.50 per hour of process time. Two different budgets for electricity cost are shown in Exhibit 11–1. The static budget is based on management's predicted level of activity for September—7,500 hours of process time. This estimate is based on planned production of 2,500 multilayer fancy cakes, where each cake requires three hours of total process time. The flexible budget includes three different production activity levels within the relevant range: 6,000, 7,500, and 9,000 hours of process time.

Advantages of Flexible Budgets

Why is the distinction between static and flexible budgets so important? Suppose DCdesserts.com ultimately produced 2,000 multilayer fancy cakes during September, used 6,000 hours of process time, and incurred electricity costs of $3,200. Does this constitute good control or poor control of electricity costs? Which budget in Exhibit 11–1 is more useful in answering this question?

A manager using the static budget makes the following comparison.

Actual Electricity Cost	Budgeted Electricity Cost (static budget)	Cost Variance
$3,200	$3,750	$550 Favorable

Exhibit 11–1
Static Budget versus Flexible Budget

Static Budget		Flexible Budget			
Activity (process hours)*	7,500	Activity (process hours)	6,000	7,500	9,000
Budgeted electricity cost	$3,750	Budgeted electricity cost	$3,000	$3,750	$4,500

Static budget: based on only one anticipated activity level.

Flexible budget: includes several possible activity levels.

*Based on planned September production of 2,500 multilayer fancy cakes, at three hours of process time per cake.

This comparison suggests that operating personnel maintained excellent control over electricity costs during September, generating a favorable variance of $550. Is this a valid analysis and conclusion?

The fault with this analysis is that the manager is comparing the electricity cost incurred at the *actual* activity level, 2,000 multilayer fancy cakes, with the budgeted electricity cost at the *planned* activity level, 2,500 multilayer fancy cakes. Since these activity levels are different, we should expect the electricity cost to be different.

A more sensible approach is to compare the actual electricity cost incurred with the cost that should be incurred when 2,000 multilayer fancy cakes are produced. At this production level, 6,000 process hours should be used (3 per cake). The flexible budget in Exhibit 11–1 shows that the manager should expect $3,000 of electricity cost at the 6,000 process-hour level of activity. Therefore, an analysis based on the flexible budget gives the following comparison.

Actual Electricity Cost	Budgeted Electricity Cost (flexible budget)	Cost Variance
$3,200	$3,000	$200 Unfavorable

Now the manager's conclusion is different; the revised analysis indicates an unfavorable variance. Electricity cost was greater than it should have been, given the actual level of output. The flexible budget provides the correct basis for comparison between actual and expected costs, given actual activity.

The Activity Measure

Notice that the flexible budget for electricity cost in Exhibit 11–1 is based on hours of process time, which is an input in the production process. The process-hour activity levels shown in the flexible budget are the standard allowed process hours given various levels of output. If 2,000 multilayer fancy cakes are produced, and the standard allowance per cake is 3 process hours, then the standard allowed number of process hours is 6,000.

Why are the activity levels in the flexible budget based on process hours, an *input* measure, instead of the number of multilayer fancy cakes produced, an *output* measure? When only a single product is produced, it makes no difference whether the flexible budget is based on input or output. In our illustration, either of the flexible budgets shown in Exhibit 11–2 could be used.

Now suppose that during August, DCdesserts.com produced three different products: 1,000 multilayer fancy cakes, 1,500 single-layer sheet cakes, and 600 specialty cakes (such as wedding cakes). The following standards have been assigned to these products.

"I will give you an example of when we were supporting budgets. We would have to go out to the person and say, 'What is going on in your budget? I don't understand why you are overspending or underspending.' Now a person looks at their budget and comes to accounting and will say, 'Can you help me with this problem?'" (11a)

Abbott Laboratories

Product	Standard Process Hours per Unit
Multilayer fancy cakes	3
Single-layer sheet cakes	2
Specialty cakes	6

During August, the company's production output was 3,100 cakes. Is 3,100 cakes a meaningful output measure? Adding quantites of multilayer fancy cakes, sheet cakes, and specialty cakes, which require different amounts of productive inputs, is like adding apples and oranges. It would not make sense to base a flexible budget for electricity cost on units of output when the output consists of different products with different electricity requirements. In this case, the flexible budget must be based on an *input* measure. The standard allowed number of process hours for the August production is computed as follows:

Product	Units Produced	Standard Process Hours per Unit	Total Standard Allowed Process Hours
Multilayer fancy cakes	1,000	3	3,000
Single-layer sheet cakes	1,500	2	3,000
Specialty cakes	600	6	3,600
Total			9,600

Exhibit 11–2

Flexible Budgets: Input versus Output

Flexible Budget (based on input)			
Activity: standard allowed process hours	6,000	7,500	9,000
Budgeted electricity cost	$3,000	$3,750	$4,500
Flexible Budget (based on output)			
Activity: multilayer fancy cakes produced	2,000	2,500	3,000
Budgeted electricity cost	$3,000	$3,750	$4,500

3 standard allowed process hours per multilayer fancy cake

Recall that the controller estimates electricity cost at $.50 per process hour. Thus, the flexible-budget cost of electricity during August is computed as follows:

Standard allowed process hours given August output	9,600
Electricity cost per process hour	× $.50
Flexible budget for electricity cost	$4,800

The important point is that *units of output* usually is not a meaningful measure in a multiproduct firm, because it would require us to add numbers of unlike products. To avoid this problem, output is measured in terms of the *standard allowed input, given actual output.* The flexible overhead budget is then based on this standard input measure.

Flexible Overhead Budget Illustrated

Learning Objective 11–2

Prepare a flexible overhead budget, using both a formula and a columnar format.

DCdesserts.com's monthly flexible overhead budget is shown in the Excel spreadsheet in Exhibit 11–3. The overhead costs on the flexible budget are divided into variable and fixed costs. The total budgeted *variable*-overhead cost increases proportionately with increases in the activity. Thus, when the number of process hours increases by 50 percent, from 6,000 hours to 9,000 hours, the total budgeted variable-overhead cost also increases by 50 percent, from $30,000 to $45,000. In contrast, the total budgeted *fixed* overhead does not change with increases in activity; it remains constant at $15,000 per month.

Formula Flexible Budget

When overhead costs can be divided into variable and fixed categories, we can express the flexible overhead budget differently. The format used in Exhibit 11–3 is called a *columnar flexible budget.* The budgeted overhead cost for each overhead item is listed in a column under a particular activity level. Notice that the columnar format allows for only a limited number of activity levels. DCdesserts.com's flexible budget shows only three.

A more general format for expressing a flexible budget is called a *formula flexible budget.* In this format, we express the relationship between activity and total budgeted overhead cost by the following formula:

$$\begin{array}{c}\text{Total budgeted}\\\text{monthly overhead}\\\text{cost}\end{array} = \left(\begin{array}{c}\text{Budgeted variable-}\\\text{overhead cost per}\\\text{activity unit}\end{array} \times \begin{array}{c}\text{Total}\\\text{activity}\\\text{units}\end{array}\right) + \begin{array}{c}\text{Budgeted fixed-}\\\text{overhead cost}\\\text{per month}\end{array}$$

Exhibit 11–3

Flexible Overhead Budget

DC desserts

DCDESSERTS.COM

Monthly Flexible Overhead Budget

Budgeted Overhead Costs	Cost per Hour	Process Hours 6,000	7,500	9,000
Variable overhead costs:				
Indirect material:				
Nonstick cooking spray	$ 2.00	$ 12,000	$ 15,000	$ 18,000
Waxed paper	0.33	2,000	2,500	3,000
Other paper products	0.33	2,000	2,500	3,000
Miscellaneous supplies	1.00	6,000	7,500	9,000
Indirect labor: maintenance	0.67	4,000	5,000	6,000
Utilities				
Electricity	0.50	3,000	3,750	4,500
Natural gas	0.17	1,000	1,250	1,500
Total variable overhead cost		$ 30,000	$ 37,500	$ 45,000
Fixed overhead costs:				
Indirect labor:				
Inspection		$ 2,200	$ 2,200	$ 2,200
Production supervisors		6,000	6,000	6,000
Setup specialists		3,000	3,000	3,000
Material handling		2,000	2,000	2,000
Depreciation: plant and equipment		500	500	500
Insurance and property taxes		100	100	100
Test kitchen		1,200	1,200	1,200
Total fixed overhead cost		$ 15,000	$ 15,000	$ 15,000
Total overhead cost		$ 45,000	$ 52,500	$ 60,000

To use this formula for DCdesserts.com, we first need to compute the budgeted variable-overhead cost per process hour. Dividing total budgeted variable-overhead cost by the associated activity level yields a budgeted variable-overhead rate of $5 per process hour. Notice that this variable-overhead rate is the same for every activity level in Exhibit 11–3.

$$\frac{\$30{,}000}{6{,}000} = \frac{\$37{,}500}{7{,}500} = \frac{\$45{,}000}{9{,}000} = \$5 \text{ per process hour}$$

DCdesserts.com's formula flexible overhead budget is shown below.

$$\text{Total budgeted monthly overhead cost} = (\$5 \times \text{Total process hours}) + \$15{,}000$$

To check the accuracy of the formula, compute the total budgeted overhead cost at each of the activity levels shown in Exhibit 11–3.

Activity (process hours)	Formula Flexible Overhead Budget		Budgeted Monthly Overhead Cost
6,000	($5 × 6,000) + $15,000	=	$45,000
7,500	($5 × 7,500) + $15,000	=	$52,500
9,000	($5 × 9,000) + $15,000	=	$60,000

The budgeted monthly overhead cost computed above is the same as that shown in Exhibit 11–3 for each activity level.

The formula flexible budget is more general than the columnar flexible budget, because the formula allows managers to compute budgeted overhead costs at any activity level. Then the flexible-budgeted overhead cost can be used at the end of the period as a benchmark against which to compare the actual overhead costs incurred.

> "It's critical to understand variable and fixed overhead costs. When activity levels change, what costs will change and how?" (11b)
> **A. T. Kearney**

Overhead Application in a Standard-Costing System

Learning Objective 11–3

Explain how overhead is applied to Work-in-Process Inventory under standard costing.

Recall that *overhead application* refers to the addition of overhead cost to the Work-in-Process Inventory account as a product cost. In a normal-costing system, described in Chapter 3, overhead is applied based on the *actual* quantity of the cost driver, as shown in the top panel of Exhibit 11–4. Continuing the example from the prior section, overhead application would be based on *actual hours.* In a standard-costing system, overhead application is based on the *standard* amount of the cost driver *allowed,* given the amount of actual output. This system is depicted in the bottom panel of Exhibit 11–4 for our example, where the application is based on *standard hours allowed.* Notice that the difference between normal costing and standard costing, insofar as overhead is concerned, lies in the quantity of the cost driver used.

Both normal- and standard-costing systems use a predetermined overhead rate. In a standard-costing system, the predetermined overhead rate also is referred to as the standard overhead rate. DCdesserts.com calculates its predetermined or standard overhead rate annually. The rate for the current year, computed in Exhibit 11–5, is based on *planned* activity of 7,500 process hours per month. Notice that DCdesserts.com breaks its predetermined overhead rate into a variable rate and a fixed rate. We will discuss further the use of standard costs for product costing in Appendix A at the end of this chapter.

Exhibit 11–4
Overhead Application

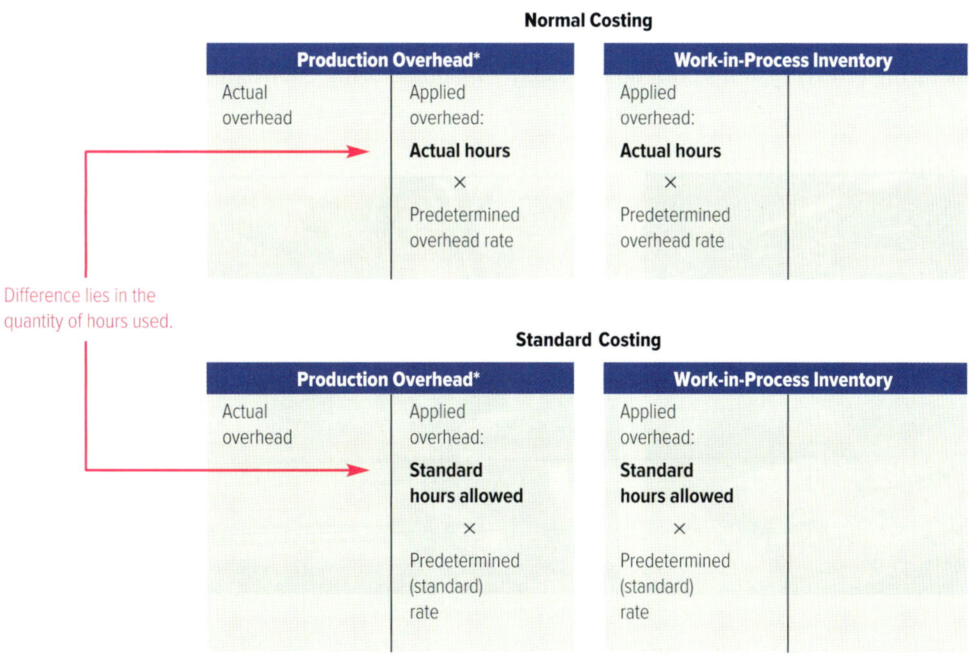

*Prior to Chapter 9, the overhead cost of the production process was usually referred to as "manufacturing overhead." Beginning with the master budget in Chapter 9, we changed to the less-specific term "production overhead" to generalize beyond manufacturing and include service and merchandising operations. A manufacturing company would still refer to production overhead as manufacturing overhead.

Exhibit 11–5
Predetermined Overhead Rate: DCdesserts.com

DC desserts

	Budgeted Overhead	Planned Monthly Activity	Predetermined Overhead Rate
Variable	$37,500*	7,500 process hours	$5.00 per process hour
Fixed	15,000*	7,500 process hours	2.00 per process hour
Total	$52,500	7,500 process hours	$7.00 per process hour

*From the flexible budget (Exhibit 11–3) for planned monthly activity of 7,500 process hours.

Choice of Activity Measure

Learning Objective 11–4

Explain the important issues in choosing an activity measure for overhead budgeting and application.

DCdesserts.com's flexible overhead budget is based on process hours. A variety of activity measures are used in practice. Machine hours, direct-labor hours, direct-labor cost, total process time, and direct-material cost are among the most common measures. Choosing the appropriate activity measure for the flexible overhead budget is important, because the flexible budget is the chief tool for managing overhead costs.

Criteria for Choosing the Activity Measure

How should a manager select the activity measure for the flexible budget? The activity measure should be one that varies in a similar pattern to the way that variable overhead varies. This means that, in practice, the activity measure for the flexible budget is the same as the cost driver in the company's costing system. As productive activity increases, both variable-overhead cost and the activity measure should increase in roughly the same proportion. As productive activity declines, both variable-overhead cost and the activity measure should decline in roughly the same proportion. In short, variable-overhead cost and the activity measure should *move together* as overall productive activity changes.

Changing Manufacturing Technology Direct-labor time has traditionally been a popular activity measure in manufacturing firms. However, as automation increases, more and more firms are switching to such measures as machine hours or process time for their flexible overhead budgets. Machine hours and process time are linked more closely than direct-labor hours to the robotic technology and computer-integrated manufacturing (CIM) systems common in today's manufacturing environment.

© Elmer Martinez/AFP/Getty Images

© Andreas Rentz/Getty Images

As manufacturing has become increasingly automated, direct labor is becoming less appropriate as an activity measure in flexible budgeting. Increased automation brings greater overhead costs while also reducing the amount of direct labor used. Left, employees inspect and pack clothes at the Zipsa industrial park near Managua, Nicaragua (a labor-intensive activity). Right, a robot assembles washing machines at the BSH Bosch und Siemens consumer appliances factory in Nauen, Germany (a high-tech process).

Cost Drivers As we discussed in Chapter 5, some companies have refined their cost management systems even further. *Cost drivers* are identified as the most significant factors affecting overhead costs. Then multiple overhead rates based on these cost drivers are used to compute product costs and control overhead expenditures. A relentless search for *non-value-added* costs is an integral part of such a cost management system. We will discuss the role of *activity-based costing* in flexible budgeting later in the chapter.

Beware of Dollar Measures Dollar measures, such as direct-labor or raw-material costs, often are used as the basis for flexible overhead budgeting. However, such measures have significant drawbacks, and they should be avoided. Dollar measures are subject to price-level changes and fluctuate more than physical measures. For example, the direct-labor *hours* required to produce a fancy dessert will be relatively stable over time. However, the direct-labor *cost* will vary as wage levels and fringe-benefit costs change with inflation and conditions in the labor market.

The choice of an activity measure upon which to base the flexible budget for variable overhead is really a cost-estimation problem, a topic that is addressed in Chapter 6.

Cost Management Using Overhead Cost Variances

Learning Objective 11–5

Compute and interpret the variable-overhead spending and efficiency variances and the fixed-overhead budget and volume variances.

The flexible overhead budget is one of a company's primary tools for the control of production-overhead costs. At the end of each accounting period, the company's managerial accountants use the flexible overhead budget to determine the level of overhead cost that should have been incurred, given the actual level of activity. They then compare the overhead cost in the flexible budget with the actual overhead cost incurred. With this information, the accountants can report to managers four separate overhead variances, each of which conveys information useful in controlling overhead costs.

To illustrate overhead variance analysis, we will continue our illustration for DCdesserts.com. Recall that the company uses process hours as the activity measure for budgeting overhead costs.

Flexible Budget DCdesserts.com's monthly flexible overhead budget, displayed in Exhibit 11–3, shows budgeted variable and fixed production-overhead costs at three levels of production output. During September, DCdesserts.com produced 2,000 multilayer fancy cakes. Since production standards allow three process hours per cake, the total standard allowed number of process hours is 6,000 hours.

Actual production output	2,000 multilayer fancy cakes
Standard allowed process hours per multilayer fancy cake	× 3
Total standard allowed process hours	6,000 process hours

From the 6,000 process-hour column in Exhibit 11–3, the budgeted overhead cost for September is as follows:

	Budgeted Overhead Cost for September
Variable overhead	$30,000
Fixed overhead	15,000

From the cost accounting records, DCdesserts.com's director of cost management determines that the following overhead cost was actually incurred during September.

	Actual Overhead Cost for September
Variable overhead	$34,650
Fixed overhead	16,100
Total overhead	$50,750

The production supervisor's records indicate that the actual total process time in September was as follows:

Actual process hours for September	6,300

Notice that the actual number of process hours used (6,300) exceeds the standard allowed number of process hours, given actual production output (6,000).

We now have assembled all of the information necessary to compute DCdesserts.com's overhead variances for September.

Variable Overhead

DCdesserts.com's total variable-overhead variance for September is computed below.

Actual variable overhead	$34,650	
Budgeted variable overhead	30,000	
Total variable-overhead variance	$ 4,650	Unfavorable

What caused the company to spend $4,650 more than the budgeted amount on variable overhead? To discover the reasons behind this performance, the financial planning and analysis system computes a **variable-overhead spending variance** and a **variable-overhead efficiency variance.** The computation of these variances is depicted in Exhibit 11–6.

Variable-Overhead Spending Variance Multiplying the actual quantity of the activity measure by the standard variable-overhead rate (AQ × SVR) gives a revised estimate of expected spending on variable overhead, given that we now know the actual quantity of the activity measure. This figure, which we designate the *projected variable overhead,* provides a benchmark against which the actual spending on variable overhead can be assessed. Any difference between the actual and projected variable-overhead cost is called the *variable-overhead spending variance.*

Two equivalent formulas for the variable-overhead spending variance are shown below.

1. $\text{Variable-overhead spending variance} = \text{Actual variable overhead} - (AQ \times SVR)$, or
2. $\text{Variable-overhead spending variance} = (AQ \times AVR) - (AQ \times SVR) = AQ(AVR - SVR)$

where

AQ denotes actual activity level (actual quantity of the activity measure)

AVR denotes actual variable-overhead rate (actual variable overhead ÷ AQ)

SVR denotes standard variable-overhead rate

These two formulas are equivalent because actual variable overhead is equal to the actual activity level times the actual variable overhead rate (AQ × AVR).

DCdesserts.com's variable-overhead spending variance for September is computed as follows (using formula 1):

$$\begin{aligned}\text{Variable-overhead spending variance} &= \text{Actual variable overhead} - (AQ \times SVR)\\ &= \$34{,}650 - (6{,}300 \times \$5.00)\\ &= \$3{,}150 \text{ Unfavorable}\end{aligned}$$

This variance is unfavorable because the actual variable-overhead cost exceeded the expected amount, after adjusting that expectation for the actual number of process hours used.

(1) Actual Variable Overhead	(2) Projected Variable Overhead	(3) Flexible Budget: Variable Overhead	(4)[†] Variable Overhead Applied to Work in Process
Actual Activity Level (AQ) × Actual Rate (AVR)	Actual Activity Level (AQ) × Standard Rate (SVR)	Standard Allowed Activity Level (SQ) × Standard Rate (SVR)	Standard Allowed Activity Level (SQ) × Standard Rate (SVR)
6,300 process hours × $5.50 per process hour*	6,300 process hours × $5.00 per process hour	6,000 process hours × $5.00 per process hour	6,000 process hours × $5.00 per process hour
$34,650	$31,500	$30,000	$30,000

$3,150 Unfavorable — Variable-overhead spending variance (between (1) and (2))

$1,500 Unfavorable — Variable-overhead efficiency variance (between (2) and (3))

No difference (between (3) and (4))

*Actual variable-overhead rate (AVR) $= \frac{\text{Actual variable-overhead cost}}{\text{Actual process hours}} = \frac{\$34{,}650}{6{,}300} = \$5.50$

[†] Column (4) is not used to compute the variances. It is included to point out that the flexible-budget amount for variable overhead, $30,000, is the amount that will be applied to Work-in-Process Inventory for product-costing purposes. For *variable* overhead, columns (3) and (4) are always equal.

Exhibit 11–6
Variable-Overhead Spending and Efficiency Variances

Variable-Overhead Efficiency Variance As Exhibit 11–6 shows, the following formula defines the variable-overhead efficiency variance.

Variable-overhead efficiency variance = (AQ × SVR) − (SQ × SVR)

where

SQ denotes standard allowed activity level (standard quantity of the activity measure)

Writing this formula more simply, we have the following expression.

Variable-overhead efficiency variance = SVR(AQ − SQ)

DCdesserts.com's variable-overhead efficiency variance for September is computed as follows:

Variable-overhead efficiency variance = SVR(AQ − SQ)
= $5.00(6,300 − 6,000)
= $1,500 Unfavorable

This variance is unfavorable because actual process hours exceeded standard allowed process hours, given actual output.

Product Costing versus Cost Management Columns (1), (2), and (3) in Exhibit 11–6 are used to compute the variances for *cost management purposes.* Column (4) in the exhibit shows the variable overhead applied to work in process for the *product-costing purpose.* Notice that the variable-overhead cost on the flexible budget, $30,000, is the same as the amount applied to work in process.

Graphing Variable-Overhead Variances Exhibit 11–7 provides a graphical analysis of DCdesserts.com's variable-overhead variances for September. The graph shows the variable-overhead rate per process hour on the vertical axis. The standard rate is $5.00 per process hour, while the actual rate is $5.50 per process hour (actual variable-overhead cost of $34,650 divided by actual process hours of 6,300). Process hours are shown on the horizontal axis.

The green area on the graph represents the flexible-budget amount for variable overhead, given actual September output of 2,000 multilayer fancy cakes. The large area on the graph enclosed by colored lines on the top and right sides represents actual variable-overhead cost. The colored area in between, representing the total variable-overhead variance, is divided into the spending and efficiency variances.

Exhibit 11–7
Graphical Analysis of Variable-Overhead Variances

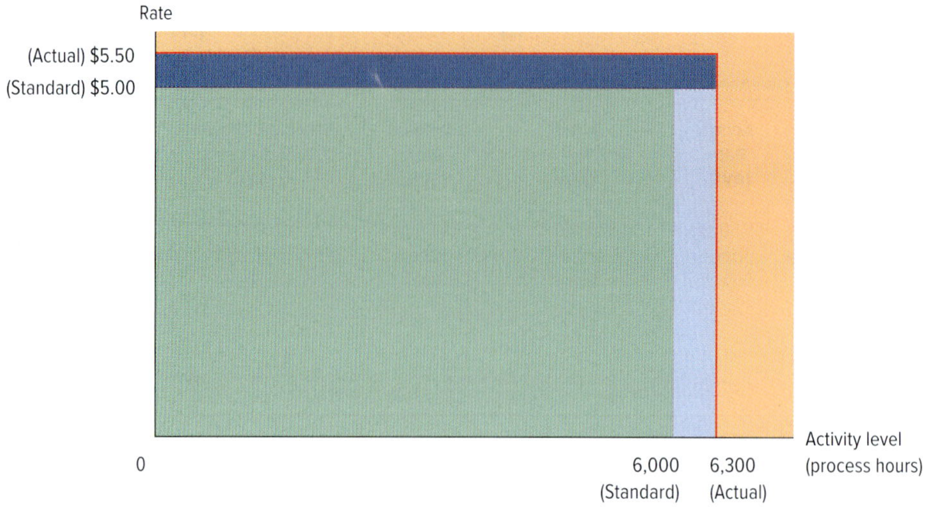

Key:
Total variable-overhead variance: blue areas
Variable-overhead spending variance: dark blue area
Variable-overhead efficiency variance: light blue area

Managerial Interpretation of Variable-Overhead Variances What do the variable-overhead variances mean? What information do they convey to management? The formulas for computing the variable-overhead variances resemble those used to compute the direct-cost variances. To see this, compare Exhibit 11–6 (variable overhead) with Exhibit 10–4 (direct labor).

Despite the similar formulas, the interpretation of the variable-overhead variances is quite different from that applicable to the direct-labor variances.

Efficiency Variance Recall that an unfavorable direct-labor efficiency variance results when more direct labor is used than the standard allowed quantity. Thus, direct labor has been used inefficiently, relative to the standard. However, that is not the proper interpretation of an unfavorable variable-overhead efficiency variance. DCdesserts.com's variable-overhead efficiency variance did *not* result from using more of the variable-overhead items, such as electricity and indirect material, than the standard allowed amount. Instead, this variance resulted when the division used *more process hours* than the standard quantity, given actual output. Recall that the company's director of cost management chose process hours as the activity measure for overhead because variable-overhead costs vary in a pattern similar to that with which process hours vary. Since 300 more process hours were used than the standard quantity, the division's management should expect that variable-overhead costs will be greater. Thus, the variable-overhead efficiency variance has nothing to do with efficient or inefficient usage of electricity, indirect material, and other variable-overhead items. This variance simply reflects an adjustment in the company's expectation about variable-overhead costs, because the division used more than the standard quantity of process hours.

What is the important difference between direct labor and variable overhead that causes this different interpretation of the efficiency variance? Direct labor is a traceable cost and is budgeted on the basis of direct-labor hours. Variable overhead, on the other hand, is a pool of *indirect* costs that are budgeted on the basis of an activity measure, *process hours*. The indirect nature of variable-overhead costs causes the different interpretation.

Spending Variance An unfavorable direct-labor rate variance is straightforward to interpret; the actual labor rate *per hour* exceeds the standard rate. Although the formula for computing the variable-overhead spending variance is similar to that for the direct-labor rate variance, its interpretation is quite different.

An unfavorable spending variance simply means that the total actual cost of variable overhead is greater than expected, after adjusting for the actual quantity of process hours used. An unfavorable spending variance could result from paying a higher-than-expected price per unit for variable-overhead items. Or the variance could result from using more of the variable-overhead items than expected.

Suppose, for example, that electricity were the only variable-overhead cost item. An unfavorable variable-overhead spending variance could result from paying a higher-than-expected price per kilowatt-hour for electricity, from using more than the expected amount of electricity, or from both.

Management of Variable-Overhead Costs Since the variable-overhead efficiency variance says nothing about efficient or inefficient usage of variable overhead, the spending variance is the real control variance for variable overhead. Managers can use the spending variance to alert them if variable-overhead costs are out of line with expectations.

Fixed Overhead

To analyze performance with regard to fixed overhead, the financial planning and analysis system calculates two fixed-overhead variances.

Fixed-Overhead Budget Variance The variance used by managers to control fixed overhead is called the **fixed-overhead budget variance.** It is defined as follows:

$$\text{Fixed-overhead budget variance} = \text{Actual fixed overhead} - \text{Budgeted fixed overhead}$$

DCdesserts.com's fixed-overhead budget variance for September is as follows:

$$\begin{aligned}\text{Fixed-overhead budget variance} &= \text{Actual fixed overhead} - \text{Budgeted fixed overhead}\\ &= \$16{,}100 - \$15{,}000^{*}\\ &= \$1{,}100\ \text{Unfavorable}\end{aligned}$$

*From the flexible budget (Exhibit 11–3).

The fixed-overhead budget variance is unfavorable, because the company spent more than the budgeted amount on fixed overhead. Notice that we need not specify an activity level to determine budgeted fixed overhead because, by definition, a *fixed* overhead cost is the same at every activity level. All three columns in the flexible budget (Exhibit 11–3) specify $15,000 as budgeted fixed overhead.

Fixed-Overhead Volume Variance The **fixed-overhead volume variance** is defined as follows:

$$\text{Fixed-overhead volume variance} = \text{Budgeted fixed overhead} - \text{Applied fixed overhead}$$

DCdesserts.com's applied fixed overhead for September is $12,000:

$$\begin{aligned}\text{Applied fixed overhead} &= \text{Predetermined fixed overhead rate} \times \text{Standard allowed activity level (quantity of the activity measure)}\\ &= \$2.00\ \text{per process hour} \times 6{,}000\ \text{process hours}\\ &= \$12{,}000\end{aligned}$$

The $2.00 predetermined fixed-overhead rate was calculated in Exhibit 11–5. The 6,000 standard allowed process hours is based on actual September production of 2,000 multilayer fancy cakes, each with a standard allowance of three process hours.

DCdesserts.com's fixed-overhead volume variance is calculated below.

$$\begin{aligned}\text{Fixed-overhead volume variance} &= \text{Budgeted fixed overhead} - \text{Applied fixed overhead} \\ &= \$15{,}000 - \$12{,}000 \\ &= \$3{,}000 \text{ Unfavorable}\end{aligned}$$

Managerial Interpretation of Fixed-Overhead Variances Exhibit 11–8 shows DCdesserts.com's two fixed-overhead variances for September. The budget variance is the real control variance for fixed overhead, because it compares actual expenditures with budgeted fixed-overhead costs.

The volume variance provides a way of reconciling two different purposes of the standard-costing system. For the *control purpose,* the system recognizes that fixed overhead does not change as production activity varies. Hence, budgeted fixed overhead is the same at all activity levels in the flexible budget. (Review Exhibit 11–3 to verify this.) Budgeted fixed overhead is the basis for controlling fixed overhead, because it provides the benchmark against which actual expenditures are compared.

For the *product-costing purpose* of the system, budgeted fixed overhead is divided by planned activity to obtain a predetermined (or standard) fixed-overhead rate. For DCdesserts.com, this rate is $2.00 per process hour (budgeted fixed overhead of $15,000 divided by planned activity of 7,500 process hours). This predetermined rate is then used to apply fixed overhead to Work-in-Process Inventory. During any period in which the standard allowed number of process hours, given actual output, differs from the planned level of process hours, the budgeted fixed overhead differs from applied fixed overhead.

Exhibit 11–9 illustrates this point graphically. Budgeted fixed overhead is constant at $15,000 for all levels of activity. However, applied fixed overhead increases with activity, since fixed overhead is applied to Work-in-Process Inventory at the rate of $2.00 per standard allowed process hour. Notice that budgeted and applied fixed overhead are equal *only* if the number of standard allowed hours equals the planned activity level of 7,500 process hours. When this happens, there is no fixed-overhead volume variance. DCdesserts.com has a $3,000 volume variance in September because the standard allowed hours and planned hours are different.

Capacity Utilization A common, but faulty, interpretation of a positive volume variance is that it measures the cost of underutilizing productive capacity. Some firms even designate a positive volume variance as unfavorable. The reasoning behind this view is

Exhibit 11–8
Fixed-Overhead Budget and Volume Variances

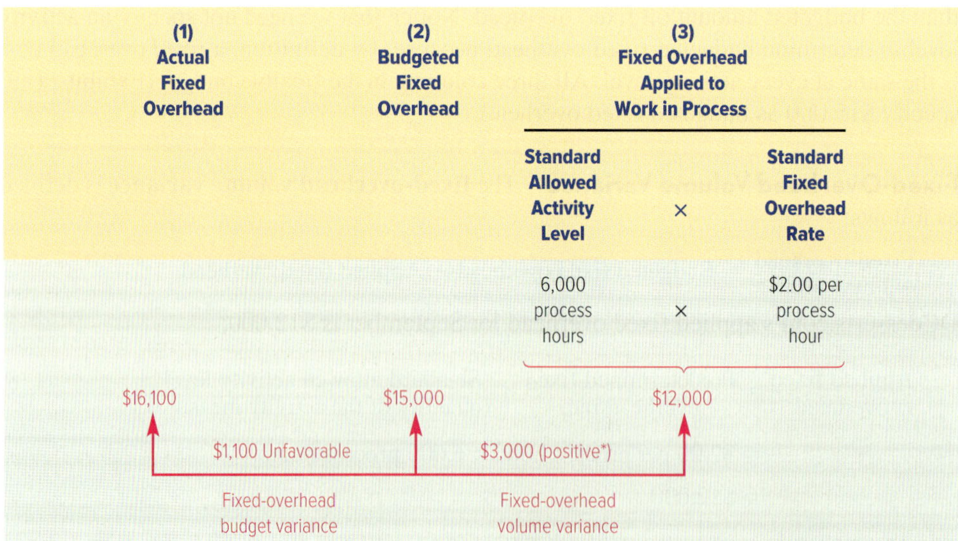

*Consistent with our discussion of the fixed-overhead volume variance, some financial planning and analysis systems would designate a positive variance as "unfavorable."

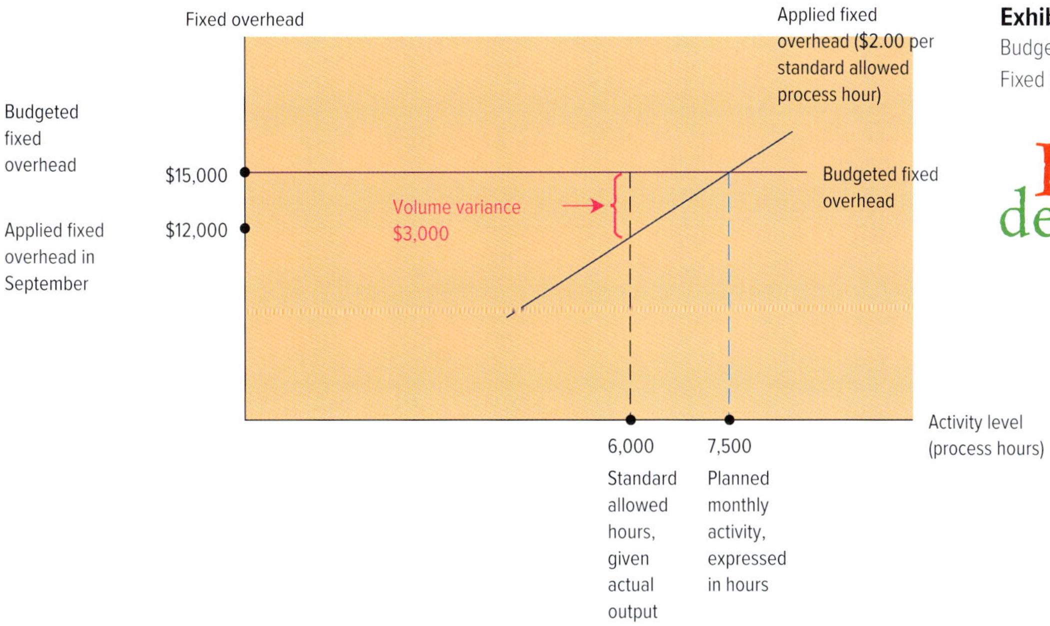

Exhibit 11–9
Budgeted versus Applied Fixed Overhead

that the planned activity level used to compute the predetermined fixed-overhead rate is a measure of normal capacity utilization. Moreover, fixed-overhead costs, such as depreciation and property taxes, are costs incurred to create productive capacity. Therefore, the predetermined fixed-overhead rate measures the cost of providing an hour of productive capacity. If 7,500 process hours are planned, but output is such that only 6,000 standard process hours are allowed, then capacity has been underutilized by 1,500 hours. Since each hour costs $2.00 (DCdesserts.com's predetermined fixed-overhead rate), the cost of underutilization is $3,000 (1,500 × $2.00), which is DCdesserts.com's volume variance.

The fault with this interpretation of the volume variance is that it ignores the real cost of underutilizing productive capacity. The real cost is due to the lost contribution margins of the products that are not produced when capacity is underutilized. Moreover, this interpretation fails to recognize that underutilizing capacity and reducing inventory may be a wise managerial response to slackening demand.

For this reason, many managers interpret the volume variance merely as a way of reconciling the two purposes of the standard-costing system. Moreover, these managers would choose not to designate the volume variance as either favorable or unfavorable. However, some designate a positive volume variance as *unfavorable*. Their reasoning is that when the volume variance is closed into Cost of Goods Sold expense at the end of the accounting period (as explained in Appendix A), the effect is to increase Cost of Goods Sold, which in turn has an *unfavorable* effect on income. In contrast, other accountants argue that no sign (favorable or unfavorable) should be assigned to the fixed-overhead volume variance.

Overhead Cost Performance Report

Learning Objective 11–6
Prepare an overhead cost performance report.

The variable-overhead spending and efficiency variances and the fixed-overhead budget variance can be computed for each overhead cost item in the flexible budget. When these itemized variances are presented along with actual and budgeted costs for each overhead item, the result is an **overhead cost performance report.** DCdesserts.com's performance report is displayed in Exhibit 11–10. This report would be used by management to exercise control over each of the division's overhead costs.

Notice that the performance report includes spending and efficiency variances for the variable items, and only a budget variance for the fixed items. Upon receiving this report, a manager might investigate the relatively large variances for indirect maintenance labor, electricity, and production supervisory labor.

	(1) Flexible Budget (for 6,000 process hr.)	(2) Standard Rate per Process Hr. [variable costs only; col. (1) ÷ 6,000 process hr.]	(3) 6,300 Actual Process Hr. × Standard Rate	(4) Actual Cost	(5) Spending Variance [col. (4) – col. (3)]	(6) Efficiency Variance [col. (3) – col. (1)]	(7) Budget Variance [col. (4) – col. (1)]
Variable costs:							
Indirect material:							
Nonstick cooking spray	$12,000	$2.00	$12,600	$12,700	$ 100 U	$ 600 U	
Waxed paper	2,000	.33	2,079	2,090	11 U	79 U	
Other paper products	2,000	.33	2,079	2,000	(79) F	79 U	
Miscellaneous supplies	6,000	1.00	6,300	6,500	200 U	300 U	
Indirect labor:							
Maintenance	4,000	.67	4,221	6,400	2,179 U	221 U	
Utilities:							
Electricity	3,000	.50	3,150	4,050	900 U	150 U	
Natural gas	1,000	.17	1,071	910	(161) F	71 U	
Total variable cost	$30,000	$5.00	$31,500	$34,650	$3,150 U	$1,500 U	
Fixed costs:							
Indirect labor:							
Inspection	$ 2,200			$ 2,210			$ 10 U
Production supervisors	6,000			7,000			1,000 U
Setup	3,000			3,000			–0–
Material handling	2,000			2,000			–0–
Depreciation:							
Plant and equipment	500			500			–0–
Insurance and property taxes	100			100			–0–
Test kitchen	1,200			1,290			90 U
Total fixed cost	$15,000			$ 16,100			$1,100 U
Total overhead cost	$45,000			$50,750			$1,100 U
Total variance between actual overhead cost and flexible budget		$5,750 U		Sum of spending, efficiency, and budget variances →		$5,750 U	

Exhibit 11–10
Overhead Cost Performance Report: DCdesserts.com

DC desserts

Learning Objective **11–7**

Explain how an activity-based flexible budget differs from a conventional flexible budget.

Activity-Based Flexible Budget

The flexible budget shown in Exhibit 11–3, which underlies our variance analysis for DCdesserts.com, is based on a single cost driver. Overhead costs that vary with respect to *process hours* are categorized as variable; all other overhead costs are treated as fixed. This approach is consistent with traditional, volume-based product-costing systems.

Under the more accurate product-costing method called activity-based costing, several cost drivers are identified.[1] Costs that may appear fixed with respect to a single volume-based cost driver, such as process hours, may be variable with respect to some other cost driver. The activity-based costing approach also can be used as the basis for a flexible budget for planning and cost management purposes. Exhibit 11–11 displays an **activity-based flexible budget** for DCdesserts.com, using the same data as Exhibit 11–3.

Compare the conventional flexible budget (Exhibit 11–3) and the activity-based flexible budget (Exhibit 11–11). The key difference lies in the costs that were categorized as fixed on the conventional flexible budget. These costs are fixed with respect to process hours but are not fixed with respect to other more appropriate cost drivers. For example,

[1]Activity-based costing is covered in Chapter 5.

Exhibit 11–11
Activity-Based Flexible Budget: DCdesserts.com

DCDESSERTS.COM
Monthly Flexible Overhead Budget

Budgeted Cost	Level of Activity		
Cost Pool I (cost driver: process hours)	**6,000**	**7,500**	**9,000**
Indirect material:			
Nonstick cooking spray	$ 12,000	$ 15,000	$ 18,000
Waxed paper	2,000	2,500	3,000
Other paper products	2,000	2,500	3,000
Miscellaneous supplies	6,000	7,500	9,000
Indirect labor: maintenance	4,000	5,000	6,000
Utilities:			
Electricity	3,000	3,750	4,500
Natural gas	1,000	1,250	1,500
Total of cost pool I	$ 30,000	$ 37,500	$ 45,000
Cost Pool II (cost driver: production runs)	**8**	**12**	**16**
Indirect labor:			
Inspection	$ 2,200	$ 3,300	$ 4,400
Setup	3,000	4,500	6,000
Total of cost pool II	$ 5,200	$ 7,800	$ 10,400
Cost Pool III (cost driver: new products tested)	**20**	**30**	**40**
Test kitchen	$ 1,200	$ 1,800	$ 2,400
Total of cost pool III	$ 1,200	$ 1,800	$ 2,400
Cost Pool IV (cost driver: pounds of material handled)	**20,000**	**30,000**	**40,000**
Material handling	$ 2,000	$ 3,000	$ 4,000
Total of cost pool IV	$ 2,000	$ 3,000	$ 4,000
Cost Pool V (facility level costs)			
Indirect labor: production supervisors	$ 6,000	$ 6,000	$ 6,000
Depreciation: plant and equipment	500	500	500
Insurance and property taxes	100	100	100
Total of cost pool V	$ 6,600	$ 6,600	$ 6,600
Total overhead cost	**$45,000**	**$56,700**	**$68,400**

cost pool II includes inspection and setup costs, which vary with respect to the number of production runs.

"ABC provides a methodology for tracking costs by product and establishing more appropriate linkages of resources to products through the use of activity analysis." (11c)
BlueCross BlueShield of North Carolina

Effect on Performance Reporting The activity-based flexible budget provides a more accurate prediction (and benchmark) of overhead costs. For example, suppose that activity in December is as follows:

December Activity	Process hours	6,000
	Production runs	12
	New products tested	40
	Direct material handled (pounds)	30,000

The following table compares the budgeted cost levels for several overhead items on the conventional and activity-based flexible budgets.

Overhead Cost Item	Conventional Flexible Budget	Activity-Based Flexible Budget
Electricity	$3,000	$3,000
Inspection	2,200	3,300
Setup	3,000	4,500
Test kitchen	1,200	2,400
Material handling	2,000	3,000
Insurance and property taxes	100	100

"In the past decade, Whirlpool has faced increasing competition, higher overhead, and greater product diversity. Managers initiated and supported ABC to obtain accurate information for dealing with these challenges." (11d)
Whirlpool

Management Accounting Practice

Stihl, Inc.

COST MANAGEMENT SYSTEMS IN GERMANY

Throughout the world, flexible budgeting is found in cost management systems as a means of controlling overhead costs. However, differences in terminology and design may be present in financial planning and control practices due to geographic variations in the evolution of management practice or accounting philosophy. In Germany, for example, *grenzplankostenrechnung* (or "flexible standard costing") exhibits many of the features illustrated in this chapter. Under the German approach, "each cost center distinguishes between variable costs (e.g., energy) and fixed costs (e.g., a manager's salary)." The number of machine hours is a common activity measure. "For purposes of cost planning and control, companies budget each cost center's expenses and then distribute the expenses to each month of the budget year. The budgeted costs are standards for efficient resource consumption. . . . " The cost and performance information "allows for effective discussions about productivity improvement" among department managers, managerial accountants, and plant managers.

Among the companies using the flexible standard costing system is **Stihl**, a well-known German manufacturer of chain saws and other landscaping equipment.[2]

The budgeted electricity cost is the same on both budgets, because both use the same cost driver (process hours). Insurance and property taxes are also the same, because both budgets recognize these as facility-level fixed costs. However, the other overhead costs are budgeted at different levels, because the conventional and activity-based flexible budgets use *different cost drivers* for these items. While the conventional budget treats inspection, setup, test kitchen, and material-handling costs as fixed, the activity-based flexible budget shows that they are all variable with respect to the appropriate cost driver.

An activity-based flexible budget is based on many cost drivers. Think about the costs that are incurred at your college. The cost of staffing the college's faculty, for example, depends on factors such as the number of students enrolled, the number of courses offered, and the average class size. The cost of operating the admissions department would depend in part on the number of applicants.[3]

© Image Source RF

These differences are important for performance reporting. The activity-based flexible budget provides a more accurate benchmark against which to compare actual costs. Suppose the actual inspection cost in December is \$3,000. Using the conventional flexible budget would result in an unfavorable variance of \$800 (\$3,000 − \$2,200). However, the activity-based flexible budget yields a favorable variance of \$300 (\$3,000 − \$3,300).

To summarize, activity-based flexible budgeting provides a richer view of cost behavior and the underlying cost drivers, and it provides a valuable tool for cost management.

[2]Kip R. Krumwiede, "Rewards and Realities of German Cost Accounting," *Strategic Finance* 86, no. 10 (April 2005), pp. 27–34; Carl S. Smith, "Going for GPK," *Strategic Finance* 86, no. 10 (April 2005), pp. 36–39; and Bernd Gaiser, "German Cost Management Systems," *Journal of Cost Management* 11, no. 5 (September/October 1997), pp. 35–41.

[3]Key cost drivers used in activity-based flexible budgeting at Cornell University include the number of students enrolled and the number of student credit hours. For further reading on activity-based budgeting, see Jay Collins, "Advanced Use of ABM: Using ABC for Target Costing, Activity-Based Budgeting, and Benchmarking," in *Activity-Based Management: Arthur Andersen's Lessons from the ABM Battlefield,* ed. Steve Player and David E. Keys (New York: John Wiley & Sons, 1999), pp. 152–58.

Exhibit 11–12
Flexible Budget: Upstate Auto Rentals

UPSTATE AUTO RENTALS

Upstate Auto Rentals - Excel

F32 =F14+F22+F30

	A	B	C	D	E	F
1	UPSTATE AUTO RENTALS					
2	Annual Flexible Budget: Operating Expenses					
3						
4			Cost			
5			Driver			
6	Budgeted Operating Expenses		Rate		Level of Activity	
7						
8	Cost Pool I *(cost driver: miles driven)*			750,000	1,000,000	1,250,000
9	Vehicle maintenance		$ 0.3200	$ 240,000	$ 320,000	$ 400,000
10	Tire replacement		0.0080	6,000	8,000	10,000
11	Vehicle insurance		0.0360	27,000	36,000	45,000
12	State registration and inspection		0.0012	900	1,200	1,500
13	Leasing costs		0.0480	36,000	48,000	60,000
14	Total - Cost Pool I			$ 309,900	$ 413,200	$ 516,500
15						
16	Cost Pool II *(cost driver: customer contracts)*			3,000	6,000	9,000
17	Reservations		$ 5.3333	$ 16,000	$ 32,000	$ 48,000
18	Registration of contract information		6.0000	$ 18,000	$ 36,000	$ 54,000
19	Inspection of vehicle by employee/customer		2.6667	$ 8,000	$ 16,000	$ 24,000
20	Employee commissions		6.6667	$ 20,000	$ 40,000	$ 60,000
21	Cleaning/washing vehicle		5.6667	$ 17,000	$ 34,000	$ 51,000
22	Total - Cost Pool II			$ 79,000	$ 158,000	$ 237,000
23						
24	Cost Pool III *(facility-level costs: fixed)*					
25	Office managers' salaries			$ 240,000	$ 240,000	$ 240,000
26	Rent: buildings			36,000	36,000	36,000
27	Utilities: buildings			13,000	13,000	13,000
28	Liability insurance: rental offices			12,000	12,000	12,000
29	Depreciation: equipment			11,000	11,000	11,000
30	Total - Cost Pool III			$ 312,000	$ 312,000	$ 312,000
31						
32	Total Operating Expenses			$ 700,900	$ 883,200	$ 1,065,500

Flexible Overhead Budget

Flexible Budgeting in the Service Industry

All kinds of organizations benefit from the concept of a flexible budget. Like manufacturing firms, service-industry organizations incur overhead costs that vary with appropriately chosen cost drivers. At Cornell University, for example, the cost of operating the admissions department depends in part on the number of applicants. At GEICO Insurance Company, the cost of administering the claims department depends in part on the number of claims. At the Mayo Clinic, the cost of operating the patient records department depends in part on the number of patients.

> "ABC has enhanced our clients' ability to manage overhead costs through flexible budgeting systems." (11e)
>
> **A. T. Kearney**

UPSTATE AUTO RENTALS

Let's briefly turn our attention to Upstate Auto Rentals, a small automobile rental company in upstate New York. The company has four rental locations in and around Syracuse and specializes in short-term car rentals, primarily for local use when a customer's car is in the repair shop. Upstate's flexible budget is displayed in Exhibit 11–12. Notice that unlike DCdesserts.com's flexible overhead budget, Upstate Auto Rentals' flexible budget lists its operating expenses. All of this service industry firm's costs are operating expenses. Upstate's management has chosen two cost drivers for its activity-based flexible budget: the number of miles driven and the number of customer contracts.

Some operating expenses (cost pool I in the flexible budget) vary with the number of miles driven by the rental cars. Automobile maintenance and tire replacement expenses increase as the cars drive more miles. Similarly, such operating expenses as insurance and leasing costs increase with the number of miles driven, because the company needs more cars on hand. Other operating expenses (cost pool II) vary with the number of customer contracts, regardless of how many miles each customer drives a rental car. Such expenses as rental reservations, filling out contracts, and cleaning up a rental car upon return depend on the number of times the cars are rented. Finally, some fixed operating expenses (cost pool III), such as the office managers' salaries and rental charges on the office locations, do not vary with any cost driver.

Upstate Auto Rentals' management can use this flexible budget to predict operating expenses at varying levels of activity, as measured by the two cost drivers.

Focus on Ethics

MISSTATED STANDARDS AFFECT ACCURACY OF REPORTS

The scenario described here, while placed in the context of a fictitious enterprise, is based on an actual situation that occurred at **NuTone Housing Group**, which at the time was a subsidiary of **Scoville, Inc.***

To set the stage, consider these facts about the standard-costing system in place at Shrood Division, a subsidiary of Gigantic Enterprises, Inc. Shrood Division manufactures a wide range of electric household products, such as lighting, fans, water pumps, and security systems. The division manufactures approximately 10,000 products, made from over 70,000 components. Tom Cleverly has run the division in what he calls a hands-on manner for over a quarter century. When Shrood Division was acquired by Gigantic Enterprises a decade ago, Cleverly was at first unhappy with the merger, but it soon became apparent that Gigantic's top management would let him run the business the way he was used to running it. Three aspects of Cleverly's management style are noteworthy. First, he insists on being involved in all major pricing decisions; he's not a delegator. Second, he has developed a second-level management that is loyal and supportive of his approach. Third, he has refused to lower the direct-labor time standards for years, even though many productivity improvements have been made. At present, the actual direct-labor times are on average only about a third of the standard times. Moreover, since production overhead is applied on the basis of direct labor, both the standard direct-labor and the standard overhead costs are inflated relative to actual costs.

*K. Merchant and L. Ferreira,"Scoville: NuTone Housing Group," a management accounting case (Boston: President and Fellows of Harvard College).

The implications of this practice are that huge favorable variances are experienced all year long in both direct labor and overhead. Cleverly has used these favorable variances to "manage the quarterly earnings" reported by Shrood Division to corporate. Cleverly has instructed his manager of accounting, Evan Twixt, to release just enough of the favorable variances into Cost of Goods Sold (CGS) on a quarterly basis to ensure that Shrood Division just meets its earnings target in the budget. Then, at the end of the year, the remainder of this large favorable variance is released into CGS, with the result that Shrood Division ends each year with fourth-quarter earnings far in excess of the target. Like a knight in shining white armor, Shrood Division saves the day for Gigantic Enterprises year after year. Shrood has come to be known in corporate circles as "the jewel in the crown of Gigantic Enterprises."

Now for the conflict. Gigantic has hired a new corporate controller, Jeffrey Fixit, whose charge is to introduce more consistency in the reporting methods of Gigantic's various divisions. When Fixit visited Shrood Division and discovered what was going on, he tried to get Tom Cleverly to instruct Evan Twixt to correct the direct-labor standards to reflect attainable results (i.e., reality). Cleverly has refused, though, and Fixit doesn't have the power to force him to do so. Meanwhile, poor Twixt is caught in the middle.

Here is what each of them had to say about the situation.

Cleverly (division manager): "I've been running this business for 25 years. And you know what? We've been profitable for 25 years! The high labor standards help me make sure that neither I nor my salespeople shave prices too much. It's like setting the clock 10 minutes ahead to make sure you're not late. We always make budget. We always report the highest profits in the company. And we are, in fact, the 'jewel in the crown.'"

Fixit (corporate controller): "This is a really bad situation. Shrood is reporting fictitious numbers to corporate on a quarterly basis, which then get rolled up into Gigantic's quarterly results. Then these numbers get published to the shareholders. We're misleading them. I don't have the authority to get Tom Cleverly to fix the problem. I can, however, go to the board of directors and explain to them that they need to get Cleverly to do what needs to be done."

Twixt (Shrood's accounting manager): "I'm caught in the middle. We basically have two sets of books: the ones based on Mr. Cleverly's labor standards, and the ones based on the more accurate results that Mr. Fixit wants. I can report either set of results. I feel like I'm serving two gods—and so far I'm getting away with it."

What do you make of this situation? Can a company that keeps two sets of books be well managed? What ethical issues do you see here? What actions should Cleverly, Twixt, and Fixit take?

Chapter Summary

LO11-1 Distinguish between static and flexible budgets and explain the advantages of a flexible overhead budget. A static budget is based on a single, predicted volume of production activity. A flexible budget allows for many possible activity levels. The flexible overhead budget is based on some activity measure that varies in a pattern similar to that of variable overhead. Management uses the amount of overhead cost specified by the flexible budget, given actual output, as a benchmark against which to compare actual overhead costs.

LO11-2 Prepare a flexible overhead budget, using both a formula and a columnar format. A columnar flexible budget is based on several distinct activity levels, while a formula flexible budget is valid for a continuous range of activity. The flexible overhead budget is based on some activity measure that varies in a pattern similar to that of variable overhead.

LO11-3 Explain how overhead is applied to Work-in-Process Inventory under standard costing. The amount of overhead cost entered into Work-in-Process Inventory is equal to the standard overhead rate multiplied by the standard allowed amount of the activity base, given actual output.

LO11-4 Explain the important issues in choosing an activity measure for overhead budgeting and application. The flexible overhead budget is based on some activity measure that varies in a pattern similar to that of variable overhead. Machine hours, process time, and direct-labor hours are common activity bases.

LO11-5 Compute and interpret the variable-overhead spending and efficiency variances and the fixed overhead budget and volume variances. The variable-overhead spending variance calculates the effect on production cost of deviations between the actual and standard variable overhead rates. The variable-overhead efficiency variance calculates the effect on production cost of deviations between actual and standard amounts of the cost driver, multiplied by the standard variable overhead rate. The fixed overhead budget variance calculates the effect on production cost of deviations between actual and budgeted fixed overhead. The fixed overhead volume variance calculates the effect of deviations between budgeted and applied fixed overhead.

LO11-6 Prepare an overhead cost performance report. The overhead cost performance report shows the actual and budgeted costs for each overhead item, along with the four overhead variances: the variable-overhead spending and efficiency variances, and the fixed-overhead budget and volume variances. These variances help management to control overhead costs.

LO11-7 Explain how an activity-based flexible budget differs from a conventional flexible budget. In an activity-based flexible budget, each overhead item may have a different cost driver identified upon which the flexible overhead budget for that cost item is based. Such a flexible budget is more accurate than conventional flexible budgets, because multiple cost drivers are identified to explain the behavior of overhead costs.

LO11-8 Prepare journal entries to record production overhead under standard costing (appendix A). The left (debit) side of the production-overhead account accumulates actual overhead costs incurred. The right (credit) side of the overhead account records production overhead applied to Work-in-Process Inventory. The cumulative difference between the amounts on the left and right sides of the overhead account is equal to the sum of the four overhead variances.

LO11-9 Compute and interpret the sales-price and sales-volume variances (appendix B). The sales-price variance is the difference between the actual and budgeted sales prices multiplied by the actual sales volume. This variance measures the effect on sales revenue of sales price deviations. The sales-volume variance is the difference between the actual and budgeted sales volumes multiplied by the budgeted sales price. This variance measures the effect on sales revenue of deviations in sales volume.

Review Problem on Flexible Budgeting and Analysis of Overhead Costs

In November, DCdesserts.com produced 3,000 multilayer fancy cakes, used 9,100 hours of process time, and incurred the following production-overhead costs.

Variable overhead	$45,955
Fixed overhead	$15,800

DCdesserts.com's monthly flexible overhead budget for November is the same as that given in Exhibit 11–3.

Compute DCdesserts.com's variable-overhead variances using the format shown in Exhibit 11–6. Compute the company's fixed-overhead variances using the format shown in Exhibit 11–8.

Solution to Review Problem

The solution to the review problem is given in Exhibits 11–13 and 11–14.

Exhibit 11–13
Variable-Overhead Spending and Efficiency Variances: Review Problem

DC desserts

(1) Actual Variable Overhead	(2) Projected Variable Overhead	(3) Flexible Budget: Variable Overhead	(4)[†] Variable Overhead Applied to Work in Process
Actual Activity Level (AQ) × Actual Rate (AVR)	Actual Activity Level (AQ) × Standard Rate (SVR)	Standard Allowed Activity Level (SQ) × Standard Rate (SVR)	Standard Allowed Activity Level (SQ) × Standard Rate (SVR)
9,100 process hours × $5.05 per process hour*	9,100 process hours × $5.00 per process hour	9,000 process hours × $5.00 per process hour	9,000 process hours × $5.00 per process hour
$45,955	$45,500	$45,000	$45,000

(1) to (2)	(2) to (3)	(3) to (4)
$455 Unfavorable	$500 Unfavorable	
Variable-overhead spending variance	Variable-overhead efficiency variance	No difference

*Actual variable-overhead rate (AVR) $= \frac{\text{Actual variable-overhead cost}}{\text{Actual process hours}} = \frac{\$45,955}{9,100} = \$5.05$

[†]Column (4) is not used to compute the variances. It is included to point out that the flexible-budget amount for variable overhead, $45,000, is the amount that will be applied to Work-in-Process Inventory for product-costing purposes.

Exhibit 11–14
Fixed-Overhead Budget and Volume Variances: Review Problem

(1) Actual Fixed Overhead	(2) Budgeted Fixed Overhead	(3) Fixed Overhead Applied to Work in Process		
		Standard Allowed Activity Level	×	Standard Fixed Overhead Rate
		9,000 process hours	×	$2.00 per process hour
$15,800	$15,000	$18,000		

$800 Unfavorable — Fixed-overhead budget variance (between $15,800 and $15,000)

$3,000 (positive*) — Fixed-overhead volume variance (between $15,000 and $18,000)

*Some financial planning and analysis systems would designate a negative fixed-overhead volume variance as "favorable."

Key Terms

For each term's definition refer to the indicated page, or turn to the glossary at the end of the text.

activity-based flexible budget, 478
fixed-overhead budget variance, 475
fixed-overhead volume variance, 475
flexible budget, 465
overhead cost performance report, 477
sales-price variance*, 488
sales-volume variance*, 488
static budget, 465
total contribution margin*, 487
unit contribution margin*, 487
variable-overhead efficiency variance, 472
variable-overhead spending variance, 472

*Term appears in Appendix B.

APPENDIX A TO CHAPTER 11

Standard Costs and Product Costing

Learning Objective 11–8

Prepare journal entries to record production overhead under standard costing.

In a standard-costing system, the standard costs are used for product costing as well as for cost control. The costs of direct material, direct labor, and production overhead are all entered into Work-in-Process Inventory at their standard costs. (Review Exhibit 11–4.)

Journal Entries under Standard Costing During September, DCdesserts.com incurred actual production-overhead costs of $50,750, which includes $34,650 of variable overhead and $16,100 of fixed overhead. A summary journal entry to record these actual expenditures follows.

Production Overhead	50,750	
Indirect-Material Inventory		23,290*
Wages Payable		20,610*
Utilities Payable		4,960
Accumulated Depreciation		500
Prepaid Insurance and Property Taxes		100
Test Kitchen Salaries Payable		1,290

*The credit amounts can be verified in column (4) of Exhibit 11-10. For example, indirect-material costs amounted to $23,290 ($12,700 + $2,090 + $2,000 + $6,500). The credit to Wages Payable is for indirect-labor costs, which amounted to $20,610 ($6,400 + $2,210 + $7,000 + $3,000 + $2,000).

The application of production overhead to Work-in-Process Inventory is based on a predetermined overhead rate of $7.00 per process hour (the total of the variable and the fixed rates) and 6,000 standard allowed process hours, given an actual output of 2,000 multilayer fancy cakes. The summary journal entry is as follows:

Work-in-Process Inventory	42,000	
Production Overhead		42,000*

*Applied overhead = $7.00 × 6,000 = $42,000

Now the Production Overhead account appears as follows:

Production Overhead			
Actual	$50,750	$42,000	Applied

The *underapplied overhead* for September is $8,750 ($50,750 − $42,000). This means that the overhead applied to Work-in-Process Inventory in September was $8,750 less than the actual overhead cost incurred. Notice that the underapplied overhead is equal to the sum of the four overhead variances for September. The total of the four overhead variances will always be equal to the overapplied or underapplied overhead for the accounting period.[4]

Disposition of Variances As explained in the preceding chapter, variances are temporary accounts, and most companies close them directly into Cost of Goods Sold at the end of each accounting period. The journal entry required to close out DCdesserts.com's underapplied overhead for September is as follows:

Cost of Goods Sold	8,750	
Production Overhead		8,750

The journal entry to close out underapplied or overapplied overhead typically is made annually, rather than monthly.

An alternative accounting treatment is to prorate underapplied or overapplied overhead among Work-in-Process Inventory, Finished-Goods Inventory, and Cost of Goods Sold, as explained in Chapter 3.

A Note on Perishable Products and JIT Production Management Systems As noted in the preceding chapter, traditional manufacturing systems typically exhibit the cost flows explained in this section. Direct-material, direct-labor, and production-overhead costs are entered in Work-in-Process Inventory, from which they flow into Finished-Goods Inventory when the goods are finished, and then on into Cost of Goods Sold. Since DCdesserts.com produces perishable goods, which are produced and sold on the same day, a simpler procedure could be used. In DCdesserts.com's case, the *standard* costs of direct material, direct labor, and production overhead could be entered directly into Cost of Goods Sold as they are incurred. This simplified procedure could be used, because the production process is very short and the goods are sold immediately. Thus, there is never any work-in-process inventory or finished-goods inventory on hand. Such situations are common with producers of perishable goods.

An analogous situation occurs in manufacturers that employ a just-in-time (JIT) production and inventory control system. In a JIT environment, raw materials are delivered just in time to be entered into production, and parts or components are manufactured in each stage of the production process just in time for the next production stage. Thus, like the case of perishable goods, there is little or no work-in-process or finished-goods inventory at any given time in a JIT environment. For this reason, many manufacturers that employ the JIT approach make use of highly simplified cost accounting procedures similar to those explained in the preceding paragraph for DCdesserts.com.

[4]Overapplied and underapplied production overhead in the manufacturing setting are discussed in Chapter 3.

APPENDIX B TO CHAPTER 11

Sales Variances

The variances discussed in Chapters 10 and 11 focus on production costs. Companies also compute variances to help management analyze the firm's sales performance. To illustrate two commonly used sales variances, we will continue our discussion of DCdesserts.com. The expected sales price and standard variable cost for a multilayer fancy cake are as follows:

Learning Objective 11–9

Compute and interpret the sales-price and sales-volume variances.

Budgeted sales price	$38
Standard variable costs:	
Direct material	$ 7
Direct labor	10
Variable overhead (3 process hours at $5 per hour)	15
Total unit variable cost	$32

The difference between the sales price and the unit variable cost is called the **unit contribution margin.** DCdesserts.com's unit contribution margin is $6 per multilayer fancy cake ($38 − $32). This is the amount that the sale of one multilayer fancy cake contributes toward covering the company's fixed costs and making a profit.

During October, DCdesserts.com's management expects to sell 1,500 multilayer fancy cakes. Based on this sales forecast, the controller computed the following budgeted **total contribution margin.**

Budgeted sales revenue (1,500 multilayered fancy cakes × $38)	$57,000
Budgeted variable costs (1,500 multilayered fancy cakes × $32)	48,000
Budgeted total contribution margin (1,500 multilayered fancy cakes × $6)	$ 9,000

The *actual* results for October were as follows:

Actual sales volume	1,600 cakes
Actual sales price	$37
Actual unit variable cost	$32

Using these actual results, the actual total contribution margin for October is as follows:

Actual sales revenue (1,600 multilayered fancy cakes × $37)	$59,200
Actual variable costs (1,600 multilayered fancy cakes × $32)	51,200
Actual total contribution margin (1,600 multilayered fancy cakes × $5)	$ 8,000

DCdesserts.com's actual and budgeted results for October are summarized in the following table. Notice that actual sales revenue exceeded budgeted sales revenue by $2,200. However, this favorable variance was more than offset by the additional $3,200 in variable costs resulting from actual sales volume exceeding budgeted sales volume. So the actual total contribution margin was $1,000 less than the budgeted total contribution margin, as the table shows.

	Budget	Actual	Variance
Revenue	$57,000	$59,200	$2,200 F
Variable costs	48,000	51,200	3,200 U
Contribution margin	$ 9,000	$ 8,000	$1,000 U

The financial planning and analysis system computes two sales variances to explain the $2,200 favorable variance in sales revenue. These variances are defined and computed as follows:

$$\text{Sales-price variance} = \left(\begin{matrix}\text{Actual}\\ \text{sales}\\ \text{price}\end{matrix} - \begin{matrix}\text{Budgeted}\\ \text{sales}\\ \text{price}\end{matrix}\right) \times \text{Actual sales volume}$$

$$= (\$37 - \$38) \times 1{,}600$$

$$= \$1{,}600 \text{ Unfavorable}$$

$$\text{Sales-volume variance} = \begin{pmatrix} \text{Actual} & & \text{Budgeted} \\ \text{sales} & - & \text{sales} \\ \text{volume} & & \text{volume} \end{pmatrix} \times \text{Budgeted sales price}$$

$$= (1{,}600 - 1{,}500) \times \$38$$

$$= \$3{,}800 \text{ Favorable}$$

Together, the **sales-price** and **sales-volume variances** explain the $2,200 favorable variance between actual and budgeted sales revenue.

Sales-price variance	$1,600 Unfavorable
Sales-volume variance	3,800 Favorable
Variance between actual and budgeted sales revenue	$2,200 Favorable

We have only just introduced sales variance analysis here. This topic is covered more extensively in cost management texts.

Review Questions

11–1. Distinguish between static and flexible budgets.

11–2. Explain the advantage of using a flexible budget.

11–3. Why are flexible overhead budgets based on activity measures, such as hours of process time, machine time, or direct-labor hours?

11–4. Distinguish between a columnar and a formula flexible budget.

11–5. Show, using T-accounts, how production overhead is added to Work-in-Process Inventory when standard costing is used.

11–6. How have advances in manufacturing technology affected overhead application?

11–7. What is the interpretation of the variable-overhead spending variance?

11–8. Jeffries Company's only variable-overhead cost is electricity. Does an unfavorable variable-overhead spending variance imply that the company paid more than the anticipated rate per kilowatt-hour?

11–9. What is the interpretation of the variable-overhead efficiency variance?

11–10. Distinguish between the interpretations of the direct-labor and variable-overhead efficiency variances.

11–11. What is the fixed-overhead budget variance?

11–12. What is the correct interpretation of the fixed-overhead volume variance?

11–13. Describe a common but misleading interpretation of the fixed-overhead volume variance. Why is this interpretation misleading?

11–14. Draw a graph showing budgeted and applied fixed overhead, and show an unfavorable (or positive) volume variance on the graph.

11–15. What types of organizations use flexible budgets?

11–16. What is the conceptual problem of applying fixed production overhead as a product cost?

11–17. Distinguish between the control purpose and the product-costing purpose of standard costing and flexible budgeting.

11–18. Why are fixed-overhead costs sometimes called capacity-producing costs?

11–19. Draw a graph showing both budgeted and applied variable overhead. Explain why the graph appears as it does.

11–20. Give one example of a plausible activity base to use in flexible budgeting for each of the following organizations: an insurance company, an express delivery service, a restaurant, and a state tax-collection agency.

11–21. Explain how an activity-based flexible budget differs from a conventional flexible budget.

Exercises

All applicable Exercises are available in Connect. connect

Exercise 11–22
Straightforward Computation of Overhead Variances
(LO 11-5)

Crystal Glassware Company has the following standards and flexible-budget data.

Standard variable-overhead rate	$6.00 per direct-labor hour
Standard quantity of direct labor	2 hours per unit of output
Budgeted fixed overhead	$100,000
Budgeted output	25,000 units

Actual results for April are as follows:

Actual output	20,000 units
Actual variable overhead	$320,000
Actual fixed overhead	$97,000
Actual direct labor	50,000 hours

Required: Use the variance formulas to compute the following variances. Indicate whether each variance is favorable or unfavorable, where appropriate.

1. Variable-overhead spending variance.
2. Variable-overhead efficiency variance.
3. Fixed-overhead budget variance.
4. Fixed-overhead volume variance.

Exercise 11–23
Diagram of Overhead Variances
(LO 11-5)

Refer to the data in the preceding exercise. Use diagrams similar to those in Exhibits 11–6 and 11–8 to compute the variable-overhead spending and efficiency variances, and the fixed-overhead budget and volume variances.

Exercise 11–24
Graphing Overhead Variances
(LO 11-5)

Refer to the data in the Exercise 11–22 for Crystal Glassware Company. Draw graphs similar to those in Exhibit 11–7 (variable overhead) and Exhibit 11–9 (fixed overhead) to depict the overhead variances.

Exercise 11–25
City or State Budget; Activity-Based Flexible Budget; Cost Drivers; Use of Internet
(LO 11-4, 11-7)

Choose a city or state in the United States (or a Canadian city or province), and use the Internet to explore the annual budget for the governmental unit you selected. For example, you could check out the annual budget for Houston, Texas at www.houstontx.gov/budget.

Required:

1. Select three items in the budget and explain how these items would be treated if the budget were converted to an activity-based flexible budget.
2. What would be appropriate cost drivers for the budgetary items you selected?

Exercise 11–26
Straightforward Computation of Overhead Variances
(LO 11-5)

The following data are the actual results for Marvelous Marshmallow Company for October.

Actual output	9,000 cases
Actual variable overhead	$405,000
Actual fixed overhead	$122,000
Actual machine time	40,500 machine hours

Standard cost and budget information for Marvelous Marshmallow Company follows:

Standard variable-overhead rate	$9.00 per machine hour
Standard quantity of machine hours	4 hours per case of marshmallows
Budgeted fixed overhead	$120,000 per month
Budgeted output	10,000 cases per month

Required:

1. Use any of the methods explained in the chapter to compute the following variances. Indicate whether each variance is favorable or unfavorable, where appropriate.
   a. Variable-overhead spending variance.
   b. Variable-overhead efficiency variance.
   c. Fixed-overhead budget variance.
   d. Fixed-overhead volume variance.
2. ***Build a spreadsheet:*** Construct an Excel spreadsheet to solve the preceding requirement. Show how the solution will change if the following information changes: actual output was 9,100 cases, and actual variable overhead was $395,000.

Exercise 11–27
Standard Hours Allowed; Flexible Budgeting; Multiple Products
(LO 11-1, 11-2)

Evening Star, Inc. produces binoculars of two quality levels: field and professional. The field model requires three direct-labor hours, while the professional binoculars require five hours. The firm uses direct-labor hours for flexible budgeting.

Required:

1. How many standard hours are allowed in May, when 200 field models and 300 professional binoculars are manufactured?
2. Suppose the company based its flexible overhead budget for May on the number of binoculars manufactured, which is 500. What difficulties would this approach cause?

Exercise 11–28
Construct a Flexible Overhead Budget; Hospital
(LO 11-1, 11-2)

The controller for Rainbow Children's Hospital, located in Munich, Germany, estimates that the hospital uses 30 kilowatt-hours of electricity per patient-day, and that the electric rate will be .10 euro per kilowatt-hour. The hospital also pays a fixed monthly charge of 1,000 euros to the electric utility to rent emergency backup electric generators.

Required: Construct a flexible budget for the hospital's electricity costs using each of the following techniques.

1. Formula flexible budget.
2. Columnar flexible budget for 30,000, 40,000 and 50,000 patient-days of activity. List variable and fixed electricity costs separately.

Exercise 11–29
Interpretation of Variable-Overhead Efficiency Variance
(LO 11-5)

You recently received the following note from the production supervisor of the company where you serve as controller. "I don't understand these crazy variable-overhead efficiency variances. My employees are very careful in their use of electricity and production supplies, and we use very little indirect labor. What are we supposed to do?" Write a brief memo responding to the production supervisor's concern.

Exercise 11–30
Reconstruct Missing Information from Partial Data
(LO 11-2, 11-5)

You brought your work home one evening, and your nephew spilled his chocolate milk shake on the variance report you were preparing. Fortunately, knowing that overhead was applied based on machine hours, you were able to reconstruct the obliterated information from the remaining data. Fill in the missing numbers below. (*Hint:* It is helpful to solve for the unknowns in the order indicated by the letters in the following table.)

Standard machine hours per unit of output	4 hours
Standard variable-overhead rate per machine hour	$8.00
Actual variable-overhead rate per machine hour	b
Actual machine hours per unit of output	d
Budgeted fixed overhead	$50,000
Actual fixed overhead	a
Budgeted production in units	25,000
Actual production in units	c
Variable-overhead spending variance	$ 72,000 U
Variable-overhead efficiency variance	$192,000 F
Fixed-overhead budget variance	$ 15,000 U
Fixed-overhead volume variance	g
Total actual overhead	$713,000
Total budgeted overhead (flexible budget)	e
Total budgeted overhead (static budget)	f
Total applied overhead	$816,000

■ **Exercise 11–31**
Activity-Based Flexible Budget
(LO 11-2, 11-7)

Refer to DCdesserts.com's activity-based flexible budget in Exhibit 11–11. Suppose that the company's activity in June is described as follows:

Process hours	7,500
Production runs	16
New products tested	30
Direct material handled (pounds)	40,000

Required:

1. Determine the flexible budgeted cost for each of the following:
   a. Indirect material
   b. Utilities
   c. Inspection
   d. Test kitchen
   e. Material handling
   f. Total overhead cost
2. Compute the variance for setup cost during the month, assuming that the actual setup cost was $3,000:
   a. Using the activity-based flexible budget.
   b. Using DCdesserts.com's conventional flexible budget (Exhibit 11–3).

■ **Exercise 11–32**
Overhead Variances
(LO 11-5)

Montoursville Control Company, which manufactures electrical switches, uses a standard-costing system. The standard production overhead costs per switch are based on direct-labor hours and are as follows:

Variable overhead (5 direct-labor hours @ $8.00 per hour)	$ 40
Fixed overhead (5 direct-labor hours @ $12.00 per hour)*	60
Total overhead	$100

*Based on capacity of 300,000 direct-labor hours per month.

The following information is available for the month of October.

- Variable-overhead costs were $2,340,000.
- Fixed-overhead costs were $3,750,000.
- 56,000 switches were produced, although 60,000 switches were scheduled to be produced.
- 275,000 direct-labor hours were worked at a total cost of $2,550,000.

Required: Compute the variable-overhead spending and efficiency variances and the fixed-overhead budget and volume variances for October. Indicate whether a variance is favorable or unfavorable where appropriate.

(CMA, adapted)

■ **Exercise 11–33**
Journal Entries for Overhead (Appendix A)
(LO 11-8)

Refer to the data in Exercise 11–22 for Crystal Glassware Company. Prepare journal entries to

- Record the incurrence of actual variable overhead and actual fixed overhead.
- Add variable and fixed overhead to Work-in-Process Inventory.
- Close underapplied or overapplied overhead into Cost of Goods Sold.

■ **Exercise 11–34**
Sales Variances (Appendix B)
(LO 11-9)

The following data pertain to Aurora Electronics for the month of February.

	Static Budget	Actual
Units sold	10,000	9,000
Sales revenue	$120,000	$103,500
Variable manufacturing cost	40,000	36,000
Fixed manufacturing cost	20,000	20,000
Variable selling and administrative cost	10,000	9,000
Fixed selling and administrative cost	10,000	10,000

Required: Compute the sales-price and sales-volume variances for February.

Problems

All applicable Problems are available in Connect.

Problem 11–35
Straightforward Overhead Variances
(LO 11-5)

Actual variable-overhead rate: $3.10 per direct-labor hour

Calgary Paper Company produces paper for photocopiers. The company has developed standard overhead rates based on a monthly capacity of 180,000 direct-labor hours as follows:

Standard costs per unit (one box of paper):	
Variable overhead (2 direct-labor hours @ $3 per hour)	$ 6
Fixed overhead (2 direct-labor hours @ $5 per hour)	10
Total	$16

During April, 90,000 units were scheduled for production: however, only 80,000 units were actually produced. The following data relate to April.

1. Actual direct-labor cost incurred was $1,567,500 for 165,000 actual hours of work.
2. Actual overhead incurred totaled $1,371,500, of which $511,500 was variable and $860,000 was fixed.

Required: Prepare two exhibits similar to Exhibits 11–6 and 11–8 in the chapter, which show the following variances. State whether each variance is favorable or unfavorable, where appropriate.

1. Variable-overhead spending variance.
2. Variable-overhead efficiency variance.
3. Fixed-overhead budget variance.
4. Fixed-overhead volume variance.

(CMA, adapted)

Problem 11–36
Standard Hours Allowed; Flexible Budget; Multiple Products; Insurance Company
(LO 11-1, 11-2, 11-4)

4. Budgeted overhead cost for July: $11,800

Gibralter Insurance Company uses a flexible overhead budget for its application-processing department. The firm offers five types of policies, with the following standard hours allowed for clerical processing.

Automobile	1 hour
Renter's	1 hour
Homeowner's	2 hours
Health	2 hours
Life	5 hours

The following numbers of insurance applications were processed during July.

Automobile	250
Renter's	200
Homeowner's	100
Health	400
Life	200

The controller estimates that the variable-overhead rate in the application-processing department is $4.00 per clerical hour, and that fixed-overhead costs will amount to $2,000 per month.

Required:

1. How many standard clerical hours are allowed in July, given actual application activity?
2. Why would it not be sensible to base the company's flexible budget on the number of applications processed instead of the number of clerical hours allowed?
3. Construct a formula flexible overhead budget for the company.
4. What is the flexible budget for total overhead cost in July?

Problem 11–37
Graphing Budgeted and Applied Overhead; Recording Studio
(LO 11-1, 11-2, 11-3)

Countrytime Studios is a recording studio in Nashville. The studio budgets and applies overhead costs on the basis of production time. Countrytime's controller anticipates 10,000 hours of production time to be available during the year. The following overhead amounts have been budgeted for the year.

Variable overhead	$40,000
Fixed overhead	90,000

Required:

1. Draw two graphs, one for variable overhead and one for fixed overhead. The variable on the horizontal axis of each graph should be production time, in hours, ranging from 5,000 to 15,000 hours. The variable on the vertical axis of each graph should be overhead cost (variable or fixed). Each graph should include two lines, one for the flexible-budget amount of overhead and one for applied overhead.
2. Write a brief memo to Countrytime Studio's general manager, explaining the graph so that she will understand the concepts of budgeted and applied overhead.

Problem 11–38
Overhead Variances
(LO 11-5)

1(d). Variable-overhead efficiency variance: $8,850 F

Newark Plastics Corporation developed its overhead application rate from the annual budget. The budget is based on an expected total output of 720,000 units requiring 3,600,000 machine hours. The company is able to schedule production uniformly throughout the year. Machine hours is the cost driver for overhead costs.

A total of 66,000 units requiring 315,000 machine hours were produced during May. Actual overhead costs for May amounted to $375,000. The actual costs, as compared to the annual budget and to one-twelfth of the annual budget, are as follows:

NEWARK PLASTICS CORPORATION
Annual Budget

	Total Amount	Per Unit	Per Machine Hour	Monthly Budget	Actual Costs for May
Variable overhead:					
Indirect material	$1,224,000	$1.70	$ .34	$102,000	$111,000
Indirect labor	900,000	1.25	.25	75,000	75,000
Fixed overhead:					
Supervision	648,000	.90	.18	54,000	51,000
Utilities	540,000	.75	.15	45,000	54,000
Depreciation	1,008,000	1.40	.28	84,000	84,000
Total	$4,320,000	$6.00	$1.20	$360,000	$375,000

Required:

1. Prepare a schedule showing the following amounts for Newark Plastics for May.
   a. Applied overhead costs.
   b. Variable-overhead spending variance.
   c. Fixed-overhead budget variance.
   d. Variable-overhead efficiency variance.
   e. Fixed-overhead volume variance.

   Where appropriate, be sure to indicate whether each variance is favorable or unfavorable.
2. Draw a graph similar to Exhibit 11–7 to depict the variable-overhead variances.
3. Why does your graph differ from Exhibit 11–7, other than the fact that the numbers differ?

(CMA, adapted)

■ **Problem 11–39**
Budgets and Performance Evaluation
(LO 11-1, 11-6)

3. Direct material used: $20.00 per unit
Variable production overhead: $6.25 per unit
Supervisory salaries: $36,000 per month

Johnson Electrical produces industrial ventilation fans. The company plans to manufacture 72,000 fans evenly over the next quarter at the following costs: direct material, $1,440,000; direct labor, $360,000; variable production overhead, $450,000; and fixed production overhead, $900,000. The $900,000 amount includes $72,000 of straight-line depreciation and $108,000 of supervisory salaries.

Shortly after the conclusion of the quarter's first month, Johnson reported the following costs:

Direct material	$432,500
Direct labor	110,600
Variable production overhead	152,000
Depreciation	24,000
Supervisory salaries	37,800
Other fixed production overhead	239,000
Total	$995,900

Dave Kellerman and his crews turned out 20,000 fans during the month—a remarkable feat given that the firm's manufacturing plant was closed for several days because of storm damage and flooding. Kellerman was especially pleased with the fact that overall financial performance for the period was favorable when compared with the budget. His pleasure, however, was very short-lived, as Johnson's general manager issued a stern warning that performance must improve, and improve quickly, if Kellerman had any hopes of keeping his job.

Required:

1. Explain the difference between a static budget and a flexible budget.
2. Which of the two budgets would be more useful when planning the company's cash needs over a range of activity?
3. Prepare a performance report that compares static budget and actual costs for the period just ended (i.e., the report that Kellerman likely used when assessing his performance).
4. Prepare a performance report that compares flexible budget and actual costs for the period just ended (i.e., the report that the general manager likely used when assessing Kellerman's performance).
5. Which of the two reports is preferred? Should Kellerman be praised for outstanding performance or is the general manager's warning appropriate? Explain, citing any apparent problems for the firm.

■ **Problem 11–40**
Linkages Between the Flexible Budget and Variances
(LO 11-1, 11-2, 11-5)

1. Medical assistants, budget: $11,060
Medical assistants, actual: $13,020
3. Variable-overhead spending variance: $20,856 F

Fall City Hospital has an outpatient clinic. Jeffrey Harper, the hospital's chief administrator, is very concerned about cost control and has asked that performance reports be prepared that compare budgeted and actual amounts for medical assistants, clinic supplies, and lab tests. Past financial studies have shown that the cost of clinic supplies used is driven by the number of medical assistant labor hours worked, whereas lab tests are highly correlated with the number of patients served.

The following information is available for June:

- *Medical assistants* Fall City's standard wage rate is $14 per hour, and each assistant is expected to spend 30 minutes with a patient. Assistants totaled 840 hours in helping the 1,580 patients seen, at an average pay rate of $15.50 per hour.
- *Clinic supplies* The cost of clinic supplies used is budgeted at $12 per labor hour, and the actual cost of supplies used was $9,150.
- *Lab tests* Each patient is anticipated to have three lab tests, at an average budgeted cost of $65 per test. Actual lab tests for June cost $318,054 and averaged 3.3 per patient.

Required:

1. Prepare a report that shows budgeted and actual costs for the 1,580 patients served during June. Compute the differences (variances) between these amounts and label them as favorable or unfavorable.
2. On the basis of your answer to requirement (1), determine whether Fall City has any significant problems with respect to clinic supplies and lab tests. Briefly discuss your findings.
3. By performing a detailed analysis, determine the spending and efficiency variances for lab tests. Does it appear that Fall City has any significant problems with the cost of its lab tests? Briefly

explain. (*Hint:* In applying the overhead variance formulas, think of the number of tests as the activity level, and think of the cost per test as analogous to the variable overhead rate.)

4. Compare the lab test variance computed in requirement (1), a flexible-budget variance, with the sum of the variances in requirement (3). Discuss your findings and explain the relationship of flexible-budget variances and standard cost variances for variable overhead.

Problem 11–41
Overhead Calculations; Variance Interpretation
(LO 11-5)

2. Variable-overhead spending variance: $2,310 F
5. Variable-overhead is underapplied by $42,065

Maxwell Company uses a standard cost accounting system and applies production overhead to products on the basis of machine hours. The following information is available for the year just ended:

Standard variable-overhead rate per hour: $2.50
Standard fixed-overhead rate per hour: $4.00
Planned activity during the period: 20,000 machine hours
Actual production: 10,700 finished units
Machine-hour standard: Two completed units per machine hour
Actual variable overhead: $55,440
Actual total overhead: $155,900
Actual machine hours worked: 23,100

Required:

1. Calculate the budgeted fixed overhead for the year.
2. Compute the variable-overhead spending variance.
3. Calculate the company's fixed-overhead volume variance.
4. Did Maxwell spend more or less than anticipated for fixed overhead? How much?
5. Was variable overhead underapplied or overapplied during the year? By how much?
6. On the basis of the data presented, does it appear that Maxwell suffered a lengthy strike during the year by its production workers? Briefly explain.

Problem 11–42
Flexible Budget; Performance Report
(LO 11-1, 11-6)

2. Advertising, flexible budget: $1,650,000

Mark Fletcher, president of SoftGro, Inc., was looking forward to seeing the performance reports for November because he knew the company's sales for the month had exceeded budget by a considerable margin. SoftGro, a distributor of educational software packages, had been growing steadily for approximately two years. Fletcher's biggest challenge at this point was to ensure that the company did not lose control of expenses during this growth period. When Fletcher received the November reports, he was dismayed to see the large unfavorable variance in the company's Monthly Selling Expense Report that follows.

SOFTGRO, INC.
Monthly Selling Expense Report
for the Month of November

	Annual Budget	November Budget	November Actual	November Variance
Unit sales	2,000,000	280,000	310,000	30,000
Dollar sales	$80,000,000	$11,200,000	$12,400,000	$1,200,000
Orders processed	54,000	6,500	5,800	(700)
Sales personnel per month	90	90	96	(6)
Advertising	$19,800,000	$ 1,650,000	$ 1,660,000	$ 10,000 U
Staff salaries	1,500,000	125,000	125,000	—
Sales salaries	1,296,000	108,000	115,400	7,400 U
Commissions	3,200,000	448,000	496,000	48,000 U
Per diem expense	1,782,000	148,500	162,600	14,100 U
Office expenses	4,080,000	340,000	358,400	18,400 U
Shipping expenses	6,750,000	902,500	976,500	74,000 U
Total expenses	$38,408,000	$ 3,722,000	$ 3,893,900	$ 171,900 U

Fletcher called in the company's new controller, Susan Porter, to discuss the implications of the variances reported for November and to plan a strategy for improving performance. Porter suggested that the company's reporting format might not be giving Fletcher a true picture of the company's operations. She proposed that SoftGro implement flexible budgeting. Porter offered to redo the Monthly Selling Expense Report for November using flexible budgeting so that Fletcher could compare the two reports and see the advantages of flexible budgeting.

Porter discovered the following information about the behavior of SoftGro's selling expenses.

- The total compensation paid to the sales force consists of a monthly base salary and a commission; the commission varies with sales dollars.
- Sales office expense is a semivariable cost with the variable portion related to the number of orders processed. The fixed portion of office expense is $3,000,000 annually and is incurred uniformly throughout the year.
- Subsequent to the adoption of the annual budget for the current year, SoftGro decided to open a new sales territory. As a consequence, approval was given to hire six additional salespeople effective November 1. Porter decided that these additional six people should be recognized in her revised report.
- Per diem reimbursement to the sales force, while a fixed amount per day, is variable with the number of sales personnel and the number of days spent traveling. SoftGro's original budget was based on an average sales force of 90 people throughout the year with each salesperson traveling 15 days per month.
- The company's shipping expense is a semivariable cost with the variable portion, $3.00 per unit, dependent on the number of units sold. The fixed portion is incurred uniformly throughout the year.

Required:

1. Citing the benefits of flexible budgeting, explain why Susan Porter would propose that SoftGro use flexible budgeting in this situation.
2. Prepare a revised Monthly Selling Expense Report for November that would permit Mark Fletcher to more clearly evaluate SoftGro's control over selling expenses. The report should have a line for each selling expense item showing the appropriate budgeted amount, the actual selling expense, and the monthly dollar variance.

(CMA, adapted)

Problem 11–43
Flexible Budgeting; Variances; Impact on Behavior
(LO 11-1, 11-2, 11-5)

1. Operating income: $122,400
2. Operating income, flexible budget variance: $45,400 U

LawnMate Company manufactures power mowers that are sold throughout the United States and Canada. The company uses a comprehensive budgeting process and compares actual results to budgeted amounts on a monthly basis. Each month, LawnMate's accounting department prepares a variance analysis and distributes the report to all responsible parties. Al Richmond, production manager, is upset about the results for May. Richmond, who is responsible for the cost of goods manufactured, has implemented several cost-cutting measures in the manufacturing area and is discouraged by the unfavorable variance in variable costs.

LAWNMATE COMPANY
Operating Results
For the Month of May

	Master Budget	Actual	Variance
Units sold	5,000	4,800	200 U
Revenue	$1,200,000	$1,152,000	$48,000 U
Variable cost	760,000	780,000	20,000 U
Contribution margin	$ 440,000	$ 372,000	$68,000 U
Fixed production overhead	180,000	180,000	—
Fixed general and administrative cost	120,000	115,000	5,000 F
Operating income	$ 140,000	$ 77,000	$63,000 U

When the master budget was prepared, LawnMate's cost accountant, Joan Ballard, supplied the following unit costs: direct material, $60; direct labor, $44; variable production overhead, $36; and variable selling expenses, $12.

The total variable costs of $780,000 for May include $320,000 for direct material, $192,000 for direct labor, $176,000 for variable production overhead, and $92,000 for variable selling expenses. Ballard believes that LawnMate's monthly reports would be more meaningful to everyone if the company adopted flexible budgeting and prepared more detailed analyses.

Required:

1. Prepare a flexible budget for LawnMate Company for the month of May that includes separate variable-cost budgets for each type of cost (direct material, etc.).
2. Determine the variance between the flexible budget and actual cost for each cost item.
3. Discuss how the revised budget and variance data are likely to impact the behavior of Al Richmond, the production manager.
4. ***Build a spreadsheet:*** Construct an Excel spreadsheet to solve requirements (1) and (2) above. Show how the solution will change if the following information changes: actual sales amounted to 4,700 units, and actual fixed overhead was $179,000.

(CMA, adapted)

Problem 11–44
Finding Missing Data; Overhead Accounting
(LO 11-1, 11-5)

2. Case A: $7.00 per direct-labor hour
5. Case B: $18,000
14. Case B: 1,000 units

For each of the following independent Cases A and B, fill in the missing information. The company budgets and applies production overhead costs on the basis of direct-labor hours. (U denotes *unfavorable variance;* F denotes *favorable variance.*)

	Case A	Case B
1. Standard variable-overhead rate	$2.50 per hour	? per hour
2. Standard fixed-overhead rate	? per hour	? per hour
3. Total standard overhead rate	? per hour	$13.00 per hour
4. Flexible budget for variable overhead	$90,000	?
5. Flexible budget for fixed overhead	$210,000	?
6. Actual variable overhead	?	?
7. Actual fixed overhead	$207,000	?
8. Variable-overhead spending variance	$5,550 U	$2,000 U
9. Variable-overhead efficiency variance	?	$400 F
10. Fixed-overhead budget variance	?	$1,080 U
11. Fixed-overhead volume variance	?	$3,600 U
12. Under- (or over-) applied variable overhead	?	?
13. Under- (or over-) applied fixed overhead	?	?
14. Budgeted production (in units)	5,000 units	?
15. Standard direct-labor hours per unit	6 hours per unit	2 hours per unit
16. Actual production (in units)	?	?
17. Standard direct-labor hours allowed, given actual production	36,000 hours	1,600 hours
18. Actual direct-labor hours	37,000 hours	1,500 hours
19. Applied variable overhead	?	?
20. Applied fixed overhead	?	?

Problem 11–45
Preparing and Using a Columnar Flexible Budget; Tour Company; Ethical Issues
(LO 11-1, 11-2, 11-6)

Total variable expenses, activity level (air miles), 38,000: $93,100
4. Total variable expenses, flexible budget: $78,400

Flaming Foliage Sky Tours is a small sightseeing tour company in New Hampshire. The firm specializes in aerial tours of the New England countryside during September and October, when the fall color is at its peak. Until recently, the company had not had an accounting department. Routine bookkeeping tasks, such as billing, had been handled by an individual who had little formal training in accounting. As the business began to grow, however, the owner recognized the need for more formal accounting procedures. Jacqueline Frost has recently been hired as the new controller, and she will have the authority to hire an assistant.

During her first week on the job, Frost was given the following performance report. The report was prepared by Red Leif, the company's manager of aircraft operations, who was planning to present it to the owner the next morning. "Look at these favorable variances for fuel and so forth," Leif pointed out, as he showed the report to Frost. "My operations people are really doing a great job." Later that day, Frost looked at the performance report more carefully. She immediately realized that it was improperly prepared and would be misleading to the company's owner.

FLAMING FOLIAGE SKY TOURS
Performance Report
for the Month of September

	Formula Flexible Budget (per air mile)	Actual (32,000 air miles)	Static Budget (35,000 air miles)	Variance
Passenger revenue	$ 3.50	$112,000	$122,500	$10,500 U
Less: Variable expenses:				
Fuel	$ .50	$ 17,000	$ 17,500	$ 500 F
Aircraft maintenance	.75	23,500	26,250	2,750 F
Flight crew salaries	.40	13,100	14,000	900 F
Selling and administrative	.80	24,900	28,000	3,100 F
Total variable expenses	$ 2.45	$ 78,500	$ 85,750	$ 7,250 F
Contribution margin	$ 1.05	$ 33,500	$ 36,750	$ 3,250 U
	Per Month			
Less: Fixed expenses:				
Depreciation on aircraft	$ 2,900	$ 2,900	$ 2,900	$ 0
Landing fees	900	1,000	900	100 U
Supervisory salaries	9,000	8,600	9,000	400 F
Selling and administrative	11,000	12,400	11,000	1,400 U
Total fixed expenses	$23,800	$ 24,900	$ 23,800	$ 1,100 U
Operating income		$ 8,600	$ 12,950	$ 4,350 U

Required:

1. Prepare a columnar flexible budget for Flaming Foliage Sky Tours' expenses, using air miles as the cost driver at the following activity levels: 32,000 air miles, 35,000 air miles, and 38,000 air miles.
2. In spite of several favorable expense variances shown on the report above, the company's September operating income was only about two-thirds of the expected level. Why?
3. Write a brief memo to the manager of aircraft operations explaining why the original variance report is misleading.
4. Prepare a revised expense variance report for September, which is based on the flexible budget prepared in requirement (1).
5. Jacqueline Frost presented the revised expense report to Leif along with the memo explaining why the original performance report was misleading. Leif did not take it well. He complained of Frost's "interference" and pointed out that the company had been doing just fine without her. "I'm taking my report to the owner tomorrow," Leif insisted. "Yours just makes us look bad." What are Frost's ethical obligations in this matter? What should she do?

Problem 11–46
Interactions Between Variances; Flexible Manufacturing System
(LO 11-5)

Eastern Auto Parts Company manufactures replacement parts for automobile repair. The company recently installed a flexible manufacturing system, which has significantly changed the production process. The installation of the new FMS was not anticipated when the current year's budget and cost structure were developed. The installation of the new equipment was hastened by several major breakdowns in the company's old production machinery.

The new equipment was very expensive, but management expects it to cut the labor time required by a substantial amount. Management also expects the new equipment to allow a reduction in direct-material waste. On the negative side, the FMS requires a more highly skilled labor force to operate it than the company's old equipment.

The following cost variance report was prepared for the month of July, the first full month after the equipment was installed.

EASTERN AUTO PARTS COMPANY
Cost Variance Report
for the Month of July

Direct material:	
Standard cost	$602,450
Actual cost	598,700
Direct-material price variance	150 U
Direct-material quantity variance	3,900 F
Direct labor:	
Standard cost	393,000
Actual cost	383,800
Direct-labor rate variance	4,800 U
Direct-labor efficiency variance	14,000 F
Production overhead:	
Applied to work in process	400,000
Actual cost	408,000
Variable-overhead spending variance	8,000 U
Variable-overhead efficiency variance	10,000 F
Fixed-overhead budget variance	30,000 U
Fixed-overhead volume variance	(20,000)†

†The sign of the volume variance is negative; applied fixed overhead exceeded budgeted fixed overhead.

Required: Comment on the possible interactions between the variances listed in the report. Which ones are likely to have been caused by the purchase of the new production equipment? The company budgets and applies production overhead on the basis of direct-labor hours. (You may find it helpful to review the discussion of variance interactions in Chapter 10.)

Problem 11–47
Flexible Budget; Improved Performance Report; Behavioral Issues
(LO 11-1, 11-6)

Contribution margin, actual: $59,400

WoodCrafts, Inc. is a manufacturer of furniture for specialty shops throughout the Northeast and has an annual sales volume of $12 million. The company has four major product lines: bookcases, magazine racks, end tables, and bar stools. Each line is managed by a production manager. Since production is spread fairly evenly over the 12 months of operation, Sara McKinley, WoodCrafts' controller, has prepared an annual budget divided into 12 periods for monthly reporting purposes.

WOODCRAFTS, INC.
Bookcase Production Performance Report
for the Month of November

	Actual	Budget	Variance
Units	3,000	2,500	500 F
Revenue	$161,000	$137,500	$23,500 F
Variable production costs:			
Direct material	$ 23,100	$ 20,000	$ 3,100 U
Direct labor	18,300	15,000	3,300 U
Machine time	19,200	16,250	2,950 U
Production overhead	41,000	35,000	6,000 U
Fixed production costs:			
Indirect labor	9,400	6,000	3,400 U
Depreciation	5,500	5,500	—
Property taxes	2,400	2,300	100 U
Insurance	4,500	4,500	—
Administrative expenses	12,000	9,000	3,000 U
Marketing expenses	8,300	7,000	1,300 U
Research and development	6,000	4,500	1,500 U
Total expenses	$149,700	$125,050	$24,650 U
Operating income	$ 11,300	$ 12,450	$ 1,150 U

WoodCrafts uses a standard-costing system and applies variable overhead on the basis of process hours. Fixed production cost is allocated on the basis of square footage occupied using a predetermined plantwide rate; the size of the space occupied varies considerably among the product lines. All other costs are assigned on the basis of revenue dollars earned. At the monthly meeting to review November performance, Steve Clark, manager of the bookcase line, received the following report.

While distributing the monthly reports at the meeting, McKinley remarked to Clark, "We need to talk about getting your division back on track. Be sure to see me after the meeting."

Clark had been so convinced that his division did well in November that McKinley's remark was a real surprise. He spent the balance of the meeting avoiding the looks of his fellow managers and trying to figure out what could have gone wrong. The monthly performance report was no help.

Required:

1. *a.* Identify three weaknesses in WoodCrafts, Inc.'s monthly Bookcase Production Performance Report.
   b. Discuss the behavioral implications of Sara McKinley's remarks to Steve Clark during the meeting.
2. WoodCrafts, Inc. could do a better job of reporting monthly performance to the production managers.
   a. Recommend how the report could be improved to eliminate weaknesses, and revise it accordingly.
   b. Discuss how the recommended changes in reporting are likely to affect Steve Clark's behavior.

(CMA, adapted)

Problem 11–48
Using a Flexible Budget
(LO 11-1, 11-2, 11-5)

3. $11 per machine hour
5. Standard variable-overhead rate per machine hour: $10.10 per machine hour
8. Variable-overhead efficiency variance: $10,100 U
11. Fixed overhead cost: $324,000

Rutherford Wheel and Axle, Inc. has an automated production process, and production activity is quantified in terms of machine hours. A standard-costing system is used. The annual static budget for 20x1 called for 6,000 units to be produced, requiring 30,000 machine hours. The standard overhead rate for the year was computed using this planned level of production. The 20x1 manufacturing cost report follows.

RUTHERFORD WHEEL AND AXLE, INC.
Manufacturing Cost Report
For 20x1
(In thousands of dollars)

	Static Budget	Flexible Budget		
Cost Item	**30,000 Machine Hours**	**31,000 Machine Hours**	**32,000 Machine Hours**	**Actual Cost**
Direct material:				
G27 aluminum	$ 252.0	$ 260.4	$ 268.8	$ 270.0
M14 steel alloy	78.0	80.6	83.2	83.0
Direct labor:				
Assembler	273.0	282.1	291.2	287.0
Grinder	234.0	241.8	249.6	250.0
Production overhead:				
Maintenance	24.0	24.8	25.6	25.0
Supplies	129.0	133.3	137.6	130.0
Supervision	80.0	82.0	84.0	81.0
Inspection	144.0	147.0	150.0	147.0
Insurance	50.0	50.0	50.0	50.0
Depreciation	200.0	200.0	200.0	200.0
Total cost	$1,464.0	$1,502.0	$1,540.0	$1,523.0

Rutherford develops flexible budgets for different levels of activity for use in evaluating performance. A total of 6,200 units was produced during 20x1, requiring 32,000 machine hours. The preceding manufacturing cost report compares the company's actual cost for the year with the static budget and the flexible budget for two different activity levels.

Required: Compute the following amounts. For variances, indicate whether favorable or unfavorable where appropriate. Answers should be rounded to two decimal places when necessary.

1. The standard number of machine hours allowed to produce one unit of product.
2. The actual cost of direct material used in one unit of product.
3. The cost of material that should be processed per machine hour.
4. The standard direct-labor cost for each unit produced.
5. The variable-overhead rate per machine hour in a flexible budget formula. (*Hint:* Use the high-low method to estimate cost behavior.)
6. The standard fixed-overhead rate per machine hour used for product costing.
7. The variable-overhead spending variance. (Assume management has determined that the actual fixed-overhead cost in 20x1 amounted to $324,000.)
8. The variable-overhead efficiency variance.
9. The fixed-overhead budget variance.
10. The fixed-overhead volume variance. [Make the same assumption as in requirement (7).]
11. The total budgeted manufacturing cost (in thousands of dollars) for an output of 6,050 units. (*Hint:* Use the flexible-budget formula.)

(CMA, adapted)

Problem 11–49
Complete Analysis of Cost Variances; Review of Chapters 10 and 11
(LO 11–5)

Direct-labor efficiency variance: $13,500 U
Fixed-overhead budget variance: $1,000 U

Chillco Corporation produces containers of frozen food. During April, Chillco produced 1,450 cases of food and incurred the following actual costs.

Variable overhead	$ 11,000
Fixed overhead	26,000
Actual labor cost (8,000 direct-labor hours)	151,200
Actual material cost (30,000 pounds purchased and used)	66,000

Overhead is budgeted and applied using direct-labor hours in a standard costing system. Standard cost and annual budget information are as follows:

Standard Costs per Case

Direct labor (5 hours at $18 per hour)	$ 90.00
Direct material (20 pounds at $2 per pound)	40.00
Variable overhead (5 direct-labor hours at $1.50 per hour)	7.50
Fixed overhead (5 direct-labor hours at $3 per hour)	15.00
Total	$152.50

Annual Budget Information

Variable overhead	$150,000
Fixed overhead	$300,000
Planned activity for year	100,000 direct-labor hours

Required:

1. Prepare as complete an analysis of cost variances as is possible from the available data.
2. ***Build a spreadsheet:*** Construct an Excel spreadsheet to solve the preceding requirement. Show how the solution will change if the following information changes: the standard rates were $17.50 per hour for direct labor, and $1.60 per direct-labor hour for variable overhead.

Problem 11–50
Overhead Variances; Journal Entries (Appendix A)
(LO 11-5, 11-8)

1(a). Variable-overhead spending variance: $173,000 U
2. Cost of goods sold (debit): $218,000

Montreal Scholastic Supply Company uses a standard-costing system. The firm estimates that it will operate its manufacturing facilities at 800,000 machine hours for the year. The estimate for total budgeted overhead is $2,000,000. The standard variable-overhead rate is estimated to be $2 per machine hour or $6 per unit. The actual data for the year are presented below.

Actual finished units	250,000
Actual machine hours	764,000
Actual variable overhead	$1,701,000
Actual fixed overhead	$ 392,000

Required:

1. Compute the following variances. Indicate whether each is favorable or unfavorable, where appropriate.
   a. Variable-overhead spending variance.
   b. Variable-overhead efficiency variance.
   c. Fixed-overhead budget variance.
   d. Fixed-overhead volume variance.
2. Prepare journal entries to
   - Record the incurrence of actual variable overhead and actual fixed overhead.
   - Add variable and fixed overhead to Work-in-Process Inventory.
   - Close underapplied or overapplied overhead into Cost of Goods Sold.

(CMA, adapted)

Problem 11–51
Comprehensive Problem on Overhead Accounting under Standard Costing; Journal Entries (Appendix A)
(LO 11-2, 11-3, 11-5, 11-8)

2. Flexible budget, variable overhead: $18,000
5. Fixed overhead applied to work in process: $25,000
8. Cost of goods sold (debit): $14,130

College Memories, Inc. publishes college yearbooks. A monthly flexible overhead budget for the firm follows.

COLLEGE MEMORIES, INC.
Monthly Flexible Overhead Budget

	Direct-Labor Hours		
Budgeted Cost	**1,500**	**1,750**	**2,000**
Variable costs:			
Indirect material:			
Glue	$ 750	$ 875	$ 1,000
Tape	300	350	400
Miscellaneous supplies	3,000	3,500	4,000
Indirect labor	7,500	8,750	10,000
Utilities:			
Electricity	1,500	1,750	2,000
Natural gas	450	525	600
Total variable cost	$13,500	$15,750	$18,000
Fixed costs:			
Supervisory labor	12,500	12,500	12,500
Depreciation	3,400	3,400	3,400
Property taxes and insurance	4,100	4,100	4,100
Total fixed cost	$20,000	$20,000	$20,000
Total overhead cost	$33,500	$35,750	$38,000

The planned monthly production is 6,400 yearbooks. The standard direct-labor allowance is .25 hour per book and overhead is budgeted and applied on the basis of direct-labor hours. During February, College Memories, Inc. produced 8,000 yearbooks and actually used 2,100 direct-labor hours. The actual overhead costs for the month were as follows:

Actual variable overhead	$19,530
Actual fixed overhead	37,600

Required:

1. Determine the formula-style flexible overhead budget for College Memories, Inc.
2. Prepare a display similar to Exhibit 11–6, which shows College Memories' variable-overhead variances for February. Indicate whether each variance is favorable or unfavorable.
3. Draw a graph similar to Exhibit 11–7, which shows College Memories' variable-overhead variances for February.
4. Interpret each of the variances computed in requirement (2).
5. Prepare a display similar to Exhibit 11–8, which shows College Memories' fixed-overhead variances for February.
6. Draw a graph similar to Exhibit 11–9, which depicts the company's applied and budgeted fixed overhead for February. Show the firm's February volume variance on the graph.
7. Interpret each of the variances computed in requirement (5).
8. Prepare journal entries to record each of the following:
   - Incurrence of February's actual overhead cost.
   - Application of February's overhead cost to Work-in-Process Inventory.
   - Close underapplied or overapplied overhead into Cost of Goods Sold.
9. Draw T-accounts for all of the accounts used in the journal entries of requirement (8). Then post the journal entries to the T-accounts.

Problem 11–52
Sales Variances (Appendix B)
(LO 11-9)

2. Sales volume variance: $50,000 U

White Mountain Sled Company manufactures children's snow sleds. The company's performance report for November is as follows.

	Actual	Budget
Sleds sold	5,000	6,000
Sales	$240,000	$300,000
Variable costs	150,000	180,000
Contribution margin	$ 90,000	$120,000
Fixed costs	84,000	80,000
Operating income	$ 6,000	$ 40,000

The company uses sales variance analysis to explain the difference between budgeted and actual sales revenue.

Required: Compute the following variances and indicate whether each is favorable or unfavorable.

1. November sales price variance.
2. November sales volume variance.

(CMA, adapted)

Problem 11–53
Analyzing Sales Variances (Appendix B)
(LO 11-9)

1. Sales price variance: $456,000 U

Cleveland Computer Accessory Company (CCAC) distributes keyboard trays to computer stores. The keyboard trays can be attached to the underside of a desk, effectively turning it into a computer table. The keyboard trays are purchased from a manufacturer that attaches CCAC's private label to the trays. The wholesale selling prices to the computer stores are $120 for the business-grade keyboard tray and

$60 for the residential-grade product. The 20x2 budget and actual results are as follows. The budget was adopted in late 20x1 and was based on CCAC's estimated share of the market for the two types of keyboard trays.

CLEVELAND COMPUTER ACCESSORY COMPANY
Income Statement
For the Year Ending December 31, 20x2
(In thousands)

	Business Grade		Residential Grade		Total		
	Budget	Actual	Budget	Actual	Budget	Actual	Variance
Sales in units	80	74	120	86	200	160	40
Revenue	$9,600	$8,510	$7,200	$5,074	$16,800	$13,584	$3,216 U
Cost of goods sold	6,400	6,068	6,000	4,300	12,400	10,368	2,032 F
Gross margin	$3,200	$2,442	$1,200	$ 774	$ 4,400	$ 3,216	$1,184 U
Unallocated costs:							
Selling					$ 1,000	$ 1,000	$ —
Advertising					1,000	1,060	60 U
Administrative					400	406	6 U
Income taxes (45%)					900	338	562 F
Total unallocated costs					$ 3,300	$ 2,804	$ 496 F
Net income					$ 1,100	$ 412	$ 688 U

During the first quarter of 20x2, management estimated that the total market for these products actually would be 10 percent below the original estimates. In an attempt to prevent unit sales from declining as much as industry projections, management implemented a marketing program. Included in the program were dealer discounts and increased direct advertising. The business-grade line was emphasized in this program.

Required:

1. Compute the sales-price and sales-volume variances for each product line. Indicate whether each variance is favorable or unfavorable.
2. Discuss the apparent effect of CCAC's special marketing program (i.e., dealer discounts and additional advertising) on the 20x2 operating results.

(CMA, adapted)

Cases

Case 11–54
Integrative Case on Chapters 10 and 11; Drawing Conclusion from Missing Data
(LO 11-1, 11-3, 11-5)

3. Actual fixed overhead: $43,250
7. Actual variable-overhead rate: $6.30 per direct-labor hour
10. Applied fixed overhead: $36,000

Your next-door neighbor recently began a new job as assistant controller for Conundrum Corporation. As her first assignment, she prepared a performance report for January. She was scheduled to present the report to management the next morning, so she brought it home to review. As the two of you chatted in the backyard, she decided to show you the report she had prepared. Unfortunately, your dog thought the report was an object to be fetched. The pup made a flying leap and got a firm grip on the report. After chasing the dog around the block, you managed to wrest the report from its teeth. Needless to say, it was torn to bits. Only certain data are legible on the report. This information follows:

CONUNDRUM CORPORATION
Performance Report For the Month of January

	Direct Material	Direct Labor	Variable Overhead	Fixed Overhead
Standard allowed cost given actual output	? (? kilograms at $12 per kilogram)	? (2 hours at $14 per hour)		
Flexible overhead budget			?	$40,000
Actual cost	$189,000 (14,000 kilograms at $13.50 per kilogram)	? (8,800 hours at ? per hour)	?	?
Direct-material price variance	?			
Direct-material quantity variance	$6,000 U			
Direct-labor rate variance		$8,800 U		
Direct-labor efficiency variance		2,800 F		
Variable-overhead spending variance			$2,640 U	
Variable-overhead efficiency variance		1,200 F		
Fixed-overhead budget variance			$3,250 U	
Fixed-overhead volume variance			?	

In addition to the fragmentary data still legible on the performance report, your neighbor happened to remember the following facts.

- Planned production of Conundrum's sole product was 500 units more than the actual production.
- All of the direct material purchased in January was used in production.
- There were no beginning or ending inventories.
- Variable and fixed overhead are applied on the basis of direct-labor hours. The fixed-overhead rate is $4.00 per hour.

Required: Feeling guilty, you have agreed to help your neighbor reconstruct the following facts, which will be necessary for her presentation.

1. Planned production (in units).
2. Actual production (in units).
3. Actual fixed overhead.
4. Total standard allowed direct-labor hours.
5. Actual direct-labor rate.
6. Standard variable-overhead rate.
7. Actual variable-overhead rate.
8. Standard direct-material quantity per unit.
9. Direct-material price variance.
10. Applied fixed overhead.
11. Fixed-overhead volume variance.

Case 11–55
Comprehensive Variance Analysis Used to Explain Operational Results; Review of Chapters 10 and 11; Activity-Based Costing; Sales Variances (Appendix B)
(LO 11-4, 11-5, 11-7, 11-9)

4(a). Direct-material price variance, total: $133,000 U
4(e). Variable-overhead spending variance: $75,000 U
4(g). Sales-price variance: $45,000 U

Aunt Molly's Old Fashioned Cookies bakes cookies for retail stores. The company's best-selling cookie is chocolate nut supreme, which is marketed as a gourmet cookie and regularly sells for $8.00 per pound. The standard cost per pound of chocolate nut supreme, based on Aunt Molly's normal monthly production of 400,000 pounds, is as follows:

Cost Item	Quantity	Standard Unit Cost	Total Cost
Direct materials:			
Cookie mix	10 oz.	$ .02 per oz.	$ .20
Milk chocolate	5 oz.	.15 per oz.	.75
Almonds	1 oz.	.50 per oz.	.50
			$1.45
Direct labor:*			
Mixing	1 min.	$14.40 per hr.	$ .24
Baking	2 min.	18.00 per hr.	.60
			$ .84
Variable overhead†	3 min.	$32.40 per direct-labor hr.	$1.62
Total standard cost per pound			$3.91

*Direct-labor rates include employee benefits.
†Applied on the basis of direct-labor hours.

Aunt Molly's management accountant, Karen Blair, prepares monthly budget reports based on these standard costs. April's contribution report, which compares budgeted and actual performance, is shown in the following schedule.

Contribution Report for April

	Static Budget	Actual	Variance
Units (in pounds)	400,000	450,000	50,000 F
Revenue	$3,200,000	$3,555,000	$355,000 F
Direct material	$ 580,000	$ 865,000	$285,000 U
Direct labor	336,000	348,000	12,000 U
Variable overhead	648,000	750,000	102,000 U
Total variable costs	$1,564,000	$1,963,000	$399,000 U
Contribution margin	$1,636,000	$1,592,000	$ 44,000 U

Justine Madison, president of the company, is disappointed with the results. Despite a sizable increase in the number of cookies sold, the product's expected contribution to the overall profitability of the firm decreased. Madison has asked Blair to identify the reason why the contribution margin decreased. Blair has gathered the following information to help in her analysis of the decrease.

Usage Report for April

Cost Item	Quantity	Actual Cost
Direct materials:		
Cookie mix	4,650,000 oz.	$ 93,000
Milk chocolate	2,660,000 oz.	532,000
Almonds	480,000 oz.	240,000
Direct labor:		
Mixing	450,000 min.	108,000
Baking	800,000 min.	240,000
Variable overhead		750,000
Total variable costs		$1,963,000

Required:

1. Prepare a new contribution report for April, in which:
   - The static budget column in the contribution report is replaced with a flexible budget column.
   - The variances in the contribution report are recomputed as the difference between the flexible budget and actual columns.
2. What is the total contribution margin in the flexible budget column of the new report prepared for requirement (1)?
3. Explain (i.e., interpret) the meaning of the total contribution margin in the flexible budget column of the new report prepared for requirement (1).
4. What is the total variance between the flexible budget contribution margin and the actual contribution margin in the new report prepared for requirement (1)? Explain this total contribution margin variance by computing the following variances. (Assume that all materials are used in the month of purchase.)
   a. Direct-material price variance.
   b. Direct-material quantity variance.
   c. Direct-labor rate variance.
   d. Direct-labor efficiency variance.
   e. Variable-overhead spending variance.
   f. Variable-overhead efficiency variance.
   g. Sales-price variance.
5. *a.* Explain the problems that might arise in using direct-labor hours as the basis for applying overhead.
   b. How might activity-based costing (ABC) solve the problems described in requirement (5a)?

(CMA, adapted)

12 Responsibility Accounting, Operational Performance Measures, and the Balanced Scorecard

FOCUS COMPANY >>>

© tomas del amo/123RF.com

THIS CHAPTER'S FOCUS COMPANY is Aloha Hotels and Resorts, a chain of luxury hotels and resorts in Hawaii. In this chapter, we will explore this hospitality company's responsibility-accounting system. Responsibility accounting refers to the various concepts and tools used to measure the performance of both people and departments in an organization. The management of Aloha Hotels and Resorts uses detailed performance reports about the company's divisions, hotels, and departments to help ensure that everyone in the organization is working toward the same overall corporate goals.

© PhotoLink/Getty Images RF

<<< IN CONTRAST

Forest Home
National Bank

In contrast to the hospitality setting of Aloha Hotels and Resorts, we will turn our attention to the financial-services industry. Here we will explore how Forest Home National Bank (FHNB), first introduced in Chapter 10, uses the balanced scorecard to measure and direct performance. FHNB's balanced scorecard helps management and employees focus on the customer, internal operations, and learning and growth areas of the business, so that ultimately the bank's long-term financial goals will be attained.

After completing this chapter, you should be able to:

12-1 Explain the role of responsibility accounting in fostering goal congruence.

12-2 Define and give an example of a cost center, a revenue center, a profit center, and an investment center.

12-3 Prepare a performance report and explain the relationships between the performance reports for various responsibility centers.

12-4 Use a cost allocation base to allocate costs.

12-5 Prepare a segmented income statement.

12-6 Describe the operational performance measures appropriate for today's production environment.

12-7 Describe the balanced scorecard concept and explain the reasoning behind it.

Learning Objective **12–1**

Explain the role of responsibility accounting in fostering goal congruence.

Most organizations are divided into smaller units, each of which is assigned particular responsibilities. These units are called by various names, including divisions, segments, business units, and departments. Each department is composed of individuals who are responsible for particular tasks or managerial functions. The managers of an organization should ensure that the people in each department are striving toward the same overall goals. **Goal congruence** results when the managers of subunits throughout an organization strive to achieve the goals set by top management.

How can an organization's managerial accounting system promote goal congruence? **Responsibility accounting** refers to the various concepts and tools used by managers to measure the performance of people and departments in order to foster goal congruence.

Responsibility Centers

Learning Objective **12–2**

Define and give an example of a cost center, a revenue center, a profit center, and an investment center.

The basis of a responsibility-accounting system is the designation of each subunit in the organization as a particular type of *responsibility center*. A **responsibility center** is a subunit in an organization whose manager is held accountable for specified financial results of the subunit's activities. There are four common types of responsibility centers.

Cost Center A **cost center** is an organizational subunit, such as a department or division, whose manager is held accountable for the costs incurred in the subunit while accomplishing the department's organizational functions at a specified level of performance. The Painting Department in an automobile plant and the Supply-Chain Management Department of an online retailer are examples of cost centers.

"Responsibility accounting is an integral part of our reporting process in this company. Always has been. Always will." (12a)

Chrysler

Revenue Center The manager of a **revenue center** is held accountable for the revenue generated by the subunit. In addition to the amount of revenue, this often includes the timing of when revenues are received, the mix of products and services sold, discounts awarded, and the creditworthiness of customers. For example, the Reservations Department of an airline and the Advertising Sales Department of a mobile app developer are revenue centers.

Profit Center A **profit center** is an organizational subunit whose manager is held accountable for profit. Since profit is equal to revenue minus costs, profit-center managers are held accountable for both the revenue and costs attributed to their subunits. This gives profit center managers that ability, and the responsibility, for balancing conflicting opportunities to maximize profit for the organization. For example, the manager of an automobile dealership located in suburban Cincinnati, a profit center, has been authorized to spend $50,000 on facility improvements. As a profit center manager, he has the authority to decide if the dealership's profits will be increased more by adding an additional service lift or by renovating the service customer waiting area. Other examples of profit centers include a company-owned restaurant in a fast-food chain and a local office of an investment brokerage firm.

Investment Center The manager of an **investment center** is held accountable for the subunit's profit *and the return on invested capital* used by the subunit to generate its profit. An investment-center manager also decides whether the profits of the investment center are paid as bonuses, reinvested in research and development, used for expansion, distributed to shareholders, and so forth. A small start-up company and a geographic division of a large corporation are both typically designated as investment centers. The large

© Jim West/The Image Works

© BananaStock RF

© Brand X Pictures/PunchStock RF

© McGraw-Hill Education/Barry Barker, photographer

Clockwise from upper left: This aircraft maintenance department in Gwinn, Michigan, is a cost center. However, a telemarketing center like the one shown next is usually treated as a revenue center. This McDonald's in Riyadh, Saudi Arabia, is a profit center. And this power plant in the Loire Valley, France, is an investment center. What sort of responsibility center designation would be appropriate for your local sandwich shop, gas station/convenience store, and dry cleaner?

Exhibit 12–1
Organization Chart: Aloha Hotels and Resorts

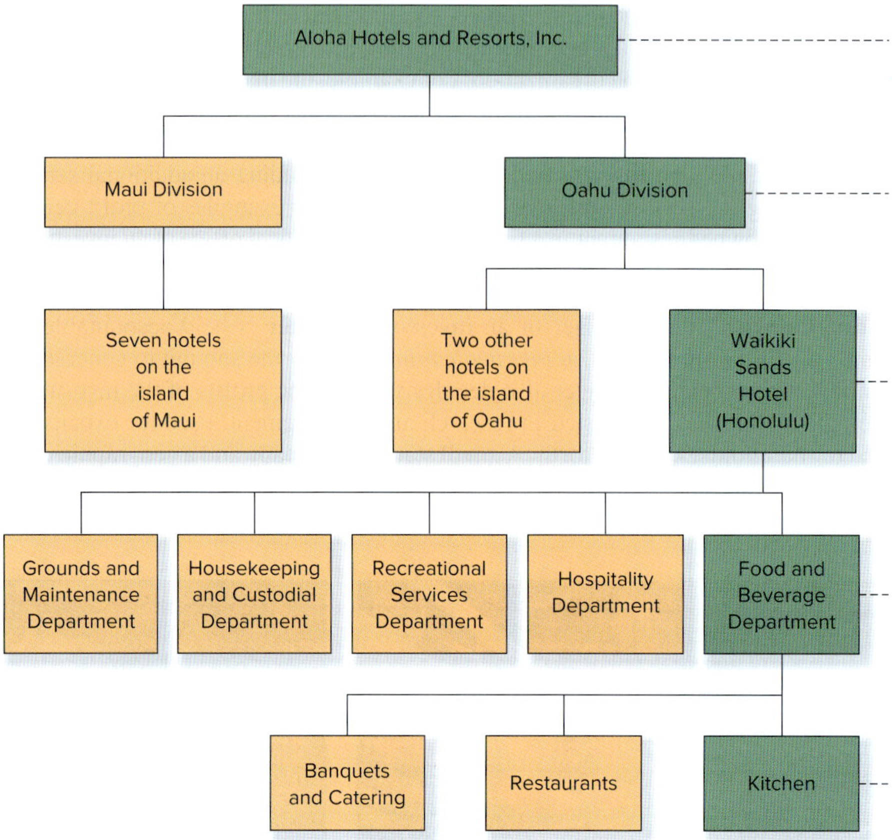

corporation itself is also an investment center, accountable to shareholders and lenders for the return on the capital that they have provided.[1]

Illustration of Responsibility Accounting

To illustrate the concepts used in responsibility accounting, we will focus on a hotel chain. Aloha Hotels and Resorts operates 10 luxury hotels in the state of Hawaii. The company is divided into the Maui Division, which operates seven hotels on the island of Maui, and the Oahu Division, with three properties on the island of Oahu. Exhibit 12–1 shows the company's organization chart, and Exhibit 12–2 depicts the responsibility-accounting system.

> "You have to wear the hat of the management team you are on to help them achieve the goals. You also have to wear the corporate finance hat to recognize that you have a duty, to the corporate finance function, to do things right and do them correctly, to stand up for what has to be done, and to say no when no is the appropriate thing to say." (12b)
>
> **Abbott Laboratories**

Corporate Level The chief executive officer of Aloha Hotels and Resorts, Inc., is the company's president. The president, who is responsible to the company's stockholders, is accountable for corporate profit in relation to the capital (assets) invested in the company. Therefore, the entire company is an *investment center.* The president has the autonomy to make significant decisions that affect the company's profit and invested capital. For example, the final decision to add a new luxury tower to any of the company's resort properties would be made by the president.

Division Level The vice president of the Oahu Division is accountable for the profit earned by the three resort hotels on Oahu in relation to the capital invested in those properties. Hence, the Oahu Division is also an *investment center.* The vice president has the authority to make major investment decisions regarding the properties on Oahu, up to a limit of $300,000. For example, the vice president could decide to landscape a swimming pool at one of the Oahu resort hotels, but could not decide to add a new wing.

[1]Although there is an important conceptual difference between profit centers and investment centers, the latter term is not always used in practice. Some managers use the term *profit center* to refer to both types of responsibility centers. Hence, when businesspeople use the term *profit center,* they may be referring to a true profit center (as defined in this chapter) or to an investment center. However, for correct incentive and control decisions, it is important to understand the difference.

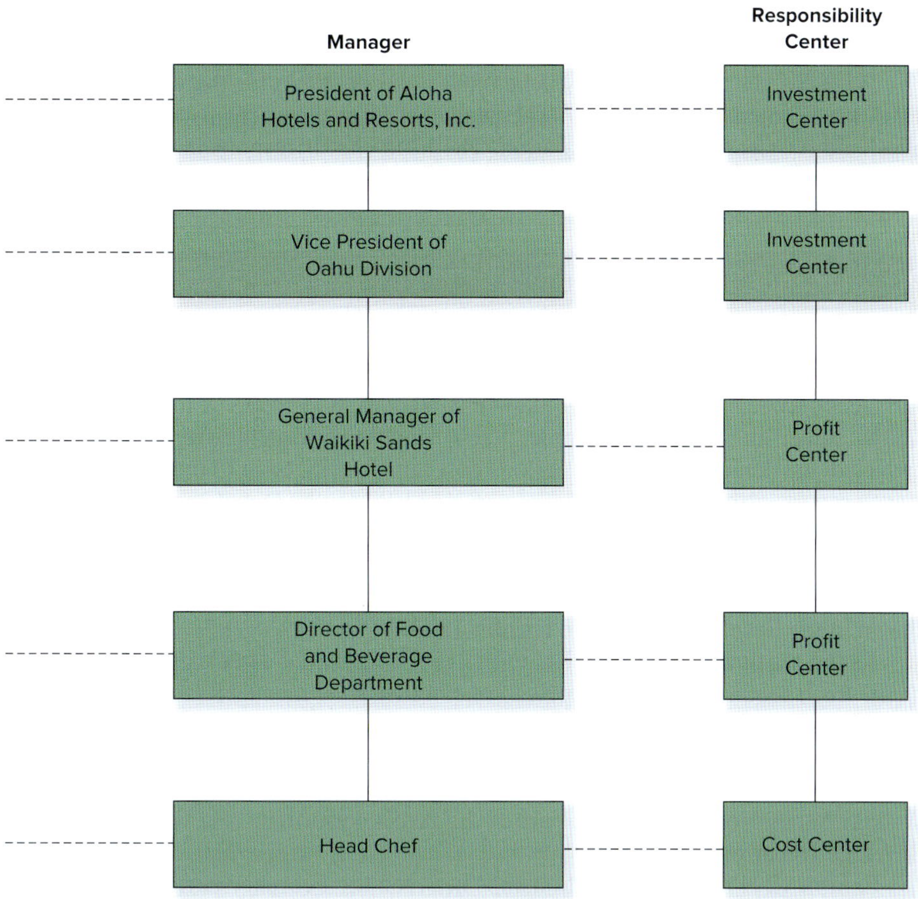

Exhibit 12–2
Responsibility Accounting System: Aloha Hotels and Resorts

Hotel Level The Waikiki Sands Hotel, in Honolulu, is one of the properties in the Oahu Division. The general manager of the Waikiki Sands Hotel is accountable for the profit earned by the hotel. The general manager does not have the authority to make major investment decisions, but is responsible for operational decisions. For example, the general manager hires all of the hotel's departmental managers, sets wage rates, determines procedures and standards for operations, approves decorating decisions, and generally oversees the hotel's operation. The hotel's general manager has no authority to make major investment decisions, and can only make improvements with authorization from the division. Accordingly, she is held accountable only for the hotel's profit, not the capital invested in the property. Thus, the Waikiki Sands Hotel is a *profit center.*

Departmental Level The Waikiki Sands Hotel has five departments, as shown in Exhibit 12–1. The Grounds and Maintenance Department includes landscaping, building and equipment maintenance, and hotel security. The Housekeeping and Custodial Services Department covers laundry and janitorial services. These two departments are called service departments, since they provide services to the hotel's other departments but do not deal directly with hotel guests. The Recreational Services Department operates the hotel's swimming pools, saunas, fitness center, and tennis courts. The Hospitality Department includes the hotel's reservations desk, rooms, bell staff, and shopping facilities. Finally, the Food and Beverage Department operates the resort's restaurants, coffee shop, lounges, poolside snack bar, banquet operations, and catering service.

The director of the Food and Beverage Department is accountable for the profit earned on all food and beverage operations. Therefore, this department is a *profit center.* The director has the authority to approve the menu, set food and beverage prices, hire the wait staff, schedule entertainers, and generally oversee all food and beverage operations.

Kitchen Level The Food and Beverage Department is divided further into subunits responsible for Banquets and Catering, Restaurants, and the Kitchen.

The head chef manages the kitchen and is accountable for the costs incurred there. Thus, the Kitchen is a *cost center.* The head chef hires the kitchen staff, orders food supplies, and oversees all food preparation. The head chef is responsible for providing safe, innovative, and high-quality food, but at the lowest possible cost.

Performance Reports

Learning Objective **12–3**

Prepare a performance report and explain the relationships between the performance reports for various responsibility centers.

The performance of each responsibility center is summarized periodically on a *performance report.* A **performance report** shows the budgeted and actual amounts, and the variances between these amounts, of key financial results appropriate for the type of responsibility center involved. For example, a cost center's performance report concentrates on budgeted and actual amounts for various cost items attributable to the cost center. Performance reports also typically show the variance between budgeted and actual amounts for the financial results conveyed in the report. The data in a performance report help managers use *management by exception* to control an organization's operations effectively.

The performance report for the kitchen of the Waikiki Sands Hotel for February is shown in the Excel spreadsheet in Exhibit 12–3.

As the organization chart in Exhibit 12–1 shows, Aloha Hotels and Resorts is a *hierarchy.* Each subunit manager reports to one higher-level manager, from the head chef all the way up to the president. In such an organization, there is also a hierarchy of performance reports, since the performance of each subunit constitutes part of the performance of the next higher-level subunit. For example, the cost performance in the kitchen of the Waikiki Sands Hotel constitutes part of the profit performance of the hotel's Food and Beverage Department.

Exhibit 12–4 shows the relationships between the February performance reports for several subunits of Aloha Hotels and Resorts. Notice that the numbers for the Grounds and Maintenance Department, the Housekeeping and Custodial Department, and the Kitchen are in parentheses. These subunits are cost centers, so the numbers shown are expenses. All of the other subunits shown in Exhibit 12–4 are either profit centers or

Exhibit 12–3

Performance Report for February: Kitchen, Waikiki Sands Hotel

Aloha Hotels and Resorts - Excel

H8 =ABS(B8-E8)

ALOHA HOTELS & RESORTS

Waikiki Sands Hotel, department: Food & Beverage: Kitchen

Performance Report, month: February

	Flexible Budget		Actual Results		Variance*			
	February	Year to Date	February	Year to Date	February		Year to Date	
Kitchen staff wages	$ 80,000	$ 168,000	$ 78,000	$ 169,000	$ 2,000	F	$ 1,000	U
Food	675,000	1,420,000	678,000	1,421,000	3,000	U	1,000	U
Paper products	120,000	250,000	115,000	248,000	5,000	F	2,000	F
Variable overhead	70,000	150,000	71,000	154,000	1,000	U	4,000	U
Fixed overhead	85,000	180,000	83,000	181,000	2,000	F	1,000	U
Total expense	$1,030,000	$2,168,000	$1,025,000	$2,173,000	$ 5,000	F	$ 5,000	U

*F denotes favorable variance; U denotes unfavorable variance.

RecreationalSvcs | Hospitality | Food&Beverage

	Flexible Budget*		Actual Results*		Variance†	
	February	Year to Date	February	Year to Date	February	Year to Date
Company	$30,660	$ 64,567	$ 30,716	$64,570	$56 F	$ 3 F
Maui Division	$ 18,400	$ 38,620	$ 18,470	$38,630	$70 F	$10 F
Oahu Division	12,260	25,947	12,246	25,940	14 U	7 U
Total profit	$ 30,660	$ 64,567	$ 30,716	$64,570	$56 F	$ 3 F
Oahu Division						
Waimea Beach Resort	$ 6,050	$ 12,700	$ 6,060	$12,740	$10 F	$40 F
Diamond Head Lodge	2,100	4,500	2,050	4,430	50 U	70 U
Waikiki Sands Hotel	4,110	8,747	4,136	8,770	26 F	23 F
Total profit	$ 12,260	$ 25,947	$ 12,246	$25,940	$14 U	$ 7 U
Waikiki Sands Hotel						
Grounds and Maintenance	$ (45)	$ (90)	$ (44)	$ (90)	$ 1 F	—
Housekeeping and Custodial	(40)	(90)	(41)	(90)	1 U	—
Recreational Services	40	85	41	88	1 F	$ 3 F
Hospitality	2,800	6,000	2,840	6,030	40 F	30 F
Food and Beverage	1,355	2,842	1,340	2,832	15 U	10 U
Total profit	$ 4,110	$ 8,747	$ 4,136	$ 8,770	$26 F	$23 F
Food and Beverage Department						
Banquets and Catering	$ 600	$ 1,260	$ 605	$ 1,265	$ 5 F	$ 5 F
Restaurants	1,785	3,750	1,760	3,740	25 U	10 U
Kitchen	(1,030)	(2,168)	(1,025)	(2,173)	5 F	5 U
Total profit	$ 1,355	$ 2,842	$ 1,340	$ 2,832	$15 U	$10 U
Kitchen						
Kitchen staff wages	$ (80)	$ (168)	$ (78)	$ (169)	$ 2 F	$ 1 U
Food	(675)	(1,420)	(678)	(1,421)	3 U	1 U
Paper products	(120)	(250)	(115)	(248)	5 F	2 F
Variable overhead	(70)	(150)	(71)	(154)	1 U	4 U
Fixed overhead	(85)	(180)	(83)	(181)	2 F	1 U
Total expense	$ (1,030)	$ (2,168)	$ (1,025)	$ (2,173)	$ 5 F	$ 5 U

*Numbers without parentheses denote profit; numbers with parentheses denote expenses; numbers in thousands.

†F denotes favorable variance; U denotes unfavorable variance.

Exhibit 12–4

Performance Reports for February: Selected Subunits of Aloha Hotels and Resorts (numbers in thousands)

investment centers. The numbers shown for these subunits are profits, so they are not enclosed in parentheses. In addition to the profit figures shown, the performance reports for the investment centers should include data about invested capital. The Maui Division, the Oahu Division, and the company as a whole are investment centers. Performance evaluation in investment centers is covered in the next chapter.

Notice the relationships between the performance reports in Exhibit 12–4. The kitchen is the lowest-level subunit shown, and its performance report is the same as that displayed in Exhibit 12–3. The *total expense* line from the kitchen performance report is included as one line in the performance report for the Food and Beverage Department. Also included are the total profit figures for the department's other two subunits: Banquets and Catering, and Restaurants. How is the *total profit* line for the Food and Beverage Department used in the performance report for the Waikiki Sands Hotel? Follow the relationships emphasized with arrows in Exhibit 12–4.

The hierarchy of performance reports starts at the bottom and builds toward the top, just as the organization structure depicted in Exhibit 12–1 builds from the bottom upward. Each manager in the organization receives the performance report for his or her own subunit in addition to the performance reports for the major subunits in the next lower level. For example, the general manager of the Waikiki Sands Hotel receives the reports for the hotel, and each of its departments: Grounds and Maintenance, Housekeeping and Custodial, Recreational Services, Hospitality, and Food and Beverage. With these reports, the hotel's general manager can evaluate her subordinates as well as her own performance. This will help the general manager in improving the hotel's performance, motivating employees, and planning future operations.

"It is real important for accountants or finance people, when you get into the numbers, to be able to take a spreadsheet that has a zillion numbers on it and then turn around and present that to somebody at a high enough level in a meaningful manner that they can understand. I think probably in the last five years that is what I spend most of my time on—working on communications." (12c)

Caterpillar

Budgets, Variance Analysis, and Responsibility Accounting

Notice that the performance reports in Exhibit 12–4 make heavy use of budgets and variance analysis. Thus, the topics of budgeting, variance analysis, and responsibility accounting are closely interrelated. The flexible budget provides the benchmark against which actual revenues, expenses, and profits are compared. As we saw in Chapter 11, it is important to use a flexible budget so that appropriate comparisons can be made. It would make no sense, for example, to compare the actual costs incurred in the kitchen at Waikiki Sands Hotel with budgeted costs established for a different level of hotel occupancy.

The performance reports in Exhibit 12–4 also show variances between budgeted and actual performance. These variances often are broken down into smaller components to help management pinpoint responsibility and diagnose performance. Variance analysis, which was discussed in detail in Chapters 10 and 11, is an important tool in a responsibility-accounting system.

Cost Allocation

Learning Objective 12–4

Use a cost allocation base to allocate costs.

Many costs incurred by an organization are the joint result of several subunits' activities. For example, the property taxes and utility costs incurred by Aloha Hotels and Resorts for the Waikiki Sands Hotel are the joint result of all of the hotel's activities. One function of a responsibility-accounting system is to assign all of an organization's costs to the subunits that cause them to be incurred.

A collection of costs to be assigned is called a **cost pool.** At the Waikiki Sands Hotel, for example, all utility costs are combined into a *utility cost pool,* which includes the costs of electricity, water, sewer, trash collection, television cable, and telephone. The responsibility centers, products, or services to which costs are to be assigned are called **cost objects.** The Waikiki Sands' cost objects are its major departments. (See the organization chart in Exhibit 12–1.) The process of assigning the costs in the *cost pool* to the *cost objects* is called **cost allocation** or **cost distribution.**

Cost Allocation Bases

To distribute (or allocate) costs to responsibility centers, the company's managerial accountant chooses an *allocation base* for each cost pool. An **allocation base** is a measure of activity, physical characteristic, or economic characteristic that is associated with the responsibility centers, which are the cost objects in the allocation process. The allocation base chosen for a cost pool should reflect some characteristic of the various responsibility centers that is related to the incurrence of costs. An allocation base also may be referred to as a *cost driver.*

Exhibit 12–5 shows the Waikiki Sands Hotel's February cost distribution for selected cost pools. Each cost pool is distributed to each responsibility center in proportion to that center's relative amount of the allocation base. For example, the Food and Beverage Department receives 30 percent of the total administrative costs, $25,000, because that department's 36 employees constitute 30 percent of the hotel's employees. Notice that no marketing costs are allocated to either the Grounds and Maintenance Department or the Housekeeping and Custodial Department. Neither of these responsibility centers generates any sales revenue.

Cost Pool	Responsibility Center	Allocation Base	Percentage of Total	Costs Distributed
Administration	Grounds and Maintenance	12 employees	10.0%	$ 2,500
	Housekeeping and Custodial	24 employees	20.0	5,000
	Recreational Services	12 employees	10.0	2,500
	Hospitality	36 employees	30.0	7,500
	Food and Beverage	36 employees	30.0	7,500
	Total	120 employees	100.0%	$25,000
Facilities	Grounds and Maintenance	2,000 sq. ft.	1.0%	$ 300
	Housekeeping and Custodial	2,000 sq. ft.	1.0	300
	Recreational Services	5,000 sq. ft.	2.5	750
	Hospitality	175,000 sq. ft.	87.5	26,250
	Food and Beverage	16,000 sq. ft.	8.0	2,400
	Total	200,000 sq. ft.	100.0%	$30,000
Marketing	Grounds and Maintenance	—	—	—
	Housekeeping and Custodial	—	—	—
	Recreational Services	$ 20,000 of sales	4.0%	$ 2,000
	Hospitality	400,000 of sales	80.0	40,000
	Food and Beverage	80,000 of sales	16.0	8,000
	Total	$500,000 of sales	100.0%	$50,000

Exhibit 12–5
Cost Distribution to Responsibility Centers: Waikiki Sands Hotel

Allocation Bases Based on Budgets

At the Waikiki Sands Hotel, administrative and marketing costs are distributed on the basis of *budgeted* amounts of the relevant allocation bases, rather than *actual* amounts. The managerial accountant should design an allocation procedure so that the behavior of one responsibility center does not affect the costs allocated to other responsibility centers.

Suppose, for example, that the budgeted and actual February sales revenues for the hotel were as shown in Exhibit 12–6. Notice that the Hospitality Department's actual sales revenue is close to the budget. However, the actual sales of the Recreational Services Department and the Food and Beverage Department are substantially below the budget. If the distribution of marketing costs is based on actual sales, instead of budgeted sales, then the cost distributed to the Hospitality Department jumps from $40,000 to $45,000, an increase of 12.5 percent. Why does this happen? As a result of a sales performance substantially below the budget for the *other two departments,* the Hospitality Department is penalized with a hefty increase in its cost distribution. This is misleading and unfair to the Hospitality Department manager. A preferable cost distribution procedure is to use budgeted sales revenue as the allocation base, rather than actual sales revenue. Then the marketing costs distributed to each department do not depend on the performance in the other two departments.

			Marketing Cost Distribution	
Responsibility Center	Budgeted Sales Revenue	Actual Sales Revenue	Based on Budget	Based on Actual
Recreational Services	$ 20,000 (4%)*	$ 4,500 (1%)*	$ 2,000	$ 500
Hospitality	400,000 (80%)	405,000 (90%)	40,000	45,000
Food and Beverage	80,000 (16%)	40,500 (9%)	8,000	4,500
Total	$500,000	$450,000	$50,000	$50,000

*Percentage of column total.

Exhibit 12–6
Cost Distribution: Budgeted versus Actual Allocation Bases

Activity-Based Responsibility Accounting

Traditional responsibility-accounting systems tend to focus on the financial performance measures of cost, revenue, and profit for the *subunits* of an organization. Contemporary cost management systems, however, focus more on *activities*. Costs are incurred in organizations and their subunits because of activities. *Activity-based costing (ABC)* systems associate costs with the activities that drive those costs. The database created by an ABC system, coupled with nonfinancial measures of operational performance for each activity, enables management to employ **activity-based responsibility accounting.** Under this approach, management's attention is directed not only to the cost incurred in an activity but also to the activity itself. Is the activity necessary? Does it add value to the organization's product or service? Can the activity be improved? By seeking answers to these questions, managers can eliminate non-value-added activities and increase the cost-effectiveness of the activities that do add value.[2]

Behavioral Effects of Responsibility Accounting

Responsibility-accounting systems can influence behavior significantly. Whether the behavioral effects are positive or negative, however, depends on how responsibility accounting is implemented.

Information versus Blame

The proper focus of a responsibility-accounting system is *information*. The system should identify the individual in the organization who is in the best position to explain each particular event or financial result. The emphasis should be on providing that individual and higher-level managers with information to help them understand the reasons behind the organization's performance. When properly used, a responsibility-accounting system *does not emphasize blame*. If managers feel they are beaten over the head with criticism and rebukes when unfavorable variances occur, they are unlikely to respond in a positive way. Instead, they will tend to undermine the system and view it with skepticism. But when the responsibility-accounting system emphasizes its informational role, managers tend to react constructively, and strive for improved performance.

Controllability

> "[P]rofitability improved sufficiently to absorb uncontrollable cost. . . . [This] was accomplished through continuous improvement activities . . . that enhance efficiency and productivity." (12d)
>
> **Univar N.V.**

Some organizations use performance reports that distinguish between controllable and uncontrollable costs or revenues. For example, the head chef at the Waikiki Sands Hotel can influence the hours and efficiency of the kitchen staff, but he probably cannot change the wage rates. A performance report that distinguishes between the financial results influenced by the head chef and those he does not influence has the advantage of providing complete information to the head chef. Yet the report recognizes that certain results are beyond his control.

Identifying costs as controllable or uncontrollable is not always easy. Many cost items are influenced by more than one person. The time frame also may be important in determining controllability. Some costs are controllable over a long time frame, but not within a short time period. To illustrate, suppose the Waikiki Sands' head chef has signed a one-year contract with a local seafood supplier. The cost of seafood can be influenced by the head chef if the time period is a year or more, but the cost cannot be controlled on a weekly basis.

---

[2]Activity-based costing is covered in Chapter 5. Activity analysis and the elimination of non-value-added activities are also covered in Chapter 5.

Motivating Desired Behavior

Management often uses the responsibility-accounting system to motivate actions they consider desirable. Sometimes the responsibility-accounting system can solve behavioral problems as well. As a case in point, consider the problem of rush orders. To accept or reject a rush order is a cost-benefit decision:

Costs of Accepting Rush Order	Benefits of Accepting Rush Order
Disrupted production	Satisfied customers
More setups	Greater future sales
Higher costs	

The following real-world example involving rush orders provides a case in point.

The production scheduler in a manufacturing firm was frequently asked to interrupt production of one product with a rush order for another product. Rush orders typically resulted in greater costs because more product setups were required. Since the production scheduler was evaluated on the basis of costs, he was reluctant to accept rush orders. The sales manager, on the other hand, was evaluated on the basis of sales revenue. By agreeing to customers' demands for rush orders, the sales manager satisfied his customers. This resulted in more future sales and favorable performance ratings for the sales manager.

As the rush orders became more and more frequent, the production manager began to object. The sales manager responded by asking if the production scheduler wanted to take the responsibility for losing a customer by refusing a rush order. The production scheduler did not want to be blamed for lost sales, so he grudgingly accepted the rush orders. However, considerable ill will developed between the sales manager and production scheduler.

The company's managerial accountant came to the rescue by redesigning the responsibility-accounting system. The system was modified to accumulate the extra costs associated with rush orders and charge them to the sales manager's responsibility center, rather than the production scheduler's center. The ultimate result was that the sales manager chose more carefully which rush-order requests to make, and the production manager accepted them gracefully.

The problem described in the preceding illustration developed because two different managers were considering the costs and benefits of the rush-order decision. The production manager was looking only at the costs, while the sales manager was looking only at the benefits. The modified responsibility-accounting system made the sales manager look at *both the costs and the benefits* associated with each rush order. Then the sales manager could make the necessary trade-off between costs and benefits in considering each rush order. Some rush orders were rejected, because the sales manager decided the costs exceeded the benefits. Other rush orders were accepted, when the importance of the customer and potential future sales justified it.

This example illustrates how a well-designed responsibility-accounting system can make an organization run more smoothly and achieve higher performance.

Segmented Reporting

Learning Objective 12–5

Prepare a segmented income statement.

Subunits of an organization are often called *segments. Segmented reporting* refers to the preparation of accounting reports by segment and for the organization as a whole. Many organizations prepare **segmented income statements,** which show the income for major segments and for the entire enterprise.

In preparing segmented income statements, management must decide how to treat costs that are incurred to benefit more than one segment. Such costs are called **common costs.** The salary of the president of Aloha Hotels and Resorts is a common cost. The president manages the entire company. Some of her time is spent on matters related specifically

> "Senior management wants to know yesterday. So the pace has quickened and there's more pressure to get information much sooner and at the same time there is so much more information there." (12e)
>
> **Qwest** (now **CenturyLink**)

to the Maui Division or the Oahu Division, but much of it is spent on tasks that are not traced easily to either division. The president works with the company's board of directors, develops strategic plans for the company, and helps set policy and goals for the entire enterprise. Thus, the president's compensation is a common cost, which is not related easily to any segment's activities.

Many managerial accountants believe that it is misleading to allocate common costs to an organization's segments. Since these costs are not traceable to the activities of segments, they can be allocated to segments only on the basis of some highly arbitrary allocation base. Consider the salary of Aloha Hotels and Resorts' president. What allocation base would you choose to reflect the contribution of the president's managerial efforts to the company's two divisions? The possible allocation bases include budgeted divisional sales revenue, the number of hotels or employees in each division, or some measure of divisional size, such as total assets. However, all of these allocation bases would yield arbitrary cost allocations and possibly misleading segment profit information. For this reason, many organizations choose not to allocate common costs on segmented income statements.

Exhibit 12–7 shows February's segmented income statement (on a budgeted basis) for Aloha Hotels and Resorts. Each segment's income statement is presented in the *contribution format* discussed in Chapter 8. Notice that Exhibit 12–7 shows income statements for the following segments.

- Aloha Hotels and Resorts
  - Maui Division
  - Oahu Division
    - Waimea Beach Resort
    - Daimond Head Lodge
    - Waikiki Sands Hotel

Three numbers in Exhibit 12–7 require special emphasis. First, the $10,000,000 of common fixed expenses in the left-hand column is not allocated to the company's two divisions. Included in this figure are such costs as the company president's salary. These costs cannot be allocated to the divisions, except in some arbitrary manner.

Exhibit 12–7

Segmented Income Statements: Aloha Hotels and Resorts (in thousands)

		Segment of Company		Segment of Oahu Division			
	Aloha Hotels and Resorts	**Maui Division**	**Oahu Division**	**Waimea Beach Resort**	**Diamond Head Lodge**	**Waikiki Sands Hotel**	**Not Allocated**
Sales revenue	$2,500,000	$1,600,000	$900,000	$450,000	$150,000	$300,000	—
Variable operating expenses:							
Personnel	$ 820,900	$ 510,400	$310,500	$155,500	$ 50,000	$105,000	—
Food, beverages, and supplies	738,000	458,600	279,400	139,700	46,400	93,300	—
Other	83,000	58,000	25,000	12,500	4,000	8,500	—
Total	$1,641,900	$1,027,000	$614,900	$307,700	$100,400	$206,800	—
Segment contribution margin	$ 858,100	$ 573,000	$285,100	$142,300	$ 49,600	$ 93,200	—
Less: Fixed expenses controllable by segment manager	30,000	21,000	9,000	4,000	1,000	3,000	$ 1,000
Profit margin controllable by segment manager	$ 828,100	$ 552,000	$276,100	$138,300	$ 48,600	$ 90,200	$ (1,000)
Less: Fixed expenses, traceable to segment, but controllable by others	750,000	500,000	250,000	26,000	8,000	16,000	200,000
Segment profit margin	$ 78,100	$ 52,000	$ 26,100	$112,300	$ 40,600	$ 74,200	$(201,000)
Less: Common fixed expenses	10,000						
Income before taxes	$ 68,100						
Less: Income tax expense	37,440						
Net income	$ 30,660						

Second, $1,000,000 of controllable fixed expense in the right-hand column constitutes part of the Oahu Division's $9,000,000 of controllable fixed expense. All $9,000,000 of expense is controllable by the vice president of the Oahu Division. However, $1,000,000 of these expenses cannot be traced to the division's three hotels, except on an arbitrary basis. For example, this $1,000,000 of expense includes the salary of the Oahu Division's vice president. Therefore, the $1,000,000 of expense is *not allocated* among the division's three hotels. This procedure illustrates an important point. Costs that are traceable to segments at one level in an organization may become common costs at a lower level in the organization. The vice president's salary is traceable to the Oahu Division, but it cannot be allocated among the division's three hotels except arbitrarily. Thus, the vice president's salary is a traceable cost at the divisional level, but it becomes a common cost at the hotel level.

Third, the $200,000,000 of fixed expenses controllable by others in the right-hand column constitutes part of the Oahu Division's $250,000,000 of fixed expenses controllable by others. However, the $200,000,000 portion cannot be allocated among the division's three hotels, except arbitrarily.

Segments versus Segment Managers

One advantage of segmented reports like the one in Exhibit 12–7 is that they make a distinction between segments and segment managers. Some costs that are traceable to a segment may be completely beyond the influence of the segment manager. Property taxes on the Waikiki Sands Hotel, for example, are traceable to the hotel, but the hotel's general manager cannot influence them. To properly evaluate the *Waikiki Sands Hotel as an investment* of the company's resources, the property taxes should be included in the hotel's costs. However, in evaluating the general manager's performance, the property-tax cost should be *excluded,* since the manager has no control over it.

Key Features of Segmented Reporting

To summarize, Exhibit 12–7 illustrates three important characteristics of segmented reporting:

1. ***Contribution format.*** These income statements use the contribution format. The statements subtract variable expenses from sales revenue to obtain the *contribution margin.*
2. ***Controllable versus uncontrollable expenses.*** The income statements in Exhibit 12–7 highlight the costs that can be controlled, or heavily influenced, by each segment manager. This approach is consistent with *responsibility accounting.*
3. ***Segmented income statement.*** *Segmented reporting* shows income statements for the company as a whole and for its major segments.

Customer-Profitability Analysis and Activity-Based Costing

Analyzing profitability by segments of the company can help managers gain insight into the factors that are driving the company's performance. In addition to focusing on the major organizational subunits in the company, profitability analysis can focus on major market segments, geographical regions, distribution channels, or customers.

Customer-profitability analysis uses the concept of activity-based costing to determine how serving particular customers causes activities to be performed and costs to be incurred. Suppose, for example, that customer A frequently changes its orders after they are placed, but customer B typically does not. Then the costs incurred in updating sales orders for changes should be recorded in a manner that reflects the fact that customer A is more responsible for those activities and costs than is customer B.

Operational Performance Measures in Today's Production Environment

Learning Objective 12–6

Describe the operational performance measures appropriate for today's production environment.

In today's production environment, operational performance measures carry great importance. Under the philosophy of *activity-based management,* the goal is to focus on continually improving each activity. As a result, the emerging operational control measures focus on the key *activities* in which the organization engages. For example, Zappos.com, the Internet shoe retailer owned by Amazon, measures the percentage of time that each customer service representative spends on the telephone, because customer service is the cornerstone of its strategy.

Exhibit 12–8 lists some commonly-used operational performance measures. The measures listed in Exhibit 12–8 are representative, but not exhaustive, of those used in practice. In using these measures to control operations, management emphasizes trends over time. The goal is to continually improve all critical aspects of production.

Raw Material and Scrap Raw material continues to be a significant cost element in any manufacturing process, whether labor-intensive or highly automated. Worldwide material sourcing and international competition have resulted in the purchasing function

Exhibit 12–8

Operational Performance Measures for the Modern Production Environment

Raw Material and Scrap
- Number of vendors
- Raw material as a percentage of total cost
- Lead time for material delivery
- Percentage of orders received on time
- Material purchase-price variances
- Scrap as a percentage of raw-material cost
- Quality of raw material

Inventory
- Average value of inventory
- Average amount of time various inventory items are held
- Ratio of inventory value to sales revenue
- Number of inventoried parts

Machinery
- Hours of machine downtime
- Percentage of machine availability
- Percentage of bottleneck machine availability
- Percentage of on-time routine maintenance procedures
- Setup time
- Product switchover times

Product and Service Quality
- Customer acceptance measures:
  - Number of customer complaints
  - Number of warranty claims
  - Cost of repeat service visits
  - Number of products returned
  - Cost of repairing returned products
- In-process quality measures:
  - Number of defects found
  - Cost of rework
- Quality costs

Production and Delivery
- Manufacturing cycle time
- Velocity
- Manufacturing cycle efficiency
- Percentage of on-time deliveries
- Percentage of orders filled
- Delivery cycle time

Productivity
- Financial measures:
  - Aggregate or total productivity (output in dollars ÷ total input in dollars)
  - Partial or component productivity (output in dollars ÷ a particular input in dollars)
- Operational (physical) measures:
  - Partial or component productivity measures. These measures express relationships between inputs and outputs, in physical terms. For example:
    - Service visits made per day per employee
    - Square feet of floor space required per finished product per day
    - Electricity required per finished product

Innovation and Learning
- New products or services:
  - Percentage of sales from new products
  - New services introduced by this firm versus introductions by competitors
- Process improvements:
  - Number of process improvements made
  - Cost savings from process improvements

taking on greater importance in many firms. As a result, purchasing performance has become an important area of measurement; criteria include total raw-material cost, deviations between actual and budgeted material prices, the quality of raw materials, and the delivery performance of vendors.

Inventory Inventory is a significant investment for any manufacturing or distribution company. The essence of the just-in-time production environment is low inventories at every stage of production. Thus, inventory control is of paramount importance in achieving the benefits of the JIT philosophy. Inventory control measures include the average value of inventory, the average amount of time various inventory items are held, and other inventory turnover measures, such as the ratio of inventory value to sales revenue.

Machinery If inventories are to be kept low while still keeping customers satisfied, the production process must be capable of producing and delivering goods and services quickly. This goal requires that machinery must work when it is needed, which means that routine maintenance schedules must be adhered to scrupulously. Performance controls in this area include measures of machine downtime and machine availability, and detailed maintenance records. Some companies make a distinction between *bottleneck machinery* and nonbottleneck machinery. A bottleneck operation is one that limits the production capacity of the entire facility. It is vital that the machinery in bottleneck operations be available 100 percent of the time, excluding time for routine required maintenance. This emphasis on bottleneck operations is consistent with the management philosophy known as the **theory of constraints (TOC),** which seeks to maximize long-run profit through proper management of organizational bottlenecks or constrained resources. The key idea in TOC is to identify the constraints in a system that are preventing the organization from achieving a higher level of success and then to seek to relieve or relax those constraints. Moreover, TOC recommends subordinating all other management goals to the objective of solving the constraint problems.[3]

Product and Service Quality The competitive market demands adherence to strict quality standards for raw materials, manufactured components, and products and services sold. Various nonfinancial data are vital for assessing a company's effectiveness in maintaining product and service quality. **Customer acceptance measures** focus on the extent to which a firm's customers perceive its outputs to be of high quality. Typical performance measures include the number of customer complaints, the number of warranty claims, the number of products returned, and the cost of repeat service visits. **In-process quality controls** refer to procedures designed to assess product and service quality before production is completed. For example, in a *quality audit program,* partially completed jobs are inspected at various stages of production. Defect rates are measured, and corrective actions are suggested.

Production and Delivery A company will achieve little success if it produces a great product but delivers it to the customer a week late. World-class companies are striving toward a goal of filling 100 percent of their orders on time. Common measures of delivery performance include the percentage of on-time deliveries and the percentage of orders filled. Another measure is **delivery cycle time,** the average time between the receipt of a customer order and delivery of the goods.

Delivering goods on time requires that they be produced on time. Various operational performance measures have been developed to assess the timeliness of the production process. For example, in a manufacturing firm, **manufacturing cycle time** is the total amount of production time (or throughput time) required per unit. It can be computed by dividing the total time required to produce a batch (*not* including the time the order spends waiting before production begins) by the number of units in the batch. **Velocity** is defined as the number of units produced in a given time period. Perhaps an

"We have to be the best in cost throughout the world. And cycle time is also very important." (12f)

MiCRUS
(joint venture of **IBM** and **Cirrus Logic**, now part of **NXP Semiconductor**)

[3]Eliyahu M. Goldratt, *Theory of Constraints* (Croton-on-Hudson, New York: North River Press, 1990).

even more important operational measure is the **manufacturing cycle efficiency (MCE),** defined as follows:

$$\text{Manufacturing cycle efficiency} = \frac{\text{Processing time}}{\text{Processing time} + \text{Inspection time} + \text{Waiting time after production begins} + \text{Move time}}$$

MCE represents the percent of time that products are actually being worked on after the production process begins. The value of the MCE measure lies in its comparison between value-added time (processing) and non-value-added time (inspection, waiting, and moving) during the production process. Competitive manufacturing firms strive for as high an MCE measure as possible.

Productivity Global competitiveness has forced virtually all companies to strive for greater productivity. One *financial* productivity measure is **aggregate (or total) productivity,** defined as total output divided by total input. A firm's total output is measured as the sum, across all of the goods and services produced, of those products and services times their sales prices. Total input is the sum of the direct-material, direct-labor, and overhead costs incurred in production. Another financial measure is a **partial (or component) productivity** measure, in which total output (in dollars) is divided by the cost of a particular input.

A preferable approach to productivity measurement is to record multiple physical measures that capture the most important determinants of a company's productivity. These *operational* (or *physical*) measures are also partial productivity measures, since each one focuses on a particular input. For example, a large automobile manufacturer routinely records the following data for one of its plants: the number of engines produced per day per employee and the number of square feet of floor space required per engine produced in a day. Data such as these convey more information to management than a summary financial measure such as aggregate productivity.

Innovation and Learning Global competition requires that companies continually improve and innovate. New products must be developed and introduced to replace those that have become obsolete. New processes must continually be developed to make production more efficient. In a world-class manufacturer or service firm, the one thing that is most constant is change.

Improvement Targets To summarize, nonfinancial measures are being used increasingly to augment financial planning and analysis systems. These operational performance measures assist management in its goal of continuous process improvement. To be most effective, operational controls should be tied to the strategic objectives of the organization. Specific improvement targets can be set for various measures to provide motivation for improvement in the areas deemed most important by management.

One widely used method to improve operational efficiency is **benchmarking.** This is the continual search for the most effective method of accomplishing a task by comparing existing methods and performance levels with those of other organizations, or with other subunits within the same organization. For example, hospitals routinely benchmark their costs of patient care by diagnostic-related groups (such as circulatory disorders) by comparing them with the costs of other hospitals.

Gain-Sharing Plans

One widely used method of providing incentives to employees to improve their performance on various operational control measures is gain sharing. A **gain-sharing plan** is an incentive system that specifies a formula by which cost or productivity gains achieved by a company are shared with the workers who helped accomplish the improvements. For example, suppose an Internet retailer reduced its returns due to late shipment by 2 percent for a savings of $100,000. A gain-sharing formula might call for 25 percent of the savings to be shared with the employees in the distribution center.

The Balanced Scorecard

Learning Objective 12–7

Describe the balanced scorecard concept and explain the reasoning behind it.

Managers of the most successful organizations do not rely on either financial or nonfinancial performance measures alone. They recognize that financial performance measures summarize the results of past actions. These measures are important to a firm's owners, creditors, employees, and so forth. Thus, they must be watched carefully by management. But nonfinancial performance measures are important too because they focus on *current* activities, which will be the drivers of *future* financial performance. Thus, effective management requires a balanced perspective on performance measurement, a viewpoint that some call the *balanced scorecard* perspective.

To illustrate the **balanced scorecard,** we will explore its use by Forest Home National Bank (FHNB), located in Boise, Idaho. The bank's balanced scorecard, which is depicted in Exhibit 12–9, integrates performance measures in four key areas: financial, internal business process, customer, and learning and growth.[4]

Exhibit 12–9

Balanced Scorecard: Forest Home National Bank

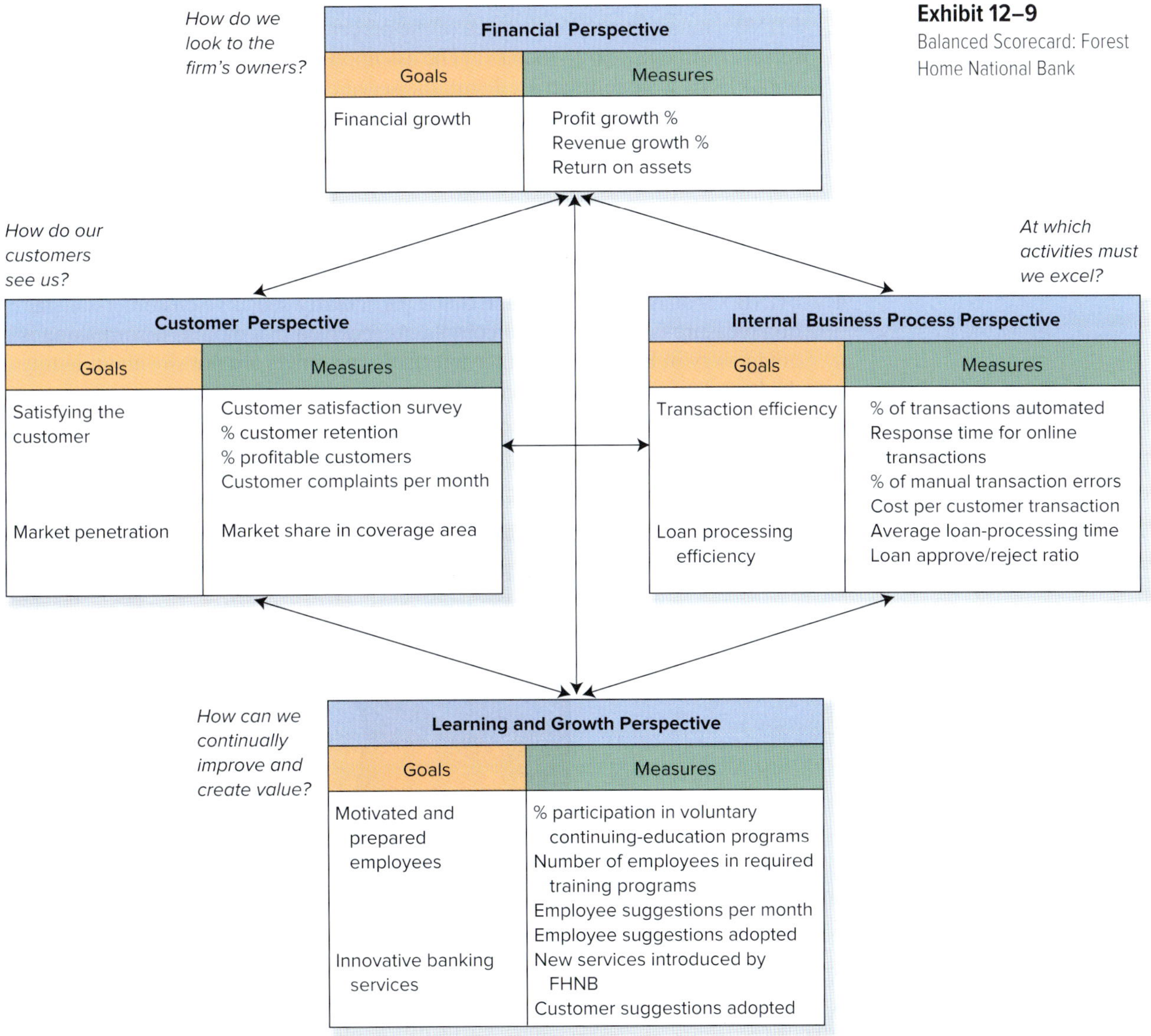

[4]Many banking institutions have developed a balanced scorecard. This balanced scorecard is an amalgamation of bank scorecards from a number of sources, including the authors' research as well as the following resources: Robert S. Kaplan and David P. Norton, *The Strategy-Focused Organization: How Balanced Scorecard Companies Thrive in the New Business Environment* (Boston: Harvard Business School Press, 2001); Norman Klein and Robert S. Kaplan, "Chemical Bank: Implementing the Balanced Scorecard," an HBS management case (Boston: President and Fellows of Harvard College, 1995); and Robert L. Simons and Antonio Davila, "Citibank: Performance Evaluation," an HBS management case (Boston: President and Fellows of Harvard College, 1997).

What is the rationale behind FHNB's balanced scorecard? The bank's overarching, *long-term* goal is financial growth. This goal will be assessed by the following financial measures: profit growth percentage, revenue growth percentage, and return on assets.

This begs the question, though, as to what FHNB should be doing right now to ensure that its long-term financial goals will be met. The bank's management has decided on several key goals that must be achieved in the near term in order for the company's long-term financial goals to be met.

"Because of the balanced scorecard, the nature of the monthly financial meetings changed from a focus on the things Pitney Bowes is doing well to the three things we need to improve, with the emphasis on an appropriate action plan." (12g)
Pitney Bowes

Let's first look at the customer perspective in the balanced scorecard. The question for FHNB's management is "How do the bank's customers see us?" Management has expressed its customer-perspective goal as "satisfying the customer." How, then, can management measure progress on this short-term, day-to-day objective? Management has chosen five measures:

1. A customer satisfaction survey is conducted annually among all the bank's customers. Moreover, a more detailed customer satisfaction survey is aimed at the bank's key customers, which account for about 20 percent of the customer base.
2. FHNB's management keeps track of the percentage of its customers that it retains from one year to the next. The assumption is that a customer who stays with FHNB is largely satisfied with the service.
3. Not all of FHNB's customers are profitable. (This is true of almost all banks.) For example, customers that keep low account balances, pay off their credit cards each month, and avoid service charges tend to be unprofitable. Therefore, the percentage of profitable customers is a very important measure. A trend in the wrong direction here would almost certainly spell trouble for the company's financial goals in the future.
4. FHNB's management has found that a particularly sensitive customer-satisfaction measure is the number of complaints received in a month. If something is going awry in FHNB's customer interface, customers are not shy about letting the bank know about it—and quickly.
5. FHNB's market share in its coverage area is a key measure of market penetration. Increasing this key measure would most likely translate into revenue and profit growth in the future.

A company's balanced scorecard should measure the aspects of its performance that are most important for its success. In a retail bank, such as ***Ulster Bank*** *pictured here in Dublin, Ireland, the customer dimension of the scorecard would be likely to include measures of satisfaction that are influenced by customer-facing services such as ATM availability. In addition, the internal business processes dimension can reflect the strategic use of technological innovations such as ATMs, as we see in the Forest Home National Bank example.*

© Chuck Burton, file/AP Photo

What about Forest Home National Bank's internal operations? In what business processes must FHNB excel in order to achieve its long-term financial goals? Management has decided to focus on two important goals: completing routine bank transactions efficiently and processing loan applications efficiently. For routine bank transactions (e.g., making deposits, withdrawals, or loan payments), FHNB's management focuses on three key measures:

1. Customers can complete automated transactions in three ways. They can bank online, use an ATM, or use a touch-tone telephone to make phone-automated

inquiries. FHNB's management believes that the greater the percentage of automated transactions, as opposed to transactions involving a bank teller, the more efficient will be the bank's transaction operations.

2. Another measure of transaction efficiency is the average time that it takes a customer to complete an online transaction. The smaller this time interval is, FHNB's management believes, the more likely customers will be to use online banking.
3. For manual, teller-assisted transactions, FHNB's management keeps track of the percentage of these transactions that exhibit errors.

On the loan side of FHNB's internal operations, management tracks two measures of loan processing efficiency:

1. The average time to process a loan application is a key indicator of how smoothly this aspect of the bank's operations is running.
2. FHNB's management also believes that the higher the ratio of approved to rejected loans, the more successful the bank has been in communicating its loan criteria to the bank's customer base.

Finally, let's look at the learning and growth perspective in Forest Home National Bank's balanced scorecard. Management has highlighted two goals: motivated and prepared employees and innovative banking services. To assess the goal of motivated and prepared employees, FHNB's management has established three measures:

1. The bank's human resource management team believes that the percentage of employees participating in voluntary continuing education programs is an indicator of both employee motivation and preparation.
2. On the other hand, employee absenteeism is measured because it may indicate problems such as poor management, incorrect hiring practices, and problems with culture in a particular branch office.
3. The number of employee suggestions per month, as well as the number of those suggestions adopted, also speaks to both employee motivation and preparation. A motivated employee is more likely to submit a suggestion, and a well-prepared employee is more likely to make an adoptable suggestion.

The second goal under learning and growth on FHNB's scorecard involves innovative banking services.

1. Measuring the percent of net interest earned that was generated from banking products and services introduced by FHNB in the past five years is a way of directly measuring the success of innovation in the bank's operations. Even if a particular type of checking account is highly successful, and thus contributing well toward performance on the financial perspective of FHNB's balanced scorecard, it will not count toward this percentage measure if more than five years have passed since it was introduced. A reduction in this percentage signals a possible reduction in innovation that may threaten future financial results.
2. Long-term employees are important to most organizations, for their knowledge of company processes, relationships with customers, and increasing alignment of incentives with those of the company. Moreover, only after considerable experience with FHNB are they typically knowledgeable and confident enough to be able to make especially innovative suggestions. So FHNB measures employee turnover (percent of employees who leave in a given measurement period) as a way of making sure that employees are satisfied with the bank as a place to work.

All in all, FHNB's management team believes that if the bank meets its current goals for its customer, internal business process, and learning and growth perspectives, the bank will ultimately be successful in achieving its long-term goal of financial growth.

Management Accounting Practice

Bain & Company, UPS

THE BALANCED SCORECARD

For many companies, the balanced scorecard plays a key role in formulating strategy. According to a survey by Bain & Company, approximately 50 percent of Fortune 1000 companies in North America and roughly 40 percent in Europe use some version of the balanced scorecard (often abbreviated as BSC). Among them are both manufacturers and service industry companies.[5]

Managers at UPS believe that its balanced scorecard has played a critical strategic role in moving the organization forward. The company's scorecard was widely accepted by its employees, who felt that the BSC helped them link their jobs to the big picture of overall company success. UPS includes the following key measures in the four perspectives of its balanced scorecard.[6]

Financial
- Profit
- Revenue
- Cost
- Volume

Customer
- Customer claims (e.g., lost parcels)
- Customer concerns
- Data integrity (e.g., accuracy of the parcel tracking process)

Internal Business Process
- Quality (e.g., timeliness of delivery, care in handling parcels)
- Operations (i.e., operational efficiency)

Learning and Growth*
- Employee injuries
- Employee retention
- Employee relation index

*Referred to as "People" in the UPS scorecard.

Lead and Lag Measures: The Key to the Balanced Scorecard

Key to understanding the value and construction of the balanced scorecard is the distinction between lead and lag indicators of performance. **Lead indicators** of performance are measures of nonfinancial and financial outcomes that guide management in making current decisions that will result in desirable results in the future. In other words, lead indicators guide management to take actions *now* that will have positive effects on enterprise performance *later*. For example, Forest Home National Bank's scorecard includes the bank's market share in its coverage area as an indicator of future market growth, which will ultimately translate into growth of the bank's profitability. By including this key lead indicator in its scorecard, management is directed to take actions now that will increase the bank's market share.

Lag indicators are measures of the final outcomes of earlier management decisions. Examples of lag indicators are a company's profit and cash flow. These key financial measures, while important, only change well after management has already made the important decisions that affect key operational results. As such, lag indicators are less useful for performance management and control.

The whole idea of the balanced scorecard is to *use lead indicators to communicate with, motivate, and evaluate individuals* with the expectation that their current actions

[5]Raef Lawson, William Stratton, and Toby Hatch, "Scorecarding Goes Global," *Strategic Finance* 87, no. 9 (March 2006), pp. 35–41; and Thomas Wunder, "New Strategy Alignment in Multinational Corporations," *Strategic Finance* 87, no. 5 (November 2005), pp. 35–41.

[6]Robert S. Kaplan and David P. Norton, *The Strategy-Focused Organization: How Balanced Scorecard Companies Thrive in the New Business Environment* (Boston: Harvard Business School Press, 2001); and Bruce Stanley, "UPS Battles Traffic Jams to Gain Ground in India," *The Wall Street Journal*, January 25, 2008, p. B1.

Exhibit 12–10
Selected Performance Measures Used in Balanced Scorecards

Financial Perspective	
Earnings	Cash flow
Earnings per share	Cash flow from operations
Customer Perspective	
Customer contacts	Customer satisfaction (surveyed)
Repeat customers	Customer complaints
New customers	Market share
Internal Business Process Perspective	
Product quality/defect rates	Finished products per day per employee
Number of vendors	Floor space per finished product
Cycle time	Cost of inventories held
Throughput	Number of common parts
Machine downtime	Number of part numbers
Learning and Growth Perspective	
Employee training hours	New processes
Employee promotion rate	Employee suggestions
New products or services	Employee retention

will result in improvements in the company's important lag measures (e.g., profitability) in the future. Exhibit 12–10 shows this relationship and gives examples of several key lead and lag measures used in a variety of organizations' balanced scorecards. In addition, note that most of the operational performance measures listed in Exhibit 12–8 could be (and are) used in balanced scorecards.

Many companies, in all types of industries, have developed a balanced scorecard to help management and employees understand the important lead indicators of performance that will ultimately bring success on the company's key long-term goals. Among the many service-industry firms that have developed a balanced scorecard are Bank of America, CIGNA, Citigroup, Duke Children's Hospital & Health Center, Fannie Mae, JPMorgan Chase, Northwestern Mutual, and UPS. Retailers have made use of the balanced scorecard as well. Among them are Ann Taylor (part of Ascena Retail Group), IKEA, and Tesco.

Among the well-known manufacturers making use of the balanced score card concept are Anheuser-Busch, Apple, Caterpillar, Chrysler, ExxonMobil, General Motors, Microsoft, Motorola, Phillips Electronics, and Pfizer. Finally, governmental units also have benefited from a balanced scorecard, among them the city of Charlotte, North Carolina, the state of Washington, and the U.S. Department of Defense.

Linking the Balanced Scorecard to Organizational Strategy

A key to making successful use of the balanced scorecard is linking the scorecard's lead and lag measures to the organization's strategy. As depicted in the diagram in Exhibit 12–11, the organization's vision and strategy drive the specification of both goals and metrics in the scorecard's financial, customer, internal business process, and learning and growth perspectives.[8]

The precise form of the linkage between strategy and the goals and measures in the balanced scorecard will, of course, depend on the nature of the organization and its strategy. However, the linkage can be visualized as a *chain of cause and effect* between the company's scorecard elements and its strategy and goals. The chain of cause and effect occurs because an important change may not directly result in the company's reaching its

> "Defining our [balanced scorecard] measures, aligning our initiatives, and providing greater visibility into our performance objectives has enabled us to make better management decisions for our future growth." (12h)
>
> **Columbia Sportswear**

[7]Robert S. Kaplan and David P. Norton, *The Strategy-Focused Organization: How Balanced Scorecard Companies Thrive in the New Business Environment* (Boston: Harvard Business School Press, 2001).

[8]Robert S. Kaplan and David P. Norton, *The Strategy-Focused Organization: How Balanced Scorecard Companies Thrive in the New Business Environment* (Boston: Harvard Business School Press, 2001). See also Raef Lawson, William Stratton, and Toby Hatch, "Scorecarding Goes Global," *Strategic Finance* 87, no. 9 (March 2006), pp. 35–41.

Exhibit 12–11
Linkage between the Balanced Scorecard and Organizational Strategy

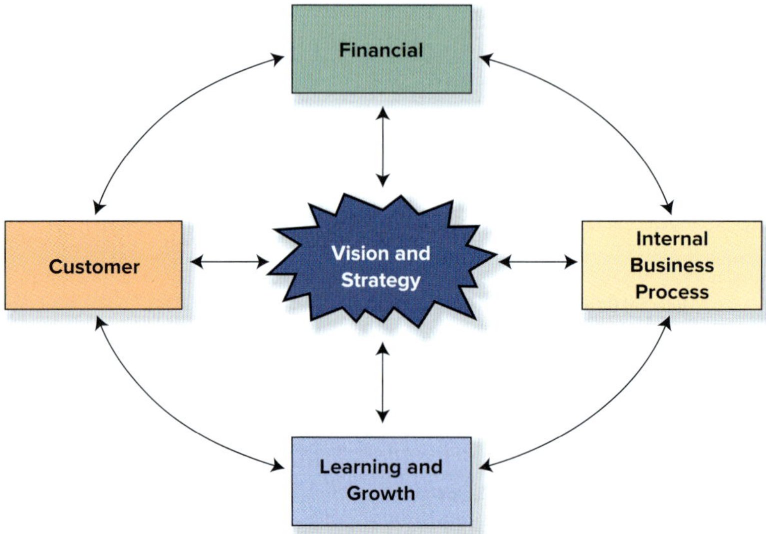

strategic goal. Instead, that change may be necessary before another type of organizational change can occur. And the second change may be the one that leads to the strategic goal.[9]

Using the balanced scorecard model, we can define the chain of cause and effect by following the sequence of lead or lag relationships in the scorecard's measures. For example, Sears once confronted challenges to its strategic profitability goals by constructing a balanced scorecard to measure the links between employee training and profits. The path to the profitability goal flowed through a chain of cause and effect: an increase in employee training hours (learning and growth) led to an increase in service quality (internal business process), which led in turn to increased repeat customers (customer) which finally led to the strategic goal of profitability (financial).[10] Notice that the learning and growth measure of increased employee training did not lead directly to increased profits: training so many employees cost a lot of money, so its direct effect was actually to reduce profits! But through the chain of cause and effect it eventually helped the company achieve its strategic profitability goals.

The following case in point explores this linkage for Amazon, which is arguably one of the most successful companies of our time.

Management Accounting Practice
Amazon

LINKING THE BALANCED SCORECARD TO ORGANIZATIONAL STRATEGY

One key to successfully using the balanced scorecard is linking the scorecard's lead and lag measures to the organization's strategy. According to the **Amazon**, website, the company's strategy is "to be Earth's most customer-centric company; to build a place where people can come to find and discover anything they might want to buy online."[11]

Leaving aside the issue of whether there might be a more customer-centric company on another planet elsewhere in the universe, Amazon's strategy of providing unparalleled customer service via its online-only sales model drives the company's efforts in each of the perspectives that comprise a balanced scorecard.

(continues)

[9]This material is based on Peter Brewer, "Putting Strategy into the Balanced Scorecard," *Strategic Finance* 83, no. 7 (January 2002), pp. 44–52. Further development is found in Wilhelm Schmeisser et al, "5: Balanced Scorecard as an Indicator System," *Controlling and Berlin Balanced Scorecard Approach* (Munich: Oldenberg Verlag, 2011) pp. 68–94.
[10]Anthony J. Rucci, Steven P. Kirn, and Richard T. Quinn, "The Employee-Customer-Profit Chain at Sears," *Harvard Business Review*, January–February 1998, pp. 82–97.
[11]This example is derived from Amazon.com's mission and strategy. For more information, refer to the Investor Relations section of the Amazon.com website at http://www.amazon.com/ir.

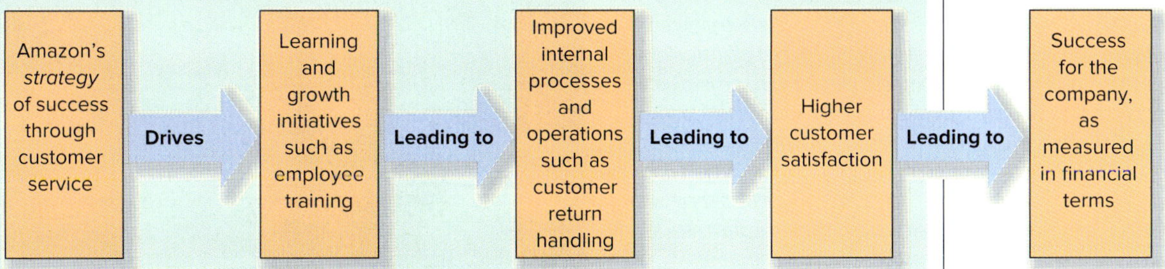

The following selected balanced scorecard measures are among those that would be relevant for Amazon to successfully implement its strategy. Notice the frequency of the word "customer" in these measures. Amazon strategy and the relevant balanced scorecard measures are dominated by its customer-focused online sales business model.

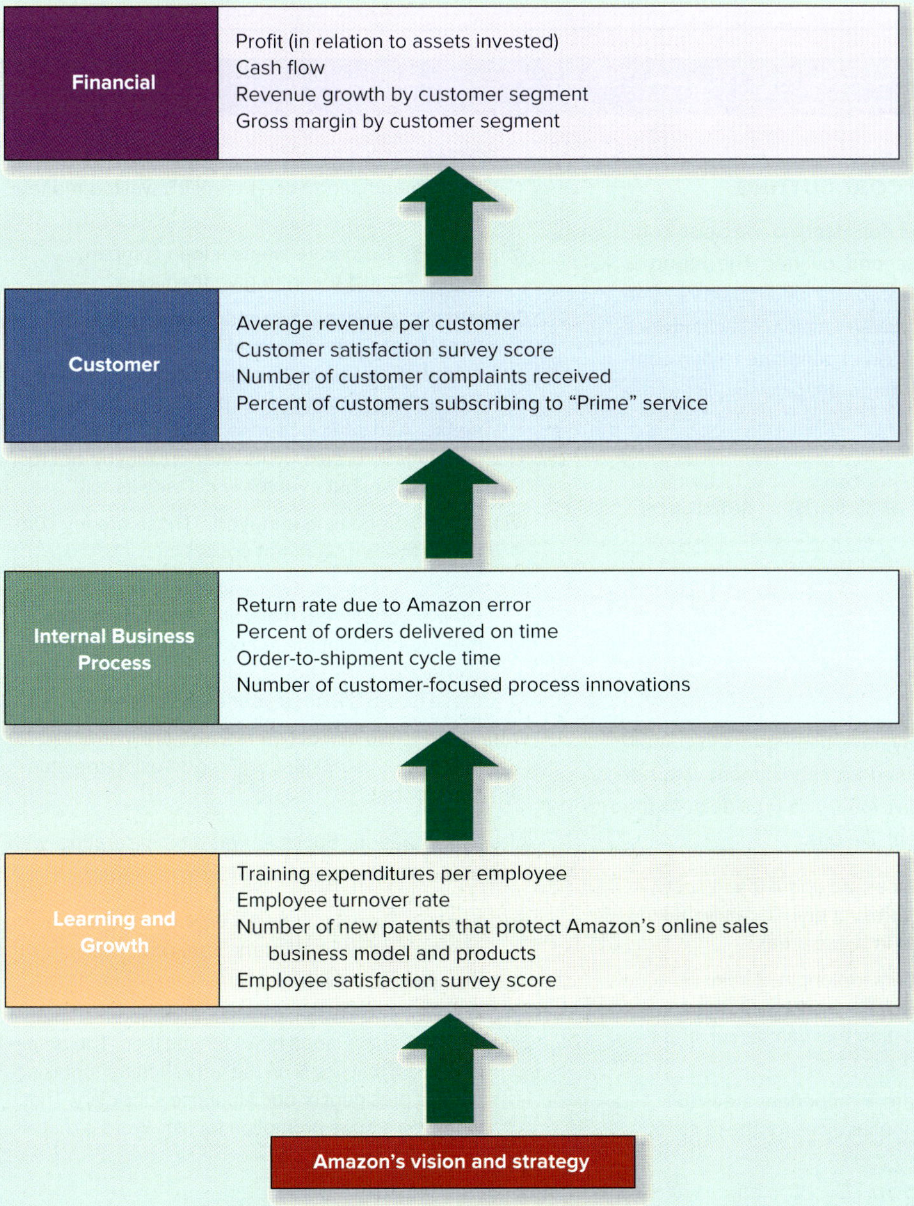

Rockwater, owned by Halliburton, is a global undersea oil services company headquartered in Aberdeen, Scotland. Doing the undersea engineering and construction for drilling rigs such as the one pictured here requires diverse technical operations, both on- and offshore. Rockwater's management found the balanced scorecard to be an invaluable tool in clarifying the company's goals and communicating them to the employees. Among the measures in Rockwater's balanced scorecard are the following: cash flow and project profitability (financial); project pricing and customer satisfaction (customer); safety index and hours spent with customers on new work (internal); percentage of revenue from new services and number of employee suggestions (learning and growth).[7]

Focus on Ethics

SHORT-SIGHTED VIEW OF COST CUTTING

Jamie Ericsson, the controller for Handico, has just compiled a cost report for the second quarter. The report is prepared each quarter for corporate headquarters. She has taken particular notice of several major cost categories that show significant reductions in expenditures when compared to the first quarter. She made the following list of the major cost cuts:

Cost Item	Cost Reduction ($)	Cost Reduction (%)
General employee training	$12,000	25%
Routine machine maintenance	13,500	20
Process improvement	12,000	12
Quality training	18,000	8
Raw-material inspection	6,500	9

Concerned that there may have been errors in compiling the data, Ericsson scheduled an appointment with her supervisor, Les Winters, the divisional vice president. At the meeting, the conversation went like this.

Ericsson (C): "Les, I'm concerned about these cost cuts. Are these mistakes, or are we really making such substantial cuts in these areas?"

Winters (VP): "Your numbers look right, Jamie. I ordered these cutbacks myself. I think there's a lot of fat in this operation that can be cut, and I'm just getting started."

Ericsson (C): "But these are all important areas to invest in, Les. I see the invoices for these costs every month, and I don't think it's wasted money at all."

Winters (VP): "Corporate wants a lean company, Jamie. I'm just trying to give them one."

Ericsson (C): "Have you thought through the implications, Les? Cutting general employee training will eventually take a toll on our productivity gains. Same thing for the cuts in process improvements. And cutting routine machine maintenance could mean breakdowns later on. Maybe not for a year or so, but eventually it'll take its toll."

Winters (VP): Becoming annoyed, "Those are my concerns, Ms. Ericsson, not yours."

Ericsson (C): "Look, Les, we're all on the same team. I'm just concerned, that's all. I feel as though I need to highlight these cost cuts in my report to corporate. They should at least be made aware of these issues. I'll need your authorization for that."

Winters (VP): "No can do, Jamie. You are instructed to make your usual quarterly report using the standard format."

After the meeting, Ericsson was commiserating with her close friend, Amy Ling, the chief of engineering.

Ericsson (C): "Amy, I just had a very unsatisfactory meeting with Les Winters. I shouldn't go into the details, but I'm concerned about some things."

Ling (E): "Well, I have good news for you then. The grapevine has it that Les is on the very short list for taking over as president of our Japanese subsidiary. That would be a huge promotion for him. Word is that all he's got to do is turn in a good performance for the year here. If he does that, the job's his."

Ericsson (C): "That explains a lot, Amy. Thanks for the heads up. I've got some thinking to do."

What do you think is going on here? What is the VP, Les Winters, up to? Is he acting ethically? What steps should the controller, Jamie Ericsson, take? (Refer to the "Resolution of Ethical Conflict" section of the **IMA Statement of Ethical Professional Practice**, printed at the end of Chapter 1.) How could a balanced scorecard help mitigate the problems apparent in this scenario?

Chapter Summary

LO12-1 Explain the role of responsibility accounting in fostering goal congruence. Responsibility-accounting systems are designed to foster goal congruence among the managers in decentralized organizations by specifying the performance measures upon which managers of various organizational subunits will be evaluated.

LO12-2 Define and give an example of a cost center, a revenue center, a profit center, and an investment center. A cost center is an organizational subunit, the manager of which is held accountable for the subunit's costs. Examples include the assembly department of an auto manufacturer and the maintenance department of a hotel. A revenue center is an organizational subunit, the manager of which is held accountable for the subunit's revenue. Examples include the sales departments of a cruise line or an insurance company. A profit center is an organizational subunit, the manager of which is held accountable for the subunit's profit. Examples include an individual branch bank or an individual fast food restaurant. An investment center is an organizational subunit, the manager of which is held accountable for the relationship between the subunit's profit and its invested capital. A division of a large corporation (manufacturing, service, or retail) is usually designated as an investment center.

LO12-3 Prepare a performance report and explain the relationships between the performance reports for various responsibility centers. The performance of each of an organization's responsibility accounting centers is summarized periodically on a performance report. This report shows the budgeted and actual performance results for a specified time period for each responsibility accounting center.

LO12-4 Use a cost allocation base to allocate costs. A cost allocation base is a measure of activity, physical characteristic, or economic characteristic associated with a group of organizational subunits or activities, which is the basis for allocating costs among those subunits or activities.

LO12-5 Prepare a segmented income statement. Segmented income statements often are included in a responsibility-accounting system to show the performance of the organization and its various segments. To be most effective, such reports should distinguish between the performance of segments and segment managers.

LO12-6 Describe the operational performance measures appropriate for today's production environment. Nonfinancial measures of operational performance are widely used to augment the control information provided by the accounting system. These measures typically focus on raw material and scrap, inventory, machinery, product and service quality, production and delivery, productivity, and innovation and learning.

LO12-7 Describe the balanced scorecard concept and explain the reasoning behind it. The balanced scorecard is an important tool designed to focus management's attention on key current goals which, if achieved, will facilitate the attainment of the organization's long-term goals. By achieving current goals in the customer, internal business process, and learning and growth perspectives, the company will ultimately achieve its long-term financial goals.

Review Problems on Responsibility Accounting and Operational Performance Measures

Problem 1

James Madison National Bank has a division for each of the two counties in which it operates, Cayuga and Oneida. Each divisional vice president is held accountable for both profit and invested capital. Each division consists of two branch banks, East and West. Each branch manager is responsible for that bank's profit. The Cayuga Division's East Branch has a Deposit Department, a Loan Department, and an Administrative Services Department. The department supervisors of the Loan and Deposit Departments are accountable for departmental revenues; the Administrative Services Department supervisor is accountable for costs.

All of James Madison National Bank's advertising and promotion is done centrally. The advertising and promotion cost pool for the year just ended, which amounted to $40,000, is allocated across the four branch banks on the basis of budgeted branch revenue. Budgeted revenue for the year is shown below.

Cayuga Division:	West Branch	$400,000
	East Branch	200,000
Oneida Division:	West Branch	250,000
	East Branch	150,000

Required:

1. Draw an organization chart for James Madison National Bank that shows each subunit described above, its manager's title, and its designation as a responsibility center.
2. Distribute (allocate) the bank's advertising cost pool to the four branch banks.

Problem 2

Tuscarora Door Company manufactures high-quality wooden doors used in home construction. The following information pertains to operations during April. (Times are average per batch.)

Waiting time before production begins	24 hours
Processing time	6 hours
Inspection time	1 hour
Waiting time after production begins	4 hours
Move time	5 hours
Units per batch	40 units

Compute the following operational measures: (1) average value-added time per batch; (2) average non-value-added time per batch; (3) manufacturing cycle efficiency; (4) manufacturing cycle time; (5) velocity.

Solutions to Review Problems

Problem 1

1. Organization chart (subunits, managers, responsibility center designation) is shown below.

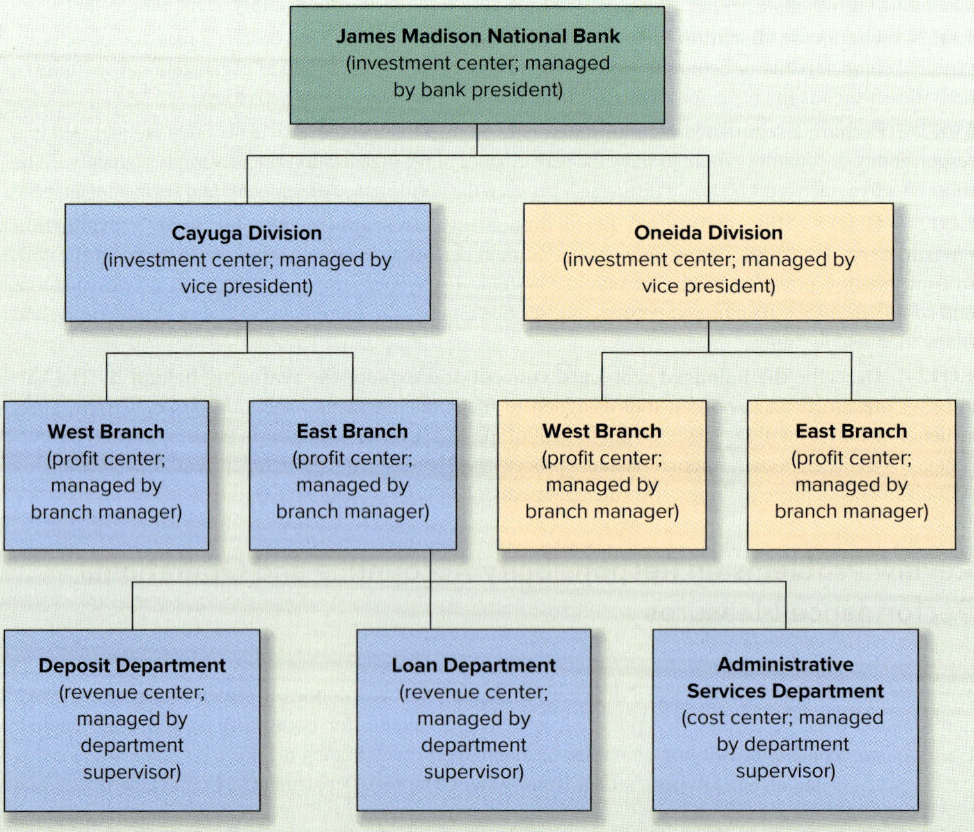

2. Cost distribution (or allocation):

Cost Pool	Responsibility Center	Allocation Base: Revenue	Percentage of Total*	Costs Distributed
Advertising	Cayuga, West Branch	$ 400,000	40%	$16,000
and	Cayuga, East Branch	200,000	20	8,000
promotion	Oneida, West Branch	250,000	25	10,000
costs	Oneida, East Branch	150,000	15	6,000
	Total	$1,000,000	100%	$40,000

*Branch revenue as a percentage of total revenue, $1,000,000.

Problem 2

1. Average value-added time per batch = Processing time = 6 hours

2. Average non-value-added time per batch = Inspection time + Waiting time (total) + Move time
$$= 1 + (4 + 24) + 5 \text{ hours} = 34 \text{ hours}$$

3.
$$\text{Manufacturing cycle efficiency} = \frac{\text{Processing time}}{\text{Processing time} + \text{Inspection time} + \text{Waiting time after production begins} + \text{Move time}}$$
$$= \frac{6 \text{ hours}}{6 + 1 + 4 + 5 \text{ hours}} = 37.5\%$$

4.
$$\text{Manufacturing cycle time} = \frac{\text{Total production time per batch}}{\text{Units per batch}}$$
$$= \frac{16 \text{ hours}}{40 \text{ units per batch}} = .4 \text{ hour (or 24 minutes) per unit}$$

5.
$$\text{Velocity} = \frac{\text{Units per batch}}{\text{Total production time per batch}}$$
$$= \frac{40 \text{ units}}{16 \text{ hours}} = 2.5 \text{ units per hour}$$

Key Terms

For each term's definition refer to the indicated page, or turn to the glossary at the end of the text.

activity-based responsibility accounting, 518
aggregate (total) productivity, 524
allocation base, 516
balanced scorecard, 525
benchmarking, 524
common costs, 519
cost allocation (or cost distribution), 516
cost center, 510
cost objects, 516
cost pool, 516
customer acceptance measures, 523
customer profitability analysis, 521
delivery cycle time, 523
gain-sharing plan, 524
goal congruence, 510
in-process quality controls, 523
investment center, 511
lag indicators, 528
lead indicators, 528
manufacturing cycle efficiency (MCE), 524
manufacturing cycle time, 523
partial (component) productivity, 524
performance report, 514
profit center, 510
responsibility accounting, 510
responsibility center, 510
revenue center, 510
segmented income statement, 519
theory of constraints (TOC), 523
velocity, 523

Review Questions

12–1. Why is goal congruence important to an organization's success? How does a responsibility-accounting system foster goal congruence?

12–2. Define and give examples of the following terms: *cost center, revenue center, profit center,* and *investment center.*

12–3. Under what circumstances would it be appropriate to change the Waikiki Sands Hotel from a profit center to an investment center?

12–4. Explain the relationship between performance reports and flexible budgeting.

12–5. What is the key feature of activity-based responsibility accounting? Briefly explain.

12–6. Explain how to get positive behavioral effects from a responsibility-accounting system.

12–7. "Performance reports based on controllability are impossible. Nobody really *controls* anything in an organization!" Do you agree or disagree? Explain your answer.

12–8. Define and give examples of the following terms: *cost pool, cost object,* and *cost allocation* (or *distribution*).

12–9. Give an example of a common resource in an organization. List some of the opportunity costs associated with using the resource. Why might allocation of the cost of the common resource to its users be useful?

12–10. Explain how and why cost allocation might be used to assign the costs of a mainframe computer system used for research purposes in a university.

12–11. Define the term *cost allocation base.* What would be a sensible allocation base for assigning advertising costs to the various components of a large theme park?

12–12. Referring to Exhibit 12–5, why are marketing costs distributed to the Waikiki Sands Hotel's departments on the basis of *budgeted* sales dollars?

12–13. Explain what is meant by a *segmented income statement.*

12–14. Why do some managers and accountants choose not to allocate common costs in segmented reports?

12–15. Why is it important in responsibility accounting to distinguish between segments and segment managers?

12–16. List and explain three key features of the segmented income statement shown in Exhibit 12–7.

12–17. Can a common cost for one segment be a traceable cost for another segment? Explain your answer.

12–18. What is meant by *customer profitability analysis?* Give an example of an activity that might be performed more commonly for one customer than for another.

12–19. List seven areas in which nonfinancial, operational performance measures are receiving increased emphasis in today's manufacturing environment.

12–20. Define the term *manufacturing cycle efficiency.*

12–21. List four examples of customer acceptance measures.

12–22. What is meant by *aggregate productivity,* and what are its limitations?

12–23. Give an example of a gain sharing plan that could be implemented by an airline.

12–24. Using the Internet, identify the organizational strategy for a company of your choosing and suggest two performance measures in each of the four balanced scorecard categories.

12–25. Using the measures selected in question 12–24, explain the difference between lead and lag measures.

12–26. Explain how an improvement in employee retention (a Learning and Growth measure) could flow through each of the balanced scorecard perspectives to result in improved financial performance.

Exercises

All applicable Exercises are available in Connect. connect

Exercise 12–27
Designating Responsibility Centers
(LO 12-2)

For each of the following organizational subunits, indicate the type of responsibility center that is most appropriate.

1. A movie theater in a company that operates a chain of theaters.
2. A radio station owned by a large broadcasting network.
3. The claims department in an insurance company.
4. The ticket sales division of a major airline.
5. A bottling plant of a soft drink company.
6. An orange juice factory operated by a large orange grower.
7. The College of Engineering at a large state university.
8. The European Division of a multinational manufacturing company.
9. The outpatient clinic in a for-profit hospital.
10. The Mayor's Office in a large city.

Exercise 12–28
Responsibility Accounting; Equipment Breakdown
(LO 12-1, 12-2)

How should a responsibility-accounting system handle each of the following scenarios?

1. Department A manufactures a component, which is then used by Department B. Department A recently experienced a machine breakdown that held up production of the component. As a result, Department B was forced to curtail its own production, thereby incurring large costs of idle time. An investigation revealed that Department A's machinery had not been properly maintained.
2. Refer to the scenario above, but suppose the investigation revealed the machinery in Department A had been properly maintained.

Exercise 12–29
Assigning Responsibility for Skilled Employees' Wages
(LO 12-1)

Saddle River Electronics Company manufactures complex circuit boards for the aerospace industry. Demand for the company's products has fallen in recent months, and the firm has cut its production significantly. Many unskilled workers have been temporarily laid off. Top management has made a decision, however, not to lay off any highly skilled employees, such as inspectors and machinery operators. Management was concerned that these highly skilled employees would easily find new jobs elsewhere and not return when production returned to normal levels.

To occupy the skilled employees during the production cutback, they have been reassigned temporarily to the Maintenance Department. Here they are performing general maintenance tasks, such as repainting the interior of the factory, repairing the loading dock, and building wooden storage racks for the warehouse. The skilled employees continued to receive their normal wages, which average $22 per hour. However, the normal wages for Maintenance Department employees average $12 per hour.

The supervisor of the Maintenance Department recently received the March performance report, which indicated that his department's labor cost exceeded the budget by $19,360. The department's actual labor cost was approximately 90 percent over the budget. The department supervisor complained to the controller.

Required: As the controller, how would you respond? Would you make any modification in Saddle River's responsibility-accounting system? If so, list the changes you would make. Explain your reasoning.

Exercise 12–30
Responsibility-Accounting Centers; Xerox Corporation
(LO 12-1, 12-2)

Xerox Corporation has been an innovator in its responsibility-accounting system. In one initiative, management changed the responsibility-center orientation of its Logistics and Distribution Department from a cost center to a profit center. The department manages the inventories and provides other logistical services to the company's Business Systems Group. Formerly, the manager of the Logistics and Distribution Department was held accountable for adherence to an operating expense budget. Now the department "sells" its services to the company's other segments, and the department's manager is evaluated partially on the basis of the department's profit. Xerox Corporation's management feels that the change has been beneficial. The change has resulted in more innovative thinking in the department and has moved decision making down to lower levels in the company.

Required: Comment on the new responsibility-center designation for the Logistics and Distribution Department.

Exercise 12–31
Performance Report; Hotel
(LO 12-3)

The following data pertain to the Waikiki Sands Hotel for the month of March.

	Flexible Budget March (in thousands)*	Actual Results March (in thousands)*
Banquets and Catering	$ 650	$ 658
Restaurants	1,800	1,794
Kitchen staff wages	(85)	(86)
Food	(690)	(690)
Paper products	(125)	(122)
Variable overhead	(75)	(78)
Fixed overhead	(90)	(93)

*Numbers without parentheses denote profit; numbers with parentheses denote expenses.

Required: Prepare a March performance report similar to the lower portion of Exhibit 12–4. The report should have six numerical columns with headings analogous to those in Exhibit 12–4. Your performance report should cover only the Food and Beverage Department and the Kitchen. Draw arrows to show the relationships between the numbers in the report. Refer to Exhibit 12–4 for guidance. For the year-to-date columns in your report, use the data given in Exhibit 12–4. You will need to update those figures using the March data given above.

Exercise 12–32
Cost Allocation in a College
(LO 12-4)

Lackawanna Community College has three divisions: Liberal Arts, Sciences, and Business Administration. The college's comptroller is trying to decide how to allocate the costs of the Admissions Department, the Registrar's Department, and the Computer Services Department. The comptroller has compiled the following data for the year just ended.

Department	Annual Cost
Admissions	$ 90,000
Registrar	150,000
Computer Services	320,000

Division	Budgeted Enrollment	Budgeted Credit Hours	Planned Courses Requiring Computer Work
Liberal Arts	1,000	30,000	12
Sciences	800	28,000	24
Business Administration	700	22,000	24

Required:

1. For each department, choose an allocation base and distribute the departmental costs to the college's three divisions. Justify your choice of an allocation base.
2. Would you have preferred a different allocation base than those available using the data compiled by the comptroller? Why?
3. ***Build a spreadsheet:*** Construct an Excel spreadsheet to solve requirement (1) above. Show how the solution will change if the following information changes: the costs incurred by the departments were $120,000, $160,000, and $360,000, for Admissions, Registrar, and Computer Services, respectively.

Exercise 12–33
Segmented Income Statement; TV Cable Company
(LO 12-5)

Countywide Cable Services, Inc. is organized with three segments: Metro, Suburban, and Outlying. Data for these segments for the year just ended follow.

	Metro	Suburban	Outlying
Service revenue	$1,000,000	$800,000	$400,000
Variable expenses	200,000	150,000	100,000
Controllable fixed expenses	400,000	320,000	150,000
Fixed expenses controllable by others	230,000	200,000	90,000

In addition to the expenses listed above, the company has $95,000 of common fixed expenses. Income-tax expense for the year is $145,000.

Required:

1. Prepare a segmented income statement for Countywide Cable Services, Inc. Use the contribution format.
2. ***Build a spreadsheet:*** Construct an Excel spreadsheet to solve the preceding requirement. Show how the solution will change if the following information changes: the sales revenues were $950,000 and $815,000 for Metro and Suburban, respectively.

Exercise 12–34
Responsibility Accounting; Use of Internet
(LO 12-1, 12-2)

Visit the website for one of the following companies, or a different company of your choosing.

Marriott	www.marriott.com	Yum Brands	www.yum.com
McDonald's	www.mcdonalds.com	Wyndham Hotels	www.wyndhamworldwide.com
Bank of America	www.bankofamerica.com	Xerox	www.xerox.com

Required: Read about the company's activities and operations. Then do as good a job as you can in preparing an organization chart for the firm. For each subunit in the organization chart, indicate what type of responsibility accounting center designation you believe would be most appropriate. (Refer to Exhibits 12–1 and 12–2 for guidance.)

Exercise 12–35
Operational Performance Measures; JIT/FMS Setting
(LO 12-6)

Hiawatha Hydrant Company manufactures fire hydrants in Oswego, New York. The following information pertains to operations during May.

Processing time (average per batch)	8.5 hours
Inspection time (average per batch)	.5 hour
Waiting time (average per batch)	.5 hour
Move time (average per batch)	.5 hour
Units per batch	20 units

Required: Compute the following operational measures: (1) manufacturing cycle efficiency; (2) manufacturing cycle time; (3) velocity.

Exercise 12–36
Performance Measures for Production and Delivery
(LO 12-6)

Data Screen Corporation is a highly automated manufacturing firm. The vice president of finance has decided that traditional standards are inappropriate for performance measures in an automated environment. Labor is insignificant in terms of the total cost of production and tends to be fixed, material quality is considered more important than minimizing material cost, and customer satisfaction is the number one priority. As a result, production and delivery performance measures have been chosen to evaluate performance. The following information is considered typical of the time involved to complete and ship orders.

Waiting time:	
From order being placed to start of production	8.0 days
From start of production to completion	7.0 days
Inspection time	1.5 days
Processing time	3.0 days
Move time	2.5 days

Required:

1. Calculate the manufacturing cycle efficiency.
2. Calculate the delivery cycle time.

(CMA, adapted)

Exercise 12–37
Productivity Measurement
(LO 12-6)

Managerial accounting procedures developed for the manufacturing industry often are applied in non-manufacturing settings also. Ontario Bank and Trust Company's total output of financial services during the year just ended was valued at $10 million. The total cost of the firm's inputs, primarily direct labor and overhead, was $8 million.

Required:

1. Compute Ontario's aggregate (or total) productivity for the year.
2. Do you believe this is a useful measure? Why? Suggest an alternative approach that Ontario Bank and Trust might use to measure productivity.

Exercise 12–38
Balanced Scorecard; NGO
(LO 12-7)

Think carefully about the overall mission and goals of a non-governmental organization (NGO), such as Doctors Without Borders or The Nature Conservancy.

Required:

1. How does the task of building a balanced scorecard for an NGO differ from that for a profit-seeking enterprise?
2. Choose an NGO that interests you and design a simple balanced scorecard for them, with a minimum of two measures in each of the scorecard's perspectives.

Problems

All applicable Problems are available in Connect. connect

Problem 12–39
Create an Organization
(LO 12-1, 12-2)

Here is your chance to be a tycoon. Create your own company. You will be the president and chief executive officer. It could be a manufacturer, retailer, or service industry firm, but *not* a hotel or bank. Draw an organization chart for your company, similar to the one in Exhibit 12–1. Identify divisions and departments at all levels in the organization. Then prepare a companion chart similar to the one in Exhibit 12–2. This chart should designate the title of the manager of a subunit at each level in the organization. It also should designate the type of responsibility center appropriate for each of these subunits. Finally, write a letter to your company's stockholders summarizing the major responsibilities of each of the managers you identified in your chart. For guidance, refer to the discussion of Exhibits 12–1 and 12–2 in the chapter. (Have some fun, and be creative.)

Problem 12–40
Design Performance Reports; Continuation of Preceding Problem
(LO 12-3)

After designing your company, design a set of performance reports for the subunits you identified in your chart. Make up numbers for the performance reports, and show the relationship between the reports. Refer to Exhibit 12–4 for guidance.

Problem 12–41
Designating Responsibility Centers; Hotel
(LO 12-2)

The following partial organization chart is an extension of Exhibit 12–1 for Aloha Hotels and Resorts.

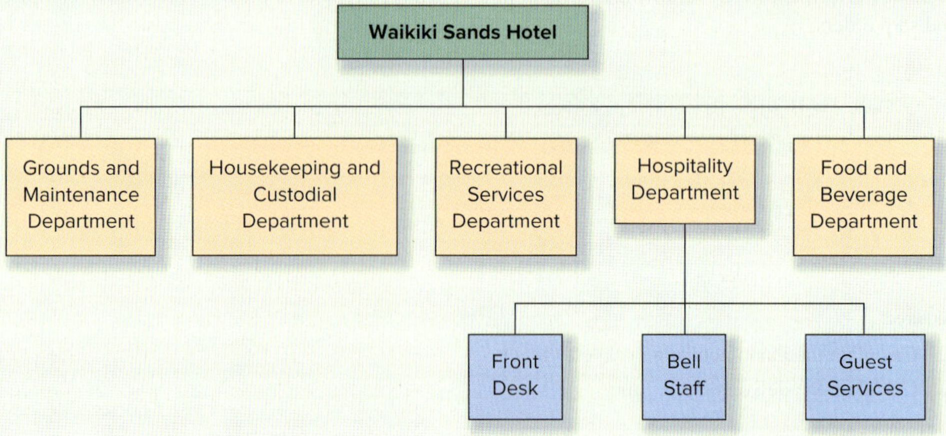

Each of the hotel's five main departments is managed by a director (e.g., director of hospitality). The Front Desk subunit, which is supervised by the front desk manager, handles the hotel's reservations, room assignments, guest payments, and key control. The Bell Staff, managed by the bell captain, is responsible for greeting guests, front door service, assisting guests with their luggage, and delivering room-service orders. The Guest Services subunit, supervised by the manager of Guest Services, is responsible for assisting guests with local transportation arrangements, advising guests on tourist attractions, and such conveniences as valet and floral services.

Required: As an outside consultant, write a memo to the hotel's general manager suggesting a responsibility-center designation for each of the subunits shown in the organization chart above. Justify your choices.

Problem 12–42
Preparation of Performance Reports; Hospital
(LO 12-3)

1. Rocky Mountain General Hospital, total cost, flexible budget, August: $582,700

Rocky Mountain General Hospital serves three counties in Colorado. The hospital is a nonprofit organization that is supported by patient billings, county and state funds, and private donations. The hospital's organization is shown in the following chart.

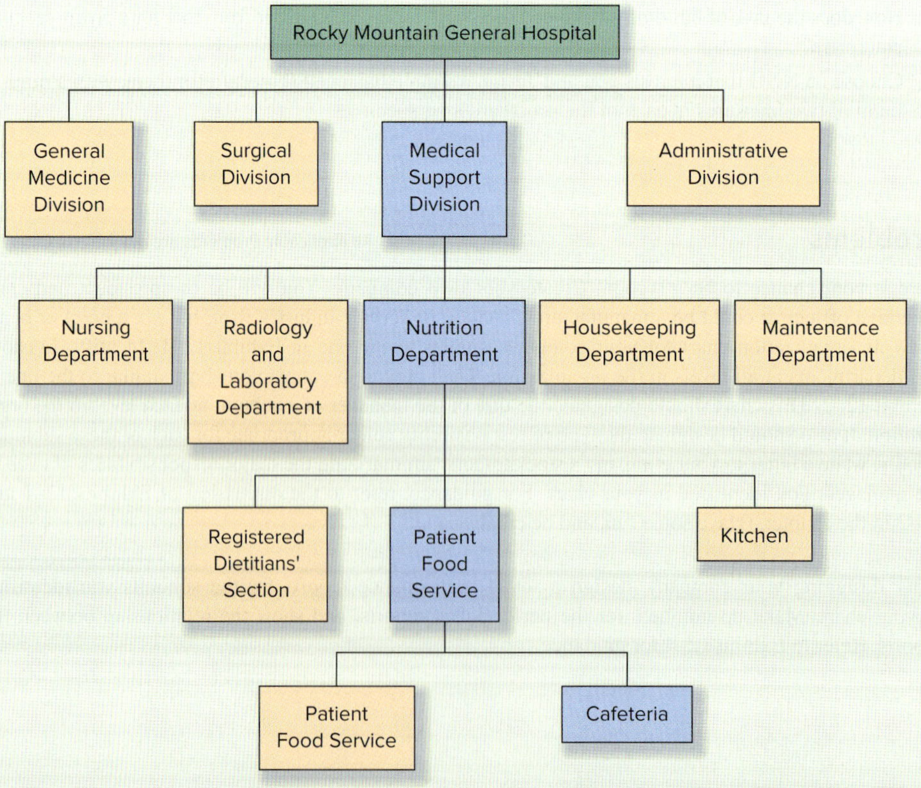

The following cost information has been compiled for August.

	Budget		Actual	
	August	**Year to Date**	**August**	**Year to Date**
Cafeteria:				
Food servers' wages	$ 8,000	$ 64,000	$ 9,000	$ 72,000
Paper products	4,500	36,000	4,400	36,200
Utilities	1,000	8,000	1,050	8,100
Maintenance	400	3,200	100	1,100
Custodial	1,100	8,800	1,100	8,600
Supplies	1,200	9,600	900	9,600
Patient Food Service	17,000	136,000	18,500	137,000
Registered Dietitians' Section	7,500	60,000	7,500	60,000
Kitchen	31,000	248,000	29,400	246,000
Nursing Department	70,000	560,000	75,000	580,000
Radiology and Laboratory Department	18,000	144,000	18,100	144,000
Housekeeping Department	10,000	80,000	11,600	86,000
Maintenance Department	13,000	104,000	6,000	77,000
General Medicine Division	210,000	1,680,000	204,000	1,670,900
Surgical Division	140,000	1,120,000	141,000	1,115,800
Administrative Division	50,000	400,000	53,500	406,000

Required:

1. Prepare a set of cost performance reports similar to Exhibit 12–4. The report should have six columns, as in Exhibit 12–4. The first four columns will have the same headings as those used above. The last two columns will have the following headings: Variance—August, Variance—Year to Date.

Since all of the information in the performance reports for Rocky Mountain General Hospital is cost information, you do not need to show these data in parentheses. Use F or U to denote whether each variance in the reports is favorable or unfavorable.

2. Using arrows, show the relationships between the numbers in your performance reports for Rocky Mountain General Hospital. Refer to Exhibit 12–4 for guidance.

3. Put yourself in the place of the hospital's administrator. Which August variances in the performance reports would you want to investigate further? Why?

Problem 12–43
Cost Distribution Using Allocation Bases; Hospital
(LO 12-4)

Facilities, General Medicine: $71,250

Refer to the organization chart for Rocky Mountain General Hospital given in the preceding problem. Ignore the rest of the data in that problem. The following table shows the cost allocation bases used to distribute various costs among the hospital's divisions.

Cost Pool	Cost Allocation Base	Annual Cost
Facilities:	Square feet of space	$190,000
Building depreciation		
Equipment depreciation		
Insurance		
Utilities:	Cubic feet of space	24,000
Electricity		
Waste disposal		
Water and sewer		
Cable TV and phone		
Heat		
General administration:	Budgeted number of employees	220,000
Administrator		
Administrative staff		
Office supplies		
Community outreach:	Budgeted dollars of patient billings	40,000
Public education		
School physical exams		

Shown below are the amounts of each cost allocation base associated with each division.

	Square Feet	Cubic Feet	Number of Employees	Patient Billings
General Medicine Division	15,000	135,000	30	$2,000,000
Surgical Division	8,000	100,000	20	1,250,000
Medical Support Division	9,000	90,000	20	750,000
Administrative Division	8,000	75,000	30	0
Total	40,000	400,000	100	$4,000,000

Required:

1. Prepare a table similar to Exhibit 12–5 that distributes each of the costs listed in the preceding table to the hospital's divisions.
2. Comment on the appropriateness of patient billings as the basis for distributing community outreach costs to the hospital's divisions. Can you suggest a better allocation base?
3. Is there any use in allocating utilities costs to the divisions? What purposes could such an allocation process serve?
4. ***Build a spreadsheet:*** Construct an Excel spreadsheet to solve requirement (1) above. Show how the solution will change if the following information changes: the costs incurred were $200,000, $25,000, $200,000, and $50,000, for facilities, utilities, general administration, and community outreach, respectively.

Problem 12–44
Segmented Income Statement; Responsibility Accounting
(LO 12-3, 12-5)

1. Segment profit margin, Las Vegas: $161,560

Show-Off, Inc. sells merchandise through three retail outlets—in Las Vegas, Reno, and Sacramento—and operates a general corporate headquarters in Reno. A review of the company's income statement indicates a record year in terms of sales and profits. Management, though, desires additional insights about the individual stores and has asked that Judson Wyatt, a newly hired intern, prepare a segmented income statement. The following information has been extracted from Show-Off's accounting records:

- The sales volume, sales price, and purchase price data follow:

	Las Vegas	Reno	Sacramento
Sales volume	37,000 units	41,000 units	46,000 units
Unit selling price	$12.00	$11.00	$9.50
Unit purchase price	5.50	5.50	6.00

- The following expenses were incurred for sales commissions, local advertising, property taxes, management salaries, and other noncontrollable (but traceable) costs:

	Las Vegas	Reno	Sacramento
Sales commissions	6%	6%	6%
Local advertising	$11,000	$22,000	$48,000
Local property taxes	4,500	2,000	6,000
Sales manager salary	—	—	32,000
Store manager salaries	31,000	39,000	38,000
Other noncontrollable costs	5,800	4,600	17,800

Local advertising decisions are made at the store manager level. The sales manager's salary in Sacramento is determined by the Sacramento store manager; in contrast, store manager salaries are set by Show-Off's vice president.

- Nontraceable fixed corporate expenses total $192,300.
- The company uses a responsibility accounting system.

Required:

1. Assume the role of Judson Wyatt and prepare a segmented income statement for Show-Off.
2. Determine the weakest-performing store and present an analysis of the probable causes of poor performance.

3. Assume that an opening has arisen at the Reno corporate headquarters and the company's chief executive officer (CEO) desires to promote one of the three existing store managers. In evaluating the store managers' performance, should the CEO use a store's segment contribution margin, the profit margin controllable by the store manager, or a store's segment profit margin? Justify your answer.

Problem 12–45
Prepare Segmented Income Statement; Contribution-Margin Format; Retail
(LO 12-5)

Profit margin traceable to segment, Olentangy store: $845,000

Buckeye Department Stores, Inc. operates a chain of department stores in Ohio. The company's organization chart appears below. Operating data for 20x1 follow.

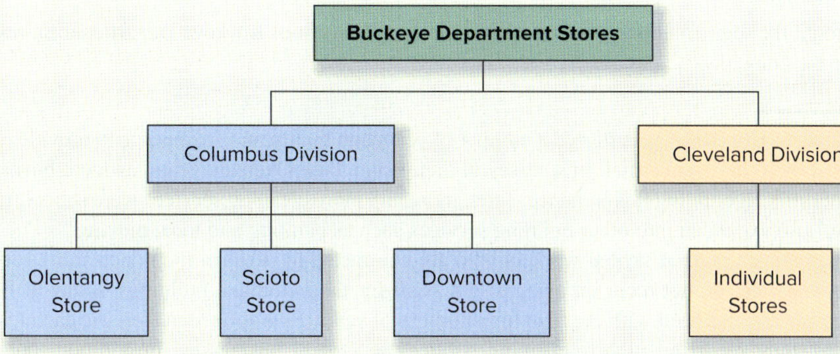

BUCKEYE DEPARTMENT STORES, INC.
Operating Data for 20x1
(in thousands)

	Columbus Division			
	Olentangy Store	**Scioto Store**	**Downtown Store**	**Cleveland Division (total for all stores)**
Sales revenue	$5,000	$2,400	$11,000	$21,000
Variable expenses:				
Cost of merchandise sold	3,000	2,000	6,000	12,000
Sales personnel—salaries	400	300	750	1,600
Sales commissions	50	40	90	200
Utilities	80	60	150	300
Other	60	35	120	250
Fixed expenses:				
Depreciation—buildings	120	90	250	470
Depreciation—furnishings	80	50	140	290
Computing and billing	40	30	75	160
Warehouse	70	60	200	450
Insurance	40	25	90	200
Property taxes	35	20	80	170
Supervisory salaries	150	100	400	900
Security	30	30	80	210

The following fixed expenses are controllable at the divisional level: depreciation—furnishings, computing and billing, warehouse, insurance, and security. In addition to these expenses, each division annually incurs $50,000 of computing costs, which are not allocated to individual stores.

The following fixed expenses are controllable only at the company level: depreciation—building, property taxes, and supervisory salaries. In addition to these expenses, each division incurs costs for supervisory salaries of $100,000, which are not allocated to individual stores.

Buckeye Department Stores incurs common fixed expenses of $120,000, which are not allocated to the two divisions. Income-tax expense for 20x1 is $1,950,000.

Required:

1. Prepare a segmented income statement similar to Exhibit 12–7 for Buckeye Department Stores, Inc. The statement should have the following columns:

	Segments of Company		Segments of Columbus Division			
Buckeye Department Stores, Inc.	Cleveland Division	Columbus Division	Olentangy Store	Scioto Store	Downtown Store	Not Allocated

   Prepare the statement in the contribution format, and indicate the controllability of expenses. Subtract all variable expenses, including cost of merchandise sold, from sales revenue to obtain the contribution margin.

2. How would the segmented income statement help the president of Buckeye Department Stores manage the company?

Problem 12–46
Responsibility Accounting; Participation; Behavioral Issues
(LO 12-1, 12-2, 12-3)

Building Services, Co. (BSC) was started a number of years ago by Jim and Joan Forge to provide cleaning services to both large and small businesses in their home city. Over the years, as local businesses reduced underutilized building maintenance staffs, more and more cleaning services were subcontracted to BSC. BSC also expanded into other building services such as painting and local moving.

BSC maintains a pool of skilled workers who are contracted to perform the noncleaning services because these services do not recur on a day-to-day basis for the individual buildings. Many of BSC's full-time employees have been with the firm for a number of years. Five zone managers are each responsible for furnishing recurring nightly cleaning services to several businesses. In addition, the zone manager sells and schedules noncleaning service jobs for the company's central pool of skilled employees. Informal meetings are held periodically to discuss BSC's performance, personnel allocations, and scheduling problems. BSC's budgeting and planning have been done by the Forges, who also manage variations from budgets.

The Forges recently decided to retire and sold the business to Commercial Maintenance Inc. (CMI), which provides similar services in a number of metropolitan locations that surround BSC's business area. After news of the sale, several of BSC's long-term employees appeared resentful of the change in ownership and did not know what to expect.

CMI's senior management met with BSC's managers and announced that George Fowler would become president of BSC and that BSC would continue to operate as a separate subsidiary of CMI. Furthermore, in accordance with CMI's management philosophy, a responsibility-accounting system is to be implemented at BSC. Also, in line with other CMI subsidiaries, a participatory budgeting process is being considered. However, no decision will be made until an evaluation of BSC's existing policies, operational culture, and management is completed. In view of the significant change in management philosophy, CMI has taken considerable time in explaining how each system operates and assuring BSC's managers that they are expected and encouraged to participate in both the planning and implementation of any of the systems that are to be adopted.

Required: Two new systems are being considered at Building Services Co.:

- Responsibility-accounting system
- Participatory budgeting system

For each of these systems:

1. Identify at least two behavioral advantages that could arise.
2. Identify at least two potential problems that could arise.
3. Discuss the likelihood that the system will contribute to the alignment of organizational and personal goals.

(CMA, adapted)

Problem 12–47
Designing a Responsibility-Accounting System
(LO 12-1, 12-2)

Warriner Equipment Company, which is located in Ontario, Canada, manufactures heavy construction equipment. The company's primary product, an especially powerful bulldozer, is among the best produced in North America. The company operates in a very price-competitive industry, so it has little control over the price of its products. It must meet the market price. To do so, the firm has to keep production costs in check by operating as efficiently as possible. Mathew Basler, the company's president, has stated that, to be successful, the company must provide a very high-quality product and meet its delivery commitments to customers on time. Warriner Equipment Company is organized as shown below.

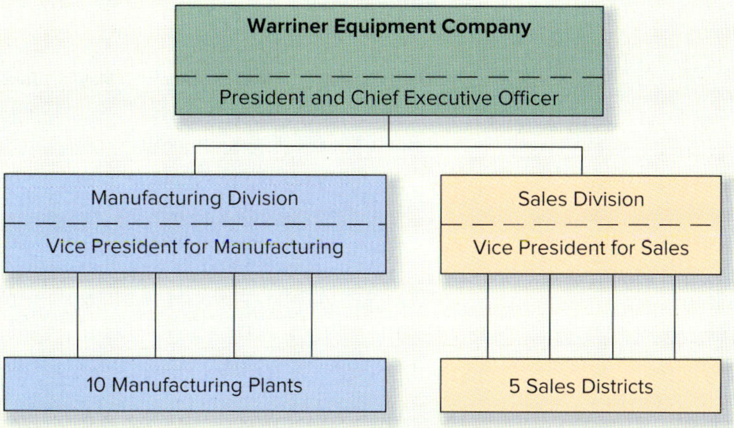

There is currently a disagreement between the company's two vice presidents regarding the responsibility-accounting system. The vice president for manufacturing claims that the 10 plants should be cost centers. He recently expressed the following sentiment: "The plants should be cost centers because the plant managers do not control the sales of our products. Designating the plants as profit centers would result in holding the plant managers responsible for something they can't control." A contrary view is held by the vice president for marketing. He recently made the following remarks: "The plants should be profit centers. The plant managers are in the best position to affect the company's overall profit."

Required: As the company's new controller, you have been asked to make a recommendation to Mathew Basler, the company president, regarding the responsibility center issue. Write a memo to the president making a recommendation and explaining the reasoning behind it. In your memo, address the following points.

1. Assuming that Warriner Equipment Company's overall goal is profitability, what are the company's critical success factors? A *critical success factor* is a variable that meets these two criteria: It is largely under the company's control and the company must succeed in this area in order to reach its overall goal of profitability.
2. Which responsibility-accounting arrangement is most consistent with achieving success on the company's critical success factors?
3. What responsibility-center designation is most appropriate for the company's sales districts?
4. As a specific example, consider the rush-order problem illustrated in the chapter. Suppose that Warriner Equipment Company often experiences rush orders from its customers. Which of the two proposed responsibility-accounting arrangements is best suited to making good decisions about accepting or rejecting rush orders? Specifically, should the plants be cost centers or profit centers?

Problem 12–48
Production Efficiency Report; Operational Performance Measures
(LO 12-6)

Pittsburgh Plastics Corporation manufactures a range of molded plastic products, such as kitchen utensils and desk accessories. The production process in the North Hills plant is a JIT system, which operates in four flexible manufacturing cells. An automated material handling system is used to transport products between production operations. Each month, the controller prepares a production efficiency report, which is sent to corporate headquarters. The data compiled in these reports, for the first six months of the year, are as follows:

PRODUCTION EFFICIENCY REPORT
Pittsburgh Plastics Corporation
North Hills Plant
January through June

	Jan.	Feb.	Mar.	Apr.	May	June	Average
Overtime hours	60	70	75	80	85	105	79.2
Total setup time	70	70	65	64	62	62	65.5
Cycle time (average in hours)	20	20	19	18	19	17	18.8
Manufacturing-cycle efficiency	95%	94%	96%	90%	89%	90%	92.3%

(continues)

PRODUCTION EFFICIENCY REPORT
Pittsburgh Plastics Corporation
North Hills Plant
January through June

	Jan.	Feb.	Mar.	Apr.	May	June	Average
Percentage of orders filled	100%	100%	100%	100%	100%	100%	100%
Percentage of on-time deliveries	99%	98%	99%	100%	96%	94%	97.7%
Inventory value/sales revenue	5%	5%	5%	4%	5%	5%	4.8%
Number of defective units, finished goods	80	82	75	40	25	22	54
Number of defective units, in process	10	30	35	40	60	60	39.2
Number of raw-material shipments with defective materials	3	3	2	0	0	0	1.3
Number of products returned	0	0	0	0	0	0	0
Aggregate productivity	1.3	1.3	1.2	1.25	1.2	1.15	1.23
Power consumption (thousands of kilowatt-hours)	800	795	802	801	800	800	800
Machine downtime (hours)	30	25	25	20	20	10	21.7
Bottleneck machine downtime	0	0	2	0	15	2	3.2
Number of unscheduled machine maintenance calls	0	0	1	0	2	3	1

Required:

1. Write a memo to the company president evaluating the North Hills plant's performance. Structure your report by dividing it into the following parts: (*a*) production processing and productivity; (*b*) product quality and customer acceptance; (*c*) delivery performance; (*d*) raw material, scrap, and inventory; and (*e*) machine maintenance.
2. If you identify any areas of concern in your memo, indicate an appropriate action for management.

Problem 12–49
Manufacturing Performance Measurement
(LO 12-6)

MedTech, Inc. manufactures diagnostic testing equipment used in hospitals. The company practices JIT production management and has a state-of-the-art manufacturing system, including an FMS and an AMHS. The following nonfinancial data were collected biweekly in the Harrisburg plant during the first quarter of the current year.

	Biweekly Measurement Period					
	1	2	3	4	5	6
Cycle time (days)	1.5	1.3	1.3	1.2	1.2	1.1
Number of defective finished products	4	4	3	4	3	3
Manufacturing-cycle efficiency	94%	94%	96%	96%	97%	96%
Customer complaints	6	7	6	5	7	8
Unresolved complaints	2	1	0	0	0	0
Products returned	3	3	2	2	1	1
Warranty claims	2	2	2	0	1	0
In-process products rejected	5	5	7	9	10	10
Aggregate productivity	1.5	1.5	1.5	1.5	1.4	1.5
Number of units produced per day per employee	410	405	412	415	415	420
Percentage of on-time deliveries	94%	95%	95%	97%	100%	100%
Percentage of orders filled	100%	100%	100%	98%	100%	100%
Inventory value/sales revenue	2%	2%	2%	1.5%	2%	1.5%
Machine downtime (minutes)	80	80	120	80	70	75
Bottleneck machine downtime (minutes)	25	20	15	0	60	10
Overtime (minutes) per employee	20	0	0	10	20	10
Average setup time (minutes)	120	120	115	112	108	101

Required:

1. For each nonfinancial performance measure, indicate which of the following areas of manufacturing performance is involved: (*a*) production processing, (*b*) product quality, (*c*) customer acceptance, (*d*) in-process quality control, (*e*) productivity, (*f*) delivery performance, (*g*) raw material and scrap, (*h*) inventory, (*i*) machine maintenance. Some measures may relate to more than one area.
2. Write a memo to management commenting on the performance data collected for the Harrisburg plant. Be sure to note any trends or other important results you see in the data. Evaluate the Harrisburg plant in each of the areas listed in requirement (1).

Problem 12–50
Gain-Sharing; Operational Performance Measures; Cost Reduction
(LO 12-6)

1. Charter Division, total bonus awarded for the year: $6,600

MedLine Equipment Corporation specializes in the manufacture of medical equipment, a field that has become increasingly competitive. Approximately two years ago, Ben Harrington, president of MedLine, became concerned that the company's bonus plan, which focused on division profitability, was not helping MedLine remain competitive. Harrington decided to implement a gain-sharing plan that would encourage employees to focus on operational areas that were important to customers and that added value without increasing cost. In addition to a profitability incentive, the revised plan also includes incentives for reduced rework costs, reduced sales returns, and on-time deliveries. Bonuses are calculated and awarded semiannually on the following basis. The bonuses are distributed among the relevant employees according to a formula developed by the division manager.

- Profitability: Two percent of operating income.
- Rework: Costs in excess of 2 percent of operating income are deducted from the bonus amount.
- On-time delivery: $5,000 if over 98 percent of deliveries are on time, $2,000 if 96 to 98 percent of deliveries are on time, and no increment if on-time deliveries are below 96 percent.
- Sales returns: $3,000 if returns are less than 1.5 percent of sales. Fifty percent of any amount in excess of 1.5 percent of sales is deducted from the bonus amount.
- *Note:* If the calculation of the bonus results in a negative amount for a particular period, there is no bonus, and the negative amount is not carried forward to the next period.

The revised bonus plan was implemented on January 1, 20x1. Presented in the following table are the results for two of Medline's divisions, Charter and Mesa Divisions, for the first year under the new bonus plan. Both of these divisions had similar sales and operating income results for the prior year, when the old bonus plan was in effect. Based on the 20x0 results, the employees of the Charter Division earned a bonus of $27,060 while the employees of the Mesa Division earned $22,440.

	Charter Division		Mesa Division	
	January 20x1– June 20x1	July 20x1– December 20x1	January 20x1– June 20x1	July 20x1– December 20x1
Sales	$4,200,000	$4,400,000	$2,850,000	$2,900,000
Operating income	$ 462,000	$ 440,000	$ 342,000	$ 406,000
On-time delivery	95.4%	97.3%	98.2%	94.6%
Rework costs	$ 11,500	$ 11,000	$ 6,000	$ 8,000
Sales returns	$ 84,000	$ 70,000	$ 44,750	$ 42,500

Required:

1. For the Charter Division:
   a. Compute the semiannual installments and total bonus awarded for 20x1.
   b. Discuss the likely behavior of the Charter Division employees under the revised bonus plan.
2. For the Mesa Division:
   a. Compute the semiannual installments and total bonus awarded for 20x1.
   b. Discuss the likely behavior of the Mesa Division employees under the revised bonus plan.
3. Citing specific examples, evaluate whether or not Harrington's revisions to the bonus plan at MedLine Equipment Corporation have achieved the desired results, and recommend any changes that might improve the plan.

(CMA, adapted)

■ **Problem 12–51**
Balanced scorecard; Banking; Use of Internet
(LO 12-7)

Visit the website of a major bank, e.g., Citibank at www.citibank.com. Explore the website to learn about the bank's services and operations.

Required:

1. What do you think the bank's overall, long-term goals are?
2. Develop a balanced scorecard for the bank. Include two to five measures in each of the scorecard's perspectives.
3. How would the balanced scorecard affect the way managers develop the bank's strategy?
4. Explain the concept of lead and lag measures in the context of the scorecard you have developed.

Cases

■ **Case 12–52**
Segmented Income Statement; Responsibility Accounting; Bonuses; Motivation; Ethics
(LO 12-1, 12-2, 12-5)

1. Operating income, Boston store: $91,275
2. Portland store's operating income for May: $12,375

Cathy's Classic Clothes is a retailer that sells to professional women in the northeast. The firm leases space for stores in upscale shopping centers, and the organizational structure consists of regions, districts, and stores. Each region consists of two or more districts; each district consists of three or more stores. Each store, district, and region has been established as a profit center. At all levels, the company uses a responsibility-accounting system focusing on information and knowledge rather than blame and control. Each year, managers, in consultation with their supervisors, establish financial and nonfinancial goals, and these goals are integrated into the budget. Actual performance is measured each month.

The New England Region consists of the Coastal District and the Inland District. The Coastal District includes the New Haven, Boston, and Portland stores. The Coastal District's performance has not been up to expectations in the past. For the month of May, the district manager has set performance goals with the managers of the New Haven and Boston stores, who will receive bonuses if certain performance measures are exceeded. The manager in Portland decided not to participate in the bonus scheme. Since the district manager is unsure what type of bonus will encourage better performance, the New Haven manager will receive a bonus based on sales in excess of budgeted sales of $570,000, while the Boston manager will receive a bonus based on operating income in excess of budget. The company's operating income goal for each store is 12 percent of sales. The budgeted sales revenue for the Boston store is $530,000.

Other pertinent data for May are as follows:

- Coastal District sales revenue was $1,500,000, and its cost of goods sold amounted to $633,750.
- The Coastal District spent $75,000 on advertising.
- General and administrative expenses for the Coastal District amounted to $180,000.
- At the New Haven store, sales were 40 percent of Coastal District sales, while sales at the Boston store were 35 percent of district sales. The cost of goods sold in both New Haven and Boston was 42 percent of sales.
- Variable selling expenses (sales commissions) were 6 percent of sales for all stores, districts, and regions.
- Variable administrative expenses were 2.5 percent of sales for all stores, districts, and regions.
- Maintenance cost includes janitorial and repair services and is a direct cost for each store. The store manager has complete control over this outlay. Maintenance costs were incurred as follows: New Haven, $7,500; Boston, $600; and Portland, $4,500.
- Advertising is considered a direct cost for each store and is completely under the control of the store manager. The New Haven store spent two-thirds of the Coastal District total outlay for advertising, which was 10 times the amount spent in Boston on advertising.
- Coastal District rental expense amounted to $150,000.
- The rental expenses at the New Haven store were 40 percent of the Coastal District's total, while the Boston store incurred 30 percent of the district total.
- District expenses were allocated to the stores based on sales.
- New England Region general and administrative expenses of $165,000 were allocated to the Coastal District. These expenses were, in turn, allocated equally to the district's three stores.

Required:

1. Prepare the May segmented income statement for the Coastal District and for the New Haven and Boston stores.
2. Compute the Portland store's operating income for May.
3. Discuss the impact of the responsibility-accounting system and bonus structure on the managers' behavior and the effect of their behavior on the financial results for the New Haven store and the Boston store.
4. The assistant controller for the New England Region, Jack Isner, has been a close friend of the New Haven store manager for over 20 years. When Isner saw the segmented income statement [as prepared in requirement (1)], he realized that the New Haven store manager had really gone overboard on advertising expenditures. To make his friend look better to the regional management, he reclassified $25,000 of the advertising expenditures as miscellaneous expenses, and buried them in rent and other costs. Comment on the ethical issues in the assistant controller's actions. (Refer to specific ethical standards that were given in Chapter 1.)

(CMA, adapted)

Case 12–53
Segmented Income Statement; International Operations
(LO 12-1, 12-5)

1. Operating income (loss), Canada: $421,000

Pacific Rim Industries is a diversified company whose products are marketed both domestically and internationally. The company's major product lines are furniture, sports equipment, and household appliances. At a recent meeting of Pacific Rim's board of directors, there was a lengthy discussion on ways to improve overall corporate profitability. The members of the board decided that they required additional financial information about individual corporate operations in order to target areas for improvement.

Danielle Murphy, the controller, has been asked to provide additional data that would assist the board in its investigation. Murphy believes that income statements, prepared along both product lines and geographic areas, would provide the directors with the required insight into corporate operations. Murphy had several discussions with the division managers for each product line and compiled the following information from these meetings.

	Product Lines			
	Furniture	Sports	Appliances	Total
Production and sales in units	160,000	180,000	160,000	500,000
Average selling price per unit	$8.00	$20.00	$15.00	
Average variable manufacturing cost per unit	4.00	9.50	8.25	
Average variable selling expense per unit	2.00	2.50	2.25	
Fixed manufacturing overhead, excluding depreciation				$ 500,000
Depreciation of plant and equipment				400,000
Administrative and selling expense				1,160,000

1. The division managers concluded that Murphy should allocate fixed manufacturing overhead to both product lines and geographic areas on the basis of the ratio of the variable costs expended to total variable costs.
2. Each of the division managers agreed that a reasonable basis for the allocation of depreciation on plant and equipment would be the ratio of units produced per product line (or per geographical area) to the total number of units produced.
3. There was little agreement on the allocation of administrative and selling expenses, so Murphy decided to allocate only those expenses that were traceable directly to a segment. For example, manufacturing staff salaries would be allocated to product lines, and sales staff salaries would be allocated to geographic areas. Murphy used the following data for this allocation.

Manufacturing Staff	
Furniture	$120,000
Sports	140,000
Appliances	80,000

Sales Staff	
United States	$ 60,000
Canada	100,000
Asia	250,000

4. The division managers were able to provide reliable sales percentages for their product lines by geographical area.

	Percentage of Unit Sales		
	United States	**Canada**	**Asia**
Furniture	40%	10%	50%
Sports	40%	40%	20%
Appliances	20%	20%	60%

Murphy prepared the following product-line income statement based on the data presented above.

PACIFIC RIM INDUSTRIES
Segmented Income Statement by Product Lines
For the Fiscal Year Ended April 30, 20x0

	Product Lines				
	Furniture	**Sports**	**Appliances**	**Unallocated**	**Total**
Sales in units	160,000	180,000	160,000		
Sales	$1,280,000	$3,600,000	$2,400,000	—	$7,280,000
Variable manufacturing and selling costs	960,000	2,160,000	1,680,000	—	4,800,000
Contribution margin	$ 320,000	$1,440,000	$ 720,000	—	$2,480,000
Fixed costs:					
Fixed manufacturing overhead	$ 100,000	$ 225,000	$ 175,000	$ —	$ 500,000
Depreciation	128,000	144,000	128,000	—	400,000
Administrative and selling expenses	120,000	140,000	80,000	820,000	1,160,000
Total fixed costs	$ 348,000	$ 509,000	$ 383,000	$ 820,000	$2,060,000
Operating income (loss)	$ (28,000)	$ 931,000	$ 337,000	$(820,000)	$ 420,000

Required:

1. Prepare a segmented income statement for Pacific Rim Industries based on the company's geographical areas. The statement should show the operating income for each segment.
2. As a result of the information disclosed by both segmented income statements (by product line and by geographic area), recommend areas where Pacific Rim Industries should focus its attention in order to improve corporate profitability.

(CMA, adapted)

13 Investment Centers and Transfer Pricing

FOCUS COMPANY >>>

© Daniel Koebe/Corbis RF

THIS CHAPTER'S FOCUS COMPANY is Suncoast Food Centers, a chain of retail grocery stores in Florida. The company has three divisions. The Gulf and Atlantic divisions operate individual grocery stores in six coastal Floridian cities. The Food Processing Division operates dairy plants, bakeries, and meat-processing facilities in Miami, Orlando, and Jacksonville in order to supply the Suncoast grocery stores with fresh food products. In this chapter, we will explore how companies evaluate the performance of investment centers, such as Suncoast's three divisions. Investment centers are organizational subunits whose managers have the authority to make significant investment decisions, such as building a new store or expanding an existing one.

© Brand X Pictures/PunchStock RF

<<< IN CONTRAST

In contrast to the evaluation of investment center performance explored in the first part of the chapter, we will turn our attention to transfer pricing. The amount charged when one division of a company sells products or services to another division is called a transfer price. We can continue to use Suncoast Food Centers for our illustration, because the Suncoast food processing facilities sell their dairy, bakery, and meat products to the Suncoast grocery stores at a transfer price. We will explore different ways to set such transfer prices.

After completing this chapter, you should be able to

13-1 Explain the role of managerial accounting in achieving goal congruence.

13-2 Compute an investment center's return on investment (ROI), residual income (RI), and economic value added (EVA).

13-3 Explain how a manager can improve ROI by increasing either the sales margin or capital turnover.

13-4 Describe some advantages and disadvantages of both ROI and residual income as divisional performance measures.

13-5 Explain how to measure a division's income and invested capital.

13-6 Use the general economic rule to set an optimal transfer price.

13-7 Explain how to base a transfer price on market prices, costs, or negotiations.

13-8 Understand the behavioral issues of incentives, goal congruence, and internal controls.

How do the top managers of large companies such as Allstate Insurance Company and General Electric Company evaluate their divisions and other major subunits? The largest subunits within these and similar organizations usually are designated as **investment centers.** The manager of this type of *responsibility center* is held accountable not only for the investment center's *profit* but also for the *capital invested* to earn that profit. Invested capital refers to assets, such as buildings and equipment, used in a subunit's operations. In this chapter, we will study the methods that managerial accountants use to evaluate investment centers and the performance of their managers.[1]

In many organizations, one subunit manufactures a product or produces a service that is then transferred to another subunit in the same organization. For example, automobile parts manufactured in one division of General Motors are then transferred to another GM division that assembles vehicles.

The price at which products or services are transferred between two subunits in an organization is called a **transfer price.** Since a transfer price affects the profit of both the buying and selling divisions, the transfer price affects the performance evaluation of these responsibility centers. Later in this chapter, we will study the methods that managerial accountants use to determine transfer prices.

Delegation of Decision Making

Learning Objective 13-1

Explain the role of managerial accounting in achieving goal congruence..

Most large organizations are decentralized. Managers throughout these organizations are given autonomy to make decisions for their subunits. Decentralization takes advantage of the specialized knowledge and skills of managers, permits an organization to

[1]Recall from Chapter 12 that in practice the term *profit center* sometimes is used interchangeably with the term *investment center.* To be precise, however, the term *profit center* should be reserved for a subunit whose manager is held accountable for profit but not for invested capital.

respond quickly to events, and relieves top management of the need to direct the organization's day-to-day activities. The biggest challenge in making a decentralized organization function effectively is to obtain *goal congruence* among the organization's autonomous managers.

Obtaining Goal Congruence: A Behavioral Challenge

Goal congruence is obtained when the managers of subunits throughout an organization strive to achieve the goals set by top management. This desirable state of affairs is difficult to achieve for a variety of reasons. Managers often are unaware of the effects of their decisions on the organization's other subunits. Also, it is only human for people to be more concerned with the performance of their own subunit than with the effectiveness of the entire organization. The behavioral challenge in designing any management control system is to come as close as possible to obtaining goal congruence.

To obtain goal congruence, the behavior of managers throughout an organization must be directed toward top management's goals. Successful managers not only have their sights set on these organizational goals, but also have been given positive incentives to achieve them. *The managerial accountant's objective* in designing a responsibility-accounting system is to provide these incentives to the organization's subunit managers. *The key factor in deciding how well the responsibility-accounting system works is the extent to which it directs managers' efforts toward organizational goals.* Thus, the accounting measures used to evaluate investment-center managers should provide them with incentives to act in the interests of the overall organization.

Management by Objectives (MBO) An emphasis on obtaining goal congruence is consistent with a broad managerial approach called **management by objectives,** or MBO**.** Under the MBO philosophy, managers participate in setting goals that they then strive to achieve. The goals usually are expressed in financial or other quantitative terms, and the responsibility-accounting system is used to evaluate performance in achieving them.

Adaptation of Management Control Systems

When an organization begins its operations, it is usually small and decision making generally is centralized. The chief executive can control operations without a formal responsibility-accounting system. It is relatively easy in a small organization for managers to keep in touch with routine operations through face-to-face contact with employees.

As an organization grows, however, its managers need more formal information systems, including managerial accounting information, in order to maintain control. Accounting systems are established to record events and provide the framework for internal and external financial reports. Budgets become necessary to plan the organization's activity. As the organization gains experience in producing its goods or services, cost standards and flexible budgets often are established to help control operations. As the organization continues to grow, some delegation of decision making becomes necessary. Decentralization is often the result of this tendency toward delegation. Ultimately, a fully developed responsibility-accounting system emerges. Managerial accountants designate cost centers, revenue centers, profit centers, and investment centers, and develop appropriate performance measures for each subunit.

Thus, an organization's accounting and managerial control systems usually adapt and become more complex as the organization grows and changes.

Measuring Performance in Investment Centers

In our study of investment-center performance evaluation, we will focus on Suncoast Food Centers. This Florida chain of retail grocery stores has three divisions, as depicted by the organization chart in Exhibit 13–1.

The Gulf and Atlantic divisions consist of individual grocery stores located in six coastal cities. The company's Food Processing Division operates dairy plants, bakeries, and meat-processing plants in Miami, Orlando, and Jacksonville. These facilities provide all Suncoast Food Centers with milk, ice cream, yogurt, cheese, breads and desserts, and packaged meat. These Suncoast-brand food products are transferred to the company's Gulf and Atlantic divisions at transfer prices established by the corporate controller's office.

"Accounting is changing. You're no longer sitting behind a desk just working on a computer, just crunching the numbers. You're actually getting to be a part of the day to day functions of the business." (13a)

Abbott Laboratories

Suncoast Food Centers' three divisions are investment centers. This responsibility-center designation is appropriate, because each division manager has the authority to make decisions that affect both profit and invested capital. For example, the Gulf Division manager approves the overall pricing policies in the Gulf Division's stores, and also has the autonomy to sign contracts to buy food and other products for resale. These actions influence the division's profit. In addition, the Gulf Division manager has the authority to build new Suncoast Food Centers, rent space in shopping centers, or close existing stores. These decisions affect the amount of capital invested in the division.

The primary goals of any profit-making enterprise include maximizing its profitability and using its invested capital as effectively as possible. Managerial accountants use three different measures to evaluate the performance of investment centers: return on investment (ROI), residual income (RI), and economic value added (EVA®). (EVA® is a registered trademark of Stern Stewart & Co.) We will illustrate each of these measures for Suncoast Food Centers.

Return on Investment

Learning Objective **13-2**

Compute an investment center's return on investment (ROI), residual income (RI), and economic value added (EVA).

The most common investment-center performance measure is **return on investment,** or **ROI,** which is defined as follows:

$$\text{Return on investment (ROI)} = \frac{\text{Income}}{\text{Invested capital}}$$

Exhibit 13–1

Organization Chart: Suncoast Food Centers

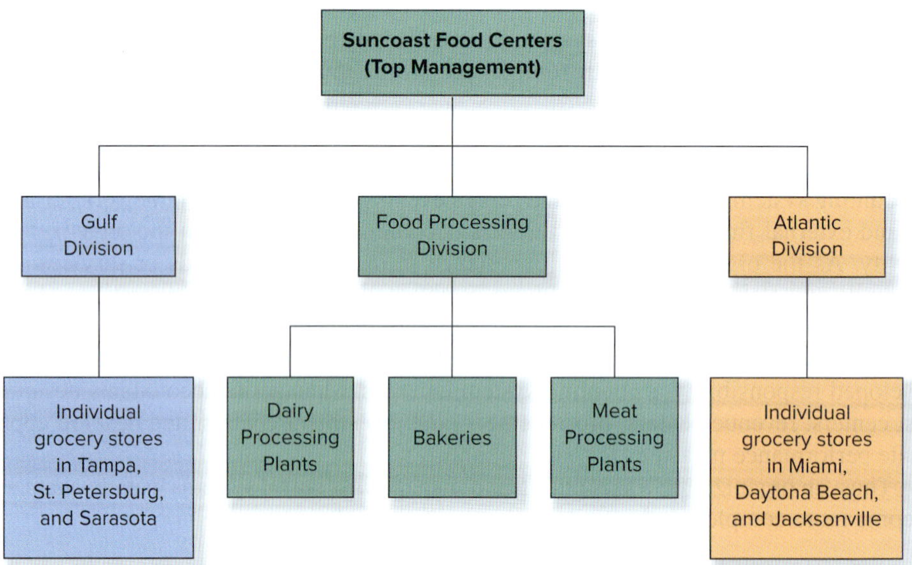

The most recent year's ROI calculations for Suncoast Food Centers' three divisions are:

	$\frac{\text{Income}}{\text{Invested capital}}$	=	Return on investment (ROI)
Gulf Division	$\frac{\$3{,}000{,}000}{\$20{,}000{,}000}$	=	15%
Food Processing Division	$\frac{\$3{,}600{,}000}{\$18{,}000{,}000}$	=	20%
Atlantic Division	$\frac{\$6{,}750{,}000}{\$45{,}000{,}000}$	=	15%

Notice how the ROI calculation for each division takes into account *both divisional income and the capital invested* in the division. Why is this important? Suppose each division were evaluated only on the basis of its divisional profit. The Atlantic Division reported a higher divisional profit than the Gulf Division. Does this mean the Atlantic Division performed better than the Gulf Division? The answer is no. Although the Atlantic Division's profit exceeded the Gulf Division's profit, the Atlantic Division used a much larger amount of invested capital to earn its profit. The Atlantic Division's assets are more than two times the assets of the Gulf Division.

Considering the relative size of the two divisions, we should expect the Atlantic Division to earn a larger profit than the Gulf Division. The important question is not how much profit each division earned, but rather how effectively each division used its invested capital to earn a profit.

Factors Underlying ROI We can rewrite the ROI formula as follows:

$$\text{Return on investment} = \frac{\text{Income}}{\text{Invested capital}} = \frac{\text{Income}}{\text{Sales revenue}} \times \frac{\text{Sales revenue}}{\text{Invested capital}}$$

Notice that the *sales revenue* term cancels out in the denominator and numerator when the two right-hand fractions are multiplied.

Writing the ROI formula in this way highlights the factors that determine a division's return on investment. Income divided by sales revenue is called the **sales margin.** This term measures the percentage of each sales dollar that remains as profit after all expenses are covered. Sales revenue divided by invested capital is called the **capital turnover.** This term focuses on the number of sales dollars generated by every dollar of invested capital. The sales margin and capital turnover for Suncoast Food Centers' three divisions are calculated below for the most recent year.

"The ROI of pollution prevention rises radically when 'hidden' environmental management costs are revealed." (13b)

Kestrel Management Services

(an environmental consulting firm)

	Sales margin	×	Capital turnover	=	ROI
	$\frac{\text{Income}}{\text{Sales revenue}}$	×	$\frac{\text{Sales revenue}}{\text{Invested capital}}$	=	ROI
Gulf Division	$\frac{\$3{,}000{,}000}{\$60{,}000{,}000}$	×	$\frac{\$60{,}000{,}000}{\$20{,}000{,}000}$	=	15%
Food Processing Division	$\frac{\$3{,}600{,}000}{\$9{,}000{,}000}$	×	$\frac{\$9{,}000{,}000}{\$18{,}000{,}000}$	=	20%
Atlantic Division	$\frac{\$6{,}750{,}000}{\$135{,}000{,}000}$	×	$\frac{\$135{,}000{,}000}{\$45{,}000{,}000}$	=	15%

The Gulf Division's sales margin is 5 percent ($3,000,000 of profit ÷ $60,000,000 of sales revenue). Thus, each dollar of divisional sales resulted in a five-cent profit. The division's capital turnover was 3 ($60,000,000 of sales revenue ÷ $20,000,000 of invested capital). Thus, three dollars of sales revenue were generated by each dollar of capital invested in the division's assets, such as store buildings, display shelves, checkout equipment, and inventory.

Learning Objective **13-3**

Explain how a manager can improve ROI by increasing either the sales margin or capital turnover.

Improving ROI How could the Gulf Division manager improve the division's return on investment? Since ROI is the product of the sales margin and the capital turnover, ROI can be improved by increasing either or both of its components. For example, if the Gulf Division manager increased the division's sales margin to 6 percent while holding the capital turnover constant at 3, the division's ROI would climb from 15 percent to 18 percent, as follows:

$$\begin{aligned}\text{Gulf Division's improved ROI} &= \text{Improved sales margin} \times \text{Same capital turnover}\\ &= 6\% \times 3 = 18\%\end{aligned}$$

To bring about the improved sales margin, the Gulf Division manager would need to increase divisional profit to \$3,600,000 on sales of \$60,000,000 (\$3,600,000 ÷ \$60,000,000 = 6%). How could profit be increased without changing total sales revenue? There are two possibilities: increase sales prices while selling less quantity, or decrease expenses. Neither of these is necessarily easy to do. In increasing sales prices, the division manager must be careful not to lose sales to the extent that total sales revenue declines. Similarly, reducing the expenses must not diminish product quality, customer service, or overall store atmosphere. Any of these changes could also result in lost sales revenue.

An alternative way of increasing the Gulf Division's ROI would be to increase its capital turnover. Suppose the Gulf Division manager increased the division's capital turnover to 4 while holding the sales margin constant at 5 percent. The division's ROI would climb from 15 percent to 20 percent:

$$\begin{aligned}\text{Gulf Division's improved ROI} &= \text{Same sales margin} \times \text{Improved capital turnover}\\ &= 5\% \times 4 = 20\%\end{aligned}$$

To obtain the improved capital turnover, the Gulf Division manager would need to either increase sales revenue or reduce the division's invested capital. For example, the improved ROI could be achieved by reducing invested capital to \$15,000,000 while maintaining sales revenue of \$60,000,000. This would be a very tall order. The division manager can lower invested capital somewhat by reducing inventories and can increase sales revenue by using store space more effectively. But reducing inventories may lead to stockouts and lost sales, and crowded aisles may drive customers away.

Improving ROI is a balancing act that requires all the skills of an effective manager. The ROI analysis above merely shows the arena in which the balancing act is performed.

Residual Income

Learning Objective **13-2**

Compute an investment center's return on investment (ROI), residual income (RI), and economic value added (EVA).

Although ROI is the most popular investment-center performance measure, it has one major drawback. To illustrate, suppose Suncoast's Food Processing Division manager can buy a new food processing machine for \$500,000, which will save \$80,000 in operating expenses and thereby raise divisional profit by \$80,000. The return on this investment in new equipment is 16 percent:

$$\text{Return on investment in new equipment} = \frac{\text{Increase in divisional profit}}{\text{Increase in invested capital}} = \frac{\$80{,}000}{\$500{,}000} = 16\%$$

Now suppose it costs Suncoast Food Centers 12 cents for each dollar of capital to invest in operational assets. What is the optimal decision for the Food Processing

Division manager to make, *viewed from the perspective of the company as a whole?* Since it costs Suncoast Food Centers 12 percent for every dollar of capital, and the return on investment in new equipment is 16 percent, the equipment should be purchased. For goal congruence, the autonomous division manager should decide to buy the new equipment.

Now consider what is likely to happen. The Food Processing Division manager's performance is evaluated on the basis of his division's ROI. Without the new equipment, the divisional ROI is 20 percent ($3,600,000 of divisional profit ÷ $18,000,000 of invested capital). If he purchases the new equipment, his divisional ROI will decline:

Food Processing Division's Return on Investment

Without Investment in New Equipment	With Investment in New Equipment
$\frac{\$3{,}600{,}000}{\$18{,}000{,}000} = 20\%$	$\frac{\$3{,}600{,}000 + \$80{,}000}{\$18{,}000{,}000 + \$500{,}000} < 20\%$

Why did this happen? Even though the investment in new equipment earns a return of 16 percent, which is greater than the company's cost of raising capital (12 percent), the return is less than the division's ROI without the equipment (20 percent). Averaging the new investment with those already in place in the Food Processing Division merely reduces the division's ROI. Since the division manager is evaluated using ROI, he will be reluctant to decide in favor of acquiring the new equipment.

The problem is that the ROI measure leaves out an important piece of information: it ignores the firm's cost of raising investment capital. For this reason, many managers prefer to use a different investment-center performance measure instead of ROI.

Computing Residual Income An investment center's **residual income (RI)** is defined as follows:

$$\text{Residual income} = \text{Investment center's profit} - \left(\text{Investment center's invested capital} \times \text{Imputed interest rate}\right)$$

where the imputed interest rate is the firm's cost of acquiring investment capital.

Residual income is a dollar amount, not a ratio like ROI. It is the amount of an investment center's profit that remains (as a residual) after subtracting an imputed interest charge. The term *imputed* means that the interest charge is estimated by the managerial accountant. This charge reflects the firm's minimum required rate of return on invested capital. In some firms, the imputed interest rate depends on the riskiness of the investment for which the funds will be used. Thus, divisions that have different levels of risk sometimes are assigned different imputed interest rates.

© Royalty-Free/Corbis

ROI and residual income are common performance measures for investment centers. Both measures relate the profit earned from selling the final product to the capital required to carry out production operations. Here the product is orange juice, and this bottling equipment represents the capital investment.

The residual income of Suncoast's Food Processing Division is computed below, both with and without the investment in the new equipment. The imputed interest rate is 12 percent.

Food Processing Division's Residual Income

	Without Investment in New Equipment		With Investment in New Equipment	
Divisional profit		$3,600,000		$3,680,000
Less imputed interest charge:				
Invested capital	$18,000,000		$18,500,000	
× Imputed interest rate	× .12		× .12	
Imputed interest charge	→	2,160,000	→	2,220,000
Residual income		$1,440,000		$1,460,000

Investment in new equipment raises residual income by $20,000.

Notice that the Food Processing Division's residual income will *increase* if the new equipment is purchased. What will be the division manager's incentive if he is evaluated on the basis of residual income instead of ROI? He will want to make the investment because that decision will increase his division's residual income. Thus, goal congruence is achieved when the managerial accountant uses residual income to measure divisional performance.

Learning Objective 13-4

Describe some advantages and disadvantages of both ROI and residual income as divisional performance measures

Why does residual income facilitate goal congruence while ROI does not? Because the residual-income formula incorporates an important piece of data that is excluded from the ROI formula: the firm's minimum required rate of return on invested capital. To summarize, ROI and residual income are compared as follows:

$$\text{ROI} = \frac{\text{Investment center's profit}}{\text{Investment center's invested capital}}$$

Two pieces of data

$$\text{Residual income} = \text{Investment center's profit} - \left(\text{Investment center's invested capital} \times \text{Imputed interest rate}\right)$$

Three pieces of data

Unfortunately, residual income also has a serious drawback: It should not be used to compare the performance of different-sized investment centers because it incorporates a bias in favor of the larger investment center. To illustrate, the following table compares the residual income of Suncoast Food Centers' Gulf and Atlantic divisions. Notice that the Atlantic Division's residual income is considerably higher than the Gulf Division's. This is entirely due to the much greater size of the Atlantic Division, as evidenced by its far greater invested capital.

Comparison of Residual Income: Two Divisions

	Gulf Division		Atlantic Division	
Divisional profit		$3,000,000		$6,750,000
Less imputed interest charge:				
Invested capital	$20,000,000		$45,000,000	
× Imputed interest rate	× .12		× .12	
Imputed interest charge	→	2,400,000	→	5,400,000
Residual income		$ 600,000		$1,350,000

The Atlantic Division's residual income is much higher simply because it is larger than the Gulf Division.

In short, neither ROI nor residual income provides a perfect measure of investment-center performance. ROI can undermine goal congruence. Residual income distorts comparisons between investment centers of different sizes. As a result, some companies routinely use both measures for divisional performance evaluation.

Shareholder Value Analysis Some companies apply the residual income concept to individual product lines. **Shareholder value analysis** calculates the residual income for a major product line, with the objective of determining how the product line affects the firm's value to the shareholders. Suppose, for example, that Suncoast Food Centers offers in-store, one-hour film development in selected stores. Let's say that the company's investment in this service is $200,000 and the annual profit is $40,000. Then the residual income on one-hour film development is $16,000 [$40,000 − ($200,000 × 12%)].

Economic Value Added

The most contemporary measure of investment center performance is **economic value added (EVA),** which is defined as follows:

$$\text{Economic value added} = \text{Investment center's after-tax operating income} - \left[\left(\text{Investment center's total assets} - \text{Investment center's current liabilities}\right) \times \text{Weighted-average cost of capital}\right]$$

Like residual income, the economic value added is a dollar amount. However, it differs from residual income in two important ways. First, an investment center's current liabilities are subtracted from its total assets. Second, the weighted-average cost of capital is used in the calculation.

Weighted-Average Cost of Capital Suncoast Food Centers has two sources of long-term capital: debt and equity. The cost to Suncoast of issuing debt is the after-tax cost of the interest payments on the debt, taking account of the fact that the interest payments are tax deductible. The cost of Suncoast's equity capital is the investment opportunity rate of Suncoast Food Centers' investors, that is, the rate they could earn on investments of similar risk to that of investing in Suncoast Food Centers. The **weighted-average cost of capital (WACC)** is defined as follows:

$$\text{Weighted-average cost of capital} = \frac{\left(\text{After-tax cost of debt capital}\right)\left(\text{Market value of debt}\right) + \left(\text{Cost of equity capital}\right)\left(\text{Market value of equity}\right)}{\text{Market value of debt} + \text{Market value of equity}}$$

The interest rate on Suncoast Food Centers' $40 million of debt is 9 percent, and the company's tax rate is 30 percent. Therefore, Suncoast's after-tax cost of debt is 6.3 percent [9% × (1 − 30%)]. Let's assume that the cost of Suncoast's equity capital is 12 percent. Moreover, the market value of the company's equity is $60 million.[2] The following calculation shows that Suncoast Food Centers' WACC is 9.72 percent.

$$\text{Weighted-average cost of capital} = \frac{(.063)(\$40{,}000{,}000) + (.12)(\$60{,}000{,}000)}{\$40{,}000{,}000 + \$60{,}000{,}000} = .0972$$

[2]The *book value* of Suncoast Food Centers' equity is $41 million, but that amount does not reflect the current value of the company's assets or the value of intangible assets such as the Suncoast Food Centers name.

Finally, Suncoast Food Centers had an average balance of $2 million in current liabilities, distributed as follows:

Division	Current Liabilities
Gulf Division	$ 400,000
Food Processing Division	1,000,000
Atlantic Division	600,000

Now we can compute the economic value added (or EVA) for each of Suncoast's three divisions.

Division	After-tax operating income (in millions)	−	[(Total assets (in millions)	−	Current liabilities (in millions))	× WACC]	=	Economic value added
Gulf	$3.00 × (1 − .30)	−	[($20	−	$ .4)	×.0972]	=	$194,880
Food Processing	$3.60 × (1 − .30)	−	[($18	−	$1.0)	×.0972]	=	867,600
Atlantic	$6.75 × (1 − .30)	−	[($45	−	$ .6)	×.0972]	=	409,320

The EVA analysis reveals that all three of Suncoast Food Centers' divisions are contributing substantially to the company's economic value.

What does an EVA analysis tell us? EVA indicates how much shareholder wealth is being created, as Roberto Goizueta, Coca-Cola's former CEO, explained: "We raise capital to make concentrate and sell it at an operating profit. Then we pay the cost of that capital. Shareholders pocket the difference (EVA amount)."

Management Accounting Practice

Siemens and Royal Bank of Canada

PAY FOR PERFORMANCE BASED ON EVA

"Company directors say they pay CEOs based on performance. Now the numbers show they mean it." In the wake of the excesses in top management compensation over the past few years, at many companies pay for performance is back in vogue. Top executives earn hefty bonuses when times are good, but are expected to share in the pain during a decline in business.

Siemens, a global electronics firm, links the compensation of its top 500 managers to their business units' economic value added (EVA) measure. Similarly, the **Royal Bank of Canada (RBC)**, upon observing that its lower-level managers were not acting in accordance with the bank's overall strategy, links their compensation to the bank's EVA and revenue growth.[3]

[3]S. Thurm, "Pay for Performance No Longer a Punchline," *The Wall Street Journal* (on line), March 20, 2013; J. Greenwood, "RBC Boosts CEO's Pay 25%" *Financial Post,* February 4, 2013, p. 1; K. Seannell and J. Lublin, "SEC Unhappy with Answers on Executive Pay," *The Wall Street Journal,* January 29, 2008, p. 31; Louis Lavelle, "The Gravy Train Just Got Derailed—'Pay for Performance' Is Back in Vogue," *BusinessWeek,* November 19, 2001; and T. Leahy, "All the Right Moves," *Business Finance* 6, no. 1 (April 2000), p. 32.

Measuring Income and Invested Capital

The ROI, residual-income, and economic value added (EVA) measures of investment-center performance all use profit and invested capital in their formulas. This raises the question of how to measure divisional profit and invested capital. This section will illustrate various approaches to resolving these measurement issues.

Invested Capital

Learning Objective **13-5**

Explain how to measure a division's income and invested capital.

We will focus on Suncoast Food Centers' Food Processing Division to illustrate several alternative approaches to measuring an investment center's capital. Exhibit 13–2 lists the assets and liabilities associated with the Food Processing Division. Notice that Exhibit 13–2 does not constitute a complete balance sheet. First, there are no long-term liabilities, such as bonds payable, associated with the Food Processing Division. Although Suncoast Food Centers may have such long-term debt, it would not be meaningful to assign portions of that debt to the company's individual divisions. Second, there is no stockholders' equity associated with the Food Processing Division. The owners of the company own stock in Suncoast Food Centers, not in its individual divisions.

Average Balances ROI, residual income, and EVA are computed for a period of time, such as a year or a month. Asset balances, on the other hand, are measured at a point in time, such as December 31. Since divisional asset balances generally will change over time, we use average balances in calculating ROI, residual income, and EVA. For example, if the Food Processing Division's balance in invested capital was $19,000,000 on January 1 and $17,000,000 on December 31, we would use the year's average invested capital of $18,000,000 in the ROI, residual income, and EVA calculations.

Should Total Assets Be Used? Exhibit 13–2 shows that the Food Processing Division had average balances during the year of $2,000,000 in current assets, $15,000,000 in long-lived assets, and $1,000,000 tied up in a plant under construction. (Suncoast Food Centers is building a new high-tech dairy plant in Orlando to produce its innovative zero-calorie ice cream.) In addition, Exhibit 13–2 discloses that the Food Processing Division's average balance of current liabilities was $1,000,000.

Assets*		
Current assets (cash, accounts receivable, inventories, etc.)		$ 2,000,000
Long-lived assets (land, buildings, equipment, vehicles, etc.):		
Gross book value (acquisition cost)	$19,000,000	
Less: Accumulated depreciation	4,000,000	
Net book value		15,000,000
Plant under construction		1,000,000
Total assets		$18,000,000
Liabilities		
Current liabilities (accounts payable, salaries payable, etc.)		$ 1,000,000

*This is not a balance sheet, but rather a listing of certain assets and liabilities associated with the Food Processing Division.

Exhibit 13–2
Assets and Liabilities Associated with Food Processing Division

What is the division's invested capital? Several possibilities exist.

1. ***Total assets***. The management of Suncoast Food Centers has decided to use *average total assets* for the year in measuring each division's invested capital. Thus, $18,000,000 is the amount used in the ROI, residual-income, and EVA calculations discussed earlier in this chapter. This measure of invested capital is appropriate if the division manager has considerable authority in making decisions about *all* of the division's assets, *including nonproductive assets.* In this case, the Food Processing Division's partially completed dairy plant is a nonproductive asset. Since the division manager had considerable influence in deciding to build the new plant and he is responsible for overseeing the project, average total assets provides an appropriate measure.
2. ***Total productive assets***. In other companies, division managers are directed by top management to keep nonproductive assets, such as vacant land or construction in progress. In such cases, it is appropriate to exclude nonproductive assets from the measure of invested capital. Then *average total productive assets* is used to measure invested capital. If Suncoast Food Centers had chosen this alternative, $17,000,000 would have been used in the ROI, residual-income, and EVA calculations (total assets of $18,000,000 less $1,000,000 for the plant under construction).
3. ***Total assets less current liabilities***. Some companies allow division managers to secure short-term bank loans and other short-term credit. In such cases, invested capital often is measured by *average total assets less average current liabilities.* This approach encourages investment-center managers to minimize resources tied up in assets and maximize the use of short-term credit to finance operations. If this approach had been used by Suncoast Food Centers, the Food Processing Division's invested capital would have been $17,000,000, total assets of $18,000,000 less current liabilities of $1,000,000. (Note that current liabilities are always subtracted from total assets for the measure of invested capital used in the EVA measure.)

Gross or Net Book Value Another decision to make in choosing a measure of invested capital is whether to use the *gross book value (acquisition cost)* or the *net book value* of long-lived assets. (Net book value is the acquisition cost less accumulated depreciation.) Suncoast Food Centers' management has decided to use the average net book value of $15,000,000 to value the Food Processing Division's long-lived assets. If gross book value had been used instead, the division's measure of invested capital would have been $22,000,000, as the following calculation shows.

Current assets	$ 2,000,000
Long-lived assets (at gross book value)	19,000,000
Plant under construction	1,000,000
Total assets (at gross book value)	$22,000,000

There are advantages and disadvantages associated with both gross and net book value as a measure of invested capital. The advantages of net book value are:

1. Using net book value maintains consistency with the balance sheet prepared for external reporting purposes. This allows for more meaningful comparisons of return-on-investment measures across different companies.
2. Using net book value to measure invested capital is also more consistent with the definition of income, which is the numerator in ROI calculations. In computing income, the current period's depreciation on long-lived assets is deducted as an expense.

Exhibit 13-3
Increase in ROI over Time (when net book value is used)

Acquisition cost of equipment	$500,000
Useful life	5 years
Salvage value at end of useful life	0
Annual straight-line depreciation	$100,000
Annual income generated by asset (before deducting depreciation)	$150,000

Year	Income before Depreciation	Annual Depreciation	Income Net of Depreciation	Average Net Book Value*	ROI Based on Net Book Value†	Average Gross Book Value	ROI Based on Gross Book Value
1	$150,000	$100,000	$50,000	$450,000	11.1%	$500,000	10%
2	150,000	100,000	50,000	350,000	14.3	500,000	10
3	150,000	100,000	50,000	250,000	20.0	500,000	10
4	150,000	100,000	50,000	150,000	33.3	500,000	10
5	150,000	100,000	50,000	50,000	100.0	500,000	10

*Average net book value is the average of the beginning and ending balances for the year in net book value. In year 1, for example, the average net book value is

$$\frac{\$500{,}000 + \$400{,}000}{2}$$

†ROI rounded to nearest tenth of 1 percent.

The following two advantages are often associated with using gross book value:

1. The usual methods of computing depreciation, such as the straight-line and the declining-balance methods, are arbitrary. Hence, they should not be allowed to affect ROI, residual-income, or EVA calculations.
2. When long-lived assets are depreciated, their net book value declines over time. This results in a misleading increase in ROI, residual income, and EVA across time. Exhibit 13–3 provides an illustration of this phenomenon for the ROI calculated on an equipment purchase under consideration by the Food Processing Division manager. Notice that the ROI rises steadily across the five-year horizon if invested capital is measured by net book value. However, using gross book value eliminates this problem. If an accelerated depreciation method were used instead of the straight-line method, the increasing trend in ROI would be even more pronounced.

A Behavioral Problem The tendency for net book value to produce a misleading increase in ROI over time can have a serious effect on the incentives of investment-center managers. Investment centers with old assets will show much higher ROIs than investment centers with relatively new assets. This can discourage investment-center managers from investing in new equipment. If this behavioral tendency persists, a division's assets can become obsolete, making the division uncompetitive.

Allocating Assets to Investment Centers Some companies control certain assets centrally, although these assets are needed to carry on operations in the divisions. Common examples are cash and accounts receivable. Divisions need cash in order to operate, but many companies control cash balances centrally in order to minimize their total cash holdings. Some large retail firms manage accounts receivable centrally. A credit customer of some national department store chains can make a payment either at the local store or by mailing the payment to corporate headquarters.

When certain assets are controlled centrally, some allocation basis generally is chosen to allocate these asset balances to investment centers, for the purpose of measuring invested capital. For example, cash may be allocated based on the budgeted cash needs in each division or on the basis of divisional sales. Accounts receivable usually are allocated on the basis of divisional sales. Divisions with less stringent credit terms are allocated proportionately larger balances of accounts receivable.

Measuring Investment-Center Income

Learning Objective 13-5

Explain how to measure a division's income and invested capital.

In addition to choosing a measure of investment-center capital, an accountant must also decide how to measure a center's income. The key issue is controllability; the choice involves the extent to which uncontrollable items are allowed to influence the income measure. The Excel spreadsheet in Exhibit 13–4 illustrates several different possibilities for measuring the income of Suncoast Food Centers' Food Processing Division.

Suncoast Food Centers' top management uses the *profit margin controllable by division manager,* $3,600,000, to evaluate the Food Processing Division manager. This profit measure is used in calculating ROI, residual income, or EVA. Some fixed costs traceable to the division have not been deducted from this $3,600,000 amount, but the division manager cannot control or significantly influence these costs. Hence they are excluded from the ROI calculation in evaluating the division manager. In calculating EVA, the $3,600,000 profit-margin amount is converted to an after-tax basis by multiplying it by 1 minus the tax rate of 30 percent.

Pay for Performance Some companies reward investment-center managers with **cash bonuses** if they meet a predetermined target on a specified performance criterion, such as residual income, ROI, or EVA. Such payments often are referred to as **pay for performance, merit pay,** or **incentive compensation.** These cash bonuses generally are single payments, independent of a manager's base salary.

As the result of public outrage over the recent nearly catastrophic financial meltdown, as well as other perceived corporate excesses, many companies are beginning to rein in top management compensation packages. The U.S. government also reacted to the negative public mood by appointing a "pay czar" whose job it was to oversee top management compensation for the various companies that received "bailout" funds from government coffers during the recent financial crisis. Eventually, though, the office of the pay czar itself came under fire for its controversial decisions about executive compensation.[4]

Exhibit 13–4

Divisional Income Statement: Food Processing Division

Suncoast Food Centers - Excel

H17 =H15-H16

SUNCOAST FOOD CENTERS
DIVISION: Food Processing
Divisional Income Statement

5		Sales revenue	$9,000,000
6		Variable expenses	3,800,000
7	(1)	Divisional contribution margin	$5,200,000
8		Fixed expenses controllable by division manager	1,600,000
9	(2)	Profit margin controllable by division manager	$3,600,000
10		Fixed expenses, traceable to division, but controlled by others	1,200,000
11	(3)	Profit margin traceable to division	$2,400,000
12		Common fixed expenses, allocated from corporate headquarters	400,000
13	(4)	Divisional income before interest and taxes	$2,000,000
14		Interest expense allocated from corporate headquarters	250,000
15	(5)	Divisional income before taxes	$1,750,000
16		Income taxes allocated from corporate headquarters	700,000
17	(6)	Divisional net income	$1,050,000

Divisional Income Statement

[4]"TARP Pay Czar Permitted Excessive Executive Pay at Bailed-Out Companies," *Huffington Post,* January, 28, 2013. See also G. Chazan, "Shell Plans to Reduce Executive Salaries," *The Wall Street Journal,* February 17, 2010, p. B1; and D. Brady, "The Pay Czar on the End of His Empire," *Bloomberg Businessweek,* January 4, 2010, p. 15.

Managers versus Investment Centers It is important to make a distinction between an investment center and its manager. In evaluating the *manager's* performance, only revenues and costs that the manager can control or significantly influence should be included in the profit measure. Remember that the overall objective of the performance measure is to provide incentives for goal-congruent behavior. No performance measure can motivate a manager to make decisions about costs he or she cannot control. This explains why Suncoast Food Centers' top management relies on the profit margin controllable by division manager to compute the manager's ROI performance measure.

Evaluating the Food Processing Division as a viable economic investment is a different matter altogether. In this evaluation, traceability of costs, rather than controllability, is the issue. For this purpose, Suncoast Food Centers' top management uses the profit margin traceable to division to compute the divisional ROI, residual income, or EVA. As Exhibit 13–4 shows, this amount is $2,400,000.

Other Profit Measures The other measures of divisional profit shown in Exhibit 13–4 (lines 4, 5, and 6) also are used by some companies. The rationale behind these divisional income measures is that all corporate costs have to be covered by the operations of the divisions. Allocating corporate costs, interest, and income taxes to the divisions makes division managers aware of these costs.

Inflation: Historical-Cost versus Current-Value Accounting

Whether measuring investment-center income or invested capital, the impact of price-level changes should not be forgotten. During periods of inflation, historical-cost asset values soon cease to reflect the cost of replacing those assets. Therefore, some accountants argue that investment-center performance measures based on historical-cost accounting are misleading. Yet surveys of corporate managers indicate that an accounting system based on current values would not alter their decisions. Most managers believe that measures based on historical-cost accounting are adequate when used in conjunction with budgets and performance targets. As managers prepare those budgets, they build their expectations about inflation into the budgets and performance targets.

Another reason for using historical-cost accounting for internal purposes is that it is required for external reporting. Thus, historical-cost data already are available, while installing current-value accounting would add substantial incremental costs to the organization's information system.

Other Issues in Segment Performance Evaluation

Alternatives to ROI, Residual Income, and Economic Value Added (EVA)

ROI, residual income, and EVA are short-run performance measures. They focus on only one period of time. Yet an investment center is really a collection of assets (investments), each of which has a multiperiod life. Exhibit 13–5 portrays this perspective of an investment center.

To evaluate any one of these individual investments correctly requires a multiperiod viewpoint, which takes into account the timing of the cash flows from the investment. For example, investment E in Exhibit 13–5 may start out slowly in years 4 and 5, but it may be economically justified by its expected high performance in years 8, 9, and 10. Any evaluation of the investment center in year 5 that ignores the long-term performance of its various investments can result in a misleading conclusion. Thus, single-period

Exhibit 13–5
Investment Center Viewed as a Collection of Investments

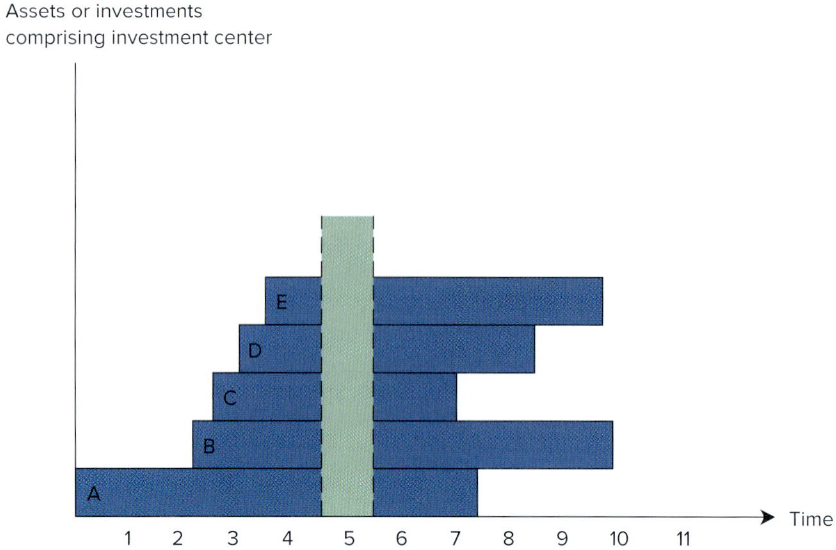

performance measures suffer from myopia. They focus on only a short time segment that slices across the division's investments as portrayed in Exhibit 13–5.

To avoid this short-term focus, some organizations downplay ROI, residual income, and EVA in favor of an alternative approach. Instead of relating profit to invested capital in a single measure, these characteristics of investment-center performance are evaluated separately. Actual divisional profit for a time period is compared to a flexible budget, and variances are used to analyze performance. The division's major investments are evaluated through a *postaudit* of the investment decisions. For example, investment E may have been undertaken because of expected high performance in years 8, 9, and 10. When that time comes, a review will determine whether the project lived up to expectations.

Evaluating periodic profit through flexible budgeting and variance analysis, coupled with postaudits of major investment decisions, is a more complicated approach to evaluating investment centers. However, it does help management avoid the myopia of single-period measures such as ROI, residual income, and EVA.

Importance of Nonfinancial Information

Although financial measures such as segment profit, ROI, residual income, and EVA are widely used in performance evaluation, nonfinancial measures are important also. Manufacturers collect data on rates of defective products, airlines record information on lost bags and aircraft delays, and hotels keep track of occupancy rates. The proper evaluation of an organization and its segments requires that multiple performance measures be defined and used. The *balanced scorecard,* with its *lead* and *lag measures* of performance, is one tool that is more and more widely used as a means of introducing nonfinancial measures into performance evaluation. See Chapter 10 for a discussion of the balanced scorecard.

Measuring Performance in Nonprofit Organizations

Management control in a nonprofit organization presents a special challenge. Such organizations often are managed by professionals, such as physicians in a hospital. Moreover, many people participate in a nonprofit organization at some personal sacrifice, motivated by humanitarian or public service ideals. Often, such people are less receptive to formal control procedures than their counterparts in business.

The goals of nonprofit organizations often are less clear-cut than those of businesses. Public service objectives may be difficult to specify with precision and even more difficult to measure in terms of achievement. For example, one community health center was established in an economically depressed area with three stated goals:

1. To reduce costs in a nearby hospital by providing a clinic for people to use instead of the hospital emergency room.
2. To provide preventive as well as therapeutic care, and establish outreach programs in the community.
3. To become financially self-sufficient.

There is some conflict between these objectives, since goal 2 does not provide revenue to the center, while goals 1 and 3 focus on financial efficiency. Moreover, the health center was staffed with physicians who could have achieved much greater incomes in private practice. The management control tools described in this and the preceding three chapters can be used in nonprofit organizations. However, the challenges in doing so effectively often are greater.

Transfer Pricing

Measuring performance in profit centers or investment centers is made more complicated by transfers of goods or services between responsibility centers. The amount charged when one division sells goods or services to another division is called a *transfer price*. This price affects the profit measurement for both the selling division and the buying division. A high transfer price results in high profit for the selling division and low profit for the buying division. A low transfer price has the opposite effect. Consequently, the transfer-pricing policy *can* affect the *incentives* of autonomous division managers as they decide whether to make the transfer. Exhibit 13–6 depicts this scenario.

Goal Congruence

What should be management's goal in setting transfer prices for internally transferred goods or services? In a decentralized organization, the managers of profit centers and investment centers often have considerable autonomy in deciding whether to accept or reject orders and whether to buy inputs from inside the organization or from outside. For example, a large manufacturer of farm equipment allows its Assembly Division managers to buy parts either from another division of the company or from independent manufacturers. The goal in setting transfer prices is to establish incentives for autonomous division managers to make decisions that support the overall goals of the organization.

Suppose it is in the best interests of Suncoast Food Centers for the baked goods produced by the Food Processing Division's Orlando Bakery to be transferred to the Gulf Division's stores in the Tampa Bay area. Thus, if the firm were centralized, bakery products would be transferred from the Food Processing Division to the Gulf Division. However, Suncoast Food Centers is a decentralized company, and the Gulf Division manager is free to buy baked goods either from the Food Processing Division or from an outside bakery company. Similarly, the Food Processing Division manager is free to accept or reject an order for baked goods, at any given price, from the Gulf Division. The goal of the company's controller in setting the transfer price is to provide incentives for each of these division managers to act in the company's best interests.

© Jim West/Alamy

Transfer pricing is widely used in all kinds of businesses. When the chassis for this GM Corvette Stingray was transferred from the manufacturing division to the assembly division, a transfer price was specified.

Exhibit 13–6
The Transfer-Pricing Scenario

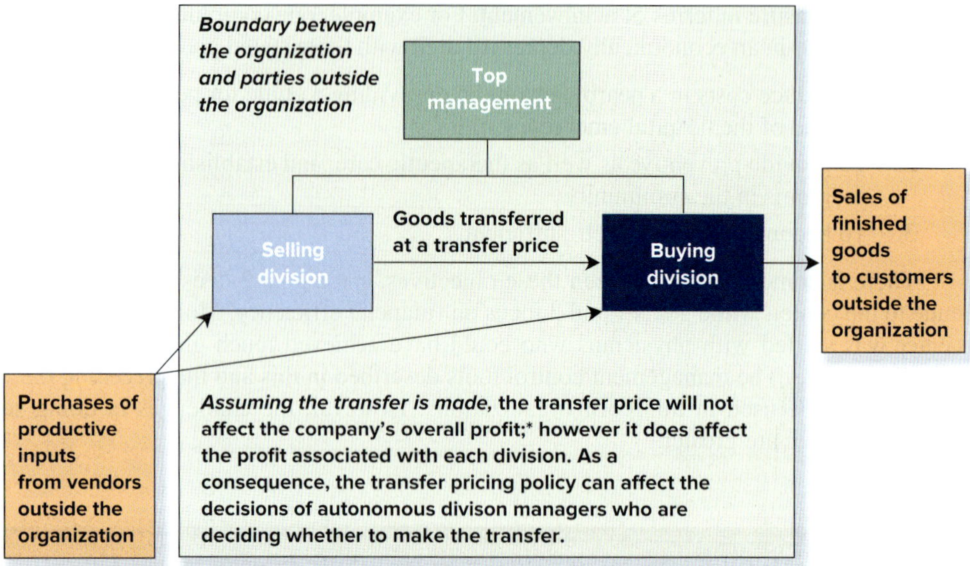

*Assumes no tax complexities involving multinational companies. This issue is addressed later in the chapter.

The transfer price should be chosen so that each division manager, when striving to maximize his or her own division's profit, makes the decision that maximizes the company's profit.

General Transfer-Pricing Rule

Learning Objective **13-6**

Use the general economic rule to set an optimal transfer price.

Management's objective in setting a transfer price is to encourage goal congruence among the division managers involved in the transfer. A general rule that will ensure goal congruence is given below.

$$\text{Transfer price} = \begin{array}{c}\text{Additional } \textit{outlay cost} \\ \text{per unit incurred because} \\ \text{goods are transferred}\end{array} + \begin{array}{c}\textit{Opportunity cost} \text{ per unit} \\ \text{to the organization} \\ \text{because of the transfer}\end{array}$$

The general rule specifies the transfer price as the sum of two cost components. The first component is the outlay cost incurred by the division that produces the goods or services to be transferred. Outlay costs will include the direct variable costs of the product or service and any other outlay costs that are incurred only as a result of the transfer. The second component in the general transfer-pricing rule is the opportunity cost incurred by the organization as a whole because of the transfer. Recall from Chapter 2 that an *opportunity cost* is a benefit that is forgone as a result of taking a particular action.

> "Transfer pricing is a business issue as well as a tax issue that should be considered in the board room." (13c)
> **EY (formerly Ernst & Young)**

We will illustrate the general transfer-pricing rule for Suncoast Food Centers. The company's Food Processing Division produces bread in its Orlando Bakery. The division transfers some of its products to the company's Gulf and Atlantic divisions, and sells some of its products to other companies in the *external market* under different labels.

Bread is transported to stores in racks containing one dozen loaves of packaged bread. In the Orlando bakery, the following variable costs are incurred to produce bread and transport it to a buyer.

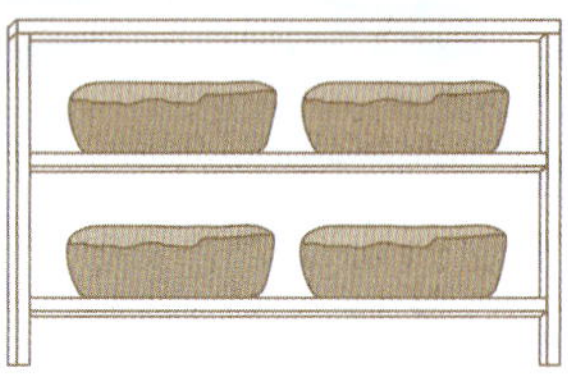

Production:	
Standard variable cost per rack (including packaging)	$7.00
Transportation:	
Standard variable cost per rack to transport bread	.25

In applying the general transfer-pricing rule, we will distinguish between two different scenarios.

Scenario I: No Excess Capacity Suppose the Food Processing Division can sell all the bread it can produce to outside buyers at a market price of $11 per rack. Since the division can sell all of its production, it has *no excess capacity. Excess capacity* exists only when more goods can be produced than the producer is able to sell, due to low demand for the product.

What transfer price does the general rule yield under this scenario of no excess capacity? The transfer price is determined as follows:

Outlay Cost:	
Standard variable cost of production	$ 7.00 per rack
Standard variable cost of transportation	.25 per rack
Total outlay cost	$ 7.25 per rack
Opportunity cost:	
Selling price per unit in external market	$11.00 per rack
Less: Variable cost of production and transportation	7.25 per rack
Opportunity cost (forgone contribution margin)	$ 3.75 per rack
General transfer-pricing rule:	

Transfer price	=	Outlay cost	+	Opportunity cost
$11.00	=	$7.25	+	$3.75

The *outlay cost* incurred by the Food Processing Division in order to transfer a rack of bread includes the standard variable production cost of $7.00 and the standard variable transportation cost of $.25. The *opportunity cost* incurred by Suncoast Food Centers when its Food Processing Division transfers a rack of bread to the Gulf Division *instead* of selling it in the external market is the forgone contribution margin from the lost sale, equal to $3.75. Why does the company lose a sale in the external market for every rack of bread transferred to the Gulf Division? The sale is lost because there is *no excess capacity* in the Food Processing Division. Every rack of bread transferred to another company division results in one less rack of bread sold in the external market.

Goal Congruence How does the general transfer-pricing rule promote goal congruence? Suppose the Gulf Division's grocery stores can sell a loaf of bread for $1.50, or $18 for a rack of 12 loaves ($18 = 12 × $1.50). What is the best way for Suncoast Food Centers to use the limited production capacity in the Food Processing Division's Orlando bakery? The answer is determined as follows:

Contribution to Suncoast Food Centers from Sale in External Market		Contribution to Suncoast Food Centers from Transfer to Gulf Division	
Wholesale selling price per rack	$11.00	Retail selling price per rack	$18.00
Less: Variable costs	7.25	Less: Variable costs	7.25
Contribution margin	$ 3.75	Contribution margin	$10.75

The best use of the bakery's limited production capacity is to produce bread for transfer to the Gulf Division. If the transfer price is set at $11.00, as the general rule specifies, goal congruence is maintained. The Food Processing Division manager is willing to transfer bread to the Gulf Division, because the transfer price of $11.00 is equal to the external market price. The Gulf Division manager is willing to buy the bread, because her division will have a contribution margin of $7.00 on each rack of bread transferred ($18.00 sales price minus the $11.00 transfer price).

Now consider a different situation. Suppose a local organization makes a special offer to the Gulf Division manager to buy several hundred loaves of bread to sell in a promotional campaign. The organization offers to pay $.80 per loaf, which is $9.60 per rack of a dozen loaves. What will the Gulf Division manager do? She must pay a transfer price of $11.00 per rack, so the Gulf Division would lose $1.40 per rack if the special offer were accepted ($1.40 = $11.00 − $9.60). The Gulf Division manager will decline the special offer. Is this decision in the best interests of Suncoast Food Centers as a whole? If the offer were accepted, the company as a whole would make a positive contribution of $2.35 per rack, as shown below.

Contribution to Suncoast Food Centers If Special Offer Is Accepted

Special price per rack	$9.60 per rack
Less: Variable cost to company	7.25 per rack
Contribution to company, per rack	$2.35 per rack

However, the company can make even more if its Food Processing Division sells bread directly in its external market. Then the contribution to the company is $3.75, as we have just seen. (The external market price of $11.00 per rack minus a variable cost of $7.25 per rack equals $3.75 per rack.) Thus, Suncoast Food Centers is better off, as a whole, if the Gulf Division's special offer is rejected. Once again, the general transfer-pricing rule results in goal-congruent decision making.

Scenario II: Excess Capacity Now let's change our basic assumption, and suppose the Food Processing Division's Orlando bakery has excess production capacity. This means that the total demand for its bread from all sources, including the Gulf and Atlantic divisions and the external market, is less than the bakery's production capacity. Under this scenario of excess capacity, what does the general rule specify for a transfer price?

$$\begin{array}{ccccc} \text{Transfer price} & = & \text{Outlay cost} & + & \text{Opportunity cost} \\ \$7.25 & = & \$7.25 & + & 0 \end{array}$$

The *outlay cost* in the Food Processing Division's Orlando bakery is still $7.25, since it does not depend on whether there is idle capacity or not. The *opportunity cost,* however, is now zero. There is no opportunity cost to the company when a rack of bread is transferred to the Gulf Division, because the Food Processing Division can still satisfy all of its external demand for bread. Thus, the general rule specifies a transfer price of $7.25, the total standard variable cost of production and transportation.

"It is difficult for people 'doing the business' to stop and consult about the transfer pricing implications of their moves, but they have to." (13d)

Respondent, EY Survey

Goal Congruence Let's reconsider what will happen when the Gulf Division manager receives the local organization's special offer to buy bread at $9.60 per rack. The Gulf Division will now show a positive contribution of $2.35 per rack on the special order.

Special price per rack	$9.60 per rack
Less: Transfer price paid by Gulf Division	7.25 per rack
Contribution to Gulf Division	$2.35 per rack

The Gulf Division manager will accept the special offer. This decision is also in the best interests of Suncoast Food Centers. The company, as a whole, also will make a contribution of $2.35 per rack on every rack transferred to the Gulf Division to satisfy the special order. Once again, the general transfer-pricing rule maintains goal-congruent decision-making behavior.

Notice that the general rule yields a transfer price that leaves the Food Processing Division manager indifferent as to whether the transfer will be made. At a transfer price of \$7.25, the contribution to the Food Processing Division will be zero (transfer price of \$7.25 less variable cost of \$7.25). To avoid this problem, we can view the general rule as providing a lower bound on the transfer price. Some companies allow the producing division to add a markup to this lower bound in order to provide a positive contribution margin. This in turn provides a positive incentive to make the transfer.

Difficulty in Implementing the General Rule The general transfer-pricing rule will always promote goal-congruent decision making *if the rule can be implemented.* However, the rule is often difficult or impossible to implement due to the difficulty of measuring opportunity costs. Such a cost-measurement problem can arise for a number of reasons. One reason is that the external market may not be perfectly competitive. Under **perfect competition,** the market price does not depend on the quantity sold by any one producer. Under **imperfect competition,** a single producer or group of producers can affect the market price by varying the amount of product available in the market. In such cases, the external market price depends on the production decisions of the producer. This in turn means that the opportunity cost incurred by the company as a result of internal transfers depends on the quantity sold externally. These interactions may make it impossible to measure accurately the opportunity cost caused by a product transfer.

Other reasons for difficulty in measuring the opportunity cost associated with a product transfer include uniqueness of the transferred goods or services, a need for the producing division to invest in special equipment in order to produce the transferred goods, and interdependencies among several transferred products or services. For example, the producing division may provide design services as well as production of the goods for a buying division. What is the opportunity cost associated with each of these related outputs of the producing division? In many such cases, it is difficult to sort out the opportunity costs.

The general transfer-pricing rule provides a good conceptual model for the managerial accountant to use in setting transfer prices. Moreover, in many cases, it can be implemented. When the general rule cannot be implemented, organizations turn to other transfer-pricing methods, as we shall see next.

Transfers Based on the External Market Price

Learning Objective **13-7**

Explain how to base a transfer price on market prices, costs, or negotiations.

A common approach is to set the transfer price equal to the price in the external market. In the Suncoast Food Centers illustration, the Food Processing Division would set the transfer price for bread at \$11.00 per rack, since that is the price the division can obtain in its external market. When the producing division has no excess capacity and perfect competition prevails, where no single producer can affect the market price, the general transfer-pricing rule and the external market price yield the same transfer price. This fact is illustrated for Suncoast Food Centers as follows:

Transfer price =	Outlay cost	+	Opportunity cost		
=	Variable cost of production and transportation	+	Forgone contribution margin of an external sale		
=	\$7.25	+	(\$11.00 − \$7.25)	= \$11.00	

Transfer price = External market price = \$11.00

If the producing division has excess capacity or the external market is imperfectly competitive, the general rule and the external market price will not yield the same transfer price.

If the transfer price is set at the market price, the producing division should have the option of either producing goods for internal transfer or selling in the external market. The buying division should be required to purchase goods from inside its organization if the producing division's goods meet the product specifications. Otherwise, the buying division should have the autonomy to buy from a supplier outside its own organization. To handle pricing disputes that may arise, an arbitration process should be established.

Transfer prices based on market prices are consistent with the responsibility-accounting concepts of profit centers and investment centers. In addition to encouraging division managers to focus on divisional profitability, market-based transfer prices help to show the contribution of each division to overall company profit. Suppose the Food Processing Division of Suncoast Food Centers transfers bread to the Gulf Division at a market-based transfer price of $11.00 per rack. The following contribution margins will be earned by the two divisions and the company as a whole.

Food Processing Division		Gulf Division	
Transfer price	$11.00 per rack	Retail sales price	$18.00 per rack
Less: Variable costs	7.25 per rack	Less: Transfer price	11.00 per rack
Contribution margin	$ 3.75 per rack	Contribution margin	$ 7.00 per rack

Suncoast Food Centers	
Retail sales price	$18.00 per rack
Less: Variable costs	7.25 per rack
Contribution margin	$10.75 per rack

When aggregate divisional profits are determined for the year, and ROI and residual income are computed, the use of a market-based transfer price helps to assess the contributions of each division to overall corporate profits.

Distress Market Prices Occasionally an industry will experience a period of significant excess capacity and extremely low prices. For example, when gasoline prices soared due to a foreign oil embargo, the market prices for recreational vehicles and power boats fell temporarily to very low levels.

Under such extreme conditions, basing transfer prices on market prices can lead to decisions that are not in the best interests of the overall company. Basing transfer prices on artificially *low distress market prices* could lead the producing division to sell or close the productive resources devoted to producing the product for transfer. Under distress market prices, the producing division manager might prefer to move the division into a more profitable product line. While such a decision might improve the division's profit in the short run, it could be contrary to the best interests of the company overall. It might be better for the company as a whole to avoid divesting itself of any productive resources and to ride out the period of market distress. To encourage an autonomous division manager to act in this fashion, some companies set the transfer price equal to the long-run average external market price, rather than the current (possibly depressed) market price.

Negotiated Transfer Prices

Many companies use negotiated transfer prices. Division managers or their representatives actually negotiate the price at which transfers will be made. Sometimes they start with the external market price and then make adjustments for various reasons. For example, the producing division may enjoy some cost savings on internal transfers that are not obtained on external sales. Commissions may not have to be paid to sales personnel on internally transferred products. In such cases, a negotiated transfer price may split the cost savings between the producing and buying divisions.

In other instances, a negotiated transfer price may be used because no external market exists for the transferred product.

Two drawbacks sometimes characterize negotiated transfer prices. First, negotiations can lead to divisiveness and competition between participating division managers. This can undermine the spirit of cooperation and unity that is desirable throughout an organization. Second, although negotiating skill is a valuable managerial talent, it should not be the sole or dominant factor in evaluating a division manager. If, for example, the producing division's manager is a better negotiator than the buying division's manager, then the producing division's profit may look better than it should, simply because of its manager's superior negotiating ability.

Cost-Based Transfer Prices

Organizations that do not base prices on market prices or negotiations often turn to a cost-based transfer-pricing approach.

Variable Cost One approach is to set the transfer price equal to the standard variable cost. The problem with this approach is that even when the producing division has excess capacity, it is not allowed to show any contribution margin on the transferred products or services. To illustrate, suppose the Food Processing Division has excess capacity and the transfer price is set at the standard variable cost of $7.25 per rack of bread. There is no positive incentive for the division to produce and transfer bread to the Gulf Division. The Food Processing Division's contribution margin from a transfer will be zero (transfer price of $7.25 minus variable costs of $7.25 equals zero). Some companies avoid this problem by setting the transfer price at standard variable cost plus a markup to allow the producing division a positive contribution margin.

Full Cost An alternative is to set the transfer price equal to the *full cost* of the transferred product or service. **Full (or absorption) cost** is equal to the product's variable cost plus an allocated portion of fixed overhead.

Suppose the Food Processing Division's Orlando bakery has budgeted annual fixed overhead of $500,000 and budgeted annual production of 200,000 racks of bread. The full cost of the bakery's product is computed as follows:

$$\begin{aligned}\text{Full cost} &= \text{Variable cost} + \text{Allocated fixed overhead}\\ &= \$7.25 \text{ per rack} + \frac{\$500{,}000 \text{ budgeted fixed overhead}}{200{,}000 \text{ budgeted racks of bread}}\\ &= \$7.25 + \$2.50\\ &= \$9.75 \text{ per rack}\end{aligned}$$

Under this approach, the transfer price is set at $9.75 per rack of bread.

Dysfunctional Decision-Making Behavior Basing transfer prices on full cost entails a serious risk of causing dysfunctional decision-making behavior. Full-cost-based transfer prices lead the buying division to view costs that are fixed for the company as a whole as variable costs to the buying division. This can cause faulty decision making.

To illustrate, suppose the Food Processing Division has excess capacity, and the transfer price of bread is equal to the full cost of $9.75 per rack. What will happen if the Gulf Division receives the special offer discussed previously, where it can sell bread to a local organization at a special price of $9.60 per rack? The Gulf Division manager will reject the special order, since otherwise her division would incur a loss of $.15 per rack.

Special price per rack	$ 9.60 per rack
Less: Transfer price based on full cost	9.75 per rack
Loss	$(.15) per rack

What is in the best interests of the company as a whole? Suncoast Food Centers would make a positive contribution of $2.35 per rack on the bread sold in the special order.

Special price per rack	$9.60 per rack
Less: Variable cost in Food Processing Division	7.25 per rack
Contribution to company as a whole	$2.35 per rack

What has happened here? Setting the transfer price equal to the full cost of $9.75 has turned a cost that is fixed in the Food Processing Division, and hence is fixed for the company as a whole, into a variable cost from the viewpoint of the Gulf Division manager. The manager would tend to reject the special offer, even though accepting it would benefit the company as a whole.

Although the practice is common, transfer prices should not be based on full cost. The risk is too great that the cost behavior in the producing division will be obscured. This can all too easily result in poor decisions in the buying division.

Standard versus Actual Costs

Throughout our discussion of transfer prices, we have used standard costs rather than actual costs. This was true in our discussion of the general transfer-pricing rule as well as for cost-based transfer prices. Transfer prices should not be based on actual costs, because such a practice would allow an inefficient producing division to pass its excess production costs on to the buying division in the transfer price. When standard costs are used in transfer-pricing formulas, the buying division is not forced to pick up the tab for the producer's inefficiency. Moreover, the producing division is given an incentive to control its costs, since any costs of inefficiency cannot be passed on.

Undermining Divisional Autonomy

Suppose the manager of Suncoast Food Centers' Food Processing Division has excess capacity but insists on a transfer price of $9.75, based on full cost. The Gulf Division manager is faced with the special offer for bread at $9.60 per rack. She regrets that she will have to decline the offer because it would cause her division's profit to decline, even though the company's interests would be best served by accepting the special order. The Gulf Division manager calls the company president and explains the situation. She asks the president to intervene and force the Food Processing Division manager to lower his transfer price.

"[Transfer pricing] affects nearly every aspect of multinational operations—R&D, manufacturing, marketing and distribution, after-sale services." (13e)

EY

As the company president, what would you do? If you stay out of the controversy, your company will lose the contribution on the special order. If you intervene, you will run the risk of undermining the autonomy of your division managers. You established a decentralized organization structure for Suncoast Centers and hired competent managers because you believed in the benefits of decentralized decision making.

There is no obvious answer to this dilemma. In practice, central managers are reluctant to intervene in such disputes unless the negative financial consequences to the organization are quite large. Most managers believe the benefits of decentralized decision making are important to protect, even if it means an occasional dysfunctional decision.

An International Perspective

Two international issues arise in the case of multinational firms setting transfer prices between divisions in different countries.

Income-Tax Rates Multinational companies often consider domestic and foreign income-tax rates when setting transfer prices. For example, suppose a company based in

TRANSFER PRICING AND TAX ISSUES

The most difficult transfer-pricing issues arise in multinational corporations because of the complexity of the tax issues involved. According to a survey by **EY (formerly Ernst, & Young)**, "transfer pricing is the top tax issue facing multinational corporations. Of the international tax directors at 582 multinational organizations polled in the survey, 75 percent expect their company to face a transfer-pricing audit within the next two years. Respondents cited related-party transactions (including the intercompany transfer of goods, services, properties, loans, and leases) involving administrative and management services as the most likely to be audited. Moreover, there has been an increase in transfer pricing audit activity in recent years."[5]

"The **Internal Revenue Service (IRS)** is concerned that companies could use transfer prices to shift profits between related entities through cost of goods sold. Thus, transfer pricing manipulation could be used by taxpayers to shift income from high tax jurisdictions like the U.S. to low tax jurisdictions. The right price from the IRS's perspective is the market value price. Because it's difficult to prove that the transfer price was equal to the market price, companies often find themselves in disputes with the IRS. But now there's help. The IRS's Advanced Pricing Agreement Program provides companies an opportunity to avoid costly audits and litigation by allowing them to negotiate a prospective agreement with the IRS regarding the facts, the transfer pricing methodology, and an acceptable range of results. The program is aimed at multinational corporations interested in avoiding penalties, managing risk, and determining their tax liability with certainty."[6]

Management **A**ccounting **P**ractice

EY, IRS

Europe also has a division in Asia. A European division produces a subassembly, which is transferred to the Asian division for assembly and sale of the final product. Suppose also that the income-tax rate for the company's European division is higher than the rate in the Asian division's country. How would these different tax rates affect the transfer price for the subassembly?

The company's management has an incentive to set a low transfer price for the subassembly. This will result in relatively low profits for the company's European division and a relatively high income for the Asian division. Since the tax rate is lower in the Asian country, the overall company will save on income tax. By setting a low transfer price, the company will shift a portion of its income to a country with a lower tax rate. Tax laws vary among countries with regard to flexibility in setting transfer prices. Some countries' tax laws prohibit the behavior described in our example, while other countries' laws permit it.

"Transfer pricing has become the most difficult area of international taxation." (13f)

EY

Import Duties Another international issue that can affect a firm's transfer pricing policy is the imposition of import duties, or tariffs. These are fees charged to an importer, generally on the basis of the reported value of the goods being imported. Consider again the example of a firm with divisions in Europe and Asia. If the Asian country imposes an import duty on goods transferred in from the European division, the company has an incentive to set a relatively low transfer price on the transferred goods. This will minimize the duty to be paid and maximize the overall profit for the company as a whole. As in the

5 *2012 Transfer Pricing Global Reference Guide*, Ernst & Young (London: 2012); *2010 Global Transfer Pricing Surveys*, Ernst & Young (London: 2010). See also M. Gujarathi, "GlaxoSmithkline Plc.: International Transfer Pricing and Taxation," *Issues in Accounting Education* 22, no. 4 (November 2007), pp. 749–759; and E. Krell, "Scrutiny of Transfer Pricing Grows," *Business Finance* 6, no. 4 (August 2000), p. 12.

6 S. C. Wrappe, K. Milani, and J. Joy, "The Transfer Price Is Right," *Strategic Finance* 81, no. 1 (July 1999), p. 40.

Transfer prices are used in the service industry as well as in manufacturing. Cornell University, for example, charges an accessory instruction fee to a campus unit when one of its students enrolls in a course offered in a different unit.

© Dennis Macdonald/Getty Images

case of taxation, countries sometimes pass laws to limit a multinational firm's flexibility in setting transfer prices for the purpose of minimizing import duties.

Transfer Pricing in the Service Industry

Service industry firms and nonprofit organizations also use transfer pricing when services are transferred between responsibility centers. In banks, for example, the interest rate at which depositors' funds are transferred to the loan department is a form of transfer price. At Cornell University, if a student in the law school takes a course in the business school, a transfer price is charged to the law school for the credit hours of instruction provided to the law student. Since the transfer price is based on tuition charges, it is a market-price-based transfer price.

Behavioral Issues: Risk Aversion and Incentives

Learning Objective 13-8

Understand the behavioral issues of incentives, goal congruence, and internal controls.

The designer of a performance-evaluation system for responsibility-center managers must consider many factors. Trade-offs often must be made between competing objectives. The overall objective is to achieve goal congruence by providing *incentives* for managers to act in the best interests of the organization as a whole. Financial performance measures such as divisional income, ROI, and residual income go a long way toward achieving this objective. However, these measures do have the disadvantage of imposing *risk* on a manager, because the measures also are affected by factors beyond the manager's control. For example, the income of an orange-growing division of an agricultural company will be affected not only by the manager's diligence and ability, but also by the weather and insect infestations.

Since most people exhibit *risk aversion,* managers must be compensated for the risk they must bear. This compensation comes in the form of higher salaries or bonuses. Thus, the design of a managerial performance evaluation and reward system involves a trade-off between the following two factors:

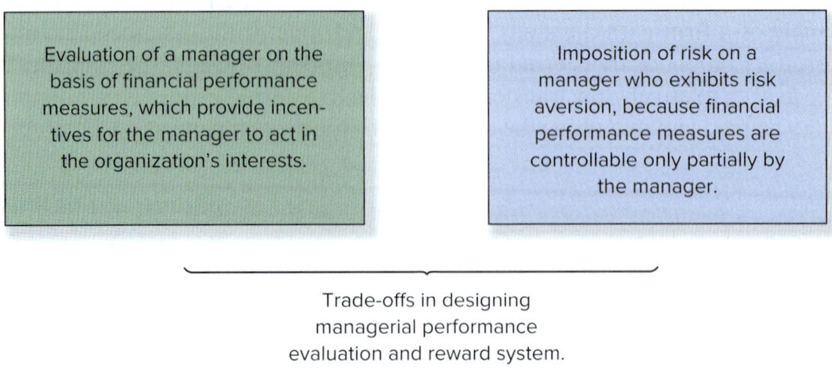

Achieving the optimal trade-off between risk and incentives is a delicate balancing act that requires the skill and experience of top management.

Goal Congruence and Internal Control Systems

Although most business professionals have high ethical standards, there are unfortunately those who will cut corners. An **internal control system** is designed to provide reasonable assurance of the achievement of objectives in: (1) the effectiveness and efficiency of operations; (2) reliability of financial reporting; and (3) compliance with laws and regulations. Internal control procedures are designed to prevent the major lapses in responsible behavior described below.

Fraud Theft or misuse of an organization's resources constitutes *fraud.* To prevent and detect fraud, organizations establish well-defined procedures that prescribe how valuable resources will be handled. For example, many organizations require all checks above a particular amount to be authorized by two people.

Financial Misrepresentation Internal control systems also are designed to prevent managers from intentionally (or accidentally) misstating an organization's financial records. Most companies have an *internal audit* staff, which reviews financial records throughout the organization to ensure their accuracy. (Appendix I explores the Sarbanes-Oxley Act and internal controls over financial reporting).[7]

Corruption Activities such as bribery, deceit, illegal political campaign contributions, and kickbacks constitute *corruption.* Most organizations have internal control procedures and codes of conduct to prevent and detect corrupt practices. For example, many organizations forbid their purchasing personnel from accepting gifts or gratuities from the sales personnel with whom they conduct business. The Foreign Corrupt Practices Act, passed by the U.S. Congress in 1977, prohibits a variety of corrupt practices in foreign business operations. For example, the law prohibits a company's management from bribing officials of a foreign government in return for favorable treatment of their company.

Unauthorized Action Sometimes a well-meaning employee is tempted to take an action that is not illegal or even unethical, but it is contrary to the organization's policies. Internal control procedures also are designed to detect and prevent unauthorized actions by an organization's employees, when those actions could reflect unfavorably on the organization. For example, a company may prohibit its employees from using company facilities for a rally in support of a controversial social cause.

An internal control system constitutes an integral part of an organization's efforts to achieve its goals. To be effective, internal control procedures require top management's full support and intolerance of intentional violations.

[7]The Sarbanes-Oxley Act, passed by the U.S. Congress in 2002, is designed to ensure that a company's financial statements accurately portray its financial condition. See Appendix I (pp 768–772) for coverage of the Sarbanes-Oxley Act.

Chapter Summary

LO13-1 Explain the role of managerial accounting in achieving goal congruence. An important objective of any organization's managerial accounting system is to promote goal congruence among its employees. Thus, the primary criterion for judging the effectiveness of performance measures for responsibility-center managers is the extent to which the measures promote goal congruence.

LO13-2 Compute an investment center's return on investment (ROI), residual income (RI), and economic value added (EVA). An investment center's ROI is equal to its income divided by its invested capital. The investment center's RI is equal to its profit minus the product of its invested capital and an imputed interest rate. The investment center's EVA is computed as follows: After-tax operating income − [(Total assets − Current liabilities) × Weighted-average cost of capital].

LO13-3 Explain how a manager can improve ROI by increasing either the sales margin or capital turnover. An investment center's ROI equals sales margin multiplied by capital turnover. Therefore, an investment center's ROI may be improved by increasing either the sales margin or capital turnover.

LO13-4 Describe some advantages and disadvantages of both ROI and residual income as divisional performance measures. Each of these performance measures relates an investment center's income to the capital invested to earn it. However, residual income and EVA have the additional advantage of incorporating the organization's cost of acquiring capital in the performance measure.

LO13-5 Explain how to measure a division's income and invested capital. There are several ways that investment centers' invested capital is measured in practice. Among the commonly observed measures are: total assets, total productive assets, and total assets less current liabilities. Similarly, several measures of investment center income are observed in practice. As explained in the chapter, these income measures differ on the degree to which certain expenses are controllable at the investment center level.

LO13-6 Use the general economic rule to set an optimal transfer price. The general rule states that the transfer price should be equal to the outlay cost incurred to make the transfer plus the organization's opportunity cost associated with the transfer.

LO13-7 Explain how to base a transfer price on market prices, costs, or negotiations. Due to difficulties in implementing the general transfer pricing rule, most companies base transfer prices on external market prices, costs, or negotiations. Market prices may be the best practical measure, as long as an external market for the transferred product exists. Alternatively, transfer prices may be based on full, absorption product costs or variable product costs. Negotiation, although widely used in setting transfer prices, can be time-consuming and divisive.

LO13-8 Understand the behavioral issues of incentives, goal congruence, and internal controls. In general, companies use investment center performance measures and transfer pricing methods to provide incentives to managers to make goal-congruent decisions. In some cases, both investment center performance measures and transfer prices may result in dysfunctional decisions by mid-level managers. Top management then must weigh the benefits of intervening to prevent suboptimal decisions and the costs of undermining divisional autonomy. Internal controls also are used in organizations to promote the effectiveness and efficiency of operations, the reliability of financial reporting, and compliance with laws and regulations.

Review Problems on Investment Centers and Transfer Pricing

Problem 1

Stellar Systems Company manufactures guidance systems for rockets used to launch commercial satellites. The company's Software Division reported the following results for 20x7.

Income	$ 300,000
Sales revenue	2,000,000
Invested capital (total assets)	3,000,000
Average balance in current liabilities	20,000

Stellar Systems' weighted-average cost of capital (WACC) is 9 percent, and the company's tax rate is 40 percent. Moreover, the company's required rate of return on invested capital is 9 percent.

Required:

1. Compute the Software Division's sales margin, capital turnover, return on investment (ROI), residual income, and economic value added (EVA) for 20x7.
2. If income and sales remain the same in 20x8, but the division's capital turnover improves to 80 percent, compute the following for 20x8: (*a*) invested capital and (*b*) ROI.

Problem 2

Stellar Systems Company's Microprocessor Division sells a computer module to the company's Guidance Assembly Division, which assembles completed guidance systems. The Microprocessor Division has no excess capacity. The computer module costs $10,000 to manufacture, and it can be sold in the external market to companies in the computer industry for $13,500.

Required: Compute the transfer price for the computer module using the general transfer-pricing rule.

Solutions to Review Problems

Problem 1

1. Sales margin $= \frac{\text{Income}}{\text{Sales revenue}} = \frac{\$300{,}000}{\$2{,}000{,}000} = 15\%$

   Capital turnover $= \frac{\text{Sales revenue}}{\text{Invested capital}} = \frac{\$2{,}000{,}000}{\$3{,}000{,}000} = 67\%$

   Return on investment $= \frac{\text{Income}}{\text{Invested capital}} = \frac{\$300{,}000}{\$3{,}000{,}000} = 10\%$

Residual income:

Divisional income		$300,000
Less: Imputed interest charge:		
Invested capital	$3,000,000	
× Imputed interest rate	× .09	
Imputed interest charge		270,000
Residual income		$ 30,000

Economic value added (EVA):

$$\text{EVA} = \begin{pmatrix}\text{Investment center's}\\\text{after-tax}\\\text{operating income}\end{pmatrix} - \left[\left(\begin{matrix}\text{Investment center's}\\\text{total assets}\end{matrix} - \begin{matrix}\text{Investment center's}\\\text{current liabilities}\end{matrix}\right) \times \begin{matrix}\text{Weighted-average}\\\text{cost of capital}\end{matrix}\right]$$

$$= \$300{,}000\,(1 - .40) - [(\$3{,}000{,}000 - \$20{,}000) \times .09]$$

$$= \$(88{,}200)$$

2. *a.* Capital turnover $= \frac{\text{Sales revenue}}{\text{Invested capital}} = \frac{\$2{,}000{,}000}{?} = 80\%$

   Therefore: Invested capital $= \frac{\$2{,}000{,}000}{.80} = \$2{,}500{,}000$

   b. New ROI = 15% × 80% = 12%

Problem 2

Transfer price = Outlay cost + Opportunity cost

= $10,000 + ($13,500 − $10,000)

= $13,500

The $3,500 opportunity cost of a transfer is the contribution margin that will be forgone if a computer module is transferred instead of sold in the external market.

Key Terms

For each term's definition refer to the indicated page, or turn to the glossary at the end of the text.

capital turnover, 557
cash bonus, 566
economic value added (EVA), 561
full (or absorption) cost, 575
goal congruence, 555
imperfect competition, 573
incentive compensation, 566
internal control system, 579
investment center, 554
management by objectives (MBO), 555
merit pay, 566
pay for performance, 566
perfect competition, 573
residual income (RI), 559
return on investment (ROI), 556
sales margin, 557
shareholder value analysis, 561
transfer price, 554
weighted-average cost of capital (WACC), 561

Review Questions

13–1. What is the managerial accountant's primary objective in designing a responsibility-accounting system?

13–2. Define *goal congruence,* and explain why it is important to an organization's success.

13–3. Describe the managerial approach known as *management by objectives* or *MBO.*

13–4. Define and give three examples of an *investment center.*

13–5. Write the formula for ROI, showing sales margin and capital turnover as its components.

13–6. Explain how the manager of the Automobile Division of an insurance company could improve her division's ROI.

13–7. Create an example showing how residual income is calculated. What information is used in computing residual income that is not used in computing ROI?

13–8. What is the chief disadvantage of ROI as an investment-center performance measure? How does the residual-income measure eliminate this disadvantage?

13–9. Why is there typically a rise in ROI or residual income across time in a division? What undesirable behavioral implications could this phenomenon have?

13–10. Define the term *economic value added.* How does it differ from residual income?

13–11. Distinguish between the following measures of invested capital, and briefly explain when each should be used: (*a*) total assets, (*b*) total productive assets, and (*c*) total assets less current liabilities.

13–12. Why do some companies use gross book value instead of net book value to measure a division's invested capital?

13–13. Explain why it is important in performance evaluation to distinguish between investment centers and their managers.

13–14. How do organizations use pay for performance to motivate managers?

13–15. Describe an alternative to using ROI or residual income to measure investment-center performance.

13–16. How does inflation affect investment-center performance measures?

13–17. List three nonfinancial measures that could be used to evaluate a division of an insurance company.

13–18. Discuss the importance of nonfinancial information in measuring investment-center performance.

13–19. Identify and explain the managerial accountant's primary objective in choosing a transfer-pricing policy.

13–20. Describe four methods by which transfer prices may be set.

13–21. Explain the significance of excess capacity in the transferring division when transfer prices are set using the general transfer-pricing rule.

13–22. Why might income-tax laws affect the transfer-pricing policies of multinational companies?

13–23. Explain the role of import duties, or tariffs, in affecting the transfer-pricing policies of multinational companies.

Exercises

All applicable Exercises are available in Connect. connect

Exercise 13–24
Components of ROI
(LO 13-2)

The following data pertain to Dakota Division's most recent year of operations.

Income	$ 4,000,000
Sales revenue	50,000,000
Average invested capital	20,000,000

Required: Compute Dakota Division's sales margin, capital turnover, and return on investment for the year.

Exercise 13–25
Improving ROI
(LO 13-3)

Refer to the preceding exercise.

Required: Demonstrate two ways Dakota Division's manager could improve the division's ROI to 25 percent.

Exercise 13–26
Residual Income
(LO 13-2)

Refer to the data for Exercise 13–24. Assume that the company's minimum desired rate of return on invested capital is 11 percent.

Required: Compute Dakota Division's residual income for the year.

Exercise 13–27
Calculate Weighted-Average Cost of Capital for EVA
(LO 13-2)

Golden Gate Construction Associates, a real estate developer and building contractor in San Francisco, has two sources of long-term capital: debt and equity. The cost to Golden Gate of issuing debt is the after-tax cost of the interest payments on the debt, taking into account the fact that the interest payments are tax deductible. The cost of Golden Gate's equity capital is the investment opportunity rate of Golden Gate's investors, that is, the rate they could earn on investments of similar risk to that of investing in Golden Gate Construction Associates. The interest rate on Golden Gate's $60 million of long-term debt is 10 percent, and the company's tax rate is 40 percent. The cost of Golden Gate's equity capital is 15 percent. Moreover, the market value (and book value) of Golden Gate's equity is $90 million.

Required: Calculate Golden Gate Construction Associates' weighted-average cost of capital.

Exercise 13–28
Economic Value Added (EVA); Continuation of Preceding Exercise
(LO 13-2)

Refer to the data in the preceding exercise for Golden Gate Construction Associates. The company has two divisions: the real estate division and the construction division. The divisions' total assets, current liabilities, and before-tax operating income for the most recent year are as follows:

Division	Total Assets	Current Liabilities	Before-Tax Operating Income
Real estate	$100,000,000	$6,000,000	$20,000,000
Construction	60,000,000	4,000,000	18,000,000

Required: Calculate the economic value added (EVA) for each of Golden Gate Construction Associates' divisions. (You will need to use the weighted-average cost of capital, which was computed in the preceding exercise.)

Exercise 13–29
ROI; Residual Income
(LO 13-1, 13-2)

Wyalusing Industries has manufactured prefabricated houses for over 20 years. The houses are constructed in sections to be assembled on customers' lots. Wyalusing expanded into the precut housing market when it acquired Fairmont Company, one of its suppliers. In this market, various types of lumber are precut into the appropriate lengths, banded into packages, and shipped to customers' lots for assembly. Wyalusing designated the Fairmont Division as an investment center. Wyalusing uses return on investment (ROI) as a performance measure with investment defined as average productive assets. Management bonuses are based in part on ROI. All investments are expected to earn a minimum return of 15 percent before income taxes. Fairmont's ROI has ranged from 19.3 to 22.1 percent since it was acquired. Fairmont had an investment opportunity in 20x1 that had an estimated ROI of 18 percent. Fairmont's management decided against the investment because it believed the investment would decrease the division's overall ROI. The 20x1 income statement for Fairmont Division follows. The division's productive assets were $12,600,000 at the end of 20x1, a 5 percent increase over the balance at the beginning of the year.

FAIRMONT DIVISION
Income Statement
For the Year Ended December 31, 20x1
(in thousands)

Sales revenue		$24,000
Cost of goods sold		15,800
Gross margin		$ 8,200
Operating expenses:		
Administrative	$2,140	
Selling	3,600	5,740
Income from operations before income taxes		$ 2,460

Required:

1. Calculate the following performance measures for 20x1 for the Fairmont Division.
   a. Return on investment (ROI).
   b. Residual income.
2. Would the management of Fairmont Division have been more likely to accept the investment opportunity it had in 20x1 if residual income were used as a performance measure instead of ROI? Explain your answer.
3. ***Build a spreadsheet:*** Construct an Excel spreadsheet to solve requirement (1) above. Show how the solution will change if income from operations was $2,700,000.

(CMA, adapted)

Exercise 13–30
ROI and Residual Income; Annual Reports; Use of Internet
(LO 13-2)

Select one of the following companies (or any company of your choosing) and use the Internet to explore the company's most recent annual report.

American Airlines	www.aa.com
Deere and Company	www.deere.com
IBM	www.ibm.com
Wyndham Hotels	www.wyndham.com
Walmart	www.walmart.com

Required:

1. Calculate the company's overall return on investment (ROI). Also, calculate the company's overall residual income. (Assume an imputed interest rate of 10 percent.) List and explain any assumptions you make.
2. Does the company include a calculation of ROI in its online annual report? If it does, do your calculations agree with those of the company? If not, what would be some possible explanations?

Exercise 13–31
Increasing ROI over Time
(LO 13-2, 13-4, 13-5)

Refer to Exhibit 13–3. Assume that you are a consultant who has been hired by Suncoast Food Centers.

Required: Write a memorandum to the company president explaining why the ROI based on net book value (in Exhibit 13–3) behaves as it does over the five-year time horizon.

Exercise 13–32
Internal Control
(LO 13-8)

Dryden Company is an auto parts supplier. At the end of each month, the employee who maintains all of the inventory records takes a physical inventory of the firm's stock. When discrepancies occur between the recorded inventory and the physical count, the employee changes the physical count to agree with the records.

Required:

1. What problems could arise as a result of Dryden Company's inventory procedures?
2. How could the internal control system be strengthened to eliminate the potential problems?

Exercise 13–33
Improving ROI
(LO 13-2, 13-3)

The following data pertain to British Isles Aggregates Company, a producer of sand, gravel, and cement, for the year just ended.

Sales revenue	£2,000,000
Cost of goods sold	1,100,000
Operating expenses	800,000
Average invested capital	1,000,000

£ denotes the British pound sterling, the national monetary unit of Great Britain.

Required:

1. Compute the company's sales margin, capital turnover, and ROI.
2. If the sales and average invested capital remain the same during the next year, to what level would total expenses have to be reduced in order to improve the firm's ROI to 15 percent?
3. Assume expenses are reduced, as calculated in requirement (2). Compute the firm's new sales margin. Show how the new sales margin and the old capital turnover together result in a new ROI of 15 percent.

Exercise 13–34
General Transfer-Pricing Rule
(LO 13-6)

Illinois Metallurgy Corporation has two divisions. The Fabrication Division transfers partially completed components to the Assembly Division at a predetermined transfer price. The Fabrication Division's standard variable production cost per unit is $300. The division has no excess capacity, and it could sell all of its components to outside buyers at $380 per unit in a perfectly competitive market.

Required:

1. Determine a transfer price using the general rule.
2. How would the transfer price change if the Fabrication Division had excess capacity?

Exercise 13–35
Cost-Based Transfer Pricing
(LO 13-7)

Refer to the preceding exercise. The Fabrication Division's full (absorption) cost of a component is $340, which includes $40 of applied fixed-overhead costs. The transfer price has been set at $374, which is the Fabrication Division's full cost plus a 10 percent markup.

The Assembly Division has a special offer for its product of $465. The Assembly Division incurs variable costs of $100 in addition to the transfer price for the Fabrication Division's components. Both divisions currently have excess production capacity.

Required:

1. What is the Assembly Division's manager likely to do regarding acceptance or rejection of the special offer? Why?
2. Is this decision in the best interests of the company as a whole? Why?
3. How could the situation be remedied using the transfer price?

Problems

All applicable Problems are available in Connect. connect

Problem 13–36
Comparing the Performance of Two Divisions
(LO 13-2, 13-4)

Long Beach Pharmaceutical Company has two divisions, which reported the following results for the most recent year.

	Division I	Division II
Income	$ 900,000	$ 200,000
Average invested capital	$6,000,000	$1,000,000
ROI	15%	20%

Required: Which was the more successful division during the year? Think carefully about this, and explain your answer.

Problem 13–37
ROI and Residual Income; Missing Data
(LO 13-2)

Residual income, division A: $240,000

The following data pertain to three divisions of Nevada Aggregates, Inc. The company's required rate of return on invested capital is 8 percent.

	Division A	Division B	Division C
Sales revenue	?	$10,000,000	?
Income	$400,000	$2,000,000	?
Average investment	?	$2,500,000	?
Sales margin	20%	?	25%
Capital turnover	1	?	?
ROI	?	?	20%
Residual income	?	?	$120,000

Required: Fill in the blanks above.

Problem 13–38
Improving ROI
(LO 13-3)

2. ROI: 25%

Refer to the preceding problem about Nevada Aggregates, Inc.

Required:

1. Explain three ways the Division B manager could improve her division's ROI. Use numbers to illustrate these possibilities.
2. Suppose Division A's sales margin increased to 25 percent, while its capital turnover remained constant. Compute the division's new ROI.

Problem 13–39
Residual Income
(LO 13-2, 13-4)

Refer to the data for problem 13–36 regarding Long Beach Pharmaceutical Company.

Required: Compute each division's residual income for the year under each of the following assumptions about the firm's cost of acquiring capital.

1. 12 percent.
2. 15 percent.
3. 18 percent.

Which division was more successful? Explain your answer.

Problem 13–40
Increasing ROI over Time; Accelerated Depreciation
(LO 13-2, 13-4, 13-5)

Year 2, ROI based on net book value: 12.5%

Refer to Exhibit 13–3. Prepare a similar table of the changing ROI assuming the following accelerated depreciation schedule. Assume the same income before depreciation as shown in Exhibit 13–3. (If there is a loss, leave the ROI column blank.)

Year	Depreciation
1	$200,000
2	120,000
3	72,000
4	54,000
5	54,000
Total	$500,000

Required:

1. How does your table differ from the one in Exhibit 13–3? Why?
2. What are the implications of the ROI pattern in your table?

Problem 13–41
Increasing Residual Income over Time
(LO 13-2, 13-4, 13-5)

Year 1, residual income (based on net book value): $5,000

Prepare a table similar to Exhibit 13–3, which focuses on residual income. Use a 10 percent rate to compute the imputed interest charge. The table should show the residual income on the investment during each year in its five-year life. Assume the same income before depreciation and the same depreciation schedule as shown in Exhibit 13–3.

Problem 13–42
ROI and Residual Income; Investment Evaluation
(LO 13-2, 13-3, 13-4, 13-8)

3. Income: $150,000
5. Current residual income of the Northeast Division: $148,000

Megatronics Corporation, a massive retailer of electronic products, is organized in four separate divisions. The four divisional managers are evaluated at year-end, and bonuses are awarded based on ROI. Last year, the company as a whole produced a 13 percent return on its investment.

During the past week, management of the company's Northeast Division was approached about the possibility of buying a competitor that had decided to redirect its retail activities. (If the competitor is acquired, it will be acquired at its book value.) The data that follow relate to recent performance of the Northeast Division and the competitor:

	Northeast Division	Competitor
Sales	$8,400,000	$5,200,000
Variable costs	70% of sales	65% of sales
Fixed costs	$2,150,000	$1,670,000
Invested capital	$1,850,000	$625,000

Management has determined that in order to upgrade the competitor to Megatronics' standards, an additional $375,000 of invested capital would be needed.

Required: As a group, complete the following requirements.

1. Compute the current ROI of the Northeast Division and the division's ROI if the competitor is acquired.
2. What is the likely reaction of divisional management toward the acquisition? Why?
3. What is the likely reaction of Megatronics' corporate management toward the acquisition? Why?
4. Would the division be better off if it didn't upgrade the competitor to Megatronics' standards? Show computations to support your answer.
5. Assume that Megatronics uses residual income to evaluate performance and desires a 12 percent minimum return on invested capital. Compute the current residual income of the Northeast Division and the division's residual income if the competitor is acquired. Will divisional management be likely to change its attitude toward the acquisition? Why?

Problem 13–43
ROI and Performance Evaluations
(LO 13-2, 13-4, 13-8)

1. Capital turnover: 80%

Kenneth Washburn, head of the Sporting Goods Division of Reliable Products, has just completed a miserable nine months. "If it could have gone wrong, it did. Sales are down, income is down, inventories are bloated, and quite frankly, I'm beginning to worry about my job," he moaned. Washburn is evaluated on the basis of ROI. Selected figures for the past nine months follow.

Sales	$4,800,000
Operating income	360,000
Invested capital	6,000,000

In an effort to make something out of nothing and to salvage the current year's performance, Washburn was contemplating implementation of some or all of the following four strategies:

a. Write off and discard $60,000 of obsolete inventory. The company will take a loss on the disposal.

b. Accelerate the collection of $80,000 of overdue customer accounts receivable.

c. Stop advertising through year-end and drastically reduce outlays for repairs and maintenance. These actions are expected to save the division $150,000 of expenses and will conserve cash resources.

d. Acquire two competitors that are expected to have the following financial characteristics:

	Projected Sales	Projected Operating Expenses	Projected Invested Capital
Anderson Manufacturing	$3,000,000	$2,400,000	$5,000,000
Palm Beach Enterprises	4,500,000	4,120,000	4,750,000

Required:

1. Briefly define sales margin, capital turnover, and return on investment and then compute these amounts for Reliable's Sporting Goods Division over the past nine months.
2. Evaluate each of the first two strategies listed, with respect to its effect on the Reliable's last nine months' performance, and make a recommendation to Washburn regarding which, if any, to adopt.
3. Are there possible long-term problems associated with strategy (c)? Briefly explain.
4. Determine the ROI of the investment in Anderson Manufacturing and do the same for the investment in Palm Beach Enterprises. Should Washburn reject both acquisitions, acquire one company, or acquire both companies? Assume that sufficient capital is available to fund investments in both organizations.

Problem 13–44
Weighted-Average Cost of Capital; Economic Value Added (EVA)
(LO 13-2)

1. Weighted-average cost of capital: .1056

Cape Cod Lobster Shacks, Inc. (CCLS) is a seafood restaurant chain operating throughout the northeast. The company has two sources of long-term capital: debt and equity. The cost to CCLS of issuing debt is the after-tax cost of the interest payments on the debt, taking into account the fact that the interest payments are tax deductible. The cost of CCLS's equity capital is the investment opportunity rate of CCLS's investors, that is, the rate they could earn on investments of similar risk to that of investing in Cape Cod Lobster Shacks, Inc. The interest rate on CCLS's $80 million of long-term debt is 9 percent, and the company's tax rate is 40 percent. The cost of CCLS's equity capital is 14 percent. Moreover, the market value (and book value) of CCLS's equity is $120 million.

Cape Cod Lobster Shacks, Inc. consists of two divisions, the properties division and the food service division. The divisions' total assets, current liabilities, and before-tax operating income for the most recent year are as follows:

Division	Total Assets	Current Liabilities	Before-Tax Operating Income
Properties	$145,000,000	$3,000,000	$29,000,000
Food Service	64,000,000	6,000,000	15,000,000

Required:

1. Calculate the weighted-average cost of capital for Cape Cod Lobster Shacks, Inc.
2. Calculate the economic value added (EVA) for each of CCLS's divisions.

   Build a spreadsheet: Construct an Excel spreadsheet to solve both of the preceding requirements. Show how the solution will change if the following information changes: before-tax operating income was $30,000,000 and $14,000,000 for Properties and Food Service, respectively.

Problem 13–45
Weighted-Average Cost of Capital; Economic Value Added (EVA)
(LO 13-2)

1. The weighted-average cost of capital: .0972
2. Atlantic Division, economic value added: $(12,181,200)

All-Canadian, Ltd. is a multiproduct company with three divisions: Pacific Division, Plains Division, and Atlantic Division. The company has two sources of long-term capital: debt and equity. The interest rate on All-Canadian's $400 million debt is 9 percent, and the company's tax rate is 30 percent. The cost of All-Canadian's equity capital is 12 percent. Moreover, the market value of the company's equity is $600 million. (The book value of All-Canadian's equity is $430 million, but that amount does not reflect the current value of the company's assets or the value of intangible assets.)

The following data (in millions) pertain to All-Canadian's three divisions.

Division	Operating Income	Current Liabilities	Total Assets
Pacific	$14	$6	$70
Plains	45	5	300
Atlantic	48	9	480

Required:

1. Compute All-Canadian's weighted-average cost of capital (WACC).
2. Compute the economic value added (or EVA) for each of the company's three divisions.
3. What conclusions can you draw from the EVA analysis?

Problem 13–46
Comprehensive Transfer-Pricing Problem; Ethics
(LO 13-6, 13-7, 13-8)

2(a). Transfer price: $65

Clearview Window Company manufactures windows for the home-building industry. The window frames are produced in the Frame Division. The frames are then transferred to the Glass Division, where the glass and hardware are installed. The company's best-selling product is a three-by-four-foot, doublepaned operable window.

The Frame Division also can sell frames directly to custom home builders, who install the glass and hardware. The sales price for a frame is $80. The Glass Division sells its finished windows for $190. The markets for both frames and finished windows exhibit perfect competition.

The standard variable cost of the window is detailed as follows:

	Frame Division	Glass Division
Direct material	$15	$30*
Direct labor	20	15
Variable overhead	30	30
Total	$65	$75

*Not including the transfer price for the frame.

Required:

1. Assume that there is no excess capacity in the Frame Division.

   a. Use the general rule to compute the transfer price for window frames.

   b. Calculate the transfer price if it is based on standard variable cost with a 10 percent markup.

2. Assume that there is excess capacity in the Frame Division.
   a. Use the general rule to compute the transfer price for window frames.
   b. Explain why your answers to requirements (1*a*) and (2*a*) differ.
   c. Suppose the predetermined fixed-overhead rate in the Frame Division is 125 percent of direct-labor cost. Calculate the transfer price if it is based on standard full cost plus a 10 percent markup.
   d. Assume the transfer price established in requirement (2c) is used. The Glass Division has been approached by the U.S. Army with a special order for 1,000 windows at $155. From the perspective of Clearview Window Company as a whole, should the special order be accepted or rejected? Why?
   e. Assume the same facts as in requirement (2d). Will an autonomous Glass Division manager accept or reject the special order? Why?
   f. Comment on any ethical issues you see in the questions raised in requirements (2*d*) and (2*e*).
3. Comment on the use of full cost as the basis for setting transfer prices.

Problem 13–47
Transfer Pricing; Negotiation
(LO 13-7, 13-8)

4. Produce diode and sell externally, contribution margin: $275

Cortez Enterprises has two divisions: Birmingham and Tampa. Birmingham currently sells a diode reducer to manufacturers of aircraft navigation systems for $775 per unit. Variable costs amount to $500, and demand for this product currently exceeds the division's ability to supply the marketplace.

Despite this situation, Cortez is considering another use for the diode reducer, namely, integration into a satellite positioning system that would be made by Tampa. The positioning system has an anticipated selling price of $1,400 and requires an additional $670 of variable manufacturing costs. A transfer price of $750 has been established for the diode reducer.

Top management is anxious to introduce the positioning system; however, unless the transfer is made, an introduction will not be possible because of the difficulty of obtaining needed diode reducers. Birmingham and Tampa are in the process of recovering from previous financial problems, and neither division can afford any future losses. The company uses responsibility accounting and ROI in measuring divisional performance, and awards bonuses to divisional management.

Required:

1. How would Birmingham's divisional manager likely react to the decision to transfer diode reducers to Tampa? Show computations to support your answer.
2. How would Tampa's divisional management likely react to the $750 transfer price? Show computations to support your answer.
3. Assume that a lower transfer price is desired. Should top management lower the price or should the price be lowered by another means? Explain.
4. From a contribution margin perspective, does Cortez benefit more if it sells the diode reducers externally or transfers the reducers to Tampa? By how much?

Problem 13–48
Setting a Transfer Price; International Setting; Differential Tax Rates
(LO 13-6, 13-7)

2. U.S. operation, income after tax: $24.00
3. German operation, income after tax: $36.00

Alpha Communications, Inc., which produces telecommunications equipment in the United States, has a very strong local market for its circuit board. The variable production cost is $130, and the company can sell its entire supply domestically for $170. The U.S. tax rate is 40 percent.

Alternatively, Alpha can ship the circuit board to its division in Germany, to be used in a product that the German division will distribute throughout Europe. Information about the German product and the division's operating environment follows.

Selling price of final product: $360

Shipping fees to import circuit board: $20

Labor, overhead, and additional material costs of final product: $115

Import duties levied on circuit board (to be paid by the German division): 10% of transfer price

German tax rate: 60%

Assume that U.S. and German tax authorities allow a transfer price for the circuit board set at either U.S. variable manufacturing cost or the U.S. market price. Alpha's management is in the process of exploring which transfer price is better for the firm as a whole.

Required:

1. Compute overall company profitability per unit if all units are transferred and U.S. variable manufacturing cost is used as the transfer price. Show separate calculations for the U.S. operation and the German division.
2. Repeat requirement (1), assuming the use of the U.S. market price as the transfer price. Which of the two transfer prices is better for the firm?
3. Assume that the German division can obtain the circuit board in Germany for $155.
   a. If you were the head of the German division, would you rather do business with your U.S. division or buy the circuit board locally? Why?
   b. Rather than proceed with the transfer, is it in the best interest of Alpha to sell its goods domestically and allow the German division to acquire the circuit board in Germany? Why? Show computations to support your answer.
4. Generally speaking, when tax rates differ between countries, what strategy should a company use in setting its transfer prices?
5. ***Build a spreadsheet:*** Construct an Excel spreadsheet to solve requirements (1) and (2) above. Show how the solution will change if the following information changes: the U.S. tax rate is 35 percent, the German tax rate is 55 percent, and the import duties are 8 percent of the transfer price.

Problem 13–49
Transfer Pricing; Management Behavior
(LO 13-6, 13-7, 13-8)

2. Total contribution margin, Mining Division: $15,200,000

Provo Consolidated Resources Company (PCRC) has several divisions. However, only two divisions transfer products to other divisions. The Mining Division refines toldine, which is then transferred to the Metals Division. The toldine is processed into an alloy by the Metals Division, and the alloy is sold to customers at a price of $150 per unit. The Mining division is currently required by PCRC to transfer its total yearly output of 400,000 units of toldine to the Metals Division at total actual manufacturing cost plus 10 percent. Unlimited quantities of toldine can be purchased and sold on the open market at $90 per unit. While the Mining Division could sell all the toldine it produces at $90 per unit on the open market, it would incur a variable selling cost of $5 per unit.

Brian Jones, manager of the Mining Division, is unhappy with having to transfer the entire output of toldine to the Metals Division at 110 percent of cost. In a meeting with the management of Provo, he said, "Why should my division be required to sell toldine to the Metals Division at less than market price? For the year just ended in May, Metals' contribution margin was over $19 million on sales of 400,000 units, while Mining's contribution was just over $5 million on the transfer of the same number of units. My division is subsidizing the profitability of the Metals Division. We should be allowed to charge the market price for toldine when transferring to the Metals Division."

The following table shows the detailed unit cost structure for both the Mining and Metals divisions during the most recent year.

	Mining Division	Metals Division
Transfer price from Mining Division	—	$ 66
Direct material	$12	6
Direct labor	16	20
Manufacturing overhead	32*	25†
Total cost per unit	$60	$117

*Manufacturing-overhead cost in the Mining Division is 25 percent fixed and 75 percent variable.
†Manufacturing-overhead cost in the Metals Division is 60 percent fixed and 40 percent variable.

Required:

1. Explain why transfer prices based on total actual costs are not appropriate as the basis for divisional performance measurement.
2. Using the market price as the transfer price, determine the contribution margin for both the Mining Division and the Metals Division.
3. If Provo Consolidated Resources Company were to institute the use of negotiated transfer prices and allow divisions to buy and sell on the open market, determine the price range for toldine that would be acceptable to both the Mining Division and the Metals Division. Explain your answer.

4. Use the general transfer-pricing rule to compute the lowest transfer price that would be acceptable to the Mining Division. Is your answer consistent with your conclusion in requirement (3)? Explain.
5. Identify which one of the three types of transfer prices (cost-based, market-based, or negotiated) is most likely to elicit desirable management behavior at PCRC. Explain your answer.

(CMA, adapted)

Cases

Case 13–50
ROI versus Residual Income; Incentive Effects
(LO 13-1, 13-2, 13-4, 13-8)

2. Residual income, RLI: $120,000

Holiday Entertainment Corporation (HEC), a subsidiary of New Age Industries, manufactures go-carts and other recreational vehicles. Family recreational centers that feature not only go-cart tracks but miniature golf, batting cages, and arcade games as well have increased in popularity. As a result, HEC has been receiving some pressure from New Age's management to diversify into some of these other recreational areas. Recreational Leasing, Inc. (RLI), one of the largest firms that leases arcade games to family recreational centers, is looking for a friendly buyer. New Age's top management believes that RLI's assets could be acquired for an investment of $3.2 million and has strongly urged Bill Grieco, division manager of HEC, to consider acquiring RLI.

Grieco has reviewed RLI's financial statements with his controller, Marie Donnelly, and they believe the acquisition may not be in the best interest of HEC. "If we decide not to do this, the New Age people are not going to be happy," said Grieco. "If we could convince them to base our bonuses on something other than return on investment, maybe this acquisition would look more attractive. How would we do if the bonuses were based on residual income, using the company's 15 percent cost of capital?"

New Age Industries traditionally has evaluated all of its divisions on the basis of return on investment. The desired rate of return for each division is 20 percent. The management team of any division reporting an annual increase in the ROI is automatically eligible for a bonus. The management of divisions reporting a decline in the ROI must provide convincing explanations for the decline in order to be eligible for a bonus. Moreover, this bonus is limited to 50 percent of the bonus paid to divisions reporting an increase in ROI.

In the following table are condensed financial statements for both HEC and RLI for the most recent year.

	RLI	HEC
Sales revenue	–	$9,500,000
Leasing revenue	$3,100,000	–
Variable expenses	(1,300,000)	(6,000,000)
Fixed expenses	(1,200,000)	(1,500,000)
Operating income	$ 600,000	$2,000,000
Current assets	$1,900,000	$2,300,000
Long-lived assets	1,100,000	5,700,000
Total assets	$3,000,000	$8,000,000
Current liabilities	$ 850,000	$1,400,000
Long-term liabilities	1,200,000	3,800,000
Stockholders' equity	950,000	2,800,000
Total liabilities and stockholders' equity	$3,000,000	$8,000,000

Required:

1. If New Age Industries continues to use ROI as the sole measure of divisional performance, explain why Holiday Entertainment Corporation would be reluctant to acquire Recreational Leasing, Inc.
2. If New Age Industries could be persuaded to use residual income to measure the performance of HEC, explain why HEC would be more willing to acquire RLI.
3. Discuss how the behavior of division managers is likely to be affected by the use of the following performance measures: (*a*) return on investment and (*b*) residual income.

(CMA, adapted)

Case 13–51
Interdivisional Transfers; Pricing the Final Product
(LO 13-6, 13-7, 13-8)

1. Increase in net income before taxes: $132,000
3. Increase in net income before taxes for InterGlobal Industries: $312,500

InterGlobal Industries is a diversified corporation with separate operating divisions. Each division's performance is evaluated on the basis of profit and return on investment.

The Air Comfort Division manufactures and sells air-conditioner units. The coming year's budgeted income statement, which follows, is based upon a sales volume of 15,000 units.

AIR COMFORT DIVISION
Budgeted Income Statement
(In thousands)

	Per Unit	Total
Sales revenue	$400	$6,000
Manufacturing costs:		
Compressor	$70	$1,050
Other direct material	37	555
Direct labor	30	450
Variable overhead	45	675
Fixed overhead	32	480
Total manufacturing costs	$214	$3,210
Gross margin	$186	$2,790
Operating expenses:		
Variable selling	$ 18	$270
Fixed selling	19	285
Fixed administrative	38	570
Total operating expenses	$ 75	$1,125
Net income before taxes	$111	$1,665

Air Comfort's division manager believes sales can be increased if the price of the air-conditioners is reduced. A market research study by an independent firm indicates that a 5 percent reduction in the selling price would increase sales volume 16 percent, or 2,400 units. The division has sufficient production capacity to manage this increased volume with no increase in fixed costs.

The Air Comfort Division uses a compressor in its units, which it purchases from an outside supplier at a cost of $70 per compressor. The Air Comfort Division manager has asked the manager of the Compressor Division about selling compressor units to Air Comfort. The Compressor Division currently manufactures and sells a unit to outside firms that is similar to the unit used by the Air Comfort Division. The specifications of the Air Comfort Division compressor are slightly different, which would reduce the Compressor Division's direct material cost by $1.50 per unit. In addition, the Compressor Division would not incur any variable selling costs in the units sold to the Air Comfort Division. The manager of the Air Comfort Division wants all of the compressors it uses to come from one supplier and has offered to pay $50 for each compressor unit.

The Compressor Division has the capacity to produce 75,000 units. Its budgeted income statement for the coming year, which follows, is based on a sales volume of 64,000 units without considering Air Comfort's proposal.

COMPRESSOR DIVISION
Budgeted Income Statement
(In thousands)

	Per Unit	Total
Sales revenue	$100	$6,400
Manufacturing costs:		
Direct material	$ 12	$ 768
Direct labor	8	512
Variable overhead	10	640
Fixed overhead	11	704
Total manufacturing costs	$ 41	$2,624
Gross margin	$ 59	$3,776

(continued)

COMPRESSOR DIVISION
Budgeted Income Statement
(In thousands)

	Per Unit	Total
Operating expenses:		
Variable selling	$ 6	$ 384
Fixed selling	4	256
Fixed administrative	7	448
Total operating expenses	$ 17	$1,088
Net income before taxes	$ 42	$2,688

Required:

1. Should the Air Comfort Division institute the 5 percent price reduction on its air-conditioner units even if it cannot acquire the compressors internally for $50 each? Support your conclusion with appropriate calculations.
2. Independently of your answer to requirement (1), assume the Air Comfort Division needs 17,400 units. Should the Compressor Division be willing to supply the compressor units for $50 each? Support your conclusions with appropriate calculations.
3. Independently of your answer to requirement (1), assume Air Comfort needs 17,400 units. Suppose InterGlobal's top management has specified a transfer price of $50. Would it be in the best interest of *InterGlobal Industries* for the Compressor Division to supply the compressor units at $50 each to the Air Comfort Division? Support your conclusions with appropriate calculations.
4. Is $50 a goal-congruent transfer price? [Refer to your answers for requirements (2) and (3).]

(CMA, adapted)

Case 13–52
Minimum and Maximum Acceptable Transfer Prices; Multinational
(LO 13-6, 13-7, 13-8)

2. Unit contribution margin, LDP: $6
5. Net savings if TCH-320 is produced using an HDP: $112.00

General Instrumentation Company manufactures dashboard instruments for heavy construction equipment. The firm is based in Baltimore, but operates several divisions in the United States, Canada, and Europe. The Hudson Bay Division manufactures complex electrical panels that are used in a variety of the firm's instruments. There are two basic types of panels. The high-density panel (HDP) is capable of many functions and is used in the most sophisticated instruments, such as tachometers and pressure gauges. The low-density panel (LDP) is much simpler and is used in less-complicated instruments. Although there are minor differences among the different high-density panels, the basic manufacturing process and production costs are the same. The high-density panels require considerably more skilled labor than the low-density panels, but the unskilled labor needs are about the same. Moreover, the direct materials in the high-density panel run substantially more than the cost of materials in the low-density panels. Production costs are summarized as follows:

	LDP	HDP
Unskilled labor (.5 hour @ $10)	$ 5	$ 5
Skilled labor:		
LDP (.25 hour @ $20)	5	
HDP (1.5 hours @ $20)		30
Raw material	3	8
Purchased components	4	12
Variable overhead	5	15
Total variable cost	$22	$70

The annual fixed overhead in the Hudson Bay Division is $1,000,000. There is a limited supply of skilled labor available in the area, and the division must constrain its production to 40,000 hours of skilled labor each year. This has been a troublesome problem for Jacqueline Ducharme, the division manager. Ducharme has successfully increased demand for the LDP line to the point where it is essentially unlimited. Each LDP sells for $28. Business also has increased in recent years for the HDP, and Ducharme estimates the division could now sell anywhere up to 6,000 units per year at a price of $115.

On the other side of the Atlantic, General Instrumentation operates its Volkmar Tachometer Division in Berlin. A recent acquisition of General Instrumentation, the division was formerly a German company known as Volkmar Construction Instruments. The division's main product is a sophisticated tachometer used in heavy-duty cranes, bulldozers, and backhoes. The instrument, designated as a TCH–320, has the following production costs.

TCH–320

Unskilled labor (.5 hour @ $9)	$ 4.50
Skilled labor (3 hours @ $17)	51.00
Raw material	11.50
Purchased components	150.00
Variable overhead	11.00
Total variable cost	$228.00

The cost of purchased components includes a $145 control pack currently imported from an Asian electronics company. Fixed overhead in the Volkmar Tachometer Division runs about $800,000 per year. Both skilled and unskilled labor are in abundant supply. The TCH–320 sells for $270.

Bertram Mueller, the division manager of the Volkmar Tachometer Division, recently attended a high-level corporate meeting in Baltimore. In a conversation with Jacqueline Ducharme, it was apparent that Hudson Bay's high-density panel might be a viable substitute for the control pack currently imported from Japan and used in Volkmar's TCH–320. Upon returning to Berlin, Mueller asked his chief engineer to look into the matter. Hans Schmidt obtained several HDP units from Hudson Bay, and a minor R&D project was mounted to determine if the HDP could replace the Japanese control pack. Several weeks later, the following conversation occurred in Mueller's office:

Schmidt: There's no question that Hudson Bay's HDP unit will work in our TCH–320. In fact, it could save us some money.

Mueller: That's good news. If we can buy our components within the company, we'll help Baltimore's bottom line without hurting ours. Also, it will look good to the brass at corporate if they see us working hard to integrate our division into General Instrumentation's overall production program.

Schmidt: I've also been worried about the reliability of supply of the control pack. I don't like being dependent on such a critical supplier that way.

Mueller: I agree. Let's look at your figures on the HDP replacement.

Schmidt: I got together with the controller's people, and we worked up some numbers. If we replace the imported control pack with the HDP from Canada, we'll avoid the $145 control pack cost we're now incurring. In addition, I figure we'll save $5.50 on the basic raw materials. There is one catch, though. The HDP will require some adjustments in order to use it in the TCH–320. We can make the adjustments here in Berlin. I'm guessing it will require an additional two hours of skilled labor to make the necessary modifications. I don't think variable overhead would be any different. Then there is the cost of transporting the HDPs to Berlin. Let's figure on $4.50 per unit.

Mueller: Sounds good. I'll give Jacqueline Ducharme a call and talk this over. We can use up to 10,000 of the HDP units per year given the demand for the TCH–320. I wonder what kind of a transfer price Hudson Bay will want.

Required:

1. Draw a simple diagram depicting the two divisions and their products. Also show the two alternatives that the Volkmar Tachometer Division has in the production of its TCH–320.
2. From the perspective of General Instrumentation's top management, should any of the TCH–320 units be produced using the high-density panel? If so, how many?
3. Suppose Hudson Bay transfers 10,000 HDP units per year to Volkmar. From the perspective of General Instrumentation's top management, what effect will the transfer price have on the company's income?
4. What is the minimum transfer price that the Hudson Bay Division would find acceptable for the HDP?
5. What is the maximum transfer price that the Volkmar Tachometer Division would find acceptable for the HDP?
6. As the corporate controller for General Instrumentation, recommend a transfer price.

14 Decision Making: Relevant Costs and Benefits

FOCUS COMPANY >>>

© Compassionate Eye Foundation/Getty Images RF

THIS CHAPTER'S FOCUS COMPANY is Worldwide Airways, an international airline based in Atlanta, Georgia. Using this service-industry company for our illustration, we will explore a variety of decisions that managers make routinely. Examples of such decisions are accepting or rejecting a special offer for the company's services, outsourcing a service, and adding or dropping a service or department. We will find in this chapter that different kinds of cost information are relevant, depending on the type of decision to be made.

© Ilene MacDonald/Alamy RF

In contrast to the transportation-services setting of Worldwide Airways, we will explore certain types of decisions that most often arise in a manufacturing setting. Our illustration will be based on International Chocolate Company, which produces a variety of chocolate products. In addition to producing chocolate candy, the company processes cocoa beans into cocoa powder and cocoa butter. The cocoa powder can then be processed further into instant cocoa mix. We will explore a variety of decisions faced by International Chocolate Company's management.

© Agencja Fotograficzna Caro/Alamy

After completing this chapter, you should be able to:

14-1 Describe seven steps in the decision-making process and the managerial accountant's role in that process.

14-2 Explain the relationship between quantitative and qualitative analyses in decision making.

14-3 List and explain two criteria that must be satisfied by relevant information.

14-4 Identify relevant costs and benefits, giving proper treatment to sunk costs, opportunity costs, and unit costs.

14-5 Prepare analyses of various special decisions, properly identifying the relevant costs and benefits.

14-6 Analyze manufacturing decisions involving joint products and limited resources.

14-7 Explain the impact of an advanced manufacturing environment and activity-based costing on a relevant-cost analysis.

14-8 Formulate a linear program to solve a product-mix problem with multiple constraints (appendix).

Decision making is a fundamental part of management. Decisions about the acquisition of equipment, mix of products, methods of production, and pricing of products and services confront managers in all types of organizations. This chapter covers the role of managerial accounting information in a variety of common decisions. The next chapter examines pricing decisions.

The Managerial Accountant's Role in Decision Making

Managerial accountants are increasingly playing important roles as full-fledged members of cross-functional management teams. These management teams face a broad array of decisions, including production, marketing, financial, and other decisions. All managers

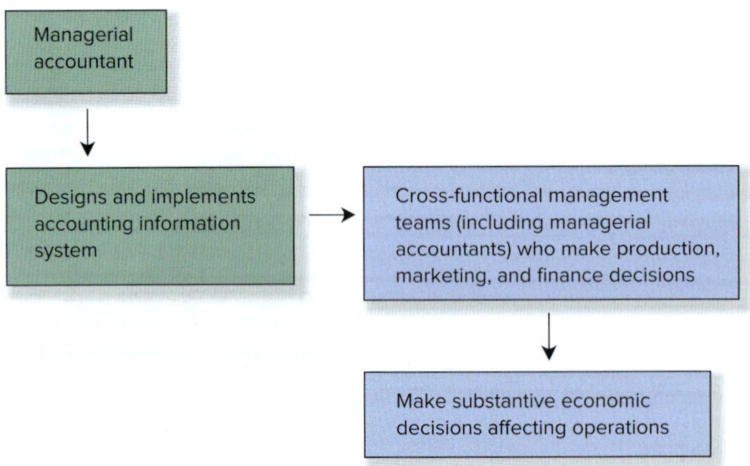

and management teams need information pertinent to their decisions. In support of the decision-making process, managerial accountants play a specific role in providing relevant information. Thus, the managerial accountant must have a good understanding of the decisions faced by managers throughout the organization.

Steps in the Decision-Making Process

Seven steps characterize the decision-making process:

Learning Objective **14-1**

Describe seven steps in the decision-making process and the managerial accountant's role in that process.

1. ***Clarify the decision problem.*** Sometimes the decision to be made is clear. For example, if a company receives a special order for its product at a price below the usual price, the decision problem is to accept or reject the order. But the decision problem is seldom so clear and unambiguous. Perhaps demand for a company's most popular product is declining. What exactly is causing this problem? Increasing competition? Declining quality control? A new alternative product on the market? Before a decision can be made, the problem needs to be clarified and defined in more specific terms. Considerable managerial skill is required to define a decision problem in terms that can be addressed effectively.
2. ***Specify the criterion.*** Once a decision problem has been clarified, the manager should specify the criterion upon which a decision will be made. Is the objective to maximize profit, increase market share, minimize cost, or improve public service? Sometimes the objectives are in conflict, as in a decision problem where production cost is to be minimized but product quality must be maintained. In such cases, one objective is specified as the decision criterion—for example, cost minimization. The other objective is established as a constraint—for example, product quality must not be worse than one defective part in 1,000 manufactured units.
3. ***Identify the alternatives.*** A decision involves selecting between two or more alternatives. If a machine breaks down, what are the alternative courses of action? The machine can be repaired or replaced, or a replacement can be leased. But perhaps repair will turn out to be more costly than replacement. Determining the possible alternatives is a critical step in the decision process.
4. ***Develop a decision model.*** A *decision model* is a simplified representation of the choice problem. Unnecessary details are stripped away, and the most important elements of the problem are highlighted. Thus, the decision model brings together the elements listed above: the criterion, the constraints, and the alternatives.
5. ***Collect the data.*** Although the managerial accountant often is involved in steps 1 through 4, he or she is chiefly responsible for step 5. Selecting data pertinent to decisions is one of the managerial accountant's most important roles in an organization.
6. ***Select an alternative.*** Once the decision model is formulated and the pertinent data are collected, the appropriate manager makes a decision.
7. ***Evaluate decision effectiveness.*** After a decision has been implemented, the results of the decision are evaluated with the objective of improving future decisions.

"We are looked upon as more business advisors than just accountants, and that has a lot to do with the additional analysis and the forward looking goals we are setting." (14a)

Caterpillar

Quantitative versus Qualitative Analysis

Learning Objective **14-2**

Explain the relationship between quantitative and qualitative analyses in decision making.

Decision problems involving accounting data typically are specified in quantitative terms. The criteria in such problems usually include objectives such as profit maximization or cost minimization. When a manager makes a final decision, however, the qualitative characteristics of the alternatives can be just as important as the quantitative measures. **Qualitative characteristics** are the factors in a decision problem that cannot be expressed effectively in numerical terms. To illustrate, suppose Worldwide Airways' top management is considering the elimination of its hub operation in London. Airlines establish hubs at airports where many of their routes intersect. Hub operations include facilities for in-flight food preparation, aircraft maintenance and storage, and administrative offices. A careful quantitative analysis indicates that Worldwide Airways' profit-maximizing alternative

Exhibit 14–1
The Decision-Making Process

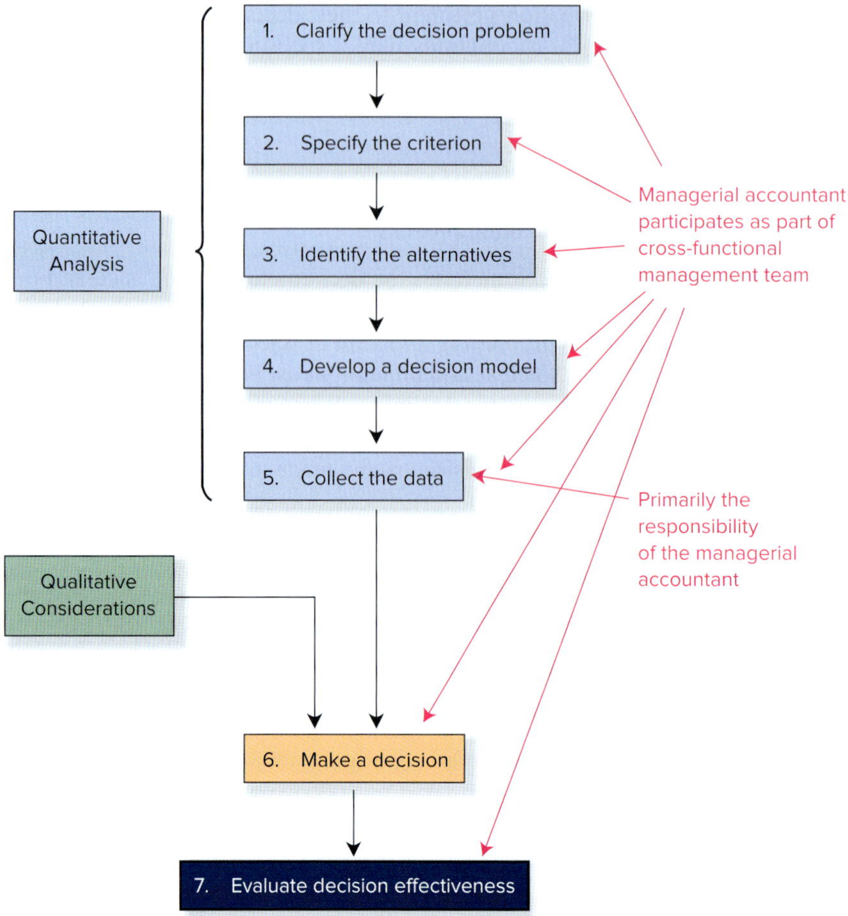

is to eliminate the London hub. In making its decision, however, the company's managers will consider such qualitative issues as the effect of the closing on its London employees and on the morale of its remaining employees in the airline's Paris, Atlanta, and Tokyo hubs.

To clarify what is at stake in such qualitative analyses, quantitative analysis can allow the decision maker to put a "price" on the sum total of the qualitative characteristics. For example, suppose Worldwide Airways' controller gives top management a quantitative analysis showing that elimination of the London hub will increase annual profits by $2,000,000. However, the qualitative considerations favor the option of continuing the London operation. How important are these qualitative considerations to the top managers? If they decide to continue the London operation, the qualitative considerations must be worth at least $2,000,000 to them. Weighing the quantitative and qualitative considerations in making decisions is the essence of management. The skill, experience, judgment, and ethical standards of managers all come to bear on such difficult choices.

Exhibit 14–1 depicts the seven steps in the decision process, and the relationship between quantitative and qualitative analysis.

Obtaining Information: Relevance, Accuracy, and Timeliness

What criteria should the managerial accountant use in designing the accounting information system that supplies data for decision making? Three characteristics of information determine its usefulness.

Relevance Information is **relevant** if it is *pertinent* to a decision problem. Different decisions typically will require different data. The primary theme of this chapter is how to decide what information is relevant to various common decision problems.

Accuracy Information that is pertinent to a decision problem also must be **accurate,** or it will be of little use. This means the information must be precise. For example, the cost incurred by Worldwide Airways to rent facilities at London's Heathrow Airport is relevant to a decision about eliminating the airline's London hub. However, if the rental cost data are imprecise, due to incomplete or misplaced records, the usefulness of the information will be diminished.

Conversely, highly accurate but irrelevant data are of no value to a decision maker. Suppose Worldwide Airways will continue its daily round-trip flight between New York and London regardless of its decision about eliminating the London hub. Precise data about fuel consumption on the New York–London route are irrelevant to the decision about closing down the London hub.

Timeliness Relevant and accurate data are of value only if they are **timely,** that is, available in time for a decision. Thus, timeliness is the third important criterion for determining the usefulness of information. Some situations involve a trade-off between the accuracy and the timeliness of information. More accurate information may take longer to produce. Therefore, as accuracy improves, timeliness suffers, and vice versa. For example, a company may test-market a potential new product in a particular city. The longer the test-marketing program runs, the more accurate will be the marketing data generated. However, a long wait for the accurate marketing report may unduly delay management's decision to launch the new product nationally.

To summarize, the managerial accountant's primary role in the decision-making process is twofold:

1. Decide what information is *relevant* to each decision problem.
2. Provide *accurate* and *timely* data, keeping in mind the proper balance between these often-conflicting criteria.

Relevant Information

What makes information relevant to a decision problem? Two criteria are important.

Learning Objective 14-3

List and explain two criteria that must be satisfied by relevant information.

Bearing on the Future The consequences of decisions are borne in the future, not the past. To be relevant to a decision, cost or benefit information must involve a future event. The cost information relevant to Worldwide Airways' decision concerning its London operations involves the costs that *will be incurred in the future* under the airline's two alternatives. Costs incurred in the past in the airline's London operations will not change regardless of management's decision, and they are irrelevant to the decision at hand.

Since relevant information involves future events, the managerial accountant must predict the amounts of the relevant costs and benefits. In making these predictions, the accountant often will use estimates of cost behavior based on historical data. There is an important and subtle issue here. *Relevant* information must involve costs and benefits to be realized in the *future*. However, the accountant's *predictions* of those costs and benefits often are based on data from the *past.*

"You have to try to summarize numbers. You can't just give numbers. People in marketing are going to make decisions based on your numbers. They have to understand what those numbers mean." (14b)
Abbott Laboratories

Different under Competing Alternatives Relevant information must involve costs or benefits that *differ among the alternatives.* Costs or benefits that are the same across all the available alternatives have no bearing on the decision. For example, suppose Worldwide Airways' management decides to keep its reservations and ticketing office in London regardless of whether its London hub is eliminated. Then the costs of the reservations and ticketing office will not differ between the two alternatives regarding elimination of the London hub. Hence, those costs are irrelevant to that decision.

Unique versus Repetitive Decisions

Unique decisions arise infrequently or only once. Worldwide Airways' decision regarding its London hub is an example. Compiling data for unique decisions usually requires a special analysis by the managerial accountant. The relevant information often will be found in many diverse places in the organization's overall information system.

In contrast, *repetitive decisions* are made over and over again, at either regular or irregular intervals. For example, Worldwide Airways makes route-scheduling decisions every six months. Such a routine decision makes it worthwhile for the managerial accountant to keep a special file of the information relevant to the scheduling decision.

Cost predictions relevant to repetitive decisions typically can draw on a large amount of historical data. Since the decisions have been made repeatedly in the past, the data from those decisions should be readily available. Information relevant to unique decisions is harder to generate. The managerial accountant typically will have to give more thought to deciding which data are relevant, and will have less historical data available upon which to base predictions.

Importance of Identifying Relevant Costs and Benefits

Why is it important for the managerial accountant to isolate the relevant costs and benefits in a decision analysis? The reasons are twofold. First, generating information is a costly process. The relevant data must be sought, and this requires time and effort. By focusing on only the relevant information, the managerial accountant can simplify and shorten the data-gathering process.

Second, people can effectively use only a limited amount of information. Beyond this, they experience **information overload,** and their decision-making effectiveness declines. By routinely providing only information about relevant costs and benefits, the managerial accountant can reduce the likelihood of information overload.

Identifying Relevant Costs and Benefits

Learning Objective 14-4

Identify relevant costs and benefits, giving proper treatment to sunk costs, opportunity costs, and unit costs.

To illustrate how managerial accountants determine relevant costs and benefits, we will consider several decisions faced by the management of Worldwide Airways. Based in Atlanta, the airline flies routes between the United States and Europe, between various cities in Europe, and between the United States and several Asian cities.

Sunk Costs

Sunk costs are costs that have already been incurred. They do not affect any future cost and cannot be changed by any current or future action. Sunk costs are irrelevant to decisions, as the following two examples show.

Book Value of Equipment At Charles de Gaulle Airport in Paris, Worldwide Airways has a three-year-old loader truck used to load in-flight meals onto airplanes. The box on the truck can be lifted hydraulically to the level of a jumbo jet's side doors. The *book value* of this loader, defined as the asset's acquisition cost less the accumulated depreciation to date, is computed as follows:

Acquisition cost of old loader	$100,000
Less: Accumulated depreciation	75,000
Book value	$ 25,000

The loader has one year of useful life remaining, after which its salvage value will be zero. However, it could be sold now for $5,000. In addition to the annual depreciation of $25,000, Worldwide Airways annually incurs $80,000 in variable costs to operate the loader. These include the costs of operator labor, gasoline, and maintenance.

John Orville, Worldwide Airways' ramp manager at Charles de Gaulle Airport, faces a decision about replacement of the loader. A new kind of loader uses a conveyor belt to move meals into an airplane. The new loader is much cheaper than the old hydraulic loader and costs less to operate. However, the new loader would be operable for only one year before it would need to be replaced. Pertinent data about the new loader are as follows:

Acquisition cost of new loader	$15,000
Useful life	1 year
Salvage value after one year	0
Annual depreciation	$15,000
Annual operating costs	$45,000

Orville's initial inclination is to continue using the old loader for another year. He exclaims, "We can't dump that equipment now. We paid $100,000 for it, and we've only used it three years. If we get rid of that loader now, we'll lose $20,000 on the disposal." Orville reasons that the old loader's book value of $25,000, less its current salvage value of $5,000, amounts to a loss of $20,000.

Fortunately, Orville's comment is overheard by Joan Wilbur, the managerial accountant in the company's Charles de Gaulle Airport administrative offices. Wilbur points out to Orville that the book value of the old loader is a *sunk cost*. It cannot affect any future cost the company might incur. To convince Orville that she is right, Wilbur prepares the analysis shown in Exhibit 14–2.

Regardless of which alternative is selected, the $25,000 book value of the old loader will be an expense or loss in the next year. If the old loader is kept in service, the $25,000 will be recognized as depreciation expense; otherwise, the $25,000 cost will be incurred by the company as a write-off of the asset's book value. Thus, the current book value of the old loader is a *sunk cost* and irrelevant to the replacement decision.

Notice that the *relevant* data in the equipment replacement decision are items (2), (3), and (4). Each of these items meets the two tests of relevant information:

1. The costs or benefits relate to the future.
2. The costs or benefits differ between the alternatives.

The proceeds from selling the old loader, item (2), will be received in the future only under the "replace" alternative. Similarly, the acquisition cost (depreciation) of the new

"[We are continually moving] from being the scorekeeper to being an active, involved participant in crafting business solutions." (14c)

Boeing

Exhibit 14–2
Equipment Replacement Decision: Worldwide Airways

		Costs of Two Alternatives		
		(a) Do Not Replace Old Loader*	(b) Replace Old Loader*	(c) Differential Cost: (a) − (b)
Sunk cost	(1a) Depreciation of old loader	$ 25,000		
	OR			–0–
	(1b) Write-off of old loader's book value		$25,000	
Relevant data	(2) Proceeds from disposal of old loader	–0–	(5,000)†	$ 5,000
	(3) Depreciation (cost) of new loader	–0–	15,000	(15,000)
	(4) Operating costs	80,000	45,000	35,000
	Total cost	$105,000	$80,000	$25,000

*Since costs are the focus of the analysis in this exhibit, costs are shown in columns (a) and (b) without parentheses.
†Parentheses denote a cash inflow in this case.

loader, item (3), is a future cost incurred only under the "replace" alternative. The operating cost, item (4), is also a future cost that differs between the two alternatives.

Differential Costs Exhibit 14–2 includes a column entitled *Differential Cost.* A **differential cost** is the difference in a cost item under two decision alternatives. The computation of differential costs is a convenient way of summarizing the relative advantage of one alternative over the other. John Orville can make a correct equipment-replacement decision in either of two ways: (1) by comparing the total cost of the two alternatives, shown in columns (a) and (b); or (2) by focusing on the total differential cost, shown in column (c), which favors the "replacement" option.

Cost of Inventory on Hand Never having taken a managerial accounting course in college, John Orville is slow to learn how to identify sunk costs. The next week he goofs again.

The inventory of spare aircraft parts held by Worldwide Airways at Charles de Gaulle includes some obsolete parts originally costing $20,000. The company no longer uses the planes for which the parts were purchased. The obsolete parts include spare passenger seats, luggage racks, and galley equipment. The spare parts could be sold to another airline for $17,000. However, with some modifications, the obsolete parts could still be used in the company's current fleet of aircraft. Using the modified parts would save Worldwide Airways the cost of purchasing new parts for its airplanes.

John Orville decides not to dispose of the obsolete parts, because doing so would entail a loss of $3,000. Orville reasons that the $20,000 book value of the parts, less the $17,000 proceeds from disposal, would result in a $3,000 loss on disposal. Joan Wilbur, the managerial accountant, comes to the rescue again, demonstrating that the right decision is to dispose of the parts. Wilbur's analysis is shown in Exhibit 14–3.

Notice that the book value of the obsolete inventory is a sunk cost. If the parts are modified, the $20,000 book value will be an expense during the period when the parts are used. Otherwise, the $20,000 book value of the asset will be written off when the parts are sold. As a sunk cost, the book value of the obsolete inventory will not affect any future cash flow of the company.

As the managerial accountant's analysis reveals, the relevant data include the $17,000 proceeds from disposal, the $12,000 cost to modify the parts, and the $26,000 cost to buy new parts. All of these data meet the two tests of relevance: they affect future cash flows and they differ between the two alternatives. As Joan Wilbur's analysis shows, Worldwide Airways' cost will be $3,000 less if the obsolete parts are sold and new parts are purchased.

Exhibit 14–3

Obsolete Inventory Decision: Worldwide Airways

		Costs of Two Alternatives		
		(a) Modify and Use Parts*	(b) Dispose of Parts*	(c) Differential Cost: (a) − (b)
Sunk cost	Book value of parts inventory: asset value written off whether parts are used or not	$20,000	$20,000	$ –0–
Relevant data	Proceeds from disposal of parts	–0–	(17,000)†	17,000
	Cost to modify parts	12,000	–0–	12,000
	Cost incurred to buy new parts for current aircraft fleet	–0–	26,000	(26,000)
	Total cost	$32,000	$29,000	$ 3,000

*Since costs are the focus of the analysis in this exhibit, costs are shown in columns (a) and (b) without parentheses.

†Parentheses denote a cash inflow in this case.

Exhibit 14–4
Flight-Route Decision: Worldwide Airways

			Revenues and Costs under Two Alternatives		
Relevant or Irrelevant			(a) Nonstop Route*	(b) With Stop in San Francisco*	(c) Differential Amount†: (a) − (b)
Relevant		(1) Passenger revenue	$240,000	$258,000	$(18,000)
	Irrelevant	(2) Cargo revenue	80,000	80,000	–0–
Relevant		(3) Landing fee in San Francisco	–0–	(5,000)	5,000
Relevant		(4) Use of airport gate facilities	–0–	(3,000)	3,000
Relevant		(5) Flight crew cost	(2,000)	(2,500)	500
Relevant		(6) Fuel	(21,000)	(24,000)	3,000
Relevant		(7) Meals and services	(4,000)	(4,600)	600
	Irrelevant	(8) Aircraft maintenance	(1,000)	(1,000)	–0–
		Total revenue less costs	$292,000	$297,900	$ (5,900)

*In columns (a) and (b), parentheses denote costs and numbers without parentheses are revenues.
†In column (c), parentheses denote differential items favoring option (b).

Irrelevant Future Costs and Benefits

At Worldwide Airways' headquarters in Atlanta, Amy Earhart, manager of flight scheduling, is in the midst of making a decision about the Atlanta to Honolulu route. The flight is currently nonstop, but she is considering a stop in San Francisco. She feels that the route would attract additional passengers if the stop is made, but there also would be additional variable costs. Her analysis appears in Exhibit 14–4.

The analysis indicates that the preferable alternative is the route that includes a stop in San Francisco. Notice that the cargo revenue [item (2)] and the aircraft maintenance cost [item (8)] are irrelevant to the flight-route decision. Although these data do affect future cash flows, they *do not differ between the two alternatives.* All of the other data in Exhibit 14–4 are relevant to the decision, because they do differ between the two alternatives. The analysis in Exhibit 14–4 could have ignored the irrelevant data; the same decision would have been reached. (Exercise 14–30, at the end of the chapter, will ask you to prove this assertion by redoing the analysis without the irrelevant data.)

Opportunity Costs

Another decision confronting Amy Earhart is whether to add two daily round-trip flights between Atlanta and Montreal. Her initial analysis of the relevant costs and benefits indicates that the additional revenue from the flights will exceed their costs by $30,000 per month. Hence, she is ready to add the flights to the schedule. However, Chuck Lindbergh, Worldwide Airways' hangar manager in Atlanta, points out that Earhart has overlooked an important consideration.

Worldwide Airways currently has excess space in its hangar. A commuter airline has offered to rent the hangar space for $40,000 per month. However, if the Atlanta-to-Montreal flights are added to the schedule, the additional aircraft needed in Atlanta will require the excess hangar space.

If Worldwide Airways adds the Atlanta-to-Montreal flights, it will forgo the opportunity to rent the excess hangar space for $40,000 per month. Thus, the $40,000 in rent forgone is an *opportunity cost* of the alternative to add the new flights. An **opportunity cost** is the potential benefit given up when the choice of one action precludes a different action. Although people tend to overlook or underestimate the importance of opportunity costs, they are just as relevant as out-of-pocket costs in evaluating decision alternatives. In Worldwide Airways' case, the best action is to rent the excess hangar space to the commuter airline, rather than adding the new flights. The analysis in Exhibit 14–5 supports this conclusion.

Exhibit 14–5
Decision to Add Flights: Worldwide Airways

	(a) Add Flights	(b) Do Not Add Flights	(c) Differential Amount: (a) − (b)
Additional revenue from new flights less additional costs	$30,000	–0–	$ 30,000
Rental of excess hangar space	–0–	$40,000	(40,000)*
Total	$30,000	$40,000	$(10,000)

*Parentheses denote that differential benefit favors option (b).

It is a common mistake for people to overlook or underweigh opportunity costs. The $40,000 hangar rental, which will be forgone if the new flights are added, is an *opportunity cost* of the option to add the flights. It is a *relevant cost* of the decision, and it is just as important as any out-of-pocket expenditure.

Summary

Relevant costs and benefits satisfy the following two criteria:

1. They affect the future.
2. They differ between alternatives.

"I would say that they [line managers] view us as business partners." (14d)
Boeing

Sunk costs are *not* relevant costs, because they do not affect the future. An example of a sunk cost is the book value of an asset, either equipment or inventory. *Future costs or benefits that are identical across all decision alternatives are not relevant.* They can be ignored when making a decision. *Opportunity costs are relevant costs.* Such costs deserve particular attention because many people tend to overlook them when making decisions.

Analysis of Special Decisions

Learning Objective 14-5

Prepare analyses of various special decisions, properly identifying the relevant costs and benefits.

What are the relevant costs and benefits when a manager must decide whether to add or drop a product or service? What data are relevant when deciding whether to produce or buy a service or component? These decisions and certain other nonroutine decisions merit special attention in our discussion of relevant costs and benefits.

Accept or Reject a Special Offer

Jim Wright, Worldwide Airways' vice president for operations, has been approached by a Japanese tourist agency about flying chartered tourist flights from Japan to Hawaii. The tourist agency has offered Worldwide Airways $150,000 per round-trip flight on a jumbo jet. Given the airline's usual occupancy rate and air fares, a round-trip jumbo-jet flight between Japan and Hawaii typically brings in revenue of $250,000. Thus, the tourist agency's specially priced offer requires a special analysis by Jim Wright.

Wright knows that Worldwide Airways has two jumbo jets that are not currently in use. The airline has just eliminated several unprofitable routes, freeing these aircraft for other uses. The airline was not currently planning to add any new routes, and therefore the two jets were idle. To help make his decision, Wright asks for cost data from the controller's office. The controller provides the information in Exhibit 14–6, which pertains to a typical round-trip jumbo-jet flight between Japan and Hawaii.

The variable costs cover aircraft fuel and maintenance, flight-crew costs, in-flight meals and services, and landing fees. The fixed costs allocated to each flight cover Worldwide Airways' fixed costs, such as aircraft depreciation, maintenance and depreciation of facilities, and fixed administrative costs.

Revenue:		
Passenger	$250,000	
Cargo	30,000	
Total revenue		$280,000
Expenses:		
Variable expenses of flight	$ 90,000	
Fixed expenses allocated to each flight	100,000	
Total expenses		190,000
Profit		$ 90,000

Exhibit 14–6
Data for Typical Flight Between Japan and Hawaii: Worldwide Airways

If Jim Wright had not understood managerial accounting, he might have done the following *incorrect analysis.*

Special price for charter	$150,000
Total cost per flight	190,000
Loss on charter flight	$ (40,000)

This calculation suggests that the special charter offer should be rejected. What is the error in this analysis? The mistake is the inclusion of allocated fixed costs in the cost per flight. This is an error, because the *fixed costs will not increase in total* if the charter flight is added. Since the fixed costs will not change under either of the alternate choices, they are irrelevant.

Fortunately, Jim Wright does not make this mistake. He knows that only the variable costs of the proposed charter are relevant. Moreover, Wright determines that the variable cost of the charter would be less than that of a typical flight, because Worldwide Airways would not incur the variable costs of reservations and ticketing. These variable expenses amount to $5,000 for a scheduled flight. Thus, Wright's analysis of the charter offer is as shown below.

Assumes excess capacity (idle aircraft)

Special price for charter		$150,000
Variable cost per routine flight	$90,000	
Less: Savings on reservations and ticketing	5,000	
Variable cost of charter		85,000
Contribution from charter		$ 65,000

Wright's analysis shows that the special charter flight will contribute $65,000 toward covering the airline's fixed costs and profit. Since the airline has excess flight capacity, due to the existence of idle aircraft, the optimal decision is to accept the special charter offer.

"I've seen it (managerial accounting) evolve to become more of a team player and being involved in major projects and being looked to as a business advisor or consultant to help leverage our expertise on profitability of certain products or sourcing decisions." (14e)

Caterpillar

No Excess Capacity Now let's consider how Wright's analysis would appear if Worldwide Airways had no idle aircraft. Suppose that in order to fly the charter between Japan and Hawaii, the airline would have to cancel its least profitable route, which is between Japan and Hong Kong. This route contributes $80,000 toward covering the airline's fixed costs and profit. Thus, if the charter offer is accepted, the airline will incur an opportunity cost of $80,000 from the forgone contribution of the Japan–Hong Kong route. Now Wright's analysis should appear as shown below.

Assumes no excess capacity (no idle aircraft)

Special price for charter		$150,000
Variable cost per routine flight	$90,000	
Less: Savings on reservations and ticketing	5,000	
Variable cost of charter	$85,000	
Add: Opportunity cost, forgone contribution on canceled Japan–Hong Kong route	80,000	165,000
Loss from charter		$ (15,000)

Thus, if Worldwide Airways has no excess flight capacity, Jim Wright should reject the special charter offer.

Summary The decision to accept or reject a specially priced order is common in both service-industry and manufacturing firms. Manufacturers often are faced with decisions about selling products in a special order at less than full price. The correct analysis of such decisions focuses on the relevant costs and benefits. Fixed costs, which often are allocated to individual units of product or service, are usually irrelevant. Fixed costs typically will not change in total, whether the order is accepted or rejected.

When excess capacity exists, the only relevant costs usually will be the variable costs associated with the special order. When there is no excess capacity, the opportunity cost of using the firm's facilities for the special order is also relevant to the decision.

Outsource a Product or Service

Ellie Rickenbacker is Worldwide Airways' manager of in-flight services. She supervises the airline's flight attendants and all of the firm's food and beverage operations. Rickenbacker currently faces a decision regarding the preparation of in-flight dinners at the airline's Atlanta hub. In the Atlanta flight kitchen, full-course dinners are prepared and packaged for long flights that pass through Atlanta. In the past, all of the desserts were baked and packaged in the flight kitchen. However, Rickenbacker has received an offer from an Atlanta bakery to bake the airline's desserts. Thus, her decision is whether to *outsource* the dessert portion of the in-flight dinners. An **outsourcing decision,** also called a **make-or-buy decision,** entails a choice between producing a product or service in-house and purchasing it from an outside supplier. To help guide her decision, Rickenbacker has assembled the cost information in Exhibit 14–7, which shows a total cost per dessert of 25 cents.

The Atlanta bakery has offered to supply the desserts for 21 cents each. Rickenbacker's initial inclination is to accept the bakery's offer, since it appears that the airline would save 4 cents per dessert. However, the controller reminds Rickenbacker that not all of the costs listed in Exhibit 14–7 are relevant to the outsourcing decision. The controller modifies Rickenbacker's analysis as shown in Exhibit 14–8.

If Worldwide Airways stops making desserts, it will save all of the variable costs but only 1 cent of fixed costs. The 1-cent saving in supervisory salaries would result because the airline could get along with two fewer kitchen supervisors. The remainder of the fixed costs would be incurred even if the desserts were purchased. These remaining fixed costs of supervision and depreciation would have to be reallocated to the flight kitchen's other products. In light of the controller's revised analysis, Rickenbacker realizes that the airline should continue to make its own desserts. To outsource the desserts would require an expenditure of 21 cents per dessert, but only 15 cents per dessert would be saved.

To clarify her decision further, Rickenbacker asks the controller to prepare an analysis of the *total costs* per month of making or buying desserts. The controller's report,

Exhibit 14–7
Cost of In-Flight Desserts: Worldwide Airways

	Cost per Dessert
Variable costs:	
Direct material (food and packaging)	$.06
Direct labor	.04
Variable overhead	.04
Fixed costs (allocated to products):	
Supervisory salaries	.04
Depreciation of flight-kitchen equipment	.07
Total cost per dessert	$.25

INSOURCING MAKES A COME-BACK

After many years of outsourcing key business processes and offshoring of domestic jobs to overseas manufacturers, the trend may finally be reversing. **K'Nex Brands** is a small, family-owned manufacturer of snap-together building toys in the Philadelphia suburb of Hatfield, Pennsylvania. "Over the past few years, K'Nex has brought most of its production of its plastic building toys back to its factory in Hatfield from subcontractors in China." To carry out this decision, the company has redesigned some of its toys. "In the long run, it's much better for us to manufacture here," said K'Nex Brands' chairman. "By moving production closer to U.S. retailers, K'Nex said it can react faster to the fickle shifts in toy demand and deliver hot-selling items to stores faster. It also has greater control over quality and materials, often a critical safety issue for toys. And as wages and transport costs rise in China, the advantages of producing there for the U.S. market are waning."

On the other end of the company-size continuum is **General Electric**. "After years of offshore production, the company is moving much of its appliance-manufacturing operations back home." GE's Appliance Park in Louisville, Kentucky, is one of the company's focal points for its new insourcing (or onshoring) strategy. GE is "spending some $800 million to bring the place back to life," after years of decline as the company had been pursuing an outsourcing strategy for its appliance manufacturing.[1]

What has happened to cause K'Nex, GE, and many other companies to choose an insourcing strategy? Here are some of the factors in this all-important decision: "Oil prices are three times what they were in 2000, making cargo-ship fuel much more expensive now than it was then. The natural-gas boom in the U.S. has dramatically lowered the cost for running something as energy-intensive as a factory." Moreover, "Wages in China are some five times what they were in 2000, and they are expected to keep rising." In addition to these key cost drivers in the economy at large, every company faces many cost and operational issues that are more specific to its own operations.

The key point, from a managerial accounting perspective, is that whether a company chooses to outsource or insource key business processes or production operations is an important decision that will rely heavily on managerial accounting information.

Management **A**ccounting **P**ractice

General Electric and K'Nex Brands

[1]See J. R. Hagerty, "A Toy Maker Comes Home to U.S.A.," *The Wall Street Journal,* March 11, 2013, p. B1, for the information and quotations presented here about K'nex Brands. The information and quotations about GE's insourcing trend are from C. Fishman, "The Insourcing Boom," *The Atlantic,* December 2012, p. 45. There is considerable confusion of terms in the popular business press, where the terms *outsourcing and offshoring* are often used synonymously, and similarly, *insourcing and onshoring* tend to be used interchangeably. The key distinction being made in both sets of terms, though, is whether business functions or production operations are performed in-country or otherwise.

Exhibit 14–8
Cost Savings from Buying In-Flight Desserts: Worldwide Airways

	Cost per Dessert	Costs Saved by Purchasing Desserts
Variable costs:		
Direct material	$ .06	$ .06
Direct labor	.04	.04
Variable overhead	.04	.04
Fixed costs (allocated to products):		
Supervisory salaries	.04	.01
Depreciation of flight-kitchen equipment	.07	–0–
Total cost per dessert	$ .25	$ .15
Cost of purchasing desserts (per dessert)		$ .21
Loss per dessert if desserts are purchased (savings per dessert minus purchase cost per dessert, or $.15 − $.21)		$(.06)

© PhotoLink/Getty Images RF

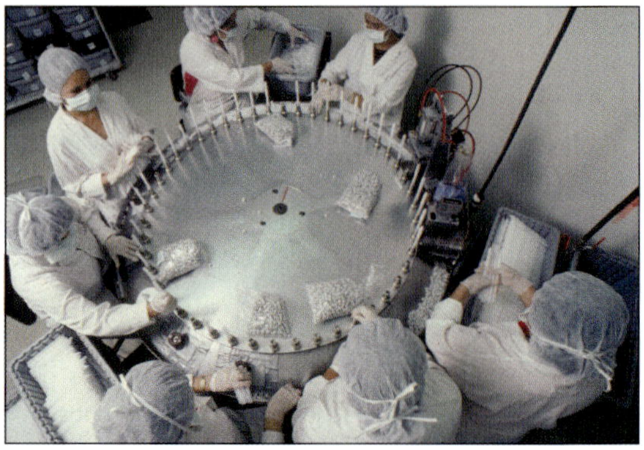

© Royalty-Free/Corbis

In today's global economy, many companies outsource significant products and services. Gallo Winery, for example, buys a significant portion of its grapes from other vintners. Cummins Engine outsources many of its pistons, and Intel Corporation buys microchips. Chase Bank outsources its cafeteria and legal services. Many pharmaceutical companies, such as Japan's Yamanouchi Pharmaceutical, have outsourced much of their production to cut costs.[2] Pictured here are grape harvesting and pharmaceutical production.

displayed in Exhibit 14–9, shows the total cost of producing 1,000,000 desserts, the flight kitchen's average monthly volume.

The total-cost analysis confirmed Rickenbacker's decision to continue making desserts in the airline's flight kitchen.

Beware of Unit-Cost Data Fixed costs often are allocated to individual units of product or service for product-costing purposes. For decision-making purposes, however, unitized fixed costs can be misleading. As the total-cost analysis in Exhibit 14–9 shows, only $10,000 in fixed monthly cost will be saved if the desserts are purchased. The remaining $100,000 in monthly fixed cost will continue whether the desserts are made or purchased. Rickenbacker's initial cost analysis in Exhibit 14–7 implies that each dessert costs the airline 25 cents, but that 25-cent cost includes 11 cents of unitized fixed costs. Most of these costs will remain unchanged regardless of the outsourcing decision. By allocating fixed costs to individual products or services, they are made to appear variable even though they are not.

Exhibit 14–9
Total-Cost Analysis of Outsourcing Decision: Worldwide Airways

	Cost per Month	Costs Saved by Purchasing Desserts
Variable costs:		
Direct material	$ 60,000	$ 60,000
Direct labor	40,000	40,000
Variable overhead	40,000	40,000
Fixed costs (allocated to products):		
Supervisory salaries	40,000	10,000*
Depreciation of flight-kitchen equipment	70,000	–0–
Total cost per month	$250,000	$150,000
Cost of purchasing desserts (per month)		$210,000
Total loss if desserts are purchased (total savings minus total cost of purchasing, or $150,000 − $210,000)		$ (60,000)

*Cost of monthly compensation for two kitchen supervisors, who will not be needed if desserts are purchased.

[2]Peter Landers, "Japan's Local Drug Makers to Outsource to Suppliers," *The Wall Street Journal,* March 26, 2002, p. A20.

Add or Drop a Service, Product, or Department

Worldwide Airways offers its passengers the opportunity to join its World Express Club. Club membership entitles a traveler to use the club facilities at the airport in Atlanta. Club privileges include a private lounge and restaurant, discounts on meals and beverages, and use of a small health spa.

Jayne Wing, the president of Worldwide Airways, is worried that the World Express Club might not be profitable. Her concern is caused by the statement of monthly operating income shown in the Excel spreadsheet in Exhibit 14–10.

In her weekly staff meeting, Wing states her concern about the World Express Club's profitability. The controller responds by pointing out that not all of the costs on the club's income statement would be eliminated if the club were discontinued. The vice president for sales adds that the club helps Worldwide Airways attract passengers who it might otherwise lose to a competitor. As the meeting adjourns, Wing asks the controller to prepare an analysis of the relevant costs and benefits associated with the World Express Club. The controller's analysis is displayed in Exhibit 14–11.

The controller's analysis in Exhibit 14–11 contains two parts. Part I focuses on the relevant costs and benefits of the World Express Club only, while ignoring any impact of the club on other airline operations. In column (a), the controller has listed the club's revenues and expenses from the income statement presented in Exhibit 14–10. Column (b) in Exhibit 14–11 lists the expenses that will continue if the club is eliminated. These expenses are called **unavoidable expenses.** In contrast, the expenses appearing in column (a) but not column (b) are **avoidable expenses.** The airline will no longer incur these expenses if the club is eliminated.

Notice that all of the club's variable expenses are avoidable. The depreciation expense, $30,000, is an allocated portion of the depreciation on a Worldwide Airways building, part of which is used by the World Express Club. If the Club is discontinued, the airline will continue to own and use the building, and the depreciation expense will continue. Thus, it is an unavoidable expense. The fixed supervisory salaries are avoidable, since these employees will no longer be needed if the club is eliminated. The fixed insurance expense of $10,000 is not avoidable; the $5,000 fee paid to the airport for the

Exhibit 14–10
World Express Club Monthly Operating Income Statement: Worldwide Airways

Worldwide Airways - Excel

F17 =F10-F16

	A–D	E	F
1	WORLDWIDE AIRWAYS		
2	DEPARTMENT: World Express Club		
3	Monthly Operating Income Statement		
4			
5	Sales revenue		$ 200,000
6	Variable expenses:		
7	Food and beverages	$ 70,000	
8	Personnel	40,000	
9	Variable overhead	25,000	135,000
10	Contribution margin		$ 65,000
11	Fixed expenses:		
12	Depreciation	$ 30,000	
13	Supervisory salaries	20,000	
14	Insurance	10,000	
15	Airport fees	5,000	
16	General overhead (allocated)	10,000	75,000
17	Operating Income (Loss)		$ (10,000)

Operating Income Statement

Exhibit 14–11
Relevant Costs and Benefits of World Express Club: Worldwide Airways

Worldwide Airways

	(a) Keep Club	(b) Eliminate Club	(c) Differential Amount: (a) − (b)
Part I:			
Sales revenue	$200,000	–0–	$200,000
Less: Variable expenses:			
Food and beverages	(70,000)	–0–	(70,000)
Personnel	(40,000)	–0–	(40,000)
Variable overhead	(25,000)	–0–	(25,000)
Contribution margin	$ 65,000	–0–	$ 65,000
Less: Fixed expenses:			
Depreciation	$ (30,000)	$(30,000)	$ –0–
Supervisory salaries	(20,000)	–0–	(20,000)
Insurance	(10,000)	(10,000)	–0–
Airport fees	(5,000)	–0–	(5,000)
General overhead (allocated)	(10,000)	(10,000)	–0–
Total fixed expenses	$ (75,000)	$(50,000)	$ (25,000)
Profit (loss)	$ (10,000)	$(50,000)	$ 40,000*
		Expenses in the column above are **unavoidable** expenses	Expenses in the column above are **avoidable** expenses
Part II:			
Contribution margin from general airline operations that will be forgone if club is eliminated	$ 60,000	–0–	$ 60,000

*The positive $40,000 differential amount reflects the fact that the company is $40,000 better off by keeping the club.

privilege of operating the club is avoidable. Finally, the club's allocated portion of general overhead expenses, $10,000, is not avoidable. Worldwide Airways will incur these expenses regardless of its decision about the World Express Club.

The conclusion shown by Part I of the controller's report is that the club should not be eliminated. If the club is closed, the airline will lose more in contribution margin, $65,000, than it saves in avoidable fixed expenses, $25,000. Thus, the club's $65,000 contribution margin is enough to cover the avoidable fixed expenses of $25,000 and still contribute $40,000 toward covering the overall airline's fixed expenses.

World Express Club's contribution margin	$65,000
Avoidable fixed expenses	25,000
Contribution of club toward covering overall airline's fixed expenses	$40,000

Now consider Part II of the controller's analysis in Exhibit 14–11. As the vice president for sales pointed out, the World Express Club is an attractive feature to many travelers. The controller estimates that if the club were discontinued, the airline would lose $60,000 each month in forgone contribution margin from general airline operations. This loss in contribution margin would result from losing to a competing airline current passengers who are attracted to Worldwide Airways by its World Express Club. This $60,000 in forgone contribution margin is an *opportunity cost* of the option to close down the club.

Considering both Parts I and II of the controller's analysis, Worldwide Airways' monthly profit will be greater by $100,000 if the club is kept open. Recognition of two issues is key to this conclusion:

1. Only the avoidable expenses of the club will be saved if it is discontinued.
2. Closing the club will adversely affect the airline's other operations.

ADDING A SERVICE

Management Accounting Practice

FedEx and Caterpillar

Changing business conditions can cause a company to rethink its business model and add new services. A classic case of this phenomenon occurred when **Federal Express** found that a sizable portion of its overnight letter delivery business was eliminated by e-mail. Customers no longer needed to ship a hard-copy document overnight, when the same document could be sent instantaneously via e-mail. FedEx also found a decline in the need for overnight repair parts shipments. Many customers' improved supply chain systems resulted in better spare parts preparedness and less need for last-minute overnight shipments. FedEx responded by adding slower ground shipment services to compete more directly with UPS and the U.S. Postal Service. While FedEx still excels when an overnight shipment is needed, its ground transport business has become an increasingly important part of its operations. And FedEx has recently added new express package services in China, where the company has invested in a new hub for its business to and from Asia.

Caterpillar has added heavy equipment overhaul services to its already successful manufacturing operations. The company uses available capacity in its manufacturing plants to disassemble and rebuild heavy diesel engines, after cleaning, inspecting, and repairing them. This new service component of Caterpillar's operations has become one of the company's fastest-growing business units.[3]

Special Decisions in Manufacturing Firms

Learning Objective 14-6

Analyze manufacturing decisions involving joint products and limited resources.

Some types of decisions are more likely to arise in manufacturing companies than in service-industry firms. We will examine two of these decisions.

Joint Products: Sell or Process Further

A **joint production process** results in two or more products, called *joint products.* An example is the processing of cocoa beans into cocoa powder and cocoa butter. Cocoa beans constitute the input to the joint production process, and the two joint products are cocoa powder and cocoa butter. The point in the production process where the joint products are identifiable as separate products is called the **split-off point.** Other examples of joint production processes include the slaughtering of animals for various cuts of meat and the processing of petroleum into various products, such as kerosene and gasoline.

Manufacturers with joint production processes sometimes must decide whether a joint product should be sold at the split-off point or processed further before being sold. Such a decision recently confronted Bill Candee, the president of International Chocolate Company. Candee's firm imports cocoa beans and processes them into cocoa powder and cocoa butter. Only a portion of the cocoa powder is used by International Chocolate Company in the production of chocolate candy. The remainder of the cocoa powder is sold to an ice cream producer. Candee is considering the possibility of processing his remaining cocoa powder into an instant cocoa mix to be marketed under the brand name ChocoTime. Data pertaining to Candee's decision are displayed in Exhibit 14–12.

[3] B. Sechler, "FedEx, UPS Get a Toehold in China's Express Delivery," *The Wall Street Journal,* September 11, 2012, p. B1; J. Hagerty and B. Tita, "Caterpillar Builds Optimism," *The Wall Street Journal,* January 27, 2012, p. B3. D. Foust, "The Ground War at FedEx," *BusinessWeek,* November 28, 2005, pp. 42, 43; "Overnight, Everything Changed for FedEx; Can It Reinvent Itself?" *The Wall Street Journal,* November 4, 1999, p. A1; and M. Arndt, "Cat Sinks Its Claws into Services," *BusinessWeek,* December 5, 2005, pp. 56–59.

Exhibit 14–12
Joint Processing of Cocoa Beans: International Chocolate Company

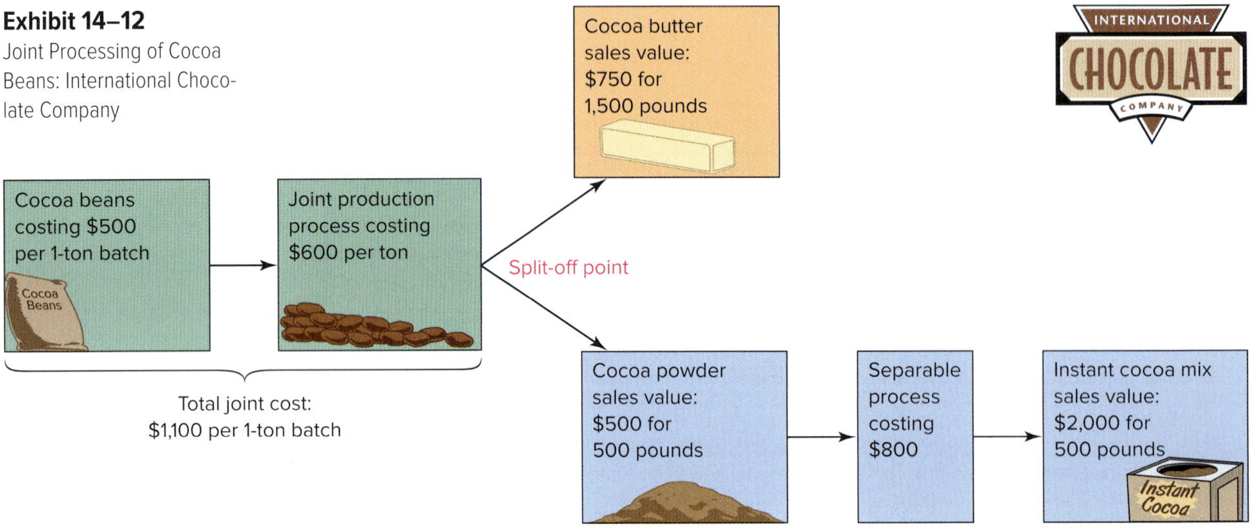

Notice from the diagram that cocoa beans are processed in 1-ton batches. The total cost of the cocoa beans and the joint processing is $1,100. This is called the **joint cost.** The output of the joint process is 1,500 pounds of cocoa butter and 500 pounds of cocoa powder.

How should Bill Candee approach the decision about processing the cocoa powder into instant cocoa mix? What are the relevant costs and benefits? First, let's consider the joint cost of $1,100. Is this a relevant cost in the decision at hand? *The joint cost is not a relevant cost,* because it will not change regardless of the decision Candee makes.

Suppose the $1,100 joint cost had been allocated to the two joint products for product-costing purposes. A common method of allocating a joint cost is the **relative-sales-value method,** in which the joint cost is allocated between the joint products in proportion to their sales value at the split-off point.[4] International Chocolate Company would make the following joint cost allocation.

Joint Cost	Joint Products	Sales Value at Split-Off Point	Relative Proportion	Allocation of Joint Cost
$1,100	Cocoa butter	$750	.60	$ 660
	Cocoa powder	500	.40	440
	Total joint cost allocated			$1,100

Does this allocation of the $1,100 joint cost make it relevant to the decision about processing cocoa powder into instant cocoa mix? The answer is no. *The $1,100 joint cost still does not change in total,* whether the cocoa powder is processed further or not. The joint cost is irrelevant to the decision at hand.

The only costs and benefits relevant to Candee's decision are those that differ between the two alternatives. The proper analysis is shown in Exhibit 14–13.

There is a shortcut method that arrives at the same conclusion as Exhibit 14–13. In this approach, the incremental revenue from the further processing of cocoa powder is compared with the **separable processing cost,** which is the cost incurred after the split-off point, as follows:

Sales value of instant cocoa mix	$2,000
Sales value of cocoa powder	500
Incremental revenue from further processing	$1,500
Less: Separable processing cost	(800)
Net benefit from further processing	$ 700

[4]Other methods of allocating joint costs are covered in Chapter 17.

Exhibit 14–13
Decision to Sell or Process Further: International Chocolate Company

Relevant or Irrelevant		(a) Process Cocoa Powder into Instant Cocoa Mix	(b) Sell Cocoa Powder at Split-Off Point	(c) Differential Amount: (a) − (b)
	Sales revenue:			
Irrelevant	Cocoa butter	$ 750	$ 750	–0–
Relevant	Instant cocoa mix	2,000		
Relevant	Cocoa powder		500	→ $1,500
	Less: Costs:			
Irrelevant	Joint cost	(1,100)	(1,100)	–0–
Relevant	Separable cost of processing cocoa powder into instant cocoa mix	(800)	–0–	(800)
	Total	$ 850	$ 150	$ 700

Both analyses indicate that Bill Candee should process his excess cocoa powder into instant cocoa mix. The same conclusion is reached if the analysis is done on a per-unit basis rather than a total basis:

Sales value of instant cocoa mix ($2,000 ÷ 500 pounds)	$4.00	per pound
Sales value of cocoa powder ($500 ÷ 500 pounds)	1.00	per pound
Incremental revenue from further processing	$3.00	per pound
Less: Separable processing cost ($800 ÷ 500 pounds)	(1.60)	per pound
Net benefit from further processing	$1.40	per pound

Once again, the analysis shows that Bill Candee should decide to process the cocoa powder into instant cocoa mix.

Decisions Involving Limited Resources

Organizations typically have limited resources. Limitations on floor space, machine time, labor hours, or raw materials are common. Operating with limited resources, a firm often must choose between sales orders, deciding which orders to fill and which ones to decline. In making such decisions, managers must decide which product or service is the most profitable.

To illustrate, suppose International Chocolate Company's Phoenix plant makes two candy-bar products, Chewies and Chompo Bars. The contribution margin for a case of each of these products is computed in Exhibit 14–14.

A glance at the contribution-margin data suggests that Chompo Bars are more profitable than Chewies. It is true that a case of Chompo Bars contributes more toward covering the company's fixed cost and profit. However, an important consideration has been ignored in the analysis so far. The Phoenix plant's capacity is limited by its available

Exhibit 14–14
Contribution Margin per Case: International Chocolate Company

	Chewies	Chompo Bars
Sales price	$10.00	$14.00
Less: Variable costs:		
Direct material	$ 3.00	$ 3.75
Direct labor	2.00	2.50
Variable overhead	3.00	3.75
Variable selling and administrative costs	1.00	2.00
Total variable costs	$ 9.00	$12.00
Contribution margin per case	$ 1.00	$ 2.00

Exhibit 14–15
Contribution Margin per Machine Hour: International Chocolate Company

		Chewies	Chompo Bars
(a)	Contribution margin per case	$1.00	$2.00
(b)	Machine hours required per case	.02	.05
(a) ÷ (b)	Contribution margin per machine hour	$50	$40

machine time. Only 700 machine hours are available in the plant each month. International Chocolate Company can sell as many cases of either candy bar as it can produce, so production is limited only by the constraint on machine time.

To maximize the plant's total contribution toward covering fixed cost and profit, management should strive to use each machine hour as effectively as possible. This realization alters the analysis of product profitability. The relevant question is *not,* Which candy bar has the highest contribution margin *per case?* The pertinent question is, Which product has the highest contribution margin *per machine hour?* This question is answered with the calculation in Exhibit 14–15.

A machine hour spent in the production of Chewies will contribute $50 toward covering fixed cost and profit, while a machine hour devoted to Chompo Bars contributes only $40. Hence, the Phoenix plant's most profitable product is Chewies, when the plant's scarce resource is taken into account.

Suppose International Chocolate Company's Phoenix plant manager, Candace Barr, is faced with a choice between two sales orders, only one of which can be accepted. Only 100 hours of unscheduled machine time remains in the month, and it can be used to produce either Chewies or Chompos. The analysis in Exhibit 14–16 shows that Barr should devote the 100-hour block of machine time to filling the order for Chewies.

As Exhibit 14–16 demonstrates, a decision about the best use of a limited resource should be made on the basis of the *contribution margin per unit of the scarce resource.*

Multiple Scarce Resources Suppose the Phoenix plant had a limited amount of *both* machine hours *and* labor hours. Now the analysis of product profitability is more complicated. The choice as to which product is most profitable typically will involve a trade-off between the two scarce resources. Solving such a problem requires a powerful mathematical tool called *linear programming,* which is covered in the appendix to this chapter.

Theory of Constraints As the previous analysis suggests, a binding constraint can limit a company's profitability. For example, a manufacturing company may have a *bottleneck operation,* through which every unit of a product must pass before moving on to other operations. The *theory of constraints (TOC)* calls for identifying such limiting constraints and seeking ways to relax them. Also referred to as *managing constraints,* this management approach can significantly improve an organization's level of goal attainment. Among the ways that management can relax a constraint by expanding the capacity of a bottleneck operation are the following:

- *Outsourcing* (subcontracting) all or part of the bottleneck operation.
- Investing in additional production equipment and employing *parallel processing,* in which multiple product units undergo the same production operation simultaneously.

Exhibit 14–16
Total Contribution from 100 Machine Hours: International Chocolate Company

	Chewies	Chompo Bars
Contribution margin per case	$1.00	$2.00
Number of cases produced in 100 hours of machine time	× 5,000*	× 2,000†
Total contribution toward covering fixed cost and profit	$5,000	$4,000

*Chewies: 100 hours ÷ .02 hour per case = 5,000 cases
†Chompo Bars: 100 hours ÷ .05 hour per case = 2,000 cases

		Chewies	Chompo Bars
Original Analysis			
(a)	Contribution margin per case predicted	$1.00	$2.00
(b)	Machine hours required per case	.02	.05
(a) ÷ (b)	Contribution per machine hour	$50.00	$40.00
Sensitivity Analysis			
(c)	Contribution margin per case hypothesized in sensitivity analysis	$.80	
(d)	Machine hours required per case	.02	same
(c) ÷ (d)	Contribution per machine hour	$40.00	

Exhibit 14–17
Sensitivity Analysis: International Chocolate Company

- Working *overtime* at the bottleneck operation.
- *Retraining* employees and shifting them to the bottleneck.
- Eliminating any *non-value-added activities* at the bottleneck operation.

Uncertainty

Our analyses of the decisions in this chapter assumed that all relevant data were known with certainty. In practice, of course, decision makers are rarely so fortunate. One common technique for addressing the impact of uncertainty is *sensitivity analysis.* **Sensitivity analysis** is a technique for determining what would happen in a decision analysis if a key prediction or assumption proved to be wrong.

To illustrate, let's return to Candace Barr's decision about how to use the remaining 100 hours of machine time in International Chocolate Company's Phoenix plant. The calculation in Exhibit 14–15 showed that Chewies have the higher contribution margin per machine hour. Suppose Barr is uncertain about the contribution margin per case of Chewies. A sensitivity analysis shows how sensitive her decision is to the value of this uncertain parameter. As Exhibit 14–17 shows, the Chewies contribution margin could decline to $.80 per case before Barr's decision would change. As long as the contribution margin per case of Chewies exceeds $.80 per case, the 100 hours of available machine time should be devoted to Chewies.

Sensitivity analysis can help the managerial accountant decide which parameters in an analysis are most critical to estimate accurately. In this case, the managerial accountant knows that the contribution margin per case of Chewies could be as much as 20 percent lower than the original $1.00 prediction without changing the outcome of the analysis.

Expected Values Another approach to dealing explicitly with uncertainty is to base the decision on expected values. The **expected value** of a random variable is equal to the sum of the possible values for the variable, each weighted by its probability. To illustrate, suppose the contribution margins per case for Chewies and Chompos are uncertain, as shown

	Chewies			Chompo Bars	
	Possible Values of Contribution Margin	Probability		Possible Values of Contribution Margin	Probability
	$ .75	.5		$1.50	.3
	1.25	.5		2.00	.4
				2.50	.3
Expected value	(.5)($.75) + (.5)($1.25) = $1.00			(.3)($1.50) + (.4)($2.00) + (.3)($2.50) = $2.00	
Machine hours required per case		.02			.05
Expected value of contribution per machine hour		$50	>		$40

Exhibit 14–18
Use of Expected Values: International Chocolate Company

in Exhibit 14–18. As the exhibit shows, the choice as to which product to produce with excess machine time may be based on the *expected value* of the contribution per machine hour. Statisticians have developed many other methods for dealing with uncertainty in decision making. These techniques are covered in statistics and decision analysis courses.

Activity-Based Costing and Today's Advanced Manufacturing Environment

Learning Objective 14-7

Explain the impact of an advanced manufacturing environment and activity-based costing on a relevant-cost analysis.

In this chapter we have explored how to identify the relevant costs and benefits in various types of decisions. How will the relevant-costing approach change in an advanced manufacturing environment, characterized by just-in-time (JIT) production methods and flexible manufacturing systems (FMS)? How would a relevant-costing analysis change if a company uses an activity-based costing (ABC) system?[5]

The *concepts* underlying a relevant-costing analysis continue to be completely valid in an advanced manufacturing setting and in a situation where activity-based costing is used. The objective of the decision analysis is to determine the costs and benefits that are relevant to the decision. As we found earlier in this chapter, relevant costs and benefits *have a bearing on the future and differ among the decision alternatives.*

What *will* be different in a setting where activity-based costing is used is the decision maker's ability to determine what costs are relevant to a decision. Under ABC, the decision maker typically can associate costs with the activities that drive them much more accurately than under a conventional product-costing system. Let's explore these issues with an illustration.

Conventional Outsourcing (Make-or-Buy) Analysis

International Chocolate Company makes fine chocolates in its Savannah plant. The chocolates are packaged in two-pound and five-pound gift boxes. The company also manufactures the gift boxes in the Savannah plant. The plant manager, Marsha Mello, was approached recently by a packaging company with an offer to supply the gift boxes at a price of $.45 each. Mello concluded that the offer should be rejected on the basis of the relevant-costing analysis in Exhibit 14–19. International Chocolate Company's traditional, volume-based product-costing system showed a unit product cost of $.80 per box. However, Mello realized that not all of the costs would be avoided. She reasoned that all of the direct material, direct labor, and variable overhead would be avoided, but only a small part of the assigned fixed overhead would be saved. She concluded that $60,000 of supervisory salaries and $20,000 of machinery depreciation could be traced directly to gift package production. These costs would be avoided, she felt, but the remaining fixed costs would not. Mello concluded that only $430,000 of costs would be avoided by purchasing, while $450,000 would be spent to buy the boxes. The decision was clear; the supplier's offer should be rejected.

Activity-Based Costing Analysis of the Outsourcing Decision

At a staff meeting, Mello mentioned her tentative decision to Dave Mint, the plant controller. Mint then explained to Mello that he was completing a pilot project using activity-based costing. Mint offered to analyze the outsourcing decision using the new ABC database. Mello agreed, and Mint proceeded to do the ABC analysis shown in Exhibit 14–20.

In stage one of the ABC analysis, Mint designated 11 activity cost pools corresponding to the major items in the Savannah plant's overhead budget. These activity cost pools

[5]This section can be studied most effectively after completing Chapter 5, in which activity-based costing (ABC) is covered. Also, just-in-time (JIT) production and inventory systems are explored in Appendix III at the end of the text.

Exhibit 14–19
Conventional Product-Costing Data and Outsourcing Analysis: International Chocolate Company

A. Manufacturing Overhead Budget for Savannah Plant	
Variable overhead:	
Electricity	$ 700,000
Oil and lubricants	120,000
Equipment maintenance	180,000
Total variable overhead	$1,000,000
Variable overhead rate: $1,000,000 ÷ 100,000 direct-labor hours = $10 per hour	
Fixed overhead:	
Plant depreciation	$1,650,000
Product development	300,000
Supervisory salaries	600,000
Material handling	800,000
Purchasing	250,000
Inspection	300,000
Setup	400,000
Machinery depreciation	200,000
Total fixed overhead	$4,500,000
Fixed overhead rate: $4,500,000 ÷ 100,000 direct-labor hours = $45 per hour	
B. Conventional Product-Costing Data: Gift Boxes	
Direct material	$ 100,000
Direct labor (10,000 hr. at $15 per hr.)	150,000
Variable overhead ($10 per direct-labor hr.)	100,000
Fixed overhead ($45 per direct-labor hr.)	450,000
Total cost	$ 800,000
Unit cost: $800,000 ÷ 1,000,000 boxes = $.80 per box	
C. Conventional Outsourcing Analysis: Gift Boxes	
Relevant costs (costs that will be avoided if the gift boxes are purchased):	
Direct material	$ 100,000
Direct labor	150,000
Variable overhead	100,000
Fixed overhead:	
Supervision	60,000
Machinery depreciation	20,000
Total costs to be avoided by purchasing	$ 430,000
Total cost of purchasing (1,000,000 boxes × $.45 per box)	$ 450,000

were categorized as facility-level, product-sustaining level, batch-level, or unit-level activities. In stage two of the ABC project, cost drivers were identified and pool rates were computed. The ABC analysis showed that $243,000 of overhead should be assigned to the gift boxes, rather than $550,000 as the conventional product-costing system had indicated.

Using the ABC database, Mint completed a new relevant-costing analysis of the outsourcing decision. Mint felt that all of the overhead costs assigned to the gift box operation could be avoided if the boxes were purchased. Notice that none of the facility-level costs are relevant to the analysis. They will not be avoided by purchasing the gift boxes. Mint's ABC analysis showed that a total of $493,000 of costs could be avoided by purchasing the boxes at a cost of $450,000. This would result in a net saving of $43,000.

Mint showed the ABC relevant-costing analysis to Mello. After some discussion, they agreed that various qualitative issues needed to be explored before a final decision was made. For example, would the new supplier be reliable, and would the gift boxes be of good quality? Nevertheless, Mello and Mint agreed that the ABC data cast an entirely different light on the decision.

A. Activity Cost Pools and Pool Rates

Activity Cost Pools	Budgeted Cost	Pool Rate and Cost Driver	Cost Assigned to Gift Boxes	
Facility level:				
Plant depreciation	$1,650,000	—		
Product-sustaining level:				
Product development	300,000	$600 per product spec	$600 × 5* =	$ 3,000
Supervisory salaries	600,000	$40 per supervisory hour	$40 × 1,500 =	60,000
Batch level:				
Material handling	800,000	$8 per material-handling hour	$8 × 5,000 =	40,000
Purchasing	250,000	$250 per purchase order	$250 × 40 =	10,000
Inspection	300,000	$300 per inspection	$300 × 20 =	6,000
Setup	400,000	$400 per setup	$400 × 10 =	4,000
Unit level:				
Electricity	700,000	$1.40 per machine hour	$1.40 × 50,000 =	70,000
Oil and lubrication	120,000	$.24 per machine hour	$.24 × 50,000 =	12,000
Equipment maintenance	180,000	$.36 per machine hour	$.36 × 50,000 =	18,000
Machinery depreciation	200,000	$.40 per machine hour	$.40 × 50,000 =	20,000
Total overhead for Savannah plant	$5,500,000			
Total overhead assigned to gift box production				$243,000

B. ABC Outsourcing Analysis: Gift Boxes

Relevant costs (costs that will be avoided if the gift boxes are purchased):	
Direct material	$100,000
Direct labor	150,000
Overhead (from ABC analysis in panel A, above)	243,000
Total costs to be avoided by purchasing	$493,000
Total cost of purchasing (1,000,000 boxes × $.45 per box)	$450,000

*The numbers in this column are the quantities of each cost driver required for gift box production.

Exhibit 14–20
Activity-Based Costing Analysis of Outsourcing Decision: International Chocolate Company

The Key Point What has happened here? Why did the conventional and ABC analyses of this decision reach different conclusions? Is the relevant-costing concept faulty?

The answer is no; the relevant-costing idea is alive and well. Both analyses sought to identify the relevant costs as those that would be avoided by purchasing the gift boxes. That approach is valid. The difference in the analyses lies in the superior ability of the ABC data to properly identify what the avoidable costs are. This is the key point. The conventional analysis relied on a traditional, volume-based product-costing system. That system lumps all of the fixed overhead costs together and assigns them using a single, unit-based cost driver (i.e., direct-labor hours). That analysis simply failed to note that many of the so-called fixed costs are *not* really fixed with respect to the appropriate cost driver. The more accurate ABC system correctly showed this fact, and identified additional costs that could be avoided by purchasing.

To summarize, under activity-based costing, the concepts underlying relevant-costing analysis remain valid. However, the ABC system does enable the decision maker to apply the relevant-costing decision model more accurately.

Other Issues in Decision Making

Incentives for Decision Makers

In this chapter, we studied how managers should make decisions by focusing on the relevant costs and benefits. In previous chapters, we covered accounting procedures for evaluating managerial performance. There is an important link between *decision making* and *managerial performance evaluation.* Managers typically will make decisions that maximize their perceived performance evaluations and rewards. This is human nature. If we want managers to make optimal decisions by properly evaluating the relevant costs and benefits, then the performance evaluation system and reward structure had better be consistent with that perspective.

The proper treatment of sunk costs in decision making illustrates this issue. Earlier in this chapter, we saw that sunk costs should be ignored as irrelevant. For example, the book value of an outdated machine is irrelevant in making an equipment-replacement decision. Suppose, however, that a manager correctly ignores an old machine's book value and decides on early replacement of the machine he purchased a few years ago. Now suppose the hapless manager is criticized by his superior for "taking a loss" on the old machine, or for "buying a piece of junk" in the first place. What is our manager likely to do the next time he faces a similar decision? If he is like many people, he will tend to keep the old machine in order to justify his prior decision to purchase it. In so doing, he will be compounding his error. However, he also may be avoiding criticism from a superior who does not understand the importance of goal congruence.

The point is simply that if we want managers to make optimal decisions, we must give them incentives to do so. This requires that managerial performance be judged on the same factors that should be considered in making correct decisions.

Short-Run versus Long-Run Decisions

The decisions we have examined in this chapter were treated as short-run decisions. *Short-run decisions* affect only a short time period, typically a year or less. In reality, many of these decisions would have longer-term implications. For example, managers usually make a decision involving the addition or deletion of a product or service with a relatively long time frame in mind. The process of identifying relevant costs and benefits is largely the same whether the decision is viewed from a short-run or long-run perspective. One important factor that does change in a long-run analysis, however, is the *time value of money.* When several time periods are involved in a decision, the analyst should account for the fact that a \$1.00 cash flow today is different from a \$1.00 cash flow in five years. A dollar received today can be invested to earn interest, while the dollar received in five years cannot be invested over the intervening time period. The analysis of long-run decisions requires a tool called *capital budgeting,* which is covered in Chapter 16.

Pitfalls to Avoid

Identification of the relevant costs and benefits is an important step in making any economic decision. Nonetheless, analysts often overlook relevant costs or incorrectly include irrelevant data. In this section, we review four common mistakes to avoid in decision making.

1. ***Sunk costs.*** The book value of an asset, defined as its acquisition cost less the accumulated depreciation, is a sunk cost. Sunk costs cannot be changed by any current or future course of action, so they are irrelevant in decision making. Nevertheless, a common behavioral tendency is to give undue importance to book values in decisions that involve replacing an asset or disposing of obsolete inventory. People often seek to justify their past decisions by refusing to dispose of an asset, even if a better alternative has been identified. *The moral: Ignore sunk costs.*
2. ***Unitized fixed costs.*** For product-costing purposes, fixed costs often are divided by some activity measure and assigned to individual units of product. The result is to make a fixed cost appear variable. While there are legitimate reasons for this practice from a *product-costing* perspective, it can create havoc in *decision making.* Therefore, in a decision analysis, it is usually wise to include a fixed cost in its total amount, rather than as a per-unit cost. *The moral: Beware of unitized fixed costs in decision making.*
3. ***Allocated fixed costs.*** It is also common to allocate fixed costs across divisions, departments, or product lines. A possible result is that a product or department may appear unprofitable when in reality it does make a contribution toward covering fixed costs and profit. Before deciding to eliminate a department, be

sure to ask which costs will be *avoided* if a particular alternative is selected. A fixed cost that has been allocated to a department may continue, in total or in part, even after the department has been eliminated. *The moral: Beware of allocated fixed costs; identify the avoidable costs.*

4. ***Opportunity costs.*** People tend to overlook opportunity costs, or to treat such costs as less important than out-of-pocket costs. Yet opportunity costs are just as real and important to making a correct decision as are out-of-pocket costs. *The moral: Pay special attention to identifying and including opportunity costs in a decision analysis.*

Focus on Ethics

EFFECTS OF A DECISION TO CLOSE A DEPARTMENT AND OUTSOURCE

Outsourcing has become a common way of reducing costs in many organizations. Such decisions, though, often have repercussions that may not be captured "by the numbers." Employee morale, product quality, and vendor reliability are some of the issues that should be considered. Let's revisit the scenario described earlier at the International Chocolate Company. Recall that the Savannah plant manager, Marsha Mello (M), was considering outsourcing the production of gift boxes for the company's fine chocolates. A conventional analysis of the decision pointed toward keeping the production operation in-house. Now let's change the scenario a bit, and consider the following conversation between Dave Mint, plant controller (C), and Jack Edgeworth, supervisor of the gift box production department (SG). The conversation takes place after the two friends' weekly tennis game.

Mint (C): "Well, you took me again, Jack. I'm starting to feel old."

Edgeworth (SG): "It was a close match, Dave. Always is. Fortunately, it looks like we'll be able to keep our matches up, too."

Mint (C): "What do you mean?"

Edgeworth (SG): "I'm talking about the outsourcing decision Marsha was considering. Fortunately, the analysis showed her that we should keep making our own gift boxes. So my department stays in business. And I won't have to consider a transfer. My wife's very happy about that, with the twins in middle school and all."

Mint (C): "Uh, Jack, I think there's something you need to know about."

Edgeworth (SG): "What's that?"

Mint (C): "I've been doing some preliminary studies using a technique called activity-based costing. I think it could improve our decision making in a lot of areas."

Edgeworth (SG): "So?"

Mint (C): "That outsourcing decision is one of the areas where I tried out the new ABC approach. I just finished the analysis yesterday. I was going to schedule an appointment with Marsha and you next week to discuss it."

Edgeworth (SG): "I'm getting queasy about where this is going, Jack. What did your analysis show?"

Mint (C): "It changes the conclusion—pretty dramatically, in fact. The ABC study shows that we'd save over $40,000 each year by outsourcing."

Edgeworth (SG): "Is that really all that much, Dave? Among friends, I mean?"

Mint (C): "It's not a trivial amount, Jack."

Edgeworth (SG): "Look, Dave, I don't think I've ever asked anything of you before. But can't you bury this one for me? Our family really doesn't need another move. And I've got people working for me who will probably lose their jobs. We've done a good job for the company. Our product is top notch. Nobody's ever complained about a thing."

Mint (C): "I don't see how I can withhold the analysis from Marsha, Jack. She has a right to all the information I have."

Edgeworth (SG): "But you said you were just doing preliminary studies, Dave. Marsha doesn't know anything about this one, does she?"

Mint (C): "Not yet, Jack, but I've got a professional obligation to show it to her."

Edgeworth (SG): "You're opening a Pandora's box, Dave. What about employee morale if you close my department? And what about product quality, and reliability of the supply?"

Mint (C): "Those are valid issues, Jack. But they need to be addressed on their own merits, in a full and open discussion."

Edgeworth (SG): "Could you at least share this so-called ABC study with me before you show it to Marsha? Maybe I'll see something you've missed."

Mint (C): "I don't see why not, Jack. Come by my office tomorrow morning—say about 10:00."

Identify any ethical issues you see in this scenario. How would you resolve them? What should the controller do?

Chapter Summary

LO14-1 Describe seven steps in the decision-making process and the managerial accountant's role in that process. The decision-making steps are: (1) clarify the decision problem; (2) specify the criterion; (3) identify the alternatives; (4) develop a decision model; (5) collect the data; (6) select an alternative; and (7) evaluate decision effectiveness.

LO14-2 Explain the relationship between quantitative and qualitative analyses in decision making. The managerial accountant's key role in the decision-making process is to provide data relevant to the decision. Managers can then use these data in preparing a quantitative analysis of the decision. Qualitative factors also are considered in making the final decision.

LO14-3 List and explain two criteria that must be satisfied by relevant information. In order to be relevant to a decision, a cost or benefit must (1) bear on the future and (2) differ under the various decision alternatives.

LO14-4 Identify relevant costs and benefits, giving proper treatment to sunk costs, opportunity costs, and unit costs. Sunk costs, such as the book value of equipment or inventory, are not relevant to decisions. Such costs do not have any bearing on the future. Opportunity costs frequently are relevant to decisions, but they often are overlooked by decision makers. Unit costs bear particular scrutiny in decision-making situations. Fixed costs often are unitized and assigned to products or services for product-costing purposes. For decision-making purposes, however, unit costs can be misleading, since the total fixed cost will not increase as the total number of units produced increases.

LO14-5 Prepare analyses of various special decisions, properly identifying the relevant costs and benefits. To analyze any special decision, the proper approach is to determine all of the costs and benefits that will differ among the alternatives. Common decisions include the following: (1) accept or reject a special offer; (2) outsource a product or service; and (3) add or drop a service, product, or department.

LO14-6 Analyze manufacturing decisions involving joint products and limited resources. A common decision that arises in a joint-product environment is whether to sell a joint product at the split-off point or process it further. This decision should be based on the incremental costs and benefits occurring after the split-off point. A common decision involving limited resources is which of several products to produce. The correct decision is to produce the product with the highest contribution margin per unit of the scarce resource.

LO14-7 Explain the impact of an advanced manufacturing environment and activity-based costing on a relevant-cost analysis. The concepts underlying a relevant-cost analysis remain valid in an advanced manufacturing environment and in situations where activity-based costing is used. However, an ABC system typically enables a decision maker to estimate the relevant costs in a decision problem more accurately.

LO14-8 Formulate a linear program to solve a product-mix problem with multiple constraints (appendix). A linear program can be used to solve a firm's product-mix problem when the production process is constrained by scarce resources. A linear program consists of a linear objective function and a set of linear constraints. The solution to the optimization problem consists of finding the optimal solution point within the feasible region, as determined by the constraints.

Review Problem on Relevant Costs

Lansing Camera Company has received a special order for photographic equipment it does not normally produce. The company has excess capacity, and the order could be manufactured without reducing production of the firm's regular products. Discuss the relevance of each of the following items in computing the cost of the special order.

1. Equipment to be used in producing the order has a book value of $2,000. The equipment has no other use for Lansing Camera Company. If the order is not accepted, the equipment will be sold for $1,500. If the equipment is used in producing the order, it can be sold in three months for $800.

2. If the special order is accepted, the operation will require some of the storage space in the company's plant. If the space is used for this purpose, the company will rent storage space temporarily in a nearby warehouse at a cost of $18,000. The building depreciation allocated to the storage space to be used in producing the special order is $12,000.
3. If the special order is accepted, it will require a subassembly. Lansing Camera can purchase the subassembly for $24 per unit from an outside supplier or make it for $30 per unit. The $30 cost per unit was determined as follows:

Direct material	$10.00
Direct labor	6.00
Variable overhead	6.00
Allocated fixed overhead	8.00
Total unit cost of subassembly	$30.00

Solution to Review Problem

1. The book value of the equipment is a sunk cost, irrelevant to the decision. The relevant cost of the equipment is $700, determined as follows:

Sales value of equipment now	$1,500
Sales value after producing special order	800
Differential cost	$ 700

2. The $12,000 portion of building depreciation allocated to the storage space to be used for the special order is irrelevant. First, it is a sunk cost. Second, any costs relating to the company's factory building will continue whether the special order is accepted or not. The relevant cost is the $18,000 rent that will be incurred only if the special order is accepted.
3. Lansing Camera should make the subassembly. The subassembly's relevant cost is $22 per unit.

Relevant Cost of Making Subassembly (per unit)		Relevant Cost of Purchasing Subassembly (per unit)	
Direct material	$10.00	Purchase price	$24.00
Direct labor	6.00		
Variable overhead	6.00		
Total	$22.00		

Notice that the unitized fixed overhead, $8, is not a relevant cost of the subassembly. Lansing Camera Company's *total* fixed cost will not change, whether the special order is accepted or not.

Key Terms

For each term's definition refer to the indicated page, or turn to the glossary at the end of the text.

accurate information, 601
avoidable expenses, 611
constraints,* 625
decision variables,* 625
differential cost, 604
expected value, 617
feasible region,* 625
information overload, 602
joint cost, 614
joint production process, 613
make-or-buy decision, 608
objective function,* 625
opportunity cost, 605
outsourcing decision, 608
qualitative characteristics, 599
relative-sales-value method, 614
relevant information, 600
sensitivity analysis, 617
separable processing cost, 614
split-off point, 613
sunk costs, 602
timely information, 601
unavoidable expenses, 611

*Term appears in the appendix.

APPENDIX TO CHAPTER 14

Linear Programming

Learning Objective **14-8**

Formulate a linear program to solve a product-mix problem with multiple constraints.

When a firm produces multiple products, management must decide how much of each output to produce. In most cases, the firm is limited in the total amount it can produce, due to constraints on resources such as machine time, direct labor, or raw materials. This situation is known as a *product-mix problem.*

To illustrate, we will use International Chocolate Company's Phoenix plant, which produces Chewies and Chompo Bars. Exhibit 14–21 provides data pertinent to the problem.

Linear programming is a powerful mathematical tool, well suited to solving International Chocolate Company's product-mix problem. The steps in constructing the linear program are as follows:

1. Identify the **decision variables,** which are the variables about which a decision must be made. International Chocolate's decision variables are as follows:

   Decision variables X = Number of cases of Chewies to produce each month
   Y = Number of cases of Chompo Bars to produce each month

2. Write the **objective function,** which is an algebraic expression of the firm's goal. International Chocolate's goal is to *maximize its total contribution margin.* Since Chewies bring a contribution margin of \$1 per case, and Chompos result in a contribution margin of \$2 per case, the firm's objective function is the following:

   Objective function Maximize $Z = X + 2Y$

3. Write the **constraints,** which are algebraic expressions of the limitations faced by the firm, such as those limiting its productive resources. International Chocolate has a constraint for machine time and a constraint for direct labor.

   Machine-time constraint $.02X + .05Y \leq 700$
   Labor-time constraint $.20X + .25Y \leq 5{,}000$

Suppose, for example, that management decided to produce 20,000 cases of Chewies and 6,000 cases of Chompos. The machine-time constraint would appear as follows:

$$(.02)(20{,}000) + (.05)(6{,}000) = 700$$

Thus, at these production levels, the machine-time constraint would just be satisfied, with no machine hours to spare.

Graphical Solution

To understand how the linear program described above will help International Chocolate's management solve its product-mix problem, examine the graphs in Exhibit 14–22. The two colored lines in panel A represent the constraints. The colored arrows indicate that the production quantities, X and Y, must lie on or below these lines. Since the production quantities must be nonnegative, colored arrows also appear on the graphs' axes. Together, the axes and constraints form an area called the **feasible region,** in which the solution to the linear program must lie.

The purple slanted line in panel A represents the objective function. Rearrange the objective function equation as follows:

$$Z = X + 2Y \rightarrow Y = \frac{Z}{2} - \frac{1}{2}X$$

	Chewies	Chompo Bars
Contribution margin per case	\$1.00	\$2.00
Machine hours per case	.02	.05
Direct-labor hours per case	.20	.25
	Machine Hours	**Direct-Labor Hours**
Limited resources: hours available per month	700	5,000

Exhibit 14–21
Data for Product-Mix Problem: International Chocolate Company

Exhibit 14–22
Product-Mix Problem Expressed as Linear Program: International Chocolate Company

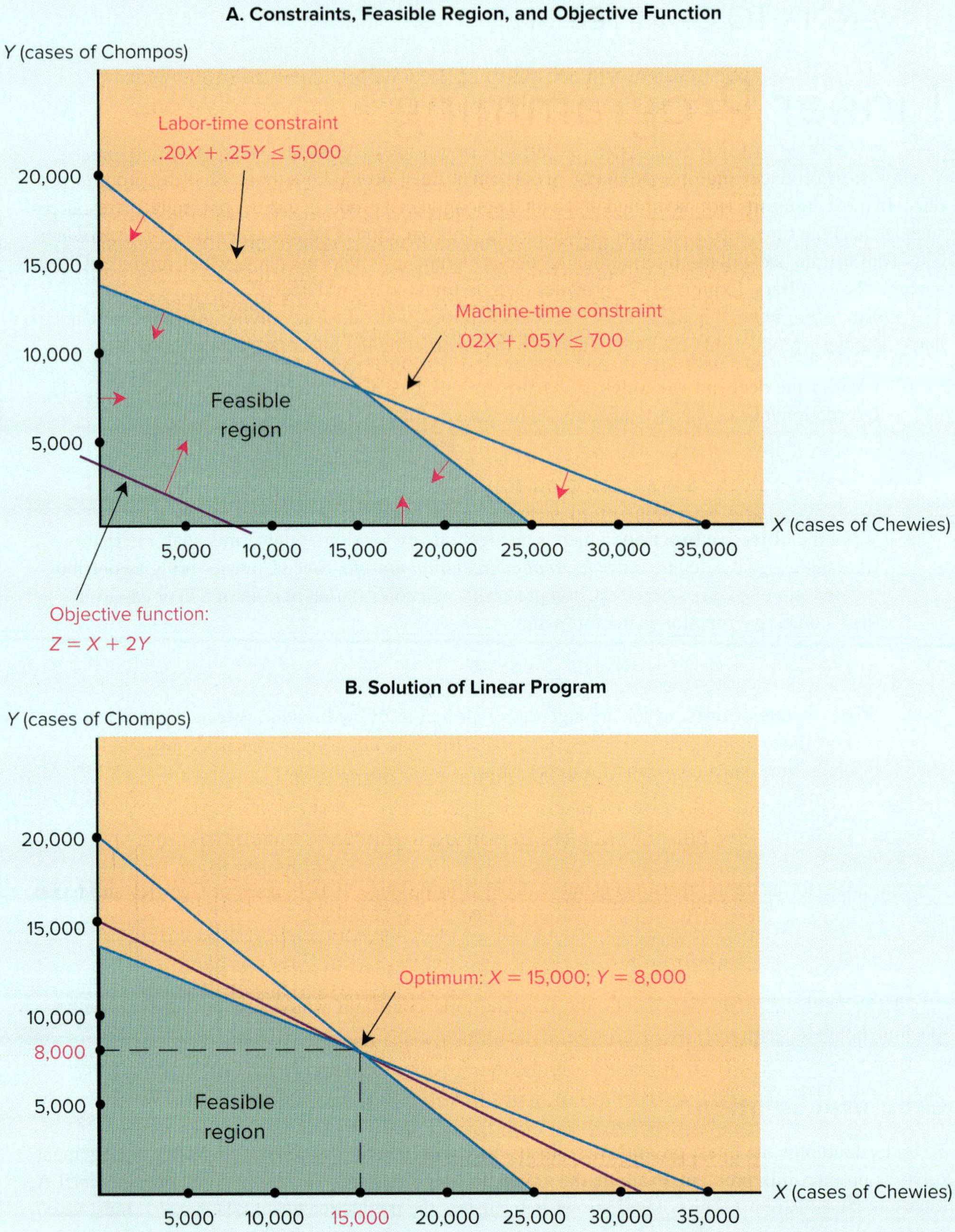

This form of the objective function shows that the slope of the equation is −½, which is the slope of the objective-function line in the exhibit. Management's goal is to maximize total contribution margin, denoted by *Z*. To achieve the maximum, the objective-function line must be moved as far outward and upward in the feasible region as possible, while maintaining the same slope. This goal is represented in panel A by the arrow that points outward from the objective-function line.

Solution The result of moving the objective-function line as far as possible in the indicated direction is shown in panel B of the exhibit. The objective-function line intersects the feasible region at exactly one point, where *X* equals 15,000 and *Y* equals 8,000. Thus, International Chocolate's optimal product mix is 15,000 cases of Chewies and 8,000 cases of Chompos per month. The total contribution margin is calculated as shown below.

Total contribution margin = (15,000)($1) + (8,000)($2) = $31,000

Simplex Method and Sensitivity Analysis Although the graphical method is instructive, it is a cumbersome technique for solving a linear program. Fortunately, mathematicians have developed a more efficient solution method called the *simplex algorithm.* A computer can apply the algorithm to a complex linear program and determine the solution in seconds. In addition, most linear programming computer packages provide a sensitivity analysis of the problem. This analysis shows the decision maker the extent to which the estimates used in the objective function and constraints can change without changing the solution.

Managerial Accountant's Role

What is the managerial accountant's role in International Chocolate's product-mix decision? The production manager in the company's Phoenix plant makes this decision, with the help of a linear program. However, the linear program uses *information supplied by the managerial accountant.* The coefficients of X and Y in the objective function are unit contribution margins. Exhibit 14–14 shows that calculating these contribution margins requires estimates of direct-material, direct-labor, variable-overhead, and variable selling and administrative costs. These estimates were provided by a managerial accountant, along with estimates of the machine time and direct-labor time required to produce a case of Chewies or Chompos. All of these estimates were obtained from the standard-costing system, upon which the Phoenix plant's product costs are based. Thus, the managerial accountant makes the product-mix decision possible by providing the relevant cost data.

Linear programming is widely used in business decision making. Among the applications are blending in the petroleum and chemical industries; scheduling of personnel, railroad cars, and aircraft; and the mixing of ingredients in the food industry. In all of these applications, managerial accountants provide information crucial to the analysis.

Review Questions

14–1. List the seven steps in the decision-making process.

14–2. Describe the managerial accountant's role in the decision-making process.

14–3. Distinguish between qualitative and quantitative decision analyses.

14–4. Explain what is meant by the term *decision model.*

14–5. A quantitative analysis enables a decision maker to put a "price" on the sum total of the qualitative characteristics in a decision situation. Explain this statement, and give an example.

14–6. What is meant by each of the following potential characteristics of information: relevant, accurate, and timely? Is objective information always relevant? Accurate?

14–7. List and explain two important criteria that must be satisfied in order for information to be relevant.

14–8. Explain why the book value of equipment is not a relevant cost.

14–9. Is the book value of inventory on hand a relevant cost? Why?

14–10. Why might a manager exhibit a behavioral tendency to inappropriately consider sunk costs in making a decision?

14–11. Give an example of an irrelevant future cost. Why is it irrelevant?

14–12. Define the term *opportunity cost,* and give an example of one.

14–13. What behavioral tendency do people often exhibit with regard to opportunity costs?

14–14. How does the existence of excess production capacity affect the decision to accept or reject a special order?

14–15. What is meant by the term *differential cost analysis?*

14–16. Briefly describe the proper approach for making a decision about adding or dropping a product line.

14–17. What is a *joint production process?* Describe a special decision that commonly arises in the context of a joint production process. Briefly describe the proper approach for making this type of decision.

14–18. Are allocated joint processing costs relevant when making a decision to sell a joint product at the split-off point or process it further? Why?

14–19. Briefly describe the proper approach to making a production decision when limited resources are involved.

14–20. What is meant by the term *contribution margin per unit of scarce resource?*

14–21. How is sensitivity analysis used to cope with uncertainty in decision making?

14–22. There is an important link between *decision making* and *managerial performance evaluation.* Explain.

14–23. List four potential pitfalls in decision making, which represent common errors.

14–24. Why can unitized fixed costs cause errors in decision making?

14–25. Give two examples of sunk costs, and explain why they are irrelevant in decision making.

14–26. "Accounting systems should produce only relevant data and forget about the irrelevant data. Then I'd know what was relevant and what wasn't!" Comment on this remark by a company president.

14–27. Are the concepts underlying a relevant-cost analysis still valid in an advanced manufacturing environment? Are these concepts valid when activity-based costing is used? Explain.

14–28. List five ways that management can seek to relax a constraint by expanding the capacity of a bottleneck operation.

Exercises

All applicable Exercises are available in Connect.

Exercise 14–29
Steps in Decision-Making Process
(LO 14-1)

Choose an organization and a particular decision situation. Then give examples, using that decision context, of each step illustrated in Exhibit 14–1. For example, you could choose a decision that would be made by a retailer, such as Best Buy or Dick's Sporting Goods. Or you could focus on a service provider, such as Hertz rent-a-car or Marriott Hotels. Alternatively, select a manufacturer, such as Nike or Nokia. Or consider a decision to be made by your college or home city.

Exercise 14–30
Irrelevant Future Costs and Benefits
(LO 14-3, 14-4)

Redo Exhibit 14–4 without the irrelevant data.

Exercise 14–31
Machine Replacement
(LO 14-4, 14-5)

Valley Pizza's owner bought his current pizza oven two years ago for $9,000, and it has one more year of life remaining. He is using straight-line depreciation for the oven. He could purchase a new oven for $1,900, but it would last only one year. The owner figures the new oven would save him $2,600 in annual operating expenses compared to operating the old one. Consequently, he has decided against buying the new oven, since doing so would result in a "loss" of $400 over the next year.

Required:

1. How do you suppose the owner came up with $400 as the loss for the next year if the new pizza oven were purchased? Explain.
2. Criticize the owner's analysis and decision.
3. Prepare a correct analysis of the owner's decision.

Exercise 14–32
Joint Products
(LO 14-4, 14-5, 14-6)

Lamont Industries produces chemicals for the swimming pool industry. In one joint process, 10,000 gallons of GSX are processed into 7,000 gallons of xenolite and 3,000 gallons of banolide. The cost of the joint process, including the GSX, is $19,000. The firm allocates $13,300 of the joint cost to the xenolite and $5,700 of the cost to the banolide. The 3,000 gallons of banolide can be sold at the split-off point for $2,500, or be processed further into a product called kitrocide. The sales value of 3,000 gallons of kitrocide is $10,000, and the additional processing cost is $8,100.

Required: Lamont's president has asked your consulting firm to make a recommendation as to whether the banolide should be sold at the split-off point or processed further. Write a letter providing an analysis and a recommendation.

Exercise 14–33
Drop Product Line
(LO 14-4, 14-5)

Day Street Deli's owner is disturbed by the poor profit performance of his ice cream counter. He has prepared the following profit analysis for the year just ended.

Sales		$45,000
Less: Cost of food		20,000
Gross profit		$25,000
Less: Operating expenses:		
Wages of counter personnel	$12,000	
Paper products (e.g., napkins)	4,000	
Utilities (allocated)	2,900	
Depreciation of counter equipment and furnishings	2,500	
Depreciation of building (allocated)	4,000	
Deli manager's salary (allocated)	3,000	
Total		28,400
Loss on ice cream counter		$(3,400)

Required: Criticize and correct the owner's analysis.

Exercise 14–34
Outsourcing Decision; Use of Internet
(LO 14-1, 14-2, 14-5)

Visit the website of one of the following companies, or a different company of your choosing.

Burger King	www.burgerking.com
Corning	www.corning.com
Walmart	www.walmart.com
Apple	www.apple.com
NBC	www.nbc.com

Required: Read about the company's activities and operations. Choose an activity that is necessary for the company's operations, and then discuss the pros and cons of outsourcing that activity.

Exercise 14–35
Obsolete Inventory
(LO 14-4, 14-5)

Armstrong Corporation manufactures bicycle parts. The company currently has a $21,000 inventory of parts that have become obsolete due to changes in design specifications. The parts could be sold for $9,000, or modified for $12,000 and sold for $22,300.

Required:

1. Which of the data above are relevant to the decision about the obsolete parts?
2. Prepare an analysis of the decision.

Exercise 14–36
Special Order
(LO 14-4, 14-5)

Intercontinental Chemical Company, located in Buenos Aires, Argentina, recently received an order for a product it does not normally produce. Since the company has excess production capacity, management is considering accepting the order. In analyzing the decision, the assistant controller is compiling the relevant costs of producing the order. Production of the special order would require 8,000 kilograms of theolite. Intercontinental does not use theolite for its regular product, but the firm has 8,000 kilograms of the chemical on hand from the days when it used theolite regularly. The theolite could be sold to a chemical wholesaler for 14,500 *p*. The book value of the theolite is 2.00 *p* per kilogram. Intercontinental could buy theolite for 2.40 *p* per kilogram. (*p* denotes the peso, Argentina's national monetary unit. Many countries use the peso as their unit of currency. On the day this exercise was written, Argentina's peso was worth .104 U.S. dollar.)

Required:

1. What is the relevant cost of theolite for the purpose of analyzing the special-order decision? (Remember to express your answer in terms of Argentina's peso.)
2. Discuss each of the numbers given in the exercise with regard to its relevance in making the decision.

Exercise 14–37
Continuation of Preceding Exercise
(LO 14-4, 14-5)

Intercontinental's special order also requires 1,000 kilograms of genatope, a solid chemical regularly used in the company's products. The current stock of genatope is 8,000 kilograms at a book value of 8.10 *p* per kilogram. If the special order is accepted, the firm will be forced to restock genatope earlier than expected, at a predicted cost of 8.70 *p* per kilogram. Without the special order, the purchasing manager predicts that the price will be 8.30 *p* when normal restocking takes place. Any order of genatope must be in the amount of 5,000 kilograms.

Required:

1. What is the relevant cost of genatope?
2. Discuss each of the figures in the exercise in terms of its relevance to the decision.

Exercise 14–38
Closing a Department
(LO 14-4, 14-5)

Fusion Metals Company is considering the elimination of its Packaging Department. Management has received an offer from an outside firm to supply all Fusion's packaging needs. To help her in making the decision, Fusion's president has asked the controller for an analysis of the cost of running Fusion's Packaging Department. Included in that analysis is $9,100 of rent, which represents the Packaging Department's allocation of the rent on Fusion's factory building. If the Packaging Department is eliminated, the space it used will be converted to storage space. Currently Fusion rents storage space in a nearby warehouse for $11,000 per year. The warehouse rental would no longer be necessary if the Packaging Department were eliminated.

Required:

1. Discuss each of the figures given in the exercise with regard to its relevance in the department-closing decision.
2. What type of cost is the $11,000 warehouse rental, from the viewpoint of the costs of the Packaging Department?

Exercise 14–39
Continuation of Preceding Exercise
(LO 14-4, 14-5)

Fusion Metals Company needs a new manager for its Cutting Department. It is considering closing its Packaging Department, and if it does the Packaging Department manager will be appointed manager of the Cutting Department. The Packaging Department manager makes $45,000 per year. To hire a new Cutting Department manager from outside the company will cost Fusion $60,000 per year.

Required: Discuss the relevance of each of these salary figures to the department-closing decision.

Exercise 14–40
Joint Products; Relevant Costs; Cost-Volume-Profit Analysis
(LO 14-4, 14-6)

Zytel Corporation produces cleaning compounds and solutions for industrial and household use. While most of its products are processed independently, a few are related. Grit 337, a coarse cleaning powder with many industrial uses, costs $1.60 a pound to make and sells for $2.00 a pound. A small portion of the annual production of this product is retained for further processing in the Mixing Department, where it is combined with several other ingredients to form a paste, which is marketed as a silver polish selling for $4.00 per jar. This further processing requires ¼ pound of Grit 337 per jar. Costs of other ingredients, labor, and variable overhead associated with this further processing amount to $2.50 per jar. Variable selling costs are $.30 per jar. If the decision were made to cease production of the silver polish, $5,600 of Mixing Department fixed costs could be avoided. Zytel has limited production capacity for Grit 337, but unlimited demand for the cleaning powder.

Required: Calculate the minimum number of jars of silver polish that would have to be sold to justify further processing of Grit 337.

(CMA, adapted)

Exercise 14–41
Limited Resource
(LO 14-6)

Duo Company manufactures two products, Uno and Dos. Contribution margin data follow.

	Uno	Dos
Unit sales	$13.00	$31.00
Less variable cost:		
Direct material	$ 7.00	$ 5.00
Direct labor	1.00	6.00
Variable overhead	1.25	7.50
Variable selling and administrative cost	.75	.50
Total variable cost	$10.00	$19.00
Unit contribution margin	$ 3.00	$12.00

Duo company's production process uses highly skilled labor, which is in short supply. The same employees work on both products and earn the same wage rate.

Required: Which of Duo Company's products is more profitable? Explain.

Exercise 14–42
Linear Programming (Appendix)
(LO 14-6, 14-8)

Refer to the data given in the preceding exercise for Duo Company. Assume that the direct-labor rate is $24 per hour, and 10,000 labor hours are available per year. In addition, the company has a short supply of machine time. Only 8,000 hours are available each year. Uno requires 1 machine hour per unit, and Dos requires 2 machine hours per unit.

Required: Formulate the production planning problem as a linear program. Specifically identify (1) the decision variables, (2) the objective function, and (3) the constraints.

Exercise 14–43
Linear Programming; Formulate and Solve Graphically (Appendix)
(LO 14-8)

Southern California Chemical Company manufactures two industrial chemical products, called kreolite-red and kreolite-blue. Two machines are used in the process, and each machine has 24 hours of capacity per day. The following data are available:

	Kreolite-Red	Kreolite-Blue
Selling price per drum	$36	$42
Variable cost per drum	$28	$28
Hours required per drum on machine I	2 hr	2 hr
Hours required per drum on machine II	1 hr	3 hr

The company can produce and sell partially full drums of each chemical. For example, a half drum of kreolite-red sells for $18.

Required:

1. Formulate the product-mix problem as a linear program.
2. Solve the problem graphically.

Problems

All applicable Problems are available in Connect.

connect

Problem 14–44
Production Decisions; Limited Capacity
(LO 14-5, 14-6)

Kitchen Magician, Inc. has assembled the following data pertaining to its two most popular products.

	Blender	Electric Mixer
Direct material	$ 6	$11
Direct labor	4	9
Manufacturing overhead @ $16 per machine hour	16	32
Cost if purchased from an outside supplier	20	38
Annual demand (units)	20,000	28,000

Past experience has shown that the fixed manufacturing overhead component included in the cost per machine hour averages $10. Kitchen Magician's management has a policy of filling all sales orders, even if it means purchasing units from outside suppliers.

Required:

1. If 50,000 machine hours are available, and management desires to follow an optimal strategy, how many units of each product should the firm manufacture? How many units of each product should be purchased?
2. With all other things constant, if management is able to reduce the direct material for an electric mixer to $6 per unit, how many units of each product should be manufactured? Purchased?
3. ***Build a spreadsheet:*** Construct an Excel spreadsheet to solve requirement (1) above. Show how the solution will change if the following information changes: the unit cost if purchased from an outside supplier is $22 for the blender and $40 for the electric mixer.

(CMA, adapted)

Problem 14–45
Special Order; Financial and Production Considerations
(LO 14-4, 14-5)

1. Net contribution to profit: $34,050

Jupiter Corporation manufactures skateboards. Several weeks ago, the firm received a special-order inquiry from Venus, Inc. Venus desires to market a skateboard similar to one of Jupiter's and has offered to purchase 11,000 units if the order can be completed in three months. The cost data for Jupiter's model no. 43 skateboard follow.

Direct material	$ 8.20
Direct labor: .25 hour at $9.00	2.25
Total manufacturing overhead:	
.5 hour at $20	10.00
Total	$20.45

Additional data:

- The normal selling price of model no. 43 is $26.50; however, Venus has offered Jupiter only $15.75 because of the large quantity it is willing to purchase.
- Venus requires a modification of the design that will allow a $2.10 reduction in direct-material cost.
- Jupiter's production supervisor notes that the company will incur $3,700 in additional setup costs and will have to purchase a $2,400 special device to manufacture these units. The device will be discarded once the special order is completed.
- Total manufacturing overhead costs are applied to production at the rate of $20 per machine hour. This figure is based, in part, on budgeted yearly fixed overhead of $750,000 and planned production activity of 60,000 machine hours (5,000 per month).
- Jupiter will allocate $1,800 of existing fixed administrative costs to the order as ". . . part of the cost of doing business."

Required:

1. Assume that present sales will not be affected. Should the order be accepted from a financial point of view (i.e., is it profitable)? Why? Show calculations.
2. Assume that Jupiter's current production activity consumes 70 percent of planned machine-hour activity. Can the company accept the order and meet Venus' deadline?
3. What options might Jupiter consider if management truly wanted to do business with Venus in hopes of building a long-term relationship with the firm?

Problem 14–46
Introducing a New Product
(LO 14-4, 14-5)

1. Unit contribution margin, Enhanced Model, $200

Johnson and Gomez, Inc. is a small firm involved in the production and sale of electronic business products. The company is well known for its attention to quality and innovation.

During the past 15 months, a new product has been under development that allows users improved access to e-mail and video images. Johnson and Gomez code named the product the Wireless Wizard and has been quietly designing two models: Basic and Enhanced. Development costs have amounted to $121,000 and $175,000, respectively. The total market demand for each model is expected to be 40,000 units, and management anticipates being able to obtain the following market shares: Basic, 25 percent; Enhanced, 20 percent. Forecast data follow.

	Basic	Enhanced
Projected selling price	$ 250	$ 330
Per-unit production costs:		
Direct material	28	45
Direct labor	15	20
Variable overhead	24	32
Marketing and advertising (fixed but avoidable)	130,000	200,000
Sales commissions*	10%	10%

*Computed on the basis of sales dollars.

Since the start of development work on the Wireless Wizard, advances in technology have altered the market somewhat, and management now believes that the company can introduce only one of the two models. Consultants confirmed this fact not too long ago, with Johnson and Gomez paying $23,000 for an in-depth market study. Sales salaries (excluding commission) will be $57,000 no matter which product is sold. The marketing and advertising costs indicated for each product are incurred only if that product is sold. Other fixed overhead is expected to be the same, regardless of which product is introduced.

Required:

1. Compute the unit contribution margin for both models.
2. Which of the data in the table above should be ignored in making the product-introduction decision? For what reason?
3. Prepare a financial analysis and determine which of the two models should be introduced.
4. What other factors should Johnson and Gomez, Inc. consider before a final decision is made?

Problem 14–47
Closing an Unprofitable Department
(LO 14-4, 14-5)

1. Income (loss) from closure: $(12,800)

Tipton One-Stop Decorating sells paint and paint supplies, carpet, and wallpaper at a single-store location in suburban Des Moines. Although the company has been very profitable over the years, management has seen a significant decline in wallpaper sales and earnings. Much of this decline is attributable to the Internet and to companies that advertise deeply discounted prices in magazines and offer customers free shipping and toll-free telephone numbers. Recent figures follow.

	Paint and Supplies	Carpeting	Wallpaper
Sales	$380,000	$460,000	$140,000
Variable costs	$228,000	$322,000	$112,000
Fixed costs	56,000	75,000	45,000
Total costs	$284,000	$397,000	$157,000
Operating income (loss)	$ 96,000	$ 63,000	$ (17,000)

Tipton is studying whether to drop wallpaper because of the changing market and accompanying loss. If the line is dropped, the following changes are expected to occur:

- The vacated space will be remodeled at a cost of $12,400 and will be devoted to an expanded line of high-end carpet. Sales of carpet are expected to increase by $120,000, and the line's overall contribution margin ratio will rise by five percentage points.
- Tipton can cut wallpaper's fixed costs by 40 percent. Remaining fixed costs will continue to be incurred.
- Customers who purchased wallpaper often bought paint and paint supplies. Sales of paint and paint supplies are expected to fall by 20 percent.
- The firm will increase advertising expenditures by $25,000 to promote the expanded carpet line.

Required:

1. Should Tipton close its wallpaper operation? Show computations to support your answer.
2. Assume that Tipton's wallpaper inventory at the time of the closure decision amounted to $23,700. How would you have treated this additional information in making the decision?
3. What advantages might Internet- and magazine-based firms have over Tipton that would allow these organizations to offer deeply discounted prices—prices far below what Tipton can offer?
4. ***Build a spreadsheet:*** Construct an Excel spreadsheet to solve requirement (1) above. Show how the solution will change if the following information changes: sales were $400,000, $450,000, and $130,000, for paint and supplies, carpeting, and wallpaper, respectively.

Problem 14–48
Excess Production Capacity
(LO 14-5, 14-6)

2. Contribution margin per direct-labor hour, Deluxe Model: $12

Carpenter's Mate, Inc. manufactures electric carpentry tools. The Production Department has met all production requirements for the current month and has an opportunity to produce additional units of product with its excess capacity. Unit selling prices and unit costs for three different drill models are as follows:

	Home Model	Deluxe Model	Pro Model
Selling price	$58	$65	$80
Direct material	16	20	19
Direct labor ($10 per hour)	10	15	20
Variable overhead	8	12	16
Fixed overhead	16	5	15

Variable overhead is applied on the basis of direct-labor dollars, while fixed overhead is applied on the basis of machine hours. There is sufficient demand for the additional production of any model in the product line.

Required:

1. If Carpenter's Mate, Inc. has excess machine capacity and can add more labor as needed (i.e., neither machine capacity nor labor is a constraint), the excess production capacity should be devoted to producing which product? (Assume that the excess capacity will be used for a single product line.)
2. If Carpenter's Mate has excess machine capacity but a limited amount of labor time, the excess production capacity should be devoted to producing which product or products?

(CMA, adapted)

Problem 14–49
Make or Buy
(LO 14-4, 14-5)

Casting Technology Resources (CTR) has purchased 10,000 pumps annually from Kobec, Inc. Because the price keeps increasing and reached $68.00 per unit last year, CTR's management has asked for an estimate of the cost of manufacturing the pump in CTR's facilities. CTR makes stampings and castings and has little experience with products requiring assembly.

The engineering, manufacturing, and accounting departments have prepared a report for management that includes the following estimate for an assembly run of 10,000 pumps. Additional production employees would be hired to manufacture the pumps but no additional equipment, space, or supervision would be needed.

The report states that total costs for 10,000 units are estimated at $957,000, or $95.70 per unit. The current purchase price is $68.00 per unit, so the report recommends continued purchase of the product.

Components (outside purchases)	$120,000
Assembly labor*	300,000
Manufacturing overhead†	450,000
General and administrative overhead‡	87,000
Total costs	$957,000

*Assembly labor consists of hourly production workers.

†Manufacturing overhead is applied to products on a direct-labor-dollar basis. Variable-overhead costs vary closely with direct-labor dollars.

Fixed overhead	50% of direct-labor dollars
Variable overhead	100% of direct-labor dollars
Manufacturing-overhead rate	150% of direct-labor dollars

‡General and administrative overhead is applied at 10 percent of the total cost of material (or components), assembly labor, and manufacturing overhead.

Required: Was the analysis prepared by Casting Technology Resources' engineering, manufacturing, and accounting departments and their recommendation to continue purchasing the pumps correct? Explain your answer and include any supporting calculations you consider necessary.

(CMA, adapted)

Problem 14–50
Outsourcing Decision; Relevant Costs; Ethics
(LO 14-3, 14-4, 14-5)

1(a). Savings if purchased from Marley: $(15,440)

The Midwest Division of the Paibec Corporation manufactures subassemblies that are used in the corporation's final products. Lynn Hardt of Midwest's Profit Planning Department has been assigned the task of determining whether a component, MTR–2000, should continue to be manufactured by Midwest or purchased from Marley Company, an outside supplier. MTR–2000 is part of a subassembly manufactured by Midwest.

Marley has submitted a bid to manufacture and supply the 32,000 units of MTR–2000 that Paibec will need for 20x1 at a unit price of $17.30. Marley has assured Paibec that the units will be delivered according to Paibec's production specifications and needs. While the contract price of $17.30 is only applicable in 20x1, Marley is interested in entering into a long-term arrangement beyond 20x1.

Hardt has gathered the following information regarding Midwest's cost to manufacture MTR–2000 in 20x0. These annual costs will be incurred to manufacture 30,000 units.

Direct material	$195,000
Direct labor	120,000
Factory space rental	84,000
Equipment leasing costs	36,000
Other manufacturing overhead	225,000
Total manufacturing costs	$660,000

Hardt has collected the following additional information related to manufacturing MTR–2000.

- Direct materials used in the production of MTR–2000 are expected to increase 8 percent in 20x1.
- Midwest's direct-labor contract calls for a 5 percent increase in 20x1.
- The facilities used to manufacture MTR–2000 are rented under a month-to-month rental agreement. Thus, Midwest can withdraw from the rental agreement without any penalty. Midwest will have no need for this space if MTR–2000 is not manufactured.
- Equipment leasing costs represent special equipment that is used in the manufacture of MTR–2000. This lease can be terminated by paying the equivalent of one month's lease payment for each year left on the lease agreement. Midwest has two years left on the lease agreement, through the end of the year 20x2.

- Forty percent of the other manufacturing overhead is considered variable. Variable overhead changes with the number of units produced, and this rate per unit is not expected to change in 20x1. The fixed manufacturing overhead costs are expected to be the same across a relevant range of zero to 50,000 units. Equipment other than the leased equipment can be used in Midwest's other manufacturing operations.

John Porter, divisional manager of Midwest, stopped by Hardt's office to voice his concern regarding the outsourcing of MTR–2000. Porter commented, "I am really concerned about outsourcing MTR–2000. I have a son-in-law and a nephew, not to mention a member of our bowling team, who work on MTR–2000. They could lose their jobs if we buy that component from Marley. I really would appreciate anything you can do to make sure the cost analysis comes out right to show we should continue making MTR–2000. Corporate is not aware of the material increases and maybe you can leave out some of those fixed costs. I just think we should continue making MTR–2000!"

Required:

1. *a.* Prepare an analysis of relevant costs that shows whether or not the Midwest Division of Paibec Corporation should make MTR–2000 or purchase it from Marley Company for 20x1.

b. Based solely on the financial results, recommend whether the 32,000 units of MTR–2000 for 20x1 should be made by Midwest or purchased from Marley.

2. Identify and briefly discuss three qualitative factors that the Midwest Division and Paibec Corporation should consider before agreeing to purchase MTR–2000 from Marley Company.

3. By referring to the standards of ethical conduct for managerial accountants given in Chapter 1, explain why Lynn Hardt would consider the request of John Porter to be unethical.

(CMA, adapted)

Problem 14–51
Joint Products; Sell or Process Further
(LO 14-6)

Total revenue from further processing $460,000

Connecticut Chemical Company is a diversified chemical processing company. The firm manufactures swimming pool chemicals, chemicals for metal processing, specialized chemical compounds, and pesticides.

Currently, the Noorwood plant is producing two derivatives, RNA–1 and RNA–2, from the chemical compound VDB developed by the company's research labs. Each week, 1,200,000 pounds of VDB are processed at a cost of $246,000 into 800,000 pounds of RNA–1 and 400,000 pounds of RNA–2. The proportion of these two outputs cannot be altered, because this is a joint process. RNA–1 has no market value until it is converted into a pesticide with the trade name Fastkil. Processing RNA–1 into Fastkil costs $240,000. Fastkil wholesales at $50 per 100 pounds.

RNA–2 is sold as is for $80 per hundred pounds. However, management has discovered that RNA–2 can be converted into two new products by adding 400,000 pounds of compound LST to the 400,000 pounds of RNA–2. This joint process would yield 400,000 pounds each of DMZ–3 and Pestrol, the two new products. The additional direct-material and related processing costs of this joint process would be $120,000. DMZ–3 and Pestrol would each be sold for $57.50 per 100 pounds. The company's management has decided not to process RNA–2 further based on the analysis presented in the following schedule.

		Process Further		
	RNA–2	**DMZ–3**	**Pestrol**	**Total**
Production in pounds	400,000	400,000	400,000	
Revenue	$320,000	$230,000	$230,000	$460,000
Costs:				
VDB costs	$ 82,000*	$ 61,500	$ 61,500	$123,000†
Additional direct materials (LST) and processing of RNA–2	—	60,000	60,000	120,000
Total costs	$ 82,000	$121,500	$121,500	$243,000
Weekly gross profit	$238,000	$108,500	$108,500	$217,000

*$82,000 is one-third of the $246,000 cost of processing VDB. When RNA–2 is not processed further, one-third of the final output is RNA–2 (400,000 out of a total of 1,200,000 pounds).

†$123,000 is one-half of the $246,000 cost of processing VDB. When RNA–2 is processed further, one-half of the final output consists of DMZ–3 and Pestrol. The final products then are: 800,000 pounds of RNA–1; 400,000 pounds of DMZ–3; and 400,000 pounds of Pestrol.

Required: Evaluate Connecticut Chemical Company's analysis, and make any revisions that are necessary. Your critique and analysis should indicate:

a. Whether management made the correct decision.

b. The gross savings or loss per week resulting from the decision not to process RNA–2 further, if different from management's analysis.

(CMA, adapted)

Problem 14–52
Add a Product Line
(LO 14-4, 14-5)

1. Incremental contribution margin: $42,945

Manhattan Fashions, Inc., a high-fashion dress manufacturer, is planning to market a new cocktail dress for the coming season. Manhattan Fashions supplies retailers in the east and mid-Atlantic states.

Four yards of material are required to lay out the dress pattern. Some material remains after cutting, which can be sold as remnants. The leftover material also could be used to manufacture a matching cape and handbag. However, if the leftover material is to be used for the cape and handbag, more care will be required in the cutting operation, which will increase the cutting costs.

The company expects to sell 1,250 dresses. Market research reveals that dress sales will be 20 percent higher if a matching cape and handbag are available. The market research indicates that the cape and handbag will be salable only as accessories with the dress. The combination of dresses, capes, and handbags expected to be sold by retailers are as follows:

	Percent of Total
Complete sets of dress, cape, and handbag	70%
Dress and cape	6
Dress and handbag	15
Dress only	9
Total	100%

The material used in the dress costs $12.50 a yard, or $50.00 for each dress. The cost of cutting the dress if the cape and handbag are not manufactured is estimated at $20.00 a dress, and the resulting remnants can be sold for $5.00 per dress. If the cape and handbag are manufactured, the cutting costs will be increased by $9.00 per dress and there will be no salable remnants. The selling prices and the costs to complete the three items once they are cut are as follows:

	Selling Price per Unit	Unit Cost to Complete (excludes costs of material and cutting operation)
Dress	$200.00	$80.00
Cape	27.50	19.50
Handbag	9.50	6.50

Required:

1. Calculate Manhattan Fashions' incremental profit or loss from manufacturing the capes and handbags in conjunction with the dresses.
2. Identify any qualitative factors that could influence the company's management in its decision to manufacture capes and handbags to match the dresses.

(CMA, adapted)

Problem 14–53
Outsourcing Decision
(LO 14-4, 14-5)

1. Total variable cost per unit: $10.50
2. Quantity of component B81 to be purchased: 4,000 units

Upstate Mechanical, Inc. has been producing two bearings, components T79 and B81, for use in production. Data regarding these two components follow.

	T79	B81
Machine hours required per unit	2.5	3.0
Standard cost per unit:		
Direct material	$ 2.25	$ 3.75
Direct labor	4.00	4.50
Manufacturing overhead		
Variable*	2.00	2.25
Fixed†	3.75	4.50
Total	$12.00	$15.00

*Variable manufacturing overhead is applied on the basis of direct-labor hours.

†Fixed manufacturing overhead is applied on the basis of machine hours.

Upstate Mechanical's annual requirement for these components is 8,000 units of T79 and 11,000 units of B81. Recently, management decided to devote additional machine time to other product lines, leaving only 41,000 machine hours per year for producing the bearings. An outside company has offered to sell Upstate Mechanical its annual supply of bearings at prices of $11.25 for T79 and $13.50 for B81. Management wants to schedule the otherwise idle 41,000 machine hours to produce bearings so that the firm can minimize costs (maximize net benefits).

Required:

1. Compute the net benefit (loss) per machine hour that would result if Upstate Mechanical accepts the supplier's offer of $13.50 per unit for component B81.
2. Choose the correct answer. Upstate Mechanical will maximize its net benefits by:
   a. purchasing 4,800 units of T79 and manufacturing the remaining bearings.
   b. purchasing 8,000 units of T79 and manufacturing 11,000 units of B81.
   c. purchasing 11,000 units of B81 and manufacturing 8,000 units of T79.
   d. purchasing 4,000 units of B81 and manufacturing the remaining bearings.
   e. purchasing and manufacturing some amounts other than those given above.
3. Suppose management has decided to drop product T79. Independently of requirements (1) and (2), assume that the company's idle capacity of 41,000 machine hours has a traceable, avoidable annual fixed cost of $44,000, which will be incurred only if the capacity is used. Calculate the maximum price Upstate Mechanical should pay a supplier for component B81.

(CMA, adapted)

Problem 14–54
Outsource a Component; Relevant Costs, Opportunity Costs, and Quality Control
(LO 14-3, 14-4, 14-5)

2. Increase in monthly cost: $23,000

Chenango Industries uses 10 units of part JR63 each month in the production of radar equipment. The cost of manufacturing one unit of JR63 is the following:

Direct material	$ 1,000
Material handling (20% of direct-material cost)	200
Direct labor	8,000
Manufacturing overhead (150% of direct labor)	12,000
Total manufacturing cost	$21,200

Material handling represents the direct variable costs of the Receiving Department that are applied to direct materials and purchased components on the basis of their cost. This is a separate charge in addition to manufacturing overhead. Chenango Industries' annual manufacturing overhead budget is one-third variable and two-thirds fixed. Scott Supply, one of Chenango Industries' reliable vendors, has offered to supply part number JR63 at a unit price of $15,000.

Required:

1. If Chenango Industries purchases the JR63 units from Scott, the capacity Chenango Industries used to manufacture these parts would be idle. Should Chenango Industries decide to purchase the parts from Scott, the unit cost of JR63 would increase (or decrease) by what amount?
2. Assume Chenango Industries is able to rent out all its idle capacity for $25,000 per month. If Chenango Industries decides to purchase the 10 units from Scott Supply, Chenango's monthly cost for JR63 would increase (or decrease) by what amount?
3. Assume that Chenango Industries does not wish to commit to a rental agreement but could use its idle capacity to manufacture another product that would contribute $52,000 per month. If Chenango's management elects to manufacture JR63 in order to maintain quality control, what is the net amount of Chenango's cost from using the space to manufacture part JR63?

(CMA, adapted)

Problem 14–55
Analysis of Special Order
(LO 14-4, 14-5)

2. Contribution from sale to Kaytell: $53,848

Miami Industries received an order for a piece of special machinery from Jay Company. Just as Miami completed the machine, Jay Company declared bankruptcy, defaulted on the order, and forfeited the 10 percent deposit paid on the selling price of $72,500.

Miami's manufacturing manager identified the costs already incurred in the production of the special machinery for Jay Company as follows:

Direct material		$16,600
Direct labor		21,400
Manufacturing overhead applied:		
Variable	$10,700	
Fixed	5,350	16,050
Fixed selling and administrative costs		5,405
Total		$59,455

Another company, Kaytell Corporation, will buy the special machinery if it is reworked to Kaytell's specifications. Miami Industries offered to sell the reworked machinery to Kaytell as a special order for $68,400. Kaytell agreed to pay the price when it takes delivery in two months. The additional identifiable costs to rework the machinery to Kaytell's specifications are as follows:

Direct material	$ 6,200
Direct labor	4,200
Total	$10,400

A second alternative available to Miami's management is to convert the special machinery to the standard model, which sells for $62,500. The additional identifiable costs for this conversion are as follows:

Direct material	$2,850
Direct labor	3,300
Total	$6,150

A third alternative for Miami Industries is to sell the machine as is for a price of $52,000. However, the potential buyer of the unmodified machine does not want it for 60 days. This buyer has offered a $7,000 down payment, with the remainder due upon delivery.

The following additional information is available regarding Miami's operations.

- The sales commission rate on sales of standard models is 2 percent, while the rate on special orders is 3 percent.
- Normal credit terms for sales of standard models are 2/10, net/30. This means that a customer receives a 2 percent discount if payment is made within 10 days, and payment is due no later than 30 days after billing. Most customers take the 2 percent discount. Credit terms for a special order are negotiated with the customer.
- The allocation rates for manufacturing overhead and fixed selling and administrative costs are as follows:

Manufacturing costs:	
Variable	50% of direct-labor cost
Fixed	25% of direct-labor cost
Fixed selling and administrative costs	10% of the total of direct-material, direct-labor, and manufacturing-overhead costs

- Normal time required for rework is one month.

Required:

1. Determine the dollar contribution each of the three alternatives will add to Miami Industries' before-tax profit.
2. If Kaytell makes Miami Industries a counteroffer, what is the lowest price Miami should accept for the reworked machinery from Kaytell? Explain your answer.
3. Discuss the influence fixed manufacturing-overhead cost should have on the sales price quoted by Miami Industries for special orders.

(CMA, adapted)

Problem 14–56
Special Order; Ethics
(LO 14-3, 14-4, 14-5)

2. Accepting the special order will result in a total additional contribution margin of $37,500

Winner's Circle, Inc. manufactures medals for winners of athletic events and other contests. Its manufacturing plant has the capacity to produce 10,000 medals each month. Current monthly production is 7,500 medals. The company normally charges $175 per medal. Variable costs and fixed costs for the current activity level of 75 percent of capacity are as follows:

Production Costs

Variable costs:	
Manufacturing:	
Direct labor	$ 375,000
Direct material	262,500
Marketing	187,500
Total variable costs	$ 825,000
Fixed costs:	
Manufacturing	$ 275,000
Marketing	175,000
Total fixed costs	$ 450,000
Total costs	$1,275,000
Variable cost per unit	$110
Fixed cost per unit	60
Average unit cost	$170

Winner's Circle has just received a special one-time order for 2,500 medals at $100 per medal. For this particular order, no variable marketing costs will be incurred. Cathy Donato, a management accountant with Winner's Circle, has been assigned the task of analyzing this order and recommending whether the company should accept or reject it. After examining the costs, Donato suggested to her supervisor, Gerard LePenn, who is the controller, that they request competitive bids from vendors for the raw material as the current quote seems high. LePenn insisted that the prices are in line with other vendors and told her that she was not to discuss her observations with anyone else. Donato later discovered that LePenn is a brother-in-law of the owner of the current raw-material supply vendor.

Required:

1. Identify and explain the costs that will be relevant to Cathy Donato's analysis of the special order being considered by Winner's Circle, Inc.
2. Determine if Winner's Circle should accept the special order. In explaining your answer, compute both the new average unit cost and the incremental unit cost for the special order.
3. Discuss any other considerations that Donato should include in her analysis of the special order.
4. What steps could Donato take to resolve the ethical conflict arising out of the controller's insistence that the company avoid competitive bidding?
5. ***Build a spreadsheet:*** Construct an Excel spreadsheet to solve requirement (2). Show how the solution will change if the sales price is $170 per medal.

(CMA, adapted)

Problem 14–57
Production Planning
(LO 14-5, 14-6)

2. Contribution margin, product M07: $93
2. Total contribution margin: $113,250

Ozark Industries manufactures and sells three products, which are manufactured in a factory with four departments. Both labor and machine time are applied to the products as they pass through each department. The machines and labor skills required in each department are so specialized that neither machines nor labor can be switched from one department to another.

Ozark Industries' management is planning its production schedule for the next few months. The planning is complicated, because there are labor shortages in the community and some machines will be down several months for repairs.

Management has assembled the following information regarding available machine and labor time by department and the machine hours and direct-labor hours required per unit of product. These data should be valid for the next six months.

	Department			
Monthly Capacity Availability	**1**	**2**	**3**	**4**
Normal machine capacity in machine hours	3,500	3,500	3,000	3,500
Capacity of machines being repaired in machine hours	(500)	(400)	(300)	(200)
Available machine capacity in machine hours	3,000	3,100	2,700	3,300
Available labor in direct-labor hours	3,700	4,500	2,750	2,600

Labor and Machine Specifications per Unit of Product

Product	Labor and Machine Time				
M07	Direct-labor hours	2	3	3	1
	Machine hours	1	1	2	2
T28	Direct-labor hours	1	2	—	2
	Machine hours	1	1	—	2
B19	Direct-labor hours	2	2	2	1
	Machine hours	2	2	1	1

The sales department believes that the monthly demand for the next six months will be as follows:

Product	Monthly Unit Sales
M07	500
T28	400
B19	1,000

Inventory levels are satisfactory and need not be increased or decreased during the next six months. Unit price and cost data that will be valid for the next six months are as follows:

	Product		
	M07	**T28**	**B19**
Unit costs:			
Direct material	$ 7	$ 13	$ 17
Direct labor:			
Department 1	12	6	12
Department 2	21	14	14
Department 3	24	—	16
Department 4	9	18	9
Variable overhead	27	20	25
Fixed overhead	15	10	32
Variable selling expenses	3	2	4
Unit selling price	196	123	167

Required:

1. Calculate the monthly requirement for machine hours and direct-labor hours for the production of products M07, T28, and B19 to determine whether the monthly sales demand for the three products can be met by the factory.
2. What monthly production schedule should Ozark Industries select in order to maximize its dollar profits? Explain how you selected this production schedule, and present a schedule of the contribution to profit that would be generated by your production schedule.
3. Identify the alternatives Ozark Industries might consider so it can supply its customers with all the product they demand.

(CMA, adapted)

Problem 14–58
Conventional versus Activity-Based-Costing Analyses; Relevant Costs
(LO 14-5, 14-7)

2. Costs to be avoided by purchasing (ABC analysis), total: $810,750

In addition to fine chocolate, International Chocolate Company also produces chocolate-covered pretzels in its Savannah plant. This product is sold in five-pound metal canisters, which also are manufactured at the Savannah facility. The plant manager, Marsha Mello, was recently approached by Catawba Canister Company with an offer to supply the canisters at a price of $1.00 each. International Chocolate's traditional product-costing system assigns the following costs to canister production.

Direct material	$ 300,000
Direct labor (12,000 hrs. at $15 per hr.)	180,000
Variable overhead ($10 per direct-labor hr.)	120,000
Fixed overhead ($45 per direct-labor hr.)	540,000
Total cost	$1,140,000

Unit costs: $1,140,000 ÷ 760,000 canisters = $1.50 per canister

Mello's conventional make-or-buy analysis indicated that Catawba's offer should be rejected, since only $708,000 of costs would be avoided (including $80,000 of supervisory salaries and $28,000 of machinery depreciation). In contrast, the firm would spend $760,000 buying the canisters. The controller, Dave Mint, came to the rescue with an activity-based costing analysis of the decision. Mint concluded that the cost driver levels associated with canister production are as follows:

10 product specs	30 inspections
2,000 supervisory hours	15 setups
6,000 material-handling hours	70,000 machine hours
55 purchase orders	

Additional conventional and ABC data from the Savannah plant are given in Exhibits 14–19 and 14–20.

Required:

1. Show how Mello arrived at the $708,000 of cost savings in her conventional make-or-buy analysis.
2. Determine the costs that will be saved by purchasing canisters, using Mint's ABC data.
3. Complete the ABC relevant-costing analysis of the make-or-buy decision. Should the firm buy from Catawba?
4. If the conventional and ABC analyses yield different conclusions, briefly explain why.

Problem 14–59
Linear Programming; Formulate and Solve Graphically (Appendix)
(LO 14-8)

3. Total contribution margin: $55,000

Deru Chocolate Company manufactures two popular candy bars, the Venus bar and the Comet bar. Both candy bars go through a mixing operation where the various ingredients are combined, and the Coating Department where the bars from the Mixing Department are coated with chocolate. The Venus bar is coated with both white and dark chocolate to produce a swirled effect. A material shortage of an ingredient in the Comet bar limits production to 300 batches per day. Production and sales data are presented in the following table. Both candy bars are produced in batches of 200 bars.

	Use of Capacity in Hours per Batch of Product		
Department	**Available Daily Capacity in Hours**	**Venus**	**Comet**
Mixing	525	1.5	1.5
Coating	500	2.0	1.0

Management believes that Deru Chocolate can sell all of its daily production of both the Venus and Comet bars. Other data follow.

	Venus	**Comet**
Selling price per batch	$ 300	$ 350
Variable cost per batch	100	225
Monthly fixed costs (allocated evenly between both products)	375,000	375,000

Required:

1. Formulate the objective function and all of the constraints in order to maximize contribution margin. Be sure to define the variables.
2. How many batches of each type of candy bar (Venus and Comet) should be produced to maximize the total contribution margin?
3. Calculate the contribution margin at the optimal solution.

(CMA, adapted)

Problem 14–60
Linear Programming (Appendix)
(LO 14-8)

4. Contribution margin at the optimal solution: $4,500

Meals for Professionals, Inc. offers monthly service plans providing prepared meals that are delivered to the customers' homes. The target market for these meal plans includes double-income families with no children and retired couples in upper income brackets. The firm offers two monthly plans: Premier Cuisine and Haute Cuisine. The Premier Cuisine plan provides frozen meals that are delivered twice each month; this plan generates a contribution margin of $120 for each monthly plan sold. The Haute Cuisine plan provides freshly prepared meals delivered on a daily basis and generates a contribution margin of $90 for each monthly plan sold. The company's reputation provides a market that will purchase all the meals that can be prepared. All meals go through food preparation and cooking steps in the company's kitchens. After these steps, the Premier Cuisine meals are flash frozen. The time requirements per monthly meal plan and hours available per month are as follows:

	Preparation	Cooking	Freezing
Hours required:			
Premier Cuisine	2	2	1
Haute Cuisine	1	3	0
Hours available	60	120	45

For planning purposes, Meals for Professionals, Inc. uses linear programming to determine the most profitable number of Premier Cuisine and Haute Cuisine monthly meal plans to produce.

Required:

1. Using the notation P for Premier Cuisine and H for Haute Cuisine, state the objective function and the constraints that management should use to maximize the total contribution margin generated by the monthly meal plans.
2. Graph the constraints on the meal preparation process. Be sure to clearly label the graph.
3. Using the graph prepared in requirement (2), determine the optimal solution to the company's production planning problem in terms of the number of each type of meal plan to produce.
4. Calculate the value of the objective function at the optimal solution.
5. If the constraint on preparation time could be eliminated, determine the revised optimal solution.

(CMA, adapted)

Problem 14–61
Linear Programming; Formulate and Discuss (Appendix)
(LO 14-8)

2(a). Contribution margin, R_L: $10.30

Colonial Corporation manufactures two types of electric coffeemakers, Regular and Deluxe. The major difference between the two appliances is capacity. Both are considered top-quality units and sell for premium prices. Both coffeemakers pass through two manufacturing departments: Plating and Assembly. Colonial has two assembly operations, one automated and one manual. The Automated Assembly Department has been in operation for one year and was intended to replace the Labor Assembly Department. However, Colonial's business has expanded rapidly in recent months, and both assembly operations are still being used. Workers have been trained for both operations and can be used in either department. The only difference between the two departments is the proportion of machine time versus direct labor used. Data regarding the two coffeemakers are presented in the following schedule.

Sales Data

	Regular Model	Deluxe Model
Selling price per unit	$ 45.00	$ 60.00
Variable selling cost per unit	3.00	3.00
Annual allocated fixed overhead	900,000	900,000

Unit Variable Manufacturing Costs

	Plating Department		Labor Assembly	Automated Assembly
	Regular	Deluxe		
Raw material:				
Casing	$7.75	$14.50	—	—
Heating element	6.00	6.00	—	—
Other	8.25	8.25	—	—
Direct labor:				
At $10 per hour	2.00	2.00	—	—
At $12 per hour	—	—	$3.00	$ .60
Manufacturing overhead:				
Supplies	1.25	1.25	1.50	1.50
Power	1.20	1.20	.75	1.80

Machine Hour Data

	Plating	Labor Assembly	Automated Assembly
Machine hours required per unit	.15	.02	.05
Machine hours available per month	25,000	1,500	5,000
Annual machine hours available	300,000	18,000	60,000

Colonial produced and sold 600,000 Deluxe coffeemakers and 900,000 Regular coffemakers last year. Management estimates that total unit sales could increase by 20 percent or more if the units can be produced. Colonial already has contracts to produce and sell 35,000 units of each model each month. Colonial has a monthly maximum labor capacity of 30,000 direct-labor hours in the Plating Department and 40,000 direct-labor hours for the assembly operation (Automated Assembly and Labor Assembly, combined). Sales, production, and costs occur uniformly throughout the year.

Required:

1. Colonial Corporation's management believes that linear programming could be used to determine the optimum mix of Regular and Deluxe coffeemakers to produce and sell. Explain why linear programming is appropriate to use in this situation.
2. Management has decided to use linear programming to determine the optimal product mix.

   Formulate and label the following:

   a. Objective function

   b. Constraints

   Be sure to define your variables.

(CMA, adapted)

Cases

Case 14–62
Adding a Product Line
(LO 14-4, 14-5)

1. Contribution per hour, tackle boxes: $26.40
2. Improvement in contribution margin: $236,250

Bo Vonderweidt, the production manager for Sportway Corporation, had requested to have lunch with the company president. Vonderweidt wanted to put forward his suggestion to add a new product line. As they finished lunch, Meg Thomas, the company president, said, "I'll give your proposal some serious thought, Bo. I think you're right about the increasing demand for skateboards. What I'm not sure about is whether the skateboard line will be better for us than our tackle boxes. Those have been our bread and butter the past few years."

Vonderweidt responded with, "Let me get together with one of the controller's people. We'll run a few numbers on this skateboard idea that I think will demonstrate the line's potential."

Sportway is a wholesale distributor supplying a wide range of moderately priced sports equipment to large chain stores. About 60 percent of Sportway's products are purchased from other companies while the remainder of the products are manufactured by Sportway. The company has a Plastics Department that is currently manufacturing molded fishing tackle boxes. Sportway is able to manufacture and sell 8,000 tackle boxes annually, making full use of its direct-labor capacity at available work stations. The selling price and costs associated with Sportway's tackle boxes are as follows:

Selling price per box		$86.00
Costs per box:		
Molded plastic	$ 8.00	
Hinges, latches, handle	9.00	
Direct labor ($15.00 per hour)	18.75	
Manufacturing overhead	12.50	
Selling and administrative cost	17.00	65.25
Profit per box		$20.75

Because Sportway's sales manager believes the firm could sell 12,000 tackle boxes if it had sufficient manufacturing capacity, the company has looked into the possibility of purchasing the tackle boxes for distribution. Maple Products, a steady supplier of quality products, would be able to provide up to 9,000 tackle boxes per year at a price of $68.00 per box delivered to Sportway's facility.

Bo Vonderweidt, Sportway's production manager, has come to the conclusion that the company could make better use of its Plastics Department by manufacturing skateboards. Vonderweidt has a market study that indicates an expanding market for skateboards and a need for additional suppliers. Vonderweidt believes that Sportway could expect to sell 17,500 skateboards annually at a price of $45.00 per skateboard.

After his lunch with the company president, Vonderweidt worked out the following estimates with the assistant controller.

Selling price per skateboard		$45.00
Costs per skateboard:		
Molded plastic	$5.50	
Wheels, hardware	7.00	
Direct labor ($15.00 per hour)	7.50	
Manufacturing overhead	5.00	
Selling and administrative cost	9.00	34.00
Profit per skateboard		$11.00

In the Plastics Department, Sportway uses direct-labor hours as the application base for manufacturing overhead. Included in the manufacturing overhead for the current year is $50,000 of factorywide, fixed manufacturing overhead that has been allocated to the Plastics Department. For each unit of product that Sportway sells, regardless of whether the product has been purchased or is manufactured by Sportway, there is an allocated $6.00 fixed overhead cost per unit for distribution that is included in the selling and administrative cost for all products. Total selling and administrative costs for the purchased tackle boxes would be $10.00 per unit.

Required: In order to maximize the company's profitability, prepare an analysis that will show which product or products Sportway Corporation should manufacture or purchase.

1. First determine which of Sportway's options makes the best use of its scarce resources. How many skateboards and tackle boxes should be manufactured? How many tackle boxes should be purchased?
2. Calculate the improvement in Sportway's total contribution margin if it adopts the optimal strategy rather than continuing with the status quo.

(CMA, adapted)

Case 14–63
Drop a Product Line
(LO 14-4, 14-5)

Unit contribution, E-gauge: $19.00

Alberta Gauge Company, Ltd., a small manufacturing company in Calgary, Alberta, manufactures three types of electrical gauges used in a variety of machinery. For many years the company has been profitable and has operated at capacity. However, in the last two years, prices on all gauges were reduced and selling expenses increased to meet competition and keep the plant operating at capacity. Second-quarter results for the current year, which follow, typify recent experience.

ALBERTA GAUGE COMPANY, LTD.
Income Statement
Second Quarter
(in thousands)

	Q-Gauge	E-Gauge	R-Gauge	Total
Sales	$1,600	$900	$ 900	$3,400
Cost of goods sold	1,048	770	950	2,768
Gross margin	$ 552	$130	$ (50)	$ 632
Selling and administrative expenses	370	185	135	690
Income before taxes	$ 182	$ (55)	$(185)	$ (58)

Alice Carlo, the company's president, is concerned about the results of the pricing, selling, and production prices. After reviewing the second-quarter results, she asked her management staff to consider the following three suggestions:

- Discontinue the R-gauge line immediately. R-gauges would not be returned to the product line unless the problems with the gauge can be identified and resolved.
- Increase quarterly sales promotion by $100,000 on the Q-gauge product line in order to increase sales volume by 15 percent.

- Cut production on the E-gauge line by 50 percent, and cut the traceable advertising and promotion for this line to $20,000 each quarter.

Jason Sperry, the controller, suggested a more careful study of the financial relationships to determine the possible effects on the company's operating results of the president's proposed course of action. The president agreed and assigned JoAnn Brower, the assistant controller, to prepare an analysis. Brower has gathered the following information.

- All three gauges are manufactured with common equipment and facilities.
- The selling and administrative expense is allocated to the three gauge lines based on average sales volume over the past three years.
- Special selling expenses (primarily advertising, promotion, and shipping) are incurred for each gauge as follows:

	Quarterly Advertising and Promotion	Shipping Expenses
Q-gauge	$210,000	$10 per unit
E-gauge	100,000	4 per unit
R-gauge	40,000	10 per unit

- The unit manufacturing costs for the three products are as follows:

	Q-Gauge	E-Gauge	R-Gauge
Direct material	$ 31	$17	$ 50
Direct labor	40	20	60
Variable manufacturing overhead	45	30	60
Fixed manufacturing overhead	15	10	20
Total	$131	$77	$190

- The unit sales prices for the three products are as follows:

Q-gauge	$200
E-gauge	90
R-gauge	180

- The company is manufacturing at capacity and is selling all the gauges it produces.

Required:

1. JoAnn Brower says that Alberta Gauge Company's product-line income statement for the second quarter is not suitable for analyzing proposals and making decisions such as the ones suggested by Alice Carlo. Write a memo to Alberta Gauge's president that addresses the following points.
   a. Explain why the product-line income statement as presented is not suitable for analysis and decision making.
   b. Describe an alternative income-statement format that would be more suitable for analysis and decision making, and explain why it is better.
2. Use the operating data presented for Alberta Gauge Company and assume that the president's proposed course of action had been implemented at the beginning of the second quarter. Then evaluate the president's proposal by specifically responding to the following points.
   a. Are each of the three suggestions cost-effective? Support your discussion with an analysis that shows the net impact on income before taxes for each of the three suggestions.
   b. Was the president correct in proposing that the R-gauge line be eliminated? Explain your answer.
   c. Was the president correct in promoting the Q-gauge line rather than the E-gauge line? Explain your answer.
   d. Does the proposed course of action make effective use of the company's capacity? Explain your answer.
3. Are there any qualitative factors that Alberta Gauge Company's management should consider before it drops the R-gauge line? Explain your answer.

(CMA, adapted)

15 Target Costing and Cost Analysis for Pricing Decisions

FOCUS COMPANY >>>

THIS CHAPTER'S FOCUS COMPANY is Sydney Sailing Supplies, a manufacturer of sailing supplies and equipment in Sydney, Australia. One of the company's most popular products is the Wave Darter, a two-person sailboat. In this chapter, we will explore a variety of issues surrounding how Sydney Sailing Supplies' management could set a price for the Wave Darter. We also will study a pricing method called target costing. Under this approach, management determines what consumers are willing to pay for a particular product. Then management must find a way to produce the product at a low enough cost to justify the price that consumers are willing to pay.

<<< IN CONTRAST

In contrast to the product-pricing setting explored in the first part of the chapter, we turn our attention to competitive bidding on projects, services, or products. In a competitive-bidding situation, two or more companies submit sealed bids for a job, and the buyer selects from among the bids. We will explore competitive bidding in the context of Sydney Sailing Supplies' Marine Services Division. The company's Marine Services Division specializes in marina maintenance and construction, and its management is preparing a bid to build a new marina in Sydney harbor.

© Comstock Images/Getty Images RF

After completing this chapter, you should be able to:

15-1 List and describe the four major influences on pricing decisions.

15-2 Explain and use the economic, profit-maximizing pricing model.

15-3 Set prices using cost-plus pricing formulas.

15-4 Discuss the issues involved in the strategic pricing of new products.

15-5 List and discuss the key principles of target costing.

15-6 Explain the role of activity-based costing in setting a target cost.

15-7 Explain how product-cost distortion can undermine a firm's pricing strategy.

15-8 Explain the process of value engineering and its role in target costing.

15-9 Determine prices using the time and material pricing approach.

15-10 Set prices in special-order or competitive-bidding situations by analyzing the relevant costs.

15-11 Describe the legal restrictions on setting prices.

Setting the price for an organization's product or service is one of the most important decisions a manager faces. It is also one of the most difficult, due to the number and variety of factors that must be considered. The pricing decision arises in virtually all types of organizations. Manufacturers set prices for the products they manufacture; merchandising companies set prices for their goods; service firms set prices for such services as insurance policies, train tickets, theme park admissions, and bank loans. Nonprofit organizations often set prices also. For example, governmental units price vehicle registrations, park-use fees, and utility services. Art museums and symphonies set admission and ticket prices. The optimal approach to pricing often depends on the situation. Pricing a mature product or service that a firm has sold for a long time may be quite different from pricing a new product or service. Public utilities and TV cable companies face political considerations in pricing their products and services, since their prices often must be approved by a governmental commission.

In this chapter, we will study pricing decisions, with an emphasis on the role of managerial accounting information. The setting for our discussion is Sydney Sailing Supplies, a manufacturer of sailing supplies and equipment located in Sydney, Australia.

Major Influences on Pricing Decisions

Four major influences govern the prices set by Sydney Sailing Supplies:

1. Customer demand.
2. Actions of competitors.
3. Costs.
4. Political, legal, and image-related issues.

Customer Demand

Learning Objective 15-1

List and describe the four major influences on pricing decisions.

The demands of customers are of paramount importance in all phases of business operations, from the design of a product to the setting of its price. Product-design issues and pricing considerations are interrelated, so they must be examined simultaneously. For example, if customers want a high-quality sailboat, this will entail greater production time and more expensive raw materials. The result almost certainly will be a higher price. On the other hand, management must be careful not to price its product out of the market. Discerning customer demand is a critically important and continuous process. Companies routinely obtain information from market research, such as customer surveys and test-marketing campaigns, and through feedback from sales personnel. To be successful, Sydney Sailing Supplies must provide the products its customers want at a price they perceive to be appropriate.

Actions of Competitors

Although Sydney Sailing Supplies' managers would like the company to have the sailing market to itself, they are not so fortunate. Domestic and foreign competitors are striving to sell their products to the same customers. Thus, as Sydney Sailing Supplies' management designs products and sets prices, it must keep a watchful eye on the firm's competitors. If a competitor reduces its price on sailboats of a particular type, Sydney Sailing Supplies may have to follow suit to avoid losing its market share Yet the company cannot follow its competitors blindly either. Predicting competitive reactions to its product-design and pricing strategy is a difficult but important task for Sydney Sailing Supplies' management.

In considering the reactions of customers and competitors, management must be careful to properly define its product. Should Sydney Sailing Supplies' management define its product narrowly as sailing supplies, or more broadly as boating supplies? For example, if the company raises the price of its two-person sailboat, will this encourage potential customers to switch to canoes, rowboats, and small motorboats? Or will most potential sailboat customers react to a price increase only by price-shopping among competing sailboat manufacturers? The way in which Sydney Sailing Supplies' management answers these questions can profoundly affect its marketing and pricing strategies.

Costs

The role of costs in price setting varies widely among industries. In some industries, prices are determined almost entirely by market forces. An example is the agricultural industry, where grain and meat prices are market-driven. Farmers must meet the market price. To make a profit, they must produce at a cost below the market price. This is not always possible, so some periods of loss inevitably result. In other industries, managers set prices at least partially on the basis of production costs. For example, cost-based pricing is used in the aircraft, household appliance, and gasoline industries. Prices are set by adding a markup to production costs. Managers have some latitude in determining the markup, so market forces influence prices as well. In public utilities, such as electricity and natural gas companies, prices generally are set by a regulatory agency of the state government. Production costs are of prime importance in justifying utility rates. Typically, a public utility will make a request to the Public Utility Commission for a rate increase on the basis of its current and projected production costs.

Balance of Market Forces and Cost-Based Pricing In most industries, both market forces and cost considerations heavily influence prices. No organization or industry can price its products below their production costs indefinitely. And no company's management can set prices blindly at cost plus a markup without keeping an eye on the market. In most cases, pricing can be viewed in either of the following ways.

How Are Prices Set?

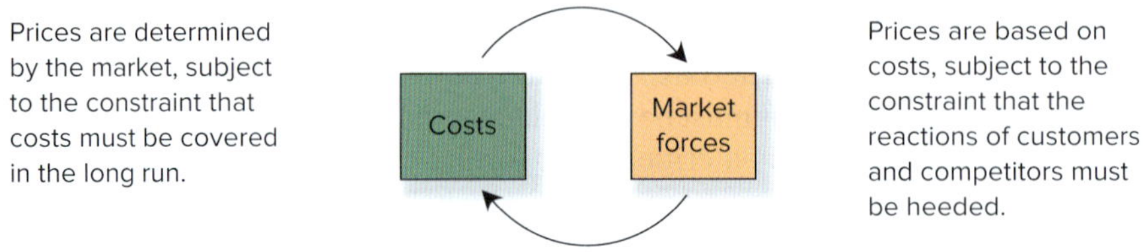

"You're looked to for business expertise. You're looked to also [for] business perspective, pricing strategies, manufacturing strategies, to see if they make sense financially." (15a)
Caterpillar

In our illustration of Sydney Sailing Supplies' pricing policies, we will assume the company responds to both market forces and costs.

Political, Legal, and Image-Related Issues

© Mary Altaffer/AP Photo

Setting prices requires a balance between cost considerations and market forces. A good example is provided by the airlines, which keep a close eye on the fares of their competitors, while striving to cover operating costs.

Beyond the important effects on prices of market forces and costs are a range of environmental considerations. In the *legal* area, managers must adhere to certain laws. The law generally prohibits companies from discriminating among their customers in setting prices. Also prohibited is collusion in price setting, where the major firms in an industry all agree to set their prices at high levels.

Political considerations also can be relevant. For example, if the firms in an industry are *perceived* by the public as reaping unfairly large profits, there may be political pressure on legislators to tax those profits differentially or to intervene in some way to regulate prices.

Companies also consider their *public image* in the price-setting process. A firm with a reputation for very-high-quality products may set the price of a new product high to be consistent with its image. As we have all discovered, the same brand-name product may be available in a discount store at half the price charged in a more exclusive store.

Economic Profit-Maximizing Pricing

Learning Objective 15-2

Explain and use the economic, profit-maximizing pricing model.

Companies are sometimes **price takers,** which means their products' prices are determined totally by the market. Some agricultural commodities and precious metals are examples of such products. In most cases, however, firms have some flexibility in setting prices. Generally speaking, as the price of a product or service is increased, the quantity demanded declines, and vice versa.

Total Revenue, Demand, and Marginal Revenue Curves

The trade-off between a higher price and a higher sales quantity can be shown in the shape of the firm's **total revenue curve,** which graphs the relationship between total sales revenue and quantity sold. Sydney Sailing Supplies' total revenue curve for its two-person sailboat, the Wave Darter, is displayed in Exhibit 15–1, panel A. The total revenue

Exhibit 15–1
Total Revenue, Demand, and Marginal Revenue Curves

A. Total Revenue Curve

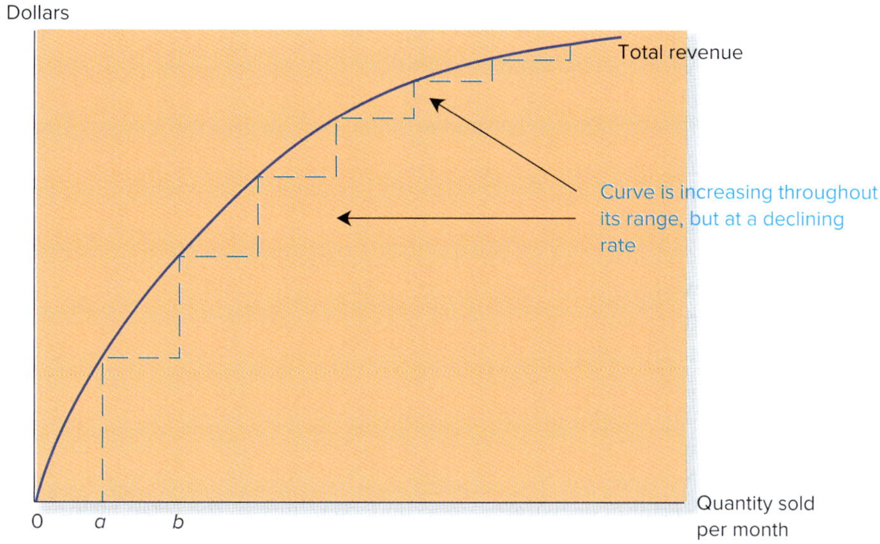

B. Demand (or Average Revenue) Curve and Marginal Revenue Curve

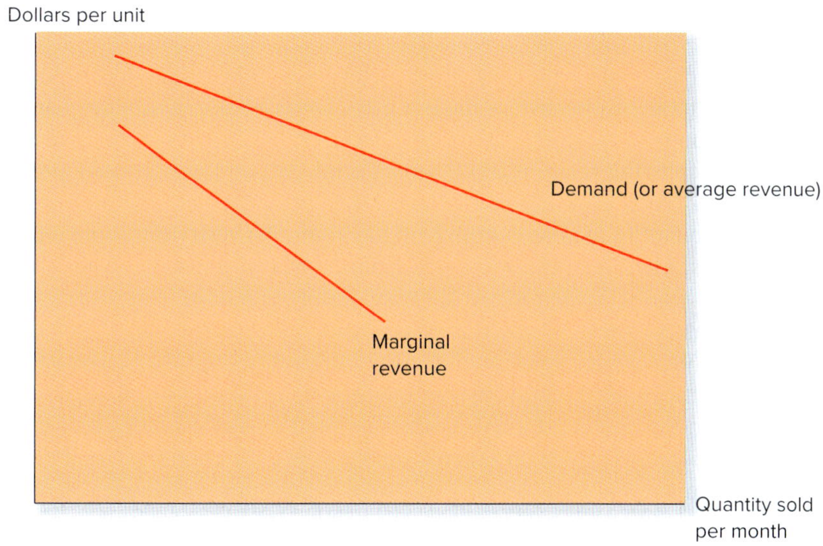

C. Tabulated Price, Quantity, and Revenue Data

Quantity Sold per Month	Unit Sales Price	Total Revenue per Month	Changes in Total Revenue
10	$1,000	$10,000	
			$9,500
20	975	19,500	
			9,000
30	950	28,500	
			8,500
40	925	37,000	
			8,000
50	900	45,000	
			7,500
60	875	52,500	

Related to demand curve — Related to total revenue curve — Related to marginal revenue curve

curve increases throughout its range, but the rate of increase declines as monthly sales quantity increases. To see this, notice that the increase in total revenue when the sales quantity increases from zero to *a* units is greater than the increase in total revenue when the sales quantity increases from *a* units to *b* units.

Closely related to the total revenue curve are two other curves, which are graphed in panel B of Exhibit 15–1. The **demand curve** shows the relationship between the sales price and the quantity of units demanded. The demand curve decreases throughout its range, because any decrease in the sales price brings about an increase in the monthly sales quantity. The demand curve is also called the **average revenue curve,** since it shows the average price at which any particular quantity can be sold.

The **marginal revenue curve** shows the *change* in total revenue that accompanies a *change* in the quantity sold. The marginal revenue curve is decreasing throughout its range to show that total revenue increases at a declining rate as monthly sales quantity increases.

A tabular presentation of the price, quantity, and revenue data for Sydney Sailing Supplies is displayed in panel C of Exhibit 15–1. Study this table carefully to see how the data relate to the graphs shown in panels A and B of the exhibit. No matter what approach a manager takes to the pricing decision, a good understanding of the relationships shown in Exhibit 15–1 will lead to better decisions. Before we can fully use the revenue data, however, we must examine the cost side of Sydney Sailing Supplies' business.

Total Cost and Marginal Cost Curves

Understanding cost behavior is important in many business decisions, and pricing is no exception. How does total cost behave as the number of Wave Darters produced and sold by Sydney Sailing Supplies changes? Panel A of Exhibit 15–2 displays the firm's **total cost curve,** which graphs the relationship between total cost and the quantity produced and sold each month.[1] Total cost increases throughout its range. The rate of increase in total cost declines as quantity increases from zero to *c* units. To verify this, notice that the increase in total costs when quantity increases from zero to *a* units is greater than the increase in total costs when quantity increases from *a* units to *b* units.

The rate of increase in total costs increases as quantity increases from *c* units upward. To verify this, notice that the increase in total costs as quantity increases from *c* units to *d* units is less than the increase in total costs as quantity increases from *d* units to *e* units.

Closely related to the total cost curve is the marginal cost curve, which is graphed in panel B of Exhibit 15–2. The **marginal cost curve** shows the change in total cost that accompanies a change in quantity produced and sold. Marginal cost declines as quantity increases from zero to *c* units; then it increases as quantity increases beyond *c* units.

A tabular presentation of the cost and quantity data for Sydney Sailing Supplies is displayed in panel C of Exhibit 15–2. Examine this table carefully, and trace the relationships between the data and the graphs shown in panels A and B of the exhibit.

Profit-Maximizing Price and Quantity

Now we have the tools we need to determine the profit-maximizing price and quantity. In Exhibit 15–3, we combine the revenue and cost data presented in Exhibits 15–1 and 15–2. Sydney Sailing Supplies' profit-maximizing sales quantity for the Wave Darter is determined by the intersection of the marginal cost and marginal revenue curves. (See panel B of Exhibit 15–3.) This optimal quantity is denoted by q^* on the graph. The profit-maximizing price, denoted by p^*, is determined from the demand curve for the quantity, q^*.

[1]Notice that the demand and revenue curves are based on the quantity sold, while the cost curves are based on the quantity produced. We will assume for simplicity that Sydney Sailing Supplies' monthly sales and production quantities are the same. This assumption tends to be true in the pleasure boat industry.

Exhibit 15–2
Total Cost and Marginal Cost Curves

A. Total Cost Curve

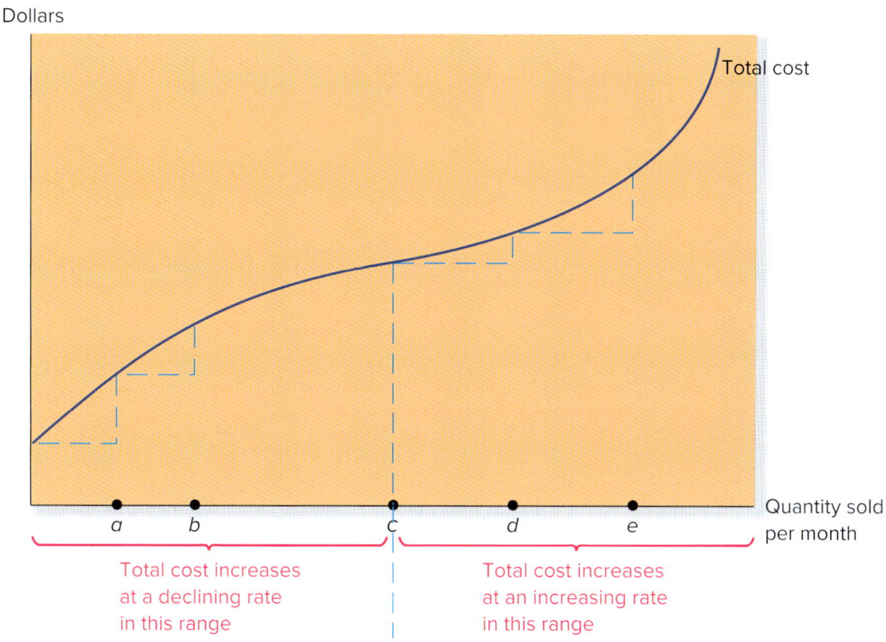

B. Marginal Cost Curve

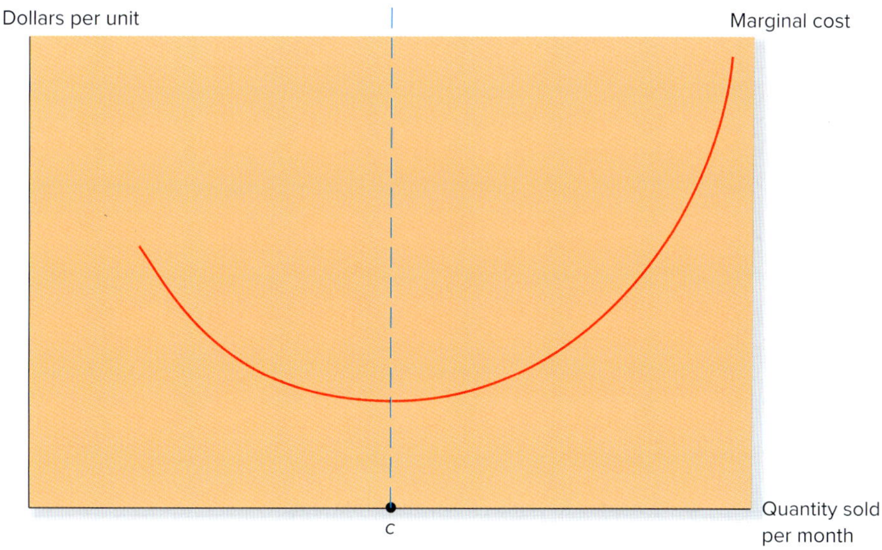

C. Tabulated Cost and Quantity Data

Quantity Produced and Sold per Month	Average Cost per Unit	Total Cost per Month	Changes in Total Cost
10	$1,920	$19,200	
			$ 5,600
20	1,240	24,800	
			4,300
30	970	29,100	
			2,900
40	800	32,000	
			9,000
50	820	41,000	
			15,400
60	940	56,400	

Related to total cost curve

Related to marginal cost curve

Exhibit 15–3
Determining the Profit-Maximizing Price and Quantity

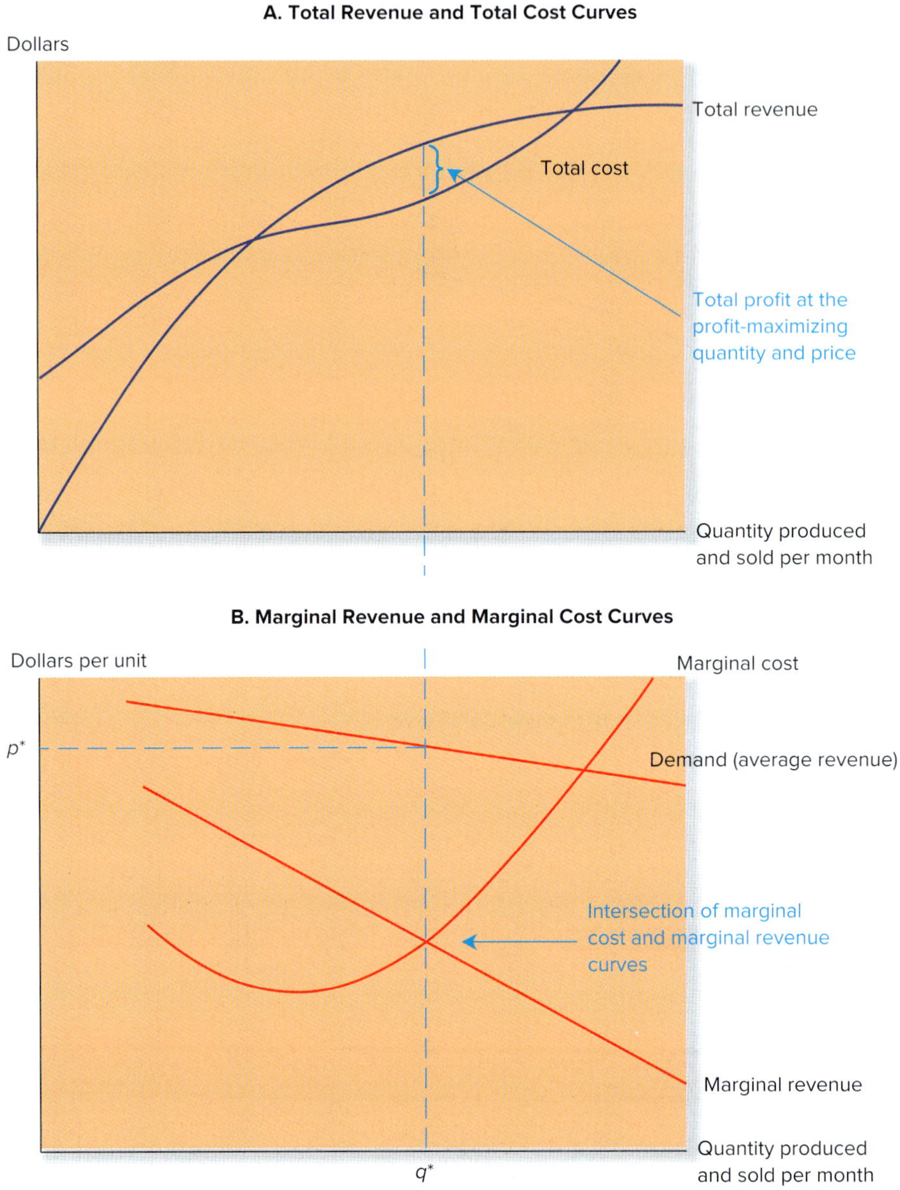

C. Tabulated Revenue, Cost, and Profit Data

	Quantity Produced and Sold per Month	Unit Sales Price	Total Revenue per Month	Total Cost per Month	Profit (Loss) per Month
	10	$1,000	$10,000	$19,200	$(9,200)
	20	975	19,500	24,800	(5,300)
	30	950	28,500	29,100	(600)
Profit-maximizing quantity and price	40	925	37,000	32,000	5,000
	50	900	45,000	41,000	4,000
	60	875	52,500	56,400	(3,900)

Examine the total revenue and total cost curves in panel A of Exhibit 15–3. At the profit-maximizing quantity (and price), the distance between these curves, which is equal to total profit, is maximized.

A tabular presentation of the revenue, cost, and profit data is shown in panel C of Exhibit 15–3. Notice that monthly profit is maximized when the price is set at $925 and 40 Wave Darters are produced and sold each month.

Price Elasticity

The impact of price changes on sales volume is called the **price elasticity.** Demand is *elastic* if a price increase has a large negative impact on sales volume, and vice versa. Demand is *inelastic* if price changes have little or no impact on sales quantity. **Cross-elasticity** refers to the extent to which a change in a product's price affects the demand for other *substitute products.* For example, if Sydney Sailing Supplies raises the price of its two-person sailboat, there may be an increase in demand for substitute recreational craft, such as small powerboats, canoes, or windsurfers.

Measuring price elasticity and cross-elasticity is an important objective of market research. Having a good understanding of these economic concepts helps managers to determine the profit-maximizing price.

Limitations of the Profit-Maximizing Model

The economic model of the pricing decision serves as a useful framework for approaching a pricing problem. However, it does have several limitations. First, the firm's demand and marginal revenue curves are difficult to discern with precision. Although market research is designed to gather data about product demand, it rarely enables management to predict completely the effects of price changes on the quantity demanded. Many other factors affect product demand in addition to price. Product design and quality, advertising and promotion, and company reputation also significantly influence consumer demand for a product.

Second, the marginal-revenue, marginal-cost paradigm is not valid for all forms of market organization. In an **oligopolistic market,** where a small number of sellers compete among themselves, the simple economic pricing model is no longer appropriate. In an *oligopoly,* such as the automobile industry, the reactions of competitors to a firm's pricing policies must be taken into account. While economists have studied oligopolistic pricing, the state of the theory is not sufficient to provide a thorough understanding of the impact of prices on demand.

The third limitation of the economic pricing model involves the difficulty of measuring marginal cost. Cost accounting systems are not designed to measure the marginal changes in cost incurred as production and sales increase unit by unit. To measure marginal costs would entail a very costly information system. Most managers believe that any improvements in pricing decisions made possible by marginal-cost data would not be sufficient to defray the cost of obtaining the information.

Costs and Benefits of Information

Managerial accountants always face a cost-benefit trade-off in the production of cost information for pricing and other decisions. As Exhibit 15–4 shows, only a sophisticated information system can collect marginal-cost data. However, such information is more costly to obtain. The result is that the optimal approach to pricing and other decisions is likely to lie in between the extremes shown in Exhibit 15–4. For this reason, most managers make pricing decisions based on a combination of economic considerations and accounting product-cost information.

In spite of its limitations, the marginal-revenue, marginal-cost paradigm of pricing serves as a useful conceptual framework for the pricing decision. Within this overall framework, managers typically rely heavily on a cost-based pricing approach, as we shall see next.

Exhibit 15–4
Cost-Benefit Trade-Off in Information Production

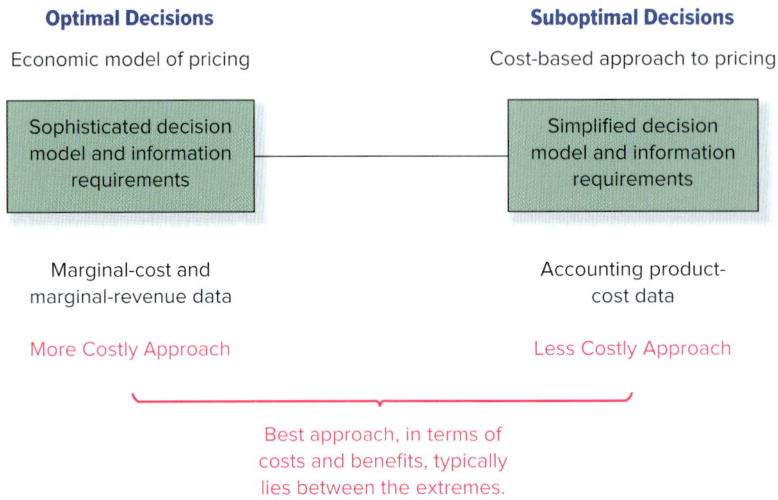

Role of Accounting Product Costs in Pricing

> "Today we spend more of our time analyzing and understanding . . . our margins, understanding our prices, understanding the markets in which we do business." (15b)
> **Caterpillar**

Most managers base prices on accounting product costs, at least to some extent. There are several reasons for this. First, most companies sell many products or services. There simply is not enough time to do a thorough demand and marginal-cost analysis for every product or service. Managers must rely on a quick and straightforward method for setting prices, and cost-based pricing formulas provide it. Second, even though market considerations ultimately may determine the final product price, a cost-based pricing formula gives the manager a place to start. Finally, and most importantly, the cost of a product or service provides a floor below which the price cannot be set in the long run. Although a product may be "given away" initially, at a price below cost, a product's price ultimately must cover its costs in order for the firm to remain in business. Even a nonprofit organization, unless it is heavily subsidized, cannot forever price products or services below their costs.

Cost-Plus Pricing

Learning Objective 15-3
Set prices using cost-plus pricing formulas.

Cost-based pricing formulas typically have the following general form.

Price = Cost + (Markup percentage × Cost)

Such a pricing approach often is called **cost-plus pricing,** because the price is equal to *cost plus a markup*. Depending on how cost is defined, the markup percentage may differ. Several different definitions of cost, each combined with a different markup percentage, can result in the same price for a product or service.

Exhibit 15–5 illustrates how Sydney Sailing Supplies' management could use several different cost-plus pricing formulas and arrive at a price of $925 for the Wave Darter. Cost-plus formula (1) is based on variable manufacturing cost. Formula (2) is based on absorption (or full) manufacturing cost, which includes an allocated portion of fixed manufacturing costs. Formula (3) is based on all costs: both variable and fixed costs of the manufacturing, selling, and administrative functions. Formula (4) is based on all variable costs, including variable manufacturing, selling, and administrative costs. Notice that all four pricing formulas are based on a linear representation of the cost function, in which all costs are categorized as fixed or variable.

As Sydney Sailing Supplies includes more costs in the cost base of the pricing formula, the required markup percentage declines. This reflects the fact that, one way or another, the price must cover all costs as well as a normal profit margin. If only variable manufacturing costs are included explicitly in the cost base, as in formula (1), then all of the other costs (and the firm's profit) must be covered by the markup. However, if the

Each of the following cost-plus pricing formulas yields the same $925 price for the Wave Darter.

Price and Cost Data			Cost-Plus Pricing Formulas
Variable manufacturing cost	$400	**1**	$\$925 = \$400 + (131.25\% \times \$400) = \text{Variable manufacturing cost} + \left(\text{Markup percentage} \times \text{Variable manufacturing cost}\right)$
Applied fixed manufacturing cost	250*		
Absorption manufacturing cost	650	**2**	$\$925 = \$650 + (42.3\%^{\dagger} \times \$650) = \text{Absorption manufacturing cost} + \left(\text{Markup percentage} \times \text{Absorption manufacturing cost}\right)$
Variable selling and administrative cost	50		
Allocated fixed selling and administrative cost	100*		
Total cost	$800	**3**	$\$925 = \$800 + (15.63\%^{\dagger} \times \$800) = \text{Total cost} + \left(\text{Markup percentage} \times \text{Total cost}\right)$
Variable manufacturing cost	$400		
Variable selling and administrative cost	50		
Total variable cost	$450	**4**	$\$925 = \$450 + (105.56\%^{\dagger} \times \$450) = \text{Total variable cost} + \left(\text{Markup percentage} \times \text{Total variable cost}\right)$

*Based on planned monthly production of 40 units (or 480 units per year).
† Rounded.

Exhibit 15–5
Alternative Cost-Plus Pricing Formulas

cost base used in the pricing formula includes all costs, as in formula (3), the markup can be much lower, since it need cover only the firm's normal profit margin.

A company typically uses only one of the four cost-plus pricing formulas illustrated in Exhibit 15–5. Which formula is best? Let's examine the advantages and disadvantages of each approach.

Absorption-Cost Pricing Formulas

Most companies that use cost-plus pricing use either absorption manufacturing cost or total cost as the basis for pricing products or services. [See formulas (2) and (3) in Exhibit 15–5.] The reasons generally given for this tendency are as follows:

1. In the long run, the price must cover *all* costs and a normal profit margin. Basing the cost-plus formula on only variable costs could encourage managers to set too low a price in order to boost sales. This will not happen if managers understand that a variable cost-plus pricing formula requires a higher markup to cover fixed costs and profit. Nevertheless, many managers argue that people tend to view the cost base in a cost-plus pricing formula as the floor for setting prices. If prices are set too close to variable manufacturing cost, the firm will fail to cover its fixed costs. Ultimately, such a practice could result in the failure of the business.
2. Absorption-cost or total-cost pricing formulas provide a justifiable price that tends to be perceived as equitable by all parties. Consumers generally understand that a company must make a profit on its product or service in order to remain in business. Justifying a price as the total cost of production, sales, and administrative activities, plus a reasonable profit margin, seems reasonable to buyers.
3. When a company's competitors have similar operations and cost structures, cost-plus pricing based on full costs gives management an idea of how competitors may set prices.
4. Absorption-cost information is provided by a firm's cost accounting system, because it is required for external financial reporting under generally accepted

accounting principles. Since absorption-cost information already exists, it is cost-effective to use it for pricing. The alternative would involve preparing special product-cost data specifically for the pricing decision. In a firm with hundreds of products, such data could be expensive to produce.

The primary disadvantage of absorption-cost or total-cost pricing formulas is that they obscure the cost behavior pattern of the firm. Since absorption-cost and total-cost data include allocated fixed costs, it is not clear from these data how the firm's total costs will change as volume changes. Another way of stating this criticism is that absorption-cost data are not consistent with cost-volume-profit analysis. CVP analysis emphasizes the distinction between fixed and variable costs. This approach enables managers to predict the effects of changes in prices and sales volume on profit. Absorption-cost and total-cost information obscures the distinction between variable and fixed costs.

"An indemnity [insurance] company prices products by looking at existing costs and at what the trends have been. The company then predicts, or forecasts, costs for the next year and uses this information to set the price." (15c)

BlueCross BlueShield of North Carolina

Variable-Cost Pricing Formulas

To avoid blurring the effects of cost behavior on profit, some managers prefer to use cost-plus pricing formulas based on either variable manufacturing costs or total variable costs. [See formulas (1) and (4) in Exhibit 15–5.] Three advantages are attributed to this pricing approach:

1. Variable-cost data do not obscure the cost behavior pattern by unitizing fixed costs and making them appear variable. Thus, variable-cost information is more consistent with cost-volume-profit analysis often used by managers to see the profit implications of changes in price and volume.
2. Variable-cost data do not require allocation of common fixed costs to individual product lines. For example, the annual salary of Sydney Sailing Supplies' vice president of sales is a cost that must be borne by all of the company's product lines. Arbitrarily allocating a portion of her salary to the Wave Darter product line is not meaningful.
3. Variable-cost data are exactly the type of information managers need when facing certain decisions, such as whether to accept a special order. This decision, examined in detail in the preceding chapter, often requires an analysis that separates fixed and variable costs.

The primary disadvantage of the variable-cost pricing formula was described earlier. If managers perceive the variable cost of a product or service as the floor for the price, they may tend to set the price too low for the firm to cover its fixed costs. Eventually this can spell disaster. Therefore, if variable-cost data are used as the basis for cost-plus pricing, managers must understand the need for higher markups to ensure that all costs are covered.

Determining the Markup

Regardless of which cost-plus formula is used, Sydney Sailing Supplies must determine its markup on the Wave Darter. If management uses a variable-cost pricing formula, the markup must cover all fixed costs and a reasonable profit. If management uses an absorption-costing formula, the markup still must be sufficient to cover the firm's profit on the Wave Darter product line. What constitutes a reasonable or normal profit margin?

Return-on-Investment Pricing A common approach to determining the profit margin in cost-plus pricing is to base profit on the firm's target return on investment (ROI). To illustrate **return-on-investment pricing,** suppose Sydney Sailing Supplies' production plan calls for 480 Wave Darters to be manufactured during the year. Based on the cost data shown in Exhibit 15–5, this production plan will result in the following total costs.

Variable costs:		
Manufacturing	$192,000	
Selling and administrative	24,000	
Total variable costs		$216,000
Fixed costs:		
Manufacturing	$120,000	
Selling and administrative	48,000	
Total fixed costs		168,000
Total costs		$384,000

Suppose the year's average amount of capital invested in the Wave Darter product line is $300,000. If Sydney Sailing Supplies' target return on investment for the Wave Darter line is 20 percent, the required annual profit is computed as follows:

$$\text{Average invested capital} \times \text{Target ROI} = \text{Target profit}$$
$$\$300{,}000 \times 20\% = \$60{,}000$$

The markup percentage required to earn Sydney Sailing Supplies a $60,000 profit on the Wave Darter line depends on the cost-plus formula used. We will compute the markup percentage for two cost-plus formulas.

1. ***Cost-plus pricing based on total costs.*** The total cost of a Wave Darter is $800 per unit (Exhibit 15–5). To earn a profit of $60,000 on annual sales of 480 sailboats, the company must make a profit of $125 per boat ($125 = $60,000 ÷ 480). This entails a markup percentage of 15.63 percent *above* total cost of $800.

$$15.63\% = \frac{\$925}{\$800} - 100\%$$

A shortcut to the same conclusion uses the following formula.

$$\text{Markup percentage on total cost} = \frac{\text{Target profit}}{\text{Annual volume} \times \text{Total cost per unit}}$$
$$15.63\% = \frac{\$60{,}000}{480 \times \$800}$$

2. ***Cost-plus pricing based on total variable costs.*** The total variable cost of a Wave Darter is $450 per unit (Exhibit 15–5). The markup percentage applied to variable cost must be sufficient to cover *both* annual profit of $60,000 *and* total annual fixed costs of $168,000. The required markup percentage is computed as follows:

$$\text{Markup percentage on total variable cost} = \frac{\text{Target profit} + \text{Total annual fixed cost}}{\text{Annual volume} \times \text{Total variable cost per unit}}$$
$$105.56\% = \frac{\$60{,}000 + \$168{,}000}{480 \times \$450}$$

General Formula The general formula for computing the markup percentage in cost-plus pricing to achieve a target ROI is as follows:

$$\text{Markup percentage applied to cost base in cost-plus pricing formula} = \frac{\text{Profit required to achieve target ROI} + \text{Total annual costs } \textit{not} \text{ included in cost base}}{\text{Annual volume} \times \text{Cost base per unit used in cost-plus pricing formula}}$$

Exercise 15–34 at the end of the chapter gives you an opportunity to employ this formula to compute the markup percentage for the other two cost-plus pricing formulas in Exhibit 15–5.

M anagement
A ccounting
P ractice

Target, Best Buy, and Amazon

REAL TIME PRICE WARS

Intense price competition, sometimes referred to as a price war, can occur in any industry. Now price wars are taking on a new flavor, though, as they play out in real time. As *The Wall Street Journal* reported, this phenomenon is happening in the retail industry, particularly around the all-important year-end holiday shopping period. "The historical race between e-commerce retailers and their physical-store rivals continues. But in a new development, bricks-and-mortar retailers are turning the tables, using their websites to match rivals' marquee discounts more aggressively than ever. When **Target** advertised plans to sell a $400 Dyson Ball vacuum cleaner for $269, **Best Buy** responded by cutting its online price." And Best Buy was not immune from the pricecutting either. "When the electronics retailer published a circular advertising it would sell a $1,500 Nikon camera for $1,000, **Amazon**" immediately responded by "cutting its price for the same camera to $997."

The fact that various retailers were responding in kind to their competitors' price cuts is not new. What is new, though, is the retailers' near instant reaction to their competitors' prices through the use of technology. "The fast price changes during the year's most competitive shopping period highlight a sea change in how retailing is done. The rise of e-commerce, along with an explosion in data and the power of technology for analyzing it, has made it possible for retailers of all stripes to monitor their rivals' pricing strategies and react in seconds."

Consumers may be the beneficiaries in such a real-time price war, as prices decline. "For retailers, however, the risk is profit-killing discounting" as they compete ever more aggressively to stand out in the pack. Therefore, "to fight online competition, retailers try to shift as much as possible to exclusive gear that can't easily be matched. They're also matching more of their offline deals in their online stores."

In general, "the spread of e-commerce means that most retailers will have to get used to flexible pricing."[2]

Cost-Plus Pricing: Summary and Evaluation

We have examined two different approaches to setting prices: (1) the economic, profit-maximizing approach and (2) cost-plus pricing. Although the techniques involved in these methods are quite different, the methods complement each other. In setting prices, managers cannot ignore the market, nor can they ignore costs. Cost-plus pricing is used widely in practice to establish a starting point in the process of determining a price. Cost-plus formulas are simple; they can be applied mechanically without taking the time of top management. They make it possible for a company with hundreds of products or services to cope with the tasks of updating prices for existing products and setting initial prices for new products.

Cost-plus pricing formulas can be used effectively with a variety of cost definitions, but the markup percentage must be appropriate for the type of cost used. It is imperative that price-setting managers understand that ultimately the price must cover all costs and a normal profit margin. Absorption-cost-plus or total-cost-plus pricing has the advantage of keeping the manager's attention focused on covering total costs. The variable-cost-plus formulas have the advantage of not obscuring important information about cost behavior.

Cost-plus pricing formulas establish a starting point in setting prices. Then the price setter must weigh market conditions, likely actions of competitors, and general business conditions. Thus, effective price setting requires a constant interplay of market considerations and cost awareness.

---

[2]Dana Mattioli, "Price War Rages in Real Time," *The Wall Street Journal,* November 23, 2012, p. B1.

Strategic Pricing of New Products

Learning Objective **15-4**

Discuss the issues involved in the strategic pricing of new products.

Pricing a new product is an especially challenging decision problem. The newer the concept of the product, the more difficult the pricing decision is. For example, if Sydney Sailing Supplies comes out with a new two-person sailboat, its pricing problem is far easier than the pricing problem of a company that first markets products using a radically new technology. Genetic engineering, superconductivity, artificial hearts, and space-grown crystals are all examples of such frontier technologies.

Pricing a new product is harder than pricing a mature product because of the magnitude of the uncertainties involved. New products entail many uncertainties. For example, what obstacles will be encountered in manufacturing the product, and what will be the costs of production? Moreover, after the product is available, will anyone want to buy it, and at what price? If Sydney Sailing Supplies decides to market a new two-person sailboat, management can make a good estimate of both the production costs and the potential market for the product. The uncertainties here are far smaller than the uncertainties facing a company developing artificial hearts.

In addition to the production and demand uncertainties, new products pose another sort of challenge. There are two widely differing strategies that a manufacturer of a new product can adopt. One strategy is called **skimming pricing,** in which the initial product price is set high, and short-term profits are reaped on the new product. The initial market will be small, due in part to the high initial price. This pricing approach often is used for unique products, where there are people who "must have it" whatever the price. As the product gains acceptance and its appeal broadens, the price is lowered gradually. Eventually the product is priced in a range that appeals to several kinds of buyers. An example of a product for which skimming pricing was used is the high-definition television. Initially HDTVs were priced quite high and were affordable by only a few buyers. Eventually the price was lowered, and HDTVs were purchased by a wide range of consumers.

"HMOs go to the marketplace and ask what is the competitive market rate to sell business. Through market pricing, they determine what the rate has to be and then manage their costs accordingly." (15d)

BlueCross BlueShield of North Carolina

An alternative initial pricing strategy is called **penetration pricing,** in which the initial price is set relatively low. By setting a low price for a new product, management hopes to penetrate a new market deeply, quickly gaining a large market share. This pricing approach often is used for products that are of good quality, but do not stand out as vastly better than competing products.

The decision between skimming and penetration pricing depends on the type of product and involves trade-offs of price versus volume. Skimming pricing results in much slower acceptance of a new product, but higher unit profits. Penetration pricing results in greater initial sales volume, but lower unit profits.

Regardless of the pricing strategy used, companies must closely monitor and manage costs in order to remain price competitive.

Target Costing

Learning Objective **15-5**

List and discuss the key principles of target costing.

Earlier in this chapter, we described product pricing as a process whereby the cost of the product is determined, and then an appropriate price is chosen. Increasingly, the opposite approach is being taken. The company first uses market research to determine the price at which a new product can be sold. Given the likely sales price, management computes the cost for which the product must be manufactured in order to provide the firm with an acceptable profit margin. Finally, engineers and cost analysts work together to design a product that can be manufactured for the allowable cost. This process, called **target costing,** is used widely by companies in the development stages of new products. A new product's **target cost** is the projected long-run cost that will enable a firm to enter and remain in the market for the product and compete successfully with the firm's competitors.

Management Accounting Practice

Amazon

DYNAMIC PRICING ON THE INTERNET BY "E-TAILERS"

Pricing on the Internet "was expected to offer retailers a number of advantages." First, "it would be far easier to raise or lower prices in response to demand, without the need of a clerk running through a store with a pricing gun. Online prices could be changed in far smaller increments—even by just a penny or two—as frequently as a merchant desired, making it possible to fine-tune pricing strategies."

The real payoff, though, "was supposed to be better information on exactly how price-conscious customers are. For instance, knowing that customer A doesn't care whether the latest popular DVD in her shopping basket costs $21.95 or $25.95 would leave an enterprising merchant free to charge the higher price on the spot. By contrast, knowing that customer B is going to put author John Le Carre's latest thriller back on the shelf unless it's priced at $20, instead of $28, would open an opportunity for a bookseller to make the sale by cutting the price in real time." However, putting this concept "into practice online has turned out to be exceptionally difficult, in part because the Internet also has empowered consumers to compare prices to find out if other merchants are offering a better deal or if other consumers are getting a bigger break." It has also made it easier for consumers to register a complaint. For example, "**Amazon** raised a furor . . . when customers learned they were paying different prices for the same DVD movies, the result of a marketing test in which the retailer varied prices to gauge the effect on demand." After receiving many complaints from irate consumers, "Amazon announced it would refund the difference between the highest and lowest prices in the test."[3]

A Strategic Profit and Cost Management Process

Target costing can be a critical tool for management as it seeks to strategically manage the company's costs and profits. By ensuring that products are designed so that they can be produced at a low enough cost to be priced competitively, management can achieve and maintain a sustainable competitive position in the market.

Key Principles of Target Costing Target costing involves seven key principles.[4]

- *Price-led costing.* Target costing sets the target cost by *first* determining the price at which a product can be sold in the marketplace. Subtracting the *target profit margin* from this *target price* yields the *target cost,* that is, the cost at which the product must be manufactured. This simple, but strategically important, relationship can be expressed in the following equation.

  $$\text{Target cost} = \text{Target price} - \text{Target profit}$$

  Notice that in a target costing approach, the price is set *first,* and *then* the target product cost is determined. This is opposite from the order in which the product cost and selling price are determined under traditional cost-plus pricing.
- *Focus on the customer.* To be successful at target costing, management must listen to the company's customers. What products do they want? What features are important? How much are they willing to pay for a certain level of product quality? Management needs to aggressively seek customer feedback, and then products must be designed to satisfy customer demand and be sold at a price they are willing to pay. In short, the target costing approach is market driven.

[3]David P. Hamilton, "The Price Isn't Right: Internet Pricing Has Turned Out to Be a Lot Trickier Than Retailers Expected," *The Wall Street Journal,* February 12, 2001, p. R8; Also see Kate Kaye, "Retailers Embrace Data Tools for Rapid-Fire Price Changes," Ad Age Digital (online), January 24, 2013, p. 1.

[4]This section is based on Shahid L. Ansari, Jan E. Bell, and the CAM-I Target Cost Core Group, *Target Costing: The Next Frontier in Strategic Cost Management* (Burr Ridge, IL: Irwin, 1997).

- *Focus on product design.* Design engineering is a key element in target costing. Engineers must design a product from the ground up so that it can be produced at its target cost. This design activity includes specifying the raw materials and components to be used as well as the labor, machinery, and other elements of the production process. In short, a product must be designed for manufacturability.
- *Focus on process design.* As indicated in the preceding point, every aspect of the production *process* must be examined to make sure that the product is produced as efficiently as possible. The use of touch labor, technology, global sourcing in procurement, and every aspect of the production process must be designed with the product's target cost in mind.
- *Cross-functional teams.* Manufacturing a product at or below its target cost requires the involvement of people from many different functions in an organization: market research, sales, design engineering, procurement, production engineering, production scheduling, material handling, and cost management. Individuals from all these diverse areas of expertise can make key contributions to the target costing process. Moreover, "a cross-functional team is not a set of specialists who contribute their expertise and then leave; they are responsible for the entire product."[5]
- *Life-cycle costs.* In specifying a product's target cost, analysts must be careful to incorporate all of the product's *life-cycle costs.* These include the costs of product planning and concept design, preliminary design, detailed design and testing, production, distribution, and customer service. Traditional cost-accounting systems have tended to focus only on the production phase and have not paid enough attention to the product's other life-cycle costs.[6]
- *Value-chain orientation.* Sometimes the projected cost of a new product is above the target cost. Then efforts are made to eliminate *non-value-added costs* to bring the projected cost down.[7] In some cases, a close look at the company's entire *value chain* can help managers identify opportunities for cost reduction. For example, Procter & Gamble placed order-entry computers in Walmart stores. This resulted in substantial savings in order-processing costs for both companies.[8]

"Target costing is neither easily nor quickly done." (15e)
U.S. Navy Acquisition Center

"Target costing with suppliers involves developing detailed cost models of both existing products and those in development. This necessitates the open sharing of cost information in an ethical and professional manner." (15f)
Eastman Kodak Company

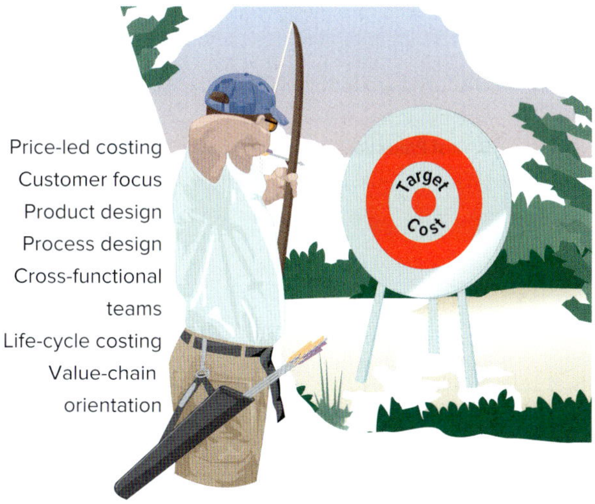

[5]Ibid., p. 15.

[6]See Chapter 9 for further discussion of product life-cycle costing.

[7]The elimination of non-value-added costs is covered in Chapter 5 as part of the discussion of activity-based management.

[8]J. Shank and V. Govindarajan, "Strategic Cost Management and the Value Chain," *Journal of Cost Management* 5, no. 4 (Winter 1992), p. 10. See also T. Tanaka, "Target Costing at Toyota," *Journal of Cost Management* 7, no. 1 (Spring 1993), pp. 4–12.

Activity-Based Costing and Target Costing

Learning Objective **15-6**

Explain the role of activity-based costing in setting a target cost.

An activity-based costing (ABC) system can be particularly helpful as product design engineers try to achieve a product's target cost. ABC enables designers to break down the production process for a new product into its component activities. Then designers can attempt cost improvement in particular activities to bring a new product's projected cost in line with its target cost.

To illustrate, Sydney Sailing Supplies' Marine Instruments Division, located in Perth, Australia, wants to introduce a new depth finder. Target costing studies indicate that a target cost of $340 must be met in order to successfully compete in this market. Exhibit 15–6 shows how ABC was used to bring the depth finder's initial cost estimate of $399 down to $337, just below the target cost. The company's design engineers were able to focus on key activities in the production process, such as material handling and inspection, and reduce the projected costs.

"A key Honda philosophy is that 'cost is a result.' To get better results, you must manage the cost drivers." (15g)

Honda of America Manufacturing, Inc.

Computer-Integrated Manufacturing When a computer-integrated manufacturing (CIM) system is used, the process of target costing sometimes is computerized. A manufacturer's computer-aided design and cost-accounting software are interconnected. An engineer can try out many different design features and immediately see the product-cost implications, without ever leaving the computer terminal.

Product-Cost Distortion and Pricing: The Role of Activity-Based Costing

Learning Objective **15-7**

Explain how product-cost distortion can undermine a firm's pricing strategy.

Use of a traditional, volume-based product-costing system may result in significant cost distortion among product lines. In many cases, high-volume and relatively simple

Exhibit 15–6

Target Costing and Cost Improvement for a New Product

SYDNEY SAILING SUPPLIES

A. Activity-Based Costing System

Activity Cost Pool	Cost Driver	Pool Rate
Purchasing	Number of parts	$1 per part
Material handling	Dollar value of parts	$.20 per direct-material dollar
Inspection	Inspection hours	$28 per inspection hour

This is a highly simplified example of activity-based costing (ABC), which is covered in Chapter 5.

B. Cost Projections for a New Product: Depth Finder

	Original Cost Projection		Improved Cost Projection
Direct material	$200		$190
Direct labor	100		70
Purchasing:			
$1 per part (45 parts)	45		
$1 per part (32 parts)			32
Material handling:			
$.20 per direct-material dollar ($200)	40		
$.20 per direct-material dollar ($190)			38
Inspection:			
$28 per inspection hour (.5 hour)	14		
$28 per inspection hour (.25 hour)			7
Total projected cost	$399		$337
Target cost		$340	

products are overcosted while low-volume and complex products are undercosted. This results from the fact that high-volume and relatively simple products require proportionately less activity per unit for various manufacturing-support activities than do low-volume and complex products. Yet a traditional product-costing system, in which all overhead is assigned on the basis of a single unit-level activity like direct-labor hours, fails to capture the cost implications of product diversity. In contrast, an activity-based costing (ABC) system does measure the extent to which each product line drives costs in the key production-support activities.

Managers should be aware that cost distortion can result in overpricing high-volume and relatively simple products, while low-volume and complex products are undercosted. This can undermine any effort to set prices competitively, even under the target-costing approach. The competitive implications of such strategic pricing errors can be disastrous.[9]

Value Engineering and Target Costing

Learning Objective **15-8**

Explain the process of value engineering and its role in target costing.

Target costing is an outgrowth of the concept of **value engineering,** which is a cost-reduction and process-improvement technique that utilizes information collected about a product's design and production processes and then examines various attributes of the design and processes to identify candidates for improvement efforts.

Much of the historical development of the target-costing approach has taken place in Japanese industry, where "more than 80 percent of all assembly industries in Japan use target costing. Some of the best practitioners of target costing are leading Japanese companies."[10] In recent years, however, many other companies, including Caterpillar, Fiat Chrysler (FCA), and Boeing have made significant contributions to target costing theory and practice.

Isuzu Motors, Ltd. is a leading Japanese manufacturer of automobiles, buses, and both light- and heavy-duty trucks. "At Isuzu, value engineering (VE) has been developed to cover all stages of product design and manufacture. Indeed, three different stages of VE—zeroth, first, and second 'looks'—are used in the design phase to increase the functionality of new products."[11]

- *Zeroth look VE* is applied at the earliest stages of new product design—"the concept proposal stage, when the basic concept of the product is developed and its preliminary quality, cost, and investment targets are established."
- *First look VE* is applied during the last half of the concept proposal stage and throughout the product planning phase. During this stage, a product's quality, functionality, and selling price are determined; a design plan is submitted; and target costs are determined for each of the new vehicle's major functions (e.g., engine and transmission). Also, the degree of component commonality is set. "First look VE is used at this stage to increase the value of the product by increasing its functionality without increasing its cost."
- *Second look VE* is applied during the last half of the product planning stage and the first half of the product development and preparation stage. "The components of the vehicle's major functions are identified, and hand-made prototypes are assembled. At this stage, VE works to improve the value and functionality of existing components, not to create new ones."

---

[9]This whole issue of cost distortion and the role of ABC in product pricing is covered extensively in Chapter 5.

[10]Shahid L. Ansari, Jan E. Bell, and the CAM-I Target Cost Core Group, *Target Costing: The Next Frontier in Strategic Cost Management* (Burr Ridge, IL: Irwin, 1997). See also Y. Kato, "Target Costing Support Systems: Lessons from Leading Japanese Companies," *Management Accounting Research* 4 (1992), pp. 33–47; and T. Tani, H. Okano, N. Shimizu, Y. Iwabuchi, J. Fukuda, and S. Cooray, "Target Cost Management in Japanese Companies: Current State of the Art," *Management Accounting Research* 6 (1994), pp. 67–81.

[11]This description of Isuzu's target costing and value-engineering methods is drawn from Robin Cooper, *When Lean Enterprises Collide* (Boston, MA: Harvard Business School Press, 1995), pp. 165–83.

In addition, various *tear-down methods* are used by Isuzu, and many other companies, "to analyze competitive products in terms of materials they contain, parts they use, ways they function, and ways they are manufactured." At Isuzu, for example, *dynamic tear-down* focuses on reducing the number of vehicle assembly operations or the time required to perform them. *Cost tear-down* examines ways to reduce the cost of the components used in a vehicle. *Material tear-down* compares the materials and surface treatments of the components used by Isuzu with those of its competitors. *Static tear-down* disassembles a competitor's product into its components to enable Isuzu's engineers to compare Isuzu's components with those used in the competitor's product.

> "An old Japanese saying states that 'there are many ways to the top of a mountain.' Analogously, there is no one right way to do target costing." (15h)
> **Honda of America Manufacturing, Inc.**

Although the Isuzu approach is illustrative of target costing methods, many different approaches are used by the thousands of companies now engaged in target costing programs. However, the Isuzu target costing and value-engineering process is indicative of the seriousness with which companies approach the problem of reducing costs in order to meet a product's target cost and remain competitive in an ever more difficult market.

Time and Material Pricing

Learning Objective 15-9

Determine prices using the time and material pricing approach.

Another cost-based approach to pricing is called **time and material pricing.** Under this approach, the company determines one charge for the labor used on a job and another charge for the materials. The labor typically includes the direct cost of the employee's time and a charge to cover various overhead costs. The material charge generally includes the direct cost of the materials used in a job plus a charge for material handling and storage. Time and material pricing is used widely by construction companies, printers, repair shops, and professional firms, such as engineering, law, and public accounting firms.

To illustrate, we will examine a special job undertaken by Sydney Sailing Supplies. The company's vice president for sales, Richard Moby, was approached by a successful local physician about refurbishing her yacht. She wanted an engine overhaul, complete refurbishment and redecoration of the cabin facilities, and stripping and repainting of the hull and deck. The work would be done in the Repair Department of the company's Yacht Division, located in Melbourne, Australia.

Data regarding the operations of the Repair Department are as follows:

Labor rate, including fringe benefits	$18.00 per hour
Hourly charge to cover profit margin	$7.00 per hour
Annual labor hours	10,000 hours
Annual overhead costs:	
Material handling and storage	$40,000
Other overhead costs (supervision, utilities, insurance, and depreciation)	$200,000
Annual cost of materials used in Repair Department	$1,000,000

Based on these data, the Repair Department computed its time and material prices as follows:

Time Charges

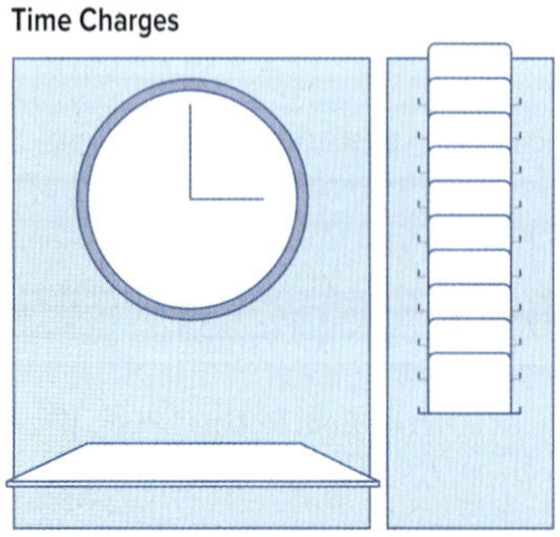

$$\text{Hourly labor cost} + \frac{\text{Annual overhead (excluding material handling and storage)}}{\text{Annual labor hours}} + \text{Hourly charge to cover profit margin}$$

$$\$18 \text{ per hour} + \frac{\$200,000}{10,000 \text{ hours}} + \$7 \text{ per hour} = \$45 \text{ per labor hour}$$

Material Charges

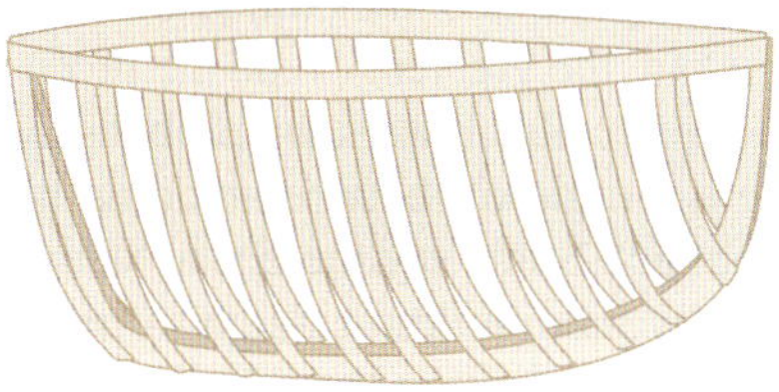

$$\text{Material cost incurred on job} + \left(\text{Material cost incurred on job} \times \frac{\text{Material handling and storage costs}}{\text{Annual cost of materials used in Repair Department}}\right)$$

$$\text{Material cost incurred on job} + \left(\text{Material cost incurred on job} \times \frac{\$40{,}000}{\$1{,}000{,}000}\right)$$

$.04 per dollar of material cost

The effect of the material-charge formula is to include a charge for the costs incurred in the handling and storage of materials.

Richard Moby estimates that the yacht refurbishment job will require 200 hours of labor and $8,000 in materials. Moby's price quotation for the job is shown in the Excel spreadsheet in Exhibit 15–7.

Included in the $17,320 price quotation for the yacht refurbishment are charges for labor costs, overhead, material costs, material handling and storage costs, and a normal profit margin. Some companies also charge an additional markup on the materials used in a job in order to earn a profit on that component of their services. Sydney Sailing Supplies' practice is to charge a high enough profit charge on its labor to earn an appropriate profit for the Repair Department.

Competitive Bidding

In a **competitive bidding** situation, two or more companies submit sealed bids (or prices) for a project, service, or product to a potential buyer. The buyer selects one of the companies for the job on the basis of the bid price and the design specifications for the job. Competitive bidding complicates a manager's pricing problem, because now the manager

Learning Objective 15-10

Set prices in special-order or competitive-bidding situations by analyzing the relevant costs.

Exhibit 15–7

Time and Material Pricing

Sydney Sailing Supplies - Excel

G15 =G13+G14

	A	B–E	F	G	H
1		SYDNEY SAILING SUPPLIES			
2		Price Quotation			
3		Yacht Division: Repair Department			
4					
5	Time charges	Labor time		200	hours
6		x Rate	x	$ 45	per hour
7		Total		$ 9,000	
8					
9	Material charges	Cost of materials for job		$ 8,000	
10		+ Charge for material handling and storage*		320	
11		Total		$ 8,320	
12					
13	Total price of job	Time		$ 9,000	
14		Material		8,320	
15		Total		$17,320	
16					
17	*Charge for material handling and storage:				
18	($8,000 material cost) x ($.04 per dollar of material cost) = $320				

Price Quotation

READY

is in direct competition with one or more competitors. If all of the companies submitting bids offer a roughly equivalent product or service, the bid price becomes the sole criterion for selecting the contractor. The higher the price that is bid, the greater will be the profit on the job, *if* the firm gets the contract. However, a higher price also lowers the probability of obtaining the contract to perform the job. Thus, there is a trade-off between bidding high, to make a good profit, and bidding low, to land the contract. Some say there is a "winner's curse" in competitive bidding, meaning that the company bidding low enough to beat out its competitors probably bid too low to make an acceptable profit on the job. Despite the winner's curse, competitive bidding is a common form of selecting contractors in many types of business.

Richard Moby was approached recently by the city of Sydney about building a new marina for moderate-sized sailing vessels. Moby decided that his company's Marine Services Division should submit a bid on the job. The Marine Services Division specializes in marina maintenance and construction. The city announced that three other firms also would be submitting bids. Since all four companies were equally capable of building the marina to the city's specifications, Moby assumed that the bid price would be the deciding factor in selecting the contractor.

Moby consulted with the controller and chief engineer of the Marine Services Division, and the following data were compiled.

Estimated direct-labor requirements, 1,500 hours at $12.00 per hour	$18,000
Estimated direct-material requirements	30,000
Estimated variable overhead (allocated on the basis of direct labor), 1,500 direct-labor hours at $5.00 per hour	7,500
Total estimated variable costs	$55,500
Estimated fixed overhead (allocated on the basis of direct labor), 1,500 direct-labor hours at $8.00 per hour	12,000
Estimated total cost	$67,500

The Marine Services Division allocates variable-overhead costs to jobs on the basis of direct-labor hours. These costs consist of indirect-labor costs, such as the wages of equipment-repair personnel, gasoline and lubricants, and incidental supplies such as rope, chains, and drill bits. Fixed-overhead costs, also allocated to jobs on the basis of direct-labor hours, include such costs as workers'compensation insurance, depreciation on vehicles and construction equipment, depreciation of the division's buildings, and supervisory salaries.

It was up to Richard Moby to decide on the bid price for the marina. In his meeting with the divisional controller and the chief engineer, Moby argued that the marina job was important to the company for two reasons. First, the Marine Services Division had been operating well below capacity for several months. The marina job would not preclude the firm from taking on any other construction work, so it would not entail an opportunity cost. Second, the marina job would be good advertising for Sydney Sailing Supplies. City residents would see the firm's name on the project, and this would promote sales of the company's boats and sailing supplies.

Based on these arguments, Moby pressed for a bid price that just covered the firm's variable costs and allowed for a modest contribution margin. The chief engineer was obstinate, however, and argued for a higher bid price that would give the division a good profit on the job. "My employees work hard to do an outstanding job, and their work is worth a premium to the city," was the engineer's final comment on the issue. After the threesome tossed the problem around all morning, the controller agreed with Moby. A bid price of $60,000 was finally agreed upon.

This is a typical approach to setting prices for special jobs and competitively bid contracts. When a firm has excess capacity, a price that covers the incremental costs incurred because of the job will contribute toward covering the company's fixed cost and profit. None of the Marine Services Division's fixed costs will increase as a result of taking on the marina job. Thus, a bid price of $60,000 will cover the $55,500 of variable costs on the job and contribute $4,500 toward covering the division's fixed costs.

Bid price	$60,000
Variable costs of marina job (incremental costs incurred only if job is done)	55,500
Contribution from marina job (contribution to covering the division's fixed costs)	$ 4,500

Naturally, Sydney Sailing Supplies' management would like to make a larger profit on the marina job, but bidding a higher price means running a substantial risk of losing the job to a competitor.

No Excess Capacity What if the Marine Services Division has no excess capacity? If management expects to have enough work to fully occupy the division, a different approach is appropriate in setting the bid price. The fixed costs of the division are capacity-producing costs, which are costs incurred in order to create productive capacity. Depreciation of buildings and equipment, supervisory salaries, insurance, and property taxes are examples of fixed costs incurred to give a company the capacity to carry on its operations. When such costs are allocated to individual jobs, the cost of each job reflects an estimate of the opportunity cost of using limited capacity to do that particular job. For this reasoning to be valid, however, the organization must be at full capacity. If there is excess capacity, there is no opportunity cost in using that excess capacity.

If the Marine Services Division has no excess capacity, it would be appropriate to focus on the estimated full cost of the marina job, $67,500, which includes an allocation of the division's fixed capacity-producing costs. Now Richard Moby might legitimately argue for a bid price in excess of $67,500. If the division is awarded the marina contract by the city, a price above $67,500 will cover all the costs of the job and make a contribution toward the division's profit.

However, as Richard Moby pointed out, there will be valuable promotional benefits to Sydney Sailing Supplies if its Marine Services Division builds the marina. This is a qualitative factor, because these potential benefits are difficult to quantify. Moby will have to make a judgment regarding just how important the marina job is to the company. The greater the perceived qualitative benefits, the lower the bid price should be set to maximize the likelihood that the company will be awarded the contract.

Summary of Competitive-Bidding Analysis The Marine Services Division's pricing problem is summarized in Exhibit 15–8. As you can see, the final pricing decision requires managerial judgment to fully consider the quantitative cost data, the qualitative promotional benefits, and the trade-off between a higher profit and a greater likelihood of getting the marina contract.

Accept or Reject a Special Order In the preceding chapter, we examined in detail the decision as to whether a special order should be accepted or rejected. The analysis focused on identifying the relevant costs of the special order. The existence of excess capacity was an important factor in that analysis. Accepting a special order when excess capacity exists entails no opportunity cost. But when there is no excess capacity, one relevant cost of accepting a special order is the opportunity cost incurred by using the firm's limited capacity for the special order instead of some other job. After all relevant costs of the order have been identified, the decision maker compares the total relevant cost of the order with the price offered. If the price exceeds the relevant cost, the order generally should be accepted.

The decision is conceptually very similar to the bid-pricing problem discussed in this chapter. Setting a price for a special order or competitive bid also entails an analysis of the relevant costs of the job. Whether the decision maker is setting a price or has been offered a price, he or she must identify the relevant costs of providing the product or service requested.

Effect of Antitrust Laws on Pricing

Learning Objective 15-11

Describe the legal restrictions on setting prices.

Companies are not free to set any price they wish for their products or services. U.S. antitrust laws, including the Robinson-Patman Act, the Clayton Act, and the Sherman Act, restrict certain types of pricing behavior. These laws prohibit **price discrimination,** which means quoting different prices to different customers for the same product or service. Such price differences are unlawful unless they can be clearly justified by differences in the costs incurred to produce, sell, or deliver the product or service. Managers should keep careful records justifying such cost differences when they exist, because the records may be vital to a legal defense if price differences are challenged in court.

Another pricing practice prohibited by law is **predatory pricing.** This practice involves temporarily cutting a price to broaden demand for a product with the intention of later restricting the supply and raising the price again. In determining whether a price is predatory, the courts examine a business's cost records. If the product is sold below cost, the pricing is deemed to be predatory. The laws and court cases are ambiguous as to the appropriate definition of cost. However, various court decisions make it harder to prove predatory pricing. Nevertheless, this is one area where a price-setting decision maker is well advised to have an accountant on the left and a lawyer on the right before setting prices that could be deemed predatory.

Exhibit 15–8

Summary of Competitive-Bidding Analysis

Estimated variable costs of marina job:	
Direct labor	$18,000
Direct material	30,000
Variable overhead (allocated)	7,500
Total estimated variable cost	$55,500
Estimated fixed cost (allocated)	12,000
Estimated total cost	$67,500

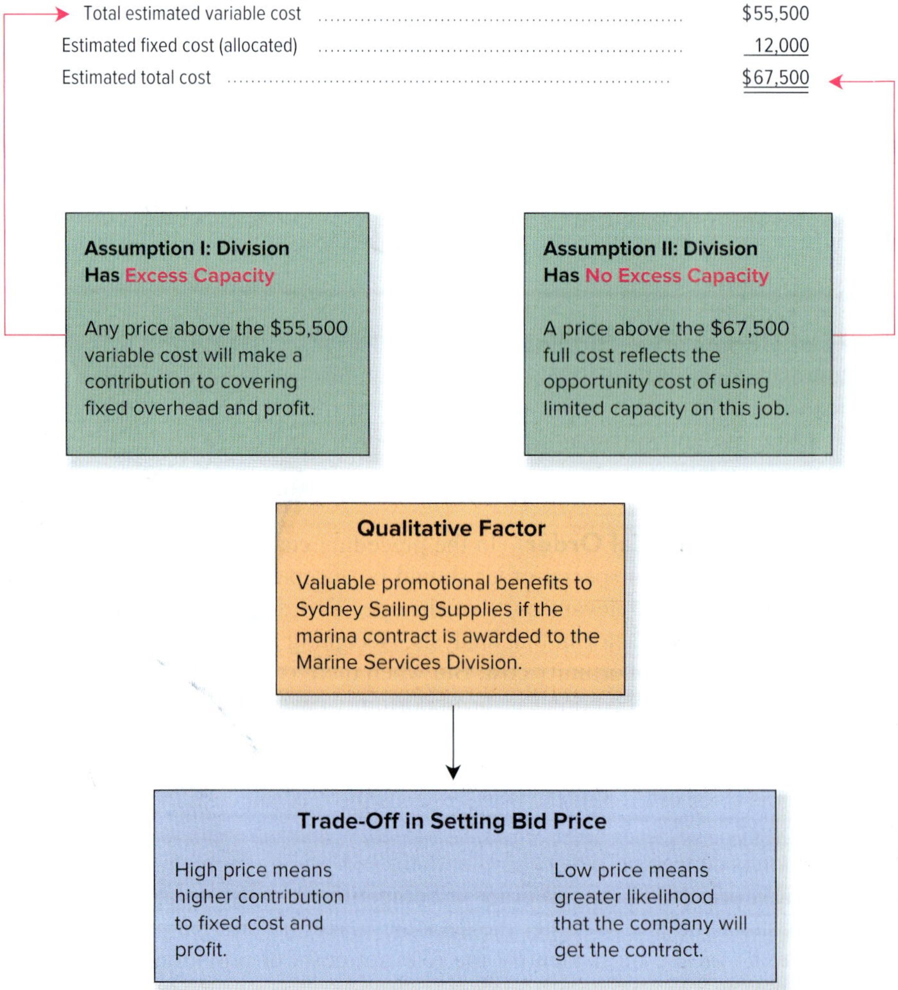

Chapter Summary

LO15-1 List and describe the four major influences on pricing decisions. Many influences affect pricing decisions. Chief among these are: customer demand; the actions of competitors; the costs of the products or services; and political, legal, and image-related issues.

LO15-2 Explain and use the economic, profit-maximizing pricing model. Under this approach to pricing, the profit-maximizing quantity is determined by the intersection of the marginal revenue and marginal cost curves. At this optimal sales quantity level, the profit-maximizing price is determined from the demand (or average-revenue) curve.

LO15-3 Set prices using cost-plus pricing formulas. Cost-plus pricing formulas are commonly based on four product-cost measures: (1) variable manufacturing cost; (2) absorption manufacturing cost; (3) total cost; and (4) total variable cost. Markups often are set to earn the company a target profit on its products, based on a target rate of return on investment.

LO15-4 Discuss the issues involved in the strategic pricing of new products. Strategic pricing of new products is an especially challenging problem for management. Various pricing approaches, such as skimming pricing or penetration pricing, may be appropriate depending on the product.

LO15-5 List and discuss the key principles of target costing. Target costing often is used to design a new product that can be produced at a cost that will enable the firm to sell it at a competitive price. Value engineering and activity-based costing are valuable tools used in the target costing process.

LO15-6 Explain the role of activity-based costing in setting a target cost. Activity-based costing helps to avoid product cost distortion, in which relatively high-volume and relatively simple products tend to be overcosted by traditional product-costing systems, and relatively low-volume and relatively complex products tend to be undercosted.

LO15-7 Explain how product-cost distortion can undermine a firm's pricing strategy. Product-cost distortion occurs when relatively high-volume and relatively simple products tend to be overcosted by traditional product-costing systems, and relatively low-volume and relatively complex products tend to be undercosted. This phenomenon can lead a company to lose sales by overpricing certain products and lose profit by selling other products at too low a price.

LO15-8 Explain the process of value engineering and its role in target costing. Value engineering analyzes a product's design and production process to identify areas for cost reduction and process improvement. By reducing a product's cost, management can bring a product's production cost down to meet its target cost.

LO15-9 Determine prices using the time and material pricing approach. In industries such as construction, repair, printing, and professional services, time and material pricing often is used. Under this approach, the price is determined as the sum of a labor-cost component and a material-cost component. Either or both of these components may include a markup to ensure that the company earns a profit on its services.

LO15-10 Set prices in special-order or competitive-bidding situations by analyzing the relevant costs. Pricing special orders and determining competitive bid prices entail an analysis of the relevant costs to be incurred in completing the job. The relevant-cost analysis should incorporate the existence of excess capacity or the lack of it.

LO15-11 Describe the legal restrictions on setting prices. The law prohibits price discrimination, which means quoting different prices to different customers for the same product or service. Also outlawed is predatory pricing, which involves temporarily cutting a price to broaden demand for a product with the intention of later restricting the supply and raising the price again.

Review Problem on Cost-Plus Pricing

Kitchenware Corporation manufactures high-quality copper pots and pans. Greta Cooke, one of the company's price analysts, is involved in setting a price for the company's new Starter Set. This set consists of seven of the most commonly used pots and pans. During the next year, the company plans to produce 10,000 Starter Sets, and the controller has provided Cooke with the following cost data.

Predicted Costs of 10,000 Starter Sets

Direct material per set	$60
Direct labor per set, 2 hours at $10.00 per hr	20
Variable selling cost per set	5
Total	$85
Variable-overhead rate	$ 8.00 per direct-labor hour
Fixed-overhead rate	$12.00 per direct-labor hour

In addition, the controller indicated that the Accounting Department would allocate $20,000 of fixed administrative expenses to the Starter Set product line.

Required:

1. Compute the cost of a Starter Set using each of the four cost definitions commonly used in cost-plus pricing formulas.
2. Determine the markup percentage required for the Starter Set product line to earn a target operating income of $317,500 before taxes during the next year. Use the total cost as the cost definition in the cost-plus formula.

Solution to Review Problem

1.

Variable manufacturing cost*	$ 96	1	
Applied fixed-overhead cost†	24		
Absorption manufacturing cost	$120	2	
Variable selling cost	5		
Allocated fixed administrative cost‡	2		
Total cost	$127	3	
Variable manufacturing cost	$ 96		
Variable selling cost	5		
Total variable cost	$101	4	
*Direct material	$ 60		
Direct labor	20		
Variable overhead	16		(2 × $8.00 per hour)
Total variable manufacturing cost	$ 96		
†Applied fixed overhead cost	$ 24		(2 × $12 per hour)
‡Allocated fixed administrative cost	$ 2		($20,000 ÷ 10,000 sets)

2. Markup percentage on total cost $= \dfrac{\$317,500}{10,000 \times \$127} = 25\%$

Proof: Price = Total cost + (.25 × Total cost) = $127 + (.25)($127) = $158.75

Income Statement

Sales revenue (10,000 × $158.75)		$1,587,500
Less: Variable costs:		
Direct material	$600,000	
Direct labor	200,000	
Variable overhead	160,000	
Variable selling cost	50,000	
Total variable costs		1,010,000
Contribution margin		$ 577,500
Less: Fixed costs:		
Manufacturing overhead	$240,000	
Administrative cost	20,000	
Total fixed costs		260,000
Operating income		$ 317,500

Key Terms

For each term's definition refer to the indicated page, or turn to the glossary at the end of the text.

competitive bidding, 667
cost-plus pricing, 656
cross-elasticity, 655
demand curve (average revenue curve), 652
marginal cost curve, 652
marginal revenue curve, 652
oligopolistic market, 655
penetration pricing, 661
predatory pricing, 670
price discrimination, 670
price elasticity, 655
price taker, 650
return-on-investment pricing, 658
skimming pricing, 661
target cost, 661
target costing, 661
time and material pricing, 666
total cost curve, 652
total revenue curve, 650
value engineering, 665

Review Questions

15–1. Comment on the following remark made by a bank president: "The prices of our banking services are determined by the financial-services market. Costs are irrelevant."

15–2. "All this marginal revenue and marginal cost stuff is just theory. Prices are determined by production costs." Evaluate this assertion.

15–3. List and briefly describe four major influences on pricing decisions.

15–4. Explain what is meant by the following statement: "In considering the reactions of competitors, it is crucial to define your product."

15–5. Explain the following assertion: "Price setting generally requires a balance between market forces and cost considerations."

15–6. Briefly explain the concept of *economic, profit-maximizing pricing.* It may be helpful to use graphs in your explanation.

15–7. Define the following terms: *total revenue, marginal revenue, demand curve, price elasticity,* and *cross-elasticity.*

15–8. Briefly define *total cost* and *marginal cost.*

15–9. Describe three limitations of the economic, profit-maximizing model of pricing.

15–10. Determining the best approach to pricing requires a cost-benefit trade-off. Explain.

15–11. Write the general formula for cost-plus pricing, and briefly explain its use.

15–12. List the four common cost bases used in cost-plus pricing. How can they all result in the same price?

15–13. List four reasons often cited for the widespread use of absorption cost as the cost base in cost-plus pricing formulas.

15–14. What is the primary disadvantage of basing the cost-plus pricing formula on absorption cost?

15–15. List three advantages of pricing based on variable cost.

15–16. Explain the behavioral problem that can result when cost-plus prices are based on variable cost.

15–17. Briefly explain the concept of *return-on-investment pricing.*

15–18. Explain the phrase *price-led costing.*

15–19. Why is a focus on the customer such a key principle of target costing?

15–20. Explain the role of value engineering in target costing.

15–21. Could *tear-down* methods be used effectively for target pricing in a service-industry company, such as a hotel or an airline? Explain.

15–22. Briefly describe the *time-and-material pricing approach.*

15–23. Explain the importance of the excess-capacity issue in setting a competitive bid price.

15–24. The decision to accept or reject a special order and the selection of a price for a special order are very similar decisions. Explain.

15–25. Describe the following approaches to pricing new products: skimming pricing, penetration pricing, and target costing.

15–26. Explain what is meant by unlawful price discrimination and predatory pricing.

15–27. Briefly explain the potential negative consequences in pricing decisions from using a traditional, volume-based product-costing system.

Exercises

All applicable Exercises are available in Connect. connect

Exercise 15–28
Demand and Revenue Data
(LO 15-1, 15-2)

Spectrum Sound, Inc. manufactures compact disc players with unusual features in its St. Louis Division. The divisional sales manager has estimated the following demand-curve data.

Quantity Sold per Month	Unit Sales Price
20	$1,000
40	950
60	900
80	850
100	800

Required:

1. Prepare a table similar to panel C of Exhibit 15–1 summarizing Spectrum Sound's price, quantity, and revenue data.
2. Draw a graph similar to panel A of Exhibit 15–1 reflecting the data tabulated in requirement (1).

Exercise 15–29
Continuation of Preceding Exercise; Cost Data
(LO 15-1, 15-2)

Refer to the preceding exercise. The divisional controller at Spectrum Sound's St. Louis Division has estimated the following cost data for the division's CD players. (Assume there are no fixed costs.)

Quantity Produced and Sold per Month	Average Cost per Unit
20	$900
40	850
60	820
80	860
100	890

Required:

1. Prepare a table similar to panel C of Exhibit 15–2 summarizing Spectrum Sound's cost relationships.
2. Draw a graph similar to panel A of Exhibit 15–2 reflecting the data tabulated in requirement (1).

Exercise 15–30
Continuation of Preceding Two Exercises; Profit-Maximizing Price
(LO 15-1, 15-2)

Refer to the data given in the preceding two exercises.

Required:

1. Prepare a table of Spectrum Sound's revenue, cost, and profit relationships. For guidance, refer to panel C of Exhibit 15–3.
2. Draw a graph similar to panel A of Exhibit 15–3 reflecting the data tabulated in requirement (1).
3. To narrow down the pricing decision, the St. Louis Division's sales manager has decided to price the CD player at one of the following prices: $800, $850, $900, $950, or $1,000. Which price do you recommend? Why?

Exercise 15–31
Marginal Revenue and Marginal Cost Curves
(LO 15-1, 15-2)

The marginal cost, marginal revenue, and demand curves for Houston Home and Garden's deluxe wheelbarrow are shown in the graph below.

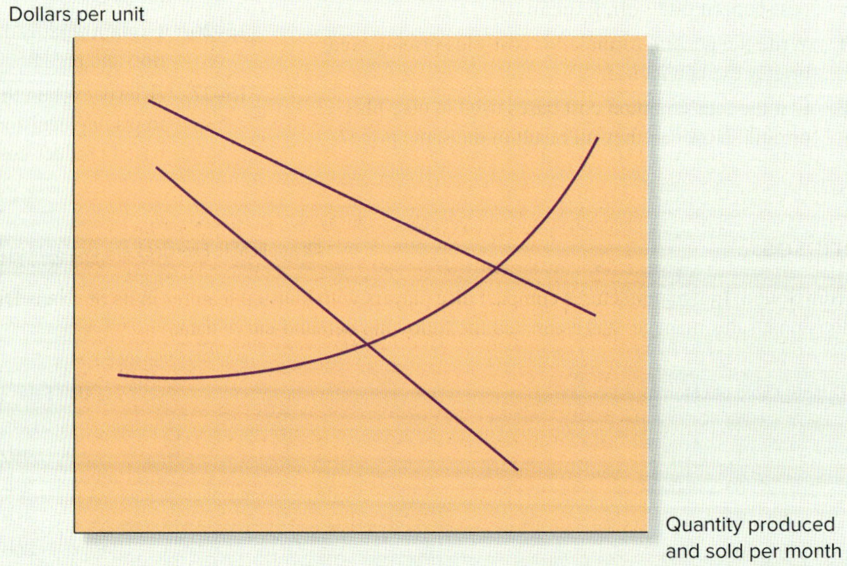

Required: Before completing any of the following requirements, read over the entire list.

1. Trace the graph onto a blank piece of paper, and label all parts of the graph.
2. Draw a companion graph directly above the traced graph. Use this graph to draw the firm's total revenue and total cost curves.
3. Show the company's profit-maximizing price on the lower graph and its profit-maximizing quantity on both graphs.

Exercise 15–32
Pricing, Advertising, and Special-Order Decisions
(LO 15-10)

Corrientes Company produces a single product in its Buenos Aires plant that currently sells for 5.00 *p* per unit. Fixed costs are expected to amount to 60,000 *p* for the year, and all variable manufacturing and administrative costs are expected to be incurred at a rate of 3.00 *p* per unit. Corrientes has two salespeople who are paid strictly on a commission basis. Their commission is 10 percent of the sales revenue they generate. (Ignore income taxes.) (*p* denotes the peso, Argentina's national currency. Many countries use the peso as their national currency. On the day this exercise was written, Argentina's peso was worth .104 U.S. dollar.)

Required:

1. Suppose management alters its current plans by spending an additional amount of 5,000 *p* on advertising and increases the selling price to 6.00 *p* per unit. Calculate the profit on 60,000 units.
2. The Sorde Company has just approached Corrientes to make a special one-time purchase of 10,000 units. These units would not be sold by the sales personnel, and, therefore, no commission would have to be paid. What is the price Corrientes would have to charge per unit on this special order to earn additional profit of 20,000 *p?*

(CMA, adapted)

Exercise 15–33
Target Costing for a New Product; Use of Internet
(LO 15-5, 15-8)

Visit the website of one of the following companies, or a different company of your choosing.

Apple Computer	www.apple.com
Carnival Cruise Lines	www.carnivalcorp.com
Chase Bank	www.chase.com
General Electric Company	www.ge.com
Intel Corporation	www.intel.com
Nintendo	www.nintendo.com
Procter & Gamble	www.pg.com

Required: Read about a new product or service to be offered by the company. Then explain how the firm could use target costing to price the new product or service.

Exercise 15–34
Determining Markup Percentage; Target ROI
(LO 15-3)

Refer to the cost and production data for the Wave Darter in Exhibit 15–5. The target profit is $60,000.

Required: Use the general formula for determining a markup percentage to compute the required markup percentages with the following two cost-plus formulas:

1. Variable manufacturing costs [formula (1) in Exhibit 15–5].
2. Absorption manufacturing cost [formula (2) in Exhibit 15–5].

Exercise 15–35
Cost-Plus Pricing Formulas; Missing Data
(LO 15-3)

The following data pertain to Lawn Master Corporation's top-of-the-line lawn mower.

Variable manufacturing cost	$250
Applied fixed manufacturing cost	50
Variable selling and administrative cost	60
Allocated fixed selling and administrative cost	?

To achieve a target price of $450 per lawn mower, the markup percentage is 12.5 percent on total unit cost.

Required:

1. What is the fixed selling and administrative cost allocated to each unit of Lawn Master's top-of-the-line mower?
2. For each of the following cost bases, develop a cost-plus pricing formula that will result in a target price of $450 per mower: (*a*) variable manufacturing cost, (*b*) absorption manufacturing cost, and (*c*) total variable cost.

Exercise 15–36
Cost-Plus Pricing Formulas
(LO 15-3)

The following data pertain to Royal Lighting Company's oak-clad, contemporary chandelier.

Variable manufacturing cost	$200
Applied fixed manufacturing cost	70
Variable selling and administrative cost	30
Allocated fixed selling and administrative cost	50

Required: For each of the following cost bases, develop a cost-plus pricing formula that will result in a price of $400 for the oak chandelier.

1. Variable manufacturing cost.
2. Absorption manufacturing cost.
3. Total cost.
4. Total variable cost.

Exercise 15–37
Time and Material Pricing
(LO 15-9)

Refer to Exhibit 15–7. Suppose the Repair Department of Sydney Sailing Supplies adds a markup of 5 percent on the material charges of a job (including the cost of material handling and storage).

Required:

1. Rewrite the material component of the time and material pricing formula to reflect the markup on material cost.
2. Compute the new price to be quoted on the yacht refurbishment described in Exhibit 15–7.

Problems

All applicable Problems are available in Connect. connect

Note: Several of the problems and cases in Chapter 5 relate to pricing and may be assigned with Chapter 15 as well. These problems emphasize the impact of cost distortion on pricing decisions. They stress the differences between traditional, volume-based costing systems and activity-based costing systems with respect to their role in pricing. These problems should be assigned only after Chapter 5 has been completed. The following problems are relevant: 5–46, 5–47, 5–49, 5–56, 5-57, 5-59, 5-60, and 5–61. Also relevant is case 5-69.

Problem 15–38
Pricing a Special Order; International
(LO 15-10)

2. Total incremental profit: $552,000

Badger Valve and Fitting Company, located in southern Wisconsin, manufactures a variety of industrial valves and pipe fittings that are sold to customers in nearby states. Currently, the company is operating at about 70 percent capacity and is earning a satisfactory return on investment. Management has been approached by Glasgow Industries Ltd. of Scotland with an offer to buy 120,000 units of a pressure valve. Glasgow Industries manufactures a valve that is almost identical to Badger's pressure valve; however, a fire in Glasgow Industries' valve plant has shut down its manufacturing operations. Glasgow needs the 120,000 valves over the next four months to meet commitments to its regular customers. Glasgow is prepared to pay $19 each for the valves. Badger's total product cost, based on current attainable standards, for the pressure valve is $20, calculated as follows:

Direct material	$ 5.00
Direct labor	6.00
Manufacturing overhead	9.00
Total product cost	$20.00

Manufacturing overhead is applied to production at the rate of $18 per standard direct-labor hour. This overhead rate is made up of the following components.

Variable manufacturing overhead	$ 6.00
Fixed manufacturing overhead (traceable)	8.00
Fixed manufacturing overhead (allocated)	4.00
Applied manufacturing overhead rate	$18.00

Additional costs incurred in connection with sales of the pressure valve include sales commissions of 5 percent and freight expense of $1.00 per unit. However, the company does not pay sales commissions on special orders that come directly to management. In determining selling prices, Badger adds a 40 percent markup to total product cost. This provides a $28 suggested selling price for the pressure valve. The Marketing Department, however, has set the current selling price at $27 in order to maintain market share. Production management believes that it can handle the Glasgow Industries order without disrupting its scheduled production. The order would, however, require additional fixed factory overhead of $12,000 per month in the form of supervision and clerical costs. If management accepts the order, 30,000 pressure valves will be manufactured and shipped to Glasgow Industries each month for the next four months. Glasgow's management has agreed to pay the shipping charges for the valves.

Required:

1. Determine how many direct-labor hours would be required each month to fill the Glasgow Industries order.
2. Prepare an analysis showing the impact of accepting the Glasgow Industries order.
3. Calculate the minimum unit price that Badger Valve and Fitting Company's management could accept for the Glasgow Industries order without reducing net income.
4. Identify the factors, other than price, that Badger's management should consider before accepting the Glasgow Industries order.
5. ***Build a spreadsheet:*** Construct an Excel spreadsheet to solve requirements (2) and (3) above. Show how the solution will change if the following information changes: the direct material and direct labor per unit are $4.90 and $6.10, respectively.

(CMA, adapted)

Problem 15–39
Cost-Plus Pricing; Bidding
(LO 15-3, 15-10)

2. Total bid price: $14,950

North American Pharmaceuticals, Inc. specializes in packaging bulk drugs in standard dosages for local hospitals. The company has been in business for seven years and has been profitable since its second year of operation. Don Greenway, Assistant Controller, installed a standard costing system after joining the company three years ago.

Wyant Memorial Hospital has asked North American Pharmaceuticals to bid on the packaging of one million doses of medication at total cost plus a return on total cost of no more than 15 percent. Wyant defines total cost as including all variable costs of performing the service, a reasonable amount of fixed overhead, and reasonable administrative costs. The hospital will supply all packaging materials and ingredients. Wyant has indicated that any bid over $.015 per dose will be rejected.

Greenway has accumulated the following information prior to the preparation of the bid.

Direct labor	$8.00 per direct-labor hour (DLH)
Variable overhead	$6.00 per DLH
Fixed overhead	$10.00 per DLH
Incremental administrative costs	$1,000 for the order
Production rate	2,000 doses per DLH

Required:

1. Calculate the minimum price per dose that North American Pharmaceuticals could bid for the Wyant Memorial Hospital job that would not reduce the pharmaceutical company's income.
2. Calculate the bid price per dose using total cost and the maximum allowable return specified by Wyant Memorial Hospital.
3. Independent of your answer to requirement (2), suppose that the price per dose that North American Pharmaceuticals, Inc. calculated using the cost-plus criterion specified by Wyant Memorial Hospital is greater than the maximum bid of $.015 per dose allowed by Wyant. Discuss the factors that the pharmaceutical company's management should consider before deciding whether or not to submit a bid at the maximum price of $.015 per dose that Wyant allows.

(CMA, adapted)

Problem 15–40
Target Costing
(LO 15-3, 15-5, 15-6, 15-8)

4. Target profit: $2,520,000

MPE, Inc. will soon enter a very competitive marketplace in which it will have limited influence over the prices that are charged. Management and consultants are currently working to fine-tune the company's sole service, which hopefully will generate a 12 percent first-year return (profit) on the firm's $18,000,000 asset investment. Although the normal return in MPE's industry is 14 percent, executives are willing to accept the lower figure because of various start-up inefficiencies. The following information is available for first-year operations:

Hours of service to be provided: 25,000
Anticipated variable cost per service hour: $22
Anticipated fixed cost: $1,900,000 per year

Required:

1. Assume that management is contemplating what price to charge in the first year of operation. The company can take its cost and add a markup to achieve a 12 percent return; alternatively, it can use target costing. Given MPE's marketplace, which approach is probably more appropriate? Why?
2. How much profit must MPE generate in the first year to achieve a 12 percent return?
3. Calculate the revenue per hour that MPE must generate in the first year to achieve a 12 percent return.
4. Assume that prior to the start of business in year 1, management conducted a planning exercise to determine if MPE could attain a 14 percent return in year 2. Can the company achieve this return if (*a*) competitive pressures dictate a maximum selling price of $175 per hour and (*b*) service hours and the variable cost per service hour are the same as the amounts anticipated in year 1? Show calculations.
5. If your answer to requirement (4) is no, suggest and briefly describe a procedure that MPE might use to achieve the desired results.

Problem 15–41
Cost-Plus Pricing vs. Target Costing
(LO 15-1, 15-3, 15-5, 15-6, 15-8)

3. Required cost reduction: $24

For many years, Leno Corporation has used a straightforward cost-plus pricing system, marking its goods up approximately 25 percent of total cost. The company has been profitable; however, it has recently lost considerable business to foreign competitors that have become very aggressive in the marketplace. These firms appear to be using target costing.

An example of Leno's problem is typified by item no. 8976, which has the following unit-cost characteristics:

Direct material	$30
Direct labor	75
Manufacturing overhead	50
Selling and administrative expenses	25

The going market price for an identical product of comparable quality is $195, which is significantly below what Leno is charging.

Required:

1. Contrast cost-plus pricing and target costing. Which of the two approaches could be aptly labeled price-led costing? Why?
2. What is Leno's current selling price of item no. 8976?
3. If Leno used target costing for item no. 8976, what must happen to costs if the company desires to meet the market price and maintain its current rate of profit *on sales?* By how much?
4. Would the identification of value-added and non-value-added costs assist Leno in this situation? Briefly explain.
5. Suppose that by previous cost-cutting drives, costs had already been "pared to the bone" on item no. 8976. What might Leno be forced to do with its markup on cost to remain competitive? By how much?
6. Early in this chapter, the text noted that in many industries, prices are the result of an interaction between market forces and costs. Explain what is meant by this statement.
7. ***Build a spreadsheet:*** Construct an Excel spreadsheet to solve requirements (2) and (3) above. Show how the solution will change if the following information changes: the direct material and direct labor per unit are $25 and $85, respectively.

Problem 15–42
Target Costing; Selection of Product Features
(LO 15-5, 15-8)

3. Maximum allowable cost: $76.00

Danish Furniture (DF) manufactures easy-to-assemble wooden furniture for home and office. The firm is considering modification of a table to make it more attractive to individuals and businesses that buy products through outlets such as Office Max, Office Depot, and Staples stores. The table is small, can be used to hold a computer printer or fax machine, and has several shelves for storage.

The company's marketing department surveyed potential buyers of the table regarding five proposed modifications. The 200 survey participants were asked to evaluate the modifications by using a five-point scale that ranged from 1 (strongly disagree) to 5 (strongly agree). Their responses, along with DF's related unit costs for the modifications, follow.

	1 Strongly Disagree	2 Disagree	3 Neutral	4 Agree	5 Strongly Agree
Add cabinet doors in storage area ($6.00)	10	20	30	60	80
Expand storage area ($2.50)	10	40	70	50	30
Add security lock to storage area ($1.65)	30	60	50	40	20
Give table top a more rich, marble appearance ($4.25)	10	20	50	60	60
Extend warranty to five years ($5.10)	40	70	30	35	25

The table currently costs $64 to produce and distribute, and DF's selling price for this unit averages $80. An analysis of competitive tables in the marketplace revealed a variety of features, with some models having all of the features that DF is considering and other models having only a few. The current manufacturers' selling prices for these tables averages $95.

Required:

1. Why is there a need in target costing to (*a*) focus on the customer and (*b*) have a marketing team become involved with product design?
2. DF's marketing team will evaluate the survey responses by computing a weighted-average rating of each of the modifications. This will be accomplished by weighting (multiplying) the point values (1, 2, etc.) by the frequency of responses, summing the results, and dividing by 200. Rank the popularity of the five modifications using this approach.
3. Management desires to earn approximately the same rate of profit on sales that is being earned with the current design.
   a. If DF uses target costing and desires to meet the current competitive selling price, what is the maximum cost of the modified table?
   b. Which of the modifications should DF consider?
4. Assume that DF wanted to add a modification or two that you excluded in your answer to requirement (3*b*). What process might management adopt to allow the company to make its target profit for the table? Briefly explain.

Problem 15–43
Pricing of Special Order
(LO 15-10)

1. The order will boost Graydon's net income by: $27,900

Graydon, Inc. manufactures food blending machinery according to customer specifications. The company operated at 75 percent of practical capacity during the year just ended, with the following results (in thousands):

Sales revenue	$25,000
Less: Sales commissions (10%)	2,500
Net sales	$22,500
Expenses:	
Direct material	$6,000
Direct labor	7,500
Manufacturing overhead—variable	2,250
Manufacturing overhead—fixed	1,500
Corporate administration—fixed	750
Total costs	$18,000
Income before taxes	$ 4,500
Income taxes (40%)	1,800
Net income	$ 2,700

Graydon, which expects continued operations at 75 percent of capacity, recently submitted a bid of $165,000 on some custom-designed machinery for Premier Foods, Inc. Graydon used a pricing formula in deriving the bid amount, the formula being based on last year's operating results. The formula follows.

Estimated direct material	$ 29,200
Estimated direct labor	56,000
Estimated manufacturing overhead at 50% of direct labor	28,000
Estimated corporate overhead at 10% of direct labor	5,600
Estimated total costs excluding sales commissions	$118,800
Add 25% for profit and taxes	29,700
Suggested price (with profit) before sales commissions	$148,500
Suggested total price: $148,500 ÷ 0.9 to adjust for 10% commission	$165,000

Required:

1. Calculate the impact the order would have on Graydon's net income if the $165,000 bid were accepted by Premier Foods, Inc.
2. Assume that Premier has rejected Graydon's bid but has stated it is willing to pay $127,000 for the machinery. Should Graydon manufacture the machinery for the counteroffer of $127,000? Explain your answer and show calculations.
3. At what bid price will Graydon break even on the order?
4. Explain how the profit performance in the coming year would be affected if Graydon accepted all of its work at prices similar to Premier's $127,000 counteroffer described in requirement (2).
5. ***Build a spreadsheet:*** Construct an Excel spreadsheet to solve requirements (1) and (2) above. Show how the solution will change if the following information changes: the direct material and direct labor for the year just ended were $5,900 and $7,800, respectively; and sales commissions were 8 percent.

(CMA, adapted)

Problem 15–44
Target Costing; Value Engineering; ABC; JIT
(LO 15-5, 15-6, 15-8)

3. Pharsalia Electronics' current profit on sales is 10 percent

Alexis Kunselman, president of Pharsalia Electronics (PE), is concerned about the prospects of one of its major products. The president has been reviewing a marketing report with Jeff Keller, marketing product manager, for their 10-disc car compact disc (CD) changer. The report indicates another price reduction is needed to meet anticipated competitors' reductions in sales prices. The current selling price for their 10-disc car CD changer is $350 per unit. It is expected that within three months PE's two major competitors will be selling their 10-disc car CD changers for $300 per unit. This concerns Kunselman because their current cost of producing the CD changer is $315, which yields a $35 profit on each unit sold.

The situation is especially disturbing because PE had implemented an activity-based costing (ABC) system about two years ago. The ABC system helped them better identify costs, cost pools, cost drivers, and cost reduction opportunities. Changes made when adopting ABC reduced costs on this product by approximately 15 percent during the last two years. Now it appears that costs will need to be reduced considerably more to remain competitive and to earn a profit on the 10-disc car CD changers. Total costs to produce, sell, and service the CD changer units are as follows:

10-Disc Car CD Changer

		Per Unit
Material	Purchased components	$110
	All other material	40
Labor	Manufacturing, direct	65
	Setups	9
	Material handling	18
	Inspection	23
Machining	Cutting, shaping, and drilling	21
	Bending and finishing	14
Other	Finished-goods warehousing	5
	Warranty	10
	Total unit cost	$315

Kunselman has decided to hire Donald Collins, a consultant, to help decide how to proceed. After two weeks of review, discussion, and value engineering analysis, Collins suggested that PE adopt a just-in-time (JIT) cell manufacturing process to help reduce costs. He also suggested that using target costing would help in meeting the new target price.

By changing to a JIT cell manufacturing system, PE expects that manufacturing direct labor will increase by $15 per finished unit. However, setup, material handling, inspection, and finished goods warehousing will all be eliminated. Machining costs will be reduced from $35 to $30 per unit, and warranty costs are expected to be reduced by 40 percent.

Required:

1. Define *target costing.*
2. Define *value engineering.*
3. Determine Pharsalia Electronics' unit target cost at the $300 competitive sales price while maintaining the same percentage of profit on sales as is earned on the current $350 sales price.
4. If the just-in-time cell manufacturing process is implemented with the changes in costs noted, will Pharsalia Electronics meet the unit target cost you determined in requirement (3)? Prepare a schedule detailing cost reductions and the unit cost under the proposed JIT cell manufacturing process.

(CMA, adapted)

Problem 15–45
Time and Material Pricing
(LO 15-9)

2. Total price of job: $77,600

Southern Tier Heating, Inc. installs heating systems in new homes built in the southern tier counties of New York state. Jobs are priced using the time and materials method. The president of Southern Tier Heating, B. T. Ewing, is pricing a job involving the heating systems for six houses to be built by a local developer. He has made the following estimates.

Material cost	$60,000
Labor hours	400

The following predictions pertain to the company's operations for the next year.

Labor rate, including fringe benefits	$16.00 per hour
Annual labor hours	12,000 hours
Annual overhead costs:	
Material handling and storage	$25,000
Other overhead costs	$108,000
Annual cost of materials used	$250,000

Required: Southern Tier Heating adds a markup of $4.00 per hour on its time charges, but there is no markup on material costs.

1. Develop formulas for the company's (*a*) time charges and (*b*) material charges.
2. Compute the price for the job described above.
3. What would be the price of the job if Southern Tier Heating also added a markup of 10 percent on all material charges (including material handling and storage costs)?

Problem 15–46
Bidding on a Special Order
(LO 15-10)

2. Bid price: $29.90

Omaha Synthetic Fibers Inc. specializes in the manufacture of synthetic fibers that the company uses in many products such as blankets, coats, and uniforms for police and firefighters. The company has been in business for 20 years and has been profitable each of the past 15 years. Omaha Synthetic Fibers uses a standard-costing system and applies overhead on the basis of direct-labor hours. Management has recently received a request to bid on the manufacture of 800,000 blankets scheduled for delivery to several military bases. The bid must be stated at full cost per unit plus a return on full cost of no more than 15 percent before income taxes. Full cost has been defined as including all variable costs of manufacturing the product, a reasonable amount of fixed overhead, and reasonable incremental administrative costs associated with the manufacture and sale of the product. The contractor has indicated that bids in excess of $25 per blanket are not likely to be considered.

In order to prepare the bid for the 800,000 blankets, Andrea Lightner, director of cost management, has gathered the following information about the costs associated with the production of the blankets.

Direct material	$1.50 per pound of fibers
Direct labor	$7.00 per hour
Direct machine costs*	$10.00 per blanket
Variable overhead	$3.00 per direct-labor hour
Fixed overhead	$8.00 per direct-labor hour
Incremental administrative costs	$2,500 per 1,000 blankets
Special fee†	$.50 per blanket
Material usage	6 pounds per blanket
Production rate	4 blankets per direct-labor hour

*Direct machine costs consist of items such as special lubricants, replacement of needles used in stitching, and maintenance costs. These costs are not included in the normal overhead rates.

†Omaha Synthetic Fibers recently developed a new blanket fiber at a cost of $750,000. In an effort to recover this cost, management has instituted a policy of adding a $.50 fee to the cost of each blanket using the new fiber. To date, the company has recovered $125,000. Lightner knows that this fee does not fit within the definition of full cost as it is not a cost of manufacturing the product.

Required:

1. Calculate the minimum price per blanket that Omaha Synthetic Fibers Inc. could bid without reducing the company's net income.
2. Using the full cost criteria and the maximum allowable return specified, calculate Omaha Synthetic Fibers Inc.'s bid price per blanket.
3. Independent of your answer to requirement (2), assume that the price per blanket that Omaha Synthetic Fibers Inc. calculated using the cost-plus criteria specified is greater than the maximum bid of $25 per blanket allowed. Discuss the factors that management should consider before deciding whether to submit a bid at the maximum acceptable price of $25 per blanket.

(CMA, adapted)

Problem 15–47
Product Cost Distortion and Product Pricing; Departmental Overhead Rates
(LO 15-3, 15-7)

1. Predetermined overhead rate: $10 per direct-labor hour
5. Price, Advanced Model: $588.80

Sounds Fine, Inc. manufactures two models of stereo speakers. Cost estimates for the two models for the coming year are as follows:

	Basic Model	Advanced Model
Direct material	$160	$260
Direct labor (10 hours at $14 per hour)	140	140
Manufacturing overhead*	100	100
Total cost	$400	$500

*The predetermined overhead rate is $10 per direct-labor hour.

Each stereo speaker requires 10 hours of direct labor. Each Basic Model unit requires two hours in Department I and eight hours in Department II. Each unit of the Advanced Model requires eight hours in Department I and two hours in Department II. The manufacturing overhead costs expected during the coming year in Departments I and II are as follows:

	Department I	Department II
Variable overhead	$8 per direct-labor hour	$4 per direct-labor hour
Fixed overhead	$150,000	$150,000

The expected operating activity for the coming year is 37,500 direct-labor hours in each department.

Required:

1. Show how Sounds Fine, Inc. derived its plantwide predetermined overhead rate of $10 per direct-labor hour.
2. What will be the price of each model stereo speaker if the company prices its products at absorption manufacturing cost plus 15 percent?
3. Suppose Sounds Fine, Inc. were to use departmental overhead rates. Compute these rates for Departments I and II for the coming year.

4. Compute the absorption cost of each model stereo speaker using the departmental overhead rates computed in requirement (3).
5. Suppose management sticks with its policy of setting prices equal to absorption cost plus 15 percent. Compute the new price for each speaker model using the product costs developed in requirement (4).
6. Should Sounds Fine, Inc. use plantwide or departmental overhead rates? Explain your answer.

Cases

Case 15–48
Pricing in a Tight Market; Possible Plant Closing
(LO 15-1, 15-10)

2(a). Contribution margin, Standard: $350

Gargantuan Industries is a multiproduct company with several manufacturing plants. The Boise Plant manufactures and distributes two household cleaning and polishing compounds, standard and commercial, under the Super Clean label. The forecasted operating results for the first six months of the current year, when 100,000 cases of each compound are expected to be manufactured and sold, are presented in the following statement.

SUPER CLEAN COMPOUNDS—BOISE PLANT
Forecasted Results of Operations
For the Six-Month Period Ending June 30
(in Thousands)

	Standard	Commercial	Total
Sales	$2,000	$3,000	$5,000
Cost of goods sold	1,600	1,900	3,500
Gross profit	$ 400	$1,100	$1,500
Selling and administrative expenses:			
Variable	$ 400	$ 700	$1,100
Fixed*	240	360	600
Total selling and administrative expenses	$ 640	$1,060	$1,700
Income (loss) before taxes	$ (240)	$ 40	$ (200)

*The fixed selling and administrative expenses are allocated between the two products on the basis of dollar sales volume.

The standard compound sold for $20 a case and the commercial compound sold for $30 a case during the first six months of the year. The manufacturing costs, by case of product, are presented in the schedule below. Each product is manufactured on a separate production line. Annual normal manufacturing capacity is 200,000 cases of each product. However, the plant is capable of producing 250,000 cases of standard compound and 350,000 cases of commercial compound annually.

	Cost per Case	
	Standard	Commercial
Direct material	$ 7.00	$ 8.00
Direct labor	4.00	4.00
Variable manufacturing overhead	1.00	2.00
Fixed manufacturing overhead*	4.00	5.00
Total manufacturing cost	$16.00	$19.00
Variable selling and administrative costs	$ 4.00	$ 7.00

*Depreciation charges are 50 percent of the fixed manufacturing overhead of each line.

The following schedule reflects the consensus of top management regarding the price-volume alternatives for the Super Clean products for the last six months of the current year. These are essentially the same alternatives management had during the first six months of the year.

Standard Compound		Commercial Compound	
Alternative Prices (per case)	**Sales Volume (in cases)**	**Alternative Prices (per case)**	**Sales Volume (in cases)**
$18	120,000	$25	175,000
20	100,000	27	140,000
21	90,000	30	100,000
22	80,000	32	55,000
23	50,000	35	35,000

Gargantuan's top management believes the loss for the first six months reflects a tight profit margin caused by intense competition. Management also believes that many companies will leave this market by next year and profit should improve.

Required:

1. What unit selling price should Gargantuan Industries select for each of the Super Clean compounds for the remaining six months of the year? Support your selection with appropriate calculations.
2. Independently of your answer to requirement (1), assume the optimum alternatives for the last six months were as follows: a selling price of $23 and volume of 50,000 cases for the standard compound, and a selling price of $35 and volume of 35,000 cases for the commercial compound.
   a. Should Gargantuan Industries consider closing down its operations until January 1 of the next year in order to minimize its losses? Support your answer with appropriate calculations.
   b. Identify and discuss the qualitative factors that should be considered in deciding whether the Boise Plant should be closed down during the last six months of the current year.

(CMA, adapted)

Case 15–49
Bidding on a Special Order; Ethics
(LO 15-10)

2. Variable overhead rate: $5.40

Zylar Industries is a manufacturer of standard and custom-designed bottling equipment. Early in December 20x0, Lyan Company asked Zylar to quote a price for a custom-designed bottling machine to be delivered in April. Lyan intends to make a decision on the purchase of such a machine by January 1, so Zylar would have the entire first quarter of 20x1 to build the equipment.

Zylar's pricing policy for custom-designed equipment is 50 percent markup on absorption manufacturing cost. Lyan's specifications for the equipment have been reviewed by Zylar's Engineering and Cost Management Departments, which made the following estimates for direct material and direct labor.

Direct material	$256,000
Direct labor (11,000 hours at $15)	165,000

Manufacturing overhead is applied on the basis of direct-labor hours. Zylar normally plans to run its plant at a level of 15,000 direct-labor hours per month and assigns overhead on the basis of 180,000 direct-labor hours per year. The overhead application rate for 20x1 of $9.00 per hour is based on the following budgeted manufacturing overhead costs for 20x1.

Variable manufacturing overhead	$ 972,000
Fixed manufacturing overhead	648,000
Total manufacturing overhead	$1,620,000

Zylar's production schedule calls for 12,000 direct-labor hours per month during the first quarter. If Zylar is awarded the contract for the Lyan equipment, production of one of its standard products would have to be reduced. This is necessary because production levels can only be increased to 15,000 direct-labor hours each month on short notice. Furthermore, Zylar's employees are unwilling to work overtime.

Sales of the standard product equal to the reduced production would be lost, but there would be no permanent loss of future sales or customers. The standard product for which the production schedule would be reduced has a unit sales price of $12,000 and the following cost structure.

Direct material	$2,500
Direct labor (250 hours at $15)	3,750
Manufacturing overhead (250 hours at $9)	2,250
Total cost	$8,500

Lyan needs the custom-designed equipment to increase its bottle-making capacity so that it will not have to buy bottles from an outside supplier. Lyan Company requires 5,000,000 bottles annually. Its present equipment has a maximum capacity of 4,500,000 bottles with a directly traceable cash outlay cost of 15 cents per bottle. Thus, Lyan has had to purchase 500,000 bottles from a supplier at 40 cents each. The new equipment would allow Lyan to manufacture its entire annual demand for bottles at a direct-material cost savings of 1 cent per bottle. Zylar estimates that Lyan's annual bottle demand will continue to be 5,000,000 bottles over the next five years, the estimated life of the special-purpose equipment.

Required: Zylar Industries plans to submit a bid to Lyan Company for the manufacture of the special-purpose bottling equipment.

1. Calculate the bid Zylar would submit if it follows its standard pricing policy for special-purpose equipment.
2. Calculate the minimum bid Zylar would be willing to submit on the Lyan equipment that would result in the same total contribution margin as planned for the first quarter of 20x1.
3. Suppose Zylar Industries has submitted a bid slightly above the minimum calculated in requirement (2). Upon receiving Zylar's bid, Lyan's assistant purchasing manager telephoned his friend at Tygar Corporation: "Hey Joe, we just got a bid from Zylar Industries on some customized equipment. I think Tygar would stand a good chance of beating it. Stop by the house this evening, and I'll show you the details of Zylar's bid and the specifications on the machine."
   Is Lyan Company's assistant purchasing manager acting ethically? Explain.

(CMA, adapted)

16 Capital Expenditure Decisions

FOCUS COMPANY >>>

THIS CHAPTER'S FOCUS is on the City of Mountainview, New Mexico. Mountainview's mayor and city council face a variety of decisions that involve cash flows over several periods of time. The decision tool used in making such multiperiod decisions is called discounted-cash-flow analysis, because it takes account of the timing of cash flows that occur in different time periods. Among the decisions that Mountainview's leadership makes is whether to purchase a new computer system for the city government. Since the City of Mountainview is not a profit-seeking enterprise, income taxes play no role in the decisions faced by the city's leadership.

Source: NPS Photo by Robb Hannawacker

<<< IN CONTRAST

HIGH COUNTRY
DEPARTMENT STORES

In contrast to the Mountainview city government setting, in which income taxes play no role in decisions, we turn our attention to High Country Department Stores. This chain of retail department stores, located in Mountainview, also faces some significant decisions involving multiperiod cash flows. Since High Country is a profit-seeking enterprise, it does pay income taxes. Therefore, when the company's management uses discounted-cash-flow analysis, it must take taxes into account. Among the decisions faced by High Country's management is whether to purchase a new computerized checkout system.

After completing this chapter, you should be able to:

16-1 Use the net-present-value method and the internal-rate-of-return method to evaluate an investment proposal.

16-2 Compare the net-present-value and internal-rate-of-return methods, and state the assumptions underlying each method.

16-3 Use both the total-cost approach and the incremental-cost approach to evaluate an investment proposal.

16-4 Determine the after-tax cash flows in an investment analysis.

16-5 Use the Modified Accelerated Cost Recovery System to determine an asset's depreciation schedule for tax purposes.

16-6 Evaluate an investment proposal using a discounted-cash-flow analysis, giving full consideration to income-tax issues.

16-7 Discuss the difficulty of ranking investment proposals, and use the profitability index.

16-8 Use the payback method and accounting-rate-of-return method to evaluate capital investment projects.

16-9 Describe the impact of activity-based costing and advanced manufacturing technology on capital-budgeting decisions.

16-10 Explain the impact of inflation on a capital-budgeting analysis (Appendix B).

Managers in all organizations periodically face major decisions that involve cash flows over several years. Decisions involving the acquisition of machinery, vehicles, buildings, or land are examples of such decisions. Other examples include decisions involving significant changes in a production process or adding a major new line of products or services to the organization's activities.

Decisions involving cash inflows and outflows beyond the current year are called **capital-budgeting decisions.** Managers encounter two types of capital-budgeting decisions.

Acceptance-or-Rejection Decisions In **acceptance-or-rejection decisions,** managers must decide whether they should undertake a particular capital investment project. In such a decision, the required funds are available or readily obtainable, and management must decide whether the project is worthwhile. For example, the controller for the city of Mountainview is faced with a decision as to whether to replace one of the city's oldest street-cleaning machines. The funds are available in the city's capital budget. The question is whether the cost savings with the new machine will justify the expenditure.

Capital-Rationing Decisions In **capital-rationing decisions,** managers must decide which of several worthwhile projects makes the best use of limited investment funds. To illustrate, suppose the voters in the city of Mountainview have recently passed a proposition mandating the city government to undertake a cost-reduction program to trim administrative expenses. The voters also passed a bond issue, which enables the city government to raise \$100,000 through the sale of bonds, to provide capital to finance the cost-reduction program. The mayor has in mind three cost-reduction programs, each of which would reduce administrative costs significantly over the next five years. However, the city can afford only two of the programs with the \$100,000 of investment capital available. The mayor's decision problem is to decide which projects to pursue.

Focus on Projects Capital-budgeting problems tend to focus on specific projects or programs. Is it best for Mountainview to purchase the new street cleaner or not? Which cost-reduction programs will provide the city with the greatest benefits? Should a university buy a new electron microscope? Should a manufacturing firm acquire a computer-integrated manufacturing system?

Over time, as managers make decisions about a variety of specific programs and projects, the organization as a whole becomes the sum total of its individual investments, activities, programs, and projects. The organization's performance in any particular year is the combined result of all the projects under way during that year.

Chapter Organization This chapter is divided into three modular sections, each of which explores a particular aspect of capital expenditure decisions. Section 1 should be studied first, after which either Section 2 or Section 3 may be studied.

- Section 1: Discounted-Cash-Flow Analysis
- Section 2: Income Taxes and Capital Budgeting
- Section 3: Alternative Methods for Making Investment Decisions

Section 1: Discounted-Cash-Flow Analysis

How do managers evaluate capital investment projects? Our discussion will be illustrated by several decisions made by the Mountainview city government. The controller of Mountainview routinely advises the mayor and city council on major capital-investment decisions.

CITY OF MOUNTAINVIEW

Learning Objective 16-1

Use the net-present-value method and the internal-rate-of-return method to evaluate an investment proposal.

Currently under consideration is the purchase of a new street cleaner. The controller has estimated that the city's old street-cleaning machine would last another five years. A new street cleaner, which also would last for five years, can be purchased for \$50,470. It would cost the city \$14,000 less each year to operate the new equipment than it costs to operate the old machine. The expected cost savings with the new machine are due to lower expected maintenance costs. Thus, the new street cleaner will cost \$50,470 and save \$70,000 over its five-year life (\$70,000 = 5 × \$14,000 savings per year). Since the \$70,000 in cost savings exceeds the \$50,470 acquisition cost, one might be tempted to conclude that the new machine should be purchased. However, *this analysis is flawed, since it does not account for the time value of money.* The \$50,470 acquisition cost will occur now, but the cost savings are spread over a five-year period. It is a mistake to add cash flows occurring at different points in time. The proper approach is to use **discounted-cash-flow analysis,** which takes into account the timing of the cash flows. There are two widely used methods of discounted-cash-flow analysis: the net-present-value method and the internal-rate-of-return method. [Those who wish to review the basic concept of present value should read Appendix II (on pages 766–772) before continuing.]

Net-Present-Value Method

The following four steps constitute a net-present-value analysis of an investment proposal:

1. Prepare a table showing the cash flows during each year of the proposed investment.
2. Compute the present value of each cash flow, using a discount rate that reflects the cost of acquiring investment capital. This discount rate is often called the **hurdle rate** or **minimum desired rate of return.**
3. Compute the **net present value,** which is the sum of the present values of the cash flows.
4. If the net present value (NPV) is equal to or greater than zero, accept the investment proposal. Otherwise, reject it.

> "We're key members of the decision making team when it comes to significant capital expenditure decisions." (16a)
>
> **Ford Motor Company**

Exhibit 16–1 displays these four steps for the Mountainview controller's street-cleaner decision. In step (2) the controller used a discount rate of 10 percent. Notice that the cost savings are \$14,000 in each of the years 1 through 5. Thus, the cash flows in those years comprise a five-year, \$14,000 annuity. The controller used the annuity discount factor to compute the present value of the five years of cost savings. (The discount factors are found in Table IV in Appendix A at the end of this chapter.)

The net-present-value analysis indicates that the city should purchase the new street cleaner. The present value of the cost savings exceeds the new machine's acquisition cost.

Internal-Rate-of-Return Method

An alternative discounted-cash-flow method for analyzing investment proposals is the internal-rate-of-return method. An asset's **internal rate of return** (or **time-adjusted rate of return**) is the true economic return earned by the asset over its life. Another way of stating the definition is that an asset's *internal rate of return (IRR)* is the discount rate that would be required in a net-present-value analysis in order for the asset's net present value to be exactly *zero.*

What is the internal rate of return on Mountainview's proposed street-cleaner acquisition? Recall that the asset has a positive net present value, given that the city's cost of acquiring investment capital is 10 percent. Would you expect the asset's IRR to be higher or lower than 10 percent? Think about this question intuitively. The higher the discount rate used in a net-present-value analysis, the lower the present value of all future cash

Exhibit 16–1
Net-Present-Value Method

CITY OF MOUNTAINVIEW

MOUNTAINVIEW CITY GOVERNMENT
Purchase of Street Cleaner
($r = .10, n = 5$)

Step 1	**Time 0**	**Time 1**	**Time 2**	**Time 3**	**Time 4**	**Time 5**
Acquisition cost	\$(50,470)					
Annual cost savings		\$14,000	\$14,000	\$14,000	\$14,000	\$14,000

Step 2 Present value of annuity = \$14,000(3.791)

Annuity discount factor for $r = .10$ and $n = 5$ from Table IV in Appendix A

	Time 0			Time 3
Present value	\$(50,470)			\$53,074

Step 3 Net present value \$2,604

Step 4 Accept proposal, since net present value is positive.

flows will be. This is true because a higher discount rate means that it is even more important to have the money earlier instead of later. Thus, a discount rate higher than 10 percent would be required to drive the new street cleaner's net present value down to zero.

Finding the Internal Rate of Return How can we find this rate? One way is trial and error. We could experiment with different discount rates until we find the one that yields a zero net present value. We already know that a 10 percent discount rate yields a positive NPV. Let's try 14 percent. Discounting the five-year, $14,000 cost-savings annuity at 14 percent yields a negative NPV of $(2,408).

(3.433)($14,000) − $50,470 = ($2,408)

↑ Annuity discount factor for $r = .14$ and $n = 5$ from Table IV in Appendix A.

What does this negative NPV at a 14 percent discount rate mean? We increased the discount rate too much. Therefore, the street cleaner's internal rate of return must lie between 10 percent and 14 percent. Let's try 12 percent:

(3.605)($14,000) − $50,470 = 0

↑ Annuity discount factor for $r = .12$ and $n = 5$ from Table IV in Appendix A.

That's it. The new street cleaner's internal rate of return is 12 percent. With a 12 percent discount rate, the investment proposal's net present value is zero, since the street cleaner's acquisition cost is equal to the present value of the cost savings.

We could have found the internal rate of return more easily in this case, because the street cleaner's cash flows exhibit a very special pattern. The cash inflows in years 1 through 5 are identical, as shown below.

Time	0	1	2	3	4	5
Cash flow	$(50,470)	$14,000	$14,000	$14,000	$14,000	$14,000
	↑ Initial cash outflow (acquisition cost)	Equal cash inflows (operating-cost savings)				

When we have this special pattern of cash flows, the internal rate of return is determined in two steps, as follows:

1. Divide the initial cash outflow by the equivalent annual cash inflows:

$$\frac{\$50,470}{\$14,000} = 3.605 = \text{Annuity discount factor}$$

2. In Table IV, find the discount rate associated with the annuity discount factor computed in step (1), given the appropriate number of years in the annuity.

From Table IV of Appendix A

	r		
	10%	12%	14%
$n = 5$	3.791	3.605	3.433

Decision Rule Now that we have determined the investment proposal's internal rate of return to be 12 percent, how do we use this fact in making a decision? The decision rule in the internal-rate-of-return method is to accept an investment proposal if its internal rate of return is greater than the organization's cost of capital (or hurdle rate). Thus, Mountainview's controller should recommend that the new street cleaner be purchased. The internal rate of return on the proposal, 12 percent, exceeds the city's hurdle rate, 10 percent.

To summarize, the internal-rate-of-return method of discounted-cash-flow analysis includes the following three steps:

1. Prepare a table showing the cash flows during each year of the proposed investment. This table will be identical to the cash-flow table prepared under the net-present-value method. (See Exhibit 16–1.)
2. Compute the internal rate of return (IRR) for the proposed investment. This is accomplished by finding a discount rate that yields a zero net present value for the proposed investment.
3. If the IRR is equal to or greater than the hurdle rate (cost of acquiring investment capital), accept the investment proposal. Otherwise, reject it.

> "Our role is to be internal management consultants for the key decisions facing management." (16b)
> **Hewlett-Packard**

Recovery of Investment The reason for purchasing an asset is an expectation that it will provide benefits in the future. Thus, Mountainview may purchase the new street cleaner because of expected future operating-cost savings. For a capital investment proposal to be accepted, the expected future benefits must be sufficient for the purchaser to recover the investment and earn a return on the investment equal to or greater than the cost of acquiring capital. We can illustrate this point with Mountainview's street-cleaner acquisition.

Exhibit 16–2 examines the investment proposal's cash flows from the perspective of recovering the investment and earning a return on the investment. Focus on the Year 1 column in the exhibit. The street cleaner costs \$50,470, so this is the unrecovered investment at the beginning of year 1. The operating-cost savings in year 1 are \$14,000. Since the asset's internal rate of return is 12 percent, it must earn \$6,056 during the first year (12% × \$50,470). Therefore, \$6,056 of the \$14,000 cost savings represents a *return on* the unrecovered investment. This leaves \$7,944 as a *recovery of* the investment during year 1 (\$14,000 − \$6,056). Subtracting the year 1 recovery of investment from the unrecovered investment at the beginning of the year leaves an unrecovered investment of \$42,526 at year-end (\$50,470 − \$7,944).

Exhibit 16–2
Recovery of Investment and Return on Investment

MOUNTAINVIEW CITY GOVERNMENT
Purchase of Street Cleaner
($r = .12, n = 5$)

	Year 1	Year 2	Year 3	Year 4	Year 5
1. Unrecovered investment at beginning of year	\$50,470	\$42,526	\$33,629	\$23,664	\$12,504
2. Cost savings during year	14,000	14,000	14,000	14,000	14,000
3. Return on unrecovered investment [12% × amount in row (1)]	6,056	5,103	4,035	2,840	1,500
4. Recovery of investment during year [row (2) amount minus row (3) amount]	7,944	8,897	9,965	11,160	12,500
5. Unrecovered investment at end of year [row (1) amount minus row (4) amount]	42,526	33,629	23,664	12,504	4*

* We are left with an unrecovered investment of \$4 because of accumulated rounding errors in the table. If we had carried out each number to cents, the table would have finished up with an unrecovered investment of zero.

Uneven Cash Flows A complication that often arises in finding a project's internal rate of return is an uneven pattern of cash flows. In Mountainview's proposed street-cleaner acquisition, the cost savings are $14,000 per year for all five years of the machine's life. Suppose, instead, that the pattern of cost savings is as follows:

Cost savings	$14,000	$14,000	$12,000	$10,000	$8,000	
Year	1	2	3	4	5	Time

Such an uneven cost-savings pattern is quite plausible, since the maintenance costs could rise in the machine's latter years. When the cash-flow pattern is uneven, iteration must be used to find the internal rate of return. You can try various discount rates iteratively until you find the one that yields a zero net present value for the investment proposal. This sort of computationally intensive work is the kind of task for which computers are designed. Numerous computer software packages are available to find a project's IRR almost instantaneously.

Learning Objective 16-2

Compare the net-present-value and internal-rate-of-return methods, and state the assumptions underlying each method.

Comparing the NPV and IRR Methods

The decision to accept or reject an investment proposal can be made using either the net-present-value method or the internal-rate-of-return method. The different approaches used in the methods are summarized as follows:

Net-Present-Value Method

1. Compute the investment proposal's net present value, using the organization's hurdle rate as the discount rate.
2. Accept the investment proposal if its net present value is equal to or greater than zero; otherwise reject it.

Internal-Rate-of-Return Method

1. Compute the investment proposal's internal rate of return, which is the discount rate that yields a zero net present value for the project.
2. Accept the investment proposal if its internal rate of return is equal to or greater than the organization's hurdle rate; otherwise reject it.

Notice that the hurdle rate is used in each of the two methods.

Advantages of Net-Present-Value Method The net-present-value method exhibits two potential advantages over the internal-rate-of-return method. First, if the investment analysis is carried out by hand, it is easier to compute a project's NPV than its IRR. For example, if the cash flows are uneven across time, trial and error must be used to find the IRR. This advantage of the NPV approach is not as important, however, when a computer is used.

A second potential advantage of the NPV method is that the analyst can adjust for risk considerations. For some investment proposals, the further into the future that a cash flow occurs, the less certain the analyst can be about the amount of the cash flow. Thus, the later a projected cash flow occurs, the riskier it may be. It is possible to adjust a net-present-value analysis for such risk factors by using a higher discount rate for later cash flows than earlier cash flows. It is not possible to include such a risk adjustment in the internal-rate-of-return method, because the analysis solves for only a single discount rate, the project's IRR.

Assumptions Underlying Discounted-Cash-Flow Analysis

As is true of any decision model, discounted-cash-flow methods are based on assumptions. Four assumptions underlie the NPV and IRR methods of investment analysis.

1. In the present-value calculations used in the NPV and IRR methods, all cash flows are treated as though they occur at year-end. If the city of Mountainview were to acquire the new street cleaner, the $14,000 in annual operating-cost savings actually would occur uniformly throughout each year. The additional computational complexity that would be required to reflect the exact timing of all cash flows would complicate an investment analysis considerably. The error introduced by the year-end cash-flow assumption generally is not large enough to cause any concern.
2. Discounted-cash-flow analyses treat the cash flows associated with an investment project as though they were known with certainty. Although methods of capital budgeting under uncertainty have been developed, they are not used widely in practice. Most decision makers do not feel that the additional benefits in improved decisions are worth the additional complexity involved. As mentioned above, however, risk adjustments can be made in an NPV analysis to partially account for uncertainty about the cash flows.
3. Both the NPV and IRR methods assume that each cash inflow is immediately reinvested in another project that earns a return for the organization. In the NPV method, each cash inflow is assumed to be reinvested at the same rate used to compute the project's NPV, the organization's hurdle rate. In the IRR method, each cash inflow is assumed to be reinvested at the same rate as the project's internal rate of return.

   What does this reinvestment assumption mean in practice? In the case of Mountainview's proposed new street cleaner, the city must instantly reinvest the money saved each year either in some interest-bearing investment or in some other capital project.
4. A discounted-cash-flow analysis assumes a perfect capital market. This implies that money can be borrowed or lent at an interest rate equal to the hurdle rate used in the analysis.

In practice, these four assumptions rarely are satisfied. Nevertheless, discounted-cash-flow models provide an effective and widely used method of investment analysis. The improved decision making that would result from using more complicated models seldom is worth the additional cost of information and analysis.

Choosing the Hurdle Rate

The choice of a hurdle rate is a complex problem in finance. The hurdle rate is determined by management based on the **investment opportunity rate.** This is the rate of return the organization can earn on its best alternative investments of equivalent risk. In general, the greater a project's risk is, the higher the hurdle rate should be.

Investment versus Financing Decisions In capital-expenditure decisions, the investment decision should be separated from the financing decision. The decision as to whether to invest in a project should be made first using a discounted-cash-flow approach with a hurdle rate based on the investment opportunity rate. If a project is accepted, then a separate analysis should be made as to the best way to finance the project.

Cost of Capital How do organizations generate investment capital? Nonprofit organizations, such as local, city, and state governments and charitable organizations, often acquire capital through special bond issues or borrowing from financial institutions. In such cases, the cost of capital is based on the interest rate paid on the debt.

Another source of capital for both nonprofit and profit-oriented organizations is invested funds, such as a university's endowment fund. In this case, the cost of using the capital for an investment project is the interest rate forgone on the original investment. For example, suppose your university's endowment earns interest at the rate of

10 percent. If the university uses a portion of these funds to buy new laboratory equipment, the cost of capital is the 10 percent interest rate that is no longer earned on the funds removed from the endowment.

Profit-oriented enterprises fund capital projects by borrowing, by issuing stock, or by using invested funds. In most cases, capital projects are funded by all of these sources. Then the cost of capital should be a combination of the costs of obtaining money from each of these sources.

Depreciable Assets

When a long-lived asset is purchased, its acquisition cost is allocated to the time periods in the asset's life through depreciation charges. However, we did not include any depreciation charges in our discounted-cash-flow analysis. Both the NPV and IRR methods focus on cash flows, and *periodic depreciation charges are not cash flows.* Suppose that the controller for the city of Mountainview depreciates assets using the straight-line method. If the city purchases the new street cleaner for $50,470, the depreciation charges will be recorded as follows:

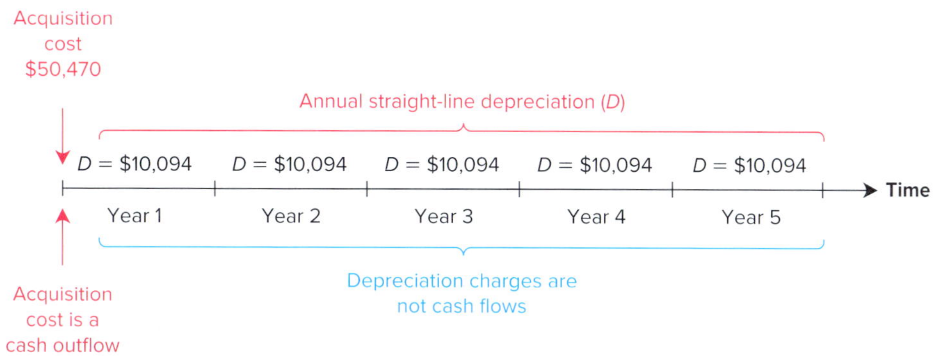

The only cash flow in the diagram above is the $50,470 cash outflow incurred to acquire the street cleaner. The $10,094 annual depreciation charges are not cash flows. Thus, the acquisition cost is recorded as a cash flow in our investment analysis (Exhibit 16–1), but the annual depreciation charges are not.

Nonprofit versus Profit-Oriented Organizations Suppose our illustration had focused on a profit-seeking enterprise instead of the city of Mountainview. For example, if the street-cleaner acquisition is contemplated by a theme-park company, would this change our treatment of the annual depreciation charges for the street cleaner? The depreciation charges still are not cash flows. However, in a profit-seeking enterprise, depreciation expense is deductible for income-tax purposes. Since tax payments *are* cash flows, the reduction in tax due to depreciation expense is a legitimate cash flow that should be included in an investment analysis. In Section 2 of this chapter, we will study the tax implications of depreciable assets in detail. For now, let's return to our focus on the city of Mountainview. As a nonprofit enterprise, the city pays no income tax. Therefore, depreciation is irrelevant in our discounted-cash-flow analysis.

Comparing Two Investment Projects

Learning Objective 16-3

Use both the total-cost approach and the incremental-cost approach to evaluate an investment proposal.

We have developed all of the tools and concepts required to use discounted-cash-flow analysis in an investment decision. Now we can expand on our discussion using an illustration that combines the net-present-value method of investment analysis with the concepts of relevant costs and benefits studied in Chapter 14. The first step in any investment analysis is to determine the cash flows that are relevant to the analysis.

The computing system used by the city of Mountainview is outdated. The city council has voted to purchase a new computing system to be funded through municipal bonds. The mayor has asked the city's controller to make a recommendation as to which of two computing systems should be purchased. The two systems are equivalent in their ability to meet the city's needs and in their ease of use. The mainframe system consists of one large mainframe computer with remote terminals and printers located throughout the city offices. The personal computer system consists of a much smaller mainframe computer, a few remote terminals, and a dozen personal computers, which will be networked to the small mainframe. Each system would last five years. The controller has decided to use a 12 percent hurdle rate for the analysis.

Exhibit 16–3 presents data pertinent to the decision. Examine these data carefully. Most of the items are self-explanatory. Item (9) is the annual cost of a data-link service. This service enables Mountainview to participate in a nationwide computer network, which allows cities to exchange information on such issues as crime rates, demographic data, and economic data. Item (10) is the revenue the city will receive from two time-sharing customers. The Mountainview City School District and the county legislature each has agreed to pay the city in return for a limited amount of time on the city's computer.

Before we begin the steps of the net-present-value method, let's examine the cash-flow data in Exhibit 16–3 to determine if any of the data can be ignored as irrelevant. Notice that items (1) and (9) do not differ between the two alternatives. Regardless of which new computing system is purchased, certain components of the old system can be sold now for $25,000. Moreover, the data-link service will cost $20,000 annually, regardless of which system is acquired. If the only purpose of the NPV analysis is to determine

Exhibit 16–3
Data for Extended Illustration of Net-Present-Value Analysis

MOUNTAINVIEW CITY GOVERNMENT
Purchase of Computing System

		Mainframe System	Personal Computer System
(1)	Salvage value of city's old computer (time 0)*	$ 25,000	$ 25,000
(2)	Acquisition cost of new system (time 0)	(400,000)	(300,000)
(3)	Acquisition cost of software (time 0)	(40,000)	(75,000)
(4)	Cost of updating system (time 3)	(40,000)	(60,000)
(5)	Salvage value of new system (time 5)	50,000	30,000
	Operating costs (times 1,2,3,4,5):		
(6)	Personnel	(300,000)	(220,000)
(7)	Maintenance	(25,000)	(10,000)
(8)	Other	(10,000)	(5,000)
(9)	Data-link service (times 1,2,3,4,5)	(20,000)	(20,000)
(10)	Revenue from time-share customers (times 1,2,3,4,5)	20,000	-

*Time 0 denotes "immediately." Time 1 denotes the end of year 1, etc.

which computer system is the least-cost alternative, items (1) and (9) can be ignored as irrelevant, since they will affect both alternatives' NPVs equally.

Total-Cost Approach Exhibit 16–4 displays a net-present-value analysis of the two alternative computing systems. The exhibit uses the *total-cost approach,* in which all of the relevant costs of each computing system are included in the analysis. Then the net present value of the cost of the mainframe system is compared with that of the personal computer system. Since the NPV of the costs is lower with the personal computer system, that will be the controller's recommendation to the Mountainview City Council.

A decision such as Mountainview's computing-system choice, in which the objective is to select the alternative with the lowest cost, is called a *least-cost decision.* Rather than maximizing the NPV of cash inflows minus cash outflows, the objective is to *minimize the NPV of the costs to be incurred.*

Incremental-Cost Approach Exhibit 16–5 displays a different net-present-value analysis of the city's two alternative computing systems. This exhibit uses the *incremental-cost approach,* in which the difference in the cost of each relevant item under the two alternative systems is included in the analysis. For example, the incremental computer acquisition cost is shown in Exhibit 16–5 as $(100,000). This is the amount by which the acquisition cost of the mainframe system exceeds that of the personal computer system.

Exhibit 16–4
Net-Present-Value Analysis: Total-Cost Approach

CITY OF MOUNTAINVIEW

MOUNTAINVIEW CITY GOVERNMENT
Purchase of Computing System
(r = .12, n = 5)

Item Number (from Exhibit 16–3)	Time 0	Time 1	Time 2	Time 3	Time 4	Time 5
Mainframe System						
(2) Acquisition cost: computer	$(400,000)					
(3) Acquisition cost: software	(40,000)					
(4) System update				$ (40,000)		
(5) Salvage value						$ 50,000
(6), (7), (8) Operating costs		$(335,000)	$(335,000)	(335,000)	$(335,000)	(335,000)
(10) Time-sharing revenue		20,000	20,000	20,000	20,000	20,000
Total cash flow	$(440,000)	$(315,000)	$(315,000)	$(355,000)	$(315,000)	$(265,000)
× Discount factor	× 1.000	× .893	× .797	× .712	× .636	× .567
Present value	$(440,000)	$(281,295)	$(251,055)	$(252,760)	$(200,340)	$(150,255)
Net present value of costs			Sum = $(1,575,705)			
Personal Computer System						
(2) Acquisition cost: computer	$(300,000)					
(3) Acquisition cost: software	(75,000)					
(4) System update				$ (60,000)		
(5) Salvage value						$ 30,000
(6), (7), (8) Operating costs		$(235,000)	$(235,000)	(235,000)	$(235,000)	(235,000)
(10) Time-sharing revenue		–0–	–0–	–0–	–0–	–0–
Total cash flow	$(375,000)	$(235,000)	$(235,000)	$(295,000)	$(235,000)	$(205,000)
× Discount factor	× 1.000	× .893	× .797	× .712	× .636	× .567
Present value	$(375,000)	$(209,855)	$(187,295)	$(210,040)	$(149,460)	$(116,235)
Net present value of costs			Sum = $(1,247,885)			
Difference in NPV of costs (favors personal computer system)			$ (327,820)			

MOUNTAINVIEW CITY GOVERNMENT Purchase of Computing System ($r = .12, n = 5$)						
Item Number (from Exhibit 16–3)	**Time 0**	**Time 1**	**Time 2**	**Time 3**	**Time 4**	**Time 5**
Incremental Cost of Mainframe System over Personal Computer System						
(2) Acquisition cost: computer	$(100,000)					
(3) Acquisition cost: software	35,000					
(4) System update				$ 20,000		
(5) Salvage value						$ 20,000
(6), (7), (8) Operating costs		$(100,000)	$(100,000)	(100,000)	$(100,000)	(100,000)
(10) Time-sharing revenue		20,000	20,000	20,000	20,000	20,000
Incremental cash flow	$ (65,000)	$ (80,000)	$ (80,000)	$ (60,000)	$ (80,000)	$ (60,000)
× Discount factor	× 1.000	× .893	× .797	× .712	× .636	× .567
Present value	$ (65,000)	$ (71,440)	$ (63,760)	$ (42,720)	$ (50,880)	$ (34,020)
Net present value of incremental costs (favors personal computer system)				Sum = $(327,820)		

Exhibit 16–5

Net-Present-Value Analysis: Incremental-Cost Approach

CITY OF MOUNTAINVIEW

The result of this analysis is that the NPV of the costs of the mainframe system exceeds that of the personal computer system by $327,820. Notice that this is the same as the difference in NPVs shown at the bottom of Exhibit 16–4.

The total-cost and incremental-cost approaches always will yield equivalent conclusions. Choosing between them is a matter of personal preference.

Managerial Accountant's Role

To use discounted-cash-flow analysis in deciding about investment projects, managers need accurate cash-flow projections. This is where the managerial accountant plays a role. The accountant often is asked to predict cash flows related to operating-cost savings, additional working-capital requirements, or incremental costs and revenues. Such predictions are difficult in a world of uncertainty. The managerial accountant often draws upon historical accounting data to help in making cost predictions. Knowledge of market conditions, economic trends, and the likely reactions of competitors also can be important in projecting cash flows.

Postaudit

"We make considerable use of discounted-cash-flow analysis when we're considering facility upgrades. We realize that we need to continually invest in our research facilities in order to do the kind of research that is needed." (16c)

Cornell University

The discounted-cash-flow approach to evaluating investment proposals requires cash-flow projections. The desirability of a proposal depends heavily on those projections. If they are highly inaccurate, they may lead the organization to accept undesirable projects or to reject projects that should be pursued. Because of the importance of the capital-budgeting process, most organizations systematically follow up on projects to see how they turn out. This procedure is called a **postaudit** (or **reappraisal**).

In a postaudit, the managerial accountant gathers information about the actual cash flows generated by a project. Then the project's actual net present value or internal rate of return is computed. Finally, the projections made for the project are compared with the actual results. If the project has not lived up to expectations, an investigation may be warranted to determine what went awry. Sometimes a postaudit will reveal shortcomings in the cash-flow projection process. In such cases, action may be taken to improve future cash-flow predictions. Two types of errors can occur in discounted-cash-flow analyses: undesirable projects may be accepted, and desirable projects may be rejected. The postaudit is a tool for following up on accepted projects. Thus, a postaudit helps to detect only the first kind of error, not the second.

As in any performance-evaluation process, a postaudit should not be used punitively. The focus of a postaudit should provide information to the capital-budgeting staff, the project manager, and the management team.

Capital-investment decisions go through an elaborate capital-budgeting process. This robotic arm packages candy at the chocolate factory of Lindt & Sprüngli in Zurich, Switzerland. Due to this equipment's significant cost, the capital expenditure decision was carefully analyzed. For what types of decisions would capital budgeting be used by the administration of the college you attend?

Real Option Analysis

One way managerial accountants can assist the management team is by assessing the consequences of changes in an investment decision that may develop after the project has been approved. In long-term projects, there is often considerable uncertainty about the future cash flows, due to uncertainty about future economic, political, or cultural events. As a project unfolds, management may decide to alter the course of the project or even postpone it. Suppose, for example, that the city of Mountainview decides to build a new municipal water system that will take 5 years to build and is expected to last 75 years. The project involves collaboration with several private enterprises, other municipalities, and the state and federal governments. As the project develops and various uncertainties are resolved, it may be desirable to make changes in the water system or postpone certain parts of it. A capital-budgeting tool called *real option analysis* can be used to quantify and analyze the merits of such changes. Real option analysis is covered in advanced cost management and finance courses.

Section 2: Income Taxes and Capital Budgeting

Learning Objective **16-4**

Determine the after-tax cash flows in an investment analysis.

When a business makes a profit, it usually must pay income taxes, just as individuals do. Since many of the cash flows associated with an investment proposal affect the company's profit, they also affect the firm's income-tax liability. The following equation shows the four types of items that appear on an income statement.

Income = Revenue − Expenses + Gains − Losses

Any aspect of an investment project that affects any of the items in this equation generally will affect the company's income-tax payments. These income-tax payments are cash flows, and they must be considered in any discounted-cash-flow analysis. In some cases, tax considerations are so crucial in a capital-investment decision that they dominate all other aspects of the analysis.

After-Tax Cash Flows

The first step in a discounted-cash-flow analysis for a profit-seeking enterprise is to determine the after-tax cash flows associated with the investment projects under consideration. An **after-tax cash flow** is the cash flow expected after all tax implications have been taken into account. Each financial aspect of a project must be examined carefully to determine its potential tax impact.

HIGH COUNTRY
DEPARTMENT STORES

To illustrate the tax implications of various types of financial items, we will focus on a retail business. High Country Department Stores, Inc. operates two department stores in the city of Mountainview. The firm has a large downtown store and a smaller branch store in the suburbs. The company is quite profitable, and management is considering several capital projects that will enhance the firm's future profit potential. Before analyzing these projects, let's pause to consider the tax issues the company is likely to face. For the purposes of our discussion, we will assume that High Country Department Stores' income tax rate is 40 percent. Thus, if the company's net income is $1,000,000, its income-tax payment will be $400,000 ($1,000,000 × 40%).

Cash Revenue Suppose High Country's management is considering the purchase of an additional delivery truck. The sales manager estimates that a new truck will allow the company to increase annual sales revenue by $110,000. Further suppose that this incremental sales revenue will be received in cash during the year of sale. Any credit sales will be paid in cash within a short time period. High Country's additional annual sales revenue will result in an increase of $60,000 per year in cost of goods sold. Moreover, the additional merchandise sold will be paid for in cash during the same year as the related sales. Thus, the net incremental cash inflow resulting from the sales increase is $50,000 per year ($110,000 − $60,000).

What is High Country's *after-tax cash flow* from the incremental sales revenue, net of cost of goods sold? As the following calculation shows, the firm's incremental cash inflow from the additional sales is only $30,000.

Incremental sales revenue, net of cost of goods sold (cash inflow)	$50,000
Incremental income tax (cash outflow), $50,000 × 40%	(20,000)
After-tax cash flow (net inflow after taxes)	$30,000

Although the incremental sales amounted to an additional net cash inflow of $50,000, the cash outflow for income taxes also increased by $20,000. Thus, the after-tax cash inflow from the incremental sales, net of cost of goods sold, is $30,000.

A quick method for computing the after-tax cash inflow from incremental sales is the following:

$$\begin{array}{ccccc} \text{Incremental sales revenue, net of cost of goods sold} & \times & (1 - \text{Tax rate}) & = & \text{After-tax cash inflow} \\ \$50{,}000 & \times & (1 - .40) & = & \$30{,}000 \end{array}$$

Cash Expenses What are the tax implications of cash expenses? Suppose the addition of the delivery truck under consideration by High Country's management will involve hiring an additional employee, whose annual compensation and fringe benefits will amount to $30,000. As the following computation shows, the company's incremental cash outflow is only $18,000.

Incremental expense (cash outflow)	$(30,000)
Reduction in income tax (reduced cash outflow), $30,000 × 40%	12,000
After-tax cash flow (net outflow after taxes)	$(18,000)

Although the incremental employee compensation is $30,000, this expense is tax-deductible. Thus, the firm's income-tax payment will be reduced by $12,000. As a result, the after-tax cash outflow from the additional compensation is $18,000.

A quick method for computing the after-tax cash outflow from an incremental cash expense is given in the following equation:

$$\begin{array}{ccccc} \text{Incremental cash expense} & \times & (1 - \text{Tax rate}) & = & \text{After-tax cash inflow} \\ \$(30{,}000) & \times & (1 - .40) & = & \$(18{,}000) \end{array}$$

Noncash Expenses Not all expenses represent cash outflows. The most common example of a noncash expense is depreciation expense. Suppose High Country Department Stores' management is considering the purchase of a delivery truck that costs $40,000 and has no salvage value. We will discuss the specific methods of depreciation allowed under the tax law later in the chapter, but for now assume the truck will be depreciated as follows:

The only cash flow shown in the diagram above is the truck's acquisition cost of $40,000 at time zero. The depreciation expense in each of the next five years is *not a cash flow.* However, *depreciation is an expense* on the income statement, and it reduces the firm's income. For example, the $5,000 depreciation expense in year 1 will reduce High Country's income by $5,000. As a result, the company's year 1 income-tax payment will decline by $2,000 (40% × $5,000).

The annual depreciation expense associated with the truck provides a reduction in income-tax expense equal to the firm's tax rate times the depreciation deduction. This reduction in income taxes is called a **depreciation tax shield.**

To summarize, depreciation is a noncash expense. Although depreciation is not a cash flow, it does cause a reduced cash outflow through the depreciation tax shield.

Depreciation or any other noncash expense × Tax rate = Reduced cash outflow for income taxes

Year 1 depreciation of $5,000 × 40% = $2,000

↑ Is not a cash flow (Year 1 depreciation of $5,000)

↑ Is a cash flow ($2,000)

The following schedule shows High Country Department Stores' depreciation tax shield over the depreciable life of the proposed delivery truck.

Year	Depreciation Expense	Tax Rate	Cash Flow: Reduced Tax Payment	
1	$ 5,000	40%	$2,000	Depreciation tax shield
2	10,000	40	4,000	
3	10,000	40	4,000	
4	10,000	40	4,000	
5	5,000	40	2,000	

The cash flows constituting the depreciation tax shield occur in five different years. Thus, in a discounted-cash-flow analysis, we still must discount these cash flows to find their present value.

Cash Flows Not on the Income Statement Some cash flows do not appear on the income statement. They are not revenues, expenses, gains, or losses. A common example of such a cash flow is the purchase of an asset. If High Country Department Stores purchases the delivery truck, the $40,000 acquisition cost is a cash outflow but not an expense. A purchase is merely the exchange of one asset (cash) for another (a delivery truck). The expense associated with the truck's purchase is recognized through depreciation expense recorded throughout the asset's depreciable life. Thus, the cash flow resulting from the purchase of an asset does not affect income and has no direct tax consequences.

Net-Present-Value Analysis Now let's complete our example by preparing a net-present-value analysis of the proposed delivery-truck acquisition. The company's after-tax hurdle rate is 10 percent. Exhibit 16–6 displays the net-present-value analysis. Since the NPV is positive, the delivery truck should be purchased.

Timing of Tax Deductions We have assumed in our analysis of High Country Department Stores' delivery-truck purchase that the cash flows resulting from income taxes occur during the same year as the related before-tax cash flows. This assumption is realistic, as most businesses must make estimated tax payments throughout the tax year. They generally cannot wait until the following year and pay their prior year's taxes in one lump sum.

Inflation Our discussion of discounted-cash-flow analysis has assumed no inflation. The additional complexity of inflation is discussed in Appendix B at the end of this chapter.

Accelerated Depreciation

The main concept underlying discounted-cash-flow analysis is the time value of money. We discount each cash flow to find its present value. Since money has a time value, it is advantageous for a business to take tax deductions as early as allowable under the tax law.

Although federal and state income tax laws are changed periodically by the appropriate governmental legislative bodies, income-tax laws usually permit some form of accelerated depreciation for tax purposes. An *accelerated depreciation method* is any method under which an asset is depreciated more quickly in the early part of its life than it would be by using straight-line depreciation. For example, suppose High Country Department Stores purchased a personal computer and peripheral devices for $10,000. The equipment's useful life is four years with no salvage value. Exhibit 16–7 shows the pattern

Exhibit 16–6
Net-Present-Value Analysis: with After-Tax Cash Flows

HIGH COUNTRY
DEPARTMENT STORES

HIGH COUNTRY DEPARTMENT STORES, INC.
Purchase of Delivery Truck
($r = .10, n = 5$)

	Time 0	Time 1	Time 2	Time 3	Time 4	Time 5
Acquisition cost	$(40,000)					
After-tax cash flow from incremental sales revenue, net of cost of goods sold $50,000 × (1 − .40)		$30,000	$30,000	$30,000	$30,000	$30,000
After-tax cash flow from incremental compensation expense, $30,000 × (1 − .40)		(18,000)	(18,000)	(18,000)	(18,000)	(18,000)
After-tax cash flow from depreciation tax shield, depreciation expense × .40		2,000	4,000	4,000	4,000	2,000
Total cash flow	$(40,000)	$14,000	$16,000	$16,000	$16,000	$14,000
× Discount factor	× 1.000	× .909	× .826	× .751	× .683	× .621
Present value	$(40,000)	$12,726	$13,216	$12,016	$10,928	$ 8,694
Net present value			Sum = $17,580			

Exhibit 16–7

Present Value of Depreciation Tax Shield: Alternative Depreciation Methods

HIGH COUNTRY
DEPARTMENT STORES

Depreciation Expense (Double-Declining-Balance*)	Depreciation Tax Shield (Depreciation × 40%)	Depreciation Expense (Sum-of-the-Years'-Digits)	Depreciation Tax Shield (Depreciation × 40%)	Depreciation Expense (Straight-Line)	Depreciation Tax Shield (Depreciation × 40%)
$5,000	$2,000	$4,000	$1,600	$2,500	$1,000
2,500	1,000	3,000	1,200	2,500	1,000
1,250	500	2,000	800	2,500	1,000
1,250	500	1,000	400	2,500	1,000
Present value of depreciation tax shield (10% discount rate)	$3,361		$3,320		$3,170

*Steps in applying the double-declining-balance (DDB) method:

To apply the double-declining-balance depreciation method, use the following steps:

1. Divide 100% by the number of years of depreciation to be taken.
2. Multiply the answer obtained in step (1) by 200%.
3. Compute the asset's depreciation each year by applying the percentage obtained in step (2) to the asset's underpreciated cost at the beginning of the year.
4. Switch to straight-line depreciation during the first year in which the straight-line amount, computed for the asset's remaining life, is greater than the double-declining-balance amount.

of depreciation deductions, the associated after-tax cash flows, and the present value of the depreciation tax shield under three different depreciation methods. Notice that both the double-declining-balance method and the sum-of-the-years'-digits method result in a greater present value for the depreciation tax shield than the straight-line method does. Thus, it usually is desirable for a business to use accelerated depreciation for tax purposes whenever the tax law permits. The current tax law does not require that the same depreciation method be used for both the tax purpose and the external-reporting purpose. Thus, management could use straight-line depreciation when preparing published financial statements but use an accelerated method for tax purposes.

"It's clear that we have an important role to play in the decision-making process. We bring a perspective that is different from the other functions." (16d)

Boeing

Modified Accelerated Cost Recovery System (MACRS)

Learning Objective **16-5**

Use the Modified Accelerated Cost Recovery System to determine an asset's depreciation schedule for tax purposes.

Under U.S. tax laws, most depreciable assets acquired after December 31, 1980, have been depreciated for tax purposes in accordance with the Accelerated Cost Recovery System (ACRS). The Tax Reform Acts of 1986, 1989, and 1993 modified the ACRS depreciation program. Under the **Modified Accelerated Cost Recovery System**, or **MACRS**, every asset is placed in one of eight classes, depending on the asset's expected useful life. These eight classes, along with examples of the assets included, are shown in columns (a) and (b) of Exhibit 16–8. For each class, the Internal Revenue Code specifies the number of years over which the asset may be depreciated, and the depreciation method to be used. These specifications are shown in column (c) of Exhibit 16–8. Notice that the number of years of depreciation specified by the tax code is not the same as an asset's useful life. Thus, each asset's useful life is used only to place the asset in its appropriate MACRS class. Then the tax code specifies the appropriate number of years of depreciation.[1]

[1]The U.S. tax law changes almost every year. Occasionally, changes are made in the assignment of assets to property classes and in the associated depreciation schedules. Moreover, the terminology frequently changes. The tax act of 1980 established the Accelerated Cost Recovery System, which then was referred to as ACRS. Since the tax act of 1986, the program has been referred to in various publications by a variety of names. Among these are the Modified Accelerated Cost Recovery System (MACRS), the ACRS as modified, the CRS, or simply the ACRS. We will follow the common convention of referring to the current system as MACRS. Our discussion incorporates the latest tax law changes known as this book went to press. Regardless of what minor changes the tax laws may make in terminology or depreciation schedules, it is likely that the tax code will continue to allow depreciation by an accelerated schedule similar to MACRS.

(a) Asset's Useful Life*	(b) Types of Assets in MACRS Class	(c) MACRS Class and Depreciation Method
Up to 4 years	Industrial tools	3-year class; double-declining-balance
Between 4 and 10 years	Automobiles, trucks, office equipment, computers, research equipment	5-year class; double-declining-balance
Between 10 and 16 years	Most industrial equipment and machinery; office furniture	7-year class; double-declining-balance
Between 16 and 20 years	Equipment and machinery for specified purposes	10-year class; double-declining-balance
Between 20 and 25 years	Land improvements; some industrial machinery	15-year class; 150%-declining-balance
25 years or longer	Specified real property, such as farm buildings	20-year class; 150%-declining-balance
—	Residential rental property	27.5-year class; straight-line
—	Nonresidential real property	39-year class; straight-line

*In the tax law, an asset's useful life is referred to as the Asset Depreciation Range (ADR) Midpoint Life.

Exhibit 16–8

Modified Accelerated Cost Recovery System (as modified by the Tax Reform Acts of 1986, 1989, and 1993)

Depreciation Methods As Exhibit 16–8 indicates, assets in the 3-year, 5-year, 7-year, and 10-year MACRS property classes are depreciated using the double-declining-balance (DDB) method. Assets in the 15-year and 20-year MACRS property classes are depreciated using the 150%-declining-balance method. To apply this depreciation method, use the same steps as those listed in Exhibit 16–7 for the DDB method, except change 200% in step (2) to 150%. Assets in the 27.5-year and 39-year MACRS property classes are depreciated using the straight-line method.

The utility company that owns this truck uses an accelerated method of depreciation for its utility equipment. The truck is categorized in the five-year property class under the Modified Accelerated Cost Recovery System (MACRS).

Source: Walt Jennings/FEMA

Half-Year Convention An asset may be purchased at any time during the tax year. MACRS assumes that, on average, assets will be placed in service halfway through the tax year. Thus, the tax code allows only a half-year's depreciation during the tax year in which an asset is placed in service. The other half of the first year's depreciation is picked up in the second tax year in which the asset is in service. The following diagram shows the pattern with which a five-year asset's depreciation is recorded, for tax purposes, under MACRS.

MACRS Depreciation Tables To assist taxpayers, the Internal Revenue Service has published tables of the MACRS depreciation percentages for each MACRS property class. The IRS tables use the depreciation method specified in Exhibit 16–8 and incorporate the half-year convention. Exhibit 16–9 provides a convenient table of the MACRS percentages, as computed by the IRS, for selected property classes. In the 5-year column, we see 20 percent for year 1. This results from the half-year convention, since 20 percent is half of the double-declining balance rate of 40 percent.

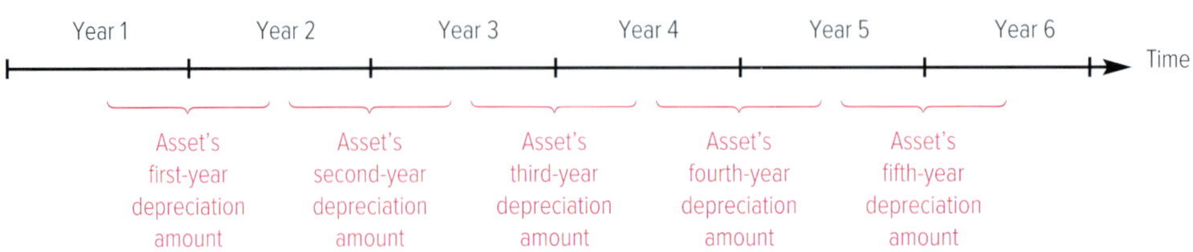

	MACRS Property Class			
Year	**3-year**	**5-year**	**7-year**	**10-year**
1	33.33%	20.00%	14.29%	10.00%
2	44.45	32.00	24.49	18.00
3	14.81*	19.20	17.49	14.40
4	7.41	11.52*	12.49	11.52
5		11.52	8.93*	9.22
6		5.76	8.92	7.37
7			8.93	6.55*
8			4.46	6.55
9				6.56
10				6.55
11				3.28

*Denotes the year during which the depreciation method switches to the straight-line method.

Source: IRS Publication 946, entitled "How to Depreciate Property."

Exhibit 16–9
Selected MACRS Depreciation Percentages as Computed by the IRS (incorporates half-year convention; also incorporates recent modifications in the tax laws)

No Salvage Values Under MACRS, an asset's estimated salvage value is not subtracted in computing the asset's depreciation basis. Thus, for an asset costing $10,000 with an estimated salvage value of $1,000, the full $10,000 cost is depreciated over the asset's life.

Optional Straight-Line Depreciation The tax law permits a business to depreciate any asset using the straight-line method instead of the method prescribed in Exhibit 16–8. A business with a loss might prefer this approach for tax reasons. If the straight-line method is used, the business may depreciate the asset over either the MACRS life or the asset's estimated useful life. Thus, businesses have considerable flexibility in choosing a depreciation schedule for tax purposes. Regardless of the depreciation method chosen, the half-year convention still must be followed.

Income-Tax Complexities The U.S. tax code is a complex document with a multitude of provisions. It is not possible to cover all of these provisions in this text, so it is wise to consult a tax expert regarding the complexities that may apply in a particular investment decision. Since the tax code is changed frequently by Congress, a tax rule that applied last year may not apply this year. For example, the *investment tax credit* is one important tax-code provision that has been switched on and off repeatedly by Congress. During periods when the investment tax credit has been in effect, a company has been allowed a substantial reduction in its income taxes when particular types of investments are made. The intent of the investment credit was to stimulate the economy by giving businesses an incentive to make new investments. The status of the investment tax credit is always subject to change. If there is a moral to the changing-tax-code story, it is this: When making an important investment decision, a manager should have a managerial accountant on one side and a tax accountant on the other.

"The tax issues can often drive a client's business decision." (16e)
A. T. Kearney

Gains and Losses on Disposal

Learning Objective **16-6**

Evaluate an investment proposal using a discounted-cash-flow analysis, giving full consideration to income-tax issues.

When a business sells an asset, there often is a gain or loss on the sale. Since gains and losses are included in income, the business's income taxes generally are affected. Capital investment decisions frequently involve the disposal of assets, and sometimes gains or losses are recorded on those sales. Thus, the tax effects of gains and losses on disposal of assets can be an important feature of an investment decision.

The *book value* of an asset is defined as the asset's acquisition cost minus the accumulated depreciation on the asset. When an asset is sold for more than its current book value, a *gain on disposal* is recorded. The gain is defined as the difference between the sales proceeds and the asset's book value. A loss on disposal is recorded when an asset is sold for less than its current book value. The loss is equal to the difference between the asset's current book value and the sales proceeds.

To illustrate, suppose High Country Department Stores owns a forklift, which cost $10,000 and currently has accumulated depreciation of $6,000. The forklift's book value is computed as follows:

Book value	=	Acquisition cost	−	Accumulated depreciation
$4,000	=	10,000	−	$6,000

Scenario I: Gain on Disposal Suppose High Country sells the forklift for $5,000. The gain on the sale is $1,000 ($5,000 proceeds minus $4,000 book value). If High Country's income-tax rate is 40 percent, the following cash flows will occur at the time of the sale.

Cash inflow: proceeds from sale	$5,000
Cash outflow: incremental income tax due to the gain, $1,000 × 40%	(400)
Net cash flow	$4,600

Although High Country sold the forklift for $5,000, the company's net cash benefit is only $4,600. The firm will have to pay the other $400 in increased income taxes on the $1,000 gain.

Scenario II: Loss on Disposal Now assume instead that High Country Department Stores sells the forklift for $3,200. The *loss* on the sale is $800 ($3,200 proceeds minus $4,000 book value). If High Country's income-tax rate is 40 percent, the following cash flows will occur at the time of the sale.

Cash inflow: proceeds from sale	$3,200
Reduced cash outflow: reduction in income tax due to the loss, $800 × 40%	320
Total cash flow	$3,520

Although High Country sold the forklift for only $3,200, the company's total benefit from the sale is $3,520. The extra $320 comes in the form of a reduction in income taxes due to the loss on the sale.

Tax Rates on Gains and Losses Another complexity of the tax code that changes from time to time is that capital gains and losses may be taxed at different rates than ordinary income (i.e., revenue minus expenses). Thus, before preparing an NPV analysis, it is wise to check with a tax expert to obtain the proper income-tax rate to apply to a gain or loss on disposal.

Investment in Working Capital

Learning Objective 16-6

Evaluate an investment proposal using a discounted-cash-flow analysis, giving full consideration to income-tax issues.

Some investment proposals require additional outlays for working capital. **Working capital,** defined as the excess of current assets over current liabilities, often increases as the result of higher balances in accounts receivable or inventory necessary to support a project. Such increases are uses of cash and should be included in a discounted-cash-flow analysis. To illustrate, suppose the city of Mountainview has offered High Country Department Stores a contract to sell special T-shirts and mementos commemorating the city's bicentennial. The contract covers the three-year period leading up to the bicentennial celebration. The cash flows associated with the proposal are displayed in panel A of Exhibit 16–10. Notice that the sales proposal would require a $2,000 outlay for additional working capital throughout the three-year period. The increased working capital is largely due to a higher balance in merchandise inventory. Panel B of Exhibit 16–10 analyzes the contract proposal. Notice that the time 0 cash investment in working capital is included as a $2,000 cash outflow. Since the increase in working capital is not released

Exhibit 16–10
Investment in Working Capital

HIGH COUNTRY
DEPARTMENT STORES

HIGH COUNTRY DEPARTMENT STORES, INC.
Contract Proposal for the City's Bicentennial

A. Data for Illustration

Annual sales revenue from T-shirts and mementos		$25,000
Annual expenses		(12,000)
Annual contract fee to city		(3,000)
Investment in working capital (time 0)		(2,000)
Release of working capital (end of year 3)		2,000
Tax rate		40%
After-tax hurdle rate		10%
B. Discounted-Cash-Flow Analysis		
Investment in working capital (time 0)		$ (2,000)
Release of working capital:		
Working capital released (end of year 3)	$ 2,000	
Discount factor (n = 3, r = .10)	× .751*	
Present value of working capital released	→	1,502
Annual revenue and expenses:		
Sales revenue	$25,000	
Expenses	(12,000)	
Contract fee	(3,000)	
Before-tax annual income	10,000	
× (1 − tax rate)	× .60	
After-tax annual income	6,000	
× Annuity discount factor	× 2.487†	
Present value of after-tax annual income	→	14,922
Net present value of contract proposal		$14,424

* From Table III of Appendix A.
† From Table IV of Appendix A.

until the end of year 3, that $2,000 inflow is discounted. The city's proposal has a positive net present value, so it should be accepted.

Notice that the presentation format used for the analysis in Exhibit 16–10 is different from the format we used previously. Instead of listing the cash flows for each item by year and then adding the columns, we have computed the present value of each financial item pertinent to the decision. The one-time cash flows at time zero then are added to the present value of the cost-savings annuity to determine the net present value. This alternative presentation format will yield the same conclusion as the year-by-year, columnar approach. The choice of format is a matter of personal preference.

Extended Illustration of Income-Tax Effects in Capital Budgeting

Learning Objective **16-6**

Evaluate an investment proposal using a discounted-cash-flow analysis, giving full consideration to income-tax issues.

Now we have covered all of the most important concepts for analyzing an investment proposal in a profit-seeking enterprise. A comprehensive illustration will help you solidify your understanding of these concepts. High Country Department Stores' management is considering the installation of a new checkout system for its suburban store. The new computerized system would include new cash registers at each checkout station. In addition, the new checkout system would include an updated bar-code reading system. The new system will be faster and more accurate, and it will minimize the annoyance of the reader failing to recognize a product's bar code. Among the advantages of the new system are accuracy in the checkout process, automatic updating of computerized inventory records, and the ability to gather data about customers' buying patterns and trends.

Exhibit 16–11 presents the data pertinent to the decision. Notice that the old equipment has been fully depreciated already. However, its useful life can be extended to six more years if an overhaul is done in year 2. The new equipment also has an expected useful life of six years, so its MACRS classification is the 5-year property class.

Most of the data in Exhibit 16–11 are self-explanatory. The last two items in the exhibit under annual data relate to the new checkout system's ability to gather data about customer demand patterns. The extra data analysis will cost \$4,500 annually, but it is expected to generate another \$40,000 in annual sales, net of cost of goods sold.

A net-present-value analysis of the checkout equipment proposal is presented in Exhibit 16–12. A total-cost approach is used. The present value of each financial item is computed for both alternatives; then these present values are added to determine each alternative's net present value. An explanation of each line in the exhibit follows.

(1) Line (1) in Exhibit 16–12 records the acquisition cost of the new checkout equipment. This cash flow has no tax impact and does not need to be discounted since it occurs at time 0.

(2), (3) These one-time cash flows are required to retrain checkout personnel and retag merchandise to accommodate the new bar-code readers. Since these costs are expenses, we multiply by (1 − .40).

(4), (5) Since the old equipment has a current book value of zero, there is a \$1,200 gain on the sale. The \$1,200 proceeds are not taxed [line (4)], but the \$1,200 gain on the sale is taxed [line (5)].

(6) The cost of updating the software in year 3 is an expense, so we multiply by (1 − .40).

(7), (8) The new equipment can be sold in year 6 for \$1,000. Since it will be fully depreciated, there will be a \$1,000 gain. The \$1,000 proceeds are not taxed [line (7)], but the \$1,000 gain is taxed [line (8)].

(9) The depreciation tax shield on the new equipment is computed using the MACRS depreciation schedule for the 5-year property class. The annual

Exhibit 16–11

Data for Extended Illustration

HIGH COUNTRY DEPARTMENT STORES

HIGH COUNTRY DEPARTMENT STORES, INC.
Computerized Checkout Equipment Decision

Old checkout equipment:	
Remaining useful life, assuming overhaul in year 2	6 years
Cost of overhaul in year 2	\$3,500
Current book value (fully depreciated)	–0–
Current salvage value	\$1,200
Salvage value in six more years	–0–
New checkout equipment:	
Useful (ADR midpoint) life	6 years
MACRS property classification	5-year class
Acquisition cost of new equipment	\$50,000
Update of software required in year 3	\$4,000
Salvage value of new equipment in six years	\$1,000
Cost to retrain checkout personnel	\$5,000
Cost to retag merchandise	\$3,000
Annual data:	
Annual operating-cost savings	\$15,000
Annual cost of computer-system operator	\$30,000
Annual cost of marketing-data analysis	\$4,500
Annual incremental sales resulting from marketing analysis, net of cost of goods sold	\$40,000
After-tax hurdle rate	10%
Tax rate	40%

depreciation deductions are not cash flows, but they do cause a reduction in income taxes. Each cash flow is then discounted using the appropriate discount factor from Table III in Appendix A.

(10), (11), (12), (13) These items are annual cash flows. The flows are summed, and then the $20,500 annuity is multiplied by (1 − .40) because each of the cash flows will be on the income statement. The after-tax cash-flow annuity of $12,300 is then discounted using the annuity discount factor for $n = 6$ and $r = .10$.

(14) The net present value of the new equipment is $13,482.

(15) The only specific cash flow related to the alternative of keeping the old equipment is the $3,500 overhaul in year 2. This will be an expense, so we multiply by (1 − .40). Then the after-tax cash flow is discounted.

(16) The net present value of the alternative to keep the old equipment is $(1,735).

Exhibit 16–12

Net-Present-Value Analysis for Extended Illustration

HIGH COUNTRY DEPARTMENT STORES

HIGH COUNTRY DEPARTMENT STORES, INC.
Computerized Checkout Equipment Decision

	Year	Amount	Income-Tax Impact	After-Tax Cash Flow	Discount Factor (10%)	Present Value of Cash Flow
Purchase New Equipment						
(1) Acquisition cost of new equipment	Time 0	$50,000	None	$(50,000)	1.000	$(50,000)
(2) Cost to retrain checkout personnel	Time 0	5,000	(1 −.40)*	(3,000)	1.000	(3,000)
(3) Cost to retag merchandise	Time 0	3,000	(1 −.40)	(1,800)	1.000	(1,800)
(4) Proceeds from sale of old equipment	Time 0	1,200	None	1,200	1.000	1,200
(5) Gain on sale of old equipment	Time 0	1,200	.40	(480)	1.000	(480)
(6) Update of software	Year 3	4,000	(1 −.40)	(2,400)	.751	(1,802)
(7) Salvage value of new equipment	Year 6	1,000	None	1,000	.564	564
(8) Gain on sale of new equipment	Year 6	1,000	.40	(400)	.564	(226)
(9) Depreciation tax shield:						

Year	Cost	MACRS Percentage (rounded)	Depreciation Expense	Amount	Income-Tax Impact	After-Tax Cash Flow	Discount Factor (10%)	Present Value of Cash Flow
1	$50,000	20.0%	$10,000	10,000	.40	4,000	.909	3,636
2	50,000	32.0%	16,000	16,000	.40	6,400	.826	5,286
3	50,000	19.2%	9,600	9,600	.40	3,840	.751	2,884
4	50,000	11.5%	5,750	5,750	.40	2,300	.683	1,571
5	50,000	11.5%	5,750	5,750	.40	2,300	.621	1,428
6	50,000	5.8%	2,900	2,900	.40	1,160	.564	654
Total			$50,000					

Annual incremental costs and benefits (years 1 through 6):		Amount	Income-Tax Impact	After-Tax Cash Flow	Discount Factor (10%)	Present Value of Cash Flow
(10) Annual operating cost savings	$15,000					
(11) Annual cost of computer operator	(30,000)					
(12) Annual cost of marketing analysis	(4,500)				Annuity discount factor for $n = 6, r = .10$	
(13) Annual incremental sales revenue, net of cost of goods sold	40,000					
Total annual amount	$20,500	$20,500	(1 −.40)	$12,300	4.355	53,567
(14) Net present value						$13,482
Keep Old Equipment†						
(15) Cost of overhaul	Year 2	$3,500	(1 −.40)	$(2,100)	.826	$ (1,735)
(16) Net present value						$ (1,735)

*High Country Department Stores' tax rate is 40%.

†There is no depreciation tax shield if the old equipment is kept, since it has been depreciated fully already.

Management Accounting Practice

AstraZeneca, Pfizer, GlaxoSmithKline, Eli Lilly, and Merck

BIG PHARMA USES CAPITAL BUDGETING IN DEVELOPING NEW DRUGS

Among the many large companies making extensive use of capital budgeting are the big pharmaceutical companies. It can take 10 years or more to develop a new drug. It takes huge outlays of cash to develop a drug, test it, and then shepherd it through the governmental approval process. Yet much of what the drug companies claim as the cost of a new drug is actually the opportunity cost of tying up these big dollar outlays for many years before any revenue stream begins.

"The average drug developed by a major pharmaceutical company costs at least $4 billion, and it can be as much as $11 billion." Estimates of the R&D spending *per new drug* for some of the biggest pharmaceuticals (in billions) are: "AstraZeneca, $11.790; GlaxoSmithKline, $8.170; Pfizer, $7.727; Eli Lilly, $4.577; and Merck, $4.209." There are many costs included here. "A single clinical trial can cost $100 million at the high end." And manufacturing costs are significant as well. "But the main expense is failure." Most new drug ideas never make it to market.

The uncertainties big pharmaceutical companies confront are a large part of the problem. First, only a small percentage of drugs under development ever make it as far as human trials. And only 1 in 10 of those makes it through to wide-scale testing. Then there's the pricing uncertainty as well. How much will people pay for a new drug treatment? To take account of these uncertainties, many drug companies use simulation in conjunction with capital budgeting to decide whether to proceed with a drug's development. A discounted-cash-flow analysis is run many times with differing assumptions about the drug's success, its development costs, and its eventual pricing. Then a probability distribution is generated for the drug's NPV. Management can then make a decision about proceeding with development given the likelihood of a profitable drug.[2]

Decision Rule The analysis indicates that High Country Department Stores should purchase the new checkout equipment. The NPV of the new equipment exceeds that of the old equipment.

Ranking Investment Projects

Learning Objective 16-7

Discuss the difficulty of ranking investment proposals, and use the profitability index.

Suppose a company has several potential investment projects, all of which have positive net present values. If a project has a positive net present value, this means that the return projected for the project exceeds the company's cost of capital. In this case, every project with a positive NPV should be accepted. In spite of the theoretical validity of this argument, practice often does not reflect this viewpoint. In practice, managers often attempt to rank investment projects with positive net present values. Then only a limited number of the higher-ranking proposals are accepted.

The reasons for this common practice are not clear. If a discount rate is used that accurately reflects the firm's cost of capital, then any project with a positive NPV will earn a return greater than the cost of obtaining capital to fund it. One possible explanation for the practice of ranking investment projects is a limited supply of scarce resources, such as managerial talent. Thus, a form of *capital rationing* takes place, not because of a limited supply of investment capital, but because of limitations on other resources. A manager may feel that he or she simply cannot devote sufficient attention to all of the desirable projects. The solution, then, is to select only some of the positive-NPV proposals, which implies a ranking.

[2] Based on M. Herper, "The Truly Staggering Cost of Inventing New Drugs," *Forbes* (online), February 10, 2012, p. 1; J. Carey and A. Barrett, "Drug Pricees: What's Fair," *BusinessWeek*, December 10, 2001, pp. 61–70; and the authors' research.

Unfortunately, no valid method exists for ranking independent investment projects with positive net present values. To illustrate, suppose the management of High Country Department Stores has the following two investment opportunities:

1. Proposal A: Open a gift shop at the Mountainview Convention Center. High Country's management believes the benefits of this proposal would last only six years. High Country's management expects that after six years, the firm's competitors will move into the Convention Center and eliminate High Country's current advantageous position.
2. Proposal B: Open a small gift shop at the Mountainview Airport. The airport gift concession would belong to High Country Department Stores for 10 years under a contract with the city.

The predicted cash flows for these investment proposals are as follows:

	Cash Outflow	After-Tax Cash Inflows		Present Value of Inflows	Net Present	Internal Rate of
Investment Proposal	Time 0	Years 1–6	Years 7–10	(10% Discount Rate)	Value	Return
A (Convention Center)	$ (54,450)	$14,000	—	$ 60,970	$6,520	14%
B (Airport)	(101,700)	18,000	$18,000	110,610	8,910	12%

Both investment proposals have positive net present values. Suppose, however, that due to limited managerial time, High Country's management has decided to pursue only one of the projects. Which proposal should be ranked higher? This is a difficult question to answer. Proposal B has a higher net present value, but it also requires a much larger initial investment. Proposal A exhibits a higher internal rate of return. However, proposal A's return of 14 percent applies only to its six-year time horizon. If management accepts proposal A, what will happen in years 7 through 10? Will the facilities and equipment remain idle? Or could they be used profitably for some other purpose? These questions are left unanswered by the analysis above.

The main reason that the NPV and IRR methods of analysis yield different rankings for these two proposals is that the projects have different lives. Without making an assumption about what will happen in years 7 through 10 if proposal A is accepted, the NPV and IRR methods simply are not capable of ranking the proposals in any sound manner. The only theoretically correct answer to the problem posed in this illustration is that both projects are desirable, and both should be accepted. Each proposal exhibits a positive NPV and an IRR greater than the hurdle rate of 10 percent.

Profitability Index One criterion that managers sometimes apply in ranking investment proposals is called the **profitability index** (or **excess present value index**), which is defined as follows:

$$\text{Profitability index} = \frac{\text{Present value of cash flows, exclusive of initial investment}}{\text{Initial investment}}$$

The profitability indices for High Country's two investment proposals are computed as follows:

Investment Proposal	Calculation	Profitability Index	Net Present Value	Internal Rate of Return
A	$\frac{\text{Present value of inflows}}{\text{Initial investment}} = \frac{\$60{,}970}{\$54{,}450} =$	1.12	$6,520	14%
		>	<	>
B	$\frac{\text{Present value of inflows}}{\text{Initial investment}} = \frac{\$110{,}610}{\$101{,}700} =$	1.09	$8,910	12%

Although proposal A has a lower NPV than proposal B, proposal A exhibits a higher profitability index. Proposal A's higher profitability index is due to its considerably lower initial investment than that required for proposal B. Is the profitability index a foolproof method for ranking investment proposals? Unfortunately, it too suffers from the same drawbacks as those associated with the NPV or IRR method. Both proposals exhibit a profitability index greater than 1.00, which merely reflects their positive NPVs. Thus, both projects are desirable. The unequal lives of the two proposals prevent the profitability index from indicating a theoretically correct ranking of the proposals. The relative desirability of proposals A and B simply depends on what will happen in years 7 through 10 if proposal A is selected.

In summary, the problem of ranking investment projects with positive NPVs has not been solved in a satisfactory manner. This lack of resolution is due to an inconsistency inherent to the problem. The inconsistency is that if several projects have positive NPVs, they all are desirable. They all will earn a return greater than the cost of capital. If a manager chooses not to accept all projects with positive NPVs, then the required ranking ultimately must be made on the basis of subjective criteria.

Section 3: Alternative Methods for Making Investment Decisions

Learning Objective 16-8

Use the payback method and accounting-rate-of-return method to evaluate capital investment projects.

HIGH COUNTRY
DEPARTMENT STORES

The best way to decide whether to accept an investment project is to use discounted-cash-flow analysis, as described in Sections 1 and 2 of this chapter. Both the net-present-value and the internal-rate-of-return methods will yield the correct accept-or-reject decision. The strength of these methods lies in the fact that they properly account for the time value of money. In spite of the conceptual superiority of discounted-cash-flow decision models, managers sometimes use other methods for making investment decisions. In some cases, these alternative methods are used in conjunction with a discounted-cash-flow analysis. Two of these alternative decision methods are described next.

Our discussion is based on decisions faced by the management of High Country Department Stores. The firm operates two department stores in the city of Mountainview.

Payback Method

The **payback period** of an investment proposal is the amount of time it will take for the after-tax cash inflows from the project to accumulate to an amount that covers the original investment. The following formula defines an investment project's payback period.

$$\text{Payback period} = \frac{\text{Initial investment}}{\text{Annual after-tax cash inflow}}$$

There is no adjustment in the payback method for the time value of money. A cash inflow in year 5 is treated the same as a cash inflow in year 1.

To illustrate the payback method, suppose High Country Department Stores' management is considering the purchase of a new conveyor system for its warehouse. The two alternative machines under consideration have the following projected cash flows.

Conveyor System	Initial Investment	After-Tax Cash Flows: Years 1 through 7	After-Tax Cash Flow When System Is Sold
I	$(20,000)	$4,000	–0–
II	(27,000)	4,500	$14,000

The payback period for each conveyor system is computed below. Notice that *after-tax cash flows are used* in the payback method, just as they are in discounted-cash-flow methods of analysis.

Conveyor System	Initial Investment / Annual After-Tax Cash Inflow	Payback Period
I	$\frac{\$20{,}000}{\$4{,}000}$	5 years
II	$\frac{\$27{,}000}{\$4{,}500}$	6 years

According to the payback method, system I is more desirable than system II. System I will "pay back" its initial investment in five years, while system II requires six years. This conclusion is too simplistic, however, because it ignores the large salvage value associated with system II. Indeed, the NPV of system I is negative, while the NPV of system II is positive, as shown in the following analysis.

	Present Value of Cash Flows (10% Discount Factor)	
After-Tax Cash Flows	**System I**	**System II**
Initial investment	\$(20,000) × 1.000 = \$(20,000)	\$(27,000) × 1.000 = \$(27,000)
Years 1–7	4,000 × 4.868 = 19,472	4,500 × 4.868 = 21,906
Cash inflow from sale	–0–	14,000 × .513 = 7,182
Net present value	\$ (528)	\$ 2,088

The net-present-value analysis demonstrates that only system II can generate cash flows sufficient to cover the company's cost of capital. The payback method makes it appear as though system I "pays back" its initial investment more quickly, but the method fails to consider the time value of money.

Another shortcoming of the payback method is that it fails to consider an investment project's profitability beyond the payback period. Suppose High Country Department Stores' management has a third alternative for its warehouse conveyor system. System III requires an initial investment of only \$12,000 and will generate after-tax cash inflows of \$6,000 in years 1 and 2. Thus, System III's payback period is two years, as computed below.

$$\text{System III payback period} = \frac{\$12{,}000}{\$6{,}000} = 2 \text{ years}$$

Strict adherence to the payback method would rank system III above systems I and II, due to its shorter payback period. However, suppose we add another piece of information. System III's useful life is only two years, and it has no salvage value after two years. It is true that system III will "pay back" its initial investment in only two years if we ignore the time value of money. But then what? System III provides no further benefits beyond year 2. In spite of system III's short payback period, it is not a desirable investment proposal. The NPV of system III, \$(1,584), is negative [\$(1,584) = (1.736 × \$6,000) − \$12,000].

Payback Period with Uneven Cash Flows The simple payback formula previously provided will not work if a project exhibits an uneven pattern of cash flows. Instead, the after-tax cash flows must be accumulated on a year-to-year basis until the accumulation equals the initial investment. Suppose High Country Department Stores' management is considering the expansion of the downtown store's parking facilities. Management expects that the additional parking will result in much greater sales initially. However, this benefit will gradually taper off, due to the reactions of competitors. The projected after-tax cash flows are shown in Exhibit 16–13, which also presents the payback calculation for the parking lot proposal. The project's payback period is five years.

Exhibit 16–13
Payback Period with Uneven Cash Flows

HIGH COUNTRY DEPARTMENT STORES

HIGH COUNTRY DEPARTMENT STORES, INC.
Parking Lot Expansion

		After-Tax Cash Flows			
Year	**Type of Cash Flow**	**Outflows**	**Inflows**	**Accumulated Cash Flows (excluding initial investment)**	
0	Initial investment	$(200,000)		—	
1	Incremental sales*		$60,000	$ 60,000	
2	Incremental sales*		50,000	110,000	
3	Incremental sales*		45,000	155,000	
4	Incremental sales*		35,000	190,000	
4	Repave parking lot	(20,000)		170,000	Payback
5	Incremental sales*		30,000	200,000 ←	period:
6	Incremental sales*		30,000	230,000	5 years
7	Incremental sales*		30,000	260,000	
8	Incremental sales*		30,000	290,000	

*Incremental sales, net of cost of goods sold.

Payback: Pro and Con In summary, the payback method of evaluating investment proposals has two serious drawbacks. First, the method fails to consider the time value of money. Second, it does not consider a project's cash flows beyond the pay-back period. Despite these shortcomings, the payback method is used widely in practice, for two legitimate reasons.

First, the payback method provides a tool for roughly screening investment proposals. If a project does not meet some minimal criterion for the payback period, management may wish to reject the proposal regardless of potential large cash flows predicted well into the future. Second, a young firm may experience a shortage of cash. For such a company, it may be crucial to select investment projects that recoup their initial investment quickly. A cash-poor firm may not be able to wait for the big payoff of a project with a long payback period. Even in these cases, it is wise not to rely on the payback method alone. If the payback method is used, it should be in conjunction with a discounted-cash-flow analysis.

Accounting-Rate-of-Return Method

Discounted-cash-flow methods of investment analysis focus on *cash flows and incorporate the time value of money. The* **accounting-rate-of-return method** focuses on the incremental *accounting income* that results from a project. Accounting income is based on accrual accounting procedures. Revenue is recognized during the period of sale, not necessarily when the cash is received; expenses are recognized during the period they are incurred, not necessarily when they are paid in cash. The following formula is used to compute the accounting rate of return on an investment project.

$$\text{Accounting rate of return} = \frac{\begin{pmatrix}\text{Average}\\ \text{incremental}\\ \text{revenue}\end{pmatrix} - \begin{pmatrix}\text{Average incremental expenses}\\ \text{(including depreciation}\\ \text{and income taxes)}\end{pmatrix}}{\text{Initial investment}}$$

To illustrate the accounting-rate-of-return method, suppose High Country Department Stores' management is considering the installation of a small lunch counter in its downtown store. The required equipment and furnishings cost $210,000 and are in the MACRS 7-year property class. The company has elected to use the optional straight-line depreciation method with the half-year convention. The Excel spreadsheet shown in Exhibit 16–14 displays management's revenue and expense projections for the lunch

Exhibit 16–14
Accounting-Rate-of-Return Method

HIGH COUNTRY DEPARTMENT STORES

HIGH COUNTRY DEPARTMENT STORES, INC.
Revenue and Expense Projection: Lunch Counter for Downtown Store

Year	Sales Revenue	Cost of Goods Sold	Operating Expenses	MACRS Depreciation*	Income Before Taxes	Income Taxes @ 40%	Net Income
1	$ 200,000	$ 100,000	$ 50,000	$ 15,000	$ 35,000	$ 14,000	$ 21,000
2	200,000	100,000	50,000	30,000	20,000	8,000	12,000
3	200,000	100,000	50,000	30,000	20,000	8,000	12,000
4	200,000	100,000	50,000	30,000	20,000	8,000	12,000
5	200,000	100,000	50,000	30,000	20,000	8,000	12,000
6	200,000	100,000	50,000	30,000	20,000	8,000	12,000
7	200,000	100,000	50,000	30,000	20,000	8,000	12,000
8	200,000	100,000	50,000	15,000	35,000	14,000	21,000
9	200,000	100,000	50,000	-	50,000	20,000	30,000
10	200,000	100,000	50,000	-	50,000	20,000	30,000
Total				$ 210,000			$ 174,000

*Annual straight-line depreciation = ($210,000 / 7) = $30,000

Note: In accordance with the half-year convention, only half a year's depreciation is recorded in years 1 & 8

counter. The total income projected over the project's 10-year useful life is $174,000. Thus, the average annual income is $17,400. The accounting rate of return on the lunch-counter proposal is computed as follows:

$$\text{Accounting rate of return} = \frac{\$17,400}{\$210,000} = 8.3\%\text{ (rounded)}$$

To compute the lunch-counter project's internal rate of return, let's assume that each year's sales revenue, cost of goods sold, operating expenses, and income taxes are cash flows in the same year that they are recorded under accrual accounting. Recall that the depreciation expense is not a cash flow. These assumptions imply the following cash-flow pattern for the project.

Net After-Tax Cash Inflows

Year	Amount	Year	Amount
Initial investment	$(210,000)		
1	36,000	6	$42,000
2	42,000	7	42,000
3	42,000	8	36,000
4	42,000	9	30,000
5	42,000	10	30,000

The internal rate of return on the lunch-counter proposal is approximately 13.5 percent. That is, if we compute the present value of the cash flows using a discount rate of 13.5 percent, we obtain approximately a zero NPV.[3] Notice that the project's accounting rate of return, at 8.3 percent, is much lower than its IRR of 13.5 percent.

[3] You can verify the IRR of 13.5% using Table III in Appendix A. You will need to interpolate to find the discount factors for 13.5%, which lie between the 12% and 14% discount factors. For example, .881 is the approximate discount factor for 13.5% and $n = 1$ [.881 = .877 + (.25)(.893 − .877)]. Alternatively, you can calculate the discount factor for 13.5% using the formula given in Table III.

Use of the Average Investment Some managers prefer to compute the accounting rate of return using the average amount invested in a project for the denominator, rather than the project's full cost. The formula is modified as follows:

$$\begin{array}{c}\text{Accounting rate of return}\\ \text{(using average invesment)}\end{array} = \frac{\begin{pmatrix}\text{Average}\\ \text{incremental}\\ \text{revenue}\end{pmatrix} - \begin{pmatrix}\text{Average incremental expenses}\\ \text{(including depreciation}\\ \text{and income taxes)}\end{pmatrix}}{\text{Average investment}}$$

A project's average investment is the average accounting book value over the project's life.

Refer again to High Country Department Stores' lunch-counter data given in Exhibit 16–14. The project's book value at the beginning of each year is tabulated as follows:

Year	(a) Book Value at Beginning of Year	MACRS Depreciation	(b) Book Value at End of Year	$\frac{(a) + (b)}{2}$ Average Book Value During Year
1	$210,000	$15,000	$195,000	$202,500
2	195,000	30,000	165,000	180,000
3	165,000	30,000	135,000	150,000
4	135,000	30,000	105,000	120,000
5	105,000	30,000	75,000	90,000
6	75,000	30,000	45,000	60,000
7	45,000	30,000	15,000	30,000
8	15,000	15,000	–0–	7,500
9	–0–	–0–	–0–	–0–
10	–0–	–0–	–0–	–0–

The average investment over the project's useful life is the average of the amounts in the right-hand column, which is $84,000. Thus, the modified version of the project's accounting rate of return is 20.7 percent. (The average annual income of $17,400 divided by the average investment of $84,000 equals 20.7 percent, rounded.)

Notice that this modified version of the accounting rate of return yields a significantly higher return than the project's internal rate of return, which we computed as 13.5 percent. As a general rule of thumb, the following relationships will be observed.

$$\begin{array}{c}\text{Accounting rate of return}\\ \text{(using initial investment)}\end{array} < \begin{array}{c}\text{Internal rate}\\ \text{of return}\end{array} < \begin{array}{c}\text{Accounting rate of return}\\ \text{(using average investment)}\end{array}$$

Accounting Rate of Return: Pro and Con Like the payback method, the accounting-rate-of-return method is a simple way of screening investment proposals. Some managers use this method because they believe it parallels financial accounting statements, which also are based on accrual accounting. However, like the payback method, the accounting-rate-of-return method does not consider the time value of money.

Inconsistent Terminology Many different terms for the accounting rate of return are used in practice. Among these terms are *simple rate of return, rate of return on assets,* and the *unadjusted rate of return.*

Estimating Cash Flows: The Role of Activity-Based Costing

The validity of any discounted-cash-flow analysis is dependent on the accuracy of the cash-flow estimates. Activity-based-costing (ABC) systems generally improve the ability of an analyst to estimate the cash flows associated with a proposed project. By separating costs into activity cost pools and identifying a cost driver for each pool, the analyst can more accurately determine the levels of various costs that will be incurred if the project is implemented. Costs that are treated as fixed under a traditional, volume-based costing system often are seen to be variable, with respect to the appropriate cost driver, under an ABC system.[4]

Learning Objective **16-9**

Describe the impact of activity-based costing and advanced manufacturing technology on capital-budgeting decisions.

Accuracy in estimating cash flows is particularly important in evaluating a proposed investment in advanced manufacturing equipment. These decisions are complex, involving many peripheral cash flows besides the actual purchase of the equipment. Flexible manufacturing systems (FMSs) generally require cash outlays for software, retraining of employees, realignment of the production line, and engineering. The benefits of such systems often are difficult to quantify also. Intangible benefits such as greater production flexibility are important considerations in making these investment decisions.

In today's manufacturing environment, it is crucial that companies make the best decisions possible regarding huge investments such as those in flexible manufacturing systems. Flawed decisions can spell disaster in today's globally competitive arenas.

Justification of Investments in Advanced Manufacturing Technology

Learning Objective **16-9**

Describe the impact of activity-based costing and advanced manufacturing technology on capital-budgeting decisions.

The manufacturing industry is changing dramatically as firms adopt a just-in-time (JIT) inventory management approach and move toward computer-integrated-manufacturing (CIM) systems. Many firms have found that JIT and CIM, coupled with a revised managerial accounting system, have provided a competitive edge in the marketplace. In many cases, however, managers have been frustrated when an NPV analysis projects a negative net present value for a proposed investment in a CIM system. Managers often believe intuitively that such an investment is justified, but they are stymied when the NPV analysis points to rejection of the proposal.

What is the problem here? Are managers overly optimistic about the advantages of CIM? Or is the NPV approach inappropriate for such an investment decision? Most likely neither of these conjectures is true. Managers often are right when their intuition tells them that the company would benefit from advanced manufacturing technology. And it is difficult to find fault with the NPV investment decision model. It is economically and mathematically sound. The problem lies in the difficulties of applying the NPV approach in a CIM investment decision. Some of these difficulties are listed here.[5]

1. *Hurdle rates that are too high.* Sometimes managers have a tendency to set hurdle rates that are too high in a CIM investment analysis. They tend to forget that the purpose of discounting in the NPV model is to account for the time value of money. The appropriate hurdle rate for any investment decision is the investment opportunity rate for alternative investment projects of equivalent risk. In many cases managers tend to overstate this rate.
2. *Time horizons that are too short.* Another common mistake is to evaluate a CIM investment proposal with too short a time horizon. The acquisition cost of a CIM system can be enormous, and the benefits may be realized over a lengthy period of time.
3. *Bias toward incremental projects.* Most firms require that large investments be authorized by managers at higher levels than are required for smaller investments. One result of this sensible practice is an incentive for lower-level

[4]Activity-based-costing systems are covered extensively in Chapter 5.

[5]This section is based on discussions in R. Kaplan, "Must CIM Be Justified by Faith Alone?" *Harvard Business Review* 64, no. 2 (March 1986), pp. 87–95; Callie Berliner and James A. Brimson, eds., *Cost Management for Today's Advanced Manufacturing* (Boston: Harvard Business School Press, 1988), pp. 16–18, 36–38, 150; and Jean L. Noble, "A New Approach for Justifying Computer-Integrated Manufacturing," *Journal of Cost Management* 3, no. 4 (Winter 1990), pp. 14–19.

Focus on Ethics

DYSFUNCTIONAL FOCUS ON EARLY CASH FLOWS

The timing of cash flows in investment decisions can sometimes create behavioral incentives to make dysfunctional decisions. The following hypothetical scenario presents such a situation.

The Institute for Environmental Studies (IES) is a privately funded, nonprofit scientific organization based in Montreal. The organization's director of field research is scheduled to retire in two years, and the assistant director, Marie Fenwar, is hoping to be appointed to the post at that time. In her current position, Fenwar has significant administrative responsibilities, including the approval of research proposals and equipment acquisitions. Fenwar has developed a reputation for carefully scrutinizing every proposed project and keeping the institute's field research branch within its budget. Fenwar has been so successful in her job that she has been quietly assured by several members of the IES board of directors that she is in line for her boss's job. She knows, however, that her prospects depend on her continued success in keeping the field research branch in solid financial shape.

IES recently signed a contract with the U.S. and Canadian governments to do a five-year study of the effects of global warming on the migration of water fowl. The contract fee is $500,000, payable in equal annual installments over the contract term. Fenwar is now considering two alternative proposals for carrying out the study. Each proposal entails the purchase of equipment and the incurrence of various operating costs throughout the term of the contract. Fenwar's normal procedure for project evaluation is to calculate each proposal's NPV, using an 8 percent hurdle rate. The projected costs follow:

Year	Type of Cost	Research Proposal I	Research Proposal II
Time 0	Equipment acquisition*	$ 40,000	$70,000
Year 1	Operating costs	150,000	75,000
Year 2	Operating costs	120,000	75,000
Year 3	Operating costs	75,000	95,000
Year 4	Operating costs	40,000	95,000
Year 5	Operating costs	40,000	95,000

*The equipment will be obsolete at the end of the contract term.

Fenwar calculated an NPV of $1,370 for Proposal I and $(14,375) for Proposal II. After completing her NPV analysis, however, Fenwar was tempted to ignore it. These thoughts ran through her mind as she drove to work: "If I approve Proposal I, the financial picture for the field research branch is going to pieces for the next two years. After a $40,000 initial investment in equipment, I'm going to show losses of $50,000 and $20,000 in the first two years. That's not going to look very good when the board considers my promotion." When she arrived at the office, Fenwar wrote a memo approving Proposal II.

Which research proposal should Fenwar have accepted? Why? Comment on the ethical issues in this scenario.

managers to request relatively small, incremental improvements in the manufacturing process rather than a large, comprehensive improvement, such as a move to CIM. In many cases, a series of such incremental improvements will not bring about the benefits that could be attained with a full commitment to advanced manufacturing technology.

4. *Greater uncertainty about operating cash flows.* Managers often have greater uncertainty about the cash flows that will result when an advanced manufacturing system is implemented. This increased uncertainty is due to the complexity of the machinery and the firm's inexperience with such advanced technology.
5. *Exclusion of benefits that are difficult to quantify.* The benefits to the firm from JIT and CIM systems are extensive. Some are easy to estimate, such as lower inventory levels, less floor space, and improved product quality. Others that can be even more significant are often difficult to quantify. Some of these benefits are as follows:

   a. *Greater flexibility in the production process.* A flexible manufacturing system cell often can produce runs of several distinct products in the same day. Flexible manufacturing systems also allow engineering changes to be made more easily as products are adapted to changing customer preferences.

b. *Shorter cycle times and reduced lead times* are possible with an FMS. This enables the firm to fill customer orders more quickly.

c. *Reduction of non-value-added costs* often results when JIT and FMS systems are adopted. Part of the philosophy of these systems is to encourage employees to seek out activities that can be made more efficient or eliminated.

d. *Reduced inventory levels* result in savings on working capital investment, less storage space, and reduced obsolescence.

e. *Lower floor-space requirements* in a flexible manufacturing system require less space than several stand-alone machines.

f. *Product quality* becomes higher and more constant because of advanced manufacturing systems.

Although it is difficult to quantify these benefits, few managers doubt their existence. Excluding them from an NPV analysis means they are being valued at zero. In many cases it would be preferable to make some estimate of these benefits, however crude it may be, than to ignore them. If a manager believes it is impossible to make such an estimate, then the investment criteria should be expanded to consider these intangible benefits along with a proposal's NPV.

Chapter Summary

LO16-1 Use the net-present-value method and the internal-rate-of-return method to evaluate an investment proposal. Under the net-present-value method, an investment proposal should be accepted if its net present value is zero or positive. A project's net present value is the present value of the project's future cash flows, less its initial acquisition cost. In computing the present value of the cash flows, the discount rate is the organization's cost of acquiring investment capital. Under the internal-rate-of-return method, an investment proposal should be accepted if its internal rate of return equals or exceeds the organization's hurdle rate. A project's internal rate of return is the discount rate required to make the project's net present value equal to zero.

LO16-2 Compare the net-present-value and internal-rate-of-return methods, and state the assumptions underlying each method. The net-present-value method is somewhat easier to apply. It also has the advantage of allowing the decision maker to adjust the discount rate upward for highly uncertain cash flows. Both the net-present-value method and the internal-rate-of-return method are based on important assumptions, including the following: (1) All cash flows are assumed to occur at year-end. (2) Cash flow amounts are assumed to be certain. (3) Cash flows are assumed to be reinvested immediately in another return-generating project. (4) A perfect capital market is assumed.

LO16-3 Use both the total-cost approach and the incremental-cost approach to evaluate an investment proposal. Under the total-cost approach, all projects' cash flows are included in the analysis at their total amounts. Under the incremental-cost approach, the differences in each cash flow, between alternatives, are included in the analysis.

LO16-4 Determine the after-tax cash flows in an investment analysis. For financial items that are both cash flows and on the income statement, the cash flow is multiplied by 1 minus the tax rate to compute the after-tax cash flow. For financial items that are not cash flows but are on the income statement, the cash flow is multiplied by the tax rate to compute the relevant after-tax cash flow. For financial items that are cash flows but are not on the income statement, the cash flow is multiplied by 1 to determine the after-tax cash flow. (In other words, for these items, the cash flow is already on an after-tax basis.)

LO16-5 Use the Modified Accelerated Cost Recovery System to determine an asset's depreciation schedule for tax purposes. This tax-law-based depreciation schedule, known as MACRS, places every asset in one of eight classes and then states the depreciation rate for each year in the asset's depreciable life.

LO16-6 Evaluate an investment proposal using a discounted-cash-flow analysis, giving full consideration to income-tax issues. For any organization subject to income taxes, the first step in a discounted-cash-flow analysis is to determine the after-tax cash flows related to the investment proposal under consideration. Then these after-tax cash flows are discounted in accordance with the net-present-value method or the internal-rate-of-return method.

LO16-7 Discuss the difficulty of ranking investment proposals, and use the profitability index. No valid method exists for ranking independent investment projects with positive net present values. In theory, *all* projects with positive net present values should be accepted, because the returns expected for the projects exceed the company's cost of capital. Nevertheless, in practice, managers often do attempt to rank investment projects. One commonly used criterion for such rankings is the profitability index, which is defined as follows: present value of a project's cash flows, exclusive of the initial investment, divided by the project's initial investment.

LO16-8 Use the payback method and accounting-rate-of-return method to evaluate capital investment projects. A project's payback period is its initial investment divided by the annual after-tax cash inflow. As explained in the chapter, for projects with uneven cash flows, the payback period requires a more complex calculation. A project's accounting rate of return is computed as follows: (the project's average incremental revenue minus its average incremental expenses, including depreciation and income taxes) divided by the project's initial investment. Since these methods do not account for the time value of money, they are conceptually inferior to discounted-cash-flow methods. However, many organizations use these methods in conjunction with the NPV or IRR method.

LO16-9 Describe the impact of activity-based costing and advanced manufacturing technology on capital-budgeting decisions. The validity of any discounted-cash-flow analysis depends on the accuracy of the cash-flow estimates. Activity-based costing systems generally improve the cost analyst's ability to accurately estimate projects' cash flows. Some observers argue that, for a variety of reasons, discounted-cash-flow analyses tend to underestimate the benefits of investing in advanced manufacturing technology.

LO16-10 Explain the impact of inflation on a capital-budgeting analysis (Appendix B). Inflation (a decline in the purchasing power of a monetary unit) can be incorporated in a discounted-cash-flow analysis in either of two ways: (1) The cash flows are measured in nominal dollars, and the nominal interest rate is used to compute the nominal discount rate. (2) The cash flows are measured in real dollars, and the real interest rate is used to compute the real discount rate.

Review Problems on Investment Centers and Transfer Pricing

Problem 1

Bay City's Department of Public Works (DPW) is considering the replacement of some machinery. This machinery has zero book value but its current market value is $960. One possible alternative is to invest in new machinery, which has a cost of $46,800. This new machinery would produce estimated annual operating cash savings of $15,000. The estimated useful life of the new machinery is four years. The DPW uses straight-line depreciation. The new machinery has an estimated salvage value of $2,400 at the end of four years. The investment in the new machinery would require an additional investment in working capital of $3,600, which would be recovered after four years.

If the DPW accepts this investment proposal, disposal of the old machinery and investment in the new equipment will take place on December 31, 20x4. The cash flows from the investment will occur during the calendar years 20x5 through 20x8.

Required: Prepare a net-present-value analysis of the DPW's machinery replacement decision. The city has a 10 percent hurdle rate.

Problem 2

River City Pool Company recently purchased a truck for $40,000. The first year's depreciation was $8,000. The truck driver's salary in the first year of operation was $42,000.

Required: Show how each of the amounts mentioned above should be converted to an after-tax amount. The company's tax rate is 35 percent.

Solutions to Review Problems

Problem 1

	Time 0	Time 1	Time 2	Time 3	Time 4
Acquisition cost	$(46,800)				
Investment in working capital	(3,600)				
Recovery of working capital					$ 3,600
Salvage value of old machinery	960				
Salvage value of new machinery					2,400
Annual operating cash savings		$15,000	$15,000	$15,000	15,000
Total cash flow	$(49,440)	$15,000	$15,000	$15,000	$21,000
Discount factor*	× 1.000	× .909	× .826	× .751	× .683
Present value	$(49,440)	$13,635	$12,390	$11,265	$14,343
Net present value			Sum = $2,193		

*The discount factors are from Table III in Appendix A (r = .10)

Conclusion: The DPW's proposed investment in new machinery has a positive net present value and should be accepted.

Problem 2

a. Acquisition cost = $40,000

After-tax cash outflow = $(40,000)

b. Depreciation expense = $8,000

After-tax cash flow = $8,000(.35) = $2,800 savings in cash outflow for taxes

c. Salary expense = $42,000

After-tax cash outflow = ($42,000)(1 − .35) = $(27,300)

Key Terms

For each term's definition refer to the indicated page, or turn to the glossary at the end of the text.

acceptance-or-rejection decision, 688
accounting-rate-of-return method, 714
after-tax cash flow, 699
capital-budgeting decision, 688
capital-rationing decision, 688
depreciation tax shield, 701
discounted-cash-flow analysis, 689
hurdle rate (or minimum desired rate of return), 690
internal rate of return (or time-adjusted rate of return), 690
investment opportunity rate, 694
Modified Accelerated Cost Recovery System (MACRS), 703
net present value, 690
nominal dollars*, 724
nominal interest rate*, 724
payback period, 712
postaudit (or reappraisal), 698
profitability index (or excess present value index), 711
real dollars*, 724
real interest rate*, 724
working capital, 706

*Terms appear in Appendix B.

APPENDIX A TO CHAPTER 16

Future Value and Present Value Tables

Table I

Future Value of $\$1.00(1 + r)^n$

Period	4%	6%	8%	10%	12%	14%	20%
1	1.040	1.060	1.080	1.100	1.120	1.140	1.200
2	1.082	1.124	1.166	1.210	1.254	1.300	1.440
3	1.125	1.191	1.260	1.331	1.405	1.482	1.728
4	1.170	1.263	1.361	1.464	1.574	1.689	2.074
5	1.217	1.338	1.469	1.611	1.762	1.925	2.488
6	1.265	1.419	1.587	1.772	1.974	2.195	2.986
7	1.316	1.504	1.714	1.949	2.211	2.502	3.583
8	1.369	1.594	1.851	2.144	2.476	2.853	4.300
9	1.423	1.690	1.999	2.359	2.773	3.252	5.160
10	1.480	1.791	2.159	2.594	3.106	3.707	6.192
11	1.540	1.898	2.332	2.853	3.479	4.226	7.430
12	1.601	2.012	2.518	3.139	3.896	4.818	8.916
13	1.665	2.133	2.720	3.452	4.364	5.492	10.699
14	1.732	2.261	2.937	3.798	4.887	6.261	12.839
15	1.801	2.397	3.172	4.177	5.474	7.138	15.407
20	2.191	3.207	4.661	6.728	9.646	13.743	38.338
30	3.243	5.744	10.063	17.450	29.960	50.950	237.380
40	4.801	10.286	21.725	45.260	93.051	188.880	1,469.800

Table II

Future Value of a Series of $1.00 Cash Flows (Ordinary Annuity)

$$\frac{(1 + r)^n - 1}{r}$$

Period	4%	6%	8%	10%	12%	14%	20%
1	1.000	1.000	1.000	1.000	1.000	1.000	1.000
2	2.040	2.060	2.080	2.100	2.120	2.140	2.220
3	3.122	3.184	3.246	3.310	3.374	3.440	3.640
4	4.247	4.375	4.506	4.641	4.779	4.921	5.368
5	5.416	5.637	5.867	6.105	6.353	6.610	7.442
6	6.633	6.975	7.336	7.716	8.115	8.536	9.930
7	7.898	8.394	8.923	9.487	10.089	10.730	12.916
8	9.214	9.898	10.637	11.436	12.300	13.233	16.499
9	10.583	11.491	12.488	13.580	14.776	16.085	20.799
10	12.006	13.181	14.487	15.938	17.549	19.337	25.959
11	13.486	14.972	16.646	18.531	20.655	23.045	32.150
12	15.026	16.870	18.977	21.385	24.133	27.271	39.580
13	16.627	18.882	21.495	24.523	28.029	32.089	48.497
14	18.292	21.015	24.215	27.976	32.393	37.581	59.196
15	20.024	23.276	27.152	31.773	37.280	43.842	72.035
20	29.778	36.778	45.762	57.276	75.052	91.025	186.690
30	56.085	79.058	113.283	164.496	241.330	356.790	1,181.900
40	95.026	154.762	259.057	442.597	767.090	1,342.000	7,343.900

Table III

Present Value of $1.00

$$\frac{1}{(1+r)^n}$$

Period	4%	6%	8%	10%	12%	14%	16%	18%	20%	22%	24%	26%	28%	30%	32%
1	.962	.943	.926	.909	.893	.877	.862	.847	.833	.820	.806	.794	.781	.769	.758
2	.925	.890	.857	.826	.797	.769	.743	.718	.694	.672	.650	.630	.610	.592	.574
3	.889	.840	.794	.751	.712	.675	.641	.609	.579	.551	.524	.500	.477	.455	.435
4	.855	.792	.735	.683	.636	.592	.552	.516	.482	.451	.423	.397	.373	.350	.329
5	.822	.747	.681	.621	.567	.519	.476	.437	.402	.370	.341	.315	.291	.269	.250
6	.790	.705	.630	.564	.507	.456	.410	.370	.335	.303	.275	.250	.227	.207	.189
7	.760	.665	.583	.513	.452	.400	.354	.314	.279	.249	.222	.198	.178	.159	.143
8	.731	.627	.540	.467	.404	.351	.305	.266	.233	.204	.179	.157	.139	.123	.108
9	.703	.592	.500	.424	.361	.308	.263	.225	.194	.167	.144	.125	.108	.094	.082
10	.676	.558	.463	.386	.322	.270	.227	.191	.162	.137	.116	.099	.085	.073	.062
11	.650	.527	.429	.350	.287	.237	.195	.162	.135	.112	.094	.079	.066	.056	.047
12	.625	.497	.397	.319	.257	.208	.168	.137	.112	.092	.076	.062	.052	.043	.036
13	.601	.469	.368	.290	.229	.182	.145	.116	.093	.075	.061	.050	.040	.033	.027
14	.577	.442	.340	.263	.205	.160	.125	.099	.078	.062	.049	.039	.032	.025	.021
15	.555	.417	.315	.239	.183	.140	.108	.084	.065	.051	.040	.031	.025	.020	.016
20	.456	.312	.215	.149	.104	.073	.051	.037	.026	.019	.014	.010	.007	.005	.004
30	.308	.174	.099	.057	.033	.020	.012	.007	.004	.003	.002	.001	.001	—	—
40	.208	.097	.046	.022	.011	.005	.003	.001	.001	—	—	—	—	—	—

Table IV

Present Value of Series of $1.00 Cash Flows

$$\frac{1}{r}\left(1-\frac{1}{(1+r^n)}\right)$$

Period	4%	6%	8%	10%	12%	14%	16%	18%	20%	22%	24%	25%	26%	28%	30%
1	0.962	0.943	0.926	0.909	0.893	0.877	0.862	0.847	0.833	0.820	0.806	0.800	0.794	0.781	0.769
2	1.886	1.833	1.783	1.736	1.690	1.647	1.605	1.566	1.528	1.492	1.457	1.440	1.424	1.392	1.361
3	2.775	2.673	2.577	2.487	2.402	2.322	2.246	2.174	2.106	2.042	1.981	1.952	1.923	1.868	1.816
4	3.630	3.465	3.312	3.170	3.037	2.914	2.798	2.690	2.589	2.494	2.404	2.362	2.320	2.241	2.166
5	4.452	4.212	3.993	3.791	3.605	3.433	3.274	3.127	2.991	2.864	2.745	2.689	2.635	2.532	2.436
6	5.242	4.917	4.623	4.355	4.111	3.889	3.685	3.498	3.326	3.167	3.020	2.951	2.885	2.759	2.643
7	6.002	5.582	5.206	4.868	4.564	4.288	4.039	3.812	3.605	3.416	3.242	3.161	3.083	2.937	2.802
8	6.733	6.210	5.747	5.335	4.968	4.639	4.344	4.078	3.837	3.619	3.421	3.329	3.241	3.076	2.925
9	7.435	6.802	6.247	5.759	5.328	4.946	4.607	4.303	4.031	3.786	3.566	3.463	3.366	3.184	3.019
10	8.111	7.360	6.710	6.145	5.650	5.216	4.833	4.494	4.192	3.923	3.682	3.571	3.465	3.269	3.092
11	8.760	7.887	7.139	6.495	5.938	5.453	5.029	4.656	4.327	4.035	3.776	3.656	3.544	3.335	3.147
12	9.385	8.384	7.536	6.814	6.194	5.660	5.197	4.793	4.439	4.127	3.851	3.725	3.606	3.387	3.190
13	9.986	8.853	7.904	7.103	6.424	5.842	5.342	4.910	4.533	4.203	3.912	3.780	3.656	3.427	3.223
14	10.563	9.295	8.244	7.367	6.628	6.002	5.468	5.008	4.611	4.265	3.962	3.824	3.695	3.459	3.249
15	11.118	9.712	8.559	7.606	6.811	6.142	5.575	5.092	4.675	4.315	4.001	3.859	3.726	3.483	3.268
20	13.590	11.470	9.818	8.514	7.469	6.623	5.929	5.353	4.870	4.460	4.110	3.954	3.808	3.546	3.316
30	17.292	13.765	11.258	9.427	8.055	7.003	6.177	5.517	4.979	4.534	4.160	3.995	3.842	3.569	3.332
40	19.793	15.046	11.925	9.779	8.244	7.105	6.234	5.548	4.997	4.544	4.166	3.999	3.846	3.571	3.333

APPENDIX B TO CHAPTER 16

Impact of Inflation

Learning Objective 16-10

Explain the impact of inflation on a capital-budgeting analysis.

Most countries have experienced inflation to some degree over the past 30 years. *Inflation* is defined as a decline in the general purchasing power of a monetary unit, such as a dollar, across time. Since capital-budgeting decisions involve cash flows over several time periods, it is worthwhile to examine the impact of inflation in capital-budgeting analyses.

Inflation can be incorporated in a discounted-cash-flow analysis in either of two ways. Both approaches yield correct results, but the analyst must be careful to be consistent in applying either approach. The two approaches are distinguished by the use of either *nominal* or *real* interest rates and dollars. These terms are defined below.

Interest Rates: Real or Nominal The **real interest rate** is the underlying interest rate, which includes compensation to investors for the *time value of money* and the *risk* of an investment. The **nominal interest rate** includes the real interest rate, plus an additional premium to compensate investors for inflation. Suppose the real interest rate is 10 percent, and inflation of 5 percent is projected. Then the nominal interest rate is determined as follows:[6]

Real interest rate	.10
Inflation rate	.05
Combined effect (.10 × .05)	.005
Nominal interest rate	.155

Dollars: Real or Nominal A cash flow measured in **nominal dollars** is the actual cash flow we observe. For example, a particular model of automobile cost $10,000 in year 1 but it cost $12,155 in year 5. Both the $10,000 cash flow in year 1 and $12,155 cash flow in year 5 are measured in *nominal dollars.* A cash flow measured in **real dollars** reflects an adjustment for the dollar's purchasing power. The following table shows the relationship between nominal and real dollars, assuming an inflation rate of 5 percent.

Year	(a) Cash Flow in Nominal Dollars	(b) Price Index	(c) = (a) ÷ (b) Cash Flow in Real Dollars
Year 1	$10,000	1.0000	$10,000
Year 2	10,500	$(1.05)^1 = 1.0500$	10,000
Year 3	11,025	$(1.05)^2 = 1.1025$	10,000
Year 4	11,576	$(1.05)^3 = 1.1576$	10,000
Year 5	12,155	$(1.05)^4 = 1.2155$	10,000

As the table shows, cash flows in nominal dollars must be deflated, which means dividing by the price index, to convert them to cash flows in real dollars. The real-dollar cash flows are expressed in year 1 dollars.

Two Capital-Budgeting Approaches under Inflation

A correct capital-budgeting analysis may be done using either of the following approaches.

1. Use cash flows measured in *nominal dollars* and a nominal interest rate to determine the *nominal discount rate.*
2. Use cash flows measured in *real dollars* and a real interest rate to determine the *real discount rate.*

[6]An alternative way to compute the nominal interest rate is: $(1.10 \times 1.05) - 1.00 = .155$.

To illustrate these two approaches, we will focus on an equipment-replacement decision faced by the management of High Country Department Stores. The company operates an appliance-repair service for the household appliances it sells. Management is considering the replacement of a sophisticated piece of testing equipment used in repairing TVs and VCRs. The new equipment costs $5,000 and will have no salvage value. Over its four-year life, the new equipment is expected to generate the cost savings and depreciation tax shield shown below. The cash flows in column (f) of the table are the total after-tax cash inflows, measured in *nominal dollars*.

HIGH COUNTRY
DEPARTMENT STORES

Measured in Nominal Dollars

Year	(a) Acquisition Cost	(b) Cost Savings	(c) After-Tax Cost Savings [(b) × (1 − .40)]	(d) MACRS Depreciation (3-year class)	(e) Depreciation Tax Shield [(d) × .40]	(f) Total After-Tax Cash Flow [(c) + (e)]
Year 1	$(5,000)					
Year 2		$1,900	$1,140	$1,667	$667	$1,807
Year 3		2,000	1,200	2,223	889	2,089
Year 4		2,100	1,260	740	296	1,556
Year 5		2,500	1,500	370	148	1,648

Approach 1: Nominal Dollars and Nominal Discount Rate Under this capital-budgeting approach, we discount the nominal-dollar cash flows in the preceding table using the nominal discount rate of 15.5 percent. The net-present-value analysis is as follows:

Year	(a) Cash Flow in Nominal Dollars	(b) Discount Factor for Nominal Discount Rate of 15.5%	(c) = (a) × (b) Present Value
Year 1	$(5,000)	1.000	$(5,000)
Year 2	1,807	.8658 [1/(1.155)]*	1,564
Year 3	2,089	.7496 [$1/(1.155)^2$]	1,565
Year 4	1,556	.6490 [$1/(1.155)^3$]	1,009
Year 5	1,648	.5619 [$1/(1.155)^4$]	926
Net present value			$ 64

*The 15.5% discount factors are computed using the formula in Table III of Appendix A.

High Country's management should purchase the new testing equipment, since its NPV is positive.

Approach 2: Real Dollars and Real Discount Rate Under this capital-budgeting approach, we first convert the cash flows measured in nominal dollars to cash flows in real dollars, as follows:

Year	(a) After-Tax Cash Flow in Nominal Dollars	(b) Price Index	(c) = (a) ÷ (b) After-Tax Cash Flow in Real Dollars*
Year 1	$(5,000)	1.0000	$(5,000)
Year 2	1,807	1.0500	1,721
Year 3	2,089	1.1025	1,895
Year 4	1,556	1.1576	1,344
Year 5	1,648	1.2155	1,356

*Real-dollar cash flows expressed in terms of year 1 dollars.

Now we discount the after-tax cash flows, measured in real dollars, using the real discount rate of 10 percent. The net-present-value analysis is shown below.

Year	(a) Cash Flow in Real Dollars	(b) Discount Factor for Real Discount Rate of 10%	(c) = (a) × (b) Present Value
Year 1	$(5,000)	1.000	$(5,000)
Year 2	1,721	.909	1,564
Year 3	1,895	.826	1,565
Year 4	1,344	.751	1,009
Year 5	1,356	.683	926
Net present value			$ 64

Notice that the new testing equipment's NPV is the same under both capital-budgeting approaches. Under both approaches, we conclude that High Country Department Stores should purchase the new equipment.

Consistency Is the Key Either capital-budgeting approach will provide the correct conclusion, as long as it is applied consistently. Use either nominal dollars and a nominal discount rate or real dollars and a real discount rate. A common error in capital budgeting is to convert the after-tax cash flows to real dollars, but then use the nominal discount rate. This faulty analysis creates a bias against acceptance of worthwhile projects.

To illustrate, suppose High Country's management had made this error in its testing-equipment analysis. The following *incorrect* analysis is the result.

Incorrect Analysis of Testing-Equipment Decision

Inconsistency (between (a) and (b))

Year	(a) Cash Flow in Real Dollars	(b) Discount Factor for Nominal Discount Rate of 15.5%	(c) = (a) × (b) Present Value
Year 1	$(5,000)	1.0000	$(5,000)
Year 2	1,721	.8658	1,490
Year 3	1,895	.7496	1,420
Year 4	1,344	.6490	872
Year 5	1,356	.5619	762
Net present value			$ (456)

This inconsistent and incorrect analysis will lead High Country's management to the wrong conclusion.

Review Questions

Note: Review questions 1 through 10 relate to Section 1 of the chapter. Questions 11 through 18 relate to Section 2, and questions 19 through 22 relate to Section 3. Question 23 relates to Appendix B.

16–1. "Time is money!" is an old saying. Relate this statement to the evaluation of capital-investment projects.

16–2. Distinguish between the following two types of capital-budgeting decisions: acceptance-or-rejection decisions and capital-rationing decisions.

16–3. "The greater the discount rate, the greater the present value of a future cash flow." True or false? Explain your answer.

16–4. Briefly explain the concept of *discounted-cash-flow analysis.* What are the two common methods of discounted-cash-flow analysis?

16–5. State the decision rule used to accept or reject an investment proposal under each of these methods of analysis: (1) net-present-value method and (2) internal-rate-of-return method.

16–6. Explain the following terms: *recovery of investment* versus *return on investment.*

16–7. List and briefly explain two advantages that the net-present-value method has over the internal-rate- of-return method.

16–8. List and briefly explain four assumptions underlying discounted-cash-flow analysis.

16–9. Distinguish between the following approaches to discounted-cash-flow analysis: total-cost approach versus incremental-cost approach.

16–10. What is meant by a *postaudit* of an investment project?

16–11. Give an example of a noncash expense. What impact does such an expense have in a capital-budgeting analysis? Explain how to compute the after-tax impact of a noncash expense.

16–12. Explain how to compute the after-tax amount of a cash revenue or expense.

16–13. What is a *depreciation tax shield?* Explain the effect of a depreciation tax shield in a capital-budgeting analysis.

16–14. Give an example of a cash flow that is not on the income statement. How do you determine the after-tax amount of such a cash flow?

16–15. Why is accelerated depreciation advantageous to a business?

16–16. Explain how a gain or loss on disposal is handled in a capital-budgeting analysis.

16–17. Why may the net-present-value and internal-rate-of-return methods yield different rankings for investments with different lives?

16–18. Define the term *profitability index.* How is it used in ranking investment proposals?

16–19. What is meant by the term *payback period?* How is this criterion sometimes used in capital budgeting?

16–20. What are the two main drawbacks of the payback method?

16–21. How is an investment project's *accounting rate of return* defined? Why do the accounting rate of return and internal rate of return on a capital project generally differ?

16–22. Discuss the pros and cons of the accounting rate of return as an investment criterion.

16–23. (Appendix B) Briefly describe two correct methods of net-present-value analysis in an inflationary period.

Exercises

All applicable Exercises are available in Connect. connect

Note: Several exercises on the basics of compound interest and the concept of present value are included in Appendix II, which appears at the end of the text.

Exercise 16–24
Net Present Value (Section 1)
(LO 16-1)

Jack and Jill's Place is a nonprofit nursery school run by the parents of the enrolled children. Since the school is out of town, it has a well rather than a city water supply. Lately, the well has become unreliable, and the school has had to bring in bottled drinking water. The school's governing board is considering drilling a new well (at the top of the hill, naturally). The board estimates that a new well would cost $2,825 and save the school $500 annually for 10 years. The school's hurdle rate is 8 percent.

Required: Compute the new well's net present value. Should the governing board approve the new well?

Exercise 16–25
Internal Rate of Return (Section 1)
(LO 16-1)

Refer to the data given in the preceding exercise.

Required: Compute the internal rate of return on the new well. Should the governing board approve the new well?

Exercise 16–26
Internal Rate of Return; Uneven Cash Flows (Section 1)
(LO 16-1)

The trustees of the Danube School of Art and Music, located in Tuttlingen, Germany, are considering a major overhaul of the school's audio system. With or without the overhaul, the system will be replaced in two years. If an overhaul is done now, the trustees expect to save the following repair costs during the next two years: year 1, 3,000 *euros;* year 2, 5,000 *euros.* The overhaul will cost 6,664 *euros.* (The *euro* is used in most European markets.)

Required: Use trial and error to compute the internal rate of return on the proposed overhaul. *(Hint:* The NPV of the overhaul is positive if an 8 percent discount rate is used, but the NPV is negative if a 16 percent rate is used.)

Exercise 16–27
Use of Internet; City Government; Capital Projects (Section 1)
(LO 16-1)

Use the Internet to access the home page for the City of Chicago, www.cityofchicago.org. Use one of the links there to access the home page for one of Chicago's sister organizations, such as the following:

Chicago Housing Authority	www.thecha.org
Chicago Park District	www.chicagoparkdistrict.com
Chicago Public Schools	www.cps.edu
Chicago Transit Authority	www.transitchicago.com

Each of these linked pages contains information about the organization's budget and its capital projects. Read about one or more of these capital projects, and then discuss how the organization's managers should go about making significant decisions about expenditures for major capital projects like the one you have explored.

Exercise 16–28
New Present Value with Different Discount Rates (Section 1)
(LO 16-1)

Vancouver Shakespearean Theater's board of directors is considering the replacement of the theater's lighting system. The old system requires two people to operate it, but the new system would require only a single operator. The new lighting system will cost $129,750 and save the theater $27,000 annually for the next eight years.

Required:

1. Prepare a table showing the proposed lighting system's net present value for each of the following discount rates: 8 percent, 10 percent, 12 percent, 14 percent, and 16 percent. Use the following headings in your table. Comment on the pattern in the right-hand column.

Discount Rate	Annuity Discount Factor	Annual Savings	Present Value of Annual Savings	Acquisition Cost	Net Present Value

2. *Build a spreadsheet:* Construct an Excel spreadsheet to solve the preceding requirement. Show how the solution will change if the following information changes: the new lighting system will cost $131,000, and the annual savings amount to $27,500.

Exercise 16–29
Sensitivity Analysis; NPV (Section 1)
(LO 16-1)

Refer to the data given in the preceding exercise. Suppose the Vancouver Shakespearean Theater's board is uncertain about the cost savings with the new lighting system.

Required: How low could the new lighting system's annual savings be and still justify acceptance of the proposal by the board of directors? Assume the theater's hurdle rate is 12 percent.

Exercise 16–30
After-Tax Cash Flows (Section 2)
(LO 16-4)

Daly Publishing Corporation recently purchased a truck for $30,000. Under MACRS, the first year's depreciation was $6,000. The truck driver's salary in the first year of operation was $32,000.

Required: Show how each of the amounts mentioned above should be converted to an after-tax amount. The company's tax rate is 30 percent.

Exercise 16–31
Using the Modified Accelerated Cost Recovery System (Section 2)
(LO 16-5)

For each of the following assets, indicate the MACRS property class and depreciation method.

1. A pharmaceutical company bought a new microscope to use in its Research and Development Division.
2. A midwestern farmer constructed a new barn to house beef cattle.
3. A steel fabrication company bought a machine, which is expected to be useful for 18 years.
4. The president of an insurance company authorized the purchase of a new desk for her office.
5. A pizza restaurant purchased a new delivery car.

Exercise 16–32
Gain or Loss on Disposal (Section 2)
(LO 16-4)

In December of 20x4, Atlas Chemical Corporation sold a forklift for $9,255. The machine was purchased in 20x1 for $50,000. Since then $38,845 in depreciation has been recorded on the forklift.

Required:

1. What was the forklift's book value at the time of sale?
2. Compute the gain or loss on the sale.
3. Determine the after-tax cash flow at the time the forklift was sold. The firm's tax rate is 45 percent.

Exercise 16–33
Depreciation Tax Shield (Section 2)
(LO 16-4, 16-5)

Sharpe Machining Company purchased industrial tools costing $100,000, which fall in the 3-year property class under MACRS.

Required:

1. Prepare a schedule of depreciation deductions assuming:
   a. The firm uses the accelerated depreciation schedule specified by MACRS.
   b. The firm uses the optional straight-line depreciation method and the half-year convention.
2. Calculate the present value of the depreciation tax shield under each depreciation method listed in requirement (1). Sharpe Machining Company's after-tax hurdle rate is 12 percent, and the firm's tax rate is 30 percent.

Exercise 16–34
Profitability Index; Taxes (Section 2)
(LO 16-7)

The owner of Atlantic City Confectionary is considering the purchase of a new semiautomatic candy machine. The machine will cost $25,000 and last 10 years. The machine is expected to have no salvage value at the end of its useful life. The owner projects that the new candy machine will generate $4,000 in after-tax savings each year during its life (including the depreciation tax shield).

Required: Compute the profitability index on the proposed candy machine, assuming an after-tax hurdle rate of: (*a*) 8 percent, (*b*) 10 percent, and (*c*) 12 percent.

Exercise 16–35
Payback Period; Even Cash Flows (Section 3)
(LO 16-1, 16-6, 16-8)

The management of Niagra National Bank is considering an investment in automatic teller machines. The machines would cost $124,200 and have a useful life of seven years. The bank's controller has estimated that the automatic teller machines will save the bank $27,000 after taxes during each year of their life (including the depreciation tax shield). The machines will have no salvage value.

Required:

1. Compute the payback period for the proposed investment.
2. Compute the net present value of the proposed investment assuming an after-tax hurdle rate of: (*a*) 10 percent, (*b*) 12 percent, and (*c*) 14 percent.
3. What can you conclude from your answers to requirements (1) and (2) about the limitations of the payback method?
4. ***Build a spreadsheet:*** Construct an Excel spreadsheet to solve requirements (1) and (2) above. Show how the solution will change if the following information changes: the machines would cost $134,400, and the annual savings amount to $28,000.

Exercise 16–36
Payback Period; Uneven Cash Flows (Section 3)
(LO 16-1, 16-6, 16-8)

Allegience Insurance Company's management is considering an advertising program that would require an initial expenditure of $165,500 and bring in additional sales over the next five years. The projected additional sales revenue in year 1 is $75,000, with associated expenses of $25,000. The additional sales revenue and expenses from the advertising program are projected to increase by 10 percent each year. Allegience's tax rate is 40 percent. (*Hint:* The $165,500 advertising cost is an expense.)

Required:

1. Compute the payback period for the advertising program.
2. Calculate the advertising program's net present value, assuming an after-tax hurdle rate of 10 percent.

Exercise 16–37
Payback, Accounting Rate of Return; Net Present Value; Taxes (Sections 1, 2, and 3)
(LO 16-1, 16-6, 16-8)

Metro Car Washes, Inc. is reviewing an investment proposal. The initial cost as well as the estimate of the book value of the investment at the end of each year, the net after-tax cash flows for each year, and the net income for each year are presented in the following schedule. The salvage value of the investment at the end of each year is equal to its book value. There would be no salvage value at the end of the investment's life.

Year	Initial Cost and Book Value	Annual Net After-Tax Cash Flows	Annual Net Income
0	$105,000		
1	70,000	$50,000	$15,000
2	42,000	45,000	17,000
3	21,000	40,000	19,000
4	7,000	35,000	21,000
5	0	30,000	23,000

Management uses a 16 percent after-tax target rate of return for new investment proposals.

Required: For requirement (1) *only,* assume that the cash flows in years 1 through 5 occur uniformly throughout each year.

1. Compute the project's payback period.
2. Calculate the accounting rate of return on the investment proposal. Base your calculation on the initial cost of the investment.
3. Compute the proposal's net present value.

(CMA, adapted)

Exercise 16–38
Inflation and Capital Budgeting (Appendix B)
(LO 16-10)

The state's Secretary of Education is considering the purchase of a new computer for $100,000. A cost study indicates that the new computer should save the Department of Education $30,000, measured in real dollars, during each of the next eight years.

The real interest rate is 20 percent and the inflation rate is 10 percent. As a governmental agency, the Department of Education pays no taxes.

Required:

1. Prepare a schedule of cash flows measured in real dollars. Include the initial acquisition and the cost savings for each of the next eight years.
2. Using cash flows measured in real dollars, compute the net present value of the proposed computer. Use a real discount rate equal to the real interest rate.

Exercise 16–39
Inflation and Capital Budgeting (Appendix B)
(LO 16-10)

Refer to the data in the preceding exercise.

Required:

1. Compute the nominal interest rate.
2. Prepare a schedule of cash flows measured in nominal dollars.
3. Using cash flows measured in nominal dollars, compute the net present value of the proposed computer. Use a nominal discount rate equal to the nominal interest rate.

Problems

All applicable Problems are available in Connect. connect

Problem 16–40
County Government; Net-Present-Value Analysis (Section 1)
(LO 16-1, 16-3, 16-6)

Net present value: $1,829

The supervisor of the county Department of Transportation (DOT) is considering the replacement of some machinery. This machinery has zero book value but its current market value is $800. One possible alternative is to invest in new machinery, which has a cost of $39,000. This new machinery would produce estimated annual operating cash savings of $12,500. The estimated useful life of the new machinery is four years. The DOT uses straight-line depreciation. The new machinery has an estimated salvage value of $2,000 at the end of four years. The investment in the new machinery would require an additional investment in working capital of $3,000, which would be recovered after four years.

If the DOT accepts this investment proposal, disposal of the old machinery and investment in the new equipment will take place on December 31, 20x1. The cash flows from the investment will occur during the calendar years 20x2 through 20x5.

Required: Prepare a net-present-value analysis of the county DOT's machinery replacement decision. The county has a 10 percent hurdle rate.

(CMA, adapted)

Problem 16–41
Net Present Value; Total-Cost Approach (Section 1)
(LO 16-1, 16-3)

Difference in NPV of costs: $(2,270,200)

The chief ranger of the state's Department of Natural Resources is considering a new plan for fighting forest fires in the state's forest lands. The current plan uses eight fire-control stations, which are scattered throughout the interior of the state forest. Each station has a four-person staff, whose annual compensation totals $200,000. Other costs of operating each base amount to $100,000 per year. The equipment at each base has a current salvage value of $120,000. The buildings at these interior stations have no other use. To demolish them would cost $10,000 each.

The chief ranger is considering an alternative plan, which involves four fire-control stations located on the perimeter of the state forest. Each station would require a six-person staff, with annual compensation costs of $300,000. Other operating costs would be $110,000 per base. Building each perimeter station would cost $200,000. The perimeter bases would need helicopters and other equipment costing $500,000 per station. Half of the equipment from the interior stations could be used at the perimeter stations. Therefore, only half of the equipment at the interior stations would be sold if the perimeter stations were built.

The state uses a 10 percent hurdle rate for all capital projects.

Required:

1. Use the total-cost approach to prepare a net-present-value analysis of the chief ranger's two fire-control plans. Assume that the interior fire-control stations will be demolished if the perimeter plan is selected. The chief ranger has decided to use a 10-year time period for the analysis.
2. What qualitative factors would the chief ranger be likely to consider in making this decision?

Problem 16–42
Net Present Value; Incremental-Cost Approach (Section 1)
(LO 16-1, 16-3)

Net present value of excess cash outflows with interior stations: $(2,270,200)

Refer to the data in the preceding problem.

Required: Use the incremental-cost approach to prepare a net-present-value analysis of the chief ranger's decision between the interior fire-control plan and the perimeter fire-control plan.

Problem 16–43
Net-Present-Value Analysis; Hospital (Section 1)
(LO 16-1, 16-3)

Net present value: $239,410

Allegheny Community Hospital is a nonprofit hospital operated by the county. The hospital's administrator is considering a proposal to open a new outpatient clinic in the nearby city of New Castle. The administrator has made the following estimates pertinent to the proposal.

1. Construction of the clinic building will cost $780,000 in two equal installments of $390,000, to be paid at the end of 20x0 and 20x1. The clinic will open on January 2, 20x2. All staffing and operating costs begin in 20x2.
2. Equipment for the clinic will cost $150,000, to be paid in December of 20x1.
3. Staffing of the clinic will cost $800,000 per year.
4. Other operating costs at the clinic will be $200,000 per year.
5. Opening the clinic is expected to increase charitable contributions to the hospital by $250,000 per year.
6. The clinic is expected to reduce costs at Allegheny Community Hospital. Annual cost savings at the hospital are projected to be $1,000,000.
7. A major refurbishment of the clinic is expected to be necessary toward the end of 20x5. This work will cost $180,000.
8. Due to shifting medical needs in the county, the administrator doubts the clinic will be needed after 20x9.
9. The clinic building and equipment could be sold for $290,000 at the end of 20x9.
10. The hospital's hurdle rate is 12 percent.

Required:

1. Compute the cash flows for each year relevant to the analysis.
2. Prepare a table of cash flows, by year, similar to Exhibit 16–4.
3. Compute the net present value of the proposed outpatient clinic.
4. Should the administrator recommend to the hospital's trustees that the clinic be built? Why?
5. ***Build a spreadsheet:*** Construct an Excel spreadsheet to solve requirements (1), (2), and (3) above. Show how the solution will change if the following information changes: staffing will cost $790,000 per year, and the increased charitable contributions will be $265,000.

Problem 16–44
Net Present Value; Qualitative Issues (Section 1)
(LO 16-1, 16-3)

1. Old machine, net present value: $(494,605)

Special People Industries (SPI) is a nonprofit organization that employs only people with physical or mental disabilities. One of the organization's activities is to make cookies for its snack food store. Several years ago, Special People Industries purchased a special cookie-cutting machine. As of December 31, 20x0, this machine will have been used for three years. Management is considering the purchase of a newer, more efficient machine. If purchased, the new machine would be acquired on December 31, 20x0. Management expects to sell 300,000 dozen cookies in each of the next six years. The selling price of the cookies is expected to average $1.15 per dozen.

Special People Industries has two options: continue to operate the old machine or sell the old machine and purchase the new machine. No trade-in was offered by the seller of the new machine. The following information has been assembled to help management decide which option is more desirable.

	Old Machine	New Machine
Original cost of machine at acquisition	$80,000	$120,000
Remaining useful life as of December 31, 20x0	6 years	6 years
Expected annual cash operating expenses:		
Variable cost per dozen	$.38	$.29
Total fixed costs	$21,000	$ 11,000
Estimated cash value of machines:		
December 31, 20x0	$40,000	$120,000
December 31, 20x6	$ 7,000	$ 20,000

Assume that all operating revenues and expenses occur at the end of the year.

Required:

1. Use the net-present-value method to determine whether Special People Industries should retain the old machine or acquire the new machine. The organization's hurdle rate is 16 percent.
2. Independent of your answer to requirement (1), suppose the quantitative differences are so slight between the two alternatives that management is indifferent between the two proposals. Write a memo to the president of SPI that identifies and discusses any nonquantitative factors that management should consider.

(CMA, adapted)

Problem 16–45
Internal Rate of Return; Even Cash Flows (Section 1)
(LO 16-1, 16-3)

1. Initial cost of investment: $(429,440)

Washington County's Board of Representatives is considering the construction of a longer runway at the county airport. Currently, the airport can handle only private aircraft and small commuter jets. A new, long runway would enable the airport to handle the midsize jets used on many domestic flights. Data pertinent to the board's decision appear below.

Cost of acquiring additional land for runway	$ 70,000
Cost of runway construction	200,000
Cost of extending perimeter fence	29,840
Cost of runway lights	39,600
Annual cost of maintaining new runway	28,000
Annual incremental revenue from landing fees	40,000

In addition to the preceding data, two other facts are relevant to the decision. First, a longer runway will require a new snowplow, which will cost $100,000. The old snowplow could be sold now for $10,000. The new, larger plow will cost $12,000 more in annual operating costs. Second, the County Board of Representatives believes that the proposed long runway, and the major jet service it will bring to the county, will increase economic activity in the community. The board projects that the increased economic activity will result in $64,000 per year in additional tax revenue for the county.

In analyzing the runway proposal, the board has decided to use a 10-year time horizon. The county's hurdle rate for capital projects is 12 percent.

Required:

1. Compute the initial cost of the investment in the long runway.
2. Compute the annual net cost or benefit from the runway.
3. Determine the IRR on the proposed long runway. Should it be built?

Problem 16–46
Net Present Value (Section 1)
(LO 16-1, 16-3)

1. Present value of annual benefits: $361,600

Refer to the data given in the preceding problem.

Required:

1. Prepare a net-present-value analysis of the proposed long runway.
2. Should the County Board of Representatives approve the runway?
3. Which of the data used in the analysis are likely to be most uncertain? Least uncertain? Why?

Problem 16–47
Internal Rate of Return; Sensitivity Analysis (Section 1)
(LO 16-1, 16-3)

Initial cost of investment: $429,440

Refer to the data given in Problem 16–45. The County Board of Representatives believes that if the county conducts a promotional effort costing $20,000 per year, the proposed long runway will result in substantially greater economic development than was projected originally. However, the board is uncertain about the actual increase in county tax revenue that will result.

Required: Suppose the board builds the long runway and conducts the promotional campaign. What would the increase in the county's annual tax revenue need to be in order for the proposed runway's internal rate of return to equal the county's hurdle rate of 12 percent?

Problem 16–48
MACRS Depreciation; Present Value of Tax Shield (Section 2)
(LO 16-4, 16-5)

Computer-controlled printing press, present value of tax shield: $72,126

Mind Challenge, Inc. publishes innovative science textbooks for public schools. The company's management recently acquired the following two new pieces of equipment.

- Computer-controlled printing press: cost, $250,000; expected useful life, 12 years.
- Duplicating equipment to be used in the administrative offices: cost, $60,000; expected useful life, six years.

The company uses straight-line depreciation for book purposes and the MACRS accelerated depreciation schedule for tax purposes. The firm's tax rate is 40 percent; its after-tax hurdle rate is 10 percent. Neither machine has any salvage value.

Required: For each of the publishing company's new pieces of equipment:

1. Prepare a schedule of the annual depreciation expenses for book purposes.
2. Determine the appropriate MACRS property class.
3. Prepare a schedule of the annual depreciation expenses for tax purposes.
4. Compute the present value of the depreciation tax shield.

Problem 16–49
After-Tax Cash Flows; NPV (Section 2)
(LO 16-3, 16-4, 16-5, 16-6)

1. Total initial cash outflow: $(312,000)

Philadelphia Fastener Corporation manufactures nails, screws, bolts, and other fasteners. Management is considering a proposal to acquire new material-handling equipment. The new equipment has the same capacity as the current equipment but will provide operating efficiencies in labor and power usage. The savings in operating costs are estimated at $150,000 annually.

The new equipment will cost $300,000 and will be purchased at the beginning of the year when the project is started. The equipment dealer is certain that the equipment will be operational during the second quarter of the year it is installed. Therefore, 60 percent of the estimated annual savings can be obtained in the first year. The company will incur a one-time expense of $30,000 to transfer production activities from the old equipment to the new equipment. No loss of sales will occur, however, because the processing facility is large enough to install the new equipment without interfering with the operations of the current equipment. The equipment is in the MACRS 7-year property class. The firm would depreciate the machinery in accordance with the MACRS depreciation schedule.

The current equipment has been fully depreciated. Management has reviewed its condition and has concluded that it can be used an additional eight years. The company would receive $10,000, net of removal costs, if it elected to buy the new equipment and dispose of its current equipment at this time. The new equipment will have no salvage value at the end of its life. The company is subject to a 40 percent income-tax rate and requires an after-tax return of at least 12 percent on any investment.

Required:

1. Calculate the annual incremental after-tax cash flows for Philadelphia Fastener Corporation's proposal to acquire the new equipment.
2. Calculate the net present value of the proposal to acquire the new equipment using the cash flows calculated in requirement (1), and indicate what action management should take. Assume all cash flows take place at the end of the year.

(CMA, adapted)

Problem 16–50
After-Tax Cash Flows; Robotic Equipment (Section 2)
(LO 16-4, 16-5, 16-6)

Computer expert's salary and fringe benefits (after-tax): $(56,000)

Tax effect of gain on sale: $(15,000)

Scientific Frontiers Corporation manufactures scientific equipment for use in elementary schools. In December of 20x0 the company's management is considering the acquisition of robotic equipment, which would radically change its manufacturing process. The controller has collected the following data pertinent to the decision.

1. The robotic equipment would cost $1,000,000, to be paid in December of 20x0. The equipment's useful life is projected to be eight years. The equipment is in the MACRS 5-year property class. The company will use the MACRS accelerated depreciation schedule.
2. The robotic equipment requires software, which will be developed over a two-year period in 20x1 and 20x2. Each software expenditure, which will amount to $25,000 per year, will be expensed during the year incurred.
3. A computer systems operator will be hired immediately to oversee the operation of the new robotic equipment. The computer expert's annual salary will be $60,000. Fringe benefits will cost $20,000 annually.

4. Maintenance technicians will be needed. The total cost of their wages and fringe benefits will be $150,000 per year.
5. The changeover of the manufacturing line will cost $90,000, to be expensed in 20x1.
6. Several employees will need retraining to operate the new robotic equipment. The training costs are projected as follows:

20x1	$35,000
20x2	25,000
20x3	10,000

7. An inventory of spare parts for the robotic equipment will be purchased immediately at a cost of $60,000. This investment in working capital will be maintained throughout the eight-year life of the equipment. At the end of 20x8, the parts will be sold for $60,000.
8. The robotic equipment's salvage value at the end of 20x8 is projected to be $50,000. It will be fully depreciated at that time.
9. Aside from the costs specifically mentioned above, management expects the robotic equipment to save $480,000 per year in manufacturing costs.
10. Switching to the robotic equipment will enable Scientific Frontiers Corporation to sell some of its manufacturing machinery over the next two years. The following sales schedule is projected.

	Acquisition Cost of Equipment Sold	Accumulated Depreciation at Time of Sale	Sales Proceeds
20x1	$150,000	$100,000	$ 20,000
20x2	305,000	215,000	140,000

11. Scientific Frontiers Corporation's tax rate is 30 percent.
12. The company's after-tax hurdle rate is 12 percent.

Required: Prepare a year-by-year columnar schedule including all of the after-tax cash flows associated with the robotic-equipment decision. Assume that each cash flow will occur at year-end.

Problem 16–51
Robotic Equipment; Taxes
Net Present Value (Section 2)
(LO 16-3, 16-4, 16-6)

Net present value: $68,098

Refer to the data given in the preceding problem.

Required: Compute the net present value of Scientific Frontiers Corporation's proposed acquisition of robotic equipment.

Problem 16–52
Net Present Value; Internal Rate of Return; Payback; Sensitivity Analysis; Taxes (Sections 2, 3)
(LO 16-3, 16-4, 16-6, 16-8)

Total after-tax cash flow, 20x1: $(964,000)
3. Total after-tax cash inflow (years 20x2, 20x3, 20x4): $910,360

The management of Tri-County Air Taxi, Inc. is considering the replacement of an old machine used in its helicopter repair facility. It is fully depreciated but it can be used by the corporation through 20x5. If management decides to replace the old machine, James Transportation Company has offered to purchase it for $60,000 on the replacement date. The old machine would have no salvage value in 20x5. If the replacement occurs, a new machine would be acquired from Hillcrest Industries on December 31, 20x1. The purchase price of $1,000,000 for the new machine would be paid in cash at the time of replacement. Due to the increased efficiency of the new machine, estimated annual cash savings of $300,000 would be generated through 20x5, the end of its expected useful life. The new machine is not expected to have any salvage value at the end of 20x5. Tri-County's management requires all investments to earn a 12 percent after-tax return. The company's tax rate is 40 percent. The new machine would be classified as three-year property for MACRS purposes.

Required:

1. Compute the net present value of the machine replacement investment.
2. Between which of the following two percentages is the internal rate of return on the machine replacement: 4 percent, 6 percent, 8 percent, 10 percent, 12 percent, and 14 percent?
3. Between what two whole numbers of years is the machine replacement's payback period?
4. How much would the salvage value of the new machine have to be on December 31, 20x5, in order to turn the machine replacement into an acceptable investment?

(CMA, adapted)

■ **Problem 16–53**
Ranking Investment Proposals; NPV versus Profitability Index; Taxes (Section 2)
(LO 16-4, 16-6, 16-7)

1(a). Mall restaurant, net present value: $25,700
2(b). Downtown restaurant, profitability index: 1.10 (rounded)

The owner of Waco Waffle House is considering an expansion of the business. He has identified two alternatives, as follows:

- Build a new restaurant near the mall.
- Buy and renovate an old building downtown for the new restaurant.

The projected cash flows from these two alternatives are shown below. The owner of the restaurant uses a 10 percent after-tax discount rate.

Investment Proposal	Cash Outflow: Time 0	Net After-Tax Cash Inflows* Years 1–10	Years 11–20
Mall restaurant	$400,000	$50,000	$50,000
Downtown restaurant	200,000	35,800	—

* Includes after-tax cash flows from all sources, including incremental revenue, incremental expenses, and depreciation tax shield.

Required:

1. Compute the net present value of each alternative restaurant site.
2. Compute the profitability index for each alternative.
3. How do the two sites rank in terms of (*a*) NPV and (*b*) the profitability index?
4. Comment on the difficulty of ranking the owner's two options for the new restaurant site.

■ **Problem 16–54**
Payback; Accounting Rate of Return (Section 3)
(LO 16-8)

1(a). Payback period, mall restaurant: 8 years

Refer to the data given in the preceding problem. The owner of Waco Waffle House will consider capital projects only if they have a payback period of six years or less. The owner also favors projects that exhibit an accounting rate of return of at least 15 percent. The owner bases a project's accounting rate of return on the initial investment in the project.

Required:

1. Compute the payback period for each of the proposed restaurant sites.
2. Compute the accounting rate of return for each proposed site. Assume the average annual incremental income is $50,000 for the mall restaurant and $35,800 for the downtown restaurant.
3. If the owner of the restaurant sticks to his criteria, which site will he choose?
4. Comment on the pros and cons of the restaurant owner's investment criteria.

■ **Problem 16–55**
Payback; Accounting Rate of Return; Ethics (Section 3)
(LO 16-8)

2. Accounting rate of return (ARR) using initial investment: .125

Liberty Bell Theater is a nonprofit enterprise in downtown Philadelphia. The board of directors is considering an expansion of the theater's seating capacity, which will entail significant renovations to the existing facilities. The board has been promised by the city government that in five years the city will build a new building for the theater, so the proposed expansion is only a temporary solution to the theater's strained seating capacity. The seating expansion project will cost $120,000. The following table lists the incremental ticket revenue, the incremental operating expenses, the depreciation expense, and the incremental operating income over the five-year life of the investment expected as a result of the theater expansion. The theater's revenue and operating expenses are in cash. Thus, depreciation is the only noncash expense. As a nonprofit enterprise, the theater company is not subject to income taxes.

Year	Incremental Revenue	Incremental Operating Expenses	Net Incremental Cash Flow	Annual Straight-Line Depreciation
1	$70,000	$30,000	$40,000	$24,000
2	72,000	32,000	40,000	24,000
3	74,000	34,000	40,000	24,000
4	76,000	38,000	38,000	24,000
5	78,000	41,000	37,000	24,000

Required:

1. Compute the payback period for the proposed expansion of the theater's seating capacity.
2. Compute the project's accounting rate of return using the project's initial investment.
3. Compute the project's accounting rate of return using the project's average investment.
4. Explain why many managerial accountants believe that discounted-cash-flow methods of evaluating investment proposals are superior to the payback and accounting-rate-of-return methods.
5. Suppose the chairperson of the theater's board, who was formerly a managerial accountant, has calculated the seating expansion project's internal rate of return to be lower than the project's accounting rate of return. Moreover, the theater's cost of acquiring expansion capital is above the expansion project's internal rate of return but below its accounting rate of return. As a champion of the theater, and a strong proponent of the expansion, the board chairperson has decided to present only the project's accounting rate of return to the board for its approval of the project. Is this ethical on the part of the board's chairperson? Explain.

Problem 16–56
Sensitivity Analysis; NPV with Taxes (Section 2)
(LO 16-6)

The increase in annual before-tax sales revenue could fall to: $34,840

Refer to the data for High Country Department Stores' computerized checkout equipment decision given in Exhibit 16–11. Also refer to the net-present-value analysis presented in Exhibit 16–12.

Required: The annual incremental sales revenue resulting from the marketing analysis is estimated at $40,000. How low could this amount be and still result in a nonnegative net present value for the new equipment?

Problem 16–57
Inflation; NPV; Nominal Dollars (Appendix B)
(LO 16-4, 16-6, 16-10)

1. Time 0 cash outflow: $(188,000)
3. Net present value: $56,204

Pensacola Cablevision Company provides television cable service to two counties in the Florida panhandle. The firm's management is considering the construction of a new satellite dish in December of 20x0. The new antenna would improve reception and the service provided to customers. The dish antenna and associated equipment will cost $200,000 to purchase and install. The company's old equipment, which is fully depreciated, can be sold now for $20,000. The company president expects the firm's improved capabilities to result in additional revenue of $80,000 per year during the dish's useful life of seven years. The incremental operating expenses associated with the new equipment are projected to be $10,000 per year. These incremental revenues and expenses are in real dollars.

The new satellite dish will be depreciated under the MACRS depreciation schedule for the 5-year property class. The company's tax rate is 40 percent.

Pensacola Cablevision's president expects the real rate of interest in the economy to remain stable at 10 percent. She expects the inflation rate, currently running at 20 percent, to remain unchanged.

Required:

1. Prepare a schedule of cash flows projected over the next eight years (20x0 through 20x7), measured in nominal dollars. The schedule should include the initial costs of purchase and installation, the after-tax incremental revenue and expenses, and the depreciation tax shield. Remember to express the incremental revenues and expenses in nominal dollars.
2. Compute the nominal interest rate.
3. Prepare a net-present-value analysis of the proposed new satellite dish. Use cash flows measured in nominal dollars and a nominal discount rate equal to the nominal interest rate.

Problem 16–58
Inflation; NPV; Real Dollars (Appendix B)
(LO 16-4, 16-6, 16-10)

Time 0 cash outflow: $(188,000)

Refer to the data given in the preceding problem for Pensacola Cablevision Company.

Required:

1. Compute the price index for each year from 20x1 through 20x7, using 1.0000 as the index for 20x0.
2. Prepare a schedule of after-tax cash flows measured in real dollars.
3. Compute the net present value of the proposed new satellite dish using cash flows measured in real dollars. Use a real discount rate equal to the real interest rate.

Cases

Case 16–59
Decision Problem with Sub-options; NPV; IRR; Ethics (Section 1)
(LO 16-1, 16-2, 16-3)

4. Present value of incremental annual cash flows: $129,780
Acquisition cost of minibuses: $(216,000)
5. Initial cost if the minibuses are purchased: $(231,250)

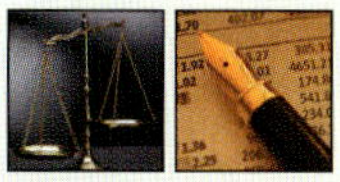

The board of education for the Central Catskill School District is considering the acquisition of several minibuses for use in transporting students to school. Five of the school district's bus routes are underpopulated, with the result that the full-size buses on those routes are not fully utilized. After a careful study, the board has decided that it is not feasible to consolidate these routes into fewer routes served by full-size buses. The area in which the students live is too large for that approach, since some students' bus ride to school would exceed the state maximum of 45 minutes.

The plan under consideration by the board is to replace five full-size buses with eight minibuses, each of which would cover a much shorter route than a full-size bus. The bus drivers in this rural school district are part-time employees whose compensation costs the school district $18,000 per year for each driver. In addition to the drivers' compensation, the annual costs of operating and maintaining a full-size bus amount to $50,000. In contrast, the board projects that a minibus will cost only $20,000 annually to operate and maintain. A minibus driver earns the same wages as a full-size bus driver. The school district controller has estimated that it will cost the district $15,250, initially, to redesign its bus routes, inform the public, install caution signs in certain hazardous locations, and retrain its drivers.

A minibus costs $27,000, whereas a full-size bus costs $90,000. The school district uses straight-line depreciation for all of its long-lived assets. The board has two options regarding the five full-size buses. First, the buses could be sold now for $15,000 each. Second, the buses could be kept in reserve to use for field trips and out-of-town athletic events and to use as backup vehicles when buses break down. Currently, the board charters buses from a private company for these purposes. The annual cost of chartering buses amounts to $30,000. The school district controller has estimated that this cost could be cut to $5,000 per year if the five buses were kept in reserve. The five full-size buses have five years of useful life remaining, either as regularly scheduled buses or as reserve buses. The useful life of a new minibus is projected to be five years also.

Central Catskill School District uses a hurdle rate of 12 percent on all capital projects.

Required:

1. Think about the decision problem faced by the board of education. What are the board's two main alternatives?
2. One of these main alternatives has two options embedded within it. What are those two options?
3. Before proceeding, check the hint given at the end of the chapter, which explains and diagrams the school board's alternatives. Suppose the board of education chooses to buy the minibuses. Prepare a net-present-value analysis of the two options for the five full-size buses. Should these buses be sold now or kept in reserve?
4. From your answer to requirement (3), you know the best option for the board to choose regarding the full-size buses *if* the minibuses are purchased. Now you can ignore the other option. Prepare a net-present-value analysis of the school board's two *main alternatives: (a)* continue to use the full-size buses on regular routes or *(b)* purchase the minibuses. Should the minibuses be purchased?
5. Compute the internal rate of return on the proposed minibus acquisition.
6. What information given in this case was irrelevant to the school board's decision problem? Explain why the information was irrelevant.
7. Independent of requirements (1) through (6), suppose the NPV analysis favors keeping the full-size buses. Michael Jeffries, the business manager for the Central Catskill School District, was prepared to recommend that the board not purchase the minibuses. Before doing so, however, Jeffries ran into a long-time friend at the racquet club. Peter Reynolds was the vice president for sales at a local automobile dealership from which the minibuses would have been purchased. Jeffries broke the bad news about his impending recommendation about the minibuses to his friend. The two talked for some time about the pros and cons of the minibus alternative. Finally, Reynolds said, "Michael, you and I go back a long time. I know you're not paid all that well at the school district. Our top financial person is retiring next year. How would you like to come to work for the dealership?"

   "That's pretty tempting, Peter. Let me think it over," was Jeffries' response.

   "Sure, Michael, take all the time you want. In the meantime, how about rethinking that minibus decision? It's no big deal to you, and I could sure use the business."

   "But Peter, I told you what the figures say about that," responded Jeffries.

   "Come on, Michael. What are friends for?"

   Discuss the ethical issues in this situation. What should Michael Jeffries do?

■ **Case 16–60**
Investment in Robotic Manufacturing Equipment; Net Present Value; Payback (Sections 2, 3)
(LO 16-6, 16-8)

1. Net present value: $47,359

Office King Corporation manufactures three different models of paper shredders including the waste container that serves as the base. While the shredder heads are different for the three models, the waste container is the same. The number of waste containers that Office King will need during the next five years is estimated as follows:

20x1	50,000
20x2	50,000
20x3	52,000
20x4	55,000
20x5	55,000

The equipment used to manufacture the waste container must be replaced because it is broken and cannot be repaired. Management is considering the purchase of robotic equipment to replace the old machinery. The new equipment would have a purchase price of $945,000. There will be a 2 percent discount if payment is made within 10 days. Company policy is to take all purchase discounts. The freight on the equipment would be $11,000, and installation costs would total $22,900. Freight and installation costs will be included in the equipment's cost basis for MACRS depreciation purposes. The equipment would be purchased in December of the current year and placed into service on January 1, 20x1. It would have a five-year useful life but would be treated as three-year property under MACRS because of the nature of the equipment. This equipment is expected to have a salvage value of $12,000 at the end of its useful life in 20x5. The new equipment will result in a 25 percent reduction in both direct labor and variable overhead. There will be an additional one-time permanent decrease in working capital requirements of $2,500, resulting from a reduction in direct-material inventories. This working capital reduction would be recognized in the analysis at the time of equipment acquisition. The old equipment is fully depreciated, and it can be sold for a salvage amount of $1,500.

Rather than replace the equipment, one of Office King's production managers has suggested that the waste containers be purchased. Office King has no alternative use for the manufacturing space at this time, so if the waste containers are purchased, the old equipment would be left in place. One supplier has quoted a price of $27 per container. This price is $8 less than Office King's current manufacturing cost, which is as follows:

Direct material		$ 8.00
Direct labor		10.00
Variable overhead		6.00
Fixed overhead:		
Supervision	$2.00	
Facilities	5.00	
General	4.00	11.00
Total manufacturing cost per unit		$35.00

Office King employs a plantwide fixed overhead rate in its operations. If the waste containers are purchased outside, the salary and benefits of one supervisor, included in the fixed overhead budget at $45,000, would be eliminated. There would be no other changes in the other cash and noncash items included in fixed overhead, except depreciation on the new equipment. Office King is subject to a 40 percent income tax rate. Management assumes that all annual cash flows and tax payments occur at the end of the year and uses a 12 percent after-tax discount rate.

Required:

1. Office King must decide whether to purchase the waste containers from an outside supplier or purchase the equipment to manufacture the waste containers. Calculate the net present value of the estimated after-tax cash flows and determine which of these two options to pursue.
2. Explain why some companies calculate the payback period of an investment in addition to determining the net present value.
3. Between what two consecutive whole number amounts is the payback period for the new equipment?

(CMA, adapted)

Hint for Case 16–59

The school board's two main alternatives are as follows: (1) continue to use the five full-size buses on regular routes or (2) purchase eight minibuses to cover the regular bus routes. Under alternative (2), the board has two options. The full-size buses could be *(a)* sold now or *(b)* kept in reserve.

Thus, the board's decision problem can be diagrammed as follows:

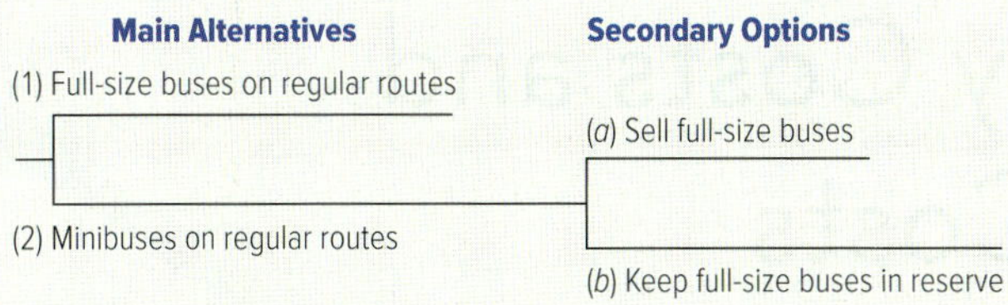

17 Allocation of Support Activity Costs and Joint Costs

FOCUS COMPANY >>>

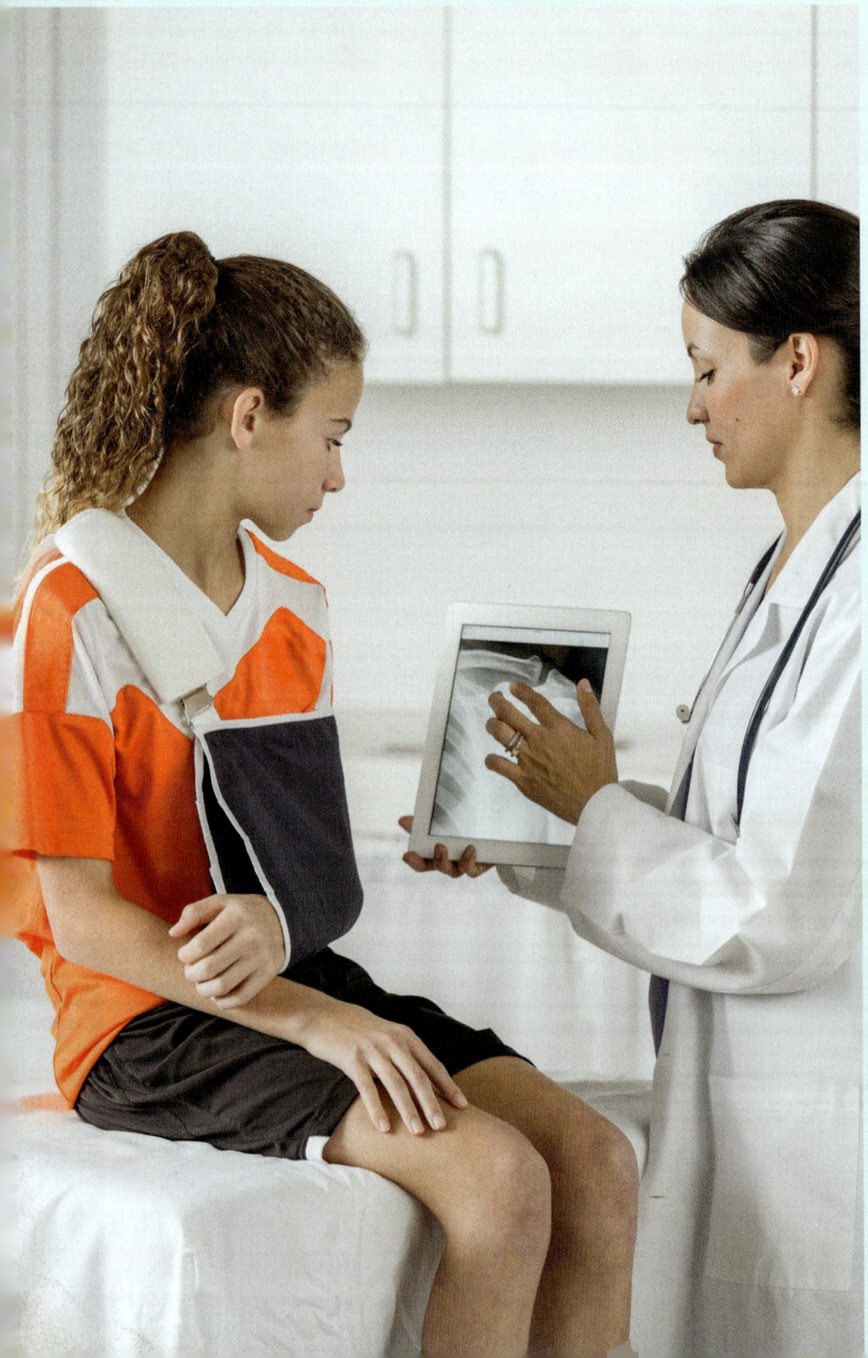

© Terry Vine/Blend Images RF

RIVERSIDE CLINIC

THIS CHAPTER'S FOCUS COMPANY is Riverside Clinic, an outpatient medical facility in Louisville, Kentucky. The clinic has two direct-patient-care departments: Orthopedics and Internal Medicine. In these two departments, patients are treated by medical professionals. Riverside Clinic also has three service departments, which are not directly involved in patient care. The clinic's Patient Records, Human Resources, and Administration and Accounting departments are necessary for the clinic to function, but they operate in a support role to the two direct-patient-care departments. In this chapter, we explore several methods for allocating the costs of the clinic's service departments to the direct-patient-care departments.

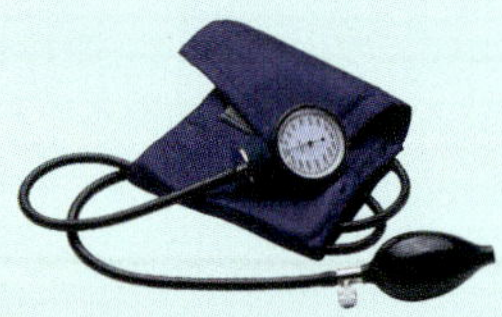

© Siede Preis/Getty Images RF

<<< IN CONTRAST

In contrast to the health care services setting of Riverside Clinic, we explore a different type of allocation issue in the context of International Chocolate Company. This company uses a joint production process to turn cocoa beans into cocoa butter and cocoa powder. The cocoa powder can be processed further into instant cocoa mix. A joint production process results in two or more products, which are called joint products. We will discuss several different methods that International Chocolate Company could use to allocate the costs of its joint production process to its two joint products.

After completing this chapter, you should be able to:

17-1 Allocate service department costs using the direct method and the step-down method.

17-2 Use the dual approach to service department cost allocation.

17-3 Explain the difference between two-stage cost allocation with departmental overhead rates and activity-based costing (ABC).

17-4 Allocate joint costs among joint products using each of the following techniques: physical-units method, relative-sales-value method, and net-realizable-value method.

17-5 Describe the purposes for which joint cost allocation is useful and those for which it is not.

17-6 Allocate service department costs using the reciprocal-services method (appendix).

In earlier chapters, we studied cost allocation and explored its role in an organization's overall managerial accounting system. We also examined several purposes of cost allocation. The goal of cost allocation is to ensure that all costs incurred by the organization ultimately are assigned to its products or services. This is important for several purposes, including cost-based pricing and bidding, cost reimbursements from outside parties such as insurance companies, valuation of inventory, and determination of cost of goods sold. In addition, the allocation of all costs to departments serves to make departmental managers aware of the costs incurred to produce services their departments use.

This chapter is divided into two sections, each of which explores a particular cost-allocation topic in greater detail. The two sections, which may be studied separately, cover the following topics:

- Service department cost allocation[1]
- Joint product cost allocation[2]

Section 1: Service Department Cost Allocation

Learning Objective 17-1

Allocate service department costs using the direct method and the step-down method.

A **service department** is a unit in an organization that is not involved *directly* in producing the organization's goods or services. However, a service department does provide a service that enables the organization's production process to take place. For example, the Maintenance Department in an automobile plant does not make automobiles, but if it did not exist, the production process would stop when the manufacturing machines broke down. Thus, the Maintenance Department is crucial to the production operation even though the repair personnel do not work directly on the plant's products.

[1]The section on service department cost allocation is written as a module, which can be studied separately from the rest of the chapter. This material may be studied after the completion of Chapter 3, which covers basic issues in product costing.

[2]The section on joint cost allocation is written as a module, which can be studied separately from the rest of the chapter. This material may be studied after the completion of Chapter 3.

Service departments are important in nonmanufacturing organizations also. For example, a hospital's Human Resources Department is responsible for staffing the hospital with physicians, nurses, lab technicians, and other employees. The Human Resources Department never serves the patients, yet without it the hospital would have no staff to provide medical care.

A service department such as the Maintenance Department or the Human Resources Department must exist in order for an organization to carry out its primary function. Therefore, the cost of running a service department is part of the cost incurred by the organization in producing goods or services. In order to determine the cost of those goods or services, all service department costs must be allocated to the production departments in which the goods or services are produced. For this reason, the costs incurred in an automobile plant's Maintenance Department are allocated to all of the production departments that have machinery. The costs incurred in a hospital's Human Resources Department are allocated to all of the departments that have personnel. Direct-patient-care departments, such as Surgery and Physical Therapy, are allocated their share of the Human Resources Department's costs.

To see how service department cost allocation fits into the overall picture of product and service costing, it may be helpful to review Exhibit 3–12. The exhibit shows three types of allocation processes, as follows:

1. *Cost distribution.* Costs in various cost pools are distributed to all departments, including both service and production departments.
2. *Service department cost allocation.* Service department costs are allocated to production departments.
3. *Cost application.* Costs are assigned to the goods or services produced by the organization.

RIVERSIDE CLINIC

It is the second type of allocation process listed above that we are focusing on now. The context for our discussion is Riverside Clinic, an outpatient medical facility in Louisville, Kentucky.

The clinic is organized into three service departments and two direct-patient-care departments. Exhibit 17–1 displays a simple organization chart for Riverside Clinic. Since the clinic is not a manufacturing organization, we refer to *direct-patient-care departments* instead of *production departments.* These two departments, Orthopedics and Internal Medicine, directly provide the health care that is the clinic's primary objective. Thus, the clinic's direct-patient-care departments are like the production departments in a manufacturing firm.

"Support, or service, department costs are becoming a greater and greater percentage of our cost structure."(17a)
Fiat Chrysler

Notice that the Human Resources Department and the Administration and Accounting Department provide services to each other. When this situation occurs, the two service departments exhibit *reciprocal services.*

Exhibit 17–2 provides some of the details for our illustration of service department cost allocation. Panel A shows the proportion of each service department's output that is consumed by each of the departments using its services. Panel B shows the allocation

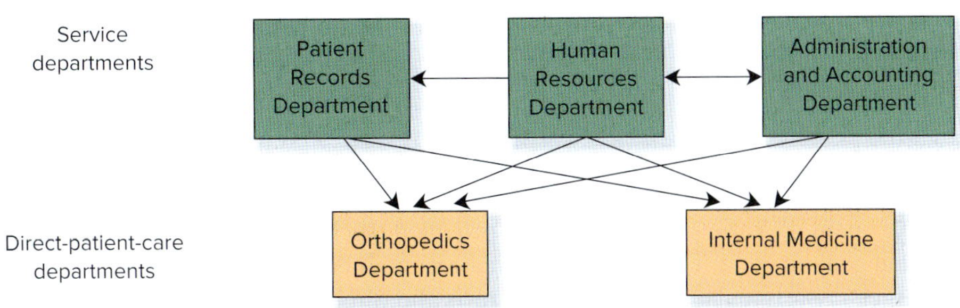

Exhibit 17–1
Organization Chart for Riverside Clinic*

RIVERSIDE CLINIC

*The arrows in the organization chart depict the provision of service by the three service departments. For example, the Human Resources Department serves the Patient Records Department, but not vice versa.

Exhibit 17–2
Provision of Services by Service Departments in 20x1: Riverside Clinic

RIVERSIDE CLINIC

A. Percentage of Service Output Consumed by Using Departments

		Provider of Service		
User of Service		**Patient Records**	**Human Resources**	**Administration and Accounting**
Service departments	Patient Records	—	5%	—
	Human Resources	—	—	5%
	Administration and Accounting	—	20%	—
Direct-patient-care departments	Orthopedics	30%	25%	35%
	Internal Medicine	70%	50%	60%

B. Allocation Bases

Service Department	Allocation Base
Patient Records	Annual patient load
Human Resources	Number of employees
Administration and Accounting	Size of department (measured in square feet of space)

C. Service Department Costs

Service Department	Variable Cost	Fixed Cost	Total Cost to Be Allocated
Patient Records	$24,000	$ 76,000	$100,000
Human Resources	15,000	45,000	60,000
Administration and Accounting	47,500	142,500	190,000
Total	$86,500	$263,500	$350,000

bases, which are used to determine the proportions shown in panel A. Further explanation of the information in Exhibit 17–2 follows.

Patient Records The service output of the Patient Records Department is consumed only by the Orthopedics and Internal Medicine Departments. *Annual patient load* is the *allocation base* used to determine that 30 percent of the Patient Records Department's services were consumed by Orthopedics and 70 percent by Internal Medicine.

Human Resources The Human Resources Department serves each of the clinic's other departments, including the other two service departments and the two direct-patient-care departments. The *allocation base* used to determine the proportions of the Human Resources Department's output consumed by the four using departments is the *number of employees* in the using departments. For example, 5 percent of the clinic's employees (excluding those in the Human Resources Department) work in the Patient Records Department.

Administration and Accounting This service department provides services only to the Human Resources Department, the Orthopedics Department, and the Internal Medicine Department. A variety of services are provided, such as computer support, patient billing, and general administration. Since greater amounts of these services are provided to the larger departments, departmental size is the allocation base used to determine the proportion of service output consumed by each department. Since the space devoted to each department is a convenient measure of departmental size, square footage is the measure used in Exhibit 17–2. For example, 5 percent of the clinic's space (excluding that occupied by Administration and Accounting and Patient Records) is devoted to the Human Resources Department.

Panel C of Exhibit 17–2 shows the total budgeted cost of each service department that is to be allocated among the using departments.

There are two widely used methods of service department cost allocation, the direct method and the step-down method. These methods are discussed and illustrated next, using the data for Riverside Clinic.

Direct Method

Under the **direct method,** each service department's costs are allocated among *only the direct-patient-care departments* that consume part of the service department's output. This method ignores the fact that some service departments provide services to other service departments. Thus, even though Riverside Clinic's Human Resources Department provides services to two other service departments, none of its costs are allocated to those departments. Exhibit 17–3 presents Riverside Clinic's service department cost allocations under the direct method.

Notice that the proportion of each service department's costs to be allocated to each direct-patient-care department is determined by the *relative proportion* of the service department's output consumed by each direct-patient-care department. For example, a glance at Exhibit 17–2 shows that the Human Resources Department provides 25 percent of its services to Orthopedics and 50 percent to Internal Medicine. Summing these two percentages yields 75 percent. Thus, 25/75 is the fraction of the Human Resources Department's cost allocated to Orthopedics and 50/75 is the fraction allocated to Internal Medicine.

Step-Down Method

As stated above, the direct method ignores the provision of services by one service department to another service department. This shortcoming is overcome partially by the **step-down method** of service department cost allocation. Under this method, the managerial accountant first chooses a sequence in which to allocate the service departments' costs. A common way to select the first service department in the sequence is to choose the one that serves the largest number of other service departments. The service departments are ordered in this manner, with the last service department being the one that serves the smallest number of other service departments.[3] Then the managerial accountant

Exhibit 17–3
Direct Method of Service Department Cost Allocation: Riverside Clinic

RIVERSIDE CLINIC

		Direct-Patient-Care Departments Using Services			
		Orthopedics		Internal Medicine	
Provider of Service	**Cost to Be Allocated**	**Proportion**	**Amount**	**Proportion**	**Amount**
Patient Records	$100,000	3/10	$ 30,000	7/10	$ 70,000
Human Resources	60,00	25/75	20,000	50/75	40,000
Administration and Accounting	190,000	35/95	70,000	60/95	120,000
Total	$350,000		$120,000		$230,000
			Grand total= $350,000		

[3] A tie occurs when two or more service departments serve the same number of other service departments. Then the sequence among the tied service departments usually is an arbitrary choice.

allocates each service department's costs among the direct-patient-care departments and all of the other service departments that follow it in the sequence. Note that the ultimate cost allocations assigned to the direct-patient-care departments will differ depending on the sequence chosen.

The step-down method is best explained by way of an illustration. Riverside Clinic's Human Resources Department serves two other service departments: Patient Records, and Administration and Accounting. The Administration and Accounting Department serves only one other service department: Human Resources. Finally, the Patient Records Department serves no other service departments. Thus, Riverside Clinic's service department sequence is as follows:

(1) Human Resources	(2) Administration and Accounting	(3) Patient Records

In accordance with this sequence, each service department's costs are allocated to the other departments as follows:

"Allocating service department costs to the academic units serves a variety of purposes. For one thing, it makes the [academic] units aware that their activities result in those costs being incurred behind the scenes." (17b)
Cornell University

Cost Allocated from This Service Department →	To These Departments
Human Resources	Administration and Accounting
	Patient Records
	Orthopedics
	Internal Medicine
Administration and Accounting	Orthopedics
	Internal Medicine
Patient Records	Orthopedics
	Internal Medicine

Notice that even though Administration and Accounting serves Human Resources, there is no cost allocation in that direction. This results from the placement of Human Resources before Administration and Accounting in the allocation sequence. Moreover, no costs are allocated from Patient Records to either of the other service departments, because Patient Records does not serve those departments.

Exhibit 17–4 presents the results of applying the step-down method at Riverside Clinic. First, the Human Resources Department's $60,000 in cost is allocated among the four departments using its services. Second, the cost of the Administration and Accounting Department is allocated. The total cost to be allocated is the department's original $190,000 *plus* the $12,000 allocated from the Human Resources Department. The new total of $202,000 is allocated to the Orthopedics and Internal Medicine Departments according to the *relative proportions* in which these two departments use the services of the Administration and Accounting Department. Finally, the Patient Records Department's cost is allocated.

Reciprocal-Services Method

The direct method and the step-down method both ignore the fact that the Administration and Accounting Department serves the Human Resources Department. Neither of these methods allocates any of the costs incurred in Administration and Accounting back to Human Resources.

Review the relationships between the service departments depicted in Exhibit 17–1. Notice that the Administration and Accounting Department and the Human Resources

	Service Department			Direct-Patient-Care Department	
	Human Resources	Administration and Accounting	Patient Records	Orthopedics	Internal Medicine
Costs prior to allocation	$60,000	$190,000	$100,000		
Allocation of Human Resources Department costs	$60,000 →	12,000 (20/100)†	3,000 (5/100)	$ 15,000 (25/100)	$ 30,000 (50/100)
Allocation of Administration and Accounting Department costs		$202,000 →		74,421* (35/95)	127,579* (60/95)
Allocation of Patient Records Department costs			$103,000 →	30,900 (30/100)	72,100 (70/100)
Total cost allocated to each department				$120,321	$229,679
Total cost allocated to direct-patient-care departments				$350,000	

*Rounded.

†Fractions in parentheses are relative proportions of service department's output consumed by departments to which costs are allocated.

Exhibit 17–4

Step-Down Method of Service Department Cost Allocation: Riverside Clinic

RIVERSIDE CLINIC

Department *serve each other*. This mutual provision of service is called reciprocal service. A more accurate method of service department cost allocation, called the **reciprocal-services method,** fully accounts for the mutual provision of services. This method, which is more complex than the direct and step-down methods, is covered in the appendix at the end of this chapter.

Fixed versus Variable Costs

In our allocation of Riverside Clinic's service department costs, we did not distinguish between fixed and variable costs. Under some circumstances, this simple approach can result in an unfair cost allocation among the using departments. To illustrate, we will use the data about Riverside Clinic's fixed and variable costs given in panel C of Exhibit 17–2. Consider the cost data for the Patient Records Department, which serves only the Orthopedics and Internal Medicine departments. Under the *direct method* of service department cost allocation, the Patient Records Department's costs were allocated as follows:

Cost Allocation for 20x1: Direct Method

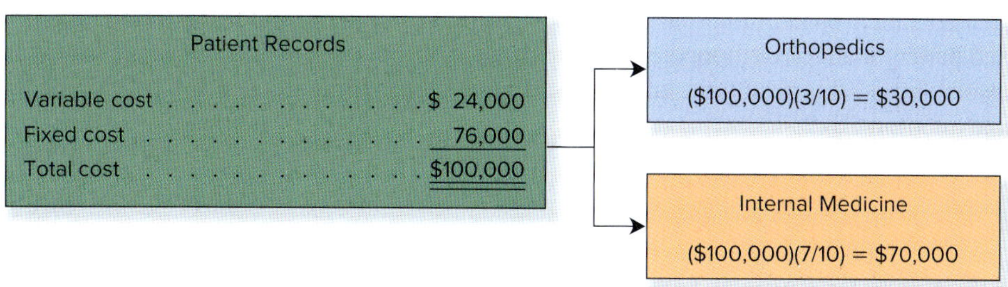

The allocation base used in this cost allocation is the annual patient load in the Orthopedics and Internal Medicine departments. Let's assume the following patient loads in 20x1, the year for which the cost allocation has been done.

Department	Patient Load	Proportion of Total
Orthopedics	30,000	(30,000/100,000) = 3/10
Internal Medicine	70,000	(70,000/100,000) = 7/10
Total	100,000	

Now suppose the projections for 20x2 are as follows:

Department	Projected Patient Load	Projected Proportion of Total
Orthopedics	30,000	(30,000/80,000) = 3/8
Internal Medicine	50,000	(50,000/80,000) = 5/8
Total	80,000	

Department	Budgeted Variable Cost	Budgeted Fixed Cost	Budgeted Total Cost
Patient Records	$19,200	$76,000	$95,200

The projections for 20x2 include a stable patient load in the Orthopedics Department but a decline in the patient load of the Internal Medicine Department. Since the projected total patient load is lower for 20x2, the projected variable cost in the Patient Records Department is lower also.

What will be the effect of these changes on the 20x2 allocation of the Patient Records Department's costs? Using the direct method, we obtain the following allocation.

Cost Allocation for 20x2: Direct Method

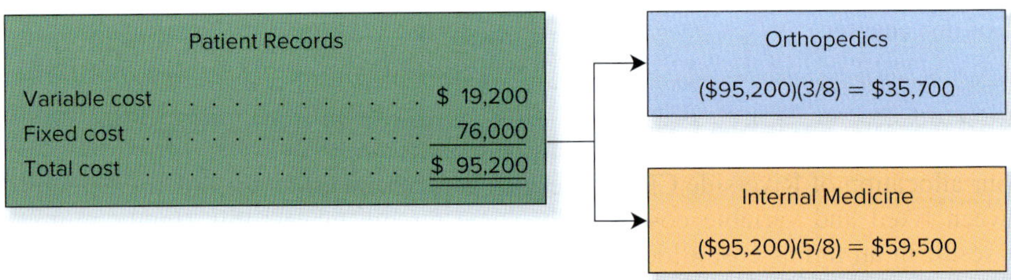

Compare the costs allocated to the two direct-patient-care departments in 20x1 and 20x2. Notice that the cost allocated to the Orthopedics Department *increased by* $5,700 (from $30,000 to $35,700), even though Orthopedics' patient load is projected to remain constant. What has happened here? The projected decline in the Internal Medicine Department's volume resulted in lower budgeted variable costs for the Patient Records Department, but the budgeted *fixed costs* did not change. At the same time, the lower projected patient load in Internal Medicine resulted in a higher proportion of the total projected patient load for Orthopedics (from 3/10 in 20x1 up to 3/8 in 20x2). As the following analysis shows, this results in an increased allocation of fixed costs to the Orthopedics Department in 20x2.

	20x1	20x2
Fixed cost in Patient Records Department	$76,000	$76,000
Orthopedics Department's proportion of total patient load	3/10	3/8
Orthopedics Department's allocation of fixed cost	$22,800	$28,500
	Difference = $5,700	

This difference of $5,700 is equal to the increase in the Orthopedics Department's total cost allocation from the Patient Records Department in 20x2.

COST REIMBURSEMENT IN THE HEALTH CARE INDUSTRY

Medicare uses a system called relative value units (RVUs) to set payment rates for physicians. "RVUs are supposed to measure how much time and physical effort a doctor requires to perform different clinical endeavors. Medicare assigns each clinical procedure a different RVU and then multiplies this figure by a fixed amount of money to arrive at how much it will pay a doctor for a given task. A routine office visit has an RVU of about 1.68. Setting a finger fracture rates a 3.48." There is much argument in the press about the effectiveness of this system in managing health care costs. One observer argues, "This system misses all the intangible factors that help gauge the quality and efficiency of the health care being delivered."[4]

Additionally, there is much uncertainty in the minds of many as to how Medicare payments will be affected by the U.S. Patient Protection and Affordable Care Act enacted in 2010. And, of course, many observers argue that the entire Medicare system is in jeopardy of running out of money as the baby boom generation retires and adds to the ranks of Medicare recipients. Most observers agree that the entire U.S. health care system is in need of reform as costs continue to explode.

Management **A**ccounting **P**ractice

Medicare

To summarize, the projected decline in Internal Medicine's 20x2 patient load will result in an increased cost allocation from the Patient Records Department to the Orthopedics Department in 20x2. The cause of this increased allocation is our failure to distinguish between fixed and variable costs in the allocation process.

Dual Cost Allocation

Learning Objective **17-2**

Use the dual approach to service department cost allocation.

The problem illustrated in the preceding section can be resolved by allocating fixed and variable costs separately. This approach, called **dual cost allocation,** works with either the direct method or the step-down method of allocation. Under dual cost allocation, *variable costs* are allocated on the basis of *short-run usage* of the service department's output; *fixed costs* are allocated on the basis of *long-run average usage* of the service department's output. The rationale for this approach is that fixed costs are capacity-producing costs. When service departments are established, their size and scale usually are determined by the projected long-run needs of the using departments.

To illustrate dual cost allocation for Riverside Clinic, we need estimates of the long-run average usage of each service department's output by each using department. These estimates are given in Exhibit 17–5.

Exhibit 17–5
Provision of Services by Service Departments: Long-Run Average Usage, Riverside Clinic

RIVERSIDE CLINIC

		Provider of Service		
User of Service		**Patient Records**	**Human Resources**	**Administration and Accounting**
Service departments	Patient Records	—	10%	—
	Human Resources	—	—	10%
	Administration and Accounting	—	10%	—
Direct-patient-care departments	Orthopedics	40%	20%	45%
	Internal Medicine	60%	60%	45%

[4]Scott Gottlieb, "The Doctor Won't See You Now. He's Clocked Out," *The Wall Street Journal,* March 15, 2013, p. A13; and the authors' research.

To combine the dual cost allocation approach with either the direct method or the step-down method, we simply apply the allocation method twice, as follows:

Costs to Be Allocated	Basis for Allocation	Allocation Method	
Variable costs in 20x1 (Exhibit 17–2, panel C)	Short-run usage in 20x1 (Exhibit 17–2, panel A)	Direct method	Step-down method
		OR	
Fixed costs in 20x1 (Exhibit 17–2, panel C)	Long-run average usage (Exhibit 17–5)	Direct method	Step-down method

After both of these allocation procedures have been completed, the resulting variable- and fixed-cost allocations for each direct-patient-care department are summed. Exhibit 17–6 presents the allocation computations when the dual approach is combined with the direct method. Compare the final direct allocations with those in Exhibit 17–3, where the dual approach was not used. Notice that the final allocations are different. Exhibit 17–7 presents the computations for the step-down method. Compare the final step-down allocations with those in Exhibit 17–4, where dual cost allocation was not used. Again, the final allocations are different.

A Behavioral Problem Dual cost allocation prevents a change in the short-run activity of one using department from affecting the cost allocated to another using department. However, the approach sometimes presents a problem of its own. In order to implement the technique, we need accurate projections of the long-run average usage of each service department's output by each using department. This is the information in Exhibit 17–5. Typically, these estimates come from the managers of the departments that consume the services. The problem is that the higher a manager's estimate of the department's long-run average usage is, the greater will be the department's allocation of fixed service department costs. This creates an incentive for using-department managers to understate their expected long-run service needs. Ultimately, such understatements can result in building service facilities that are too small.

> "Our clients are realizing to an ever-greater extent that they have to understand and manage their support service costs." (17c)
>
> **American Management Systems**

How can we prevent this behavioral problem? First, we can rely on the professionalism and integrity of the managers who provide the estimates. Second, we can reward managers through promotions and pay raises for making accurate estimates of their departments' service needs.

Exhibit 17–6
Dual Allocation Combined with Direct Method: Riverside Clinic

RIVERSIDE CLINIC

		Direct-Patient-Care Department Using Services			
		Orthopedics		Internal Medicine	
Provider of Service	Cost to Be Allocated	Proportion	Amount	Proportion	Amount
I. Variable Costs					
Patient Records	$ 24,000	3/10	$ 7,200	7/10	$ 16,800
Human Resources	15,000	25/75	5,000	50/75	10,000
Administration and Accounting	47,500	35/95	17,500	60/95	30,000
Total variable cost	$ 86,500		$ 29,700		$ 56,800
II. Fixed Costs					
Patient Records	$ 76,000	4/10	$ 30,400	6/10	$ 45,600
Human Resources	45,000	20/80	11,250	60/80	33,750
Administration and Accounting	142,500	45/90	71,250	45/90	71,250
Total fixed cost	$263,500		$112,900		$150,600
Total cost (variable + fixed)	$350,000		$142,600		$207,400

Grand total = $350,000

	Service Department			Direct-Patient-Care Department	
	Human Resources	Administration and Accounting	Patient Records	Orthopedics	Internal Medicine
I. Variable Costs					
Variable cost prior to allocation	$15,000	$ 47,500	$24,000		
Allocation of Human Resources Department costs	$15,000	3,000 (20/100)†	750 (5/100)	$ 3,750 (25/100)	$ 7,500 (50/100)
Allocation of Administration and Accounting Department costs		$ 50,500		18,605* (35/95)	31,895* (60/95)
Allocation of Patient Records Department costs			$24,750	7,425 (30/100)	17,325 (70/100)
Total variable cost allocated to each department				$ 29,780	$ 56,720
II. Fixed Costs					
Fixed cost prior to allocation	$45,000	$142,500	$76,000		
Allocation of Human Resources Department costs	$45,000	4,500 (10/100)	4,500 (10/100)	$ 9,000 (20/100)	$ 27,000 (60/100)
Allocation of Administration and Accounting Department costs		$147,000		73,500 (45/90)	73,500 (45/90)
Allocation of Patient Records Department costs			$80,500	32,200 (40/100)	48,300 (60/100)
Total fixed cost allocated to each department				$114,700	$148,800
Total cost allocated to each department (variable + fixed)				$144,480	$205,520
				Grand total = $350,000	

*Rounded

† Fractions in parentheses are relative proportions of service department's output consumed by departments to which costs are allocated. Variable costs allocated on basis of short-run proportions. Fixed costs allocated on basis of long-run average proportions.

Exhibit 17–7

Dual Allocation Combined with Step-Down Method: Riverside Clinic

RIVERSIDE CLINIC

Allocate Budgeted Costs

When service department costs are allocated to production departments, such as the direct-patient-care departments of Riverside Clinic, *budgeted* service department costs should be used. If actual costs are allocated instead, any operating inefficiencies in the service departments are passed along to the using departments. This reduces the incentive for service department managers to control the costs in their departments. The proper approach is as follows:

1. Compare budgeted and actual service department costs and compute any variances.
2. Use these variances to help control costs in the service departments.
3. Close out the service department cost variances against the period's income.
4. Allocate the service departments' budgeted costs to the departments that directly produce goods or services.

Today's Advanced Manufacturing Environment

In traditional manufacturing environments, service department costs are allocated to production departments to ensure that all manufacturing costs are assigned to products. For example, the costs incurred in a machine-maintenance department typically are allocated to the other service departments and the production departments that use maintenance services. Service department cost allocation continues to be used in the new manufacturing environment, characterized by JIT inventory management and CIM systems. However, the extent of such allocations is diminished in advanced manufacturing systems, because more costs are directly traceable to product lines. In a flexible manufacturing system, almost all operations are performed in the FMS cell. Even machine maintenance is done largely by the FMS cell operators rather than a separate maintenance department. Inspection often is performed by FMS cell operators, eliminating the need for a separate inspection department. In short, as more and more costs become directly traceable to products, the need for allocation of indirect costs declines.

The Rise of Activity-Based Costing

Learning Objective 17-3

Explain the difference between two-stage cost allocation with departmental overhead rates and activity-based costing (ABC).

Service department cost allocation is one type of allocation procedure used in two-stage allocation with departmental overhead rates. (See Exhibit 3–12 on page 108.) Under this approach, costs first are distributed to *departments;* then they are allocated from service *departments* to production *departments.* Finally, they are assigned from production *departments* to products or services. *Departments* play a key role as intermediate cost objects under this approach.

In an activity-based costing (ABC) system, on the other hand, the key role is played by *activities,* not departments. (See Exhibit 5–4 on page 173.) First, the costs of various *activities* are assigned to *activity* cost pools; then these costs are assigned to products or services.

The breakdown of costs by activity in an ABC system is much finer than a breakdown by departments. For example, under the service department cost allocation approach, the Purchasing Department might be one of the service departments identified. However, under ABC, the various activities engaged in by purchasing personnel would be separately identified. Activities such as part specification, vendor identification, vendor selection, price negotiation, ordering, expediting, receiving, inspection, and invoice paying might be identified separately under ABC. Then the costs of each of these activities would be assigned to products or services on the basis of the appropriate cost drivers. The ABC approach generally will provide a much more accurate cost for each of the organization's products or services.[5]

Section 2: Joint Product Cost Allocation

Learning Objective 17-4

Allocate joint costs among joint products using each of the following techniques: physical-units method, relative-sales-value method, and net-realizable-value method.

A **joint production process** results in two or more products, which are termed **joint products.** The cost of the input and the joint production process is called a *joint product cost.* The point in the production process where the individual products become separately identifiable is called the **split-off point.** To illustrate, International Chocolate Company produces cocoa powder and cocoa butter by processing cocoa beans in the joint production process depicted in Exhibit 17–8.

As the diagram shows, cocoa beans are processed in 1-ton batches. The beans cost \$500 and the joint process costs \$600, for a total *joint cost* of \$1,100. The process results in 1,500 pounds of cocoa butter and 500 pounds of cocoa powder. Each of these two joint products can be sold at the split-off point or processed further. Cocoa butter can be separately processed into a sun screen, and cocoa powder can be separately processed into instant cocoa mix.

Milk processing provides an example of joint product cost allocation in the agriculture industry. The cost of producing raw milk must be allocated among such joint products as heavy cream, light cream, whole milk, 2 percent milk, and skim milk.

Allocating Joint Costs

For product-costing purposes, a joint product cost usually is allocated to

[5]Activity-based costing (ABC) is covered extensively in Chapter 5.

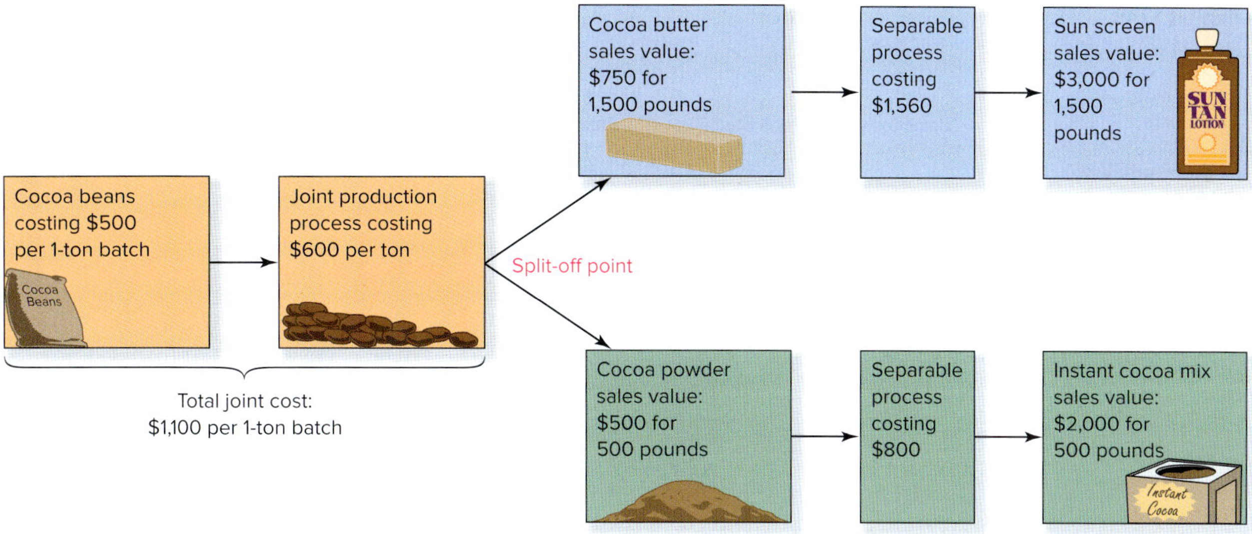

Exhibit 17–8
Joint Processing of Cocoa Beans: International Chocolate Company

the joint products that result from the joint production process. Such allocation *is necessary* for inventory valuation and income determination, among other reasons.[6] As we discussed in Chapter 14, however, joint cost allocation is *not useful* for making substantive economic decisions about the joint process or the joint products. For example, Chapter 14 shows that joint cost allocation is not useful in deciding whether to process a joint product further. There are three commonly used methods for allocating joint product costs. Each of these is explained next.

Learning Objective 17-5

Describe the purposes for which joint cost allocation is useful and those for which it is not.

Physical-Units Method The **physical-units method** allocates joint product costs on the basis of some physical characteristic of the joint products at the split-off point. Panel A of Exhibit 17–9 illustrates this allocation method for International Chocolate Company using the *weight* of the joint products as the allocation basis.

Exhibit 17–9
Methods for Allocating Joint Product Costs

A. Physical-Units Method

Joint Cost	Joint Products	Weight at Split-off Point	Relative Proportion	Allocation of Joint Cost
$1,100	Cocoa butter	1,500 pounds	3/4	$ 825
	Cocoa powder	500 pounds	1/4	275
	Total joint cost allocated			$1,100

B. Relative-Sales-Value Method

Joint Cost	Joint Products	Sales Value at Split-off Point	Relative Proportion	Allocation of Joint Cost
$1,100	Cocoa butter	$750	3/5	$ 660
	Cocoa powder	500	2/5	440
	Total joint cost allocated			$1,100

(continued)

[6]The purposes of product costing are covered in Chapter 3.

Exhibit 17–9
Methods for Allocating Joint Product Costs
(concluded)

INTERNATIONAL CHOCOLATE COMPANY

C. Net-Realizable-Value Method

Joint Cost	Joint Products	Sales Value of Final Product	Separable Cost of Processing	Net Realizable Value	Relative Proportion	Allocation of Joint Cost
$1,100	Sun screen	$3,000	$1,560	$1,440*	6/11†	$600
	Instant cocoa mix	2,000	800	1,200*	5/11†	500
	Total joint cost allocated					$1,100

*Sales value of final product	–	Separable cost of processing	=	Net realizable value
$3,000	–	$1,560	=	$1,440
2,000	–	800	=	1,200

†Calculation of relative proportions:

$1,440	+	$1,200	=	$2,640
1,440	÷	2,640	=	6/11
1,200	÷	2,640	=	5/11

Relative-Sales-Value Method The **relative-sales-value method** is based on the relative sales value of each joint product *at the split-off point.* In the International Chocolate Company illustration, these joint products are cocoa butter and cocoa powder. This method is illustrated in Exhibit 17–9 (panel B).

Net-Realizable-Value Method Under the **net-realizable-value method,** the relative value of the final products is used to allocate the joint cost. International Chocolate Company's final products are sun screen and instant cocoa mix. The **net realizable value** of each final product is its sales value less any separable costs incurred *after* the split-off

Management **A**ccounting **P**ractice

ExxonMobil

JOINT COST ALLOCATION IN THE PETROLEUM INDUSTRY

One of the most complicated problems in joint cost allocation routinely occurs in the petroleum industry. When an oil company, such as ExxonMobil, drills a successful oil well, the well almost always produces natural gas in addition to crude oil. Moreover, the crude oil produced by a typical oil well is of various grades. Lighter crude oils suitable for production of such products as gasoline are generally near the top of an oil reservoir, while the heavier crudes are near the bottom. The heavier crude oils are used to make such products as fuel oil for heating homes and businesses and for the generation of electricity.

All of these products obtained from a successful oil well are joint products: the various grades of crude oil and the natural gas. Most of these products will require further processing before they will be salable products such as gasoline, diesel fuel, or home heating oil. Thus, substantial separable costs will be incurred in processing the joint products in addition to the joint costs incurred in the oil field operations. Millions of dollars of joint costs are incurred in the development of an off-shore oil field. The costs of locating the oil field, building the drilling platforms, and the drilling itself are all joint costs. Then there are the costs of crewing the oil rigs and the ongoing costs of bringing oil and natural gas to the surface.

Oil companies such as ExxonMobil typically use the net realizable value of the products manufactured as the basis for allocating the joint production costs. The full costs of the company's various products then become the basis for pricing and product-mix decisions.

The next time you pump gas for your automobile, think about the salaries of the helicopter pilots who bring food and other supplies to the many off-shore oil platforms. Those costs comprise a part of the joint cost allocated to the gasoline you obtain from the pump.

point. The joint cost is allocated according to the relative magnitudes of the final products' net realizable values. Panel C of Exhibit 17–9 illustrates this allocation method.

Notice how different the cost allocations are under the three methods, particularly the physical-units method. Since the physical-units approach is not based on the *economic* characteristics of the joint products, it is the least preferred of the three methods.

> "Joint costing problems crop up more often than you might think. They're among the thornier [cost management] issues our clients have to deal with." (17d)
>
> **A. T. Kearney**

By-Products A joint product with minimal value relative to the other joint products is termed a **by-product.** For example, whey is a by-product in the production of cheese. A common practice in accounting is to subtract a by-product's net realizable value from the cost of the joint process. Then the remaining joint cost is allocated among the major joint products.

An alternative procedure is to inventory the by-product at its sales value at the split-off point. Then the by-product's sales value is deducted from the production cost of the main products.

Chapter Summary

LO17-1 Allocate service department costs using the direct method and the step-down method. Under the direct method, the costs of each service department are allocated directly to each production department in proportion to each production department's usage of each service department's output. Under the step-down method, the service departments are first ranked by the number of other service departments that each one serves. Then the costs of each service department in the ranked sequence are allocated among all of the remaining service departments in the sequence together with all of the production departments.

LO17-2 Use the dual approach to service department cost allocation. Either the direct or the step-down method may be combined with dual cost allocation, in which variable and fixed costs are allocated separately.

LO17-3 Explain the difference between two-stage cost allocation with departmental overhead rates and activity-based costing (ABC). Two-stage allocation with departmental overhead rates involves the following three steps: (1) All overhead costs are allocated among all service and production departments. (2) Service-department costs are allocated to production departments. (3) Production department costs are applied to products or services. In contrast, two-stage allocation under ABC involves the following two steps: (1) Resource costs are assigned to activity cost pools. (2) The costs in these activity cost pools are assigned to cost objects (e.g., products or services) using appropriate cost drivers.

LO17-4 Allocate joint costs among joint products using each of the following techniques: physical units method, relative-sales-value method, and net-realizable-value method. In the physical-units method, the joint cost is allocated to the joint products in proportion to some physical characteristic of the joint products, such as weight or volume. In the relative-sales-value method, the joint cost is allocated to the joint products in proportion to the joint products' sales values at the split-off point. In the net-realizable-value method, the joint cost is allocated to the joint products in proportion to the joint products' net realizable values.

LO17-5 Describe the purposes for which joint cost allocation is useful and those for which it is not. Joint cost allocation is useful for product-costing purposes, but the allocated costs should not affect substantive economic decisions.

LO17-6 Allocate service department costs using the reciprocal-services method (appendix). Under the reciprocal-services method, simultaneous equations are specified to show how each service and production department uses the services of the various service departments. When these equations are solved simultaneously, the result is the amount of service department cost to be allocated to each production department. Unlike the direct and step-down methods, the reciprocal-services method fully accounts for all reciprocal services among service departments.

Review Problem on Service Department Cost Allocation

Renaissance School of Music and Art provides classes for school-age children. The students are enrolled in two departments: Music Education and Art Education. The school also has two service departments: Administration and Human Resources (A&HR) and Maintenance (M). The budgeted costs in the two service departments are as follows:

Administration and Human Resources	$342,000
Maintenance	171,000

The usage of the service department's output for the year is as follows:

	Provider of Service	
User of Service	**Administration & Human Resources**	**Maintenance**
Administration & Human Resources	—	5%
Maintenance	10%	—
Music Education	40%	40%
Art Education	50%	55%

Required: Allocate the two services departments' costs to the Music Education and Art Education departments using each of the following allocation methods.

1. Direct method.
2. Step-down method (Since each service department serves one other service department, allocate the cost of A&HR first.)

Solution to Review Problem

1. Cost allocation using direct method:

		Departments Using Services			
		Music Education		Art Education	
Provider of Service	**Cost to Be Allocated**	**Proportion**	**Amount**	**Proportion**	**Amount**
A&HR	$342,000	(4/9)	$152,000	(5/9)	$190,000
M*	171,000	(8/19)	72,000	(11/19)	99,000
Total	$513,000		$224,000		$289,000

*(8/19) = [40/(40 + 55)]; (11/19) = [55/(40 + 55)].

2. Cost allocation using step-down method:

	Service Departments		Departments Using Services	
	A&HR	**M**	**Music Education**	**Art Education**
Costs prior to allocation	$342,000	$171,000		
Allocation of A&HR costs*	$342,000	34,200 (10%)	$136,800 (40%)	$171,000 (50%)
Allocation of M costs*		$205,200	86,400 (8/19)	118,800 (11/19)
Total costs allocated to each department			$223,200	$289,800
Total cost allocated to academic departments			$513,000	

*(8/19) = [40/(40 + 55)]; (11/19) = [55/(40 + 55)].

Key Terms

For each term's definition refer to the indicated page, or turn to the glossary at the end of the text.

by-product, 755
direct method, 745
dual cost allocation, 749
joint production process, 752
joint products, 752
net realizable value, 754
net-realizable-value method, 754
physical-units method, 753
reciprocal-services method, 747
relative-sales-value method, 754
service department, 742
split-off point, 752
step-down method, 745

APPENDIX TO CHAPTER 17

Reciprocal-Services Method

RIVERSIDE CLINIC

Learning Objective 17-6

Allocate service department costs using the reciprocal services method.

The reciprocal-services method of service department cost allocation fully accounts for the mutual provision of services among all the service departments. The relationships between Riverside Clinic's three service departments are portrayed in the following diagram.

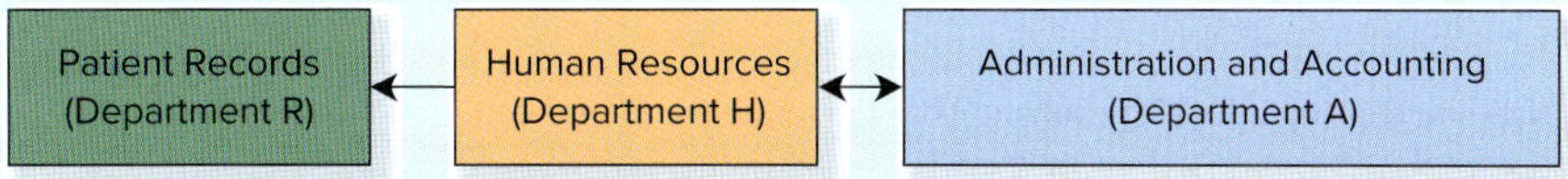

The first step in the technique is to specify a set of equations that express the relationships between the departments. The following equations, which express these relationships for Riverside Clinic, are based on the data in Exhibit 17–2.

$$R = 100{,}000 + .05H \tag{1}$$

$$H = 60{,}000 + .05A \tag{2}$$

$$A = 190{,}000 + .20H \tag{3}$$

where R denotes the total cost of the Patient Records Department
H denotes the total cost of the Human Resources Department
A denotes the total cost of the Administration and Accounting Department

Equation (1) says that the *total cost* of operating the Patient Records Department (R) is \$100,000 *plus* 5 percent of the total cost of operating the Human Resources Department (H). The \$100,000 comes from Exhibit 17–2 (panel C) and is the total cost *traceable* to the Patient Records Department. We add to this amount 5 percent of the total cost of operating the Human Resources Department. Why? Because Exhibit 17–2 (panel A) tells us that the Patient Records Department used 5 percent of the Human Resources Department's services. Similar explanations underlie equations (2) and (3).

The second step in the reciprocal-services method is to solve the simultaneous equations.[7] Let's begin by substituting the expression for A from equation (3) into equation (2), and solving for H as follows:

$$\begin{aligned} H &= 60{,}000 + .05(190{,}000 + .20H) \\ &= 60{,}000 + 9{,}500 + .01H \\ .99H &= 69{,}500 \\ H &= 70{,}202 \text{ (rounded)} \end{aligned}$$

[7]Simultaneous equations are more quickly solved by computers than by people. Numerous software packages are available for this purpose.

	Service Department			Direct-Patient-Care Department	
	Human Resources	**Administration and Accounting**	**Patient Records**	**Orthopedics**	**Internal Medicine**
Traceable costs	$60,000	$190,000	$100,000		
Allocation of Human Resources Department costs	(70,202)	14,040* (.20)	3,510* (.05)	$17,551*(.25)	$ 35,101 (.50)
Allocation of Administration and Accounting Department costs	10,202 (.05)†	(204,040)	–0– (0)	71,414 (.35)	122,424 (.60)
Allocation of Patient Records Department costs	–0– (0)	–0– (0)	(103,510)	31,053 (.30)	72,457 (.70)
Total cost allocated to each direct-patient-care department				$120,018	$229,982
Total costs allocated				$350,000	

*Rounded.

†Percentages in parentheses are relative proportions of a service department's output consumed by departments to which costs are allocated (from Exhibit 17–2, panel A).

Exhibit 17–10
Reciprocal-Services Method of Service Department Cost Allocation: Riverside Clinic

RIVERSIDE CLINIC

Then we substitute the value for H we just obtained into equation (3), and solve for A as follows:

$$A = 190{,}000 + .20H$$
$$= 190{,}000 + (.20)(70{,}202)$$
$$= 204{,}040 \text{ (rounded)}$$

Now we can solve for R by substituting the value for H into equation (1) as follows:

$$R = 100{,}000 + .05H$$
$$= 100{,}000 + (.05)(70{,}202)$$
$$= 103{,}510 \text{ (rounded)}$$

Thus, we have determined that $H = 70{,}202$, $A = 204{,}040$, and $R = 103{,}510$.

The final step in the reciprocal-services method is to allocate the *total cost* of operating each service department (R, H, and A) to the various departments that use its services. For example, we will allocate the total cost of operating the Human Resources Department (H) among all four of Riverside Clinic's other departments, because they all use services from Human Resources. This allocation is made in proportion to the use of Human Resources's services by the other departments, as given in Exhibit 17–2 (panel A).

The allocations are shown in Exhibit 17–10. Focus on the second row of numbers, which refers to the Human Resources Department. The $70,202 shown in parentheses in the Human Resources column is that department's total cost, as computed using the simultaneous equations. This $70,202 total cost is allocated as follows:

- 20 percent (or $14,040) to Administration and Accounting, because that department uses 20 percent of the Human Resources Department's services.
- 5 percent (or $3,510) to Patient Records, because that department uses 5 percent of the Human Resources Department's services.
- 25 percent (or $17,551) to Orthopedics, because that department uses 25 percent of the Human Resources Department's services.
- 50 percent (or $35,101) to Internal Medicine, because that department uses 50 percent of the Human Resources Department's services.

A similar explanation underlies the Administration and Accounting row and the Patient Records row in Exhibit 17–10.

The total costs allocated to Riverside Clinic's two direct-patient-care departments are as follows: $120,018 to Orthopedics and $229,982 to Internal Medicine. Notice that these two amounts add up to $350,000, which is the total of the original traceable costs for the three service departments. Thus, all service department costs have been fully allocated.

The reciprocal-services method is more accurate than the direct and step-down methods, because it fully accounts for reciprocal services. To make the reciprocal-services method even more accurate, it can be combined with dual cost allocation. In this approach, variable and fixed costs are allocated separately. This method is explored in Problem 17–34.

Review Questions

17–1. Distinguish between a service department and a production department. Give an example of the counterpart of a manufacturer's "production" department in a bank.

17-2. Define the term *reciprocal services.*

17-3. Explain briefly the main differences between the direct, step-down, and reciprocal-services methods of service department cost allocation.

17-4. How does the managerial accountant determine the department sequence in the step-down method? How are ties handled?

17-5. Why does dual cost allocation improve the resulting allocation of service department costs?

17-6. What potential behavioral problem can result when dual cost allocation is used?

17-7. Should actual or budgeted service department costs be allocated? Why?

17-8. Explain the difference between two-stage allocation with departmental overhead rates and activity-based costing. Which approach generally results in more accurate product costs?

17-9. Define the following terms: joint production process, joint costs, joint products, split-off point, separable costs, and by-product.

17-10. Briefly explain how to use the physical-units method of joint cost allocation.

17-11. Describe the relative-sales-value method of joint cost allocation.

17-12. Define the term *net realizable value,* and explain how this concept can be used to allocate joint costs.

17-13. Are joint cost allocations useful? If they are, for what purpose?

17-14. For what purpose should the managerial accountant be careful to not use joint cost allocations?

Exercises

All applicable Exercises are available in Connect.

connect

Exercise 17–15
Direct Method of Service Department Cost Allocation; College
(LO 17-1)

Hudson Community College enrolls students in two departments, Liberal Arts and Sciences. The college also has two service departments, the Library and the Computing Services Department. The usage of these two service departments' output for the year is as follows:

	Provider of Service	
User of Service	**Library**	**Computing Services**
Library	—	20%
Computing Services	—	—
Liberal Arts	60%	30%
Sciences	40%	50%

The budgeted costs in the two service departments for the year are as follows:

Library	$600,000
Computing Services	240,000

Required:

1. Use the direct method to allocate the budgeted costs of the Library and Computing Services Department to the college's Liberal Arts and Sciences departments.
2. *Build a spreadsheet:* Construct an Excel spreadsheet to solve the preceding requirement. Show how the solution will change if the following information changes: the budgeted costs of the Library and Computing Services are $590,000 and $280,000, respectively.

Exercise 17–16
Step-Down Method of Service Department Cost Allocation; College
(LO 17-1)

Refer to the data given in the preceding exercise.

Required:

1. Use the step-down method to allocate Hudson Community College's service department costs to the Liberal Arts and Sciences departments.
2. *Build a spreadsheet:* Construct an Excel spreadsheet to solve the preceding requirement. Show how the solution will change if the following information changes: the budgeted costs of the Library and Computing Services are $590,000 and $280,000, respectively.

Exercise 17–17
Direct Method of Service Department Cost Allocation; Bank
(LO 17-1)

Tuscaloosa National Bank has two service departments, the Human Resources (HR) Department and the Computing Department. The bank has two other departments that directly service customers, the Deposit Department and the Loan Department. The usage of the two service departments' output for the year is as follows:

	Provider of Service	
User of Service	**HR**	**Computing**
HR	—	15%
Computing	10%	—
Deposit	60%	50%
Loan	30%	35%

The budgeted costs in the two service departments for the year are as follows:

HR	$153,000
Computing	229,500

Required: Use the direct method to allocate the budgeted costs of the HR and Computing departments to the Deposit and Loan departments.

Exercise 17–18
Step-Down Method of Service Department Cost Allocation; Bank
(LO 17-1)

Refer to the data given in the preceding exercise.

Required: Use the step-down method to allocate the budgeted costs of the HR and Computing departments to the Deposit and Loan departments. Tuscaloosa National Bank allocates the costs of the HR Department first.

Exercise 17–19
Service Department Cost Allocation; Use of Internet
(LO 17-1)

Visit the website of one of the following organizations, or a different organization of your choosing.

Allstate	www.allstate.com
Gallo Winery	www.gallo.com
Mayo Clinic	www.mayoclinic.org
Starwood Hotels	www.starwoodhotels.com
Walt Disney Studios	www.disney.com

Required: Read about the organization's activities and operations. Then list three activities that you think the organization would need that would likely be established as service departments. For what purposes would it be relevant to allocate those service department costs to nonservice departments within the organization?

Exercise 17–20
Physical-Units Method; Joint Cost Allocation
(LO 17-4)

Breakfasttime Cereal Company manufactures two breakfast cereals in a joint process. Cost and quantity information is as follows:

Joint Cost	Cereal	Quantity at Split-Off Point	Sales Price per Kilogram
$30,000	Yummies	12,000 kilograms	$2.00
	Crummies	8,000 kilograms	2.50

Required: Use the physical-units method to allocate the company's joint production cost between Yummies and Crummies.

Exercise 17–21
Relative-Sales-Value Method; Joint Cost Allocation
(LO 17-4)

Refer to the data given in the preceding exercise.

Required: Use the relative-sales-value method to allocate Breakfasttime Cereal Company's joint production cost between Yummies and Crummies.

Exercise 17–22
Net-Realizable-Value Method; Joint Cost Allocation
(LO 17-4)

Refer to the data given in Exercise 17–20. Breakfasttime Cereal Company has an opportunity to process its Crummies further into a mulch for ornamental shrubs. The additional processing operation costs $.50 per kilogram, and the mulch will sell for $3.50 per kilogram.

Required:

1. Should Breakfasttime's management decide to process Crummies into the mulch? Why?
2. Suppose the company does process Crummies into the mulch. Use the net-realizable-value method to allocate the joint production cost between the mulch and the Yummies.

Exercise 17–23
Reciprocal-Services Method; Bank (Appendix)
(LO 17-6)

Refer to the data given in Exercise 17–17 for Tuscaloosa National Bank.

Required: Use the reciprocal-services method to allocate the budgeted costs of the HR and Computing departments to the Deposit and Loan departments.

Problems

All applicable Problems are available in Connect.

connect

Problem 17–24
Direct and Step-Down Methods of Service Department Cost Allocation
(LO 17-1)

1. HR department cost allocated to assembly: $138,889
3. HR department cost allocated to CAD: $12,500

Tampa Instrument Company manufactures gauges for construction machinery. The company has two production departments: Machining and Assembly. There are three service departments: Maintenance, Human Resources (HR), and Computer Aided Design (CAD). The usage of these service departments' output during the year just completed is as follows:

Provision of Service Output (in hours of service)

	Provider of Service		
User of Service	**HR**	**Maintenance**	**CAD**
HR	—	—	—
Maintenance	500	—	—
CAD	500	500	—
Machining	4,000	3,500	4,500
Assembly	5,000	4,000	1,500
Total	10,000	8,000	6,000

The budgeted costs in Tampa Instrument Company's service departments during the year are as follows:

	HR	**Maintenance**	**CAD**
Variable	$ 50,000	$ 80,000	$ 50,000
Fixed	200,000	150,000	300,000
Total	$250,000	$230,000	$350,000

Required:

1. Use the direct method to allocate Tampa Instrument Company's service department costs to its production departments.
2. Determine the proper sequence to use in allocating the firm's service department costs by the step-down method.
3. Use the step-down method to allocate the company's service department costs.
4. ***Build a spreadsheet:*** Construct an Excel spreadsheet to solve requirements (1) and (3) above. Show how the solution will change if the following information changes: the budgeted variable costs in the three departments are $60,000, $70,000, and $55,000, for Human Resources, Maintenance, and CAD, respectively.

Problem 17–25
Dual Allocation of Service Department Costs
(LO 17-1, 17-2)

1(a). Variable costs, CAD, allocated to machining: $37,500
1(b). Fixed costs, HR department, allocated to assembly: $117,647

Refer to the data given in the preceding problem. When Tampa Instrument Company established its service departments, the following long-run needs were anticipated.

Long-Run Service Needs (in hours of service)

	Provider of Service		
User of Service	**HR**	**Maintenance**	**CAD**
HR	—	—	—
Maintenance	500	—	—
CAD	1,000	800	—
Machining	3,500	4,800	4,800
Assembly	5,000	2,400	1,200
Total	10,000	8,000	6,000

Required: Use dual cost allocation in conjunction with each of the following methods to allocate Tampa Instrument Company's service department costs: (1) direct method and (2) step-down method.

Problem 17–26
Service Department Cost Allocation
(LO 17-1)

1. Overhead rate per hour, etching: $10.602 (rounded)
2. Maintenance department costs allocated to finishing: $87,111

Celestial Artistry Company is developing departmental overhead rates based on direct-labor hours for its two production departments, Etching and Finishing. The Etching Department employs 20 people and the Finishing Department employs 80 people. Each person in these two departments works 2,000 hours per year. The production-related overhead costs for the Etching Department are budgeted at $200,000, and the Finishing Department costs are budgeted at $320,000. Two service departments, Maintenance and Computing, directly support the two production departments. These service departments have budgeted costs of $48,000 and $250,000, respectively. The production departments' overhead rates cannot be determined until the service departments' costs are allocated. The following schedule reflects the use of the Maintenance Department's and Computing Department's output by the various departments.

	Using Department			
Service Department	**Maintenance**	**Computing**	**Etching**	**Finishing**
Maintenance (maintenance hours)	0	1,000	1,000	8,000
Computing (minutes)	240,000	0	840,000	120,000

Required:

1. Use the direct method to allocate service department costs. Calculate the overhead rates per direct-labor hour for the Etching Department and the Finishing Department.
2. Use the step-down method to allocate service department costs. Allocate the Computing Department's costs first. Calculate the overhead rates per direct-labor hour for the Etching Department and the Finishing Department.

(CMA, adapted)

Problem 17–27
Joint Costs
(LO 17-4, 17-5)

2. CBL, allocation of joint cost: $225,000
3. MSB, net realizable value: $200,000

Snake River Sawmill manufactures two lumber products from a joint milling process. The two products developed are mine support braces (MSB) and unseasoned commercial building lumber (CBL). A standard production run incurs joint costs of $300,000 and results in 60,000 units of MSB and 90,000 units of CBL. Each MSB sells for $2, and each unit of CBL sells for $4.

Required:

1. Calculate the amount of joint cost allocated to commercial building lumber (CBL) on a physical-units basis.
2. Calculate the amount of joint cost allocated to the mine support braces (MSB) on a relative-sales-value basis.
3. Assume the commercial building lumber is not marketable at split-off but must be further planed and sized at a cost of $200,000 per production run. During this process, 10,000 units are unavoidably lost; these spoiled units have no value. The remaining units of commercial building lumber are saleable at $10 per unit. The mine support braces, although saleable immediately at the split-off point, are coated with a tarlike preservative that costs $100,000 per production run. The braces are then sold for $5 each. Using the net-realizable-value basis, compute the completed cost assigned to each unit of commercial building lumber.
4. If Snake River Sawmill chose not to process the mine support braces beyond the split-off point, the contribution from the joint milling process would increase or decrease by what amount?
5. Did you use the joint cost allocation results in answering requirement (4)? If so, how? Why did you use or not use the allocation results?

(CMA, adapted)

Problem 17–28
Service Department Cost Allocation; Plantwide versus Departmental Overhead Rates; Cost Drivers
(LO 17-1, 17-2, 17-3)

1. Plantwide overhead rate: $20.55 per direct-labor hour
2(c). Rate, molding: $37.44 per MH

Travelcraft Company manufactures a complete line of fiberglass suitcases and attaché cases. The firm has three manufacturing departments: Molding, Component, and Assembly. There are also two service departments: Power and Maintenance.

The sides of the cases are manufactured in the Molding Department. The frames, hinges, and locks are manufactured in the Component Department. The cases are completed in the Assembly Department. Varying amounts of materials, time, and effort are required for each of the cases. The Power Department and Maintenance Department provide services to the three manufacturing departments.

Travelcraft has always used a plantwide overhead rate. Direct-labor hours are used to assign overhead to products. The predetermined overhead rate is calculated by dividing the company's total estimated overhead by the total estimated direct-labor hours to be worked in the three manufacturing departments.

Karen Mason, director of cost management, has recommended that Travelcraft use departmental overhead rates. The planned operating costs and expected levels of activity for the coming year have been developed by Mason and are presented by department in the following schedules. (All numbers are in thousands.)

	Service Departments	
	Power	**Maintenance**
Departmental activity measures:		
Maximum capacity	1,000 kilowatt-hours	Adjustable
Estimated usage for the coming year	800 kilowatt-hours	125 hours
Departmental costs:		
Materials and supplies	$ 5,000	$1,500
Variable labor	1,400	2,250
Fixed overhead	12,000	250
Total service department costs	$18,400	$4,000

	Manufacturing Departments		
	Molding	**Component**	**Assembly**
Department activity measures:			
Direct-labor hours	500	2,000	1,500
Machine hours	875	125	–0–
Departmental costs:			
Direct material	$12,400	$30,000	$ 1,250
Direct labor	3,500	20,000	12,000
Variable overhead	3,500	10,000	16,500
Fixed overhead	17,500	6,200	6,100
Total departmental costs	$36,900	$66,200	$35,850
Use of service departments:			
Maintenance:			
Estimated usage in labor hours for the coming year	90	25	10
Power (in kilowatt-hours):			
Estimated usage for the coming year	360	320	120
Maximum allotted capacity	500	350	150

Required:

1. Calculate the plantwide overhead rate for Travelcraft Company for the coming year using the same method as used in the past.
2. Karen Mason has been asked to develop departmental overhead rates for comparison with the plantwide rate. The following steps are to be followed in developing the departmental rates.
   a. The Maintenance Department costs should be allocated to the three manufacturing departments using the direct method.
   b. The Power Department costs should be allocated to the three manufacturing departments using dual cost allocation combined with the direct method of service department cost allocation.

Fixed costs are to be allocated according to maximum allotted capacity, and variable costs are to be allocated according to planned usage for the coming year.

c. Calculate departmental overhead rates for the three manufacturing departments using a machine-hour cost driver for the Molding Department and a direct-labor-hour cost driver for the Component and Assembly departments.

3. As Karen Mason's assistant, draft a memo for her to send to Travelcraft's president recommending whether the company should use a plantwide rate or departmental rates to assign overhead to products.

(CMA, adapted)

Problem 17–29
Joint Costs; Allocation and Production Decisions
(LO 17-4, 17-5)

1. HTP-3, net realizable value: $1,926,000
3. Additional processing costs per gallon: $2.33 (rounded)

Biondi Industries is a manufacturer of chemicals for various purposes. One of the processes used by Biondi produces HTP–3, a chemical used in hot tubs and swimming pools; PST–4, a chemical used in pesticides; and RJ–5, a product that is sold to fertilizer manufacturers. Biondi uses the net-realizable-value method to allocate joint production costs. The ratio of output quantities to input quantities of direct material used in the joint process remains consistent from month to month. Biondi Industries uses FIFO (first-in, first-out) in valuing its finished-goods inventories.

Data regarding Biondi's operations for the month of October are as follows. During this month, Biondi incurred joint production costs of $1,700,000 in the manufacture of HTP–3, PST–4, and RJ–5.

	HTP–3	PST–4	RJ–5
Finished goods inventory in gallons (October 1)	18,000	52,000	3,000
October sales in gallons	650,000	325,000	150,000
October production in gallons	700,000	350,000	170,000
Additional processing costs	$874,000	$816,000	$60,000
Final sales value per gallon	$ 4.00	$ 6.00	$ 5.00

Required:

1. Determine Biondi Industries' allocation of joint production costs for the month of October. (Carry calculation of relative proportions to four decimal places.)
2. Determine the dollar values of the finished-goods inventories for HTP–3, PST–4, and RJ–5 as of October 31. (Round the cost per gallon to the nearest cent.)
3. Suppose Biondi Industries has a new opportunity to sell PST–4 at the split-off point for $3.80 per gallon. Prepare an analysis showing whether the company should sell PST–4 at the split-off point or continue to process this product further.

(CMA, adapted)

Problem 17–30
Joint Cost Allocation; Missing Data
(LO 17-4)

1. Omega, joint cost allocation: $9,000
3. Kappa, net realizable value: $20,000

Berger Company manufactures products Delta, Kappa, and Omega from a joint process. Production, sales, and cost data for July follow.

	Delta	Kappa	Omega	Total
Units produced	4,000	2,000	1,000	7,000
Joint cost allocation	$36,000	?	?	$ 60,000
Sales value at split-off	?	?	$15,000	$100,000
Additional costs if processed further	$ 7,000	$ 5,000	$ 3,000	$ 15,000
Sales value if processed further	$70,000	$25,000	$20,000	$115,000

Required:

1. Assuming that joint costs are allocated using the relative-sales-value method, what were the joint costs allocated to products Kappa and Omega?
2. Assuming that joint costs are allocated using the relative-sales-value method, what was the sales value at split-off for product Delta?
3. Use the net-realizable-value method to allocate the joint production costs to the three products.

(CPA, adapted)

Problem 17–31
Joint Products; Sell or Process Further
(LO 17-4, 17-5)

2. Joint cost allocation, VX-4: $900,000

Winchester Chemicals uses a joint process to produce VX-4, a chemical used in the manufacture of paints and varnishes; HD-10, a chemical used in household cleaning products; and FT-5, a by-product that is sold to fertilizer manufacturers. Joint production costs are allocated to the main products on the basis of net realizable value. The by-product is inventoried at its net realizable value, and this value is used to reduce the joint production cost before allocation to the main products.

During the month of November, Winchester incurred joint production costs of $1,568,000. Data regarding Winchester's November operations are as follows:

	VX-4	HD-10	FT-5
November production in gallons	600,000	320,000	85,000
Sales value per gallon at split-off	None	$3.00	$.90*
Separable processing cost	$720,000	$920,000	None
Final sales value per gallon	$4.00	$6.375	None
Finished-goods inventory in gallons on November 30 (all produced during November)	9,000	26,000	1,500

*Disposal costs of $.10 per gallon will be incurred in order to sell the by-product.

Required:

1. Define the terms *joint costs* and *split-off point.*
2. Determine the dollar values of Winchester Chemicals' finished-goods inventories on November 30 for VX-4 and HD-10.
3. Winchester Chemicals has an opportunity to sell HD-10 for its sales value at the split-off point. Determine if Winchester should sell HD-10 at the split-off point or continue to process it further.

(CPA, adapted)

Problem 17–32
Joint Costs; Allocation and Production Decisions; Ethics
(LO 17-4, 17-5)

3(b). Ultrasene, separable cost of processing: $88,000

Lafayette Company manufactures two products out of a joint process: Compod and Ultrasene. The joint costs incurred are $250,000 for a standard production run that generates 120,000 gallons of Compod and 80,000 gallons of Ultrasene. Compod sells for $2.00 per gallon while Ultrasene sells for $3.25 per gallon.

Required:

1. If there are no additional processing costs incurred after the split-off point, calculate the amount of joint cost of each production run allocated to Compod on a physical-units basis.
2. If there are no additional processing costs incurred after the split-off point, calculate the amount of joint cost of each production run allocated to Ultrasene on a relative-sales-value basis.
3. Suppose the following additional processing costs are required beyond the split-off point in order to obtain Compod and Ultrasene: $.10 per gallon for Compod and $1.10 per gallon for Ultrasene.
   a. Calculate the amount of joint cost of each production run allocated to Ultrasene on a physical-units basis.
   b. Calculate the amount of joint cost of each production run allocated to Compod on a net-realizable-value basis.
4. Assuming the same data as in requirement (3), suppose Compod can be processed further into a product called Compodalene, at an additional cost of $.40 per gallon. Compodalene will be sold for $2.60 per gallon by independent distributors. The distributors' commission will be 10% of the sales price. Should Lafayette sell Compod or Compodalene?
5. Independent of your answer to requirement (4), suppose Christine Dalton, the assistant controller, has completed an analysis showing that Compod should not be processed further into Compodalene. Before presenting her analysis to top management, however, she got a visit from Jack Turner, Lafayette's director of research. Turner was upset upon learning that Compodalene, a product he had personally developed, would not be manufactured.

   Turner: "The company's making a big mistake if it passes up this opportunity. Compodalene will be a big seller and get us into new markets."

   Dalton: "But the analysis shows that we'd be losing money on every gallon of Compod that we process further."

Turner: "I know, Christine, but that's a temporary problem. Eventually, we'll bring down the cost of making Compodalene."

Dalton: "Can you find me some estimates on the cost reduction you expect?"

Turner: "I don't have a crystal ball, Christine. Look, if you could just fudge the numbers a little bit to help me get approval to produce some Compodalene, I can get this product off the ground. I know the cost reduction will come."

Comment on the ethical issues in this scenario. What should Christine Dalton do?

6. Assume the same data as given in requirements (3) and (4). The industrial chemical industry has experienced a downturn, which has left Lafayette with idle capacity. Suppose Lafayette can sell only half of the Compod made in each production run, but the remainder could be sold as Compodalene. Should Lafayette process the remaining Compod into Compodalene?

(CMA, adapted)

Problem 17–33
Reciprocal-Service Method (Appendix)
(LO 17-6)

M = $100,000, where M denotes the "total" cost of the Maintenance Department; Service Department costs allocated to Etching: $192,000

Refer to the data given in Problem 17–26 for Celestial Artistry Company.

Required:

1. Use the reciprocal-services method to allocate service department costs. Calculate the overhead rates per direct-labor hour for the Etching Department and the Finishing Department.
2. Which of the three methods of service department cost allocation results in the most accurate overhead rates? Why?

Problem 17–34
Reciprocal-Services Method; Dual Allocation (Appendix)
(LO 17-2, 17-6)

1. Variable costs: H = $17,551 (rounded), where H denotes the "total" cost of the HR Department; total variable cost allocated to Orthopedics: $29,705
2. H = $59,848 (rounded), where H denotes the "total" cost of the HR Department; total fixed cost allocated to Internal Medicine: $151,918

Refer to the data for Riverside Clinic given in Exhibits 17–2 and 17–5.

Required: Use the reciprocal-services method in combination with the dual-allocation approach to allocate Riverside's service department costs. *Hint:* You will need to apply the reciprocal-services method twice. First, allocate the three service departments' variable costs using the short-run usage proportions in Exhibit 17–2 (panel A). Second, allocate the three service departments' fixed costs using the long-run average usage proportions in Exhibit 17–5. Finally, add the variable costs and fixed costs allocated to each direct-patient-care department.

Cases

Case 17–35
Joint Cost Allocation; By-Product
(LO 17-4)

2. Juice, net realizable value: $17,000
3. Allocation of joint cost, slices: $30,160

Top Quality Fruit Company, based on Oahu, grows, processes, cans, and sells three main pineapple products: sliced, crushed, and juice. The outside skin is cut off in the Cutting Department and processed as animal feed. The feed is treated as a by-product. The company's production process is as follows:

- Pineapples first are processed in the Cutting Department. The pineapples are washed and the outside skin is cut away. Then the pineapples are cored and trimmed for slicing. The three main products (sliced, crushed, juice) and the by-product (animal feed) are recognizable after processing in the Cutting Department. Each product then is transferred to a separate department for final processing.
- The trimmed pineapples are sent to the Slicing Department, where the pineapples are sliced and canned. Any juice generated during the slicing operation is packed in the cans with the slices.

- The pieces of pineapple trimmed from the fruit are diced and canned in the Crushing Department. Again, the juice generated during this operation is packed in the can with the crushed pineapple.
- The core and surplus pineapple generated from the Cutting Department are pulverized into a liquid in the Juicing Department. There is an evaporation loss equal to 8 percent of the weight of the good output produced in this department that occurs as the juices are heated.
- The outside skin is chopped into animal feed in the Feed Department.

Top Quality Fruit Company uses the net-realizable-value method to assign the costs of the joint process to its main products. The net realizable value of the by-product is subtracted from the joint cost before the allocation.

A total of 270,000 pounds were entered into the Cutting Department during June. The following schedule shows the costs incurred in each department, the proportion by weight transferred to the four final processing departments, and the selling price of each end product.

Processing Data and Costs for June

Department	Costs Incurred	Proportion of Product by Weight Transferred to Departments	Selling Price per Pound of Final Product
Cutting	$60,000	—	none
Slicing	4,700	35%	$.60
Crushing	10,580	28	.55
Juicing	3,250	27	.30
Animal feed	700	10	10
Total	$79,230	100%	

Required: Compute each of the following amounts.

1. The number of pounds of pineapple that result as output for pineapple slices, crushed pineapple, pineapple juice, and animal feed.
2. The net realizable value at the split-off point of the three main products.
3. The amount of the cost of the Cutting Department allocated to each of the three main products.

(CMA, adapted)

■ **Case 17–36**
Comprehensive Case on Joint Cost Allocation
(LO 17-4, 17-5)

1. Total joint cost: $210,000
2(b). Resoline, sales value at split-off point: $200,000

Valdosta Chemical Company manufactures two industrial chemical products in a joint process. In May, 10,000 gallons of input costing $60,000 were processed at a cost of $150,000. The joint process resulted in 8,000 pounds of Resoline and 2,000 pounds of Krypto. Resoline sells for $25 per pound, and Krypto sells for $50 per pound. Management generally processes each of these chemicals further in separable processes to produce more refined chemical products. Resoline is processed separately at a cost of $5 per pound. The resulting product, Resolite, sells for $35 per pound. Krypto is processed separately at a cost of $15 per pound. The resulting product, Kryptite, sells for $95 per pound.

Required:

1. Draw a diagram similar to Exhibit 17–8 to depict Valdosta Chemical Company's joint production process.
2. Allocate the company's joint production costs for May using
   a. The physical-units method.
   b. The relative-sales-value method.
   c. The net-realizable-value method.
3. Valdosta's management is considering an opportunity to process Kryptite further into a new product called Omega. The separable processing will cost $40 per pound. Packaging costs for Omega are projected to be $6 per pound, and the anticipated sales price is $130 per pound. Should Kryptite be processed further into Omega? Why?
4. In answering requirement (3), did you use your joint cost allocation from requirement (2)? If so, how did you use it?
5. ***Build a spreadsheet:*** Construct an Excel spreadsheet to solve requirements (2) and (3) above. Show how the solution will change if the following information changes: the joint cost is $245,000, and the sales price of Omega is $125 per pound.

Appendix I

The Sarbanes-Oxley Act, Internal Controls, and Management Accounting

After completing this appendix, you should be able to:

I-1 Understand and discuss the concept of internal controls over financial reporting.

I-2 Understand and discuss the role of the PCAOB and the implications of Sarbanes-Oxley Sections 302 and 404.

The Sarbanes-Oxley Act (often abbreviated as SOX) was enacted by the U.S. Congress in 2002 in the aftermath of several corporate accounting scandals. Accounting problems at Enron and Worldcom, and other debacles, resulted in a precipitous drop in the investing public's confidence in companies' published financial statements. SOX was enacted to bring about reform in companies' financial reporting processes, as well as the internal and external auditing of the financial reporting process. Under SOX, a company's top executives, including the CEO (chief executive officer) and the CFO (chief financial officer), can be held criminally responsible if their firm's financial statements prove to be fraudulent or materially misstate the firm's financial condition.

The SOX act runs 66 pages long and consists of 11 major parts (called titles), each of which is organized into several sections. SOX is a very complicated piece of legislation, and most of it relates primarily to corporate governance, financial accounting, auditing, and the penalties that the courts can invoke for violations of the law.[1] Three sections of SOX are germane to management accounting, because they address aspects of *internal controls* over financial reporting. Before covering these three sections of SOX, let's digress for a brief discussion of internal controls.

[1]The entire Sarbanes-Oxley Act is available at http://news.findlaw.com/hdocs/docs/gwbush/sarbanesoxley072302.pdf.

Internal Controls over Financial Reporting

Learning Objective I-1

Understand and discuss the concept of internal controls over financial reporting.

Internal control is defined as "a process, effected by an entity's board of directors, management, and other personnel, designed to provide reasonable assurance regarding the achievement of objectives relating to operations, reporting, and compliance."[2]

Included in this definition of internal control is a reference to "reasonable assurance regarding reporting," which is often referred to as *internal controls over financial reporting*. This refers to the broad set of policies, processes, and procedures that enable both the organization's management and interested outside parties to have confidence in the organization's financial reports. These reports include the financial statements in the organization's annual report, the 10K filed with the SEC (Securities and Exchange Commission), tax returns filed with tax authorities, and other public financial disclosures. Even a moderately large company has thousands of procedures that can properly be viewed as internal controls. They include a diverse range of activities such as the following:

- Physical control over raw-material, work-in-process, and finished-goods inventories to prevent loss due to theft.
- Maintenance of adequate cost records to justify inventory valuations.
- Limitations on who is authorized to make purchases of various types and value.
- Requirement that two individuals sign checks to reduce the possibility of fraudulent expenditures.[3]

This list could go on and on. Moreover, in the age of computerized accounting systems, many internal control procedures are automated. When you make a purchase from a major retailer, for example, the sale is entered into a computerized cash register by the salesperson. All sales are then accumulated across time by the retailer's accounting software system, and the result is a sales revenue figure on the firm's income statement. Suppose, though, that there was a glitch in the company's accounting software such that this sales accumulation process was not accurate. Among the retailer's internal controls would be safeguards to ensure that the software is working properly and doing what it is supposed to do.[4] Other important software controls include limits on who in the organization has the authority to access computer programs and data.

To summarize, a large company's internal controls over financial reporting comprise a vast array of policies and procedures involving potentially hundreds of individuals. Since accounting information is used by both managers inside the company and interested parties outside the organization, internal controls are crucial to the integrity of both managerial and financial accounting. Now let's turn our attention to the three sections of the Sarbanes-Oxley Act that address internal controls.

---

[2] *Internal Control–Integrated Framework: Executive Summary*, COSO (Committee of Sponsoring Organizations of the Treadway Commission), May 2013. See http://www.coso.org/documents/990025p_executive_summary_final_may20_e.pdf.

[3] Ibid. The Executive Summary contains a detailed discussion of the activities involved in internal control.

[4] There are many anecdotes of software glitches that resulted in flawed financial information or other mistakes. In one such incident, a company's billing software was incorrectly designed to express amounts in cents, rather than dollars, resulting in the company sending out bills for, say 10,000 dollars rather than the correct amount of 100 dollars (which is equivalent to 10,000 cents).

Public Company Accounting Oversight Board

Learning Objective **I-2**

Understand and discuss the role of the PCAOB and the implications of Sarbanes-Oxley Sections 302 and 404.

Title I, Section 101 of SOX established the **Public Company Accounting Oversight Board (PCAOB).** With five full-time board members operating under the auspices of the SEC, the PCAOB's mission is to "oversee and investigate the audits and auditors of public companies, and sanction both firms and individuals for violations of laws, rules, and regulations."[5] The PCAOB's *Auditing Standard No. 5,* entitled *An Audit of Internal Control Over Financial Reporting That Is Integrated With an Audit of Financial Statements,* details the board's requirements for auditors as they assess and attest to a client's internal control system.

SOX Sections 302 and 404

The SOX sections most relevant to managerial accounting are sections 302 and 404.

SOX 302 Entitled *Corporate Responsibility for Financial Reports,* SOX section 302 requires the signing officers of a company's financial reports to establish, maintain, and periodically evaluate the effectiveness of the company's internal controls over financial reporting. The following is an excerpt from SOX section 302, part (a).

> (4) The signing officers:
> (A) are responsible for establishing and maintaining internal controls;
> (B) have designed such internal controls to ensure that material information relating to the issuer [of the financial reports] and its consolidated subsidiaries is made known to such officers by others within those entities . . .;
> (C) have evaluated the effectiveness of the issuer's internal controls as of a date within 90 days prior to the report;
> (D) have presented in the report their conclusions about the effectiveness of their internal controls based on their evaluation as of that date.[6]

Section 302 goes on to require that the signing officers must disclose to the company's auditors any material weaknesses or changes in the company's internal control system.

SOX 404 Entitled *Management Assessment of Internal Controls,* SOX section 404 requires a company to include in its annual report an internal control report. SOX section 404, part (a) states that the internal control report shall:

> (1) state the responsibility of management for establishing and maintaining an adequate internal control structure and procedures for financial reporting; and
> (2) contain an assessment, as of the end of the most recent fiscal year of the issuer, of the effectiveness of the internal control structure and procedures of the issuer for financial reporting.[7]

Implications of SOX Sections 302 and 404

SOX section 302(a)(4)(C), excerpted earlier in this appendix, is "one of the most serious and onerous requirements imposed by SOX. The CEO and CFO are expected to be able to demonstrate that there is a reliable process in place to evaluate, at least quarterly, the internal controls in place to ensure the reliability of the data being produced."[8] SOX

[5]"How the Sarbanes-Oxley Act of 2002 Impacts the Accounting Profession" (New York: AICPA), p. 1, available at http://www.aicpa.org/info/Sarbanes-Oxley2002.asp.

[6]Excerpt from the Sarbanes-Oxley Act, p. 33, available at http://files.findlaw.com/news.findlaw.com/hdocs/docs/gwbush/sarbanesoxley072302.pdf.

[7]Ibid., p. 45.

[8]T. J. Leech, "Sarbanes-Oxley Sections 302 and 404: A White Paper Proposing Practical, Cost Effective Compliance Strategies," CARDdecisions, April 2003, p. 1, available at http://www.sec.gov/rules/proposed/s74002/card941503.pdf.

section 404 then adds the requirement that the company's annual report include a report assessing the company's internal controls over financial reporting.

To summarize, SOX sections 302 and 404 go hand in hand. Section 302 essentially requires that management establish, maintain, and periodically assess the company's internal controls over financial reporting. Section 404 then requires that management include in the company's annual report a separate report that assesses those internal controls. Moreover, the company's auditors are required to attest as to the effectiveness of the internal controls.

After its enactment, SOX sections 302 and 404 initially caused a firestorm of controversy in business and accounting. Managers of many companies complained about the onerous requirements imposed by sections 302 and 404 for detailed reporting on internal controls, as well as the extensive documentation required to back up the internal control reports. Others defend sections 302 and 404 as necessary reforms in the wake of Enron and other corporate scandals.

The concept of controlling substantial risk exposure may well be the key to making SOX sections 302 and 404 more effective. It is probably not reasonable to require companies to report on the minutia of their internal controls over financial reporting. If management maintains, assesses, and reports on the internal control areas where the greatest risk of fraud or material misstatement occurs, that may be enough to achieve the objectives of SOX.

The first decade of the SOX legislation was characterized by controversy, Congressional hearings, and court rulings. In recent years, however, some of the controversy has died down as small businesses have been absolved of the most onerous reporting requirements. Most observers believe the law will remain in some form, at least for the foreseeable future. As the pros and cons of SOX continue to be debated, one perspective holds that "the impact of Sarbanes-Oxley isn't necessarily found in the collective impact of its substantive provisions. Rather, it is found in the profound way the law has reshaped attitudes toward corporate governance. The need for fundamental change in boardroom behavior was a message that transcended the text of the Sarbanes-Oxley law. The old ways weren't working. That idea lit the corporate responsibility movement,"[9] resulting in greater fiduciary responsibility to shareholders and to corporate ethical behavior in general. And, as another observer put it, "SOX has been successful in increasing corporate focus on a strong ethical culture in publicly-owned companies."[10]

Key Terms

For each term's definition refer to the indicated page, or turn to the glossary at the end of the text.

internal control, 769

Public Company Accounting Oversight Board (PCAOB), 770

SOX 302, 770

SOX 404, 770

Review Questions

I–1. Briefly describe the overall intent of the Sarbanes-Oxley Act of 2002.

I–2. Explain the nature and importance of internal controls over financial reporting.

I–3. What is the PCAOB? Describe its mission.

I–4. What does SOX section 302 require of management?

I–5. What does SOX section 404 require of management?

I–6. Why did some managers complain about the requirements imposed by SOX sections 302 and 404?

[9] M. W. Peregrine, "The Law Changed Corporate America," *The New York Times,* July 25, 2012. See also K. Drawbaugh and D. Aubin, "A Decade On, Is Sarbanes-Oxley Working," *Reuters,* July 30, 2012.

[10] C. Verschoor, "Has SOX Been Successful?" *Strategic Finance,* September 2012, p. 17.

Exercises

Exercise I–7
Internal Controls
(LO I-1)

Can you describe any internal controls you observed in a job you have held? Alternatively, what kinds of internal controls do you think are in place at your college?

Exercise I–8
Need for Internal Controls; Accountability
(LO I-1)

Can the CEO of a large company really be expected to know what is going on at all levels in the organization? In various court cases, CEOs have argued that they could not be held accountable for the actions of others in their companies. As a group, stage an in-class debate about this issue.

Exercise I–9
Implications of Sarbanes-Oxley
(LO I-2)

Go online and use Google or another search engine to find several current news articles about SOX. Read three of these articles, and then summarize them for your classmates.

Exercise I–10
Implications of Sarbanes-Oxley
(LO I-2)

As a group, stage an in-class debate about the future of the Sarbanes-Oxley Act. At least three positions can be staked out: leave SOX as is, repeal SOX, and modify SOX.

Exercise I–11
Implications of Sarbanes-Oxley
(LO I-2)

What does it mean to say that the concept of risk exposure may be the key to making SOX sections 302 and 404 more effective?

Exercise I–12
Internal Controls and Sarbanes-Oxley
(LO I-1, I-2)

Read Exercise 13–32. Instead of answering the requirements listed in the exercise, discuss the implications of SOX sections 302 and 404 for the company's internal control issues.

Exercise I–13
Internal Controls and Sarbanes-Oxley
(LO I-1, I-2)

Read Problem 9–43. Instead of answering the requirements listed in the problem, discuss the implications of SOX sections 302 and 404 regarding John Winslow's contemplated actions.

Appendix II

Compound Interest and the Concept of Present Value

After completing this appendix, you should be able to:

II-1 Explain the importance of the time value of money in capital-budgeting decisions.

II-2 Compute the future value and present value of cash flows occurring over several time periods.

Learning Objective II-1

Explain the importance of the time value of money in capital-budgeting decisions.

Before we can study the methods used to make capital-budgeting decisions, we must examine the basic tools used in those methods. The fundamental concept in a capital-budgeting decision analysis is the *time value* of money. Would you rather receive a \$100 gift check from a relative today, or would you rather receive a letter promising the \$100 in a year? Most of us would rather have the cash now. There are two possible reasons for this attitude. First, if we receive the money today, we can spend it on that new sweater now instead of waiting a year. Second, as an alternative strategy, we can invest the \$100 received today at 10 percent interest. Then, at the end of one year, we will have \$110. Thus, there is a time value associated with money. A \$100 cash flow today is not the same as a \$100 cash flow in 1 year, 2 years, or 10 years.

Compound Interest Suppose you invest \$100 today (time 0) at 10 percent interest for one year. How much will you have after one year? The answer is \$110, as the following analysis shows.

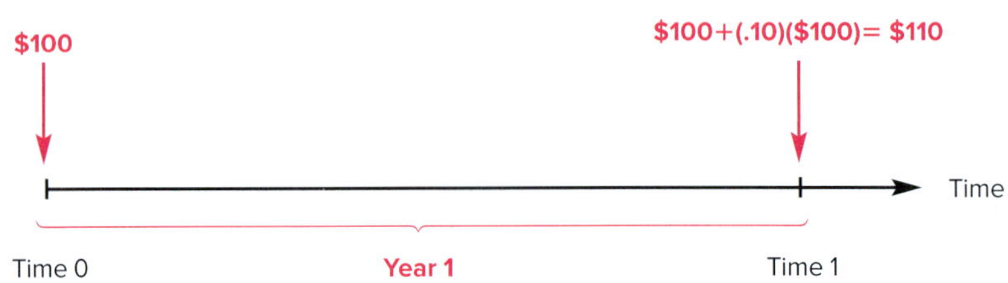

The $110 at time 1 (end of one year) is composed of two parts, as shown below.

Principal, time 0 amount	$100
Interest earned during year 1 (.10 × $100)	10
Amount at time 1	$110

Learning Objective II-2

Compute the future value and present value of cash flows occurring over several time periods.

Thus, the $110 at time 1 consists of the $100 at time 0, called the **principal,** plus the $10 of interest earned during the year.

Now suppose you leave your $110 invested during the second year. How much will you have at the end of two years? As the following analysis shows, the answer is $121.

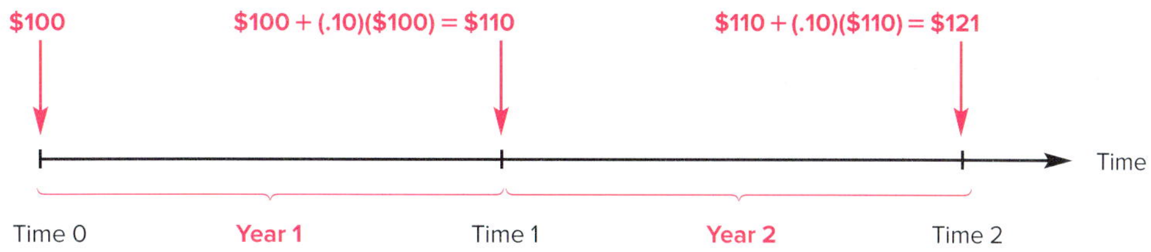

We can break down the $121 at time 2 into two parts as follows:

Amount at time 1	$110
Interest earned during year 2 (.10 × $110)	11
Amount at time 2	$121

Notice that you earned more interest in year 2 ($11) than you earned in year 1 ($10). Why? During year 2, you earned 10 percent interest on the original principal of $100 *and* you earned 10 percent interest on the year 1 interest of $10. Interest earned on prior periods' interest is called **compound interest.** Exhibit II-1 shows how your invested funds grow over the five-year period of the investment. As the exhibit shows, the **future value** of your initial $100 investment is $161.05 after five years.

As the number of years in an investment increases, it becomes more cumbersome to compute the future value of the investment using the method in Exhibit II–1.

Exhibit II–1
Compound Interest and Future Value

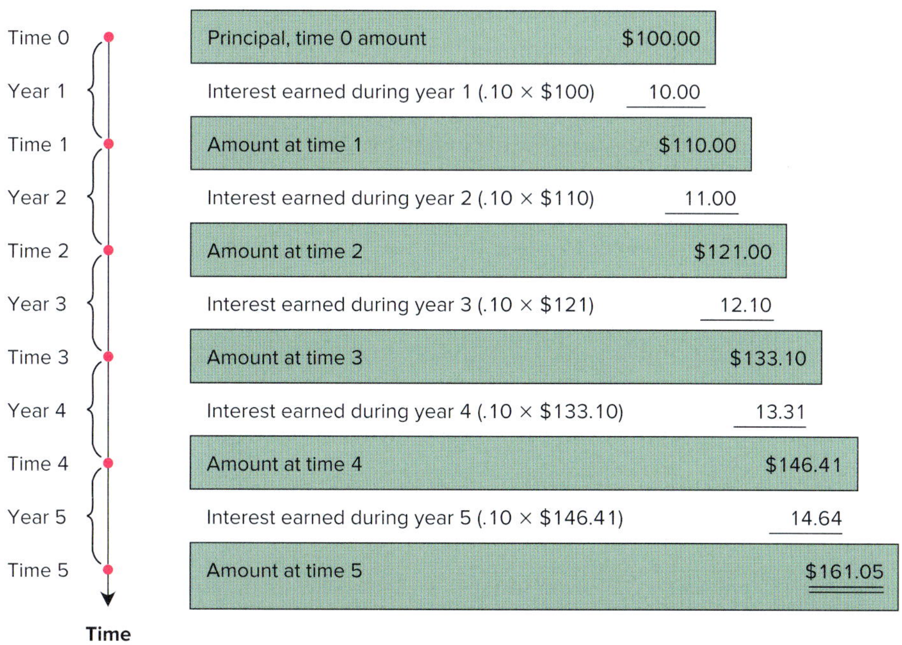

Fortunately, the simple formula shown below may be used to compute the future value of any investment.

$$F_n = P(1 + r)^n \quad (1)$$

where P denotes principal
r denotes interest rate per year
n denotes number of years

Using formula (1) to compute the future value after five years of your \$100 investment, we have the following computation.

$$\begin{aligned} F_n &= P(1 + r)^n \\ &= \$100(1 + .10)^5 \\ &= \$100(1.6105) = \$161.05 \end{aligned}$$

The value of $(1 + r)^n$ is called the **accumulation factor.** The values of $(1 + r)^n$, for various combinations of r and n, are tabulated in Table I of Appendix A to Chapter 16.

Use formula (1) and the tabulated values in Table I to compute the future value after 10 years of an \$800 investment that earns interest at the rate of 12 percent per year.[1]

Present Value In the discussion above, we computed the future value of an investment when the original principal is known. Now consider a slightly different problem. Suppose you know how much money you want to accumulate at the end of a five-year investment. Your problem is to determine how much your initial investment needs to be in order to accumulate the desired amount in five years. To solve this problem, we start with formula (1):

$$F_n = P(1 + r)^n$$

Now divide each side of the preceding equation by $(1 + r)^n$

$$P = F_n \left(\frac{1}{(1 + r)^n} \right) \quad (2)$$

In formula (2), P denotes what is commonly referred to as the **present value** of the cash flow F_n, which occurs after n years when the interest rate is r.

Let's try out formula (2) on your investment problem, which we analyzed in Exhibit II–1. Suppose you did not know the value of the initial investment required if you want to accumulate \$161.05 at the end of five years in an investment that earns 10 percent per year. We can determine the present value of the investment as follows:

$$\begin{aligned} P &= F_n \left(\frac{1}{(1 + r)^n} \right) \\ &= \$161.05 \left(\frac{1}{(1 + .10)^5} \right) \\ &= \$161.05(.6209) = \$100 \end{aligned}$$

[1]Using formula (1): $F = \$800(1 + .12)^{10}$. From Table I, $(1 + .12)^{10} = 3.106$. (Note that the values in Table I are rounded.) Thus, the future value of the investment is (\$800)(3.106) = \$2,484.80. Compound interest will more than triple the original \$800 investment in 10 years.

Thus, as we knew already, you must invest \$100 now in order to accumulate \$161.05 after five years in an investment earning 10 percent per year. The *present value* of \$100 and the *future value* of \$161.05 at time 5 are *economically equivalent,* given that the annual interest rate is 10 percent. If you are planning to invest the \$100 received now, then you should be indifferent between receiving the present value of \$100 now or receiving the future value of \$161.05 at the end of five years.

When we used formula (2) to compute the present value of the \$161.05 cash flow at time 5, we used a process called *discounting*. The interest rate used when we discount a future cash flow to compute its present value is called the **discount rate.** The value of $1/(1 + r)^n$, which appears in formula (2), is called the *discount factor*. Discount factors, for various combinations of r and n, are tabulated in Table III of Appendix A to Chapter 16.

Suppose you want to accumulate \$18,000 to buy a car in four years, and you can earn interest at the rate of 8 percent per year on an investment you make now. How much do you need to invest now? Use formula (2) and the discount factors in Table III of Appendix A to Chapter 16 to compute the present value of the required \$18,000 amount needed at the end of four years.[2]

Present Value of a Cash-Flow Series The present-value problem we just solved involved only a single future cash flow. Now consider a slightly different problem. Suppose you just won \$5,000 in the state lottery. You want to spend some of the cash now, but you have decided to save enough to rent a beach condominium during spring break of each of the next three years. You would like to deposit enough in a bank account now so that you can withdraw \$1,000 from the account at the end of each of the next three years. The money in the bank account will earn 8 percent per year. The question, then, is how much do you need to deposit? Another way of asking the same question is, what is the *present value* of a series of three \$1,000 cash flows at the end of each of the next three years, given that the discount rate is 8 percent?

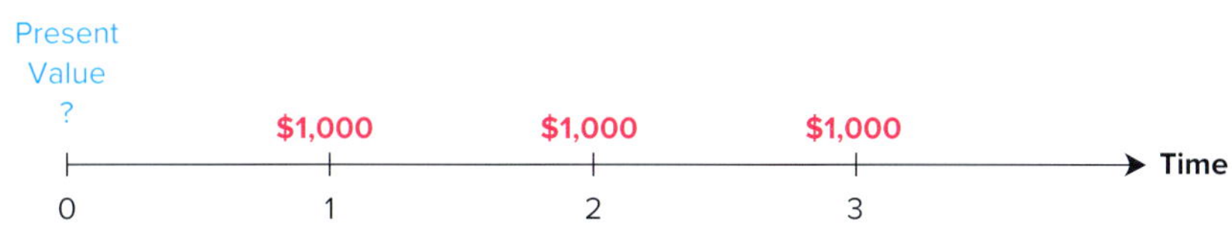

One way to figure out the answer to the question is to compute the present value of each of the three \$1,000 cash flows and add the three present-value amounts. We can use formula (2) for these calculations, as shown in panel A of Exhibit II–2. Notice that the present value of each of the \$1,000 cash flows is different, because the timing of the cash flows is different. The earlier the cash flow will occur, the higher is its present value.

Examine panel A of Exhibit II–2 carefully. We obtained the \$2,577 total present value by adding three present-value amounts. Each of these amounts is the result of multiplying \$1,000 by a discount factor. Notice that we can obtain the same final result by adding the three discount factors first, and then multiplying by \$1,000. This approach is taken in panel B of Exhibit II–2. The sum of the three discount factors is called an *annuity discount factor,* because a series of equivalent cash flows is called an **annuity.** Annuity discount factors for various combinations of r and n are tabulated in Table IV of Appendix A to Chapter 16.

---

[2]Using formula (2): $P = \$18{,}000 \times [1/(1 + .08)^4]$. From Table III, $1/(1 + .08)^4 = .735$. (Note that the values in Table III are rounded.) Thus, the present value of the required \$18,000 amount is (\$18,000)(.735) = \$13,230. An investment of \$13,230 made now, earning annual interest at 8 percent, will accumulate to \$18,000 at the end of four years.

Exhibit II–2
Present Value of a Series of Cash Flows

A. Present Value of Cash-Flow Series Using Three Independent Present-Value Calculations

Present-value formula [formula (2)]: $P = F_n\left(\frac{1}{(1+r)^n}\right)$

Present value of time 1 cash flow: $\$1{,}000\left(\frac{1}{(1+.08)^1}\right) = \$1{,}000(.9259) =$ $ 925.90

Present value of time 2 cash flow: $\$1{,}000\left(\frac{1}{(1+.08)^2}\right) = \$1{,}000(.8573) =$ $ 857.30

Present value of time 3 cash flow: $\$1{,}000\left(\frac{1}{(1+.08)^3}\right) = \$1{,}000(.7938) =$ $ 793.80

Total: present value of series of three cash flows $2,577.00

Sum of Three Discount Factors is the Annuity Discount Factor

B. Present Value of Cash-Flow Series Using the Annuity Discount Factor

Present value of series of three cash flows = $1,000(2.5770) = $2,577.00

Now let's verify that $2,577 is the right amount to finance your three spring-break vacations. Exhibit II–3 shows how your bank account will change over the three-year period as you earn interest and then withdraw $1,000 each year.

Future Value of a Cash-Flow Series To complete our discussion of present-value and future-value concepts, let's consider the series of $1,000 condo rental payments from

Exhibit II–3
Verification of Present-Value Calculation for Cash-Flow Series

Time	Year		
Time 0		Deposit $2,577	$2,577.00
	Year 1	Earn interest of $2,577(.08)	206.16*
Time 1		Accumulation at time 1	$2,783.16
		Withdrawal to cover time 1 beach trip	1,000.00
		Amount remaining to earn interest in year 2	$1,783.16
	Year 2	Earn interest of $1,783.16(.08)	142.65*
Time 2		Accumulation at time 2	$1,925.81
		Withdrawal to cover time 2 beach trip	1,000.00
		Amount remaining to earn interest in year 3	$ 925.81*
	Year 3	Earn interest of $925.81(.08)	74.06
Time 3		Accumulation at time 3	$ 999.87†
		Withdrawal to cover time 3 beach trip	$ 999.87†

Time

*Rounded
†This amount does not equal $1,000 exactly because of rounding error in the computation of each year's interest.

Exhibit II–4
Future Value of a Series of Cash Flows

A. Future Value of Cash-Flow Series Using Three Independent Future-Value Calculations

Future-value formula [formula (1)]: $F_n = P(1 + r)^n$

Future value of time 1 cash flow: $\$1,000(1 + .08)^2 = \$1,000(1.1664) = \$1,166.40$

Future value of time 2 cash flow: $\$1,000(1 + .08)^1 = \$1,000(1.0800) = \$1,080.00$

Future value of time 3 cash flow: $\$1,000 = \$1,000(1.0000) = \$1,000.00$

Total: future value of series of three cash flows $3,246.40

Sum of Three Accumulation Factors is the Annuity Accumulation Factor

B. Future Value of Cash-Flow Series Using the Annuity Accumulation Factor

Future value of series of three cash flows $= \$1,000(3.2464) = \$3,246.40$

the condo owner's perspective. Suppose the owner invests each $1,000 rental payment in a bank account that pays 8 percent interest per year. How much will the condo owner accumulate at the end of the three-year period? An equivalent question is, What is the future value of the three-year series of $1,000 cash flows, given an annual interest rate of 8 percent? Exhibit II–4 answers the question in two ways. In panel A of the exhibit, three separate future-value calculations are made using formula (1). Notice that the $1,000 cash flow at time 1 is multiplied by (1.08)2, since it has two years to earn interest. The $1,000 cash flow at time 2 has only one year to earn interest, and the time 3 cash flow has no time to earn interest.

In panel B of the exhibit, the three-year *annuity accumulation factor* is used. This factor is the sum of the three accumulation factors used in panel A of the exhibit. The annuity accumulation factors for various combinations of *r* and *n* are tabulated in Table II of Appendix A to Chapter 16.

Using the Tables Correctly When using the tables in Appendix A to Chapter 16 to solve future-value and present-value problems, be sure to select the correct table. Table I is used to find the *future value* of a *single* cash flow, and Table III is used to find the *present value* of a *single* cash flow. Table II is used in finding the *future value* of a *series* of identical cash flows; Table IV is used in finding the *present value* of a *series* of identical cash flows. Be careful not to confuse future value with present value or to confuse a single cash flow with a series of identical cash flows.

If you have a calculator that will exponentiate (raise a number to a power), you can forget the tables altogether. Just use the pertinent formula and compute the appropriate factor yourself.

Key Terms

For each term's definition refer to the indicated page, or turn to the glossary at the end of the text.

accumulation factor, 776
annuity, 777
compound interest, 775
discount rate, 777
future value, 775
present value, 776
principal, 775

Review Questions

II–1. What is meant by the term *compound interest?*

II–2. Explain in words the following future-value formula: $F_n = P(1 + r)^n$.

II–3. Define the term *present value.*

II–4. "The greater the discount rate, the greater the present value of a future cash flow." True or false? Explain your answer.

II–5. "If the interest rate is 10 percent, a present value of $100 and a future value of $161.10 at the end of five years are *economically equivalent.*" Explain.

II–6. What is an *annuity?*

Exercises

All applicable Exercises are available in Connect.

Exercise II–7
Future Value and Present Value
(LO II-1, II-2)

Answer each of the following independent questions. Ignore personal income taxes.

1. Suppose you invest $2,500 in an account bearing interest at the rate of 14 percent per year. What will be the future value of your investment in six years?
2. Your best friend won the state lottery and has offered to give you $10,000 in five years, after he has made his first million dollars. You figure that if you had the money today, you could invest it at 12 percent annual interest. What is the present value of your friend's future gift?
3. In four years, you would like to buy a small cabin in the mountains. You estimate that the property will cost you $52,500 when you are ready to buy. How much money would you need to invest each year in an account bearing interest at the rate of 6 percent per year in order to accumulate the $52,500 purchase price?
4. You have estimated that your educational expenses over the next three years will be $13,000 per year. How much money do you need in your account now in order to withdraw the required amount each year? Your account bears interest at 10 percent per year.

Exercise II–8
Continuation of Preceding Exercise
(LO II-1, II-2)

Refer to the answers given for the preceding exercise.

Required:

1. Refer to requirement (1) of the preceding exercise. Prepare a display similar to Exhibit II-1 to show how your accumulation grows each year to equal $5,487.50 after six years.
2. Refer to requirement (4) of the preceding exercise. Prepare a display similar to Exhibit II-3 to verify that $32,331 is the amount you need to fund your educational expenses.

Exercise II–9
Future Value and Present Value
(LO II-1, II-2)

You plan to retire at age 40 after a highly successful but short career. You would like to accumulate enough money by age 40 to withdraw $225,000 per year for 40 years. You plan to pay into your account 15 equal installments beginning when you are 25 and ending when you are 39. Your account bears interest of 12 percent per year.

Required:

1. How much do you need to accumulate in your account by the time you retire?
2. How much do you need to pay into your account in each of the 15 equal installments?
3. Is this a future-value problem or a present-value problem? Explain.

Appendix III

Inventory Management

After completing this appendix, you should be able to:

III-1 Calculate the economic order quantity (EOQ) using the EOQ decision model.

III-2 Understand the differences between the economic-order-quantity and just-in-time approaches to inventory management.

Learning Objective III-1

Calculate the economic order quantity (EOQ) using the EOQ decision model.

A key decision in manufacturing, retail, and some service industry firms is how much inventory to keep on hand. Moreover, inventory policy is a key part of the budgeting process. This appendix covers two alternative approaches to inventory management. Section 1 covers the traditional approach, known as the economic order quantity decision model. Section 2 covers a more contemporary approach, known as the just-in-time inventory management system.

Section 1: Economic Order Quantity

Inventory decisions involve a delicate balance between three classes of costs: ordering costs, holding costs, and shortage costs. Examples of costs in each of these categories are given in Exhibit III–1. The following illustration emphasizes the benefits of a sound inventory policy.

cozycamps.com

Cozycamps.com, a camping equipment manufacturer, has recently expanded its product line into winter sports equipment. The company's newest product is a fiberglass snowboard. One of the raw materials is a special resin used to bind the fiberglass in the molding phase of production. The production manager, Hi Mogul, uses an **economic order quantity (EOQ)** decision model to determine the size and frequency with which resin is ordered. The EOQ model is a mathematical tool for determining the order quantity that minimizes the costs of ordering and holding inventory.

Resin is purchased in 50-gallon drums, and 9,600 drums are used each year. Each drum costs $400. The controller estimates that the cost of placing and receiving a typical resin order is $225. The controller's estimate of the annual cost of carrying resin in inventory is $3 per drum.

Exhibit III–1
Inventory Ordering, Holding, and Shortage Costs

Ordering Costs
- Clerical costs of preparing purchase orders
- Time spent finding suppliers and expediting orders
- Transportation costs
- Receiving costs (e.g., unloading and inspection)

Holding Costs
- Costs of storage space (e.g., warehouse depreciation)
- Security
- Insurance
- Forgone interest on working capital tied up in inventory
- Deterioration, theft, spoilage, or obsolescence

Shortage Costs
- Disrupted production when raw materials are unavailable:
- Idle workers
- Extra machinery setups
- Lost sales resulting in dissatisfied customers
- Loss of quantity discounts on purchases

Tabular Approach Suppose Mogul orders 800 drums of resin in each order placed during the year. The total annual cost of ordering and holding resin in inventory is calculated as follows:

$$\frac{\text{Annual requirement}}{\text{Quantity per order}} = \frac{9{,}600}{800} = 12 = \text{Number of orders}$$

$$\text{Annual ordering cost} = 12 \text{ orders} \times \$225 \text{ per order} = \$2{,}700$$

$$\text{Average quantity in inventory} = \frac{\text{Quantity per order}}{2} = \frac{800}{2} = 400 \text{ drums}$$

$$\begin{aligned}\text{Annual holding cost} &= (\text{Average quantity in inventory}) \times (\text{Annual carrying cost per drum}) \\ &= 400 \times \$3 = \$1{,}200\end{aligned}$$

$$\begin{matrix}\text{Total annual cost} \\ \text{of inventory policy}\end{matrix} = \text{Ordering cost} + \text{Holding cost} = \$2{,}700 + \$1{,}200 = \$3{,}900$$

Notice that the $3,900 cost does not include the purchase cost of the resin at $400 per drum. We are focusing only on the costs of *ordering* and *holding* resin inventory.

Can Mogul do any better than $3,900 for the annual cost of his resin inventory policy? Exhibit III–2, which tabulates the inventory costs for various order quantities, indicates that Mogul can lower the costs of ordering and holding resin inventory. Of the five order quantities listed, the 1,200-drum order quantity yields the lowest total annual cost. Unfortunately, this tabular method for finding the least-cost order quantity is cumbersome. Moreover, it does not necessarily result in the optimal order quantity. It is possible that some order quantity other than those listed in Exhibit III–2 is the least-cost order quantity.

Equation Approach The total annual cost of ordering and holding inventory is given by the following equation.

$$\begin{aligned}\text{Total annual cost} = &\left(\frac{\text{Annual requirement}}{\text{Order quantity}}\right)\left(\begin{matrix}\text{Cost per} \\ \text{order}\end{matrix}\right) \\ &+ \left(\frac{\text{Order quantity}}{2}\right)\left(\begin{matrix}\text{Annual holding} \\ \text{cost per unit}\end{matrix}\right)\end{aligned}$$

Exhibit III–2
Tabulation of Inventory Ordering and Holding Costs

cozycamps.com

Order size	800	960	1,200	1,600	2,400
Number of orders (9,600 ÷ order size)	12	10	8	6	4
Ordering costs ($225 × number of orders)	$2,700	$2,250	$1,800	$1,350	$ 900
Average inventory (order size ÷ 2)	400	480	600	800	1,200
Holding costs ($3 × average inventory)	$1,200	$1,440	$1,800	$2,400	$3,600
Total annual cost (ordering cost + holding cost)	$3,900	$3,690	$3,600 ↑ Minimum	$3,750	$4,500

The following formula for the least-cost order quantity, called the economic order quantity (or EOQ), has been developed using calculus.

$$\text{Economic order quantity} = \sqrt{\frac{(2)(\text{Annual requirement})(\text{Cost per order})}{(\text{Annual holding cost per unit})}}$$

The EOQ formula in Cozycamp.com's problem yields the following EOQ for resin.

$$\text{EOQ} = \sqrt{\frac{(2)(9{,}600)(225)}{3}} = 1{,}200$$

Graphical Approach Another method for solving the EOQ problem is the graphical method, which is presented in Exhibit III–3. Notice that the ordering-cost line slants down to the right. This indicates a decline in these costs as the order size increases and the order frequency decreases. However, as the order size increases, so does the average inventory on hand. This results in an increase in holding costs, as indicated by the positive slope of the holding-cost line. The EOQ falls at 1,200 units, where the best balance is struck between these two costs. Total costs are minimized at $3,600.

Timing of Orders The EOQ model helps management decide how much to order at a time. Another important decision is when to order. This decision depends on the **lead time,** which is the length of time it takes for the material to be received after an order is placed. Suppose the lead time for resin is one month. Since Cozycamps.com uses 9,600 drums of resin per year, and the production rate is constant throughout the year, this implies that 800 drums are used each month. Production manager Mogul should order resin, in the economic order quantity of 1,200 drums, when the inventory falls to 800 drums. By the time the new order arrives, one month later, the 800 drums in inventory will have been used in production. Exhibit III–4 depicts this pattern of ordering and using inventory. By placing an order early enough to avoid a stockout, management takes into account the potential costs of shortages.

Safety Stock Our example assumed that the usage of resin is constant at 800 drums per month. Suppose instead that monthly usage fluctuates between 600 and 1,000 drums. Although average monthly usage still is 800 drums, there is the potential for an excess usage of 200 drums in any particular month. In light of this uncertainty, management may wish to keep a safety stock of resin equal to the potential excess monthly usage of 200 drums. With a safety stock of 200 drums, the reorder point is 1,000 drums. Thus, Mogul should order the EOQ of 1,200 drums whenever resin inventory falls to 1,000 drums. During the one-month lead time, another 600 to 1,000 drums of resin will be consumed in production. Although a safety stock will increase inventory holding costs, it will minimize the potential costs caused by shortages.

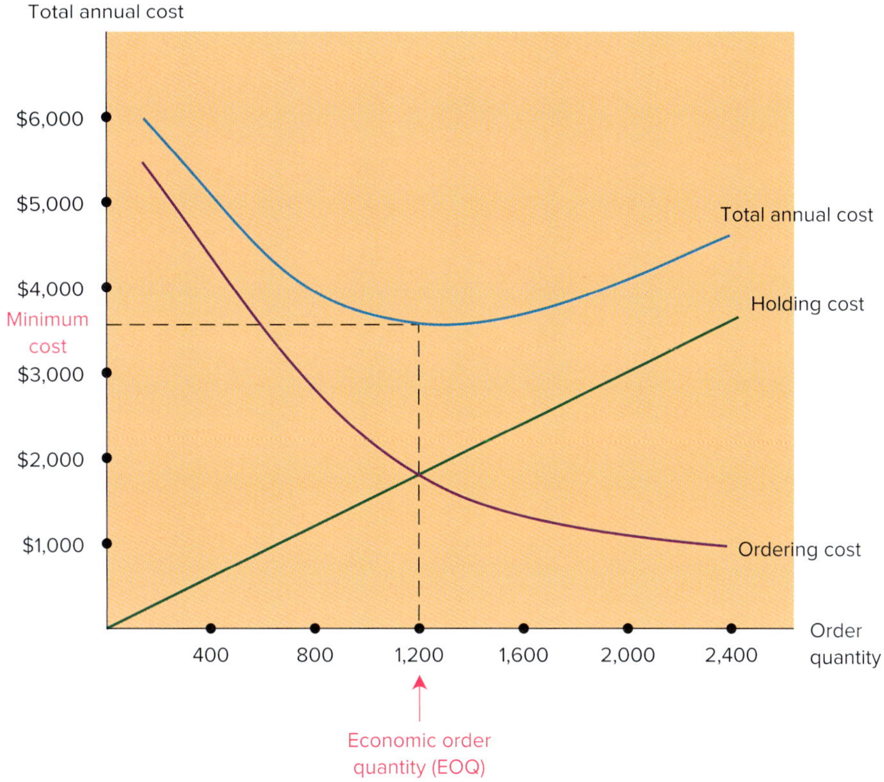

Exhibit III–3
Graphical Solution to Economic Order Quantity Decision

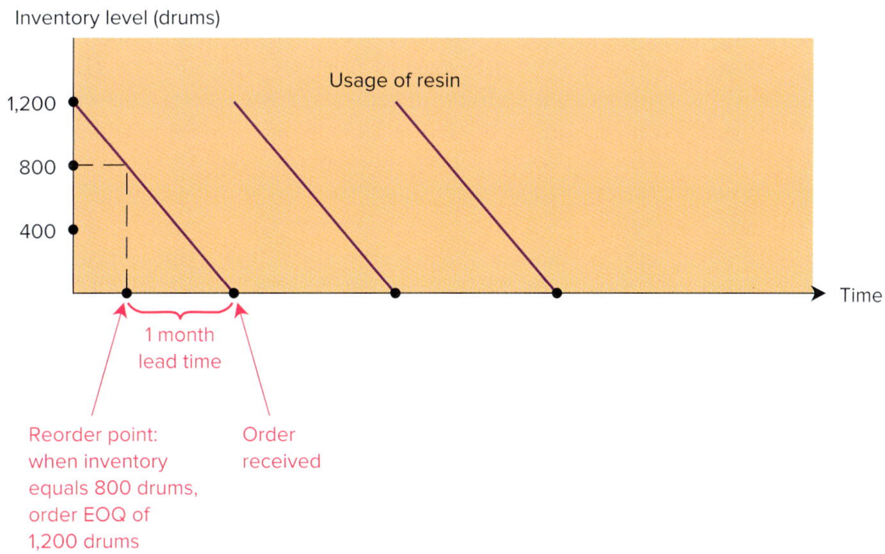

Exhibit III–4
Ordering, Lead Time, and Usage of inventory.

Section 2: Just-in-Time Inventory Management

In traditional manufacturing settings, inventories of raw materials and parts, partially completed components, and finished goods were kept as a buffer against the possibility of running out of a needed item. However, large buffer inventories consume valuable resources and generate hidden costs. Consequently, many companies have changed their approach to production and inventory management. These manufacturers have adopted a strategy for controlling the flow of manufacturing in a multistage production process. In a **just-in-time (JIT) production and inventory management system,** raw materials and

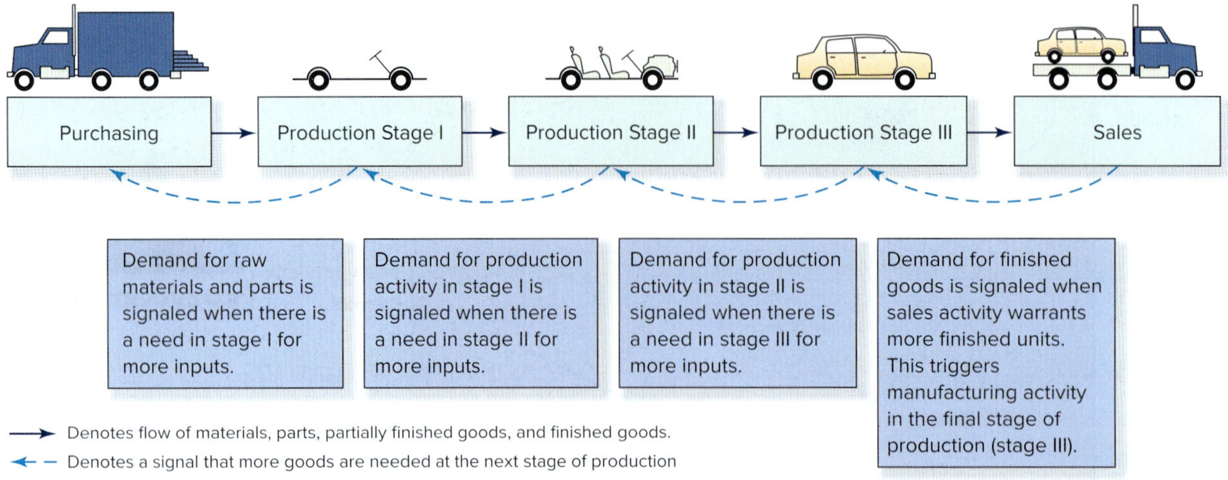

Exhibit III–5
Just-in-Time (JIT) Production and Inventory Management System

parts are purchased or produced just in time to be used at each stage of the production process. This approach to inventory and production management brings considerable cost savings from reduced inventory levels.

The key to the JIT system is the "pull" approach to controlling manufacturing. To visualize this approach, look at Exhibit III–5, which displays a simple diagram of a multistage production process. The flow of manufacturing activity is depicted by the solid arrows running across the page from one stage of production to the next. However, the signal that triggers more production activity in each stage comes from the *next* stage of production. These signals, depicted by the dashed-line arrows, run from right to left. We begin with sales at the right-hand side of the exhibit. When sales activity warrants more production of finished goods, the goods are "pulled" from production stage III by sending a signal that more goods are needed. Similarly, when production employees in stage III need more inputs, they send a signal back to stage II. This triggers production activity in stage II. Working our way back to the beginning of the process, purchases of raw materials and parts are triggered by a signal that they are needed in stage I. This pull system of production management, which characterizes the JIT approach, results in a smooth flow of production and significantly reduced inventory levels. The result is considerable cost savings for the manufacturer.

Learning Objective III-2

Understand the differences between the economic-order-quantity and just-in-time approaches to inventory management.

JIT Implications for EOQ The EOQ model minimizes the total cost of ordering and holding purchased inventory. Thus, this inventory management approach seeks to balance the cost of ordering against the cost of storing inventory. Under the JIT philosophy, the goal is to keep *all* inventories as low as possible. *Any* inventory holding costs are seen as inefficient and wasteful. Moreover, under JIT purchasing, ordering costs are minimized by reducing the number of vendors, negotiating long-term supply agreements, making less frequent payments, and eliminating inspections. The implication of the JIT philosophy is that inventories should be minimized by more frequent deliveries in smaller quantities. This result can be demonstrated using the EOQ formula, as shown in Exhibit III–6. As the cost of holding inventory increases, the EOQ decreases. Moreover, as the cost of placing an order declines, the EOQ decreases.

The economics underlying the EOQ model support the JIT viewpoint that inventory should be purchased or produced in small quantities, and inventories should be kept to the absolute minimum. However, the basic philosophies of JIT and EOQ are quite different.

Exhibit III–6
Economic Order Quantity with Different Ordering and Holding Costs

cozycamps.com

Holding Costs per Unit	Ordering Costs per Order $225	$150	$100	$50	
$3	1,200*	980	800	566	EOQ declines →
4	1,039	849	693	490	
5	930	759	620	438	
6	849	693	566	400	
	EOQ declines ↓				

*The annual requirement is assumed to be 9,600 units for each case in this table. This was the annual requirement for drums of resin in the cozycamps.com illustration. (Several of the EOQs in the table are rounded.)

The EOQ approach takes the view that some inventory is necessary, and the goal is to optimize the order quantity in order to balance the cost of ordering against the cost of holding inventory. In contrast, the JIT philosophy argues that holding costs tend to be higher than may be apparent because of the inefficiency and waste of storing inventory. Thus, inventory should be minimized, or even eliminated completely, if possible. Moreover, under the JIT approach, orders typically will vary in size, depending on needs. The EOQ model, in contrast, results in a constant order quantity.

Key Terms

For each term's definition refer to the indicated page, or turn to the glossary at the end of the text.

economic order quantity (EOQ), 782
just-in-time (JIT) production and inventory management system, 785
lead time, 784

Review Questions

III–1. Define and give examples of *inventory ordering, holding,* and *shortage costs.*

III–2. Explain the differences in the basic philosophies underlying the JIT and EOQ approaches to inventory management.

Exercises

All applicable Exercises are available in Connect.

Exercise III–3
Economic Order Quantity
(LO III-1)

For each of the following independent cases, use the equation method to compute the economic order quantity.

	Case A	Case B	Case C
Annual requirement (in units)	13,230	1,681	560
Cost per order	$250	$40	$10
Annual holding cost per unit	6	20	7

Exercise III–4
Lead Time and Safety Stock
(LO III-1)

Andrew and Fulton, Inc., uses 780 tons of a chemical bonding agent each year. Monthly demand fluctuates between 50 and 80 tons. The lead time for each order is one month, and the economic order quantity is 130 tons.

Required:

1. Determine the safety stock appropriate for the chemical bonding agent.
2. At what order point, in terms of tons remaining in inventory, should Andrew and Fulton, Inc., order the bonding agent?

Exercise III–5
Economic Order Quantity Equation Approach; JIT Purchasing
(LO III-1, III-2)

Fiber Technology, Inc., manufactures glass fibers used in the communications industry. The company's materials and parts manager is currently revising the inventory policy for XL-20, one of the chemicals used in the production process. The chemical is purchased in 10-pound canisters for $95 each. The firm uses 4,800 canisters per year. The controller estimates that it costs $150 to place and receive a typical order of XL-20. The annual cost of storing XL-20 is $4 per canister.

Required:

1. Write the formula for the total annual cost of ordering and storing XL-20.
2. Use the EOQ formula to determine the optimal order quantity.
3. What is the total annual cost of ordering and storing XL-20 at the economic order quantity?
4. How many orders will be placed per year?
5. Fiber Technology's controller, Jay Turnbull, recently attended a seminar on JIT purchasing. Afterward he analyzed the cost of storing XL-20, including the costs of wasted space and inefficiency. He was shocked when he concluded that the real annual holding cost was $19.20 per canister. Turnbull then met with Doug Kaplan, Fiber Technology's purchasing manager. Together they contacted Reno Industries, the supplier of XL-20, about a JIT purchasing arrangement. After some discussion and negotiation, Kaplan concluded that the cost of placing an order for XL-20 could be reduced to just $20. Using these new cost estimates, Turnbull computed the new EOQ for XL-20.
   a. Use the equation approach to compute the new EOQ.
   b. How many orders will be placed per year?

Exercise III–6
Economic Order Quantity; Tabular Approach
(LO III-1)

Refer to the *original* data given in the preceding exercise for Fiber Technology, Inc.

Required:

1. Prepare a table showing the total annual cost of ordering and storing XL-20 for each of the following order quantities: 400, 600, and 800 canisters.
2. What are the weaknesses in the tabular approach?

Exercise III–7
Economic Order Quantity; Graphical Approach
(LO III-1)

Refer to the *original* data given in Exercise III–5 for Fiber Technology, Inc.

Required: Prepare a graphical analysis of the economic order quantity decision for XL-20.

Exercise III–8
Economic Order Quantity; Lead Time and Safety Stock
(LO III-1)

Refer to the *original* data given in Exercise III–5 for Fiber Technology, Inc. The lead time required to receive an order of XL-20 is one month.

Required:

1. Assuming stable usage of XL-20 each month, determine the reorder point for XL-20.
2. Draw a graph showing the usage, lead time, and reorder point for XL-20.
3. Suppose that monthly usage of XL-20 fluctuates between 300 and 500 canisters, although annual demand remains constant at 4,800 canisters. What level of safety stock should the materials and parts manager keep on hand for XL-20? What is the new reorder point for the chemical?

References for "In Their Own Words"

Chapter One

(1a)* Gary Siegel and James E. Sorensen, principal investigators for the Gary Siegel Organization, *Counting More, Counting Less: Transformations in the Management Accounting Profession* (Montvale, NJ: Institute of Management Accountants, 1999).

(1b) Kimberly S. Johnson, "Wanted: Versatile Accountants," *The Wall Street Journal,* May 19, 2015, p. B7.

(1c) Ibid. (1a)

(1d) Ibid.

(1e) Ibid.

(1f) Noelle Knox, "A CFO's Role in a Fast-Growing Company," *The Wall Street Journal,* October 20, 2014, p. R7.

(1g) Ibid. (1a)

(1h) Matthew Quinn, "CFO Journal: For CFOs, a Move Past Finance," *The Wall Street Journal,* July 31, 2012.

(1i) Ibid.

(1j) Ibid. (1a)

(1k) Matthew Quinn and Alix Stuart, "Not Just Bean Counters," *The Wall Street Journal,* July 31, 2012.

(1l) Quoted on CMA Certification web page at http://www.imanet.org/cma-certification/cma-certification-overview. December 13, 2015.

(1m) Vipal Monga, "Mylan's Hostile Offer Puts Perrigo CFO to the Test," *The Wall Street Journal,* November 9, 2015.

Chapter Two

(2a) Gary Siegel and James E. Sorensen, principal investigators for the Gary Siegel Organization, *Counting More, Counting Less: Transformations in the Management Accounting Profession* (Montvale, NJ: Institute of Management Accountants, 1999).

(2b) Ruth Porat, CFO of Google Inc, quoted in Alistair Barr, "Google Shares Surge on Results, Tough Talk," *The Wall Street Journal*, July 16, 2015.

(2c) Greg Foran, Walmart CEO, quoted in Loretta Chao, Wal-Mart Reins Back Inventory in a Revamped Supply Chain," *The Wall Street Journal*, August 18, 2015.

(2d) Benjamin Mulling, Tente Casters CFO, quoted in Kimberly S. Johnson, "The Plain-Vanilla Accountant Goes Out of Style," *The Wall Street Journal*, May 18,

(2e) *Activity-Based Management: Part I,* a management education video (Boston: President and Fellows of Harvard College, 1993).

(2f) Gary Siegel, project director, *The Practice Analysis of Management Accounting* (Montvale, NJ: Institute of Management Accountants, 1996), p. 18.

(2g) Bain and Company describing client Kraft Foods, in Michael Heric et al, "How to break out from the G&A cost treadmill," at www.bain.com/publications/articles/break-out-from-the-g-and-a-cost-treadmill.aspx, July 10, 2013.

(2h) Gary Siegel and James E. Sorensen, principal investigators for the Gary Siegel Organization, *Counting More, Counting Less: Transformations in the Management Accounting Profession* (Montvale, NJ: Institute of Management Accountants, 1999).

Chapter Three

(3a) Jeff Woodbury, Exxon's head of investor relations, quoted in Ernest Scheyder and Anna Driver, "Tumbling Oil Prices Slam Profit at Exxon Mobil, Chevron," *Reuters,* July 31, 2015.

(3b) Nell Edgington, "Overcoming The Nonprofit Starvation Cycle: An Interview With Ann Goggins Gregory," *Social Velocity* website, November 14, 2014.

(3c) Danny Hakim, "Aboard a Cargo Colossus," *New York Times,* October 5, 2014. p. BU4.

(3d) Interview with a DaimlerChrysler accountant conducted during research by the author.

(3e) Interview with an accountant for The Walt Disney Company conducted during research by the author.

(3f) Interview with a DaimlerChrysler accountant conducted during research by the author.

(3g) Jay Goltz, "The Price of Bad Pricing," *The New York Times,* July 6, 2011.

(3h) Interview with a Cornell University accountant conducted during research by the author.

Chapter Four

(4a) Steve Player and Carol Cobble, *Cornerstones of Decision Making: Profiles of Enterprise ABM* (Greensboro, NC: Oakhill Press, 1999), p. 161.

(4b) Ibid., p. 12.

(4c) Ibid., p. 168.

Chapter Five

(5a) *Activity-Based Management: Part I,* a management education video (Boston: The President and Fellows of Harvard College, 1993).

(5b) Joyce R. Ochs and Kenneth L. Parkinson, "Moving to Activity-Based Cost Analysis," *Business Finance* 5, no. 11 (November 1999), p. 101.

(5c) Steve Player and Carol Cobble, *Cornerstones of Decision Making: Profiles of Enterprise ABM* (Greensboro, NC: Oakhill Press, 1999), p. 167.

(5d) Ibid., p. 119.

(5e) Tad Leahy, "The A to Z of ABC Dictionaries," *Business Finance* 5, no. 12 (December 1999), p. 82.

(5f) Mike Esterl, "How Dr Pepper Cuts Costs. And Then Cuts Costs Some More," *The Wall Street Journal,* February 22, 2016, p. R4.

(5g) Richard Hayes, Ranjit Singh, Ajit Kambil, and Lori Calabro, "Pricing for Profitability: What's in Your Pocket?" *Deloitte CFO Insights,* 2013.

(5h) Scott Smith, in Steve Player and Carol Cobble, *Cornerstones of Decision Making: Profiles of Enterprise ABM* (Greensboro, NC: Oakhill Press, 1999), p. 187.

(5i) Melinda Beck, "Here's What Your Operation Will Really Cost," *The Wall Street Journal,* November 17, 2013.

*The references are organized by chapter. Thus, reference (1a) relates to the first quote in Chapter 1, and so forth.

Chapter Six

(6a) Paulo Salgado,Margarida Bajanca, and Nuno Belo, in Steve Player and Carol Cobble, *Cornerstones of Decision Making: Profiles of Enterprise ABM* (Greensboro, NC: Oakhill Press, 1999), p. 172.

(6b) Steve Player and Carol Cobble, *Cornerstones of Decision Making: Profiles of Enterprise ABM* (Greensboro, NC: Oakhill Press, 1999), p. 214.

(6c) Interview with a Ford Motor Company accountant conducted during research by the author.

(6d) Steve Player and Carol Cobble, *Cornerstones of Decision Making: Profiles of Enterprise ABM* (Greensboro, NC: Oakhill Press, 1999), p. 78.

(6e) Interview with a Cornell University administrator conducted during research by the author.

Chapter Seven

(7a) Gary Siegel and James E. Sorensen, principal investigators for the Gary Siegel Organization, *Counting More, Counting Less: Transformations in the Management Accounting Profession* (Montvale, NJ: Institute of Management Accountants, 1999).

(7b) Interview with a Cornell University accountant conducted during research by the author.

(7c) Interview with a Delta Air Lines accountant conducted during research by the author.

(7d) Gary Siegel and James E. Sorensen, principal investigators for the Gary Siegel Organization, *Counting More, Counting Less: Transformations in the Management Accounting Profession* (Montvale, NJ: Institute of Management Accountants, 1999).

(7e) Steve Player and Carol Cobble, *Cornerstones of Decision Making: Profiles of Enterprise ABM* (Greensboro, NC: Oakhill Press, 1999), p. 78.

Chapter Eight

(8a) Timothy Aeppel, "Firms Race to Regain Control Over Inventories," *The Wall Street Journal,* February 9, 2009.

(8b) ASQ website, http://asq.org/learn-about-quality/cost-of-quality/overview/overview.html (2012).

(8c) Michael Arndt, "Quality Isn't Just for Widgets," *BusinessWeek,* July 22, 2002, p. 72.

(8d) Marc J Epstein, Adriana Rejc Buhovac, and Kristi Yuthas, "Managing Social, Environmental and Financial Performance Simultaneously: What Can We Learn from Corporate Best Practices," *IMA Research Foundation Report Series* (2009).

(8e) Richard Anderson, "Puma First to Publish Environmental Impact Costs," *BBC News,* May 16, 2011.

Chapter Nine

(9a) Matthew Quinn, "CFO Journal: For CFOs, a Move Past Finance," *The Wall Street Journal,* July 31, 2012.

(9b) *The Management Accounting Video,* a management education video (New York: McGraw-Hill, 1997). Best Foods introduced several well-known brands, such as Skippy peanut butter, Hellman's mayonnaise, and Thomas' English Muffins. Best Foods has since been acquired by Unilever.

(9c) Steve Player, "FP&A Talent in High Demand," *bigfatfinanceblog.com* (February 23, 2010).

(9d) Anne Stuart, "The Importance of Accurate Forecasting: A CFO's Perspective," *Sales Performance Journal,* March 2006.

(9e) Jay Collins, "Advanced Use of ABM: Using ABC for Target Costing, Activity-Based Budgeting, and Benchmarking," in *Activity-Based Management: Arthur Andersen's Lessons from the ABM Battlefield,* ed.Steve Player and David E. Keys (New York: John Wiley & Sons, 1999), p. 153.

(9f) Steve Hornyak, "Budgeting Made Easy," *Management Accounting* 80, no. 4 (October 1998), pp. 18–23.

(9g) "A Survey of Corporate IT: Let It Rise," *The Economist,* October 23, 2008.

Chapter Ten

(10a) Bill Gates, "My Plan to Fix the World's Biggest Problems," *The Wall Street Journal,* January 26-27, 2013, pp. C1–C2.

(10b) *The Management Accounting Video,* a management education video (New York: McGraw-Hill, 1997).

(10c) African Performance Specialists, "Purchasing Efficiency Improvement Project," *APS NewsLetter,* October 2008, http://www.africanwizard.co.za/files/purchasing_efficiency_oct_08.pdf.

(10d) Simon Osmer, Rachel Woods, and Jeremy Thomas, "Standard Costing: Insights from Leading Companies," *KPMG Financial Management Advisory,* February 2010.

(10e) Rockwell Collins, "Engineer of the Year Awards," *Horizons Online* 15, Issue 2 (2010).

(10f) David Johnsen and Parvez Sopariwala, "Standard Costing Is Alive and Well at Parker Brass," *Management Accounting Quarterly* 1, no. 2 (Winter 2000), p. 13.

Chapter Eleven

(11a) Gary Siegel and James E. Sorensen, principal investigators for the Gary Siegel Organization, *Counting More, Counting Less: Transformations in the Management Accounting Profession* (Montvale, NJ: Institute of Management Accountants, 1999).

(11b) Interview with an A. T. Kearney consultant conducted during research by the author.

(11c) Steve Player and Carol Cobble, *Cornerstones of Decision Making: Profiles of Enterprise ABM* (Greensboro, NC: Oakhill Press, 1999), p. 79.

(11d) Cynthia Beier Greeson and Mehmet C. Kocakulah, "Implementing an ABC Pilot at Whirlpool," *Journal of Cost Management* 11, no. 2 (March/April 1997), pp. 16–21.

(11e) Interview with an A. T. Kearney consultant conducted during research by the author.

Chapter Twelve

(12a) Interview with Chrysler accountant conducted during research by the author.

(12b) Gary Siegel and James E. Sorensen, principal investigators for the Gary Siegel Organization, *Counting More, Counting Less: Transformations in the Management Accounting Profession* (Montvale, NJ: Institute of Management Accountants, 1999).

(12c) Ibid.

(12d) Company presentation at www.univarcorp.com/040506/UKUnivarAGM-1.ppt (May 2004).

(12e) Ibid. (12b)

(12f) *The Management Accounting Video,* a management education video (New York: McGraw-Hill, 1997).

(12g) Mark Green, Jeanine Garrity, Andra Gumbus, and Bridget Lyons, "Pitney Bowes Calls for New Metrics," *Strategic Finance* 83, no. 11 (May 2002), p. 34.

(12h) Quoted in Palladium Group, "Strategy Management," http://www.thepalladiumgroup.com/Solutions/strategy/Pages/overview.aspx (February 16, 2013).

Chapter Thirteen

(13a) Gary Siegel and James E. Sorensen, principal investigators for the Gary Siegel Organization, *Counting More, Counting Less: Transformations in the Management Accounting Profession* (Montvale, NJ: Institute of Management Accountants, 1999).

(13b) Thomas P. Kunes, "Environmental Cost Management," *Strategic Finance,* February 2001, p. 83.

(13c) *Current Practices, Perceptions and Trends: Transfer Pricing—1997 Global Survey* (Chicago: Ernst & Young, 1997), p. 1.

(13d) Ibid., p. 4.

(13e) Ibid., p. 11.

(13f) Ibid., p. 11.

Chapter Fourteen

(14a) Gary Siegel and James E. Sorensen, principal investigators for the Gary Siegel Organization, *Counting More, Counting Less: Transformations in the Management Accounting Profession* (Montvale, NJ: Institute of Management Accountants, 1999).

(14b) Ibid.

(14c) Ibid.

(14d) Ibid.

(14e) Ibid.

Chapter Fifteen

(15a) Gary Siegel and James E. Sorensen, principal investigators for the Gary Siegel Organization, *Counting More, Counting Less: Transformations in the Management Accounting Profession* (Montvale, NJ: Institute of Management Accountants, 1999).

(15b) Ibid.

(15c) Steve Player and Carol Cobble, *Cornerstones of Decision Making: Profiles of Enterprise ABM* (Greensboro, NC: Oakhill Press, 1999), p. 80.

(15d) Ibid.

(15e) Presentation by U.S. Navy Acquisition Center, *The Second Annual International Conference on Target Costing,* sponsored by the Consortium for Advanced Manufacturing—International, Arthur Andersen, Ernst & Young, and the University of Akron (Washington, DC: CAM-I, 1998).

(15f) Presentation by Eastman Kodak Company, *The Second Annual International Conference on Target Costing,* sponsored by the Consortium for Advanced Manufacturing—International, Arthur Andersen, Ernst & Young, and the University of Akron (Washington, DC: CAM-I, 1998).

(15g) Presentation by Honda of America, *The Second Annual International Conference on Target Costing,* sponsored by the Consortium for Advanced Manufacturing—International, Arthur Andersen, Ernst & Young, and the University of Akron (Washington, DC: CAM-I, 1998).

(15h) Ibid.

Chapter Sixteen

(16a) Interview with a Ford Motor Company accountant conducted during research by the author.

(16b) Interview with a Hewlett-Packard accountant conducted during research by the author.

(16c) Interview with a Cornell University accountant conducted during research by the author.

(16d) Interview with a Boeing Company accountant conducted during research by the author.

(16e) Interview with an A. T. Kearney consultant conducted during research by the author.

Chapter Seventeen

(17a) Interview with a Chrysler accountant conducted during research by the author.

(17b) Interview with a Cornell University accountant conducted during research by the author.

(17c) Interview with an American Management Systems consultant conducted during research by the author.

Glossary

absorption costing (or full costing) A method of product costing in which both variable and fixed manufacturing overhead are included in the product costs that flow through the manufacturing accounts (i.e., Work-in-Process Inventory, Finished-Goods Inventory, and Cost of Goods Sold).

Accelerated Cost Recovery System (ACRS) The depreciation schedule specified by the United States tax code. Since it has been modified by recent tax law changes, the system also is called the Modified Accelerated Cost Recovery System (MACRS).

acceptance-or-rejection decision A decision as to whether or not a particular capital investment proposal should be accepted.

account-classification method (also called account analysis) A cost-estimation method involving a careful examination of the ledger accounts for the purpose of classifying each cost as variable, fixed, or semivariable.

accounting-rate-of-return method A percentage formed by taking a project's average incremental revenue minus its average incremental expenses (including depreciation and income taxes) and dividing by the project's initial investment.

accumulation factor The value of $(1 + r)^n$, in a future value calculation, where r denotes the interest rate per year and n denotes the number of years.

accurate information Precise and correct data.

activity accounting The collection of financial or operational performance information about significant activities in an enterprise.

activity analysis The detailed identification and description of the activities conducted in an enterprise.

activity base (or cost driver) A measure of an organization's activity that is used as a basis for specifying cost behavior. The activity base also is used to compute a predetermined overhead rate. The current trend is to refer to the activity base as a volume-based cost driver.

activity-based budgeting (ABB) The process of developing a master budget using information obtained from an activity-based costing (ABC) analysis.

activity-based costing (ABC) system A two-stage procedure used to assign overhead costs to products or services produced. In the first stage, significant activities are identified, and overhead costs are assigned to activity cost pools in accordance with the way resources are consumed by the activities. In the second stage, the overhead costs are allocated from each activity cost pool to each product line in proportion to the amount of the cost driver consumed by the product line.

activity-based flexible budget A flexible budget based on several cost drivers rather than on a single, volume-based cost driver.

activity-based management (ABM) Using an activity-based costing system to improve the operations of an organization.

activity-based responsibility accounting A system for measuring the performance of an organization's people and subunits, which focuses not only on the cost of performing activities but on the activities themselves.

activity cost pool A grouping of overhead costs assigned to various similar activities identified in an activity-based costing system.

actual costing A product-costing system in which actual direct material, direct labor, and *actual* manufacturing-overhead costs are added to Work-in-Process Inventory.

activity dictionary A complete listing of the activities included in an organization's ABC analysis.

actual manufacturing overhead The actual costs incurred during an accounting period for manufacturing overhead. Includes actual indirect material, indirect labor, and other manufacturing costs.

actual overhead rate The rate at which overhead costs are actually incurred during an accounting period. Calculated as follows: actual manufacturing overhead ÷ actual cost driver (or activity base). Supp*

after-tax cash flow The cash flow expected after all tax implications have been taken into account.

after-tax net income An organization's net income after its income-tax expense is subtracted.

aggregate (or total) productivity Total output divided by total input.

allocation base A measure of activity, physical characteristic, or economic characteristic that is associated with the responsibility centers that are the cost objects in an allocation process.

annuity A series of equivalent cash flows.

applied manufacturing overhead The amount of manufacturing-overhead costs added to Work-in-Process Inventory during an accounting period.

appraisal costs Costs of determining whether defective products exist.

attention-directing function The function of managerial accounting information in pointing out to managers issues that need their attention.

average cost per unit The total cost of producing a particular quantity of product divided by the number of units produced.

average revenue curve *See* **demand curve.**

avoidable expenses Expenses that will no longer be incurred if a particular action is taken.

balanced scorecard A model of business performance evaluation that includes several types of financial and nonfinancial performance measures, typically comprising the following perspectives: financial, customer, internal business process, and learning and growth.

batch-level activity An activity that must be accomplished for each batch of products rather than for each unit.

batch manufacturing High-volume production of several product lines that differ in some important ways but are nearly identical in others.

before-tax income An organization's income before its income tax expense is subtracted.

benchmarking (or competitive benchmarking) The continual search for the most effective method of accomplishing a task, by comparing existing methods and performance levels with those of other organizations or with other subunits within the same organization.

best practices The most effective methods of accomplishing various tasks in a particular industry, often discovered through benchmarking. Supp

big data A massive volume of both structured and unstructured data that is so large it is difficult to process using traditional methods.

bill of activities (for a product or service) A complete listing of the activities required for that product or service to be produced.

bill of materials A list of all the materials needed to manufacture a product or product component.

break-even point The volume of activity at which an organization's revenues and expenses are equal. May be measured either in units or in sales dollars.

budget A detailed plan, expressed in quantitative terms, that specifies how resources will be acquired and used during a specified period of time.

budget administration The procedures used to prepare a budget, secure its approval, and disseminate it to the people who need to know its contents. Supp

budget committee A group of top-management personnel who advise the budget director during the preparation of the budget.

budget director (or chief budget officer) The individual designated to be in charge of preparing an organization's budget.

budget manual A set of written instructions that specify who will provide budgetary data, when and in what form the data will be provided, how the master budget will be prepared and approved, and who should receive the various schedules constituting the budget.

budget period The time period covered by a budget. Supp

budgetary slack The difference between the budgetary projection provided by an individual and his or her best estimate of the item being projected. (For example, the difference between a supervisor's expected departmental utility cost and his or her budgetary projection for utilities.)

budgeted balance sheet Shows the expected end-of-period balances for the company's assets, liabilities, and owners' equity.

budgeted financial statements (or pro forma financial statements) A set of planned financial statements showing what an organization's overall financial condition is expected to be at the end of the budget period if planned operations are carried out.

budgeted income statement Shows the expected revenue and expenses for a budget period, assuming that planned operations are carried out.

budgeted schedule of cost of goods manufactured and sold Details the direct material, direct labor, and manufacturing overhead costs to be incurred and shows the cost of the goods to be sold during a budget period.

budgeted statement of cash flows A budget schedule providing information about the expected sources and uses of cash for operating activities, investing activities, and financing activities during a particular period of time.

by-product A joint product with very little value relative to the other joint products.

CAD/CAM system *See* **computer-aided design** and **computer-aided manufacturing.**

capacity The upper limit on the amount of goods or services that an organization can produce in a specified period of time.

capital budget A long-term budget that shows planned acquisition and disposal of capital assets, such as land, buildings, and equipment.

capital-budgeting decision A decision involving cash flows beyond the current year.

capital-intensive A production process accomplished largely by machinery. Supp

capital-rationing decision A decision in which management chooses which of several investment proposals to accept to make the best use of limited investment funds.

capital turnover Sales revenue divided by invested capital.

cash bonus *See* **pay for performance.**

cash budget Details the expected cash receipts and disbursements during a budget period.

cash disbursements budget A schedule detailing expected cash payments during a budget period.

cash equivalents Short-term, highly liquid investments that are treated as equivalent to cash in the preparation of a statement of cash flows. Supp

cash provided by (or used by) operations The difference between the cash receipts and cash disbursements that are related to operating activities. Supp

cash receipts budget A schedule detailing the expected cash collections during the budget period.

cellular manufacturing The organization of a production facility into FMS cells. Supp

Certified Management Accountant (CMA) An accountant who has earned professional certification in managerial accounting.

chief financial officer (CFO) The executive responsible for all accounting and finance functions in an organization.

coefficient of determination A statistical measure of goodness of fit; a measure of how closely a regression line fits the data on which it is based.

committed cost A cost that results from an organization's ownership or use of facilities and its basic organization structure.

common costs Costs incurred to benefit more than one organizational segment.

common-size financial statements Financial statements prepared in terms of percentages of a base amount. Supp

comparative financial statements Financial statements showing the results of two or more successive years. Supp

competitive benchmarking *See* **benchmarking.**

competitive bidding A situation where two or more companies submit bids (prices) for a product, service, or project to a potential buyer.

compound interest The interest earned on prior periods' interest.

comptroller *See* **controller.**

computer-aided design (CAD) system Computer software used by engineers in the design of a product. Supp

computer-integrated manufacturing (CIM) system The most advanced form of automated manufacturing, in which virtually all parts of the production process are accomplished by computer-controlled machines and automated material-handling equipment. Supp

computer-numerically-controlled (CNC) machines Standalone machines controlled by a computer via a numerical, machine- readable code. Supp

constraints Algebraic expressions of limitations faced by a firm, such as those limiting its productive resources.

consumption ratio The proportion of an activity consumed by a particular product.

continual (or continuous) improvement The constant effort to eliminate waste, reduce response time, simplify the design of both products and processes, and improve quality and customer service.

contribution income statement An income statement on which fixed and variable expenses are separated.

contribution margin Sales revenue minus variable expenses. The amount of sales revenue, which is left to cover fixed expenses and profit after paying variable expenses. Supp

contribution margin per unit The difference between the unit sales price and the unit variable expense. The amount that each unit contributes to covering fixed expenses and profit. Supp

contribution-margin ratio The unit contribution margin divided by the sales price per unit. Also may be expressed in percentage form; then it is called the contribution-margin percentage.

controllability The extent to which managers are able to control or influence a cost or cost variance.

controllable cost A cost that is subject to the control or substantial influence of a particular individual.

controller (or comptroller) The top managerial and financial accountant in an organization. Supervises the accounting department and assists management at all levels in interpreting and using managerial-accounting information.

controlling Ensuring that an organization operates in the intended manner and achieves its goals. Supp

conversion costs Direct-labor cost plus production-overhead cost or, more generally, the costs of the resources needed to convert purchased inputs into a marketable product or service.

cost The sacrifice made, usually measured by the resources given up, to achieve a particular purpose.

Cost Accounting Standards Board (CASB) A federal agency chartered by Congress in 1970 to develop cost-accounting standards for large government contractors. Supp

cost accounting system Part of the core accounting system that accumulates data about the costs of producing goods and services for use in both managerial and financial accounting.

cost allocation The process of assigning costs in a cost pool to the appropriate cost objects. *See also* **cost distribution.**

cost behavior The relationship between cost and activity.

cost center A responsibility center whose manager is accountable for its costs of operation, while accomplishing the department's organizational functions at a specified level of performance.

cost distribution The cost of storing and transporting finished goods for sale.

cost distribution (sometimes called cost allocation) The first step in assigning manufacturing-overhead costs. Overhead costs are assigned to all departmental overhead centers.

cost driver A characteristic of an activity or event that results in the incurrence of costs by that activity or event.

cost estimation The process of determining how a particular cost behaves.

cost hierarchy The classification of activities into levels, such as unit-level, batch-level, product-sustaining level, and facility-level activities.

cost management system (CMS) A management planning and controlling system that measures the cost of significant activities, identifies non-value-added costs, and identifies activities that will improve organizational performance.

cost objects Responsibility centers, products, or services to which costs are assigned.

cost of capital The cost of acquiring resources for an organization, either through debt or through the issuance of stock. Supp

cost of goods manufactured The total cost of direct material, direct labor, and manufacturing overhead transferred from Work-in-Process Inventory to Finished-Goods Inventory during an accounting period.

cost of goods sold The expense measured by the cost of the finished goods sold during a period of time.

cost-plus pricing A pricing approach in which the price is equal to cost plus a markup.

cost pool A collection of costs to be assigned to a set of cost objects.

cost prediction Forecast of cost at a particular level of activity.

cost structure The relative proportions of an organization's fixed and variable costs.

cost variance The difference between actual and standard cost.

cost variance analysis The process of systematically comparing expected costs (standards) against actual costs, analyzing the differences, and explaining significant deviations.

cost-volume-profit (CVP) analysis A study of the relationships between sales volume, expenses, revenue, and profit.

cost-volume-profit (CVP) graph A graphical expression of the relationships between sales volume, expenses, revenue, and profit.

cross-elasticity The extent to which a change in a product's price affects the demand for substitute products.

curvilinear cost A cost with a curved line for its graph.

customer acceptance measures The extent to which a firm's customers perceive its product to be of high quality.

customer profitability analysis Using the concepts of activity- based costing to determine the activities, costs, and profit associated with serving particular customers.

customer-profitability profile A graphical portrayal of a company's customer profitability analysis.

cycle time *See* **throughput time.**

decentralization A form of organization in which subunit managers are given authority to make substantive decisions. Supp

decision making Choosing between alternatives. Supp

decision variables The variables in a linear program about which a decision is made.

delivery cycle time The average time between the receipt of a customer order and delivery of the goods.

demand curve A graph of the relationship between sales price and the quantity of units sold.

departmental overhead center Any department to which overhead costs are assigned via overhead cost distribution.

departmental overhead rate An overhead rate calculated for a single production department.

departmental production report The key document in a process-costing system. This report summarizes the physical flow of units, equivalent units of production, cost per equivalent unit, and analysis of total departmental costs.

dependent variable A variable whose value depends on other variables, called *independent variables.*

depreciation tax shield The reduction in a firm's income-tax expense due to the depreciation expense associated with a depreciable asset.

differential cost The difference in a cost item under two decision alternatives.

direct cost A cost that can be traced to a particular department or other subunit of an organization.

direct-exchange (or noncash) transaction A significant investing or financing transaction involving accounts other than cash, such as a transaction where land is obtained in exchange for the issuance of capital stock. Supp

directing operational activities Running an organization on a day-to-day basis. Supp

direct-labor budget A schedule showing the number of hours and cost of direct labor to be used in production of services or goods during a budget period.

direct-labor cost The cost of salaries, wages, and fringe benefits for personnel when they are working directly on the production of goods or services.

direct-labor efficiency variance The difference between actual and standard hours of direct labor multiplied by the standard hourly labor rate.

direct-labor rate variance The difference between actual and standard hourly labor rate multiplied by the actual hours of direct labor used.

direct material Raw material that is physically incorporated in the finished product.

direct-material budget A schedule showing the number of units and the cost of material to be purchased during a budget period.

direct-material price variance The difference between actual and standard price of direct material used in production, multiplied by the actual quantity of material used.

direct-material purchase price variance The difference between the standard price and the actual price paid for direct material purchased, multiplied by the actual quantity of material purchased.

direct-material quantity variance The difference between actual and standard quantity of materials allowed, given actual output, multiplied by the standard price.

direct method (of preparing the statement of cash flows) A method of preparing the operating activities section of a statement of cash flows. A cash-basis income statement is constructed in which operating cash disbursements are subtracted from operating cash receipts. Supp

direct method (of service department cost allocation) A method of service department cost allocation in which service department costs are allocated directly to the production departments.

discounted-cash-flow analysis An analysis of an investment proposal that takes into account the time value of money.

discount rate The interest rate used in computing the present value of a cash flow.

discretionary cost A cost that results from a discretionary management decision to spend a particular amount of money.

dual cost allocation An approach to service department cost allocation in which variable costs are allocated in proportion to short-term usage and fixed costs are allocated in proportion to long-term usage.

e-budgeting An electronic and enterprisewide budgeting process in which employees throughout the organization can submit and retrieve budget information electronically via the Internet.

economic order quantity (EOQ) The order size that minimizes inventory ordering and holding costs.

economic value added (EVA) An investment center's after-tax operating income minus the investment center's total assets (net of its current liabilities) times the company's weighted-average cost of capital.

electronic data interchange (EDI) The direct exchange between organizations of data via a computer-to-computer interface. Supp

engineered cost A cost that results from a definitive physical relationship with the activity measure.

engineering method A cost-estimation method in which a detailed study is made of the process that results in cost incurrence.

environmental cost management The strategic implementation of systems for identifying, measuring, controlling, and reducing environmental costs.

environmental costs Costs incurred in dealing with environmental issues.

equivalent unit A measure of the amount of production effort applied to a physical unit of production. For example, a physical unit that is 50 percent completed represents one-half of an equivalent unit.

estimated manufacturing overhead The amount of manufacturing-overhead cost expected for a specified period of time. Used as the numerator in computing the predetermined overhead rate. Supp

expected value The sum of the possible values for a random variable, each weighted by its probability.

expense The consumption of assets for the purpose of generating revenue.

experience curve A graph (or other mathematical representation) that shows how a broad set of costs decline as cumulative production output increases.

external failure costs Costs incurred because defective products have been sold.

facility-(or general-operations) level activity An activity that is required for an entire production process to occur.

favorable variance Sometimes abbreviated F, a cost variance is designated as favorable when spending on that element of cost is lower than the spending anticipated during the planning process.

feasible region The possible values for decision variables that are not ruled out by constraints.

FIFO (first-in, first-out) method A method of process costing in which the cost assigned to the beginning work-in-process inventory is not added to current-period production costs. The cost per equivalent unit calculated under FIFO relates to the current period only. Supp

financial accounting The use of accounting information for reporting to parties outside the organization.

financial leverage The concept that a relatively small increase in income can provide a proportionately much larger increase in return to the common stockholders. Supp

financial planning and analysis (FP&A) system A coordinated set of tools that helps managers assess the company's future and know if they are reaching their performance goals; includes subsystems for (1) planning, (2) measuring and recording results, and (3) evaluating performance.

financial planning model A set of mathematical relationships that express the interactions among the various operational, financial, and environmental events that determine the overall results of an organization's activities.

financing activities Transactions involving a company's debt or equity capital. Supp

financing budget A schedule that outlines how an organization will acquire financial resources during the budget period (for example, through borrowing or sale of capital stock).

finished goods Completed products awaiting sale.

fixed cost A cost that does not change in total as activity changes.

fixed-overhead budget variance The difference between actual and budgeted fixed overhead.

fixed-overhead volume variance The difference between budgeted and applied fixed overhead.

flexible budget A budget that is valid for a range of activity.

flexible manufacturing system (FMS) A series of manufacturing machines, controlled and integrated by a computer, which is designed to perform a series of manufacturing operations automatically. Supp

FMS cell A group of machines and personnel within a flexible manufacturing system (FMS). Supp

full (or absorption) cost A product's variable cost plus an allocated portion of fixed overhead.

future value The amount to which invested funds accumulate over a specified period of time.

gain-sharing plan An incentive system that specifies a formula by which the cost savings from productivity gains achieved by a company are shared with the workers who helped accomplish the improvements.

goal congruence A meshing of objectives, where managers throughout an organization strive to achieve the goals set by top management.

goodness of fit The closeness with which a regression line fits the data upon which it is based.

grade The extent of a product's capability in performing its intended purpose, viewed in relation to other products with the same functional use.

gross margin *See* **gross profit**

gross profit Revenues left after deducting cost of sales (cost of goods sold), without considering any other costs of operating the company.

high-low method A cost estimation method in which a cost line is fit using exactly two data points—the high and low activity levels.

homogeneous cost pool A grouping of overhead costs in which each cost component is consumed in roughly the same proportion by each product line. Supp

horizontal analysis An analysis of the year-to-year change in each financial statement item. Supp

hurdle rate The minimum desired rate of return used in a discounted-cash-flow analysis.

hybrid product-costing system A system that incorporates features from two or more alternative product-costing systems, such as job-order and process costing.

idle time Unproductive time spent by employees due to factors beyond their control, such as power outages and machine breakdowns.

imperfect competition A market in which a single producer or group of producers can affect the market price.

incentive compensation *See* **pay for performance.**

incremental cost The increase in cost from one alternative to another.

independent variable The variable upon which an estimate is based in least-squares regression analysis.

indirect cost A cost that cannot be traced to a particular department.

indirect labor All costs of compensating employees who do not work directly on the firm's product but who are necessary for production to occur.

indirect-labor budget A schedule showing the amount and cost of indirect labor to be used during a budget period. Supp

indirect materials Materials that either are required for the production process to occur but do not become an integral part of the finished product, or are consumed in production but are insignificant in cost.

indirect method (or reconciliation method) A method of preparing the operating activities section of a statement of cash flows, in which the analyst begins with net income. Then adjustments are made to convert from an accrual-basis income statement to a cash-basis income statement. Supp

information overload The provision of so much information that, due to human limitations in processing information, managers cannot effectively use it.

in-process quality controls Procedures designed to assess product quality before production is completed.

inspection time The time spent on quality inspections of raw materials, partially completed products, or finished goods. Supp

internal auditor An accountant who reviews the accounting procedures, records, and reports in both the controller's and treasurer's areas of responsibility.

internal failure costs Cost of correcting defects found prior to product sale.

internal control system A process designed to provide reasonable assurance regarding the achievement of objectives in the following categories: effectiveness and efficiency of operations, reliability of financial reporting, and compliance with applicable laws and regulations.

internal failure costs Costs of correcting defects found prior to product sale.

internal rate of return The discount rate required for an investment's net present value to be zero; also known as the *time-adjusted rate of return.*

inventoriable cost Cost incurred to purchase or manufacture goods. *See also* **product cost.**

inventoriable goods Goods that can be stored before sale, such as durable goods, mining products, and some agricultural products. Supp

inventory budgets Schedules that detail the amount and cost of finished-goods, work-in-process, and direct-material inventories expected at the end of a budget period. Supp

investing activities Transactions involving the extension or collection of loans, acquisition or disposal of investments, and purchase or sale of productive, long-lived assets. Supp

investment center A responsibility center whose manager is accountable for its profit and for the return on capital invested to generate that profit.

investment opportunity rate The rate of return an organization can earn on its best alternative investments that are of equivalent risk.

ISO 9000 standards International quality-control standards issued by the International Standards Organization. Supp

job-cost record A document that records the costs of direct material, direct labor, and manufacturing overhead for a particular production job or batch. The job-cost record is a subsidiary ledger account for the Work-in-Process Inventory account in the general ledger.

job-order costing A product-costing system in which costs are assigned to batches or job orders of production. Used by firms that produce relatively small numbers of dissimilar products.

joint cost The cost incurred in a joint production process before the joint products become identifiable as separate products.

joint production process A production process that results in two or more joint products.

joint products The outputs of a joint production process.

just-in-time (JIT) production and inventory management system A comprehensive inventory and manufacturing control system in which no materials are purchased and no products are manufactured until they are needed.

kaizen costing The process of cost reduction during the manufacturing phase of a product. Refers to continual and gradual improvement through small betterment activities.

labor-intensive A production process accomplished largely by manual labor. Supp

lag indicators Measures of the final, usually financial, outcomes of earlier management decisions.

lead indicators Performance measures that identify future nonfinancial and financial outcomes to guide management decision making.

lead time The time required to receive inventory after it has been ordered.

learning curve A graphical expression of the decline in the average labor time required per unit as cumulative output increases.

least-squares regression method A cost estimation method in which the cost line is fit to the data by statistical analysis. The method minimizes the sum of the squared deviations between the cost line and the data points.

line positions Positions held by managers who are directly involved in providing the goods or services that constitute an organization's primary goals.

make-or-buy (or outsourcing) decision A decision as to whether a product or service should be produced in-house or purchased from an outside supplier.

management by exception A managerial technique in which only significant deviations from expected performance are investigated.

management by objectives (MBO) The process of designating the objectives of each subunit in an organization and planning for the achievement of these objectives. Managers at all levels participate in setting goals, which they then will strive to achieve.

managerial accountants Specialists in using the tools of managerial accounting to help the organization and its managers operate effectively.

managerial accounting The process of identifying, measuring, analyzing, interpreting, and communicating information in pursuit of an organization's goals.

manufacturing The process of converting raw materials into finished products. Supp

manufacturing costs Costs incurred in a manufacturing process, which consist of direct material, direct labor, and manufacturing overhead. Supp

manufacturing cycle efficiency (MCE) The ratio of process time to the sum of processing time, inspection time, waiting time, and move time.

manufacturing cycle time The total amount of production time (or throughput time) required per unit.

manufacturing overhead All manufacturing costs other than direct-material and direct-labor costs.

manufacturing-overhead budget Shows the cost of overhead expected to be incurred in the manufacturing process during the budget period.

manufacturing-overhead variance The difference between actual overhead cost and the amount specified in the flexible budget. Supp

marginal cost The extra cost incurred in producing one additional unit of output.

marginal cost curve A graph of the relationship between the change in total cost and the quantity produced and sold.

marginal revenue curve A graph of the relationship between the change in total revenue and the quantity sold.

marketing cost The cost incurred in selling goods or services. Includes order-getting costs and order-filling or distribution costs. Supp

mass customization A manufacturing environment in which many standardized components are combined to produce custom-made products to customer order.

master budget (or profit plan) A comprehensive set of budgets that covers all phases of an organization's operations for a specified period of time.

material-requirements planning (MRP) An operations- management tool that assists managers in scheduling production in each stage of a complex manufacturing process. Supp

material requisition form A document used by the production department supervisor to request the release of raw materials for production.

merchandise cost The cost of acquiring goods for resale. Includes purchasing and transportation costs. Supp

merchandising The business of acquiring finished goods for resale, either in a wholesale or a retail operation. Supp

merit pay *See* **pay for performance.**

minimum desired rate of return The net present value is the sum of the present values of the cash flows.

mixed cost *See* **semivariable cost.**

Modified Accelerated Cost Recovery System (MACRS) The depreciation schedule specified by the United States tax code, as modified by recent changes in the tax laws. *See also* **Accelerated Cost Recovery System (ACRS).**

move time The time spent moving raw materials, subassemblies, or finished products from one production operation to another. Supp

multiple regression A statistical method in which a linear (straight-line) relationship is estimated between a dependent variable and two or more independent variables.

multistage cost allocation The three-step process in which costs are assigned to products or services: (1) cost distribution (or allocation), (2) service department cost allocation, and (3) cost application. Supp

net present value The present value of a project's future cash flows less the cost of the initial investment.

net realizable value A joint product's final sales value less any separable costs incurred after the split-off point.

net-realizable-value method A method in which joint costs are allocated to the joint products in proportion to the net realizable value of each joint product.

nominal dollars The measure used for an actual cash flow that is observed.

nominal interest rate The real interest rate plus an additional premium to compensate investors for inflation.

non-value-added activities Operations that are either (1) unnecessary and dispensable or (2) necessary, but inefficient and improvable.

non-value-added costs The costs of activities that can be eliminated without deterioration of product quality, performance, or perceived value.

normal costing A product-costing system in which actual direct-materials, actual direct-labor, and applied manufacturing-overhead costs are added to Work-in-Process Inventory.

normalized overhead rate An overhead rate calculated over a relatively long time period. Supp

objective function An algebraic expression of the firm's goal.

off-line quality control Activities during the product design and engineering phases that will improve the manufacturability of the product, reduce production costs, and ensure high quality. Supp

oligopolistic market (or oligopoly) A market with a small number of sellers competing among themselves.

operating activities All activities that are not investing or financing activities. Generally speaking, operating activities include all cash transactions that are involved in the determination of net income. Supp

operating expenses The costs incurred to produce and sell services, such as transportation, repair, financial, or medical services.

operating income Profits from operations, excluding nonoperating items such as interest income, interest expense, and taxes.

operating leverage The extent to which an organization uses fixed costs in its cost structure. The greater the proportion of fixed costs, the greater the operating leverage.

operating leverage factor A measure of operating leverage at a particular sales volume. Computed by dividing an organization's total contribution margin by its net income.

operating profit *See* **operating income**

operational budgets A set of budgets that specify how operations will be carried out to produce an organization's services or goods.

operation costing A hybrid of job-order and process costing. Direct material is accumulated by batch of products using job-order costing methods. Conversion costs are accumulated by department and assigned to product units by process-costing methods.

opportunity cost The potential benefit given up when the choice of one action precludes selection of a different action.

organizational culture The mindset of employees, including their shared beliefs, values, and goals. Supp

outlier A data point that falls far away from the other points in a scatter diagram and is not representative of the data.

out-of-pocket costs Costs incurred that require the expenditure of cash or other assets.

outsourcing (or make-or-buy) decision A decision as to whether a product or service should be produced in-house or purchased from an outside supplier.

overapplied overhead The amount by which the period's applied manufacturing overhead exceeds actual manufacturing overhead.

overhead application (or absorption) The third step in assigning manufacturing-overhead costs. All costs associated with each production department are assigned to the product units on which a department has worked.

overhead budget A schedule showing the cost of overhead expected to be incurred in the production of services or goods during a budget period. Supp

overhead cost performance report A report showing the actual and flexible-budget cost levels for each overhead item, together with variable-overhead spending and efficiency variances and fixed-overhead budget variances.

overtime premium The extra compensation paid to an employee who works beyond the normal period of time.

padding the budget The process of building budgetary slack into a budget by overestimating expenses and underestimating revenue.

partial (or component) productivity Total output (in dollars) divided by the cost of a particular input.

participative budgeting The process of involving people throughout an organization in the budgeting process.

payback period The amount of time required for a project's after-tax cash inflows to accumulate to an amount that covers the initial investment.

pay for performance A one-time cash payment to an investment-center manager as a reward for meeting a predetermined criterion on a specified performance measure.

penetration pricing Setting a low initial price for a new product in order to penetrate the market deeply and gain a large and broad market share.

percentage of completion The extent to which a physical unit of production has been finished with respect to direct material or conversion activity. Supp

perfect competition A market in which the price does not depend on the quantity sold by any one producer.

perfection (or ideal) standard The cost expected under perfect or ideal operating conditions.

performance report A report showing the budgeted and actual amounts, and the variances between these amounts, of key financial results for a person or subunit.

period costs Costs that are expensed during the time period in which they are incurred.

physical unit An actual item of production, fully or partially completed. Supp

physical-units method A method in which joint costs are allocated to the joint products in proportion to their physical quantities.

planning Developing a detailed financial and operational description of anticipated operations. Supp

plantwide overhead rate An overhead rate calculated by averaging manufacturing-overhead costs for the entire production facility.

pool rate The cost per unit of the cost driver for a particular activity cost pool.

postaudit (or reappraisal) A systematic follow-up of a capital-budgeting decision to see how the project turned out.

practical capacity The upper limit on the amount of goods or services that an organization can produce in a specified period of time, allowing for normal occurrences such as machine downtime and employee fatigue or illness.

practical (or attainable) standard The cost expected under normal operating conditions.

predatory pricing An illegal practice in which the price of a product is set low temporarily to broaden demand. Then the product's supply is restricted and the price is raised.

predetermined overhead rate The rate used to apply manufacturing overhead to Work-in-Process Inventory, calculated as: estimated manufacturing overhead cost ÷ estimated amount of cost driver (or activity base).

present value The economic value now of a cash flow that will occur in the future.

prevention costs Costs of preventing defective products.

price discrimination The illegal practice of quoting different prices for the same product or service to different buyers, when the price differences are not justified by cost differences.

price elasticity The impact of price changes on sales volume.

price takers Firms whose products or services are determined totally by the market.

prime costs The costs of direct material and direct labor.

principal The amount originally invested, not including any interest earned.

process A set of linked activities.

process-costing system A product-costing system in which production costs are averaged over a large number of product units. Used by firms that produce large numbers of nearly identical products.

process time The amount of time during which a product is actually undergoing conversion activity. Supp

process value analysis (PVA) Another term for *activity analysis,* which is the detailed identification and description of the activities conducted in an enterprise.

product cost Cost associated with goods for sale until the time period during which the products are sold, at which time the costs become expenses. *See also* **inventoriable cost.**

product costing The process of assigning production costs to an organization's outputs.

product-costing system The process of accumulating the costs of a production process and assigning them to the products and services that constitute the organization's output.

production budget A schedule showing the number of units of services or goods that are to be produced during a budget period.

production department A department in which work is done directly on a firm's products. Supp

production overhead budget Shows the cost of overhead expected to be incurred in the production process (either manufacturing or nonmanufacturing) during the budget period.

product life-cycle costing The accumulation of costs that occur over the entire life cycle of a product. Supp

product-sustaining-level activity An activity that is needed to support an entire product line but is not always performed every time a new unit or batch of products is produced.

profitability index (or excess present value index) The present value of a project's future cash flows (exclusive of the initial investment), divided by the initial investment.

profit center A responsibility center whose manager is accountable for its profit and for making decisions where revenues and costs must be balanced.

profit plan (or master budget) A comprehensive set of budgets that cover all phases of an organization's operations during a specified period of time.

profit-volume graph A graphical expression of the relationship between profit and sales volume.

project costing The process of assigning costs to projects, cases, contracts, programs, or missions in nonmanufacturing organizations. Supp

proration The process of allocating underapplied or overapplied overhead to Work-in-Process Inventory, Finished-Goods Inventory, and Cost of Goods Sold.

Public Company Accounting Oversight Board (PCAOB) An organization operating under the auspices of the SEC, whose mission is to oversee and investigate the audits and auditors of public companies, and sanction both firms and individuals for violations of laws, rules, and regulations.

purchases budget A schedule showing the company's plan for the resources they will need to acquire from outside the organization in order to produce the goods and services they plan to sell during the budget period.

qualitative characteristics Factors in a decision analysis that cannot be expressed easily in numerical terms.

quality of conformance The extent to which a product meets the specifications of its design.

quality of design The extent to which a product is designed to perform well in its intended use.

quick assets Cash, marketable securities, accounts receivable, and current notes receivable. Excludes inventories and prepaid expenses, which are current assets but not quick assets. Supp

raw material Material entered into a manufacturing process.

real dollars A measure that reflects an adjustment for the purchasing power of a monetary unit.

real interest rate The underlying interest rate in the economy, which includes compensation to an investor for the time value of money and the risk of an investment.

reciprocal-services method A method of service department cost allocation that accounts for the mutual provision of reciprocal services among all service departments.

reengineering The complete redesign of a process, with an emphasis on finding creative new ways to accomplish an objective. Supp

regression line A line fit to a set of data points using least-squares regression.

relative-sales-value method A method in which joint costs are allocated to the joint products in proportion to their total sales values at the split-off point.

relevant information Data that are pertinent to a decision.

relevant range The range of activity within which management expects the organization to operate.

research and development (R&D) costs Costs incurred to develop and test new products or services. Supp

residual income (RI) Profit minus an imputed interest charge, which is equal to the invested capital times an imputed interest rate.

responsibility accounting Tools and concepts used by managerial accountants to measure the performance of an organization's people and subunits.

responsibility center A subunit in an organization whose manager is held accountable for specified financial results of its activities.

return-on-investment pricing A cost-plus pricing method in which the markup is determined by the amount necessary for the company to earn a target rate of return on investment.

return on investment (ROI) Income divided by invested capital.

revenue center A responsibility center whose manager is accountable for the revenues that the unit generates.

rolling budget (also revolving or continuous budget) A budget that is continually updated by adding another incremental time period and dropping the most recently completed period.

safety margin Difference between budgeted sales revenue and break-even sales revenue.

safety stock Extra inventory consumed during periods of above-average usage in a setting with fluctuating demand. Supp

sales budget A schedule that shows the expected sales of services or goods during a budget period, expressed in both monetary terms and units.

sales forecasting The process of predicting sales of services or goods. The initial step in preparing a master budget.

sales margin Income divided by sales revenue.

sales mix Relative proportion of sales of each of an organization's multiple products.

sales-price variance The difference between actual and expected unit sales price multiplied by the actual quantity of units sold.

sales-volume variance The difference between actual sales volume and budgeted sales volume multiplied by the budgeted unit contribution margin.

scatter diagram A set of plotted cost observations at various activity levels.

schedule of cost of goods manufactured A detailed schedule showing the manufacturing costs incurred during an accounting period and the change in work-in-process inventory.

schedule of cost of goods sold A detailed schedule showing the cost of goods sold and the change in finished-goods inventory during an accounting period.

segmented income statement A financial statement showing the income for an organization and its major segments (subunits).

selling costs Costs of obtaining and filling sales orders, such as advertising costs, compensation of sales personnel, and product promotion costs. Supp

selling, general, and administrative (SG&A) expense budget A schedule showing the planned amounts of selling, general, and administrative expenses during a budget period.

semivariable (or mixed) cost A cost with both a fixed and a variable component.

sensitivity analysis A technique for determining what would happen in a decision analysis if a key prediction or assumption proves to be wrong.

separable processing cost Cost incurred on a joint product after the split-off point of a joint production process.

sequential production process A manufacturing operation in which partially completed products pass in sequence through two or more production departments. Supp

service department cost allocation The second step in assigning manufacturing-overhead costs. All costs associated with a service department are assigned to the departments that use the services it produces.

service-industry firm A firm engaged in production of a service that is consumed as it is produced, such as air transportation service or medical service. Supp

service (or support) departments Subunits in an organization that are not involved directly in producing the organization's output of goods or services.

shareholder value analysis Calculation of the residual income associated with a major product line, with the objective of determining how the product line affects a firm's value to its shareholders.

simple regression A regression analysis based on a single independent variable.

Six Sigma An analytical method that aims at achieving near perfect results in a production process.

skimming pricing Setting a high initial price for a new product in order to reap short-run profits. Over time, the price is reduced gradually.

source document A document that is used as the basis for an accounting entry. Examples include material requisition forms and direct-labor time tickets.

SOX 302 A section of the Sarbanes-Oxley Act that requires the signing officers of a company's financial reports to establish, maintain, and periodically evaluate the effectiveness of the company's internal controls over financial reporting.

SOX 404 A section of the Sarbanes-Oxley Act that requires a company to include in its annual report an internal control report.

split-off point The point in a joint production process at which the joint products become identifiable as separate products.

staff positions Positions held by managers who are only indirectly involved in producing an organization's product or service.

standard cost A predetermined cost for the production of goods or services that serves as a benchmark against which to compare the actual cost.

standard-costing system A cost-control and product-costing system in which cost variances are computed and production costs are entered into work-in-process inventory at their standard amounts.

standard direct-labor quantity The number of labor hours normally needed to manufacture one unit of product.

standard direct-labor rate Total hourly cost of compensation, including fringe benefits.

standard direct-material price The total delivered cost, after subtracting any purchase discounts taken.

standard direct-material quantity The total amount of material normally required to produce a finished product, including allowances for normal waste and inefficiency.

standard quantity allowed The standard quantity per unit of output multiplied by the number of units of actual output.

statement of cash flows A major financial statement that shows the change in an organization's total cash and cash equivalents and explains that change in terms of the organization's operating, investing, and financing activities during a period. Supp

static budget A budget that is valid for only one planned activity level.

statistical control chart A plot of cost variances across time, with a comparison to a statistically determined critical value.

step-down method A method of service department cost allocation in which service department costs are allocated first to service departments and then to production departments.

step-fixed cost A cost that remains fixed over wide ranges of activity, but jumps to a different amount for activity levels outside that range.

step-variable cost A cost that is nearly variable, but increases in small steps instead of continuously.

storage time The time during which raw materials or finished products are stored in stock. Supp

storyboarding A procedure used to develop a detailed process flowchart, which visually represents activities and the relationships among the activities.

strategic cost analysis A broad-based managerial-accounting analysis that supports strategic management decisions. Supp

strategic cost management Overall recognition of the cost relationships among the activities in the value chain, and the process of managing those cost relationships to a firm's advantage.

summary cash budget A combination of the cash receipts and cash disbursements budgets. Supp

sunk costs Costs that were incurred in the past and cannot be altered by any current or future decision.

supply chain The flow of all goods, services, and information into and out of an organization.

sustainable development Business activity that produces the goods and services needed in the present without limiting the ability of future generations to meet their needs.

target cost The projected long-run product cost that will enable a firm to enter and remain in the market for the product and compete successfully with the firm's competitors.

target costing The design of a product, and the processes used to produce it, so that ultimately the product can be manufactured at a cost that will enable a firm to make a profit when the product is sold at an estimated market-driven price. This estimated price is called the *target price,* the desired profit margin is called the *target profit,* and the cost at which the product must be manufactured is called the *target cost.*

target profit (or income) The profit level set as management's objective.

task analysis Setting standards by analyzing the production process.

theoretical capacity The upper limit on production of goods or services, during a specified period of time, if everything works perfectly (i.e., no employees miss time for illness, no machines break down, there are no unexpected interruptions such as power outages or severe storms, and so forth). Supp

theory of constraints (TOC) A management approach that focuses on identifying and relaxing the constraints that limit an organization's ability to reach a higher level of goal attainment.

throughput time The average amount of time required to convert raw materials into finished goods ready to be shipped to customers.

time-driven activity-based costing (TDABC) A version of ABC that has found wide acceptance in service-industry settings.

time and material pricing A cost-plus pricing approach that includes components for labor cost and material cost, plus markups on either or both of these cost components.

timely information Data that are available in time for use in a decision analysis.

time record A document that records the amount of time an employee spends on each production job.

total contribution margin Total sales revenue less total variable expenses.

total cost curve Graphs the relationship between total cost and total quantity produced and sold.

total manufacturing cost The combined costs of direct material, direct labor, and manufacturing overhead incurred during a defined period of time.

total quality management (TQM) The broad set of management and control processes designed to focus an entire organization and all of its employees on providing products or services that do the best possible job of satisfying the customer.

total revenue curve Graphs the relationship between total sales revenue and quantity sold.

transfer price The price at which products or services are transferred between two divisions in an organization.

transferred-in costs Costs assigned to partially completed products that are transferred into one production department from a prior department.

treasurer An accountant in a staff position who is responsible for managing an organization's relationships with investors and creditors and maintaining custody of the organization's cash, investments, and other assets.

trend analysis A comparison across time of three or more observations of a particular financial item, such as net income. Supp

two-dimensional ABC model A combination of the cost assignment view of the role of activity-based costing with its process analysis and evaluation role. Two-dimensional ABC is one way of depicting activity-based management.

two-stage cost allocation A two-step procedure for assigning overhead costs to products or services produced. In the first stage, all production costs are assigned to the production departments. In the second stage, the costs that have been assigned to each production department are applied to the products or services produced in those departments.

unavoidable expenses Expenses that will continue to be incurred even if a subunit or activity is eliminated.

underapplied overhead The amount by which the period's actual manufacturing overhead exceeds applied manufacturing overhead.

unfavorable variance Sometimes abbreviated U, a cost variance is designated as unfavorable when spending on that element of cost is higher than the spending anticipated during the planning process.

unit contribution margin Sales price minus the unit variable cost.

unit-level activity An activity that must be done for each unit of production.

value analysis *See* **value engineering.**

value chain An organization's set of linked, value-creating activities, ranging from securing basic raw materials and energy to the ultimate delivery of products and services.

value engineering (or value analysis) A cost-reduction and process improvement technique that utilizes information collected about a product's design and production processes and then examines various attributes of the design and processes to identify candidates for improvement efforts.

variable cost A cost that changes in total in direct proportion to a change in an organization's activity.

variable costing (or direct costing) A method of product costing in which only variable manufacturing overhead is included as a product cost that flows through the manufacturing accounts (i.e., Work-in-Process Inventory, Finished-Goods Inventory, and Cost of Goods Sold). Fixed manufacturing overhead is treated as a period cost.

variable-overhead efficiency variance The difference between actual and standard hours of an activity base (e.g., machine hours) multiplied by the standard variable-overhead rate.

variable-overhead spending variance The difference between actual variable-overhead cost and the product of the standard variable-overhead rate and actual hours of an activity base (e.g., machine hours).

variance The difference between actual and standard cost. *See* **cost variance.**

variance analysis *See* **cost variance analysis.**

velocity The number of units produced in a given time period.

vertical analysis An analysis of the relationships among various financial items on a particular financial statement. Generally presented in terms of common-size financial statements. Supp

visual-fit method A method of cost estimation in which a cost line is drawn through a scatter diagram according to the visual perception of the analyst.

volume-based cost driver (or activity base) A cost driver that is closely associated with production volume, such as direct-labor hours or machine hours.

volume-based costing system A product-costing system in which costs are assigned to products on the basis of a single activity base related to volume (e.g., direct-labor hours or machine hours).

waiting time The time during which partially completed products wait for the next phase of production. Supp

weighted-average cost of capital (WACC) A weighted average of the after-tax cost of debt capital and the cost of equity capital.

weighted-average method A method of process costing in which the cost assigned to beginning work-in-process inventory is added to the current-period production costs. The cost per equivalent unit calculated under this process-costing method is a weighted average of the costs in the beginning work in process and the costs of the current period.

weighted-average unit contribution margin Average of a firm's several products' unit contribution margins, weighted by the relative sales proportion of each product.

working capital Current assets minus current liabilities.

work in process Partially completed products that are not yet ready for sale.

Index of Companies and Organizations

Index of Subjects

Page numbers followed by n refer to footnotes.

Focus on Ethics

IMA STATEMENT OF ETHICAL PROFESSIONAL PRACTICE

Members of IMA shall behave ethically. A commitment to ethical professional practice includes overarching principles that express our values and standards that guide our conduct.

Principles

IMA's overarching ethical principles include: Honesty, Fairness, Objectivity, and Responsibility. Members shall act in accordance with these principles and shall encourage others within their organizations to adhere to them.

Standards

A member's failure to comply with the following standards may result in disciplinary action.

I. Competence

Each member has a responsibility to:

1. Maintain an appropriate level of professional expertise by continually developing knowledge and skills.
2. Perform professional duties in accordance with relevant laws, regulations, and technical standards.
3. Provide decision support information and recommendations that are accurate, clear, concise, and timely.
4. Recognize and communicate professional limitations or other constraints that would preclude responsible judgment or successful performance of an activity.

II. Confidentiality

Each member has a responsibility to:

1. Keep information confidential except when disclosure is authorized or legally required.
2. Inform all relevant parties regarding appropriate use of confidential information. Monitor subordinates' activities to ensure compliance.
3. Refrain from using confidential information for unethical or illegal advantage.

III. Integrity

Each member has a responsibility to:

1. Mitigate actual conflicts of interest. Regularly communicate with business associates to avoid apparent conflicts of interest. Advise all parties of any potential conflicts.
2. Refrain from engaging in any conduct that would prejudice carrying out duties ethically.
3. Abstain from engaging in or supporting any activity that might discredit the profession.

IV. Credibility

Each member has a responsibility to:

1. Communicate information fairly and objectively.
2. Disclose all relevant information that could reasonably be expected to influence an intended user's understanding of the reports, analyses, or recommendations.
3. Disclose delays or deficiencies in information, timeliness, processing, or internal controls in conformance with organization policy and/or applicable law.

Resolution of Ethical Conflict

In applying the Standards of Ethical Professional Practice, you may encounter problems identifying unethical behavior or resolving an ethical conflict. When faced with ethical issues, you should follow your organization's established policies on the resolution of such conflict. If these policies do not resolve the ethical conflict, you should consider the following courses of action:

1. Discuss the issue with your immediate supervisor except when it appears that the supervisor is involved. In that case, present the issue to the next level. If you cannot achieve a satisfactory resolution, submit the issue to the next management level. If your immediate superior is the chief executive officer or equivalent, the acceptable reviewing authority may be a group such as the audit committee, executive committee, board of directors, board of trustees, or owners. Contact with levels above the immediate superior should be initiated only with your superior's knowledge, assuming he or she is not involved. Communication of such problems to authorities or individuals not employed or engaged by the organization is not considered appropriate, unless you believe there is a clear violation of the law.
2. Clarify relevant ethical issues by initiating a confidential discussion with an IMA Ethics Counselor or other impartial advisor to obtain a better understanding of possible courses of action.
3. Consult your own attorney as to legal obligations and rights concerning the ethical conflict.